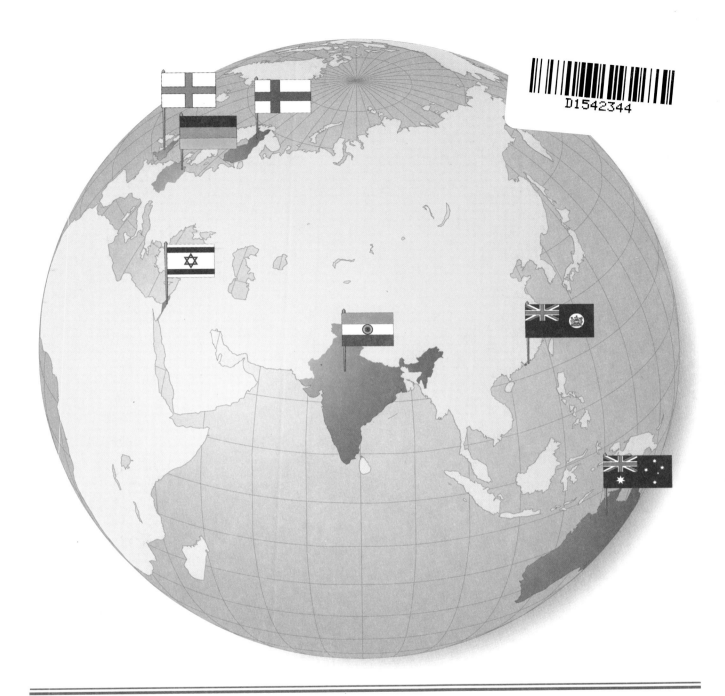

D1542344

About the Authors

Kenneth C. Laudon is a Professor of Information Systems at New York University's Stern School of Business. He holds a B.A. in Economics from Stanford and a Ph.D. from Columbia University. He has authored eleven books dealing with information systems, organizations, and society. Professor Laudon has also written over forty articles concerned with the social, organizational, and management impacts of information systems, privacy, ethics, and multimedia technology.

Professor Laudon's current research is on the planning and management of large-scale information systems for the 1990s and multimedia information technology. He has received grants from the National Science Foundation to study the evolution of national information systems at the Social Security Administration, the IRS, and the FBI. A part of this research is concerned with computer-related organizational and occupational changes in large organizations, changes in management ideology, changes in public policy, and understanding productivity change in the knowledge sector.

Ken Laudon has testified as an expert before the United States Congress. He has been a researcher and consultant to the Office of Technology Assessment (United States Congress) and to the Office of the President, several executive branch agencies, and Congressional Committees. Professor Laudon also acts as a consultant on systems planning and strategy to several Fortune 500 firms.

Ken Laudon's hobby is sailing

Jane Price Laudon is a management consultant in the information systems area and the author of seven books. Her special interests include systems analysis, data management, MIS auditing, software evaluation, and teaching business professionals how to design and use information systems.

Jane received her Ph.D. from Columbia University, her M.A. from Harvard University, and her B.A. from Barnard College. She has taught at Columbia University and the New York University Graduate School of Business. She maintains a lifelong interest in Oriental languages and civilizations.

The Laudons have two daughters, Erica and Elisabeth.

Management Information Systems: Organization and Technology reflects a deep understanding of MIS research and teaching as well as practical experience designing and building real world systems.

Management Information Systems

Organization and Technology **Fourth Edition**

Kenneth C. Laudon
New York University

Jane Price Laudon
Azimuth Corporation

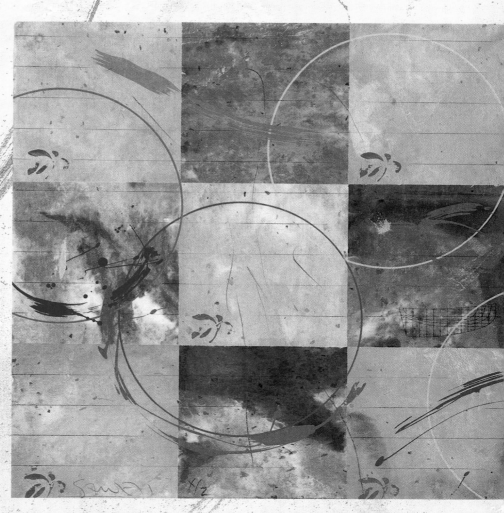

PRENTICE HALL
Upper Saddle River, New Jersey 07458

Library of Congress Cataloging-in-Publication Data

Laudon, Kenneth C.
 Management information systems : organization and technology /
Kenneth C. Laudon, Jane Price Laudon. -- 4th ed.
   p.   cm.
 Includes bibliographical references and index.
 ISBN 0-13-213778-X
   1. Management information systems.   I. Laudon, Jane Price.
 II. Title.
 T58.6.L376   1996
 658.4'038--dc20   95-43663
                                                                      CIP

Acquisitions Editors: PJ Boardman and Richard Wohl
Editorial Assistants: Jane Avery and Linda Albelli
Production Editor: Elaine Lynch
Design Director: Patricia Wosczyk
Interior Design: Ox & Company
Cover Design: Ox & Company
Cover Image: "Oceanworks" Scott Sandell/John Szoke Graphics, Inc.
Manufacturing Buyer: Paul Smolenski
Compositor: Carlisle Communications, Ltd.

Screen shots [various] Lotus Development Corporation. Used with permission of Lotus
Development Corporation. Lotus and Lotus Notes are registered trademarks and Notes is a
trademark of Lotus Development Corporation.

 © 1996 by Prentice-Hall, Inc.
A Simon & Schuster Company
Upper Saddle River, New Jersey 07458

Printed in the United States of America

10   9   8   7   6   5   4   3   2   1

ISBN 0-13-213778-X

Prentice-Hall International (UK) Limited, *London*
Prentice-Hall of Australia Pty. Limited, *Sydney*
Prentice-Hall Canada Inc., *Toronto*
Prentice-Hall Hispanoamericana, S.A., *Mexico*
Prentice-Hall of India Private Limited, *New Delhi*
Prentice-Hall of Japan, Inc., *Tokyo*
Simon & Schuster Asia Pte. Ltd., *Singapore*
Editora Prentice-Hall do Brasil, Ltda., *Rio de Janeiro*

for

Erica

and

Elisabeth

Brief Table
of Contents

Contents

Windows
on MIS

Preface

Management Information Systems: Organization and Technology (Fourth Edition) is based on the premise that professional managers, in both the private and public sectors, cannot afford to ignore information systems. In today's business environment, professional managers must learn how to use information technology to create competitive firms, manage global corporations, and provide useful products and services to customers. Information systems have become so vital to the management, organization, operation, and products of large organizations that they are too important to be left only to technicians. A few years ago, this statement was not true. Briefly, it is difficult—if not impossible—to manage a modern organization without at least some grounding in the fundamentals of what information systems are, how they affect the organization and its employees, and how they can make businesses more competitive and efficient.

Accordingly, this book has been written for nontechnical undergraduate and MBA students in finance, accounting, management, and the liberal arts who will find a knowledge of information systems vital for their professional success. This book may also serve as a first course for students who subsequently major in information systems at either the undergraduate or graduate level. We have made every effort to provide a comprehensive and current survey of research and literature on organizations and systems and to present it in a highly readable style.

THE CONTEMPORARY ENVIRONMENT

This book reflects three related trends in the contemporary business environment. First, globalization of markets puts new emphasis on organizational design and management control. When your parts originate in Korea, your assembly occurs in Mexico, and your finance, marketing and general counsel are in New York, then you know you face tough challenges in designing the proper organization and in managing the work.

Second, the transformation of the American and other advanced industrial economies into full-fledged knowledge and information economies puts new emphasis on time-based competition, productivity of knowledge workers, short product life cycles, and employee training. When 70% of the gross national product is an output of the information sector, then the productivity of information workers is a central societal concern. When your firm's future depends on having a new product in the marketplace in nine months, then you face a difficult challenge as a manager in speeding up the work of engineers and other knowledge workers. The demand for information, for communications, has never been so great.

Third, the development of powerful microprocessors and telecommunications networks has brought forth a new information architecture based on powerful desktop computers and communications networks. We can now put what used to be called a mainframe computer on every desktop, and we can now design organizations with powerful information networks to instantly link factories, offices, and desktops within the company and with other companies around the world. A few years ago this was a dream.

The work of an organization—and its employees—depends increasingly on what its information systems are capable of doing. Increasing market share, becoming the high-quality or low-cost producer, developing new products, and increasing employee productivity, depend more and more on the kinds and quality of information systems in the organization. Information systems can lead to more efficient and effective organizations, new styles and procedures of management, new strategies, and new organizational roles. Organizations innovating with information systems have transformed the way they operate and even changed the face of an entire industry.

Today's managers are not only expected to use systems but are also expected to:

- Know how to use information technology to design competitive and efficient organizations.
- Understand the business and system requirements of a global environment.
- Use information systems to ensure quality throughout the firm.
- Make choices about technology platforms—hardware, software, and communications technologies—to enhance their firm's productivity and overall performance.
- Manage and control the influence of systems on employees and customers.
- Understand the ethical dilemmas and controversies which surround the use of advanced information systems.

In essence, contemporary managers are expected to know enough about information technology to use it in the design and management of their organizations. These new management responsibilities require a deeper understanding of information technology and systems than ever before. Although this book primarily deals with private organizations, public sector managers are no less susceptible to these trends and changes in management and organization.

UNIQUE FEATURES OF THIS TEXT

Management Information Systems: Organization and Technology (Fourth Edition) has many unique features designed to create an active, dynamic learning environment.

- **Interactive Multimedia Edition:** The textbook is available in a new multimedia interactive format on CD-ROM. The Multimedia Edition features the full 19 chapters of the printed text plus 19 additional videos explaining key concepts, audio clips, line art, research articles, simulations, and interactive exercises. With specially prepared "BulletText" summaries, hyperlinked graphics, and complete hypertext linking of concepts, definitions, and applications, the multimedia version can be used independently of the hard cover version or in conjunction with the hard cover text as an interactive study guide. All supplements for the printed version may be used with the Multimedia Edition.

- **An integrated framework for describing and analyzing information systems.** An integrated framework portrays information systems as being composed of management, organization, and technology elements. This framework is used throughout the text to describe and analyze information systems and information system problems. A special diagram accompanying each chapter-opening vignette graphically illustrates how management, organization, and technology elements work together to create an information system solution to the business challenges discussed in the vignette. The diagram can be used as a starting point to analyze any information system problem.

- **Real-World Examples:** Real-world examples drawn from business and public organizations are used throughout to illustrate text concepts. Each chapter opens with a vignette illustrating the themes of the chapter by showing how a real-world organization meets a business challenge using information systems. More than 100 companies in the United States and over 100 organizations in Canada, Europe, Australia, Asia, and Africa are discussed (see the Organization and International Organization indexes.)

Each chapter contains three WINDOW ON boxes (WINDOW ON MANAGEMENT, WINDOW ON ORGANIZATIONS, WINDOW ON TECHNOLOGY) that present real-world examples illustrating the management, organization, and technology issues in the chapter. Each WINDOW ON box includes a section called *To Think About* containing questions for students to apply chapter concepts to management problem solving. The themes for each box are:

WINDOW ON MANAGEMENT: Management problems raised by systems and their solution; management strategies and plans; careers and experiences of managers using systems.

WINDOW ON TECHNOLOGY: Hardware, software, telecommunications, data storage, standards, and systems-building methodologies.

WINDOW ON ORGANIZATIONS: Activities of private and public organizations using information systems; experiences of people working with systems.

- **Coverage of new leading-edge topics.** Full chapters address the challenges posed by today's competitive global business environment. Enterprise-Wide Computing and Networking (Chapter 10); Managing International Information Systems (Chapter 19); Ensuring Quality with Information Systems (Chapter 13); and Ethical and Social Impact of Information Systems (Chapter 5) address these themes. The text includes up-to-date coverage of topics such as:
  - The Internet and the information superhighway
  - Electronic commerce
  - Business re-engineering
  - Intelligent agents
  - Wireless networks
  - Case-based reasoning
  - Fuzzy logic
  - Genetic algorithms
  - Client/server computing
  - Multimedia

- **A truly international perspective:** In addition to a full chapter on Managing International Information Systems, all chapters of the text are illustrated with real-world examples from one hundred corporations in Canada, Europe, Asia, Latin America, Africa, Australia, and the Middle East. Each chapter contains at least one, and often more, WINDOW ON box, case study, or opening vignette drawn from a non-U.S. firm. The text concludes with five major international case studies contributed by leading MIS experts in Canada, Europe, and Australia—Andrew Boynton, University of North Carolina at Chapel Hill and the

International Institute for Management Development (Switzerland) and Michael E. Shank, Renaissance Vision; Len Fertuck, University of Toronto (Canada); Helmut Krcmar and Bettina Schwarzer, Hohenheim University (Germany); Tapio Reponen, Turku School of Economics and Business Administration (Finland); and Peter Weill and Joel B. Barolsky, University of Melbourne (Australia).

■ **Activist pedagogy to teach management problem-solving:** *Management Information Systems: Organization and Technology* contains many features that encourage students to actively learn and to engage in management problem solving.

GROUP PROJECTS.   At the end of each chapter is a group project that encourages students to develop teamwork and oral and written presentation skills. The group project exercise asks students to work in groups of three or four to research a specific topic, analyze the pros and cons of an issue, write about it, and orally present the group's findings to the class. For instance, students might be asked to work in small groups to analyze a business and to suggest appropriate strategic information systems for that particular business or to develop a corporate ethics code on privacy that considers E-mail privacy and employers' use of information systems to monitor work sites.

MANAGEMENT CHALLENGES SECTION.   Each chapter concludes with several challenges, relating to the chapter topic, that managers are likely to encounter. These challenges are multi-faceted and sometimes pose dilemmas. They make excellent springboards for class discussion. Some of these Management Challenges are the organizational obstacles to building a database environment and the major risks and uncertainties in systems development.

TO THINK ABOUT QUESTIONS.   Included in every WINDOW ON box, these questions require students to apply chapter concepts to real-world scenarios. These questions frequently ask students to assume the role of managers, use multiple perspectives, consider different alternatives, and think creatively. The questions can be used for class discussion or for short written projects.

CASE STUDIES.   Each chapter concludes with a case study based on a real-world organization. These cases help students synthesize chapter concepts and apply this new knowledge to real-world problems and scenarios. Major case studies at the end of each part of the text and international case studies concluding the text provide additional opportunities for management problem solving. Professors can assign these case studies for class discussion or for term projects.

NEW TO THE FOURTH EDITION

This edition maintains the strengths of earlier editions, but puts even more emphasis on showing managers the opportunities for reshaping and enhancing their organizations using information technology. The Internet and other global networks have opened up exciting new avenues for expediting the flow of knowledge, organizational coordination, and electronic commerce. More and more companies are trying to use information technology to redesign their business processes and to fundamentally change the way they work. Small businesses, as well as large, can benefit from understanding the capabilities—and the limitations—of today's information technologies. The fourth edition was reworked from start to finish to more fully integrate the issues surrounding the growing use of the Internet, business re-engineering, and the system requirements of small businesses into the MIS course. These concerns are reflected in the following changes:

THE INTERNET.   An entirely new chapter on the Internet and enterprise-wide computing (Chapter 10) describes the underlying technology, capabilities, and benefits of the Internet with numerous illustrations from real-world companies. The chapter carefully analyzes the benefits and liabilities of this world-wide network. Internet topics such as intelligent agents, Internet security, digital commerce, and the information superhighway are integrated into other chapters of the book.

The Internet Connection can be found in each chapter of the text and in each of the major part-ending case studies. The Internet Connection interactively shows students how to use the Internet for research and management problem-solving and helps professors integrate the Internet into the MIS course.

The Internet Connection icon in the text directs the reader to additional materials and resources on the World Wide Web of the Internet dealing with topics and organizations discussed in the chapter or case, interactive software demonstrations, or in-depth descriptions of Internet capabilities and tools. These Web resources can be used to illustrate concepts such as multimedia, strategic information systems, telecommunications-based transaction processing, decision-support systems, or Total Quality Management. The user first links to Prentice-Hall's World Wide Web Site [http://www,prenhall.com] via either a university or home Internet service. Once the user is attached to the Prentice Hall Web site, he or she will be directed to a Laudon-Laudon Home Page. From the Laudon-Laudon Home Page the user can link directly to the Web resources specified for each Internet Connection session.

ATTENTION TO SMALL BUSINESSES AND ENTREPRENEURS. We have expanded the text to devote more attention to the specific management, organization, and technology issues relevant to small businesses and entrepreneurs using information systems. Specially designated chapter-opening vignettes, Window On boxes, and ending case studies highlight the experiences of small businesses using information systems.

EXPANDED TREATMENT OF BUSINESS RE-ENGINEERING, ORGANIZATIONAL CHANGE, AND ORGANIZATIONAL DESIGN USING INFORMATION TECHNOLOGY. Chapter 11 contains a detailed discussion of redesigning businesses processes using information technology. Experiences of real-world organizations performing business re-engineering are described in this chapter and integrated throughout the text. The entire text reflects a new emphasis on showing the potential for organizational change and organizational design using information technology.

EXPANDED TREATMENT OF INFORMATION SYSTEMS AND QUALITY. The text now puts more emphasis on showing the various ways that information systems can be used to promote quality throughout the business. Quality issues are addressed in Chapter 13 (Ensuring Quality with Information Systems) and integrated throughout the text.

INTERACTIVE LEARNING. The CD-ROM version provides an interactive, computer-managed instruction component that lets students learn at their own pace. Students apply text concepts to management problems in on-line interactive exercises. They can select and access material using powerful electronic indices for subjects, names, and organizations and they can review key terms with an electronic glossary. Each chapter of the text contains a bulletized summary of the key points for immediate on-line access and review through hot buttons and on-line glossaries and indexes. Videos and audio clips for each chapter illustrate real-world applications of key concepts. An interactive study guide provides helpful question-and-answer sessions, which can be automatically graded and handed to the professor.

BOOK OVERVIEW

The five parts of the book are designed to be relatively independent of each other. Each instructor may choose to emphasize different parts.

Part One is concerned with the organizational foundations of systems and their emerging strategic role. It provides an extensive introduction to real-world systems, focusing on their relationship to organizations, management, and important ethical and social issues. This section is important for understanding the larger environment in which systems operate and for showing students how they relate to organizational design, strategy, operations, and accountability.

Part Two provides the technical foundation for understanding information systems, describing hardware, software, storage, and telecommunications technologies. The section concludes by describing the challenge of making all of the information technologies work together in a new information architecture based on enterprise-wide networking and internetworking with other organizations.

Part Three focuses on the process of redesigning organizations using information systems, showing how new information systems can be used to engineer varying degrees of organizational change, including re-engineering of critical business processes. Because information systems and organizations are so closely intertwined, we see systems analysis and design as an exercise in organizational design, one that requires great sensitivity to the right tools and techniques, quality assurance, and change management.

Part Four describes the role of information systems in capturing and distributing organizational knowledge and intelligence and in enhancing management decision-making. It shows how knowledge creation and distribution, work group collaboration, and individual and group decision making can be supported by the use of knowledge work systems, decision support systems, and executive support systems. Organizational performance can also be enhanced by the use of carefully chosen artificial intelligence applications.

Part Five concludes the text by examining the special management challenges and opportunities created by the pervasiveness and power of contemporary information systems: ensuring security and control and developing global systems. Throughout the text, emphasis is placed on using information technology to redesign the organization's products, services, procedures, jobs and management structures. Numerous examples, drawn from multinational systems and global business environments, are presented.

Chapter Outline

Each chapter contains the following:

- A detailed outline at the beginning to provide an overview.
- An opening vignette, describing a real-world organization, to establish the theme and importance of the chapter.
- A diagram analyzing the opening vignette in terms of the management, organization, and technology model used throughout the text.
- A list of learning objectives.
- Marginal glosses of key terms in the text.
- Management challenges.
- An Internet Connection icon directing students to related material on the Internet.
- A chapter summary keyed to the learning objectives.
- A list of key terms that the students can use to review concepts.
- Review questions for students to test their comprehension of chapter material.
- A set of discussion questions that can be used for class discussion or for research topics.
- A group project to develop teamwork and presentation skills.
- A chapter-ending case study that illustrates important themes.
- A list of references for further research on topics.

INSTRUCTIONAL SUPPORT MATERIALS:

Software

A series of optional management software cases called *Solve it! Management Problem Solving with PC Software* has been developed to support the text. *Solve it!*

consists of 10 spreadsheet and 10 database cases drawn from real-world businesses, plus a data diskette with the files required by the cases. The cases are graduated in difficulty. The case book contains complete tutorial documentation showing how to use spreadsheet and database software to solve the problems. There are separate *Solve it!* case books for Windows and DOS software tools. A new version of *Solve it!* with all new cases is published every year. *Solve it!* must be adopted for an entire class. It can be purchased directly from the supplier, Azimuth Corporation, 124 Penfield Ave., Croton-on-Hudson, New York 10520 (Telephone 914-271-6321).

Instructor's Manual/Test Bank and Videocases

The *Instructor's Resource Manual,* written by Ken and Jane Laudon and Marshall R. Kaplan, includes lecture outlines as well as answers to review questions, discussion questions, group project exercises, case study questions, video cases, and To Think About questions. The Test Bank has been expanded to include 25 true-false questions, 25 multiple choice questions, and 25 fill in the blank questions for each chapter.

Video Cases

Ten video cases based on the real-world corporations and organizations used in the text are available to adopters. The video cases illustrate the concepts in each section and can be used for class discussion or written projects. The video cases are analyzed in the *Instructor's Resource Manual.*

Computerized Test Bank

All test bank questions are available in computerized form.

Transparency Acetates

A set of approximately 100 full-color transparency acetates is available to illuminate key concepts.

The New York Times "Themes of the Times"

Information systems is a constant theme in the news, both because of developments in the IT industry itself and because of the ways business uses it on a day-to-day basis. To enhance access to important news items, the *New York Times* and Prentice Hall are sponsoring "Themes of the Times." Twice a year, Prentice Hall will deliver complimentary copies of a "mini newspaper" containing reprints of selected *Times* articles to instructors who use this book for their classes. "Themes of the Times" is an excellent way of keeping students abreast of the ever-changing world of MIS.

Prentice Hall Video Library

Prentice Hall is fortunate to have an exclusive contract with Computer Chronicles, a premier TV program in its 12th season. It airs each week on 289 public television stations and in over 200 foreign cities. Stewart Cheifet, the host, takes an in-depth look each week at cutting-edge topics in new technology. Prentice Hall has selected clips from the most innovative programs and included them in our MIS Video Library for adopters of Laudon/Laudon's MIS 4E. In addition, Prentice Hall provides company footage from case studies highlighted in the text.

Powerpoint Transparencies

Prentice Hall provides you with PowerPoint electronic transparencies, for all of the figures and tables in the text, to support lectures. Instructors can customize these 4-color images adding information to suit their presentation style and to personalize their lectures.

ACKNOWLEDGMENTS

The production of any book involves many valuable contributions from a number of persons. We would like to thank all of our editors for encouragement, insight, and strong support for many years. We are grateful to P. J. Boardman for her energy and enthusiasm in guiding the development of this edition and to Charles Stewart for his vision and encouragement in the preparation of earlier editions of this text. We thank Amy Cohen for directing the preparation of ancillary materials and commend Elaine Lynch of Prentice Hall's Production Department for guiding production of this text under a very ambitious schedule.

We are deeply indebted to Marshall R. Kaplan for his invaluable assistance in the preparation of this edition and for his work on the *Instructor's Resource Manual*.

The Stern School of Business at New York University and the Information Systems Department provided a very special learning environment, one in which we and others could rethink the MIS field. Special thanks to Vasant Dhar, Ajit Kambil, Robert Kauffman, and Stephen Slade for providing critical feedback and support where deserved. Professor Norm White was especially helpful in commenting on the technical chapters in Part II and we thank him. Professor William H. Starbuck of the Management Department at NYU provided valuable comments and insights.

The late Professor James Clifford of Stern's Information Systems Department made valuable recommendations for improving our discussion of files and databases. Jim was a wonderful friend and colleague, and we will miss him deeply.

Professors Al Croker and Michael Palley of Baruch College and NYU, Professor Kenneth Marr of Hofstra University, Professor Edward Roche of Seton Hall University, Professor Sassan Rahmatian of California State University, Fresno, Ashok Malhotra and Emilio Collar of IBM, Jiri Rodovsky, and Russell Polo provided additional suggestions for improvement.

We are truly grateful to our colleagues in the MIS field who shared their expertise and comments with us. We want to thank Len Fertuck, Andrew Boynton, Michael E. Shank, Helmut Krcmar, Tapio Reponen, Bettina Schwarzer, Joel B. Barolski, and Peter Weill for contributing case studies. They deeply enrich the text.

One of our goals for *Management Information Systems,* 4E was to write a book which was authoritative, synthesized diverse views in the MIS literature, and helped define a common academic field. A large number of leading scholars in the field were contacted and assisted us in this effort. Reviewers and consultants for *Management Information Systems: Organization and Technology* took considerable time and care to examine individual chapters as specialists and the entire manuscript as instructors in the MIS course. Insofar as time and space allowed, we tried to incorporate their ideas in the text. We deeply appreciate their work and their suggestions for improving the text. These consultants are listed in the front end papers of the book. It is our hope that this group endeavor contributes to a shared vision and understanding of the MIS field.

Management Information Systems

one

Organizational Foundations of Information Systems

Contemporary information systems are both technical and social in nature. Managers must understand the relationship between the technical components of an information system and the structure, functions, and politics of organizations. Builders of information systems should consider management objectives and decision-making as well as the impact these systems will have on the well-being of people and society. Part One places information systems in the context of organizations, highlighting their strategic role and their ethical and social implications.

Chapter 1
The Challenge of Information Systems

Chapter 1 introduces the concept of an information system and illustrates the critical role that information systems play in organizations with examples of the key information system applications in the firm. Information systems literacy embraces both technical and behavioral perspectives, emphasizing awareness of the management, organization, and technology dimensions of information systems. Information systems pose five key challenges to today's managers.

Chapter 2
The Strategic Role of Information Systems

Chapter 2 highlights how businesses can use information systems to gain a competitive advantage. Strategic information systems have transformed organizations' products and services; marketing strategies; relationships with customers and suppliers; and internal operations. To use information systems strategically, organizations have to undergo both technical and social change.

Chapter 3
Information Systems and Organizations

Chapter 3 explores the relationship between information systems and organizations. Information systems are shaped by organizational structure, culture, political processes, and management, but information technology can influence organizations as well. The chapter uses both economic and behavioral theories to explain how information systems have affected organizations.

Chapter 4
Information, Management, and Decision Making

Chapter 4 examines how information systems can support management decision making. It examines how managers actually make decisions, and discusses the different levels, types, and stages of decision making. The chapter compares individual and organizational models of decision making and shows how information systems should be designed to support managerial decision making.

Chapter 5
Ethical and Social Impact of Information Systems

Chapter 5 describes the ethical dimensions of information systems in contemporary society. The widespread use of information systems has created new ethical and social problems. The issues of information rights (including privacy), intellectual property rights, accountability, liability, system quality, and quality of life must be carefully examined in light of the new power of information technology.

Part One Case Study:
Chrysler and GM: Can Information Technology Save the U.S. Auto Industry?

This case illustrates how two giant American corporations, Chrysler and General Motors, have tried to use information technology to combat foreign and domestic competitors. The case explores the relationship between each firm's management strategy, organizational characteristics, and information systems, posing the question: To what extent can information technology solve the problems confronting the U.S. automobile industry?

Chapter 1

The Challenge of Information Systems

From Teaspoons to Satellites

In 1984, two young women and a man sat on their living room floor, using teaspoons to fill jars and containers with skin care products. They were the founders of Nu Skin International, a producer of additive-free skin care products aimed at aging baby boomers. Initially Nu Skin's founders Blake Roney and Sandie Tillotson promoted Nu Skin products themselves. They sold their wares at malls and airports and to family and friends—wherever people congregated.

Demand for the product spread like wildfire. Ten years later, Nu Skin's revenues have soared to over $500 million. Roney and Tillotson preside over a vast network of Nu Skin distributors in Canada, Mexico, Hong Kong, Taiwan, Japan, Australia, and New Zealand. While one Nu Skin distributor hosts a live satellite broadcast to thousands of distributors all across North America, his Taiwanese counterpart can transmit an order via voice mail on high-speed links to Nu Skin's headquarters in Provo, Utah. New technologies and information systems have made that spectacular growth possible.

Without the cash or resources of giant cosmetics companies, Roney, Tillotson, and other co-founders decided that they could build their company through network marketing. Nu Skin created networks of distributors who would be responsible for promoting and selling Nu Skin products on a commission basis. Distributors in turn could create "downlines," or networks of distributors working under them. Some distributors have tens of thousands of people working under them on three continents.

To keep the distributors happy and the sales and distribution network humming, Nu Skin's managers believed that it was all-important to get distributors their commission checks on time. Nu

Skin built a seamless compensation system. No matter how many people or how many different countries were in a distributor's "downline" empire, Nu Skin paid the distributor once a month with one check. (Most other multi-level marketing companies write their distributors one check for each market.)

Nu Skin continually upgraded its information systems to make sure that it could handle its skyrocketing volume of sales transactions and commission checks as the company grew monthly at double-digit rates. Nu Skin upgraded its computer hardware and software multiple times. The company now runs a $3.5 million Sequoia mainframe computer that keeps records of every sales transaction for the past 14 months and calculates commissions for 250,000 active distributors. Each distributor is eligible for commissions on six levels of sales. The information system crunches the numbers and transmits the results

back to each Nu Skin market. It cuts checks in U.S. dollars, Australian dollars, yen, pesos—whatever the local currency is.

Nu Skin also developed an application that translates prompts on the computer screen into various foreign languages. If a distributor in Tokyo or Mexico City needs to check personal and group sales volumes, he or she simply calls the local office. An agent accesses the company's mainframe computer, pulls up a screen in the appropriate language, and relays the requested information directly back to the distributor. No translations are needed.

Nu Skin developed a Voice Information Program (VIP) to connect distributors to its downlines. A distributor can use telephone, voice mail, or fax for prospecting, recruiting, and keeping in touch with its downlines. A feature called Business Card lets a prospective distributor call an 800 number and listen

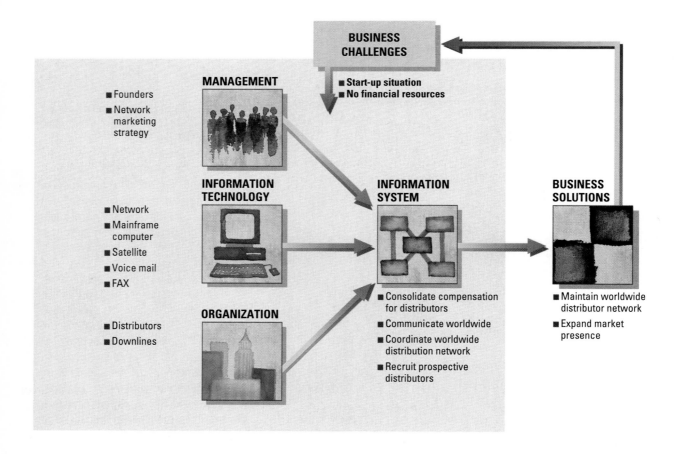

BUSINESS CHALLENGES
- Start-up situation
- No financial resources

MANAGEMENT
- Founders
- Network marketing strategy

INFORMATION TECHNOLOGY
- Network
- Mainframe computer
- Satellite
- Voice mail
- FAX

ORGANIZATION
- Distributors
- Downlines

INFORMATION SYSTEM
- Consolidate compensation for distributors
- Communicate worldwide
- Coordinate worldwide distribution network
- Recruit prospective distributors

BUSINESS SOLUTIONS
- Maintain worldwide distributor network
- Expand market presence

to a tape about Nu Skin business opportunities. The system captures the prospect's phone number so that the distributor can immediately make a follow-up call. Some distributors, such as Lien Yu Shing in Taiwan, use VIP every month to place their orders.

Within three years, Nu Skin plans to move into at least six to twelve new countries, with the main push in Europe. The technological infrastructure is in place. With its far-reaching information systems, Nu Skin can open a new market in 90 days—without a teaspoon in sight. ■

Source: Niklas von Daehne, "Techno-Boom," *Success*, December 1994.

Nu Skin's reliance on information systems to drive its basic operations demonstrates how information systems can help both small and large companies compete in today's global business environment. Information systems help firms like Nu Skin extend their reach to faraway locations, offer new products and services, reshape jobs and work flows, and perhaps profoundly change the way they conduct business. Information systems understanding is essential for today's managers.

Like Nu Skin, most organizations will need information systems to survive and prosper. This chapter starts our investigation of information systems and organizations by describing information systems from both technical and behavioral perspectives, surveying the role of information systems in the organization.

After completing this chapter, you will be able to:

Learning Objectives

1. Define an information system.
2. Explain the difference between computer literacy and information systems literacy.
3. Describe the information needs of different organizational levels.
4. Describe the role played by the six major types of information systems in organizations and the relationship between these systems.
5. Explain why information systems are so important today.
6. Identify the major management challenges to building and using information systems in organizations.

1.1   WHY INFORMATION SYSTEMS?

Until the 1980s, there was little need for this textbook or course. Managers generally did not need to know much about how information was collected, processed, and distributed in their organizations, and the technology involved was minimal. Information itself was not considered an important asset for the firm. The management process was considered a face-to-face, personal art and not a far-flung, global coordination process. But today few managers can afford to ignore how information is handled by their organization.

THE COMPETITIVE BUSINESS ENVIRONMENT

Three powerful worldwide changes have altered the environment of business. The first change is the emergence and strengthening of the global economy. The second change is the transformation of industrial economies and societies into knowledge- and information-based service economies. The third is the transformation of the business enterprise. These changes in the business environment and climate, summarized in Table 1.1, pose a number of new challenges to business firms and their management.

Emergence of the Global Economy

A growing percentage of the American economy—and other advanced industrial economies in Europe and Asia—depends on imports and exports. Foreign trade, both exports and imports, accounts for a little over 25 percent of the goods and services produced in the United States, and even more in countries like Japan and Germany.

| **Table 1.1** | **The Changing Contemporary Business Environment** |

Globalization

- Management and control in a global marketplace
- Competition in world markets
- Global work groups
- Global delivery systems

Transformation of Industrial Economies

- Knowledge- and information-based economies
- Productivity
- New products and services
- Leadership
- Time-based competition
- Shorter product life
- Turbulent environment
- Limited employee knowledge base

Transformation of the Enterprise

- Flattening
- Decentralization
- Flexibility
- Location independence
- Low transaction and coordination costs
- Empowerment
- Collaborative work and teamwork

This percentage will grow in the future. The success of firms today and in the future depends on their ability to operate globally.

Globalization of the world's industrial economies greatly enhances the value of information to the firm and offers new opportunities to businesses. Today, information systems provide the communication and analytic power that firms need for conducting trade and managing businesses on a global scale. To coordinate its worldwide network of distributors, companies like Nu Skin had to develop global information systems that can track orders, deliveries, and payments, communicate with distributors and suppliers, operate 24 hours a day in different national environments, and service local as well as international management reporting needs. In short, controlling the far-flung global corporation is a major business challenge that requires powerful information system responses.

Globalization and information technology also bring new threats to domestic business firms: Because of global communication and management systems, customers now can shop in a worldwide marketplace, obtaining price and quality information reliably, 24 hours a day. This phenomenon heightens competition and forces firms to play in open, unprotected worldwide markets. To become effective and profitable participants in international markets, firms need powerful information and communication systems.

Transformation of Industrial Economies

The United States, Japan, Germany, and other major industrial powers are experiencing a third economic revolution. In the first revolution, the United States had by 1890

FIGURE 1.1

The growth of the information economy. Since the turn of the century, the United States has experienced a steady decline in the number of farm workers and blue-collar workers who are employed in factories. At the same time, the country is experiencing a rise in the number of white-collar workers who produce economic value using knowledge and information.

Sources: Adapted from U.S. Department of Commerce, Bureau of the Census, Statistical Abstract of the United States, 1994, *Table 644 and* Historical Statistics of the United States, Colonial Times to 1970, *Vol. 1, Series D 182-232.*

transformed itself from a colonial backwater to an agrarian powerhouse capable of feeding large segments of the world population. In the second revolution, the United States had by 1920 transformed itself from an agrarian nineteenth-century society to a first-class industrial power. In the third revolution, now in progress, the country is transforming itself into a knowledge- and information-based service economy.

The knowledge and information revolution began at the turn of the twentieth century and has gradually accelerated. By 1976 the number of white-collar workers employed in offices surpassed the number of farm workers, service workers, and blue-collar workers employed in manufacturing. Today, most people no longer work in farms or factories but instead are found in sales, education, health care, banks, insurance firms, and law firms; they also provide business services like copying, computer software, or deliveries. These jobs primarily involve working with, distributing, or creating new knowledge and information. In fact, knowledge and information work now account for a significant 75 percent of the American gross national product, and nearly 70 percent of the labor force.

In a knowledge- and information-based economy, information technology and systems take on great importance. For instance, information technology constitutes more than 70 percent of the invested capital in service industries like finance, insurance, and real estate. This means that for many managers—perhaps for most—decisions about information technology will be the most common investment decisions.

Because the productivity of employees will depend on the quality of the systems serving them, management decisions about information technology are critically important to the prosperity and survival of a firm. Consider also that the growing power of information technology makes possible new services of great economic value. Credit cards, overnight package delivery, and worldwide reservation systems are examples of services that are based on new information technologies. Information and the technology that delivers it have become critical, strategic resources for business firms and their managers.

Transformation of the Business Enterprise

The third major change in the business environment is the very nature of organization and management. There has been a transformation in the possibilities for organizing and managing. Some firms have begun to take advantage of these new possibilities.

The purpose of a business firm is to show a profit by creating value through the production of services and products based on resources that cost less than the price of its services and products. The purpose of management is to plan, organize, coordinate, and lead the members of the firm in order to achieve profitable value creation. Information technology has transformed how the firm creates value and how managers manage (see Table 1.2).

The traditional business firm was—and still is—a hierarchical, centralized, structured arrangement of specialists that typically relies on a fixed set of standard operating procedures to deliver a mass produced product (or service). The new style of business firm is a flattened (less hierarchical), decentralized, flexible arrangement of generalists who rely on real time (nearly instant) information to deliver mass-customized products and services uniquely suited to specific markets or customers. This new style of organization is not yet firmly entrenched, it is still evolving. Nevertheless, the direction is clear. This new direction would be unthinkable without information technology.

The traditional management group relied—and still does—on formal plans, a rigid division of labor, formal rules, and appeals to loyalty to ensure the proper operation of a firm. The new manager relies on informal commitments and networks to establish goals (rather than formal planning), a flexible arrangement of teams and individuals working in task forces, a customer orientation to achieve coordination among employees, and appeals to professionalism and knowledge to ensure proper operation of the firm. Once again, information technology makes this style of management possible.

Table 1.2	How Information Technology Can Transform Organizations
Information Technology	**Organizational Change**
Global networks	International division of labor: the operations of a firm are no longer determined by location; the global reach of firms is extended; costs of global coordination decline. Transaction costs decline.
Enterprise networks	Collaborative work and teamwork: the organization of work can now be coordinated across divisional boundaries; a customer and product orientation emerges; widely dispersed task forces become the dominant work group. The costs of management (agency costs) decline. Business processes are changed.
Distributed computing	Empowerment: individuals and work groups now have the information and knowledge to act. Business processes are redesigned, streamlined. Management costs decline. Hierarchy and centralization decline.
Portable computing	Virtual organizations: work is no longer tied to geographic location. Knowledge and information can be delivered anywhere they are needed, anytime. Work becomes portable. Organizational costs decline as real estate is less essential for business.
Graphical user interfaces	Accessibility: everyone in the organization—even senior executives—can access information and knowledge; work flows can be automated, contributed to by all from remote locations. Organizational costs decline as work flows move from paper to digital image, documents, and voice.

Information technology is bringing about changes in organization that make the firm even more dependent than in the past on the knowledge, learning, and decision making of individual employees. Throughout the book, we describe the role that information technology is now playing in the transformation of the business enterprise form.

WHAT IS AN INFORMATION SYSTEM?

An **information system** can be defined technically as a set of interrelated components that collect (or retrieve), process, store, and distribute information to support decision making and control in an organization. In addition to supporting decision making, coordination, and control, information systems may also help managers and workers analyze problems, visualize complex subjects, and create new products.

Information systems contain information about significant people, places, and things within the organization or in the environment surrounding it (see Figure 1.2). By **information** we mean data that have been shaped into a form that is meaningful and useful to human beings. **Data**, in contrast, are streams of raw facts representing events occurring in organizations or the physical environment before they have been organized and arranged into a form that people can understand and use.

Three activities in an information system produce the information organizations need for making decisions, controlling operations, analyzing problems, and creating new products or services. These activities are input, processing, and output. **Input** captures or collects raw data from within the organization or from its external environment. **Processing** converts this raw input into a more meaningful form. **Output** transfers the processed information to the people or activities where it will be used. Information systems also require **feedback**, which is output that is returned to appropriate members of the organization to help them evaluate or correct the input stage. In the information system used by Nu Skin to calculate commissions for distributors, the raw input consists of data from each sales transaction of Nu Skin products. The central computer processes these data into paychecks for distributors and reports that become output. The system thus provides meaningful information such as the amount of sales for each product, distributor, region, and downline and the size of payments to distributors.

Our interest in this book is in formal, organizational computer-based information systems (CBIS) like those designed and used by Nu Skin. Formal systems rest on accepted and fixed definitions of data and procedures for collecting, storing, processing, disseminating, and using these data. The formal systems we describe in this text are structured, that is, they operate in conformity with predefined rules that are relatively fixed and not easily changed. For instance, Nu Skin's commission payment system requires that all sales transactions be identified with the name of the distributor responsible for the sale and the number of units and type of each Nu Skin product that was sold.

Informal information systems (such as office gossip networks) rely, by contrast, on implicit agreements and unstated rules of behavior. There is no agreement on what is information, or on how it will be stored and processed. They are essential for the life of an organization, but an analysis of their qualities is beyond the scope of this text.

Formal information systems can be either computer-based or manual. Manual systems use paper and pencil technology. These manual systems serve important needs, but they too are not the subject of this text. **Computer-based information systems (CBIS)**, in contrast, rely on computer hardware and software technology to process and disseminate information. From this point on, when we use the term *information systems* we will be referring to computer-based information systems—formal organizational systems that rely on computer technology. The Window on Technology describes some of the typical technologies used in computer-based information systems today.

---

information system Interrelated components working together to collect, process, store, and disseminate information to support decision making, coordination, control, analysis, and visualization in an organization.

information Data that have been shaped into a form that is meaningful and useful to human beings.

data Streams of raw facts representing events occurring in organizations or the physical environment before they have been organized and arranged into a form that people can understand and use.

input The capture or collection of raw data from within the organization or from its external environment for processing in an information system.

processing The conversion, manipulation, and analysis of raw input into a form that is more meaningful to humans.

output The distribution of processed information to the people or activities where it will be used.

feedback Output that is returned to the appropriate members of the organization to help them evaluate or correct input.

computer-based information systems (CBIS) Information systems that rely on computer hardware and software for processing and disseminating information.

FIGURE 1.2
Functions of an information system. An information system contains information about an organization and its surrounding environment. Three basic activities—input, processing, and output—produce the information organizations need. Feedback is output returned to appropriate people or activities in the organization to evaluate and refine the input.

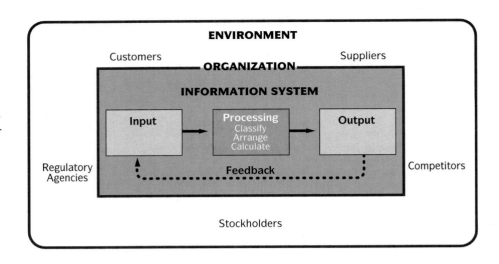

Although computer-based information systems use computer technology to process raw data into meaningful information, there is a sharp distinction between a computer and a computer program on the one hand, and an information system on the other. Electronic computers and related software programs are the technical foundation, the tools and materials, of modern information systems. Computers provide the equipment for storing and processing information. Computer programs, or software, are sets of operating instructions that direct and control computer processing. Knowing how computers and computer programs work is important in designing solutions to organizational problems, but computers are only part of an information system.

Housing provides an appropriate analogy. Houses are built with hammers, nails, and wood, but these do not make a house. The architecture, design, setting, landscaping, and all of the decisions that lead to the creation of these features are part of the house and are crucial for finding a solution to the problem of putting a roof over one's head. Computers and programs are the hammer, nails, and lumber of CBIS, but alone they cannot produce the information a particular organization needs. To understand information systems, one must understand the problems they are designed to solve, their architectural and design elements, and the organizational processes that lead to these solutions. Today's managers must combine computer literacy with information systems literacy.

A BUSINESS PERSPECTIVE ON INFORMATION SYSTEMS

From a business and management perspective, information systems are far more than just input-process-output machines operating in a vacuum. *From a business perspective, an information system is an organizational and management solution, based on information technology, to a challenge posed by the environment.* Examine this definition closely because it emphasizes the organizational and management nature of information systems: Information systems provide a major organizational solution to challenges and problems created in the business environment. To understand information systems—to be information systems literate as opposed to computer literate—a manager must understand the broader organization, management, and information technology dimensions of systems (see Figure 1.3) and their power to provide solutions to the business challenges described in this text.

Review the diagram at the beginning of the chapter, which reflects this expanded definition of an information system. The diagram shows how Nu Skin's information systems provide a solution to the business challenges posed by intense global competition and the company's limited resources. The diagram also illustrates how management, technology, and organization elements work together to create these systems.

UPS COMPETES GLOBALLY WITH INFORMATION TECHNOLOGY

United Parcel Service, the world's largest air and ground package distribution company, started out in 1907 in a closet-sized basement office. Jim Casey and Claude Ryan—two teenagers from Seattle with two bicycles and one phone—promised the "best service and lowest rates." UPS has used this formula successfully for nearly 90 years.

UPS still lives up to that promise today, delivering close to 3 billion parcels and documents each year to any address in the United States and to more than 185 countries and territories. The company not only excels at traditional package delivery but is competing against Federal Express in the overnight delivery business as well. Critical to the firm's success has been its investment in advanced information technology. Between 1992 and 1996, UPS expects to invest $1.8 billion in information technology that will keep it a worldwide market leader. Technology has helped UPS boost customer service while keeping costs low and streamlining its overall operations.

Using a hand-held computer called a Delivery Information Acquisition Device (DIAD), UPS drivers automatically capture cutomers' signatures along with pickup, delivery, and time-card information. The drivers then place the DIAD into their truck's vehicle adapter, an information transmitting device that is connected to the cellular telephone network. Package tracking information is then transmitted to UPS's computer network for storage and processing in UPS's main computer in Mahwah, New Jersey. From there, the information can be accessed worldwide to provide proof of delivery to the customer. The system can also generate a printed response to queries for the customer.

Through TotalTrack, its automated package-tracking system, UPS can monitor packages throughout the delivery process. At various points along the route from sender to receiver, a bar code device scans shipping information on the package label; the information is then fed into the central computer. Customer service representatives can check the status of any package from desktop computers linked to the central computer and are able to respond immediately to inquiries from customers. UPS customers can also access this information directly from their own microcomputers, using special package tracking software supplied by UPS.

UPS's Inventory Express, launched in 1991, warehouses customers' prod-

> *To Think About:* What are the inputs, processing, and outputs of UPS's package tracking system? What technologies are used? How are these technologies related to UPS's business strategy? What would happen if these technologies were not available?

ucts and ships them overnight to any destination the customer requests. Customers using this service can transmit electronic shipping orders to UPS by 1:00 A.M. and expect delivery by 10:30 that same morning.

In 1988, UPS moved aggressively into overseas markets and set up its own global communications network, UPSnet, as the information processing pipeline for worldwide operations. UPSnet extends the system's capabilities internationally by providing access to information for billing and delivery confirmation, tracking international shipments, and expediting customs clearance. UPS uses its network to transmit documentation electronically on each shipment directly to customs officials prior to the arrival of shipments. The customs officials clear the shipment or flag it for inspection.

UPS is enhancing its information system capabilities so that it can guarantee that a particular package or group of packages will arrive at its destination at a specified time. If requested by the customer, UPS will be able to intercept a package prior to delivery and have it returned or rerouted. Eventually UPS may even use its systems to transmit electronic messages directly between customers.

Sources: Jeff Moad, "Can High Performace Be Cloned? Should It Be?" *Datamation,* March 1, 1995; Linda Wilson, "Stand and Deliver," *InformationWEEK,* November 23, 1992; and UPS Public Relations, "High Tech Advances Lead UPS into the Paperless Age," April 1992.

PPING & RECEIVING

United Parcel

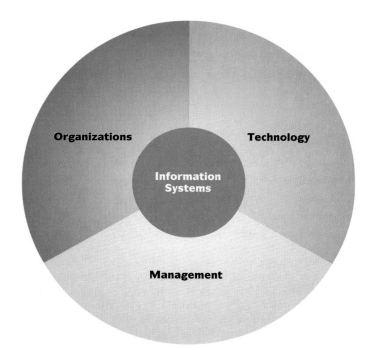

FIGURE 1.3
Information systems are more than computers. Using information systems effectively requires an understanding of the organization, management, and information technology shaping the systems. All information systems can be described as organizational and management solutions to challenges posed by the environment.

We begin each chapter of the text with a diagram like this one to help you analyze the opening case. You can use this diagram as a starting point for analyzing any information system or information system problem you encounter.

To design and use information systems effectively, you must first understand the environment, structure, function, and politics of organizations, as well as the role of management and management decision making. Then you must examine the capabilities and opportunities provided by contemporary information technology to provide solutions. This text is organized to fulfill this plan.

Organizations

Information systems are a part of organizations. Indeed, for some companies, such as credit reporting firms, without the system there would be no business. The key elements of an organization are its people, structure and operating procedures, politics, and culture. We introduce these components of organizations here and describe them in greater detail in Chapter 3. Formal organizations are composed of different levels and specialties. Their structures reveal a clear-cut division of labor. Experts are employed and trained for different functions, including sales and marketing, manufacturing, finance, accounting, and human resources. Table 1.3 describes these functions.

An organization coordinates work through a structured hierarchy and formal, standard operating procedures. The hierarchy arranges people in a pyramidal structure of rising authority and responsibility. The upper levels of the hierarchy consist of managerial, professional, and technical employees, while the lower levels consist of operational personnel.

Standard operating procedures (SOPs) are formal rules for accomplishing tasks that have been developed over a long time; these rules guide employees in a variety of procedures, from writing an invoice to responding to complaining customers. Most procedures are formalized and written down, but many others are informal work practices. Many of a firm's SOPs are incorporated into information systems—such as how to pay a supplier or how to correct an erroneous bill.

Organizations require many different kinds of skills and people. In addition to managers, **knowledge workers** (such as engineers, architects, or scientists) design products or services, and **data workers** (such as secretaries, bookkeepers, or clerks)

standard operating procedures (SOPs) Formal rules for accomplishing tasks that have been developed to cope with expected situations.

knowledge workers People such as engineers or architects who design products or services and create knowledge for the organization.

data workers People such as secretaries or bookkeepers who process the organization's paperwork.

Table 1.3	Major Organizational Functions
Function	Purpose
Sales and marketing	Selling the organization's products and services
Manufacturing	Producing products and services
Finance	Managing the organization's financial assets (cash, stocks, bonds, etc.)
Accounting	Maintaining the organization's financial records (receipts, disbursements, paychecks, etc.); accounting for the flow of funds
Human resources	Attracting, developing, and maintaining the organization's labor force; maintaining employee records

production or **service workers** People who actually produce the products or services of the organization.

process the organization's paperwork. **Production** or **service workers** (such as machinists, assemblers, or packers) actually produce the products or services of the organization.

Each organization has a unique culture, or fundamental set of assumptions, values, and ways of doing things, that has been accepted by most of its members. Parts of an organization's culture can always be found embedded in its information systems. For instance, the concern with putting service to the customer first is an aspect of the organizational culture of United Parcel Service that can be found in the company's package tracking systems.

Different levels and specialties in an organization create different interests and points of view. These views often conflict. Conflict is the basis for organizational politics. Information systems come out of this cauldron of differing perspectives, conflicts, compromises, and agreements that are a natural part of all organizations. In Chapter 3 we will examine these features of organizations in greater detail.

Management

Managers perceive business challenges in the environment; they set the organizational strategy for responding, and they allocate the human and financial resources to achieve the strategy and coordinate the work. Throughout, they must exercise responsible leadership. The business information systems described in this book reflect the hopes, dreams, and realities of real-world managers. These are managers' conventional responsibilities.

But less understood is the fact that managers must do more than manage what already exists. They must also create new products, services, and even re-create the organization from time to time. A substantial part of management is creative work driven by new knowledge and information. Information technology can play a powerful role in redirecting and redesigning the organization.

senior managers People occupying the topmost hierarchy in an organization who are responsible for making long-range decisions.

middle managers People in the middle of the organizational hierarchy who are responsible for carrying out the plans and goals of senior management.

operational managers People who monitor the day-to-day activities of the organization.

Chapter 4 describes the activities of managers and management decision making in detail. It is important to note that managerial roles and decisions vary at different levels of the organization. **Senior managers** make long-range strategic decisions about products and services to produce. **Middle managers** carry out the programs and plans of senior management. **Operational managers** are responsible for monitoring the firm's daily activities. All levels of management are expected to be creative: to develop novel solutions to a broad range of problems. Each level of management has different information needs and information system requirements.

Technology

Information systems technology is one of many tools available to managers for coping with change. More important today, information technology is the glue that

computer hardware Physical equipment used for input, processing, and output activities in an information system.

computer software Detailed, preprogrammed instructions that control and coordinate the work of computer hardware components in an information system.

storage technology Physical media and software governing the storage and organization of data for use in an information system.

telecommunications technology Physical devices and software that link various computer hardware components and transfer data from one physical location to another.

holds the organization together. It is the instrument through which management controls and creates, and it is an arrow in the manager's quiver. CBIS utilize computer hardware, software, storage, and telecommunications technologies.

Computer hardware is the physical equipment used for input, processing, and output activities in an information system. It consists of the following: the computer processing unit; various input, output, and storage devices; and physical media to link these devices together. Chapter 6 describes computer hardware in greater detail.

Computer software consists of the detailed preprogrammed instructions that control and coordinate the computer hardware components in an information system. Chapter 7 explains the importance of computer software in information systems.

Storage technology includes both the physical media for storing data, such as magnetic or optical disk or tape, and the software governing the organization of data on these physical media. More detail on physical storage media can be found in Chapter 6, whereas Chapter 8 treats data organization and access methods.

Telecommunications technology, consisting of both physical devices and software, links the various pieces of hardware and transfers data from one physical location to another. Chapter 9 covers telecommunications technology and issues.

Returning to UPS's package tracking system in the Window on Technology, let us identify the organization, management, and technology elements. The organization element anchors the package tracking system in UPS's sales and production functions (the main product of UPS is a service—package delivery). It identifies the required procedures for identifying packages with both sender and recipient information, taking inventory, tracking the packages en route, and providing package status reports for UPS customers and customer service representatives. The system must also provide information to satisfy the needs of managers and workers. UPS drivers need to be trained in both package pickup and delivery procedures and in how to use the package tracking system so that they can work more efficiently and effectively. UPS's management is responsible for monitoring service levels and costs and for promoting the company's strategy combining low cost and superior service. Management decided to use automation to increase the ease of sending a package via UPS and of checking its delivery status, thereby reducing delivery costs and increasing sales revenues. The technology supporting this system consists of hand-held computers, bar code scanners, wired and wireless telecommunications networks, desktop computers, UPS's central computer, and storage technology for the package delivery data. The result is an information system solution to a business challenge.

1.2 CONTEMPORARY APPROACHES TO INFORMATION SYSTEMS

Multiple perspectives on information systems show that the study of information systems is a multidisciplinary field; no single theory or perspective dominates. Figure 1.4 illustrates the major disciplines that contribute problems, issues, and solutions in the study of information systems. In general, the field can be divided into technical and behavioral approaches. Information systems are sociotechnical systems. Though they are composed of machines, devices, and "hard" physical technology, they require substantial social, organizational, and intellectual investments to make them work properly.

TECHNICAL APPROACH

The technical approach to information systems emphasizes mathematically based, normative models to study information systems, as well as the physical technology and formal capabilities of these systems. The disciplines that contribute to the technical approach are computer science, management science, and operations research. Computer science is concerned with establishing theories of computability, methods of computation, and methods of efficient data storage and access. Management science emphasizes the development of models for decision making and management practices. Operations

FIGURE 1.4
Contemporary approaches to information systems. The study of information systems deals with issues and insights contributed from technical and behavioral disciplines.

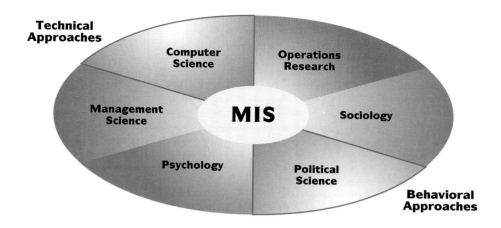

research focuses on mathematical techniques for optimizing selected parameters of organizations such as transportation, inventory control, and transaction costs.

BEHAVIORAL APPROACH

A growing part of the information systems field is concerned with behavioral problems and issues. Many behavioral problems, such as system utilization, implementation, and creative design, cannot be expressed with the normative models used in the technical approach. Other behavioral disciplines also play a role. Sociologists focus on the impact of information systems on groups, organizations, and society. Political science investigates the political impacts and uses of information systems. Psychology is concerned with individual responses to information systems and cognitive models of human reasoning.

The behavioral approach does not ignore technology. Indeed, information systems technology is often the stimulus for a behavioral problem or issue. But the focus of this approach is generally not on technical solutions; it concentrates rather on changes in attitudes, management and organizational policy, and behavior (Kling and Dutton, 1982).

APPROACH OF THIS TEXT: SOCIOTECHNICAL SYSTEMS

The study of management information systems (MIS) arose in the 1960s to focus on computer-based information systems aimed at managers (Davis and Olson, 1985). MIS combines the theoretical work of computer science, management science, and operations research with a practical orientation toward building systems and applications. It also pays attention to behavioral issues.

Our experience as academics and practitioners leads us to believe that no single perspective effectively captures the reality of information systems. Problems with systems—and their solutions—are rarely all technical or all behavioral. Our best advice to students is to understand the perspectives of all disciplines. Indeed, the challenge and excitement of the information systems field is that it requires an appreciation and tolerance of many different approaches.

A sociotechnical systems perspective helps to avoid a purely technological approach to information systems. For instance, the fact that information technology is rapidly declining in cost and growing in power does not necessarily or easily translate into productivity enhancement or bottom-line profits.

In this book, we stress the need to optimize the performance of the system as a whole. Both the technical and behavioral components need attention. This means that technology must be changed and designed in such a way as to fit organizational and individual needs. At times, the technology may have to be "de-optimized" to accomplish this fit. Organizations and individuals must also be changed through training,

FIGURE 1.5
A sociotechnical perspective on information systems. In a sociotechnical perspective, the performance of a system is optimized when both the technology and the organization mutually adjust to one another until a satisfactory fit is obtained.
Source: Tornatsky et al., 1983.

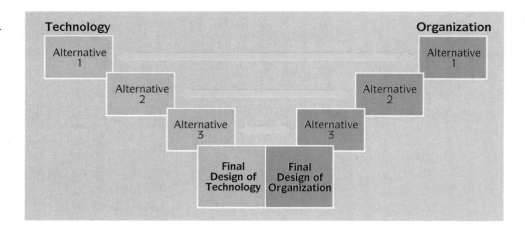

learning, and planned organizational change in order to allow the technology to operate and prosper (see, for example Liker et al., 1987). Figure 1.5 illustrates this process of mutual adjustment in a sociotechnical system.

1.3   KEY SYSTEM APPLICATIONS IN THE ORGANIZATION

Because there are different interests, specialties, and levels in an organization, there are different kinds of systems. No single system can provide all the information an organization needs. Figure 1.6 illustrates one way to depict the kinds of systems found in an organization. In the illustration, the organization is divided into strategic, management, knowledge, and operational levels and then is further divided into functional areas such as sales and marketing, manufacturing, finance, accounting, and human resources. Systems are built to serve these different organizational interests (Anthony, 1965).

DIFFERENT KINDS OF SYSTEMS

There are four main types of information systems serving different organizational levels: operational-level systems, knowledge-level systems, management-level systems, and strategic-level systems. **Operational-level systems** support operational managers by keeping track of the elementary activities and transactions of the organization, such as sales, receipts, cash deposits, payroll, credit decisions, and the flow of materials in a factory. The principal purpose of systems at this level is to answer routine questions and to track the flow of transactions through the organization. How many parts are in inventory? What happened to Mr. Williams' payment? What is the size of the payroll this month? To answer these kinds of questions, information generally must be easily available, current, and accurate. Examples of operational-level systems include a system to record bank deposits from automatic teller machines or one that tracks the number of hours worked each day by employees on a factory floor.

Knowledge-level systems support knowledge and data workers in an organization. The purpose of knowledge-level systems is to help the business firm integrate new knowledge into the business and to help the organization control the flow of paperwork. Knowledge-level systems, especially in the form of workstations and office systems, are the fastest-growing applications in business today.

Management-level systems are designed to serve the monitoring, controlling, decision-making, and administrative activities of middle managers. The principal question addressed by such systems is: Are things working well? These systems compare the current day's output with that of a month or a year ago. Management-level systems typically provide periodic reports rather than instant information on opera-

operational-level systems
Information systems that monitor the elementary activities and transactions of the organization.

knowledge-level systems
Information systems that support knowledge and data workers in an organization.

management-level systems
Information systems that support the monitoring, controlling, decision-making, and administrative activities of middle managers.

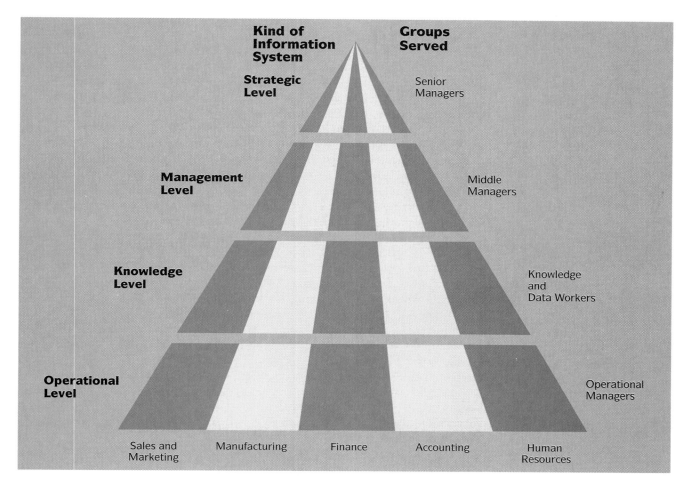

Kind of Information System

Groups Served

Strategic Level — Senior Managers

Management Level — Middle Managers

Knowledge Level — Knowledge and Data Workers

Operational Level — Operational Managers

Sales and Marketing Manufacturing Finance Accounting Human Resources

FIGURE 1.6
Types of information systems. Organizations and information systems can be divided into strategic, management, knowledge, and operational levels. They can be divided further into five functional areas: sales and marketing, manufacturing, finance, accounting, and human resources. Information systems serve each of these levels and functions. Strategic-level systems help senior managers with long-term planning. Management-level systems help middle managers monitor and control. Knowledge-level systems help knowledge and data workers design products, distribute information, and cope with paperwork. Operational-level systems help operational managers keep track of the firm's day-to-day activities.

tions. There is less need for instant information, but periodic reports are still required. An example is a relocation control system that reports on the total moving, house-hunting, and home financing costs for employees in all company divisions, noting wherever actual costs exceed budgets.

Some management-level systems support nonroutine decision making (Keen and Morton, 1978). They tend to focus on less structured decisions for which information requirements are not always clear. These systems often answer "what if" questions: What would be the impact on production schedules if we were to double sales in the month of December? What would happen to our return on investment if a factory schedule were delayed for six months? Answers to these questions frequently require new data from outside the organization, as well as data from inside that cannot be drawn from existing operational-level systems.

strategic-level systems
Information systems that support the long-range planning activities of senior management.

Strategic-level systems help senior management tackle and address strategic issues and long-term trends, both in the firm and in the external environment. Their principal concern is matching changes in the external environment with existing organizational capability. What will employment levels be in five years? What are the long-term industry cost trends, and where does our firm fit in? What products should we be making in five years?

Information systems may also be differentiated by functional specialty. Major organizational functions, such as sales and marketing, manufacturing, finance, accounting, and human resources, are each served by their own information systems. In large organizations, subfunctions of each of these major functions also have their own information systems. For example, the manufacturing function might have systems for inventory management, process control, plant maintenance, computer-aided engineering, and material requirements planning.

A typical organization has operational-, management-, knowledge-, and strategic-level systems for each functional area. For example, the sales function generally has a sales system on the operational level to record daily sales figures and to process orders. A knowledge-level system designs promotional displays for the firm's products. A management-level system tracks monthly sales figures by sales territory and reports on territories where sales exceed or fall below anticipated levels. A system to forecast sales trends over a five-year period serves the strategic level.

Finally, different organizations have different information systems for the same functional areas. Because no two organizations have exactly the same objectives, structures, or interests, information systems must be custom-made to fit the unique characteristics of each. There is no such thing as a universal information system that can fit all organizations, even in such standard areas as payroll or accounts receivable. Every organization does the job somewhat differently.

Information systems can thus be classified by functional specialty or by the organizational level they serve. Throughout this text are examples of systems supporting the various functional areas—sales systems, manufacturing systems, human resources systems, finance and accounting systems. For professors and students requiring deeper analysis of information systems from a functional perspective, we have included additional material in Appendix A. This chapter analyzes the key applications of the organization primarily in terms of the organizational level and types of decisions they support.

SIX MAJOR TYPES OF SYSTEMS

In this section we describe the specific categories of systems serving each organizational level and their value to the organization. Figure 1.7 shows the specific types of information systems that correspond to each organizational level. The organization has executive support systems (ESS) at the strategic level; management information systems (MIS) and decision-support systems (DSS) at the management level; knowledge work systems (KWS) and office automation systems (OAS) at the knowledge level; and transaction processing systems (TPS) at the operational level. Systems at each level in turn are specialized to serve each of the major functional areas. Thus, the typical systems found in organizations are designed to assist workers or managers at each level and in the functions of sales and marketing, manufacturing, finance, accounting, and human resources.

Table 1.4 summarizes the features of the six types of information systems. It should be noted that each of the different kinds of systems may have components that are used by organizational levels and groups other than their main constituencies. A secretary may find information on an MIS, or a middle manager may need to extract data from a TPS.

Transaction Processing Systems

transaction processing systems (TPS) Computerized systems that perform and record the daily routine transactions necessary to conduct the business; they serve the operational level of the organization.

Transaction processing systems (TPS) are the basic business systems that serve the operational level of the organization. A transaction processing system is a computerized system that performs and records the daily routine transactions necessary to the conduct of the business. Examples are sales order entry, hotel reservation systems, client information (for public agencies), payroll, employee recordkeeping, and shipping.

At the operational level, tasks, resources, and goals are predefined and highly structured. The decision to grant credit to a customer, for instance, is made by a lower-level

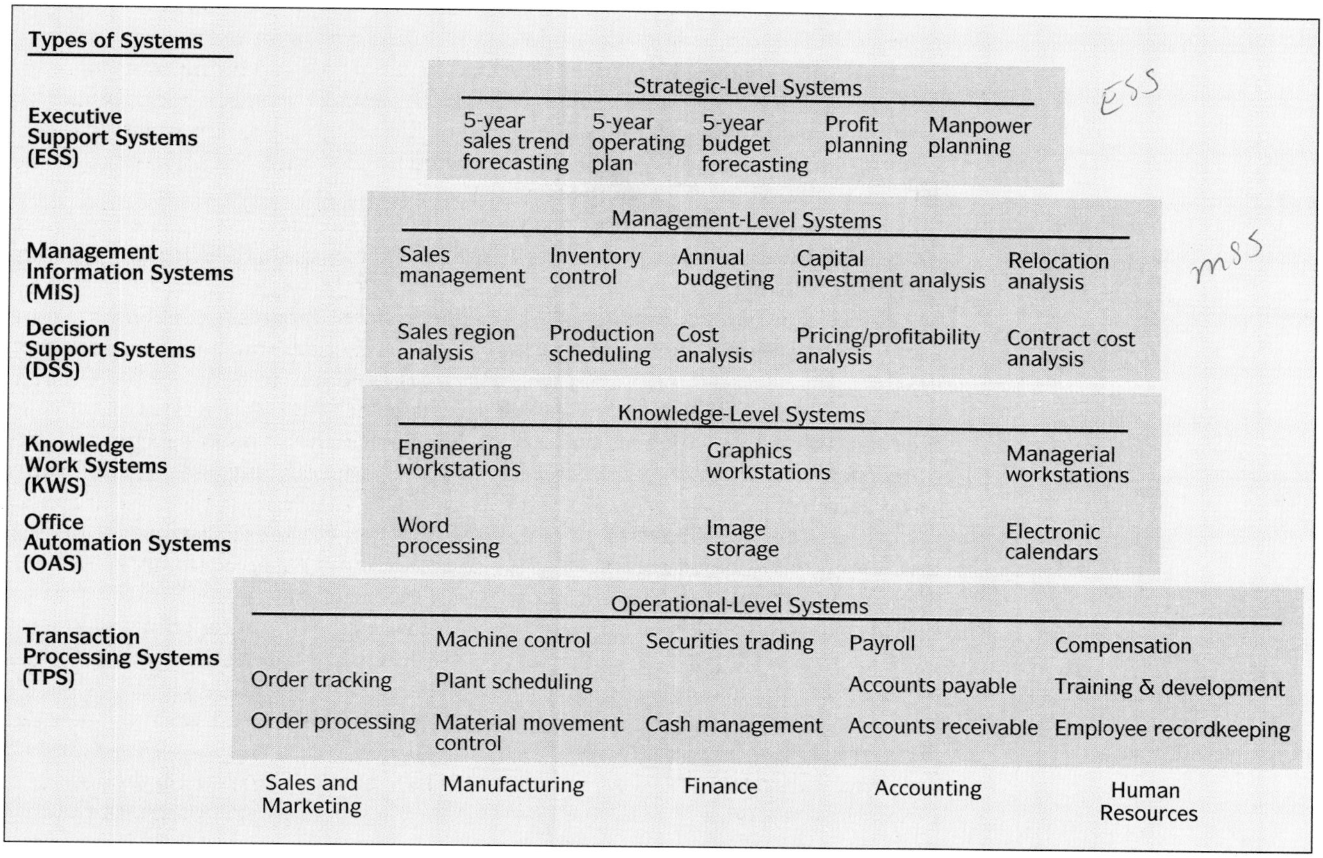

Types of Systems

Strategic-Level Systems — *ESS*

| Executive Support Systems (ESS) | 5-year sales trend forecasting | 5-year operating plan | 5-year budget forecasting | Profit planning | Manpower planning |

Management-Level Systems — *mss*

| Management Information Systems (MIS) | Sales management | Inventory control | Annual budgeting | Capital investment analysis | Relocation analysis |
| Decision Support Systems (DSS) | Sales region analysis | Production scheduling | Cost analysis | Pricing/profitability analysis | Contract cost analysis |

Knowledge-Level Systems

| Knowledge Work Systems (KWS) | Engineering workstations | Graphics workstations | Managerial workstations |
| Office Automation Systems (OAS) | Word processing | Image storage | Electronic calendars |

Operational-Level Systems

Transaction Processing Systems (TPS)		Machine control	Securities trading	Payroll	Compensation
	Order tracking	Plant scheduling		Accounts payable	Training & development
	Order processing	Material movement control	Cash management	Accounts receivable	Employee recordkeeping
	Sales and Marketing	Manufacturing	Finance	Accounting	Human Resources

FIGURE 1.7

The six major types of information systems needed for the four levels of an organization. Information systems are built to serve each of the four levels of an organization. Transaction processing systems (TPS) serve the operational level of an organization. Knowledge work systems (KWS) and office automation systems (OAS) serve the knowledge level of an organization. Decision-support systems (DSS) and management information systems (MIS) serve the management level of the organization. Executive support systems (ESS) serve the strategic level of an organization.

Table 1.4 Characteristics of Information Processing Systems

Type of System	Information Inputs	Processing	Information Outputs	Users
ESS	Aggregate data; external, internal	Graphics; simulations; interactive	Projections; responses to queries	Senior managers
DSS	Low-volume data; analytic models	Interactive; simulations, analysis	Special reports; decision analyses; responses to queries	Professionals; staff managers
MIS	Summary transaction data; high-volume data; simple models	Routine reports; simple models; low-level analysis	Summary and exception reports	Middle managers
KWS	Design specifications; knowledge base	Modeling; simulations	Models; graphics	Professionals; technical staff
OAS	Documents; schedules	Document; management; scheduling; communication	Documents; schedules; mail	Clerical workers
TPS	Transactions; events	Sorting; listing; merging; updating	Detailed reports; lists; summaries	Operations personnel; supervisors

supervisor according to predefined criteria. The decision, in that sense, has been "programmed." All that must be determined is whether the customer meets the criteria.

Figure 1.8 depicts a payroll TPS, which is a typical accounting transaction processing system found in most firms. A payroll system keeps track of the money paid to employees. The master file is composed of discrete pieces of information (such as a name, address, or employee number) called data elements. Data are keyed into the system, updating the data elements. The elements on the master file are combined in different ways to make up reports of interest to management and government agencies and paychecks sent to employees. These TPS can generate other report combinations of existing data elements.

Other typical TPS appplications are identified in Figure 1.9. The figure shows that there are five functional categories of TPS : sales/marketing, manufacturing/production, finance/accounting, human resources, and other types of TPS that are unique to a particular industry. The UPS package tracking system is an example of a manufacturing TPS. UPS sells package delivery services; the system keeps track of all of its package shipment transactions. Nu Skin's compensation system is an example of an accounting TPS.

All organizations have these five kinds of TPS (even if the systems are manual). It is difficult to imagine a modern organization without a transaction processing system. These systems are often so central to a business that in the 1960s it was estimated that organizations might survive for only a day without functioning computer systems. In the 1990s, TPS failure for a few hours can spell the demise of a firm and perhaps other firms linked to it. Imagine what would happen to UPS if its package tracking system were not working! What would the airlines do without their computerized reservation systems?

Two features of TPS are noteworthy. First, many TPS span the boundary between the organization and its environment. They connect customers to the firm's

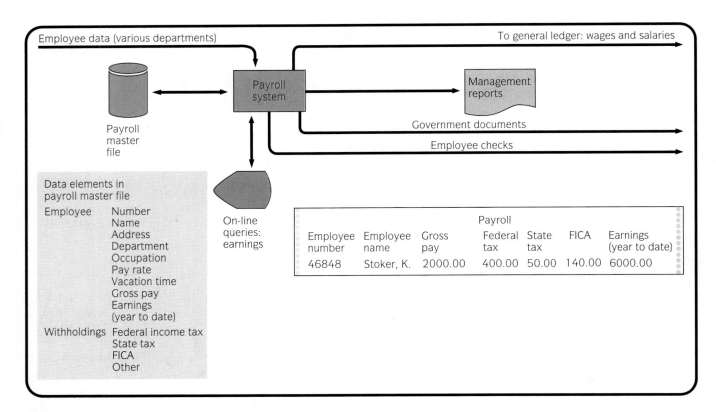

FIGURE 1.8
A symbolic representation for a payroll system TPS.

	Type of TPS System				
	Sales/ marketing systems	Manufacturing/ production systems	Finance/ accounting systems	Human resources systems	Other types (e.g., university)
Major functions of system	Sales management	Scheduling	Budgeting	Personnel records	Admissions
	Market research	Purchasing	General ledger	Benefits	Grade records
	Promotion	Shipping/receiving	Billing	Compensation	Course records
	Pricing	Engineering	Cost accounting	Labor relations	Alumni
	New products	Operations		Training	
Major application systems	Sales order information system	Materials resource planning systems	General ledger	Payroll	Registration system
	Market research system	Purchase order control systems	Accounts receivable/payable	Employee records	Student transcript system
	Pricing system	Engineering systems	Budgeting	Benefit systems	Curriculum class control systems
		Quality control systems	Funds management systems	Career path systems	Alumni benefactor system
				Personnel planning systems	

FIGURE 1.9

Typical applications of TPS. There are five functional categories of TPS: sales/marketing, manufacturing/production, finance/accounting, human resources, and other types of systems specific to a particular industry. TPS support most business functions in most organizations. Within each of these major functions are subfunctions. For each of these subfunctions (e.g., sales management) there is a major application system.

warehouse, factory, and management. If TPS do not work well, the organization fails either to receive inputs from the environment (orders) or to deliver outputs (assembled goods). Second, TPS are major producers of information for the other types of systems. (For example, the payroll system illustrated here along with other accounting TPS supplies data to the company's General Ledger System, which is responsible for maintaining records of the firm's income and expenses and for producing reports such as income statements and balance sheets.) Because TPS track relations with the environment, they are the only place where managers can obtain both up-to-the-minute assessments of organizational performance and long-term records of past performance. (See the discussion of MIS below.) TPS can be viewed as "organizational message processing systems" (Huber, 1984), informing managers about the status of internal operations and about the firm's relations with the external environment, and supporting other information systems that facilitate management decision making (Culnan, 1989).

Knowledge Work and Office Automation Systems

Knowledge work systems (KWS) and **office automation systems (OAS)** serve the information needs at the knowledge level of the organization. Knowledge work systems aid knowledge workers, whereas office automation systems primarily aid data workers (although they are also used extensively by knowledge workers).

In general, *knowledge workers* are people who hold formal university degrees and who are often members of a recognized profession, like engineers, doctors, lawyers, and scientists. Their jobs consist primarily of creating new information and knowledge. Knowledge work systems, such as scientific or engineering design workstations, promote the creation of new knowledge and ensure that new knowledge and technical expertise are properly integrated into the business. One example of a

knowledge work systems (KWS) Information systems that aid knowledge workers in the creation and integration of new knowledge in the organization.

office automation systems (OAS) Computer systems, such as word processing, electronic mail systems, and scheduling systems, that are designed to increase the productivity of data workers in the office.

KWS is the computer-aided-design system used by Odense Shipyards described in the Window on Management.

Data workers typically have less formal, advanced educational degrees and tend to process rather than create information. They consist primarily of secretaries, accountants, filing clerks, or managers whose jobs are principally to use, manipulate, or disseminate information. Office automation systems are information technology applications designed to increase the productivity of data workers in the office by supporting the coordinating and communicating activities of the typical office. Office automation systems coordinate diverse information workers, geographic units, and functional areas: The systems communicate with customers, suppliers, and other organizations outside the firm, and serve as a clearinghouse for information and knowledge flows.

Typical office automation systems handle and manage documents (through word processing, desktop publishing, and digital filing), scheduling (through electronic calendars), and communication (through electronic mail, voice mail, or videoconferencing). **Word processing** refers to the software and hardware that creates, edits, formats, stores, and prints documents (see Chapters 7 and 15). Word processing systems represent the single most common application of information technology to office work, in part because producing documents is what offices are all about. **Desktop publishing** produces professional publishing–quality documents by combining output from word processing software with design elements, graphics, and special layout features.

Knowledge workers, who create and produce knowledge, have traditionally utilized office automation technology as well. Now, however, they also have new technologies available to support their role in the firm. Powerful desktop computers called **workstations** with graphic, analytic, document management, and communications capabilities can pool together information from diverse perspectives and sources both inside and outside the firm. In the engineering field, knowledge work systems might use such tools to run thousands of calculations before designers are satisfied that a specific part is safe. Designers and drafting experts such as those at Odense Shipyards might want to use workstations with 3-D graphics software to vi-

word processing Office automation technology that facilitates the creation of documents through computerized text editing, formatting, storing, and printing.

desktop publishing Technology that produces professional-quality documents combining output from word processors with design, graphics, and special layout features.

workstations Powerful desktop computers that combine high-quality graphics, analytical capabilities, document management, and communications capabilities. Generally used in engineering and design applications.

Automobile manufacturers can use software to simulate an assembly line to make sure that welding robots can maneuver. Computer-aided design (CAD) systems eliminate many manual steps in design and production by performing much of the design work on the computer.

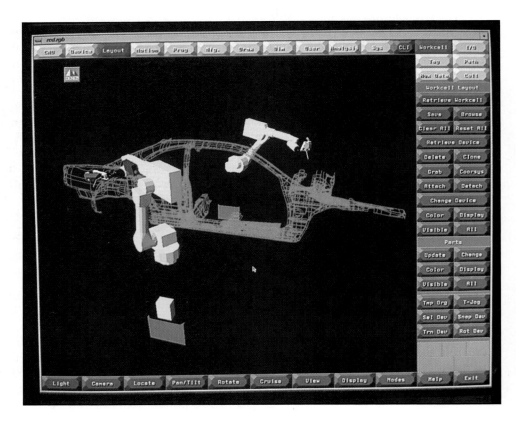

ODENSE SHIPYARDS SPEEDS UP PRODUCT DESIGN

Odense Steel Shipyards in Denmark is not one of the world's larger shipyards, but it specializes in building the world's biggest ships. Since its founding in 1917 Odense has been a subsidiary of the A. P. Moeller Group, a $12 billion holding company that includes cargo shipping, oil, and gas businesses and a supermarket chain. After the mid-1970s, competition in the shipbuilding industry reached new heights. The oil crisis created gross overcapacity in the oil tanker industry and Japanese and South Korean shipbuilders made a concerted push to become global leaders. These companies had a huge advantage over Odense because their labor costs were much lower and shipbuilding is a highly labor-intensive industry. Other companies from Italy and East Germany tried to keep competitive by having their governments subsidize their shipbuilding industries.

By 1979 Odense had laid off all but 800 of its 6000 workers. It decided to make a comeback by becoming a leader in building double-hulled oil tankers that would be more resistant to oil spills in collisions and in building giant ships holding metal cargo containers. To keep costs low and competitive, Odense turned to information systems.

Today, only 15 people run its main steel-construction facility, a gigantic shed the size of 12 football fields. A less automated facility would require 300 people to do the same job. Most of the work on the steel parts is performed by computer-controlled machines. Metal arms slice prepro-

grammed curves into the steel. Eighty-foot-wide radio-programmed lifters swoop down from ceilings to grab lawn-size plates and position them between machines. Dozens of robots the size of trash cans move across the plates, performing some 150 miles of welds for each ship. Workstations throughout the facility display windows showing the progress of jobs.

The data driving all of this automation come from computer-aided design models. Odense does all of its design work on 150 Data General workstations. Computer-aided design (CAD) eliminates much of the manual drafting and building of physical prototypes that used to slow down the design process by performing much of the design work on the computer. Before CAD, Odense designers used to spend six months building a one-fifteenth scale model of the pumping arrangement in the engine room and surrounding maze of pipes to make sure everything was connected properly and fit the space. Now, a designer merely needs to indicate two endpoints and the function of the pipe, and the CAD system picks out the appropriate type of pipe and lays a path for it—all on the computer. The process takes one-sixth the time of building a physical model. The prototyped designs can automatically feed the design specifications to Odense's computerized manufacturing systems. According to Odense CEO Kurt Andersen, Odense can now generate six different designs that meet the speed and size requirements of the customer and select the one that is the most efficient and durable.

The CAD software is tied into software that assists with inventory and labor logistics. When the CAD model for a ship is complete, the sys-

To Think About: What are the management benefits of such systems? How did implementing a computer-aided design system change the way Odense Shipyards conducted its business?

tem generates a complete list of the 400,000 parts needed, ranging from steel plates to butterfly valves. The system breaks down the list according to supplier and required delivery date and monitors shipment schedules. When part items arrive, they are logged in and taken straight to the building site; only the smallest and largest-quantity items, such as rivets, are kept in inventory. The system helps Odense schedule parts deliveries for the precise date when they will be used. It also helps Odense schedule its labor force, listing every manual task required by a new ship with an estimate of how much time each task will take. Odense can move several hundred people from one task to another with a precise estimate of costs. The company would like to further leverage its information system technology by putting more automation into finished ships. It's aiming for ships that steer and maintain themselves.

Source: David Freedman, "Bits to Ships," *Forbes ASAP,* December 5, 1994.

sualize a model of a product more fully (see the Window on Management). Lawyers, in turn, may want to scan thousands of legal findings on their desktop before recommending a strategy. More details on these powerful desktop tools can be found in Chapter 15.

The role of knowledge work and office automation systems in the firm cannot be underestimated. As the economy shifts from relying on manufactured goods to producing services, knowledge, and information, the productivity of individual firms and the entire economy will increasingly depend on knowledge-level systems. This is one reason knowledge-level systems have been the fastest-growing applications over the last decade and are likely to grow in the future. Knowledge-level systems also have become tied in more closely with the other systems in the firm.

Management Information Systems

management information systems (MIS) Information systems at the management level of an organization that serve the functions of planning, controlling, and decision making by providing routine summary and exception reports.

Management information systems (MIS) serve the management level of the organization, providing managers with reports and, in some cases, with on-line access to the organization's current performance and historical records. Typically, they are oriented almost exclusively to internal, not environmental or external, events. MIS primarily serve the functions of planning, controlling, and decision making at the management level. Generally, they are dependent on underlying transaction processing systems for their data (see the Window on Organizations).

MIS summarize and report on the basic operations of the company. The basic transaction data from TPS are compressed and are usually presented in long reports that are produced on a regular schedule. Figure 1.10 shows how a typical MIS transforms transaction level data from inventory, production, and accounting into MIS files that are used to provide managers with reports. Figure 1.11 shows a sample report from this system.

MIS usually serve managers interested in weekly, monthly, and yearly results—not day-to-day activities. MIS address structured questions that are known well in advance. These systems are generally not flexible and have little analytical capability. For instance, one cannot instruct an MIS to "take the monthly sales figures by ZIP code and correlate with the Bureau of the Census estimates of income by ZIP code." First, a typical MIS contains only corporate internal data, not external data like the U.S. Census figures. Second, most MIS use simple routines such as summaries and comparisons, as opposed to sophisticated mathematical models or statistical techniques. Third, data on sales by ZIP code would not be available on a typical MIS

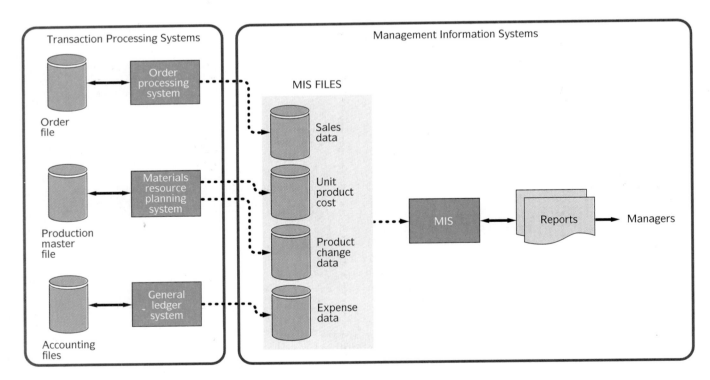

FIGURE 1.10
How management information systems obtain their data from the organization's TPS. In the system illustrated by this diagram, three TPS supply summarized transaction data at the end of the time period to the MIS reporting system. Managers gain access to the organizational data through the MIS, which provides them with the appropriate reports.

CALIFORNIA PIZZA CONTROLS COSTS WITH PIZAZZ

California Pizza Kitchen (CPK) started out in 1985 as a venture by two former federal prosecutors who wanted to do something different. They decided to sell "designer pizza" in which the pizza dough is a "canvas" for exotic food toppings such as Thai chicken, shrimp pesto, Peking duck, or southwestern burritos. By offering stylish entrees costing less than $10 in a sit-down setting, CPK mushroomed into a national chain of 70 restaurants in only nine years, with PepsiCo buying half-ownership in 1992.

Success did not come easily to this Los Angeles–headquartered chain. The restaurant business is a high-risk industry presenting restaurants and fast food chains with many factors that are beyond their control—swelling competition, fickle customer tastes, and rising real estate costs. Thus, restaurants need to tightly control food and labor costs to remain profitable—without affecting the quality of their food or service.

Now CPK company is poised for another take-off. It hopes to expand to 700 restaurants by using information systems to control food costs and make employees more productive. Since diners are turned away by high prices, the only way to contain costs is through inventory and portion control—keeping precise track of the amount of ingredients used in each menu item and stocking only as much of these ingredients as each restaurant actually needs.

All California Pizza Kitchen restaurants contain point-of-sale (POS) devices, which capture data about each item sold at the time the sale takes place. The sales data and inventory reports prepared by restaurant managers are transmitted from each restaurant to the company's central computer, where the information is consolidated and analyzed. An application called Inventory Express "remembers" ordering patterns, such as the amount of lettuce a restaurant needs each week, and also compares the amount of each item used to what each restaurant actually sold. If, for example, a restaurant sold 100 Thai shrimp pizzas in one week, it should have used a predetermined amount of shrimp, such as 40 pounds, based on portion measurements established by CPK management. Using more shrimp would indicate a problem with overportioning or waste. Restaurants with out-of-line portions would be told to take corrective action.

The POS-derived data is used for other purposes besides portion control. CPK's restaurant operations group uses the data to determine peak sales at each location so that they can schedule employee work shifts. The data tell food and beverage specialists how well each item sells. CPK found that it should get rid of its egg-salad pizza, for instance, when the item registered poor sales. CPK can also use its information systems to calculate the relative costs of different markets so it can determine if it

has a lower profit margin on Hawaiian pizza in Bethesda, Maryland, than in Waikiki. (Pineapple should be less expensive in Hawaii than in the northeast-

> *To Think About:* Is this a typical MIS? Why or why not? Where does it obtain its data? What does it do with its data? How is this system related to CPK's business strategy?

ern United States.) CPK's corporate accounting department can use the aggregated sales data to tally revenue and can manage the accounts payable and accounts receivable processes by combining that data with financial data residing on a central CPK computer.

California Pizza now has pilot projects to move to more state-of-the-art information system technology. Waiters and waitresses are experimenting with hand-held point-of-sale devices, which management hopes will boost productivity by reducing the amount of time employees spend with customers. The devices use radio frequencies to transmit orders to a computer in the back of the restaurant, eliminating the need for employees to run back and forth to a stationary POS device to place orders.

Source: Mary Hayes, "Getting a Slice of the Action," *InformationWEEK*, December 12, 1994.

unless a user had informed the designer several years earlier that this arrangement of data might be useful.

Table 1.5 describes the characteristics of typical management information systems.

Newer MIS are more flexible and may include software that lets managers structure their own reports and combine data from separate files and TPS. For instance, suppose a director of sales wanted to know if prices charged to major customers this year are keeping pace with cost increases. An MIS could tell the sales director if the customer bought as much this year as last year and could compare the profit margin between this year and last. Many older MIS do not have these features.

Some researchers use the term *MIS* to include all of the information systems that support the functional areas of the organization (Davis and Olson, 1985). However,

FIGURE 1.11
A sample report that might be produced
by the MIS system in Figure 1.10.

Consolidated Consumer Products Corporation
Sales by Product and Sales Region: 1995

PRODUCT CODE	PRODUCT DESCRIPTION	SALES REGION	ACTUAL SALES	PLANNED	ACTUAL VS. PLANNED
4469	Carpet Cleaner	Northeast	4,066,700	4,800,000	0.85
		South	3,778,112	3,750,000	1.01
		Midwest	4,867,001	4,600,000	1.06
		West	4,003,440	4,400,000	0.91
		TOTAL	16,715,253	17,550,000	0.95
5674	Room Freshener	Northeast	3,676,700	3,900,000	0.94
		South	5,608,112	4,700,000	1.19
		Midwest	4,711,001	4,200,000	1.12
		West	4,563,440	4,900,000	0.93
		TOTAL	18,559,253	17,700,000	1.05

in this book we prefer to use *computer-based information systems (CBIS)* as the umbrella term for all information systems and to consider management information systems as those that are specifically dedicated to management-level functions.

Decision-Support Systems

decision-support systems (DSS)
Information systems at the management level of an organization that combine data and sophisticated analytical models to support semistructured and unstructured decision making.

Any system that supports a decision is a **decision-support system (DSS)**. Like MIS, DSS serve the management level of the organization. Information systems support decisions in vastly different ways, and DSS are a class of systems that supports decisions in a unique way (at least when compared to the past). Table 1.6 shows how contemporary decision-support systems (DSS) differ from MIS and TPS systems.

DSS help managers make decisions that are semistructured, unique, or rapidly changing, and not easily specified in advance. DSS have to be responsive enough to run several times a day in order to correspond to changing conditions. While DSS use internal information from TPS and MIS, they often bring in information from external sources, such as current stock prices or product prices of competitors.

Clearly, by design, DSS have more analytical power than other systems; they are built explicitly with a variety of models to analyze data. Second, DSS are designed so

Table 1.5   Characteristics of Management Information Systems

1. MIS support structured and semistructured decisions at the operational and management control levels. However, they are also useful for planning purposes of senior management staff.

2. MIS are generally reporting and control oriented. They are designed to report on existing operations and therefore to help provide day-to-day control of operations.

3. MIS rely on existing corporate data and data flows.

4. MIS have little analytical capability.

5. MIS generally aid in decision making using past and present data.

6. MIS are relatively inflexible.

7. MIS have an internal rather than an external orientation.

8. Information requirements are known and stable.

9. MIS require a lengthy analysis and design process (on the order of one to two years).

Table 1.6 | **Characteristics of Decision-Support Systems**

1. DSS offer users flexibility, adaptability, and a quick response.

2. DSS allow users to initiate and control the input and output.

3. DSS operate with little or no assistance from professional programmers.

4. DSS provide support for decisions and problems whose solutions cannot be specified in advance.

5. DSS use sophisticated analysis and modeling tools.

that users can work with them directly; these systems explicitly include user-friendly software. This requirement follows both from their purpose (to inform personal decision making by key actors) and from the method of design (see Chapter 16). Third, these systems are interactive; the user can change assumptions and include new data.

An interesting, small, but powerful DSS is the voyage-estimating system of a subsidiary of a large American metals company that exists primarily to carry bulk cargoes of coal, oil, ores, and finished products for its parent company. The firm owns some vessels, charters others, and bids for shipping contracts in the open market to carry general cargo. A voyage-estimating system calculates financial and technical voyage details. Financial calculations include ship/time costs (fuel, labor, capital), freight rates for various types of cargo, and port expenses. Technical details include a myriad of factors such as ship cargo capacity (dead-weight tons, tons per inch immersion, etc.), speed, port distances, fuel and water consumption, and loading patterns (location of cargo for different ports).

An existing system to calculate only operating costs, freight rates, and profit was run on the company mainframe computer. The reports could not be understood by the managers because of the wealth of technical details they contained; only one person in the MIS department could run the program; and it took several weeks to make changes in assumptions (cost of fuel, speed). Moreover, the system could not answer questions such as the following: Given a customer delivery schedule and an offered freight rate, which vessel should be assigned at what rate to maximize profits? What is the optimum speed at which a particular vessel can optimize its profit and still meet its delivery schedule? What is the optimal loading pattern for a ship bound for the U.S. West Coast from Malaysia?

Senior and middle management wanted a more interactive system that they could control and run themselves, with as many changes in data and models as they needed and with little interference from data processing professionals. Management also needed information immediately to respond to bidding opportunities. Figure 1.12 illustrates the DSS built for this company. The system operates on a powerful desktop microcomputer, provides a system of menus that makes it easy for users to enter data or obtain information, is totally under management control, and required about 160 person-days to build.

Executive Support Systems

executive support systems (ESS)
Information systems at the strategic level of an organization designed to address unstructured decision making through advanced graphics and communications.

Senior managers use a category of information systems called **executive support systems (ESS)** to make decisions. ESS serve the strategic level of the organization. They address unstructured decisions and create a generalized computing and communications environment rather than providing any fixed application or specific capability. ESS are designed to incorporate data about external events such as new tax laws or competitors, but they also draw summarized information from internal MIS and DSS. They filter, compress, and track critical data, emphasizing the reduction of time and effort required to obtain information useful to executives. Although they have limited analytical capabilities, ESS employ the most advanced graphics software and can deliver graphs and data from many sources immediately to a senior executive's office or to a board room.

FIGURE 1.12
Voyage estimating decision-support system. This DSS operates on a powerful microcomputer. It is used daily by managers who must develop bids on shipping contracts.

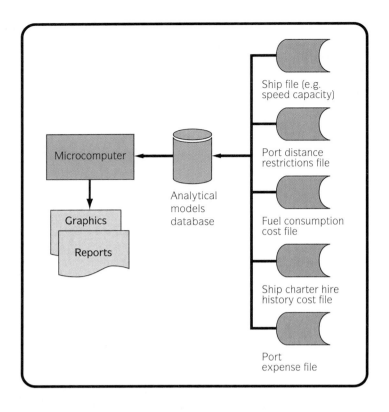

Unlike the other types of information systems, ESS are not designed primarily to solve specific problems. Instead, ESS provide a generalized computing and telecommunications capacity that can be applied to a changing array of problems. While DSS are designed to be highly analytical, ESS tend to make less use of analytical models. Instead, they deliver information to managers on demand and on a highly interactive basis.

Questions ESS must assist in answering include the following: What business should we be in? What are the competitors doing? What new acquisitions would protect us from cyclical business swings? Which units should we sell to raise cash for acquisitions? What is the impact on earnings of proposed changes in the investment tax credit? (Rockart and Treacy, 1982; Keen, 1991). Figure 1.13 illustrates a model of

Executive support systems (ESS) are being used by the executives in this boardroom meeting. Videoconferencing and advanced graphic software create an integrated computing and comunications environment to enhance decision making.

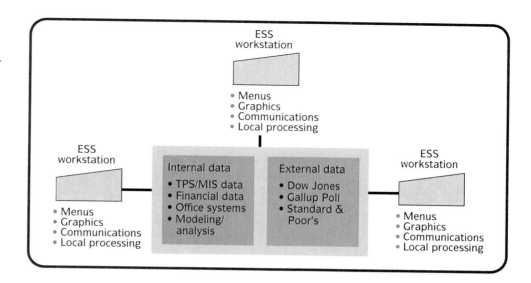

an ESS. It consists of workstations with menus, interactive graphics, and communications capabilities that can access historical and competitive data from internal corporate systems and external databases such as Dow Jones News/Retrieval or the Gallup Poll.

Senior executives differ in their personal styles, and all face radically changing environments and questions. Systems must be built that can adapt to these new conditions. ESS are one response to this challenge. Because ESS are designed to be used by senior managers who often have little, if any, direct contact or experience with computer-based information systems, they incorporate easy-to-use graphic interfaces. More details on leading-edge applications of DSS and ESS can be found in Chapter 16.

RELATIONSHIP OF SYSTEMS TO ONE ANOTHER: INTEGRATION

Figure 1.14 illustrates how the various types of systems in the organization are related to one another. TPS is typically a major source of data for other systems (for

FIGURE 1.14
Interrelationships among systems. The various types of systems in the organization do not work independently; rather, there are interdependencies between the systems. TPS are a major producer of information that is required by the other systems which, in turn, produce information for other systems. These different types of systems are only loosely coupled in most organizations.

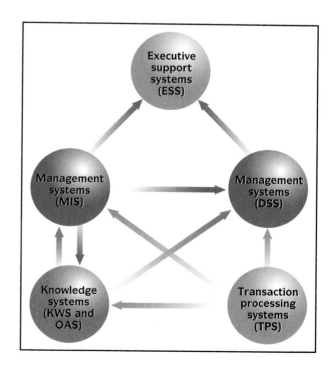

instance, sales transaction data feed California Pizza Kitchen's MIS), whereas ESS is primarily a recipient of data from lower-level systems. The other types of systems may exchange data among one another as well.

But how much can or should these systems be integrated? Should organizations have a single information system that serves the entire organization and coordinates all of the special systems we previously outlined? Would it not be best to have such a single, total system to ensure that information can flow where it is needed, that it is uniform, and that all new systems are coordinated? Unfortunately, no organization builds systems this way, and it would be foolish to try. The activities of a Sears, a General Motors, or a California Pizza Kitchen are so diverse that in all but the tiniest organizations, many different specialists are needed to build different systems serving different purposes.

Yet systems should be integrated with one another—that is, they should provide for the systematic flow of information among different systems. But integration costs money, and it would be foolish to build bridges among systems simply for the sake of building bridges.

In the real world, managers provide the level of integration needed to operate the business. Connections among systems evolve over time. Most systems are built in isolation from other systems (unless some business reason suggests a different approach). Organizations do not build all systems at once; the resources required to do so would be enormous, the management problems insurmountable.

Organizations pay a penalty for this evolutionary approach to systems. Systems are often not as integrated as they sometimes need to be. This situation creates bottlenecks and inefficiencies in a firm's essential business activities. Occasionally, an organization must mount a massive effort to integrate its systems. General Motors purchased Electronic Data Systems (EDS) to develop a seamless, interconnected set of systems to replace its hodgepodge of uncoordinated computer-aided design, computer-aided manufacturing, word processing, and various other systems, plus one hundred telecommunications networks. GM needed to integrate its manufacturing, ordering, and delivery operations to remain globally competitive.

As organizations move toward centralizing, coordinating, and controlling system evolution, however, they create more layers of management approval for systems and more bureaucracy in the process. Eventually, centralization reaches a saturation point, and organizations start allowing their divisions or operating units to develop systems on their own. In short, decisions to integrate systems, to centralize control, are like the tides—they ebb and flow in accordance with business conditions and values. There is no "one right level" of integration or centralization (Allen and Boynton, 1991; King, 1984).

1.4   THE CHANGING MANAGEMENT PROCESS

The information systems we have described cannot be ignored by managers because they play such a critical role in contemporary organizations. The first information systems of the 1950s were operational systems that automated such clerical processes as check processing. These were followed by management-level systems in the 1970s and strategic-level systems in the 1980s. Today, information systems are helping to create and disseminate knowledge and information throughout the organization through new knowledge work systems, applications providing company-wide access to data, and company-wide communications networks.

Because early systems addressed largely technical operational issues, managers could afford to delegate authority and concern to lower-level technical workers. But because today's systems directly affect how managers decide, how senior managers plan, and in many cases what products and services are produced (and how), responsibility for information systems cannot be delegated to technical decision makers. Information systems today play a strategic role in the life of the firm.

THE NEW ROLE OF INFORMATION SYSTEMS IN ORGANIZATIONS

Figure 1.15 illustrates the new relationship between organizations and information systems. There is a growing interdependence between business strategy, rules, and procedures, on the one hand, and information systems software, hardware, data, and telecommunications, on the other. A change in any of these components often requires changes in other components. This relationship becomes critical when management plans for the future. What a business would like to do in five years is often dependent on what its systems will be able to do.

A second change in the relationship of information systems and organizations results from the growing complexity and scope of system projects and applications. Building systems today involves a much larger part of the organization than it did in the past (see Figure 1.16). Whereas early systems produced largely technical changes that affected few people, contemporary systems bring about managerial changes (who has what information about whom, when, and how often) and institutional "core" changes (what products and services are produced, under what conditions, and by whom).

In the 1950s, employees in the treasurer's office, a few part-time programmers, a single program, a single machine, and a few clerks utilized a computerized payroll system. The change from a manual to a computer system was largely technical. The computer system simply automated an existing procedure. In contrast, today's integrated human resources system (which includes payroll processing) may involve all major corporate divisions, the human resources department, dozens of full-time programmers, a flock of external consultants, multiple machines (or remote computers linked by telecommunications networks), and perhaps hundreds of end users in the organization who use payroll data to make calculations about benefits and pensions and to answer a host of other questions. The data, instead of being located in and controlled by the treasurer's office, are now available to hundreds of employees via desktop computers, each of which is as powerful as the large computers of the mid-1980s. This contemporary system embodies both managerial and institutional changes.

FIGURE 1.15
The interdependence between organizations and information systems. In contemporary systems there is a growing interdependence between organizational business strategy, rules, and procedures and the organization's information systems. Changes in strategy, rules, and procedures increasingly require changes in hardware, software, databases, and telecommunications. Existing systems can act as a constraint on organizations. Often, what the organization would like to do depends on what its systems will permit it to do.

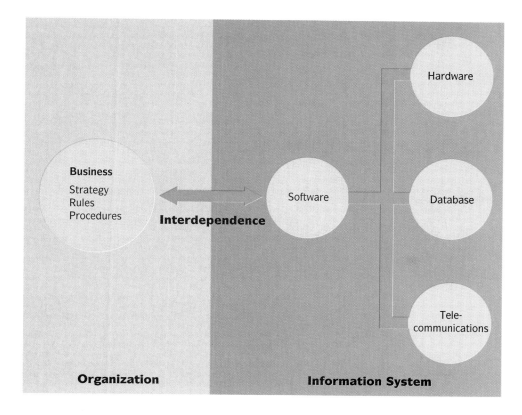

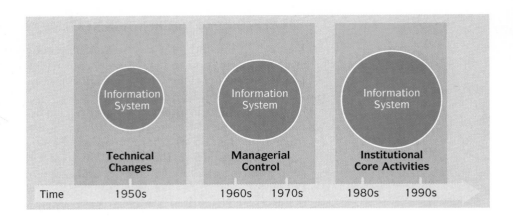

FIGURE 1.16
The widening scope of information systems. Over time, information systems have come to play a larger role in the life of organizations. Early systems brought about largely technical changes that were relatively easy to accomplish. Later systems affected managerial control and behavior; ultimately systems influenced "core" institutional activities concerning products, markets, suppliers, and customers.

THE CHANGING NATURE OF INFORMATION TECHNOLOGY

One reason why systems play a larger role in organizations, and why they affect more people, is the growing power and declining cost of information technology—the computers and peripheral devices that make up the core of information systems. Although the details are covered in later chapters, here it is sufficient to note that it is now possible to put the power of a large mainframe computer, which took up nearly an entire floor of a company in the 1970s, on every desktop in today's organization. This new hardware power makes powerful, easy-to-use software available to complete novices. In a few hours, relatively unskilled employees can be taught word processing, project scheduling, spreadsheet preparation, and telecommunications applications on a microcomputer. The skills needed for these activities once belonged exclusively to employees who had been through extensive specialized training. Now it is conceivable that everyone in an organization may be using a computer simultaneously in some way during the workday.

In addition, it is now possible for end users to design their own applications and simple systems without the help of professional programmers. A good manager cannot afford to ignore the fact that many of his or her employees are using information technology much of the time. Is this use productive? Could it be made more productive? Where are the major bottlenecks? How can we measure the benefits of investing in the technology? When should professional help be sought, and when can end users design their own solutions?

THE CHANGING CHARACTER OF APPLICATIONS

Both the changing role of systems and the new technology have brought about new kinds of systems and applications that are much more deeply embedded in the fundamental activities of the firm. Whether they are massive transaction processing or reporting systems or customized systems for one or a few groups in the organization, the new kinds of applications require direct, close interaction between technical support personnel and managers who will use the system, plus senior management support. Managers need some computer understanding to maximize the benefit from such applications.

THE NEED TO PLAN THE INFORMATION ARCHITECTURE OF AN ORGANIZATION

It is not enough for managers to be computer literate. Systems today require that a manager have an understanding of major islands or constellations of technologies: data processing systems, telecommunications, and office technologies (see the articles by McKenney and McFarlan, 1982; McFarlan et al., 1983a, 1983b). As the scope of information systems widens, these previously separate islands of technology must be closely coordinated. Managers today must know how to track, plan, and

information architecture The particular form that information technology takes in a specific organization to achieve selected goals or functions.

manage the many islands of technology in a way best suited to their organization. This systems knowledge is important.

In addition, managers must know how to recognize organizational problems and find a systems solution. For this, knowledge of the organization is required. Together, systems knowledge and organizational understanding shape the information architecture of the organization. **Information architecture** is the particular form that information technology takes in an organization to achieve selected goals or functions. Information architecture includes the extent to which data and processing power are centralized or distributed. Managers increasingly play the critical role in determining the information architecture of their organizations. There is no one else to do the job.

Figure 1.17 illustrates the major elements of information architecture that a student will have to understand today if he or she is to become an effective manager. Although the computer systems base is typically operated by technical personnel, general management must decide how to allocate the resources it has assigned to hardware, software, and telecommunications. Increasingly, the top managers of systems and communications departments are also general managers. Resting upon the computer systems base are the major business application systems, or the major islands of applications. Because managers and employees directly interact with these systems, it is critical for the success of the organization that these systems meet business functional requirements now and in the future. In many service industries—such

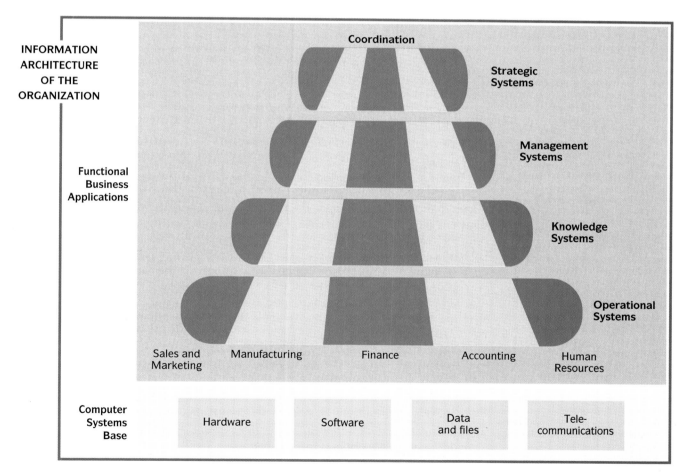

FIGURE 1.17
The information architecture of the firm. Today's managers must know how to arrange and coordinate the various computer technologies and business system applications to meet the information needs of each level of their organization, as well as the needs of the organization as a whole.

as airlines, hotels, banks, insurance firms, and brokerages—the major business applications provide unique competitive advantages. Failure to develop these systems can lead to business failure.

The following are some typical questions regarding information architecture that today's managers should be able to answer: Should the corporate sales data and function be distributed to each corporate remote site, or should they be centralized at headquarters? Should the organization purchase stand-alone microcomputers or build a more powerful centralized mainframe environment within an integrated telecommunications network? Should the organization build its own data communications utility to link remote sites or rely on external providers like the telephone company? Although there is no one right answer to these questions (see Allen and Boynton, 1991), a manager today should at least have the knowledge to deal with them.

1.5   THE CHALLENGE OF INFORMATION SYSTEMS: KEY MANAGEMENT ISSUES

Increasingly, information systems are bringing about changes in business goals, relationships with customers and suppliers, and internal operations. Creating a new system now means much more than installing a new machine in the basement. Today, this process typically places thousands of terminals or microcomputers on the desks of employees who have little experience with them, connecting the devices to powerful communications networks, rearranging social relations in the office and work locations, changing reporting patterns, and asking employees to achieve higher levels of productivity. Briefly, new systems today often require redesigning the organization and developing a new information architecture.

One message of this text is that despite, or perhaps because of, the rapid development of computer technology, there is nothing easy or mechanical about building workable information systems. Building, operating, and maintaining information systems are challenging activities for a number of reasons. We believe there are five key challenges that managers should heed:

1. *The Strategic Business Challenge: How can businesses use information technology to design organizations that are competitive and effective?*

Investment in information technology amounts to over half of the annual capital expenditures of most large, service sector firms. Yet despite investing more in computers than any other country, the United States is grappling with a serious productivity challenge. Until recently, America's productivity growth rate of just under 2 percent per year has been far below that of other industrial countries. The productivity lag has been especially pronounced in the service sector. During the 1980s, white-collar productivity increased at an annual rate of only .28 percent (Roach, 1991).

Technical change moves much faster than humans and organizations are changing. The power of computer hardware and software has grown much more rapidly than the ability of organizations to apply and use this technology. To stay competitive, many organizations actually need to be redesigned. They will need to use information technology to simplify communication and coordination, eliminate unnecessary work, and eliminate the inefficiencies of outmoded organizational structures. If organizations merely automate what they are doing today, they are largely missing the potential of information technology. Organizations need to rethink and redesign the way they design, produce, deliver, and maintain goods and services.

2. *The Globalization Challenge: How can firms understand the business and system requirements of a global economic environment?*

The rapid growth in international trade and the emergence of a global economy call for information systems that can support both producing and selling goods in many different countries. In the past, each regional office of a multinational corporation focused on solving its own unique information problems. Given language, cultural, and political differences among countries, this focus frequently resulted in chaos and the failure of central management controls. To develop integrated multinational information systems, businesses must develop global hardware, software, and communications standards and create cross-cultural accounting and reporting structures (Roche, 1992; Buss, 1982).

3. *The Information Architecture Challenge: How can organizations develop an information architecture that supports their business goals?*

While information technology can suggest some new ways of doing business, firms still need to have a clear idea of their business goals and how these can best be supported by information systems. Many organizations cannot meet their goals because they are crippled by fragmented and incompatible computer hardware, software, telecommunications networks, and information systems. Integrating these "islands of information" into a coherent architecture is now a priority.

4. *The Information Systems Investment Challenge: How can organizations determine the business value of information systems?*

A major problem raised by the development of powerful inexpensive computers involves not technology but rather management and organizations. It's one thing to use information technology to design, produce, deliver, and maintain new products. It's another thing to make money doing it. How can organizations obtain a sizable payoff from their investment in information systems?

Engineering massive organizational and system changes in the hope of positioning a firm strategically is complicated and expensive. Is this an investment that pays off? How can you tell? Senior management can be expected to ask these questions: Are we receiving the kind of return on investment from our systems that we should be? Do our competitors get more? While understanding the costs and benefits of building a single system is difficult enough, it is daunting to consider whether the entire systems effort is "worth it." Imagine, then, how a senior executive must think when presented with a major transformation in information architecture, a bold venture in organizational change costing tens of millions of dollars and taking many years.

5. *The Responsibility and Control Challenge: How can organizations design systems that people can control and understand? How can organizations ensure that their information systems are used in an ethically and socially responsible manner?*

Information systems are so essential to business, government, and daily life that organizations must take special steps to ensure that they are accurate, reliable, and secure. Automated or semi-automated systems that malfunction or are poorly operated can have extremely harmful consequences. A firm invites disaster if it uses systems that don't work as intended, that don't deliver information in a form that people can interpret correctly and use, or that have control rooms where controls don't work or where instruments give false signals. The potential for massive fraud, error, abuse, and destruction is enormous.

Information systems must be designed so that they function as intended and so that humans can control the process. When building and using information systems, health, safety, job security, and social well-being should be considered as carefully as meeting an organization's business goals. Managers will need to ask: Can we apply high quality assurance standards to our information systems as well as to our products and services? Can we build information systems that respect people's rights of privacy while still pursuing our organization's goals? Should information systems monitor employees? What do we do when an information system designed to increase efficiency and productivity eliminates people's jobs?

This text is designed to provide future managers with the knowledge and understanding required to deal with these challenges. To further this objective, each chapter concludes with a Management Challenges box that outlines the key issues managers should be aware of.

Summary

1. Define an information system. The purpose of a CBIS is to collect, store, and disseminate information from an organization's environment and internal operations for the purpose of supporting organizational functions and decision making, communication, coordination, control, analysis, and visualization. Information systems transform raw data into useful information through three basic activities: input, processing, and output.

2. Explain the difference between computer literacy and information systems literacy. Information systems literacy requires an understanding of the organizational and management dimensions of information systems as well as the technical dimensions addressed by computer literacy. Information systems literacy draws on both technical and behavioral approaches to studying information systems. Both perspectives can be combined into a sociotechnical approach to systems.

3. Describe the information needs of different organizational levels. To be useful, a CBIS must faithfully reflect the organization's requirements for information. It must fit the needs of the specific organizational level and the business function that it is intended to support. Operational-level systems keep track of the firm's day-to-day activities. Knowledge-level systems support the integration of new knowledge throughout the firm; they also exist to manage paperwork. Management-level systems support the planning, controlling, and monitoring activities of middle management. Strategic-level systems support long-term planning. Each functional specialty, such as sales and marketing, manufacturing, finance, accounting, and human resources, typically has all four types of systems.

4. Describe the role played by the six major types of information systems in organizations and the relationship between these systems. There are six major types of information systems in contemporary organizations: (1) transaction processing systems (TPS) at the operational level; (2) knowledge work systems (KWS) and (3) office automation systems (OAS) at the knowledge level; (4) management information systems (MIS) and (5) decision-support systems (DSS) at the management level; and (6) executive support systems (ESS) at the strategic level.

The six types of systems are designed for different purposes and different audiences: Transaction processing systems (TPS) perform and record the daily routine transactions that are necessary to conduct business. They also produce information for the other systems. Many organizations today would come to a standstill if their TPS failed for a day or even a few hours. Examples are systems for order processing, airline reservations, and payroll.

Knowledge-level systems support clerical, managerial, and professional workers. They consist of office automation systems for increasing the productivity of data workers (word processing, desktop publishing, document storage, facsimile transmission, electronic mail, videoconferencing) and knowledge work systems for enhancing the productivity of knowledge workers (professional workstations, graphics, analytical models, document preparation, and communication). Knowledge work systems are increasingly tied to other systems in the firm.

Management systems (MIS and DSS) provide the management control level with reports and access to the organization's current performance and historical records. Most MIS reports condense information from TPS and are not highly analytical. Decision-support systems (DSS) support management decisions when these decisions are unique, rapidly changing, and not specified easily in advance. They have more advanced analytical models than MIS and often draw on information from external as well as internal sources.

Executive support systems (ESS) support the strategic level by providing a generalized computing and communications environment to assist senior management's decision making. They have limited analytical capabilities but can draw on sophisticated graphics software and many sources of internal and external information.

The various types of systems in the organization exchange data with one another. TPS are a major source of data for other systems, especially MIS and DSS. ESS are primarily a recipient of data from lower-level systems. However, the different systems in an organization are only loosely integrated. The information needs of the various functional areas and organizational levels are too specialized to be served by a single system.

5. Explain why information systems are so important today. In general, there is a much greater need to plan for the overall information architecture of the organization. The kinds of systems built today are more important for the overall performance of the organization, especially in today's highly globalized and information-based economy; technologies have become more powerful and more difficult to implement; and new applications require intense interaction between professional technical experts and general management.

6. Identify the major management challenges to building and using information systems in organizations. There are five key management challenges in building and using information systems: (1) designing systems that are competitive and efficient; (2) understanding the system requirements of a global business environment; (3) creating an information architecture that supports the organization's goals; (4) determining the business value of information systems; and (5) designing systems that people can control, understand, and use in a socially and ethically responsible manner.

Key Terms

Information system
Information
Data
Input
Processing
Output
Feedback
Computer-based informa-
tion systems (CBIS)
Standard operating proce-
dures (SOPs)
Knowledge workers

Data workers
Production or service
workers
Senior managers
Middle managers
Operational managers
Computer hardware
Computer software
Storage technology
Telecommunications tech-
nology
Operational-level systems

Knowledge-level systems
Management-level systems
Strategic-level systems
Transaction processing
systems (TPS)
Knowledge work systems
(KWS)
Office automation systems
(OAS)
Word processing
Desktop publishing
Workstations

Management information
systems (MIS)
Decision-support system
(DSS)
Executive support systems
(ESS)
Information architecture

Review Questions

1. Distinguish between a computer, a computer pro-gram, and an information system. Between data and information.
2. What activities convert raw data to usable informa-tion in information systems? What is their relation-ship to feedback?
3. What is information systems literacy?
4. What are the organization, management, and tech-nology dimensions of information systems?
5. Distinguish between a behavioral and a technical approach to information systems in terms of the questions asked and the answers provided.
6. What major disciplines contribute to an under-standing of information systems?
7. Identify and describe the four levels of the organiza-tional hierarchy. What types of information systems serve each level?
8. List and briefly describe the major types of systems in organizations. How are they related to one another?

9. What are the five major types of TPS in business or-ganizations? What functions do they perform? Give examples of each.
10. Describe the functions performed by knowledge work and office automation systems and the tools used for each.
11. What are the characteristics of MIS? How do MIS differ from TPS? From DSS?
12. What are the characteristics of DSS? How do they differ from ESS?
13. Why should managers study information systems?
14. What is the relationship between an organization and its information systems? How is this relation-ship changing over time?
15. What do we mean by the information architecture of the organization?
16. What are the key management challenges involved in building, operating, and maintaining information systems today?

Discussion Questions

1. Some people argue that the creation of CBIS is fun-damentally a social process. Hence, a person who is an expert in information technology may not be suited to design a CBIS. Discuss and comment.
2. Most of the problems we have with information sys-tems will disappear when computers become faster and cheaper. Discuss and comment.
3. In what way are the United Parcel Service package tracking systems illustrated here examples of trans-

action processing systems? Describe the transactions that power these systems. What data do they cap-ture? What do they do with these data? How could these data be used in a MIS?
4. Discuss the major factors that may prevent an orga-nization from building a totally integrated informa-tion system that combines all six major types of sys-tems into a single design effort.

Group Projects

1. In a group with three or four classmates, find a de-scription in a computer or business magazine of an in-formation system used by an organization. Describe the system in terms of its inputs, processes, and outputs

and in terms of its organization, management, and technology features. Present your analysis to the class.

2. In a group with three or four other classmates, research a business firm using annual reports or publications such as *Fortune* or *Business Week*. Describe some of the TPS, MIS, DSS, KWS, OAS, and ESS that might be found in the firm. Suggest appropriate strategic information systems for that particular business. Present your group's findings to the class.

THE CASE OF THE SHOEMAKER'S CHILD

Does a company that sells high-tech services need to rely on computerized information systems if it is to be a success? DataTec Industries Inc., of Fairfield, New Jersey, grew from revenues of $500,000 and nine employees in 1976 to $31 million in revenues and 300 employees by 1991, all with no real attention to information systems for its own internal processes. The company, owned and run by Christopher Carey, aids retailers in installing and linking electronic cash-register systems, coupon machines, and traffic-tracking equipment. The company's customers include large nationwide chains that can have 1000 or more sites. Carey's attitude, according to his own words, has always been "Why do we need them?" His focus on his customers has caused him to spend most of his time on the road. This customer focus, combined with DataTec's reputation for the quality of its 1200 road teams, has been the reason the company has prospered.

It is not that DataTec did not own and make extensive use of computers. Its staff had about 200 desktop computers of all ages in its eight field offices, while the headquarters had its own computer as well. The staff ran customer, invoice, job assignment, and inventory systems, among others, on these computers. Nonetheless, DataTec was essentially a case of the proverbial shoemaker's child. There was no corporate computer planning—no one focused on these systems for the company. As a result DataTec found itself with a real hodgepodge of computers and software with little or no coordination and all of them unable to "talk" to one another. Much of the work that could have been automated was still being done by pencil and paper.

In time, problems began to emerge. Work crew assignment errors often resulted in fully one sixth of the company's 200 crews being sent to the wrong place. Without up-to-date warehouse data, even Carey found himself purchasing equipment costing tens of thousands of dollars later found to be in the warehouse in abundance. Job costing took up to two months, which meant that in many cases the company did not know what its cost projections were until the work was completed. In other words, DataTec did not know whether or not a job was profitable until weeks too late. Invoicing was taking ten days to two weeks, compared with the norm of same-day invoicing. Fifteen percent of its invoices were sent out with errors as compared to the norm of less than 1 percent. The billing situation deteriorated so badly that one customer, responding to a survey on the company, praised its service and support but had one complaint: "Your billing sucks."

The lack of a unified computer system in such an expanding company created other problems as well. Employees often worked 12 hours per day just to keep up with their growing business. Because many of DataTec's customers spanned the country, customer information was also scattered, and with no networking to connect the various sites, needed customer information was very difficult to obtain. The situation first gained management attention in 1988, at which time the company realized it had to do something. Carey spent $100,000 to upgrade some of the company's computers, expecting the upgraded systems to last the company for ten more years. Therefore, the shock was particularly great when two years later, in 1991, someone walked into Carey's office and declared that "the file is full," that the main office computer had run out of room. It appeared that the problems could be avoided no longer and that things could not get worse, but they did.

Billing problems had become so great that one longtime million-dollar customer walked out on DataTec even though it realized that the company had done good work. The customer had become disgusted with DataTec's repeated but unfulfilled promises to fix the billing problems. Few companies can easily take the loss of such a major customer. This time it appeared that DataTec had received a real wake-up call, and so management decided to carry out a thorough review of the company's computer systems. They found more than just the problems described above. They also realized that DataTec was often months late in collecting its accounts receivable, a "luxury" few companies can afford.

Even this did not force the final showdown, however. Independent action taken by two employees in the Atlanta office gave the company some relief. Fed up with all the problems they faced every day at work, the two reprogrammed their office desktop computers to better process work orders and inventory. They used a spreadsheet that had been sitting unused on a computer to cross-reference their customer and inventory information. The result was dramatic. The time needed to produce invoices, financial statements, and other documents fell sharply. For example, job costing fell to less than two weeks. One result was that Atlanta quickly became the most profitable DataTec office. Another was that the whole company wanted Atlanta's system, and they got it. The two Atlanta staffers spent the next six months spreading their systems to the other offices all around the country.

One major problem still was obvious. Data stored in computers around the country were isolated because these computers were not connected. The way the company handled this problem was to have each office overnight their data on floppy diskettes to the Fairfield office via Federal Express. Updated disks were then "Fedexed" back to the field offices so each office could be up-to-date. Meanwhile the company continued to grow, and within a year, because of DataTec's larger size, the efficiencies began to disappear.

Before long the company was in as much trouble as before. The "fixes" from the Atlanta office and the massive use of Federal Express were only fingers in the dike. The water continued to rise.

Today DataTec is finally in the process of building new computer systems, at a cost of about $1 million. The company clearly can afford them because its revenues are still growing at 20 percent per year—revenues for 1995 are projected to be $60 million. Elements of the new computer systems include a minicomputer in company headquarters, networks to connect all the computers within each office, and a network to connect the eight field offices to each other and to headquarters. In addition DataTec is replacing the fax machines it had installed in the dashboard of each of its trucks with portable computers so that each crew can have immediate access to the most up-to-date information about its current and upcoming assignments. The company has even more plans for the near future, including teleconferencing, companywide electronic messaging, and even a service that enables customers to leave detailed messages about their problems in the DataTec computer and to schedule their own customer-service calls.

Source: Leslie Cauley, "Computer Makeover," *The Wall Street Journal*, June 27, 1994.

Case Study Questions

1. How important a role did information systems play at DataTec?

2. DataTec information systems are used by many people at different locations who need different kinds of information. What kinds of organizational decisions and functions do the systems support? You may find it helpful to organize your answers in tabular form.

   Organizational level
   Function
   Decision

3. Why do you think the company did not pay more attention to its computer systems? How harmful was this lack of attention? Categorize their problems as management, organization, and/or technology problems, and explain your reasoning.

4. What are the costs and effects of not embracing this technology? Are there benefits to companies like DataTec continuing their work in a traditional way?

5. How important are information systems in solving the problems of companies like DataTec? What are some problems that technology cannot address?

References

Ackoff, R. L. "Management Misinformation System." *Management Science* 14, no. 4 (December 1967), B140–B116.

Alavi, Maryam, and Patricia Carlson. "A Review of MIS Research and Disciplinary Development." *Journal of Management Information Systems* 8, no. 4 (Spring 1992).

Allen, Brandt R., and Andrew C. Boynton. "Information Architecture: In Search of Efficient Flexibility." *MIS Quarterly* 15, no. 4 (December 1991).

Anthony, R. N. *Planning and Control Systems: A Framework for Analysis*. Cambridge, MA: Harvard University Press (1965).

Buss, Martin D. J., "Managing International Information Systems," *Harvard Business Review* (September 1982).

Cash, James I., F. Warren McFarlan, James L. McKenney, and Lynda M. Applegate. *Corporate Information Systems Management*, 3rd ed. Homewood, IL: Irwin (1992).

Clark, Thomas D. Jr., "Corporate Systems Management: An Overview and Research Perspective." *Communications of the ACM* 35, no. 2 (February 1992).

Culnan, Mary J. "Transaction Processing Applications as Organizational Message Systems: Implications for the Intelligent Organization." Working paper no. 88-10, Twenty-second Hawaii International Conference on Systems Sciences (January 1989).

Davis, Gordon B., and Margrethe H. Olson. *Management Information Systems: Conceptual Foundations, Structure, and Development*, 2nd ed. New York: McGraw-Hill (1985).

Fedorowicz, Jane, and Benn Konsynski. "Organization Support Systems: Bridging Business and Decision Processes." *Journal of Management Information Systems* 8, no. 4 (Spring 1992).

Gorry, G. A., and M. S. Scott Morton. "A Framework for Management Information Systems." *Sloan Management Review* 13, no. 1 (1971).

Houdeshel, George, and Hugh J. Watson. "The Management Information and Decision Support (MIDS) System at Lockheed Georgia." *MIS Quarterly* 11, no. 1 (March 1987).

Huber, George P. "Organizational Information Systems: Determinants of Their Performance and Behavior." *Management Science* 28, no. 2 (1984).

Keen, Peter G. W. *Shaping the Future: Business Design through Information Technology.* Cambridge, MA: Harvard Business School Press (1991).

Keen, P. G. W., and M. S. Morton. *Decision Support Systems: An Organizational Perspective.* Reading, MA: Addison-Wesley (1978).

King, John. "Centralized vs. Decentralized Computing: Organizational Considerations and Management Options." *Computing Surveys* (October 1984).

Kling, Rob, and William H. Dutton. "The Computer Package: Dynamic Complexity," in *Computers and Politics,* edited by James Danziger, William H. Dutton, Rob Kling, and Kenneth Kraener. New York: Columbia University Press (1982).

Laudon, Kenneth C. "A General Model for Understanding the Relationship Between Information Technology and Organizations." Working paper, Center for Research on Information Systems, New York University (1989).

Liker, Jeffrey K., David B. Roitman, and Ethel Roskies. "Changing Everything All at Once: Work Life and Technological Change." *Sloan Management Review* (Summer 1987).

Lucas, Henry C., Jr. and Jack Baroudi. "The Role of Information Technology in Organization Design." *Journal of Management Information Systems* 10, no. 4 (Spring 1994).

McFarlan, F. Warren, James L. McKenney, and Philip Pyburn. "The Information Archipelago—Plotting a Course." *Harvard Business Review* (January–February 1983a).

McFarlan, F. Warren, James L. McKenney, and Philip Pyburn. "Governing the New World." *Harvard Business Review* (July–August 1983b).

McKenney, James L., and F. Warren McFarlan. "The Information Archipelago—Maps and Bridges." *Harvard Business Review* (September–October 1982).

Niederman, Fred, James C. Brancheau, and James C. Wetherbe. "Information Systems Management Issues for the 1990s." *MIS Quarterly* 15, no. 4 (December 1991).

Orlikowski, Wanda J., and Jack J. Baroudi. "Studying Information Technology in Organizations: Research Approaches and Assumptions." *Information Systems Research* 2, no. 1 (March 1991).

Roach, Stephen S. "Technology and the Services Sector: The Hidden Competitive Challenge." *Technological Forecasting and Social Change* 34 (1988).

Roach, Stephen S. "Services Under Siege—The Restructuring Imperative." *Harvard Business Review* (September–October, 1991).

Roche, Edward M. "Planning for Competitive Use of Information Technology in Multinational Corporations." AIB UK Region, Brighton Polytechnic, Brighton, UK, Conference Paper, March 1992. Edward M. Roche, W. Paul Stillman School of Business, Seton Hall University.

Rockart, John F., and Michael E. Treacy. "The CEO Goes On-Line." *Harvard Business Review* (January–February 1982).

Scott Morton, Michael, Ed. *The Corporation in the 1990s.* New York: Oxford University Press (1991).

Sprague, Ralph H., Jr., and Eric D. Carlson. *Building Effective Decision Support Systems.* Englewood Cliffs, NJ: Prentice Hall (1982).

Strassman, Paul. *The Information Payoff—The Transformation of Work in the Electronic Age.* New York: Free Press (1985).

Tornatsky, Louis G., J. D. Eveland, Myles G. Boylan, W. A. Hertzner, E. C. Johnson, D. Roitman, and J. Schneider. *The Process of Technological Innovation: Reviewing the Literature.* Washington, DC: National Science Foundation (1983).

Watson, Hugh D., R. Kelly Rainer, Jr., and Chang E. Koh. "Executive Information Systems: A Framework for Development and a Survey of Current Practices." *MIS Quarterly* 15, no. 1 (March 1991).

Chapter 2

The Strategic Role of Information Systems

Information Systems Keep Gillette on the Cutting Edge

In the early 1900s, when The Gillette Company introduced the first safety razor, it recognized right away that its products were vulnerable to competition. Anyone could obtain a piece of steel at a reasonable price. The way to stay ahead of the pack was to shape that same piece of steel into a sharper, sturdier blade at the lowest possible cost and to be the first to bring a superior product to market. Gillette has pursued this strategy ever since.

Gillette has 64 percent of the U.S. wet-shaving market and is a market leader in the rest of the world as well. Gillette has 70 percent of the market share in Europe and 80 percent in Latin America. This is a cutthroat market where a price difference of a few pennies can spell the difference between success and failure, especially since razors and blades have accounted for nearly 40 percent of Gillette's sales and 70 percent of its operating profit.

Information systems have helped Gillette stay ahead as both a low-cost, high-quality producer and as an innovator of new shaving products. With advanced technology, Gillette can cut fractions of a cent off the cost of manufacturing a blade cartridge, yet produce a high-quality product. When you're making a billion razor blades a year, shaving a few tenths of a cent off the cost of each blade creates many millions of dollars in savings.

Virtually everything in Gillette's Boston manufacturing plant is automated. The firm's 3000 workers spend most of their time monitoring equipment, checking report printouts, or searching for bottlenecks in the production process.

With computerized process control devices, Gillette can control temperature, pressure, and other machine settings more precisely while optimizing output. The result: Both blade cartridge and razor parts can be fashioned much faster and with higher quality than five or ten years ago. A "cycle" in the production process that used to take ten seconds is now down to seven or eight.

Gillette uses information systems to enforce scrupulous quality control standards. For instance, a high-resolution microscopic camera linked to a minicomputer examines every mounted twin blade for Gillette's Sensor razor. The minicomputer compares the images captured by the camera with the image of correctly mounted blades stored in its memory, rejecting blades that are not absolutely parallel. Since an infinitesimal change in angle will give an unsatisfactory shave, the system rejects blades that are off by a couple of microns.

Information systems help detect weak links in the production process as well. Gillette increased output of its Sensor razors by 4 percent by improving a small clip resembling a staple that anchors the cartridge assembly. Engineers found out that the gap in the clip was too narrow by analyzing computerized data from millions of cartridge assemblies.

Information systems have also helped Gillette capture market share with innovative new razors and speed its product development process. Ten Gillette designers used three-dimensional computer-aided design software running on networked workstations to design the Sensor cartridge that uses independently suspended twin blades to deliver a closer shave. Sensor became an instant hit and the top seller in the nondisposable razor market, with 43 percent of market share. Gillette wants to increase this market share even more, and is rolling out an improved version of the Sensor, called the SensorExcel, that features tiny rubber fins that stretch the skin so that hair jumps out of the follicle. ■

Sources: Barbara Carton, "Gillette Looks Beyond Whiskers to Big Hair and Stretchy Floss," *The Wall Street Journal*, December 14, 1994; and Lawrence Ingrassia, "The Cutting Edge," *The Wall*

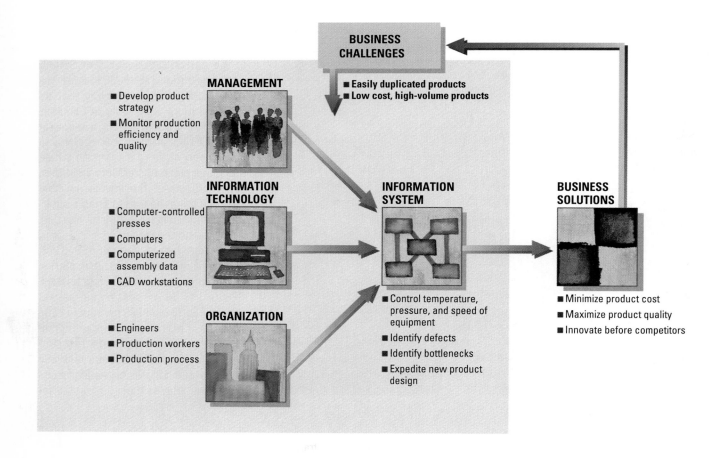

MANAGEMENT
- Develop product strategy
- Monitor production efficiency and quality

INFORMATION TECHNOLOGY
- Computer-controlled presses
- Computers
- Computerized assembly data
- CAD workstations

ORGANIZATION
- Engineers
- Production workers
- Production process

BUSINESS CHALLENGES
- Easily duplicated products
- Low cost, high-volume products

INFORMATION SYSTEM
- Control temperature, pressure, and speed of equipment
- Identify defects
- Identify bottlenecks
- Expedite new product design

BUSINESS SOLUTIONS
- Minimize product cost
- Maximize product quality
- Innovate before competitors

Street Journal, April 6, 1992; and "Gillette Holds Its Edge by Endlessly Searching for a Better Shave," *The Wall Street Journal,* December 10, 1992.

Gillette's use of information systems to stay ahead of the competition is one example of the strategic use of information systems. In this case, information systems enabled the firm to pursue strategies to maximize the quality and innovation of its products while minimizing costs. Information systems can be used to pursue other competitive strategies as well.

In this chapter we look at the problems firms face from competition and the ways the information systems can help businesses stay ahead of competitors. Information systems can help businesses develop new products and services, market products more accurately, forge new relationships with suppliers and customers, and reduce internal operating costs.

After completing this chapter you will be able to:

Learning Objectives

1. Explain why information is now considered a strategic resource.

2. Define a strategic information system.

3. Describe how the competitive forces and value chain models can be used to identify opportunities for strategic information systems.

4. Describe how information systems contribute to the four competitive strategies that businesses can pursue.

5. Explain why it is difficult to build strategic information systems and to sustain strategic advantage.

2.1   INFORMATION AS A STRATEGIC RESOURCE

In the last few decades there has been a revolution in the way that organizations treat information and information systems. Today, leading companies are using information and information systems as tools for staying ahead of competitors. Organizations have developed a special category of information systems called strategic information systems for this purpose.

WHAT IS A STRATEGIC INFORMATION SYSTEM?

strategic information systems
Computer systems at any level of the organization that change the goals, operations, products, services, or environmental relationships to help the organization gain a competitive advantage.

Strategic information systems change the goals, operations, products, services, or environmental relationships of organizations to help them gain an edge over competitors. Systems that have these effects may even change the business of organizations. Merrill Lynch, for instance, used information systems to change from the stock brokerage business to the financial services business. In the 1980s, State Street Bank and Trust Co. of Boston transformed its core business from traditional banking services, such as customer checking and savings accounts and loans, to electronic recordkeeping, providing data processing services for securities and mutual funds. Now it is moving beyond computerized recordkeeping into a broad array of financial information services, including a monitoring service that allows pension funds to keep better tabs on their money managers (Rebello, 1995).

Strategic information systems often change the organization as well as its products, services, and internal procedures, driving the organization into new behavior patterns. As we will see, organizations may need to change their internal operations to take advantage of the new information systems technology. Such changes often require new managers, a new work force, and a much closer relationship with customers and suppliers.

Behind the growing strategic uses of information systems is a changing conception of the role of information in organizations. Organizations now consider information a resource, much like capital and labor. This was not always the case.

Information as a Paper Dragon

In the past, information was often considered a necessary evil associated with the bureaucracy of designing, manufacturing, and distributing a product or service. Information was a "paper dragon" that could potentially strangle the firm and prevent it from doing its real work (see Table 2.1). Information systems of the 1950s focused on reducing the cost of routine paper processing, especially in accounting. The first information systems were semi-automatic check-processing, issuing, and canceling machines—so-called electronic accounting machines (EAM). The term *electronic data processing (EDP)* dates from this period.

Information for General Support

By the 1960s, organizations started viewing information differently, recognizing that information could be used for general management support. The information systems of the 1960s and 1970s were frequently called management information systems (MIS) and were thought of as an information factory churning out reports on weekly production, monthly financial information, inventory, accounts receivable, accounts payable, and the like. To perform these tasks, organizations acquired general-purpose computing equipment that could support many functions rather than simply canceling checks.

Information for Management

In the 1970s and early 1980s information—and the systems that collected, stored, and processed it—were seen as providing fine-tuned, special-purpose, customized management control over the organization. The information systems that emerged during this period were called decision-support systems (DSS) and executive support systems (ESS). Their purpose was to improve and speed up the decision-making process of specific managers and executives in a broad range of problems.

Information as a Strategic Resource

By the mid-1980s, the conception of information changed again. Information has since then been regarded as a strategic resource, a potential source of competitive ad-

Table 2.1	Changing Concepts of Information Systems		
Time Period	**Conception of Information**	**Information Systems**	**Purpose**
1950–1960	Necessary evil Bureaucratic requirement A paper dragon	Electronic accounting machines (EAM)	Speed accounting and paper processing
1960s–1970s	General-purpose support	Management information systems (MIS) Information factory	Speed general reporting requirements
1970s–1980s	Customized management control	Decision-support systems (DSS) Executive support systems (ESS)	Improve and customize decision making
1985–2000	Strategic resource Competitive advantage Strategic weapon	Strategic systems	Promote survival and prosperity of the organization

vantage, or a strategic weapon to defeat and frustrate the competition. These changing conceptions of information reflect advances in strategic planning and theory (Porter, 1985). The types of systems being built to support this concept of information are called strategic systems, and their purpose is to ensure the survival and prosperity of the organization in the near future.

Strategic information systems should be distinguished from strategic-level systems for senior managers that focus on long-term decision-making problems. Strategic information systems can be used at all levels of the organization and are more far-reaching and deep-rooted than the other kinds of systems we have described. Strategic information systems fundamentally change the firm's goals, products, services, or internal and external relationships. Strategic information systems profoundly alter the way a firm conducts its business or the very business of the firm itself.

2.2 HOW INFORMATION SYSTEMS CAN BE USED FOR COMPETITIVE ADVANTAGE

In order to use information systems as competitive weapons, one must first understand where strategic opportunities for businesses are likely to be found. Two models of the firm and its environment have been used to identify areas of the business where information systems can provide advantages over competitors. These are the competitive forces model and the value chain model.

COUNTERING COMPETITIVE FORCES

competitive forces model Model used to describe the interaction of external influences, specifically threats and opportunities, that affect an organization's strategy and ability to compete.

To identify where information systems can provide a competitive advantage, one must first understand the firm's relationship to its surrounding environment. In the **competitive forces model**, which is illustrated in Figure 2.1 (Porter, 1980), a firm faces a number of external threats and opportunities: the threat of new entrants into its market; the pressure from substitute products or services; the bargaining power of customers; the bargaining power of suppliers; and the positioning of traditional industry competitors.

Competitive advantage can be achieved by enhancing the firm's ability to deal with customers, suppliers, substitute products and services, and new entrants to its market, which in turn may change the balance of power between a firm and other competitors in the industry in the firm's favor. Businesses can use four basic competitive strategies to deal with these competitive forces:

product differentiation Competitive strategy for creating brand loyalty by developing new and unique products and services that are not easily duplicated by competitors.

- **Product differentiation:** Firms can develop brand loyalty by creating unique new products and services that can easily be distinguished from those of competitors, and that existing competitors or potential new competitors can't duplicate.

focused differentiation Competitive strategy for developing new market niches for specialized products or services where a business can compete in the target area better than its competitors.

- **Focused differentiation:** Businesses can create new market niches by identifying a specific target for a product or service that it can serve in a superior manner. The firm can provide a specialized product or service that serves this narrow target market better than existing competitors and that discourages potential new competitors.

switching costs The expense a customer or company incurs in lost time and expenditure of resources when changing from one supplier or system to a competing supplier or system.

- *Developing tight linkages to customers and suppliers:* Firms can create ties to customers and suppliers that "lock" customers into the firm's products and that tie suppliers into a delivery timetable and price structure shaped by the purchasing firm. This raises **switching costs** (the cost for customers to switch to competitors' products and services) and reduces customers' bargaining power and the bargaining power of suppliers.

- *Becoming the low-cost producer:* To prevent new competitors from entering their markets, businesses can produce goods and services at a lower price than competitors without sacrificing quality and level of service.

FIGURE 2.1

The competitive forces model. There are various forces that affect an organization's ability to compete and therefore greatly influence a firm's business strategy. There are threats from new market entrants and from substitute products and services. Customers and suppliers wield bargaining power. Traditional competitors constantly adapt their strategies to maintain their market positioning.

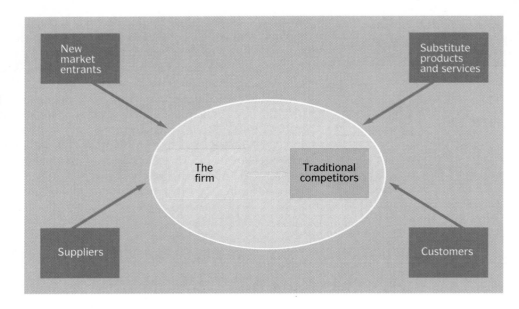

A firm may achieve competitive advantage by pursuing one of these strategies or by pursuing several strategies simultaneously. For instance, the Gillette Company described earlier is competing on quality, innovation, and cost. We now describe how information systems can support these competitive strategies.

INFORMATION SYSTEMS PRODUCTS AND SERVICES

When businesses use information systems to provide products or services that cannot be easily duplicated or that serve highly specialized markets, they can raise the market entry costs for competitors. These strategic information systems can prevent the competition from responding in kind so that firms with these differentiated products and services no longer have to compete on the basis of cost.

Financial institutions have led the way in using information systems to create new products and services. Citibank developed automatic teller machines (ATM) and bank debit cards in 1977. Seeking to tap the largest retail depository market in the United States, Citibank installed its ATM machines throughout the New York metropolitan area, everywhere a depositor might find the time to use them to deposit or withdraw money. As a leader in this area, Citibank became at one time the largest bank in the United States. Citibank ATMs were so successful that Citibank's competitors, large and small, were forced to counterstrike with a technological effort of their own called the New York Cash Exchange (NYCE).

Creating innovative information systems-based products and services does not necessarily require the most advanced or sophisticated information systems technology. The Window on Technology illustrates how the Israeli Discount Bank developed competitive advantage by designing new kinds of banking services using older information systems technology.

In 1978, Merrill Lynch, the nation's largest retail brokerage firm, developed a new financial product called a Cash Management Account, which permitted customers to transfer money freely from stocks to bonds to money market funds, and to write checks against these funds cost-free. Such flexibility in a single financial product brought Merrill Lynch into the banking industry and broadened its retail market appeal. It also forced other leading brokerage firms to offer a similar service and large banking institutions such as Citibank to counterstrike with their own flexible cash management systems.

In the retail world, manufacturers are starting to use information systems to create products and services that are custom-tailored to fit the precise specifications of

OLDER TECHNOLOGY FOR MORE MODERN CUSTOMER SERVICE

 Is having the latest information technology the most important factor in developing strategic information systems? Or is the quality of customer service more important? While many companies strive as a general policy to keep up with the latest technology, the Israeli Discount Bank (IDB) has shown that the age of the technology is less important than the strategic value of the applications developed with that technology.

IDB is headquartered in Tel Aviv, Israel, but has branches in other countries. It has $17 billion in assets competing with larger Israeli banks such as Bank Leumi and Bank Hapolaim. IDB's strategic view can be summed up as customer service. Its information technology is about 15 years old—and yet it has been a leader in offering its customers services that are only dreamed of in banks with flashier information infrastructures.

IDB has not yet installed graphics-based workstations, distributed databases, or multimedia. Most of the data are stored on mainframes in old-fashioned flat files (see Chapter 8), and the data are stored centrally (a necessity given the age of the technology) at IDB's Tel Aviv headquarters. Its old Unisys 286 terminals do not have graphical user interfaces. However, not only does the bank offer its customers the cash ATMs seen in many banks around the world, but it also has available about 400 on-line self-service terminals or SSTs (to service a country about the size of New Jersey) that offer a dazzling array of functions. The SSTs offer more than 40 kinds of financial service transactions. Using an SST, customers can produce statements of their bank accounts; obtain real-time stock market quotes; buy and sell stocks; print out a history of their credit-card purchases; check their foreign exchange accounts; transfer funds between accounts; produce account statements;

arrange for automatic check deposits; and even monitor their pension funds. In addition, the SSTs allow the customers to work in Hebrew, Arabic, or Russian. As Coopers & Lybrand banking system specialist Peter Robin says, "It's far ahead of what you would find in London, Paris, or New York." One customer's comment was "I can't believe how primitive banking was in the United States. It seems you really can't do anything there."

Customers use either a bank credit card or a self-service card to sign on to a SST, manually entering their personal identification numbers. When someone signs on, the system automatically checks to see if that customer has a monthly statement pending. If so, the customer can request it and it will be printed on the spot (all SST kiosks contain a printer). IDB claims that 44 percent of its bank statements are obtained this way, reducing the cost of stamps, envelopes, and mailing staff by nearly 50 percent. The customer gets the statement quicker as well.

IDB's SSTs and ATMs are well-utilized. A 1992 survey of IDB activity showed that 84 percent of cash withdrawals, 65 percent of all account information requests, and 44 percent of all bank statements originated from its automated services. In case customers have questions or problems, IDB stations customer service representatives at many branches to assist them.

Because of the intricate trilingual requirements, the software is developed within IDB, causing its IS department to have more than 200 developers, engineers, and other staff members. The annual IT bill is about $10 million. However, the system allows IDB to do business with more customers and keep the customers it has.

Other banks in Israel offer the same services, a competitive necessity. In the United States, according to Deborah Williams of the Tower Group in Wellesley, Massachusetts, "Some

banks. . . . have toyed with the idea of buying and selling mutual funds from automated teller systems. But none have done it so far."

> **To Think About:** Analyze IDB in terms of the competitive forces model. How well do its information systems support its competitive strategy? How has the use of information systems technology changed the way this bank does business? Why do you think IDB staff is now beginning to consider more modern technology? What management, organization, and technology factors should they consider?

IDB first started installing the SSTs in 1984, which may explain why the technology is so old. It is not that the IT staff is uninterested in modern technology. Rather staff members have not moved on into new technology because the system is working so well and performing the strategic business functions the bank wants. IDB management is conservative, cautious about tinkering with something that works so well. However, senior managers are beginning to look at more state-of-the-art technology for their network. But, according to Cooper & Lybrand's Robin, "Many banks are missing the point: The customer is number one. You have to understand what the customers need." His point is well taken. Customers do not care about the technology being used to deliver a service. They only care about the service itself. IDB may be looking at new technology. But if its longstanding record of technological conservatism combined with a strategic focus on customer service is any indication, the bank will move into new technology only slowly and in a way that will enhance, but definitely not disrupt, customer service.

Source: Joshua M. Greenbaum, "Taking It to the Streets," *InformationWEEK*, August 8, 1994.

individual customers. Levi Strauss began equipping retail stores with an option called Personal Pair, which allows customers to design jeans to their own specifications, rather than picking them off the rack. Customers enter their measurements into a microcomputer, which then transmits the customer's specification to Levi's plants. Levi Strauss is able to produce the custom jeans on the same lines that manufacture its standard items. Analysts believe that Personal Pair could become a key feature of Levi-owned stores by the year 2000. Along similar lines, Andersen Windows created a "Window of Knowledge" system that allows customers in hardware stores and retail outlets to design their own windows. Microcomputers transmit customers' window specifications to Andersen's manufacturing plant in Bayport, Minnesota. The system has given such a boost to Andersen's business that competitors are trying to copy the system (Moad, 1995). In both of these companies, information systems technology is creating customized products and services while retaining the cost efficiencies of mass production techniques, an approach called custom manufacturing. We explore custom manufacturing in greater detail in the next chapter.

SYSTEMS TO FOCUS ON MARKET NICHE

An information system can give companies a competitive advantage by producing data to improve their sales and marketing techniques. Such systems treat existing information as a resource that can be "mined" by the organization to increase profitability and market penetration. Classic examples are the sophisticated data mining systems developed by American Express, General Motors, and other companies described in the Window on Organizations.

Sears, Roebuck and Company continually mines its computerized data on its 40 million retail customers—the largest retail customer base in the United States—to target groups such as appliance buyers, tool buyers, gardening enthusiasts, and mothers-to-be. For instance, when a customer buys a washer-dryer from Sears, either on credit or for cash, Sears mails a postcard advertising an annual maintenance contract. If the contract is not purchased, Sears still maintains a record of who purchased the machine, using the information the customer supplies on the written guarantee. Each year, Sears will send out an annual maintenance contract renewal form or will

By providing a wide range of electronic financial services in self-service terminals with menu options in different foreign languages, banks such as Citibank or Israel Discount Bank can achieve a competitive advantage.

phone customers to keep its maintenance business humming. At the same time, Sears routinely sends out notices about special sales and products for these machines (such as soap and replacement parts). Likewise with electric hand tools: Purchasers routinely receive fliers on sales and products put out by Sears.

Sears also uses its customer information database to track the purchases made by credit-card customers. This information is then used to target direct mail inserts that accompany the monthly credit-card bill. In addition, information obtained on the initial credit application, as well as the history of credit purchases, can be used by the Sears marketing staff to target specific subgroups such as males between the ages of 40 and 50 who have a family and live in affluent ZIP code areas.

The cost of acquiring a new customer has been estimated to be five times that of retaining an existing customer. By carefully examining transactions of customer purchases and activities, firms can identify profitable customers, win more of their business, and develop flexible pricing, products, and services to defend their customer base against inroads from competitors. Likewise, companies can use these data to identify nonprofitable customers (Clemons and Weber, 1994).

LINKING WITH CUSTOMERS AND SUPPLIERS

Information systems can counter competitive forces by "locking in" customers and suppliers. Strategic information systems can make the costs of switching from one product to a competing product prohibitive for customers. For example, the Federal Express Corporation provides its 20,000 best customers with free personal computers linked to its Memphis headquarters. Shippers using FedEx can use the machines to check the status of the packages they send each day. Even customers that are not large enough to qualify for free computers can receive free FedEx Ship Software to use with their own microcomputers for this purpose. The software connects their computers directly to Fed Ex, creates shipping labels, prints them on customers' laster printers, schedules pickups, and tracks and confirms package delivery. The ease and convenience of using Fed Ex's package tracking system discourages customers from defecting to rivals like the United Parcel Service.

Baxter International's "stockless inventory" and ordering system is another information system that locks in customers. Participating hospitals become unwilling to switch to another supplier because of the system's convenience and low cost. Baxter Healthcare International Inc. supplies nearly two thirds of all products used by U.S. hospitals. It uses an information system originally developed by American Hospital Supply Corporation (which Baxter acquired in 1985) to become a full-line supplier for

Wal-Mart's continuous inventory replenishment system uses sales data captured at the checkout counter to transmit orders to restock merchandise directly to its suppliers. The system enables Wal-Mart to keep costs low while fine-tuning its merchandise to meet customer demands.

MINING DATA FOR PROFITS

Although it is difficult for many to imagine, organizations as large as American Express, with millions of customers worldwide, have refined their ability to target their marketing to the point where they may make a targeted promotional offer to as few as 20 customers. Marketing has come a long way from its early exclusive reliance on mass marketing, where the same message is directed at virtually everyone. Many years ago, marketers developed the concept of market segmentation, in which advertisers directed their messages at smaller, more targeted though still anonymous, massive groups. We see targeted marketing at work today when we receive an offer in the mail for products that go to residents only in certain ZIP codes, or when we see beer advertising on television during major sports events. The newest approach, commonly known as *data mining*, consists of personal or individualized messages based upon likely individual preferences. Many of us have been the target of relatively unsophisticated, obvious examples of such campaigns when we have received mail offers timed for our birthday or a magazine to which we subscribed with advertisements that carry our name in them.

Data mining has a primary goal of better understanding current and potential customers in order to boost sales and build customer loyalty. Many companies are trying to recreate the small town atmosphere where customers will feel comfortable and loyal because they are known and understood by their "local" merchants. Other companies turn to data mining because they believe they have no choice if they wish to remain competitive. For example, the competition for shelf space in supermarkets can be so fierce that retailers will demand that the distributors of brand name products carry out targeted marketing campaigns if they wish to retain a large allocation of shelf space in the store.

Some practitioners of data mining even claim the lofty goal of killing off junk mail by targeting mailings so finely that they will only reach people who want to receive the offers.

What is data mining? It is based on the idea that past behavior is the best indicator of the purchasing interests of consumers. Massive quantities of data are gathered on consumers and then analyzed to locate customers with specific interests or to determine the interests of a specific group of customers. The data come from a range of sources. For example, every time we purchase by credit or credit card, the seller or the credit-card company adds another piece of information about where and when we shop, the kinds of goods that interest us, the prices we are willing to pay, the type of stores we frequent, where and when we travel. Companies also will gather specific personal and preference information from us whenever we apply for credit, fill out product warranties, or respond to promotional offers that require filling out forms requesting personal information. They will also purchase personal information from other companies and from public agencies such as state motor vehicle departments. The data from the various sources are combined, and then analyzed usually using new, powerful technology, including massively parallel supercomputers (discussed in Chapter 6) and neural network software (examined in Chapter 17).

A simple example of how data can tell businesses about us is the case of an existing bank customer who suddenly applies for a joint bank account. If the bank knows it is the first joint account, the bank might conclude the customer is about to get married and so will attempt to market him or her life insurance and long-term investments in order to save for buying a house, paying children's college costs, or prepare for retirement. The bank might also sell the information to a company that markets goods related to marriages.

Data mining systems have become strategic to many companies who use it

to generate sales. American Express has a gigantic database that can store over 500 billion characters or numbers culled from $350 billion in spending

> **To Think About:**   Describe effects the use of data mining would have upon organizations such as those described here. What benefits does data mining provide? What problems does it create?

during 1991 and continually updated since. One way it uses this data is in *relationship billing*. With this concept, if, for example, a customer purchases a dress at Saks Fifth Avenue department store, American Express might include in her next billing an offer of a discount on a pair of shoes purchased at the same store and charged on her American Express card. The two goals are to increase the customer's use of her American Express card and also to expand the presence of American Express at Saks. Customers will often receive a customized newsletter. A card holder residing in London, England, who recently took a British Airways flight to Paris might find an offer in the newsletter for a special discounted "getaway" weekend to New York. The resident of New York City who just purchased a suit on his card will find a different offer in that place in the same newsletter.

Fingerhut Co., a catalog retailer headquartered in Minnetonka, Minnesota, has a database with 25 million customers. Fingerhut might search through the data to locate all who bought patio furniture this season to attempt to sell them a gas barbecue grill. Kraft General Foods has built a database of 30 million customers who have responded to coupons and other promotions. Kraft augments the data by surveying customers and learning about their interests and tastes. Then based upon their profiles, Kraft sends them selected coupons with appropriate tips on nutrition and exercise, as well as recipes that include Kraft-branded products. Reader's Digest owns one of the largest such databases in the world. Started 40 years ago, today it has information on over 100 million families worldwide. The database is running 24 hours per day, seven days per week, and is constantly being updated. Reader's Digest guards these data jealously and will neither rent nor sell its lists. The company considers them so important that when it moved into the specialty magazine business in 1989 by acquiring four magazines, Reader's Digest management stated that the most important reason for the acquisitions was to strengthen its database. They use the data to make all kinds of special marketing appeals of magazines, books, tapes, videos, and CDs, all of which are produced by Reader's Digest.

Some companies find themselves in new businesses primarily to gain and control a key database. General Motors has joined with a credit-card company, MasterCard, to offer a GM credit card. Simply by applying for this credit card, these credit-card holders are expressing a strong interest in purchasing General Motors vehicles because they know that bonus points earned by charging with this card are used to reduce the price of a GM vehicle. GM surveys 12 million card holders regularly to learn of their current driving habits, the types of vehicles that interest them, and when a purchase is likely. At the suitable time, the customer information is passed on to the appropriate GM division to attempt to sell them a vehicle.

Philip Morris Co. has a different reason for building a database—survival. With the increasing restrictions on smoking and on smoking advertising, the company has been forced to find new ways to market to smokers and to maintain their loyalty. It uses offerings of other products, such as free shirts or sales of items in a catalog to learn who are smokers and which ones smoke Philip Morris brands. The com-

pany then sends the appropriate customers coupons and special offers. It also enlists its customers in the tobacco industry's continuing political battle against further restrictions on smoking and on tobacco advertising.

Falling hardware and software costs have allowed small businesses to use data mining. Yuri Radzievsky of YAR Communications used a Macintosh personal computer to collect a list of 50,000 Russians, 75,000 Poles, and 30,000 Israelis living in the United States. He sells his lists to clients like AT&T who mail offers for discount telephone service on calls home to these prospective customers in Hebrew and Russian. Health Valley Foods, a small Irwindale, California, maker of health cereals, soups, and snacks sold to health-food stores, built a database using names from letters of complaint and inquiry and from calls to the company's 800 number providing tips on health eating. Health Valley Foods then used its database to create mailing lists for special promotions of its products, developing enough customer loyalty to move on to supermarket shelves. Between 1989 and 1993 its sales doubled to more than $100 million.

Organizations that use data mining have encountered many problems. The technology can be expensive, often requiring supercomputers, vast amounts of data storage, and expensive software. The user must be certain that the returns are worth the costs. Alan Gottesman, an analyst at Paine-Webber, put it this way, "If it costs $1.35 to get someone to try a 75 cent product and there's only a 30 percent chance he's going to buy it again, forget it." Some companies find their managers are reluctant to use the output of data mining analysis, preferring to rely instead on their traditional "gut" instinct in making marketing decisions. The data can also be managed improperly, as Reader's Digest discovered. The various divisions of Reader's Digest all used these data to issue their

own special offers in the early 1990s. The company neither limited the offers nor coordinated them. As a result, a person with an interest in travel might in quick succession have received offers for a special travel magazine (*Travel Holiday*), language CDs, language tapes, travel videotapes, and travel books. Inundated customers tended to overbuy for a while, and then sales fell off, resulting in a sharp drop in the price of the stock. Recovery of the stock price took several years.

Perhaps the most pervasive problem in the use of data mining techniques is the potential for abuse of the lists and a negative reaction from customers as if the use of the information itself is an abuse. Customers often feel their privacy has been invaded when companies know so much about them or sell their names to other businesses for their lists. In one case, a policeman kept his address and telephone number private out of fear of retribution from crooks he had arrested. However, he totally lost his privacy when the hospital where his new baby was born sold his name to a range of companies who market to families of newborns. In a common reaction, Mary Culnan, an associate professor of business at Georgetown University, closed down her credit-card account when she received a telephone sales pitch for a dental insurance plan soon after paying her dental bill on her credit card. Many people fear the government or businesses knowing too much about them, using such terms at *creepy* to describe how much others know or *big brother* to describe the fear of power others might have over them.

Sources: Jonathan Berry, John Verity, Kathleen Kerwin, and Gail DeGeorge, "Database Marketing," *Business Week*, September 5, 1994; Deirdre Carmody, "Lifeblood at Reader's Digest Is a 40-Year-Old Data Base," *The New York Times*, May 17, 1994; Laurie Hays, "Using Computers to Divine Who Might Buy a Gas Grill," *The Wall Street Journal*, August 16, 1994.

hospitals, a one-stop source for all hospital needs. This effort requires an inventory of more than 120,000 items. Maintaining a huge inventory is very costly. However, it is also costly *not* to have items in stock, because hospitals switch to competitors.

Terminals tied to Baxter's own computers are installed in hospitals. When hospitals want to place an order, they do not need to call a salesperson or send a purchase order—they simply use a Baxter computer terminal on-site to order from the full Baxter supply catalog. The system generates shipping, billing, invoicing, and inventory information, and the hospital terminals provide customers with an estimated delivery date. With more than 80 distribution centers in the United States, Baxter can make daily deliveries of its products, often within hours of receiving an order.

This system is similar to the just-in-time delivery systems developed in Japan and now being used in the American automobile industry. In these systems, automobile manufacturers such as GM or Chrysler enter the quantity and delivery schedules of specific automobile components into their own information systems. Then these requirements are automatically entered into a supplier's order entry information system. The supplier must respond with an agreement to deliver the materials at the time specified. Thus, automobile companies can reduce the cost of inventory, the space required for warehousing components or raw materials, and construction time.

Baxter has even gone one step further. Delivery personnel no longer drop off their cartons at a loading dock to be placed in a hospital storeroom. Instead, they deliver orders directly to the hospital corridors, dropping them at nursing stations, operating rooms, and stock supply closets. This has created in effect a "stockless inventory," with Baxter serving as the hospitals' warehouse. Stockless inventory substantially reduces the need for hospital storage space and personnel and lowers holding and handling costs (Caldwell, 1991). New Textron Automotive Interiors plants in Columbia, Missouri, and the Netherlands, which build instrument panels for Fords, use a similar stockless inventory system. Textron's suppliers deliver parts directly to its assembly lines.

Figure 2.2 compares stockless inventory with the just-in-time supply method and traditional inventory practices. While just-in-time inventory allows customers to reduce their inventories, stockless inventory allows them to eliminate their inventories entirely. All inventory responsibilities shift to the distributor, who manages the sup-

FIGURE 2.2
A comparison of traditional inventory and delivery practices to the *just-in-time supply method* and the *stockless inventory method.* Strategic systems for linking customers and suppliers have changed the way in which some companies handle the supply and inventory requirements of their businesses. The just-in-time supply method reduces inventory requirements of the customer while stockless inventory allows the customer to eliminate inventories entirely, resulting in a decided competitive advantage. *Adapted from "Removing the Warehouse from Cost-Conscious Hospitals,"* The New York Times, *March 3, 1991. Copyright © 1991 by The New York Times Company. Reprinted by permission.*

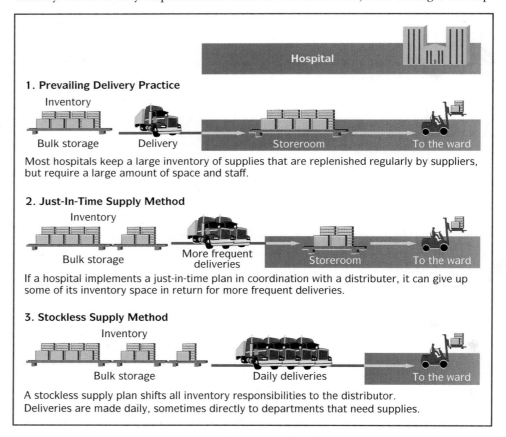

1. **Prevailing Delivery Practice**

Inventory

Bulk storage   Delivery   Storeroom   To the ward

Most hospitals keep a large inventory of supplies that are replenished regularly by suppliers, but require a large amount of space and staff.

2. **Just-In-Time Supply Method**

Inventory

Bulk storage   More frequent deliveries   Storeroom   To the ward

If a hospital implements a just-in-time plan in coordination with a distributer, it can give up some of its inventory space in return for more frequent deliveries.

3. **Stockless Supply Method**

Inventory

Bulk storage   Daily deliveries   To the ward

A stockless supply plan shifts all inventory responsibilities to the distributor.
Deliveries are made daily, sometimes directly to departments that need supplies.

ply flow. The stockless inventory is a powerful instrument for binding customers, giving the supplier a decided competitive advantage.

Strategic systems aimed at suppliers, such as the automobile manufacturers' ordering systems described above or Wal-Mart's "continuous replenishment section" described in the following section, are designed to maximize the firm's purchasing power (and minimize costs) by having suppliers interact with its information system to satisfy the firm's precise business needs. If suppliers are unwilling to go along with this system, they may lose business to other suppliers who can meet these demands.

On the other hand, these information systems also provide benefits for suppliers. Suppliers can continually monitor product requirements, factory scheduling, and commitments of their customers against their own schedule to ensure that enough inventory will be available. The manufacturers and retailers are their customers. Once these systems are in place and working smoothly, their efficiency and convenience may help discourage the vendors' customers from switching to competitors.

Interorganizational Systems and Electronic Markets

interorganizational systems
Information systems that automate the flow of information across organizational boundaries and link a company to its customers, distributors, or suppliers.

The systems that link a company to its customers, distributors, or suppliers are termed **interorganizational systems** because they automate the flow of information across organizational boundaries (Barrett, 1986–1987; Johnston and Vitale, 1988). Such systems allow information or processing capabilities of one organization to improve the performance of another or to improve relationships among organizations. In addition to tightening linkages to customers or suppliers, interorganizational systems can lower costs and increase product differentiation.

electronic market A marketplace that is created by computer and communication technologies which link many buyers and sellers via interorganizational systems.

Interorganizational systems that provide services to multiple organizations by linking together many buyers and sellers create an **electronic market**. Through computers and telecommunications, these systems function like electronic middlemen (Malone, Yates, and Benjamin, 1987).

Electronic markets are growing because computer and communication technologies can lower the costs of typical marketplace transactions such as selecting suppliers, establishing prices, ordering goods, and paying bills. For example, Charles Schwab and Company, a discount brokerage service, sells investors software for their personal computers to obtain current price quotes for stocks, bonds, and mutual funds; to access research reports from firms such as Standard & Poor's; and to execute trades themselves. Schwab customers can also place orders to trade and obtain price quotes from a touch-tone telephone. By using information systems to provide a single low-cost channel for securities trading and specialized banking services, Schwab is revolutionizing the way financial services are being sold to the public.

Computerized airline reservation systems are used by airline reservation agents and also by independent travel agents (about 80 percent of all airline tickets issued in the United States are sold by travel agents using these computerized reservation systems). Although there are rival systems from other airlines, American Airlines' SABRE system and United Airlines' Apollo system control 75 percent of the computerized reservation system market.

While these systems provide unparalleled convenience to airline travelers, as well as to travel agents who must book flights (e.g., SABRE enables travel agents to serve their customers with reservations for airlines, hotels, and cars), they also confer formidable market power on the two airlines. Medium-size air carriers claimed unfair treatment by SABRE and Apollo because these reservation systems were listing American and United Airlines flights first. This example indicates how a strategic system gives a supplier a market advantage over a distributor and a customer.

Because computerized reservation systems cost tens of millions of dollars to develop, smaller carriers were discouraged from building their own systems. The smaller carriers have their flights listed on their bigger competitors' systems but must pay a fee to the airline owning the system every time a ticket is sold through the computerized reservation system. (Small airlines such as Southwest and Kiwi have claimed success in using inexpensive off-the-shelf information system technology to build their own low-cost reservation systems. It remains to be seen whether travel agents will accept working with many disparate reservation systems.) SABRE and Apollo have been major sources of revenue for their owners.

Public policy, through the courts or the legislature, has acted to set limits on the uses of information technology to preserve fairness and competition. After a congressional investigation, the Civil Aeronautics Board in 1984 forced American Airlines to remove any bias in the display of flights on SABRE screens. Eleven other airlines joined in an antitrust suit against both United and American. Consumer advocates, competing airlines, and the U.S. Department of Transportation asked the Justice Department to consider blocking a proposed merger of American and Delta Airlines' computerized reservation systems because the combined system would control 46 percent of the market for ticket reservations.

Chapter 9 covers the technologies underlying interorganizational systems and electronic markets.

SYSTEMS TO LOWER COSTS

The strategic systems we described change the strategic relationship between an organization and its markets, customers, and suppliers. Other strategically oriented information systems facilitate internal operations, management control, planning, and personnel. These systems are strategic because they help firms significantly lower their internal costs, allowing them to deliver products and services at a lower price (and sometimes with higher quality) than their competitors can provide. By lowering operating costs, raising profits, and making firms more efficient, such systems contribute to the survival and prosperity of the firm. The following examples describe information uses that are much more dynamic and intensive than mere management support tools.

The Wizard system developed by Avis, the car rental company, is an example of a strategic internal MIS designed to improve the firm's overall productivity. This system keeps track of the location, costs, and performance of Avis car rental fleet. This capability, in turn, has permitted Avis to compete effectively against Hertz, National, and other car rental firms by optimizing the distribution of its car rental fleet to ensure that cars are available where there is a demand for them and that costs are kept to a minimum.

By keeping prices low and shelves well-stocked, Wal-Mart has become the leading retail business in the United States. Wal-Mart uses a legendary inventory replenishment system triggered by point-of-sale purchases that is considered the best in the industry. The "continuous replenishment system" sends orders for new merchandise directly to suppliers as soon as consumers pay for their purchases at the cash register. Point-of-sale terminals record the bar code of each item passing the checkout counter and send a purchase transaction directly to a central computer at Wal-Mart headquarters. The computer collects the orders from all of the Wal-Mart stores and transmits them to suppliers. Because the system can replenish inventory with lightning speed, Wal-Mart does not need to spend much money on maintaining large inventories of goods in its own warehouses. The system also allows Wal-Mart to adjust purchases of store items to meet customer demands. Competitors such as Sears spend nearly 30 percent of each dollar in sales to pay for overhead (that is, expenses for salaries, advertising, warehousing, and building upkeep). Kmart spends 21 percent of sales on overhead. But by using systems to keep operating costs low, Wal-Mart pays only 15 percent of sales revenue for overhead.

Airlines have used information systems strategically to lower costs so that they can counter competitors' discount fares. Information systems have automated a technique called yield management that allows carriers to match any discount fare that arises as efficiently and sparingly as possible. Yield management is the process of wringing the most profit out of every airline seat and determining when to drop or increase prices or offer promotions. On average, every airline seat is booked one and one-half times and canceled one and one-half times during the three months before a flight. Yield management develops a spot price for any seat at any time. For example, a Sunday evening flight from New York to London might show 70 empty seats a week from departure. Rather than offer cut-rate fares to fill up the plane, the yield management system examines the historical pattern of that flight and determines how many seats the airline should set aside for executives willing to pay full fares at the last moment.

The Window on Management shows how information systems for controlling costs and boosting efficiency can help entrepreneurs maintain their profitability in a difficult competitive environment.

All of the examples in this section show that information systems can have strategic implications for the organization's internal operations and can alter critical balances with external environmental factors such as new products and services, customers, and suppliers. Together these internal and external strategic changes alter the firm's competitive advantage. Strategic systems counter competitive forces by rapidly changing the basis of competition.

LEVERAGING TECHNOLOGY IN THE VALUE CHAIN

value chain model Model that highlights the primary or support activities that add a margin of value to a firm's products or services where information systems can best be applied to achieve a competitive advantage.

The **value chain model** highlights specific activities in the business where competitive strategies can be best applied (Porter, 1985) and where information systems are most likely to have a strategic impact. The value chain model can supplement the competitive forces model by identifying specific, critical leverage points where a firm can use information technology most effectively to enhance its competitive position. Exactly where can it obtain the greatest benefit from strategic information systems— what specific activities can be used to create new products and services, enhance market penetration, lock in customers and suppliers, and lower operational costs? This model views the firm as a series or "chain" of basic activities that add a margin of value to a firm's products or services. These activities can be categorized as either primary activities or support activities.

primary activities Activities most directly related to the production and distribution of a firm's products or services.

Primary activities are most directly related to the production and distribution of the firm's products and services that create value for the customer. Primary activities include inbound logistics, operations, outbound logistics, sales and marketing, and service. Inbound logistics include receiving and storing materials for distribution to production. Operations transforms inputs into finished products. Outbound logistics entail storing and distributing products. Marketing and sales includes promoting and selling the firm's products. The service activity includes maintenance and repair of the firm's goods and services. **Support activities** make the delivery of the primary activities possible and consist of organization infrastructure (administration and management), human resources (employee recruiting, hiring, and training), technology (improving products and the production process), and procurement (purchasing input).

support activities Activities that make the delivery of the primary activities of a firm possible. Consist of the organization's infrastructure, human resources, technology, and procurement.

Organizations have competitive advantage when they provide more value to their customers or when they provide the same value to customers at a lower price. An information system could have strategic impact if it helped the firm provide products or services at a lower cost than competitors or if it provided products and services at the same cost as competitors but with greater value. Gillette's systems described in the chapter-opening vignette create value by both lowering production costs and raising the level of quality of Gillette razors and blades. The value activities that add the most value to products and services depend on the features of each particular firm. Businesses should try to develop strategic information systems for the value activities that add the most value to their particular firm. Wal-Mart, for example, found it could achieve competitive advantage by focusing on logistics. Figure 2.3 illustrates the activities of the value chain, showing examples of strategic information systems that could be developed to make each of the value activities more cost effective.

CAN A SMALL BUSINESS COMPETE UNDER PRICE PRESSURE?

How can a small business survive when being squeezed by pricing competition? Five-million-dollar (1994) Header Die & Tool Inc. found a way—using information technology to help the company better control its costs and so compete at lower prices. Header's customers are fastener manufacturers that sell to the automobile industry. According to Header executive vice president, Pat Derry, his labor, insurance, and tax costs keep rising while competition is becoming more intense, particularly given the growing economic globalization. And, of course, his customers are demanding higher quality and more service. Large companies are squeezing labor and parts costs while asking smaller companies to provide more customization, service, and preassembly work than in the past. As Michael S. Flynn, the associate director of the Office for the Study of Automotive Transportation at the University of Michigan, put it, "The pressure from auto makers . . . is being passed all the way down through the chain. . . ."

These problems are particularly difficult for small businesses. Large corporations often temporarily use higher profits in one product line to subsidize profits in another product line. Small businesses have no such option. Yet Header does not want to raise prices because its management believes that would simply cause its customers to go elsewhere. To remain competitive, Header management decided on a three-pronged strategy: increased understanding of the costs in order to be able to reduce them; helping customers to redesign their products to be less expensive; and improved customer service.

To help Header price aggressively yet profitably, Derry bought two off-the-shelf microcomputer applications at a total cost of $27,000 (including the computer hardware needed to run them). Machine Shop Estimating System (Micro Estimating Systems Inc., Franklin, Wisconsin) produces a time and cost estimate for products that are manufactured using manually controlled equip-

ment. The other, MasterCam (CNC Software, Tolland, Connecticut), does the same for products that will be built using equipment controlled by computer-aided-manufacturing (CAM) software.

Here's how the Machine Shop Estimating System works. When a customer asks for a price quote on a job that is to be produced on manually set machinery, the estimator inputs a detailed description of the most efficient process for manufacturing the product. The software analyzes various possibilities for manufacturing the product and calculates how much time operators and their equipment will have to spend making it. By trying several different approaches to manufacturing the product, the software can provide comparative costs, allowing Header to identify and use the lowest cost method of manual production. Moreover, the software enables the company to price the product more accurately than previous manual methods. The company is now much less likely to set the bid price higher than needed to cover its costs and expected profit; such pricing can result in the unnecessary loss of some contracts. Similarly, the company is less likely to bid too low, which will result in the company taking an unexpected loss if it is awarded the contract.

MasterCam performs similar functions for CAM-controlled manufacturing, allowing Header staff to predict how much time and labor will be required to produce a specified product and to adjust the process speed or improve the product's surface finish. An operator selects the tools (center drill, drill, bore, turn, cut-off) needed to produce a given product, then instructs the computer on how far the tools should move and how far and fast they should cut. The system generates the programs for Header's computer-controlled machinery.

MasterCam sometimes can produce big savings because the CAM-controlled production process can achieve higher precision than can manual methods. In one case, for example, Header decided to bid on a job to manufacture a punch for a large fastener manufacturer that

was already its customer. In the past Header had bid the product at $27 and won the contract, producing it with manually controlled equipment. How-

> *To Think About:* Use the competitive forces model to analyze Header Die & Tool. How did its manufacturing software support its competitive strategy? How did information systems change the way Header conducted its business? Suggest other types of software that might help a small business like Header reduce its costs.

ever, Derry knew that this time the bid had to be much lower because the company's main competition was to be the customer's own in-house tool shop. Using MasterCam, and playing with the process to find the least costly approach, Header was able to bid—and win—the job at $21. The reason for the lower price was Header's ability to make the punch faster and with more precision using CAM machines. Derry claims that Header can usually reduce its costs by 8 to 10 percent using MasterCam.

Using the software, Header engineers are also often able to modify designs in order to identify ways of making products less expensively. Derry will then suggest the new design to the customer, urging the customer to "make certain that everything you are paying us to do is necessary." The result, of course, often is a satisfied customer and another winning bid.

Derry also finds that he is able to use these two pieces of software to service his customers more quickly. In the automobile industry, customers are often in a hurry. When Header's customers offer a contract for bidding, they want a response quickly. Derry finds that using the estimating software, he is able to submit an accurate bid to the prospective customer rapidly enough that he now requires his company to fax back its bid within 24 hours of having received the specifications.

Source: Jeannie Mandelker, "Pricing with Precision," *Profit,* September–October 1994.

FIGURE 2.3
Activities of the value chain. Various examples of strategic information systems for the primary and support activities of a firm that would add a margin of value to a firm's products or services.

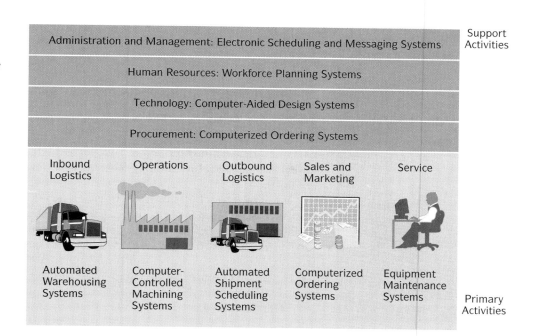

For instance, a firm could save money in the inbound logistics activity by having suppliers make daily deliveries of goods to the factory, thereby lowering the costs of warehousing and inventory. A computer-aided design system might support the technology activity, helping a firm to reduce costs and perhaps to design more high-quality products than the competition produces. Gillette's computer-controlled machining supports the operations activity, reducing costs and boosting quality. Such systems would be more likely to have strategic impact in a manufacturing firm, whereas an electronic scheduling and messaging system or office automation technology would more likely have strategic value in a law firm or consulting firm.

A strategic analysis might identify the sales and marketing activity as an area where information systems would provide the greatest productivity boost. The analysis might recommend a system similar to those used by American Express, Fingerhut, or Reader's Digest for bringing together and analyzing data (described in this chapter's Window on Organizations) to reduce marketing costs by targeting marketing campaigns more efficiently. The system might also provide information that lets the firm develop products more finely attuned to its target market as well. Many different projects, or a series of linked systems, may be required to create a strategic advantage.

2.3   IMPLICATIONS FOR MANAGERS AND ORGANIZATIONS

The strategic information systems that we have described leverage information systems technology and technology impacts. Until recently, information systems played a relatively minor role in the production, distribution, and sale of products and services. Vast increases in the productivity of information processing made relatively little difference in the firm's productivity or bottom-line balance sheet. Now, however, as the operations of an organization have come to depend heavily on information systems, and as these systems penetrate the organization, increases in the productivity of information processing can have dramatic implications for the overall productivity of the corporation. This leveraging effect is important when we consider recommendations for management.

The corporate alliance between Northwest Airlines and First Bank led to this marketing campaign where flyers are awarded bonus travel miles on Northwest for using First Bank's Visa credit card.

information partnership Cooperative alliance formed between two corporations for the purpose of sharing information to gain strategic advantage.

In general, strategic information systems provide significant, although generally temporary, market advantages, principally by raising the entry costs of competitors. If short-term advantages are repeated, however, a firm that gains an advantage for five years can utilize the time and the additional resources that leadership brings to ensure that it maintains a technological advantage for the next five years, and so on. Firms can thus build on their initial successes and can develop a stream of innovative applications if they have the staff to support their information systems and if they understand the strategic importance of information. For instance, a company can parlay a series of innovations into a valuable market image of it as a consistent leader at the cutting edge of technology. This image alone can help maintain the firm's market position.

Firms may also find that a single, generic strategy such as cost leadership will not be sufficient to combat competitors. The low cost of information systems technology has made it much easier for new, opportunistic, and nimble competitors to finely tune their products and prices to win away a firm's customer base. Firms that pursue a strategy of being the low cost leader may find that they also have to compete on quality; to remain competitive they may have to implement multiple strategies simultaneously (Clemons and Weber, 1994).

Sometimes systems that first provide an exclusive advantage to one company are worth more if they are shared with others. For instance, American Airlines jealously guarded its yield management system (described earlier in this chapter). But beginning in 1986, it started selling its yield management expertise to any firm that wanted to buy it. American even set up a subsidiary, AA Decision Technologies, to build yield management systems for airlines, railroads, and other companies (Hopper, 1990). Mrs. Fields Cookies is marketing its Retail Operations Intelligence system, an automated store management network, to other retail chains.

STRATEGIC ALLIANCES AND INFORMATION PARTNERSHIPS

Companies are increasingly using information systems for strategic advantage by entering into strategic alliances with other companies where both firms cooperate by sharing resources or services. Such alliances are often **information partnerships** in which two or more firms share data for mutual advantage (Konsynski and McFarlan, 1990). They can join forces without actually merging. American Airlines has an arrangement with Citibank to award one mile in its frequent flier program for every dollar spent using Citibank credit cards. American benefits from increased customer loyalty, while Citibank gains new credit-card subscribers and a highly creditworthy customer base for cross-marketing. Northwest Airlines has a similar arrangement with First Bank of Minneapolis. American and Northwest have also allied with MCI, awarding frequent flier miles for each dollar of long-distance billing.

Although falling sales caused Sears, Roebuck and Co. to close its "big book" general mail order catalog, it set up joint ventures with six partners to produce 14 smaller catalogs catering to specialized market niches such as work wear and auto accessories. Sears provides its partners access to its database of 24 million credit-card customers and database mining analysis. Its partners then select the merchandise, mail the catalogs, and fill the orders using their own merchandise. Although the Sears name goes on the cover, the catalogs produced by the partners are similar to those mailed to their own customers, except that the partners tailor the merchandise selection to the buying patterns of Sears customers. Sears shares the profits from each catalog. Sears partners, such as Hanover Direct Inc. in Weehawken, New Jersey, benefit from the powerful Sears merchandising name and access to Sears' customer base. This information partnership allows Sears to make money in the mail order business even though it is no longer in catalogs (Chandler, 1994).

Such partnerships help firms gain access to new customers, creating new opportunities for cross-selling and targeting products. They can share investments in computer hardware and software. Sometimes traditional competitors (such as Sears and competing catalog companies) can benefit from some of these partnerships. Baxter Healthcare International offers its customers medical supplies from competitors and office supplies through its electronic ordering channel. Even companies that were traditional competitors have found such alliances to be mutually advantageous.

MANAGING STRATEGIC TRANSITIONS

strategic transitions A movement from one level of sociotechnical system to another. Often required when adopting strategic systems that demand changes in the social and technical elements of an organization.

Adopting the kinds of systems described in this chapter generally requires changes in business goals, relationships with customers and suppliers, internal operations, and information architecture. These sociotechnical changes, affecting both social and technical elements of the organization, can be considered **strategic transitions**—a movement between levels of sociotechnical systems.

How much sociotechnical change occurs depends on the specific circumstances. Clearly, however, there is a connection between the strategy of an organization and its internal structure. As companies move to make information systems part of the overall corporate strategy, their internal structure must also change to reflect these new developments. Managers struggling to boost competitiveness will need to redesign various organizational processes to make effective use of leading-edge information systems technology.

Such changes often entail blurring of organizational boundaries, both external and internal. This is especially true of telecommunications-based strategic systems (Cash and Konsynski, 1985; Keen, 1986). Suppliers and customers must become intimately linked and may share each other's responsibilities. For instance, in Baxter International's stockless inventory system, Baxter has assumed responsibility for managing its customers' inventories (Johnston and Vitale, 1988). With the help of information systems, the supplier actually makes the inventory replenishment decisions, based on orders, point-of-sale data, or warehouse data supplied by the customer. This approach to inventory management, called **vendor-managed inventory,** is based on the theory that suppliers are the product or "category" experts and thus can do the best job of making sure that supply meets demand. Managers will need to devise new mechanisms for coordinating their firms' activities with those of customers, suppliers, and other organizations (Kambil and Short, 1994).

vendor-managed inventory Approach to inventory management that assigns the supplier the responsibility to make inventory replenishment decisions based on order, point-of-sale data, or warehouse data supplied by the customer.

Firms with successful strategic information systems have broken down organizational barriers that block the sharing of data across functions. Design, sales, and manufacturing departments must work together much more closely. Federal Express' package-tracking system shares information among operations, customer service, and accounting functions. Firestone Tire & Rubber Company has made tire design information available to quality control, production, and testing groups as well as to customers' engineers. Sundstrand Corporation has halved its warehousing staff and expedited customer-order processing by improving information systems links between spare parts ordering, warehousing, and manufacturing control in the aerospace industry. Over time, Baxter redesigned its work processes numerous times to continually improve its overall service level and business relationship to customers (Short and Venkatraman, 1992).

Other organizational changes may be required as well. Gillette found that its sophisticated new machines that produced its redesigned razors raised the level of technology so much that operators needed more training. The operators didn't understand the reports on quality and production rates produced by these machines and how to make appropriate adjustments to the equipment. Gillette revised its employee development policies to stage remedial education before introducing new equipment. Standard operating procedures may also need to be redesigned. As companies examine their value chains for strategic opportunities, looking for the activities that add the most value, they are finding many wasted steps or procedures that could be eliminated. In redesigning a Celina, Ohio plant, Reynolds & Reynolds Co. of Dayton,

Ohio, found that 90 separate steps were required to fill an order for its business forms. Using a new ordering information system that enters specifications for orders directly into the computer, Reynolds cut the steps down to 20 and the elapsed time from quoting the order to shipment from three weeks to one (Bulkeley, 1994).

In some cases, reshaping an organization to remain competitive may necessitate an entirely new organizational structure. General Motors, in order to develop a comprehensive strategic information system strategy, had to purchase Electronic Data Systems, EDS, a consulting firm specializing in data processing and communications services. And to produce the Saturn, a new low-cost car competitive with Japanese models, GM also created an entirely new automotive division with a new factory, a new sales force, and a new design team to utilize the new technologies. Not all strategic information systems require such massive change, but clearly, many do. The organizational change requirements surrounding new information systems are so important that they merit attention throughout this text. Chapters 3, 11, and 14 examine organizational change issues in great detail.

WHAT MANAGERS CAN DO

Information systems are too important to be left entirely to a small technical group in the corporation. Managers must take the initiative to identify the types of systems that would provide a strategic advantage to the firm. Although some industries are far ahead of others in their use of information technology, some of those that are far behind may be so for a good reason: The technology may not be appropriate. Other industries have simply failed to keep up with the times and thus offer considerable opportunities for vast and rapid changes. Some of the important questions managers should ask themselves are as follows:

- What are some of the forces at work in the industry? What strategies are being used by industry leaders?
- How is the industry currently using information and communication technology? Which organizations are the industry leaders in the application of information systems technology?
- What are the direction and nature of change within the industry? Where are the momentum and change coming from?
- Are significant strategic opportunities to be gained by introducing information systems technology into the industry? Can information systems alter the basis of competition, build in switching costs, generate new products, strengthen the firm's power in dealing with suppliers, or create barriers against new competitors (Cash, McFarlan, McKenney, and Applegate, 1992)?
- What kinds of systems are applicable to the industry? Does it require systems to create new products and services, supplier systems, and/or sales and marketing systems?

Once the nature of information systems technology in the industry is understood, managers should turn to their organization and ask other important questions:

- Is the organization behind or ahead of the industry in its application of information systems?
- What is the current business strategic plan, and how does that plan mesh with the current strategy for information services?
- Have the information technologies currently in use provided significant payoffs to the business? Do they largely support the business or drain its resources?
- Where would new information systems provide the greatest value to the firm?

Once these issues have been considered, managers can gain a keener insight into whether their firms are ready for strategic information systems.

Studies of successful strategic systems have found that they are rarely planned but instead evolve slowly over long periods of time, and they almost always originate with practical operational problems. For instance, SABRE, the American Airlines computerized reservation system that is often cited as a classic "strategic system," originated as a straightforward inventory control and order entry system (Copeland and McKenney, 1988; Hopper, 1990). Rather than sprouting from some magical methodology, strategic systems, like most new products, come from closely observing real-world business situations. This finding may provide a clue about how to look for powerful strategic impact systems.

Management Challenges

1. Sustainability of competitive advantage. The competitive advantages conferred by strategic systems do not necessarily last long enough to ensure long-term profits. Competitors can retaliate and copy strategic systems. Moreover, these systems are often expensive; costs saved by some systems are expended immediately to maintain the system.

Competitive advantage isn't always sustainable. Market conditions change. The business and economic environment changes. Technology and customers' expectations change. The classic strategic information systems—American Airlines' SABRE computerized reservation system, Citibank's ATM system, and Federal Express' package tracking system—benefited by being the first in their respective industries. But then rival systems emerged. NYCE banks blunted Citibank's ATM edge. United Parcel Service, described in Chapter 1, is challenging Federal Express' domination of the overnight package market. Information systems alone cannot provide an enduring business advantage (Hopper, 1990).

Systems originally intended to be strategic frequently become tools for survival, something every firm has in order to stay in business. Rather than conferring long-term competitive advantage, they become critical for a company just to keep abreast of the competition.

2. Organizational barriers to strategic transitions. Implementing strategic systems usually requires far-reaching sociotechnical changes. This goal is not easy to accomplish because organizational change is frequently resisted by middle and even senior managers. In fact, one of the greatest obstacles to strategic transitions may be resistance to change—both the changes that are imposed on an organization and those that employees experience as their jobs are reshaped. Even the identities of employees must change. One is no longer simply a salesperson or a member of the production department. These tasks become increasingly integrated through a single information network. To be successful, strategic transitions require changes in organizational culture (see Chapter 3). Interorganizational systems may also be resisted if one organization perceives that it will be worse off by closer coordination with another organization (Clemons and Row, 1993).

Summary

1. Explain why information is now considered a strategic resource. In the past, information used to be considered a bureaucratic nuisance and a limited tool for management decision making. Today, information systems can so dramatically boost a firm's productivity and efficiency that businesses view information as a weapon against competition and a strategic resource.

2. Define a strategic information system. Strategic information systems change the goals, operations, products, services, or environmental relationships of organizations to help them gain an edge over competitors.

3. Describe how the competitive forces and value chain models can be used to identify opportunities for strategic information systems. The competitive forces and value chain models can help identify areas of a business where information systems can supply a strategic advantage. The competitive forces model describes a number of external threats and opportunities faced by firms that they must counter with competitive strategies. Information systems can be developed to cope with the threat of new entrants into the market, the pressure from substitute products, the bargaining power of buyers, the bargaining power of suppliers, and the positioning of traditional industry competitors.

The value chain model highlights specific activities in the business where competitive strategies can best be applied and where information systems are most likely to have a strategic impact. This model views the firm as a series or "chain" of basic activities that add a margin of value to a firm's products or services. Information systems can have strategic impact in the activities that add the most value to the firm.

4. Describe how information systems contribute to the four competitive strategies that businesses can pursue. Information systems can help businesses pursue the four basic competitive strategies: Information systems can be used to develop new market niches; they can provide unique products and services; they can lock in customers and suppliers by raising the cost of switching; and they can help firms provide products and services at lower cost by reducing production and distribution costs.

5. **Explain why it is difficult to build strategic information systems and to sustain strategic advantage.** Not all strategic systems make a profit; they can be expensive and risky to build. Many strategic information systems are easily copied by other firms, so that strategic advantage is not always sustainable. Implementing strategic systems often requires extensive organizational change and a transition from one sociotechnical level to another. Such changes are called strategic transitions and are often difficult and painful to achieve.

Key Terms

Strategic information system	Focused differentiation	Value chain model	Strategic transitions
Competitive forces model	Switching costs	Primary activities	Vendor-managed inventory
Product differentiation	Interorganizational systems	Support activities	
	Electronic market	Information partnership	

Review Questions

1. What is a strategic information system? What is the difference between a strategic information system and a strategic-level system?
2. Identify four different conceptions of the role of information in organizations. How have information systems changed to match these differing views of information?
3. Define and compare the competitive forces and value chain models for identifying opportunities for strategic systems.
4. What are the four basic competitive strategies? How can information systems help firms pursue each of these strategies?
5. How can a firm use information systems to create new products and services? Give an example.
6. How can information systems help firms focus on a market niche? Give an example.
7. How can a firm use an information system to "lock in" customers? Give an example.
8. How can a firm use an information system to improve its bargaining power with a supplier?
9. How can a firm increase its overall operational productivity through the use of information systems?
10. Define interorganizational systems, electronic markets, and information partnerships.
11. What is meant by leveraging technology in the value chain?
12. Why are strategic information systems difficult to build?
13. What is a strategic transition?
14. How can managers find strategic applications in their firm?

Discussion Questions

1. Several information systems experts have claimed, "There is no such thing as a sustainable strategic advantage." Discuss.
2. How do the following kinds of systems give each company a strategic advantage? What competitive strategy does each support?
   a. Mazda Motors of America distributes software to its dealerships; the software compiles customer data on trade-ins and used car sales.
   b. Citibank has arranged with Federal Express to replace lost credit cards within 24 hours. Federal Express and Citibank computers networked together can track the creation and shipment of new cards to customers through the Federal Express hub in Memphis.
   c. Shell Oil Corporation in Houston introduced ATM machines in its gas stations.
   d. The Food Emporium supermarket chain is starting to use video screens attached to shopping carts. As shoppers stroll down the aisles, a sensor activates video commercials and store specials on the video screen using software attached to a computer in the store. In addition to providing information about items for sale, the video screens can give brief weather and news reports.
3. Reexamine the case concluding Chapter 1 in light of the competitive forces and value chain models. What forces are pressuring these companies to change? What information systems support value chain activities? Can you suggest other information systems that would make these firms more competitive?
4. Manufacturing firms in the United States and abroad are furiously adopting just-in-time delivery systems

whereby firms minimize inventories by requiring suppliers to deliver just enough materials to meet the day's or week's production schedule. Does this practice convey a competitive advantage or not? Discuss.

Group Project

Form a group with two or three of your classmates. Research a business using annual reports or business publications such as *Fortune, Business Week*, and *The Wall Street Journal*. Analyze the business using the competitive forces and value chain models. Suggest appropriate strategic information systems for that particular business. Present your findings to the class.

Case Study

GREYHOUND SEEKS SALVATION IN A STRATEGIC RESERVATION SYSTEM

Greyhound Lines Inc., headquartered in Dallas, Texas, has long been the leading transcontinental bus company in the United States. However, the company share of interstate travel dropped from 30 percent in 1960 to 6 percent in the late 1980s, due to the rise in ownership of automobiles and discount airline service. The following chronology lists events that appear to be relevant to the problems Greyhound underwent in the following seven years.

1987

- Dial Corporation carries out a leveraged buyout of Greyhound.

- Operations are interrupted by two violent labor strikes.

- Greyhound is forced to file for protection and reorganization under the Federal Bankruptcy Act, Chapter 11.

- J. Michael Doyle, age 39, a financial officer at Phillips Petroleum Co., joins Greyhound.

1989

- Frank Schmieder, age 47, joins Greyhound in an executive-level position from a position as a merchant banker.

JULY 1991

- Schmieder becomes Greyhound chief executive. Schmieder gained a reputation as an intelligent though volatile boss. Union negotiators found him to be affable and were pleased that he occasionally rode the bus.

- Doyle becomes chief financial officer and works closely with Schmieder to run Greyhound.

AUGUST 1991

- Schmieder begins to cut costs, upgrade buses and facilities, and settle labor disputes. Schmieder and Doyle policies included cutting the bus fleet from 3700 to 2400 and replacing current regional executives. They also replaced most terminal workers with part-time workers who were paid about $6 an hour, whether they swept floors or served customers. These part-time workers were offered little opportunity to get a raise. Ralph Borland, the VP for customer satisfaction, observed that "if people stayed around too long, they would get too sour and cynical." Over the next three years, annual staff turnover of 30 percent became common, with some terminals reaching 100 percent annual turnover.

OCTOBER 1991

- The company emerges from Chapter 11. The Greyhound business plan included a commitment to a computerized reservation system that financial market analysts focused on as the key to a revitalized Greyhound. The plan included system support for more efficient use of buses and drivers.

  Bus customers traditionally do not reserve seats in advance but rather arrive at the terminal, buy a ticket, and take the next bus. Few buses ever reserve seats. The primary use of bus customer telephone lines has been to disseminate schedule information, not for reserving seats as is the case in the airline industry. Traditionally, clerks plotted journeys manually from thick bus schedule log books (Greyhound buses stopped in several thousand towns in the United States). The process was very slow. Computerizing all of the routes and stops would theoretically greatly reduce the time needed to plot journeys and issue tickets. The goals of an automated system were not only to speed the issuing of tickets, thereby reducing company service counter costs, but also simultaneously to improve customer service and customer relations.

The need to automate assignment of buses and drivers arose both because of the volatility of demand in the bus industry and the huge resources that needed to be managed efficiently. After all, the company had to manage several thousand buses and their drivers nationwide, making certain they were in the right locations at the right time. Greyhound assigned buses and bus drivers by hand, using data that was usually months old. The company kept buses and drivers in reserve in order to meet peak period demand, thereby enabling the company to remain the premier continent-wide bus company. In Greyhound's weakened financial condition, a new system that achieved more efficient, cost-effective bus and driver allocation was seen as essential if Greyhound were to remain competitive in the national market.

The new system, called Trips, was to handle both reservations and bus and driver allocations together because they were seen as tightly linked. The traditional bus strategy of no reservations, just walk-in riders meant that many times buses departed nearly empty. Management hoped that adopting a reservation approach would allow them to reduce the number of near-empty buses. They also expected that the reservation portion of the system would provide Greyhound with reliable readership data so schedules could be more efficiently organized and so planners could determine where and when to reduce prices in order to fill seats. Doyle described the planned automated system as "probably the first piece that had to get into

place before we could do other things. It was the foundation."

Greyhound management's desire to move to reserved seats with an automated reservation system and computerized bus and driver allocation was closely tied to its financial situation. The idea was received very positively in the financial markets, giving Greyhound the ability to borrow funds and to offer new shares to raise capital.

EARLY SPRING 1992

■ The Trips project begins with staff of 40 or so and $6 million budget; Thomas Thompson, Greyhound senior VP for network planning and operations, is placed in charge of Trips development.

A bus reservation system, by the nature of the operation of buses, is far more complex than airline reservation systems. A passenger might make one or two stops on an airline flight and cross the United States with none to two stops only, whereas bus passengers may make ten or more stops on a trip, and a cross-country trip might involve scores of stops. Greyhound technicians estimated that a bus management system would need to manage ten times the number of vehicle stops per day of an airline vehicle management system.

The average bus passenger also differs from the average airline passenger. The average annual income of a bus rider is only $17,000. Several Greyhound executives later claimed to have raised the questions of how many bus passengers would have credit cards to enable them to purchase tickets in advance by telephone, and even how many have telephones available.

The American Airlines' SABRE reservation system had taken three years to develop, cost several hundred million dollars, and the project included a staff many times the size of the Trips staff.

JUNE 1992

■ Jose Oller is hired as senior VP for marketing.

JULY 1992

■ Corporate executives and directors, with spouses, spend four days at a conference at expensive Greenbrier in West Virginia. Travel policy, issued by Doyle, required "efficient and economical travel arrangements." However, executives commonly used limousines to get to and from airports, flew first class, and stayed in Ritz Carlton hotels.

Soon after becoming CEO, Schmieder ordered the upgrading of corporate offices by moving them from a Spartan high-rise near the bus terminal in Dallas to a sleek new building in a suburban mall. Interior design bills ran as high as $90,000 per month. Fixtures cost $50,000. Oller was given $10,000 to decorate his office. Doyle's office included a $6200 entertainment center.

The company paid a monthly retainer of $5000 per month to a San Francisco investor-relations firm. Bain & Co., a Boston consulting firm, was paid up to $175,000 per month to identify "the strategy and the implementation to drive the stock from $6 to $22," according to Ted Beneski, a VP of Bain. Meridian Institute of Crested Butte, Colorado, was paid $560,000 for two seminars of several days for executives where the attendees discussed their perceptions of each other and played games intended to boost their morale.

Greyhound donated $50,000 to the Dallas Museum of Art and purchased season tickets for the Texas Rangers, Dallas Cowboys, and Washington Redskins games.

NOVEMBER–DECEMBER 1992

■ Greyhound stock price reaches $13.50.

Greyhound management actively promoted Trips to investors,

lenders, and security analysts as a key to the future success of Greyhound. Management publicly promised to launch the system in time for the 1993 summer busy season.

- Oller is replaced by David Swift as senior VP for marketing.

- Trips is tested in Houston, Dallas, San Antonio, and Austin.

- Thompson decides Trips is a failure and moves to redesign it totally, to cut back its functionality, and to delay going live with the new system.

    The first version of Trips had been developed by a consulting firm. Planned users of the system such as ticket clerks required 40 hours of training to learn to use it. Clerks had to deal with many screens in order to plot a trip between any two points. The system data bank was incomplete so that clerks often had to pull out the log books and revert to plotting a ticket purchaser's planned trip manually. Clerk time to issue tickets doubled when they used the system. The system also crashed repeatedly.

    Thompson's revised plan included a gradual introduction of Trips, starting in the Northeast corridor in the spring of 1993. After that initial introduction, no new sites would be added until the autumn of 1993, when the busiest travel season would be behind Greyhound. This approach would also give the team time to work out the bugs before the system was introduced nationally.

- Greyhound reports a profit of $11 million, its first profit since 1989.

EARLY 1993

- Schmieder's salary climbs to $526,000, up from an estimated $335,000 in 1991.

- Doyle's salary is raised to $264,000, up from estimated $150,000 in 1991.

FEBRUARY 1993

- Thompson issues a warning to the executive committee that Trips failed its live test and would not be ready on time; he argues for a gradual rollout of the system but loses the argument. Thompson and several other employees present at the meeting claim that Doyle ruled out any discussion of a change in plans, saying, "We made these commitments, and by God, we're going to live up to them." According to Thompson and several others, Doyle's reference was to the commitments the company had made to the financial community. Thompson also claims that most copies of his report to the board were destroyed and that mention of it was purged from company calendars and from computer files that preceded the meeting.

    Doyle later denied cutting off discussion and claims he thought the project was on target and the problems were being solved. He said he does not recall such an incident. He claims that he gave the Trips team the opportunity to halt the rollout throughout the spring, but "They said that we ought to press on." He says that throughout the early summer "we were hearing that progress was being made and problems were being resolved."

APRIL 1993

- Doyle and other executives fly to London, Paris, and New York to promote a $90 million stock offering, basing the appeal primarily upon the coming installation of Trips.

- Phillip W. Taff, an old friend of Schmieder's, is named executive VP.

- Greyhound renews its pledge of a summer rollout of Trips in a filing with the SEC to offer 4 million shares for sale. The funds would be used for 300 new buses. The prospectus promises improved customer service and more convenient ticket buying through Trips.

MAY 1993

- Rollout of Trips begins, using the failed version because Thompson did not have enough time to develop the new version. When Trips reaches 50 locations, the computer terminals begin to freeze unpredictably.

- Greyhound stock hits a post Chapter 11 high of $22.75. Securities analysts had been praising Greyhound management for re-engineering the company and for cutting costs.

JUNE 1993

- The rollout of Trips continues.

- Doyle exercises an option to purchase 15,000 shares of Greyhound stock at $9.81.

- Greyhound stock holds above $20 as formal introduction of Trips nears.

- Doyle exercises options on 22,642 shares at $9.81 and immediately sells them at a profit of $179,000.

- A new 800 customer-service telephone number begins operating, replacing previous customer-information telephone systems; in Omaha, Nebraska, 400 operators answer the calls. The average number of calls per day prior to the new system is 60,000.

JULY 1993

- The new 800 number telephone system begins serving the 220 terminals already hooked up to Trips to be used for making reservations; over the past month calls have risen to an estimated 800,000 per day.

    According to some reports, the system could not handle all the calls, with many customers receiving busy signals. The reports claim that customers often had to call up to a dozen times to get through and that each call, including those that were not completed due to busy signals, was recorded as one call in the official count. The busy signals were caused by the switching mechanism and by the slow response time of Trips. Average time on the line with a customer rose from one minute 49 seconds to two minutes 30 seconds. The computer in Dallas sometimes took as long as 45 seconds to respond to just a single keystroke and could take up to five minutes to print a ticket. The system also crashed numerous times, causing many tickets to be written manually.

At some bus terminals, the passengers who arrived with manual tickets were told to wait in line so that they could be reissued a ticket by the computer. Long lines, delays, and confusion resulted. Many passengers missed their connections; others lost their luggage. In the New York City Port Authority bus station (the main New York City bus terminal), lines grew so long that regional bus company agents began to work the lines and lure customers away from Greyhound.

- On the same day as the initiation of the telephone system, Greyhound announces an increase in earnings per share and ridership and the introduction of a new discount-fare program; Greyhound stock rises 4.5 percent.

AUGUST 1993

- Doyle sells 15,000 shares of stock at $21.75 on August 4.
- Schmieder exercises options on 13,600 shares at $9.81 and sells them at a profit of $155,000 during the first two weeks of the month.
- Two other Greyhound VPs sell a total of 21,300 shares of stock.

SEPTEMBER 1993

- Trips is closed down west of the Mississippi River because of its continuing problems and delays. No reports had yet appeared in the press of the Greyhound problems.
- One weekend in September, the 800 phone center is ordered to

take no more calls temporarily.

- On September 23, Greyhound announces ridership down by 12 percent in August and earnings also down; the press release did not mention Trips and blames the fall in ridership on the national economic environment.
- Greyhound stock, which was down 12 percent in August, fell to $11.75 or 24 percent in one day.
- Thompson is relieved of his duties on Trips; another VP takes over responsibility.

DECEMBER 1993

- Swift is replaced as VP for marketing.

JANUARY 1994

- The VP who took over Trips in September 1993 is forced to resign; Bradley Harslem, a former American Airlines reservations executive, is hired as VP and chief information officer and takes over Trips.

APRIL 1994

- Taff is replaced as executive VP.

MAY 1994

- The company drops its 1993 nationwide image-building advertising campaign ("I go simple, I go easy, I go Greyhound") and returns instead to its 1992 campaign advertising fares in specific market areas.
- The company offers a $68 ticket for a trip anywhere in the United States with a three-day advance purchase. With the heavy travel season beginning at the end of the month, the crush of potential customers trying to take advantage of the $68 offer brings Trips to a halt. The crush of people causes some locations to stop selling tickets. Buses and drivers are not available in some cities, resulting in large numbers of frustrated passengers stranded in terminals.

JULY 1994

- Greyhound announces its traffic is down 10 percent for the first half of 1994.
- On-time bus performance falls to 59 percent versus 81 percent at its peak.
- First half operating revenues fall 12.6 percent, accompanied by a large drop-off in ridership; the nine largest regional carriers in the United States show an average rise in operating revenue of 2.6 percent.
- Greyhound announces it will abandon its long-haul business and concentrate instead on short hauls; the company announces plans to cut 1000 more jobs and cut back expenses $65 million annually.

AUGUST 1994

- Thompson resigns from Greyhound.
- Schmieder and Doyle both resign.
- Thomas G. Plaskett, a 50-year-old Greyhound director, is appointed interim CEO; Plaskett was the chairman and CEO of Pan Am Corporation and a former managing director of Fox Run Capital Associates investments.
- The stock price falls to about $6.
  One morning, Harslem bought a Greyhound ticket from his suburban home to the downtown Dallas computer center. He was not recognized and did not identify himself and so was treated like any other customer. The bus had more than its legal limit of passengers, but employees told him to get on anyway. He rode into Dallas sitting on the bus floor.

SEPTEMBER 1994

- Greyhound misses a $4.2 million payment due on debentures.
- Results of the third quarter, normally Greyhound's busiest and best season, show a net loss of $0.72 per share.

- October ridership fell nearly 16 percent from a year earlier. Only 43 percent of Greyhound's seats were filled, down 10 percent from a year earlier.

NOVEMBER 1994

- Greyhound creditors file suit to attempt to force Greyhound back into protection under Chapter 11 of the Federal Bankruptcy Act.

- Greyhound stock falls to $1.875 per share.

- Greyhound announces its fourth consecutive quarterly loss.

- A financial restructuring agreement is reached that gives creditors 45 percent ownership of Greyhound. The agreement allows the company to avoid Chapter 11 bankruptcy.

- Craig Lentzcsh is appointed Greyhound's new permanent CEO.

- Greyhound announces new systemwide fare reduction for long-haul trips. Its maximum one-way fare for interstate travel will be lowered to $149, with the Los Angeles to New York fare dropping to $129. The company also announced a 25 percent discount on tickets purchased three days in advance and for travel through December 15.

- Greyhound stock is selling at $2.1875 per share.

DECEMBER 1994

- Enough Greyhound bondholders agree to swap their debt for company stock to avoid a second bankruptcy reorganization. This move eliminates $90 million of debt, but turns more than 45 percent of the company over to the bondholders.

JANUARY 1995

- Greyhound announces the Securities and Exchange Commission is investigating the company and former directors, officers, and employees for possible securities law violations. The investigation is examining possible insider trading, the adequacy of the firm's internal accounting procedures, and the adequacy of public disclosures related to the Trips system and the company's disappointing earnings in 1993. Greyhound says that it does not believe it has violated any securities laws and is cooperating fully. In addition to the SEC investigation, Greyhound is facing a raft of investors' lawsuits involving similar allegations and a Justice Department antitrust investigation into its terminal agreements with smaller carriers.

- By January 25 Greyhound stock has dropped to $1.563 per share.

Greyhound continues trying to improve the Trips system. It has started to de-emphasize advance reservations and to use the system for more efficient dispatching.

Sources: Robert Tomsho, "Greyhound Says SEC Is Investigating Possible Violations of Securities Law," *The Wall Street Journal*, January 26, 1995; "How Greyhound Lines Re-Engineered Itself Right into a Deep Hole," *The Wall Street Journal*, October 20, 1994; "Greyhound, Debenture Holders Agree to Restructuring, Avoiding Chapter 11," *The Wall Street Journal*, November 11, 1994; "Greyhound Reduces Fares in Move to Boost Ridership," *The Wall Street Journal*, December 8, 1994, and "Debtholders Move to Drive Greyhound into Chapter 11; Stock Slumps 25%," *The Wall Street Journal*, November 4, 1994; and Wendy Zellner, "Greyhound Is Limping Badly," *Business Week*, August 22, 1994.

Case Study Questions

1. Use the competitive forces and value chain models to analyze Greyhound's situation. What competitive forces did Greyhound have to deal with? What was Greyhound's business strategy? What kinds of strategic information systems did Greyhound attempt to use?

2. How much strategic advantage would Trips have provided had it been designed and implemented successfully? Why?

3. What management, organization, and technology factors contributed to Greyhound's problems?

4. If you were a Greyhound manager, what solutions would you recommend? Would you suggest new information systems applications? If so, what would be the functions of those systems?

References

Bakos, J. Yannis. "A Strategic Analysis of Electronic Marketplaces." *MIS Quarterly* 15, no. 3 (September 1991).

Bakos, J. Yannis, and Michael E. Treacy. "Information Technology and Corporate Strategy: A Research Perspective." *MIS Quarterly* (June 1986).

Barrett, Stephanie S. "Strategic Alternatives and Interorganizational System Implementations: An Overview." *Journal of Management Information Systems* (Winter 1986–1987).

Barua, Anitesh, Charles H. Kriebel, and Tridas Mukhopadhyay. "An Economic Analysis of Strategic Information Technology Investments." *MIS Quarterly* 15, no. 5 (September 1991).

Beath, Cynthia Mathis, and Blake Ives. "Competitive Information Systems in Support of Pricing." *MIS Quarterly* (March 1986).

Betts, Mitch. "ATM Pioneers Reaped Market Share, Income." *Computerworld* (January 20, 1992).

Bower, Joseph L., and Thomas M. Hout. "Fast-Cycle Capability for Competitive Power." *Harvard Business Review* (November–December 1988).

Bulkeley, William M. "The Latest Big Thing at Many Companies Is Speed, Speed, Speed." *The Wall Street Journal* (December 23, 1994).

Caldwell, Bruce. "A Cure for Hospital Woes." *Information WEEK* (September 9, 1991).

Cash, J. I., and Benn R. Konsynski. "IS Redraws Competitive Boundaries." *Harvard Business Review* (March–April 1985).

Cash, James I., F. Warren McFarlan, James L. McKenney, and Lynda M. Applegate. *Corporate Information Systems Management*, 3rd ed. Homewood, IL: Irwin (1992).

Cash, J. I., and P. L. McLeod. "Introducing IS Technology in Strategically Dependent Companies." *Journal of Management Information Systems* (Spring 1985).

Chandler, Susan. "Strategies for the New Mail Order: Sears." *Business Week* (December 19, 1994).

Clemons, Eric K. "Evaluation of Strategic Investments in Information Technology." *Communications of the ACM* (January 1991).

Clemons, Eric K., and Michael Row. "McKesson Drug Co.: Case Study of a Strategic Information System." *Journal of Management Information Systems* (Summer 1988).

Clemons, Eric K., and Michael C. Row. "Sustaining IT Advantage: The Role of Structural Differences." *MIS Quarterly* 15, no. 3 (September 1991).

Clemons, Eric K. and Michael Row. "Limits to Interfirm Coordination through IT." *Journal of Management Information Systems* 10, no. 1 (Summer 1993).

Clemons, Eric K., and Bruce W. Weber. "Segmentation, Differentiation, and Flexible Pricing: Experience with Information Technology and Segment-Tailored Strategies." *Journal of Management Information Systems* 11, no. 2 (Fall 1994).

Connolly, James, and Elisabeth Horwitt. "American Express Sets Own Limits." *Computerworld* (December 12, 1988).

Copeland, Duncan G., and James L. McKenney. "Airline Reservations Systems: Lessons from History." *MIS Quarterly* 12, no. 3 (September 1988).

Cushman, John H., Jr. "The High-Stakes Battle for Airline Reservations." *The New York Times* (June 18, 1989).

Emmett, Arielle. "Hot or Cold, Steel Maker Forges Ahead with IS." *Computerworld* (June 15, 1992).

Feeny, David F., and Blake Ives. "In Search of Sustainability: Reaping Long-Term Advantage from Investments in Information Technology." *Journal of Management Information Systems* (Summer 1990).

Henderson, John C., and John J. Sifonis. "The Value of Strategic IS Planning: Understanding Consistency, Validity, and IS Markets." *MIS Quarterly* 12, no. 2 (June 1988).

Hopper, Max. "Rattling SABRE—New Ways to Compete on Information." *Harvard Business Review* (May–June 1990).

Ives, Blake, and Gerald P. Learmonth. "The Information System as a Competitive Weapon." *Communications of the ACM* (December 1984).

Ives, Blake, and Michael R. Vitale. "After the Sale: Leveraging Maintenance with Information Technology." *MIS Quarterly* (March 1986).

Janulaitis, M. Victor. "Gaining Competitive Advantage." *Infosystems* (October 1984).

Johnston, H. Russell, and Shelley R. Carrico. "Developing Capabilities to Use Information Strategically." *MIS Quarterly* 12, no. 1 (March 1988).

Johnston, Russell, and Paul R. Lawrence. "Beyond Vertical Integration—The Rise of the Value-Adding Partnership." *Harvard Business Review* (July–August 1988).

Johnston, Russell, and Michael R. Vitale. "Creating Competitive Advantage with Interorganizational Information Systems." *MIS Quarterly* 12, no. 2 (June 1988).

Kambil, Ajit and James E. Short. "Electronic Integration and Business Network Redesign: A Roles-Linkage Perspective." *Journal of Management Information Systems* 10, No. 4 (Spring 1994).

Keen, Peter G. W. *Competing in Time: Using Telecommunications for Competitive Advantage.* Cambridge, MA: Ballinger Publishing Company (1986).

Keen, Peter G. W. *Shaping the Future: Business Design Through Information Technology.* Cambridge, MA: Harvard Business School Press (1991).

Konsynski, Benn R., and F. Warren McFarlan. "Information Partnerships—Shared Data, Shared Scale." *Harvard Business Review* (September–October 1990).

Lindsey, Darryl, Paul H. Cheney, George M. Kasper, and Blake Ives. "Competitive Advantage in the Cotton Industry." *MIS Quarterly* 14, no. 4 (December 1990).

McFarlan, F. Warren. "Information Technology Changes the Way You Compete." *Harvard Business Review* (May–June 1984).

Maglitta, Joseph. "Lean, Mean Flying Machines." *Computerworld* (July 11, 1994).

Main, Thomas J., and James E. Short. "Managing the Merger: Building Partnership through IT Planning at the New Baxter." *MIS Quarterly* 13, no. 4 (December 1989).

Malone, Thomas W., JoAnne Yates, and Robert I. Benjamin. "Electronic Markets and Electronic Hierarchies." *Communications of the ACM* (June 1987).

Malone, Thomas W., JoAnne Yates, and Robert I. Benjamin. "The Logic of Electronic Markets." *Harvard Business Review* (May–June 1989).

Markoff, John. "American Express Goes High-Tech." *The New York Times* (July 31, 1988).

Millar, Victor E. "Decision-Oriented Information." *Datamation* (January 1984).

Miron, Michael, John Cecil, Kevin Bradcich, and Gene Hall. "The Myths and Realities of Competitive Advantage." *Datamation* (October 1, 1988).

Moad, Jeff. "Let Customers Have It Their Way." *Datamation* (April 1, 1995).

Pastore, Richard. "Coffee, Tea and a Sales Pitch." *Computerworld* (July 3, 1989).

Porter, Michael. *Competitive Advantage.* New York: Free Press (1985).

Porter, Michael. *Competitive Strategy.* New York: Free Press (1980).

Porter, Michael. "How Information Can Help You Compete." *Harvard Business Review* (August–September 1985a).

Rackoff, Nick, Charles Wiseman, and Walter A. Ullrich. "Information Systems for Competitive Advantage: Implementation of a Planning Process." *MIS Quarterly* (December 1985).

Rebello, Joseph. "State Street Boston's Allure for Investors Starts to Fade." *The Wall Street Journal* (January 4, 1995).

Scott Morton, Michael, ed. *The Corporation in the 1990s.* New York: Oxford University Press (1991).

Short, James E. and N. Venkatraman. "Beyond Business Process Redesign: Redefining Baxter's Business Network." *Sloan Management Review* (Fall 1992).

Vitale, Michael R. "The Growing Risks of Information System Success." *MIS Quarterly* (December 1986).

Wayne, Leslie. "The Next Giant in Mutual Funds?" *The New York Times* (March 20, 1994).

Wiseman, Charles. *Strategic Information Systems.* Homewood, IL: Richard D. Irwin (1988).

Chapter 3

Information Systems and Organizations

PanCanadian Awakens with Information Systems

3.1 The Relationship between Organizations and Information Systems
The Two-Way Relationship
What Is an Organization?

3.2 Salient Features of Organizations
Why Organizations Are So Much Alike: Common Features
Why Organizations Are So Different: Unique Features
Levels of Analysis

3.3 How Organizations Affect Information Systems
Decisions about the Role of Information Systems
Decisions about the Computer Package: Who Delivers Information Technology Services?
Decisions about Why Information Systems Are Built
Window on Organizations:
Schneider Responds to the New Rules of the Trucking Game

3.4 How Information Systems Affect Organizations
Economic Theories
Window on Technology:
Custom Manufacturing: The New Automation
Behavioral Theories
Window on Management:
Managing the Virtual Office

Organizational Resistance to Change
Implications for the Design and Understanding of Information Systems

Management Challenges
Summary
Key Terms
Review Questions
Discussion Questions
Group Project
Case Study: Can Sears Reinvent Itself?
References

PanCanadian Awakens with Information Systems

PanCanadian Petroleum in Calgary, Alberta, used to be known as a "sleeping giant." Although the company owned 25 million acres of potentially oil-bearing land, it drilled fewer wells, produced less oil, and took in less money than its competitors in western Canada. Today, PanCanadian drills more earth than any other Canadian oil company. Its oil production has doubled since 1990. PanCanadian has been able to produce a profit even when the price of crude oil has sunk because it uses information systems to lower the cost of finding, pumping, and distributing oil.

PanCanadian's turnaround began when David O'Brien became its CEO in January 1990. O'Brien trimmed 15 percent of the company's work force, replaced eight of the company's fifteen officers, and restructured the company geographically instead of along functional lines. O'Brien moved to computerize virtually all aspects of PanCanadian's operations, appointing David Tuer, the deputy minister of energy for the province of Alberta, in charge of the effort. Tuer assigned dozens of managers and other employees to two-year tours of duty in the information systems department as a way of breaking down the barriers between information systems and the rest of the company.

The oil industry believes that there aren't any more large pools of oil in western Canada that haven't already been discovered. The goal of oil exploration thus is to find the small pools or find ways of getting more oil out of the large pools that are nearly tapped out. Since the payoff from tapping such sources is modest, oil companies must be selective about the sites where they invest drilling resources.

One way information systems can help is by providing field geologists and engineers with seismic data that can be translated by a supercomputer into a rough picture of rock layers that includes pockets that might contain trapped oil. PanCanadian had seismic data and state-of-the-art drilling tools, but it still lacked the information that would provide the whole picture of each prospective drilling site. Each type of information was stored in a different source—different computer files as well as paper files. Tuer and his staff consolidated all of this information in a geological information system that makes all information about existing or potential well sites immediately available through the computer. Anyone researching a site merely needs to type in a location and select the kind of data desired. Tuer put microcomputers and workstations on the desks of engineers, geologists, and managers and linked them together in a network.

The system has allowed PanCanadian to push decision making further down the organization. Field geologists and engineers used to have to wait for managers to approve their choices for drilling sites. Now, with instant access to a vast array of data, PanCanadian's exploration professionals have been given the authority to make their own decisions.

PanCanadian now drills three times as many wells as before. Its success rate has risen from 85 to 93 percent. With the new access to information, management believes that the company will be able to double its rate of drilling in shallow sites and quadruple its rate of drilling in deep sites.

Besides lowering exploration costs, information systems are helping PanCanadian lower its production costs by keeping its oil pumps running at optimum rates. PanCanadian used to assign 400 people throughout western Canada to show up at regional headquarters in the morning, fan out to the wells to read pump-monitoring equipment and look

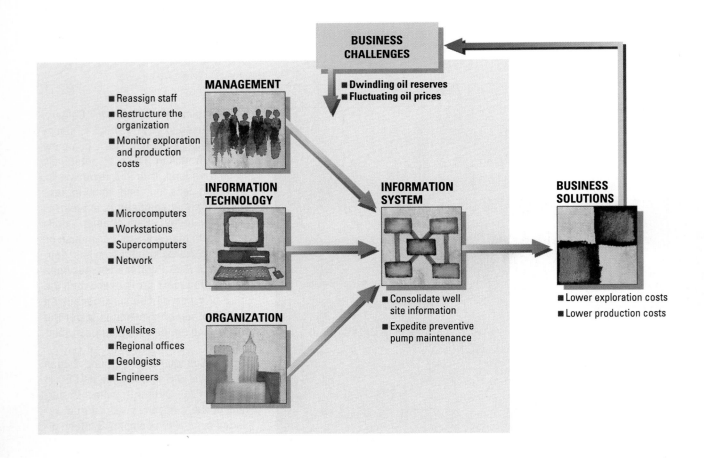

for repairs, and finally return to the office to write up four different kinds of reports. With most of their time spent doing bookkeeping (three hours daily) or traveling, the well maintenance staff spent only two hours per day working on pumps. Most of those two hours in turn was spent repairing malfunctioning pumps rather than performing preventive maintenance. PanCanadian addressed this problem by placing microcomputers with special report-writing software at its seven regional offices. When well maintenance staff return from the wells, they type in the new data that they gathered on the various wells. The software produces the four required reports and transmits them via telephone links to headquarters for consolidation and management review. This system has made information accessible and has cut bookkeeping time to one half-hour. ■

Source: David Freedman, "Savvy IT Lets PanCan Dance," *Forbes ASAP*, October 10, 1994.

The experience of PanCanadian Petroleum illustrates the interdependence of business environments, organizational structure, management, and the development of information systems. PanCanadian developed new information systems in response to changes in competitive pressures from its surrounding environment, but it needed to change its organizational structure and management before it could use its new systems successfully. The information systems in turn changed the way PanCanadian ran its business and made management decisions.

The complex relationship between organizations and information systems is explored in this chapter. Our goal is to introduce you to the features of organizations that you will need to know about as a manager when you envision, design, build, and operate information systems. First we will describe the features of organizations that are related to information systems—what we call the "salient" features. Then we will examine in greater detail precisely how information systems affect organizations, and just as important, how organizations affect information systems. The chapter concludes by describing some of the reasons why organizations are so difficult to change—with or without technology—and how you can use this knowledge to your advantage.

After completing this chapter, you will be able to:

Learning Objectives

1. Describe the salient characteristics of organizations.

2. Explain the changing role of information systems within the organization.

3. Compare models for describing the origins of systems in organizations.

4. Identify the major theories about organizations that help us understand their relationship with information systems.

5. Discuss the impact of information systems on organizational structure, culture, political processes, and management.

6. Describe the organizational implications for the design and implementation of systems.

3.1 THE RELATIONSHIP BETWEEN ORGANIZATIONS AND INFORMATION SYSTEMS

Can information systems "flatten" organizations by reducing their number of levels? Will information systems allow organizations to operate with fewer middle managers and clerical workers? Can information systems reduce paperwork? Can they be used to "re-engineer" organizations so they become lean, efficient, and hard hitting? Can organizations use information technology to decentralize power down to lower-level workers, thereby unleashing the creative talents of millions of employees?

These are among today's leading management questions. The issues raised by contemporary information systems—efficiency, creativity, bureaucracy, employment, quality of work life—are longstanding issues of industrial society, and they pre-date computers. No one can deny that information systems have contributed to organizational efficiency and effectiveness. Yet social and behavioral scientists who have studied organizations over long periods of time argue that no radical transformation of organizations has occurred except in isolated cases. Exactly what can information systems do for organizations?

The relationship between information technology and organizations is complex, and the interpretations of this relationship are controversial. In this chapter we cannot provide a complete description of this relationship. Our goal is to present an overview of the relationship and a discussion of contemporary research so that you can understand the issues and join the debate.

THE TWO-WAY RELATIONSHIP

Let us start with a simple premise based on observation and a great deal of research: Information systems and organizations have a mutual influence on each other (see Figure 3.1). On the one hand, information systems must be aligned with the organization to provide information needed by important groups within the organization. At the same time, the organization must be aware of and must open itself to the influences of information systems to benefit from new technologies. Information systems affect organizations, and organizations necessarily affect the design of systems.

It is very convenient for journalists, scholars, and managers to think about "the impact of computers" on organizations as if it were like some ship colliding with an iceberg at sea. But the actual effect is much more complex. Figure 3.1 shows a great many mediating factors that influence the interaction between information technology and organizations. These include the organization's surrounding environment, culture, structure, standard operating procedures, politics, and management decisions (Orlikowski and Robey, 1991; Orlikowski, 1992). Managers, after all, decide what systems will be built, what they will do, how they will be implemented, and so forth. To a very large extent, managers and organizations choose the "computer impacts" they want (or at least receive the impacts they deserve) (Laudon, 1986; Laudon and Marr, 1994; Laudon and Marr, 1995). Sometimes, however, the outcomes are the result of pure chance and of both good and bad luck.

Because there are many types of organizations, it stands to reason that the technology of information systems will have a different impact on different types of organizations. There is no singular effect of computers; one cannot, for example, conclude that "computers flatten hierarchies" in all organizations. Instead, different organizations in different circumstances experience different effects from the same technology. Before describing how each of these mediating factors affects information systems, we must first review the salient features of organizations.

WHAT IS AN ORGANIZATION?

An **organization** is a stable, formal social structure that takes resources from the environment and processes them to produce outputs. This technical definition focuses

organization (technical definition)
A stable, formal social structure that takes resources from the environment and processes them to produce outputs.

FIGURE 3.1
The two-way relationship between organizations and information technology. This complex two-way relationship is mediated by many factors not the least of which are the decisions made—or not made—by managers. Other factors mediating the relationship are the organizational culture, bureaucracy, politics, business fashion, and pure chance.

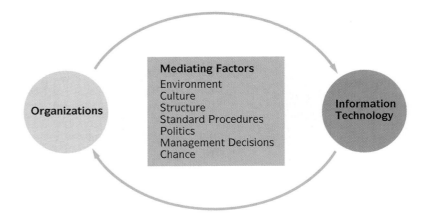

on three elements of an organization (see Figure 3.2). *Capital* and *labor* are primary production factors provided by the environment. The organization (the firm) transforms these inputs into products and services in a *production function*—a process that transforms capital and labor into a product.[1] The products and services are *consumed by environments* in return for supply inputs.

An organization is *more stable* than an informal group in terms of longevity and routineness. Organizations are *formal* because they are legal entities and must abide by laws. They have internal rules and procedures. Organizations are *social structures* because they are a collection of social elements, much as a machine has a structure—a particular arrangement of valves, cams, shafts, and other parts.

Organizations are, in part, information processing entities. However, it would be a mistake to view organizations or the human beings who work for them in this limited way. Organizations process and use information in order to produce outputs for an environment (e.g., products and services). Most organizations are not designed primarily for processing information. A newspaper delivers news and opinions to customers, not merely data or information. Even government agencies such as the Social Security Administration and the Internal Revenue Service, which are heavy users of information, have as their primary goal the delivery of pension and taxation services.

This definition of organizations is powerful and simple, but it is not very descriptive or even predictive of the real-world organizations that most of us belong to.

FIGURE 3.2
The technical microeconomic definition of the organization. In the microeconomic definition of organizations, capital and labor (the primary production factors provided by the environment) are transformed by the firm through the production process into products and services (outputs to the environment). The products and services are consumed by the environment, which supplies additional capital and labor as inputs in the feedback loop.
(B) The microeconomic view is a technical model of the firm in which the firm combines capital and labor in a production function to produce a single product of the amount Q. The firm can freely substitute the capital for labor anywhere along the curve Q.

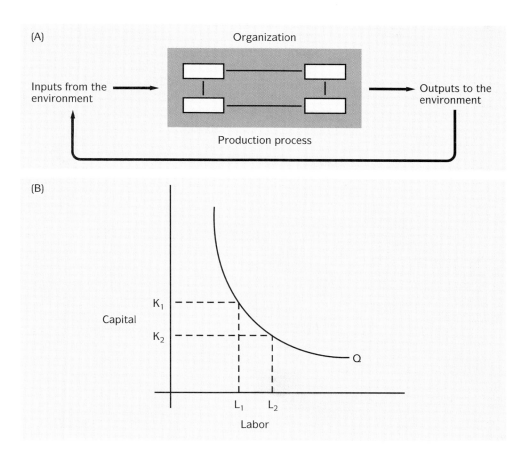

1. A typical production function is given by $Q = A * (K,L)$, where Q is the quantity of output produced by a firm; K and L are factors of production, capital, and labor. "A" represents a parameter greater than 0 reflecting the productivity of available technology—factors such as education, knowledge, and changes in technique and technology—which can alter the output Q independent of capital and labor. See any microeconomics textbook for further background. An excellent reference is Robert S. Pindyck and Daniel L. Rubinfield, *Microeconomics* (New York: Macmillan, 1992). This text has several interesting chapters on information asymmetries, although like most microeconomics texts it is limited in its coverage of technology.

FIGURE 3.3
The behavioral view of organizations. The behavioral view of organizations emphasizes group relationships, values, and structures.

Formal Organization

Structure
Hierarchy
Division of labor
Rules, procedures

Process
Rights /obligations
Privileges /responsibilities

Values
Norms
People

Environmental resources →

→ Environmental outputs

organization (behavioral definition) A collection of rights, privileges, obligations, and responsibilities that are delicately balanced over a period of time through conflict and conflict resolution.

A more realistic behavioral definition of an **organization** is that it is a collection of rights, privileges, obligations, and responsibilities that are delicately balanced over a period of time through conflict and conflict resolution (see Figure 3.3).

In this behavioral view of the firm, people who work in organizations develop customary ways of working; they gain attachments to existing relationships; and they make arrangements with subordinates and superiors about how work will be done, how much work will be done, and under what conditions. Most of these arrangements and feelings are not discussed in any formal rule book.

How do these definitions of organizations relate to information system technology? A technical microeconomic view of organizations encourages us to think that introducing new technology changes the way inputs are combined into outputs, like changing the spark plugs on an engine. The firm is seen as infinitely malleable, with capital and labor substituting for one another quite easily.

But the more realistic behavioral definition of an organization suggests that building new information systems or rebuilding old ones involves much more than a technical rearrangement of machines or workers. Instead, technological change requires changes in who owns and controls information, who has the right to access and update that information, and who makes decisions about whom, when, and how. For instance, PanCanadian's new information system empowered field geologists and engineers to make decisions about drilling sites. The more complex view forces us to look at the way work is designed and the procedures used to achieve outputs.

The technical and behavioral definitions of organizations are not contradictory. Indeed, they complement one another: The microeconomic definition tells us how thousands of firms in competitive markets combine capital and labor and information technology, whereas the behavioral model takes us inside the individual firm to see how, in fact, specific firms use capital and labor to produce outputs. Section 3.4 describes how theories based on each of these definitions of organizations can help explain the relationship between information systems and organizations.

Information systems can markedly alter life in the organization. Some information systems change the organizational balance of rights, privileges, obligations, responsibilities, and feelings that has been established over a long period of time. What this means is that managers cannot design new systems or understand existing systems without understanding organizations.

3.2   SALIENT FEATURES OF ORGANIZATIONS

In this section, we introduce and discuss the major features of organizations that managers should be aware of when building information systems. These organizational features are mediating factors (review Figure 3.1) that influence the relationship between organizations and information technology.

Some features of organizations are common to all organizations; others distinguish one organization from another. Let us look first at the features common to all organizations.

WHY ORGANIZATIONS ARE SO MUCH ALIKE: COMMON FEATURES

You might not think that Apple Computer, United Airlines, or the Aspen Colorado Police Department have much in common, but they do. In some respects, all modern organizations are alike because they share the characteristics listed in Table 3.1. German sociologist Max Weber was the first to describe these "ideal-typical" characteristics of organizations in 1911. He called organizations **bureaucracies** that have certain "structural" features (see Table 3.1).

According to Weber, all modern bureaucracies have a clear-cut *division of labor and specialization*. Organizations employ or train individuals who possess specific talents or skills. Organizations arrange specialists in a *hierarchy* of authority in which everyone is accountable to someone and authority is limited to specific actions. Authority and action are further limited by abstract *rules or procedures* (standard operating procedures or SOP) that are interpreted and applied to specific cases. These rules create a system of *impartial and universalistic decision making;* everyone is treated equally. Organizations try to hire and promote employees on the basis of *technical qualifications and professionalism* (not personal connections). The organization itself is devoted to the *principle of efficiency:* maximizing output using limited inputs.

Bureaucracies are so prevalent, according to Weber, because they are the most efficient form of organization. They are much more stable and powerful than mercurial charismatic groups or formal aristocracies held together by the right of birth. Other scholars supplemented Weber, identifying additional features of organizations. All organizations develop standard operating procedures, politics, and a culture.

Standard Operating Procedures

All organizations, over time, stabilize to produce a given number of products and services. Over long periods of time, the organizations that survive become very efficient, producing a limited number of products and services by following standard routines. In this period of time, employees develop reasonably precise rules, procedures, and practices called **standard operating procedures (SOPs)** to cope with virtually all expected situations. Some of these rules and procedures are written down as formal procedures, but most are rules of thumb to be followed in selected situations.

A great deal of the efficiency that modern organizations attain has little to do with computers but a great deal to do with the development of standard operating procedures. For instance, in the assembly of a car, thousands of motions and procedures must be planned and executed in a precise fashion to permit the finished product to roll off the line. If workers had to decide how each vehicle was to be built, or if managers had to decide how each day's product was to be built, efficiency would drop off dramatically. Instead, managers and workers develop a complex set

bureaucracy Formal organization with a clear-cut division of labor, abstract rules and procedures, and impartial decision making that uses technical qualifications and professionalism as a basis for promoting employees.

standard operating procedures (SOPs) Precise, defined rules, procedures, and practices developed by organizations to cope with virtually all expected situations.

Table 3.1	Structural Characteristics of All Organizations

Clear division of labor

Hierarchy

Explicit rules and procedures

Impartial judgments

Technical qualifications for positions

Maximum organizational efficiency

of standard procedures to handle most situations. Any change in SOPs requires an enormous organizational effort. Indeed, the organization may need to halt the entire production process, or create a new and expensive parallel system, which must then be tested exhaustively before the old SOPs can be retired. For example, difficulty in changing standard operating procedures is one reason Detroit auto makers have been slow to adopt Japanese mass-production methods. Until recently, U.S. auto makers followed Henry Ford's mass-production principles. Ford believed that the cheapest way to build cars was to churn out the largest number of autos by having workers repeatedly perform a simple task. By contrast, Japanese auto makers have emphasized "lean production" methods where a smaller number of workers, each performing several tasks, can produce cars with less inventory, less investment, and fewer mistakes. Workers have multiple job responsibilities and are encouraged to note every glitch and, if necessary, stop production to correct a problem.

Organizational Politics

Organizations are arranged so that people occupy different positions. Because these individuals have different concerns and specialties, they naturally have differences in viewpoint, perspective, and opinion about how resources, rewards, and punishments should be distributed. These differences matter to members of organizations, both managers and employees. Because of these differences, political struggle, competition, and conflict occur in every organization. Sometimes political struggles occur when individuals or interest groups seek to exercise leadership and to gain advantages. Other times, entire groups compete, leading to clashes on a large scale. In either case, politics is a normal part of organizational life.

People use politics to gain everything worth having in a job: pay, position, job conditions, respect, prestige, and ultimately careers. Because of the stakes, players take the game very seriously. Politics, as described by the famous political scientist Harold Lasswell, is who does what to whom, where, when, and how.

One of the great difficulties of bringing about change in organizations—especially concerning the development of new information systems—is the political resistance that any important organizational change seems to bring forth. "Important" changes are those that directly affect who does what to whom, where, when, and how. Virtually all information systems that bring about significant changes in goals, procedures, productivity, and personnel are politically charged.

Organizational Culture

organizational culture The set of fundamental assumptions about what products the organization should produce, how and where it should produce them, and for whom they should be produced.

All organizations have bedrock, unassailable, unquestioned (by the members) assumptions that define the goals and products of the organization. **Organizational culture** is the set of fundamental assumptions about what the organization should produce, how it should produce its products, where, and for whom. Generally, these cultural assumptions are taken totally for granted and are rarely publicly announced or spoken about. They are simply assumptions that few people, if anyone (in their right mind), would question (Schein, 1985).

Everything else—technology, values, norms, public announcements, and so on—follows from these assumptions. You can see organizational culture at work by looking around your university or college. Some bedrock assumptions of university life are that professors know more than students, the reason students attend college is to learn, the primary purpose of the university is to create new knowledge and communicate knowledge to students, classes follow a regular schedule, and libraries are repositories of knowledge in the form of books and journals. Sometimes these cultural assumptions are true. Organizational culture is a powerful unifying force, which restrains political conflict and promotes common understanding, agreement on procedures, and common practices. If we all share the same basic cultural assumptions, then agreement on other matters is more likely.

At the same time, organizational culture is a powerful restraint on change, especially technological change. Any technological change that threatens commonly held cultural assumptions will meet with a great deal of resistance. Another reason why U.S. auto makers have been slow to switch to lean production methods is because of longstanding assumptions that management should be very authoritarian and does not need to listen to the opinions of workers. Not only must U.S. companies change the standard operating procedures on their assembly lines, but they must also find ways to involve auto workers in improving factories. This hasn't been easy, because U.S. auto companies have traditionally been hierarchical and authoritarian.

In general, organizational cultures are far more powerful than information technologies. Therefore, most organizations will do almost anything to avoid making changes in basic assumptions, and new technologies are almost always used at first in ways that support existing cultures.

On the other hand, there are times when the only sensible way to employ a new technology is directly opposed to an existing organizational culture. When this occurs, the technology is often stalled or delayed while the culture slowly adjusts. Organizational change requires far more time than technological change requires. On average, it takes five to seven years for an industry's "best practice" to become the median practice (Klotz, 1966).[2] This statistic is derived from studies of industrial machine tools and may not apply to computer-based techniques. But is the information systems world really any different from other forms of technology?

WHY ORGANIZATIONS ARE SO DIFFERENT: UNIQUE FEATURES

Some features vary from one organization to another. Although all organizations have some common characteristics, no two organizations are identical. Organizations have different structures, goals, constituencies, leadership styles, tasks, and surrounding environments. These differences are listed and summarized in Table 3.2, along with the primary sources, main concepts, and sample organizations that characterize these organizational differences.

Different Organizational Types

One important way in which organizations differ is in their structure or shape. The differences among organizational structures are characterized in many ways. Mintzberg's classification is especially useful and simple (see Figure 3.4), for it identifies five basic kinds of organizations:

entrepreneurial structure Young, small firm in a fast-changing environment dominated by a single entrepreneur and managed by a single chief executive officer.

machine bureaucracy Large bureaucracy organized into functional divisions that centralizes decision making, produces standard products, and exists in a slow-changing environment.

Entrepreneurial structure: Organizations with simple structures tend to be young, small, entrepreneurial firms in fast-changing environments, dominated by a single entrepreneur and managed by a single chief executive officer. Information systems typically are poorly planned and significantly behind fast-breaking production developments.

Machine bureaucracy: The large, classic bureaucracy exists in slow-changing environments, producing standardized products. It is dominated by a strategic senior management that centralizes information flow and decision authority. It is likely to be organized into functional divisions—for example, manufacturing, finance, marketing, and human resources. Information systems tend to be mainframe-based. They are well planned, but are generally limited to accounting, finance, simple planning, and administrative applications.

2. B. Klotz, *Industry Productivity Projections: A Methodological Study* (U.S. Department of Labor, Bureau of Labor Statistics, 1966). See also T. K. Bikson and J. D. Eveland, "Integrating New Tools into Information Work. Technology Transfer as a Framework for Understanding Success," The Rand Corporation, 1992. These estimates are for industrial-sector innovations, and no one really knows how long it takes for IT innovations to become industry median practice.

Table 3.2   A Comparison of Types of Organizations

Primary Source Author	Organizational Differences	Main Concepts	Sample Organizations
Mintzberg (1979)	Have different structures	Simple structure Machine bureaucracy Professional bureaucracy Divisionalized form Adhocracy	Mom-and-Pop firms Post office Hospital Fortune 500 Research firm
Etzioni (1975)	Have different goals	Coercive goals Utilitarian goals Normative goals	Military Business Church
Blau and Scott (1962)	Benefit different groups	Members Clients Owners	Boy Scouts Welfare agency Business
Parsons (1960)	Perform different functions	Economic Pattern maintenance Integrative Political	Business Universities, schools Hospitals, courts Government
Gouldner (1954)	Have different leadership styles	Democratic Authoritarian Laissez-faire Technocratic Bureaucratic	Different types of leadership could occur in any organization
March and Simon (1958)	Make different decisions	Programmed Semi-programmed Unprogrammed decisions	Inventory reorder Production scheduling Selecting strategy
	Perform different tasks		
Blauner (1967) Woodward (1965)	Use different techniques and technology	Craft Batch routine Continuous process	Woodworker Assembly line Oil refinery
Thompson (1967)	Exist in different environments	Turbulence Complexity	Rapid technology change Multiple competitors

professional bureaucracy
Knowledge-based organization such as a law firm or a hospital that is dominated by department heads with weak centralized authority; operates in a slowly changing environment.

Professional bureaucracy: This structure is typical of law firms, school systems, accounting firms, hospitals, and other knowledge-based organizations that depend on the knowledge and expertise of professionals. Professional bureaucracies are suitable for slow-changing environments and skill sets. They are dominated by department heads and have weak centralized authority. Professional members of the organization who have considerable information and authority create the product or service. Such organizations typically have primitive central information systems for time accounting and billing for professional services, and often have very sophisticated knowledge work support systems for professionals. Knowledge work systems are described in greater detail in Chapter 15.

divisionalized bureaucracy
Combination of many machine bureaucracies, each producing a different product or service, under one central headquarters. Common form for Fortune 500 firms.

adhocracy Task force organization, such as a research organization, designed to respond to a rapidly changing environment and characterized by large groups of specialists organized into short-lived multidisciplinary task forces.

Divisionalized bureaucracy: This type of organization is the most common Fortune 500 form, a combination of many machine bureaucracies, each producing a different product or service, topped by a central headquarters. This type of organization is suited to slow-changing environments and standardized products, but because these kinds of organizations are divisionalized, they tend to operate in several different environments (one for each division or product line). Information systems typically are elaborate and complex so that they can support central headquarters' financial planning and reporting requirements on one hand, and the operational requirements of the divisions on the other hand. Typically there is a great deal of tension and conflict between central headquarters IS groups (who want to expand in the name of efficiency and cost control) and divisional IS groups (who want to expand in the name of more effective service to operations). Currently, the divisional IS groups have more prominent roles while central headquarters IS groups are shrinking.

Adhocracy: This "task force" organization is typically found in research organizations (such as the Rand Corporation), aerospace companies, medical, biomedical, electronic, and other high-tech firms that must respond to rapidly changing environments

FIGURE 3.4
Different types of organizations. Organizational types tend to be suited to specific environments: The simple entrepreneurial structure (A) and the adhocracy (E) are suited to fast-changing environments. Machine (B) and divisionalized bureaucracies (D) are more suited to slowly paced environmental changes. Professional bureaucracies (C) are suited to knowledge intensive industries where change is typically slow-paced. *Source: Parts A–E:* Henry Mintzberg, The Structuring of Organizations, © 1979, pp. 311, 328, 329, 382. Reprinted by permission of Prentice Hall, Englewood Cliffs, NJ.

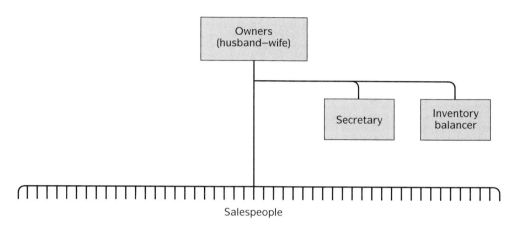

(A) Entrepreneurial structure

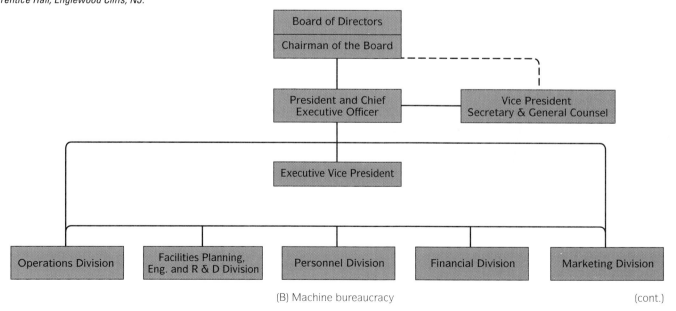

(B) Machine bureaucracy

(cont.)

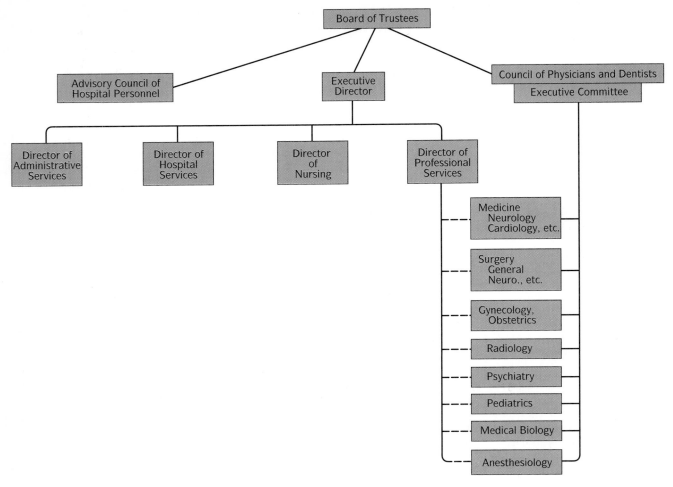

(C) Professional bureaucracy

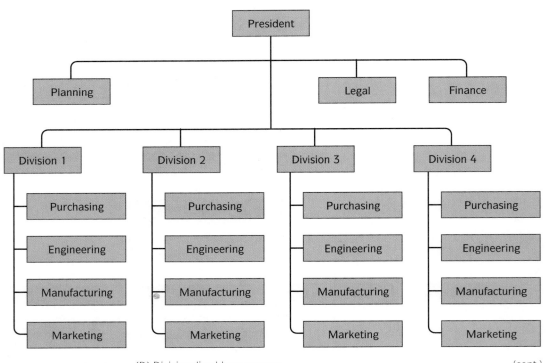

(D) Divisionalized bureaucracy

(cont.)

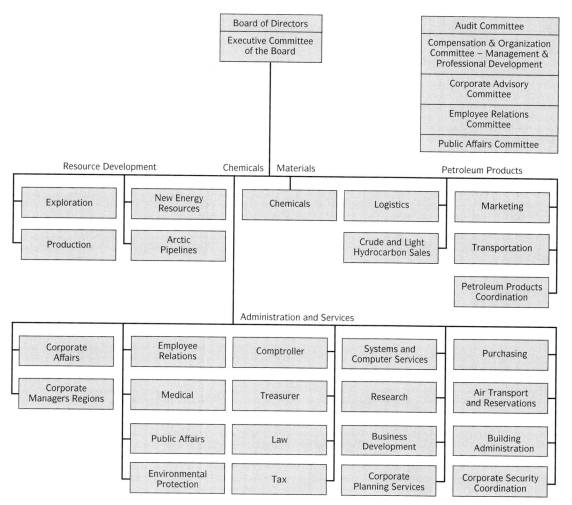

(E) Organigram of an Oil Company: An Administrative Adhocracy

and markets or that derive revenue from government contracts. Such organizations are more innovative than machine bureaucracies, more flexible than professional bureaucracies, and have more sustained, effective power than the simple entrepreneurial firm. They are characterized by large groups of specialists organized into short-lived, multidisciplinary task forces focusing on new products and by weak central management that understands little of the technical work of its employees but is nevertheless expected to manage the flow of funds from the environment and deliver products in return. Information systems are poorly developed at the central level, but are often remarkably advanced within task forces where experts build their unique systems for narrow functions.

Environments

Organizations have different environments and environments exert a powerful influence on organizational structure. Generally, organizations in fast-changing environments are more like adhocracies—they are less hierarchical, with much authority delegated to subordinates. Organizations in stable environments tend to develop into machine bureaucracies.

Most people do not realize how fragile and short-lived formal organizations really are. Consider that less than 10 percent of Fortune 500 companies in 1918 survived more than fifty years; less than 4 percent of all federal government organizations ever created are still in existence; 50 percent of all new private organizations are out of business within five years; and bigness per se is only marginally protective against extinction and may only slow the decline (Laudon, 1989).

The main reasons for organizational failure are an inability to adapt to a rapidly changing environment and the lack of resources—particularly among young firms—to sustain even short periods of troubled times (Freeman et al., 1983). New technologies, new products, and changing public tastes and values (many of which result in new government regulations) put strains on any organization's culture, politics, and people.

In general, most organizations do not cope well with large environmental shifts. The inertia built into an organization's standard operating procedures, the political conflict raised by potential change, and the threat to closely held cultural values typically inhibit organizations from making significant changes to cope with a changing environment. For this reason, corporate raiders and other outsiders are usually needed to save failing organizations and restructure them entirely.

From an organizational standpoint, technology is a major environmental factor that continually threatens existing arrangements. At times, technological changes occur so radically as to constitute a "technological discontinuity," a sharp break in industry practice that either enhances or destroys the competence of firms in an industry (Tushman and Anderson, 1986). When technological discontinuities happen, most organizations fail to adapt, go out of existence, and free up resources for new, younger organizations. Fast-changing technologies, like information technology, pose a particular threat to organizations. For instance, Wang Laboratories, a leading manufacturer of minicomputers and word processors, was a dominant force in the computer industry during the 1970s and early 1980s. But when powerful desktop microcomputers reduced the need for minicomputers, Wang nearly went out of business because it failed to adapt its products to the new technology.

As we see throughout this book, it is very difficult to identify precisely the impacts of computers on organizations. Much depends on the type of organization we are analyzing, the environment, management, and the underlying production technology. One cannot assume that information technologies will have the same effects on all organizations.

Other Differences among Organizations

There are many reasons why organizations have different shapes or structures. Organizations differ in their ultimate goals and the types of power used to achieve them. Some organizations have coercive goals (e.g., prisons); other have utilitarian goals (e.g., businesses). Still others have normative goals (universities, religious groups). The kinds of power and incentives differ accordingly, as does the overall shape of the organization: A coercive organization will be very hierarchical whereas a normative organization will be less hierarchical.

Organizations serve different groups or have different constituencies. Some primarily benefit their members; others benefit clients, stockholders, or the public. The social roles or functions of organizations differ. Some organizations are primarily interested in politics (trying to change the distribution of benefits in society), while others play primarily economic roles (seeking to optimize the utilization of resources). Some organizations play integrative roles by trying to pull together diverse groups in a common enterprise; examples include hospitals devoted to the control of disease and courts devoted to the pursuit of justice. Still other organizations, such as universities, schools, and churches, work to preserve important social values (normative roles). In general, the wider the constituency that an organization serves, the less hierarchical the organization.

Clearly, the nature of leadership differs greatly from one organization to another, even in similar organizations that are devoted to the same goal. Some of the major leadership styles are democratic, authoritarian (even totalitarian), laissez-faire (leadership is absent), technocratic (according to technical criteria, formal models), or bureaucratic (strictly according to formal rules). These kinds of leadership can occur in any type of organization and seem to depend on chance and history.

Still another way organizations differ is by the tasks they perform, and the technology they use. In some cases, organizations use routine tasks that could be programmed—that is, tasks may be reduced to formal rules that require little judgment (e.g., inventory reordering). Organizations that primarily perform routine tasks are typically like machine bureaucracies—they are hierarchical and run according to standard procedures. In other cases, organizations work with highly judgmental, nonroutine tasks (e.g., a consulting company that creates strategic plans for other companies).

In summary, both the common and the unique features of organizations exert a powerful influence on precisely how information technology can be and will be used in an organization. Because organizations are so different, it is probably wrong to conclude that information systems will have certain specific impacts on all organizations: So much depends on a number of other nontechnological factors. A wise manager will attempt to take these factors into account when building or proposing new information systems. We will deal more with this issue at the end of the chapter.

LEVELS OF ANALYSIS

We now have a basis for comparing organizations, one to another, using the features we discussed above. But what about within the organization? Within organizations, there

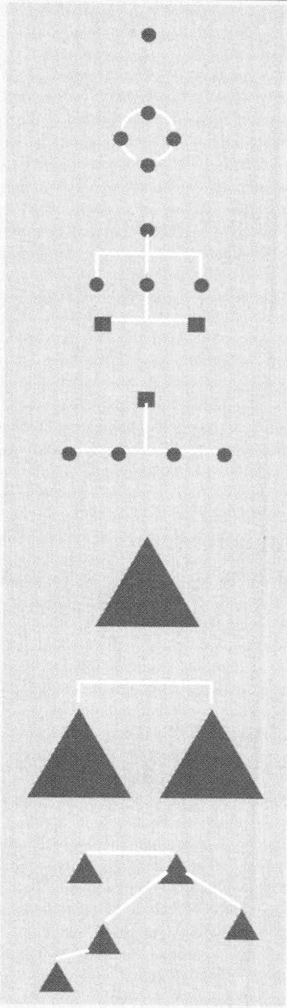

Organizational Level		Activity	Example Support System
Individual	•	Job, task	Microcomputer application; personal client database; decision-support systems
Group		Project	Product scheduling; access to mainframe data; access to external data sources; dynamic information requirements; group DSS
Department		Major function	Accounts payable; warehouse; payroll; human resources; marketing; stable information requirements; MIS; major transaction systems
Division		Major product or service	Systems to support production, marketing, administration, and human resources; access to organizational financial and planning data; MIS; major transaction systems; on-line interactive systems
Organization		Multiple products, services, and goals	Integrated financial and planning systems; MIS; on-line interactive systems; ESS
Interorganization		Alliance Competition Exchange Contact	Communication systems; intelligence, observation, and monitoring systems
Organizational network		Sector of economy: related products, services; interdependencies	Informal communication systems; industry and sector-level formal reporting systems

FIGURE 3.5
Organizational levels and support systems. Systems are designed to support various levels of the organization.

are different levels, occupations, divisions, and groups. All organizations have levels, but each organization is quite different from others in terms of what the levels are, who occupies them, and what tasks are assigned to different levels. The impact of information systems will probably be different for different levels and groups within an organization.

Each organizational level has different concerns and a different framework of analysis. This can be seen in Figure 3.5, which describes the various organizational levels and the principal concerns at each level, providing examples of information systems that are appropriate for each level.

At the individual and small-group levels of organization, information systems apply to a particular job, task, or project. At the department and division levels, information systems deal with a particular business function, product, or service. At the organization, interorganization, and organizational network levels, information systems support multiple products, services, and goals and facilitate alliances and coordination between two different organizations or groups of organizations.

Perhaps one of the most important and least heralded contributions of information systems is to support the large variety of work groups that spring up in organizations and that are not even part of the formal organization chart. While the organization chart shows the formal relationships in an organization, much of the work of an organization is done by informal task forces, interdepartmental committees, project teams, and committees. Table 3.3 presents the most important work groups and shows how systems can support them. These work groups generally have rapidly changing information needs, peak-load work schedules associated with project deadlines, and high communication requirements. Office automation systems, especially those with high-speed communication linkages, are one of the most recently developed system tools directed at work groups (see Chapter 15).

Table 3.3	Work Groups, Problems, and Systems Support		
Type of Work Group Support	Description	Problems	Systems
Hierarchical	Formal working relationship between manager and staff	Frequent meetings; dispersed work environments	Video conferencing; electronic mail (one to many)
Interdepartmental	Sequential activities; "expediters," "fixers"	Need occasional direct communication	Electronic messaging (one to one)
Project teams	Formally defined groups; close day-to-day interaction	Meeting schedules	Scheduling and communication software; meeting support tools; document interchange
Committees	Formally defined groups; occasional interaction	High peak-load; communications intermittent	Electronic bulletin boards; video conferencing; electronic mail; computer conferencing
Task force	Formally defined single-purpose group	Rapid communication; access to internal and external data	Graphics display; information utility; document interchange; meeting support tools
Peer groups/social networks	Informal groups of similar-status individuals	Intense personal communication	Telephone; electronic mail
		Problems of all work groups Making arrangements Attending meetings Long agendas Cost of meetings Between-meeting activities	

Working task forces use their combined skills to improve on the design and manufacturing of semiconductors at this Motorola research facility.

We have developed a rather long list of salient features you should know about when considering information systems in organizations (see Table 3.4). As you can see, the list of unique features of organizations is longer than the common features list. This should suggest to you that most organizations are quite unique. One consequence of this fact is that information systems are not completely portable from one organization to another. The impacts of systems will differ from one organization to

Table 3.4   A Summary of Salient Features of Organizations

Common Features	Unique Features
Formal structure	Organizational type
Standard operating procedures (SOPs)	Environments
Politics	Goals
Culture	Power
	Constituencies
	Function
	Leadership
	Tasks
	Technology
	Levels

another, and only by close analysis of a specific organization can a manager design and manage information systems.

3.3 HOW ORGANIZATIONS AFFECT INFORMATION SYSTEMS

We now can look more closely at the two-way relationship between information systems and organizations. We first need to explain how organizations affect technology and systems. Organizations have an impact on information systems through the decisions made by managers and employees. Managers make decisions about the design of systems; they also use information technology. Managers decide who will build and operate systems, and ultimately it is managers who provide the rationale for building systems. There are four important questions to consider in studying this issue:

- How have organizations actually used information systems?
- How has the organizational role of information systems changed?
- Who operates information systems?
- Why do organizations adopt information systems in the first place?

In this section, we answer these questions.

DECISIONS ABOUT THE ROLE OF INFORMATION SYSTEMS

Organizations have a direct impact on information technology by making decisions about how the technology will be used and what role it will play in the organization. (Chapters 1 and 2 have described the ever-widening role of information systems in organizations.) Supporting this changing role have been changes in the technical and organizational configuration of systems that have brought computing power and data much closer to the ultimate end users (see Figure 3.6).

Isolated "electronic accounting machines" with limited functions in the 1950s gave way to large, centralized mainframe computers that served corporate headquarters and a few remote sites in the 1960s. In the 1970s, midsized minicomputers located in individual departments or divisions of the organization were networked to large centralized computers. Desktop microcomputers first were used independently and then were linked to minicomputers and large computers in the 1980s.

In the 1990s, the architecture for a fully networked organization emerged. In this new architecture, the large central mainframe computer stores information (like a library) and coordinates information flowing among desktops and perhaps among hundreds of smaller local networks. It operates much like a telephone system. Chapter 10 provides a detailed discussion of this information architecture and the way it has reshaped the delivery of information in the firm. Information systems have become integral, on-line, interactive tools deeply involved in the minute-to-minute operations and decision making of large organizations. Organizations now are critically dependent on systems and could not survive even occasional breakdowns: In most large organizations the entire cash flow is linked to information systems.

DECISIONS ABOUT THE COMPUTER PACKAGE: WHO DELIVERS INFORMATION TECHNOLOGY SERVICES?

A second way in which organizations affect information technology is through decisions about who will design, build, and operate the technology within the organization. Computer technology is similar to other kinds of technology, including automotive technology. In order to use automobiles, a society needs highways, mechanics, gas stations, engine designers, police, and parts manufacturers. The "automobile" is a package of services, organizations, and people. Likewise, information systems require specialized organizational subunits, information specialists, and a host of other

FIGURE 3.6
The development of information architecture of organizations. The last five decades have seen dramatic changes in the technical and organizational configurations of systems. During the 1950s organizations were dependent on computers for a few critical functions. The 1960s witnessed the development of large centralized machines. By the late 1970s and into the 1980s information architecture became complex and information systems included telecommunications links to distribute information. During the 1990s information architecture is an enterprise-wide information utility.

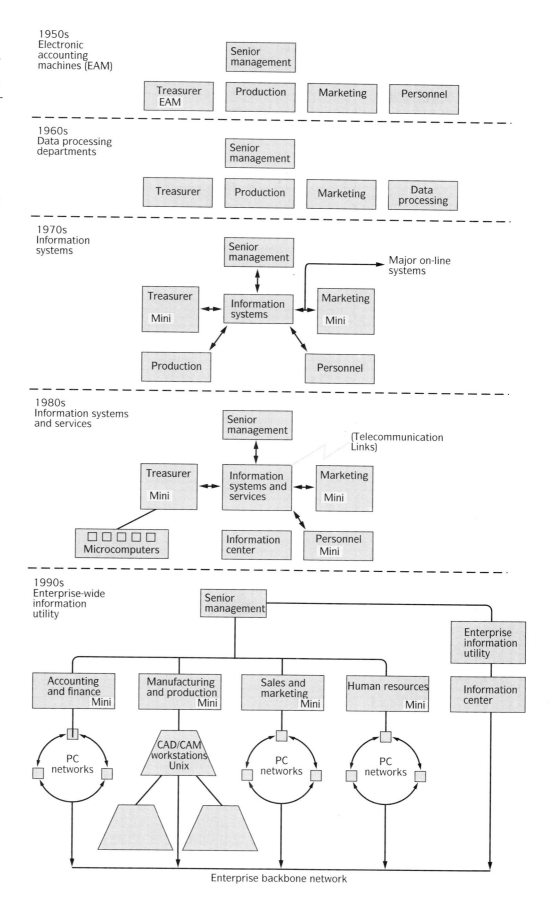

supportive groups (Kling and Dutton, 1982). Managers (and organizations in general) make the key decisions about the computer package: These decisions determine how technology services will be delivered, and by whom, how, and when.

The computer package is composed of three distinct entities (see Figure 3.7). The first is a formal organizational unit or function called an **information systems department**. The second consists of information systems specialists such as programmers, systems analysts, project leaders, and information systems managers. Also, external specialists such as hardware vendors and manufacturers, software firms, and consultants frequently participate in the day-to-day operations and long-term planning of information systems. A third element of the information systems package is the technology itself, both hardware and software.

Today the information systems group often acts as a powerful change agent in the organization, suggesting new business strategies and new information-based products and coordinating both the development of technology and the planned changes in the organization.

The size of the information systems department can vary greatly, depending on the role of information systems in the organization and on the organization's size. In most medium to large firms, the information systems group is composed of 100 to 400 people. The size of the information systems group and the total expenditures on computers and information systems are largest in service organizations (especially those that sell information products like Dow Jones News), where information systems can consume over 40 percent of gross revenues.

In the early years of the computer, when the role of information systems was limited, the information systems group was composed mostly of **programmers**, highly trained technical specialists who wrote the software instructions for the computer. Today, in most information systems groups, a growing proportion of staff members are systems analysts. **Systems analysts** constitute the principal liaison between the information systems group and the rest of the organization. It is the system analyst's job to translate business problems and requirements into information requirements and systems.

Information systems managers are leaders of teams of programmers and analysts, project managers, physical facility managers, telecommunications managers, heads of office automation groups, and, finally, managers of computer operations and data entry staff.

End users are representatives of departments outside of the information systems group for whom applications are developed. These users are playing an increasingly large role in the design and development of information systems.

The last element of the computer package is the technology itself, the hardware and software instructions. Chapters 6 and 7 provide detailed discussions of these topics.

DECISIONS ABOUT WHY INFORMATION SYSTEMS ARE BUILT

Managers provide the public and private rationales for building information systems. Managers can choose to use systems primarily to achieve economies, or to provide better service, or to provide a better workplace. The "impact" of computers in any organization depends in part on how managers make decisions.

At first glance, the answer to the question, "Why do organizations adopt information systems?" seems very simple. Obviously, organizations adopt information systems to become more efficient, to save money, and to reduce the work force. Although this response may have been generally true in the past, it no longer comprises the only or even the primary reason for adopting systems.

Systems today are, of course, built with efficiency in mind, but they have become vitally important simply for staying in business. Information systems are as vital as are capital improvements such as modern buildings or corporate headquarters. Improvements in decision making (speed, accuracy, comprehensiveness), serving ever higher customer and client expectations, coordinating dispersed groups in an organization, complying with governmental reporting regulations, and exercising tighter

information systems department The formal organizational unit that is responsible for the information systems function in the organization.

programmers Highly trained technical specialists who write computer software instructions.

systems analysts Specialists who translate business problems and requirements into information requirements and systems, acting as liaison between the information systems department and the rest of the organization.

information systems managers Leaders of the various specialists in the information systems department.

end users Representatives of departments outside the information systems group for whom information systems applications are developed.

FIGURE 3.7
The computer package. Many groups, individuals, and organizations are involved in the design and management of information systems.

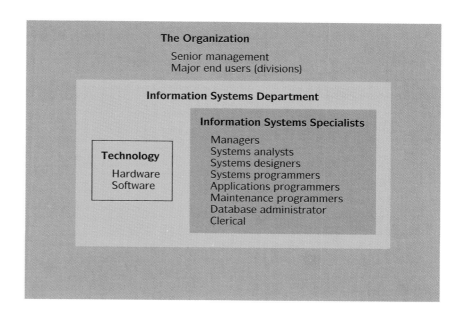

The Organization
Senior management
Major end users (divisions)

Information Systems Department

Information Systems Specialists
Managers
Systems analysts
Systems designers
Systems programmers
Applications programmers
Maintenance programmers
Database administrator
Clerical

Technology
Hardware
Software

control over personnel and expenditures have become important reasons for building systems (Huff and Munro, 1985).

More recently, organizations have been seeking the competitive benefits of systems described in Chapter 2. Hence, what seems like an easy question to answer—*Why do organizations adopt systems?*—is really quite complex. Some organizations are simply more innovative than others. They have values that encourage any kind of innovation, regardless of its direct economic benefit to the company. In other cases, information systems are built because of the ambitions of various groups within an organization and the anticipated effect on existing organizational conflicts. And in some cases such as PanCanadian Railways, described in the chapter-opening vignette and Schneider National, described in the Window on Organizations, changes in an organization's environment—including changes in government regulations, competitors' actions, and costs—demand a computer system response.

Figure 3.8 illustrates a model of the systems development process that includes many factors other than economic considerations. This model divides the explanations for why organizations adopt systems into two groups: *external environmental factors* and *internal institutional factors* (Laudon, 1985; King et al., 1994).

environmental factors Factors external to the organization that influence the adoption and design of information systems.

Environmental factors are factors that are external to the organization that influence the adoption and design of information systems. Some external environmental factors are rising costs of labor or other resources; the competitive actions of other organizations; and changes in government regulations. In general, these can be thought of as *environmental constraints:* At the same time, the environment also provides

FIGURE 3.8
The systems development process. External environmental factors and internal institutional factors influence the types of information systems the organizations select, develop, and use.

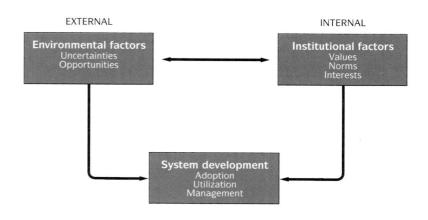

EXTERNAL

Environmental factors
Uncertainties
Opportunities

INTERNAL

Institutional factors
Values
Norms
Interests

System development
Adoption
Utilization
Management

SCHNEIDER RESPONDS TO THE NEW RULES OF THE TRUCKING GAME

Deregulation changed the whole business environment for the trucking industry overnight. Competition between trucking firms for customers heated up. Interstate truckers no longer had to follow the rules of a regulatory bureaucracy about what kinds of freight to carry and where to take it. This same regulatory red tape had also made it difficult for customers to change carriers because only certain trucking firms could meet these regulations. Large retailers and manufacturers were also trying to slash inventory costs and warehouses by installing just-in-time delivery systems. They wanted to use trucking firms that could transport their shipments right away.

To meet these new demands Schneider National, North America's biggest carrier of full-truckload cargoes, used a two-pronged strategy. First, it tried to make sweeping changes in its corporate culture. CEO Don Schneider realized he had to replace his firm's regulated-utility mentality with quick reflexes and an urgency to get things done. Schneider democratized the organization by calling all employees "associates" and removing status symbols like reserved parking places. He encouraged everyone, from drivers on up, to speak out on ways to improve operations. He also instituted an extra bonus paycheck based solely on performance.

Second, Schneider deployed new information systems to support these changes. In 1988, the firm equipped each truck with a computer and a rotating antenna. A satellite tracks every rig, making sure it adheres to schedule. When an order comes in to headquarters, often directly via the customer's computer to Schneider's computer, dispatchers know exactly which truck in the customer's vicinity should be assigned to the job. The dispatchers send an order directly by satellite to the driver's on-board terminal, complete with directions to the destination and instructions on what gate to use and papers to collect with the merchandise. Within 15 to 30 minutes of sending an order to Schneider's computer, customers know which trucks to expect and when.

> **To Think About:** Don Schneider has also said that the job of a transportation manager today requires more emphasis on management and less on transportation itself. Why? How did information systems change the way Schneider ran its business?

For example, when Procter & Gamble advises that a trailer of detergent for Omaha will be ready in Cincinnati at 4 P.M., the system lists drivers headed for Cincinnati and their arrival times, updating the information every two hours via the satellite link on each truck. The system passes over drivers such as driver 11743, who is free at 2 P.M. but who has been driving since 4 A.M. and needs a break. After selecting an appropriate driver, the system beams the time and place of pickup to the driver's cab, relieving him of the need to phone in. The computer even registers the driver's speed (drivers exceeding Schneider's 55-mile-per-hour speed limit may lose their monthly bonuses).

Schneider has started using its information systems to provide the entire logistics management function for other companies. It contracted with General Motors Corporation to manage every shipment of GM service parts, amounting to 435,000 outbound "order lines" daily to more than 9000 GM dealers, warehouse distributors, and mass merchandisers. Schneider won't carry all of the shipments on its own trucks. While other providers use only their own trucks, planes, and trains, Schneider gives solutions that use the best medium for moving freight, even if it isn't using its own trucks.

Schneider's information systems now play such a powerful role in company operations that the firm has been described as "an information system masquerading as a trucking line." Don

institutional factors Factors internal to the organization that influence the adoption and design of information systems.

organizations with *opportunities:* new technologies, new sources of capital, the development of new production processes, the demise of a competitor, or a new government program that increases the demand for certain products.

Institutional factors are factors internal to the organization that influence the adoption and design of information systems. They include values, norms, and vital interests that govern matters of strategic importance to the organization. For instance, the top management of a corporation can decide that it needs to exercise much stronger control over the inventory process and therefore decides to develop an inventory information system. The resulting system is adopted, developed, and operated for purely internal, institutional reasons (for a similar model, see Kraemer et al., 1989).

3.4   HOW INFORMATION SYSTEMS AFFECT ORGANIZATIONS

In the previous section, we described one side of a two-way relationship between information technology and organizations. Now we shall look at the other side, asking the following question: How do information systems affect organizations? To answer this question, we need to examine and quickly summarize a large body of research and theory. Some researchers base their work on economics, while others take a behavioral approach. In a single chart, Table 3.5 compares these theories and the hypothesized impacts of information technology on organizations. Table 3.5 is complex, and you should read the text first and then use the table for a convenient summary. In general, we have much more theory in this area than we have hard data and acceptable findings. We briefly now describe these theoretical models and the suggested information system technology impacts.

ECONOMIC THEORIES

Economics is the study of allocating scarce resources in markets populated by thousands of competing firms. It is also the study of national and global economies. Microeconomics focuses on individual firms and provides several models to describe the impact of information technology on organizations (see Gurbaxani and Whang, 1991).

Microeconomic Theory

microeconomic model Model of the firm that views information technology as a factor of production that can be freely substituted for capital and labor.

The most widespread theory of how information technology affects thousands of firms is the **microeconomic model** portrayed in Figure 3.9. Information system technology is viewed as a factor of production that can be freely substituted for capital and labor. As the cost of information system technology falls, it is substituted for labor that historically has a rising cost. As information system technology transforms the production function—through the use of technology to automate previously manual activities or to streamline or to rethink how work is accomplished—the entire production function shifts inward. Over time, less capital and less labor are required for a given output. Moreover, the expansion trajectory of the firm is altered more toward increasing reliance on capital, and less toward reliance on labor—which historically has risen in cost (Pindyck and Rubinfield, 1992). Hence, in microeconomic theory information technology should result in a decline in the number of middle managers and clerical workers as information technology substitutes for their labor.

Table 3.5 The Impact of Information Systems on Organizations

Theories	(A) Economic Theories			(B) Behavioral Theories		
	Micro-Econ	Transaction Cost	Agency	Decision/Control	Social Science*	Post Industrial
Unit of Analysis	The firm	Markets and the firm	The firm	The organization	The organization, sub-units, players, environments	Macro and global society and economy
Core Concepts	Substitution of factors of production	Transactions costs Markets	Agents, principals, and contracts	Decision-making process and structure	SOPs, politics, culture, social history	Knowledge and information-intense work and products
Dynamics	Capital is substituted for labor as IT costs fall	IT reduces market transaction costs	IT reduces agency costs	IT replaces humans in the information and decision process	IT reflects bureaucratic, political, and cultural forces	IT encourages growth of information-intense occupations and goods
Impacts of IT Occupational Structure	Decline in middle managers and clericals	Decline in middle managers and clerical workers	Decline in middle managers and clerical workers	Decline in middle managers and clericals; growth in information and knowledge workers	IT has little impact per se on occupational structure; specialists try to use IT to their advantage	IT creates new occupations highly dependent on information
Organizational Structure Formal: Hierarchy Div. of Labor SOPs Authority	Reduced hierarchy Centralization	Reduced org. size Centralization of authority; decentralization of decisions; Reduction in hierarchy Less reliance on SOPs	Reduced org. size Centralization of authority, reduction in hierarchy	Authority more uniform Less specialization and less reliance on SOPs Reduction in hierarchy Formalization of information functions	Groups use IT to extend their influence, stabilize their position, and optimize performance of SOPs	IT results in more flexible, self-guided work, decentralization, flattening of hierarchies, and fluid division of labor
Informal: Info. flow Decision making Intelligence	Increased info. flow, more rapid decision making, more intelligence	Information access, timeliness, accuracy increase; decision-making units fewer and more efficient	Increased surveillance Information access, timeliness, accuracy increase; decision-making units fewer and more efficient	Information access, timeliness, accuracy increase; decision-making units fewer and more efficient	IT as a formal information system has little impact on informal channels of power and influence	Rigid hierarchic decision structures replaced by rich information-intense networks
Management Strategy	Employ technology to reduce labor costs	Employ IT to increase reliance on markets and reduce org. size, middle mgmt. and clericals	Senior managers employ IT to increase surveillance, reduce costs of management	Employ IT to improve decision making and restructure organization to optimize command and control technologies	Managers should understand and use IT to achieve their agendas	Managers should assist the emergence of less rigid organizations, encourage self-manager and networked organizations

*The social science reference disciplines are sociology, political science, anthropology, and social history.

Source: Azimuth Corporation, 1992

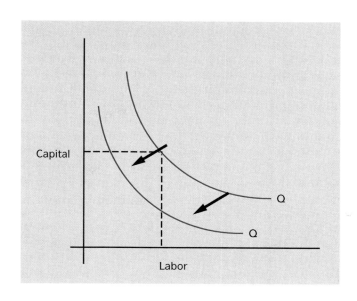

FIGURE 3.9
The microeconomic theory of the impact of information technology on the organization. Firms substitute IT for labor over time; when IT transforms the production function, the function shifts inward, lowering the amount of both capital and labor needed to produce level Q.

Transaction Cost Theory

transaction cost theory Economic theory that states that firms exist because they can conduct marketplace transactions internally more cheaply than they can with external firms in the marketplace.

Transaction cost theory is based on the idea that a firm incurs costs when it buys on the marketplace what it does not make itself. These costs are referred to as transaction costs. Transaction costs are the equivalent of friction in physical systems. Firms and individuals seek to economize on transaction costs (much as they do on production costs). Using markets is expensive (Williamson, 1985) because of coordination costs such as locating and communicating with distant suppliers, monitoring contract compliance, buying insurance, obtaining information on products, and so forth. Traditionally, firms sought to reduce transaction costs by getting bigger: hiring more employees; vertically integrating (as General Motors did—see the Part One section-ending case on Chrysler and GM); buying their own suppliers and distributors; growing horizontally by moving into new markets; taking over smaller companies; and even developing monopolies.

Information technology could help firms lower the cost of market participation (transaction costs), making it worthwhile for firms to contract with external suppliers instead of using internal sources of supply. The size of firms (measured by the number of employees) could stay constant or contract even though they increased their revenues. As transaction costs decrease, firm size (the number of employees) should shrink because it becomes easier and cheaper for the firm to contract the purchase of goods and services in the marketplace rather than to make the product or service inside. (For example, Caterpillar Inc. produces the same total output of heavy equipment it had in 1979 with 40,000 fewer employees. General Electric reduced its work force from about 400,000 people in the early 1980s to about 230,000 while increasing revenues 150%.) Why hire workers, grow bigger, and suffer rising management costs when the same volume of business and profit could be obtained if the firm contracted with outside suppliers and workers in an electronic marketplace? (See Figure 3.10.) These labor force reductions would probably affect middle managers and clerical workers in particular.

Agency Theory

agency theory Economic theory that views the firm as a nexus of contracts among self-interested individuals rather than a unified, profit-maximizing entity.

In **agency theory**, the firm is viewed as a "nexus of contracts" among self-interested individuals rather than as a unified, profit-maximizing entity (Jensen and Meckling, 1976). A principal (owner) employs "agents" (employees) to perform work on his or her behalf and delegates some decision-making authority to the agent. However, agents need constant supervision and management because they otherwise will tend to pursue their own interests rather than those of the owners. This factor introduces

FIGURE 3.10
The transaction cost theory of the impact of information technology on the organization. Firms traditionally grew in size in order to reduce transaction costs. IT potentially reduces the costs for a given size, shifting the transaction cost curve inward, opening up the possibility of revenue growth without increasing size, or even revenue growth accompanied by shrinking size.

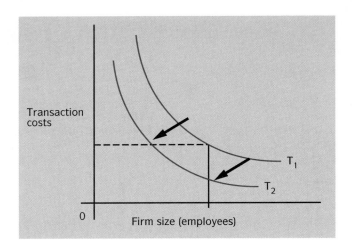

agency costs or management costs. As firms grow in size and scope, management costs rise because owners must expend more and more effort monitoring agents, acquiring information, tracking inventory, and so on. Owners must delegate more decision-making authority to agents, who in turn may be untrustworthy.

Information technology, by reducing the costs of acquiring and analyzing information, permits organizations to reduce overall management costs, and allows them to grow in revenues while shrinking the numbers of middle management and clerical workers (see Figure 3.11). We have seen examples in earlier chapters where information technology expanded the power and scope of small organizations by allowing them to perform coordinating activities such as processing orders or keeping track of inventory with very few clerks and managers. Under the right circumstances, information technology can also give large organizations some of the agility and flexibility of small organizations. The Window on Technology explores one aspect of this phenomenon—custom manufacturing.

Computer controls on machine tools and electronic exchange of data can also give small companies some of the efficiency and quality formerly reserved for giant manufacturers.

BEHAVIORAL THEORIES

Information technology has not transformed all large organizations into agile manufacturers, nor has it automatically given all small companies the powers of giants. Although microeconomic theories try to explain how large numbers of firms act in

FIGURE 3.11
The agency cost theory of the impact of information technology on the organization. As firms grow in size and complexity, traditionally they experience rising agency costs. IT shifts the agency cost curve down and to the right, allowing firms to increase size while lowering agency costs.

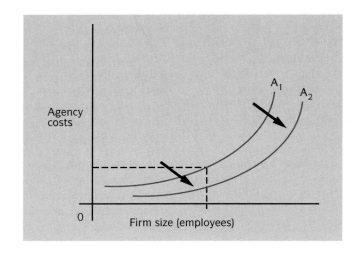

CUSTOM MANUFACTURING: THE NEW AUTOMATION

For two decades after World War II, mass production reigned supreme. Mass production techniques pushed companies into standardized one-size-fits-all products, long product life cycles, and rigid manufacturing emphasizing efficiency and low cost over flexibility. Special orders and made-to-order products cost more. But today's consumers are very choosy. They want quality, value, and products specially tailored to their needs—at the lowest possible price. Enter custom manufacturing.

Custom manufacturing uses state-of-the-art information technology to produce and deliver products and services designed to fit the specifications of individual customers. Companies can customize products in quantities as small as one with the same speed and low cost as mass production methods. In custom manufacturing, software and computer networks are used to link the plant floor tightly with orders, design, and purchasing and to finely control production machines. The result is a dynamically responsive environment in which products can be turned out in greater variety and easily customized with no added cost for small production runs. Huge manufacturers can be as agile as small firms.

Custom manufacturing systems take information from the customer and apply it behind the scenes to control the flow of goods. For example, Motorola manufactures hand-held pagers to individual customer specifications. Retailers use Macintosh microcomputers to help customers design the pager features they want. At Motorola's Boynton Beach, Florida, plant, orders stream in over 800 lines or E-mail for different colors and models. The data are digitized and flow immediately to the assembly line. Within 80 minutes, pick-and-place robots select the proper components for each order and humans assemble them into the final product. Often the customer can have his or her pager the same day or the day after. Instead of manufacturing, Motorola thinks of this process as rapidly translating data from customers into products.

The John Deere Harvester Works manufacturing plant in Moline, Illinois, produces a wide variety of crop planters, many of which sell for over $100,000. Customers can choose from scores of options, including liquid or dry fertilizer and row count, which amount to thousands of different configurations. Until a few years ago the plant was a typical mass production operation. It kept an inventory of about 300 planters, based on projected demand and production forecasts because it could not respond quickly to individual orders. In 1992, Deere equipped the factory with new manufacturing scheduling software called OptiFlex that would provide shorter lead times and greater flexibility. With this new system, the Deere plant can reschedule production each day in response to customer orders. The plant needs to keep only 20 finished machines in inventory.

Caterpillar Inc.'s Aurora, Illinois, plant used to build several different models of earth-moving vehicles on just two assembly lines, requiring frequent setup changes that wasted a great deal of time. Cat redesigned its manufacturing process, spending $250 million on new information systems and equipment. Now, as vehicles move down its assembly line, automatically guided cranes and a monorail system deliver parts as needed from one of 500 or more storage locations next to the factory floor. The redesigned factory can run eight shorter, more specialized assembly lines.

> **To Think About:** What theories about the relationship of information technology and organizations are illustrated by custom manufacturing? How does custom manufacturing change the way the companies described here did business?

Production lines at IBM's Charlotte, North Carolina, plant can turn out as many as 27 different products at once—hand-held bar code scanners, fiber-optic connectors for mainframes, portable medical computers, satellite communications devices for truck drivers. Workers are surrounded by "kits" of parts that have been assembled to match production orders. Each worker has a computer screen tied into the factory network displaying an up-to-the-minute checklist of the parts required for the product he or she is working on at the moment. The worker can ask the computer to display information to guide the assembly steps if he or she needs help. When the task is finished, the worker punches a button and the information system moves the product on a conveyor to the next bench on the line.

Sources: Jeff Moad, "Let Customers Have It Their Way," *Datamation*, April 1, 1995; Gene Bylinsky, "The Digital Factory," *Fortune*, November 14, 1994; and Peter Coy, "Start with Some High-Tech Magic," *Business Week/Enterprise* 1993.

the marketplace, most economists would agree they are quite poor at describing or predicting the actual behavior of any one particular real-world firm. In the real world, managers face unique problems such as minimizing inventory costs, meeting production schedules, devising diverse product mixes, managing a labor force, and obtaining financing. Behavioral theories from sociology, psychology, and political science generally are far more descriptive and predictive of the behavior of individual firms and managers than are economic theories.

Behavioral research has found that there is little evidence that information systems automatically transform organizations, although the systems may be instrumental in accomplishing this goal once senior management decides to pursue this end. Instead, researchers have observed an intricately choreographed relationship in which organizations and information technology mutually influence each other. Because information systems are used to promote organizational values and interests, they are deeply affected by the organization.

What looks like an impact of information technology is often a reflection of what the organization and the system designers consciously intended (or unconsciously created). In behavioral models of the firm, the influence of information systems is not as simple and direct as the economic models suggest.

Decision and Control Theory

decision and control theory
Behavioral theory stating that the function of the organization is to make decisions under conditions of uncertainty and risk and that organizations centralize decision making and create a hierarchy of decision making to reduce uncertainty and to ensure survival.

According to **decision and control theory**, the function of the organization is to make decisions under conditions of uncertainty and risk and under the constraint of bounded rationality. The theory holds that managers never have complete information and knowledge, and they can never examine all alternatives even though they would like to.[3] Organizations are decision-making structures, arranged so as to reduce uncertainty and to ensure survival. They are vitally dependent on the routine flow of information to decision makers. Because persons lower in the hierarchy do not have the information needed for making decisions, organizations must centralize decision making and create a hierarchy of decision makers. A large middle management group is necessary to gather information, analyze it, and pass it up to senior managers. In turn, senior managers require middle managers to implement policies because middle managers are in direct contact with lower-level operating units. Lower-level employees—in turn—rely on standard operating procedures designed by senior decision makers. If a situation does not fit the SOP, then senior managers must make a decision. The organization is a pyramidal structure in which authority and responsibility grow as one rises in the hierarchy.

Theoretically, information technology could change this rigid structure by lowering the costs of information acquisition and broadening the distribution of information. Information technology could bring information directly from operating units to senior managers, thereby eliminating middle managers and their clerical support workers. Information technology could permit senior managers to contact lower-level operating units directly through the use of networked telecommunications and computers, eliminating middle management intermediaries. Alternatively, information technology could distribute information to lower-level workers, who could then make their own decisions based on their own knowledge and information without management intervention (Applegate, Cash, and Mills, 1988).

Early speculation on the impact of information systems suggested that organizations would indeed become more centralized and that middle management would tend to disappear over time because computers would give central, high-level man-

---

3. See George P. Huber, "The Nature and Design of Post-Industrial Organizations." *Management Science* 30, no. 8 (August 1984). See the classic statement of this view in James G. March and Herbert A. Simon, *Organizations* (New York: John Wiley, 1958). See also Herbert A. Simon, "Applying Information Technology to Organization Design," *Public Administration Review,* May–June 1973).

agers all of the information they required to operate the organization without intervention from middle management (Leavitt and Whistler, 1958; Drucker, 1988).

Figure 3.12 illustrates this change in organizational structure. Before information technology, the organization had a triangular shape with decision making concentrated at the top. After the introduction of computer systems, the organization chart would start to look like an inverted *T*. Other research suggests that computerization gives more information to middle managers, empowering them to make more important decisions than in the past and reducing the need for large numbers of lower-level workers. Over time, this results in a diamond-like structure (Shore, 1983).

Sociological Theory: Oligarchies and Routines

sociological theory Behavioral theory stating that organizations develop hierarchical bureaucratic structures and standard operating procedures to cope in unstable environments and that organizations can't change routines when environments change.

Sociological theory focuses on the growth of hierarchical, bureaucratic structures and standard operating procedures as primary tools for organizations trying to cope in unstable environments. Robert Michels' saying that "Whoever says organization, says oligarchy (rule by a few)" (Michels, 1962) and the phrase "the iron cage of bureaucracy" (Weber, 1947; DiMaggio and Powell, 1983) suggest that organizations inherently breed inequalities of power. Organizations hone and refine routines (SOPs) until they become extremely efficient. Unfortunately, attainment of success contains the seeds of failure. Organizations find it nearly impossible to change routines when their environment changes.

Sociologists argue that information technology has little independent power to transform organizations. Information technology is embraced by managers in various subunits of the organization insofar as it furthers their own interests or the interests of their subunit. Managers are always looking for better ways to implement existing rules and SOPs. They reject information technology if it threatens existing routines or subunits. Information technology itself becomes, over time, just another SOP, just as hard to change as any other. Information technology adds little to the survivability of firms, and given reasonable time, most organizations fail. Change comes about because new organizations form around new technologies, and they incorporate the new technologies into their SOPs. Over time, these new organizations become old, bureaucratic, and brittle, and they too pass away.

The sociological view emphasizes the power of people and organizations to control the impacts of systems. Important groups in the organization determine, either consciously or unconsciously, the kinds of changes that will occur in organizational structure. Organizations adopt information technology because it suits the power interests of key subunits, divisions, and managers. Organizations can decide to centralize or decentralize power.

In recent years, many organizations have shifted authority away from central headquarters, shrinking staff and placing more power in the hands of division man-

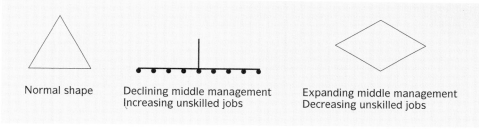

| Normal shape | Declining middle management Increasing unskilled jobs | Expanding middle management Decreasing unskilled jobs |

FIGURE 3.12

The impact of information systems on organizational structure. There are several hypotheses on how systems can change the structure of an organization. Three outcomes are represented here: Systems can have no effect; they may reduce the number of middle managers, creating an inverted "T" effect; or they may expand the capabilities and numbers of middle managers, producing the diamond effect.

agers and local factory managers. Yet many organizations still consciously seek to gather more information from operating units and to develop a large central corporate staff both for planning and for operational control purposes (Leifer, 1988). Managers make these decisions in pursuit of their own interests (Kraemer et al., 1989).

Post-Industrial Theory: Knowledge-Intensive Structures and Shapes

According to theorists of post-industrial society—often sociologists and political scientists—advanced industrial countries entered a new kind of post-industrial economy and society sometime in the 1960s (Bell, 1973; Brzezinski, 1970; Masuda, 1980; Toffler, 1970; Martin, 1981). In a "post-industrial society," the service sector dominates the economy.[4] The service sector itself favors knowledge workers (scientists, engineers, and some managers) and data workers (secretaries, accountants, sales people) over service providers like chefs and custodians. In post-industrial global economies, industrial manufacturing is shifted to low-wage countries, and high-skilled, "knowledge-based" work grows rapidly in the developed, high-wage countries.

post-industrial theory Behavioral theory stating that the transformation of advanced industrial countries into post-industrial societies creates flatter organizations dominated by knowledge workers where decision making is more decentralized.

According to **post-industrial theory**, the transformation to a post-industrial society brings with it inherent changes in organizational structure: Authority should rely more on knowledge and competence, and not on mere formal position; the shape of organizations should flatten, since professional workers tend to be self-managing; and decision making should become more decentralized as knowledge and information become more widespread throughout (Drucker, 1988).

Information technology should lead then to "task force" networked organizations in which groups of professionals come together—face-to-face or electronically—for short periods of time to accomplish a specific task (e.g., designing a new automobile); once the task is accomplished, the individuals join other task forces. Clericals are reduced because professionals maintain their own portable offices in the form of laptop and palmtop personal computers connected to powerful global networks. Firms could conceivably operate as "virtual organizations" where work is no longer tied to geographic location because knowledge and information can be delivered anywhere and anytime they are needed. Organizations should look more like Mintzberg's adhocracies depicted in Figure 3.4E.[5]

Recent discussions of information technology and organizational change have expanded on post-industrial theories by suggesting that organizations will become "flatter" and more "horizontal" not only by trimming middle managers but also by reshaping themselves around business processes instead of the traditional functional departments. Figure 3.13 shows the differences between a traditional vertical organization where groups are arranged by function and the proposed horizontal organization where teams are arranged by processes.

Business processes are sequences of logically related tasks performed to achieve a defined business outcome. Examples of processes are new product development, which turns an idea into a manufacturable prototype, or order fulfillment, which begins with the receipt of an order and ends when the customer has received and paid for the product. Processes, by nature, are generally cross-functional, transcending the boundaries between sales, marketing, manufacturing, and research and development. Processes cut across the traditional organizational structure, grouping employees from different functional specialties to complete a piece of work.

---

4. The names for this phenomenon—of societies based primarily on knowledge and information—differ, but the underlying rationale remains the same: the "technetronic society" (Brzezinski), "telematic society" (Martin), and Toffler's Future Shock and ad-hoc organizations.

5. Post-industrial themes are echoed in Drucker's 1988 formulation of how IT affects organizations: "The typical large business 20 years hence will have fewer than half the levels of management of its counterpart today, and no more than a third the managers. . . . the typical business will be knowledge-based, an organization composed largely of specialists, who direct and discipline their own performance through organized feedback from colleagues, customers, and headquarters. For this reason, it will be what I call an information based organization" (Drucker, 1988, p. 45).

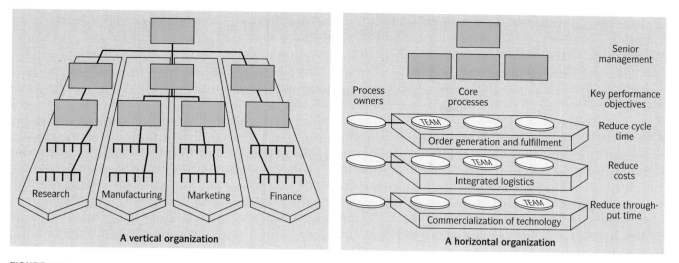

FIGURE 3.13
Some researchers and popular writers argue that information technology allows firms to reorganize themselves from vertical organizations to horizontal organizations where groups of people are arranged by processes. *Source: John Pepper, "Horizontal Organization," InformationWeek, August 17, 1992. Copyright © 1992 by CMP Publications, Inc., 600 Community Drive, Manhasset, NY 11030. Reprinted from* InformationWeek *with permission.*

The objectives for processes are more external and linked to meeting customer and market demands than are those for the traditional functional approach. Instead of evaluating how well each functional area is performing as a discrete business function, management would evaluate how well a group executes a process. For instance, instead of measuring manufacturing independently on how well it reduces the cost to produce each unit, and shipping independently on how quickly it ships out each unit, management might look at the entire logistics process from receipt of raw material to receipt by the customer.

Information systems can help organizations achieve great efficiencies by automating parts of these processes or by helping organizations rethink and streamline these processes. Chapter 11 will treat this subject in greater detail, since it is fundamental to systems analysis and design.

Who makes sure that self-managed teams do not head off in the wrong direction? Who decides which person works on what team and for how long? How can managers judge the performance of someone who is constantly rotating from team to team? How do people know where their careers are headed when there is no clear hierarchical ladder to ascend? The Window on Management explores some of these questions as it examines the impact of "virtual offices" and anytime, anywhere work environments.

No one knows the answer to these questions, and it is not clear that all modern organizations will undergo this transformation: General Motors may have many self-managed knowledge workers in certain divisions, but it still has a manufacturing division structured as a "machine bureaucracy," to use Mintzberg's category. Not all types of organizations can be "flattened." No one knows if organizations designed along process lines survive longer than traditional function-based organizations.

In general, the shape of organizations historically changes with the business cycle and with the latest management fashions. When times are good and profits are high, firms hire large numbers of supervisory and nonproduction personnel. When times are tough, they let go of many of these same people (Mintzberg, 1979). In the late 1980s, times were tough: Real incomes did not expand, although profits were restored to 1980 levels by 1990. As a result, many firms, especially those in direct competition with Japanese manufacturing, shrank their middle-level management and supervisory positions. This was also a period of extensive investment in computer technology. It is not known if the shrinkage of some firms' middle management resulted from hard times or from computerization. For firms not in direct foreign competition, and for

MANAGING THE VIRTUAL OFFICE

"Work is something you do, not a place to go" at Chiat/Day Inc., an advertising agency with operations based in Los Angeles and New York. Chiat/Day is eliminating its offices and letting its employees work from any location they choose. IBM, the consulting firms Ernst & Young and Arthur Andersen, and other firms are starting to follow suit. Some of their employees are supposed to work in "virtual offices," any place like a car, plane, train, or home where they can get work done. Virtual offices are possible because of information technology like cellular telephones, fax machines, portable computers, and other mobile computing and communications devices (see Chapter 9).

Chiat/Day armed its employees with laptop computers and cellular car telephones and eliminated private offices and assigned desks. It redesigned its work spaces to create a feeling of creative unrest. There are workrooms dedicated to specific clients; 10 small project workrooms; a library; several large open common areas for meetings, screenings, or socializing; and audio-video and print production centers. Employees keep all of their personal items in assigned lockers. Chiat/Day employees can check in whenever they want or work part of the time at home. Chiat/Day believes that this architecture and structure support the organizational need to be nimble and fast in today's fast-changing business environment.

All seven of IBM's regional U.S. markets are trying to convert to nonterritorial offices. In November 1993 IBM converted seven offices in five midwestern cities into "productivity centers," sending 700 executives into the field right away. These productivity centers replace traditional office environments with small "team rooms" that mobile executives can use when they are around. Each room contains a

round conference table, plugs for networked computers, and telephones. Eight executives are assigned to a room on a rotating basis and are expected to use the rooms as "work pods" to solve specific problems. After the problems are solved, the executives go back to the customers. IBM expects to convert all of its 30 Midwest locations into productivity centers.

Ernst & Young, the accounting firm, began moving its Chicago-based accountants and consultants, including senior managers, from offices into a "hoteling" system in June 1992 as means of reducing office space 15 to 18 percent and thereby reducing costs. Office spaces must be reserved at least one day in advance so that everything necessary to do the work, such as personal belongings and files, can be set up beforehand. Ernst & Young has targeted for elimination 1 million of the 7 million square feet of office space it rents nationwide, a savings of $40 million per year.

These companies are not alone. According to Link Resources, a New York market research firm, approximately 7 million people already do at least some of their work on the road; by 2000 this number will swell to 25 million people.

Eliminating private offices can cut down on real estate rental costs and increase the amount of time employees spend with customers. It may help firms comply with the U.S. government's Clean Air Act, which requires companies with 200 or more employees in major metropolitan areas to reduce commuter automobile mileage 25 percent by 1996. Working on the go potentially gives employees more flexibility and control over their own time. The question is, Is it a better way of working? What is the impact of virtual offices on individual identity, worker satisfaction, and corporate community?

Many employees are fearful of the virtual office. To some it sounds too much like downsizing, part-time work, or a "virtual" work force of consul-

tants. They are frightened for their jobs. Others respond to the loss of daily social contact. According to Andrea Saveri, a director at the

> *To Think About:* What management, organization, and technology issues must be addressed when converting to a virtual office? Can all companies use virtual offices?

Institute for the Future in Menlo Park, California, electronically mediated work raises questions about "the extent to which humans and human contact are needed. It also threatens to fragment an organization. People begin to wonder what's holding them together."

A Bell Telephone study done years ago on employees working from their homes found that their productivity and morale plunged precipitously unless they kept in very close personal contact with the office. Some fear the breakdown of the separation between the refuge known as home and pressure-cooker environment known as work. High-level executives may resent relinquishing offices that they spent years trying to acquire. A few recent studies have been more positive. Surveying 300 Indiana-based executives, IBM found that nearly three quarters of its mobile employees had become more productive. The company believes that customer-related activities register the largest productivity gains. Ernst & Young registered 99 percent employee approval of its hoteling arrangement, with reports of increased interaction among employees from different areas and between employees and their bosses.

Companies with virtual offices are experimenting with alternative ways of promoting a team atmosphere. IBM ran staff seminars that described how to stay in touch with peers, managers, and clients and made sure all of its mobile employees had the right equipment for the job—cellular phones, text pagers, and IBM ThinkPad laptop computers. Chiat/Day runs "team reconstruction" seminars that bring together account team members with senior management and makes computer training part of every employee review. Chiat/Day realizes that not everyone makes an easy transition to a virtual office environment. People fearful of new technology, people with trouble drawing boundaries between work and relaxation, or managers who can't deal with employees who are more empowered to make their own decisions will be slow to adapt.

Sources: Montieth M. Illingworth, "Virtual Managers," *InformationWEEK*, June 13, 1994; Phil Patton, "The Virtual Office Becomes Reality," *The New York Times,* October 28, 1993; and Mitchell Pacelle, "To Trim Their Costs, Some Companies Cut Space for Employees," *The Wall Street Journal,* June 4, 1993.

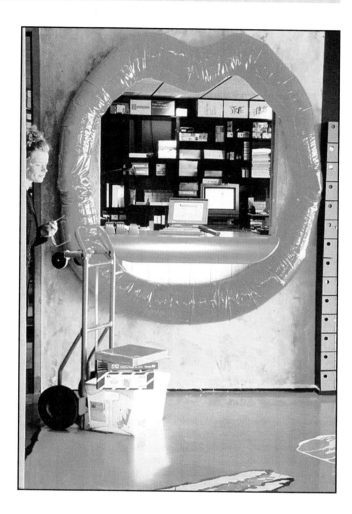

The giant lips frame an electronic dispensary where employees of Chiat/Day's virtual office sign up for work spaces and pick up their computers.

firms that experienced good business environments, employment rose throughout the 1980s even as information technology exploded. What this phenomenon suggests, then, is that the impact of information technology and systems is not limited to a simple outcome but instead will vary as a function of many behavioral factors.

Cultural Theories: IT and Fundamental Assumptions

cultural theory Behavioral theory stating that information technology must fit into an organization's culture or the technology won't be adopted.

Cultural theory (often discussed by anthropologists) argues that information technology must fit into the organization's culture or is unlikely to be adopted. The assumption at Ford, for instance, is that the company's primary activity is to make cars (rather than to operate a credit corporation), or at IBM it is the assumption that the primary purpose of the organization is to make large mainframe computers. These assumptions are rarely challenged by members, and if members do present challenges to these assumptions, the members are ostracized (Schein, 1985).

When the assumptions no longer fit reality, members of the culture may try to deny reality, ignore reality, or reinvent reality to fit the culture. Cultures change when the organizations that support them die off, or when radical fringe groups gain control and shift cultural assumptions. This feature is usually attended by massive senior management turnover because it is the senior managers who support the old culture (indeed, they were recruited and promoted for precisely this reason).

Information technology can either threaten or support organizational culture. The emergence of microcomputer technology, for instance, threatened both the manufacturers of large mainframe computers and their customers in large corporations as well—the managers of large information system departments in Fortune 1000 corporations. Resistance, denial, and efforts to redefine the reality followed in many of these organizations. On the other hand, information technology can be supportive of organizational cultures: The insurance industry welcomed computers to reduce costs in traditional claims processing.

Political Theories: Information Technology as a Political Resource

political theory Behavioral theory that describes information systems as the outcome of political competition between organizational subgroups for influence over the policies, procedures, and resources of the organization.

Organizations are divided into specialized subgroups (e.g., marketing, accounting, production). These groups have different values, and they compete for resources, producing competition and conflict. **Political theory** describes information systems as the outcome of political competition between organizational subgroups for influence over the policies, procedures, and resources of the organization (Laudon, 1974; Keen, 1981; Kling, 1980; Laudon, 1986).

Information systems inevitably become bound up in the politics of organizations because they influence access to a key resource—namely, information. Information systems can affect who does what to whom, when, where, and how in an organization. For instance, a major study of the efforts of the FBI to develop a national computerized criminal history system (a single national listing of the criminal histories, arrests, and convictions of over 36 million individuals in the United States) found that the state governments strongly resisted the FBI's efforts. The states felt that this information would give the federal government, and the FBI in particular, the ability to monitor how states use criminal histories and to control the interstate dissemination of criminal history information. This was a function that the states felt they could accomplish without federal interference. The states resisted the development of this national system quite successfully (Laudon, 1986).

ORGANIZATIONAL RESISTANCE TO CHANGE

Because information systems potentially change an organization's structure, culture, politics, and work, there is often considerable resistance to them when they are introduced. Microeconomic theories have no explanation for organizational resistance to change. In general, behavioral theories are superior for describing this phenomenon.

There are several ways to visualize organizational resistance. Leavitt (1965) used a diamond shape to illustrate the interrelated and mutually adjusting character of technology and organization (see Figure 3.14). Here, changes in technology are absorbed, deflected, and defeated by organizational task arrangements, structures, and people. In this model, the only way to bring about change is to change the technology, tasks, structure, and people simultaneously. Other authors have spoken about the need to "unfreeze" organizations before introducing an innovation, quickly implementing it, and "re-freezing" or institutionalizing the change (Kolb and Frohman, 1970; Alter and Ginzberg, 1978). (See Figure 3.15.)

Chapter 14 describes how organizational resistance causes many systems failures. Because of the difficulties of introducing new information systems, experienced systems observers approach social change through systems very cautiously. Briefly:

- Organizations do not innovate unless there is a substantial environmental change. Organizations adopt innovations only when they must do so.

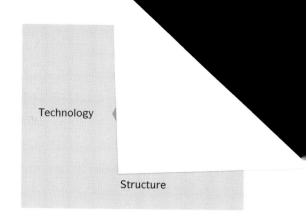

FIGURE 3.14
Organizational resistance and the mutually adjusting relationship between technology and the organization. Implementing information systems has consequences for task arrangements, structures, and people. According to this model, in order to implement change, all four components must be changed simultaneously. *Source:* Leavitt, 1965.

- Substantial forces resisting change are rooted in the organization's structures, values, and interest groups.

- Organizational innovation is difficult and complex to achieve. It involves more than simply purchasing technology. In order to reap the benefits of technology, innovations must be utilized and managed properly. This, in turn, requires changes in the values, norms, and interest-group alignments of the organization.

- The function of leaders is to take advantage of external circumstances to solidify their power. Leaders must use external opportunities to tilt the internal conflict in an organization in their favor and toward the successful development of their own agendas.

IMPLICATIONS FOR THE DESIGN AND UNDERSTANDING OF INFORMATION SYSTEMS

What is the importance of these theories of organizations? How can one take these factors into account when envisioning, designing, building, or managing information systems? The primary significance of this chapter is to show you that you should not take a narrow view of organizations and their relationship to information systems. Neither should you believe that "technology will do the job" for you—whatever that job is. For the information system to work properly, you will have to manage the process actively, adjust the technology to the situation, and accept responsibility for success as well as failure.

FIGURE 3.15
Lewin/Schein and Kolb/Frohman models of change.
Source: Keen 1981.

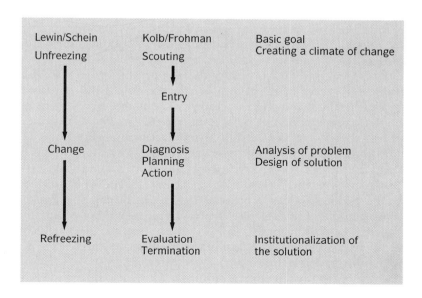

No formula takes these organizational factors into account. You can develop a checklist of factors to consider in your systems plans. In our experience, the central organizational factors in rough rank order of importance are these:

- The *environment* in which the organization must function
- The *structure* of the organization: hierarchy, specialization, standard operating procedures
- The *culture and politics* of the organization
- The *type* of organization
- The extent of support and understanding of *top management*
- The *level* of organization at which the system resides
- The principal *interest groups* affected by the system
- The *kinds of tasks and decisions* that the information system is designed to assist
- The *sentiments and attitudes* of workers in the organization who will be using the information system
- The *history of the organization:* past investments in information technology, existing skills, important programs, and human resources

Management Challenges

1. The difficulties of managing change. Bringing about change through the development of information technology and information systems is slowed considerably by the natural inertia of organizations. Of course, organizations do change, and powerful leaders are often required to bring about these changes. Nevertheless, the process, as leaders eventually discover, is more complicated and much slower than is typically anticipated.

2. Fitting technology to the organization (or vice versa). On the one hand, it is important to align information technology to the business plan, to senior management's strategic business plans, and to standard operating procedures in the business. IT is, after all, supposed to be the servant of the organization. On the other hand,

these business plans, senior managers, and SOPs may all be very outdated or incompatible with the envisioned technology. In such instances, managers will need to change the organization to fit the technology or to adjust both the organization and the technology to achieve an optimal "fit."

3. Understanding the limits of information technology. We often look to technology to solve what are fundamentally human and organizational problems. We often fail to realize that information technology is no better than the skills of the knowledge and information workers who use it. Ultimately, the impact of computers is decided by the intelligence of the user. Information technology is a mirror for both organizations and individuals.

Summary

1. Describe the salient characteristics of organizations. All modern organizations are hierarchical, specialized, and impartial. They use explicit standard operating procedures to maximize efficiency. All organizations have their own culture and politics arising from differences in interest groups. Organizations differ in goals, groups served, social roles, leadership styles, incentives, surrounding environments, and types of tasks performed. These differences create varying types of organizational structures. Mintzberg classified organizations into five structures: the simple entrepreneurial structure, machine bureaucracy, professional bureaucracy, divisionalized bureaucracy, and adhocracy.

2. Explain the changing role of information systems within the organization. Computerized information systems are supported in organizations by a "computer

package" consisting of a formal organizational unit or information systems department, information specialists, and computer technology. The roles of information systems and the computer package in the organization have become increasingly critical to both daily operations and strategic decision making.

3. Compare models for describing the origins of systems in organizations. Organizations adopt information systems for both external environmental reasons, such as to increase competition or to promote changes in government regulations, and for internal institutional reasons, such as to promote the values or interests of top management.

4. Identify the major theories about organizations that help us understand their relationship with information systems. Theories that describe the relationship between information systems and organizations can be classified as based on either economic or behavioral models of the firm. Theories based on economic models of the firm include the microeconomic model, the transaction cost model, and agency theory. Theories based on behavioral models of the firm include decision and control theory, sociological theory, post-industrial theory, cultural theories, and political theories.

5. **Discuss the impact of information systems on organizational structure, culture, political processes, and management.** The impact of information systems on organizations is not unidirectional. Information systems and the organizations in which they are used interact with and influence each other. The introduction of a new information system will affect the organizational structure, goals, work design, values, competition between interest groups, decision making, and day-to-day behavior. At the same time, information systems must be designed to serve the needs of important organizational groups and will be shaped by the structure, tasks, goals, culture, politics, and management of the organization. The power of information systems to transform organizations radically by flattening organizational hierarchies has not yet been demonstrated for all types of organizations.

6. **Describe the organizational implications for the design and implementation of systems.** Salient features of organizations that must be addressed by information systems include organizational levels, organizational structures, types of tasks and decisions, the nature of management support, and the sentiments and attitudes of workers who will be using the system. The organization's history and external environment must be considered as well.

Implementation of a new information system is often more difficult than anticipated because of organizational change requirements. Since information systems potentially change important organizational dimensions, including the structure, culture, power relationships, and work activities, there is often considerable resistance to new systems.

Key Terms

Organization (technical definition)	Entrepreneurial structure	Systems analysts	Agency theory
Organization (behavioral definition)	Machine bureaucracy	Information systems managers	Decision and control theory
	Professional bureaucracy		Sociological theory
Bureaucracy	Divisionalized bureaucracy	End users	Post-industrial theory
Standard operating procedures (SOPs)	Adhocracy	Environmental factors	Cultural theory
	Information systems department	Institutional factors	Political theory
Organizational culture	Programmers	Microeconomic model	
		Transaction cost theory	

Review Questions

1. What is an organization? How do organizations use information?
2. Compare the technical definition of organizations with the behavioral definition.
3. What features do all organizations have in common?
4. In what ways can organizations diverge?
5. Describe the five basic kinds of organizational structures.
6. Name the levels of analysis for organizational behavior.
7. Name the changing applications of organizational information systems that existed from the 1950s to the 1990s. How has the role of information systems in the organization changed over this time period?
8. Name the three elements in the computer package. How has the role of each element in the organization changed over time?
9. Describe the two factors that explain why organizations adopt information systems.
10. Describe each of the three economic theories that help explain how information systems affect organizations. What are their limitations?
11. Describe each of the behavioral theories that help explain how information systems affect organizations. What are their limitations?
12. How can information systems change organizational structure?
13. What is the relationship between information systems and organizational culture?
14. What is the relationship between information systems and organizational politics?
15. Why is there considerable organizational resistance to the introduction of information systems? Describe two models that explain this resistance.
16. What aspects of organizations addressed by various theories of organizations must be considered when designing an information system?

Discussion Questions

1. It has been said that when we design an information system, we are redesigning the organization. Discuss.
2. You are an information systems designer assigned to build a new accounts receivable system for one of your corporation's divisions. What organizational factors should you consider?
3. It has been said that implementation of a new information system is always more difficult than anticipated. Discuss.

Group Project

With a group of two or three students, examine an organization such as a local drugstore or the bookstore, cafeteria, or registrar's office in your college or university. Describe some of the features of this organization, such as its standard operating procedures, culture, structure, and interest groups. Identify an information system or series of information systems that might improve the performance of this organization, and describe the changes that the organization would have to make to use information technology successfully.

Case Study

CAN SEARS REINVENT ITSELF?

On January 25, 1993, Sears Roebuck, the nation's largest retailer, announced that it was dropping its famous "big book" catalogs, closing 113 of its stores, and eliminating 50,000 jobs. Four months earlier Sears had announced plans to dispose of its Dean Witter securities business, Discover credit card, and Coldwell Banker real estate operations and to sell up to 20 percent of the stock in its Allstate insurance subsidiary. These moves were designed to make Sears a much smaller, leaner concern that could recapture its leadership in retailing.

During the 1980s, Sears had tried to provide middle-class consumers with almost every type of banking, investment, and real estate service in addition to selling appliances, hardware, clothes, and other goods. In recent years, Sears' financial services businesses were the healthiest parts of the company, contributing up to as much as 70 percent of its profits. What is ironic is that Sears' board of directors chose to retain its underperforming operations while it got rid of the profitable parts, and that the un-

derperforming part represents the longtime core of the company.

The spotlight now falls on reinvigorating Sears' retail business. Will it sink or swim? Sears has steadily lost ground in retailing, moving from the number 1 position to number 3 behind discounters Wal-Mart Stores, Inc. and Kmart Corporation. Sears had been slow to remodel stores, trim costs, and keep pace with current trends in selling and merchandising. Sears could not keep up with the discounters and with specialty retailers, such as Toys "Я" Us, Home Depot, Inc., and Circuit City Stores, Inc., that focus on a wide selection of low-price merchandise in a single category. Nor could Sears compete with trend-setting department stores.

In recent years, Sears tried to catch up. It began initiatives such as the Store of the Future, brand-name merchandise, and "everyday low pricing." None of these changes revived the flagging retail business. In 1991, retail operations contributed to 38 percent of the corporate bottom line. The rest of the merchandising group's profits came

from the lucrative Sears credit card. Strategies that worked well for competitors fizzled at Sears. J. C. Penney successfully refocused its business to emphasize moderately priced apparel. Everyday low pricing, the pricing strategy used by Wal-Mart and other retailers, bombed at Sears because the firm's cost structure, one of the highest in the industry, did not allow for rock-bottom prices. Everyday low pricing has become "everyday fair pricing" supplemented by frequent sales.

Sears' catalog sales also stagnated. While the Sears "big book" catalog, founded in 1887, had the largest revenues of any mail order business, sales had not been profitable for 20 years; and the catalog had lost ground to specialty catalogs such as those of L. L. Bean and Lands' End.

Yet Sears is heavily computerized—it spends more on information technology and networking than other noncomputer firms in the United States except the Boeing Corporation. Why hasn't this translated into competitive advantage?

One big problem is Sears' high cost of operations. Nearly 30 percent of each dollar in sales is required to cover overhead (e.g., expenses for salaries, light bills, and advertising) compared to 15 percent for Wal-Mart and about 21 percent for Kmart. Sears now hopes to cut costs by streamlining distribution systems and by combining merchandising functions so that there are only two or three general merchandising managers instead of six. Sears also realizes that it can't compete with discounters such as Wal-Mart on price alone and hopes to build a competitive edge through superior service.

In early 1992, Sears embarked on the Store-Simplification Program, a $60 million automation project that will make Sears stores more efficient, attractive, and convenient by bringing all transactions closer to the sales floor and centralizing every store's general offices, cashiers, customer services, and credit functions. The program makes many changes in Sears' traditional retail sales efforts.

New point-of-sale (POS) terminals allow sales staff to issue new charge cards, accept charge-card payments, issue gift certificates, and report account information to card holders. These innovations will increase savings by reducing the size of Sears' charge-card group operations while making shopping more convenient for customers.

Some stores installed ATM machines to give customers cash advances against their Sears Discover credit cards. Telephone kiosks have been installed throughout the Sears retail network. Customers can use them to inquire about service, parts, and credit; check the status of their car in the tire and auto center; or call the manager.

Customer service desks will be eliminated. Sales personnel are authorized to handle refunds and returns, eliminating the need for two separate staffs. If a customer forgets his or her charge card, he or she can obtain immediate credit by telling the cashier his or her name and address and presenting identification.

Streamlining of patterns of work in back rooms and loading docks will also trim staff and create savings. The entire simplification effort is expected to eliminate $50 million in annual back office costs, 6900 jobs, and the customer service desks at all stores. Changes will also increase the ratio of selling space to nonselling space at Sears, so that more space can be used to generate revenues.

Sears has also been trying to reduce costs by moving its 6000 suppliers to an electronic ordering system similar to that described for Baxter Health Care (see Chapter 2). By linking its computerized ordering system directly to that of each supplier, Sears plans to eliminate paper throughout the order process and hopes to expedite the flow of goods into its stores.

To help turn Sears around and refocus on retailing, CEO Edward A. Brennan hired executive Arthur C. Martinez away from Saks Fifth Avenue in September 1992 (and named Martinez his successor as Sears chairman and chief executive officer two years later). Martinez ordered the company to combine its half-dozen disparate customer databases to find out who was really shopping at Sears. It turned out that Sears' biggest shoppers were not men looking for Craftsmen tool belts but women aged 25 to 50 in the market for everything from skirts to appliances.

Under Martinez, Sears stopped trying to sell everything and started focusing on six core types of merchandise—men's, women's, and children's clothing; home furnishings; home improvement; automotive services and supplies; appliances; and consumer electronics. The company is rearranging its merchandise displays to resemble those of more upscale department stores and is focusing on selling women's apparel, which is considered the most profitable segment of Sears' merchandising. Sears is stocking more upscale women's clothing and cosmetics, using advertising campaigns inviting women to see "the softer side of Sears."

Will all these efforts make customers happier with Sears? Will Sears be able to prosper? Since Martinez arrived, earnings have rebounded from their dismally low levels of 1992. The question is whether Sears can sustain this momentum. Its operating expenses are still high compared with industry leaders. Market research indicates that Sears continues to be the destination of choice for lawn mowers, wrenches, washing machines, and other "hard" goods—and its tools and appliance businesses are posting large sales gains. But Sears has not yet secured itself as a place for fashionable women's clothing. Many stylish clothing manufacturers have been unwilling to sell to Sears because they are not convinced of Sears' commitment to quality and fashion. Can Sears break out of its "retailing no-man's land," caught between fashionable apparel retailers and big-time discounters?

Martinez must also combat Sears' stodgy culture. Sears managers and executives have been indoctrinated in tales of Sears' past glories and entrenched in a massive bureaucracy in which change takes a long time. Company buyers remain too friendly with long-time suppliers, allowing them to charge high prices that can't be passed along to customers. Some observers believe that Sears' biggest challenge is to transform its culture.

Sources: Susan Chandler, "Sears' Turnaround Is for Real—For Now," *Business Week*, August 15, 1994; Stephanie Strom, "Sears Eliminating Its Catalogs and 50,000 Jobs," *The New York Times*, January 26, 1993, "Signs of Life at Sears, Roebuck," *The New York Times*, October 26, 1992, "For Sears' Stores, Do-or-Die Time," *The New York Times*, September 30, 1992, and "Further Prescriptions for the Convalescent Sears," *The New York Times*, October 1, 1992; Barnaby J. Feder, "Sears, Returning to Its Roots, Is Giving Up Allstate," *The New York Times*, November 11, 1994, and "Sears Will Return to Retailing Focus," *The New York Times*, September 30, 1992; Bruce Caldwell, "Sears Shops for Competitive Edge," *InformationWEEK*, January 13, 1992.

Case Study Questions

1. What management, organization, and technology factors were responsible for Sears' poor performance?

2. Do you believe that the Store-Simplification Program solves these problems? How successful do you think it will be? Why?

3. What management, organization, and technology factors were addressed by the Store-Simplification Program?

4. What theories about the relationship of information systems and organizations are illustrated by this case?

5. Put yourself in the place of a Sears merchandising executive. Plan five steps you would take in the next year to implement the new Sears strategy.

6. Visit a Sears store and observe sales patterns. What image or market message is being conveyed in the store? How is it implemented? How might it be improved? (You might make a comparison stop at Penney's or Wal-Mart or Kmart.)

References

Allison, Graham T. *Essence of Decision: Explaining the Cuban Missile Crisis.* Boston: Little, Brown (1971).

Alter, Steven, and Michael Ginzberg. "Managing Uncertainty in MIS Implementation." *Sloan Management Review* 20, no. 1 (Fall 1978).

Anthony, R. N. *Planning and Control Systems: A Framework for Analysis.* Cambridge, MA: Harvard University Press (1965).

Applegate, Lynda M., James Cash Jr., and D. Quin Mills. "Information Technology and Tomorrow's Manager." *Harvard Business Review* (November–December 1988).

Argyris, Chris. *Interpersonal Competence and Organizational Effectiveness.* Homewood, IL: Dorsey Press (1962).

Barnard, Chester. *The Functions of the Executive.* Cambridge, MA: Harvard University Press (1968).

Beer, Michael, Russell A. Eisenstat, and Bert Spector. "Why Change Programs Don't Produce Change." *Harvard Business Review* (November–December 1990).

Bell, Daniel. *The Coming of Post-Industrial Society.* New York: Basic Books (1973).

Bikson, T. K., and J. D. Eveland. "Integrating New Tools into Information Work." The Rand Corporation (1992). RAND/RP-106.

Blau, Peter, and W. Richard Scott. *Formal Organizations.* San Francisco: Chandler Press (1962).

Blauner, Robert. *Alienation and Freedom.* Chicago: University of Chicago Press (1967).

Brzezinski, Z. *The Technetronic Society.* New York: Viking Press (1970).

Charan, Ram. "Now Networks Reshape Organizations—For Results." *Harvard Business Review* (September–October 1991).

Clement, Andrew. "Computing at Work: Empowering Action by 'Low-Level' Users." *Communications of the ACM* 37, no. 1 (January 1994).

DiMaggio, Paul J., and Walter W. Powell. "The Iron Cage Revisited: Institutional Isomorphism and Collective Rationality in Organizational Fields." *American Sociological Review* 48 (1983).

Drucker, Peter. "The Coming of the New Organization." *Harvard Business Review* (January–February 1988).

El Sawy, Omar A. "Implementation by Cultural Infusion: An Approach for Managing the Introduction of Information Technologies." *MIS Quarterly* (June 1985).

Etzioni, Amitai. *A Comparative Analysis of Complex Organizations.* New York: Free Press (1975).

Fayol, Henri. *Administration Industrielle et Generale.* Paris: Dunods (1950) (first published in 1916).

Freeman, John, Glenn R. Carroll, and Michael T. Hannan. "The Liability of Newness: Age Dependence in Organizational Death Rates." *American Sociological Review* 48 (1983).

Gorry, G. A., and M. S. Morton. "Framework for Management Information Systems." *Sloan Management Review* 13, no. 1 (Fall 1971).

Gouldner, Alvin. *Patterns of Industrial Bureaucracy.* New York: Free Press (1954).

Gurbaxani, V., and S. Whang. "The Impact of Information Systems on Organizations and Markets." *Communications of the ACM* 34, no. 1 (January 1991).

Herzberg, Frederick. *Work and the Nature of Man.* New York: Crowell (1966).

Huber, George P. "The Nature and Design of Post-Industrial Organizations." *Management Science* 30, no. 8 (August 1984).

Huff, Sid L., and Malcolm C. Munro. "Information Technology Assessment and Adoption: A Field Study." *Management Information Systems Quarterly* (December 1985).

Jaques, Elliott. "In Praise of Hierarchy." *Harvard Business Review* (January–February 1990).

Jensen, M., and W. Meckling. "Theory of the Firm: Managerial Behavior, Agency Costs, and Ownership Structure." *Journal of Financial Economics* 3 (1976).

Keen, P. G. W. "Information Systems and Organizational Change." *Communications of the ACM* 24, no. 1 (January 1981).

King, J. L., V. Gurbaxani, K. L. Kraemer, F. W. MacFarlan, K. S. Raman, and C. S. Yap. "Institutional Factors in Information Technology Innovation." *Information Systems Research* 5, no. 2 (June 1994).

Kling, Rob. "Social Analyses of Computing: Theoretical Perspectives in Recent Empirical Research." *Computing Survey* 12, no. 1 (March 1980).

Kling, Rob, and William H. Dutton. "The Computer Package: Dynamic Complexity." In *Computers and Politics,* eds. James Danziger, William Dutton, Rob Kling, and Kenneth Kraemer. New York: Columbia University Press (1982).

Klotz, B. *Industry Productivity Projections: A Methodological Study.* U.S. Department of Labor, Bureau of Labor Statistics (1966).

Kolb, D. A., and A. L. Frohman. "An Organization Development Approach to Consulting." *Sloan Management Review* 12, no. 1 (Fall 1970).

Kraemer, Kenneth, John King, Debora Dunkle, and Joe Lane. *Managing Information Systems*. Los Angeles: Jossey-Bass (1989).

Laudon, Kenneth C. *Computers and Bureaucratic Reform*. New York: John Wiley (1974).

Laudon, Kenneth C. "Environmental and Institutional Models of Systems Development." *Communications of the ACM* 28, no. 7 (July 1985).

Laudon, Kenneth C. *The Dossier Society: Value Choices in the Design of National Information Systems*. New York: Columbia University Press (1986).

Laudon, Kenneth C. "A General Model of the Relationship Between Information Technology and Organizations." Center for Research on Information Systems, New York University. Working paper, National Science Foundation (1989).

Laudon, Kenneth C., and Kenneth L. Marr. "Productivity and the Enactment of a Macro Culture." International Conference on Information Systems, Vancouver (December 1994) and working paper, Center for Research on Information Systems, New York University (1994).

Laudon, Kenneth C., and Kenneth L. Marr. "Information Technology and Occupational Structure." Working paper, Center for Research on Information Systems, New York University (1995).

Lawrence, Paul, and Jay Lorsch. *Organization and Environment*. Cambridge, MA: Harvard University Press (1969).

Leavitt, Harold J. "Applying Organizational Change in Industry: Structural, Technological and Humanistic Approaches." In *Handbook of Organizations*, ed. James G. March. Chicago: Rand McNally (1965).

Leavitt, Harold J., and Thomas L. Whistler. "Management in the 1980s." *Harvard Business Review* (November–December 1958).

Leifer, Richard. "Matching Computer-Based Information Systems with Organizational Structures." *MIS Quarterly* 12, no. 1 (March 1988).

March, James G., and Herbert A. Simon. *Organizations*. New York: John Wiley (1958).

Martin, J. *The Telematic Society*. Englewood Cliffs, NJ: Prentice Hall (1981).

Masuda, Y. *The Information Society*. Bethesda, MD: World Future Society (1980).

Mayo, Elton. *The Social Problems of an Industrial Civilization*. Cambridge, MA: Harvard University Press (1945).

Michels, Robert. *Political Parties*. New York: Free Press (1962) (originally published in 1915).

Millman, Zeeva, and Jon Hartwick. "The Impact of Automated Office Systems on Middle Managers and Their Work." *MIS Quarterly* 11, no. 4 (December 1987).

Mintzberg, Henry. *The Nature of Managerial Work*. New York: Harper & Row (1973).

Mintzberg, Henry. *The Structuring of Organizations*. Englewood Cliffs, NJ: Prentice Hall (1979).

Orlikowski, Wanda J. "The Duality of Technology: Rethinking the Concept of Technology in Organizations." *Organization Science* 3, no. 3 (August 1992).

Orlikowski, Wanda J., and Daniel Robey. "Information Technology and the Structuring of Organizations." *Information Systems Research* 2, no. 2 (June 1991).

Parsons, Talcott. *Structure and Process in Modern Societies*. New York: Free Press (1960).

Perrow, Charles. *Organizational Analysis*. Belmont, CA: Wadsworth (1970).

Pindyck, Robert S., and Daniel L. Rubinfield. *Microeconomics*. New York: Macmillan (1992).

Porat, Marc. *The Information Economy: Definition and Measurement*. Washington, DC: U.S. Department of Commerce, Office of Telecommunications (May 1977).

Roethlisberger, F. J., and W. J. Dickson. *Management and the Worker*. Cambridge, MA: Harvard University Press (1947).

Schein, Edgar H. *Organizational Culture and Leadership*. San Francisco: Jossey-Bass (1985).

Scott Morton, Michael S., Ed. *The Corporation in the 1990s*. New York: Oxford University Press (1991).

Shore, Edwin B. "Reshaping the IS Organization." *MIS Quarterly* (December 1983).

Simon, Herbert A. "Applying Information Technology to Organization Design." *Public Administration Review* (May–June 1973).

Straub, Detmar, and James C. Wetherbe. "Information Technologies for the 1990s: An Organizational Impact Perspective." *Communications of the ACM* 32, no. 11 (November 1989).

Thompson, James. *Organizations in Action*. New York: McGraw-Hill (1967).

Toffler, Alvin. *Future Shock*. New York: Random House (1970).

Turner, Jon A. "Computer Mediated Work: The Interplay Between Technology and Structured Jobs." *Communications of the ACM* 27, no. 12 (December 1984).

Turner, Jon A., and Robert A. Karasek, Jr. "Software Ergonomics: Effects of Computer Application Design Parameters on Operator Task Performance and Health." *Ergonomics* 27, no. 6 (1984).

Tushman, Michael L., and Philip Anderson. "Technological Discontinuities and Organizational Environments." *Administrative Science Quarterly* 31 (September 1986).

Tushman, Michael L., William H. Newman, and Elaine Romanelli. "Convergence and Upheaval: Managing the Unsteady Pace of Organizational Evolution." *California Management Review* 29, no. 1 (1986).

Weber, Max. *The Theory of Social and Economic Organization*. Trans. Talcott Parsons. New York: Free Press (1947).

Williamson, Oliver E. *The Economic Institutions of Capitalism*. New York: Free Press (1985).

Woodward, Joan. *Industrial Organization: Theory and Practice*. Oxford: Oxford University Press (1965).

Chapter 4

Information, Management, and Decision Making

Keeping Belgium's Tractebel Growth on Track

To many, Tractebel SA may look like Belgium's biggest utility company, but to its chief executive officer, Philippe Bodson, it must be much more if its success is to continue. Tractebel's 1993 gross sales were 263.5 billion Belgian francs ($8.45 billion), nearly 85 percent of which came from gas and electricity. Bodson believes that the tightly regulated European energy market offers little opportunity for Tractebel growth. In addition, he points out that deregulation has changed the European energy market, allowing non-European rivals to join the competition within Europe. Bodson is targeting, instead, the emerging markets elsewhere in the world, and with over half a billion in U.S. dollars to invest, he believes he is finding opportunities for growth.

This new look at Tractebel is seen through the power lines and gas pipelines it is building in Argentina and Oman. Moreover, Bodson has already clinched other power contracts in Canada and Northern Ireland. His goal is within ten years to sell as much gas and electricity overseas as it currently sells within Belgium. He believes his company is still far from being truly global. It must compete against such giants as Duke Power (United States), PowerGen PLC (Great Britain), and Ruhrgas AG (Germany) for contracts in the rapidly expanding economies of Southeast Asia where the demand for power continues to grow. "This is a gigantic market. In Southeast Asia alone, we're talking about tens of billions of dollars," says Bodson. He is also seeking opportunities to participate in the privatization that is occurring in Eastern Europe.

Tractebel has also established a long-range strategy in communications as part of its program to identify other types of markets in which it can successfully compete. The company now owns the world's densest cable-TV network in Belgium, making Tractebel the largest private-sector cable-TV company in Europe. The company is also now active in cable TV in Switzerland, Luxembourg, and the United States. Bodson sees the liberalization of Europe's telecommunications market in 1998 as a major opportunity, although so far the company is finding it difficult to plan because of the lack of clarity on regulations that will be put in place at that time. Management has taken one step by filing an application to be allowed to offer mobile-phone services, thereby bringing Tractebel into competition with Belgacom, Belgium's state-owned telephone monopoly. To continue to grow and diversify, Bodson and his management have much to do to identify and execute new opportunities, and to expand their span of control throughout the globe.

Bodson faces a second challenge closer to home. He must tend to his existing businesses while continuing to diversify and globalize. For example, Tractebel is facing a potential challenge to its cable-TV position within Belgium, a multinational country that has recently transformed itself into a loose federation of three national states. Tractebel is viewed by the government and people of Flanders (the Dutch-speaking Flemish) to be a stronghold of the French elite within Belgium. As a result of this nationalist competitive feeling, the Flanders government has announced plans to build its own cable network to compete with Tractebel. ∎

Source: Martin du Bois, "Belgium's Tractebel Sets Atypical Goals," *The Wall Street Journal*, November 7, 1994.

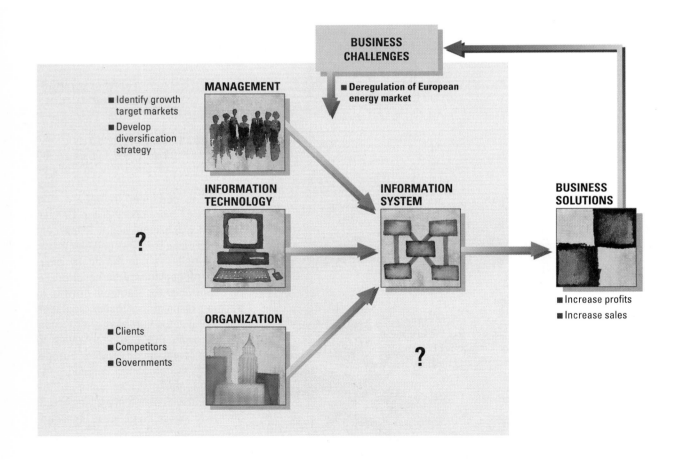

The challenges and decisions faced by Philippe Bodson and his managers are typical of those facing many senior executives. In companies both large and small, managers are asking such questions as: How can we enlarge market share? Where is our industry headed? Should we diversify? Where are we strong and where are we weak? What should our strategy be? How can we design a strategy?

There are no easy answers to these questions. In some instances, managers find solutions using infor-

mation systems; in other situations, computers may be of little or no use. The remainder of this text examines how information systems can be designed to support managers. In this chapter we scrutinize the role of a manager and try to identify areas where information systems can contribute to managerial effectiveness. We will also point out areas where information systems have limited value.

Decision making is a key task for managers at all levels in organizations large and small. Many exist-

ing systems improve or enhance management decision making, but challenges remain for systems designers seeking new forms of decision support. To identify opportunities for information systems and to understand their proper role, we first look at what managers actually do. Then we examine the types of decisions managers make and the process of decision making by individuals and organizations.

After completing this chapter you will be able to:

Learning Objectives

1. Contrast the classical and contemporary models of managerial activities and roles.

2. Describe the levels, types, and stages of decision making.

3. Identify models for describing individual and organizational decision making.

4. Explain how information systems can assist managers and improve managerial decision making.

4.1 WHAT MANAGERS DO

The responsibilities of managers might range from making decisions, to arranging birthday parties, to writing reports, to attending meetings. To determine how information systems can benefit managers, we must first examine what managers do and what information they need for decision making. We must also understand how decisions are made and what kinds of decisions can be supported by formal information systems.

In our description of what managers do, we should consider also the difference between "big business" and small entrepreneurial firms. In the U.S., only 20% of the labor force are employed by the 500 largest corporations. 80% of the labor force work in firms with fewer than 100 employees; 50% of the labor force work in firms with less than 50 employees. While managemenet in huge firms is no doubt different than management in small firms, there are many commonalities. In small firms, managers could be expected to perform many diverse functions which in larger firms could be dispersed over a number of specialists.

CLASSICAL DESCRIPTIONS OF MANAGEMENT

classical model of management
Traditional descriptions of management that focused on its formal functions of planning, organizing, coordinating, deciding, and controlling.

The **classical model of management,** which describes what managers do, was largely unquestioned for the more than 70 years since the 1920s. Henri Fayol and other early writers first described the five classical functions of managers as planning, organizing, coordinating, deciding, and controlling (see Table 4.1). This description of management activities dominated management thought for a long time and is still popular today.

But as a description of what managers actually do, these five terms are unsatisfactory. The terms do not address what managers do when they plan. How do they actually decide things? How do managers control the work of others? What is needed in a description is a more fine-grained understanding of how managers actually behave.

Table 4.1	**The Classical Model of Management Functions**

Planning

Organizing

Coordinating

Deciding

Controlling

BEHAVIORAL MODELS

Contemporary behavioral scientists have discovered from observation that managers do not behave as the classical model of management led us to believe. Kotter (1982), for example, describes the morning activities of the president of an investment management firm.

> 7:35 a.m.   Richardson arrives at work, unpacks his briefcase, gets some coffee, and begins making a list of activities for the day.
>
> 7:45 a.m.   Bradshaw (a subordinate) and Richardson converse about a number of topics and exchange pictures recently taken on summer vacations.
>
> 8:00 a.m.   They talk about a schedule of priorities for the day.
>
> 8:20 a.m.   Wilson (a subordinate) and Richardson talk about some personnel problems, cracking jokes in the process.
>
> 8:45 a.m.   Richardson's secretary arrives, and they discuss her new apartment and arrangements for a meeting later in the morning.
>
> 8:55 a.m.   Richardson goes to a morning meeting run by one of his subordinates. Thirty people are there, and Richardson reads during the meeting.
>
> 11:05 a.m.   Richardson and his subordinates return to the office and discuss a difficult problem. They try to define the problem and outline possible alternatives. He lets the discussion roam away from and back to the topic again and again. Finally, they agree on a next step.

behavioral models Descriptions of management based on behavioral scientists' observations of what managers actually do in their jobs.

Behavioral models state that the actual behavior of managers appears to be less systematic, more informal, less reflective, more reactive, and much more unorchestrated than students of information systems and decision making generally expect it to be. In our example, it is difficult to determine which activities constitute Richardson's planning, coordinating, and decision making.

A widely noted study of actual managerial behavior conducted by Mintzberg (1971) indicates that actual managerial behavior often contrasts with the classical description (see Table 4.2). First, modern researchers have found that the manager performs a great deal of work at an unrelenting pace and works at a high level of intensity. Some studies have found that managers engage in more than 600 different activities each day, with no break in their pace. Managers seem to have little free time. Even when they leave the office, general managers frequently take work home.

Table 4.2	**The Behavioral Model of Management Activities**

High-volume, high-speed work

Variety, fragmentation, brevity

Issue preference current, ad hoc, specific

Complex web of interactions, contacts

Strong preference for verbal media

Control of the agenda

Second, managerial activities are fragmented and brief. Managers simply lack the time to get deeply involved in a wide range of issues. They shift their attention rapidly from one issue to another, with very little pattern. When a problem occurs, all other matters must be dropped until the issue is solved. Mintzberg found that most activities of general managers lasted for less than nine minutes, and only 10 percent of the activities exceeded one hour in duration.

Third, managers prefer speculation, hearsay, gossip—in brief, they enjoy current, up-to-date, although uncertain, information. They pay less attention to historical, routine information. Managers want to work on issues that are current, specific, and ad hoc.

Fourth, as noted in the previous chapter, managers maintain a diverse and complex web of contacts that acts as an informal information system. Managers interact with clients, associates, peers, secretaries, outside government officials, and so forth.

Fifth, managers prefer verbal forms of communication to written forms because verbal media provide greater flexibility, require less effort, and bring a faster response. Communication is the work of the manager, and he or she uses whatever tools are available to be an effective communicator (Olson 1981).

Despite the flood of work, the press of deadlines, and the random order of crises, Mintzberg found that successful managers appear to be able to control their own affairs. To some extent, higher-level managers are at the mercy of their subordinates, who bring to their attention crises and activities that must be attended to immediately. Nevertheless, successful managers can control the activities that they choose to get involved in on a day-to-day basis. By developing their own long-term commitments, their own information channels, and their own networks, senior managers can control their personal agendas. Less successful managers tend to be overwhelmed by problems brought to them by subordinates.

MANAGERIAL ROLES: MINTZBERG

managerial roles Expectations of the activities that managers should perform in an organization.

interpersonal roles Mintzberg's classification for managerial roles where managers act as figureheads and leaders for the organization.

Managerial roles are expectations of the activities that managers should perform in an organization. Mintzberg classified managerial activities into ten roles that fall into three categories: interpersonal, informational, and decisional. Information systems, if built properly, can support these diverse managerial roles in a number of ways (see Table 4.3).

Interpersonal Roles. Managers act as figureheads for the organization when they represent their companies to the outside world and perform symbolic duties such as giving out employee awards. Managers act as leaders, attempting to motivate, counsel, and support subordinates. Lastly, managers act as a liaison between various

Table 4.3	Managerial Roles and Supporting Information Systems	
Role	**Behavior**	**Support Systems**
Interpersonal Roles		
Figurehead		$\rightarrow$ None exist
Leader	Interpersonal	$\rightarrow$ None exist
Liaison		$\rightarrow$ Electronic communication systems
Informational Roles		
Nerve center		$\rightarrow$ Management information systems
Disseminator	Information	$\rightarrow$ Mail, office systems
Spokesman	processing	$\rightarrow$ Office and professional systems Workstations
Decisional Roles		
Entrepreneur		$\rightarrow$ None exist
Disturbance handler	Decision	$\rightarrow$ None exist
Resource allocator	making	$\rightarrow$ DSS systems
Negotiator		$\rightarrow$ None exist

Source: Authors and Henry Mintzberg, "Managerial work: Analysis from Observation," *Management Science* 18 (October 1971).

informational roles Mintzberg's classification for managerial roles where managers act as the nerve centers of their organizations, receiving and disseminating critical information.

decisional roles Mintzberg's classification for managerial roles where managers initiate activities, handle disturbances, allocate resources, and negotiate conflicts.

levels of the organization; within each of these levels, they serve as a liaison among the members of the management team. Managers provide time, information, and favors, which they expect to be returned.

Informational roles. Managers act as the nerve centers of their organization, receiving the most concrete, up-to-date information and redistributing it to those who need to be aware of it. Managers are therefore disseminators and spokespersons for their organization.

Decisional roles. Managers make decisions. They act as entrepreneurs by initiating new kinds of activities; they handle disturbances arising in the organization; they allocate resources to staff members who need them; and they negotiate conflicts and mediate between conflicting groups in the organization.

Table 4.3 enables us to see where systems can help managers and where they cannot. The table shows that information systems do not as of yet contribute a great deal to many areas of management life. These areas will undoubtedly provide great opportunities for future systems and system designers.

In the area of interpersonal roles, information systems are extremely limited and currently can make only indirect contributions. The systems act largely as a communications aid with some of the newer office automation and communication-oriented applications. These systems contribute more to the field of informational roles: A manager's presentation of information is significantly improved with large-scale MIS systems, office systems, and professional workstations. In the area of decision making, DSS and microcomputer-based systems are starting to make important contributions (see Chapters 15 and 16).

The Window on Technology describes some of the ways in which information systems can help managers of small businesses and the considerations small businesses should address.

HOW MANAGERS GET THINGS DONE: KOTTER

Kotter (1982) uses the behavioral approach to modern management to describe how managers work. Building on the work of Mintzberg, Kotter argues that effective managers are involved in three critical activities. First, general managers spend significant time establishing personal agendas and goals, both short- and long-term. These personal agendas include both vague and specific topics and usually address a broad range of financial, product-oriented, and organizational issues.

Second—and perhaps most important—effective managers spend a great deal of time building an interpersonal network composed of people at virtually all levels of the organization, from warehouse staff to clerical support personnel to other managers and senior management. These networks, like their personal agendas, are generally consistent with the formal plans and networks of an organization, but they are different and apart. General managers build these networks using a variety of face-to-face, interactive tools, both formal and informal. Managers carefully nurture professional reputations and relationships with peers.

Third, Kotter found that managers use their networks to execute personal agendas. In his findings, general managers called on peers, corporate staff, subordinates three or four levels below them, and even competitors to help accomplish goals. There was no category of people that was never used.

WHAT MANAGERS DECIDE: WRAPP

Under the classical model of management, one might expect that managers make important decisions and that the more senior the manager, the more important and profound the decisions will be. Yet in a frequently cited article about general managers, H. Edward Wrapp (1984) found that good managers do not make sweeping policy decisions but instead give the organization a general sense of direction and become skilled in developing opportunities.

Table 4.4 **Some Myths About Top Managers**

Life is less complicated at the top of the organization.

The top managers also know everything, can command whatever resources are needed, and therefore can be decisive.

The top manager's job consists of making long-range plans.

The top manager's job is to meditate about the role of the company in society.

Source: H. Edward Wrapp, "Good Managers Don't Make Policy Decisions," *Harvard Business Review*, July–August 1984.

Wrapp found that good managers seldom make forthright statements of policy; often get personally involved in operating decisions; and rarely try to push through total solutions or programs for particular problems. Wrapp described a number of myths about modern managers and compared them with the reality that he came to know as a member of several corporate boards (see Table 4.4).

Wrapp was able to show that contrary to popular belief, successful managers spend much time and energy getting involved in operational decisions and problems in order to stay well informed. These managers focus time and energy on a small sub-set of organizational problems that they can directly affect successfully; they are sensitive to the power structure of the organization because any major proposal requires the support of several organizational units and actors; and they appear imprecise in setting overall organizational goals but nevertheless provide a sense of direction. In this way, managers maintain visibility but avoid being placed in a policy straitjacket.

In contrast to the classical description, in which senior managers are thought of as making grand, sweeping decisions, Wrapp found that the contemporary manager tackles organizational decisions with a purpose, and does not seek to implement comprehensive, systematic, logical, well-programmed plans. Systematic, comprehensive plans are generally unable to exploit changes in the environment, and they are just as likely to create opposition in the organization as they are to gain support. For this reason, the manager seeks to implement plans one part at a time, without drawing attention to an explicit, comprehensive design.

Figure 4.1 illustrates Wrapp's conception of a good manager. Especially critical here is the notion of general managers becoming involved in operating problems and

FIGURE 4.1
Wrapp's successful manager. According to Wrapp, successful general managers are highly involved in operating problems and decisions. Corporate strategy tends not to be systematic or comprehensive but instead is an outgrowth of day-to-day operating decisions.

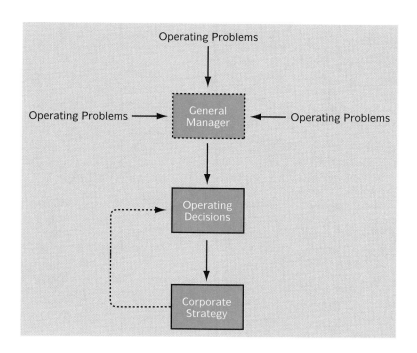

TECHNOLOGY FOR SMALL BUSINESS MANAGERS

How can managers of small businesses use information systems technology? After all, a small business will not have mainframe computers or large networks, and only very specialized businesses can afford expensive software. While more and more small businesses are starting to use information technology, small business managers often must approach the use of information technology differently than those in large firms.

While it is a given that no company should spend money on an information system unless the application has a place in that company's strategic plan, small business managers have other questions to ask: Can I accomplish the same goal more cheaply without added technology? Do I need to use the same approach as larger businesses do? Joe Little, president of $1.5 million (1994 sales) El Monte, California's Paranetics Technology Inc., often finds that technology is not the best approach. (Paranetics is best known for making parachutes.) He frequently is able to accomplish much more using the kind of personal involvement not possible in a large corporation. For example, when United States military food drops in Bosnia-Herzegovina resulted in a doubling of his company's orders for parachutes, he decided he needed to bolster productivity and quality while cutting costs. Such a small company—with only 25 employees—cannot spend $1000 a day for consultants for a quality program, or spend $20,000 on software and hardware to carry out such programs. Little compensates by using informal, inexpensive programs that seem directly applicable to what his company needs. For instance, he furnishes his workers with inexpensive pamphlets and video on how to promote quality.

On the other hand, many tasks and problems faced by small businesses are similar to those faced by big businesses, except on a smaller scale. In re-

cent years, software companies have been focusing more on developing and selling computer applications that are of appropriate size and cost for small businesses. Combine the "downsized" application with the greater functionality of low-cost computers, and small businesses will often find that carefully chosen applications will boost quality or service, generate more business, or reduce costs. Deborah Doelker of Doelker, Inc., New York, found this to be the case when she spent $2500 on a computer and several applications. Her company publishes an annual rating of African safari tours and had annual sales of $500,000 before buying the computer. Much of her work is collecting travel data and tour ratings, and she has found that she can collate it much more efficiently with a computer than doing it manually. Although Doelker says that buying the computer was "going from the Stone Age to 1993," she also says, "it was absolutely worth the money." The technology support allowed her to expand her sales to $800,000 in 1994. She was even actually able to cut costs because the accounting software she now uses meant that she no longer needed to pay a bookkeeper. High-quality, easy-to-use software available specifically for small businesses is available for many functions, including accounting and desktop publishing. Other specialty information systems technology is also available for the company that needs it. For example, if the small business actually has branches in several cities, lower cost video conferencing information technology can be cost efficient by reducing staff travel costs.

One problem that small business executives face that they often share with executives of large corporations is the lack of any computer knowledge or even a fear of computers. Many people rise to the top of medium or large businesses without computer experience or knowledge, and many small business entrepreneurs start their business in the same condition. Top executives of large

corporations can afford to buy the education they need to become computer literate. For example, CEO Institutes of New York, together with Computer

To Think About: What management, organization, and technology factors would cause small business managers to evaluate the use of information systems technology differently than those in large corporations? Do you see any circumstances under which small businesses might need to spend large amounts of their capital on information systems technology? If so, what are those circumstances?

Associates International Inc., offers a three-day seminar that teaches personal computer use for executives and also educates them in some of the key technologies their companies may be using. The seminar has attracted such executives as N. T. Widdrington, chairman of Laidlaw Inc. and the Toronto Blue Jays Baseball Club; Alexandra Penney, editor-in-chief of *Self* magazine; and Steve Duce, president of Mitsui Machinery Distribution Inc. However, the session costs $5500 plus transportation and hotel, a price not feasible for most small companies.

Small business management and employees will need to find less expensive ways to overcome their fears and to educate themselves on computer use. When Joe Little arrived at Paranetics, calculators outnumbered computers and some employees still used slide rules, signs of a lingering World War II mentality that permeated the parachute industry. Although Little could not spend much on computers, he felt it was essential to automate and to introduce new methods for running the business. He worked with his managers personally to overcome objections such as "managers don't touch a keyboard" and "that's how we always did it." Now all Paranetics managers use microcomputers for word processing and accounting. Little uses spreadsheets extensively for business planning, job costing, and forecasting and uses database management software for inventory and manufacturing resource planning. Paranetics uses computer-aided design tools to draw up new parachutes.

Sources: Mark Henricks, "Reality Checks," *Profit*, September–October 1994; Peter H.

Lewis, "Executives Unmask Computer Fears," *The New York Times*, October 5, 1994; Timothy L. O'Brien, "The Electronic Edge," *The Wall Street Journal*, October 15, 1994.

Corporate chief executives learn how to use laptop computers during a "technology retreat." Many senior managers lack computer knowledge or experience and require systems that are extremely easy to use.

decisions. Since corporate strategy derives from operating problems and decisions, it is closely tied to these problems and decisions as opposed to being an independent entity.

The classical and contemporary views of what managers do are not contradictory. Managers do, in fact, plan, organize, coordinate, decide, and control. But the contemporary view of how they manage is much more complex, more behavioral, more situational—in a word, more human—than the classical view originally suggested.

4.2 INTRODUCTION TO DECISION MAKING

The classical management theorists viewed decision making as the center of managerial activities. Although we now know that this is not exactly the case, decision making remains one of a manager's more challenging roles. Information systems have helped managers communicate and distribute information; however, they have provided only limited assistance for management decision making. Because decision making is an area that systems designers have sought most of all to affect (with mixed success), we now turn our attention to this issue. In this section we introduce the process; in the next two sections we examine models of individual and organizational decision making.

LEVELS OF DECISION MAKING

strategic decision making
Determining the long-term objectives, resources, and policies of an organization.

management control Monitoring how efficiently or effectively resources are utilized and how well operational units are performing.

knowledge-level decision making Evaluating new ideas for products, services, ways to communicate new knowledge, and ways to distribute information throughout the organization.

operational control Deciding how to carry out specific tasks specified by upper and middle management and establishing criteria for completion and resource allocation.

unstructured decisions Nonroutine decisions in which the decision maker must provide judgment, evaluation, and insights into the problem definition; there is no agreed-upon procedure for making such decisions.

structured decisions Decisions that are repetitive, routine, and have a definite procedure for handling them.

semistructured decisions Decisions where only part of the problem has a clear-cut answer provided by an accepted procedure.

Differences in decision making can be classified by organizational level. Anthony (1965) grouped decision making in an organization into three categories: strategic, management control, and operational control. We include an additional category for knowledge-level decision making because Anthony did not envision the prominent role now played by knowledge work in organizations. These categories of decisions correspond to the strategic, management, knowledge, and operational levels of the organization introduced in Chapter 1.

Strategic decision making determines the objectives, resources, and policies of the organization. A major problem at this level of decision making is predicting the future of the organization and its environment and matching the characteristics of the organization to the environment. This process generally involves a small group of high-level managers who deal with very complex, nonroutine problems.

Decision making for **management control** is principally concerned with how efficiently and effectively resources are utilized and how well operational units are performing. Management control requires close interaction with those who are carrying out the tasks of the organization; it takes place within the context of broad policies and objectives set out by strategic decision making; and, as the behavioralists have described, it requires an intimate knowledge of operational decision making and task completion.

Knowledge-level decision making deals with evaluating new ideas for products and services; ways to communicate new knowledge; and ways to distribute information throughout the organization.

Decision making for **operational control** determines how to carry out the specific tasks set forth by strategic and middle management decision makers. Determining which units in the organization will carry out the task, establishing criteria for completion and resource utilization, and evaluating outputs: All of these tasks require decisions about operational control.

TYPES OF DECISIONS: STRUCTURED VERSUS UNSTRUCTURED

Within each of these levels of decision making, Simon (1960) classified decisions as being either *programmed* or *nonprogrammed*. Other researchers refer to these types of decisions as *structured* and *unstructured,* as we do in this book. **Unstructured decisions** are those in which the decision maker must provide judgment, evaluation, and insights into the problem definition. These decisions are novel, important, and nonroutine, and there is no well-understood or agreed-upon procedure for making them (Gorry and Scott-Morton, 1971). **Structured decisions,** by contrast, are repetitive, routine, and involve a definite procedure for handling so that they do not have to be treated each time as if they were new. Some decisions are **semistructured decisions**; in such cases, only part of the problem has a clear-cut answer provided by an accepted procedure.

TYPES OF DECISIONS AND TYPES OF SYSTEMS

Combining these two views of decision making produces the grid shown in Figure 4.2. In general, operational control personnel face fairly well-structured problems. In contrast, strategic planners tackle highly unstructured problems. Many of the problems encountered by knowledge workers are fairly unstructured as well. Nevertheless, each level of the organization contains both structured and unstructured problems.

In the past, most of the success in modern information systems came in dealing with structured, operational and management control decisions. But now most of the exciting applications are occurring in the management, knowledge, and strategic planning areas, where problems are either semistructured or are totally unstructured. Examples include general DSS; microcomputer-based decision-making systems including spreadsheets and other packages; professional design workstations; and general planning and simulation systems (discussed in later chapters).

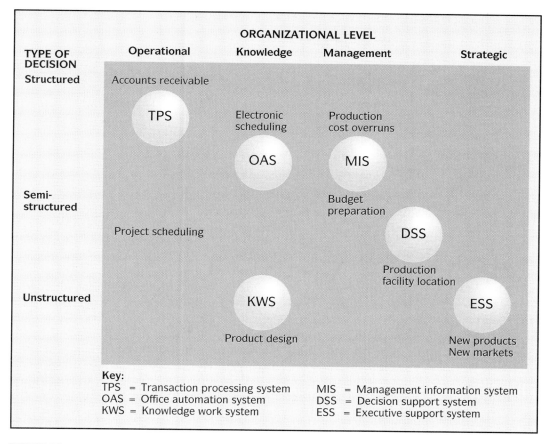

FIGURE 4.2
Different kinds of information systems at the various organization levels support different types of decisions.
Source: Gorry and Scott-Morton (1971).

STAGES OF DECISION MAKING

Making decisions is not a single activity that takes place all at once. The process consists of several different activities that take place at different times.

Take any important decision that you as a student make—for example, whether or not to attend college—and ask yourself precisely when you decided to go to college. Chances are that you made the decision over a long period of time; you were influenced by friends, counselors, and parents; and you used different information sources to find out about each alternative. Let us try to break down decision making into its component stages.

The decision maker has to perceive and understand problems. Once perceived, solutions must be designed; once solutions are designed, choices have to be made about a particular solution; finally, the solution has to be carried out and implemented. Simon (1960) described four different stages in decision making (see Table 4.5): intelligence, design, choice, and implementation.

Intelligence consists of *identifying* the problems occurring in the organization. Intelligence indicates why, where, and with what effects a situation occurs. This broad set of information-gathering activities is required to inform managers how well the organization is performing and to let them know where problems exist. Traditional MIS systems that deliver a wide variety of detailed information can help identify problems, especially if the systems report exceptions (with added ability to call up text and additional detailed information).

During **design,** the second stage of decision making, the individual designs possible solutions to the problems. This activity may require more intelligence so that

intelligence The first of Simon's four stages of decision making, when the individual collects information to identify problems occurring in the organization.

design Simon's second stage of decision making, when the individual conceives of possible alternative solutions to a problem.

Table 4.5	Stages in Decision Making, Information Requirement, and Supporting Information Systems	
Stage of Decision Making	**Information Requirement**	**Example System**
Intelligence	Exception reporting	MIS
Design	Simulation prototype	DSS, KWS
Choice	"What-if" simulation	DSS; large models
Implementation	Graphics, charts	Microcomputer and mainframe decision aids

Source: Authors and G. Anthony Gorry and Michael S. Scott-Morton, "A Framework for Management Information Systems," *Sloan Management Review* 13, no. 1 (Fall 1971).

the manager can decide if a particular solution is appropriate. The design stage may also entail more carefully specified and directed information activities. Smaller DSS systems are ideal in this stage of decision making because they operate on simple models, can be developed quickly, and can be operated with limited data.

choice Simon's third stage of decision making, when the individual selects among the various solution alternatives.

Choice, the third stage of decision making, consists of choosing among alternatives. Here a manager can use information tools that can calculate and keep track of the consequences, costs, and opportunities provided by each alternative designed in the second stage. The decision maker might require a larger DSS system to develop more extensive data on a variety of alternatives and to use complex analytic models needed to account for all of the consequences.

implementation Simon's final stage of decision making, when the individual puts the decision into effect and reports on the progress of the solution.

The last stage in decision making is **implementation**. Here managers can use a reporting system that delivers routine reports on the progress of a specific solution. The system will also report some of the difficulties that arise, will indicate resource constraints, and will suggest possible ameliorative actions. Support systems can range from full-blown MIS systems to much smaller systems as well as project-planning software operating on microcomputers.

Table 4.5 lists the stages in decision making, the general type of information required, and specific examples of information systems corresponding to each stage.

In general, the stages of decision making do not necessarily follow a linear path from intelligence, to design, choice, and implementation. Think again about your decision to attend a *specific* college. At any point in the decision-making process, you may have to loop back to a previous stage (see Figure 4.3). For instance, one can often come up with several designs but may not be certain about whether a specific design meets the requirements for the particular problem. This situation requires additional intelligence work. Alternatively, one can be in the process of implementing a decision, only to discover that it is not working. In such a case, one is forced to repeat the design or choice stage.

4.3 INDIVIDUAL MODELS OF DECISION MAKING

A number of models attempt to describe how individuals make decisions (see Table 4.6). The basic assumption behind all these models is that human beings are in some sense rational.

THE RATIONAL MODEL

rational model Model of human behavior based on the belief that people, organizations, and nations engage in basically consistent, value-maximizing calculations or adaptations within certain constraints.

The **rational model** of human behavior is based on the idea that people, organizations, and nations engage in basically consistent, value-maximizing calculations or adaptations within certain constraints. Since the time of Adam Smith, this assumption has been at the heart of consumer behavior theories and microeconomics, political philosophy (which hails the individual as a free-willed value maximizer), and social theory (which stresses the individual pursuit of prestige, money, and power).

FIGURE 4.3

FIGURE 4.3
The decision-making process. Decisions are often arrived at after a series of iterations and evaluations at each stage in the process. The decision maker often must loop back through one or more of the stages before completing the process.

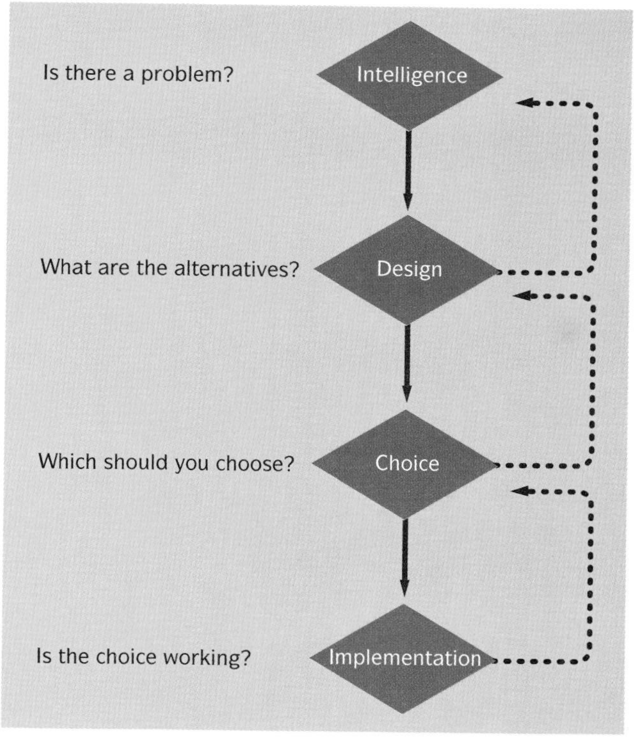

The rational model works as follows: An individual has goals or objectives and has a payoff, utility, or preference function that permits him or her to rank all possible alternative actions by their contribution to his or her goals. The actor is presented with and understands alternative courses of action. Each alternative has a set of consequences. The actor chooses the alternative (and consequences) that rank highest in terms of the payoff functions (i.e., that contribute most to the ultimate goal). In a rigorous model of rational action, the actor has comprehensive rationality (i.e., he or she can accurately rank all alternatives and consequences) and can perceive all alternatives and consequences.

There are three criticisms of the rational model. First, in a human time frame, the model is computationally impossible. In a "simple" chess game there are 10^{120}

Table 4.6 Models of Individual Decision Making

Name	Basic Concept	Inference Patterns
Rational model	Comprehensive rationality	Establish goals, examine all alternatives, and choose the best alternative.
Satisficing model	Bounded rationality	Establish goals, examine a few alternatives, and choose the first alternative that promotes the goals.
Muddling	Successive comparison	Examine alternatives to establish a mix of goals and consequences; choose policies that are marginally different from those of the past.
Psychological	Cognitive types	All decision makers choose goals, but they differ in terms of gathering and evaluating information. Systematic thinkers impose order on perceptions and evaluation; intuitive thinkers are more open to unexpected information and use multiple models and perspectives when evaluating information. Neither is more rational than the other.

moves, countermoves, and counter countermoves from start to finish, and it would take a machine 10^{95} years operating at a rate of 1 million instructions per second (MIPS) to decide the first move! Second, the model lacks realism in the sense that most individuals do not have singular goals and a consciously used payoff function, and they are not able to rank all alternatives and consequences. (To this it might be replied that realism is not required, only predictive accuracy.) Third, in real life the idea of a finite number of all alternatives and consequences makes no sense. In a maze constructed for a rat or in a game of tic-tac-toe, all alternatives and consequences can be meaningful and precise. In the real world of humans, specifying all of the alternatives and consequences is impossible.

Despite these criticisms, the rational model remains a powerful and attractive model of human decision making. It is rigorous, simple, and instructive.

BOUNDED RATIONALITY AND SATISFICING

satisficing Choosing the first available alternative in order to move closer toward the ultimate goal instead of searching for all alternatives and consequences.

bounded rationality Idea that people will avoid new uncertain alternatives and stick with tried-and-true rules and procedures.

In answer to the critics, March and Simon (1958) and Simon (1960) proposed a number of adjustments to the rigorous rational model. Rather than optimizing, which presumes comprehensive rationality, Simon argues that people **satisfice**—that is, choose the first available alternative that moves them toward their ultimate goal. Instead of searching for all of the alternatives and consequences (unlimited rationality), Simon proposes **bounded rationality**, that people limit the search process to sequentially ordered alternatives (alternatives not radically different from the current policy). Wherever possible, people avoid new, uncertain alternatives and rely instead on tried-and-true rules, standard operating procedures, and programs. Individuals have many goals—not a single consistent set—and therefore they try to divide their goals into separate programs, avoiding interdependencies wherever possible. In this way, rationality is bounded.

"MUDDLING THROUGH"

muddling through Method of decision making involving successive limited comparisons where the test of a good decision is whether people agree on it.

In an article on the "science of **muddling through**," Lindblom (1959) proposed the most radical departure from the rational model. He described this method of decision making as one of "successive limited comparisons." First, individuals and organizations have conflicting goals—they want both freedom and security, rapid economic growth and minimal pollution, faster transportation and minimal disruption due to highway construction, and so forth. People have to choose among policies that contain various mixes of conflicting goals. The values themselves cannot be discussed in the abstract; they become clear only when specific policies are considered. Everyone is against crime; there is little need to discuss this issue. But many object to permitting the police to search homes without a court order (as called for in the Fourth Amendment). Hence, values are chosen at the same time as policies, and there is no easy means-end analysis (if you believe in X, then choose policy X).

Because there is no easy means-end analysis, and because people cannot agree on values, the only test of a "good" choice is whether people agree on it. Policies cannot be judged by how much of X they provide, but rather by the agreement of the people making them. Labor and management can rarely agree on values, but they can agree on specific policies.

incremental decision making Choosing policies most like the previous policy.

Because of the limits on human rationality, Lindblom proposes **incremental decision making,** or choosing policies most like the previous policy. Nonincremental policies are apolitical (not likely to bring agreement among important groups) and are dangerous because nobody knows what they will lead to.

Finally, choices are not "made." Instead, decision making is a continuous process in which final decisions are always being modified to accommodate changing objectives, environments, value preferences, and policy alternatives provided by decision makers.

PSYCHOLOGICAL TYPES AND FRAMES OF REFERENCE

cognitive style Underlying personality disposition toward the treatment of information, selection of alternatives, and evaluation of consequences.

systematic decision makers Cognitive style that describes people who approach a problem by structuring it in terms of some formal method.

intuitive decision makers Cognitive style that describes people who approach a problem with multiple methods in an unstructured manner, using trial and error to find a solution.

Modern psychology has provided a number of qualifications to the rational model. Psychologists have rarely challenged the basic premise that human beings are value maximizers and, in that sense, that they are rational. Instead, psychologists find that humans differ *in how they maximize their values and in the frames of reference* they use to interpret information and make choices.

Cognitive style describes underlying personality dispositions toward the treatment of information, the selection of alternatives, and the evaluation of consequences. McKenney and Keen (1974) described two cognitive styles that have direct relevance to information systems: systematic versus intuitive types. **Systematic decision makers** approach a problem by structuring it in terms of some formal method. They evaluate and gather information in terms of their structured method. **Intuitive decision makers** approach a problem with multiple methods, using trial and error to find a solution, and tend not to structure information gathering or evaluation. Neither type is superior to the other, but some types of thinking are appropriate for certain tasks and roles in the organization.

The existence of different cognitive styles does not challenge the rational model of decision making. It simply says that there are different ways of being rational.

More recent psychological research poses strong challenges to the rational model by showing that humans have built-in biases that can distort decision making. Worse, people can be manipulated into choosing alternatives that they might otherwise reject simply by changing the *frame of reference*. (See the Window on Organizations).

Tversky and Kahneman (1981), summarizing a decade of work on the psychology of decision making, found that humans have a deep-seated tendency to avoid risks when seeking gains but to accept risks in order to avoid losses. In other words, people are more sensitive to negative outcomes than to positive ones. College students refuse to bet $10, for instance, on a coin flip unless they stand to win at least $30. Other biases are listed in Table 4.7.

Because losses loom larger than gains, the credit-card industry lobbied retailers aggressively to ensure that any price break given to cash customers would be presented publicly as a "cash discount" rather than a "credit-card surcharge." Consumers would be less willing to accept a surcharge than to forgo a discount.

Table 4.7   Psychosocial Biases in Decision Making

1. People are more sensitive to negative consequences than to positive ones; for example, students generally refuse to flip a coin for $10 unless they have a chance to win $30.

2. People have no sensible model for dealing with improbable events and either ignore them or overestimate their likelihood; for example, one-in-a-million lotteries are popular, and people have an exaggerated fear of shark attacks.

3. People are more willing to accept a negative outcome if it is presented as a cost rather than a loss; for example, a man will continue playing tennis at an expensive club, despite a painful tennis elbow, by accepting the pain as a cost of the game rather than quit and accept the loss of an annual membership fee.

4. People given the same information will prefer alternatives with certain gains rather than alternatives with certain losses; people will gamble to avoid certain losses. For example, students and professional health workers were given the choice between alternative programs to fight a new disease that was expected to kill 600 people. When described in terms of lives saved, a large majority preferred a program that was certain to save 200 people over a program that had a possibility—but no certainty—of saving all 600. On the other hand, when presented in terms of lives lost, a large majority rejected a program that was guaranteed to lose 400 lives and preferred to gamble, against the odds, on a program that might save everyone but probably would lose everyone.

Source: A. Tversky and D. Kahneman, "The Framing of Decisions and the Psychology of Choice," *Science* 211 (January 1981).

HOW DO JURIES DECIDE?

What is the difference between jury trials in England and the United States? In England, the trial starts once jury selection ends; in the U.S.A., the trial is already over. So goes an old lawyer's joke. Evidence is mounting that juries often hear evidence with a closed mind and reach verdicts using faulty reasoning.

Several studies have found that juries are susceptible to influence from the moment members are selected to the time of final deliberation. The research cites stories juries tell themselves to make sense of the mounds of disconnected evidence they confront. Many jurors decide on a version of events based on a preliminary story that they find convincing, often at the time of opening arguments. These stories color jurors' interpretations so much that they seize on whatever fits their verdict and dis-

count the rest. By the time such jurors enter the jury room for deliberation, they have already made up their minds.

A study conducted by Dr. Deanna Kuhn, a psychologist at the Columbia University Teachers College, attempted to simulate jury decision making by having volunteers representing a typical jury view a videotaped re-enactment of an actual murder trial and then explain how they reached their own verdicts. Close to one of third of the participants, those with the most flawed decision making, tended to be the most vehement about their certainty and argued for the most extreme verdicts as the jury deliberated. Instead of considering all alternatives, such jurors perceived their task as arguing for one version of events.

Since a trial boils down to two versions of a story—the prosecution's and the defense's—jury consultants explicitly identify the poor decision making

ers and then oppose or keep them, depending on their point of view. Both sides then compete to devise the most dramatically compelling story to appeal to this group.

> **To Think About:** What do these studies of juries reveal about the decision-making process?

Another study conducted by Dr. Nancy Pennington, a University of Colorado psychologist, found that people do not listen to all the evidence and then evaluate it at the end. Instead, they process it as they go along, creating a continuing story throughout the trial so that they can make sense of what they are hearing. Jurors have little or nothing that will enable them to tie together all the facts presented at a trial unless an attorney suggests an interpretation in an opening statement that could provide a story line for them to follow.

Dr. Pennington, along with Dr. Reid Hastie, another University of Colorado psychologist, studied people called for jury duty who were not assigned to a trial and who were asked to participate as jurors for a simulated murder trial. When Dr. Pennington interviewed jurors to find out how they reached their verdicts, 45 percent of the references they made were to events that had not been included in the courtroom testimony, including inferences about the perpetrator's and the victim's motives and psychological states, and assumptions based on jurors' personal experiences. The stories the jurors told themselves pieced together the evidence in ways that could lead to opposite verdicts.

Jurors' backgrounds played a crucial role in the assumptions they brought to their stories. Middle-class jurors were more likely to find the defendant guilty than were working-class jurors, the difference hinging mainly on how these jurors interpreted the fact that the perpetrator had a knife with

him during a struggle with the victim. Working-class jurors saw nothing incriminating about a man carrying a knife for self-protection.

Other studies of jurors by psychologists have found that many tend to focus on the ability of victims to avoid being injured. Furthermore, whites trust the honesty and fairness of the police far more than blacks, and people who favor the death penalty tend to be pro-prosecution in criminal cases.

Sources: Daniel Goleman, "Study Finds Jurors Often Hear Evidence with a Closed Mind," *The New York Times*, November 29, 1994, and Daniel Goleman, "Jurors Hear Evidence and Turn It into Stories," *The New York Times*, May 12, 1992.

4.4 ORGANIZATIONAL MODELS OF DECISION MAKING

For some purposes, it is useful to think of organizational decision making as similar to rational individual decision making. Organizations can be thought of as having singular goals, controlled by unitary rational decision makers who are completely informed, who choose among alternatives after weighing the consequences, and who act to maximize the goals of the organization. Thus, one can say, for instance, that General Motors "decided" to build a new type of automobile factory in order to make a profit on small cars.

But this simplified, shorthand way of talking about organizations should not conceal the fact that General Motors, and indeed any large organization, is composed of a number of specialized subgroups that are loosely coordinated, with each subgroup having a substantial life and capability of its own. What the organization ultimately does will be determined in large part by what the organizational subunits *can do.*

Organizations also are composed of a number of leaders who compete with each other for leadership. To a large extent, what the organization ultimately decides to do is the result of political competition among its leaders and staff.

nizational models of decision **ng** Models of decision making that take into account the structural and political characteristics of an organization.

Each of these perspectives reflects a different organizational model of decision making that is very different from the individual models previously described. (See Table 4.8; also see Allison, 1971; Laudon, 1974; and Laudon, 1986, on which our analysis draws.) **Organizational models of decision making** take into account the structural and political characteristics of an organization. Bureaucratic, political, and even "garbage can" models have been proposed to describe how decision making takes place in organizations. We shall now consider each of these models.

Table 4.8 Models of Organizational Decision Making

Name	Basic Concept	Inference Pattern
Rational actor	Comprehensive rationality	Organizations select goals, examine all alternatives and consequences, and then choose a policy that maximizes the goal or preference function.
Bureaucratic	Organizational output Standard operating procedures	Goals are determined by resource constraints and existing human and capital resources; SOPs are combined into programs, programs into repertoires; these determine what policies will be chosen. The primary purpose of the organization is to survive; uncertainty reduction is the principal goal. Policies are chosen that are incrementally different from the past.
Political	Political outcome	Organizational decisions result from political competition; key players are involved in a game of influence, bargaining, and power. Organizational outcomes are determined by the beliefs and goals of players, their skills in playing the game, the resources they bring to bear, and the limits on their attention and power.
Garbage can	Nonadaptive organizational programs	Most organizations are nonadaptive, temporary, and disappear over time. Organizational decisions result from interactions among streams of problems, potential actions, participants, and chance.

BUREAUCRATIC MODELS

bureaucratic models of decision making Models of decision making where decisions are shaped by the organization's standard operating procedures (SOPs).

The dominant idea of **bureaucratic models of decision making** is that whatever organizations do is the result of standard operating procedures honed over years of active use. The particular actions chosen by an organization are an output of one or several organizational subunits (e.g., marketing, production, finance, human resources). The problems facing any organization are too massive and too complex to be attended to by the organization as a whole. Problems are instead divided into their components and are parceled out to specialized groups. Competing with low-priced, high-quality Asian cars, for instance, is a complex problem. There are many aspects: production, labor relations, technology, marketing, finance, and even government regulation.

Each organizational subunit has a number of standard operating procedures (SOPs)—tried and proven techniques—that it invokes to solve a problem. Organizations rarely change these standard operating procedures, because they may have to change personnel and incur risks (who knows if the new techniques work better than the old ones?).

SOPs are woven into the programs and repertoires of each subunit. Taken together, these repertoires constitute the range of effective actions that leaders of organizations can take. These repertoires are what the organization can do in the short term. As a U.S. president discovered in a moment of national crisis, his actions were largely constrained not by his imagination but by what his pawns, bishops, and knights were trained to do (see the Window on Management).

The organization generally perceives problems only through its specialized subunits. These specialized subunits, in turn, are concerned only with parts of the problem. They consciously ignore information not directly relevant to their part of the problem.

Although senior management and leaders are hired to coordinate and lead the organization, they are effectively trapped by parochial subunits that feed information upward and that provide standard solutions. Senior management cannot decide to act in ways that the major subunits cannot support.

Some organizations do, of course, change; they learn new ways of behaving; and they can be led. But all of these changes require a long time. Look around and you will find many organizations doing pretty much what they did ten, twenty, or even thirty years ago. Consider the steelmakers, automakers, post office, universities, and hospitals. Have they changed radically in the last five or ten years? How about the last thirty years?

In general, organizations do not "choose" or "decide" in a rational sense; instead, they choose from among a very limited set of repertoires. The goals of organizations are multiple, not singular, and the most important goal is the preservation of the organization itself (e.g., the maintenance of budget, manpower, and territory). The reduction of uncertainty is another major goal. Policy tends to be incremental, only marginally different from the past, because radical policy departures involve too much uncertainty.

POLITICAL MODELS OF ORGANIZATIONAL CHOICE

Power in organizations is shared; even the lowest-level workers have some power. At the top, power is concentrated in the hands of a few. For many reasons, leaders differ in their opinions about what the organization should do. The differences matter, causing competition for leadership to ensue. Each individual in an organization, especially at the top, is a key player in the game of politics: Each is bargaining through a number of channels among players.

political models of decision making Models of decision making where decisions result from competition and bargaining among the organization's interest groups and key leaders.

In **political models of decision making,** what an organization does is a result of political bargains struck among key leaders and interest groups. Actions are not necessarily rational, except in a political sense, and the outcome is not what any individual necessarily wanted. Instead, policy-organizational action is a compromise, a mixture of conflicting tendencies. Organizations do not come up with "solutions"

BLOCKADE BY THE BOOK

In the evening of October 23, 1962, the Executive Committee of the President (EXCOM), a high-level working group of senior advisors to President John F. Kennedy, decided to impose a naval quarantine or blockade on Cuba in order to force the Soviet Union to remove its intermediate-range ballistic missiles from the island, located 90 miles south of Miami.

The naval blockade was chosen only after the U.S. Air Force reported that it could not conduct what the politicians in EXCOM called a "surgical air strike" to remove the missiles. Instead, the Air Force recommended a massive strategic air campaign against a number of ground, air, and naval Cuban targets. This was considered extreme by EXCOM, and the only other alternative seemed to be a blockade that would give Chairman Khrushchev plenty of time to think and several face-saving alternatives.

But EXCOM was worried that the U.S. Navy might blunder when implementing the blockade and cause an incident, which in turn could lead to World War III. Secretary of Defense Robert McNamara visited the Navy's chief of naval operations to make the point that the blockade was not intended to shoot Russians but to send a political message.

McNamara wanted to know the following: Which ship would make the first interception? Were Russian-speaking officers on board? How would submarines be dealt with? Would Russian ships be given the opportunity to turn back? What would the Navy do if Russian captains refused to answer questions about their cargo?

At that point, the chief of naval operations picked up the Manual of Naval Regulations, waved it at McNamara, and said, "It's all in there." McNamara responded, "I don't give a damn what John Paul Jones

> *To Think About:* *What does this story tell you about decision making at a time of national crisis? Is such decision making rational?*

would have done. I want to know what you are going to do tomorrow!"

The visit ended with the navy officer inviting the Secretary of Defense to go back to his office and let the Navy run the blockade.

Source: Graham T. Allison, *Essence of Decision—Explaining the Cuban Missile Crisis* (Boston: Little, Brown 1971).

that are "chosen" to solve some "problem." They come up with compromises that reflect the conflicts, the major stakeholders, the diverse interests, the unequal power, and the confusion that constitute politics.

Political models of organizations depict decision makers as having limited attention spans; participating in tens (sometimes hundreds) of games and issues; and being susceptible to misperception, extraneous influences, miscommunication, and pressures of impending deadlines. Players in the game focus almost entirely on the short-term problem: What decision must be made today? Long-term strategic thinking for the whole organization goes by the wayside as individual decision makers focus on their short-term interests and on the part of the problem they are interested in.

"GARBAGE CAN" MODEL

All of the preceding models of organizational choice take as their starting point the basic notion that organizations try to adapt, and for the most part do so successfully, to changing environmental conditions. Presumably, over the long run, organizations develop new programs and actions in order to meet their goals of profit, survival, and so on.

In Chapter 3 we pointed out that many organizations do not survive. Indeed, 30 percent of existing corporations that are 50 years old or more can be expected to disappear (Starbuck, 1983). These findings force us to recognize that organizations are not immortal and may even be temporary. When severely challenged by a changing environment, many organizations prove to be nonadaptive, incapable of learning, and unchanging.

"garbage can" model Model of decision making that states that organizations are not rational and that decisions are solutions that become attached to problems for accidental reasons.

A theory of decision making, called the **"garbage can" model**, states that organizations are not rational. Decision making is largely accidental and is the product of a stream of solutions, problems, and situations that are randomly associated. That is, solutions become attached to problems for accidental reasons: Organizations are filled with solutions looking for problems and decision makers looking for work.

If this model is correct, it should not be surprising that the wrong solutions are applied to the wrong problems in an organization, or that, over time, a large number of organizations make critical mistakes that lead to their demise. The Exxon Corporation's delayed response to the 1989 Alaskan oil spill is an example. Within an hour after the Exxon tanker *Valdez* ran aground in Alaska's Prince William Sound on March 29, 1989, workers were preparing emergency equipment; however, the aid was not dispatched. Instead of sending out emergency crews, the Alyeska Pipeline Service Company (which was responsible for initially responding to oil spill emergencies) sent the crews home. The first full emergency crew did not arrive at the spill site until at least 14 hours after the shipwreck. By the time the vessel was finally surrounded by floating oil containment booms, the oil had spread beyond effective control. Yet enough equipment and personnel had been available to respond effectively. Much of the 10 million gallons of oil fouling the Alaska shoreline in the worst tanker spill in American history could have been confined had Alyeska acted more decisively (Malcolm, 1989).

IMPLICATIONS FOR SYSTEMS DESIGN

The research on management decision making has a number of implications for information systems design and understanding. First, managers use formal information systems to plan, organize, and coordinate. However, they also use them for a variety of other less obvious (but vital) tasks such as interpersonal communication, setting and carrying out personal agendas, and establishing a network throughout the organization. This should remind information systems designers that there are multiple uses for their products and that the way systems are actually used may not, in fact, reflect the designers' original intention.

Another implication of contemporary investigations of managers is that formal information systems may have limited impact on managers. Formal systems may have an important role to play at the operational level but are less critical at the middle and senior management levels. General managers may briefly glance at the output of formal information systems, but they rarely study them in great detail. Ad hoc (less formal) information systems that can be built quickly, use more current and up-to-date information, and can be adjusted to the unique situations of a specific group of managers, are highly valued by the modern manager. Systems designers and builders should appreciate the importance of creating systems that can process information at the most general level; communicate with other sources of information, both inside and outside the organization; and provide an effective means of communication among managers and employees within the organization.

Research also shows that decision making is not a simple process, even in the rigorous rational model. There are limits to human computation, foresight, and analytical powers. Decision situations differ from one another in terms of the clarity of goals, the types of decision makers present, the amount of agreement among them, and the frames of reference brought to a decision-making situation. An important role of information systems is not to make the decision for humans but rather to support the decision-making process. How this is done will depend on the types of decisions, the decision makers, and the frames of reference.

The research on organizational decision making should alert students of information systems to the fact that decision making in a business is a group and organizational process. Systems must be built to support group and organizational decision making.

Systems must do more than merely promote decision making. They must also make individual managers better managers of existing routines, better players in the bureaucratic struggle for control of an organization's agenda, and better political

players. Finally, for those who resist the "garbage can" tendencies, systems should help bring a measure of power to those ·
solution to the right problem.

As a general rule, research on management decision ma
mation systems designers should design systems that have the

- They are flexible, with many options for handling dat
  tion, and accommodating changes in individual and c
  and growth.

- They are capable of supporting a variety of styles, skins, ..
  both individual and organizational processes of decision making.

- They are powerful in the sense of having multiple analytical and intuitive models for the evaluation of data and the ability to keep track of many alternatives and consequences.

- They reflect the bureaucratic and political requirements of systems, with features to accommodate diverse interests.

- They reflect an appreciation of the limits of organizational change in policy and in procedure and awareness of what information systems can and can't do.

Management Challenges

1. Unstructured nature of important decisions. Many important decisions, especially in the areas of strategic planning and knowledge, are not structured and require judgment and examination of many complex factors. Complete solutions cannot be provided by computerized information systems alone. System builders need to determine exactly what aspects, if any, of a solution can be computerized and exactly how systems can support the process of arriving at a decision.

2. Diversity of managerial roles. Up to now, information systems have supported only a few of the roles managers play in organizations. System builders need to determine whether new technologies can create information systems to help managers in their interpersonal and decisional roles that previously were not backed up by formal systems. In addition to helping managers plan, organize, and coordinate, it is vital that systems help managers get things done through interpersonal communication, by implementing personal agendas, and by establishing networks throughout the organization. Such systems require a different vision of information systems that are less formal, offer more communications capabilities, are adjustable to managers' unique situations, and utilize diverse sources of information inside and outside the firm.

3. Complexity of decision making. Individual decision making is not a simple rational process and is conditioned by decision makers' goals, psychological characteristics, and frames of reference. It is challenging to build systems that genuinely support decision making because they must provide multiple options for handling data and for evaluating information; they must support different personal styles, skills, and knowledge; and they should be easily modified as humans learn and clarify their values. Ideally, systems should not only be designed to support managers' predispositions but also to provide information supporting alternative points of view.

System builders must find new ways of building systems that support decision making in an organization as a group process, conditioned by bureaucratic struggles, political infighting, and the tendency to randomly attach solutions to problems.

Summary

1. Contrast the classical and contemporary models of managerial activities and roles. Early classical models of management stressed the functions of planning, organizing, coordinating, deciding, and controlling. Contemporary research has examined the actual behavior of managers to show how managers get things done.

Mintzberg (1971) found that managers' real activities are highly fragmented, variegated, and brief in duration, with managers moving rapidly and intensely from one issue to another. Other behavioral research has found that managers spend considerable time pursuing personal agendas and goals and that contemporary managers shy away from making grand, sweeping policy decisions.

2. Describe the levels, types, and stages of decision making. Decision making in an organization can be classified by organizational level: strategic, management control, knowledge, and operational control.

can be either structured, semistructured, or ~~u~~, with structured decisions clustering at the ~~al~~ level of the organization and unstructured ~~s~~ at the strategic planning level. The nature and ~~f~~ decision making are important factors in building ~~ormation~~ systems for managers.

Decision making itself is a complex activity at both the individual and the organizational level. Simon (1960) described four different stages in decision making: (1) intelligence, (2) design, (3) choice, and (4) implementation.

3. **Identify models for describing individual and organizational decision making.** Rational models of decision making assume that human beings can accurately choose alternatives and consequences based on the priority of their objectives and goals. The rigorous rational model of individual decision making has been modified by behavioral research that suggests that rationality is limited. People "satisfice," "muddle through" decisions incrementally, or select alternatives biased by their cognitive style and frame of reference.

Organizational models of decision making illustrate that real decision making in organizations takes place in arenas where many psychological, political, and bureaucratic forces are at work. Thus, organizational decision making may not necessarily be rational. The design of information systems must accommodate these realities, recognizing that decision making is never a simple process.

4. **Explain how information systems can assist managers and improve managerial decision making.** If information systems are built properly, they can support individual and organizational decision making. Up to now, information systems have been most helpful to managers for performing informational and decisional roles; the same systems have been of very limited value for managers' interpersonal roles. Information systems that are less formal and highly flexible will be more useful than large, formal systems at higher levels of the organization.

The design of information systems must accommodate these realities. Designers must recognize that decision making is never a simple process. Information systems can best support managers and decision making if such systems are flexible, with multiple analytical and intuitive models for evaluating data and the capability of supporting a variety of styles, skills, and knowledge.

Key Terms

Classical model of management	Knowledge-level decision making	Implementation	Intuitive decision makers
Behavioral models	Operational control	Rational model	Organizational models of decision making
Managerial roles	Unstructured decisions	Satisficing	Bureaucratic models of decision making
Interpersonal roles	Structured decisions	Bounded rationality	Political models of decision making
Informational roles	Semistructured decisions	Muddling through	"Garbage can" model
Decisional roles	Intelligence	Incremental decision making	
Strategic decision making	Design	Cognitive style	
Management control	Choice	Systematic decision makers	

Review Questions

1. What are the five functions of managers described in the classical model?
2. Behavioral research has identified six characteristics of the modern manager. How do these characteristics relate to the classical model?
3. What specific managerial roles can information systems support? Where are information systems particularly strong in supporting managers, and where are they weak?
4. How do managers get things done, and how can computer-based information systems (CBIS) help?
5. What did Wrapp (1984) discover about the way managers make decisions? How do these findings compare with those of the classical model?
6. What are the implications of classical and contemporary views of managers for information systems design?
7. Define structured and unstructured decisions. Give three examples of each.
8. What are the four kinds of CBIS that support decisions?
9. What are the four stages of decision making described by Simon (1960)? How can information systems support these stages?
10. Describe each of the four individual models of decision making. What is the name, basic concept, and dominant inference pattern of each? How would the design of information systems be affected by the model of decision making employed?
11. Describe each of the four organizational choice models. How would the design of systems be affected by the choice of model employed?

Discussion Questions

1. At your college or university, identify a major decision made recently by a department, an office, or a bureau. Try to apply each of the organizational models of decision making to the decision. How was information used by the various organizational participants? What are the implications for the design of information systems?

2. Identify and describe a decision that all of you have had to make (e.g., going to college, choosing a specific college, choosing a major). Use Simon's model of stages and show how an information system might have helped or hindered you in making the decision.

Group Project

Form a group with three to four of your classmates. Observe a manager for one hour. Classify the observed behavior in two ways, using the classical model and then the behavioral model. Compare the results and discuss the difficulties of coding the behavior. Present your findings to the class.

Case Study

FIDELITY MANAGES THE BUSINESS OF MANAGING OTHER PEOPLE'S MONEY

How does Fidelity Investment's management keep its company atop the highly competitive mutual fund industry? Fidelity's success is indisputable. Fidelity stock funds now manage 17.5 percent of all assets held by equity funds, a total of $280 billion in mid-1995. This percentage is growing, as nearly 25 percent of all new assets being invested in mutual funds in 1994 came to Fidelity. The firm is so large that its trading commissions amount to $300 million a year, making them the largest brokerage customer on Wall Street. On an average market day Fidelity trades about 1000 companies with a total market value of $1 billion. Many of its more than 110 funds are enormous by themselves, with Fidelity Magellan topping the list at more than $50 billion in assets alone. Confounding all the predictions that

they are too large to be good at what they do, Fidelity funds are also the most profitable of all the families of funds with a ten-year total return of 407.7 percent (Twentieth Century is second with 375.7 percent). Their five-, three-, and one-year gains also place them at or close to the top of all the families.

At the heart of Fidelity's strategy is management's philosophy of deep manager and analyst immersion into a stock market company, its strategy, plans, and operations. Fidelity managers are expected to select stocks by spotting significant changes in companies ahead of the crowd rather than by responding to the ups and downs of the stock market or the economy. Management puts this philosophy into practice in many ways. Because of its size, Fidelity managers find most corporate doors wide open to them. When Fidelity Magellan manager Jeffrey N. Vinik wanted to visit Motorola in late 1992, he was able to spend the day holding private meetings with seven top executives including Motorola's chief operating officer, George Fisher.

While both sides claim no inside information was revealed, Vinik was able to emerge with a clear enough understanding of Motorola's operations to conclude that Wall Street was not evaluating its potential properly, leaving the company's stock deeply undervalued. He quickly bought $250 million of Motorola shares, which then proceeded to triple over the next few months, reaping an enormous profit not only for the Magellan fund but for a number of other Fidelity funds as well.

Corporate executives do more than welcome Fidelity managers. They actually seek out opportunities to meet with Fidelity managers, with perhaps officers from 20 corporations visiting Fidelity (at their Boston headquarters) daily. In addition, Fidelity managers are in daily telephone contact with corporation managers. Many observers believe that this personal access is the most important single ingredient in Fidelity's formula for success. However, Fidelity information on potential and current investments is not limited to personal contacts.

Desktop workstations provide managers and analysts with virtually all available Wall Street research (resulting in enormous quantities of financial documents in Fidelity's offices). They also have modern, sophisticated market-monitoring systems. In addition, Fidelity has 50 investment analysts stationed in London, Tokyo, and Hong Kong to bring the fund managers closer to foreign markets. All in all, Fidelity fund managers certainly do not suffer from lack of information.

To add to this mountain of information, a second axiom of Fidelity's strategy is that its managers must share their information on companies with each other. They are required to write up and share summaries of their contacts with corporate managers, including even the telephone contacts. They are also required to share summaries of their trade ideas. All of this information, plus a list of Fidelity stock trades the previous day, are distributed daily to all managers. While this strategy allows managers to both sharpen their own ideas and help other managers, it also means everyone suffers from information overload. As Brian S. Posner, manager of the $7.4 billion Fidelity Equity-Income II Fund puts it, "The challenge is to stay organized." The challenging task of gathering, organizing and digesting all of this information is one that Fidelity management must make possible through their plans and decisions.

Fidelity believes in close cooperation among managers as another keystone of its philosophy. In addition to sharing information, one further way the company encourage cooperation is through its compensation policy. A manager's annual income can range from $100,000 up to $1 million, depending partially upon how one's fund has performed. Other elements in the compensation decision also stress cooperation. Managers are rated on the number of winning ideas they contribute to the company (that is, to other managers). They are also all compensated together according to how well other Fidelity funds perform as compared to

their competition, giving managers a major stake in the success of the other fund managers at Fidelity. Management encourages cooperation in yet another way—all equity fund managers and analysts are squeezed into small offices in one of two floors of a Boston bank building. They are placed so close to each other that according to Michael Gordon, manager of the $1.5 billion Blue Chip Growth Fund, "We learn here through osmosis."

One key strategy Fidelity managers follow is to make large, concentrated investments. For example, the Magellan fund had nearly 40 percent of its assets in technology stocks as of this writing. While this strategy has been successful over the years (witness the Motorola success), it presents Fidelity with a number of problems. First, a sudden drop in a concentrated area can result in enormous losses. The value of the Magellan fund fell $650 million in three days in late August 1994, when technology stocks plummeted. It simply happened too quickly for the fund to get out. Moreover, such a large quantity of stocks are not liquid—it is difficult to sell such large holdings quickly without driving down their prices. Similarly, accumulating large quantities of stock can drive the price of their purchases up. Fidelity traders also have to be very concerned with keeping all trades confidential. If it becomes known that they are taking or eliminating a position in a stock, that very knowledge will cause the stock to move sharply.

Finally, one element in Fidelity management's philosophy is their belief in hiring only top-notch young people and then training them intensely. They review about 700 applicants per year, hiring only four or five of them. The new trainees are assigned one industry to monitor, and each is placed under the tutelage of an experienced manager. Not all succeed, but those that do are usually put in charge of a sector fund such as electronics or utilities after about two years. Fidelity managers are

so well trained that they are highly sought after by competitors.

Many observers and experts have said that Fidelity cannot continue to be as successful as it has been. Their primary concern is that Fidelity is just too large, that it cannot react as quickly and as nimbly as do smaller funds that have less of an effect upon the market. Some critics believe that all stock market success is temporary, that all successful funds eventually fall back to the mean in terms of performance. To date and despite its size, this has not happened with Fidelity. What happens in the future will depend heavily upon the skills of the Fidelity managers and upon the decisions they make.

Source: Geoffrey Smith, "Inside Fidelity," *Business Week*, October 10, 1994.

Case Study Questions

1. What kinds of managerial roles, types of decisions and models of decision making are seen in this case study?

2. Fidelity management has already established and executed basic strategies that have made the company successful. What steps do senior managers of Fidelity need to take to be confident these strategies are continuing to be effective? To what extent do information systems support these strategies?

3. What kinds of decisions do Fidelity fund managers have to make? Again, suggest information systems that might help them to make these decisions. Can you suggest other systems that do not directly help them to make decisions but that will support them in their daily work?

4. In what other areas might Fidelity managers at all levels look to information systems to help them carry out their jobs?

References

Adams, Carl R., and Jae Hyon Song. "Integrating Decision Technologies: Implications for Management Curriculum." *MIS Quarterly* 13, no. 2 (June 1989).

Allison, Graham T. *Essence of Decision—Explaining the Cuban Missile Crisis*. Boston: Little, Brown (1971).

Anthony, R. N. "Planning and Control Systems: A Framework for Analysis." Harvard University Graduate School of Business Administration (1965).

Cohen, Michael, James March, and Johan Olsen. "A Garbage Can Model of Organizational Choice." *Administrative Science Quarterly* 17 (1972).

George, Joey. "Organizational Decision Support Systems." *Journal of Management Information Systems* 8, no. 3 (Winter 1991–1992).

Gorry, G. Anthony, and Michael S. Scott-Morton. "A Framework for Management Information Systems." *Sloan Management Review* 13, no. 1 (Fall 1971).

Grobowski, Ron, Chris McGoff, Doug Vogel, Ben Martz, and Jay Nunamaker. "Implementing Electronic Meeting Systems at IBM: Lessons Learned and Success Factors." *MIS Quarterly* 14, no. 4 (December 1990).

Huber, George P. "Cognitive Style as a Basis for MIS and DSS Designs: Much Ado About Nothing?" *Management Science* 29 (May 1983).

Isenberg, Daniel J. "How Senior Managers Think." *Harvard Business Review* (November–December 1984).

Ives, Blake, and Margrethe H. Olson. "Manager or Technician? The Nature of the Information Systems Manager's Job." *MIS Quarterly* (December 1981).

Jessup, Leonard M., Terry Connolly, and Jolene Galegher. "The Effects of Anonymity on GDSS Group Process with an Idea-Generating Task." *MIS Quarterly* 14, no. 3 (September 1990).

Kotter, John T. "What Effective General Managers Really Do." *Harvard Business Review* (November–December 1982).

Laudon, Kenneth C. *Computers and Bureaucratic Reform*. New York: John Wiley (1974).

Laudon, Kenneth C. *Dossier Society: Value Choices in the Design of National Information Systems*. New York: Columbia University Press (1986).

Lindblom, C. E. "The Science of Muddling Through." *Public Administration Review* 19 (1959).

McKenney, James L., and Peter G. W. Keen. "How Managers' Minds Work." *Harvard Business Review* (May–June 1974).

Malcolm, Andrew H. "How the Oil Spilled and Spread: Delay and Confusion Off Alaska." *The New York Times* (April 16, 1989).

March, James G., and Herbert A. Simon. *Organizations*. New York: John Wiley (1958).

Markus, M. L. "Power, Politics, and MIS Implementation." *Communications of the ACM* 26, no. 6 (June 1983).

Mintzberg, Henry. "Managerial Work: Analysis from Observation." *Management Science* 18 (October 1971).

Olson, Margrethe H. "The IS Manager's Job." *MIS Quarterly* (December 1981).

Simon, H. A. *The New Science of Management Decision*. New York: Harper & Row (1960).

Starbuck, William H. "Organizations as Action Generators." *American Sociological Review* 48 (1983).

Tversky, A., and D. Kahneman. "The Framing of Decisions and the Psychology of Choice." *Science* 211 (January 1981).

Wrapp, H. Edward. "Good Managers Don't Make Policy Decisions." *Harvard Business Review* (July–August 1984).

Ethical and Social Impact of Information Systems

What Price Should Workers Have to Pay for Technology?

In 1992 the order-processors employed at Pizza Pizza Ltd. began to notice that their ranks were slowly thinning, that there were fewer and fewer of them as time went by. Canada's Pizza Pizza Ltd. of Toronto, a large fast-food delivery franchising company, had employed a staff of 150 unionized order-processors, members of United Food and Commercial Workers (UFCW) Local 175-633. They worked at a Pizza Pizza office processing phone orders through terminals hooked up to Pizza Pizza's computer. Finally, in August 1992, the company informed the remaining order-processors that they would no longer have a job because Pizza Pizza simply did not have enough work for them. A union investigation quickly uncovered a different reason—that in fact the company had been slowly replacing the unionized order-processors with nonunion workers who were working out of their homes. The company supplied the new home workers with computer terminals that are linked by telephone to the corporate computer. These home workers were paid a lower wage than the unionized workers, and in addition the company saved on office expense. According to the union, the company expects to be saving $4 per hour per worker. UFCW members went out on strike to try to win those jobs back for their members who had been clandestinely replaced. In the end they were only partially successful. About 25 of the fired workers were rehired by Pizza Pizza, but only under the same conditions as the nonunion workers—they had to work at home and at the lower wage.

Once the strike was settled, the former office workers who were now working at home, discovered that their work isolated them. They had to use their own telephone lines to connect to the company's computer (the company paid for the cost of the calls), which meant that they were unable to receive outside calls. One such employee, Carol Van Helvoort, explained the dilemma succinctly: "If someone needs me immediately to discuss a problem, I can't be reached." The other issue, which the UFCW is trying to solve through talks with company officials, arises from the isolation from working at home: Do the workers have a right to use the Pizza Pizza terminals in their home for any purpose other than processing orders? The home workers are unable to use the terminal to contact anyone outside of Pizza Pizza because these terminals are dumb, only able to operate when connected to the Pizza Pizza computer.

Marc Bélanger, who runs SoliNet, Canada's nationwide labor union computer network, believes that workers should and do have such a right. "If you take people out of a social work setting, then you should have a cyberspace setting so they can interact," he argues. This social interaction aspect of many workers' jobs is sacrificed, he believes, if they are forced to work at home and given no method of interacting with other employees of the company. SoliNet itself provides computer conferencing capabilities to its members, who belong to the Canadian Union of Public Employees and 20 other unions. But the issue of isolation is one being faced by more and more workers as telecommuting becomes technologically more feasible and is adopted by more companies. ■

Source: Montieth M. Illingworth, "Workers on the Net, Unite!" *InformationWeek*, August 22, 1994.

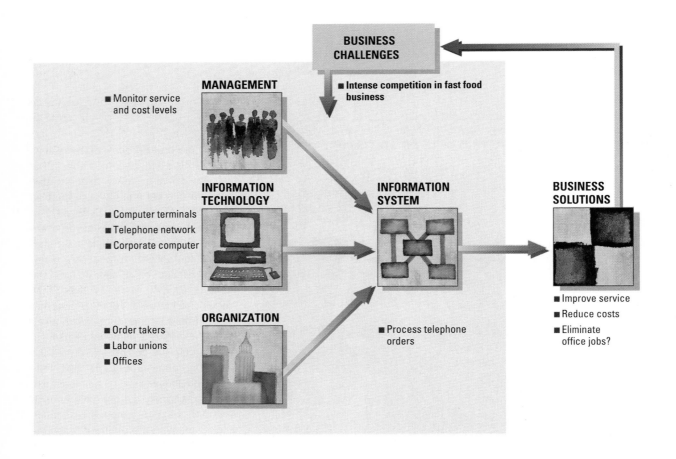

BUSINESS CHALLENGES

MANAGEMENT
- Monitor service and cost levels

■ Intense competition in fast food business

INFORMATION TECHNOLOGY
- Computer terminals
- Telephone network
- Corporate computer

INFORMATION SYSTEM

BUSINESS SOLUTIONS
- Improve service
- Reduce costs
- Eliminate office jobs?

ORGANIZATION
- Order takers
- Labor unions
- Offices

■ Process telephone orders

Pizza Pizza has a right to reduce its expenses and to use information systems technology to make that possible. However, the very telecommunications technology that allowed the company to cut expenses also cost a number of workers their jobs. In addition, those who were able to keep their jobs found themselves working at lower pay and in an environment of enforced isolation. Technology can be a double-edged sword. The choices faced by Pizza Pizza management is an example of an ethical dilemma resulting from the use of information systems, one that is shared by many organizations today.

Balancing the need for efficiency with responsibility toward employees is one of many ethical and social issues faced by organizations using information systems today. Others include establishing information rights, including the right to privacy; protecting intellectual property rights; establishing accountability for the consequences of information systems; setting standards to safeguard system quality that protects the safety of individuals and society; and preserving values and institutions considered essential to the quality of life in an information society. This chapter describes these issues and suggests guidelines for dealing with these questions.

After completing this chapter, you will be able to:

Learning Objectives

1. Understand the relation among ethical, social, and political issues raised by information systems.

2. Identify the main moral dimensions of an information society and apply them to specific situations.

3. Employ an ethical analysis to difficult situations.

4. Understand specific ethical principles for conduct.

5. Develop corporate policies for ethical conduct.

5.1   UNDERSTANDING ETHICAL AND SOCIAL ISSUES RELATED TO SYSTEMS

ethics Principles of right and wrong that can be used by individuals acting as free moral agents to make choices to guide their behavior.

In Chapter 1 we identified one of the key management challenges facing you as "the ethical and socially responsible use of information systems." Now it is time to put some flesh on that call.

Ethics refers to the principles of right and wrong that can be used by individuals acting as free moral agents to make choices to guide their behavior. Information technology and information systems pose unique problems for both individuals and societies because they create opportunities for social change. It is sometimes possible to create social change in a "socially responsible manner," one that takes into account the delicate balances among groups arrived at in the past. With new information technology it will also be possible—but not necessary—for you to decentralize power in an organization, invade the privacy of your employees while you improve service to customers, reach markets served by your global competitors and cause widespread unemployment, engage in new kinds of criminal activity as your company seeks to protect itself from information disclosures, and create new kinds of products which eliminate older products and the employment of people who make those products.

Information technology is certainly not the first technology to offer these potentials for radical social change. Steam engines, electricity, internal combustion engines, telephone, and radio—each in their day offered new opportunities for social change and for individual action. At the same time, these new technologies threatened existing distributions of power, money, rights, and obligations—in short, the things considered worth having. Likewise with information technology: The development of IT will produce losers and winners, will produce benefits for many and costs for others. In this situation, what is the ethical and socially responsible course of action?

Technology does not stand "outside" of society, acting upon it. Instead, technology—its manufacturers, benefactors, users—is a social phenomenon itself subject to all the constraints of other social actors. Among these constraints is the notion of social responsibility: corporations and individuals can and will be held accountable for their actions.

A MODEL FOR THINKING ABOUT ETHICAL, SOCIAL, AND POLITICAL ISSUES

Ethical, social, and political issues are of course tightly coupled together. The ethical dilemma you may face as a manager of information systems typically is reflected in social and political debate. One way to think about these relationships is given in Figure 5.1. Imagine society as a more or less calm pond on a summer day, a delicate ecosystem in partial equilibrium with individuals and with social and political institutions. Individuals know how to act in this pond because social institutions (family, education, organizations) have developed well-honed rules of behavior, and these are backed up by laws developed in the political sector that prescribe behavior and

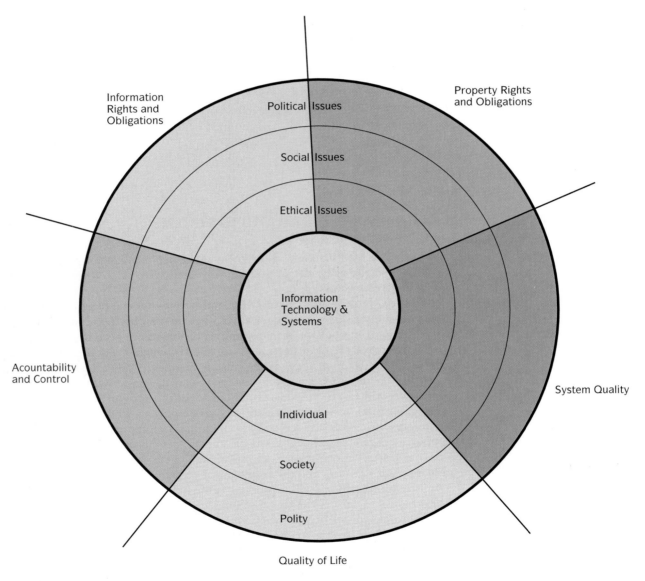

FIGURE 5.1
The relationship between ethical, social, and political issues in an information society. The introduction of new information technology has a ripple effect, raising new ethical, social, and political issues that must be dealt with on the individual, social, and political levels. These issues have five moral dimensions: information rights and obligations, property rights and obligations, system quality, quality of life, and accountability and control.

promise sanctions for violations. Now toss a rock into the center of the pond. But imagine instead of a rock that the disturbing force is a powerful shock of new information technology and systems hitting a society more or less at rest. What happens? Ripples, of course.

Suddenly individual actors are confronted with new situations often not covered by the old rules. Social institutions cannot respond overnight to these ripples—it may take years to develop etiquette, expectations, "socially responsible," "politically correct" attitudes, or approved rules. Political institutions also require time before developing new laws and often require the demonstration of real harm before they act. In the meantime, you may have to act. You may be forced to act in a legal "gray area."

We can use this model as a first approximation to the dynamics which connect ethical, social, and political issues. This model is also useful for identifying the main moral dimensions of the "information society" which cut across various levels of action—individual, social, and political.

FIVE MORAL DIMENSIONS OF THE INFORMATION AGE

A review of the literature on ethical, social and political issues surrounding systems identifies five moral dimensions of the information age that we introduce here and explore in greater detail in Section 5.3. The five moral dimensions are as follows:

information rights The rights that individuals and organizations have with respect to information which pertains to themselves.

- *Information rights and obligations:* What **information rights** do individuals and organizations possess with respect to information about themselves? What can they protect? What obligations do individuals and organizations have concerning this information?

- *Property rights:* How will traditional intellectual property rights be protected in a digital society where tracing and accounting for ownership is difficult, where ignoring such property rights is so easy?

- *Accountability and control:* Who can and will be held accountable and liable for the harm done to individual and collective information and property rights?

- *System quality:* What standards of data and system quality should we demand to protect individual rights and the safety of society?

- *Quality of life:* What values should be preserved in an information- and knowledge-based society? What institutions should we protect from violation? What cultural values and practices are supported by the new information technology?

Before going on to analyze these dimensions, we should briefly review the major technology and system trends which have heightened concern about the issues above.

KEY TECHNOLOGY TRENDS WHICH RAISE ETHICAL ISSUES

In what ways have information technology and systems created the ethical issues described above? In fact, these ethical issues long preceded information technology—they are the abiding concerns of free societies everywhere. Nevertheless, information technology has heightened ethical concerns, put stress on existing social arrangements, and made existing laws obsolete or severely crippled. There are four key technological trends responsible for these ethical stresses.

The doubling of computing power every 18 months since the early 1980s has made it possible for most organizations to utilize information systems for their core production processes. As a result, our dependence on systems and our vulnerability to system errors and poor data quality have increased. Occasional system failures heighten public concern over our growing dependence on some critical systems. Social rules and laws have not yet adjusted to this dependence. Standards for ensuring the accuracy and reliability of information systems (see Chapters 13 and 18) are not universally accepted or enforced.

The EMASS data storage system provides state of the art mass data storage and retrieval facilities for its clients.

Advances in data storage techniques and rapidly declining storage costs have been responsible for the multiplying databases on individuals—employees, customers, and potential customers—maintained by private and public organizations. These advances in data storage have made the routine violation of individual privacy both cheap and effective. For example, EMASS Storage Systems of Dallas advertises its new mass storage system as one capable of holding 55 terabytes of data in a 27-square-foot space, at a media cost of $2 a gigabyte, a data transfer rate of 15 megabytes per second, and a record access time of a few seconds (Computer Systems Policy Project, 1992; "EMASS®," 1993). This is a bit slow for on-line transaction processing, and slower than even a 600 megabyte CD-ROM with record access times of 150 milliseconds. Still, it is pretty impressive when you consider that the Social Security Master Beneficiary File requiring about one terabyte could be put on the EMASS system and take up only a fraction of the space! Already huge terabyte-size storage systems are cheap enough for regional and even local retailing firms to use in identifying customers.

Advances in data mining techniques for large databases are a third technological trend that heightens ethical concerns. The Window on Technology in Chapter 6 describes how parallel supercomputers are used by Hallmark Cards, Kmart, Wal-Mart Stores Inc., American Express, and others to very rapidly identify buying patterns of customers and suggest appropriate responses. One retailer examined customer "buying trips" as the unit of analysis. It discovered that if someone in the Midwest buys disposable diapers at 5 P.M., the most common thing purchased next is a six-pack of beer. The retailer decided, therefore, to put beer and snacks next to the diapers' rack ("Supercomputers Manage," 1992). These data mining techniques further shrink the penumbra of privacy created by older, less powerful technologies.

But the impact of widely distributed supercomputing also has equity implications for society. As with mainframes of the past, supercomputing capacity will largely be dominated by elite groups in society—large business and government organizations, and the dominant professional and business classes who dominate these institutions. In turn, these large groups may grow to become far more powerful vis-à-vis individuals and small groups than is now the case. What can be done to preserve equity, to encourage widely dispersed access to data and computing power?

Last, *advances in telecommunications infrastructure* like ISDN (Integrated Services Digital Network) and proposed national telecommunications networks like the National Research Education Network (NREN)—see the Window on Technology in Section 5.3—promise to reduce greatly the cost of moving large data sets, and open the possibility of mining large data sets remotely using smaller desktop machines. More and more regulators are moving to allow the local Bell operating companies to distribute a wide range of data services (e.g., news, sports, movies, and data along with voice, and even to own the contents of what they distribute) over the strong opposition of the Newspaper Association and the Cable Television Industry Association.

By the year 2000 it is conceivable that many homes and business offices will have communication lines with up to 100 megabits per second capacity. This capability will radically reduce the cost of mining huge terabyte-size databases, permitting the invasion of privacy on a scale and precision unimaginable to us now. Even the Census Bureau would lose its shelter: With commonly available census data on blocks, along with other data, we could easily pick out information about individuals with great regularity.

The development of national digital superhighway communication networks widely available to individuals and businesses poses many ethical and social concerns. Who will account for the flow of information over these networks? Will you be able to trace information collected about you? What will these networks do to the traditional relationships between family, work, and leisure? How will traditional job designs be altered when millions of "employees" become subcontractors using mobile offices that they themselves must pay for?

In the next section we will consider some ethical principles and analytical techniques for dealing with these kinds of ethical and social concerns.

5.2 ETHICS IN AN INFORMATION SOCIETY

Ethics is a concern of humans who have freedom of choice. Ethics is about individual choice: When faced with alternative courses of action, what is the correct moral choice? When freedom of choice is restricted or impaired for whatever reason—reasoning ability, situational factors, or forced choice—then ethical analysis is less appropriate. What are the main features of "ethical choice"?

BASIC CONCEPTS: RESPONSIBILITY, ACCOUNTABILITY, AND LIABILITY

responsibility Accepting the potential costs, duties, and obligations for the decisions one makes.

accountability The mechanisms for assessing responsibility for decisions made and actions taken.

liability The existence of laws that permit individuals to recover the damages done to them by other actors, systems, or organizations.

due process A process in which laws are well known and understood and there is an ability to appeal to higher authorities to ensure that laws are applied correctly.

Ethical choices are decisions made by individuals who are responsible for the consequences of their actions. Responsibility is a feature of individuals and is a key element of ethical action. **Responsibility** means that you accept the potential costs, duties, and obligations for the decisions you make. **Accountability** is a feature of systems and social institutions: It means that mechanisms are in place to determine who took responsible action, who is responsible. Systems and institutions where it is impossible to find out who took what action are inherently incapable of ethical analysis or ethical action. Liability extends the concept of responsibility further to the area of laws. **Liability** is a feature of political systems in which a body of law is in place which permits individuals to recover the damages done to them by other actors, systems, or organizations. **Due process** is a related feature of law-governed societies: It means a process in which laws are known and understood and there is an ability to appeal to higher authorities to ensure that the laws were applied correctly.

These basic concepts form the underpinning of an ethical analysis of information systems and those who manage them. First, as we discussed in Chapter 3 (Information Systems and Organizations), information technologies are filtered through social institutions, organizations, and individuals. Systems do not have "impacts" all by themselves. Whatever information system impacts exist are a product of institutional, organizational, and individual actions and behaviors. Second, responsibility for the consequences of technology fall clearly on the institutions, organizations, and individual managers who choose to use the technology. Using information technology in a "socially responsible" manner means that you can and will be held accountable for the consequences of your actions. Third, in an ethical political society, individuals and others can recover damages done them through a set of laws characterized by due process.

ETHICAL ANALYSIS

When confronted with a situation that seems to present ethical issues, how should you analyze and reason about the situation? Here's a five-step process that should help:

- *Identify and describe clearly the facts.* Find out who did what to whom, and where, when, and how. You will be surprised in many instances how wrong the initially reported facts typically are, and often you will find that simply getting the facts straight helps define the solution. It also helps to get the opposing parties involved in an ethical dilemma to agree on the facts.

- *Define the conflict or dilemma and identify the higher order values involved.* Ethical, social and political issues always reference higher values. The parties to a dispute all claim to be pursuing higher values (e.g., freedom, privacy, protection of property, and the free enterprise system).

  Typically, an ethical issue involves a dilemma: two diametrically opposed courses of action that support worthwhile values. In the Pizza Pizza case, you have two competing and opposing values: the right of a company to reduce its operating costs, and the rights of individuals to be employed at a living wage and to work under humane conditions.

- *Identify the stakeholders.* Every ethical, social, and political issue has stakeholders: players in the game who have an interest in the outcome, who have invested in the situation, and who usually have vocal opinions. Find out who these groups are and what they want. This will be useful later when designing a solution.

- *Identify the options that you can reasonably take.* You may find that none of the options satisfy all the interests involved, but that some options do a better job than others. Sometimes arriving at a "good" or ethical solution may not always be a "balancing" of consequences to stakeholders.

- *Identify the potential consequences of your options.* Some options may be ethically correct but disastrous from other points of view. Other options may work in this one instance, but not be generalizable to other similar instances. Always ask yourself, "What if I choose this option consistently over time?"

Once your analysis is completed, what ethical principles or rules should you use to make a decision? What higher-order values should inform your judgment?

CANDIDATE ETHICAL PRINCIPLES

While you are the only one who can decide which among many ethical principles you will follow, and how you will prioritize them, it is helpful to consider some ethical principles with deep roots in many cultures that have survived throughout recorded history.

1. Do unto others as you would have them do unto you (the Golden Rule). Putting yourself into the situation of others and thinking of yourself as the object of the decision, can help you think about "fairness" in decision making.

2. If an action is not right for everyone to take, then it is not right for anyone (**Immanuel Kant's Categorical Imperative**). Ask yourself, "If everyone did this, could the organization, or society, survive?"

3. If an action cannot be taken repeatedly, then it is not right to be taken at any time (**Descartes' rule of change**). This is the slippery-slope rule: An action may bring about a small change now that is acceptable, but if repeated would bring unac-

Immanuel Kant's Categorical Imperative A principle that states that if an action is not right for everyone to take, it is not right for anyone.

Descartes' rule of change A principle that states that if an action cannot be taken repeatedly, then it is not right to be taken at any time.

CHAPTER 5   Ethical and Social Impact of Information Systems

ceptable changes in the long run. In the vernacular, it might be stated as "once started down a slippery path you may not be able to stop."

4. Take the action that achieves the higher or greater value (the **Utilitarian Principle**). This rule assumes you can prioritize values in a rank order, and understand the consequences of various courses of action.

5. Take the action that produces the least harm or the least potential cost (**Risk Aversion Principle**). Some actions have extremely high failure costs of very low probability (e.g., building a nuclear generating facility in an urban area), or extremely high failure costs of moderate probability (speeding and automobile accidents). Avoid these high failure cost actions, with greater attention obviously to high failure cost potential of moderate to high probability.

6. Assume that virtually all tangible and intangible objects are owned by someone unless there is a specific declaration otherwise. (This is the **ethical "no free lunch" rule**.) If something created by someone else is useful to you, it has value and you should assume the creator wants compensation for this work.

None of these ethical rules can survive the detailed analytical mind of a contemporary philosopher or critical pundit. They have too many logical and substantive exceptions to be absolute guides to action. Nevertheless, actions that do not easily pass these rules deserve some very close attention and a great deal of caution if only because the appearance of unethical behavior may do as much harm to you and your company as actual unethical behavior.

PROFESSIONAL CODES OF CONDUCT

When groups of people claim to be professionals, they take on special rights and obligations. They do not cease to be moral agents—all of their actions must be justified by moral reasoning as outlined above. As professionals, they enter into special, even more constraining relationships with employers, customers, and society given their claims to knowledge, wisdom, and respect. Professional codes of conduct are promulgated by associations of professionals like the American Medical Association (AMA), the American Bar Association (ABA), and the American Society of Mechanical Engineers (ASME). These professional groups take responsibility for the partial regulation of their professions by determining entrance qualifications and competence. Codes of ethics are promises by the profession to regulate themselves in the general interest of society. In return, professionals seek to raise both the pay and the respect given their profession.

U.S. professional computer societies such as the Data Processing Management Association (DPMA), the ICP (Institute for Certification of Computer Professionals, the ITAA (Information Technology Association of America), and the Association of Computing Machinery (ACM) have drafted codes of ethics (Oz, 1992). Table 5.1 describes the code of professional conduct with moral imperatives of the ACM, the oldest of these societies.

These general moral imperatives are more fully detailed in a related and longer set of professional responsibilities and organizational imperatives. These extensions state, for instance, that ACM professions should consider the health, privacy, and general welfare of the public in the performance of their work and that professionals should express their professional opinion to their employer regarding any adverse consequences to the public (See Oz, 1994).

SOME REAL-WORLD ETHICAL DILEMMAS

The recent ethical problems described below illustrate a wide range of issues. Some of these issues are obvious ethical dilemmas. Others represent some type of breach of ethics. In either instance, there are rarely any easy solutions.

Recognition of professional status by the public depends not only on skill and dedication but also on adherence to a recognized code of professional conduct.

General Moral Imperatives

Contribute to society and human well-being

Avoid harm to others

Be honest and trustworthy

Honor property rights including copyrights and patents

Give proper credit for intellectual property

Access computing resources only when authorized

Respect the privacy of others

Source: The Association of Computing Machinery, New York, New York, 1993.

CONTINENTAL CAN.   Based in Norwalk, Connecticut, Continental Can Co. developed a human resources database with files on all of its employees. Besides the typical employee data, the system included the capability to "red flag" employees nearing retirement or approaching the age at which a pension would be vested in the individual. Throughout the 1980s, when the red flag went up, management would fire the person, even after decades of loyal service. In 1991 a federal district court in Newark, New Jersey, awarded ex-employees $445 million for wrongful dismissal (McPartlin, June 22, 1992).

COMPUTER SCIENCES CORPORATION AT THE EPA.   In 1990 the Environmental Protection Agency (EPA) signed a $347 million outsourcing contract with Computer Sciences Corporation (CSC), which essentially gave CSC the entire responsibility for running the agency's computers and information systems. Investigations by the House Subcommittee on Oversight and Investigation, and the agency's own inspector general, in 1992 claimed that CSC overcharged and double charged the agency by $13 million, engaged in wholesale fraud, and had taken over the most sensitive information at the agency including databases on bids of competitors and the systems that process orders for its own contract. According to the Inspector General, CSC practically took over the agency and in the process hired more than 1400 of its own workers working on 200 separate projects. CSC denies these allegations and claims that it is only EPA's administrative details that need cleaning up, not CSC's practices (McPartlin, March 9, 1992).

SOFTWARE BOMB AT REVLON.   In 1988 Revlon Inc., one of the world's largest cosmetics firms, contracted with a small software firm called Logisticon Inc. to develop inventory control software for the sum of $600,000. In October 1990, the Revlon vice president for systems development, Nathan Amitai, sought to terminate the contract, claiming the work had not been "up to expectations." At that point, Revlon owed Logisticon $180,000 but refused to pay this amount until work for the first phase of the project was completed. Logisticon President Donald Gallagher blamed any performance faults on bugs in Revlon's systems and demanded payment. Revlon refused.

At 2:30 A.M. on October 16, 1990, Revlon systems personnel reported systemwide breakdowns in Logisticon software. Logisticon faxed a letter to Revlon the next day, stating, "Logisticon disabled the operation of its Dispatcher System software last night but took great care to do it in an orderly fashion and not violate or corrupt your data. If you use or attempt to use Logisticon proprietary software to restart the Dispatcher System application package, we believe there is a real possibility that you could corrupt your data, and we will not be responsible. When and if agreement is reached on outstanding payments, systems can be restored in a few hours."

During the next three days, sales from the two affected distribution facilities "were brought to a standstill," resulting in the loss of millions of dollars of orders, and temporary layoffs of hundreds of workers. The systems were restored by Logisticon by October 19. On October 22, Revlon filed suit against Logisticon, charging intentional interference with contractual relations, trespass, conversion, misappropriation of trade secrets, breach of contract and warranty. One of Revlon's complaints was that Logisticon did not mention in the contract with Revlon that a "drop dead" or software bomb device had been implanted in the software. Had this been a part of the contract, Revlon would have acted differently (Caldwell, 1990).

TECHNOLOGICAL THREATS AT AT&T. In March 1992, four months before entering into contract negotiations with the Communications Workers of America (CWA) and the International Brotherhood of Electrical Workers (IBEW), AT&T announced that it was introducing technology that would replace one third of its 18,000 long-distance operators by 1994. The unions quickly branded the announcement as an "intimidation tactic" designed to soften up the unions' demands for higher wages and better working conditions.

AT&T plans to use voice recognition software to reduce the need for human operators by allowing computers to recognize a customer's responses to a series of computerized questions. New algorithms called "word spotting" allow the computer to recognize speech that is halting, stuttering, paused, or ungrammatical.

AT&T claims the new technology will permit it to eliminate 3000 to 6000 operator jobs nationwide, and 200 to 400 management positions. It will also be able to close 31 offices in 21 states. Long-distance operators earn anywhere from $10,300 to $27,100 a year, with benefits adding another third of the cost. AT&T claims not all workers will be dismissed and that many will be retrained for other positions.

Communications Workers of America officials expressed outrage at AT&T's announcement at this time, especially the announcement that entire offices will be closed. AT&T claims it made the announcement now because of leaks from the union officials and that managers only wanted to inform workers before the news spread further (Ramirez, 1992).

E-MAIL PRIVACY AT EPSON. In March 1990, E-mail administrator Alana Shoars filed a suit in Los Angeles Superior Court alleging wrongful termination, defamation, and invasion of privacy by her former employer, Epson America Inc. of Torrance, California. She sought $1 million in damages. In July 1990, Shoars filed a class-action suit seeking $75 million for 700 Epson employees and approximately 1800 outsiders whose E-mail may have been monitored. Shoars contends that she was fired because she questioned the company's policy of monitoring and printing employee's E-mail messages. Epson claims that Shoars was fired because she opened an MCI:Mail account without permission. Many firms claim that they have every right to monitor the electronic mail of their employees because they own the facilities, intend their use to be for business purposes only, and create the facility for a business purpose (Bjerklie, 1994; Rifkin, 1991).

In each instance, you can find competing values at work, with groups lined up on either side of a debate. A close analysis of the facts can sometimes produce compromised solutions that give each side "half a loaf." Try to apply some of the principles of ethical analysis described above to each of these cases. What is the right thing to do?

5.3 THE MORAL DIMENSIONS OF INFORMATION SYSTEMS

In this section, we take a closer look at the five moral dimensions of information systems first described in Figure 5.1. In each dimension we identify the ethical, social, and political levels of analysis and illustrate with real-world examples the values involved, the stakeholders, and the options chosen.

privacy The claim of individuals to be left alone, free from surveillance or interference from other individuals, organizations, or the state.

Privacy is the claim of individuals to be left alone, free from surveillance or interference from other individuals or organizations including the state. Claims to privacy are also involved at the workplace: Millions of employees are subject to electronic and other forms of hi-tech surveillance. Information technology and systems threaten individual claims to privacy by making the invasion of privacy cheap, profitable, and effective.

The claim to privacy is protected in the U.S., Canadian, and German constitutions in a variety of different ways, and in other countries through various statutes. In the United States, the claim to privacy is protected primarily by the First Amendment guarantees of freedom of speech and association and the Fourth Amendment protections against unreasonable search and seizure of one's personal documents or home, and the guarantee of due process.

Due process has become a key concept in defining privacy where absolutist claims to be left alone are not tenable. Due process requires that a set of rules or laws exist which clearly define how information about individuals will be treated, and what appeal mechanisms are available. Perhaps the best statement of the due process in recordkeeping is given by the Fair Information Practices doctrine developed in the early 1970s.

Most American and European privacy law is based on a regime called Fair Information Practices (FIP) first set forth in a report written in 1973 by a federal government advisory committee (U.S. Department of Health, Education, and Welfare, 1973). **Fair Information Practices (FIP)** is a set of principles governing the collection and use of information about individuals. The five fair information practices principles are shown in Table 5.2.

Fair Information Practices (FIP) A set of principles originally set forth in 1973 that governs the collection and use of information about individuals and forms the basis of most U.S. and European privacy law.

FIP principles are based on the notion of a "mutuality of interest" among the record holder and the individual. The individual has an interest in engaging in a transaction, and the recordkeeper—usually a business or government agency—requires information about the individual to support the transaction. Once gathered, the individual maintains an interest in the record, and the record may not be used to support other activities without the individual's consent.

Fair Information Practices form the basis of 13 federal statutes listed in Table 5.3 that set forth the conditions for handling information about individuals in such areas as credit reporting, education, financial records, newspaper records, cable communications, electronic communications, and even video rentals.

In the United States, privacy law is enforced by individuals who must sue agencies or companies in court in order to recover damages. European countries and Canada define privacy in a similar manner to that in the United States, but they have chosen to enforce their privacy laws by creating Privacy Commissions or Data Protection Agencies to pursue complaints brought by citizens.

Despite this legislation, most Americans feel there is less privacy today than ever. Public opinion polls show that when it comes to information privacy, most Americans are bewildered, fearful, confused, and increasingly distrustful about pub-

Table 5.2	Fair Information Practices Principles

1. There should be no personal record systems whose existence is secret.

2. Individuals have rights of access, inspection, review, and amendment to systems that contain information about them.

3. There must be no use of personal information for purposes other than those for which it was gathered without prior consent.

4. Managers of systems are responsible and can be held accountable, and liable for the damage done by systems, for their reliability and security.

5. Governments have the right to intervene in the information relationships among private parties.

lic policy in this area. According to a recent Harris poll, 76 percent of Americans believe they have lost all control over personal information, and 67 percent believe that computers must be restricted in the future to preserve privacy (Equifax, 1992). There are several causes of this erosion of public confidence: distrust of all institutions, the rapid growth of computer transactions not protected by any privacy legislation, and the loss of control over personal information which individuals, in fact, experience in a highly computerized transaction-oriented society. The development of law is clearly lagging far behind the reality of computer-based information.

Ethical Issues

The ethical privacy issue in this information age is as follows: Under what conditions should I (you) invade the privacy of others? What legitimates intruding into others' lives through unobtrusive surveillance, through market research, or by whatever means? Do we have to inform people we are eavesdropping? Do we have to inform people that we are using credit history information for employment screening purposes?

Social Issues

The social issue of privacy concerns the development of "expectations of privacy" or privacy norms, as well as public attitudes. In what areas of life should we as a society encourage people to think they are "in private territory" as opposed to public view? For instance, should we as a society encourage people to develop expectations of privacy when using electronic mail, cellular telephones, bulletin boards, the postal system, the workplace, the street? Should expectations of privacy be extended to criminal conspirators?

Political Issues

The political issue of privacy concerns the development of statutes which govern the relations between recordkeepers and individuals. Should we permit the FBI to prevent the commercial development of encrypted telephone transmissions so its agents can eavesdrop at will (Denning et al., 1993)? Should a law be passed to require direct marketing firms to obtain the consent of individuals before using their names in

Table 5.3	Federal Privacy Laws in the United States
(1) General Federal Privacy Laws	
Freedom of Information Act, 1968 as Amended (5 USC 552)	
Privacy Act of 1974 as Amended (5 USC 552a)	
Electronic Communications Privacy Act of 1986	
Computer Matching and Privacy Protection Act of 1988	
Computer Security Act of 1987	
Federal Managers Financial Integrity Act of 1982	
(2) Privacy Laws Affecting Private Institutions	
Fair Credit Reporting Act, 1970	
Family Educational Rights and Privacy Act of 1978	
Right to Financial Privacy Act of 1978	
Privacy Protection Act of 1980	
Cable Communications Policy Act of 1984	
Electronic Communications Privacy Act of 1986	
Video Privacy Protection Act of 1988	

The film adaptation of George Orwell's novel *1984* portrayed a frightening vision of the future. "Big Brother" kept a constant surveillance over every aspect of the daily lives of all citizens.

mass marketing (a consensus database)? Should E-mail privacy—regardless of who owns the equipment—be protected in law? In general, large organizations of all kinds, public and private, are reluctant to give up the advantages which come from the unfettered flow of information on individuals. Civil liberties and other private groups have been the strongest voices supporting restraints on large organization information-gathering activities.

PROPERTY RIGHTS: INTELLECTUAL PROPERTY

Contemporary information systems have severely challenged existing law and social practice which protects private intellectual property. In so doing, information systems have resulted in the loss of billions of dollars in software sales due to outright theft or piracy, and retarded the growth of the software industry by reducing its profitability. At the same time, the existence of so much stolen "free" software, the ease of creating perfect copies, has greatly expanded the use of software and hardware.

Intellectual property is considered to be intangible property created by individuals or corporations and is subject to a variety of protections under three different legal traditions: trade secret, copyright, and patent law. Each provides different kinds of protections for software (Graham, 1984).

Trade Secrets

Any intellectual work product—a formula, device, pattern, or compilation of data— used for a business purpose can be classified as a **trade secret**, provided it is not based on information in the public domain. Trade secrets have their basis in state law, not federal law, and protections vary from state to state. In general, trade secret laws grant a monopoly on the ideas behind a work product, but it can be a very tenuous monopoly.

Software which contains novel or unique elements, procedures, or compilations can be included as a trade secret. Trade secret law protects the actual ideas in a work product and not just their manifestation. In order to make this claim, the creator or owner must take care to bind employees and customers with nondisclosure agreements and to prevent the secret from falling into the public domain.

Here is the limitation of trade secret protection: While virtually all software programs of any complexity contain unique elements of some sort, it is difficult to prevent the ideas in the work from falling into the public domain when the software is

intellectual property Intangible property created by individuals or corporations which is subject to protections under trade secret, copyright, and patent law.

trade secret Any intellectual work or product used for a business purpose that can be classified as belonging to that business provided it is not based on information in the public domain.

widely distributed. For instance, the idea of highlighting text and then copying that text to a separate storage area called the Clipboard was an idea that quickly fell into the public domain and could not receive protection as a trade secret. However, the manner in which a proprietary direct marketing software program searches a huge national database to identify prospects can be protected as a trade secret provided the creator can show the process relies on novel or unique elements, or even that it simply provides a competitive business advantage using less well-known techniques. The key is to avoid having ideas fall into public domain.

Copyright

copyright A statutory grant which protects creators of intellectual property against copying by others for any purpose for a period of 28 years.

Copyright in the United States is a statutory grant which protects creators of intellectual property against copying by others for any purpose for a period of 28 years. Since the first Federal Copyright Act of 1790, and the creation of the copyright office to register copyrights and enforce copyright law, Congress has extended copyright protection to books, periodicals, lectures, dramas, musical compositions, maps, drawings, artwork of any kind, and motion pictures. Since the earliest days, the congressional intent behind copyright laws has been to encourage creativity and authorship by ensuring that creative people receive the financial and other benefits of their work. Copyright provides a limited monopoly on the commercial use of a work but does not protect the ideas behind a work. Most industrial nations have their own copyright laws, and there are several international conventions and bilateral agreements through which nations coordinate and enforce their laws.

In the mid-1960s the Copyright Office began registering software programs, and in 1980 Congress passed the Computer Software Copyright Act, which clearly provides protection for source and object code, for copies of the original sold in commerce, and sets forth the rights of the purchaser to use the software while the creator retains legal title. This follows a pattern in which Congress will periodically update copyright laws to take into account new forms of expression. For instance, Congress acted at the turn of the century to protect mass market sheet music, and later to protect musical works against misappropriation by radio and television, through a series of acts which ensured authors receive payments anytime their sheet music is sold or their recordings played on radios or other media.

Copyright protection is explicit and clear-cut: It protects against copying of entire programs or their parts. Damages and relief are readily obtained for infringement. The drawback to copyright protection is that the underlying ideas are not protected, only their manifestation in a work. A competitor can use your software, understand how it works, and build his or her own software that follows the same concepts without infringing on a copyright.

"Look and feel" copyright infringement lawsuits are precisely about the distinction between an idea and its expression. For instance, in the early 1990s Apple Computer sued Microsoft Corporation and Hewlett-Packard Inc. for infringement of the expression of Apple's Macintosh interface. Among other claims, Apple claimed that the defendants copied the expression of overlapping windows. The defendants counterclaimed that the idea of overlapping windows can only be expressed in a single way, and therefore was not protectable under the "merger" doctrine of copyright law. When ideas and their expression merge, the expression cannot be copyrighted. In general, courts appear to be following the reasoning of a 1989 case—*Brown Bag Software* v. *Symantec*—in which the court dissected the elements of software alleged to be infringing. The court found that neither similar concept, function, general functional features (e.g., drop-down menus), nor colors are protectable by copyright law (Brown Bag v. Symantec Corp., 1992).

Patents

patent A legal document that grants the owner an exclusive monopoly on the ideas behind an invention for 17 years; designed to ensure that inventors of new machines or methods are rewarded for their labor while making widespread use of their inventions.

The first U.S. patent was granted by Congress in 1790, and the Patent Office was established in 1836. A **patent** grants the owner an exclusive monopoly on the ideas behind an invention for 17 years. The congressional intent behind patent law was to ensure that inventors of new machines, devices, or methods receive the full financial and other rewards of their labor and yet still make widespread use of the invention possible by providing detailed diagrams for those wishing to use the idea under license from the owner of the patent. The granting of a patent is determined by the Patent Office and relies on court rulings.

The key concepts in patent law are originality, novelty, invention. The Patent Office did not accept applications for software patents routinely until a 1981 Supreme Court decision held that computer programs could be a part of a patentable process. Since then hundreds of patents have been granted and thousands await consideration.

The strength of patent protection is that it grants a monopoly on the underlying concepts and ideas of software. The difficulty is passing stringent criteria of nonobviousness (e.g., the work must reflect some special understanding and contribution), originality, and novelty, as well as years of waiting to receive protection.

Contemporary information technologies, especially software, pose a severe challenge to existing intellectual property regimes, and therefore create significant ethical, social, and political issues. Digital media differ from books, periodicals, and other media in terms of ease of replication, ease of transmission, ease of alteration, compactness, difficulty classifying a software work as a program, book, or even music—making theft easy and difficulties in establishing uniqueness. Does a hypertext document where concepts are linked via software links become unique from the original document? (See Samuelson, October 1991.)

Ethical Issues

The central ethical issue posed to individuals concerns copying software: Should I (you) copy for our own use a piece of software protected by trade secret, copyright, and/or patent law? In the information age, it is so easy to obtain perfect, functional copies of software, that the software companies themselves have abandoned software protection schemes to increase market penetration, and enforcement of the law is so rare. However, if everyone copied software, very little new software would be produced because creators could not benefit from the results of their work.

Social Issues

There are several property-related social issues raised by new information technology. Most experts agree that the current intellectual property laws are breaking down in the information age. The vast majority of Americans report in surveys that they routinely violate some minor laws—everything from speeding to taking paper clips from work to copying software. The ease with which software can be copied contributes to making us a society of lawbreakers. In 1990, the Software Publishers Association (SPA) estimated it lost $2.4 billion or half the total of $5.7 billion in software sales. Copied software is routinely found in both personal and business settings (Markoff, July 27, 1992). These routine thefts significantly threaten to reduce the speed with which new information technologies can and will be introduced, and thereby threaten further advances in productivity and social well-being.

Political Issues

The main property-related political issue concerns the creation of new property protection measures to protect investments made by creators of new software. Apple, Microsoft, and 900 other hardware and software firms formed the Software Publishers Association (SPA) to lobby for new protection laws and enforce existing laws. SPA has distributed more than 30,000 copies of SPA audit—a software inventory management tool used by corporations to establish control over software used on individual PCs; established a toll-free antipiracy hotline for employees to report on their corporations; completed 75 surprise audits or raids; sent 560 cease-and-desist letters, and filed more than 100 lawsuits since its inception (80 percent against corporations, 20 percent against bulletin board operators, training facilities, schools and universities). The SPA has developed a model Software Code of Ethics described in the Window on Organizations.

Allied against SPA are a host of groups and millions of individuals who resist efforts to strengthen antipiracy laws, and instead encourage situations where software can be copied. These groups believe that software should be free, that antipiracy laws cannot in any event be enforced in the digital age, or that software should be paid for on a voluntary basis (shareware software). According to these groups, the greater social benefit results from the free distribution of software and the "benefits" of software should accrue to the creators in the form of greater prestige perhaps, but not in the form of profits.

ACCOUNTABILITY, LIABILITY, AND CONTROL

Along with privacy and property laws, new information technologies are challenging existing liability law and social practices for holding individuals and institutions accountable. If a person is injured by a machine controlled in part by software, who should be held accountable and therefore held liable? Should public bulletin board or electronic services like Prodigy and CompuServe permit the transmission of pornographic or offensive material (as broadcasters), or should they be held harmless against any liability for what users transmit (as is true of common carriers like the telephone system)? Is Prodigy a common carrier? If you outsource your information

A CORPORATE SOFTWARE CODE OF ETHICS

This code of ethics is to state our organization's policy concerning software duplication. All employees shall use software only in accordance with the license agreement. Unless otherwise provided in the license, any duplication of licensed software except for backup and archival purposes is a violation of the law. Any unauthorized duplication of copyrighted computer software violates the law and is contrary to the organization's standards of conduct. The following points are to be followed in order to comply with software license agreements.

1. We will use all software in accordance with our license agreements.

2. Legitimate software will promptly be provided to all employees who need it. No employee of the company will make any unauthorized copies of any software under any circumstances.

Anyone found copying software other than for backup purposes is subject to termination.

3. We will not tolerate the use of any unauthorized copies of software in our company. Any person illegally reproducing software can be subject to civil and criminal penalties including fines and imprisonment. We do not condone illegal copying of software under any circumstances and anyone who makes, uses, or otherwise acquires unauthorized software shall be appropriately disciplined.

4. No employee shall give software to any outsiders (including clients, customers, and others).

5. Any employee who determines that there may be a misuse of software within the company shall notify their Department Manager or legal counsel.

6. All software used by the organization on company computers will be

properly purchased through appropriate procedures.

I have read the company's software code of ethics. I am fully aware of

To Think About: Try to find out your university's policy regarding software. Is there a software code of ethics on campus? If an employee finds routine copying of software in a firm, should he or she (1) call the firm's legal counsel or (2) call SPA on the antipiracy hotline? Are there any circumstances in which software copying should be allowed?

our software policies and agree to abide by those policies.

Source: Software Management Guide: A Guide for Software Asset Management, version 1.0. Courtesy of Software Publishers Association, 1992.

processing, can you hold the external vendor liable for injuries done to your customers? Try some real-world examples.

Some Recent Liability Problems

In February 1992, hackers penetrated the computer network of Equifax, Inc. in Atlanta, Georgia, one of the world's largest credit-reporting bureaus that sells 450 million reports annually. Consumer files, credit-card numbers, and other confidential information were accessed. The company is working with police and reviewing all files to catch the criminals. When finished, it will notify all affected customers. Who is liable for any damages done to individuals (King, 1992)?

On March 13, 1993, a blizzard hit the East Coast of the United States, knocking out an EDS (Electronic Data Systems Inc.) computer center in Clifton, New Jersey. The center operated 5200 ATM machines in 12 different networks across the country, involving more than one million card holders. In the two weeks required to recover operations, EDS informed its customers to use alternative ATM networks operated by other banks or computer centers, and offered to cover more than $50 million in cash withdrawals. Because the alternative networks did not have access to the actual customer account balances, EDS is at substantial risk of fraud. Cash withdrawals were limited to $100 per day per customer to reduce the exposure. Most service was restored by March 26. Although EDS had a disaster recovery plan, it did not have a dedicated backup facility. Who is liable for any economic harm caused individuals or businesses who could not access their full account balances in this period (Joes, 1993)?

In April 1990, a computer system at Shell Pipeline Corporation failed to detect a human-operator error. As a result, 93,000 barrels of crude oil were shipped to the wrong trader. The error cost $2 million because the trader sold oil that should not have been delivered to him. A court ruled later that Shell Pipeline was liable for the loss of the oil because the error was due to a human operator who entered erroneous information into the system. Shell was held liable for not developing a system that would prevent the possibility of misdeliveries (King, 1992). Who would you have held liable—Shell Pipeline? The trader for not being more careful about deliveries? The human operator who made the error?

Categories of Liability

These cases point out the difficulties faced by information systems executives who ultimately are responsible for the harm done by systems developed by their staffs. Traditionally, there are three categories of liability that courts use to deal with claims that products or services have caused physical or economic injury to consumers: breach of warranty, negligence, and strict liability tort.

In general, insofar as computer software is part of a machine, and the machine injures someone physically or economically, the producer of the software and the operator can be held liable for damages. Insofar as the software acts more like a book, storing and displaying information, courts have been reluctant to hold authors, publishers, and booksellers liable for contents (the exception being instances of fraud or defamation), and hence courts have been wary of holding software authors liable for "book-like" software.

The distinction between software as machine versus software as book permeates all three kinds of liability. A **warranty** can be expressly stated by the seller of goods, or implied by simply being sold on the marketplace where it is assumed by courts that the merchant is making an implied representation that the goods are of fair or average quality and fit for consumption. In either case, if software is part of a machine, it will be treated as a machine and warranty promises are enforceable. If the software is a service, warranty law does not apply unless the software author makes some specific warranties in contract about the performance of the software. If the software is a book or an information service, then it is very unlikely warranties will apply.

warranty A representation expressed by the seller of goods representing that the goods are fit for purchase and use.

negligence Finding of fault when a producer's product causes physical or economic harm to individuals that could and should have been prevented.

strict liability in tort Class of liability whenever a defective product causes injury and the manufacturer can be held liable regardless of whether or not the defect could have or should have been prevented.

Negligence also applies only to products and not, so far, to services. **Negligence** occurs when a product causes physical or economic harm to individuals, when the injury could have and should have been prevented, and when the producer has a "duty to care" about the consumer of the product. Negligence requires fault. Mere information providers have rarely been held liable no matter what media they use (the exception being professional advice of doctors or scientists and engineers). Producers of software have been found liable only in those cases where the software is part of a machine.

Strict liability in tort is a separate class of liability that arises whenever a defective product causes injury. In these cases, individuals can bring suits against the manufacturer independent of the question of fault, warranty, or duty to care. In other words, a manufacturer of a defective product that injures people can be held strictly liable regardless of whether or not he could have or should have prevented the defect. In software cases, as before, it is only when software acts as part of a defective product (rather than a service) that strict liability applies.

From this brief assessment, you should conclude that in general it is very difficult (if not impossible) to hold software producers liable for their software products when those products are considered like books, regardless of the physical or economic harm which results. Historically, print publishers, books, and periodicals have not been held liable because of fears that liability claims would interfere with First Amendment rights guaranteeing freedom of expression.

What about "software as service"? ATM machines are a service provided to bank customers. Should this service fail, customers will be inconvenienced and perhaps harmed economically if they cannot access their funds in a timely manner. Should liability protections be extended to software publishers and operators of defective financial, accounting, simulation, financial, or marketing systems?

Software is very different from books. Software users may develop expectations of infallibility about software; software is less easily inspected than a book, and more difficult to compare to other software products for quality; and software claims actually to perform a task rather than describe a task like a book; people come to depend on services essentially based on software. Given the centrality of software to everyday life, the chances are excellent that liability law will extend its reach to include software even when it merely provides an information service.

Liability and accountability are also at the heart of debates over the responsibility and freedoms of computer bulletin boards and networks. Table 5.4 illustrates the

Table 5.4	Regulatory Regimes for Various Information Providers in the United States
Provider	**Regulatory Regime**
Book publisher	None
Newspaper	None
Bookstore	None
Television broadcaster	Federal Communications Commission (FCC), courts, Congress
Radio broadcaster	FCC, courts, Congress
AT&T long lines	FCC, courts, Congress
Local Bells (BOC)	States, legislatures, commissions
Cable television operator	Congress, states, localities
Computer bulletin boards	Undecided
Public E-mail	Undecided
National computer networks	Undecided

LIABILITY ON THE PRODIGY NETWORK

Can you sue Prodigy if you think you have been libeled by a message posted on one of its on-line bulletin boards? Users of bulletin boards write and post their own messages, making them available for other bulletin board users to read. Those messages do carry the name and identification code of the writer, allowing someone who believes he or she has been libeled to sue the writer. The tricky question is, what is the legal responsibility of the marketplace that makes that message available? Courts have long ago ruled that bookstores cannot be held responsible for the content of books they sell, although authors can and are sued for libel. Similarly, telephone companies are not able to be sued for the content of telephone conversations that take place on the systems they provide. Legal experts point out that in both cases the vendors (bookstores and telephone companies) offer a means of communication but do not control the content of that communication. In 1991, in the first major computer bulletin board case, *Cubby* v. *CompuServe*, the court ruled that CompuServe acted more like a bookstore and would not be held responsible for libelous messages posted on its bulletin boards. However, Prodigy has been the object of several lawsuits that define the issues more sharply.

In a recent case, Prodigy is being sued for libel over a message that appeared on its Money Talk bulletin board under the name and identification number of David Lusby of Key West, Florida. The message, which appeared in late October 1994, made derogatory statements about Stratton Oakmont, a Lake Success, New York, investment firm. The message contended that Stratton Oakmont had just managed an initial public offering for a company while keeping confidential the information that the company had recently lost its major customer. The message stated that the president of

Stratton Oakmont is "soon to be proven criminal," and that the firm will close within the week. The message further said of the alleged Stratton Oakmont actions that "This is fraud, fraud, fraud and criminal!!!!!!!" Stratton Oakmont sued both Prodigy and Lusby, asking for $200 million. Lusby was quickly eliminated as a target of the suit. He was able to show to the satisfaction of both parties that he had not used the Prodigy account for a very long time. He had been given his account as a Prodigy employee, and when he left Prodigy's employment, the company failed to close his account. Apparently other unknown persons had gained access to it.

In *Cubby* v. *CompuServe*, CompuServe was found to be insulated from libel suits because it makes no attempt to screen messages its users post. Prodigy is expected to base its defense on this precedent. Prodigy points out that every time subscribers sign on to Money Talk, they first see a message that includes the statement "Prodigy does not verify, endorse or otherwise vouch for the contents of any note and cannot be held responsible in any way for information contained in any such note." Moreover, they say they do not censor messages for content. However, Prodigy does admit that it exercises the right to prescreen its approximately 75,000 daily messages. According to Prodigy spokeswoman Carol Wallace, "We have a machine that scans for unacceptable words," by which she apparently means obscenities. Jacob H. Samansky, the New York attorney representing Stratton Oakmont, takes the position that "Prodigy holds itself to a higher standard" because of their prescreening and should have removed the offending message.

The issues relating to on-line libel are complex. The analogy to telephone systems may be apt because vendors of bulletin board services are fast losing the ability to screen all the messages before posting them—the task is just becoming too large. However, different

from telephone services, bulletin board messages persist and so can be read over time and by many, much like material in newspapers or bookstores. The

> ***To Think About:*** *What are the implications of a monitored on-line bulletin board? Of one that has no restrictions? What measures would you take to prevent bulletin boards from being used for posting libelous statements?*

analogy to bookstores also breaks down because virtually anyone with access to a bulletin board can "publish" his or her ideas—the bulletin boards are genuinely open markets of ideas without the intervention of editors or publishers. Who then should be held accountable for the information posted on these bulletin boards? And if the service providers can be held libel for the content of messages, what kind of chilling effect will this have on the free exchange of ideas?

The problem is broader than just on-line bulletin boards. It also affects E-mail systems. Eastman Kodak Co., the Rochester, New York, multinational giant, forbids employees to post public messages on the Internet if those messages will carry a Kodak address. Robert L. Mirguet, a Kodak information security manager, says the company's concern is that employee opinions may be taken as an indication of the opinion of the company itself. False information, innuendoes, and libelous statements can even be a problem internally. Kodak E-mail systems transmit 400,000 messages every day. Kodak claims fewer than one problem a week among these messages, but it does investigate those few following standard company procedures.

Some observers of this electronic message issue see another issue emerging, that of the invasion of privacy of the users of these systems. In an earlier lawsuit related to Prodigy, Medphone Corporation, a New Jersey manufacturer of medical telecommunications devices, sued a disgruntled investor for statements he posted on a Prodigy bulletin board. As part of the lawsuit, Medphone was able to subpoena Prodigy and force the company to release the names of all the people who had read the offending messages or who had even communicated with the individual who posted them. This means that on-line system records can be used to trace communication patterns among users, perhaps further chilling the atmosphere for the free exchange of ideas.

Sources: Robert B. Charles, "On-line Libel: A $250 Million Bug." *Computerworld,* January 23, 1995. Mitch Betts, "On-line Libel Lawsuits Looming," *Computerworld,* November 28, 1994; Arthur S. Hayes, "Computer Message Prompts Libel Suit," *The Wall Street Journal,* March 26, 1993; Peter H. Lewis, "A New Twist in an On-Line Libel Case," *The New York Times,* December 19, 1994; Peter H. Lewis, "Libel Suit Against Prodigy Test On-Line Speech Limits," *The New York Times,* November 16, 1994.

different regulatory regimes of various information providers in the United States. The Window on Organizations describes recent lawsuits seeking to establish liability of bulletin board providers.

There are virtually no liabilities imposed on book publishers, bookstores, or newspapers (outside of outright defamation and certain local restrictions on pornographic materials). This is because of the historic roles these media have played in the evolution of First Amendment rights. Telephone systems are regulated "common carrier" monopolies. Corporations are granted a monopoly on telephone service with no liability for content of messages transmitted. In return they must provide access to all, at reasonable rates, and achieve acceptable reliability. Broadcasters are granted monopolies by the Federal Communications Commission, which allocates frequency spectrum according to the 1934 Communications Act and subsequent amendments. In return, broadcasters are subject to a wide variety of federal and local constraints on content and facilities. Cable television systems are directly regulated by Congress, as well as by states and localities. They too are liable for content of messages and are subject to many local regulations on content and community service.

Ethical Issues

The central liability-related ethical issue raised by new information technologies is whether or not individuals and organizations who create, produce, and sell systems (both hardware and software) are morally responsible for the consequences of their use. If so, under what conditions? What liabilities (and responsibilities) should the user assume, and what should the provider assume?

Social Issues

The central liability-related social issue concerns the expectations that society should allow to develop around service-providing information systems. Should individuals (and organizations) be encouraged to develop their own backup devices to cover likely or easily anticipated system failures, or should organizations be held strictly liable for system services they provide? If organizations are held strictly liable, what impact will this have on the development of new system services? Can society permit networks and bulletin boards to post libelous, inaccurate, and misleading information that will harm many persons? Or should information service companies become self-regulating and self-censoring?

Political Issues

The leading liability-related political issue is the debate between information providers of all kinds (from software developers to network service providers) who want to be relieved of liability insofar as possible (thereby maximizing their profits), and service users—individuals, organizations, communities—who want organizations to be held responsible for providing high-quality system services (thereby maximizing the quality of service). Service providers argue they will withdraw from the marketplace if they are held liable, while service users argue that only by holding providers liable can we guarantee a high level of service and compensate injured parties. Should legislation impose liability or restrict liability on service providers? This fundamental cleavage is at the heart of numerous political and judicial conflicts.

SYSTEM QUALITY: DATA QUALITY AND SYSTEM ERRORS

The debate over liability and accountability for unintentional consequences of system use raises a related but independent moral dimension: What is an acceptable, technologically feasible level of system quality (see Chapter 13)? At what point should system managers say, "Stop testing, we've done all we can to perfect this software. Ship it!" Obviously, individuals and organizations cannot be held responsible or liable for "acts of God" or technologically unavoidable errors. They may be held responsible for avoidable consequences, foreseeable consequences, which they have a duty to perceive and correct. And there is a gray area: Some system errors are foreseeable and correctable only at very great expense, an expense so great that pursuing this level of perfection is not feasible economically—no one could afford the product. For example, although software companies try to debug their products before releasing them for sale, they knowingly ship buggy products because the time and cost to fix all minor errors would prevent these products from ever being released (Rigdon, 1995). What if the product were not offered on the marketplace, would social welfare as a whole not advance and perhaps even decline? Carrying this further, just what is the responsibility of producers of computer services—should they withdraw the product that can never be perfect, warn the user, or forget about the risk (caveat emptor—let the buyer beware)?

As we discuss in Chapters 13, 14, and 18, three principal sources of poor system performance are software bugs and errors, hardware or facility failures due to natural or other causes, and poor input data quality. Chapter 13 establishes that zero defects in software code of any complexity cannot be achieved and the seriousness of remaining bugs cannot be estimated. Hence, there is a technological barrier to perfect software and users must be aware of the potential for catastrophic failure. The software industry has not yet arrived at testing standards for producing software of acceptable but not perfect performance (Collins et al., 1994).

System hardware and facility failures are much better documented and more easily managed. Redundancy of processors in mission-critical applications can reduce the probabilities of failure by known amounts; and even weather system patterns routinely used by civil engineers in designing buildings and bridges can be used as a rationale (by responsible system developers) to build emergency backup facilities for mission-critical and life-dependent applications.

Perhaps the single largest cause of system failure is seemingly trivial: poor input data quality. A survey of 50 CEOs of large businesses found that half of the executives believed their corporate data was less than 95 percent accurate (Bulkeley, 1992). Some of the glitches are reported in Table 5.5.

While software bugs and facility catastrophe are likely to be widely reported in the press, by far the most common source of business system failure is data quality. A total of 70 percent of IS executives in a recent survey reported data corruption as a source of business delay, 69 percent said their corporate data accuracy was unacceptable, and 44 percent said no systems were in place to check database information quality (Wilson, 1992).

Ethical Issues

The central quality-related ethical issue raised by information systems is at what point should I (or you) release software or services for consumption by others? At what point can you conclude that your software or service achieves an economically and technologically adequate level of quality? What are you obliged to know about the quality of your software, its procedures for testing, and its operational characteristics?

Table 5.5 Illustrative Reported Data Quality Problems

- An airline inadvertently corrupted its database of passenger reservations while installing new software and for months planes took off with half loads.

- A manufacturer attempted to reorganize its customer files by customer number only to discover the sales staff had been entering a new customer number for each sale because of special incentives for opening new accounts. One customer was entered 7000 times. The company scrapped the software project after spending $1 million.

- J. P. Morgan, a New York bank, discovered that 40 percent of the data in its credit-risk management database was incomplete, necessitating double-checking by users.

- Several studies have established that 5 to 12 percent of bar code sales at retail grocery and merchandise chains are erroneous and that the ratio of overcharges to undercharges runs as high as 5:1, with 4:1 as a norm. The problem tends to be human error in keeping shelf prices accurate and corporate policy which fails to allocate sufficient resources to price checking, auditing, and development of error-free policies. The cause of the high overcharge has not yet been determined, but the pattern is disturbing, suggesting intentional behavior.

Sources: William M. Bulkeley, "Databases Plagued by a Reign of Error," *The Wall Street Journal,* May 26, 1992; and Doug Bartholomew, "The Price Is Wrong," *InformationWeek,* September 14, 1992.

Social Issues

The leading quality-related social issue once again deals with expectations: Do we as a society want to encourage people to believe that systems are infallible, that data errors are impossible? Or do we instead want a society where people are openly skeptical and questioning of the output of machines, where people are at least informed of the risk? By heightening awareness of system failure, do we inhibit the development of all systems which in the end contribute to social well-being?

Political Issues

The leading quality-related political issue concerns the laws of responsibility and accountability. Should Congress establish or direct the National Institute of Science and Technology (NIST) to develop quality standards (software, hardware, data quality) and impose those standards on industry? Or should industry associations be encouraged to develop industry-wide standards of quality? Or should Congress wait for the marketplace to punish poor system quality, recognizing that in some instances this will not work (e.g., if all retail grocers maintain poor quality systems, then customers have no alternatives)?

QUALITY OF LIFE: EQUITY, ACCESS, BOUNDARIES

The negative social costs of introducing information technologies and systems are beginning to mount up as the power of the technology bounds upward. Many of these negative social consequences are neither violations of individual rights defended in the Constitution or statute nor property crimes. Nevertheless, these negative consequences can be extremely harmful to individuals, societies, and political institutions. Computers and information technologies can potentially destroy valuable elements of our culture and society even while they benefit us. If there is a balance of good and bad consequences to the use of information systems, whom do we hold responsible for the bad consequences? Below, we briefly examine some of the negative social consequences of systems, considering individual, social, and political responses.

Balancing Power Center versus Periphery

One of the earliest fears of the computer age was that huge centralized mainframe computers would centralize power at corporate headquarters and in the nation's capital, resulting in a "Big Brother" society suggested in George Orwell's novel, *1984*. The shift toward highly decentralized computing in the 1990s, coupled with an ideology of "empowerment" of thousands of workers, and the decentralization of decision making to lower organizational levels, have reduced fears of power centralization in institutions. Yet much of the empowerment and devolution described in popular business magazines is trivial. Lower-level employees may be empowered to make minor decisions about their work pace, and they may be able in some cases to stop the production line on observing defects, but the key policy decisions may be as centralized as in the past. Many of the participatory mechanisms dreamed up by consultants to tap into the profitable ideas of the work force bring unclear and inequitable rewards to employees.

Rapidity of Change: Reduced Response Time to Competition

Information systems have helped to create much more efficient national and international markets. The now more-efficient global marketplace has reduced the normal social buffers which permitted businesses many years to adjust to competition. "Time-based competition" has an ugly side: The business you work for may not have enough time to respond to global competitors and may be wiped out in a year, along with your job. We stand the risk of developing a "just-in-time society" with "just-in-time jobs" and "just-in-time" workplaces, families, and vacations.

Maintaining Boundaries: Family, Work, Leisure

Parts of this book were produced on trains, planes, as well as on family "vacations," and what otherwise might have been "family" time. The danger to ubiquitous computing, telecommuting, nomad computing, and the "do anything anywhere" computing environment is that it might actually come true. If so, the traditional boundaries that separate work from family and just plain leisure will be weakened. While authors have traditionally worked just about anywhere (typewriters have been portable for nearly a century), the advent of information systems, coupled with the growth of knowledge work occupations, means that more and more people will be working when they would have traditionally been playing or communicating with family and friends. The "work umbrella" now extends far beyond the eight-hour day.

Weakening these institutions poses clear-cut risks. Family and friends historically have provided powerful support mechanisms for individuals, and they act as balance

While people may enjoy the convenience of working at home, the "do anything anywhere" computing environment can blur the traditional boundaries between work and family time.

points in a society by preserving "private life," providing a place for one to collect one's thoughts, to think in ways contrary to one's employer, and to dream.

Dependence and Vulnerability

Our businesses, governments, schools, and private associations like churches are incredibly dependent now on information systems and therefore highly vulnerable. Table 5.6 lists the biggest system disasters culled from a list of more than 300 begun in 1987. With systems now as ubiquitous as the telephone system, it is startling to remember that there are no regulatory or standard setting forces in place similar to telephone, electrical, radio, television, or other public utility technologies. Information systems are unprecedented as a technology for their lack of societal oversight. This reflects the differences in technology: Information systems are not utilities; there are multiple providers, no natural monopolies, and a free market with many alternatives. Information systems are not as systemic as telephone systems, and their failure (when it occurs) is therefore isolated to local nodes. The evolution of a national computer network in the 1990s in the United States will be a highly decentralized network, so that no single node failure can effect the nation. Nevertheless, the absence of standards and the criticality of some system applications will probably call forth demands for national standards, perhaps regulatory oversight.

While distributed networks are seemingly more resistant to disaster than centralized mainframe installations, the terrorist attack on the World Trade Center—business home to more than 50,000 workers and hundreds of LANs—on February 26, 1993, demonstrated that it may be far easier to protect and back up a 20,000-square-foot centralized data center than to achieve similar results for over one million square feet of office space.

Computer Crime and Abuse

computer crime The commission of illegal acts through the use of a computer or against a computer system.

Many new technologies in the industrial era have created new opportunities for committing crime. Technologies, including computers, create new valuable things to steal, new ways to steal them, and new ways to harm others. **Computer crime** can be defined as the commission of illegal acts through the use of a computer or against a computer system. Computers or computer systems can be the object of the crime (destroying a company's computer center or a company's computer files) as well as the instrument of a crime (stealing computer lists by illegally gaining access to a computer system

Table 5.6	The Largest Information System Catastrophes		
Date	Event	Location	Number of Data Centers Affected
8/14/87	Flood	Chicago	64
5/8/88	Network outage	Hinsdale, Illinois	175
5/11/88	Pakistani virus	Nationwide	90+
11/2/88	Internet virus	Nationwide	500+
10/17/89	Earthquake	San Francisco	90
8/13/90	Power outage	New York	320
4/13/92	Flood	Chicago	400
5/1/92	Riot	Los Angeles	50
8/24/92	Hurricane Andrew	Southeast	150
3/15/93	Blizzard	East Coast	50

Sources: "Days of Infamy: The 10 Worst IT Disasters," *InformationWeek*, January 10, 1994; and "The Largest System Catastrophes," *InformationWeek*, March 8, 1993.

computer abuse The commission of acts involving a computer that may not be illegal but are considered unethical.

using a home microcomputer). Simply accessing a computer system without authorization, or intent to do harm, even by accident, is now a federal crime. **Computer abuse** is the commission of acts involving a computer which may not be illegal but are considered unethical.

No one knows the magnitude of the computer crime problem—how many systems are invaded, how many people engage in the practice, or what is the total economic damage. Many companies are reluctant to report computer crimes because they may involve employees and because they don't want to appear vulnerable or incompetent. The most economically damaging kinds of computer crime are the introduction of viruses, theft of services, disruption of computer systems, and theft of telecommunications services. Computer crime has been estimated to cost over $1 billion in the United States, and an additional billion dollars if corporate and cellular phone theft is included. *Hackers* is the pejorative term for persons who use computers in illegal ways. Federal law enforcement officials have estimated that 50,000 computer users "hack" at some time or another, while others put the number at a more modest 5,000 (Sterling, 1992).

Computer viruses have grown exponentially since 1987: More than 1000 viruses have been documented. The average corporate loss for a bad virus outbreak is $250,000, and the probability of a large corporation experiencing a significant computer virus infection in a single year is 50 percent according to some experts. However, examination of large-scale empirical data by IBM suggests a much lower rate of infection, on the order of 38 incidents per 100,000 microcomputers, largely because most micros are stand-alone machines or are tied into local networks that inherently limit the spread of viruses (Markoff, November 1, 1992). In a population like that of the United States, with more than 50 million microcomputers, this would suggest a total of 19,000 infections annually. This is no doubt an underestimate. While many firms now use antivirus software, the explosive growth of computer networks around the world will surely increase the probability of infections.

Below we describe some illustrative computer crimes:

- "Hacker" Robert T. Morris, a computer science student at Cornell University, unleashed a computer virus over the Internet network on November 2, 1988, jamming thousands of machines in tens of networks throughout the system. He was convicted under the Computer Fraud and Abuse Act, given three years' probation, a $10,000 fine, and 400 hours of community service.

- In July 1992, a federal grand jury indicted a national network of 1000 hackers calling themselves MOD—Masters of Deception. Theirs was one of the largest thefts of computer information and services in history. The hackers were charged with computer tampering, computer fraud, wire fraud, illegal wiretapping, and conspiracy. The group broke into over 25 of the largest corporate computer systems in the United States, including Equifax, Inc. (a credit-reporting firm with 170 million records), Southwestern Bell Corporation, New York Telephone, and Pacific Bell. The group stole and resold credit reports, credit-card numbers, and other personal information. Federal investigators used court-ordered wiretaps to monitor the calls of members. The firms blamed their own lax security and a philosophy of "openness" for not detecting the hackers themselves—all of whom were under 22 years of age. All the hackers pleaded guilty. Their convicted leader, Mark Abene, spent 10 months in prison (Gabriel, 1995; Tabor, 1992).

- At AT&T's British headquarters in London, three technicians set up their company in 1992, assigned it a 900 number, and then programmed AT&T computers to dial the number often. The loss amounted to just under $500,000 before the fraud was accidentally detected.

- In 1991, at General Dynamics corporation, Michael Lauffenburger, a disgruntled employee, created a duplicate of an inventory control program used for the Atlas missile. The duplicate was a time bomb program designed to go off just before Lauffenburger quit the company. The duplicate program would erase the original program, disrupt building the missile, then erase itself to avoid detection. Lauffenburger felt underpaid and hoped to rejoin the company as a highly paid consultant to rebuild the original inventory program.

- In 1992, the Pinkerton detective agency discovered that its employee, Marita Juse, had been siphoning off more than $1 million since 1988. Juse had been given a computer code to access Pinkerton bank accounts. She had discovered a second code that was required to provide payment authorization. The authorization code was given to her by her boss who told her to cancel it. Instead, she used it for four years without detection (Carley, 1992).

In general, it is employees—insiders—who have inflicted the most injurious computer crimes because they have the knowledge, the access, and frequently a job-related motive to commit such crimes.

Congress responded to the threat of computer crime in 1986 with the Computer Fraud and Abuse Act (1986). This act makes it illegal to access a computer system without authorization. Most of the states have corresponding laws, and nations in Europe have similar legislation. Other existing legislation covering wiretapping, fraud, conspiracy by any means, regardless of technology employed, is adequate to cover computer crimes committed so far.

Employment: Trickle Down Technology and Re-engineering Job Loss

Re-engineering work (see Chapter 11) is typically hailed in the information systems community as a major benefit of new information technology. Much less frequently noted is that redesigning business processes could potentially cause millions of middle level managers and clerical workers to lose their jobs. Worse, if re-engineering actually worked as claimed, these workers could not find similar employment in society because of an actual decline in demand for their skills. One economist has raised the possibility that we will create a society run by a small "high tech elite of corporate professionals . . . in a nation of the permanently unemployed" (Rifkin, 1993). Some have estimated that if re-engineering were seriously undertaken by the Fortune 1000 companies, about 25 percent of the U.S. labor force could be displaced. Re-engineering has being seriously used at only 15 percent of American service and manufacturing companies, and the average reduction in employment in downsizing companies is 10 percent in a year. Several surveys have documented re-engineering failure rates at from 50 to 90 percent (Cafasso, 1993). While re-engineering projects can produce 50 percent declines in employment, this is rare and likely to happen only in companies facing declining demand. However, the effects of re-engineering may be growing, leaving management with a serious ethical dilemma, as the first Window on Management illustrates.

Economists are much more sanguine about the potential job losses. They believe relieving bright, educated workers from re-engineered jobs will result in these workers moving to better jobs in fast-growth industries. Left out of this equation are blue-collar workers, and older, less well-educated middle managers. It is not clear that these groups are infinitely malleable or can be retrained easily for high-quality (high-paid) jobs. Fortunately, demographers point out, the economy tends to generate jobs to accommodate whatever the existing labor is. From 1960 to 1990, the labor force doubled because of the entrance of women and minorities. From 1990 to 2010, the labor force is expected to be stagnant or even decline in size. Re-engineering may be necessary to accommodate a no-growth labor force. Alternatively, careful planning and sensitivity to employee needs can help companies redesign work to minimize job losses.

Equity and Access: Increasing Racial and Social Class Cleavages

Does everyone have an equal opportunity to participate in the digital age? Will the social, economic, and cultural gaps which exist in American and other societies be

WHITHER THE DOWNSIZED SOCIETY?

While most people understood and expected large layoffs and downsizing during the protracted recession of the early 1990s, the fact that massive downsizing is continuing during the strong recovery that began in 1993 puzzles some and disturbs many. Observers are wondering what role technology plays in this trend. Others are perturbed that the impact of "leaner and meaner," more competitive organizations is large-scale unemployment even during a period of robust economic growth. The choice corporate managements have been facing is often productivity versus employment, and frequently the enabling tool is information technology.

Technology does appear to be key to the large corporate work-force reductions occurring in the mid-1990s. During the 1980s, United States corporations spent over $1 trillion investing in information systems technology. However, throughout that decade, analysts kept wondering what happened to the vaunted productivity gains that were supposed to accompany this investment. Technology seemed only to allow companies to do the same work faster. During the recession of the early 1990s, most downsizing began as the traditional "slash-and-burn" type—cutting staff size during hard times without re-engineering business functions. The goal of most organizations was to be trimmer; resulting in productivity gains that were the result of the remaining employees shouldering more work and putting in longer hours. Some of the jobs that were eliminated in this way did return as economic activity picked up in 1994 and beyond.

What was changing in the early 1990s was that a few companies did find ways to use technology to potently alter the ways they work, sometimes eliminating steps, oftentimes developing an entirely new approach to the function at hand. The method in large corporations was re-engineering pro-

jects with a heavy reliance upon technology. Management was finally seeing the long-promised technology-based productivity gains. While we will discuss many examples throughout this text, a few illustrations here will serve to demonstrate the point.

Pacific Bell (PacBell), a regional telephone unit of Pacific Telesis Group, has found a simple piece of technology that will save $2 million a day. The telephone company must repair all line outages for the lines it owns, but nowadays customers own the lines inside their offices and homes and usually do the repairs themselves. Until recently PacBell had to send out a truck for every customer telephone outage report in order to determine whether the outage was in PacBell's lines or the customer's lines. Twenty thousand of these reports per day, costing $140 per truck, resulted in the discovery that the problem was in the customer's line, not PacBell's line. Eliminating these unnecessary trips would save millions. The solution? PacBell is installing a $10 circuit box at every point where PacBell's lines join a customer's line. When a report of a dead line comes in, PacBell sends a test signal to the circuit box at that site. If the PacBell line is good, the circuit box will return the signal. Now PacBell will know instantly whether or not a reported problem is in the customer's line without sending out a $140 truck (unless it is a company line problem). While one result is a savings for the company of an estimated $2 million per day, another result is the loss of thousands of line repair and truck maintenance jobs.

The automotive industry has turned to computer-aided design (CAD) technology to design its automobiles. In the past, when a new automobile design was completed, a large-scale model had to be built so that the design could be tested. The models were built by skilled model makers. Once tests were complete, a modified design would be produced, requiring another test model to be built for further testing. This process continued iteratively through many designs and models until the test results were acceptable and the model would go into

> *To Think About:* Does management have any obligation to maintain jobs and the skills of its current employees when considering downsizing through technology-based productivity increases? If so, what criteria might you suggest to use in making such decisions? In either case, explain your answer.

production. However, using CAD systems, completed designs are tested on the computer rather than by a physical model. Models are built only for the final phases of design. While the process cuts months out of the new model cycle and saves a great deal of money, many model makers, skilled in working with chisels, routers, and sanders have lost their jobs. Earl Hartman, a spokesman for the United Auto Workers (UAW) local 160 union in Warren, Michigan, said during a 1994 strike against the giant General Motors Technology Center that "We understand the corporation has to maximize its use of new technology as it becomes available." He explained that "We aren't saying don't do that, just that we [the union members] should be the ones doing [the modeling.]"

GTE Corp. has turned to re-engineering in many functions. In its Garland, Texas, customer service office, workers who in the past had passed customer complaints on to repair technicians have now been authorized to resolve the problems themselves where possible, often using remote technology and telecommunications similar to the PacBell technology described above. GTE is also merging 12 operations centers into a single center to monitor the company's entire nationwide network. These and many other changes have relied upon technology to eliminate 17,000 GTE jobs by 1996. Some of these reductions will come through attrition, others by layoffs.

Apple Computer Co. has eliminated most of its receptionist jobs, replacing them with voice mail and pagers. Aetna Insurance is eliminating 4000 jobs of a total work force of 42,000 through automation of the policy issuing function. AT&T is using computer-based automation to reduce its long-distance operators to 15,000, down from 44,000 just a year earlier. Between installing automated teller machines (ATMs) and bank-by-phone computers, banks have reduced the number of tellers from 480,000 in 1983 to 301,000 in 1994. Computer and telecommunications technology are being used to read customer meters, eliminating many meter-reader jobs. Vending machine businesses are using automated sensors and a telecommunications network to check their machine inventories, eliminating many vending-machine checker jobs. All told, the evidence indicates that the work force of the 500 largest manufacturing companies in the United States has dropped by one third since 1979 (a loss of over 5 million jobs). Downsizing occurring as a result of re-engineering and of the application of information systems technology continues.

No one doubts that higher productivity as measured by increased production or company income per employee is critical to the survival of many companies and is a necessary and vital goal for management. Nonetheless, the trend toward job reduction raises problems. In many cases,

the remaining employees are angry, to the point that their loyalty to their company has been undermined because they know they could be next to go. It is unclear how this loss of motivation will affect the future effectiveness of these companies. A second problem that concerns analysts is the lack of new blood. Rex Adams, a vice president at Mobil Corp. observes that "Most of us have stopped bringing in young talent in adequate numbers to replace the talent that will be retiring over the next five to ten years."

The most fundamental question this trend raises is "What type of society are we creating when our largest organizations pursue the long-range goal of permanent job reduction?" The corollary to that question is, "What, if any, responsibility does management bear for the effects of the permanent elimination of these jobs?" The potential economic effect of this job trend is twofold. First, most of the workers whose positions are eliminated when re-engineering takes place will need other jobs—jobs which likely will not be available. During the period they are jobless and without income, the unemployed may need to be retrained or to move. Often they are without health care. How do these millions of people survive between jobs and what is the responsibility of management and society to those displaced in this way? The second question, perhaps even more fundamental, is "How will the economy survive if the total number of jobs is reduced or if high-paying skilled jobs are replaced by low-paying service

jobs?" Ultimately, for the economy to thrive, consumers must be able to purchase. One standard explanation historians offer for the coming of the Great Depression of the 1930s was that it was brought on by the loss of consumer spending power as unemployment grew during the 1920s in several key economic sectors such as agriculture. Observers raise another specter for us to reflect upon. Felix Rohatyn, the senior partner of the Lazard Frères investment bank, sees a work force with a permanent cleavage ruled by a highly trained and paid elite of 25 to 30 percent. He believes that a huge transfer of wealth has already occurred from many in the middle class to this permanent, small elite. A. M. Rosenthal, a *New York Times* columnist, adds that "the non-elite, the 70 percent or so, become the foundering, searching, angry, anxious people. They will not be qualified to find decent jobs after they are personally downsized." What is the responsibility of management and the government for replacing these lost jobs and for building the skills of our citizens so that the economy can continue to thrive and serve all the people?

Sources: Edmund L. Andrews, "A.T.&T. Will Cut 15,000 Jobs to Reduce Costs," *The New York Times*, February 11, 1994; Marc Levinson, "Thanks. You're Fired," *Newsweek*, May 23, 1994; Joan E. Rigdon, "Technological Gains Are Cutting Costs, and Jobs, in Services," *The Wall Street Journal*, February 24, 1994; A. M. Rosenthal, "The Real Revolution," *The New York Times* January 6, 1995.

reduced by information systems technology? Or will the cleavages be increased, permitting the "better off" to become still better off? When and if computing becomes ubiquitous, does this include the poor as well as the rich?

The answers to these questions are clearly not known; the differential impact of systems technology on various groups in society is not well studied. What is known is that information and knowledge, and access to these resources through educational institutions and public libraries, are inequitably distributed. (On the basis of a 1993 survey of 55,000 households, the Census Bureau estimated that 37.5 percent of whites were using computers at home, at work, or in places like public libraries, compared to 25 percent of blacks and 22 percent of Hispanic people [Williams, 1995].) Access to computers is distributed inequitably along racial and social class lines as are many other information resources. Left uncorrected, we could end up creating a society of information haves, computer literate and skilled versus a large group of information have-nots, computer illiterate and unskilled.

Poor children attending poor school districts are less likely to use computers at school. Children from wealthy homes are five times as likely to use microcomputers for schoolwork than poor children. Whites are three times more likely to use computers at home for schoolwork than African-Americans. Schools and other institutions make up for some of the social disparities in access in computing, but not all. We could potentially create a society of information haves and information have-nots.

Health Risks: RSI, CVS, and Technostress

In 1980, at the beginning of the microcomputer revolution, no one thought that by 1992 business would be paying $20 billion a year to compensate and treat victims of the most important occupational disease today: **repetitive stress injury (RSI)**. RSI occurs when muscle groups are forced through the same repetitive actions often with high-impact loads (like tennis) or tens of thousands of repetitions under low-impact loads (like working at a computer keyboard.)

The single largest source of RSI is computer keyboards. Forty-six million Americans use computers at work, and 185,000 cases of RSI are reported each year according to the National Center for Health Statistics. The most common kind of computer-related RSI is **carpal tunnel syndrome (CTS)** in which pressure on the median nerve through the wrist's bony structure called a "carpal tunnel" produces pain. The pressure is caused by constant repetition of keystrokes: In a single shift a word processor may perform 23,000 keystrokes. Symptoms of carpal tunnel syndrome include numbness, shooting pain, inability to grasp objects, and tingling. Over 1.89 million workers have been diagnosed with carpal tunnel syndrome.

RSI is avoidable. Designing workstations for a neutral wrist position (using a wrist rest to support the wrist), proper monitor stands, and footrests all contribute to proper posture and reduced RSI. New ergonomically correct keyboards are also an option, although their efficacy has yet to be clearly established. These measures should be backed up by frequent rest breaks, rotation of employees to different jobs, and moving toward voice or scanner data entry. RSI presents a serious challenge to management, as the second Window on Management illustrates.

RSI is not the only occupational illness caused by computers: Back and neck pain, leg stress, and foot pain also result from poor ergonomic designs of workstations (see Tables 5.7 and 5.8).

Computer vision syndrome (CVS) refers to any eye strain condition related to cathode ray tube (CRT) use. Its symptoms are headaches, blurred vision, dry and irritated eyes. The symptoms are usually temporary (Furger, 1993).

The newest computer-related malady is **technostress**, defined as a computer-use induced stress and whose symptoms are aggravation, hostility toward humans, impatience, and enervation. According to the National Council on Compensation

repetitive stress injury (RSI) Occupational disease that occurs when muscle groups are forced through the same, repetitive actions with high impact loads or tens of thousands of repetitions with low impact loads.

carpal tunnel syndrome (CTS) Type of RSI in which pressure on the median nerve through the wrist's bony carpal tunnel structure produces pain.

computer vision syndrome (CVS) Eye strain condition related to cathode ray tube (CRT) use, with symptoms including headaches, blurred vision, and dry, irritated eyes.

technostress Stress induced by computer use whose symptoms include aggravation, hostility toward humans, impatience, and enervation.

Table 5.7	OSHA Ergonomic Risk Factors
Intermittent keying	
Intensive keying	
Neck twisting/bending	
Wrist bending	
Prolonged mouse use	
Prolonged sitting	
Sitting without solid foot support	
Lighting (poor illumination or glare)	

Source: Mary E. Thyfault, "OSHA Clamps Down," *Information Week*, November 21, 1994.

Table 5.8	Computer-Related Diseases
Disease/Risk	Incidence
RSI	185,000 new cases a year
Other joint diseases	Unknown
Computer vision syndrome	10 million cases a year
Miscarriage	Unknown, related to manufacturing chemicals
Technostress	5 million to 10 million cases
VDT radiation	Unknown

Insurance, occupational disease claims for stress has doubled in 1980 (from 5 percent to 10 percent of claims), and in California stress claims for compensation have increased 500 percent since 1980. The California Workers Compensation Institute has concluded that exposure to computer-intense environments is a major factor in stress disease (McPartlin, 1990; Brod, 1982). The problem according to experts is that humans working continuously with computers come to expect other humans and human institutions to behave like computers, providing instant response, attentiveness, and with an absence of emotion. Computer-intense workers are aggravated when put on hold during a phone call, tend to yell or mutter at ATM machines that are slow, become incensed or alarmed when their PCs take a few seconds longer to perform a task, lack empathy for humans, and seek out friends who mirror the characteristics of their machines. Technostress is thought to be related to high levels of job turnover in the computer industry, high levels of early retirement from computer-intense occupations, and elevated levels of drug and alcohol abuse.

The incidence of technostress is not known but is thought to be in the millions in the United States and growing rapidly. Although frequently denied as a problem by management, computer-related jobs now top the list of stressful occupations based on health statistics in several industrialized countries. The costs worldwide of stress are put at $200 billion. In the United Kingdom, 10 percent of the gross national product is eaten up by the effects of stress, not all of it computer related (McPartlin, 1993).

To date the role of CRT radiation in occupational disease has not been proven. Video display terminals (VDTs) emit nonionizing electric and magnetic fields at low frequencies. These rays enter the body and have unknown effects on enzymes, molecules, chromosomes, and cell membranes. Early studies suggesting a link between low-level EMFs (electromagnetic fields) and miscarriages have been contradicted by one later, superior study published in 1991 (Schnorr, 1991; Stevens, 1991). Longer-term studies are investigating low-level electromagnetic fields and birth defects, stress, low birth weight, and other diseases. All manufacturers have reduced CRT emissions since the early 1980s, and European countries like Sweden have adopted very stiff radiation emission standards.

The computer has become a part of our lives—personally as well as socially, culturally, and politically. Like so many technologies that came before, information systems technology can be used to elevate the human spirit and well-being. But like other technologies, it often acts as a mirror, reflecting our foibles and even exaggerating them at times. We did not analyze the ethical, social, and political issues of each social impact in this section, but they should be obvious to readers. It is unlikely the issues and our choices will become easier in the near future as information technology continues to transform our world. The development of a national electronic superhighway described in the Window on Technology suggests that all the ethical and social issues we have described will be heightened further as we move into the first digital century.

MANAGING RSI

In December 1994, Chase Manhattan Bank N.A. announced a $2 million comprehensive program meant to prevent repetitive strain injuries (RSI) despite the lack of any signs of a rise in workers' compensation cases from RSI. In the same month, the Occupational Safety and Health Administration (OSHA) of the United States government began circulating a draft proposal for a new regulation forcing companies to address ergonomic issues despite the growing anti-government regulation sentiment that accompanied the Republican party electoral victory the previous month. What is behind this rise in concern over RSI, how serious is the problem, and what is management doing about it?

The Chase RSI prevention program will include a 90-minute training session on ergonomics for its 34,000 employees worldwide. All employees will be given adjustable chairs and offered the option of a telephone operator headset, an anti-glare screen for each computer, and a chair support. Chase is also experimenting with the Microsoft Corp. Natural Keyboard (which Microsoft claims was designed after extensive ergonomic and usability research). According to Craig Goldman, Chase's chief information officer, Chase "hasn't seen a rise in workers' compensation cases yet from RSI, but we're doing this to get out ahead of the curve." Through 1994 Chase was processing fewer than 35 RSI claims per year. The reason for the program is that "If we can reduce injuries and workers' compensation costs while retaining good workers and increasing morale, it will be worthwhile," according to Linda Ellwood, a Chase vice president in corporate technology and information services.

Other corporate programs have been established to address the issue. For example, US West Inc., the Englewood, Colorado, telecommunica-

tions company, has established an ergonomics team. Levi Strauss & Co., the San Francisco–based clothing manufacturer, has set up a cross-department office ergonomics team that meets monthly to implement ergonomic strategy and even publishes an ergonomics newsletter.

The proposed new OSHA regulations would require companies to identify and address ergonomic issues or face a risk of a $7000 fine for every employee. The regulations would cover more than 120 million workers. The regulation would define risky activities to include intensive typing, prolonged mouse use, sitting without foot support, and poor lighting (including glare). The proposal has generated vocal opposition. The National Association of Manufacturers is building a coalition with the goal of making certain whatever OSHA does is based on sound scientific evidence and economic impact analysis. Harold Gardner believes that the regulations "potentially . . . could have a devastating impact on companies in terms of increasing workers' compensation costs." Gardner is a physician who is also a co-founder of the Cheyenne, Wyoming, firm, Options and Choice Inc., which closely monitors health and safety issues.

Why all of this activity? One answer is the threat of lawsuits. The most serious lawsuits have been product liability cases filed against the manufacturers of computer equipment, particularly keyboard producers. Such lawsuits tend to focus on the failure of manufacturers to warn users of potential dangers in the use of their products. For example, in June 1994, Pat Piester of Providence, Rhode Island, filed a suit against IBM for $11.5 million—$1.5 million for actual damages and $10 million in punitive damages. Her lawyer, Steven Phillips of Levy Phillips & Konigsberg of New York, says he has evidence that IBM knew that its products cause RSI, but the

company did not make the information available to the purchasing public. "We have thousands of internal documents to that effect," he claims.

> **To Think About:** *If you were a corporate vice-president with responsibility for corporate safety, what policies would you recommend to your CEO regarding RSI? Explain your recommendations.*

In some cases, companies are beginning to sue equipment makers. Phillips explains the phenomenon this way, "Say you just bought a $70 million computer system, but the vendor neglected to tell you about the $100 million bill to ergonomically refit your workplace, plus union trouble. You're going to want redress." The New York Times, joined by its employees, is suing some manufacturers. At the same time they are working with IBM to develop speech-recognition terminals which would greatly reduce the amount of typing its reporting and editorial staff need to do.

In a few cases employees are suing their employers for their failure to carry workers' compensation that covers RSI-afflicted workers. In one lawsuit, Grace Budd, a 48-year-old medical transcriptionist became unemployed when she "started getting feelings like electrical shocks in [her] hands." When her doctor diagnosed her problem as carpal tunnel syndrome (CTS), she sued her former employers for lost wages, claiming that her illness was the result of poorly maintained equipment and a Draconian work schedule. Most employers, however, are shielded from any lawsuits because state workers' compensation laws remove liability from companies and pay workers directly for lost income.

Some lawyers are advocating that employees sue under the Americans with Disabilities Act of 1992 (ADA) in order to force employers to accommodate the special needs of those who have such injuries but want to continue to work. Under such lawsuits, "I don't have to prove what caused the injury," says Laura Einstein, a Washington, DC, attorney who is representing employees in a lawsuit against USAir. After all, she points out, her clients are already receiving workmen's compensation.

The effect of all of the lawsuits is unclear. Although several thousand suits have been filed, very few have made their way through the courts to a decision. In one well-known case, Compaq Computer Corp. successfully defended itself against an RSI suit. It claimed ignorance that its keyboards could cause injuries. However, this defense will not work a second time. Compaq is now planning to place warning labels on all of its keyboards urging users to pay attention to safety and comfort. The label reads, "Warning! To reduce risk of serious injury to hands, wrists or other joints, read safety & comfort guide." The guide is supplied with every keyboard it sells. In another case, Computer Consoles Inc. (now a part of Northern Telecom Ltd.) reached an out-of-court settlement with its workers. Some legal experts fear that lawsuits will proliferate and will begin to spread to chair and table manufacturers.

Despite all of this activity, the actual risk posed by computer technology is unclear. Medical experts disagree. For example, some experts claim that RSI is caused by one factor, the keyboard, however, others think it is a combination of factors. Despite its decision to place warnings on its keyboards, Compaq Computer claims there are no scientific studies proving a link between keyboards and hand and arm disorders such as CTS. Dorothy Strunk highlights the lack of adequate knowledge by asking "How many motions in a task make it a hazard? Is it the 31st, 50th, or 60th repetition?"

What about solutions? Many manufacturers are now producing ergonomic products such as keyboards, arm rests, and wrist splints. For instance, more than 20 manufacturers are producing wrist braces. Lexmark International has just introduced another ergonomic keyboard, the Select-Ease Keyboard, which is split down the middle. The user is able to set each half of the keyboard at the appropriate, comfortable angle needed for that hand. However, their efficacy is in doubt. Alan Hedge, professor of human factors at Cornell University in Ithaca, New York, has recently completed a study of forearm rests and found them to be of no help. The study

concluded that users found them too uncomfortable if they were adjusted for the correct wrist angle, and yet if adjusted for the comfort of the arm, the wrist angles were wrong. As for keyboards, Robert F. Bettenorf, the president of the Institute for Office Ergonomics, Inc., in Manchester Center, Vermont, claims "there is no scientific research to support [ergonomic keyboard] efficacy." He adds that "informed medical opinion is that [wrist braces] should not be worn while working." Despite these conclusions, a recent survey of large corporations concluded that 92 percent of such companies include wrist braces in their safety programs.

Sources: Doug Bartholomew, "OSHA Clamps Down," *Information Week*, November 21, 1994; Doug Bartholomew, "Minimizing Risks," *Information Week*, December 26, 1991; Mitch Betts, "Jury's Still Out on Worth of Stress-Injury Gadgets," *Computerworld*, June 6, 1994; Edward Cone, "Cause and Effect," *Information Week*, June 27, 1994; Edward Cone, "Keyboard Injuries, Who Should Pay?" *Information Week*, June 27, 1994; Scott McCartney, "Compaq to Put Warnings on Keyboards About Risk of Repetitive-Stress Injuries," *The Wall Street Journal*, August 17, 1994; and A. M. Rosenthal, "The Real Revolution," *The New York Times*, January 6, 1995.

Apple Computer Corporation offers an ergonomically designed keyboard and mouse. The adjustable keyboard and mouse can be positioned to meet the needs of any user.

THE COMING OF A NATIONAL DIGITAL SUPERHIGHWAY RAISES MANY ETHICAL AND SOCIAL ISSUES

In 1989, Congress passed the High Performance Computing Act that provided $3 billion in seed money to spur the development of supercomputer centers in the United States and a very high-capacity network called the National Research Education Network (NREN) to connect universities and research centers. The bill was spearheaded by then-Senator Albert Gore, who went on to become vice-president of the United States in 1993. Gore and President Bill Clinton began building on the High Performance Computing Act by suggesting a much larger-scale national computing network to connect individuals, businesses, libraries, research centers, and universities. This national computing network would be able to deliver data, voice, and video images rapidly to the household, enough to be called the "everything network of your dreams."

Here are just some of the projected benefits: Students could do research using the National Library of Congress, or any library in the country with full text retrieval possible; medical care would improve because patient records could be transferred anywhere they were needed; remote diagnosis by faraway specialists would be possible; scientists and engineers around the world could cooperate on the design of new products; video fans could call up any movie and view it; working at home would be common because there would be as much information at home as in the office; business would improve because the network could act as a huge order entry system, eliminating paper waste and slow response time.

Briefly, the social impact of a national supernetwork is likely to be as great as the building of the transcontinental railway and the interstate high-

way system combined. The cost: hundreds of billions of dollars.

The national computing network requires rewiring America with high-capacity fiberoptic cable (see Chapter 9) to the household or neighborhood switch (from which ordinary twisted wire can be used to transmit into individual households); new hardware switches and/or upgrading the existing telephone system; and new software.

Who should build the network (and pay for it)? Owners of existing networks—like AT&T and other long-distance companies—want the government to stay out and instead want to evolve the telephone network and existing technologies. Critics charge the phone companies will never invest the money needed, and existing network services are too slow anyway. Moreover, if private enterprise develops the network, they might charge so much that universities, libraries, and homeowners could not afford to use it.

The Clinton administration and groups such as the Telecommunications Policy Roundtable, a coalition of over 70 public interest organizations, think that the private sector should build the information highway but want to make sure that everyone can use the services. Vice President Al Gore has reiterated that schools should have the same access to the information superhighway as homes. The new services, including picture telephones, two-way television, and links to Library of Congress archives should be available to "virtually everyone" just as basic telephone service is now.

Universal service was not much of a problem when the telephone service was run by regulated monopolies such as AT&T. Regulations allowed carriers to charge higher rates to business customers to subsidize rural and poor residential customers who couldn't afford

to pay the actual cost of their service. Now the telecommunications industry is becoming deregulated with Congress and the administration both supporting

> *To Think About: What impact will the proposed National Computing Network have on the moral dimensions described above, especially on information rights and obligations, property rights, and accountability and control? If the network were to become as important as proponents argue, what happens if network service is disrupted, even temporarily? Who should build the national computing network? What analogies to transcontinental railroads, interstate highways, and telephone utilities seem appropriate? Is it in the interests of U.S. citizens and taxpayers to fund this network?*

the rewriting of the nation's communications laws to encourage competition. This new wave of deregulation will remove remaining restrictions that have prevented local telephone companies from offering long-distance service and have prevented telephone companies from linking their networks to those of cable television. But telecommunications companies would have trouble subsidizing money-losing network service to poor and rural customers if other companies were fiercely competing for their profitable customers. How can builders of the information highway avoid creating a society of information haves and have-nots?

Sources: Mark Lewyn, "The Information Age Isn't Just for the Elite," *Business Week,* January 10, 1994; Computer Systems Policy Project, "Perspectives on the National Information Infrastructure" (January 12, 1993), and Telecommunications Policy Roundtable, 1994.

MANAGEMENT ACTIONS: A CORPORATE CODE OF ETHICS

Many corporations have developed far-reaching corporate IS codes of ethics—Federal Express, IBM, American Express, and Merck and Co. But most firms have not developed these codes of ethics, which leaves them at the mercy of fate and their employees in the dark about expected correct behavior. There is some dispute concerning a general code of ethics (about 40 percent of the American Fortune 500 firms have such codes) versus a specific information systems code of ethics (about 40 percent of Fortune 500 firms). As managers, you should strive to develop an IS specific set of ethical standards for each of the five moral dimensions:

- *Information rights and obligations.* A code should cover topics like employee E-mail privacy, workplace monitoring, treatment of corporate information, and policies on customer information.

- *Property rights and obligations.* A code should cover topics like software licenses, ownership of firm data and facilities, ownership of software created by employees on company hardware, and software copyrights. Specific guidelines for contractual relationships with third parties should be covered as well.

- *Accountability and control.* The code should specify a single individual responsible for all information systems, and underneath this individual others who are responsible for individual rights, the protection of property rights, system quality, and quality of life (e.g., job design, ergonomics, employee satisfaction). Responsibilities for control of systems, audits, and management should be clearly defined. The potential liabilities of systems officers and the corporation should be detailed in a separate document.

- *System quality.* The code should describe the general levels of data quality and system error that can be tolerated with detailed specifications left to specific projects. The code should require that all systems attempt to estimate data quality and system error probabilities.

- *Quality of life.* The code should state that the purpose of systems is to improve the quality of life for customers and for employees by achieving high levels of product quality, customer service, and employee satisfaction and human dignity through proper ergonomics, job and work flow design, and human resource development.

Management Challenges

1. Understanding the moral risks of new technology. Rapid technological change means that all the following change as well: the choices facing individuals, the balance of risk and reward, and the probabilities of apprehension for wrongful acts. In this environment it will be important for management to conduct an ethical and social impact analysis of new technologies. One might take each of the moral dimensions described in this chapter and briefly speculate on how a new technology will impact each dimension. There will be no right answers for how to behave but there should be considered management judgment on the moral risks of new technology.

2. Establishing corporate ethics policies that include IS issues. As managers you will be responsible for developing corporate ethics policies and for enforcing them and explaining them to employees. Historically, the IS area is the last to be consulted and much more attention has been paid to financial integrity and personnel policies. But from what you now know after reading this chapter, it is clear your corporation should have an ethics policy in the IS area covering such issues as privacy, property, accountability, system quality, and quality of life. The challenge will be in educating non-IS managers to the need for these policies, as well as educating your work force.

Summary

1. Understand the relation among ethical, social, and political issues raised by information systems. Ethical, social, and political issues are closely related in an information society. Ethical issues confront individuals who must choose a course of action, often in a situation where two or more ethical principles are in conflict (a dilemma).

Social issues spring from ethical issues. Societies must develop expectations in individuals about the correct course of action, and social issues then are debates about the kinds of situations and expectations that societies should develop so that individuals behave correctly. Political issues spring from social conflict and have to do largely with laws that prescribe behavior and seek to use the law to create situations where individuals behave correctly.

2. Identify the main moral dimensions of an information society and apply them to specific situations. There are five main moral dimensions that tie together ethical, social, and political issues in an information society. These moral dimensions are information rights and obligations, property rights, accountability and control, system quality, and quality of life.

3. Employ an ethical analysis to difficult situations. An ethical analysis is a five-step methodology for analyzing a situation. The method involves identifying the facts, values, stakeholders, options, and consequences of actions. Once completed, you can begin to consider what ethical principle you should apply to a situation in order to arrive at a judgment.

4. Understand specific ethical principles for conduct. Six ethical principles are available to judge your own conduct (and that of others). These principles are derived independently from several cultural, religious, and intellectual traditions. They are not hard and fast rules and may not apply in all situations. The principles are the Golden Rule, Immanuel Kant's Categorical Imperative, Descartes' rule of change, the Utilitarian Principle, the Risk Aversion Principle, and the ethical "no free lunch" rule.

5. Develop corporate policies for ethical conduct. For each of the five moral dimensions, corporations should develop an ethics policy statement to assist individuals and to encourage the correct decisions. The policy areas are as follows. Individual information rights: Spell out corporate privacy and due process policies. Property rights and obligations: Clarify how the corporation will treat property rights of software owners. Accountability and control: Clarify who is responsible and accountable for information. System quality: Identify methodologies and quality standards to achieve. Quality of life: Identify corporate policies on family, computer crime, decision making, vulnerability, job loss, and health risks.

Key Terms

Ethics	Descartes' rule of change	Trade secret	Repetitive stress injury
Information rights	Utilitarian Principle	Copyright	(RSI)
Responsibility	Risk Aversion Principle	Patent	Carpal tunnel syndrome
Accountability	Ethical "no free lunch" rule	Warranty	(CTS)
Liability	Privacy	Negligence	Computer vision syndrome
Due process	Fair Information Practices	Strict liability in tort	(CVS)
Immanuel Kant's	(FIP)	Computer crime	Technostress
Categorical Imperative	Intellectual property	Computer abuse	

Review Questions

1. In what ways are ethical, social, and political issues connected? Give some examples.
2. What are the key technological trends which heighten ethical concerns?
3. What are the differences between responsibility, accountability, and liability?
4. What are the five steps in an ethical analysis?
5. Identify six ethical principles.
6. What is a professional code of conduct?
7. What are meant by "privacy" and "fair information practices"?
8. What are the three different regimes that protect intellectual property rights?
9. What are the three categories of liability?
10. Why is it so difficult to hold software services liable for failure or injury?
11. What is the most common cause of system quality problems?
12. Name four "quality of life" impacts of computers and information systems.
13. What is technostress, and how would you measure it?
14. Name three management actions that could reduce RSI injuries.

Discussion Questions

1. Why should anyone care about unemployment caused by re-engineering? Won't these workers be rehired at some point in the future when business gets better?
2. If everyone copied software, there would be no real market for software products, and producers of software would go out of business. Is this really true?

What ethical principle is being applied in this statement? Discuss.

3. Should producers of software-based services like ATMs be held liable for economic injuries suffered when their systems fail?

Group Projects

1. With three or four of your classmates, develop a corporate ethics code on privacy. Be sure to consider E-mail privacy, employee monitoring of work sites as well as hallways, entrances, and restrooms. You should also consider corporate use of information about employees concerning their off-job behavior (e.g., life style, marital arrangements, and so forth). Present your ethics code to the class.

2. With three or four of your classmates, interview managers of your university's information systems department concerning ethics policies in the systems area. Does your university have an ethics policy for students and employees? What is it? You could also interview a local firm rather than university officials. Present your findings to the class.

Case Study

WHO IS RESPONSIBLE?

Hopper Specialty Co.

Hopper Specialty is a retail vendor of industrial hardware located in Farmington, New Mexico. Working out of a small storefront, the company primarily serves the area's oil and gas drillers. The owner, Joe Hopper, nurtured the business during its first ten years (1978 to 1988) until it had become the largest distributor of industrial hardware in the northwest corner of the state. Oil and gas drills work 24 hours per day, and every minute a drill is shut down, the driller loses income—time truly is money. Therefore, drillers depend upon hardware dealers like Hopper Specialty to supply them with parts very quickly in order to minimize losses when problems occur. For example, Hopper Specialty's contract with its largest customer, BHP Mineral International Inc., contained a clause in which Hopper was required to fill 90 percent of any BHP parts order within 48 hours. As a result of these business conditions, in order to be competitive, Hopper Specialty must maintain a very large inventory of a wide range of products. The key to success in Hopper's business is rapid customer service.

Hopper Specialty developed a reputation for reliability, and so it thrived.

As the company grew, its inventory ballooned in size and became very comprehensive. Eventually Hopper decided he needed a computerized system to manage all of his inventory. In 1987 he began a search for software that supports the sales and inventory functions for inventory-intensive companies. One such application software package he saw demonstrated was Warehouse Manager from NCR (we will discuss NCR in more detail below). The software promised to track thousands of items in inventory, keep prices current, warn when items were running low, generate invoices automatically, and even balance the monthly books—all at the touch of a few keystrokes. Hopper was impressed with the response time of less than a second to retrieve a customer invoice and investigated the product further. At year-end 1987, he placed an order for the product. The main reason he settled on Warehouse Manager was that he had only one company to turn to for support—NCR promised support for the whole system, including hardware, the

various software components, and terminals. Additionally, he was impressed with the repeated statements by the NCR sales staff that the package was thoroughly debugged and operating smoothly at more than 200 sites. NCR began installing the product in the spring of 1988. Hopper was so excited by the prospect of the improved customer service that the computer system would bring that in May he celebrated with a large public outdoor barbecue under a circus tent, serving enough food to feed the town. The guest of honor, of course, was Warehouse Manager, and two NCR representatives attended the party, mingled with the guests, and sang the system's praises to whomever they met.

When the installation was complete in September of that year, the company turned the system on and problems immediately surfaced. The store clerks found that response times of 30 seconds to several minutes were common. In addition, the terminals would lock up 20 to 30 times per day. Delayed response times left Hopper's customers waiting in long lines. Moreover, employees soon discovered that the prices the system quoted were often in error. For example, an industrial hose that was supposed to be priced at $17 per foot was quoted on the system at $30 per foot. The company carried too many products for the clerks to know all the prices, causing Charles Brannig, Hopper Specialty's general manager, to observe that "our counter people didn't know it was the wrong price by looking at it." Moreover, the problem occurred erratically so that no one could know which prices would be wrong. Even more serious data problems occurred. The computer could indicate that the company had 50 units of an item that was actually out-of-stock with 50 on order. Or, it would show an item as out-of-stock and on order when in fact it was on the shelf. Again, where the errors would occur was unpredictable.

In early 1989 Hopper had his staff take six inventories within a two-month period, and every time the computer data differed from actual count of inventory. Lines grew longer, with customers now even waiting on the sidewalk. Hopper expressed his reaction upon seeing the lines by exclaiming, "You could pull your hair out." The computer system was often down, causing the clerks to resort to hand writing the invoices. Tracy Irwin, Hopper Specialty's office manager, found herself working 14-hour days and coming in on weekends (with her children) just to work on the problems created by the computer system.

Hopper remained in close touch with NCR throughout this ordeal. NCR representatives told him that his problems were isolated, that the system was running well elsewhere. They claimed the source of the problem was employee inexperience; their technicians even suggested that some of the problems were caused by static electricity emanating from Irwin's nylon stockings.

One problem Hopper faced was that he had plenty of competition; his customers had alternatives, if they were dissatisfied with Hopper Specialty's service. For example, just two doors down the street was Advance Supply & Pump

Co., which began to advertise its excellent inventory and top-notch service. Hopper watched his customer base dwindle as many began to patronize his competition, forcing him to reduce his stock because he could no longer afford to carry such a large and extensive inventory. The result, of course, was that he often would not have the required item in stock. "The whole thing just snowballed," exclaimed the frustrated Hopper.

In early 1992, Hopper hired an outside accounting firm to try to make sense out of his accounting books. They discovered that many numbers were missing from the company's computerized general ledger system—Warehouse Manager had randomly erased data. Britton Smith, the external accountant, explained that the "records were in terrible shape. Nothing was ever right. . . . We were continually trying to get inventory correct for financial statements and their income tax returns." To save his business, Hopper was forced to put $350,000 of his own personal funds into it.

In April, 1993 BHP canceled its contract, worth between $350,000 and $500,000 annually. Richard Richter, BHP's purchasing agent, explained that he had "met with them personally three times. They told us at that time they were trying to get a new computer system up and running. The longer it went, the worse it got." Now Hopper no longer had a choice. He began to lay off employees, and those who remained found their health-care benefits reduced. He also stopped using the computer system—the company's inventory was so low it was no longer needed. Hopper decided to sue NCR.

As of this writing, the lawsuit had not been settled. Hopper stated in the suit that his company has suffered a loss of $4.2 million in profits due to the system. NCR claims that Hopper cannot sue for that amount, that their contract limited NCR liability to the cost of the computer system, which they say was $184,567. Even here they disagreed, as Hopper claims the system cost $284,821. NCR has also asked that the suit be dismissed on the grounds that it

was filed too late. New Mexico's statute-of-limitations for this type of suit is four years, and NCR states that Hopper knew of his problems for more than four years before they filed suit.

NCR.

NCR is a $6 billion computer company headquartered in Dayton, Ohio. In 1991 the company was acquired by AT&T and was renamed AT&T Global Information Services (we refer to it as NCR throughout this case study). Overall NCR sold approximately 40 copies of Warehouse Manager from 1987 through 1992. More than two dozen of those sales ended with lawsuits being filed against NCR.

The Warehouse Manager application software was developed by Taylor Management Systems Inc. to run on Burroughs Corp. (now Unisys Corp.) computers with a Burroughs operating system. Taylor Management is now defunct. In 1987 copies of the software were running smoothly at more than 200 sites, all on computers using Burroughs computers and operating systems. The application could not run on NCR computers without being modified for the NCR operating system. In 1986 NCR licensed Warehouse Manager from Taylor, with Taylor assuming responsibility for converting the software to run under NCR operating systems. Taylor also agreed to be responsible for maintaining the software once the NCR version was released. In April 1987, Warehouse Manager began to be installed on customers' NCR computers.

Trouble began immediately. In May 1987, Vogue Tyre & Rubber Co., an auto parts distributor in Skokie, Illinois, complained to NCR of "long delays, sloppy NCR service, inattention to detail, and 'Band-Aid' solutions to problems with its system." In August 1987, E. Kinast Distributors Inc., a Franklin Park, Illinois, wood-laminating company, complained to NCR that it hadn't been able to enter a single purchase order during the entire five weeks the system had been operating. William E. Schierer, the company's president, said, "We are shocked and dismayed at this crisis that NCR and its software vendor have created," and claimed the problem was costing the company $2000 per day.

According to NCR internal documents, during that summer and autumn virtually every installation site complained. All indicated that the system response time slowed to a crawl during busy periods. Workers also all complained that if more than one user attempted to access Warehouse Manager simultaneously, all the terminals would lock up (NCR engineers dubbed this phenomenon the "deadly embrace"). All the users were then forced to log off the computer and then log back on again to be able to resume use. However, when logging back on, the users found that the data that had been saved was often inexplicably altered and invalid (NCR employees named this phenomenon the "silent death").

In December 1987, another problem was documented. John W. Shearer, president of Burgman Industries, a Jacksonville, Florida, supplier of heavy construction parts, complained that his company's general ledger was infected with inaccurate data from Warehouse Manager. For example, he reported, one machine part that had cost the company $114 was priced for sale at 54 cents. "This software is so unprofessional and is riddled with so many bugs that it may actually put us out of business," he stated in his complaint.

NCR's response was to tell virtually all of its customers that their problems were isolated, that the system was running smoothly everywhere else. Despite the denials of problems, however, NCR did keep a full record of all the complaints they received.

Internally, NCR did not refuse to acknowledge that the software was troubled. In January 1988, NCR temporarily suspended sales of Warehouse Manager in order to permit its engineers to eliminate the many critical bugs. NCR and Taylor began feuding over the cause of the problems. NCR blamed Taylor and its software, while Taylor blamed the NCR hardware and its operating system. Eventually the two companies ended up in court over this issue as it related to the distribution of royalties.

In May 1988, NCR received two internal field reports that stated that Warehouse Manager had been "inadequately tested" prior to its release and "was performing unexpectedly badly in actual business settings." Nonetheless, in mid-1988 sales of the software package resumed. NCR was disappointed to find that only four or five copies were selling each month rather than the approximately thirty-five per month that had been forecast.

In 1992 NCR released a new version of the software. It did include improvements but was nonetheless still full of bugs. Later that year, NCR finally halted sales of Warehouse Manager for good. Mark Siegel, an NCR spokesperson, later admitted that NCR "did not serve our customers well," although he says that NCR didn't "intentionally deceive" its customers. Publicly he maintains that NCR is accepting full responsibility for the problems of Warehouse Manager.

As for the suits against NCR, the company claims (in a legal document) that it "had every reason to believe" that Taylor software worked on NCR computers. As for Hopper, NCR claims that "When NCR sold Hopper its system in 1987, NCR did not know what problems would arise with T[aylor] M[anagement] S[ystem]'s software." NCR says it "had every reason to believe" that Taylor software worked on its computers at that time. NCR has settled many of the lawsuits against it and has offered to settle them all on similar terms. However, all settlements include a provision binding all parties to secrecy. Publicly they deny responsibility and blame the flaws of Warehouse Manager on the application program they licensed from Taylor Management.

Source: Milo Geyelin, "Doomsday Device," *The Wall Street Journal*, August 8, 1994.

Case Study Questions

1. What managerial, technological, and organizational factors allowed the NCR-Hopper case to develop?

2. Which of the six ethical principles apply here?

3. We have described five moral dimensions of the information age. Pick one of these dimensions and describe the ethical, social, and political aspects of this case. Include in your discussion the role of Joe Hopper.

4. Hopper Specialty was a successful and growing business prior to the installation of Warehouse Management. Some believe that software can be responsible for a company's business failure. How do you assign responsibility for the drastic decline in Hopper Specialty's business? Explain your answer.

5. If you were a manager at Hopper Specialty Company, what would or could you have done to prevent the problems described here from occurring? What could NCR have done?

References

Anderson, Ronald El., Deborah G. Johnson, Donald Gotterbarn, and Judith Perrolle. "Using the New ACM Code of Ethics in Decision Making." *Communications of the ACM* 36, no.2 (February 1993).

Barlow, John Perry. "Electronic Frontier: Private Life in Cyberspace." *Communications of the ACM* 34, no. 8 (August 1991).

Bjerklie, David. "Does E-Mail Mean Everyone's Mail?" *InformationWeek* (January 3, 1994).

Brod, Craig. *Techno Stress—The Human Cost of the Computer Revolution.* Reading MA: Addison-Wesley (1982).

Brown Bag Software v. *Symantec Corp.* 960 F2D 1465 (Ninth Circuit, 1992).

Bulkeley, William M. "Databases Plagued by a Reign of Error." *The Wall Street Journal* (May 26, 1992).

Cafasso, Rosemary. "Rethinking Reengineering." *Computerworld* (March 15, 1993).

Caldwell, Bruce, with John Soat. "The Hidden Persuader." *InformationWeek* (November 19, 1990).

Carley, William M. "Rigging Computers for Fraud or Malice Is Often an Inside Job." *The Wall Street Journal* (August 27, 1992).

Collins, W. Robert, Keith W. Miller, Bethany J. Spielman, and Phillip Wherry. "How Good Is Good Enough? An Ethical Analysis of Software Construction and Use." *Communications of the ACM* 37, no.1 (January 1994).

Computer Systems Policy Project. "Perspectives on the National Information Infrastructure." January 12, 1993.

Couger, J. Daniel. "Preparing IS Students to Deal with Ethical Issues. *MIS Quarterly,* 13, no. 2 (June 1989).

Dejoie, Roy, George Fowler, and David Paradice, eds. *Ethical Issues in Information Systems.* Boston: Boyd & Fraser (1991).

Denning, Dorothy E. et al. "To Tap or Not to Tap." *Communications of the ACM* 36, no. 3 (March 1993).

"EMASS® Is Mobil's Mass Storage Solution." *Datamation* (September 15, 1993).

"Equifax Report on Consumers in the Information Age, a National Survey." Equifax Inc. (1992).

Feder, Barnaby J. "As Hand Injuries Mount, So Do the Lawsuits." *The New York Times* (June 8, 1992).

Furger, Roberta. "In Search of Relief for Tired, Aching Eyes." *PC World* (February 1993).

Gabriel, Trip. "Reprogramming a Convicted Hacker." *The New York Times* (January 14, 1995).

Graham, Robert L. "The Legal Protection of Computer Software." *Communications of the ACM* (May 1984).

Hiramatsu, Tsuyashi. "Protecting Telecommunications Privacy in Japan." *Communications of the ACM* 36, no. 8 (August 1993).

Joes, Kathryn. "EDS Set to Restore Cash-Machine Network." *The New York Times* (March 26, 1993).

King, Julia. "It's CYA Time." *Computerworld* (March 30, 1992).

Kling, Rob. "When Organizations Are Perpetrators: The Conditions of Computer Abuse and Computer Crime." In *Computerization & Controversy: Value Conflicts & Social Choices,* eds. Charles Dunlop and Rob Kling. New York: Academic Press (1991).

McPartlin, John P. "The Terrors of Technostress." *InformationWeek* (July 30, 1990).

McPartlin, John P. "Environmental Agency 'Held Hostage' by Outsourcer." *InformationWeek* (March 9, 1992).

McPartlin, John P. "A Question of Complicity." *InformationWeek* (June 22, 1992).

McPartlin, John P. "Ten Years of Hard Labor." *InformationWeek* (March 29, 1993).

Markoff, John. "Though Illegal, Copied Software is Now Common." *The New York Times* (July 27, 1992).

Markoff, John. "Computer Viruses: Just Uncommon Colds After All?" *The New York Times* (November 1, 1992).

Mason, Richard O. "Four Ethical Issues in the Information Age. *MIS Quarterly* 10, no. 1 (March 1986).

Mykytyn, Kathleen, Peter P. Mykytyn, Jr., and Craig W. Slinkman. "Expert Systems: A Question of Liability." *MIS Quarterly* 14, no. 1 (March 1990).

Neumann, Peter G. "Inside RISKS: Computers, Ethics and Values." *Communications of the ACM* 34, no. 7 (July 1991).

Neumann, Peter G. "Inside RISKS: Fraud by Computer." *Communications of the ACM* 35, no. 8 (August 1992).

Nissenbaum, Helen. "Computing and Accountability." *Communications of the ACM* 37, no. 1 (January 1994).

Office of the Mayor, New York City. "The Trillion Dollar Gamble" (1991).

Oz, Effy. "Ethical Standards for Information Systems Professionals." *MIS Quarterly* 16, no. 4 (December 1992).

Oz, Effy. *Ethics for the Information Age.* Dubuque, Iowa: W.C. Brown (1994).

Oz, Effy. "When Professional Standards Are Lax: The Confirm Failure and Its Lessons." *Communications of the ACM* 37, no. 10 (October 1994).

Pollack, Andrew. "San Francisco Law on VDTs Is Struck Down." *The New York Times* (February 14, 1992).

Ramirez, Anthony. "AT&T to Eliminate Many Operator Jobs." *The New York Times* (March 4, 1992).

Rifkin, Glenn. "The Ethics Gap." *Computerworld* (October 14, 1991).

Rifkin, Jeremy. "Watch Out for Trickle-Down Technology." *The New York Times* (March 16, 1993).

Rigdon, Joan E. "Frequent Glitches in New Software Bug Users." *The Wall Street Journal* (January 18, 1995).

Rotenberg, Marc. "Inside RISKS: Protecting Privacy." *Communications of the ACM* 35, no. 4 (April 1992).

Rotenberg, Marc. "Communications Privacy: Implications for Network Design." *Communications of the ACM* 36, no. 8 (August 1993).

Samuelson, Pamela. "The Ups and Downs of Look and Feel." *Communications of the ACM* 36 no. 4, (April 1989).

Samuelson, Pamela. "First Amendment Rights for Information Providers?" *Communications of the ACM* 34, no. 6 (June 1991).

Samuelsu, Pamela. "Digital Media and the Law." *Communications of the ACM* 34, no. 10 (October 1991).

Samuelson, Pamela. "Updating the Copyright Look and Feel Lawsuits." *Communications of the ACM* 35, no. 9 (September 1992).

Samuelson, Pamela. "Liability for Defective Electronic Information." *Communications of the ACM* 36, no. 1 (January 1993).

Samuelson, Pamela. "Computer Programs and Copyright's Fair Use Doctrine." *Communications of the ACM* 36, no. 9 (September 1993).

Samuelson, Pamela. "Copyright's Fair Use Doctrine and Digital Data." *Communications of the ACM* 37, no. 1 (January 1994).

Samuelson, Pamela. "Self Plagiarism or Fair Use?" *Communications of the ACM* 37, no. 8 (August 1994).

Schnorr, Teresa M. "Miscarriage and VDT Exposure." *New England Journal of Medicine* (March 1991).

Smith, H. Jeff. "Privacy Policies and Practices: Inside the Organizational Maze." *Communications of the ACM* 36, no. 12 (December 1993).

Sterling, Bruce. *The Hacker Crackdown: Law and Disorder on the Computer Frontier.* New York: Bantam Books (1992).

Stevens, William K. "Major U.S. Study Finds No Miscarriage Risk from Video Terminals," *The New York Times* (March 14, 1991).

Straub, Detmar W. Jr., and William D. Nance. "Discovering and Disciplining Computer Abuse in Organizations: A Field Study." *MIS Quarterly* 14, no. 1 (March 1990).

Straub, Detmar W., Jr., and Rosann Webb Collins. "Key Information Liability Issues Facing Managers: Software Piracy, Proprietary Databases, and Individual Rights to Privacy." *MIS Quarterly* 14, no. 2 (June 1990).

"Supercomputers Manage Holiday Stock," *The Wall Street Journal* (December 23, 1992).

Tabor, Mary W., with Anthony Ramirez. "Computer Savy, with an Attitude." *The New York Times* (July 23, 1992).

The Telecommunications Policy Roundtable. "Renewing the Commitment to a Public Interest Telecommunications Policy." *Communications of the ACM* 37, no. 1 (January 1994).

Tuerkheimer, Frank M. "The Underpinnings of Privacy Protection." *Communications of the ACM* 36, no. 8 (August, 1993).

United States Department of Health, Education and Welfare. Records, Computers and the Rights of Citizens. Cambridge: M.I.T. Press (1973).

Williams, Lena. "Computer Gap Names Blacks." *The New York Times* (May 25, 1995).

Wilson, Linda. "Devil in Your Data." *Information Week* (August 31, 1992).

Wolinsky, Carol, and James Sylvester. "Privacy in the Telecommunications Age." *Communications of the ACM* 35, no. 2 (February 1992).

Chrysler and GM: Can Information Technology Turn Around the U.S. Auto Industry?

This case illustrates how two giant American corporations, Chrysler and General Motors, have tried to use information technology to combat foreign and domestic competitors. The case explores the relationship between each firm's management strategy, organizational characteristics, and information systems. It poses the following question: To what extent can information technology solve the problems confronting the U.S. automobile industry?

On October 26, 1992, Robert C. Stempel resigned as chairman and CEO of the General Motors Corporation. Stempel was pressured to resign because he had not moved quickly enough to make the changes required to ensure the automotive giant's survival. To counter massive financial losses and plummeting market share, Stempel had announced ten months earlier that GM would have to close 21 of its North American plants and cut 74,000 of its 370,000 employees over 3 years. Stempel was replaced by a more youthful and determined management team headed by Jack Smith.

GM's plight reflected the depths of the decline of the once vigorous American automobile industry in the late 1980s. Year after year, as Americans came to view American-made cars as low in quality or not stylish, car buyers purchased fewer and fewer American cars, replacing them mostly with Japanese models.

Ironically, at about the same time, the Chrysler Corporation announced strong 1992 third-quarter earnings of $202 million. During the 1980s, Chrysler had struggled with rising costs and de-

clining sales of mass market cars. However, demand was strong for its minivans and the hot Jeep Grand Cherokee. A stringent cost-cutting crusade eliminated $4 billion in operating costs in just 3 years. The rest of the U.S. auto industry was still in a slump from prolonged recession and losses of market share to the Japanese.

Ten years before, Chrysler had been battling bankruptcy and GM was flush with cash. Had Chrysler finally turned itself around? Was this the beginning of the end for the world's largest automobile maker? What is the role of information systems in this tale of two auto makers and in the future of the U.S. automobile industry?

GENERAL MOTORS

General Motors, the world's largest auto maker, has more than 710,000 employees in 35 countries, meets $22 billion in payrolls, and deals with 28,000 suppliers. In the early 1990s, GM's U.S. auto business accounted for about 1.5 percent of the U.S. economy, down from 5 percent in the 1950s. Its sheer size has proved to be one of GM's greatest burdens.

For 70 years, GM operated along the lines laid down by CEO Alfred Sloan, who rescued the firm from bankruptcy in the 1920s. Sloan separated the firm into five separate operating groups and divisions (Chevrolet, Pontiac, Oldsmobile, Buick, and Cadillac). Each division functioned as a semi-autonomous company, with its own marketing operations. GM's management was a welter of bureaucracies.

GM covered the market with low-end Chevys and high-end Caddies. At the outset, this amalgam of top-down control and decentralized execution enabled GM to build cars at lower cost than its rivals; but it could also charge more for the quality and popularity of its models. By the 1960s, GM started having trouble building smaller cars to compete with imports and started eliminating differences among divisions. By the mid 1980s, GM had reduced differences among the divisions to the point where customers could not tell a Cadillac from a Chevrolet; the engines in low-end Chevys were also found in high-end Oldsmobiles. Its own brands started to compete with each other.

Under Roger Smith, CEO from 1981 to 1990, GM moved boldly, but often in the wrong direction. GM remained a far-flung vertically integrated corporation that at one time made up to 70 percent of its parts. Its costs were much higher than either its U.S. or Japanese competitors. Like many large manufacturing firms, its organizational culture resisted change. GM has made steady improvements in car quality, but its selection and styling have lagged behind its U.S. and Japanese rivals. GM's market share plunged from a peak of 52 percent in the early 1960s to just 35 percent today. In 1979, GM's market share was 46 percent.

GM created an entirely new Saturn automobile with a totally new division, labor force, and production system based on the Japanese "lean production" model. Saturn workers and managers share information, authority, and decision making. The Saturn car was a market triumph. But Saturn took seven years to roll out the first model and drained $5 billion from other car projects. GM had been selling Saturn at a loss to build up market share.

In 1992, GM's labor costs were $2358 per car, compared to $1872 for Chrysler and $1563 for Ford. That made GM 40 percent less productive than Ford. These figures do not begin to approach those of the Japanese, whose automotive productivity surpasses all U.S. corporations.

CHRYSLER

In auto-industry downturns, Chrysler was always the weakest of Detroit's Big Three auto makers (GM, Ford, and Chrysler). Founded in the 1930s by Walter P. Chrysler through a series of mergers with smaller companies like Dodge and DeSoto, Chrysler prided itself on superior engineering, especially in engines and suspensions. In the 1940s and 1950s, Chrysler grew into a small, highly centralized firm with very little vertical integration. Unlike Ford and GM, Chrysler relied on external suppliers for 70 percent of its major components and subassemblies, be-

coming more an auto assembler than a huge vertically integrated manufacturer like GM. Unlike its larger competitors, Chrysler did not develop a global market for its cars to cushion domestic downturns. Chrysler's centralized and smaller firm could potentially move faster and be more innovative than its larger competitors.

During the late 1980s, Chrysler lost several hundred thousand units of sales annually because it did not make improvements in engine development and in its mass market cars, the small subcompacts and large rear-wheel drive vehicles. There was no new family of midpriced, midsized cars to rival Ford's Taurus or Honda's Accord. Chrysler's key car models and brands could not be distinguished from each other. Customers migrated to other brands. Chrysler's response, the Spirit and Acclaim, brought out in 1988, were ultraconservative in styling. Yet Chrysler lavished funds on specialty niches such as coupes and convertibles. By the early 1990s, fierce price cutting had upped Chrysler's breakeven point (the number of cars the firm had to sell to start making a profit) to 1.9 million units, up from 1.4 million.

GM'S INFORMATION SYSTEMS STRATEGY

Despite heavy investment in information technology, GM's information systems were virtually archaic. It had more than 100 mainframes and 34 computer centers but had no centralized system to link computer operations or to coordinate operations from one department to another. Each division and group had its own hardware and software so that the design group could not interact with production engineers via computer.

GM adopted a "shotgun" approach, pursuing several high-technology paths simultaneously in the hope that one or all of them would pay off. GM also believed it could overwhelm competitors by outspending them. GM does spend more than its competitors on information systems. It spends 2.5 percent of sales on information systems,

whereas Ford spends 1.6 percent and Chrysler 0.9 percent of sales on information systems budgets. GM also tried to use information technology to totally overhaul the way it does business.

Recognizing the continuing power of the divisions and the vast differences among them, Roger Smith, CEO of GM from 1981 to 1990, sought to integrate their manufacturing and administrative information systems by purchasing Electronic Data Systems of Dallas for $2.5 billion. EDS has supplied GM's data processing and communications services. EDS and its talented system designers were charged with conquering the administrative chaos in the divisions: more than 16 different electronic mail systems, 28 different word processing systems, and a jumble of factory floor systems that could not communicate with management. Even worse, most of these systems were running on completely incompatible equipment.

EDS consolidated its 5 computing centers and GM's 34 computing centers into 21 uniform information processing centers for GM and EDS work. EDS replaced the hundred different networks that served GM with the world's largest private digital telecommunications network. In 1993, EDS launched the Consistent Office Environment Project to replace its hodgepodge of desktop models, network operating systems and application development tools with standard hardware and software for its office technology.

GM's Integrated Scheduling Project is designed to replace 30 different materials and scheduling systems with one integrated system to handle inventory, manufacturing, and financial data. Factory managers can receive orders from the car divisions for the number and type of vehicles to build and then can create an estimated 20-week manufacturing schedule for GM and its suppliers. The system also sends suppliers schedules each morning on what materials need to be delivered to what docks at what hour during that manufacturing day.

Smith earmarked $40 billion for new plants and automation, but not all investments were fruitful. He spent heavily on robots to paint cars and install windshields, hoping to reduce GM's unionized work force. At first, however, the robots accidentally painted themselves and dropped windshields onto the front seats. While a number of these problems were corrected, some robots stand unused today. The highly automated equipment never did what was promised because GM did not train workers properly to use it and did not design its car models for easy robot assembly. Instead of reducing its work force, GM had workers stay on the line because of frequent robotic breakdowns.

CHRYSLER'S INFORMATION SYSTEMS STRATEGY

In 1980, with $2.8 billion in debt, Chrysler seemed headed for bankruptcy. Its financial crisis galvanized its management to find new ways to cut costs, increase inventory turnover, and improve quality. Its new management team led by Lee Iacocca instituted an aggressive policy to bring its computer-based systems under management control. Chrysler didn't have the money to invest in several high-technology paths at once. It adopted a "rifle" approach to systems: Build what was absolutely essential, and build what would produce the biggest returns. Chrysler focused on building common systems—systems that would work in 6000 dealer showrooms, 25 zone offices, 22 parts depots, and all of its manufacturing plants.

Chrysler built integrated systems. When an order is captured electronically at the dealer, the same order is tied to production, schedules, invoices, parts forecasts, projections, parts and inventory management, and so forth.

Chrysler's low degree of vertical integration put the company in a better position to concentrate on only a few technologies. Because it was more of an auto assembler and distributor than a manufacturer, it had less need for leading-edge manufacturing technologies such as vision systems, programmable

controllers, and robotics, all of which are far more important to GM and Ford.

Chrysler directed most of its information systems budget to corporate-wide communications systems and just-in-time inventory management. Just-in-time (JIT) inventory management is obviously critical to a company that has 70 percent of its parts made by outside suppliers. (JIT supplies needed parts to the production line on a last minute basis. This keeps factory inventory levels as low as possible and holds down production costs.) During the 1980s, Chrysler achieved a 9 percent reduction in inventory and an increase in average quarterly inventory turnover from 6.38 times to 13.9 times.

A single corporation-wide network connects Chrysler's large and mid-sized computers from various vendors and gives engineering workstations access to the large computers. This makes it easier to move data from one system, stage of production, or plant to another and facilitates just-in-time inventory management.

Even before the 1980s, Chrysler had decided it needed a centralized pool of computerized CAD specifications that was accessible to all stages of production. In 1981, it installed a system to provide managers in all work areas and in all nine Chrysler plants with the same current design specifications. Tooling and design can access this data concurrently, so that a last-minute change in design can be immediately conveyed to tooling and manufacturing engineers. Chrysler created centralized business files for inventory, shipping, marketing, and a host of other related activities. All of this centralized management information makes scheduling and inventory control much easier to coordinate. Chrysler's cars and trucks share many of the same parts.

Chrysler launched a satellite communication network in 1982 that provides one-way video and two-way data transmission to nearly 5000 of its dealerships and offices around the country. It is being expanded to sites outside the U.S.

Chrysler has set up electronic links between its computers and those of its

suppliers, such as the Budd Company of Rochester, Michigan, which supplies U.S. auto companies with sheet metal parts, wheel products, and frames. Budd can extract manufacturing releases electronically through terminals installed in all of its work areas and can deliver the parts exactly when Chrysler needs them. A new enhancement verifies the accuracy of advanced shipping notices electronically transmitted by suppliers and helps Chrysler track inventory levels and payment schedules more closely.

LEARNING FROM THE JAPANESE

In the mid 1980s, MIT researchers found that the Toyota Motor Corporation's production system represented a sharp departure from Henry Ford's mass production techniques. In "lean manufacturing," Japanese auto makers focused on minimizing waste and inventory and utilizing worker's ideas. The emphasis is on maximizing reliability and quality, and minimizing waste. The ideal "lean" factory has parts built just as they are needed and has a level of quality so high that inspection is virtually redundant.

After studying Honda, Chrysler started to cut $1 billion a year in operating costs and began to rethink virtually everything it did, from designing engines to reporting financial results. Chrysler overhauled its top-down autocratic management structure. It replaced its traditional rigid departments, such as the engine division, with nimble Honda-like "cross-functional platform teams." The teams combined experts from diverse areas such as design, manufacturing, marketing, and purchasing together in one location and were given the power to make basic decisions ranging from styling to choice of suppliers. With this new approach, Chrysler shortened its product development cycle by 18 months and increased quality. Efficiency skyrocketed.

One team of 85 people designed the Dodge Viper sports car in just 36 months, a process that traditionally had taken Chrysler 4 1/2 years. The Viper only cost $75 million to develop, compared to the $118 million Mazda Motor Corporation spent on its Miata. Chrysler's LH series of mid-sized cars went from conception to production in just 39 months, about the same time that it takes for Japanese auto makers. These newer products are considered light years ahead of the product Chrysler created in the 1980s.

Chrysler now has four separate platform teams to design its jeep, mini-vans, and cars. The cross-functional teams comprise about 750 people, half of the 1500 that were previously required for such projects.

Hourly workers are providing input to help Chrysler eliminate wasted steps in the assembly process. Toyota cut waste by diagramming every step of its assembly process. It moved tools closer to the workers and eliminated unnecessary motions. Chrysler is now redesigning its assembly lines to be more like those of Toyota. Ten years ago, it took 6000 workers to build 1000 cars a day. Now Chrysler can achieve the same output with half that many workers.

To support its new approach to product development, Chrysler built a new 3.5 million square-foot Chrysler Technology Center (CTC) 30 miles north of Detroit in Auburn Hills, Michigan. Chrysler leaders expect the CTC to further enhance productivity by providing the technology that will enable Chrysler to engineer things only once and not repeat them. For instance, a failed crash test in the past might have left engineers scratching their heads. Now they can compare crash data from a test with theoretical predictions, moving closer to a solution with each successive prediction cycle. Only when they need to test a solution would they actually have to crash another car. Since hand-built prototypes cost $250,000 to $400,000, avoiding a few crash tests has a large payoff. Using this approach, engineers designed the LH car so that it passed its crash test the first time out.

Every room in the CTC has 8-inch raised floors covering a total of 10,000 fiber optic cables that can transmit massive volumes of data at high speed. These cables link CTC's buildings to its main data center. The CTC itself is scheduled to house ten mainframe computers, two supercomputers, and control systems for all the center's data and computer networks. A total of seven thousand people work there.

With a three-story atrium, the grandiose building goes far beyond functionality. It cost the cash-strapped Chrysler over $1 billion. Chrysler management claims the CTC technology makes re-engineering of the automobile design process possible, but industry experts point out that you could put platform teams in much less elaborate quarters. Hundreds of millions of the dollars spent on the CTC could have been used to bring Chrysler cars to market even sooner. Is the CTC symbolic of Chrysler's overall predicament? While Chrysler plans to spend $3 billion annually on product development through 1997, it could not find $100 million for a full-sized wind tunnel to test car designs—less money than what the monumental features of CTC added to the building's cost.

GM similarly revamped its approach to production and product development. The company is moving away from traditional assembly lines into smaller working units called cells, where workers have more oportunity to design their own processes and improve output. To combat GM's old culture of fiefdoms and inter-divisional fighting that stifled innovation, Jack Smith replaced the old committee system with a single strategy board where GM's top executives from manufacturing, engineering, sales and marketing, finance, human resources, logistics, purchasing, and communications all work together on common goals. Every new GM car or truck must be explicitly targeted to one of 26 precisely defined market segments, such as small sporty cars or full-size pickup trucks. No two vehicles are allowed to overlap. A new launch center at GM's engineering headquarters north of Detroit acts as a filter for all design ideas. Teams of engineers, designers, and marketers evaluate car and truck proposals for cost, marketability, and compatibility with other GM products. But unlike Chrysler and Japanese automakers, GM's teams are not empowered to make the important product development decisions. The power of the functional departments such as engineering and purchasing is still maintained.

Jack Smith has put even more emphasis than his predecessors on standardizing GM's processes and parts, along with its information systems. He called for reducing the number of basic car platforms from 12 to 5. In the past, GM cars were built in plants dedicated to a single model; they seldom ran at full capacity. By reducing the potential variations of each model, GM can now build several models in the same plant; with fewer parts per car, the cars are much easier to assemble. With fewer platforms, GM can operate with fewer engineers, simpler more flexible factories, smaller inventories, more common parts, and greater economies of scale.

GM named J. Ignacio Lopez de Arriortua in April 1992 as its worldwide purchasing director to make GM's high parts costs more competitive. Before leaving the company, Arriortua consolidated 27 worldwide purchasing operations into one at Detroit. He made GM's company-owned suppliers bid against outside suppliers and pressured outside suppliers for immediate 20 percent price reductions and reductions of up to 50 percent in the next few years. At that time about 40 percent of GM parts were coming from outside suppliers, whereas 70 percent of the parts in Chrysler, Ford, and Japanese firms come from the outside.

GM is also starting to roll out a satellite network for its 9700 dealerships, racing to catch up with Chrysler and Nissan Motor Corporation, who already have such networks in place.

All of these efforts have translated into more efficient and quality-driven production and lower costs. From 1991 until the beginning of 1994, GM removed $2800 in costs, before taxes, for every vehicle it manufactured. Assembly time for the Chevrolet Cavalier and the Pontiac Sunfire takes 40 percent less than the models they replace. The number of parts for these vehicles has been cut by 29 percent.

Under Jack Smith, GM went from a $10.7 billion loss in 1991 to a $362 million profit in 1993, an $11 billion swing. Earnings improved in 1994. For the first quarter of 1995, GM posted $2.2 billion in earnings, more than 2 and 1/2 times the earnings of the first quarter of 1994. The company benefited from strong and diverse overseas operations, continued gains by nonautomotive subsidiaries such as EDS, and gradual reductions in labor and manufacturing costs in North America. More significantly, GM earned an average of $1000 for each car and light truck sold in North America, up from $500 per vehicle a year earlier. It sold relatively more high-profit vehicles.

Yet GM is still less efficient than its competitors. It still takes longer to make a Cavalier than Ford takes to make cars at its most efficient plants. The production cycle of a new model, from initial design to start-up production, still takes about 48 months, compared to 36 months for Toyota and 37 months for Chrysler. Even in the strongest automobile market in years, GM is having trouble producing earnings. It is finally introducing competitive vehicles such as the Chevrolet Cavalier and the Pontiac Sunfire in certain market segments, but engineering problems and parts shortages have crimped production. Implementing new programs and flexible manufacturing, combined with stringent cost cutting, has proved extremely difficult.

In January 1994 Chrysler set a record high, announcing an unprecedented $777 million in earnings in the final quarter of 1993. From near-collapse in the 1990s, it had become a highly profitable cash machine. It continues to dominate the minivan market, and has launched successful new models such as the Jeep Grand Cherokee, the Chrysler Neon, the Chrysler Concorde, and Eagle Vision. The question for Chrysler, too, is whether it can sustain its successes over the long haul.

Chrysler still needs to work on quality as well as productivity. While its cars and trucks are more reliable than they were a decade ago, they still do not match the competition. While Detroit appears to have stopped losing ground to Japanese autos, Japanese car makers are continuing to improve plant efficiency. Nissan and Mazda introduced assembly lines that can make half a dozen different vehicles, whereas most Big Three plants only make one or two different cars.

The principal challenge for Detroit's automakers is to keep their comeback in perspective. Some of their spectacular growth in sales and earnings was due to the increasing value of the yen in 1993 and 1994, which made some Japanese cars more expensive than comparable Big Three models. Even with enormous price gaps, Japanese cars still captured 23 percent of U.S. car and truck sales, compared to 20 percent ten years before. Can the U.S. auto industry sustain its turnaround momentum?

Sources: David Woodruff et al., "Target Chrysler," *Business Week* (April 24, 1995); Alex Taylor III, "GM's $11,000,000,000 Turnaround." *Fortune* (October 12, 1994) and "Can GM Remodel Itself? *Fortune* (January 13, 1992); Steve Lohr with James Bennet, "Lessons in Rebounds from G.M. and IBM," *The New York Times* (October 24, 1994); Kathleen Kerwin, "GM's Aurora," *Business Week* (March 21, 1994); John Greenwald, "What Went Wrong?" *Time Magazine* (November 9, 1992); Maryann Keller, *Rude Awakening: The Rise, Fall, and Struggle for Recovery of General Motors* (New York: Harper Collins Publishers, 1990); David Woodruff with Elizabeth Lesly, "Surge at Chrysler," *Business Week* (November 9, 1992); Edward Cone, "Chrysler," *Information WEEK* (September 7, 1992).

Case Study Questions

1. Compare the roles played by information systems at Chrysler and GM. How did they affect the structure of the automobile industry itself?

2. How much did information systems contribute to GM's and Chrysler's success or failure?

3. What management, organization, and technology issues explain the differences in the way Chrysler and GM used information systems?

4. What management, organization, and technology factors were responsible for Chrysler's and GM's problems?

5. How can information systems help the American automobile industry compete more effectively with the Japanese (or can they)?

6. How important are information systems in solving the problems of the American automobile industry? What are some of the problems that technology cannot address?

PART two

Technical Foundations
of Information Systems

Part Two lays out the technical foundations of information systems—hardware, software, storage, and telecommunications technologies. In today's new information architecture, the computer itself is but one of many information technologies that permit modern information systems to function. To build effective information systems, one must understand how all of these technologies can work together.

Chapter 6
Computers and Information Processing

Chapter 6 surveys the features of computer hardware which help determine the capabilities of an information system. These features include the central processing unit, primary storage, and input and output devices. Because of the soaring power of microprocessors, the capabilities of mainframes, minicomputers, microcomputers, workstations, and supercomputers are constantly expanding. Emerging technologies include parallel processing, massively parallel processing, and multimedia.

Chapter 7
Information Systems Software

Chapter 7 describes the role of computer software in processing information, showing its interdependence with the capabilities of computer hardware. It is through software that computer hardware becomes useful to people and organizations. There are two types of software: systems software and application software, each with unique functions. Selection of appropriate software and programming languages require an understanding of the organization's information needs and the capabilities of specific software products.

Chapter 8
Managing Data Resources

Chapter 8 describes how information can be organized in files and databases. Without appropriate file management techniques, organizations cannot properly access and utilize the information in their computer systems. Organizing information in databases and making effective use of database management systems can solve traditional file management problems. The chapter describes the components of a database management system and the three principal database models. Managing data as a resource requires organizational discipline as well as the appropriate data management technology.

Chapter 9
Telecommunications

Chapter 9 illustrates how advances in telecommunications technology have created new opportunities for information systems in organizations. Managers need to understand the components of a telecommunications system, the major types of telecommunications networks, the measurements of transmission capacity, and the costs and benefits of alternative telecommunications technologies, in order to plan for telecommunications systems and use them effectively. Telecommunications applications such as electronic data interchange (EDI), electronic mail, digital electronic services and videoconferencing can provide competitive advantage.

Chapter 10
Enterprise-wide Computing and Networking

Chapter 10 describes underlying technology and benefits of enterprise-wide computing, which uses organization-wide networks to distribute computer processing power to the desktop. It also examines the Internet, which links networks from many different organizations so that they can share information with each other. The key to creating networks where users can share data throughout the organization is connectivity. This chapter describes the connectivity models organizations use to link their systems and the standards that make such linkages possible.

Part Two Ending Case Study:
Can Client/Server Technology Cure Health Care?

This case explores the application of client/server technology in organizations struggling to contain health care costs. It describes the benefits and the challenges of implementing computerized patient record systems that can share information using client/server networks. The case asks students to analyze whether client/server technology should be part of the business strategy for HMOs and hospitals.

Chapter 6

Computers and Information Processing

EMI Tunes Its Information Technology

The music industry is known to lag behind many other industries in its strategic use of information systems, and the management at Thorn EMI PLC. of London decided to take advantage of that situation. EMI is a large music conglomerate, with an income of $6.2 billion in 1993 and with a major presence in a number of countries including the United States, Canada, and Great Britain. Its stars range from Garth Brooks to Megadeth to Frank Sinatra. In 1992 senior management shifted the company's strategic direction, selling off most of its non-music businesses, such as defense subsidiaries, in order to focus on its primary business, music. In shifting its focus, EMI management targeted a range of business functions. At the heart of their changes was a new emphasis upon planning and sales forecasting. Management decided to make better use of data collected at retail counters in order to more fully understand the tastes of the customers who purchase EMI products. The company could then use this information to forecast sales and link production to those forecasts, a common practice in many industries but not in the music field. Through proper planning and forecasting, the company could also significantly reduce inventory costs. Also central to the plan was improved management of the company's finances. All of this required a major redesign first of EMI's business processes and then of its computer hardware technology, its telecommunications, and its application software.

EMI had actually not redesigned its North American information technology platform for 15 years. The existing technology was centered on an IBM 3090 mainframe in Los Angeles accessed by dumb terminals at more than two dozen locations. The various company sites were linked by a range of non-compatible public networks. The new technology infrastructure looks very different. The single mainframe has been replaced by five IBM AS/400 minicomputers in a data center in New York City. These computers are accessed by 900 Compaq 486 desktop microcomputers capable of acting as minicomputer terminals and desktop computers, as well as working with other microcomputers through networking. Their many public networks were replaced by a single private network leased from AT&T that would not be subject to the public network traffic jams.

The AS/400 minicomputers now provide the processing power for EMI's financial, order entry, distribution, and royalties functions, which were previously handled by the IBM 3090 mainframe. But hardware is only part of any information systems solution. Data are critical as is the purchase of appropriate application software to support EMI's business goals. To make the data easier to access, three separate core systems were consolidated for management purposes. New software included an executive information system to support EMI's senior management. The company purchased planning and forecasting software from Demand Management Inc. of St. Louis, Missouri, and new software from Lawson Software in Minneapolis, Minnesota, to improve the management of corporate finances. Existing order entry and distribution systems were replaced by new ones from J. D. Edwards & Co. of Denver, Colorado. To support staff communications, it installed Lotus cc:Mail. Installation of the minicomputers was

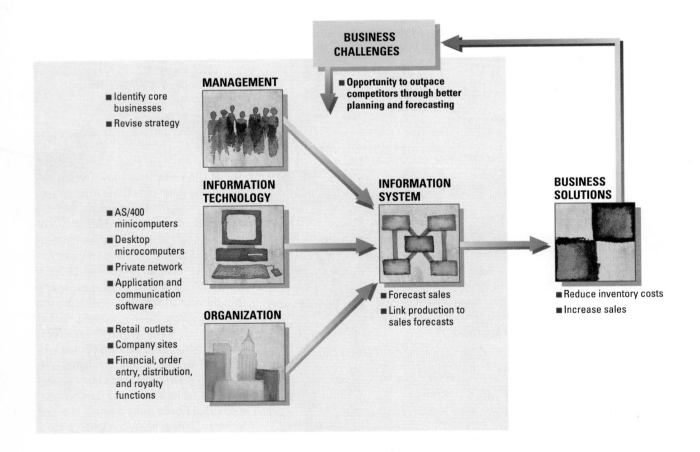

completed early in 1994, and the whole project will be completed in 1996. ■

Source: Bruce Caldwell, "EMI Puts Processes in Tune," *InformationWEEK*, October 17, 1994.

By shifting from one large mainframe computer to five midsize minicomputers, EMI was able to bring the right amount of computing power to its business operations. To implement this plan EMI's management not only had to understand the company's strategic goals and the changes to business functions necessary to achieve these goals but also needed to understand how much computer processing capacity was required by EMI's business and the performance criteria of various types of computers. They had to know why minicomputers were more appropriate for their centralized tasks rather than mainframes or supercomputers, and what role networked microcomputers could play rather than dumb terminals. Management also had to understand how the computer itself worked with related storage, input/output, and telecommunications technology.

In this chapter we describe the typical hardware configuration of a computer system, explaining how a computer works and how computer processing power and storage capacity are measured. We then compare the capabilities of various types of computers and related input, output, and storage devices.

After completing this chapter, you will be able to:

Learning Objectives

1. Identify the hardware components in a typical computer system.

2. Describe how information is represented and processed in a computer system.

3. Distinguish between generations of computer hardware.

4. Contrast the capabilities of mainframes, minicomputers, supercomputers, microcomputers, and workstations.

5. Describe the various media for storing data and programs in a computer system.

6. Compare the major input and output devices and approaches to input and processing.

7. Describe multimedia and future information technology trends.

6.1 WHAT IS A COMPUTER SYSTEM?

In order to understand how computers process data into information, you need to understand the components of a computer system and how computers work. No matter what their size, computers represent and process data using the same basic principles.

SYSTEM CONFIGURATION

A contemporary computer system consists of a central processing unit, primary storage, secondary storage, input devices, output devices, and communications devices (see Figure 6.1). The central processing unit manipulates raw data into a more useful form and controls the other parts of the computer system. Primary storage temporarily stores data and program instructions during processing, while secondary storage devices (magnetic and optical disks, magnetic tape) store data and programs when they are not being used in processing. Input devices, such as keyboards or the computer "mouse," convert data and instructions into electronic form for input into the computer. Output devices, such as printers and video display terminals, convert electronic data produced by the computer system and display it in a form that people can understand. Communications devices provide connections between the computer and communications networks. Buses are paths for transmitting data and signals between the various parts of the computer system.

FIGURE 6.1
Hardware components of a computer system. A contemporary computer system can be categorized into six major components. The central processing unit manipulates data and controls the other parts of the computer system; primary storage temporarily stores data and program instructions during processing; secondary storage feeds data and instructions into the central processor and stores data for future use; input devices convert data and instructions for processing in the computer; output devices present data in a form that people can understand; and communications devices control the passing of information to and from communications networks.

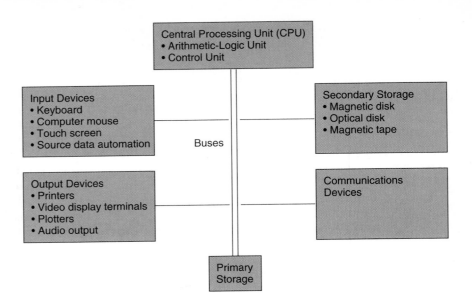

BITS AND BYTES: HOW COMPUTERS REPRESENT DATA

In order for information to flow through a computer system and be in a form suitable for processing, all symbols, pictures, or words must be reduced to a string of binary digits. A binary digit is called a **bit** and represents either a zero or a one. In the computer, the presence of an electronic or magnetic signal means *one* and its absence signifies *zero*. Digital computers operate directly with binary digits, either singly or strung together to form bytes. A string of eight bits that the computer stores as a unit is called a **byte**. Each byte can be used to store a decimal number, a symbol, a character, or part of a picture (see Figure 6.2).

Figure 6.3 shows how decimal numbers are represented using *true binary digits*. Each position in a decimal number has a certain value. Any number in the decimal system (base 10) can be reduced to a binary number. The binary number system (base 2) can express any number as a power of the number 2. The table at the bottom of the figure shows how the translation from binary to decimal works. By using a binary number system a computer can express all numbers as groups of zeroes and ones. True binary cannot be used by a computer because, in addition to representing

bit A binary digit representing the smallest unit of data in a computer system. It can only have one of two states, representing 0 or 1.

byte A string of bits, usually eight, used to store one number or character in a computer system.

FIGURE 6.2
Bits and Bytes. Bits are represented by either a 0 or 1. A string of 8 bits constitutes a byte, which represents a character. The computer's representation for the word "ALICE" is a series of five bytes, where each byte represents one character (or letter) in the name.

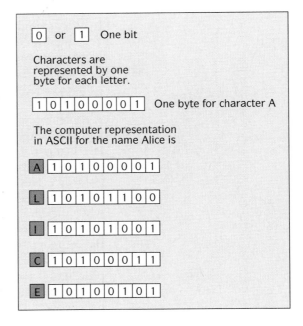

FIGURE 6.3
True binary digits. Each decimal number has a certain value that can be expressed as a binary number. The binary number system can express any number as a power of the number 2.

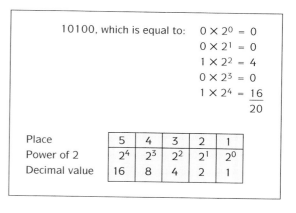

10100, which is equal to:	$0 \times 2^0 = 0$
	$0 \times 2^1 = 0$
	$1 \times 2^2 = 4$
	$0 \times 2^3 = 0$
	$1 \times 2^4 = \underline{16}$
	20

Place	5	4	3	2	1
Power of 2	2^4	2^3	2^2	2^1	2^0
Decimal value	16	8	4	2	1

numbers, a computer must represent alphabetic characters and many other symbols used in natural language, like $ and &. This requirement led manufacturers of computer hardware to develop standard *binary codes*.

There are two common codes: EBCDIC and ASCII, which are illustrated in Table 6.1. The first is the **Extended Binary Coded Decimal Interchange Code** (EBCDIC—pronounced *ib-si-dick*). This binary code, developed by IBM in the 1950s, represents every number, alphabetic character, or special character with 8 bits. EBCDIC can be used to code up to 256 different characters in one byte (2 to the eighth power equals 256).

ASCII, which stands for the **American Standard Code for Information Interchange**, was developed by the American National Standards Institute (ANSI) to provide a standard code that could be used by many different manufacturers in order to make machinery compatible. ASCII was originally designed as a 7-bit code, but most computers use 8-bit versions of ASCII. EBCDIC is used in IBM and other mainframe computers, whereas ASCII is used in data transmission, microcomputers, and some larger computers.

In actual use, EBCDIC and ASCII also contain an extra ninth **parity** or check bit. Bits can be accidentally or mistakenly changed from on to off creating errors, when data are transferred from one hardware device to another or during environmental disturbances. Parity bits are used to assist in detecting these errors. Computers are built as either *even parity* or *odd parity*. Assuming an even-parity machine, the computer expects the number of bits turned on in a byte always to be even. (If the machine were designed as an odd-parity machine, the number of bits turned on would always be odd.) When the number of bits in a byte is even, the parity bit is turned off. If the number of bits in an even-parity machine in a byte is odd, the parity bit is turned on to make the total number of "on" bits even. All computer hardware contains automatic parity checking to ensure the stability of data over time.

How can a computer represent a picture? The computer stores a picture by creating a grid overlay of the picture. In this grid or matrix, the computer measures the light or color in each box or cell, called a **pixel** (picture element). The computer then stores this information on each pixel. A high-resolution computer terminal has a 1024×768 VGA standard grid, creating more than 700,000 pixels. Whether pictures or text are stored, it is through this process of reduction that a modern computer is able to operate in a complex environment.

TIME AND SIZE IN THE COMPUTER WORLD

Table 6.2 presents some key levels of time and size that are useful in describing the speed and capacity of modern computer systems.

Processing Speed

Modern secondary storage devices generally operate at the speeds of **milliseconds** (thousandths of a second). For instance, a typical microcomputer could find your student record on a magnetic disk in about 15 milliseconds. It would take many seconds

EBCDIC (Extended Binary Coded Decimal Interchange Code)
Binary code representing every number, alphabetic character, or special character with 8 bits, used primarily in IBM and other mainframe computers.

ASCII (American Standard Code for Information Interchange) A 7- or 8-bit binary code used in data transmission, microcomputers, and some large computers.

parity An extra bit built into the EBCDIC and ASCII codes used as a check bit to ensure accuracy.

pixel The smallest unit of data for defining an image in the computer. The computer reduces a picture to a grid of pixels. The term *pixel* comes from *picture element*.

millisecond One thousandth of a second.

Table 6.1   EBCDIC and ASCII Codes

Character	EBCDIC Binary	Character	ASCII-8-Binary
A	1100 0001	A	1010 0001
B	1100 0010	B	1010 0010
C	1100 0011	C	1010 0011
D	1100 0100	D	1010 0100
E	1100 0101	E	1010 0101
F	1100 0110	F	1010 0110
G	1100 0111	G	1010 0111
H	1100 1000	H	1010 1000
I	1100 1001	I	1010 1001
J	1101 0001	J	1010 1010
K	1101 0010	K	1010 1011
L	1101 0011	L	1010 1100
M	1101 0100	M	1010 1101
N	1101 0101	N	1010 1110
O	1101 0110	O	1010 1111
P	1101 0111	P	1011 0000
Q	1101 1000	Q	1011 0001
R	1101 1001	R	1011 0010
S	1110 0010	S	1011 0011
T	1110 0011	T	1011 0100
U	1110 0100	U	1011 0101
V	1110 0101	V	1011 0110
W	1110 0110	W	1011 0111
X	1110 0111	X	1011 1000
Y	1110 1000	Y	1011 1001
Z	1110 1001	Z	1011 1010
0	1111 0000	0	0101 0000
1	1111 0001	1	0101 0001
2	1111 0010	2	0101 0010
3	1111 0011	3	0101 0011
4	1111 0100	4	0101 0100
5	1111 0101	5	0101 0101
6	1111 0110	6	0101 0110
7	11111 0111	7	0101 0111
8	11111 1000	8	0101 1000
9	11111 1001	9	0101 1001

Table 6.2 Size and Time in the Computer World

Time

Second	1	Time required to find a single record on a tape
Millisecond	1/1000 second	Time needed to find a single name on a disk, 1 to 2 milliseconds
Microsecond	1/1,000,000 second	IBM microcomputer instruction speed, .1 microseconds per instruction
Nanosecond	1/1,000,000,000 second	Mainframe instruction speed, one instruction each 15 nanoseconds
Picosecond	1/1,000,000,000,000 second	Speed of experimental devices

Size

Byte	String of 8 bits	Amount of computer storage for 1 character or number
Kilobyte	1000 bytes*	Microcomputer primary memory, 640 kilobytes
Megabyte	1,000,000 bytes	Microcomputer hard disk storage 340 megabytes; mainframe primary memory 200+ megabytes
Gigabyte	1,000,000,000 bytes	External storage disk and tape
Terabyte	1,000,000,000,000 bytes	Social security programs and records

*Actually 1024 storage positions

microsecond One millionth of a second.

nanosecond One billionth of a second.

to find your name on a much slower tape system. (The reasons for this difference are discussed later in this chapter.) A middle-range microcomputer can execute approximately 10 million program instructions per second, or .1 **microseconds** per instruction. The central processing unit in contemporary mainframe computers can execute over 200 million instructions per second (200 MIPS). At this speed, the central processor is operating at speeds of **nanoseconds** (billionths of a second), or one instruction for every 15 nanoseconds.

Storage/Memory Size

kilobyte One thousand bytes (actually 1024 storage positions). Used as a measure of microcomputer storage capacity.

megabyte Approximately one million bytes. Unit of computer storage capacity.

gigabyte Approximately one billion bytes. Unit of computer storage capacity.

Size, like speed, is an important consideration in a system. Information is stored in a computer in the form of 0s and 1s (binary digits, or bits), which are strung together to form bytes. One byte can be used to store one character, like the letter A. A thousand bytes (actually 1024 storage positions) are called a **kilobyte**. Small microcomputers used to have internal primary memories of 640 kilobytes. A large microcomputer today can store 32 megabytes of information in primary memory. Each **megabyte** is approximately one million bytes. This means, theoretically, that the machine can store up to 32 million alphabetic letters or numbers. Modern secondary storage devices, such as hard disk drives in a microcomputer or disk packs in a large mainframe, store millions of bytes of information. A microcomputer may have a 500-megabyte disk, whereas a large mainframe may have many disk drives, each capable of holding 8 gigabytes. A **gigabyte** is approximately one billion bytes. Some large organizations, like the Social Security Administration or the Internal Revenue Service, have a total storage capacity adding up all their disk drive capacities measured in trillions of bytes. And if all of their records were added together, including those stored on punched cards, paper records, and tapes, the total would be at the terabyte (thousands of billions of bytes) level of information storage.

Problems of Coordination in Computer Hardware

The vast differences in the size and speed of the major elements of computer systems introduce problems of coordination. For instance, while central processing units operate at the level of microseconds, and in some cases nanoseconds, ordinary printers operate at the level of only a few hundred to a few thousand characters per second. This means that the central processing unit can process information far faster than a printer can print it out. For this reason, additional memory and storage devices must be placed between the central processing unit and the printer so that the central processing unit is not needlessly held back from processing more information as it waits for the printer to print it out.

One of the functions of communication devices and various kinds of storage areas in the system is to stage the flow of information into and out of the machine in such a way as to maximize the utilization of the central processing unit. A major development of the last 30 years in information systems has been the creation of operating systems software (see Chapter 7) and other buffering and storage devices, all of which combine to enhance the total utilization of the central processing unit.

6.2 THE CPU AND PRIMARY STORAGE

central processing unit (CPU) Area of the computer system that manipulates symbols, numbers, and letters and controls the other parts of the computer system.

primary storage Part of the computer that temporarily stores program instructions and data being used by the instructions.

The **central processing unit (CPU)** is the part of the computer system where the manipulation of symbols, numbers, and letters occurs, and it controls the other parts of the computer system. The CPU consists of a control unit and an arithmetic-logic unit (see Figure 6.4). Located near the CPU is **primary storage** (sometimes called primary memory or main memory), where data and program instructions are stored temporarily during processing. Three kinds of buses link the CPU, primary storage, and the other devices in the computer system. The data bus moves data to and from primary storage. The address bus transmits signals for locating a given address in primary storage. The control bus transmits signals specifying whether to "read" or "write" data to or from a given primary storage address, input device, or output de-

FIGURE 6.4
The CPU and primary storage. The CPU contains an arithmetic-logic unit and a control unit. Data and instructions are stored in unique addresses in primary storage that the CPU can access during processing. The data bus, address bus, and control bus transmit signals between the central processing unit, primary storage, and other devices in the computer system.

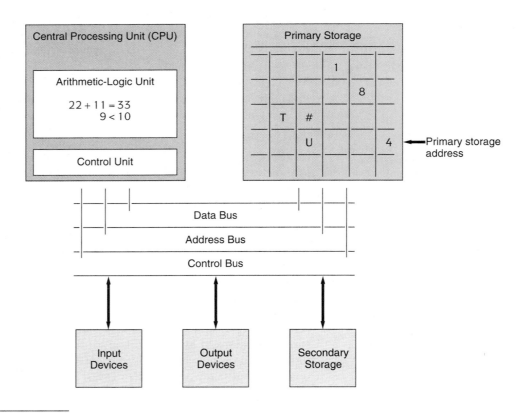

vice. The characteristics of the CPU and primary storage are very important in determining the speed and capabilities of a computer.

PRIMARY STORAGE

Primary storage has three functions. It stores all or part of the program that is being executed. Primary storage also stores the operating system programs that manage the operation of the computer. (These programs are discussed in Chapter 7.) Finally, the primary storage area holds data that are being used by the program. Data and programs are placed in primary storage before processing, between processing steps, and after processing has ended, prior to being returned to secondary storage or released as output.

How is it possible for an electronic device like primary storage to actually store information? How is it possible to retrieve this information from a known location in memory? Figure 6.5 illustrates primary storage in an electronic digital computer. Internal primary storage is often called **RAM**, or **random access memory**. It is called RAM because it can directly access any randomly chosen location in the same amount of time. The advantage of electronic information storage is the ability to store information in a precise known location in memory and to retrieve it from that same location.

Figure 6.5 shows that primary memory is divided into storage locations called bytes. Each location contains a set of eight binary switches or devices, each of which can store one bit of information. The set of eight bits found in each storage location is sufficient to store one letter, one digit, or one special symbol (such as $) using either EBCDIC or ASCII. Each byte has a unique address—similar to a mailbox, indicating where it is located in RAM. The computer can remember where the data in all of the bytes are located simply by keeping track of these addresses.

Most of the information used by a computer application is stored on secondary storage devices such as disks and tapes, located outside of the primary storage area. In order for the computer to do work on information, information must be transferred into primary memory for processing. Therefore, data are continually being read into and written out of the primary storage area during the execution of a program.

TYPES OF SEMICONDUCTOR MEMORY

Primary storage is actually composed of **semiconductors**. A semiconductor is an integrated circuit made by printing thousands and even millions of tiny transistors on a small silicon chip. There are several different kinds of semiconductor memory used

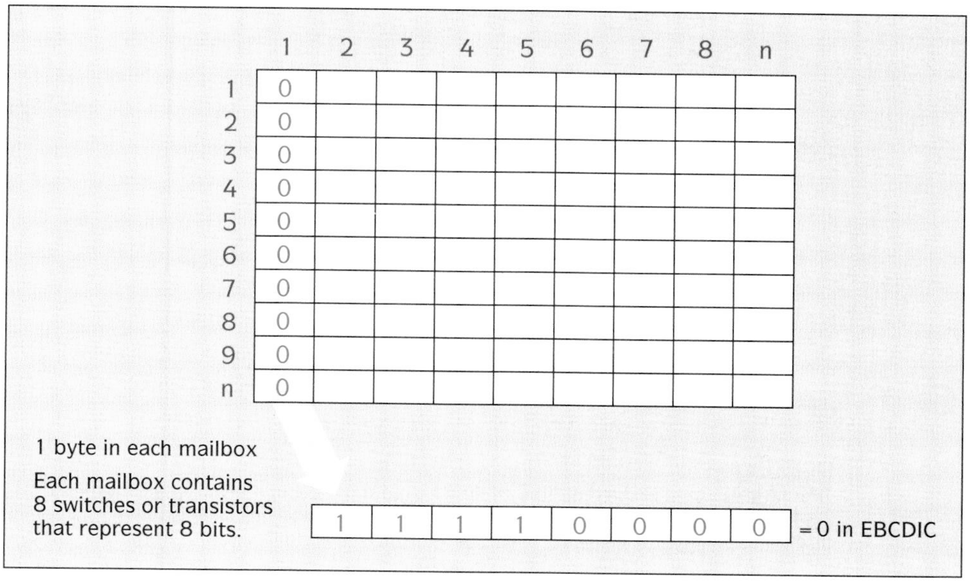

RAM (random access memory) Primary storage of data or program instructions that can directly access any randomly chosen location in the same amount of time.

semiconductor An integrated circuit made by printing thousands and even millions of tiny transistors on a small silicon chip.

FIGURE 6.5
Primary storage in the computer. Primary storage can be visualized as a matrix. Each byte represents a mailbox with a unique address. In this example, mailbox [n,1] contains 8 bits representing the number 0 (as coded in EBCDIC).

	1	2	3	4	5	6	7	8	n
1	0								
2	0								
3	0								
4	0								
5	0								
6	0								
7	0								
8	0								
9	0								
n	0								

1 byte in each mailbox

Each mailbox contains 8 switches or transistors that represent 8 bits.

| 1 | 1 | 1 | 1 | 0 | 0 | 0 | 0 | = 0 in EBCDIC |

ROM (read-only memory) Semiconductor memory chips that contain program instructions. These chips can only be read from; they cannot be written to.

PROM (programmable read-only memory) Subclass of ROM chip used in control devices because it can be programmed once.

EPROM (erasable programmable read-only memory) Subclass of ROM chip that can be erased and reprogrammed many times.

arithmetic-logic unit (ALU) Component of the CPU that performs the principal logical and arithmetic operations of the computer.

in primary storage. RAM, or random access memory, is used for short-term storage of data or program instructions. RAM is volatile: Its contents will be lost when the computer's electric supply is disrupted by a power outage or when the computer is turned off. **ROM**, or **read-only memory**, can only be read from; it cannot be written to. ROM chips come from the manufacturer with programs already "burned in" or stored. ROM is used in general-purpose computers to store important or frequently used programs (such as computing routines for calculating the square roots of numbers). Other uses for ROM chips are the storage of manufacturer-specific microcodes such as the Basic Input Output System (BIOS) chip used on an IBM Personal System/2 microcomputer, which controls the handling of data within the machine.

There are two other subclasses of ROM chips: **PROM**, or **programmable read-only memory**, and **EPROM**, or **erasable programmable read-only memory**. PROM chips are used by manufacturers as control devices in their products. They can be programmed once. In this way, manufacturers avoid the expense of having a specialized chip manufactured for the control of small motors, for instance; instead, they can program into a PROM chip the specific program for their product. PROM chips, therefore, can be made universally for many manufacturers in large production runs. EPROM chips are used for device control, such as in robots, where the program may have to be changed on a routine basis. With EPROM chips, the program can be erased and reprogrammed.

ARITHMETIC-LOGIC UNIT

The **arithmetic-logic unit (ALU)** performs the principal logical and arithmetic operations of the computer. It adds, subtracts, multiplies, and divides, determining whether a

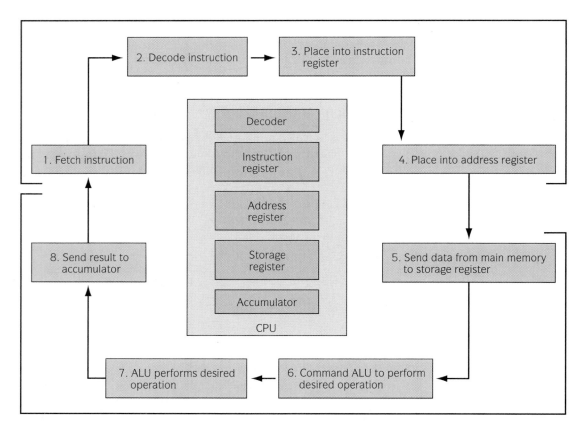

FIGURE 6.6
The various steps in the machine cycle. The machine cycle has two main stages of operation: the instruction cycle (I-cycle) and the execution cycle (E-cycle). There are several steps within each cycle required to process a single machine instruction in the CPU.

number is positive, negative, or zero. In addition to performing arithmetic functions, an ALU must be able to determine when one quantity is greater than or less than another and when two quantities are equal. The ALU can perform logical operations on the binary codes for letters as well as numbers.

CONTROL UNIT

control unit Component of the CPU that controls and coordinates the other parts of the computer system.

machine cycle Series of operations required to process a single machine instruction.

The **control unit** coordinates and controls the other parts of the computer system. It reads a stored program, one instruction at a time, and directs other components of the computer system to perform the tasks required by the program. The series of operations required to process a single machine instruction is called the **machine cycle**. As illustrated in Figure 6.6, the machine cycle has two parts: an instruction cycle and an execution cycle.

During the instruction cycle, the control unit retrieves one program instruction from primary storage and decodes it. It places the part of the instruction telling the ALU what to do next in a special instruction register and places the part specifying the address of the data to be used in the operation into an address register. (A register is a special temporary storage location in the ALU or control unit that acts like a high-speed staging area for program instructions or data being transferred from primary storage to the CPU for processing.)

During the execution cycle, the control unit locates the required data in primary storage, places it in a storage register, instructs the ALU to perform the desired operation, temporarily stores the result of the operation in an accumulator, and finally places the result in primary memory. As the execution of each instruction is completed, the control unit advances to and reads the next instruction of the program.

6.3 THE EVOLUTION OF COMPUTER HARDWARE

computer generations Major transitions in computer hardware; each generation is distinguished by a different technology for the components that do the processing.

There have been four major stages, or **computer generations**, in the evolution of computer hardware, each distinguished by a different technology for the components that do the computer's processing work. Each generation has dramatically expanded computer processing power and storage capabilities while simultaneously lowering costs (see Figure 6.7). For instance, the cost of performing 100,000 calculations plunged from several dollars in the 1950s to less than $0.025 in the 1980s and approximately $.00004 in 1995. These generational changes in computer hardware have been accompanied by generational changes in computer software (see Chapter 7) that have made computers increasingly more powerful, inexpensive, and easy to use.

GENERATIONS OF COMPUTER HARDWARE

The first and second generations of computer hardware were based on vacuum tube and transistor technology, whereas the third and fourth generations were based on semiconductor technology.

First Generation: Vacuum Tube Technology, 1946–1956

The first generation of computers relied on vacuum tubes to store and process information. These tubes consumed a great deal of power, were short-lived, and generated a great deal of heat. Colossal in size, first-generation computers had extremely limited memory and processing capability and were used for very limited scientific and engineering work. The maximum main memory size was approximately 2000 bytes (2 kilobytes), with a speed of 10 kiloinstructions per second. Rotating magnetic drums were used for internal storage and punched cards for external storage. Jobs such as running programs or printing output had to be coordinated manually.

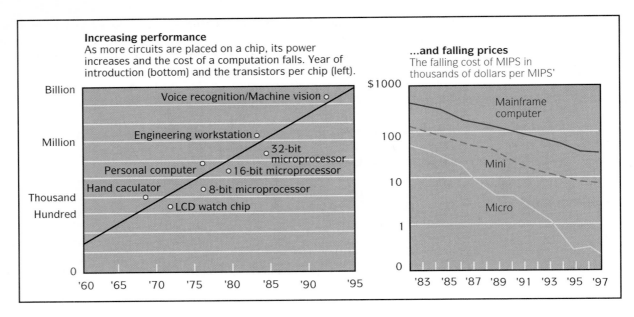

FIGURE 6.7
Increasing performance and falling prices of computers. MIPS: millions of instructions per second. *Adapted from "More Power for Less Money,"* The New York Times, *September 12, 1988. Copyright © 1988 by the New York Times Company. Reprinted by permission.*

Second Generation: Transistors, 1957–1963

In the second computer generation, transistors replaced vacuum tubes as the devices for storing and processing information. Transistors were much more stable and reliable than vacuum tubes, they generated less heat, and they consumed less power. However, each transistor had to be individually made and wired into a printed circuit board, a slow tedious process. Magnetic core memory was the primary storage technology of this period. It was composed of small magnetic doughnuts (about 1 mm in diameter), which could be polarized in one of two directions to represent a bit of data. Wires were strung along and through these cores to both write and read data. This system had to be assembled by hand and therefore was very expensive. Second-generation computers had up to 32 kilobytes of RAM memory and speeds reaching 200,000 to 300,000 instructions per second. The enhanced processing power and memory of second-generation computers enabled them to be used more widely for scientific work and for such business tasks as automating payroll and billing.

Third Generation: Integrated Circuits, 1964–1979

Third-generation computers relied on integrated circuits, which were made by printing hundreds and later thousands of tiny transistors on small silicon chips. These devices were called semiconductors. Computer memories expanded to 2 megabytes of RAM memory, and speeds accelerated to 5 MIPS. This boost to processing power made it possible to develop special software called operating systems (see Chapter 7) that automated the running of programs and communications between the CPU, printers, and other devices. Third-generation computer technology introduced software that could be used by people without extensive technical training, making it possible for computers to enlarge their role in business.

Fourth Generation: Very Large-Scale Integrated Circuits, 1980–Present

The fourth generation extends from 1980 to the present. Computers in this period use very large-scale integrated circuits (VLSIC), which are packed with as many as 200,000 to over 3 million circuits per chip. Costs have fallen to the point where desktop computers are inexpensive and widely available for use in business and everyday life. The power of a computer that once took up a large room can now reside on a small desktop. Computer memory sizes have mushroomed to over two gigabytes in large commercial machines; processing speeds have exceeded 200 MIPS. In Section 6.7, we discuss the next generation of hardware trends.

VLSIC technology has fueled a growing movement toward microminiaturization—the proliferation of computers that are so small, fast, and cheap that they have become ubiquitous. For instance, many of the "intelligent" features that have made automobiles, stereos, toys, watches, cameras, and other equipment easier to use are based on microprocessors.

WHAT IS A MICROPROCESSOR? WHAT IS A CHIP?

Very large-scale integrated circuit technology, with hundreds of thousands (or even millions) of transistors on a single chip (see Figure 6.8), integrates the computer's memory, logic, and control on a single chip; hence the name—**microprocessor**, or computer on a chip. A powerful microprocessor now widely used in personal computers is the 32-bit 66-megahertz chip such as the Intel 80486. Some popular chips are shown in Table 6.3. Chips are measured in several ways. You will often see chips labeled as 8-bit, 16-bit, or 32-bit devices. These labels refer to the **word length**, or the number of bits that can be processed at one time by the machine. An 8-bit chip can process 8 bits or 1 byte of information in a single machine cycle. A 32-bit chip can process 32 bits or 4 bytes in a single cycle. The larger the word length, the greater the speed of the computer.

A second factor affecting chip speed is cycle speed. Every event in a computer must be sequenced so that one step logically follows another. The control unit sets a beat to the chip. This beat is established by an internal clock and is measured in

microprocessor Very large-scale integrated circuit technology that integrates the computer's memory, logic, and control on a single chip.

word length The number of bits that can be processed at one time by a computer. The larger the word length, the greater the speed of the computer.

FIGURE 6.8
The Pentium microprocessor contains more than 3 million transistors and provides mainframe- and supercomputer-like processing capabilities. *From "Power PC 620 Soars" Reprinted with permission, from the November 1994 issue of* BYTE *Magazine, © by McGraw-Hill, Inc., New York, NY. All rights reserved.*

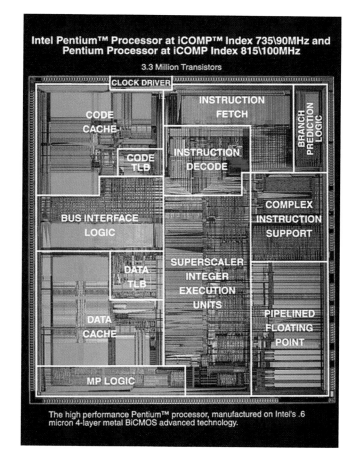

Table 6.3	Common Microprocessors				
Micro-processor Chip	Microcomputer Manufacturers	Word Length	Data Bus Width	Clock Speed (MHz)	Used in
80286	Intel	16	16	8–28	IBM AT
80386	Intel	32	32	16–33	IBM Personal System/2
68020	Motorola	32	32	12–33	Macintosh II
68030	Motorola	32	32	16–50	Macintosh IIx, IIcx
80486	Intel	32	32	20–100	Microcomputers, workstations
68040	Motorola	32	32	25–40	Mac Quadras
Pentium	Intel	32	64	60–100	High-end workstations, microcomputers
PowerPC 601	IBM, Apple, Motorola	32	64	50–100	Workstations, microcomputers
PowerPC 620	IBM, Apple, Motorola	64	128	133	High-end workstations

megahertz A measure of cycle speed, or the pacing of events in a computer; one megahertz equals one million cycles per second.

data bus width The number of bits that can be moved at one time between the CPU, primary storage, and the other devices of a computer.

reduced instruction set computing (RISC) Technology used to enhance the speed of microprocessors by embedding only the most frequently used instructions on a chip.

megahertz (abbreviated MHz, which stands for millions of cycles per second). The Intel 8088 chip, for instance, originally had a clock speed of 4.47 megahertz, whereas the Intel 80486 chip has a clock speed that ranges from 20 to 100 megahertz.

A third factor affecting speed is the **data bus width**. The data bus acts as a highway between the CPU, primary storage, and other devices, determining how much data can be moved at one time. The 8088 chip used in the original IBM personal computer, for example, had a 16-bit word length but only an 8-bit data bus width. This meant that data were processed within the CPU chip itself in 16-bit chunks but could only be moved 8 bits at a time between the CPU primary storage and external devices. On the other hand, the 80486 chip, used in IBM Personal System/2 micro-computers, and the Motorola 68040 chip used in Macintosh microcomputers, have both a 32-bit word length and a 32-bit data bus width. Obviously, in order to get a computer to execute more instructions per second and work through programs or handle users expeditiously, it is necessary to increase the word length of the processor, the data bus width, or the cycle speed—or all three.

Microprocessors can be made faster by using **reduced instruction set computing (RISC)** in their design. Some instructions that a computer uses to process data are actually embedded in the chip circuitry. Conventional chips, based on complex instruction set computing, have several hundred or more instructions hard-wired into their circuitry, and usually take several clock cycles to execute a single instruction. In many instances, only 20 percent of these instructions are needed for 80 percent of the computer's tasks. If the little-used instructions are eliminated, the remaining instructions can execute much faster.

Reduced instruction set (RISC) computers have only the most frequently used instructions embedded in them. A RISC CPU can execute most instructions in a single machine cycle and sometimes multiple instructions at the same time. RISC is most appropriate for scientific and workstation computing, where there are repetitive arithmetic and logical operations on data or applications calling for three-dimensional image rendering.

Champions of RISC claim that a microcomputer or workstation with RISC technology can offer the performance of much larger computers costing ten times as much. For example, the PowerPC microprocessors developed by IBM, Motorola, Inc. and Apple Computer Inc., can run both IBM and Macintosh applications very fast. PowerPC chip speeds range from 50 to over 100 megahertz. When used in IBM's RS/6000 workstations, the PowerPC doubled performance over some previous models. But critics believe that gains in RISC processing speed may be offset by difficulties created by dropping complex instruction set computing. Programs written for conventional processors cannot automatically be transferred to RISC machines; new software is required. Many RISC suppliers are adding more instructions to appeal to a greater number of customers, and designers of conventional microprocessors are streamlining their chips to execute instructions more rapidly.

6.4 MAINFRAMES, MINICOMPUTERS, MICROCOMPUTERS, WORKSTATIONS, AND SUPERCOMPUTERS

Computers represent and process data the same way, but there are different classifications. We can use size and processing speed to categorize contemporary computers as mainframes, minicomputers, microcomputers, workstations, and supercomputers.

MAINFRAMES, MINIS, AND MICROS

mainframe Largest category of computer, classified as having 50 megabytes to over 1 gigabyte of RAM.

minicomputer Middle-range computer with about 10 megabytes to over 1 gigabyte of RAM.

microcomputer Desktop or portable computer classified with 640 kilobytes to 64 megabytes of RAM.

workstation Desktop computer with powerful graphics and mathematical capabilities and the ability to perform several tasks at once.

supercomputer Highly sophisticated and powerful computer that can perform very complex computations extremely rapidly.

A **mainframe** is the largest computer, a powerhouse with massive memory and extremely rapid processing power. It is used for very large commercial, scientific, or military applications where a computer must handle massive amounts of data or many complicated processes. A **minicomputer** is a middle-range computer, about the size of an office desk, often used in universities, factories, or research laboratories. A **microcomputer** is one that can be placed on a desktop or carried from room to room. Microcomputers are used as personal machines as well as in business. A **workstation** also fits on a desktop but has more powerful mathematical and graphics processing capability than a microcomputer, and can perform more complicated tasks at the same time than can a microcomputer. Workstations are used for scientific, engineering, and design work that requires powerful graphics or computational capabilities. A **supercomputer** is a highly sophisticated and powerful machine that is used for tasks requiring extremely rapid and complex calculations with hundreds of thousands of variable factors. Supercomputers have traditionally been used in scientific and military work, but they are starting to be used in business as well. Representative computers in each category are listed in Table 6.4. The problem with this classification scheme is that the capacity of the machines changes so rapidly. A microcomputer today has the computing power of a mainframe from the 1980s or the minicomputer of a few years ago. Powerful microcomputers have sophisticated graphics and processing capabilities similar to workstations. Microcomputers still cannot perform as many tasks at once as mainframes, minicomputers, or workstations (see the discussion of operating systems in Chapter 7); nor can they be used by as many people simultaneously as these larger machines. Still, even these distinctions will become less pronounced in the future. In another decade, desktop micros might very well have the power and processing speed of today's supercomputers.

Generally, however, mainframes can be classified as having 50 megabytes to over 1 gigabyte of RAM; minicomputers, 10 megabytes to over 1 gigabyte of RAM; microcomputers, 640 kilobytes to 64 megabytes of RAM, and workstations, 8 to 300 megabytes of RAM. Table 6.4 illustrates the capabilities of representative commercial computers in each of these categories today. Figure 6.9 illustrates some of the capabilities of microcomputers and workstations.

The term *microcomputer* is sometimes used synonymously with personal computer, since micros were originally intended as primarily personal, single-user tools.

Table 6.4   Representative Computers

Type of Computer	Example	Memory (Megabytes)	Performance	Word Length (Bits)	Cost
Mainframe	IBM S/390 Parallel Enterprise Server	2 gigabytes	478 ITR	32	$55,000,000
Minicomputer	DEC Alpha Server Model 2100	up to 2 gigabytes	233–275 megahertz	64	$35,000
Microcomputer	Compaq Prolinea Model 4633	4–32	10.8 MIPS	32	$1600
Workstation	Sun SPARCstation 20 Model 50	32	69.2 SPEC int92 marks	32	$12,195–$40,000
Supercomputer	Cray T90	128 megawords–1,024 megawords	1.8–60 billion calculations per second	64	$2,500,000–$35,000,000

Note: Computer manufacturers do not always use the same measure of computer performance. MIPS stands for millions of instructions per second. ITR stands for Internal Throughput Ratio, a measure of the amount of work that can be put through a processor. Workstation performance is starting to be measured by SPECint92 marks, a benchmark for integer operations. Supercomputer manufacturers are starting to use additional performance measures.

However, microcomputers have become so powerful that they are no longer confined to personal information systems. Micros can operate either as individual stand-alone machines with isolated processing power or as part of a departmental or company-wide network of intelligent devices. They may be linked to other micros, telecommunications devices, workstations, or larger computers.

In either case, microcomputers are starting to do some of the work formerly performed by larger computers in business. Chapter 9 describes how microcomputers can be linked with other micros, printers, "intelligent" copy machines, and telephones to provide processing power and to coordinate the work flow without relying on mainframes. Micros can also be linked to minicomputers and mainframes, forming company-wide information networks that share hardware, software, and data resources. The use of multiple computers linked by a communication network for processing is called **distributed processing**. In contrast with **centralized processing**, in which all processing is accomplished by one large central computer, distributed processing distributes the processing work among various microcomputers, minicomputers, and mainframes linked together.

distributed processing The distribution of computer processing work among multiple computers linked by a communication network.

centralized processing Processing that is accomplished by one large central computer.

DOWNSIZING AND COOPERATIVE PROCESSING

In some firms, microcomputers have actually replaced mainframes and minicomputers. The process of transferring applications from large computers to smaller ones is called **downsizing**. Downsizing has many advantages. The cost per MIPS on a mainframe is almost 100 times greater than on a microcomputer; a megabyte of mainframe memory costs about 10 times more than the same amount of memory on a micro. For some applications, micros may also be easier for nontechnical specialists to use and maintain. Installing microcomputers can also help distribute processing power to organizations with branches in many different locations, even if they are on different parts of the globe. Often microcomputers are networked so that they can share data and communicate with each other.

downsizing The process of transferring applications from large computers to smaller ones.

The decision to downsize involves many factors beside the cost of computer hardware, including the need for new software, training, and perhaps new organizational procedures. (These issues are explored in detail in Chapters 9 and 10 and in the Part II section-ending case.) As the Window on Management illustrates, there are many applications where mainframes remain the most appropriate technology platform.

FIGURE 6.9
Workstations (top) are often used for
sophisticated CAD/CAM applications.
The IBM PS/2 (bottom) is a microcomputer capable of powerful applications
processing.

Another computing pattern divides processing work for transaction-based applications among mainframes and microcomputers. Each type of computer is assigned the functions it performs best, and each shares processing (and perhaps data) over a communications link. For example, the microcomputer might be used for data entry and validation, whereas the mainframe would be responsible for file input and

DEUTSCHE BANK DECIDES TO STAY WITH MAINFRAMES

Why would the management of a bank stay with expensive mainframe equipment when the popular wisdom is that downsizing to smaller computers will improve performance while saving money? In the case of banking giant Deutsche Bank, the answer is that its IS management was able to show that mainframes can be less expensive than networked smaller computers while allowing the bank to better serve its customers.

Deutsche Bank, headquartered in Frankfurt, is the largest bank in Germany and the second largest in Europe. It runs approximately 220 applications on its computers. Deutsche Bank's single biggest application, its branch banking system, generates by itself about 100 million transactions per month. Its financial applications serve about 1000 users and generate up to 12 million transactions per month. Its data processing department has more than 1000 employees, half of whom are writing new applications. This is a giant information systems unit by anyone's standards.

Over the years the banking business has emerged as one of the most computer-intensive and computer-dependent industries. Almost every function in banks is automated. Banks can no longer operate without fast, efficient, effective information systems. As a result, banks usually invest a great deal of capital into information technology, and IS budgets are very high. This condition is even more pronounced among German banks than among those in most other advanced countries because Germany is one of the few industrialized countries to place no restrictions on the scope of the financial services its banks are allowed to offer. The resultant competition for new products is great, and their staffs must be constantly developing large numbers of new applications just to stay competitive. One result is that information systems departments of German banks deal with more diverse information systems applications than those in other countries.

Given the size of their information systems budgets, the cost of information systems can have a major effect on a bank's bottom line. Banks usually focus heavily on reducing IS costs. Given that downsizing to networked smaller computers is widely believed to result in large cost savings while also improving computer service, why has Deutsche Bank not gone this route? Deutsche Bank IS management did examine the question of downsizing very carefully, stimulated both by the recession that hit Europe in the early 1990s and the tremendous interest in downsizing throughout the information systems field. Mathias Junger, Deutsche Bank's manager of capacity planning, gives one major reason why the bank has not downsized. After careful study, he concluded that downsizing will not result in lower costs than operating with mainframes. "Mainframes are not as expensive as networked microcomputers or workstations when you look at the whole cost," he claims. "It might be cheaper on the hardware [side], but not when you take networking, support and re-education of users into account." Another fundamental reason banks like Deutsche have not downsized is that banks "have to be able to serve their millions of customers at the cash point," according to Andrew Bird, BGS Systems Inc. managing director in the United Kingdom. "They can't afford to let response times drop," he claims. "Otherwise customers will go to another bank." He adds that to achieve the fastest retrieval times for the massive amounts of data maintained by large banks, the data must be stored on mainframes.

To examine the performance of its mainframes, Deutsche Bank turned to software from BGS Systems of Waltham, Massachusetts. BGS focuses on software to manage the performance of computers, particularly large computers, and on capacity planning for medium to large data centers. Deutsche Bank is now using a full set of BGS tools to both monitor its mainframe performance in order to tune its mainframes and to improve that performance. In addition, the bank uses BGS tools to analyze and tune the

> **To Think About:** How was computer processing power related to Deutsche Bank's business strategy? What other management, organizational, and technical factors might have contributed to management's decision not to downsize?

performance of other critical computer system elements such as the mainframe DASD, cache, and response time. According to Junger, these tools provide the bank with a comprehensive performance overview without much manual intervention. He says the bank is now better able to predict future needs and to plan for upgrades more effectively. With proper monitoring and tuning, mainframes become cost effective compared to the alternatives. BGS's Bird believes that with the help of such software to make better use of their investments in mainframes, banks not only will not be downsizing, but in the coming years will actually be consolidating their mainframes into fewer but larger machines. He also points out that mainframes provide much better data security than do minicomputers and microcomputers, a factor of prime importance to bank managements. As evidence of the effectiveness of monitoring and tuning one's hardware and software, BGS's managing director in Germany, Karl Purcz, notes that BGS sales were not affected by the global recession. He explains that the reason is that rather than being viewed as an expense, such software actually helps to lower information systems costs. "The more sensitive about costs people are," claims Purcz, "the easier it is for us to convince them to buy our products."

Source: George Black, "Deutsche Bank Gives BGS Tools Good Marks for Performance," *Software Magazine,* August 1994.

FIGURE 6.10
Cooperative processing. In cooperative processing, an application is divided into tasks that run on more than one type of computer. This example shows the tasks that a microcomputer is best at performing; the tasks that a mainframe computer is best at performing, and those tasks that each type is able to perform.

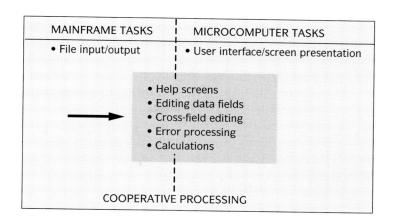

cooperative processing Type of processing that divides the processing work for transaction-based applications among mainframes and microcomputers.

output. This division of labor is called **cooperative processing**. Microcomputers are utilized because they can provide the same processing power much more economically than a mainframe or because they are superior at some tasks, such as at providing screen presentations for the user interface. Figure 6.10 illustrates cooperative processing. Cooperative processing is not always easy to implement. It may require special communications and application software and an understanding of which functions are best handled by micros and which should reside with larger machines.

MICROCOMPUTERS AND WORKSTATIONS

Since workstations are desktop machines like microcomputers, what distinguishes a microcomputer from a workstation? Workstations have more powerful graphics and mathematical processing capabilities than microcomputers, and can easily perform several tasks at the same time. They are typically used by scientists, engineers, and other knowledge workers but are spreading to the financial industry because they have the computing power to simultaneously analyze portfolios, process securities trades, and provide financial data and news services (see Chapter 15).

Workstations are especially useful for computer-aided design (CAD) and for complex simulations and modeling. They can represent fully rendered multiple views of a physical object, such as an airplane wing, rotate the object three-dimensionally, and present design history and cost factors. Workstations can easily integrate text and graphics, displaying multiple tools, applications, and types of data simultaneously.

At present, workstations have at least 8 megabytes of RAM, 32-bit microprocessors, and the capability to perform several computing tasks at the same time (see the discussion of multitasking in Chapter 7). They come with high-resolution large-screen color monitors for detailed design work and math co-processors to speed calculations.

The distinctions between workstations and microcomputers are starting to disappear. Powerful high-end microcomputers have many of the same capabilities as low-end workstations. A low-end workstation can be purchased for around $3000 to $5000. As microcomputers become increasingly graphics oriented, the distinctions between the two types of computers are likely to blur further. Moreover, workstations themselves have increased in power, so that the most sophisticated workstations have some of the capabilities of earlier mainframes and supercomputers (Thomborson, 1993).

SUPERCOMPUTERS AND PARALLEL PROCESSING

A supercomputer is an especially sophisticated and powerful type of computer that is used primarily for extremely rapid and complex computations with hundreds or thousands of variable factors. Supercomputers have traditionally been used for

---

6.4 Mainframes, Minicomputers, Microcomputers, Workstations, and Supercomputers

PARALLEL PROCESSING GOES COMMERCIAL

Parallel processing computers—often known as supercomputers—have long been viewed as tools exclusively for scientists and engineers. So what are they doing alongside commercial computers at corporations like PTT Telecom, the Dutch telephone company? The fact is, their great power is fast resulting in their finding new roles as commercial computers.

Parallel processors have not been widely used for commercial applications until recently primarily for two related reasons. First, they have been costly, so much so that they have been difficult to cost-justify for commonplace commercial uses. In addition, few corporate or IS managers have envisioned any uses for so much intense computing power—what would they do with them? Technology has progressed, resulting in the lowering of prices, while management has responded to the growing power of computers with new ideas on how the power might be used. As a result, sales of parallel processors for commercial use have been growing at an annual rate of 30 percent in recent years, and reached $400 million in 1994. The Gartner Group, a leading computer market research company, estimates sales will reach $5 billion in 1998.

Parallel processors shine when very high speeds are needed. Whereas current mainframes can handle 3 to 4 megabytes of data per second, parallel processors are able to handle 100 megabytes per second. Mainframes process several hundred MIPS (millions of instructions per second), whereas parallel processors are able to process thousands of MIPS. Parallel processors would be perfect for handling mountains of data if such data existed and needed to be processed. Therefore, critical to the emergence of the commercial use of these processing powerhouses has been the steadily falling price of

data storage. Whereas the cost of mainframe storage was about $7 per megabyte in 1989, by 1994 it had fallen to approximately $3 per megabyte and is projected to be only $1 in 1999. Similarly, microcomputer data storage costs have fallen from $2 per megabyte in 1989 to $1 in 1994 and are projected to be less than half that in 1999. As data storage costs have fallen, many companies have been storing more and more data—think of all the point-of-sale systems in supermarkets, discount stores, and department stores, collecting and storing data on every item purchased. Managers and planners have eyed all that data and have begun devising ways to use it to their organization's advantage.

Wal-Mart Stores, Inc., the Bentonville, Arkansas discounting giant and largest retailer in the United States, processes 20 million point-of-sale updates daily in its 2100 stores, storing trillions of bytes of data used to keep their inventory up to date and to spot sales trends. Wal-Mart's computers need to be able to process approximately 2300 queries per day against this massive collection of data. Trimark Investment Management, a Toronto, Canada, mutual funds company, has seen its account base shoot up from 250,000 customers in 1992 to 800,000 two years later. To post its accounts at the end of 1992, its more traditional IBM System 38 required 18 to 24 hours of processing. Today the company would not even be able to post the data for more than triple the number of customers the 1992 way— the computer simply could not handle all that data. However, in 1994, using a Pyramid Technology Niles 150 with six processors, Trimark posted all the customers in eight hours. The SABRE Group, the reservation and ticketing organization that is owned by American Airlines but also services 52 other carriers plus a large number of travel agencies, uses an IBM Parallel

Enterprise Server (PES) to price its tickets. SABRE processes a massive amount of data, normally handling about 3000 messages per second.

> **To Think About:** How is selection of parallel processor technology related to the business strategies of the firms described here? What management, organization, and technology criteria would you use in deciding whether to purchase a parallel processor?

SABRE's parallel processors have successfully processed a peak load of 4100 messages per second.

The costs of parallel processor use have declined for other reasons. One reason the SABRE Group turned to the IBM PES is that it is an air-cooled machine that requires only one-tenth the floor space of its mainframe sibling, a water-cooled IBM ES/9000; it also consumes only one-tenth the electrical power. The technology has proven to be cost effective for some small businesses as well. Medstat, the $52 million Ann Arbor, Michigan, provider of health-care services, turned to a MasPar Computer Corporation's MP-1 1104 because Medstat's management found that it could perform an analysis of a nearly 4 gigabyte statistical database in 4.5 minutes, down from nearly 38 hours with its previous computer. Medstat calculates that this speed alone will allow the MP-1 1104 to pay for itself in just 15 months, not to mention the other benefits the company expects to achieve, such as improved customer service. Users of parallel processors point out another key long-range cost benefit—these machines are flexible; they can be expanded by adding extra processors at relatively little cost should the users' needs increase.

Parallel processing computers are finding many new applications. Because graphics and video are so data-intensive, they are being used to run graphical user interfaces and to support computer-based video services. Companies are turning to them to improve their customer service. Because parallel processing computers can search large databases so rapidly, companies are finding they can answer customer queries much more rapidly than with single-processor technology. Perhaps the applications that generate the most intense interest have come to be known as data mining (see Chapter 2). Organizations mine data—search through and analyze massive pools of data—to find hidden but useful information. For example, retail companies of all types, including Wal-Mart, are now analyzing huge databases to identify changing buying patterns and customer tastes, information that can then be used to support marketing or to drive the new product development process. Others are mining data to determine the consequences of a particular action. Max D. Hopper, chairman of the SABRE Group AA, Inc., offers an example of just such an application: "If Dallas–Fort Worth has a severe weather problem that affects 50 arriving or departing flights with 5,000 passengers, the [parallel processing] technology has the power to let us see the impact on every flight, including aircraft, crew, maintenance and passengers." It might take a large mainframe several days or a week to come up with the answer, yet a parallel processing computer might deliver results within a few hours.

With all of the problems, why aren't even more companies using them? Parallel processors have their drawbacks and problems. Many users point out that not only do they require the retraining of IS staffs to be able to support and maintain them, but business staffs must also be retrained and sometimes the work flow redesigned if the organization is effectively to make full use of the increased speed and added information. More fundamental concerns include the lack of open standards for parallel processing, making application development more difficult and expensive, and resulting in applications that are neither portable nor interoperable. Because these machines have so many more components, many believe they run a higher risk of failure and feel their reliability has yet to be proven, and therefore are not yet ready to entrust their mission-critical applications to this technology.

Let us return to our original question—why does PTT Telecom, the Dutch telephone company, turn to parallel processing for a critical commercial application? PTT Telecom finds that its customers demand detailed, itemized billing, which in turn means the company must maintain and process massive quantities of data. Customers place over 30 million telephone calls per day, which averages out to about 400 calls per second. For each of these calls, PTT Telecom needs to record the call detail in a standardized format and then compute the tariff for that call. The system to perform these tasks must be able to exceed the 30-million-per-day call average, reaching 40 million calls during periods of peak traffic. Moreover, the computer has to be easily expandable to match the continuing expansion in both the number of their customers and the number of calls per customer.

To accomplish this immense yet critical task, the company determined that the only viable approach was to use parallel processing. PTT Telecom turned to two Tandem parallel processor computers. The first computer uses 48 processors and is dedicated to collecting the data and extracting it for computing. The second computer uses 16 processors to compute and store the cost of each call (using 500 gigabytes of disk storage). The Tandem computers are fully modular, allowing PTT Telecom to expand the number of processors and disk storage as needed.

Sources: "The Power of Parallelism," *Datamation*, November 15, 1994; Michael Alexander, "Mine for Gold with Parallel Systems," *Datamation*, November 15, 1994; CMP Publications, Commercial Parallel Processing," September 1994; Willie Schatz, "Out of the Lab, Into the Office," *InformationWEEK*, May 16, 1994; and Craig Stedman, "Sabre Parallel Systems Reduce Transaction Costs," *Computerworld*, November 17, 1994.

classified weapons research, weather forecasting, and petroleum and engineering applications, all of which use complex mathematical models and simulations. Although extremely expensive, supercomputers are beginning to be employed in business, as the Window on Technology demonstrates.

Supercomputers can perform complex and massive computations almost instantaneously because they can perform billions and even hundreds of billions of calculations per second—many times faster than the largest mainframes. Supercomputers do not process one instruction at a time but instead rely on **parallel processing**. As illustrated in Figure 6.11, multiple processing units (CPUs) break down a problem into smaller parts and work on it simultaneously. Some experimental supercomputers use up to 64,000 processors. Getting a group of processors to attack the same problem at once is easier said than done. It requires rethinking of the problems and special software that can divide problems among different processors in the most efficient possible way, providing the needed data, and reassembling the many subtasks to reach an appropriate solution.

parallel processing Type of processing in which more than one instruction can be processed at a time by breaking down a problem into smaller parts and processing them simultaneously with multiple processors.

FIGURE 6.11
Sequential and parallel processing. During sequential processing,
each task is assigned to one CPU
that processes one instruction at a
time. In parallel processing, multiple tasks are assigned to multiple
processing units to expedite the
result.

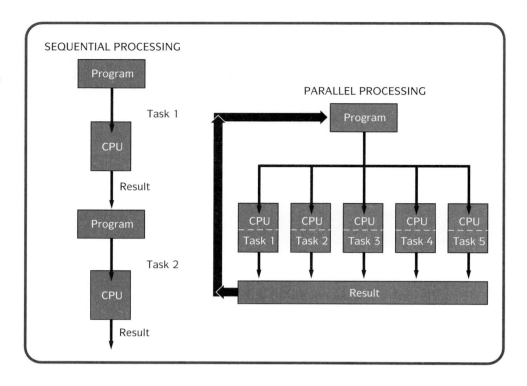

6.5 SECONDARY STORAGE

secondary storage Relatively
long-term, nonvolatile storage
of data outside the CPU and
primary storage.

register Temporary storage location in the ALU or control unit
where small amounts of data and
instructions reside for thousandths
of a second just before use.

cache High-speed storage of
frequently used instructions
and data.

In addition to primary storage, where information and programs are stored for immediate processing, modern computer systems use other types of storage in order to
accomplish their tasks. Information systems need to store information outside of the
computer in a nonvolatile state (not requiring electrical power) and to store volumes
of data too large to fit into a computer of any size today (such as a large payroll or
the U.S. census). The relatively long-term storage of data outside the CPU and primary storage is called **secondary storage**.

Primary storage is where the fastest, most expensive technology is used. As
shown in Table 6.5, there are actually three different kinds of primary memory: register, cache, and RAM. **Register** is the fastest and most expensive memory, where
small amounts of data and instructions reside for thousandths of a second just prior
to use, followed by **cache** memory (for high-speed storage of frequently used instructions and data) and RAM memory for large amounts of data. Access to infor-

Table 6.5	Data Storage Devices in a Microcomputer	
Type of Memory	**Total Storage Capacity**	**Access Time**
	Primary Storage	
Register	1 kilobyte	.01 microseconds
Cache	1 kilobyte	.1 microseconds
RAM	16 megabytes	.5 microseconds
	Secondary Storage	
Hard disk	800 megabytes	15 milliseconds
High-density diskette (3.5")	2.8 megabytes	200 milliseconds
Optical disk	660 megabytes	200–500 milliseconds
Magnetic tape (1/4" streaming tape backup)	40 megabytes	1–2 seconds

mation stored in primary memory is electronic and occurs almost at the speed of light. Secondary storage is nonvolatile and retains data even when the computer is turned off. There are many kinds of secondary storage; the most common are magnetic tape, magnetic disk, and optical disk. These media can transfer large bodies of data rapidly to the CPU. But since secondary storage requires mechanical movement to gain access to the data, in contrast to primary storage, it is relatively slow.

MAGNETIC TAPE

magnetic tape Inexpensive and relatively stable secondary storage medium in which large volumes of information are stored sequentially by means of magnetized and non-magnetized spots on tape.

Magnetic tape is an older device that is still important for secondary storage of large volumes of information. It is used primarily in mainframe batch applications and for archiving data. Generally, magnetic tape for large systems comes in 14-inch reels that are up to 2400 feet long and 0.5 inches wide. It is very similar to home cassette recording tape, but of higher quality. Figure 6.12 shows how information appears on magnetic tape using an EBCDIC coding scheme. Each byte of data utilizes one column across the width of the tape. Each column is composed of eight bits plus one check parity bit. Information can be stored on magnetic tape at different densities. Low density is 1600 bytes per inch (bpi), and densities of up to 6250 bpi are common. Tape cartridges with much higher density and storage capacity are starting to replace reel-to-reel tapes in mainframe and minicomputer systems. Microcomputers and some minicomputers use small tape cartridges resembling home audiocassettes to store information.

The principal advantages of magnetic tape are that it is very inexpensive, that it is relatively stable, and that it can store very large volumes of information. It is a reliable technology because of several self-checking features (such as parity bits), and therefore is an ideal form of backup storage for other more volatile forms of memory. Moreover, magnetic tape can be used over and over again, although it does age with time and computer users must handle it carefully.

The principal disadvantages of magnetic tape are that it stores data sequentially and is relatively slow compared to the speed of other secondary storage media. In order to find an individual record stored on magnetic tape, such as your professor's employment record, the tape must be read from the beginning up to the location of the desired record. This means that the CPU must read each name from "Abelson" all the way to your professor's name before it can locate your professor's record. Hence, magnetic tape is not a good medium when it is necessary to find information rapidly

FIGURE 6.12
Magnetic tape storage. Data can be stored on nine-track magnetic tape, which is a stable and inexpensive medium. However, data are stored sequentially and therefore access and retrieval may be slow.

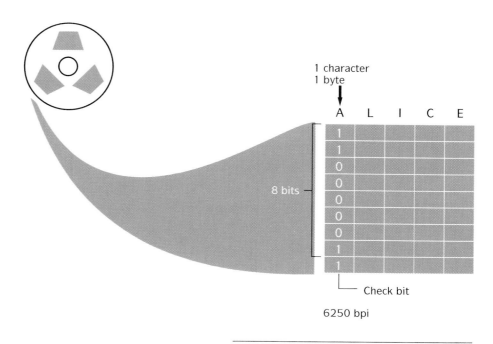

(such as for an airline reservation system). Tape can also be damaged and is labor intensive to mount and dismount. The environment in which it is stored must be carefully controlled. Since contemporary information systems call for immediate access to data, tape represents a fading technology, but it continues to exist in changing forms.

MAGNETIC DISK

magnetic disk A secondary storage medium in which data are stored by means of magnetized spots on a hard or floppy disk.

hard disk Magnetic disk resembling a thin steel platter with an iron oxide coating; used in large computer systems and in many microcomputers.

cylinder Represents circular tracks on the same vertical line within a disk pack.

track Concentric circle on the surface area of a disk on which data are stored as magnetized spots; each track can store thousands of bytes.

The most widely used secondary storage medium today is **magnetic disk**. There are two kinds of magnetic disks: floppy disks (used in microcomputers) and hard disks (used on commercial disk drives and microcomputers). **Hard disks** are thin steel platters with an iron oxide coating. In larger systems, multiple hard disks are mounted together on a vertical shaft. Figure 6.13 illustrates a commercial hard disk pack for a large system. It has 11 disks, each with two surfaces, top and bottom. However, although there are 11 disks, no information is recorded on the top or bottom surfaces; thus, there are only 20 recording surfaces on the disk pack. On each surface, data are stored on tracks. The disk pack is generally sealed from the environment and rotates at a speed of about 3500 rpm, creating an air-stream speed of about 50 mph at the disk surface.

Information is recorded on or read from the disk by read/write heads, which literally fly over the spinning disks. Unlike a home stereo, the heads never actually touch the disk (which would destroy the data and cause the system to "crash") but hover a few thousandths of an inch above it. A smoke particle or a human hair is sufficient to crash the head into the disk.

The read/write heads move horizontally (from left to right) to any of 200 positions called **cylinders**. At any one of these cylinders, the read/write heads can read or write information to any of 20 different concentric circles on the disk surface areas (called **tracks**). The cylinder represents the circular tracks on the same vertical line within the disk pack. Read/write heads are directed to a specific record using an address consisting of the cylinder number, the recording surface number, and the data record number.

The speed of access to data on a disk is a function of the rotational speed of the disk and the speed of the access arms. The read/write heads must position themselves, and the disk pack must rotate until the proper information is located. More advanced and expensive disks have access speeds of 1.5–10 milliseconds and capacities of up to 7.5 gigabytes per unit.

FIGURE 6.13
Disk pack storage. Large systems often rely on disk packs, which provide reliable storage for large amounts of data with quick access and retrieval. A typical removal disk-pack system contains 11 two-sided disks.

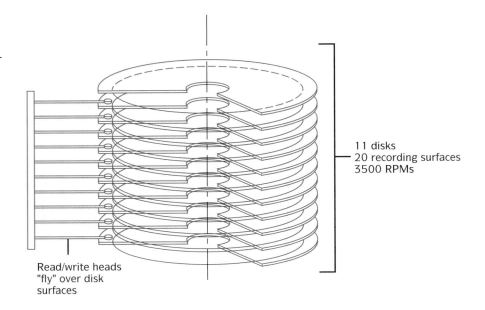

11 disks
20 recording surfaces
3500 RPMs

Read/write heads "fly" over disk surfaces

Each track contains several records. In general, 20,000 bytes of information can be stored on each track at densities of up to 12,000 bpi. If there are 20 such tracks and 200 cylinders in a disk pack, the total capacity of the illustrated disk pack is 80 megabytes. As noted previously, advanced commercial disks for large systems have much higher storage capacities over 1 billion bytes.

The entire disk pack is housed in a disk drive or disk unit. Large mainframe or minicomputer systems have multiple disk drives because they require immense disk storage capacity. Disk drive performance can be further enhanced by using a disk technology called **RAID (Redundant Array of Inexpensive Disks)**. RAID devices package more than a hundred 5.25-inch disk drives, a controller chip, and specialized software into a single large unit. While traditional disk drives deliver data from the disk drive along a single path, RAID delivers data over multiple paths simultaneously, accelerating disk access time. Smaller RAID systems provide 10 to 20 gigabytes of storage capacity, while larger systems provide over 700 gigabytes. RAID is potentially more reliable than standard disk drives because other drives are available to deliver data if one drive fails.

Microcomputers usually contain hard disks, which can store over 1.2 gigabytes, but 340 to 520 megabytes are the most common size. Microcomputers also use **floppy disks**, which are flat, 5.25-inch or 3.5-inch disks of polyester film with a magnetic coating. These disks have a storage capacity ranging from 360K to 2.8 megabytes and a much slower access rate than hard disks. Floppy disks and cartridges and packs of multiple disks use a **sector** method for storing data. As illustrated in Figure 6.14, the disk surface is divided into pie-shaped pieces, the actual number depending on the disk system used. (Some disks use eight sectors, others nine.) In most types of floppy disks, each sector has the same storage capacity (data are recorded more densely on the inner disk tracks). Each sector is assigned a unique number. Data can be located using an address consisting of the sector number and an individual data record number.

Magnetic disks on both large and small computers have several important advantages over magnetic tape. First, they permit direct access to individual records. Each record can be given a precise physical address in terms of cylinders and tracks, and the read/write head can be directed to go to that address and access the information in about 10 to 60 milliseconds. This means that the computer system does not have to search the entire file, as in a tape file, in order to find the person's record. This creates the possibility for on-line information systems providing an immediate response, such as an airline reservation or customer information system. Disk storage is often referred to as a **direct access storage device (DASD)**.

For on-line systems requiring direct access, disk technology provides the only practical means of storage today. Records can be easily and rapidly retrieved. The cost of disks has steadily declined over the years. Moreover, as we will see in Chapter 8 in

RAID (Redundant Array of Inexpensive Disks) Disk storage technology to boost disk performance by packaging more than 100 smaller disk drives with a controller chip and specialized software in a single large unit to deliver data over multiple paths simultaneously.

floppy disk Removable magnetic disk primarily used with microcomputers. The two most common standard sizes are 3.5-inch and 5.25-inch disks that are made of polyester film with magnetic coating.

sector Method of storing data on a floppy disk in which the disk is divided into pie-shaped pieces or sectors. Each sector is assigned a unique number so that data can be located using the sector number.

direct access storage device (DASD) Refers to magnetic disk technology that permits the CPU to locate a record directly, in contrast to sequential tape storage that must search the entire file.

FIGURE 6.14
The sector method of storing data. Each track of a disk can be divided into sectors. Disk storage location can be identified by sector and data record number.

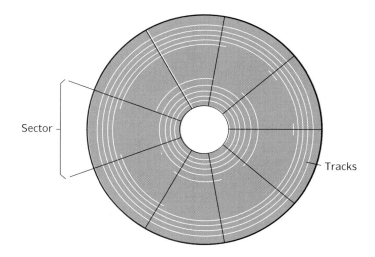

the discussion of file organization and databases, disk technology permits interrelationships among records to be built into the storage file itself. This system permits a single transaction to update or change data in a number of different files simultaneously and dramatically speeds the process of finding related records.

DASD is, however, relatively expensive compared to magnetic tape. Moreover, updating information stored on a disk destroys the old information because the old data on the disk is written over if changes are made. (In contrast, changes to data made on magnetic tape are made on a different reel of tape so that the old version of the tape can be retained and recovered.) Therefore, it becomes more difficult to back up and audit the transactions recorded on a disk. You can check this out by changing your seat selection on an airplane and then asking the clerk to tell you where you wished to sit originally. You will find that the system has no record of your previous selection because the information has been wiped off the disk.

In addition, disks can crash. The disk drives themselves are susceptible to environmental disturbances; even smoke particles can disrupt the movement of read/write heads over the disk surface. Therefore, the environment must be relatively pure and stable. That is why disk drives are sealed in a clean room.

OPTICAL DISKS

optical disk Secondary storage device on which data are recorded and read by laser beams rather than by magnetic means.

Optical disks, also called compact disks or laser optical disks, store data at densities many times greater than those of magnetic disks and are available for both microcomputers and large computers. Data are recorded on optical disks when a laser device burns microscopic pits in the reflective layer of a spiral track. Binary information is encoded by the length of these pits and the space between them. Optical disks can thus store massive quantities of data, including not only text but also pictures, sound, and full motion video, in a highly compact form. The optical disk is read by having a low-power laser beam from an optical head scan the disk (see Figure 6.15).

CD-ROM (compact disk read-only memory) Read-only optical disk storage used for imaging, reference, and database applications with massive amounts of data and for multimedia.

The most common optical disk system used with microcomputers is called **CD-ROM (compact disk read-only memory).** A 4.75-inch compact disk can store up to 660 megabytes, nearly 300 times more than a high-density floppy disk. Optical disks are most appropriate for applications where enormous quantities of unchanging data must be stored compactly for easy retrieval, or for storing graphic images and sound. CD-ROM is also less vulnerable than floppy disks to magnetism, dirt, or rough handling.

Because a single CD-ROM can store vast quantities of data, the technology is often used for storing images, sound and video, as well as text.

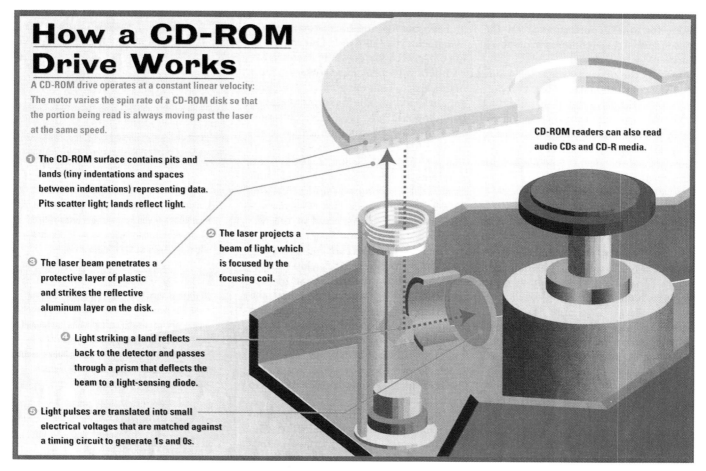

How a CD-ROM Drive Works

A CD-ROM drive operates at a constant linear velocity: The motor varies the spin rate of a CD-ROM disk so that the portion being read is always moving past the laser at the same speed.

CD-ROM readers can also read audio CDs and CD-R media.

① The CD-ROM surface contains pits and lands (tiny indentations and spaces between indentations) representing data. Pits scatter light; lands reflect light.

② The laser projects a beam of light, which is focused by the focusing coil.

③ The laser beam penetrates a protective layer of plastic and strikes the reflective aluminum layer on the disk.

④ Light striking a land reflects back to the detector and passes through a prism that deflects the beam to a light-sensing diode.

⑤ Light pulses are translated into small electrical voltages that are matched against a timing circuit to generate 1s and 0s.

FIGURE 6.15
How a CD-ROM drive works. A low-powered laser beam reads the pattern of pits and spaces representing data on the surface of the CD-ROM for translation into 0s and 1s. *From: "How a CD-ROM Drive Works," illustration by Jack Harris of Visual Logic, PC Magazine, July 1994. Reprinted by permission.*

WORM (write once/read many) Optical disk system that allows users to record data only once; data cannot be erased but can be read indefinitely.

magneto-optical disk Optical disk system that is erasable. Data are recorded by a high-powered laser beam that heats tiny spots in the magnetic media.

CD-ROM is read-only storage. No new data can be written to it; it can only be read. CD-ROM has been most widely used for reference materials with massive amounts of data, such as encyclopedias, directories, or on-line databases and for storing multimedia applications that combine text, sound, and images (see Section 6.7.) For example, financial databases from Dow Jones or Dun and Bradstreet are available on CD-ROM. The U.S. Department of Defense has initiated a system of networks and optical imaging to reduce the mountains of paper generated by technical design information and administrative data for weapons systems. The Ford Motor Company now sends its North American dealers CD-ROM disks with technical information for servicing Ford cars; it also sends a complete parts catalog and saves significantly by not having to mail a paper version.

WORM (write once/read many) optical disk systems allow users to record data only once on an optical disk. Once written, the data cannot be erased, but can be read indefinitely. WORM has been used as an alternative to microfilm for archiving digitized document images. The disadvantages of CD-ROM and WORM optical disks are that their contents cannot easily be erased and written over, as can be done with magnetic disks, and that the access speed is slower than that of magnetic disks.

Rewritable **magneto-optical disks** are starting to become cost effective for data storage. The disk surface is coated with a magnetic material that can change magnetic polarity only when heated. To record data, a high-powered laser beam heats tiny spots in the magnetic medium that allows it to accept magnetic patterns. Data can be read by shining a lower-powered laser beam at the magnetic layer and reading the reflected light. The magneto-optical disk is erasable and can be written on nearly a million times. The access speed of optical disks, while slower than that of a magnetic disk, is continuing to improve, making the optical disk a very attractive storage technology in coming years.

CD-ROM storage is likely to become more popular and more powerful in years to come. Consumer electronics companies such as Sony, Philips Electronics, Time Warner, and Toshiba are developing high-capacity compact disks that can store over 4 billion bytes of data, enough to hold two to three hours of high-resolution digital video with stereo sound. Such digital videodisks would contain 15 times more data than current CD-ROMs and would work with computers of all sizes as well as video and video-game players (Markoff, 1995).

6.6   INPUT AND OUTPUT DEVICES

Human beings interact with computer systems largely through input and output devices. Advances in information systems rely not only on the speed and capacity of the CPU but also on the speed, capacity, and design of the input and output devices. Input/output devices are often called peripheral devices.

INPUT DEVICES

The traditional method of data entry has been by keyboarding. Today, most data are entered directly into the computer using a data entry terminal and they are processed on-line. For instance, on-line airline reservation and customer information systems have reservation clerks or salespeople enter transactions directly while dealing with the customer, and their systems are updated immediately. In this manner, a business can eliminate a separate data entry staff and the associated costs.

Some batch applications developed during an earlier era in computing might still use keypunching to obtain input. Data entry clerks use a keypunch machine to code characters on an 80-column card, designating each character with a unique punch in a specific location on the card. An electromechanical card reader senses the holes and solid parts of the cards. A single card could store up to 80 bytes of information (80 columns). Key-to-tape or key-to-disk machines allowed data to be keyed directly onto magnetic tape or disk for later computer processing.

The Computer Mouse

computer mouse Hand-held input device whose movement on the desktop controls the position of the cursor on the computer display screen.

The "point-and-click" actions of the **computer mouse** have made it an increasingly popular alternative to keyboard and text-based commands. A mouse is a hand-held device that is usually connected to the computer by a cable. The computer user moves the mouse around on a desktop to control the position of the cursor on a video display screen. Once the cursor is in the desired position, the user can push a button on the mouse to select a command. The mouse can also be used to "draw" images on the screen.

Touch Screens

touch screen Input device technology that permits the entering or selecting of commands and data by touching the surface of a sensitized video display monitor with a finger or a pointer.

Touch screens are easy to use and are appealing to people who can't use traditional keyboards. Users can enter limited amounts of data by touching the surface of a sensitized video display monitor with a finger or a pointer. With colorful graphics, sound, and simple menus, touch screens allow the user to make selections by touching specified parts of the screen. Touch screens are proliferating in retail stores, restaurants, shopping malls, and even in some schools. For instance, music stores can install Intouch, touch screen–equipped kiosks produced by Muze Inc. of Brooklyn, to sell audio compact disks. Customers can use the touch screen to select 30 second samples of songs before making up their minds. Having listened to one song, a customer can again touch the screen to bring up lists of other songs by the same musicians.

Source Data Automation

source data automation Input technology that captures data in computer-readable form at the time and place the data are created.

Source data automation captures data in computer-readable form at the time and place they are created. Point-of-sale systems, optical bar-code scanners used in supermarkets, and other optical character recognition devices are examples of source data automation. One of the advantages of source data automation is that the many errors that occur when people use keyboards to enter data are almost eliminated. Bar code scanners make fewer than 1 error in 10,000 transactions, whereas skilled keypunchers make about 1 error for every 1000 keystrokes.

Moreover, source data automation permits information about events to be captured directly and immediately, with on-the-spot error correction. Businesses using these devices do not need a separate keypunch staff. The principal source data automation technologies are magnetic ink character recognition, optical character recognition, pen-based input, digital scanners, voice input, and sensors.

magnetic ink character recognition (MICR) Input technology that translates characters written in magnetic ink into digital codes for processing.

Magnetic ink character recognition (MICR) technology is used primarily in check processing for the banking industry. The bottom portion of a typical check contains characters that are preprinted using a special ink. Characters identify the bank, checking account, and check number. A MICR reader translates the characters on checks that have been cashed and sent to the bank for processing into digital form for the computer. The amount of the check, which is written in ordinary ink, must be keyed in by hand.

optical character recognition (OCR) Form of source data automation in which optical scanning devices read specially designed data off source documents and translate the data into digital form for the computer.

Optical character recognition (OCR) devices translate specially designed marks, characters, and codes into digital form. The most widely used optical code is the **bar code**, which is used in point-of-sale systems in supermarkets and retail stores. Bar codes are also used in hospitals, libraries, military operations, and transportation facilities. The codes can include time, date, and location data in addition to identification data; the information makes them useful for analyzing the movement of items and determining what has happened to them during production or other processes. (The discussion of the United Parcel Service in Chapter 1 and the case concluding this chapter show how valuable bar codes can be for this purpose.)

bar code Form of OCR technology widely used in supermarkets and retail stores in which identification data are coded into a series of bars.

Handwriting-recognition devices such as pen-based "tablets," "notebooks," and "notepads," are promising new input technologies, especially for people working in the sales or service areas or for those who have traditionally shunned computer keyboards. These **pen-based input** devices usually consist of a flat-screen display tablet and a pen-like stylus.

pen-based input Input devices such as tablets, notebooks, and notepads consisting of a flat-screen display tablet and a pen-like stylus that digitizes handwriting.

With pen-based input, users print directly onto the tablet-sized screen. The screen is fitted with a transparent grid of fine wires that detects the presence of the special stylus, which emits a faint signal from its tip. The screen can also interpret tapping and flicking gestures made with the stylus.

Pen-based input devices transform the letters and numbers written by users on the tablet into digital form, where they can be stored or processed and analyzed. For instance, the United Parcel Service replaced its drivers' familiar clipboard with a battery-powered Delivery Information Acquisition Device (DIAD) to capture signatures (see the Chapter 1 Window on Technology) along with other information required for pickup and delivery. The Gillette Corporation supplied GridPad HD pen-based computers to its store merchandisers who are responsible for stocking stores and ensuring that Gillette products, such as Right Guard, are displayed as prominently as possible. The merchandisers had never used computers before. The merchandisers enter handwritten numbers on electronic "forms" into the notebooks, and transmit the information via telephone links to Gillette. Gillette thus can receive stocking plans and information on products, pricing, and promotions immediately from the field. This technology requires special pattern-recognition software to accept pen-based input instead of keyboard input. At present, most pen-based systems cannot recognize free-hand writing very well.

digital scanners Input devices that translate images such as pictures or documents into digital form for processing.

voice input device Technology that converts the spoken word into digital form for processing.

sensors Devices that collect data directly from the environment for input into a computer system.

batch processing A method of collecting and processing data in which transactions are accumulated and stored until a specified time when it is convenient or necessary to process them as a group.

on-line processing A method of collecting and processing data in which transactions are entered directly into the computer system and processed immediately.

transaction file In batch systems, a file in which all transactions are accumulated to await processing.

master file Contains all permanent information and is updated during processing by transaction data.

video display terminal (VDT) A screen, also referred to as a cathode ray tube (CRT). Provides a visual image of both user input and computer output. Displays text or graphics as either color or monochrome images.

Digital scanners translate images such as pictures or documents into digital form, and are an essential component of image processing systems such as those described in Chapter 15. **Voice input devices** convert spoken words into digital form. Voice-recognition software (see Chapter 7) compares the electrical patterns produced by the speaker's voice to a set of prerecorded patterns. If the patterns match, the input is accepted. Most voice systems still have limited "vocabularies" of several hundred to several thousand words and can accept only very simple commands. For instance, some branches of the U.S. Postal Service are using voice-recognition systems to make sorting packages and envelopes more efficient. In one application, users can speak out ZIP codes instead of keying them in, so that both hands can manipulate a package.

Sensors are devices that collect data directly from the environment for input into a computer system. For instance, sensors are being used in General Motors cars with onboard computers and screens that display the map of the surrounding area and the driver's route. Sensors in each wheel and a magnetic compass supply information to the computer for determining the car's location. The South Coast Air Quality Management District's system uses sensors in smokestacks to supply data for monitoring pollution emissions. The sensors continuously measure emissions and are linked to microcomputers at the site of each smokestack, which send the data collected by the sensors to the district's central computer for analysis.

BATCH AND ON-LINE INPUT AND PROCESSING

The manner in which data are input into the computer affects how the data can be processed. Information systems collect and process information in one of two ways: through batch or through on-line processing. In **batch processing**, transactions such as orders or payroll time cards are accumulated and stored in a group or batch until the time when, because of some reporting cycle, it is efficient or necessary to process them. This was the only method of processing until the early 1960s, and it is still used today in older systems or some systems with massive volumes of transactions. In **on-line processing**, which is now very common, the user enters transactions into a device that is directly connected to the computer system. The transactions are usually processed immediately.

The demands of the business determine the type of processing. If the user needs periodic or occasional reports or output, as in payroll or end-of-the-year reports, batch processing is most efficient. If the user needs immediate information and processing, as in an airline or hotel reservation system, then the system should use on-line processing.

Figure 6.16 compares batch and on-line processing. Batch systems often use tape as a storage medium, whereas on-line processing systems use disk storage, which permits immediate access to specific items of information. In batch systems, transactions are accumulated in a **transaction file**, which contains all the transactions for a particular time period. Periodically this file is used to update a **master file**, which contains permanent information on entities. (An example is a payroll master file with employee earnings and deductions data. It is updated with weekly time-card transactions.) Adding the transaction data to the existing master file creates a new master file. In on-line processing, transactions are entered into the system immediately and the system usually responds immediately. The master file is updated continually. In on-line processing, there is a direct connection to the computer for input and output.

OUTPUT DEVICES

The major data output devices are **cathode ray tube (CRT)** terminals (sometimes called **video display terminals,** or **VDTs,** and printers.

The CRT is probably the most popular form of information output in modern computer systems. It works much like a television picture tube, with an electronic "gun" shooting a beam of electrons to illuminate the pixels on the screen. The more pixels per screen, the higher the resolution. CRT monitors can be classified as mono-

FIGURE 6.16
A comparison of batch and on-line processing. In batch processing, transactions are accumulated and stored in a group. Since batches are processed on a regular interval basis, such as daily, weekly, or monthly, information in the system will not always be up to date. A typical batch-processing job is payroll preparation. In on-line processing, transactions are input immediately and usually processed immediately. Information in the system is generally up to date. A typical on-line application is an airline reservation system.

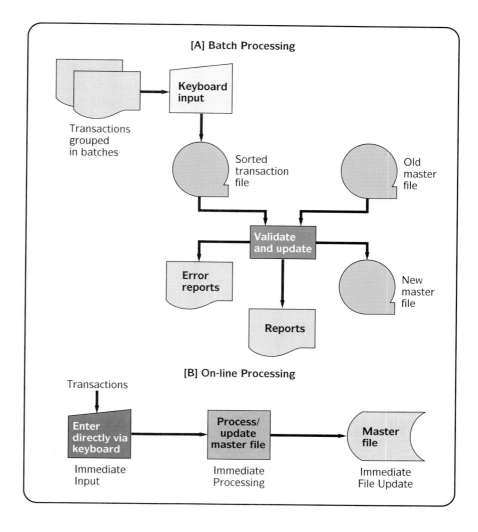

chrome or color and by their display capabilities. Some display only text, whereas others display both text and graphics. Typical CRTs display 80 columns and 24 lines of text data. Display devices for graphics often utilize **bit mapping**. Bit mapping allows each pixel on the screen to be addressed and manipulated by the computer (as opposed to blocks of pixels in character addressable displays). This requires more computer memory but permits finer detail and the ability to produce any kind of image on the display screen. Special-purpose graphics terminals used in CAD/CAM and commercial art have very high-resolution capabilities (1280 x 1024 pixels). (See Chapter 15 for further discussion.)

bit mapping The technology that allows each pixel on the screen to be addressed and manipulated by the computer.

Printers

Printers produce a printed hard copy of information output. They include impact printers (a standard typewriter or a dot matrix) and nonimpact printers (laser, inkjet, and thermal transfer printers). Most printers print one character at a time, but some commercial printers print an entire line or page at a time. Line printers capable of printing an entire line of output in a single step can print up to 3000 lines per minute. Page printers print an entire page at a time, outputting 20,000 lines per minute. Printers working with microcomputers typically provide dot-matrix print at a speed of 60 to over 400 characters per second. Much slower letter-quality printers operate in the 10 to 50 characters per-second range. In general, impact printers are slower than nonimpact printers. Laser printers for microcomputers can print 4 to 8 pages per minute. Laser printers in large computer centers can print over 100 pages per minute.

printer A computer output device that provides paper "hard copy" output in the form of text or graphics.

Dot-matrix printer quality is generally much lower than letter quality and is used for less important documents and spreadsheets. "Intelligence," or some processing ability, is built into many newer printers and other input and output devices to take over tasks that were formerly performed by the main computer. For example, many microcomputer printers, such as the Hewlett-Packard Laserjet series or the Apple LaserWriter, are programmed to store graphic elements and various type fonts, which can be used selectively by different pieces of software.

Other Devices

Microfilm and microfiche have been used to compactly store output as microscopic filmed images, and they are used mainly by insurance companies or other firms that need to output and store large numbers of documents. These media are cumbersome to search through and will be replaced by optical disk technology.

plotter Output device using multicolored pens to draw high-quality graphic documents.

High-quality graphic documents can be created using **plotters** with multicolored pens to draw (rather than print) computer output. Plotters are much slower than printers, but are useful for outputting large-size charts, maps, or drawings.

voice output device Converts digital output data into spoken words.

A **voice output device** converts digital output data back into intelligible speech. Sounds are prerecorded, coded, and stored on disk, to be translated back as spoken words. For instance, when you call for information on the telephone, you may hear a computer "voice" respond with the telephone number you requested.

6.7 INFORMATION TECHNOLOGY TRENDS

Advances in materials science, manufacturing, and concepts of computing promise to maintain the historic growth pattern in hardware power. Over the last 30 years, computing costs have dropped by a factor of 10 each decade and capacity has increased by a factor of at least 100 each decade. This momentum will most likely be maintained.

Today's microprocessors can put a mainframe on a desktop, and eventually into a briefcase or shirt pocket. Chapter 10 shows how the traditional mainframe is being supplanted by networks of powerful desktop machines, although the mainframe will never be eliminated. The future will see even more intelligence built into everyday devices, with mainframe and perhaps even supercomputer-like computing power packed in a pocket- or notebook-sized computer. Pen, notebook, and palmtop computers will be as pervasive as hand-held calculators. Computers on a chip will help guide automobiles, military weapons, robots, and everyday household devices. Computers and related information technologies will blend data, images, and sound, sending them coursing through vast networks that can process all of them with equal ease. Potentially, computer technology could be so powerful and integrated into daily experiences it would appear essentially invisible to the user (Weiser, 1993). We can see how this might be possible through the use of multimedia, superchips, and fifth-generation computers.

MULTIMEDIA

multimedia Technologies that facilitate the integration of two or more types of media such as text, graphics, sound, voice, full motion video, or animation into a computer-based application.

Multimedia is defined as the technologies that facilitate the integration of two or more types of media, such as text, graphics, sound, voice, full motion video, still video, or animation into a computer-based application. From the 1990s through the twenty-first century, multimedia will be the foundation of new consumer products and services, such as electronic books and newspapers, electronic classroom presentation technologies, full motion video conferencing, imaging, graphics design tools, and video electronic and voice mail.

By pressing a button, a person using a computer can call up a screenful of text; another button might bring up related video images. Still another might bring up related talk or music. For instance, Bell Canada, which provides residential and busi-

One of the principal applications of multimedia today is for interactive corporate training.

ness telephone services across Canada, uses a multimedia application to help diagnose and repair problems on the network. The application contains hundreds of repair manuals that have been scanned, digitized, and made available on-line to technicians and network analysts as they work on repairing off-site network components. Each multimedia workstation can display maps of the network, sound alarms when problems occur on specific equipment, and fax maps on-line to repair personnel who have trouble locating their appointments. A voice-message annotation feature lets users click on an icon to hear new information or additional comments on specific diagnostic or repair cases (DePompa, 1993).

Multimedia systems combine the elements of today's personal computers (a computer, printer, keyboard, and mouse) with two new elements: audio (sound) and video (pictures). Figure 6.17 illustrates some of the hardware components that would be required to create and run multimedia applications. Today's microcomputers can be converted to multimedia systems by purchasing special expansion boards. By the year 2000, computers will come with built-in multimedia capabilities.

The marriage of text, graphics, sound, and video data into a single application has been made possible by the advances in microprocessor and storage technologies described in this chapter. A simple multimedia system consists of a personal computer with a 32-bit microprocessor and a CD-ROM disk. A five-inch optical disk holding more than 600 megabytes of information can store an hour of music, several thousand full-color pictures, several minutes of video or animation, and millions of words. For instance, a single optical disk can store all 26 volumes of *Compton's MultiMedia Encyclopedia.* It includes 15,000 drawings, charts, photographs, and paintings, many in full color; 45 animated sequences; an hour of audio clips of famous speeches and music; and *Webster's Intermediate Dictionary,* plus about 9 million words.

The possibilities of this technology are endless, but the most promising business applications appear to be in training and presentations. For training, multimedia is appealing because it is interactive and permits two-way communication (Lambert, 1990).

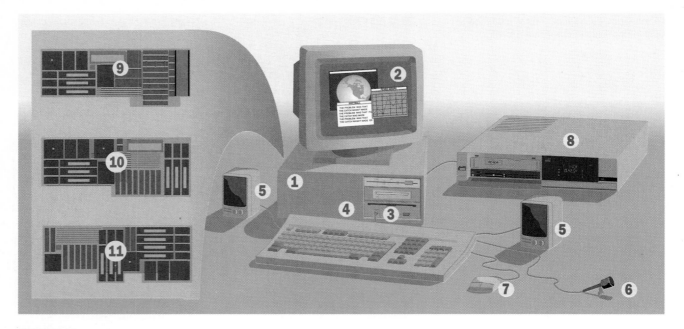

FIGURE 6.17

Multimedia applications require specially configured systems. This figure illustrates 11 components in a system used to develop a multimedia application. (1) CPU and primary storage: a minimum 80386/33 megahertz chip and 8 megabytes RAM. (2) Monitor: color monitor supporting super high resolutions from 640 × 480 to 1280 × 1024; minimum 17″ screen. (3) CD-ROM: drive with 280 millisecond access time and 150 kilobits/second data transfer rate. (4) Hard disk: minimum 300 megabytes with 15 millisecond access time. (5) Stereo speakers. (6) Microphone for voice input. (7) Mouse. (8) Video input device or video board connected to a VCR or laser video disk player. (9) Sound card. (10) Video card. (11) Video compression card. Adapter cards integrate sound and video into the computer and digitally compress full-motion video. *Adapted from: J. William Semich, "Multimedia Tools for Development Pros,"* Datamation, *August 15, 1992. Reprinted with permission from DATAMATION © 1992. Reed Publishing (USA) Inc.*

People can use multimedia training sessions any time of the day, at their own pace. Instructors can easily integrate words, sounds, pictures, and both live and animated video to produce lessons that capture students' imaginations. For example, the multimedia training material used by the salespeople at Marion Merrell Dow Pharmaceutical allows users to display an index of a video glossary by clicking a button during the presentation of a selected topic. The last term used is highlighted. The user can view the glossary clip, return to the presentation, and be quizzed by the system. Andersen Consulting Company now delivers its business practice course on three CD-ROMs with 180 minutes of digital video and interactive training and testing techniques. By replacing classroom training, this multimedia course saves the firm $10 million per year (Williamson, 1994).

Multimedia is providing powerful tools for sales presentations. For example, Honeywell, Inc., based in Minneapolis, is using video and audio on laptop computers to describe Honeywell's products and services. By providing all of its 600 sales representatives with the same multimedia presentation on their laptops, the company finds it can promote its products in a more consistent manner.

There will be numerous organizational applications of multimedia because multimedia is likely to be a major instrument for obtaining corporate information. When multimedia is coupled with the telecommunications technologies described in Chapters 9 and 10, desktop-to-desktop videoconferencing and file sharing become feasible and will likely change the way people across organizations meet and interact. People will be able to capture, store, manipulate, and transmit photos and other document images and possibly full motion video on a network as easily as they do with text. For instance, financial service firms could index a TV news report next to a related print story about a development affecting a company. The Window on Organizations focuses on kiosks, a rapidly emerging use of multimedia coupled with

DELIVERING VOTER EDUCATION VIA MULTIMEDIA KIOSKS

How can computers help educate millions of citizens who will become the rulers of their country for the first time? In the April 1994 South African elections, millions of South African blacks who had never been allowed to vote before were able to vote. That in itself was a political revolution. But to complicate the situation further, many of these new voters were illiterate. In addition, they were faced with a daunting ballot, having to select candidates from among 19 political parties. One method used to help educate these first-time voters was to place multimedia kiosks in locations throughout the country.

The Voter Education Kiosks were developed by Sandenbergh Pavon Ltd., a multimedia company located in Johannesburg, South Africa. The kiosks disseminated basic information on when and where to vote, why the citizen should vote, as well as basic information on the candidates and parties. According to Sandenbergh Pavon director Margot Sandenbergh, they "tried to make the kiosk as graphical and simple as possible since many illiterate people will be voting for the first time." The basic technology used in the kiosks was

Intel Corp. 486-based PCs using 14-inch color monitors. The kiosk screens, high-resolution graphics, animation, full motion videos, and audio components were created using IconAuthor, a multimedia application development system from AimTech Corp. in Nashua, New Hampshire. Using touch screens and political party symbols, new voters were able to listen to mission statements from each of the political parties and view digital video messages from the candidates. The kiosks even explained the role of the independent election observers from the United Nations and other organizations. A total of 30 kiosks were set up and rotated to 70 different sites around the country. According to Sandenbergh, well over one million people used the kiosks by the time the election took place.

By using IconAuthor, the developers were able to create a flexible, easily altered presentation. That flexibility proved essential due to the unstable political landscape in the newly emerging democracy where late political changes were a given. For example, because the Inkatha Freedom Party had originally refused to participate in the elections, it was not represented in the kiosk presentations. When, at the last minute, the

party agreed to compete in the elections, its information had to be added very quickly. Similarly, several parties changed their names and party messages late in the campaign, and their kiosk

> **To Think About:** *Why were multimedia kiosks so appropriate for the task of educating the new voters? What management, organization, and technology issues had to be addressed when developing this application?*

material also had to be updated rapidly.

This ground-breaking use of computer technology was funded by South Africa's Institute for Democratic Education, the European Economic Community, and the United Nations Economic, Scientific, and Cultural Organization (UNESCO). Sandenbergh says that "UNESCO is now lobbying in Paris to help create a number of similar projects using this multimedia kiosk technology across Europe and Africa."

Source: Mitch Betts, "Multimedia Kiosks Provide Voter Education in South Africa Election," *Computerworld*, May 9, 1994.

telecommunications. Throughout this text, we will be looking at the various ways multimedia will be used in information systems.

The most difficult element to incorporate into multimedia information systems has been full motion video, because so much data must be brought under the digital control of the computer. While laser videodisks and VCRs can deliver video images to microcomputers, this technology is limited to displaying images. The process of actually integrating video with other kinds of data requires special software or compression boards with dedicated video processing chips. The massive amounts of data in each video image must be digitally encoded, stored, and manipulated electronically, using techniques that "compress" the digital data.

In 1992, Apple computers were the first to come equipped with software (called QuickTime™) and some of the hardware to play back multimedia disks containing text, numbers, video, and sound. Microsoft Corporation has developed multimedia standards so that personal computers based on the IBM microcomputer model can play back and even author multimedia presentations. By the year 2000 all computers, regardless of size, will have built-in multimedia capabilities combining existing

---

text and numbers with music, full motion and still frame video (snapshots), animation, voice messages, telephone, and fax capabilities.

SUPERCHIPS

Semiconductor researchers have continued to find means of packaging circuits more densely, so that millions of transistors can be packed onto a fingernail-sized silicon wafer. Intel's P6 microprocessor squeezes 5.5 million transistors on a postage-stamp size silicon pad and can achieve twice the processing speed of the Pentium. The most powerful microprocessors—such as the P6, Pentium and PowerPC chips and Digital Equipment Corporation's Alpha chip—package mainframe and even supercomputer-like capabilities on a single chip.

In addition to improving their design, microprocessors have been made to perform faster by shrinking the distance between transistors. This process gives the electrical current less distance to travel. Figure 6.18 shows how much progress has been made. One step in fashioning microprocessors is to etch lines in silicon wafers that form the outlines of circuits. The narrower the lines forming transistors, the larger the number of transistors that can be squeezed onto a single chip, and the faster these circuits will operate. Figure 6.18 shows that line widths have shrunk from the diameter of a hair

FIGURE 6.18
The shrinking size and growth in number of transistors. *Courtesy of Intel Corporation.*

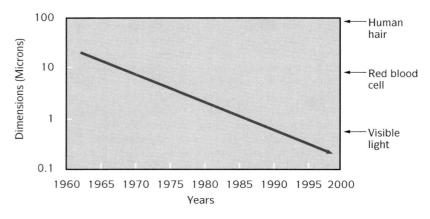

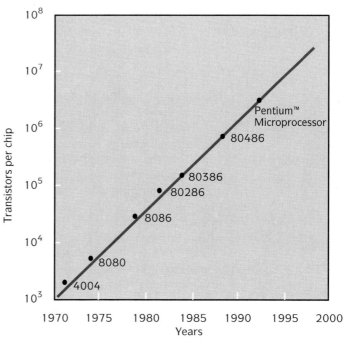

to less than one micron, and should reach one fifth of a micron by
lower part of the figure shows the number of transistors on som
processors and memory chips. Since the number of transistors t
cally onto a single silicon chip is doubling every 18 months, betv
lion transistors could conceivably be squeezed onto a single r
year 2000. There are physical limits to this approach that may
researchers are experimenting with new materials to increase r

FIFTH-GENERATION COMPUTERS

Conventional computers are based on the Von Neumann architecture, which
processes information serially, one instruction at a time. In the future, more computers will use parallel processing and massively parallel processing to blend voice,
images, and massive pools of data from diverse sources, using artificial intelligence
and intricate mathematical models.

massively parallel computers
Computers that use hundreds or
thousands of processing chips
to attack large computing problems simultaneously.

    Massively parallel computers, illustrated in Figure 6.19, have huge networks of
processor chips interwoven in complex and flexible ways. As opposed to parallel processing, where small numbers of powerful but expensive specialized chips are linked
together, massively parallel machines chain hundreds or even thousands of inexpensive, commonly used chips to attack large computing problems, attaining supercomputer speeds. For instance, Wal-Mart Stores uses a massively parallel machine to sift
through an inventory and sales trend database with 1.8 trillion bytes of data.
Massively parallel systems are said to have cost and speed advantages over conventional computers because they can take advantage of off-the-shelf chips. They may
be able to accomplish processing work for one-tenth to one-twentieth the cost of traditional mainframes or supercomputers.

    Today's supercomputers can perform hundreds of billions of calculations per sec-
ond. Now supercomputer makers are racing to harness tens of thousands of microprocessors and memory chips together to create super-supercomputers that can perform more than a trillion mathematical calculations each second—a teraflop. The
term *teraflop* comes from the Greek *teras*, which for mathematicians means one trillion, and *flop*, an acronym for floating point operations per second. (A floating point
operation is a basic computer arithmetic operation, such as addition, on numbers
that include a decimal point.) In the twenty-first century, teraflop machines could
support projects such as mapping the surface of planets, designing new computers,
or testing the aerodynamics of supersonic airplanes, where trillions of calculations
would be required.

FIGURE 6.19
Computer architecture. A comparison of traditional
serial processing, parallel processing, and massively
parallel processing. *From John Markoff, "Foray Into
Mainstream for Parallel Computing."* The New York Times,
*June 15, 1992. Copyright © 1992 by the New York Times
Corporation. Reprinted by permission.*

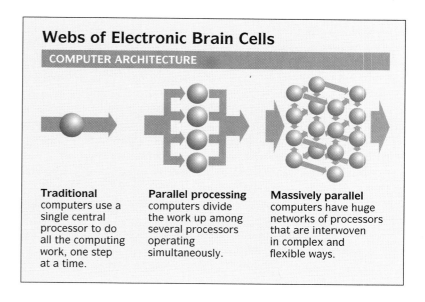

ping abreast of technological change. Because the nology is growing in power so rapidly and is changing basic patterns of information processing, managers must keep abreast of changes in the field. This requires time and resources. In medium to large firms, a person or small group must be assigned the task of tracking new technological developments and encouraging prototypes within the firm.

2. Making wise purchasing decisions. Soon after having made an investment in information technology, managers find the completed system is obsolete and too expensive given the power and lower cost of new technology. In this environment, it is very difficult to keep

one's own systems up to date. A rather considerable amount of time must be spent anticipating and planning for technological change.

3. Training the information systems staff and all employees. In the transition from the mainframe computing to desktops, enormous changes in perspective and skills and attitudes are required on the part of an organization's information systems staff. Typically, staff members must be completely retrained every five years. All employees likewise will require extensive retraining simply to keep abreast of new ways of doing business with new information technologies.

Summary

1. Identify the hardware components in a typical computer system. The modern computer system has six major components: a central processing unit (CPU), primary storage, input devices, output devices, secondary storage, and communications devices.

2. Describe how information is represented and processed in a computer system. Digital computers store and process information in the form of binary digits called *bits*. A string of 8 bits is called a *byte*. There are several coding schemes for arranging binary digits into characters. The most common are EBCDIC and ASCII. The CPU is the center of the computer, where the manipulation of symbols, numbers, and letters occurs. The CPU has two components: an arithmetic-logic unit and a control unit. The arithmetic-logic unit performs arithmetic and logical operations on data, while the control unit controls and coordinates the other components of the computer.

The CPU is closely tied to primary memory, or primary storage, which stores data and program instructions temporarily before and after processing.

Several different kinds of semiconductor memory chips are used with primary storage: RAM (random access memory) is used for short-term storage of data and program instructions, while ROM (read-only memory) permanently stores important program instructions. Other memory devices include PROM (programmable read-only memory) and EPROM (erasable programmable read-only memory.)

3. Distinguish between generations of computer hardware. Computer technology has gone through four generations, from vacuum tubes to transistors, integrated circuits, and very large-scale integrated circuits, each dramatically increasing computer processing power while shrinking the size of computing hardware.

4. Contrast the capabilities of mainframes, minicomputers, microcomputers, workstations, and supercomputers. Depending on their size and processing power,

computers are categorized as mainframes, minicomputers, microcomputers, workstations, or supercomputers. Mainframes are the largest computers with 50 megabytes to over 1 gigabyte of RAM; minicomputers are midrange machines with 10 megabytes to over 1 gigabyte of RAM; microcomputers are desktop or laptop machines with 640 kilobytes to 64 megabytes of RAM; workstations are desktop machines with powerful mathematical and graphic capabilities and 8 to 300 megabytes of RAM and supercomputers are sophisticated, powerful computers that can perform massive and complex computations because they use parallel processing. The capabilities of microprocessors used in these computers can be gauged by their word length, data bus width, and cycle speed. Because of continuing advances in microprocessor technology, the distinctions between these various types of computers are constantly changing. Microcomputers are now powerful enough to perform much of the work that was formerly limited to mainframes and minicomputers.

5. Describe the various media for storing data and programs in a computer system. The principal forms of secondary storage are magnetic tape, magnetic disk, and optical disk. Tape stores records in sequence and can only be used in batch processing. Disk permits direct access to specific records and is much faster than tape. Disk technology is used in on-line processing. Optical disks can store vast amounts of data compactly. CD-ROM disk systems can only be read from, but rewritable optical disk systems are becoming available.

6. Compare the major input and output devices and approaches to input and processing. The principal input devices are keyboards, computer mice, touch screens, magnetic ink and optical character recognition, pen-based instruments, digital scanners, sensors, and voice input. The principal output devices are video display terminals, printers, plotters, voice output devices, and microfilm and microfiche. In batch processing, transactions are accumulated and stored in a group until the time when it is efficient or necessary to process them. In on-line processing, the user enters transactions into a device that is directly connected to the computer system. The transactions are usually processed immediately.

7. **Describe multimedia and future information technology trends.** Multimedia integrates two or more types of media, such as text, graphics, sound, voice, full motion video, still video, and/or animation into a computer-based application. The future will see steady and impressive progress toward faster chips at lower cost and microprocessors with the power of today's mainframes or supercomputers. Hardware using massively parallel processing will be utilized more widely, and computers and related information technologies will be able to blend data, images, and sound.

Key Terms

Bit	PROM (programmable	Parallel processing	Source data automation
Byte	read-only memory)	Secondary storage	Magnetic ink character
EBCDIC (Extended Binary	EPROM (erasable program-	Register	recognition (MICR)
Coded Decimal	mable read-only memory)	Cache	Optical character
Interchange Code)	Arithmetic-logic unit (ALU)	Magnetic tape	recognition (OCR)
ASCII (American Standard	Control unit	Magnetic disk	Bar code
Code for Information	Machine cycle	Hard disk	Pen-based input
Interchange)	Computer generations	Cylinder	Digital scanners
Parity	Microprocessor	Track	Voice input device
Pixel	Word length	RAID (Redundant Array of	Sensors
Millisecond	Megahertz	Inexpensive Disks)	Batch processing
Microsecond	Data bus width	Floppy disk	On-line processing
Nanosecond	Reduced instruction set	Sector	Transaction file
Kilobyte	computing (RISC)	Direct access storage	Master file
Megabyte	Mainframe	device (DASD)	Cathode ray tube (CRT)
Gigabyte	Minicomputer	Optical disk	Video display terminal (VDT)
Central processing unit	Microcomputer	CD-ROM (compact disk	Bit mapping
(CPU)	Workstation	read-only memory)	Printer
Primary storage	Supercomputer	WORM (write once/read	Plotter
RAM (random access	Distributed processing	many)	Voice output device
memory)	Centralized processing	Magneto-optical disk	Multimedia
Semiconductor	Downsizing	Computer mouse	Massively parallel
ROM (read-only memory)	Cooperative processing	Touch screen	computers

Review Questions

1. What are the components of a contemporary computer system?
2. Distinguish between a bit and a byte.
3. What are ASCII and EBCDIC, and why are they used? Why can true binary not be used in a computer as a machine language?
4. Name and define the principal measures of computer time and storage capacity.
5. What problems of coordination exist in a computing environment and why?
6. Name the major components of the CPU and the function of each.
7. Describe how information is stored in primary memory.
8. What are the four different types of semiconductor memory, and when are they used?
9. Describe the major generations of computers and the characteristics of each.

10. Name and describe the factors affecting the speed and performance of a microprocessor.
11. What are downsizing and cooperative processing?
12. What is the difference between primary and secondary storage?
13. List the most important secondary storage media. What are the strengths and limitations of each?
14. List and describe the major input devices.
15. What is the difference between batch and on-line processing? Diagram the difference.
16. List and describe the major output devices.
17. Distinguish between serial, parallel, and massively parallel processing.
18. What is multimedia? What technologies are involved?

Discussion Questions

1. What is the difference between a mainframe, a mini-computer, and a microcomputer? Between a mainframe and a supercomputer? Between a microcomputer and a workstation? Why are these distinctions disappearing?

2. How are the capabilities of an information system affected by its input, output, and storage devices?

3. A firm would like to introduce computers into its order entry process but feels that it should wait for a new generation of machines to be developed. After all, any machine bought now will be quickly out of date and less expensive a few years from now. Discuss.

Group Project

It has been predicted that by the year 2000, notebook computers will be available that have 25 times the power of a current personal computer, with a touch-sensitive color screen that one can write on or draw on with a stylus or type on when a program displays a keyboard. Each will have a small compact, rewritable, removable CD-ROM disk that can store the equivalent of a set of encyclopedias. In addition, the computers will have elementary voice-recognition capabilities, including the ability to record sound and give voice responses to questions. The computer will be able to carry on a dialogue by voice, graphics, typed words, and displayed video graphics. Thus, computers will be about the size of a thick pad of letter paper and just as portable and convenient, but with the intelligence of a computer and the multimedia capabilities of a television set. Such a computer is expected to cost about $2000. Form a group with three or four of your classmates and develop an analysis of the impacts such developments would have on university education. Explain why you think the impact will or will not occur.

Case Study

BAR CODES BECOME A STRATEGIC BUSINESS WEAPON

According to most business analysts, video rental stores will soon be joining the dinosaurs—they too will be extinct. According to this view, they will be replaced by the new, interactive, fiber optic cable and telephone systems that will be in our homes in the near future. Analysts say that these systems will allow customers to call up any movie they wish and at a time of their own choosing. They will be able to play the movie, stopping and starting it, replaying and fast forwarding it, all as if they were using a tape in their own VCR. With all that function at low prices and without ever having to leave home, no one will want to bother going out to a store to rent a videotape. So why is Wayne Bailey optimistic that his Aurora, Colorado, video store business, Accurate Inventory Management (AIM), will thrive? Bailey believes that it will take many years and many hundreds of billions of dollars in technology investments before the cable business will be able to replace video stores. In the meantime, he is betting on other technology to cause his company to flourish. One key to his planned, prosperous future is the computer input device he is using—bar code scanners.

Bailey is using scanners as part of a larger business plan both to service his customers better and more efficiently and to expand his enterprise into new, related areas. First, he has redefined the business he is in from movie rentals to entertainment rentals. When video games became popular, he began renting them. Then, he moved into music video rentals, followed most recently by rentals of multimedia CD-ROM titles. Bailey also looked around and realized that many retail merchants, such as grocery stores, were also renting videos, but for them this was a sideline business. He decided he would market to these retail merchants his inventory management skills and his computerized video rental technology, managing their video rental businesses for them better than they ever could themselves. Next, he realized that video rental companies are constantly buying and selling their inventory (primarily movies), based upon their local demand. He decided to establish a national bulletin board where their videos could be bought and sold. AIM makes its money from this bulletin board by charging all users $28 per hour of connect time. AIM and Bailey have been successful in all these new businesses.

Before examining how bar code scanners have contributed to the success of AIM, we need first to understand more of Bailey's choices for bar

---

code technology. Bar coding, of course, is a form of computer data input in which bar codes are read by scanners. Bar code scanning offers the user near 100 percent accuracy as well as speed and ease of use. The user of the technology has a range of choices to make before implementing bar coding. First, Bailey had to decide what to bar code. He chose not only to bar code the rental items (such as videos and CD-ROMs), but also to bar code the customers themselves, issuing a bar-coded card customers present when renting. Thus, all the checkout counter clerk needs to do is to scan the bar code on both the customer card and the item or items being rented, and the computer has all the data needed, instantly and accurately. Next, Bailey had to decide what information he wanted the bar codes to carry. The codes can contain whatever information the user decides needs to be recorded. For example, AIM bar codes for their inventory items might include the item type (movie, CD-ROM, music), the category (adventure, comedy, horror), name (*Star Wars, Crooklyn, Frankenstein*), and copy number.

Next, the user needs to determine how to produce and affix the bar codes. Many products come with bar codes on their labels (such as pre-packaged items in grocery stores). However, a business like AIM that wants to determine the data to be carried will have to design, produce, and affix its own bar codes or go to outside specialists to do the job. The method of production is a key choice because bar codes must be printed clearly and be easily readable by the scanner. Otherwise the scanner will either fail to read the codes altogether, or else the codes will often be misread, resulting in bad data being stored. Bailey originally chose to produce his own bar codes, but he quickly found that his dot-matrix printer did not produce bar codes with the clarity needed. His checkout clerks ended up spending a great deal of time typing in information when the scanner failed, resulting in long customer waiting lines and, of course, a great many data errors. Bailey soon turned to a professional organization to print the bar codes for him.

The next choice Bailey had to make was the scanner to be used. He originally opted for pen-based scanners because they are the least expensive. However, these scanners are slow and awkward to use and in addition need to physically touch the actual code to read it. He therefore switched to charge-coupled devices (CCDs), which his clerks found much easier to use and which can read the bar code from several inches away. While more expensive, they proved to save money both because clerks were more productive and because they resulted in more accurate data—the cost of the whole system would be wasted if the data were inaccurate.

Finally, Bailey had to select or develop application software. The software needed to collect and store the data, and to secure the data from intrusions into the privacy of AIM's customers. Moreover, the application software functionality would need to support the business goals and practices of the organization.

What did Bailey want from the data collected by scanner? First, he wanted high-quality customer service. By using bar coding technology, his clerks are able to process customers quickly and accurately, keeping checkout lines small. Second, he was looking for productivity. This was achieved partially by speeding up the checkout process. However, other benefits ensued as well. Bar code scanning is very easy to do, keeping clerk training and supervision costs to a minimum. In addition, with the software he is using, Bailey has an ongoing inventory—he always knows exactly which products are out, which are on the shelves, how many of each item AIM owns, as well as the turnover rate of each item. By keeping a tight control over inventory, he keeps his inventory costs low. He also no longer needs to "take inventory" periodically, eliminating another cost. Every time an item is checked out or in, the system is automatically updated, so AIM can see how much each item is earning.

AIM also uses the data to increase business from existing customers. Because the computer shows which products are rented by whom, AIM is able to determine the tastes of its customers and then to target advertising mailings accordingly, sending literature on children's films, for example, to families that rent a large number of children's films. The company is also able to identify which customers have not rented for a long period of time (currently AIM uses a six months' threshold) so it can attempt to reactivate dormant customers. To accomplish this, AIM sends those so identified a coupon good for one free rental. Because AIM sends the coupon by first-class mail, the U.S. Post Office notifies them of addressees who are no longer at that address, enabling AIM to remove such people from their database.

Perhaps the most important use of the data, however, is AIM's market trend analysis. By having complete, up-to-date data on what items are renting and what are not, AIM is able to keep in constant touch with customer tastes. Staff spot rental trends very early and respond in time to take advantage of them. Their analyses tell them when to sell items that are no longer needed and when to purchase additional copies of items. Using computer modeling software, AIM is even able to predict with a high degree of accuracy how many copies of a new item staff need to purchase. For example, their model projected they would need 88 copies of *The Firm* when it was first released. At a purchase price of $70 each, it was important not to overbuy copies of this film. Five weeks after the release of the film, an update of the model showed that they actually could have used 89 copies, indicating the original estimate had been excellent.

Given that AIM is a small business, cost was a key factor in adopting bar coding technology. However, costs were low. AIM has found that one 486 microcomputer is powerful enough to handle all of its functions, including its own checkout and analyses functions, the same services for the 150 other video outlets serviced, and the nationwide bulletin board for buying and selling its inventories. The scanners cost $200 to $300 each but only require occasional maintenance. The technology is mature enough so as not to require updating of software and hardware so that the costs are very little beyond the initial investment. Payback was very quick, making this a viable technology, even for a small business.

However, the value to AIM cannot be calculated only in financial terms. With bar coding technology and imaginative management, the company has been able to prosper, grow, and even branch out in a market that is often considered to be difficult. Moreover, Bailey sees technology as a tool for future growth and development. He is confident his company will continue to meet its challenges as the business environment around him continues to change.

Source: Tony Seideman, "The Dream Beam," *Profit*, September–October 1994.

Case Study Questions

1. What are the advantages and disadvantages of using bar coding as the input technology over other input technologies?

2. How was the use of bar coding for input technology related to AIM's business strategy?

3. It has been observed that the challenging part of using bar codes is not collecting bar code data but designing the information systems and the business practices to use the information. Do you agree? Why or why not?

3. What management, organization, and technology changes did AIM institute in order to make bar coding effective? For each of these changes, indicate whether or not they were critical to the success of the technology and the company.

4. Name the related businesses AIM was able to expand into partly based upon the use of bar coding. Suggest additional areas the company might also expand into.

5. In what ways does bar coding improve customer service and so customer satisfaction?

6. Suggest business applications other than retail cash register and stock tracking that might find bar coding useful and explain the use and its value.

References

Bell, Gordon. "The Future of High Performance Computers in Science and Engineering." *Communications of the ACM* 32, no. 9 (September 1989).

Bell, Gordon. "Ultracomputers: A Teraflop Before Its Time." *Communications of the ACM* 35, no. 8 (August 1992).

Burgess, Brad, Nasr Ullah, Peter Van Overen, and Deene Ogden. "The PowerPC 603 Microprocessor." *Communications of the ACM* 37, no. 6 (June 1994).

Camp, W. J., S. J. Plimpton, B. A. Hendrickson, and R. W. Leland. "Massively Parallel Methods for Engineering and Science Problems." *Communications of the ACM* 37, no. 4 (April 1994).

De Pompa, Barbara. "Multimedia Isn't the Message." *InformationWEEK* (July 19, 1993).

Demasco, Patrick W., and Kathleen F. McCoy. "Generating Text from Compressed Input: An Intelligent Interface for People with Severe Motor Impairments." *Communications of the ACM* 35, no. 5 (May 1992).

Emmett, Arielle. "Simulations on Trial." *Technology Review* (May–June 1994).

Feibus, Michael, and Michael Slater. "Pentium." *PC Magazine* (April 27, 1993).

Fitzmaurice, George W. "Situated Information Spaces and Spatially Aware Palmtop Computers." *Communications of the ACM* 36, no. 7 (July 1993).

Hills, W. Daniel, and Lewis W. Tucker. "The CM-5 Connection Machine. A Scalable Supercomputer." *Communications of the ACM* 36, no. 11 (November 1993).

Jenkins, Avery. "The Right Time for RAID." *Computerworld* (March 14, 1994).

Lambert, Craig. "The Electronic Tutor." *Harvard Magazine* (November–December 1990).

Markoff, John. "Foray into Mainstream for Parallel Computing." *The New York Times* (June 15, 1992).

Markoff, John. "Battle for Influence over Insatiable Disks." *The New York Times* (January 11, 1995).

Mel, Bartlett W., Stephen M. Omohundro, Arch D. Robison, Steven S. Skiena, Kurt H. Thearling, Luke T. Young, and Stephen Wolfram. "Tablet: Personal Computer in the Year 2000." *Communications of the ACM* 31, no. 6 (June 1988).

Nelson, Neal. "The Reality of RISC." *Computerworld* (March 22, 1993).

Peled, Abraham. "The Next Computer Revolution." *Scientific American* 257, no. 4 (October 1987).

Port, Otis et al. "Wonder Chips." *Business Week* (July 4, 1994).

Press, Larry. "Compuvision or Teleputer?" *Communications of the ACM* 33, no. 3 (September 1990).

Press, Larry. "Personal Computing: Dynabook Revisited—Portable Computers Past, Present and Future." *Communications of the ACM* 35 no. 3 (March 1992).

Smarr, Larry, and Charles E. Catlett. "Metacomputing." *Communications of the ACM* 35, no. 6 (June 1992).

Thomborson, Clark D. "Does Your Workstation Computation Belong on a Vector Supercomputer?" *Communications of the ACM* 36, no. 11 (November 1993).

Thompson, Tom. "The Macintosh at 10." *Byte* (February 1994).

Thompson, Tom, and Bob Ryan. "PowerPC 620 Soars." *Byte* (November 1994).

Weiser, Mark. "Some Computer Science Issues in Ubiquitous Computing." *Communications of the ACM* 36, no. 7 (July 1993).

Williamson, Miday. "High-Tech Training." *Byte* (December 1994).

Wood, Elizabeth. "Multimedia Comes Down to Earth." *Computerworld* (August 1, 1994).

Information Systems Software

Sand Dollar Saves Many Dollars Through Mailing Software

The resort business relies heavily upon mailings of sales literature to attract clients. So it is no surprise that Sand Dollar Management Co.'s director of new-product development, Pat Simpson, decided to computerize her whole mailing list function. Sand Dollar, with 1993 sales of $20 million, manages resort property on Hilton Head Island, South Carolina. In the past this small company purchased mailing lists of potential customers, hired office temps to type labels, then paste the labels on the stuffed envelopes, and mailed them. The whole process was costly and often required several weeks or more to be completed. Now, using computerized mailing software, Simpson saves her company more than $80,000 annually.

Savings start with the mailing lists Sand Dollar receives, which now can be sent on computer disk and printed on labels or envelopes, eliminating the need for the office temps. The software also checks for duplicates, eliminating the cost of duplicate mailings. Computerized mailing lists can also be stored on the computer and reused, reducing the cost of mailing list purchases. Sand Dollar's software can also be used to check its mailing list against the United States Postal Service's (USPS) National Change of Address file, which is updated quarterly and lists all reported new addresses.

The largest saving from the software, however, comes from the fact that the software bar codes the labels and sorts them by ZIP code. Because this makes it much cheaper for the USPS to process the mail, they offer large discounts for sorted, bar-coded mail. Sand Dollar receives a USPS discount of $50,000 annually.

The software has other benefits as well. For example, Sand Dollar also uses it to capture and maintain valuable personal customer data it then uses in its marketing efforts. Moreover, the software was low cost, making it easy for a small business to adopt it. In fact, although Sand Dollar did purchase a new computer to run its new mailing software, an older computer could have run it had the company not been ready to finance a new computer. ■

Source: Mel Mandell, "Smart Mailing Techniques Deliver Postage Savings," *Profit*, May–June 1994.

In the last twenty-five years, public media have paid a great deal of attention to advances in computer hardware. But without the software to utilize the expanding capabilities of the hardware, the "computer revolution" would have been stillborn. The many businesses that rely heavily upon mailing lists, like Sand Dollar described in the opening vignette, had the names and addresses they needed and could easily have had access to computer hardware to process the addresses. What prevented them from reducing their mailing costs while more effectively reaching potential customers was the lack of appropriate software.

The usefulness of computer hardware depends a great deal on available software and the ability of

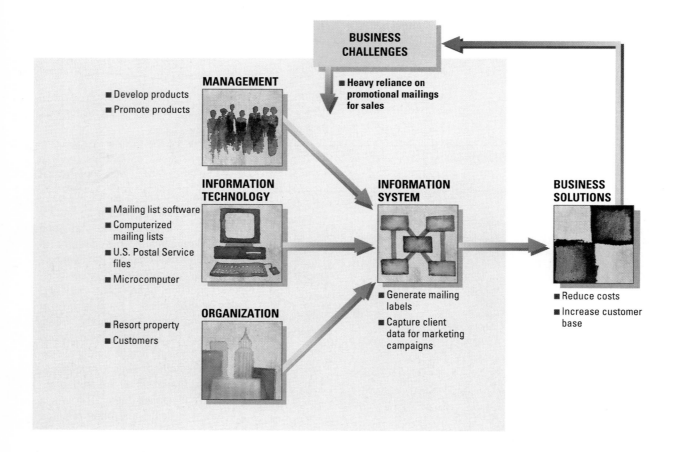

BUSINESS CHALLENGES

■ Heavy reliance on promotional mailings for sales

MANAGEMENT
■ Develop products
■ Promote products

INFORMATION TECHNOLOGY
■ Mailing list software
■ Computerized mailing lists
■ U.S. Postal Service files
■ Microcomputer

ORGANIZATION
■ Resort property
■ Customers

INFORMATION SYSTEM
■ Generate mailing labels
■ Capture client data for marketing campaigns

BUSINESS SOLUTIONS
■ Reduce costs
■ Increase customer base

management to evaluate, monitor, and control the utilization of software in the organization. This chapter shows how software turns computer hardware into useful information systems, describes the major types of software, provides criteria for selecting software, and presents new approaches to software development.

After completing this chapter you will be able to:

7.1 WHAT IS SOFTWARE?

software The detailed instructions that control the operation of a computer system.

Software is the detailed instructions that control the operation of a computer system. Without software, computer hardware could not perform the tasks we associate with computers. The functions of software are to (1) manage the computer resources of the organization; (2) provide tools for human beings to take advantage of these resources; and (3) act as an intermediary between organizations and stored information.

SOFTWARE PROGRAMS

program A series of statements or instructions to the computer.

A software **program** is a series of statements or instructions to the computer. The process of writing or coding programs is termed programming, and individuals who specialize in this task are called programmers.

stored program concept The idea that a program cannot be executed unless it is stored in a computer's primary storage along with required data.

The **stored program concept** means that a program must be stored in the computer's primary storage along with the required data in order to execute, or have its instructions performed by the computer. Once a program has finished executing, the computer hardware can be used for another task when a new program is loaded into memory.

MAJOR TYPES OF SOFTWARE

There are two major types of software: system software and application software. Each kind performs a different function. **System software** is a set of generalized programs that manage the resources of the computer, such as the central processor, communications links, and peripheral devices. Programmers who write system software are called system programmers.

system software Generalized programs that manage the resources of the computer, such as the central processor, communications links, and peripheral devices.

application software Programs written for a specific business application in order to perform functions specified by end users.

Application software describes the programs that are written for or by users to apply the computer to a specific task. Software for processing an order or generating a mailing list is application software. Programmers who write application software are called application programmers.

The types of software are interrelated and can be thought of as a set of nested boxes, each of which must interact closely with the other boxes surrounding it. Figure 7.1 illustrates this relationship. The system software surrounds and controls access to the hardware. Application software must work through the system software in order to operate. End users work primarily with application software. Each type of software must be specially designed to a specific machine in order to ensure its compatibility.

SYSTEM SOFTWARE

Operating system

   Schedules computer events
   Allocates computer resources
   Monitors events

Language translators

   Interpreters
   Compilers

Utility programs

   Routine operations (e.g., sort, list, print)
   Manage data (e.g., create files, merge files)

FIGURE 7.1
The major types of software. The relationship between the system software, application software, and users can be illustrated by a series of nested boxes. System software—consisting of operating systems, language translators, and utility programs—controls access to the hardware. Application software, such as the programming languages and "fourth-generation" languages must work through the system software to operate. The user interacts primarily with the application software.

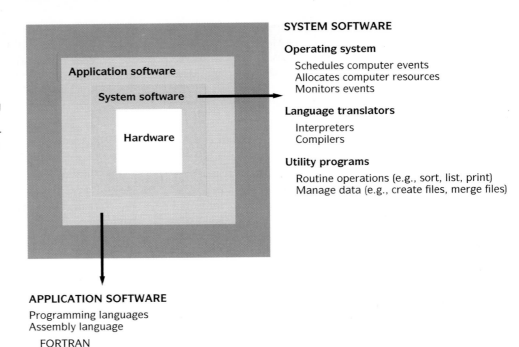

APPLICATION SOFTWARE

Programming languages
Assembly language

   FORTRAN
   COBOL
   PL /1
   BASIC
   PASCAL
   C
"Fourth-generation" languages

7.2 SYSTEM SOFTWARE

operating system The system software that manages and controls the activities of the computer.

System software coordinates the various parts of the computer system and mediates between application software and computer hardware. The system software that manages and controls the activities of the computer is called the **operating system**. Other system software consists of computer language translation programs that convert programming languages into machine language and utility programs that perform common processing tasks.

FUNCTIONS OF THE OPERATING SYSTEM

One way to look at the operating system is as the system's chief manager. Operating system software decides which computer resources will be used, which programs will be run, and the order in which activities will take place.

An operating system performs three functions. It allocates and assigns system resources; it schedules the use of computer resources and computer jobs; and it monitors computer system activities.

Allocation and Assignment

The operating system allocates resources to the application jobs in the execution queue. It provides locations in primary memory for data and programs and controls the input and output devices such as printers, terminals, and telecommunication links.

Scheduling

Thousands of pieces of work can be going on in a computer simultaneously. The operating system decides when to schedule the jobs that have been submitted and when to coordinate the scheduling in various areas of the computer so that different parts of different jobs can be worked on at the same time. For instance, while a program is executing, the operating system is scheduling the use of input and output devices. Not all jobs are performed in the order they are submitted; the operating system must schedule these jobs according to organizational priorities. On-line order processing may have priority over a job to generate mailing lists and labels.

Monitoring

The operating system monitors the activities of the computer system. It keeps track of each computer job and may also keep track of who is using the system, of what programs have been run, and of any unauthorized attempts to access the system. Information system security is discussed in detail in Chapter 18. Obviously, the operating system of a major mainframe computer is itself a very large program. For this reason, only parts of the operating system are actually stored in the primary storage area. Most of the operating system is stored in a copy on a disk, to which primary storage has very rapid access. Whenever parts of the operating system are required by a given application, they are transferred from the disk and loaded into primary storage. The device on which a complete operating system is stored is called the **system residence device**.

system residence device The secondary storage device on which a complete operating system is stored.

MULTIPROGRAMMING, VIRTUAL STORAGE, TIME SHARING, AND MULTIPROCESSING

How is it possible for 1000 or more users sitting at remote terminals to use a computer information system simultaneously if, as we stated in the previous chapter, a computer can execute only one instruction from one program at a time? How can computers run thousands of programs? The answer is that the computer has a series of specialized operating system capabilities.

Multiprogramming

The most important operating system capability for sharing computer resources is **multiprogramming**. Multiprogramming permits multiple programs to share a computer system's resources at any one time through concurrent use of a CPU. By concurrent use, we mean that only one program is actually using the CPU at any given moment but that the input/output needs of other programs can be serviced at the same time. Two or more programs are active at the same time, but they do not use the same computer resources simultaneously. With multiprogramming, a group of programs takes turns using the processor.

Figure 7.2 shows how three programs in a multiprogramming environment can be stored in primary storage. The first program executes until an input/output event is read in the program. The operating system then directs a channel (a small processor limited to input and output functions) to read the input and move the output to an output device. The CPU moves to the second program until an input/output statement occurs. At this point, the CPU switches to the execution of the third program,

multiprogramming A method of executing two or more programs concurrently using the same computer. The CPU executes only one program but can service the input/output needs of others at the same time.

FIGURE 7.2
Single-program execution versus multiprogramming. In multiprogramming, the computer can be used much more efficiently because a number of programs can be executing concurrently. Several complete programs are loaded into memory. This memory management aspect of the operating system greatly increases throughput by better management of high-speed memory and input/output devices.

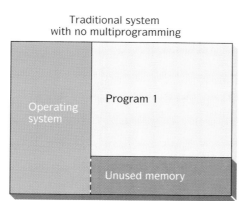

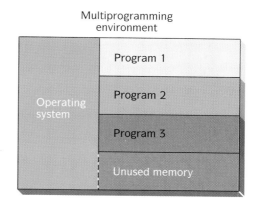

and so forth, until eventually all three programs have been executed. Notice that the interruptions in processing are caused by events that take place in the programs themselves. In this manner, many different programs can be executing at the same time, although different resources within the CPU are actually being utilized.

You can observe the advantages of multiprogramming by comparing multiprogramming systems to the first operating systems, which executed only one program at a time. Before multiprogramming, whenever a program read data off a tape or disk or wrote data to a printer, the entire CPU came to a stop. This was a very inefficient way to use the computer. With multiprogramming, the CPU utilization rate is much higher.

Multitasking

multitasking The multiprogramming capability of primarily single-user operating systems such as those for microcomputers.

Multitasking refers to multiprogramming on single-user operating systems such as those in microcomputers. One person can run two or more programs concurrently on a single computer. For example, a sales representative could write a letter to prospective clients with a word processing program while simultaneously using a database program to search for all sales contacts in a particular city or geographic area. Instead of terminating his or her session with the word processing program, returning to the operating system, and then initiating a session with the database program, multitasking allows the sales representative to display both programs on the computer screen and work with them at the same time.

Virtual Storage

virtual storage A way of handling programs more efficiently by the computer by dividing the programs into small fixed or variable-length portions with only a small portion stored in primary memory at one time.

Virtual storage was developed after some problems of multiprogramming became apparent. Virtual storage handles programs more efficiently because the computer divides the programs into small fixed or variable-length portions, storing only a small portion of the program in primary memory at one time. First, although two or three large programs can be read into memory, a certain part of main memory generally remains underutilized because the programs add up to less than the total amount of primary storage space available. Second, given the limited size of primary memory, only a small number of programs can reside in primary storage at any given time. For example, many business programs may require up to 200 K of storage, and the computer may have only 1 megabyte of primary storage. Therefore, only a few programs can reside in memory at any given time.

page Small fixed-length section of a program, which can be easily stored in primary storage and quickly accessed from secondary storage.

Only a few statements of a program actually execute at any given moment. Virtual storage takes advantage of this feature of processing. Virtual storage breaks a program into a number of fixed-length portions called **pages** or into variable-length portions called segments. Each of these portions is relatively small (a page is approximately 2 to 4 kilobytes). This permits a very large number of programs to reside in primary memory, inasmuch as only one page of each program is actually located there (see Figure 7.3).

All other program pages are stored on a peripheral disk unit until they are ready for execution. Virtual storage provides a number of advantages. First, the central processor is utilized more fully. Many more programs can be in primary storage because only one page of each program actually resides there. Second, programmers no longer have to worry about the size of the primary storage area. Before virtual storage, programs could obviously be no larger than the computer's main memory that stored them. With virtual storage, programs can be of infinite length and small machines can execute a program of any size (admittedly, small machines will take longer than big machines to execute a large program). With virtual storage, there is no limit to a program's storage requirements.

Time Sharing

time sharing The sharing of computer resources by many users simultaneously by having the CPU spend a fixed amount of time on each user's program before proceeding to the next.

Time sharing is an operating system capability that allows many users to share computer processing resources simultaneously. It differs from multiprogramming in that the CPU spends a fixed amount of time on one program before moving on to another.

FIGURE 7.3

Virtual storage. Virtual storage is based on the fact that in general, only a few statements in a program can actually be utilized at any given moment. In virtual storage, programs are broken down into small sections called pages. Individual program pages are read into memory only when needed. The rest of the program is stored on disk until it is required. In this way, very large programs can be executed by small machines, or a large number of programs can be executed concurrently by a single machine.

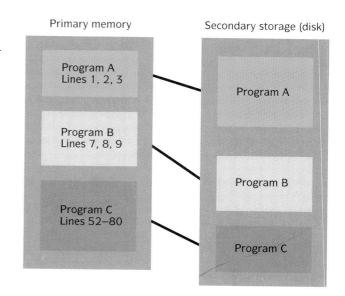

In a time-sharing environment, thousands of users are each allocated a tiny slice of computer time (2 milliseconds). In this time slot, each user is free to perform any required operations; at the end of this period, another user is given a 2-millisecond time slice of the CPU. This arrangement permits many users to be connected to a CPU simultaneously, with each receiving only a tiny amount of CPU time. But since the CPU is operating at the nanosecond level, a CPU can accomplish a great deal of work in 2 milliseconds.

Multiprocessing

multiprocessing An operating system feature for executing two or more instructions simultaneously in a single computer system by using more than one central processing unit.

Multiprocessing is an operating system capability that links together two or more CPUs to work in parallel in a single computer system. The operating system can assign multiple CPUs to execute different instructions from the same program or from different programs simultaneously, dividing the work between the CPUs. While multiprogramming uses concurrent processing with one CPU, multiprocessing uses simultaneous processing with multiple CPUs.

source code Program instructions written in a high-level language that must be translated into machine language in order to be executed by the computer.

LANGUAGE TRANSLATION AND UTILITY SOFTWARE

compiler Special system software that translates a higher-level language into machine language for execution by the computer.

When computers execute programs written in languages such as COBOL, FORTRAN, or C, the computer must convert these "human readable" instructions into a form it can understand. Computers interpret binary ones and zeros, and the language translators found in system software make the conversion. System software includes special language translator programs that translate higher-level language programs written in programming languages such as BASIC, COBOL, and FORTRAN into machine language that the computer can execute. This type of system software is called a *compiler* or *interpreter*. The program in the high-level language before translation into machine language is called **source code**. A **compiler** translates source code into machine code called **object code**. Just before execution by the computer, the object code modules are joined together with other object code modules in a process called linkage editing. The resulting load module is what is actually executed by the computer. Figure 7.4 illustrates the language translation process.

object code Program instructions that have been translated into machine language so that they can be executed by the computer.

interpreter A special translator of source code into machine code that translates each source code statement into machine code and executes it one at a time.

Some programming languages like BASIC do not use a compiler but an **interpreter**, which translates each source code statement one at a time into machine code and executes it. Interpreter languages like BASIC provide immediate feedback to the programmer if a mistake is made, but they are very slow to execute because they are translated one statement at a time.

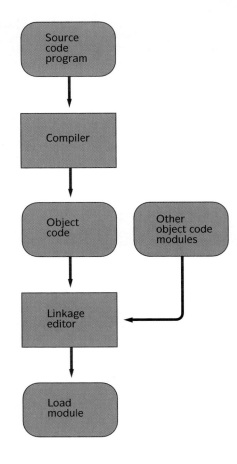

FIGURE 7.4
The language translation process. The source code, the program in a high-level language, is translated by the compiler into object code so that the instructions can be "understood" by the machine. These are grouped into modules. Prior to execution, the object code modules are joined together by the linkage editor to create the load module. It is the load module that is actually executed by the computer.

An assembler is similar to a compiler but is used to translate only assembly language (see Section 7.3) into machine code.

System software includes **utility programs** for routine, repetitive tasks, such as copying, clearing primary storage, computing a square root, or sorting. If you have worked on a computer and have performed such functions as setting up new files, deleting old files, or formatting diskettes, you have worked with utility programs. Utility programs are prewritten programs that are stored so that they can be shared by all users of a computer system and can be rapidly used in many different information system applications when requested.

utility program System software consisting of programs for routine, repetitive tasks, which can be shared by many users.

GRAPHICAL USER INTERFACES

Whenever users interact with a computer, even a microcomputer, the interaction is controlled by an operating system. The user interface is the part of an information system that users interact with. Users communicate with an operating system through the user interface of that operating system. Early microcomputer operating systems were command-driven, but the **graphical user interface**, often called a **GUI**, makes extensive use of icons, buttons, bars, and boxes to perform the same task. It has become the dominant model for the user interface of microcomputer operating systems.

graphical user interface (GUI) The part of an operating system that users interact with that uses graphic icons and the computer mouse to issue commands and make selections.

Older microcomputer operating systems, such as DOS, described below, are command-driven, requiring the user to type in text-based commands using a keyboard. For example, to perform a task such as deleting a file named DATAFILE, the user must type in a command such as *DELETE C:\DATAFILE*. Users need to remember these commands and their syntax to work with the computer effectively. As illustrated in Figure 7.5, the Macintosh computer has an operating system that uses graphical symbols called icons to depict programs, files, and activities. Commands

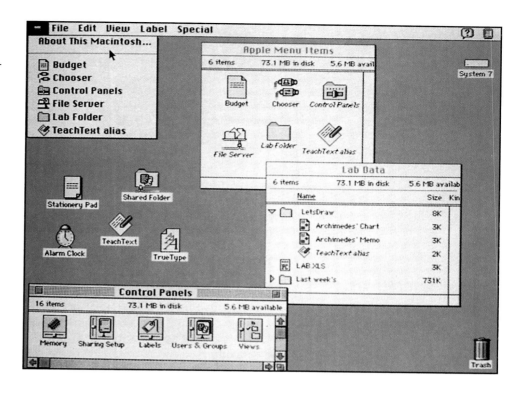

can be activated by rolling a mouse to move a cursor about the screen and clicking a button on the mouse to make selections. Icons are symbolic pictures and they are also used in GUIs to represent programs and files. For example, a file could be deleted by moving the cursor to a "Trash" icon. Many graphical user interfaces use a system of pull-down menus to help users select commands and pop-up boxes to help users select among various command options. Windowing features allow users to create, stack, size, and move around various boxes of information.

Proponents of graphical user interfaces claim that they save learning time because computing novices do not have to learn different arcane commands for each application. Common functions such as getting help, saving files, or printing output are performed the same way. A complex series of commands can be issued simply by linking icons. Commands should be standardized from one program to the next, so that using new programs is often possible without additional training or use of reference manuals. For example, the steps involved in printing a letter created by a word processing program or a financial statement generated by a spreadsheet program should be the same. Graphical user interfaces can promote superior screen and print output communicated through graphics. On the other hand, GUIs may not always simplify complex tasks if the user has to spend too much time first pointing to icons and then selecting operations to perform on those icons (Morse and Reynolds, 1993). Graphical symbols themselves are not always easy to understand unless the GUI is well-designed. Existing GUIs are modeled after an office desktop, with files documents, and actions based on typical office behavior, making them less useful for non-office applications in control rooms or processing plants (Mandelkern, 1993).

MICROCOMPUTER OPERATING SYSTEMS

Like any other software, microcomputer software is based on specific operating systems and computer hardware. A software package written for one microcomputer operating system generally cannot run on another. The microcomputer operating systems themselves have distinctive features—such as whether they support multitasking or graphics work—that determine the types of applications they are suited for.

DOS Operating system for 16-bit microcomputers based on the IBM personal computer standard.

Windows A graphical user interface shell that runs in conjunction with the DOS microcomputer operating system. Supports multitasking and some forms of networking.

Windows 95 A 32-bit operating system, with a streamlined graphical user interface that can support software written for DOS and Windows but can also run programs that take up more than 640 K of memory. Features multitasking, multithreading, and powerful networking capabilities.

Multitasking is one of the principal strengths of operating systems such as IBM's OS/2 (Operating System/2) for the IBM Personal System/2 line of microcomputers or UNIX. PC-DOS and MS-DOS, the older operating system for IBM personal computers and IBM-PC clones, do not allow multitasking, although the Microsoft Corporation markets Windows software to create a multitasking environment for DOS programs.

Table 7.1 compares the leading microcomputer operating systems—Windows 95, Windows NT, OS/2, UNIX, the Macintosh operating system, and DOS. **DOS** was the most popular operating system for 16-bit microcomputers. It is still widely used today with more powerful microcomputers based on the IBM microcomputer standard because so much available application software has been written for systems using DOS. (PC-DOS is used exclusively with IBM microcomputers. MS-DOS, developed by Microsoft, is used with other 16-bit microcomputers that function like the IBM microcomputer.) DOS itself does not support multitasking and limits the size of a program in memory to 640K.

DOS itself is command-driven, but it can present a graphical user interface by using Microsoft **Windows**, a highly popular graphical user interface shell that runs in conjunction with the DOS operating system. Windows supports multitasking and some forms of networking but shares the memory limitations of DOS. It is not considered to run very efficiently in a multitasking environment. Early versions of Windows had some problems with application crashes when multiple programs competed for the same memory space. Windows requires a minimum 386 or 486 microprocessor, 4–8 megabytes of RAM, and 80 megabytes of hard disk storage.

Microsoft's **Windows 95** is a 32-bit operating system designed to remedy many of the deficiencies of Windows sitting atop DOS. A 32-bit operating system can run faster than DOS (which could only address data in 16-bit chunks) because it can address data in 32-bit chunks. Windows 95 provides a streamlined graphical user interface that arranges icons to provide instant access to common tasks. It can support software written for DOS and Windows but it can also run programs that take up more than 640 K of memory. Windows 95 features multitasking, multithreading (the

Table 7.1	Leading Microcomputer Operating Systems
Operating System	**Features**
DOS	Operating system for IBM (PC-DOS) and IBM-compatible (MS-DOS) microcomputers. Limits program use of memory to 640 K.
Windows 95	32-bit operating system with a streamlined graphical user interface. Has multitasking and powerful networking capabilities.
Windows NT	32-bit operating system for microcomputers and workstations not limited to Intel microprocessors. Supports multitasking, multiprocessing, and networking.
OS/2 (Operating System/2)	Operating system for the IBM Personal System/2 line of microcomputers. Can take advantage of the 32-bit microprocessor. Supports multitasking and networking.
UNIX (XENIX)	Used for powerful microcomputers, workstations, and minicomputers. Supports multitasking, multi-user processing, and networking. Is portable to different models of computer hardware.
System 7	Operating system for the Macintosh computer. Supports multitasking and has powerful graphics and multimedia capabilities.

Microsoft's Windows 95 is a powerful operating system with networking capabilities and a streamlined graphical user interface.

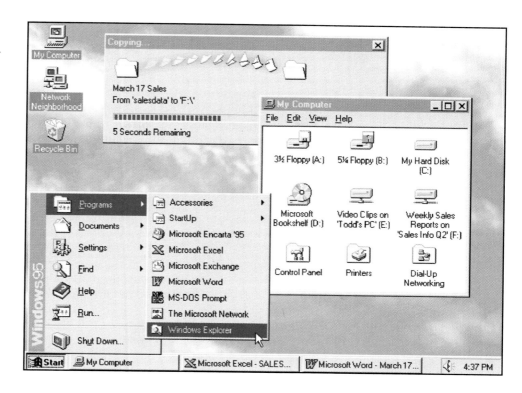

Windows NT Powerful operating system developed by Microsoft for use with 32-bit microcomputers and workstations based on Intel and other microprocessors. Supports networking, multitasking, and multiprocessing.

OS/2 Powerful operating system used with the 32-bit IBM/Personal System/2 microcomputer workstations that supports multitasking, networking, and more memory-intensive applications than DOS.

ability to manage multiple independent tasks simultaneously), and powerful networking capabilities, including the capability to integrate fax, e-mail, and scheduling programs. This operating system requires a fast 386 or 486 microprocessor, 8 megabytes of RAM, and 24–48 megabytes of hard disk storage.

Windows NT is another operating system developed by Microsoft with features that make it appropriate for critical applications in large networked organizations. Windows NT uses the same graphical user interface as Windows but it has powerful multitasking and memory management capabilities. Windows NT can support existing software written for DOS and Windows, and it can provide mainframe-like computing power for new applications with massive memory and file requirements. It can address data in 32-bit chunks if required and can even support multiprocessing with multiple CPUs. Unlike OS/2, Windows NT is not tied to computer hardware based on Intel microprocessors. It can run on microcomputers and workstations using microprocessors from Mips Computer Systems Inc. or DEC's powerful new Alpha chip. A company might choose Windows NT if it values flexibility and wants to use an operating system that can run different types of applications on a variety of computer hardware platforms using a common interface that is familiar to users. Although Windows NT can run on 80386-based microcomputers, it operates better on microcomputers or workstations with the minimum processing capacity of an 80486 microprocessor and requires 16 megabytes of RAM and a 100-megabyte hard disk.

OS/2 is a robust operating system that is used with 32-bit IBM Personal System/2 microcomputers or IBM-compatible microcomputers with Intel microprocessors. OS/2 is being used for more complex memory-intensive applications or those that require networking, multitasking or large programs. OS/2 supports multitasking, accommodates larger applications, allows applications to be run simultaneously, supports networked multimedia and pen computing applications, and is a much more protected operating system. One application that crashes is less likely to bring the whole operating system and other applications down with it. This operating system requires powerful computer hardware—a minimum 80386 or 80486 microprocessor, 4 megabytes of RAM, and 60-megabyte hard disk. OS/2 provides powerful desktop computers with mainframe operating system–like capabilities, such as multitasking and supporting multiple users in networks. Credit Industriel et Commercial de Paris, a major French bank, adopted OS/2 for its networked branch office systems because its stability and support for multitasking made it suitable for serious financial applications (Greenbaum, 1994).

OS/2 has its own graphical user interface called the Workplace Shell, which resembles the graphical user interface for the Macintosh computer. It provides users with a consistent graphical user interface across applications. OS/2 supports DOS applications and can run Windows and DOS applications at the same time in its own resizable windows.

UNIX was developed at Bell Laboratories in 1969 to help scientific researchers share data and programs while keeping other information private. It is an interactive, multi-user, multitasking operating system. Many people can use UNIX simultaneously to perform the same kind of task, or one user can run many tasks on UNIX concurrently. UNIX was developed to connect various machines together and is highly supportive of communications and networking.

UNIX was initially designed for minicomputers but now has versions for microcomputers, workstations, and mainframes. UNIX can run on many different kinds of computers and can be easily customized. It can also store and manage a large number of files. At present, UNIX is primarily used for workstations, minicomputers, and inexpensive multi-user environments in small businesses, but its use in large businesses is growing because of its machine-independence. Application programs that run under UNIX can be ported from one computer to run on a different computer with little modification.

UNIX is accused of being unfriendly to users. It is powerful but very complex. It has a legion of commands, some of which are very cryptic and terse. A typing error on a command line can easily destroy important files. UNIX cannot respond well to problems caused by the overuse of system resources such as jobs or disk space. UNIX also poses some security problems, since multiple jobs and users can access the same file simultaneously. Finally, UNIX requires huge amounts of random access memory and disk capacity, limiting its usefulness for less powerful microcomputers.

System 7, the latest version of Macintosh system software, features multitasking as well as powerful graphics capabilities, and a mouse-driven graphical user interface (illustrated in Figure 7.5). An extension of this operating system called QuickTime™ allows Macintosh users to integrate video clips, stereo sound, and animated sequences with conventional text and graphics software. (Recall the discussion of multimedia in Chapter 6.) System 7 has some features that make it attractive for global applications. For instance, it provides system-level support for Asian languages with large character sets.

SELECTING A MICROCOMPUTER OPERATING SYSTEM

How should a firm go about choosing the operating system for its microcomputer-based applications? Should the decision be made only on the basis of technical merits? Should companies look at other issues such as ease of use, training, and the cost of hardware and software that use the operating system? This brief survey suggests that there are many factors to consider.

If a firm wants an operating system for its mainstream business applications, it needs an operating system that is compatible with the software required by these applications. The operating system should be easy to use and install. The user interface features of the operating system should be easy to learn. Mission-critical applications have special operating system requirements, since businesses depend on them for their continuing operation and survival. For such applications, an operating system that provides reliable support for multitasking and memory management is essential. The operating system should be able to run multiple applications quickly without having the system crash because applications are contending for the same memory

UNIX Operating system for microcomputers, minicomputers, and mainframes that is machine-independent and supports multi-user processing, multitasking, and networking.

System 7 Operating system for the Macintosh computer which supports multitasking and has powerful graphics and multimedia capabilities.

space. Mission-critical applications typically have large volumes of transactions to process and require operating systems that can handle large complex software programs and massive files.

When selecting a microcomputer operating system, some key questions to ask are:

- What application software runs on the operating system?
- What kind of computer hardware does the operating system run on?
- How quickly does the operating system run?
- How easy is the operating system to learn and use?
- Is the operating system designed for single users or for multiple users on networks?
- Does the operating system have strong multitasking capabilities?
- How reliable is the operating system?
- How much does it cost to install the operating system?
- What technical support and assistance is required to install and run the operating system? Where is this support available?

The Window on Management shows why three different corporations each selected a different operating system based upon their individual business requirements.

7.3 APPLICATION SOFTWARE

Application software is primarily concerned with accomplishing the tasks of end users. Many different programming languages can be used to develop application software. Each has different strengths and drawbacks.

GENERATIONS OF PROGRAMMING LANGUAGES

machine language Programming language consisting of the 1s and 0s of binary code.

To communicate with the first generation of computers, programmers had to write programs in **machine language**—the 0s and 1s of binary code. End users who wanted applications had to work with specialized programmers who could understand, think, and work directly in the machine language of a particular computer. Programming in 0s and 1s, reducing all statements such as add, subtract, and divide into a series of 0s and 1s, made early programming a slow, labor-intensive process.

As computer hardware improved and processing speed and memory size increased, computer languages changed from machine language to languages that were easier for humans to understand. Generations of programming languages developed to correspond with the generations of computer hardware. Figure 7.6 shows the development of programming languages over the last 50 years as the capabilities of hardware have increased.

Machine language was the first-generation programming language. The second generation of programming languages occurred in the early 1950s with the development of assembly language. Instead of using 0s and 1s, programmers could now substitute language-like acronyms and words such as *add, sub* (subtract), and *load* in programming statements. A language translator called a *compiler* converted the English-like statements into machine language.

When the third hardware generation was underway, programming languages entered their third generation as well. From the mid-1950s to the 1970s, the first higher-level languages emerged. These languages permitted mathematicians for the first time to work with computers through the use of languages such as FORTRAN (FORmula TRANslator program). Mathematicians were now able to define variables with statements such as $Z = A + B$. The software translated these definitions and mathematical statements into a series of 0s and 1s. COBOL (COmmon Business

MANAGEMENTS SELECT OPERATING SYSTEMS

Toronto Dominion Securities Inc. of Toronto Dominion Bank in Canada decided it was time for a change. Its business in government securities had been steadily growing, and its trade volume had doubled in two years. It moved to an amphitheater-like 11,000-square-foot trading floor to give its securities traders more breathing space and a bullpen-like atmosphere for developing and discussing ideas. The new trading floor also streamlined communications that are crucial to the bank's closely related businesses. The entire project cost about $20 million Canadian.

Business heads in charge of the bank's trading operations in money market, capital market, foreign exchange, and fixed income sit in the middle of the room, surrounded by their chief traders. The proximity encourages people to interact more frequently during the trading day. For instance, a trader in the Canadian–U.S. currency market can speak to the business head in charge of the Canadian and U.S. money market. Foreign exchange traders sit near the chief money market trader. If the chief money market trader says that rates are rising, the foreign exchange trader will use this information to purchase future contracts. Toronto believes that the trading room design has boosted revenues.

For the operating system to be used on its new trading room floor, Toronto Dominion selected OS/2 Version 2.0, less than three months after this version of the operating system was formally released by IBM. There were both risks and rewards to installing this new version of the operating system so soon after its release. While there might be unforeseen bugs that often accompany new pieces of software, Toronto Dominion felt that this disadvantage was outweighed by OS/2's powerful multitasking capabilities and easier-to-use programs. The bank knew that it would not be easy to implement this new operating system

and to get existing applications to run smoothly from the start. Some modifications to the data display software, called TradeLook, had to be coded and tested. To run an application on a new operating system, new versions of that application have to be created, tested, and retested.

OS/2 has a 32-bit operating system, which promises end users more power than 16-bit operating systems such as DOS. OS/2 also runs DOS and Windows-based programs. Toronto Dominion had other hardware and software options to choose from, such as UNIX-based workstations, but opted for OS/2 because it believed this system could best meet its needs. In the old trading room, the bank's traders used more than 100 DOS-based programs on mainframes and minicomputers to handle, for instance, options analytics and trade analysis. The bank wanted to salvage its existing trading programs while allowing its traders to run more than two applications at the same time, and they wanted to let traders work with real-time data with the flick of a wrist. If systems did not work on the new version of OS/2, the bank planned to use an earlier version of OS/2. The DOS-based programs required little or no modification to run on OS/2 and run smoothly, according to Andrew K. Annett, manager of the treasury systems integration, corporate, and investment banking group. With the new technology and trading room, traders can run a Lotus 1-2-3 spreadsheet and a profit-and-loss program simultaneously instead of wasting time jumping from one application to another. The bank also feels that the OS/2 graphical user interface makes its systems easier to operate.

Before finalizing its decision, Toronto Dominion talked with over 10 technology vendors about alternative hardware and software alternatives. One was to install 30 or 40 high-end UNIX-based RISC workstations in the Toronto office, where traders make markets and take positions. But the

bank's other branches focus more on sales than on trading. There, that kind of technology would not be necessary, and using UNIX only for the trading

> **To Think About:**   Why is the selection of an operating system an important business management decision? What are the management, technology, and organization factors that should be considered when selecting an operating system? If you were in charge of selecting the operating systems for Toronto Dominion, Delta, and Groupe Colas, which would you have chosen for each firm? Why?

floor would make integration with the rest of the bank more difficult. Toronto Dominion has planned to link all six of its corporate investment banking centers in a computer network. Its long-term strategy calls for distributing trading inventory in real-time out from its Toronto trading room to its 1000 branches and for distributing trading data to its corporate group and investment banking staff. Toronto also is thinking about providing corporate clients with the capability to execute foreign exchange transactions from their own terminals.

At about the same time Toronto Dominion selected the new version of OS/2, Delta Airlines decided to pull back from a primarily OS/2 desktop strategy to one calling for a mix of operating systems. It is replacing OS/2 with Microsoft Windows for its critical, next-generation reservation system. As the most critical airline operation system, the new reservation system is mainframe-based but includes intelligent front-end workstations for reservation agents. About 900 agents will use the system initially.

In December 1991 Delta had selected OS/2 for this application as well as for another important project. Delta is not abandoning OS/2 completely but has decided not to rely on it exclusively. The airline has changed its approach to avoid locking into a particular technical platform. It evaluates software for each information system application case by case and makes its selection based on cost and functionality. Delta, like all airlines, is suffering from tight finances and is likely to look for the lowest-cost technology solution.

Delta's corporate culture is considered to be practical and somewhat conservative. The firm tends not to make pioneering, technically aggressive, or risky decisions. The firm understands that the challenge of a mixed software environment is making the software all work together. Delta is finding ways to bridge the OS/2 and Windows environments. Delta plans to continue using OS/2 for its airport traffic management system and will evaluate OS/2 for future projects.

Groupe Colas of Boulogne-Billancourt, France, is the largest road-building company in the world, with operations scattered throughout the world. Its operating environment has been based upon mainframes from Groupe Bull using networked Questar terminals. Management determined it needed to improve communications with its far-flung projects. Its goals were to give the nontechnical staff at the remote sites better information through access to applications currently running on the mainframe, and

to give headquarters better control over all aspects of its projects around the world. Headquarters expects to be more involved in management of field operations and is also interested in controlling project management, project pricing, and costs. It plans to give field engineers and managers portable computers so they can share data with headquarters. All of this dictates a change to a local area network (LAN) environment (see Chapter 9). Colas, through SPEIG (Société Parisienne d'Etudes, d'Informatique et de Gestion), its information technology arm, plans to install about 280 LANs throughout France all to be connected to two mainframes. Other sites in the world would then be connected to them.

SPEIG determined that Colas would best be served by software that combined Microsoft Windows (and its graphical user interface) with network management software. It needed an operating system that provided links to Progress, its relational database management system from Progress Software Corporation, where much of Colas' data is already stored. Finally, it wanted a system that allowed headquarters to control all of its networks rather than having 280 separate control centers. "I need to be able to control every workstation, and do remote

distribution," says SPEIG department manager Daniel Dessort. After reviewing operating systems, management decided that the answer was Microsoft's Windows NT operating system, including its Hermes network management component.

Moving to Windows NT and Hermes is a bit of a gamble for Colas. Windows NT is a new operating system and few large companies have yet adopted it. Hermes had only recently been released and had major problems. However, these two are strategic projects for Microsoft as well as for Colas. Microsoft knows that success at Colas is critical to the success of these two products. So Microsoft is throwing itself into the project. Pascal Martin, customer business unit manager at Microsoft France, says that "What we've been trying to do with these very early NT accounts is set up a structure where we share the risks."

Sources: Joshua Greenbaum, "A Key Test for Windows NT," *InformationWeek*, May 9, 1994; Greenbaum, "The Evolution Revolution," *InformationWeek*, March 14, 1994; Jenna Michaels, "Breaking in New OS/2 Technology," *Wall Street Computer Review* 9, no. 12 (July 1992); and Rosemary Hamilton, "Windows Leads Delta to Mixed Platforms," *Computerworld*, July 27, 1992.

high-level language Programming languages where each source code statement generates multiple statements at the machine-language level.

Oriented Language) permitted the use of English statements such as *print* and *sort* to be used by programmers, who did not have to think in terms of 0s and 1s.

These **high-level languages** are so called because each statement in FORTRAN or COBOL generates multiple statements at the machine-language level. The use of these higher-level languages requires much faster, more efficient compilers to translate higher-level languages into machine codes.

Fourth-generation computer languages emerged in the late 1970s, and their development is still in progress. These languages dramatically reduce programming time and make software tasks so easy that nontechnical computer users can develop applications without the help of professional programmers. Fourth-generation tools also include prewritten application software packages that can be used directly by end users. Using the software package LOTUS 1-2-3, for instance, users can create their own financial spreadsheets and manipulate data without programmer intervention. Such sophistication by nonspecialists using FORTRAN would have been impossible in the 1960s and 1970s.

There is, of course, a clear relationship between the increasing capacity of computer hardware and software. Each new generation of software requires more and more primary storage area, faster compilers, and larger secondary storage. Higher-level language programs require a huge amount of memory. For instance, to load the Statistical Package for the Social Sciences (SPSS), the program alone may require over

FIGURE 7.6

Generations of programming languages. As the capabilities of hardware increased, programming languages developed from the first generation of machine and second generation of assembly languages of the 1950s to 1960, through the third generation high-level languages such as FORTRAN and COBOL developed in the 1960s and 1970s, to the fourth-generation languages.

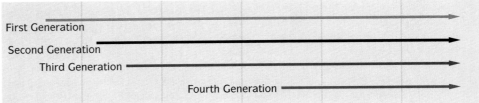

A. Generations

First Generation
Second Generation
Third Generation
Fourth Generation

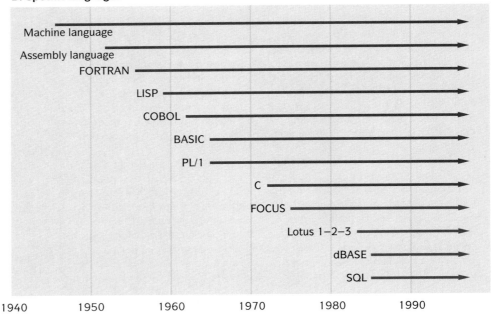

B. Specific languages

Machine language
Assembly language
FORTRAN
LISP
COBOL
BASIC
PL/1
C
FOCUS
Lotus 1–2–3
dBASE
SQL

1940   1950   1960   1970   1980   1990

200 K (200,000 bytes of primary storage). If work space is included within primary memory, up to 512 K may be required.

POPULAR PROGRAMMING LANGUAGES

Most managers need not be expert programmers, but they should understand how to evaluate software applications and to select programming languages that are appropriate for their organization's objectives. We will now briefly describe the more popular high-level languages.

Assembly Language

assembly language A programming language developed in the 1950s that resembles machine language but substitutes mnemonics for numeric codes.

Many programmers still prefer to write programs in assembly language because this language gives them close control over the hardware and very efficient execution. Like machine language, **assembly language** (Figure 7.7) is designed for a specific machine and specific microprocessors. For instance, there is a specific assembly language associated with the Intel 80386 chip used in an IBM microcomputer. In general, there is a one-to-one correspondence between machine language and assembly language. Each operation in assembly corresponds to a machine operation. On the other hand, assembly language does make use of certain mnemonics (e.g., *load, sum*) and assigns addresses and storage locations automatically. While assembly language gives programmers great control, it is costly in terms of programmer time, difficult to read and debug, and difficult to learn. Assembly language is used primarily today in system software.

FIGURE 7.7
Assembly language. This sample assembly language command adds the contents of register 3 to register 5 and stores the result in register 5.

```
AR 5, 3
```

FIGURE 7.8
FORTRAN. This sample FORTRAN program code is part of a program to compute sales figures for a particular item.

```
READ (5,100) ID, QUANT, PRICE
TOTAL = QUANT * PRICE
```

FIGURE 7.9
COBOL. This sample COBOL program code is part of a routine to compute total sales figures for a particular item.

```
MULTIPLY QUANT-SOLD BY UNIT-PRICE GIVING SALES-TOTAL.
```

FORTRAN

FORTRAN (FORmula TRANslator)
Programming language developed in 1956 for scientific and mathematical applications.

FORTRAN (FORmula TRANslator) (Figure 7.8) was developed in 1956 to provide an easier way of writing scientific and engineering applications. FORTRAN is especially useful in processing numeric data. Many kinds of business applications can be written in FORTRAN, it is relatively easy to learn, and contemporary versions (e.g., FORTRAN 77) provide sophisticated structures for controlling program logic. FORTRAN is not very good at providing input/output efficiency or in printing and working with lists. The syntax is very strict and keying errors are common, making the programs difficult to debug.

COBOL

COBOL (COmmon Business Oriented Language) Predominant programming language for business applications because it can process large data files with alphanumeric characters.

COBOL (COmmon Business Oriented Language) (Figure 7.9) came into use in the early 1960s. It was originally developed by a committee representing both government and industry because the Defense Department wished to create a common administrative language for internal and external software. Rear Admiral Grace M. Hopper was a key committee member who played a major role in COBOL development. COBOL was designed with business administration in mind, for processing large data files with alphanumeric characters (mixed alphabetic and numeric data), and for performing repetitive tasks like payroll. Its primary data structures are records, files, tables, and lists. COBOL is easily learned by business analysts. As the most widely used programming language, it is supported by external groups, and there is an abundance of productivity aids. The weakness of COBOL is a result of its virtue. It is poor at complex mathematical calculations. There are many versions of COBOL, and not all are compatible with each other. Lengthy COBOL programs—some hundreds of thousands of lines long for major payroll programs, for example—can become so complex as to be virtually incomprehensible.

BASIC

BASIC (Beginners All-purpose Symbolic Instruction Code)
General-purpose programming language used with microcomputers and for teaching programming.

BASIC (Beginners All-purpose Symbolic Instruction Code) was developed in 1964 by John Kemeny and Thomas Kurtz to teach students at Dartmouth College how to use computers. Today it is the most popular programming language on college campuses and for microcomputers. BASIC can do almost all computer processing tasks from inventory to mathematical calculations. It is easy to use, demonstrates computer capabilities well, and requires only a small interpreter. The weakness of BASIC is that it does few tasks well even though it does them all. It has no sophisticated program logic control or data structures, which makes it difficult to use in teaching good programming practices. While BASIC has only a few commands and is easily learned, subsequent versions of the language that have tried to add to the early syntax make the new versions of BASIC incompatible with the old ones. Therefore, BASIC programs often cannot be moved from one machine to another.

PL/1

PL/1 (Programming Language 1) Programming language developed by IBM in 1964 for business and scientific applications.

PL/1 (Programming Language 1) was developed by IBM in 1964. It is the most powerful general-purpose programming language because it can handle mathematical and business applications with ease, is highly efficient in input/output activities, and can handle large volumes of data.

Unfortunately, the huge volume of COBOL and FORTRAN programs written in the private sector at great cost cannot simply be jettisoned when a newer, more powerful language comes along. There are an estimated 12 billion lines of COBOL code in production in the United States. This represents an investment of over $52 trillion. PL/1 has not succeeded largely because programmers trained in COBOL could not be convinced to learn an entirely new language; and business organizations could not be convinced to spend millions of dollars rewriting their software. PL/1 is, moreover, somewhat difficult to learn in its entirety.

Pascal

Pascal Programming language used on microcomputers and to teach sound programming practices in computer science courses.

Named after Blaise Pascal, the seventeenth-century mathematician and philosopher, **Pascal** was developed by the Swiss computer science professor Niklaus Wirth of Zurich in the late 1960s. Pascal programs can be compiled using minimal computer memory, so they can be used on microcomputers. With sophisticated structures to control program logic and a simple, powerful set of commands, Pascal is used primarily in computer science courses to teach sound programming practices. The language is weak at file handling and input/output and is not easy for beginners to use.

Ada

Ada Programming language that is portable across different brands of hardware; is used for both military and nonmilitary applications.

Ada was developed in 1980 to provide the United States Defense Department with a structured programming language to serve as the standard for all of its applications. Ada was named after Ada, Countess of Lovelace, a nineteenth century mathematician whose father was the English poet Lord Byron. The Countess is sometimes called the first programmer because she developed the mathematical tables for an early calculating machine. This language was initially conceived for weapons systems where software is developed on a processor and then imbedded into the weapon. It was explicitly designed so that it could be uniformly executed in diverse hardware environments. The language also promotes structured software design. U.S. government experts hope Ada will produce more cost-effective software because it facilitates more clearly structured code than COBOL.

Congress passed legislation mandating Ada for all system development work for the U.S. Department of Defense, and Ada is used in nonmilitary government applications as well. The language can also be used for general business applications since it can operate on microcomputers and is portable across different brands of computer hardware. Will Ada emerge as a software standard for the business world? Many firms do not think so, for the same reasons they did not embrace PL/1. They are not convinced that it is worth the investment and risk to abandon COBOL as the business standard.

C

C Powerful programming language with tight control and efficiency of execution; is portable across different microprocessors and is used primarily with microcomputers.

C was developed at AT&T's Bell Labs in the early 1970s and is the language in which much of the UNIX operating system is written. C combines some of the tight control and efficiency of execution features of assembly language with machine portability. In other words, it can work on a variety of computers rather than on just one. Much commercial microcomputer software has been written in C, but C is gaining support for some minicomputer and mainframe applications. C is unlikely to dislodge COBOL for mainframe business applications, but it will be used increasingly for commercial microcomputer software and for scientific and technical applications.

LISP and Prolog

LISP (designating LISt Processor) and Prolog are widely used in artificial intelligence. LISP was created in the late 1950s by M.I.T. mathematician John McCarthy and is oriented toward putting symbols such as operations, variables, and data values into meaningful lists. LISP is better at manipulating symbols than at ordinary number crunching.

Prolog, introduced around 1970, is also well-suited to symbol manipulation and can run on general-purpose computers, whereas LISP usually runs best on machines configured especially to run LISP programs.

FOURTH-GENERATION LANGUAGES

fourth-generation language A programming language that can be employed directly by end users or less skilled programmers to develop computer applications more rapidly than conventional programming languages.

Fourth-generation languages consist of a variety of software tools that enable end users to develop software applications with minimal or no technical assistance or that enhance the productivity of professional programmers. Fourth-generation languages tend to be nonprocedural or less procedural than conventional programming languages. Procedural languages require specification of the sequence of steps, or procedures, that tell the computer what to do and how to do it. Nonprocedural languages need only to specify what has to be accomplished rather than provide details about how to carry out the task. Thus, a nonprocedural language can accomplish the same task with fewer steps and lines of program code than a procedural language.

There are seven categories of fourth-generation languages: query languages, report generators, graphics languages, application generators, very-high-level programming languages, application software packages, and microcomputer tools. Figure 7.10 illustrates the spectrum of these tools and some commercially available products in each category.

Oriented toward end users →   ← Oriented toward IS professionals

Microcomputer tools	Query languages/ report generators	Graphics languages	Application generators	Application software packages	Very high-level programming languages
Lotus 1–2–3	Easytrieve	Systat	FOCUS	MSA Payroll	APL
dBASE IV	Intellect	SAS Graph	DMS	Maxicalc	Nomad
Word Perfect	Query-By-Example	Harvard Graphics	SAS	AVP Sales/Use Tax	
	SQL		Mapper	AMAPS	
	RPG–III		Ideal		
	Inquire		Natural		
			CSP		

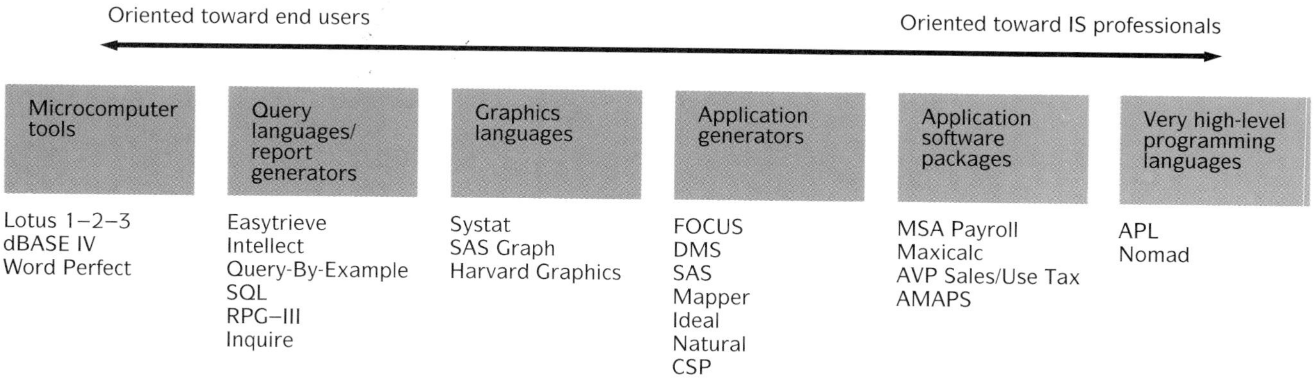

FIGURE 7.10
Fourth-generation languages. The spectrum of major categories of fourth-generation languages and commercially available products in each category is illustrated. Tools range from those that are simple and designated primarily for end users to complex tools designed for information systems professionals.

Query Languages

query language A high-level computer language used to retrieve specific information from databases or files.

Query languages are high-level languages for retrieving data stored in databases or files. They are usually interactive, on-line, and capable of supporting requests for information that are not predefined. They are often tied to database management systems (see Chapter 8) and microcomputer tools (see the following discussion). Query languages can search a database or file, using simple or complex selection criteria to display information relating to multiple records. Available query language tools have different kinds of syntax and structure, some being closer to natural language than others (Vassiliou, 1984–1985). Some support updating of data as well as retrieval. An example of a typical ad hoc query is "List all employees in the payroll department." Figure 7.11 illustrates how two different query languages, Query-By-Example and FOCUS, express this request.

Report Generators

report generator Software that creates customized reports in a wide range of formats that are not routinely produced by an information system.

Report generators are facilities for creating customized reports. They extract data from files or databases and create reports in many formats. Report generators generally provide more control over the way data are formatted, organized, and displayed than query languages. The more powerful report generators can manipulate data with complex calculations and logic before they are output. Some report generators are extensions of database or query languages. The more complex and powerful report generators may not be suitable for end users without some assistance from professional information systems specialists.

Graphics Languages

graphics language A computer language that displays data from files or databases in graphic format.

Graphics languages retrieve data from files or databases and display them in graphic format. Users can ask for data and specify how they are to be charted. Some graphics software can perform arithmetic or logical operations on data as well. SAS, Harvard Graphics, and Lotus Freelance Graphics are popular graphics tools.

Application Generators

application generator Software that can generate entire information system applications; the user needs only to specify what needs to be done and the application generator creates the appropriate program code.

Application generators contain preprogrammed modules that can generate entire applications, greatly speeding development. A user can specify what needs to be done, and the application generator will create the appropriate code for input, validation, update, processing, and reporting. Most full-function application generators consist of a comprehensive, integrated set of development tools: a database management system, data dictionary, query language, screen painter, graphics generator, report generator, decision support/modeling tools, security facilities, and a high-level program-

FIGURE 7.11
Query languages. This figure illustrates how the simple query, "List all employees in the Payroll department," would be handled by the two different query languages: Query-by-Example and FOCUS.

Query: "List all employees in the Payroll department."

Using Query-By-Example:

EMPLOYEE	EMPLOYEE #	NAME	DEPARTMENT
		P.	PAYROLL

Using FOCUS:

```
> > TABLE FILE EMPDEPT
> PRINT EMP_NAME IF DEPT EQ 'PAYROLL'
> END
```

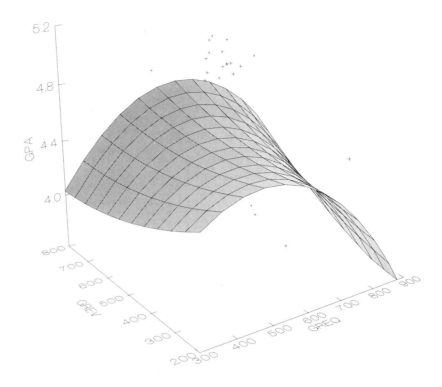

Sophisticated graphics software tools such as those from Systat Inc. can represent data in the form of three-dimensional charts.

ming language. For unique requirements that cannot be met with generalized modules, most application generators contain *user exits* where custom-programmed routines can be inserted. Some application generators are interactive, enabling users sitting at a terminal to define inputs, files, processing, and reports by responding to questions on-line.

Very-High-Level Programming Languages

very-high-level programming language Programming language using fewer instructions than conventional languages. Used primarily as a professional programmer productivity tool.

Very-high-level programming languages are designed to generate program code with fewer instructions than conventional languages such as COBOL or FORTRAN. Programs and applications based on these languages can be developed in much shorter periods of time. Simple features of these languages can be employed by end users. However, these languages are designed primarily as productivity tools for professional programmers. APL and Nomad2 are examples of these languages. The Window on Organizations illustrates how a Canadian telephone company used one such language, Magic, to solve a serious problem it faced.

Application Software Packages

software package A prewritten, precoded, commercially available set of programs that eliminates the need to write software programs for certain functions.

A **software package** is a prewritten, precoded, commercially available set of programs that eliminates the need for individuals or organizations to write their own software programs for certain functions. There are software packages for system software, but the vast majority of package software is application software.

Application software packages consist of prewritten application software that is marketed commercially. These packages are available for major business applications on mainframes, minicomputers, and microcomputers. They contain customization features so that they can be tailored somewhat to an organization's unique requirements. Although application packages for large complex systems must be installed by technical specialists, many application packages, especially those for microcomputers, are marketed directly to end users. Systems development based on application packages is discussed in Chapter 12.

BELL QUEBEC REPAIRS ITS PAY PHONES BY MAGIC

How would you react if, when you called your telephone company to report an out-of-order pay phone, you were put on hold? That was a small piece of the problem faced in 1993 by Montreal-based Bell Quebec, a division of Bell Canada. These Good Samaritan customers were put on hold because the agent had to go to another telephone line to contact the repair department to determine if someone else had already reported the problem. To make matters worse, when a technician did finally arrive at the out-of-order phone, he or she often found coins in the coin box, forcing the repairperson first to report that fact to the accounting department. Repair of the telephone then had to wait until a collector had collected those coins. Collecting the money at that point could also be a major trauma and could consume a great deal of time because each of the 40,000 pay telephones in the system had its own unique key—the correct key had to first be located and then brought to the site.

Bell Quebec did have a telephone monitoring system that polled each of the pay phones periodically to see if they were working, so out-of-service telephones were eventually identified even if no customer called to report a problem. However, the polling system itself was a nightmare. The data were transmitted to a headquarters mainframe computer where they were accumulated and then printed once a day in six-inch-thick paper reports. Workers then had to manually ferret out the out-of-order telephones so that technicians could be dispatched to repair them. All in all one might have called Bell Quebec's system for handling out-of-order pay telephones a comedy of errors except for the fact that it was an expensive comedy at a time that pay phone usage was exploding.

By early 1995 the situation had changed dramatically. The agents who take repair calls now enter the pay phone's telephone number into the computer and the telephone's repair history immediately pops up, showing the current status, including whether or not a repair truck has been dispatched, and the other information the agent needs. The previous nightmarish system had developed over the years from an application systems development history shared by most older companies—separate departments had developed their own, isolated systems as each departmental need was seen. The systems were developed in isolation without the existence of a company-wide development strategy. Within Bell Quebec, installation and support, repair services, marketing, and accounting all had stand-alone systems that shared no information and stored their own, often conflicting, data. Jean-Claude Legault, regional directory of Bell Quebec's repair operations, explained that "All those departments tried to work together, but information was never the same." To make matters worse, each of the isolated systems operated on different hardware, including IBM, Hewlett-Packard (HP) and Amdahl mainframes, Sequent, Tandem and DEC VAX minicomputers, HP9000s, Sun workstations, and various PCs and PC local-area networks. Operating systems included MVS, VMS, HP-UX, and SunOS. The data was stored in a variety of flat files and database management systems.

Claude Prouix, Bell Quebec's general manager of operator and public telecommunications services, decided in late 1992 that something had to be done, and handed the problem over to Legault. He, in turn, asked Bell Quebec's IS group, Bell Sygma, for a proposal, but they took six months to come back with a proposal for a four-staff-year project to integrate just one of the departments. "The way the public phone market is moving right now, I couldn't wait too much," was Legault's response. He immediately began to look at a range of outside solutions. The approach he finally selected was to contract for Magic Software with InterAction a value-added reseller (VAR) in Quebec, Canada. Magic Software Enterprises Ltd. is an Israeli-based company that offers a fourth-

generation tool for table-based programming. Legault selected InterAction not only because of its product (Magic) but also because the firm was bilingual, with the ability to develop systems in both French and English." With InterAction's help and the use of Magic, Bell Quebec quickly built what Legault dubbed "an information backbone," key data that needed to be shared by all the departmental systems collected from all the relevant departments and stored in one common data respository. With the data in a central location, queries quickly produced the information needed at each stage of the pay phone maintenance process. According to David Wegman, chief operating officer of Magic Software Enterprises, prior to building the information backbone, Bell Quebec had "great systems for collecting mountains of data that nobody could use." Now, however, Magic had become "data-central, able to reach out and grab the data everywhere it existed. It became the backbone for everything that was happening, a central data manipulation tool."

Magic works with no program coding by its users. Instead, users define their needs through visual programming (see this chapter's Window on Technology) and filling in tables. "Your program can literally consist of three lines because it's just like a map or instruction set for the engine to run against," says Wegman. Central to

Microcomputer Tools

Some of the most popular and productivity-promoting fourth-generation tools are the general-purpose application packages that have been developed for microcomputers, especially word processing, spreadsheet, data management, graphics, and integrated software packages.

word processing software
Software that handles electronic storage, editing, formatting, and printing of documents.

WORD PROCESSING SOFTWARE. **Word processing software** stores text data electronically as a computer file rather than on paper. The word processing software allows the user to make changes in the document electronically in memory. This eliminates the need to retype an entire page in order to incorporate corrections. The software has formatting options to make changes in line spacing, margins, character size, and column width. Microsoft Word and WordPerfect are popular word processing packages. Figure 7.12 illustrates a Microsoft Word screen for Windows displaying text, graphics, and major menu options.

Most word processing software has advanced features that automate other writing tasks: spelling checkers, style checkers (to analyze grammar and punctuation), thesaurus programs, and mail merge programs (which link letters or other text documents with names and addresses in a mailing list).

spreadsheet Software displaying data in a grid of columns and rows, with the capability of easily recalculating numerical data.

SPREADSHEETS. Electronic **spreadsheet** software provides computerized versions of traditional financial modeling tools such as the accountant's columnar pad, pencil, and calculator. An electronic spreadsheet is organized into a grid of columns and rows. The power of the electronic spreadsheet is evident when one changes a value or values, because all other related values on the spreadsheet will be automatically recomputed.

FIGURE 7.12
Text and some of the options available in Microsoft Word for Windows. Word processors provide many easy-to-use options to create and output a text document to meet a user's specifications.
Courtesy of Microsoft.

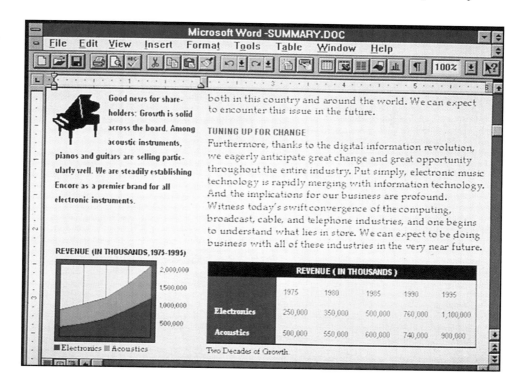

Spreadsheets are valuable for applications where numerous calculations with pieces of data must be related to each other. Spreadsheets are also useful for applications that require modeling and "what-if" analysis. After the user has constructed a set of mathematical relationships, the spreadsheet can be recalculated instantaneously using a different set of assumptions. A number of alternatives can easily be evaluated by changing one or two pieces of data without having to rekey in the rest of the worksheet. Many spreadsheet packages include graphics functions that can present data in the form of line graphs, bar graphs, or pie charts. The most popular spreadsheet packages are Lotus 1-2-3, Quattro, and Microsoft Excel.

Figure 7.13 illustrates the output from a spreadsheet for a breakeven analysis and its accompanying graph.

DATA MANAGEMENT SOFTWARE.   While spreadsheet programs are powerful tools for manipulating quantitative data, **data management software** is more suit-

data management software Software used for creating and manipulating lists, creating files and databases to store data, and combining information for reports.

FIGURE 7.13
Spreadsheet software.
Spreadsheet software organizes data into columns and rows for analysis and manipulation. Contemporary spreadsheet software provides graphing abilities for clear visual representation of the data in the spreadsheets. This sample breakeven analysis is represented as numbers in a spreadsheet as well as a line graph for easy interpretation.

Total fixed cost	19,000.00
Variable cost per unit	3.00
Average sales price	17.00
Contribution margin	14.00
Breakeven point	1357

Custom Neckties Pro Forma Income Statement				
Units Sold	0.00	679	1357	2036	2714
Revenue	0	11,536	23,071	34,607	46,143
Fixed Cost	19,000	19,000	19,000	19,000	19,000
Variable Cost	0	2,036	4,071	6,107	8,143
Total Cost	19,000	21,036	23,071	25,107	27,143
Profit/Loss	(19,000)	(9,500)	0	9,500	19,000

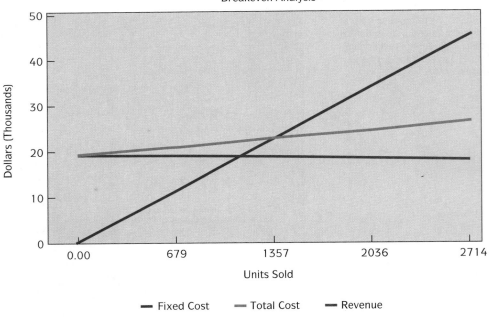

Custom Neckties
Breakeven Analysis

— Fixed Cost   — Total Cost   — Revenue

CHAPTER 7   Information Systems Software

able for creating and manipulating lists and for combining information from different files. Microcomputer database management packages have programming features and easy-to-learn menus that enable nonspecialists to build small information systems.

Data management software typically has facilities for creating files and databases and for storing, modifying, and manipulating data for reports and queries. A detailed treatment of data management software and database management systems can be found in Chapter 8. Popular database management software for the personal computer includes Microsoft Access, Paradox, and dBASE IV (R). Figure 7.14 shows a screen from Microsoft Access for Windows illustrating some of its capabilities.

integrated software package A software package that provides two or more applications, such as word processing and spreadsheets, providing for easy transfer of data between them.

INTEGRATED SOFTWARE PACKAGES. **Integrated software packages** combine the functions of the most important microcomputer software packages, such as word processing, spreadsheets, graphics, and data management. This integration provides a more general-purpose software tool and eliminates redundant data entry and data maintenance. For example, the breakeven analysis spreadsheet illustrated in Figure 7.13 could be reformatted into a polished report with word processing software without separately keying the data into both programs. Integrated packages are a compromise. While they can do many things well, they generally do not have the same power and depth as single-purpose packages.

As Chapter 12 will discuss, these advanced tools have important limitations. They are applicable only to specific areas of application development. Nevertheless, fourth-generation tools have provided many productivity and cost-cutting benefits for businesses.

7.4 NEW SOFTWARE TOOLS AND APPROACHES

A growing backlog of software projects and the need for businesses to fashion systems that are flexible and quick to build have spawned a new approach to software development with "object-oriented" programming tools.

FIGURE 7.14
Data management software. This screen from Microsoft Access for Windows illustrates some of its powerful capabilities for managing text and graphic data.

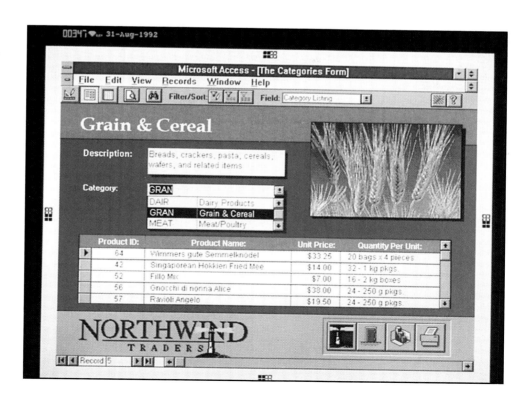

OBJECT-ORIENTED PROGRAMMING

Object-oriented concepts go back to the 1970s, but it is only recently that high-capacity hardware and iconic, graphic, windowed software (see Section 7.2 on graphical user interfaces) have made them a viable alternative.

Traditional software development methods have treated data and procedures as independent components. A separate programming procedure must be written every time someone wants to take an action on a particular piece of data. The procedures act on data that the program passes to them.

What Makes Object-Oriented Programming Different?

object-oriented programming
Approach to software development that combines data and procedures into a single object.

Object-oriented programming combines data and the specific procedures that operate on those data into one "object." The object combines data and program code. Instead of passing data to procedures, programs send a message for an object to perform a procedure that is already embedded into it. (Procedures are termed "methods" in object-oriented languages.) The same message may be sent to many different objects, but each will implement that message differently.

For example, an object-oriented financial application might have Customer objects sending debit and credit messages to Account objects. The Account objects in turn might maintain Cash-on-Hand, Accounts-Payable, and Accounts-Receivable objects.

An object's data are hidden from other parts of the program and can only be manipulated from inside the object. The method for manipulating the object's data can be changed internally without affecting other parts of the program. Programmers can focus on what they want an object to do, and the object decides how to do it.

Because an object's data are encapsulated from other parts of the system, each object is an independent software building block that can be used in many different systems without changing the program code. Thus, object-oriented programming is expected to reduce the time and cost of writing software by producing reusable program code or software "chips" that can be reused in other related systems. Future software work can draw upon a library of reusable objects, and productivity gains from object-oriented technology could be magnified if objects were stored in reusable software libraries.

visual programming Construction of software programs by selecting and arranging programming objects rather than by writing program code.

Object-oriented programming has spawned a new programming technology known as **visual programming**. With visual programming, programmers do not write code. Rather, they use a mouse to select and move around programming objects, copying an object from a library into a specific location in a program, or drawing a line to connect two or more objects. The Window on Technology more fully describes *drop-and-drag*, one visual programming method.

Object-Oriented Programming Concepts

Object-oriented programming is based on the concepts of class and inheritance. Program code is not written separately for every object but for classes, or general categories of similar objects. Objects belonging to a certain class have the features of that class. Classes of objects in turn can inherit all the structures and behaviors of a more general class and then add variables and behaviors unique to each object. New classes of objects are created by choosing an existing class and specifying how the new class differs from the existing class, instead of starting from scratch each time.

class Feature of object-oriented programming so that all objects belonging to a certain class have all of the features of that class.

Classes are organized hierarchically into superclasses and subclasses. For example, a "car" class might have a "vehicle" class for a superclass, so that it would inherit all the methods and data previously defined for "vehicle." The design of the car class would only need to describe how cars differ from vehicles. A banking application could define a Savings-Account object that is very much like a Bank-Account object with a few minor differences. Savings-Account inherits all of the Bank-Account's state and methods and then adds a few extras.

inheritance Feature of object-oriented programming in which a specific class of objects receives the features of a more general class.

We can see how class and **inheritance** work in Figure 7.15, which illustrates a tree of classes concerning employees and how they are paid. Employee is the common an-

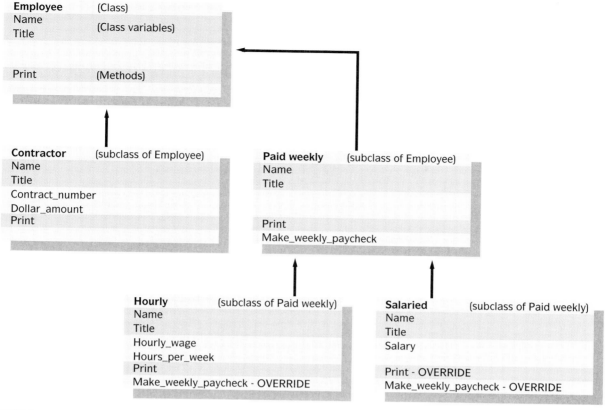

FIGURE 7.15

Class, subclasses, inheritance, and overriding. This figure illustrates how a message's method can come from the class itself or an ancestor class. Class variables and methods are shaded when they are inherited from above. © *Apple Computer, Inc. Used with permission.*

cestor of the other four classes. Contractor and Paid weekly are subclasses of Employee, while Hourly and Salaried are subclasses of Paid weekly. The variables for the class are in the top half of the box, and the methods are in the bottom half. Shaded items in each box are inherited from some ancestor class. (For example, by following the tree upward, we can see that Name and Title in the Contractor, Paid weekly, Hourly, and Salaried subclasses are inherited from the Employee superclass [ancestor class].) Unshaded methods or class variables are unique to a specific class, and they override, or redefine, existing methods. When a subclass overrides an inherited method, its object still responds to the same message, but it executes its definition of the method rather than its ancestor's. Whereas Print is a method inherited from some superclass, the method Make_weekly_paycheck is specific to the Paid weekly class, and Make_weekly_paycheck-OVERRIDE is specific to the Hourly class. The Salaried class uses its own Print-OVERRIDE method.

Object-oriented programming has not spread as rapidly as many expected. Some of the reasons why are explored in the Window on Technology.

TRENDS IN SOFTWARE CAPABILITIES

A long-term view of software shows that the major trend is to increase the ease with which users can interact with the hardware and software. The chapter-ending case illustrates one kind of software that is being designed to ease the interaction between humans and computers; the software presents and analyzes data geographically.

Software is creating more natural, seamless relationships between people and information systems, with interfaces using pointer devices such as the computer mouse, the touch screen, the graphic pad, pen-based devices, and other computer hardware

POWER SHORT CIRCUITS IN OBJECT-ORIENTED DEVELOPMENT

Ontario Hydro, the Toronto-based and government-owned utility, faces an enormous task in maintaining its 69 hydroelectric power stations, eight fossil-fuel generators, and five nuclear power plants. Whenever an unscheduled shutdown of a plant does occur, it can cost the company as much as $1 million a day. It also can affect the 8 million customers served by this $8.3 billion (Canadian) power utility. Mike Benjamin, an Ontario Hydro project manager, had an idea for an information system that would reduce unscheduled shutdowns by assisting on-site maintenance staff in their performance of plant component predictive maintenance. Much of the information the staff required to enable it to predict problems was already available, but in scattered existing systems. Benjamin launched a project that combined data from a hodgepodge of existing systems—from simulation packages to commercial databases and artificial intelligence—running on various computers so that all operators could monitor operations and even predict equipment failure. To build the system rapidly, Benjamin first developed a pilot system using object-oriented technology. As of this writing, the application was still in pilot, but it was already being judged a success, and Ontario Hydro plans to roll it out to all of its plants. This system won't prevent shutdowns, but it should decrease the frequency of shutdowns and the amount of downtime.

The key software tool Ontario Hydro used to program the objects was Xshell from Expersoft Corp., of San Diego, California, which relies on a programming technique known as drag-and-drop. Drag-and-drop is a visually oriented and easy-to-use object-oriented programming method that is gaining popularity. It relies on ORBs (or object request brokers) that are hidden to the programmer but are the elements that allow objects to communi-

cate with each other. Microcomputer users who work under Microsoft's Windows (or Apple Macintosh computer users) are familiar with two functions of ORBs. If you copy data from one Windows application to another, such as from Microsoft's Excel spreadsheet into Word Perfect's word processor, the tool that makes this transfer of data possible is an ORB called OLE (Microsoft's Object Linking and Embedding). All the user need to do is highlight the data to be copied from the first application, click the copy command with the mouse, move the cursor to the appropriate place in the other application, click the paste command, and the data is there. Similarly many Windows users easily customize their button bars in many of their applications. They do so by pointing the mouse at the button they want to add to the bar and dragging it to the bar. In fact, a Windows application button is nothing more than an object.

Benjamin's pilot system, which was developed on a Sun Microsystems workstation, is a database of plant component data that Ontario Hydro operators need if they are to do predictive and preventive maintenance. To program it, he first had to convert the relevant sections of the various Ontario Hydro applications into objects. Then, all Benjamin had to do to create the pilot application (or any future application) was to click and drag each of the needed objects to the appropriate place in the new program and then drop them there by releasing the mouse button.

While object-oriented programming is proving effective and so is expanding in use, that expansion is slowed by two technical problems. One is the use of ORBs. While programmers should not have to concern themselves with ORBs, the problem is that no ORB standard yet exists. Software developers do not have one ORB they can use to communicate with all their software applications. That problem can only be solved in time by the major

players in software development. Until then the developer is limited as to which objects can be made to communicate with which other objects.

> **To Think About:** How was object-oriented development related to Ontario Hydro's business needs? What management, technology, and organization factors would you consider before making a recommendation to use object-oriented development?

A second technical problem is the difficulties being encountered in the use of object libraries for the reuse of objects. Reuse of code is one of the major benefits of object-oriented programming, but reuse turns out to be difficult to learn to do. NationsBank-CRT, the information technology arm of the Chicago-based trading division of NationsBank Corp., found it needed almost a year before it could work out a way to reuse the objects already stored in its object library. The problem is common. James Loree, an analyst at Chrysler Financial Corporation., says "If it takes me five hours to find an object to reuse and two hours to develop it, I'll redevelop." Randee Back, a technology manager at Newark, New Jersey–based Public Service Electric & Gas Co, lists maintenance of object libraries as a major obstacle to adopting object-oriented technology, along with the cost and training involved.

The time and cost to start using the technology is another major hurdle companies must overcome. Object-oriented start-up requires a long-range commitment by management, a commitment many companies are not willing to make. Craig Fisher, a senior manager of United States distributed systems at the Bank of Montreal's Chicago office says that "Object orientation requires a significant investment in hardware, software, and retraining." John Keazirian, the executive vice-president of information technology at NationsBank-CRT claims that "after 18 months [of using object-oriented technology], we were near break-even." Developers involved with object-oriented development all agree that training is critical, yet it can be very expensive. Keazirian says that his company spent between $2,500 and $8,000 per programmer in their first year of using object-oriented development methods. He estimates that the total cost of NationsBank-CRT's first project was 50 percent higher than what it would have cost to develop in C, their traditional development technology. However, he feels the cost is worth it: Within two years, the firm achieved functionality that would not have been possible with procedural programming.

Sources: Emily Kay, "Code That's Ready to Go," *Information Week*, August 22, 1994; Lamont Wood, "The Future of Object Systems," *Information Week*, November 21, 1994.

With visual programming tools such as SQL Windows, working software programs can be created by drawing, pointing, and clicking instead of writing program code. *Source: Courtesy of the Gupta Corporation.*

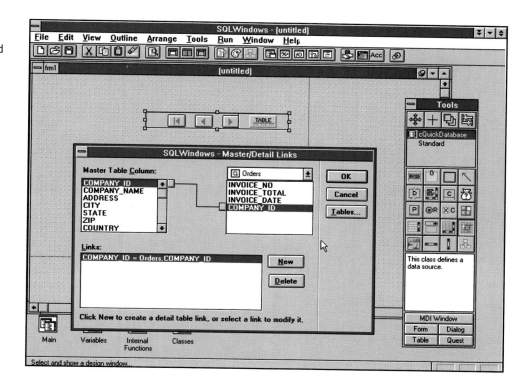

advances described in the previous chapter. People will increasingly interact with the computer in more intuitive and effortless ways—through writing, speech, touch, eye movement, and other gestures. Information systems will increasingly be able to interpret the user's actions and adapt to the user's needs (Nielsen, 1993).

For example, voice-recognition software allows people to interact with the computer by speaking. Voice-recognition software converts the spoken word into a digital form that computers can recognize. The computer responds by matching the digital translation to a vocabulary database stored in its memory, consisting of phrases, words, or phonemes (units of sound). Voice-synthesis software, on the other hand, works the opposite way, converting digitized computer data back into speech. Voice-recognition and voice-synthesis systems still work with limited vocabularies. They have been used primarily for simple, routine tasks in production-line control, computer-based telemarketing, and office dictation but are not yet sophisticated enough for information systems where tasks are complex or relatively unstructured.

Another major software trend is the development of integrated programs that support organizational needs for communication and control. Significant advances in end-user computing, as well as the advent of sophisticated on-line customer account systems like bank teller machines and brokerage firm accounts, require the development of very large, sophisticated programs to manage data for the organization

Geographic information system (GIS) software presents and analyzes data geographically, tying business data to points, lines, and areas on a map.

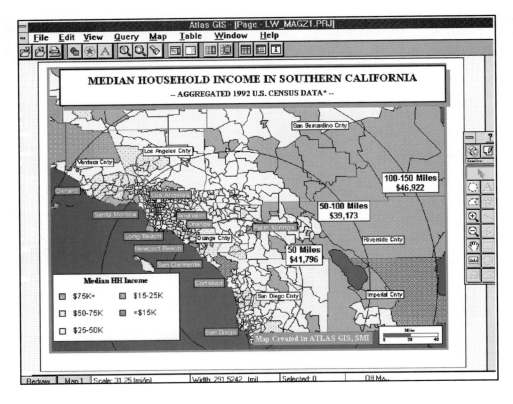

as a whole, to prepare data for end users, to integrate parts of the organization, and to permit precise control and coordination of organizational decision making. (The average size of systems in 1980 was 23,000 lines of code. By 1990, it had mushroomed to 1,246,000 lines of code. See Swanson et al., 1991.) These very large systems integrate what once were separate systems (e.g., accounts receivable and order processing) operated by separate departments (e.g., accounting and sales).

Voice recognition software converts the spoken word into digital form. Voice recognition technology is useful for applications where the input consists of simple spoken commands.

7.5 HOW TO CHOOSE SOFTWARE AND PROGRAMMING LANGUAGES

While managers need not become programming specialists, they should know the differences between programming languages and should be able to use clear criteria in deciding which language to use. The most important criteria will now be discussed.

APPROPRIATENESS

Some languages are general-purpose languages that can be used on a variety of problems, while others are special-purpose languages suitable for only limited tasks. Special-purpose graphics programs are excellent at creating tables but poor at routine processing of transactions. COBOL is excellent for business data processing but poor at mathematical calculations. Language selection involves identifying the use and the users.

SOPHISTICATION

High-level languages should have sophisticated control structures and data structures. Control structures shape the outcome of programs by providing clear, logical, structured programs that are easy to read and maintain. It may be impossible to create a table and then look up values in it unless the language has a table data structure capability. Languages should be selected that support many different data structures.

ORGANIZATIONAL CONSIDERATIONS

In order to be effective, a language must be easily learned by the firm's programming staff, easy to maintain and change, and flexible enough so that it can grow with the organization. These organizational considerations have direct long-term cost implications.

In general, sophisticated, well-structured languages are easier to learn and much easier to maintain over the long term than less sophisticated languages.

SUPPORT

It is important to purchase software that has widespread use in other organizations and is supported by many consulting firms and services. It is often less expensive to purchase software written elsewhere, or to have a service firm write it, than to develop the software internally. In these situations, it is crucial to have software that is widely used.

A different kind of support is the availability of software editing, debugging, and development aids. Because so many organizations use COBOL, there are hundreds of contemporary software development products available to assist the programming staff. The same cannot be said of Ada, a recently developed general-purpose language.

For instance, many organizations inherit poorly written, so-called spaghetti code programs that have been patched and repaired hundreds of times. After many years, perhaps decades, few people in the organization understand how such programs work. Maintenance is difficult and expensive. Now a number of new products can take poorly written COBOL programs and transform them into sophisticated, modular, documented COBOL, which is easier to maintain.

Another option is reusable software. Only a small portion of the software written is unique, novel, and specific to individual applications. Most consist of generic functions such as edit and conversion routines for Gregorian dates and edits and validation of part, employee, and account numbers. One study found that 85 percent of all programming code written in 1983 was common to many applications and theoretically could have been developed from reusable components. Firms such as the Hartford Insurance Company, Pacific Bell, and GTE Data Services have been trying to support software development by creating libraries of reusable software components.

EFFICIENCY

Although a less important feature than in the past, the efficiency with which a language compiles and executes remains a consideration when purchasing software. Languages with slow compilers, or interpreters like BASIC, can be expensive (in terms of programmer costs) to operate and maintain. In general, fourth-generation languages are very slow and expensive in terms of machine time. As discussed in later chapters, these languages are usually inappropriate for high-speed transaction systems, which must handle thousands of transactions per second.

Some programming languages are more efficient in the use of machine time than others. PL/1, for instance, requires a large section in memory for its compiler, whereas Pascal and BASIC have much simpler interpreters that require little primary memory. In any event, efficiency should be judged in terms of both machines and personnel. As machine costs fall, personnel costs become very important in choosing a language. As machines become less expensive per unit of memory, languages that are inefficient in machine time but very efficient in programmer time will grow in importance.

Management Challenges

1. Increasing complexity and software errors. While much of the software of the next decade will be rapidly generated on desktops for smaller systems and applications, a great deal of what software will be asked to do remains far-reaching and sophisticated, requiring programs that are large and complex. Citibank's automatic teller machine application required 780,000 lines of program code, written by hundreds of people, each working on small portions of the program. Large and complex systems tend to be error-prone, with software errors or "bugs" that may not be revealed for years until exhaustive testing and actual use. AT&T, for instance, found 300 errors for every 1000 lines of code in its large programs. Researchers do not know if the number of bugs grows exponentially or proportionately to the number of lines of code, nor can they tell for certain whether all segments of a complex piece of software will always work in total harmony. The process of designing and testing software that is "bug-free" is a serious quality control and management problem (see Chapter 13).

2. The application backlog. Advances in computer software have not kept pace with the breathtaking productivity gains in computer hardware. Developing software has become a major preoccupation for organizations. A great deal of software must be intricately crafted. Moreover, the software itself is only one component of a complete information system that must be carefully designed and coordinated with other people, as well as with organizational and hardware components. Managerial, procedural, and policy issues must be carefully researched and evaluated apart from the actual coding. The "software crisis" is actually part of a larger systems analysis, design, and implementation issue, which will be treated in detail in Part III. Despite the gains from fourth-generation languages, personal desktop software tools, and object-oriented programming, many businesses continue to face a backlog of two to three years in developing the information systems they need, or they will not be able to develop them at all.

Summary

1. Describe the major types of software. The major types of software are systems software and applications software. Each serves a different purpose. System software manages the computer resources and mediates between application software and computer hardware. Application software is used by application programmers and some end users to develop systems and specific business applications. Applications software works through systems software, which controls access to computer hardware.

   2. Describe the functions of system software and compare leading microcomputer operating systems. System software coordinates the various parts of the computer system and mediates between application software and computer hardware. The system software that manages and controls the activities of the computer is called the operating system. Other system software includes computer language translation programs that convert programming languages into machine language and utility programs that perform common processing tasks.

The operating system acts as the chief manager of the information system, allocating, assigning, and scheduling system resources and monitoring the use of the computer. Multiprogramming, multitasking, virtual storage, time sharing, and multiprocessing, enable system resources to be used more efficiently so that the computer can attack many problems at the same time.

Multiprogramming (multitasking in microcomputer environments) allows multiple programs to use the computer's resources concurrently. Virtual storage splits up programs into pages so that main memory can be utilized more efficiently. Time sharing enables many users to share computer resources simultaneously by allocating each user a tiny slice of computing time. Multiprocessing is the use of two or more CPUs linked together working in tandem to perform a task.

In order to be executed by the computer, a software program must be translated into machine language via special language translation software—a compiler, an assembler, or an interpreter.

Microcomputer operating systems are starting to develop sophisticated capabilities such as multitasking and support for multiple users on networks. Leading microcomputer operating systems include Windows 95, Windows NT, OS/2, UNIX, System 7, and DOS. Microcomputer operating systems with graphical user interfaces are gaining popularity over command-driven operating systems. Windows is a popular graphical user interface shell for the DOS operating system.

3. Explain how software has evolved and how it will continue to develop. Software has evolved along with hardware. The general trend is toward user-friendly high-level languages that both increase professional programmer productivity and make it possible for complete amateurs to use information systems. There have been four generations of software development: (1) machine language; (2) symbolic languages such as assembly language; (3) high-level languages such as FORTRAN and COBOL; and (4) fourth-generation languages, which are less procedural and closer to natural language than earlier generations of software. Software is starting to incorporate both sound and graphics and to support multimedia applications.

4. Compare strengths and limitations of the major application programming languages and software tools. The most popular conventional programming languages are assembly language, FORTRAN, COBOL, BASIC, PL/1, Pascal, C, and Ada. Conventional programming languages make more efficient use of computer resources than fourth-generation languages and each is designed to solve specific types of problems.

Fourth-generation languages include query languages, report generators, graphics languages, application generators, very-high-level programming languages, application software packages, and microcomputer tools. They are less procedural than conventional programming languages and enable end users to perform many software tasks that previously required technical specialists.

Object-oriented programming combines data and procedures into one "object," which can act as an independent software building block. Each object can be used in many different systems without changing program code.

5. Explain how to select appropriate software and programming languages. Choosing the right software for a particular application requires some knowledge of the strengths and weaknesses of specific software products. Equally important is the support for software packages given by vendors, the ability of the organization to absorb new software, and the efficiency of the software in executing specific tasks.

Key Terms

Software	Interpreter	COBOL (COmmon Business Oriented Language)	Very-high-level programming language
Program	Utility program	BASIC (Beginners All-purpose Symbolic Instruction Code)	Software package
Stored program concept	Graphical user interface (GUI)		Word processing software
System software	DOS	PL/1 (Programming Language 1)	Spreadsheet
Application software	Windows	Pascal	Data management software
Operating system	Windows 95	Ada	Integrated software package
System residence device	Windows NT	C	Object-oriented programming
Multiprogramming	OS/2	Fourth-generation language	Visual programming
Multitasking	UNIX	Query language	Class
Virtual storage	System 7	Report generator	Inheritance
Page	Machine language	Graphics language	
Time sharing	High-level language	Application generator	
Multiprocessing	Assembly language		
Source code	FORTRAN (FORmula TRANslator)		
Compiler			
Object code			

Review Questions

1. What are the major types of software? How do they differ in terms of users and uses?
2. What is the operating system of a computer? What does it do?
3. Describe multiprogramming, virtual storage, time sharing, and multiprocessing. Why are they important for the operation of an information system?
4. Define multitasking.
5. What is the difference between an assembler, a compiler, and an interpreter?
6. Define graphical user interfaces.
7. Compare the major microcomputer operating systems.
8. What are the major generations of software and approximately when were they developed?

9. What is a high-level language? Name three high-level languages. Describe their strengths and weaknesses.
10. Define fourth-generation languages and list the seven categories of fourth-generation tools.
11. What is the difference between fourth-generation languages and conventional programming languages?
12. What is the difference between an application generator and an application software package? Between a report generator and a query language?
13. Name and describe the most important microcomputer software tools.
14. What is object-oriented programming? How does it differ from conventional software development?
15. What are the four major trends in software? Can you think of more than the four described in the text?
16. What are the major factors to consider when selecting software and programming languages?

Discussion Questions

1. What factors should be considered in selecting microcomputer software?
2. Your firm wishes to develop a system that will process sales orders and update inventory. The programmers in your information systems department wish to use assembly language to write the programs for this system. Is this a good idea? Discuss.
3. Several authorities have claimed that fourth-generation languages will soon replace conventional programming languages such as COBOL for implementing the vast majority of information system applications. Discuss.

Group Project

OS/2 has been described as a "better Window than Windows and a better DOS than DOS." Your instructor will divide the class into two groups to debate this proposition, from both a technical and business standpoint. Use articles from computer magazines to help prepare your group's analysis.

Case Study

A GEOGRAPHIC INFORMATION SYSTEM ADDS ZEST TO SONNY'S BAR-B-Q

How does a restaurant chain know where to open new outlets? Sonny's Bar-B-Q is in the process of expanding and believes it has found a software solution to the problem. Sonny's is a chain of 83 southern United States barbecue restaurants of which eight are company owned. The company generated about $100 million in revenues in 1994. The income came from fees of $25,000 each for the about 11 new franchises, royalties of 2.5 percent of each franchisee's gross income, and the income from company-owned restaurants.

The first Sonny's was established in 1968 in Gainesville, Florida, as a low-priced barbecue restaurant, delivering quality food at 50 percent of the price of many of its competitors. Sonny's has expanded slowly ever since. According to Michael Turner, director of franchise services, the company wants to add about 100 new franchises over the next few years, with 15 to 20 to be opened in 1995 alone.

Sonny's has a well-thought-out growth plan for the company to meet their growth target. First, franchisees must be qualified to run a barbecue restaurant. Second, the company will expand only into regions where barbecued food is very common but where the number of barbecue restaurants is small. Third, the company is trying to grow in concentric circles expanding out from Florida. To date they have also established restaurants in Georgia, Alabama, South Carolina, and Tennessee. Fourth, new Sonny's sites are selected very carefully to generate the most revenue from the least number of people and the smallest area.

Turner selects location sites so that they fit in with existing restaurants. No Sonny's is closer than seven miles from any other Sonny's. Turner's view is that "if you put one restaurant in the wrong place, it doesn't just disrupt one, it can kill off two." The company looks at a range of factors when determining the suitability of a given territory, including traffic count, median age, household income, total population, and population distribution. Turner has established criteria for each of these and other factors. He requires that a franchise territory have a population of about 70,000 that meet these criteria.

Locating the data Sonny's requires in order to evaluate potential new territories is not a problem. Local authorities usually have traffic count data, and the Bureau of the Census of the U.S. Department of Commerce will supply all the rest. In fact, the census files contain up to 3000 variables, even including such items as the number of refrigerators per household. The problem Turner did face, however, was how to obtain and analyze this data at a reasonable price. According to Turner, to gather this data "the traditional way, with a large computer, it would cost from $200,000 to $500,000," a cost far too high to be cost-effective for a small business like Sonny's. Turner also faced the problem of interpreting the data—reading and understanding mountains of statistics in numeric form. To solve these problems, Turner turned to a type of software that has been growing in popularity over the last few years, geographic information systems (GIS).

Although application software has long been able to process immense amounts of data, the quantity of data is often simply too much for any human mind to absorb and effectively employ. Most of us remember (or perhaps still receive) printed reports with literally hundreds of pages of mind-numbing data. Such data usually can be understood only if it is presented through an appropriate interface. We have all become quite accustomed to one type of interface for easier grasping of the significance of large quantities of data—graphics software (such as bar and pie charts). Geographic information systems (GIS) presents masses of data by overlaying the data onto maps.

Geographic interfaces have begun to find wide acceptance, as they are proving to be quite useful. For example,

Johanna Dairies of Union, New Jersey, has been able to save $800,000 per year by using a GIS to help it plan its delivery routes. It is making available customer orders and locations through a GIS that displays customer locations on digital street maps. The user is able to zoom in on sections of the city to actually see the customer locations. With this information, Johanna was able to plan more efficient delivery routes in which delivery trucks traveled much shorter distances. As a result Johanna Dairies was able to reduce the number of delivery routes from 60 to 52 at an average annual saving of $100,000 per delivery route.

Many other creative uses have been found for this exciting and easily grasped software interface. ITT Hartford, the insurance giant, used GIS software from MapInfo of Troy, New York, to improve its response to Hurricane Andrew which devastated southern Florida in late 1992. The company tracked the hurricane using its GIS and then displayed the ZIP codes of the areas where the most damage was projected to occur. Using those ZIP codes, it was quickly able to identify policy holders in the high-damage areas. With potential claim data in hand, insurance adjusters were speedily dispatched to the hardest-hit areas, thereby expediting insurance payments to desperate customers.

A not-for-profit consumer watchdog organization named Essential Information (ESRI), located in Redlands, California, is using GIS to monitor the effectiveness of certain federal lending laws in 16 cities throughout the United States. What they have found—demonstrated with great clarity by the graphic displays of the software—is that lending institutions that are federally regulated commit a far larger percentage of their funds to minority neighborhoods than do unregulated institutions. For example, their work and the GIS software showed that in 1991 in Los Angeles, unregulated Sears Mortgage Corp. granted 12 times as many loans in white neighborhoods than in minority neighborhoods, whereas regulated Great Western Bank showed the opposite pattern,

granting 3.6 times as many loans in minority neighborhoods as they did in white neighborhoods. Police forces are now using GIS to pinpoint high crime areas in order to better deploy their police officers. They are also using GIS to alert them to changes in crime patterns. For example, if a neighborhood normally has four to eight break-ins a month, the software can be set to issue an alert whenever the monthly total of such crimes in that neighborhood rise above nine. District attorneys have even used the software to aid them in prosecuting accused criminals. In one example they were able to bolster their case by using a GIS to show that a series of neighborhood rapes that had begun after the accused moved into a neighborhood had all occurred on the accused's route to and from work.

While a GIS interface is simple and makes the data easy to grasp, a company that turns to GIS software must do a great deal of preparation prior to actually using it. GIS has four basic components users must prepare. They need to select the demographic data required, develop search-and-retrieve software to collect the required data, select the maps to be displayed, and then acquire a GIS system which will bring the data and maps together as needed.

Sonny's growth plan told them the data they would need. The traffic data had to be located locally. The census data turned out to be readily available on CD-ROM and to be relatively inexpensive. The total 1990 census is stored on 62 disks, but the customer is able to purchase the data only for the states needed. Sonny's also had to purchase the maps it needs. Map data can be rather expensive, depending partially upon the detail the user requires. Digital street maps for the entire United States can be purchased for about $15,000. To search the census data, Sonny's purchased PSearch-USA from Tetrad Computer Applications in Bellingham, Washington. It also purchased MapInfo geographic information software to do the geographic analysis and display the data. Of course, the company must have hardware capable of running the software efficiently. Sonny's is using 486 PCs.

The whole system cost Sonny's about $30,000, including the data. The MapInfo geographic information system application cost $1295. Digital street maps of the United States were $15,000, plus an additional $3995 for ZIP-code boundaries; ZIP plus four codes cost $10,000. Tetrad's census data for a state ranges from $300 to $600; for the entire country, the cost is $2000. Tetrad's PCensus and Psearch-USA search-and-retrieve software each cost $250.

For GIS to be successful, not only must a company allocate the budget to obtain the tools, but it also must allocate staff to develop the right approach for that company. In addition, the appropriate business functions must be altered to integrate the GIS software, which in the case of Sonny's, is the marketing and sales departments. Sonny's had no problem with these aspects—funding, developing and integrating—because one active and key supporter of the project was Robert Yarmuth, CEO of Sonny's. He views GIS as significant for supporting his style of quick decision making. He also uses it to aid him in providing direction to his staff. As he explains it, "The more I know and the faster I know it, the more help I can be."

Sonny's uses MapInfo to display population data, including eating habits, for a targeted area. Turner is able to bring up a map of a region and, using a mouse, outline the area in which he is interested. The computer will then display the selected population data superimposed on the map. Full color patterns quickly jump out at the user, so that, for example, it becomes easy to answer a prospective franchisee's questions in a manner the prospect has no difficulty comprehending. At the time of this writing it was too early to evaluate the overall effectiveness of GIS for Sonny's. Turner does plan to use the software to develop demographic models of successful franchises and then use the software to search for areas that fit the model. He did have one key success to point to already. One Florida county was franchised with the expectation that they could fit four restaurants in the area successfully. However, the software indicated that the county could safely absorb eight Sonny's. Ultimately they decided to open seven franchises. The unexpected additional three franchises brought in a total of $75,000 in franchise fees alone, more than covering the total cost of the GIS installation. The company will also receive its 2.5 percent royalties from these three restaurants for years to come.

Sources: Tony Seideman, "You Gotta Know the Territory," *Profit*, November–December 1994; Vera Tweed, "The Graphic Detail," *Information Week*, August 29, 1994, David Forrest, "Seeing Data in New Ways," *Computerworld*, June 29, 1993; Rick Tetzeli, "Mapping for Dollars," *Fortune*, October 18, 1993.

Case Study Questions

1. Use the competitive forces and value chain models to evaluate Sonny's business strategy. How does Sonny's use of software support that strategy?

2. Analyze the benefits obtained from Sonny's geographic information system (GIS) applications.

3. What kinds of problems can software solve for Sonny's and what kinds of problems will it not solve?

4. Name businesses for which your answer to question 3 might be different, and explain why.

5. What other applications can you suggest for geographic information systems?

6. As a manager in your company, how would you determine whether to use such software in your firm?

References

Abdel-Hamid, Tarek K. "The Economics of Software Quality Assurance: A Simulation-Based Case Study." *MIS Quarterly* 12, no. 3 (September 1988).

Apte, Uday, Chetan S. Sankar, Meru Thakur, and Joel E. Turner. "Reusability-Based Strategy for Development of Information Systems: Implementation Experience of a Bank." *MIS Quarterly* 14, no. 4 (December 1990).

Barrett, Jim, Kevin Knight, Inderject Man, and Elaine Rich. "Knowledge and Natural Language Processing." *Communications of the ACM* 33, no. 8 (August 1990).

Bochenski, Barbara. "GUI Builders Pay Price for User Productivity," *Software Magazine* (April 1992).

Borning, Alan. "Computer System Reliability and Nuclear War." *Communications of the ACM* 30, no. 2 (February 1987).

Fallows, James. "Crash-Worthy Speedster." *The Atlantic Monthly* (February 1993).

Freedman, David H. "Programming Without Tears." *High Technology* (April 1986).

Greenbaum, Joshua. "The Evolution Revolution." *Information Week* (March 14, 1994).

Haavind, Robert. "Software's New Object Lesson." *Technology Review* (February–March 1992).

Jalics, Paul J. "Cobol on a PC: A New Perspective on a Language and Its Performance." *Communications of the ACM* 30, no. 2 (February 1987).

Joyce, Edward J. "Reusable Software: Passage to Productivity?" *Datamation* (September 15, 1988).

Kim, Chai, and Stu Westin. "Software Maintainability: Perceptions of EDP Professionals." *MIS Quarterly* 12, no. 2 (June 1988).

Korson, Tim, and John D. McGregor. "Understanding Object-Oriented: A Unifying Paradigm." *Communications of the ACM* 33, no. 9 (September 1990).

Korson, Timothy D., and Vijay K. Vaishnavi. "Managing Emerging Software Technologies: A Technology Transfer Framework." *Communications of the ACM* 35, no. 9 (September 1992).

Lauriston, Robert. "OS/2 versus Windows NT." *PC World* (February 1993).

Layer, D. Kevin, and Chris Richardson. "Lisp Systems in the 1990s." *Communications of the ACM* 34, no. 9 (September 1991.)

Littlewood, Bev, and Lorenzo Strigini. "The Risks of Software." *Scientific American* 267, no. 5 (November 1992).

Mandelkern, David. "Graphical User Interfaces: The Next Generation." *Communications of the ACM* 36, no. 4 (April 1993).

Monarchi, David E., and Gretchen I. Puhr. "A Research Typology for Object-Oriented Analysis and Design." *Communications of the ACM* 35, no. 9 (September 1992).

Morse, Alan, and George Reynolds. "Overcoming Current Growth Limits in UI Development." *Communications of the ACM* 36, no. 4 (April 1993).

Mukhopadhyay, Tridas, Stephen S. Vicinanza, and Michael J. Prietula. "Examining the Feasibility of a Case-Based Reasoning Model for Software Effort Estimation." *MIS Quarterly* 16, no. 2 (June 1992).

Nance, Barry. "Windows NT and OS/2 Compared." *Byte* (June 1992).

Nerson, Jean-Marc. "Applying Object-Oriented Analysis and Design." *Communications of the ACM* 35, no. 9 (September 1992).

Nielsen, Jacob. "Noncommand User Interfaces." *Communications of the ACM* 36, no. 4 (April 1993).

Schonberg, Edmond, Mark Gerhardt, and Charlene Hayden. "A Technical Tour of Ada." *Communications of the ACM* 35, no. 11 (November 1992).

Swanson, Kent, Dave McComb, Jill Smith, and Don McCubbrey. "The Application Software Factory: Applying Total Quality Techniques to Systems Development." *MIS Quarterly* 15, no. 4 (December 1991).

Vassiliou, Yannis. "On the Interactive Use of Databases: Query Languages." *Journal of Management Information Systems* 1 (Winter 1984–1985).

White, George M. "Natural Language Understanding and Speech." *Communications of the ACM* 33, no. 8 (August 1990).

Wiederhold, Gio, Peter Wegner, and Stefano Ceri. "Toward Megaprogramming." *Communications of the ACM* 35, no. 11 (November 1992).

Wilkes, Maurice V. "The Long-Term Future of Operating Systems." *Communications of the ACM* 35, no. 11 (November 1992).

Chapter 8

Managing Data Resources

Organized Information Makes a Difference

In the 1970s, the Soviet Cosmos 954 satellite crashed in a remote section of northern Canada. On impact, it released radioactive particles from its nuclear reactor. With so many nuclear-powered satellites orbiting the globe, what can be done to prevent an incident like this or, worse, one in which the satellite hits a heavily populated area?

Scientists have been developing recovery and disposal scenarios for nuclear-powered satellites for years. In the past, these scenarios took weeks or months to develop—far too long after a crash occurred to respond effectively. The scientists prepared these simulations manually using a complex matrix, and they had to be aware of all the various options for each recovery as they made calculations.

Now scientists can generate recovery-and-disposal scenarios in minutes by using an application called Technology Hierarchy for Orbital Recovery (THOR), developed by POD Associates in Albuquerque, New Mexico. THOR uses a relational database that can store vast amounts of information collected from manufacturers and other sources on various technologies related to satellite recovery efforts. The database includes detailed data on launch sites, reactor composition, recovery vehicles, and satellite size and mass. Using menus that can be easily accessed on the computer terminal screen, scientists can input data on the type of satellite, type of reactor powering it, and whether the reactor is operational in order to design a scenario. The way the

information is organized by the database software makes it easy for scientists to access and combine the information they need to generate a solution for the recovery.

THOR automatically performs the calculations the scientists need. Using the information stored in the database, scientists can present a detailed recovery scenario, including what type of recovery vehicle to use and where to launch it from. THOR is expected to save the National Aeronautic and Space Administration (NASA), the Department of Energy, and the Department of Defense a person-year's worth of work, equivalent to between $100,000 and $200,000.

Many businesses can benefit from organized information as well. Like many banks, the San Francisco–based

Bank of America had separate systems for different financial products—checking account systems, savings account systems, IRA account systems, cash management systems, and securities account systems. But it could not tie the data from these separate systems together. It was impossible to draw together all of the information the bank maintained on a particular customer. Without the ability to easily provide customer service, marketing analysis, and managerial information, the bank was at a competitive disadvantage.

The bank eventually constructed a massive 600-gigabyte customer information database, which contains all of its customer account information including data on checking, savings, time deposit, ATM, real estate and consumer loans,

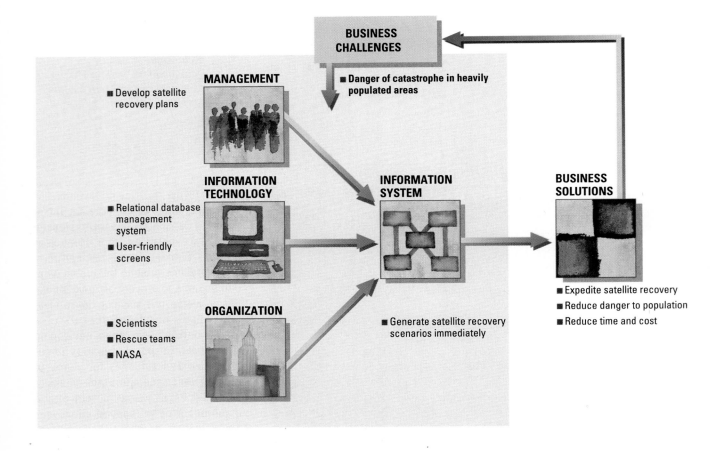

bank cards, and commercial loans. Using a system called Direct Connect, bank managers can now draw together all of the information maintained on customers, and other vital pieces of information as well. For instance, the residential lending group, which tracks the bank's $28 billion mortgage loan portfolio, was able to learn within minutes about the bank's potential loan loss resulting from the Los Angeles earthquake of January 17, 1994. They were able to see by ZIP code how many and what type of real estate loans the bank had in areas where the earthquake hit. ■

Sources: "BofA's Data Warehouse," *InformationWEEK*, July 25, 1994, and Christopher Lindquist, "RDBMS Helps Prevent Satellite Disaster," *Computerworld*, April 27, 1992.

The THOR satellite recovery system and the Direct Connect system both illustrate how much the effective use of information depends on how data are stored, organized, and accessed. Proper delivery of information not only depends on the capabilities of computer hardware and software but also on the organization's ability to manage data as an important resource.

This chapter examines the managerial and organizational requirements as well as the technologies for managing data as a resource. First we describe the traditional file management technologies that have been used for arranging and accessing data on physical storage media and the problems they have created for organizations. Then we describe the technology of database management systems, which can overcome many of the drawbacks of traditional file management. We end the chapter with a discussion of the managerial and organizational requirements for successful implementation of database management systems.

After completing this chapter, you will be able to:

Learning Objectives

1. Describe traditional file organization and management techniques.

2. Explain the problems of the traditional file environment.

3. Describe how a database management system organizes information.

4. Identify the three principal database models.

5. Explain the principles for designing a relational database.

6. Discuss new database trends.

7. Explain the managerial and organizational requirements for creating a database environment.

8.1   ORGANIZING DATA IN A TRADITIONAL FILE ENVIRONMENT

An effective information system provides users with timely, accurate, and relevant information. This information is stored in computer files. When the files are properly arranged and maintained, users can easily access and retrieve the information they need.

You can appreciate the importance of file management if you have ever written a term paper using 3 by 5 index cards. No matter how efficient your storage device (a metal box or a rubber band), if you organize the cards randomly your term paper will have little or no organization. Given enough time, you could put the cards in order, but your system would be more efficient if you set up your organizational scheme early on. If your scheme is flexible enough and well documented, you can extend it to account for any changes in your viewpoint as you write your paper.

The same need for file organization applies to firms. Well-managed, carefully arranged files make it easy to obtain data for business decisions, whereas poorly managed files lead to chaos in information processing, high costs, poor performance, and little, if any, flexibility. Despite the use of excellent hardware and software, many organizations have inefficient information systems because of poor file management. In this section we describe the traditional methods that organizations have used to arrange data in computer files. We also discuss the problems with these methods.

FILE ORGANIZATION TERMS AND CONCEPTS

field A grouping of characters into a word, a group of words, or a complete number, such as a person's name or age.

record A group of related fields.

file A group of records of the same type.

entity A person, place, thing, or event about which information must be kept.

attribute Piece of information describing a particular entity.

key field A field in a record that uniquely identifies instances of that record so that it can be retrieved, updated, or sorted.

A computer system organizes data in a hierarchy that starts with bits and bytes and progresses to fields, records, files, and databases (see Figure 8.1). A bit represents the smallest unit of data a computer can handle. A group of bits, called a byte, represents a single character, which can be a letter, a number, or another symbol. A grouping of characters into a word, a group of words, or a complete number (such as a person's name or age), is called a **field**. A group of related fields, such as the student's name, the course taken, the date, and the grade make up a **record**; a group of records of the same type is called a **file**. For instance, all of the student records in Figure 8.1 could constitute a course file. A group of related files make up a database. The student course file illustrated in Figure 8.1 could be grouped with files on students' personal histories and financial backgrounds to create a student database.

A record describes an entity. An **entity** is a person, place, thing, or event on which we maintain information. An order is a typical entity in a sales order file, which maintains information on a firm's sales orders. Each characteristic or quality describing a particular entity is called an **attribute.** For example, order number, order date, order amount, item number, and item quantity would each be an attribute of the entity order. The specific values that these attributes can have can be found in the fields of the record describing the entity *order* (see Figure 8.2).

Every record in a file should contain at least one field that uniquely identifies that record so that the record can be retrieved, updated, or sorted. This identifier field is called a **key field.** An example of a key field is the order number for the order record illustrated in Figure 8.2 or an employee number or social security number for a personnel record (containing employee data such as the employee's name, age, address, job title, and so forth).

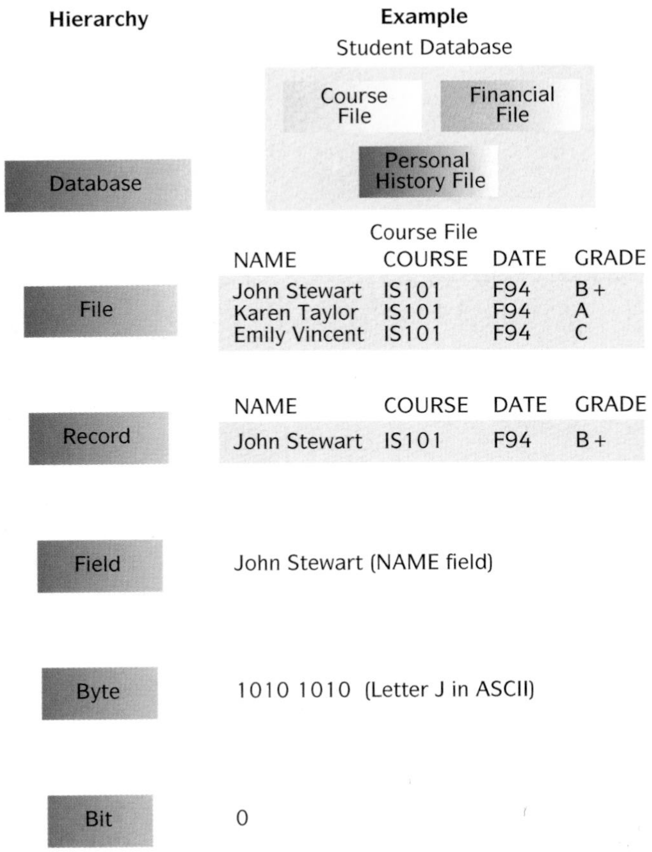

FIGURE 8.1
The data hierarchy. A computer system organizes data in a hierarchy that starts with the bit, which represents either a 0 or a 1. Bits can be grouped to form a byte to represent one character, number, or symbol. Bytes can be grouped to form a field, and related fields can be grouped to form a record. Related records can be collected to form a file, and related files can be organized into a database.

Hierarchy	Example
	Student Database
Database	Course File / Financial File / Personal History File
File	**Course File** NAME COURSE DATE GRADE John Stewart IS101 F94 B+ Karen Taylor IS101 F94 A Emily Vincent IS101 F94 C
Record	NAME COURSE DATE GRADE John Stewart IS101 F94 B+
Field	John Stewart (NAME field)
Byte	1010 1010 (Letter J in ASCII)
Bit	0

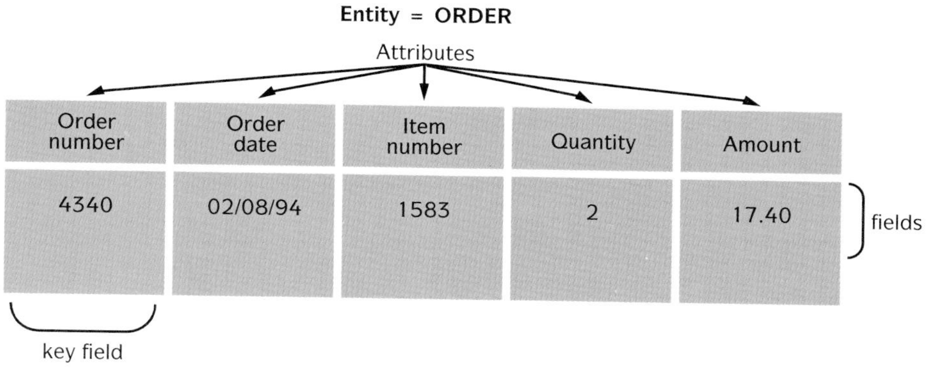

FIGURE 8.2

Entities and attributes. This record describes the entity called ORDER and its attributes. The specific values for order number, order date, item number, quantity, and amount for this particular order are the fields for this record. Order number is the key field because each order is assigned a unique identification number.

Entity = ORDER

Attributes

Order number	Order date	Item number	Quantity	Amount
4340	02/08/94	1583	2	17.40

fields

key field

ACCESSING RECORDS FROM COMPUTER FILES

Computer systems store files on secondary storage devices. Records can be arranged in several ways on storage media, and the arrangement determines the manner in which individual records can be accessed or retrieved. One way to organize records is sequentially. In **sequential file organization,** data records must be retrieved in the same physical sequence in which they are stored. In contrast, **direct** or **random file organization** allows users to access records in any sequence they desire, without regard to actual physical order on the storage media.

Sequential file organization is the only file organization method that can be used on magnetic tape. This file organization method is no longer popular, but some organizations still use it for batch processing applications in which they access and process each record sequentially. A typical application using sequential files is payroll, where all employees in a firm must be paid one by one and issued a check. Direct or random file organization is utilized with magnetic disk technology (although records can be stored sequentially on disk if desired). Most computer applications today utilize some method of direct file organization.

The Indexed Sequential Access Method

Although records may be stored sequentially on direct access storage devices, individual records can be accessed directly using the **indexed sequential access method (ISAM).** This access method relies on an index of key fields to locate individual records. An **index** to a file is similar to the index of a book, as it lists the key field of each record and where that record is physically located in storage to expedite location of that record. Figure 8.3 shows how a series of indexes identifies the location of a specific record. Records are stored on disk in their key sequence. A cylinder index shows the highest value of the key field that can be found on a specific cylinder. A track index shows the highest value of the key field that can be found on a specific track. To locate a specific record, the cylinder index and then the track index are searched to locate the cylinder and track containing the record. The track itself is then sequentially read to find the record. If a file is very large, the cylinder index might be broken down into parts and a master index created to help locate each part of the cylinder index. ISAM is employed in applications that require sequential processing of large numbers of records but that occasionally require direct access of individual records.

Direct File Access Method

The **direct file access method** is used with direct file organization. This method employs a key field to locate the physical address of a record. However, the process is accomplished using a mathematical formula called a **transform algorithm** to translate the key field directly into the record's physical storage location on disk. The algorithm

sequential file organization A method of storing data records in which the records must be retrieved in the same physical sequence in which they are stored.

direct or **random file organization** Method of storing data records in a file so that they can be accessed in any sequence without regard to their actual physical order on the storage media.

indexed sequential access method (ISAM) File access method to directly access records organized sequentially using an index of key fields.

index A table or list that relates record keys to physical locations on direct access files.

direct file access method Method of accessing records by mathematically transforming the key fields into the specific addresses for the records.

transform algorithm Mathematical formula used to translate a record's key field directly into the record's physical storage location.

FIGURE 8.3
The indexed sequential access method (ISAM). To find a record with a key field of 230, the cylinder index would be searched to find the correct cylinder (in this case, cylinder 2). The track index for cylinder 2 would then be searched to find the correct track. Since the highest key on track 2 of cylinder 2 is 238 and the highest key on track 1 of cylinder 2 is 208, track 2 must contain the record. Track 2 of cylinder 2 would then be read to find the record with key 230.

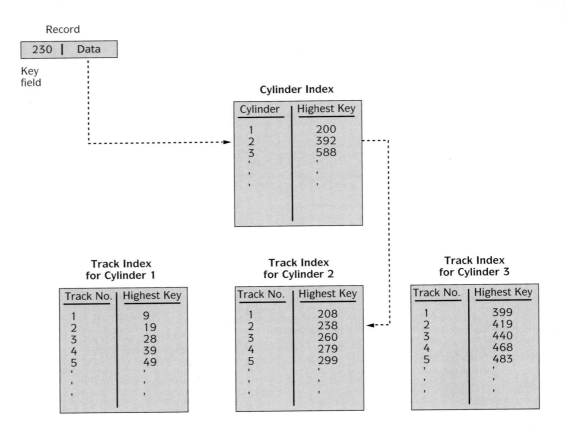

performs some mathematical computation on the record key, and the result of that calculation is the record's physical address. This process is illustrated in Figure 8.4.

This access method is most appropriate for applications where individual records must be located directly and rapidly for immediate processing only. A few records in the file need to be retrieved at one time, and the required records are found in no particular sequence. An example might be an on-line hotel reservation system.

PROBLEMS WITH THE TRADITIONAL FILE ENVIRONMENT

According to Greek legend, Gordius, King of Phrygia, tied an intricate, complex knot in a rope, of which it was said that he who untied the knot would be master of Asia. As it turned out, Alexander the Great cut the knot and went on to become master of Asia. Many organizations have found that they tied themselves into an information-system Gordian knot of their own making. Here we describe the knot. In the following section, we show how to untie parts of the knot and cut through the rest.

Most organizations began information processing on a small scale, automating one application at a time. Systems tended to grow independently, and not according to some grand plan. Typically, each division of a multidivision company developed its own applications. Within each division, each functional area tended to develop systems in isolation from other functional areas. Accounting, finance, manufacturing, and marketing all developed their own systems and data files. Figure 8.5 illustrates the traditional approach to information processing.

Each application, of course, required its own files and its own computer program in order to operate. In general, the files used in an application were some version of the functional area master file. For instance, there was one very large master personnel file containing most of the basic information on all employees in the company, including current position and salary. However, over time, a number of smaller files extracted from the larger master file were spun off for processing efficiency as well as for specialized applications. Hence, the personnel master file spawned a payroll

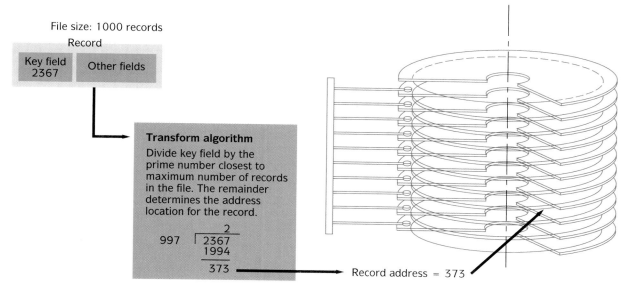

FIGURE 8.4
The direct file access method. Records are not stored sequentially on the disk but are arranged according to the results of some mathematical computation. Here, the transform algorithm divides the value in the key field by the prime number closest to the maximum number of records in the file (in this case, the prime number is 997). The remainder designates the storage location for that particular record.

FIGURE 8.5
Traditional file processing. The use of a traditional approach to file processing encourages each functional area in a corporation to develop specialized applications. Each application requires a unique data file that is likely to be a subset of the master file. These subsets of the master file lead to data redundancy, processing inflexibility, and wasted storage resources.

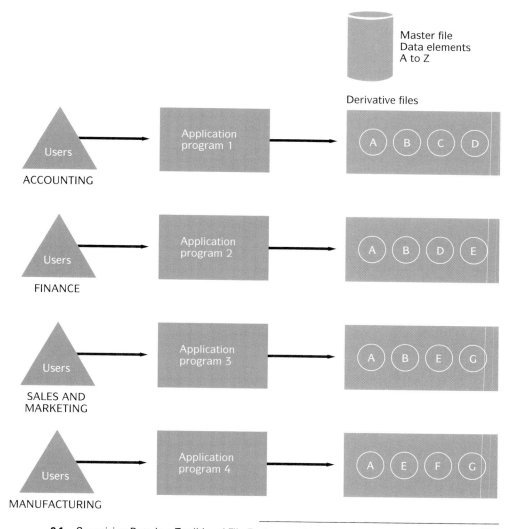

file, a medical insurance file, a pension file, a mailing list file, a list of employees who joined the company via prior acquisitions (who were paid using a different payroll program), and so forth until tens, perhaps hundreds, of files and programs existed.

In the company as a whole, this process led to multiple master files created, maintained, and operated by separate divisions or departments. Figure 8.6 shows three separate master files: customer, personnel, and sales. Creating a simple report such as that listed in this example, sales personnel by annual sales and by principal customers, required a complex "matching" program that read each of the three files, copied pertinent records, and recombined the records into an intermediate file. This intermediate file had to be sorted in the desired sequence (sales personnel ranked by highest sales) before a final report could be printed.

Of course, every data item in the various files required a set of documents to support the file and help collect information. Often the same data item, such as product code, was collected on multiple documents by different divisions and departments. In time, the file structure of the organization became so complex that programmers developed specialties by focusing on subsets of files and programs. Eventually, the programs became totally dependent on a few programmers who understood the pro-

FIGURE 8.6
Creating a report using traditional file processing. In this example, three separate files—customer, personnel, and sales—have been created and are maintained by each respective division or department. In order to create a simple report consisting of a list of sales personnel by annual sales and principal customers, the three files had to be read, and an intermediate file had to be created. This required writing several programs. The table in the figure shows the information selected from each file.

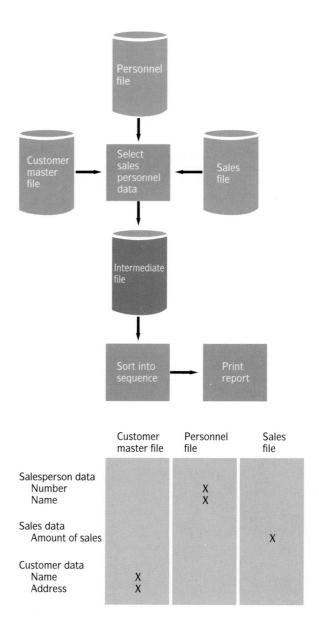

	Customer master file	Personnel file	Sales file
Salesperson data			
Number		X	
Name		X	
Sales data			
Amount of sales			X
Customer data			
Name	X		
Address	X		

grams and files. If these programmers became ill or left the company, key applications failed.

There are names for this situation: the **traditional file environment;** the flat file organization (because most of the data are organized in flat files); and the data file approach (because the data and business logic are tied to specific files and related programs). By any name, the situation results in growing inefficiency and complexity.

As this process goes on for five or ten years, the firm becomes tied up in knots of its own creation. The organization is saddled with hundreds of programs and applications, with no one who knows what they do, what data they use, and who is using the data. There is no central listing of data files, data elements, or definitions of data. The organization is collecting the same information on far too many documents. The resulting problems are data redundancy, program-data dependence, inflexibility, poor data security, and inability to share data among applications.

Data Redundancy and Confusion

Data redundancy is the presence of duplicate data in multiple data files. Data redundancy occurs when different divisions, functional areas, and groups in an organization independently collect the same piece of information. For instance, within the commercial loans division of a bank, the marketing and credit information functions might collect the same customer information. Because it is collected and maintained in so many different places, the same data item may have different meanings in different parts of the organization. Simple data items like the fiscal year, employee identification, and product code can take on different meanings as programmers and analysts work in isolation on different applications.

Program-Data Dependence

Program-data dependence is the tight relationship between data stored in files and the specific programs required to update and maintain those files. Every computer program has to describe the location and nature of the data with which it works. These data declarations can be longer than the substantive part of the program. In a traditional file environment, any change in data requires a change in all of the programs that access the data. Changes, for instance, in tax rates or ZIP code length require changes in programs. Such programming changes may cost millions of dollars to implement in each program that requires the revised data.

The development of new applications consequently takes more time and money than it would otherwise. Programmers have to write complicated programs, stripping data items from records in a variety of files to create new files. New programs require new arrangements of data. A large part of the organization's programming effort consists of updating data elements that are scattered throughout hundreds of files. In many instances, applications work with outdated data simply because of the difficulty of making updates.

Lack of Flexibility

A traditional file system can deliver routine scheduled reports after extensive programming efforts, but it cannot deliver ad hoc reports or respond to unanticipated information requirements in a timely fashion. The information required by ad hoc requests is "somewhere in the system" but is too expensive to retrieve. Several programmers would have to work for weeks to put together the required data items in a new file. Users—in particular, senior management—begin to wonder at this point why they have computers at all.

Poor Security

Because there is little control or management of data, access to and dissemination of information are virtually out of control. What limits on access exist tend to be the result of habit and tradition, as well as of the sheer difficulty of finding information.

traditional file environment A way of collecting and maintaining data in an organization that leads to each functional area or division creating and maintaining its own data files and programs.

data redundancy The presence of duplicate data in multiple data files.

program-data dependence The close relationship between data stored in files and the software programs that update and maintain those files. Any change in data organization or format requires a change in all the programs associated with those files.

Lack of Data Sharing and Availability

The lack of control over access to data in this confused environment does not make it easy for people to obtain information. Because pieces of information in different files and different parts of the organization cannot be related to one another, it is virtually impossible for information to be shared or accessed in a timely manner.

8.2 A MODERN DATABASE ENVIRONMENT

database Collection of data organized to service many applications at the same time by storing and managing data so that they appear to be in one location.

Database technology can cut through many of the problems created by traditional file organization. A more rigorous definition of a **database** is a collection of data organized to serve many applications efficiently by centralizing the data and minimizing redundant data. Rather than storing data in separate files for each application, data are stored physically to appear to users as being stored in only one location. A single database services multiple applications. For example, instead of a corporation storing employee data in separate information systems and separate files for personnel, payroll, and benefits, the corporation could create a single common Human Resources database. Figure 8.7 illustrates the database concept.

DATABASE MANAGEMENT SYSTEMS (DBMS)

database management system (DBMS) Special software to create and maintain a database and enable individual business applications to extract the data they need without having to create separate files or data definitions in their computer programs.

A **database management system (DBMS)** is simply the software that permits an organization to centralize data, manage them efficiently, and provide access to the stored data by application programs. As illustrated in Figure 8.8, the DBMS acts as an interface between application programs and the physical data files. When the application program calls for a data item such as gross pay, the DBMS finds this item in the database and presents it to the application program. Using traditional data files, the programmer would have to define the data and then tell the computer where they are. A DBMS eliminates most of the data definition statements found in traditional programs.

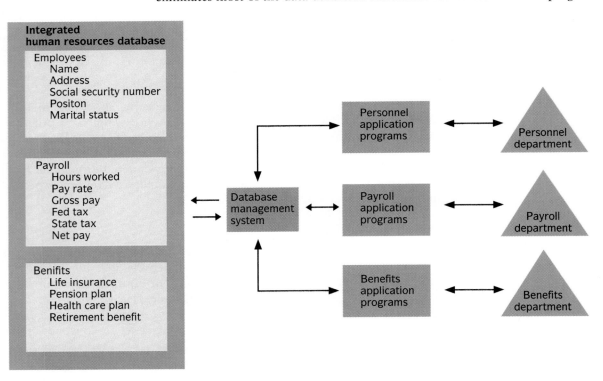

FIGURE 8.7
The contemporary database environment. A single Human Resources database serves multiple applications and also allows a corporation easily to draw together all of the information on various applications. The database management system acts as the interface between the application programs and the data.

FIGURE 8.8
Elements of a database management system. In an ideal database environment, application programs work through a database management system to obtain data from the database. This diagram illustrates a database management system with an active data dictionary that not only records definitions of the contents of the database but also allows changes in data size and format to be automatically utilized by the application programs.

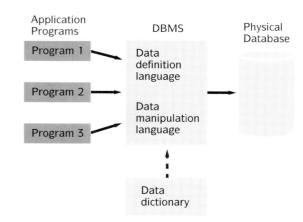

A database management system has three components:

- a data definition language
- a data manipulation language
- a data dictionary

data definition language The component of a database management system that defines each data element as it appears in the database.

data manipulation language A language associated with a database management system that is employed by end users and programmers to manipulate data in the database.

Structured Query Language (SQL) The emerging standard data manipulation language for relational database management systems.

data dictionary An automated or manual tool for storing and organizing information about the data maintained in a database.

data element A field.

The **data definition language** is the formal language used by programmers to specify the content and structure of the database. The data definition language defines each data element as it appears in the database before that data element is translated into the forms required by application programs.

Most DBMS have a specialized language called a **data manipulation language** that is used in conjunction with some conventional third- or fourth-generation programming languages to manipulate the data in the database. This language contains commands that permit end users and programming specialists to extract data from the database to satisfy information requests and develop applications. The most prominent data manipulation language today is **SQL**, or **Structured Query Language**. Complex programming tasks cannot be performed efficiently with typical data manipulation languages. However, most mainframe DBMSs are compatible with COBOL and FORTRAN, and other third-generation programming languages, permitting greater processing efficiency and flexibility.

The third element of a DBMS is a **data dictionary**. This is an automated or manual file that stores definitions of data elements and data characteristics such as usage, physical representation, ownership (who in the organization is responsible for maintaining the data), authorization, and security. Many data dictionaries can produce lists and reports of data utilization, groupings, program locations, and so on. Figure 8.9 illustrates a sample data dictionary report that shows the size, format, meaning, and uses of a data element in a Human Resources database. A **data element** represents a field. Besides listing the standard name (AMT-PAY-BASE), the dictionary lists the names that reference this element in specific systems and identifies the individuals, business functions, programs, and reports that use this data element.

By creating an inventory of all the pieces of data contained in the database, the data dictionary serves as an important data management tool. For instance, business users could consult the dictionary to find out exactly what pieces of data are maintained for the sales or marketing function or even to determine all of the information maintained by the entire enterprise. The dictionary could supply business users with the name, format, and specifications required to access data for reports. Technical staff could use the dictionary to determine what data elements and files must be changed if a program is changed.

Most data dictionaries are entirely passive; they simply report. More advanced types are active; changes in the dictionary can be automatically utilized by related programs. For instance, to change ZIP codes from five to nine digits, one could simply enter the change in the dictionary without having to modify and recompile all application programs using ZIP codes.

FIGURE 8.9
Sample data dictionary report. The sample data dictionary report for a Human Resources database provides helpful information such as the size of the data element, which programs and reports use it, and which group in the organization is the "owner" responsible for maintaining it. The report also shows some of the other names that the organization uses for this piece of data.

```
NAME:  AMT-PAY-BASE
FOCUS NAME:  BASEPAY
PC NAME:        SALARY

DESCRIPTION:  EMPLOYEE'S ANNUAL SALARY

SIZE:  9 BYTES
TYPE:  N        (NUMERIC)
DATE CHANGED:  01/01/85
OWNERSHIP:  COMPENSATION
UPDATE SECURITY:  SITE PERSONNEL
ACCESS SECURITY:  MANAGER, COMPENSATION PLANNING AND RESEARCH
                  MANAGER, JOB EVALUATION SYSTEMS
                  MANAGER, HUMAN RESOURCES PLANNING
                  MANAGER, SITE EQUAL OPPORTUNITY AFFAIRS
                  MANAGER, SITE BENEFITS
                  MANAGER, CLAIMS PAYING SYSTEMS
                  MANAGER, QUALIFIED PLANS
                  MANAGER, SITE EMPLOYMENT/EEO
BUSINESS FUNCTIONS USED BY:  COMPENSATION
                             HR PLANNING
                             EMPLOYMENT
                             INSURANCE
                             PENSION
                             ISP


PROGRAMS USING:  PI01000
                 PI02000
                 PI03000
                 PI04000
                 PI05000

REPORTS USING:   REPORT 124 (SALARY INCREASE TRACKING REPORT)
                 REPORT 448 (GROUP INSURANCE AUDIT REPORT)
                 REPORT 452 (SALARY REVIEW LISTING)
                 PENSION REFERENCE LISTING
```

In an ideal database environment, the data in the database are defined once and consistently, and used for all applications whose data reside in the database. Application programs (which are written using a combination of the data manipulation language of the DBMS and a conventional language such as COBOL) request data elements from the database. Data elements called for by the application programs are found and delivered by the DBMS. The programmer does not have to specify in detail how or where the data are to be found.

LOGICAL AND PHYSICAL VIEWS OF DATA

Perhaps the greatest difference between a DBMS and traditional file organization is that the DBMS separates the logical and physical views of the data, relieving the programmer or end user from the task of understanding where and how the data are actually stored.

The database concept distinguishes between *logical* and *physical* views of data. The **logical view** presents data as they would be perceived by end users or business specialists, whereas the **physical view** shows how data are actually organized and structured on physical storage media.

The logical description of the entire database, listing all of the data items and the relationship among them, is termed the **schema**. The specific set of data from the database that is required by each application program is termed the **subschema**. For example, for the Human Resources database illustrated in Figure 8.7, the payroll ap-

logical view Representation of data as they would appear to an application programmer or end user.

physical view The representation of data as they would be actually organized on physical storage media.

schema The logical description of an entire database, listing all the data elements in the database and the relationships among them.

subschema The logical description of the part of a database required by a particular function or application program.

With a database program that permits users to share and integrate employee health statistics, the Epidemiology group of Texaco Inc. can track unusual patterns of employee disease.

plication would have a subschema consisting of employee name, address, social security number, and would specify payroll data such as pay rate and hours worked.

Suppose, for example, that a professor of information systems wanted to know at the beginning of the semester how students performed in the prerequisite computer literacy course (Computer Literacy 101) and what their current majors are. Using a database supported by the registrar, the professor would need something like the report shown in Figure 8.10.

Ideally, for such a simple report, the professor could sit at an office terminal connected to the registrar's database and write a small application program using the data manipulation language to create this report. The professor first would create the desired logical view of the data (Figure 8.10) for the application program. The DBMS would then assemble the requested data elements, which may reside in several different files and disk locations. For instance, the student major information may be located in a file called "Student," whereas the grade data may be located in a file called "Course." Wherever they are located, the DBMS would pull these pieces of information together and present them to the professor according to the logical view requested.

The query using the data manipulation language constructed by the professor might look something like Figure 8.11. Several DBMSs working on both mainframes and microcomputers permit this kind of interactive report creation.

In the real world, there are few registration systems that permit this kind of inquiry. Many university registration systems were created in the 1960s and are of the

FIGURE 8.10
The report required by the professor. The report requires data elements that may come from different files but it can easily be pulled together with a database management system if the data are organized into a database.

Student Name	ID No.	Major	Grade in Computer Literacy 101
Lind	468	Finance	A-
Pinckus	332	Marketing	B +
Williams	097	Economics	C +
Laughlin	765	Finance	A
Orlando	324	Statistics	B

```
SELECT Stud_name, Stud.stud_id, Major, Grade

FROM Student, Course

WHERE Stud.stud_id = Course.stud_id

AND Course_id = "CL101"
```

FIGURE 8.11
The query used by the professor. This example shows how Structured Query Language (SQL) commands could be used to deliver the data required by the professor. These commands join two files, the student file (Student) and the course file (Course), and extract the specified pieces of information on each student from the combined file.

traditional, flat-file variety. In order to produce the report shown in Figure 8.10, a COBOL programmer would have to be hired to write several hundred lines of code. The final program would require at least three or four days of work, several test runs, debugging, and so forth. The labor costs alone would be around $2000. Several files would have to be accessed, stripped of the relevant information, and a third file would have to be created. With luck, no data inconsistencies would be found.

Imagine the cost to the university if all professors requested this or similar reports. If the university tried to meet the demand, its information processing costs would balloon rapidly. Instead, many universities simply say that the information is "in the system somewhere but is too expensive to retrieve." Only an information systems professor could understand this reply.

ADVANTAGES OF DATABASE MANAGEMENT SYSTEMS

The preceding discussion illustrates the advantage of a DBMS:

- Complexity of the organization's information system environment can be reduced by central management of data, access, utilization, and security.
- Data redundancy and inconsistency can be reduced by eliminating all of the isolated files in which the same data elements are repeated.
- Data confusion can be eliminated by providing central control of data creation and definitions.
- Program-data dependence can be reduced by separating the logical view of data from its physical arrangement.
- Program development and maintenance costs can be radically reduced.
- Flexibility of information systems can be greatly enhanced by permitting rapid and inexpensive ad hoc queries of very large pools of information.
- Access and availability of information can be increased.

Given all of these benefits of DBMS, one might expect all organizations to change immediately to a database form of information management. But it is not that easy, as we will see later.

8.3   DESIGNING DATABASES

There are alternative ways of organizing data and representing relationships among data in a database. Conventional DBMSs use one of three principal logical database models for keeping track of entities, attributes, and relationships. The three princi-

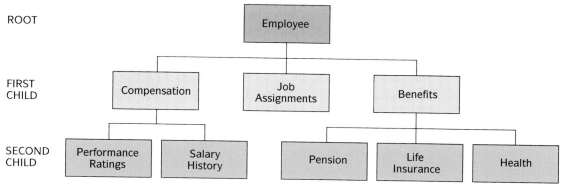

ROOT

FIRST CHILD

SECOND CHILD

FIGURE 8.12
A hierarchical database for a human resources system. The hierarchical database model looks like an organizational chart or a family tree. It has a single "root" segment (Employee) connected to lower-level segments (Compensation, Job Assignments, and Benefits). Each subordinate segment, in turn, connects to other subordinate segments. Here, Compensation connects to Performance Ratings and Salary History. Benefits connects to Pension, Life Insurance, and Health Care. Each subordinate segment is the "child" of the segment directly above it.

pal logical database models are hierarchical, network, and relational. Each logical model has certain processing advantages and certain business advantages.

HIERARCHICAL DATA MODEL

hierarchical data model One type of logical database model that organizes data in a treelike structure. A record is subdivided into segments that are connected to each other in one-to-many parent-child relationships.

The earliest DBMSs were hierarchical. The **hierarchical data model** presents data to users in a treelike structure. The most common hierarchical DBMS is IBM's IMS (Information Management System). Within each record, data elements are organized into pieces of records called segments. To the user, each record looks like an organization chart with one top-level segment called the *root*. An upper segment is connected logically to a lower segment in a parent–child relationship. A parent segment can have more than one child, but a child can have only one parent.

Figure 8.12 shows a hierarchical structure that might be used for a human resources database. The root segment is "Employee," which contains basic employee information such as name, address, and identification number. Immediately below it are three child segments: Compensation (containing salary and promotion data), Job Assignments (containing data about job positions and departments), and Benefits (containing data about beneficiaries and various benefit options.) The Compensation segment has two children below it: Performance Ratings (containing data about employee's job performance evaluations) and Salary History (containing historical data about employee's past salaries). Below the Benefits segment are child segments for Pension, Life Insurance, and Health Care, containing data about these various benefit plans.

Behind the logical view of data are a number of physical links and devices to tie the information together into a logical whole. In a hierarchical DBMS the data are physically linked to one another by a series of **pointers** that form chains of related data segments. Pointers are data elements attached to the ends of record segments on the disk directing the system to related records. In our example, the end of the Employee segment would contain a series of pointers to all of the Compensation, Job Assignments, and Benefits segments. In turn, at the end of the Compensation and Benefits segments are pointers to their respective child segments.

pointer A special type of data element attached to a record that shows the absolute or relative address of another record.

In a large database it would be convenient if the system could rapidly find the appropriate root segment, the specified employee. Rather than read each data segment (of which there might be hundreds of thousands or millions) one at a time until the right root segment is found, all employees can be stored in an index that lists each employee and its precise location on disk. Once this root segment is identified, pointers take over to guide the search of the database.

NETWORK DATA MODEL

network data model A logical database model that is useful for depicting many-to-many relationships.

The **network data model** is a variation of the hierarchical data model. Indeed, databases can be translated from hierarchical to network and vice versa in order to optimize processing speed and convenience. Whereas hierarchical structures depict one-to-many relationships, network structures depict data logically as many-to-many relationships. In other words, parents can have multiple "children" and a child can have more than one parent.

A typical many-to-many relationship in which network DBMS excels in performance is the student-course relationship (see Figure 8.13). There are many courses in a university and many students. A student takes many courses and a course has many students. The data in Figure 8.13 could be structured hierarchically. But this could result in considerable redundancy and a slowed response to certain types of information queries; the same student would be listed on the disk for each class he or she was taking instead of just once. Network structures reduce redundancy and, in certain situations (where many-to-many relationships are involved), respond more quickly. However, there is a price for this reduction in redundancy and increased speed: The number of pointers in network structures rapidly increases, making maintenance and operation potentially more complicated.

RELATIONAL DATA MODEL

relational data model A type of logical database model that treats data as if they were stored in two-dimensional tables. It can relate data stored in one table to data in another as long as the two tables share a common data element.

tuple A row or record in a relational database.

The **relational data model,** the most recent of these three database models, overcomes some of the limitations of the other two models. The relational model represents all data in the database as simple two-dimensional tables called relations. The tables appear similar to flat files, but the information in more than one file can be easily extracted and combined. Sometimes the tables are referred to as files.

Figure 8.14 shows a supplier table, a part table, and an order table. In each table, the rows are unique records and the columns are fields. Another term for a row or record in a relation is a **tuple.** Often a user needs information from a number of relations to produce a report. Here is the strength of the relational model: It can relate data in any one file or table to data in another file or table *as long as both tables share a common data element.*

To demonstrate, suppose we wanted to find in the relational database in Figure 8.14 the names and addresses of suppliers who could provide us with part number 137 or part number 152. We would need information from two tables: the supplier table and the part table. Note that these two files have a shared data element: SUPPLIER-NUMBER.

In a relational database, three basic operations are used to develop useful sets of data: select, project, and join. The *select* operation creates a subset consisting of all

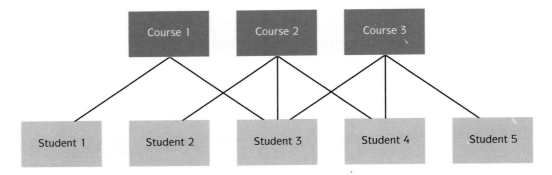

FIGURE 8.13
The network data model. This illustration of a network data model showing the relationship the students in a university have to the courses they take represents an example of logical many-to-many relationships. The network model reduces the redundancy of data representation through the increased use of pointers.

records in the file that meet stated criteria. "Select" creates, in other words, a subset of rows that meet certain criteria. In our example, we want to select records (rows) from the part table where the part number equals 137 or 152. The *join* operation combines relational tables to provide the user with more information than is available in individual tables. In our example, we want to join the now shortened part table (only parts numbered 137 or 152 will be presented) and the supplier table into a single new result table.

The *project* operation creates a subset consisting of columns in a table, permitting the user to create new tables that contain only the information required. In our example, we want to extract from the new result table only the following columns: PART-NUMBER, SUPPLIER-NUMBER, SUPPLIER-NAME, and SUPPLIER-ADDRESS.

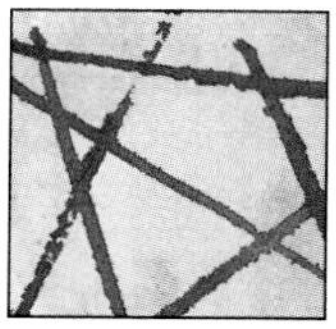

Leading mainframe relational database management systems include IBM's DB2 and Oracle from the Oracle Corporation. Microsoft Access and dBASE IV and Paradox from Borland International Inc. are examples of microcomputer relational database management systems.

ADVANTAGES AND DISADVANTAGES OF THE THREE DATABASE MODELS

The principal advantage of the hierarchical and network database models is processing efficiency. For instance, a hierarchical model is appropriate for airline reservation transaction processing systems, which must handle millions of structured routine requests each day for reservation information.

Table (Relation)   Columns (Fields)

ORDER

ORDER-NUMBER	ORDER-DATE	DELIVERY-DATE	PART-NUMBER	PART-AMOUNT	ORDER-TOTAL
1634	02/02/93	02/22/93	152	2	144.50
1635	02/12/93	02/29/93	137	3	79.70
1636	02/13/93	03/01/93	145	1	24.30

Rows (Records, Tuples)

PART

PART-NUMBER	PART-DESCRIPTION	UNIT-PRICE	SUPPLIER-NUMBER
137	Door latch	26.25	4058
145	Door handle	22.50	2038
152	Compressor	70.00	1125

SUPPLIER

SUPPLIER-NUMBER	SUPPLIER-NAME	SUPPLIER-ADDRESS
1125	CBM Inc.	44 Winslow, Gary IN 44950
2038	Ace Inc.	Rte. 101, Essex NJ 07763
4058	Bryant Corp.	51 Elm, Rochester NY 11349

FIGURE 8.14
The relational data model. Each table is a *relation* and each row or record is a *tuple.* Each column corresponds to a field. These relations can easily be combined and extracted in order to access data and produce reports, provided that any two share a common data element. In this example, the ORDER file shares the data element "PART-NUMBER" with the PART file. The PART and SUPPLIER files share the data element "SUPPLIER-NUMBER."

Hierarchical and network structures have several disadvantages. All of the access paths, directories, and indices must be specified in advance. Once specified, they are not easily changed without a major programming effort. Therefore, these designs have low flexibility. For instance, if you queried the Human Resources database illustrated in Figure 8.12 to find out the names of the employees with the job title of administrative assistant, you would discover that there is no way that the system can find the answer in a reasonable amount of time. This path through the data was not specified in advance.

Both hierarchical and network systems are programming-intensive, time-consuming, difficult to install, and difficult to remedy if design errors occur. They do not support ad hoc, English language–like inquiries for information.

The strengths of relational DBMS are great flexibility in regard to ad hoc queries, power to combine information from different sources, simplicity of design and maintenance, and the ability to add new data and records without disturbing existing programs and applications. The weakness of relational DBMSs are their relatively low processing efficiency. These systems are somewhat slower because they typically require many accesses to the data stored on disk to carry out the select, join, and project commands. Selecting one part number from among millions, one record at a time, can take a long time. Of course the database can be indexed and "tuned" to speed up prespecified queries. Relational systems do not have the large number of pointers carried by hierarchical systems.

With improvements in performance and reliability, relational databases are starting to be used for some large transaction-oriented applications, as illustrated in the Window on Organizations.

Large relational databases may be designed to have some data redundancy in order to make retrieval of data more efficient. The same data element may be stored in multiple tables. Updating redundant data elements is not automatic in many relational DBMS. For example, changing the employee status field in one table will not automatically change it in all tables. Special arrangements are required to ensure that all copies of the same data element are updated together.

Hierarchical databases remain the workhorse for intensive high-volume transaction processing. Banks, insurance companies, and other high-volume users continue to use reliable hierarchical databases such as IBM's IMS, developed in 1969. It is easier to program applications in a relational environment, but many firms do not wish to spend millions of dollars converting software from a hierarchical to a relational database management system. Many organizations have converted to DB2, IBM's relational DBMS for new applications, while retaining IMS for traditional transaction processing. For example, Dallas-based Texas Instruments depends on IMS for its heavy processing requirements. Texas Instruments bases its complete operations, including inventory, accounting, and manufacturing, on IMS. The firm has built up a huge library of IMS applications over 20 years, and a complete conversion to DB2 would take 10 more years. As relational products acquire more muscle, firms will shift away completely from hierarchical DBMS, but this will happen over a long period of time. Table 8.1 compares the characteristics of the different database models.

Table 8.1	Comparison of Database Alternatives			
Type of Database	Processing Efficiency	Flexibility	End-User Friendliness	Programming Complexity
Hierarchical	High	Low	Low	High
Network	Medium–high	Low–medium	Low–moderate	High
Relational	Lower but improving	High	High	Low

DENMARK RUNS ON DB2

One could say that the country of Denmark runs on IBM's DB2 relational database management system. That's because DB2 supports virtually all of Demark's major public service systems. All of these systems use data from Denmark's central population register, which is stored in a DB2 database. If the register were unavailable, most other systems couldn't operate, and the entire population of Denmark would be affected.

Everyone born in Denmark receives a social security number at birth. This event is registered in the system, as are all Danish marriages, divorces, deaths, and maintenance arrangements for children. When children go to kindergarten, their records are administered through the system. Citizens receive their social security payments and pay their local taxes through the system. (The system even includes all addresses and details of citizen properties and property values, as well as changes of ownership and occupation.) All of these public service applications are administered by Kommunedata, a nonprofit company jointly owned by Denmark's nine counties and 273 local governments.

Kommunedata, which is headquartered in Ballerup, runs more than 60 of Denmark's public service applications on four large mainframes at regional sites throughout the country: Aalborg, Arhus, Ballerup, and Odense. All of the transactions for these systems rely on DB2. The DB2 database handles over 500,000 transactions each day.

Denmark maintains an extensive welfare state, so the efficiency of its public service systems is critical. Its Social Democrat-led coalition government is trying to defend the welfare state against calls for budget cuts. Government users of the system believe that having a single source of information keeps overhead costs, and therefore income tax rates, to a minimum. There's less bureaucratic red tape, too, because citizens have to fill out fewer forms.

Kommunedata committed to DB2 as the underlying database management system in 1988. Freddy Hansen, its data processing manager, had helped establish Magin du Nord, Scandinavia's largest warehouse chain, as one of the world's first all-DB2 sites in 1989. When he joined Kommunedata, his main responsibility was to ensure that the DB2 database was sound.

In choosing DB2 over competing database management systems, Kommunedata believed that DB2 offered the best opportunity to achieve substantial long-term cost savings through data sharing and data reuse. However, by the end of 1990, Kommunedata's study of DB2 benefits failed to show any gains. At that point the company had only developed a few DB2-based applications because users feared excessive costs from the mainframe CPU time required for DB2. The experience of the few programmers who worked in DB2 was not widely shared. Kommunedata made too much of its initial retraining investment.

Since then, significant benefits have emerged. Kommunedata's management decided it had overestimated the amount of extra CPU time rquired by DB2. At that point the company converted more of its old flat-file systems to DB2. It retrained most of its 500 systems developers to use DB2. (Most of their programming work uses PL/1.) By the time this process was completed in 1994, cost savings had started to mate-

> **To Think About:** What are the benefits of using DB2 for Denmark's public service systems? What are the drawbacks? Was Kommunedata's selection of DB2 a sound management decision? What management, organization, and technology factors had to be addressed?

rialize. Kommunedata found that the savings in systems development costs, especially by using a data dictionary when analyzing the data required by various applications, more than offset the cost of extra CPU time.

The response time of Denmark's public systems is highly dependent on the design of the DB2 database and how programs are written. The database had to be carefully designed to support multiple systems from the same source of data. Database analysts review all SQL code before it is used.

Hansen believes that continued enhancements to DB2 make it capable of providing a solid foundation for Denmark's core public systems. It is now much more reliable than in the past. There have been no unplanned system outages caused by database problems. The quality control system developed by Kommunedata has also increased the system's reliability.

Source: George Black, "Denmark's Dependency on DB2 Pays Off in Development Time," *Software Magazine*, February 1994.

CREATING A DATABASE

In order to create a database, one must go through two design exercises, a conceptual design and a physical design. The conceptual design of a database is an abstract model of the database from a business perspective, whereas the physical design shows how the database is actually arranged on direct access storage devices.

Physical database design is performed by database specialists, whereas logical design requires a detailed description of the business information needs of actual end users of the database. Ideally, database design will be part of an overall organizational data planning effort (see Chapter 11).

The conceptual database design describes how the data elements in the database are to be grouped. The design process identifies relationships among data elements and the most efficient way of grouping data elements together to meet information requirements. The process also identifies redundant data elements and the groupings of data elements required for specific application programs. Groups of data are organized, refined, and streamlined until an overall logical view of the relationships among all of the data elements in the database emerges.

Database designers document the conceptual data model with an **entity-relationship diagram,** illustrated in Figure 8.15. The boxes represent entities and the diamonds represent relationships. The *1* or *M* on either side of the diamond represents the relationship among entities as either one-to-one, one-to-many, or many-to-many. Figure 8.15 shows that the entity ORDER can have only one PART and a PART can only have one SUPPLIER. Many parts can be provided by the same supplier. The attributes for each entity are listed next to the entity and the key field is underlined.

In order to use a relational database model effectively, complex groupings of data must be streamlined to eliminate redundant data elements and awkward many-to-many relationships. Figures 8.16 and 8.17 illustrate this process. In the particular business modeled here, an order can have more than one part but each part is provided by only one supplier. If we had built a relation called ORDER with all of the fields included here, we would have to repeat the name, description, and price of each part on the order and name and address of each part vendor. This relation contains what are called repeating groups because there can be many parts and suppliers for each order and it actually describes multiple entities—parts and suppliers as well as orders. A more efficient way to arrange the data is to break down ORDER into

entity-relationship diagram
Methodology for documenting databases illustrating the relationship between various entities in the database.

FIGURE 8.15
An entity-relationship diagram. This diagram shows the relationships between the entities ORDER, PART, and SUPPLIER that were used to develop the relational database illustrated in Figure 8.14.

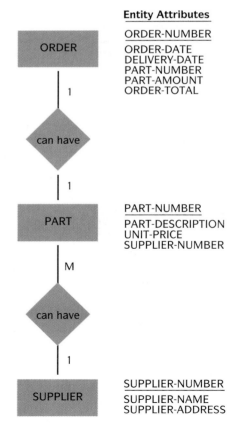

Entity Attributes

<u>ORDER-NUMBER</u>
ORDER-DATE
DELIVERY-DATE
PART-NUMBER
PART-AMOUNT
ORDER-TOTAL

<u>PART-NUMBER</u>
PART-DESCRIPTION
UNIT-PRICE
SUPPLIER-NUMBER

<u>SUPPLIER-NUMBER</u>
SUPPLIER-NAME
SUPPLIER-ADDRESS

ORDER

ORDER-NUMBER	PART-AMOUNT	PART-NUMBER	PART-DESCRIPTION	UNIT-PRICE	SUPPLIER-NUMBER	SUPPLIER-NAME	SUPPLIER-ADDRESS	ORDER-DATE	DELIVERY-DATE	ORDER-TOTAL

FIGURE 8.16
An unnormalized relation for ORDER. In an unnormalized relation there are repeating groups. For example, there can be many parts and suppliers for each order. There is only a one-to-one correspondence between ORDER-NUMBER and ORDER-DATE, ORDER-TOTAL, and DELIVERY-DATE.

normalization The process of creating small stable data structures from complex groups of data when designing a relational database.

smaller relations, each of which describes a single entity. The process of creating small, stable data structures from complex groups of data is called **normalization.** If we go step by step and normalize the relation ORDER, we emerge with the relations illustrated in Figure 8.17.

If a database has been carefully thought out, with a clear understanding of business information needs and usage, the database model will most likely be in some normalized form. Many real-world databases are not fully normalized because this may not be the most sensible way to meet business information requirements. Note that the relational database illustrated in Figure 8.14 is not fully normalized because there could be more than one part for each order. The designers chose not to use the four relations described in Figure 8.17 because this particular business has a business rule specifying that a separate order must be placed for each part. The designers might have felt that there was no business need for maintaining four different tables.

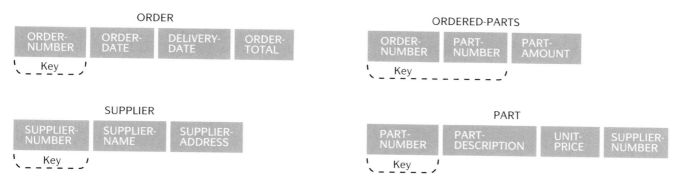

FIGURE 8.17
A normalized relation for ORDER. After normalization, the original relation ORDER has been broken down into four smaller relations. The relation ORDER is left with only three attributes and the relation ORDERED-PARTS has a combined, or concatenated, key consisting of ORDER-NUMBER and PART-NUMBER.

8.4 DATABASE TRENDS

Recent database trends include the growth of distributed databases and the emergence of object-oriented and hypermedia databases.

DISTRIBUTED PROCESSING AND DISTRIBUTED DATABASES

Beginning in the early 1970s, information processing became more distributed with the growth of powerful telecommunications networks and the decline in computer hardware costs. Instead of relying on a single centralized mainframe computer to provide service to remote terminals, organizations began to install minicomputers and microcomputers at remote sites. These distributed processors directly serve local and regional branch offices and factories and are generally linked together in networks. The dispersion and use of computers among multiple geographically or functionally separate locations so that local computers handle local processing needs is

distributed processing The distribution of computer processing among multiple geographically or functionally separate locations linked by a communications network.

distributed database A database that is stored in more than one physical location. Parts or copies of the database are physically stored in one location and other parts or copies are stored and maintained in other locations.

called **distributed processing.** Chapters 9 and 10 will describe the various network arrangements for distributed processing.

It is only a short step from distributed processing to distributed databases. Although early distributed systems worked with a single centralized database, over time the smaller local systems began to store local databases as well. It soon became obvious that the central database could be entirely distributed to local processors as long as some mechanism existed to provide proper updating, integrity of data, sharing of data, and central administrative controls.

A **distributed database** is one that is stored in more than one physical location. Parts of the database are stored physically in one location and other parts are stored and maintained in other locations. There are two main ways of distributing a database (see Figure 8.18). The central database (see Figure 8.18a) can be partitioned so that each remote processor has the necessary data on customers to serve its local area. Changes in local files can be justified with the central database on a batch basis, often at night. Another strategy is to replicate the central database (see Figure 8.18b) at all remote locations. This strategy also requires updating of the central database on off hours.

Still another possibility—one used by very large databases like the FBI's National Crime Information Center—is to maintain only a central name index and to store complete records locally (see Figure 8.18c). A query to the central name index identifies a location where the full record can be found. Here there is no central database and no updating costs. National Westminster Bank in London uses a similar approach to maintain all of its customer account information in two massive fragmented DB2 databases. Specially developed software allows each of its 22,000 users to access the data on either database with a global catalog of where the data are stored. Another variation is an ask-the-network scheme (see Figure 8.18d). There is no central index of names in this design. Instead, all remote processors are polled to find a complete record. The complete record is then transferred to whatever processor requests it (Laudon, 1986).

Both distributed processing and distributed databases have benefits and drawbacks. Distributed systems reduce the vulnerability of a single, massive central site. They permit increases in systems' power by purchasing smaller, less expensive minicomputers. Finally, they increase service and responsiveness to local users. Distributed systems, however, are dependent on high-quality telecommunications lines, which themselves are vulnerable. Moreover, local databases can sometimes depart from central data standards and definitions, and pose security problems by widely distributing access to sensitive data. The economies of distribution can be lost when remote sites buy more computing power than they need.

Despite these drawbacks, distributed processing is growing rapidly. With the advent of microcomputers and powerful telecommunications systems, more and more information services will be distributed. For large national organizations working in several regions, the question is no longer whether to distribute but how to distribute in such a way as to minimize costs and improve responsiveness without sacrificing data and system integrity.

OBJECT-ORIENTED AND HYPERMEDIA DATABASES

object-oriented database Approach to data management that stores both data and the procedures acting on the data as objects that can be automatically retrieved and shared. The objects can contain multimedia.

Conventional database management systems were designed for homogeneous data that can be easily structured into predefined data fields and records. But many applications today and in the future will require databases that can store and retrieve not only structured numbers and characters but also drawings, images, photographs, voice, and full-motion video (see Figure 8.19). Conventional DBMSs are not well-suited to handling graphics-based or multimedia applications. For instance, design data in a CAD database consist of complex relationships among many types of data. Manipulating these kinds of data in a relational system requires extensive programming to translate these complex data structures into tables and rows. An **object-oriented database,** on the other hand, stores the data and procedures as objects that can

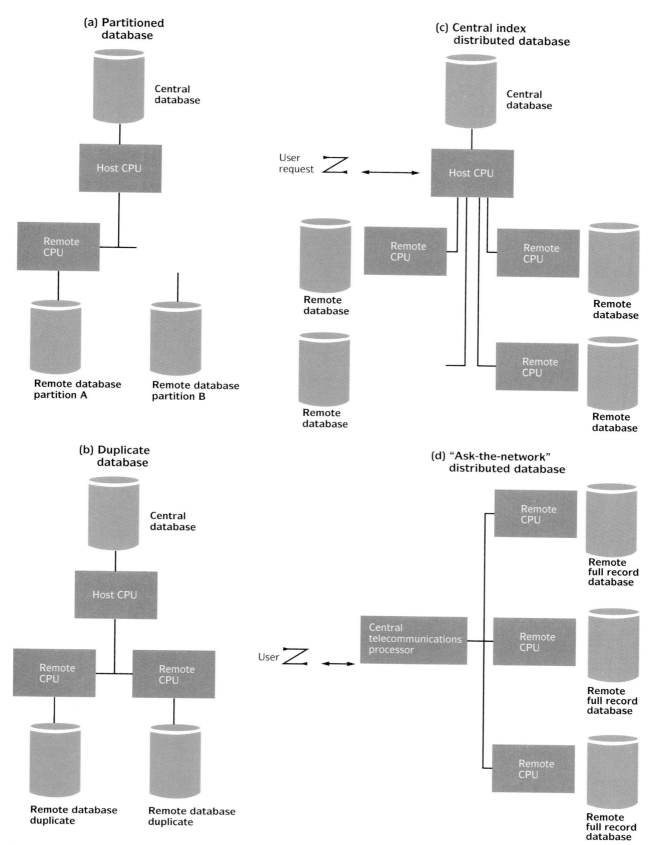

(a) Partitioned database

Central database

Host CPU

Remote CPU

Remote database partition A

Remote database partition B

(b) Duplicate database

Central database

Host CPU

Remote CPU

Remote CPU

Remote database duplicate

Remote database duplicate

(c) Central index distributed database

Central database

User request

Host CPU

Remote CPU

Remote CPU

Remote database

Remote database

Remote database

Remote CPU

Remote database

(d) "Ask-the-network" distributed database

User

Central telecommunications processor

Remote CPU

Remote full record database

Remote CPU

Remote full record database

Remote CPU

Remote full record database

FIGURE 8.18
Distributed databases. There are alternative ways of distributing a database. The central database can be partitioned (Figure 8.18a) so that each remote processor has the necessary data to serve its own local needs. The central database can also be duplicated (Figure 8.18b) at all remote locations. In the central index distributed database (Figure 8.18c) complete records are stored locally and can be located using a central name index. In an "ask-the-network" distributed database (Figure 8.18d), the network polls its remote processors to locate a record and transfers the complete record to whatever processor requests it.

FIGURE 8.19

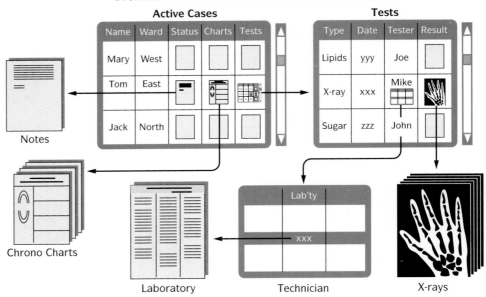

DIGITAL: BUILDING A TRUE MULTIMEDIA DATABASE

An object-oriented multimedia database. Medical data on patients in a hospital might likely be stored in a multimedia database such as this one. Doctors could access patient files including vital medical images to generate the reports and derive the information they need to deliver quality health care quickly. *Courtesy of Digital Equipment Corporation.*

hypermedia database Approach to data management that organizes data as a network of nodes linked in any pattern established by the user; the nodes can contain text, graphics, sound, full-motion video, or executable programs.

be automatically retrieved and shared. The Window on Technology describes how firms can benefit from these new capabilities.

The **hypermedia** database approach to information management transcends some of the limitations of traditional database methods by storing chunks of information in the form of nodes connected by links established by the user (see Figure 8.20). The nodes can contain text, graphics, sound, full-motion video, or executable computer programs. Searching for information does not have to follow a predetermined organization scheme. Instead, one can branch instantly to related information in any kind of relationship established by the author. The relationship between records is less structured than in a traditional DBMS.

In most systems, each node can be displayed on a screen. The screen also displays the links between the node depicted and other nodes in the database. Figure 8.21

Object-oriented database management systems can store graphic, audio, video and text data along with procedures.

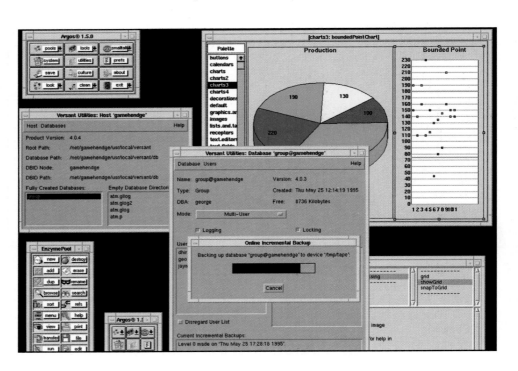

VOLKSWAGEN OPTS FOR AN OBJECT-ORIENTED DATABASE

Volkswagen has the highest sales in Europe of any automobile, and yet in 1992 it was the highest-cost high-volume car maker in the world, with a profit of only about $26 per unit. Volkswagen management clearly had a problem—they needed to find ways to cut costs. One Volkswagen subsidiary, EuroMarketing Systems, which is made up of representatives from 12 Volkswagen and Audi importers (wholesalers) across Europe, came up with an idea. According to Joseph Bayrhammer, manager of Euro-Marketing's technical team, "The idea is to build a system that all our distributors can use to track cars, from the building of them through selling and maintenance, all the way to recycling them later on." The project, named EuroElan, is targeted to 110,000 users worldwide, and will link dealerships and factories to allow all to better track every Volkswagen automobile throughout its useful life. The project will cost Volkswagen nothing. It is being financed by the wholesalers themselves. They may ultimately give the software to the 10,000 dealers in 13 countries who are part of their network.

The database must be able to hold and process an enormous amount of data. For every automobile Volkswagen produces, the dealers want to be able to determine where in the manufacturing process it is and to which dealer it will be delivered. After it is produced, they want to be able to find out which dealer currently has it. After it is sold, they want to identify the purchaser of the automobile and the dealer maintenance performed on the car. Ultimately, they even want to know the final disposition of the car at

the end of its useful life. When database design was complete, the team found that the database would contain more than 700 relational tables. They also found that the data to be stored needed to include unstructured, binary data such as automobile images. In selecting a database management system, the most fundamental criterion was the ability of the DBMS to handle all of the types of data, and to do so quickly and with efficiency.

In order to be able to test thoroughly various DBMSs, the project team spent 1 1/2 years building a prototype. Once testing began, they found that relational databases (RDBMSs) such as Ingress (from the ASK Group, Inc.) handled relatively simple queries well but that they slowed dramatically when the queries became more complicated. They also found that when using RDBMSs, they were unable to do queries on the unstructured binary fields. Object-oriented databases (OODBs), they discovered, handle complex queries much more quickly than RDBMSs, and they also allow for queries on binary objects. Thus they selected OODB as the underlying technology. The specific OODB they selected on which to build EuroElan was Versant from Versant Object Technology Corp. One reason they chose Versant was that the company promised to provide techniques to allow Volkswagen to access existing data currently stored in RDBMSs. The project team also received positive feedback from other global companies currently using the product.

The contract between Volkswagen and Versant was for $2.6 million, which Versant claims was one of the largest OODB contracts to date. The total cost of the project after the sign-

ing of the contract had already reached $8 million. Volkswagen management believes the project will help to reduce costs by reducing the size of automo-

> **To Think About:** Analyze Volkswagen using the competitive forces and value chain models. Did the use of object-oriented database technology enhance its competitive position? What management, organization, and technology issues did the selection of the Versant object-oriented database address?

bile and parts inventories. In addition, they believe customer service quality will rise while costs will go down. They point out that today when a customer asks for a specific car (such as a black Volkswagen Jetta with a sunroof, antilock brakes, and no air conditioning), the customer might have to wait a long time while the dealer does a telephone search to many of the 10,000 Volkswagen dealers worldwide in order to find the automobile. When EuroElan becomes operational, the search of the database will take only moments.

Versant (and OODBs in general) did present one major problem that Volkswagen will have to address—security. RDBMSs include better security features than do Versant and other OODBs. For example, RDBMSs usually include user authorization facilities. However, Bayrhammer concluded that even with RDBMSs, "You usually have to build more [security measures] in yourself anyway."

Source: Kim S. Nash, "Users Scout for Right Object DBMS Fit," *Computerworld*, January 10, 1994.

FIGURE 8.20

Hypermedia. In a hypermedia database, the user can choose his or her own path to move from node to node. Each node can contain text, graphics, sound, full-motion video, or executable programs.

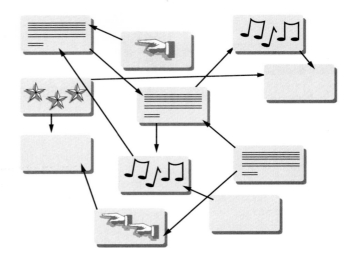

illustrates sample nodes from Apple Corporation's HyperCard, which is based on the hypermedia concept. The node for Sugar City, Montana, is linked to a node for the state of Montana and to a node showing a map of the entire United States. The node for the state of Montana illustrated in Figure 8.21 is linked to nodes for each of the cities illustrated on the map; to a node for the map of the entire United States; and to a node to return to the Home card, the first node in the HyperCard system.

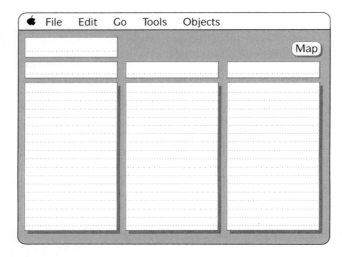

FIGURE 8.21

HyperCard. HyperCard programs are constructed as if they were stacks of individual cards, each of which can be linked to one or more other cards in any way the user chooses. The links do not have to follow the structured formulas of conventional databases or lists. HyperCard programs can contain digitized sound, drawings, and video images, as well as text. *Courtesy of Apple Computer, Inc.*

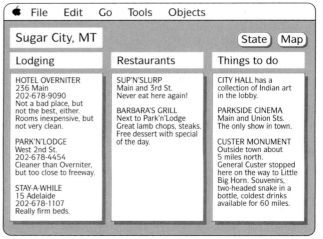

Sugar City, MT   State   Map

Lodging	Restaurants	Things to do
HOTEL OVERNITER 236 Main 202-678-9090 Not a bad place, but not the best, either. Rooms inexpensive, but not very clean.	SUP'N'SLURP Main and 3rd St. Never eat here again!	CITY HALL has a collection of Indian art in the lobby.
PARK'N'LODGE West 2nd St. 202-678-4454 Cleaner than Overniter, but too close to freeway.	BARBARA'S GRILL Next to Park'n'Lodge Great lamb chops, steaks. Free dessert with special of the day.	PARKSIDE CINEMA Main and Union Sts. The only show in town.
STAY-A-WHILE 15 Adelaide 202-678-1107 Really firm beds.		CUSTER MONUMENT Outside town about 5 miles north. General Custer stopped here on the way to Little Big Horn. Souvenirs, two-headed snake in a bottle, coldest drinks available for 60 miles.

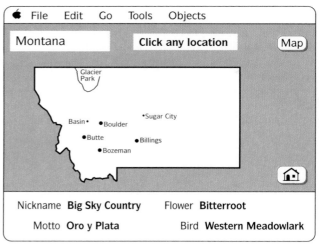

Montana   Click any location   Map

Glacier Park

Basin • • Boulder   • Sugar City
• Butte   • Billings
• Bozeman

Nickname **Big Sky Country**   Flower **Bitterroot**

Motto **Oro y Plata**   Bird **Western Meadowlark**

HyperCard is used primarily for small, single-user applications. Massive, multi-user hypermedia databases are starting to be constructed for business and military applications (Carmel et al., 1989).

8.5 MANAGEMENT REQUIREMENTS FOR DATABASE SYSTEMS

Much more is required for the development of database systems than simply selecting a logical database model. Indeed, this selection may be among the last decisions. The database is an organizational discipline, a method, rather than a tool or technology. It requires organizational and conceptual change.

Without management support and understanding, database efforts fail. The critical elements in a database environment are (1) data administration, (2) data planning and modeling methodology, (3) database technology and management, and (4) users. This environment is depicted in Figure 8.22 and will now be described.

DATA ADMINISTRATION

Database systems require that the organization recognize the strategic role of information and begin actively to manage and plan for information as a corporate resource. This means that the organization must develop a **data administration** function with the power to define information requirements for the entire company and with direct access to senior management. The chief information officer (CIO) or vice president of information becomes the primary advocate in the organization for database systems.

Data administration is responsible for the specific policies and procedures through which data can be managed as an organizational resource. These responsibilities include developing information policy, planning for data, overseeing logical database design and data dictionary development, and monitoring the usage of data by information system specialists and end-user groups.

The fundamental principle of data administration is that all data are the property of the organization as a whole. Data cannot belong exclusively to any one business area or organizational unit. All data are to be made available to any group that requires them to fulfill its mission. An organization needs to formulate an **information policy** that specifies its rules for sharing, disseminating, acquiring, standardizing, classifying, and inventorying information throughout the organization. Information policy lays out specific procedures and accountabilities, specifying which organizational

data administration A special organizational function for managing the organization's data resources, concerned with information policy, data planning, maintenance of data dictionaries, and data quality standards.

information policy Formal rules governing the maintenance, distribution, and use of information in an organization.

FIGURE 8.22
Key organizational elements in the database environment. For a database management system to flourish in any organization, data administration functions and data planning and modeling methodologies must be coordinated with database technology and management. Resources must be devoted to train end users to use databases properly.

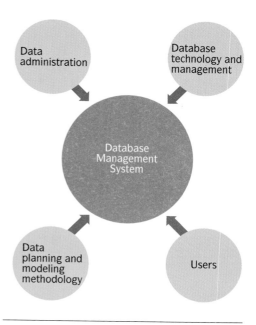

THE BATTLE TO ADMINISTER CORPORATE DATA

In the middle of the Persian Gulf War, the U.S. Navy couldn't count its own submarines. According to the General Accounting Office (GAO), "two Navy reports offered different figures for the number of submarines at sea because they did not use common data." Then Deputy Secretary of Defense William Perry (who later became Secretary of Defense) was so infuriated that he ordered "complete data standardization within three years."

The federal government's problems counting submarines are no different from those facing many businesses, especially when their data are distributed in various locations throughout a network. The need for data standardization and management has been proven over and over again—corporate executives assigning different meanings to the terms *customer* and *client* from those used by the managers who report to them, confusion over sales or profit, the inability to analyze accurately the effectiveness of an advertising campaign. It has become clear in the past few years that data are a valuable corporate resource, that they belong to the whole organization rather than to one division or one unit, and that they must be managed by the organization if the organization is fully to benefit from them. The need for the organization to manage all of its data has become urgent in recent years as more and more companies are relying on desktop computers, distributed databases, and client/server networks to create, store, and manipulate their data rather than using centralized mainframes where data have always been easy to control.

Managing data means establishing a data administration function and giving that function visible, organizationally high-level backing (such as by Deputy Secretary Perry). The problem, according to Franklin Deffer, GAO's assistant director of the accounting and information management division, is that "It's hard to get people interested in data standards." Aetna Life &

Casualty Co. of Hartford, Connecticut, has had the same experience and so has inaugurated an information resource management (IRM) group for the purpose of establishing a data administration function. The director of the IRM group, Arlene Northway, points out that in simpler centralized computing days, "everyone was very religious about following the rules," but today, in our more distributed environment, this is no longer so. She does not have the organizational clout a William Perry has within the Defense Department, so when she attempts to achieve standardization amongst various business units, she often finds "religious wars" occurring over definition and use of data elements. Northway has learned that to achieve agreement on the definition of terms and the accompanying data elements (such as the meaning of the term "participant" within various insurance policy plans), she usually has to go slow. She now phases in data standards, adding new standards to the existing ones each time a new version of an application is introduced.

One tool that is useful in managing data, including establishing and enforcing standards, is an automated data dictionary. As we indicated elsewhere in this chapter, a data dictionary is used to organize and store information about the data maintained in a database or by an organization. Today, automated data dictionaries are a standard part of database management systems. One way to achieve the complete standardization Perry ordered would be to establish a single data dictionary—a data repository—for the whole organization (or one that brings together all of the information in lower-level data dictionaries that are used only by one business unit or by a single DBMS).

The largest technical problem standing in the way of organizations using data dictionaries to manage their data is that very few vendors are offering the kind of data dictionaries needed for today's environment. With distributed data processing and reliance on

client/server technology, a useful data dictionary would need to support multiple operating systems, platforms, and DBMS. In addition it would need to

> *To Think About:* What are the management benefits of implementing enterprise-wide data administration? What management, organization, and technology issues need to be addressed? What do you think might be some of the management drawbacks?

run on a server. Few if any such software packages exist today. Some organizations have found other ways to try and accomplish similar goals. Patricia Komar, vice president of corporate data architecture at Chase Manhattan Bank N.A.'s Metrotech Center in Brooklyn, New York, is using a groupware package called Lotus Notes from Lotus Development Corp. to keep track of application usage worldwide and also to track the changes to those applications that affect data usage. Considering that she is trying to track systems and packages running on mainframes and client/servers in 40 countries around the world for a $95 billion corporation, that is some feat. At best, however, it falls well short of managing the data. (See Chapter 15 for a discussion of groupware and of Lotus Notes.)

However, most of the problems are not technical, as Aetna "religious [turf] wars" demonstrates. Michael Swanson, a development manager at United Behavioral Systems (UBS), has found that reaching agreement on common data elements, establishing common names, and managing the data at the center, is still not enough. UBS is a mental health–care subsidiary of $2.5 billion United Healthcare Corp. (UHC) of Minnetonka, Minnesota. UHC decided to build an internal network to allow three of its nine subsidiaries to access the data of all three of the subsidiaries. The project was finished in July 1993 and included complete agreement on

units share information; where information can be distributed; and who has responsibility for updating and maintaining the information.

Although data administration is a very important organizational function, it has proven very challenging to implement, as described in the Window on Management.

DATA PLANNING AND MODELING METHODOLOGY

Because the organizational interests served by the DBMS are much broader than those in the traditional file environment, the organization requires enterprise-wide planning for data. Enterprise analysis, which addresses the information requirements of the entire organization (as opposed to the requirements of individual applications), is needed to develop databases. The purpose of enterprise analysis is to identify the key entities, attributes, and relationships that constitute the organization's data. These techniques are described in greater detail in Chapter 11.

DATABASE TECHNOLOGY AND MANAGEMENT

Databases require new software and a new staff specially trained in DBMS techniques as well as new management structures. Most corporations develop a database design and management group within the corporate information system division that is responsible for the more technical and operational aspects of managing data. The functions it performs are called **database administration**. This group does the following:

database administration Refers to the more technical and operational aspects of managing data, including physical database design and maintenance.

- Defines and organizes database structure and content
- Develops security procedures to safeguard the database
- Develops database documentation
- Maintains the database management software

In close cooperation with users, the design group establishes the physical database, the logical relations among elements, and the access rules and procedures.

USERS

A database serves a wider community of users than traditional systems. Relational systems with fourth-generation query languages permit employees who are not computer specialists to access large databases. In addition, users include trained computer specialists. In order to optimize access for nonspecialists, more resources must be devoted to training end users. Professional systems workers must be retrained in the DBMS language, DBMS application development procedures, and new software practices.

Management Challenges

Hierarchical database technology first became commercially available in the late 1960s. Since then, more sophisticated database models have appeared. Nevertheless, progress in creating a true database environment in organizations has been much slower than anticipated. Why? Three challenges stand out.

1. Organizational obstacles to a database environment. Implementing a database requires widespread organizational change in the role of information (and information managers), the allocation of power at senior levels, the ownership and sharing of information, and patterns of organizational agreement. A DBMS challenges the existing arrangements in an organization and for that reason often generates political resistance. In a traditional file environment, each department constructed files and programs to fulfill its specific needs. Now, with a database, files and programs must be built that take into account the full organization's interest in data. For instance, in the past the treasurer could insulate his or her data and applications from others in the organization. Some information that once "belonged" to the treasurer is now shared through the DBMS with other users in other departments. Quite naturally, the treasurer may worry that other users will not treat financial data with the same care and concern as the treasurer's personnel.

2. Cost/benefit considerations. The costs of moving to a database environment are tangible, up front, and large in the short term (three years). Most firms buy a commercial DBMS package and related hardware. The software alone can cost one-half million dollars for a full-function package with all options. New hardware may cost an additional $1 million to $2 million annually. It soon becomes apparent to senior management that a database system is a huge investment. Although the organization has spent the money on the hardware and software for a database environment, it may not reap the benefits it should because it is unwilling to make the requisite organizational changes.

Unfortunately, the benefits of the DBMS are often intangible, back-loaded, and long term (five years). The systems that the DBMS seeks to replace generally work, although they are inefficient. Moreover, several million dollars have been spent over the years designing and maintaining existing systems. People in the organization understand the existing system after long periods of training and socialization. For all of these reasons, and despite the clear advantages of the DBMS, the short-term costs of developing a DBMS often appear to be nearly as great as the benefits. When the short-term political costs are added to the equation, it is convenient for senior management to defer the database investment. The obvious long-term benefits of the DBMS tend to be severely discounted by managers, especially those unfamiliar with (and perhaps unfriendly to) systems. Moreover, it may not be cost-effective to build organization-wide databases that integrate all of the organization's data (Goodhue et. al., September 1992).

3. Organizational placement of the data management function. Many organizations, seeking to avoid large commitments and organizational change, begin (and end) by buying a DBMS package and placing it in the hands of a low-level database group in the information systems department. Generally this leads to a piecemeal approach to database use; that is, small database systems will be developed for various divisions, functional areas, departments, and offices. Eventually this results in incompatible databases throughout the company and fails to address the key organizational issue: What is the role of information and who will manage it for the organization as a whole? Senior management must be persuaded to implement a data administration function and data planning methodology at the highest corporate level.

Summary

1. Describe traditional file organization and management techniques. In a traditional file environment, data records are organized using either a sequential file organization or a direct or random file organization. Records in a sequential file can be accessed sequentially or they can be accessed directly if the sequential file is on disk and uses an indexed sequential access method. Records on a file with direct file organization can be accessed directly without an index.

2. Explain the problems of the traditional file environment. By allowing different functional areas and groups in the organization to maintain their own files independently, the traditional file environment creates problems such as data redundancy and inconsistency, program-data dependence, inflexibility, poor security, and lack of data sharing and availability.

3. Describe how a database management system organizes information. Database management systems (DBMSs) are the software that permits centralization of data and data management. A DBMS includes a data definition language, a data manipulation language, and a data dictionary capability. The most important feature of the DBMS is its ability to separate the logical and physical views of data. The user works with a logical view of data. The DBMS software translates user queries into queries that can be applied to the physical view of the data. The DBMS retrieves information so that the user does not have to be concerned with its physical location. This feature separates programs from data and from the management of data.

4. Identify the three principal database models. There are three principal logical database models: hierarchical, network, and relational. Each has unique advantages and disadvantages. Hierarchical systems, which support one-to-many relationships, are low in flexibility but high in processing speed and efficiency. Network systems support many-to-many relationships. Relational systems are relatively slow but are very flexible for supporting ad hoc requests for information and for combining information from different sources. The choice depends on the business requirements.

5. Explain the principles for designing a relational database. Designing a database requires both a logical design and a physical design. The process of creating small, stable data structures from complex groups of data when using a relational database model is termed *normalization*.

6. Discuss new database trends. It is no longer necessary for data to be centralized in a single, massive database. A complete database or portions of the database can be distributed to more than one location to increase responsiveness and reduce vulnerability and costs. There are two major types of distributed databases: replicated databases and partitioned databases. Object-oriented databases and hypermedia databases may be alternatives to traditional database structures for certain types of applications. Both can store graphics and other types of data in addition to conventional text data to support multimedia applications. Hypermedia databases allow data to be stored in nodes linked together in any pattern established by the user.

7. Explain the managerial and organizational requirements for creating a database environment. Development of a database environment requires much more than selection of technology. It requires a change in the corporation's attitude toward information. The organization must develop a data administration function and a data planning methodology. The database environment has developed more slowly than was originally anticipated. There is political resistance in organizations to many key database concepts, especially to sharing of information that has been controlled exclusively by one organizational group. There are difficult cost/benefit questions in database management. Often, to avoid raising difficult questions, database use begins and ends as a small effort isolated in the information systems department.

Key Terms

Field	Index	Structured Query Language (SQL)	Relational data model
Record	Direct file access method	Data dictionary	Tuple
File	Transform algorithm	Data element	Entity-relationship diagram
Entity	Traditional file environment	Logical view	Normalization
Attribute	Data redundancy	Physical view	Distributed processing
Key field	Program-data dependence	Schema	Distributed database
Sequential file organization	Database	Subschema	Object-oriented database
Direct or random file organization	Database management system (DBMS)	Hierarchical data model	Hypermedia database
Indexed sequential access method (ISAM)	Data definition language	Pointer	Data administration
	Data manipulation language	Network data model	Information policy
			Database administration

Review Questions

1. Why is file management important for overall system performance?
2. Describe how indexes and key fields enable a program to access specific records in a file.
3. Define and describe the indexed sequential access method and the direct file access method.
4. List and describe some of the problems of the traditional file environment.
5. Define a database and a database management system.
6. Name and briefly describe the three components of a DBMS.
7. What is the difference between a logical and a physical view of data?
8. List some of the benefits of a DBMS.
9. Describe the three principal database models and the advantages and disadvantages of each.
10. What is normalization? How is it related to the features of a well-designed relational database?
11. What is a distributed database, and how does it differ from distributed data processing?
12. What are object-oriented and hypermedia databases? How do they differ from a traditional database?
13. What are the four key elements of a database environment? Describe each briefly.
14. Describe and briefly comment on the major management challenges in building a database environment.

Discussion Questions

1. It has been said that you do not need database management software to have a database environment. Discuss.
2. As an information system manager, you are concerned that the percentage of your staff working on maintenance of existing programs is growing and the percentage working on new applications is declining. How could a database environment change this trend?
3. To what extent should end users be involved in the selection of a database management system and in database design?

Group Project

Form a group with half of your classmates. Consider two strategies for building a database environment. One strategy recommends that a small group be created in the information systems department to begin exploring database applications throughout the firm. The other strategy recommends the creation of a vice president of information and subsequent development of important database applications. Debate the costs and benefits of each strategy with the other group.

CAN MIGRATION TO A RELATIONAL DATABASE MANAGEMENT SYSTEM HELP A GERMAN HOME LOAN LENDER?

Will moving to new database technology help a company stay competitive? Officials at BHW Bausparkasse AG thought so and gave that as the reason they moved from the IDMS database management system to the DB2 database management system. BHW, which is headquartered in Hameln, Germany, is the second largest building society (home loan association) in Germany. They had used IDMS from Computer Associates (CA) of Islandia, New York (a network database management system), for many years with upward of 2000 programs accessing it. The 1991 decision to move to IBM's DB2, a relational database management system (RDBMS), was therefore a major strategic move.

BHW was founded in 1928 and by the 1990s was offering not only mortgages but also banking, real estate, and life insurance services. Its basic business data was stored in the IDMS DBMS. It required 55 gigabytes of storage to hold its 440 separate databases encompassing about 12,000 data elements—a gigantic system by any standards. To service its nearly 3 million customers and 12 million contracts, BHW found that its 2500 employees accessed IDMS on average about 33 million times per day, a very well-used system. Any improvement in its performance was bound to have a major and positive impact on the company.

To remain competitive, home loan companies such as BHW must be able to read the market and quickly provide customers with new financial products and services to customers. According to Harry Gehlen, project manager for the database reengineering project, IDMS was not modern enough to allow BHW to react rapidly to customer needs. IDMS was a network DBMS, and BHW needed to move into the world of relational databases. For example, BHW wanted to develop an executive information system (EIS), an application that really only works well using a RDBMS. In addition Gehlen sees his company adding object-oriented databases next and then moving to distributed technology. He hopes that BHW will be able to establish total independence of its data from its application software. He believes that all these moves would be too complex to be done directly from a network DBMS. He concludes that a move to a RDBMS is a proper migration path to these other newer technologies.

BHW managers had looked at the possibility of moving to an RDBMS as early as 1987 but rejected the idea at that earlier date because they did not find any RDBMS that could meet their needs. What they did do was migrate from their longtime Unisys Corp. mainframe to IBM mainframes, thus positioning themselves very well to take advantage of RDBMS

technology as it matured. By 1991 they determined that DB2 would serve their needs. However, because they had always been pleased with CA's IDMS, they also looked at its announced release, version 12. They rejected it for several reasons. First, version 12 was only announced, not actually released (software purchasers tend to be very wary of "vaporware"). Second, BHW required that any RDBMS it purchases must include standard SQL, but again, while CA had announced that its new product would be SQL compliant, CA indicated no shipping date. Third, the BHW IS staff did not find what they considered an adequate contact for their project at CA's European headquarters at Daarmstadt, Germany, and so they became very concerned about future product support should they convert to version 12. They also reasoned that a move to any relational database, whether it be DB2, IDMS, or some other product, would take about the same amount of time, so that they would gain nothing by staying with IDMS. Thus, they made the decision to purchase DB2.

Mario Pelleschi, senior vice president of CA's European operation, disputes Gehlen's version, and particularly the last point. He claims that his product has all the functionality of DB2, and that BHW could have converted to version 12 much more quickly and inexpensively because it would not need to rewrite programs or convert the databases. Gehlen countered that BHW "wanted to have a secure system which will be maintained for many years, and Computer Associates didn't seem to be the right partner for us in the future." This seemed to indicate that the real basis for the decision to go with DB2 was the vendor rather than the product.

The conversion project lasted only about 10 months and used highly automated tools. Before converting to DB2, Gehlen decided that they needed to convert the 2000 older VS COBOL programs into the more up-to-date COBOL Ansi 85, a task for which good automated tools were available. In the process, the team also identified programs which were no longer being used and eliminated them. His team also analyzed the IDMS data and prepared an automated conversion tool to use to convert the data to DB2. Once the data was converted, they found they were able to use the upgraded programs to access and update both the DB2 and IDMS databases, enabling them to work with either one, as needed. They set up a pilot project to convert three applications to DB2. This pilot lasted four months, and Gehlen used this time to educate his IS staff on DB2. In early 1993 they began to convert programs on a mass basis.

The project was not only successfully completed, but the team also had a positive surprise. They had expected that performance would decline in the conversion from IDMS, a network database, to DB2, a relational database. However, according to Gehlen, "performance went up by a factor of three to five," thus giving BHW a clear jump in productivity.

Source: Elke Gronert, "German Financial Institution Comes Home to Database," *Software Magazine*, March 1994.

Case Study Questions

1. Analyze BHW from the standpoint of the competitive forces and value chain models.

2. To what extent is selecting a database management system an important business decision? Did BHW's selection of DB2 enhance its competitive position?

3. From what you have learned in this case study, was a relational database management system the best choice for BHW Bausparkasse AG? Why or why not?

4. In the case study, Harry Gehlen is cited as the source for future plans to move BHW into object-oriented and distributed technologies. Comment on the appropriateness of using him as the source.

5. What management, organization, and technology factors should be considered when selecting a database management system?

References

Belkin, Nicholas J., and W. Bruce Croft. "Information Filtering and Information Retrieval: Two Sides of the Same Coin?" *Communications of the ACM* 35, no. 12 (November 1992).

Burleson, Donald. "OODBMSs Gaining MIS Ground but RDBMSs Still Own the Road." *Software* (November 1994).

Butterworth, Paul, Allen Otis, and Jacob Stein. "The GemStone Object Database Management System." *Communications of the ACM* 34, no. 10 (October 1991).

Carmel, Erran, William K. McHenry, and Yeshayahu Cohen. "Building Large, Dynamic Hypertexts: How Do We Link Intelligently?" Journal of Management Information Systems 6, no. 2 (Fall 1989).

Date, C. J. *An Introduction to Database Systems*, 6th ed. Reading, MA: Addison-Wesley (1994).

Everest, G. C. *Database Management: Objectives, System Functions, and Administration.* New York: McGraw-Hill (1985).

Goldstein, R. C., and J. B. McCririck. "What Do Data Administrators Really Do?" *Datamation* 26 (August 1980).

Goodhue, Dale L., Laurie J. Kirsch, Judith A. Quillard, and Michael D. Wybo. "Strategic Data Planning: Lessons from the Field." *MIS Quarterly* 16, no. 1 (March 1992).

Goodhue, Dale L., Judith A. Quillard, and John F. Rockart. "Managing the Data Resource: A Contingency Perspective." *MIS Quarterly* (September 1988).

Goodhue, Dale L., Michael D. Wybo, and Laurie J. Kirsch. "The Impact of Data Integration on the Costs and Benefits of Information Systems." *MIS Quarterly* 16, no. 3 (September 1992).

Grover, Varun, and James Teng. "How Effective Is Data Resource Management?" *Journal of Information Systems Management* (Summer 1991).

Kahn, Beverly K. "Some Realities of Data Administration." *Communications of the ACM* 26 (October 1983).

Kahn, Beverly, and Linda Garceau. "The Database Administration Function." *Journal of Management Information Systems* 1 (Spring 1985).

Kent, William. "A Simple Guide to Five Normal Forms in Relational Database Theory." *Communications of the ACM* 26, no. 2 (February 1983).

King, John L., and Kenneth Kraemer. "Information Resource Management Cannot Work." *Information and Management* (1988).

Kroenke, David. *Database Processing*, 4th ed. New York: Macmillan (1992).

Laudon, Kenneth C. *Dossier Society: Value Choices in the Design of National Information Systems.* New York: Columbia University Press (1986).

Madnick, Stuart E., and Richard Y. Wang. "Evolution towards Strategic Application of Databases through Composite Information Systems." *Journal of Management Information Systems* 5, no. 3 (Winter 1988–1989).

March, Salvatore T., and Young-Gul Kim. "Information Resource Management: A Metadata Perspective." *Journal of Management Information Systems* 5, no. 3 (Winter 1988–1989).

Martin, James. *Managing the Data-Base Environment.* Englewood Cliffs, NJ: Prentice Hall (1983).

Silberschatz, Avi, Michael Stonebraker, and Jeff Ullman, eds. "Database Systems: Achievements and Opportunities." *Communications of the ACM* 34, no. 10 (October 1991).

Smith, John B., and Stephen F. Weiss. "Hypertext." *Communications of the ACM* 31, no. 7 (July 1988).

Chapter 9

Telecommunications

Networks Promote Global Trade

By establishing a global electronic trading network, the United Nations is attempting to address some of the problems faced by small and medium-sized businesses in developing countries as they become involved with world trade. The goal of the network is to stimulate growth in international trade by helping small businesses or firms in countries without adequate foreign trade support services find information that would help them enter global markets. A pilot version of the network, known as the Global Trade Point Network, was established in late 1994 with a messaging service that companies can use to locate trade leads, negotiate business transactions, and make shipping and payment arrangements. "Trade points" have been established in Dar es Salaam,

Tanzania, Columbus, Ohio, and about 50 other sites around the world. They act as gateways into the network and as sites to store data being made available to network users. Users in many countries can access the trade points through their national telecommunications infrastructures. Those in countries that do not have adequate infrastructures can travel to any of the trade points to utilize the network. The electronic traffic on the network uses a range of existing telecommunications networks, including General Electric Information Systems (GEIS), AT&T's EasyLink, and the Internet (see Chapter 10).

The network will quickly be adding other services. Several trade points, including one in Bangkok, Thailand, are making electronic data interchange services for exchanging business transactions available based upon the United Nation's Edifact EDI standard. The United States Department of Commerce, whose Foreign and Commercial service has joined the pilot in its overseas offices, is making accessible through the network the National Trade Database which contains import/export guides, foreign trade indices, and other foreign trade data. The Bankers Association of Foreign Trade is establishing Trade Point databases that will bring traders together with businesses that finance international trade. The trade association also will help businesses obtain letters of credit if they are operating in countries where the local currency cannot readily be used in international trade. A number of American manufacturers, such as cylinder and industrial equipment producer Worthington Industries, are making product catalogs available on-line. The network enables such catalogs to list printed product information, show product pictures, and even show short, animated product demonstrations. Plans exist to expand these services and to add others, such as a database of trade leads, data on customs regulations, information on freight forwarders, and listings of international trade insurance companies.

Small and medium-sized businesses are finding that other networks have been established that are targeted to support them as well. For example, the over 150,000 users of IndustryNet are often able to locate needed supplies quickly and easily via IndustryNet's on-line catalogs. Companies such as Livingston Products, Inc., a small diversified manufacturer in Wheeling, Illinois, use IndustryNet to enhance their bargaining power by comparing various suppliers' selections and prices. This network, free to its users, also offers message boards, new product announcements, and electronic mailboxes. The network is financed by on-line advertisements from such companies as IBM Corporation and Honeywell Inc. Small business users are particularly pleased with this serv-

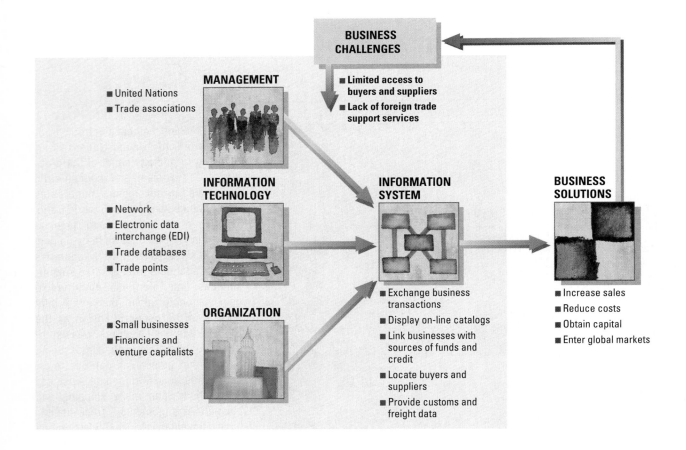

ice, and not only because it saves time and effort. They also point out that although large suppliers often will not deal with small businesses, transactions occur through this network without the supplier knowing the size of the purchaser, so smaller businesses are put on an equal footing with their larger competitors. Without such networks, only large manufacturers could link their computers directly to those of their suppliers and distributors.

Even start-up companies are finding on-line services to aid them. A number of new services have been established to facilitate bringing together entrepreneurs with venture capitalists. For example, American Venture Capital Exchange, an on-line service based in Portland, Oregon, lists entrepreneurial companies seeking investors at a flat fee of $150 each for six months. Potential investors pay $95 for 12 months of access. Ken Hamilton of Western Call & Decoy produces decoys and game calls for hunters and is a satisfied user of the ex-

change. After trying to raise investment funds through more traditional methods, he turned to the Venture Capital network, and within several months he found a venture capitalist who invested $110,000 in start-up funds. ∎

Sources: Stephanie N. Mehta, "On-Line Service Offers Fast Lane to Small Businesses," *The Wall Street Journal*, October 11, 1994; Timothy L. O'Brien, "Entrepreneurs Raise Funds Through On-line Computer Services," *The Wall Street Journal*, June 2, 1994; and Lynda Radosevich, "United Nations Launches Worldwide Network," *Computerworld*, October 24, 1994.

Many companies, large and small from all over the world, are finding they can benefit from telecommunications to locate suppliers and buyers, to negotiate contracts with them, and to service their trades. In fact, the uses of telecommunications are multiplying for research, customer support, and even

for organizational coordination and control. Many of the technical advances in computing and information systems, such as on-line processing and providing direct access to data, would be impossible without telecommunications technology.

Telecommunications has become so essential to the conduct of business life that managers will be making telecommunications-related decisions throughout their careers. This chapter describes the components of telecommunications systems, showing how they can be arranged to create various types of telecommunications networks and network-based applications that can increase the efficiency and competitiveness of an organization. It provides a method for determining the organization's telecommunications requirements.

After completing this chapter, you will be able to:

Learning Objectives

1. Describe the basic components of a telecommunications system.

2. Measure the capacity of telecommunications channels and evaluate transmission media.

3. Describe the three basic network topologies.

4. Classify the various types of telecommunications networks.

5. Identify telecommunications applications that can provide competitive advantages to organizations.

6. Explain the criteria used in planning for telecommunications systems.

9.1   THE TELECOMMUNICATIONS REVOLUTION

telecommunications
Communication of information by electronic means, usually over some distance.

Telecommunications can be defined as communication of information by electronic means, usually over some distance. We are currently in the middle of a telecommunications revolution that has two components: rapid changes in the technology of communications and equally important changes in the ownership, control, and marketing of telecommunications services. Today's managers need to understand the capabilities, costs, and benefits of alternative communications technologies and how to maximize their benefits for their organizations.

THE MARRIAGE OF COMPUTERS AND COMMUNICATIONS

For most of the last 150 years since Alexander Bell invented the first "singing telegraph" in 1876, telecommunications was a monopoly either of the state or of a regulated private firm. In the United States, American Telephone and Telegraph (AT&T) was the largest regulated monopoly, providing virtually all telecommunications services. In Europe and in the rest of the world, there is a state post, telephone, and telegraph authority (PTT). In the United States, the monopoly ended in 1984, when the Justice Department forced AT&T to give up its monopoly and allow competing firms to sell telecommunications services and equipment.

The end of AT&T's monopoly widened the market for new telecommunications technologies and devices, from cheaper long-distance service to telephone answering equipment, cellular telephones, and private satellite services. AT&T itself started marketing computing services and computing equipment.

Changes in the telecommunications industry were accompanied by changes in telecommunications technology. Previously, telecommunications meant voice transmission over telephone lines. Today, much telecommunications transmission is digital data transmission, using computers to transmit data from one location to another. On-line information systems and remote access to information would be impossible without telecommunications. Table 9.1 shows some of the common tasks performed by computer systems that would be impossible without advanced telecommunications.

THE INFORMATION SUPERHIGHWAY

information superhighway High-speed digital telecommunications networks that are national or worldwide in scope and accessible by the general public rather than restricted to use by members of a specific organization or set of organizations such as a corporation.

Deregulation and the marriage of computers and communications has also made it possible for the telephone companies to expand from traditional voice communications into new information services, such as providing transmission of news reports, stock reports, television programs, and movies. The Window on Organizations describes how the telecommunications revolution has allowed the regional Bell telephone companies created by the breakup of AT&T to move into the information service business.

The efforts described in the Window on Organizations are laying the foundation for the **information superhighway**, a vast web of high-speed digital telecommunications networks delivering information, education, and entertainment services to offices and

Table 9.1	Common Tasks Performed by Computer Systems Requiring Telecommunications	
Application	Example	Requirements
Business		
On-line data entry	Inventory control	Transactions occurring several times/second, direct response required
On-line text retrieval	Hospital information systems; library systems	Response required in real time; high character volumes
Inquiry/response	Point-of-sale system; airline reservation system; credit checking	Transactions several times/second; instant response within seconds
Administrative message switching	Electronic mail	Short response and delivery times (minutes to hours)
Process control	Computer-aided manufacturing (CAM); numeric control of machine tools	Continuous input transactions and on-line responses required
Intercomputer data exchange	International transfer of bank funds	Infrequent but high-volume bursts of information; transfer of large data blocks; on-line immediate response
Home		
Inquiry response	Home banking; shopping; ordering	On-line transactions collected with high frequency
Text-retrieval	Home education	High-volume, rapid transmission
Special entertainment	Sports; polling and political participation	High-capacity video and data capabilities

PHONE COMPANIES RACE TO PROVIDE INFORMATION SERVICES

In a dramatic move in May 1993, a federal appeals court gave the seven regional Bell telephone companies permission to provide such information services as stock quotes, sports scores, news reports, and electronic versions of books and periodicals. The ruling overturned part of a previous lower court decision and lifted a longstanding ban prohibiting the regional Bell companies from owning information services. This ruling followed a July 1992 Federal Communications Commission ruling that the Baby Bells could deliver movies and television to homes in the same way that they now deliver telephone calls.

The Bells have started by offering information from their own valuable databases—primarily lists of phone subscribers that make up their white- and yellow-page directories—as well as from their voice mail services. Pacific Telesis is testing expanded directory assistance whereby operators answering 411 calls will give callers additional information on businesses. Pacific Telesis is also developing a service for California's schools to provide access to university library data nationwide and is also planning to deliver daily customized news reports. Ameritech is testing a health-care network that provides information about patients to doctors, diagnostic clinics, and hospitals.

The Baby Bells are moving cautiously into videotext services, which electronically deliver information to a personal computer or television set. For instance, U.S. West has a Community Link service that gives customers with microcomputers or special terminals news stories, restaurant menus, theater tickets, and airline schedules. Bell

Atlantic, Nynex, and Pacific Telesis have started a joint venture to provide entertainment, information, and home shopping services delivered over the telephone lines. (Ameritech, SBC Communications, Bell South, and the Walt Disney Company have a similar venture.)

Technology developed by Bellcore, the Baby Bells' research consortium, has given this whole trend a major boost. It makes it possible to transmit high-quality video over ordinary copper telephone lines. This means that the telephone companies do not need to replace existing copper wiring with optical fiber that might cost $100 billion to $400 billion in order to transmit movies and television programs to customers at home. If shoppers at home can dial up movies or television programs over ordinary telephone lines, the Baby Bells can easily become electronic video rental stores.

The telephone companies are also joining with cable companies to gain access to the large installed base of coaxial cable that is already transmitting graphics and video. For example, regional Bell telephone company U.S. West established a joint venture with Time-Warner, the largest cable company in the United States, to build an information and entertainment service. The telephone companies bring vital switching technology to such ventures while the cable companies bring a huge installed base of coaxial cable and, of course, their entertainment expertise. When available, this network will be interactive, offer home shopping services, movies, and programs on demand and consist of up to 500 channels. MCI Communications Corp. agreed to invest up to $2 billion in News Corp. to operate and distribute electronic informa-

tion, education and entertainment through a digital network.

Similar developments are occurring within Europe also. Bell Canada and cable company Videotron Corp.

> *To Think About:* How has the business strategy of telephone companies changed as the result of deregulation? What are some of the obstacles these companies face? Should telephone companies be allowed to deliver information services?

(which owns cable companies in London, England) have joined with Nynex, Southwestern Bell, U.S. West, and Singapore Telecom to install networks that will carry voice, data and video into British homes and businesses. Together, Deutsch Bundespost Telekom and the city of Berlin are establishing a service that will begin by supplying personalized electronic newspapers. In time they expect the service to enable physicians to videoconference while viewing X-rays and other medical documentation. France has long had its Minitel videotext system for home banking and shopping. Now, France's Plaisance Television has established a service the public can operate through the telephone to shop at home or play video games.

Sources: John T. Keller and Laura Landro. "MCI Agrees to Inject as Much as $2 Billion in News Corp. in Data Highway Venture" *The Wall Street Journal*, May 11, 1995; Mark Landler, "New! Improved? TV's Bell Telephone Hour," *The New York Times*, March 19, 1995; Paula Dwyer, "Britain Races Down the Information Superhighway," *Business Week*, September 27, 1993; and Edmund L. Andrews, "Ruling Backs 'Baby Bells' on Information Services," *The New York Times*, May 29, 1993.

homes. The networks comprising the highway are national or worldwide in scope and accessible by the general public rather than restricted to use by members of a specific organization or set of organizations such as a corporation. Some analysts believe the information superhighway will have as profound an impact on economic and social life in the twenty-first century as railroads and interstate highways did in the past.

The press has stressed the home entertainment implications of this technology, extolling movies on demand with VCR-like forward and reverse controls. This technology has also been touted for its ability to offer an almost unlimited number of cable television channels—the standard number quoted is 500. Users will be able to read newspapers and magazines via these networks, and many predict the decline of paper-based news journals as a result. The technology will make possible interactive communications between the televised programs and the viewers at home. While all of this is indeed an important aspect of the information superhighway, the concept is much broader and richer than indicated in these popular press reports. It involves new ways to obtain and disseminate information that virtually eliminate the barriers of time and place. The business implications of this new superhighway are only now beginning to emerge. The most well-known and easily the largest implementation of the information superhighway is the Internet, a global web of interconnected networks described in the following chapter.

Another aspect of the information superhighway is the national computing network proposed by the U.S. federal government described in the Window on Technology in Chapter 5. The Clinton administration envisions this network linking universities, research centers, libraries, hospitals, and other institutions that need to exchange vast amounts of information while being accessible in homes and schools.

9.2 COMPONENTS AND FUNCTIONS OF A TELECOMMUNICATIONS SYSTEM

telecommunications system
Collection of compatible hardware and software arranged to communicate information from one location to another.

A **telecommunications system** is a collection of compatible hardware and software arranged to communicate information from one location to another. Figure 9.1 illustrates the components of a typical telecommunications system. Telecommunications systems can transmit text, graphic images, voice, or video information. This section describes the major components of telecommunications systems. Subsequent sections describe how the components can be arranged into various types of networks.

TELECOMMUNICATIONS SYSTEM COMPONENTS

The essential components of a telecommunications system are these:

1. Computers to process information.
2. Terminals or any input/output devices that send or receive data.
3. Communications channels, the links by which data or voice are transmitted between sending and receiving devices in a network. Communications channels use various communications media, such as telephone lines, fiber optic cables, coaxial cables, and wireless transmission.
4. Communications processors, such as modems, multiplexers, controllers, and front-end processors, which provide support functions for data transmission and reception.
5. Communications software that controls input and output activities and manages other functions of the communications network.

Functions of Telecommunications Systems

In order to send and receive information from one place to another, a telecommunications system must perform a number of separate functions. These functions are largely invisible to the people using the system. As outlined in Table 9.2, a telecom-

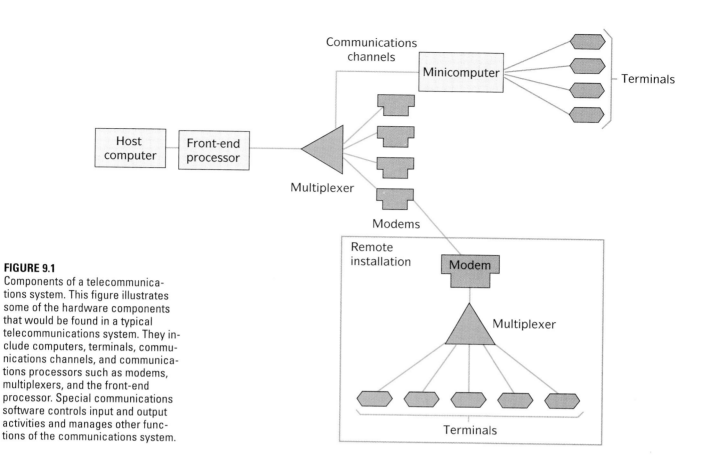

FIGURE 9.1
Components of a telecommunications system. This figure illustrates some of the hardware components that would be found in a typical telecommunications system. They include computers, terminals, communications channels, and communications processors such as modems, multiplexers, and the front-end processor. Special communications software controls input and output activities and manages other functions of the communications system.

munications system transmits information, establishes the interface between the sender and the receiver, routes messages along the most efficient paths, performs elementary processing of the information to ensure that the right message gets to the right receiver, performs editorial tasks on the data (such as checking for errors and rearranging the format), and converts messages from one speed (say, the speed of a computer) into the speed of a communications line or from one format to another. Lastly, the telecommunications system controls the flow of information. Many of these tasks are accomplished by computer.

Protocols

A telecommunications network typically contains diverse hardware and software components that need to work together to transmit information. Different compo-

Table 9.2	Functions of Telecommunications
Function	**Definition**
Transmission	Media, networks, and path
Interface	Path—sender—receiver
Routing	Choosing the most efficient path
Processing	Getting the right message to the right receiver
Editorial	Checking for errors, formats, and editing
Conversion	Changing speeds and codes from one device to another
Control	Routing messages, polling receivers, providing network structure maintenance

nents in a network can communicate by adhering to a common set of rules that enable them to "talk" to each other. This set of rules and procedures governing transmission between two points in a network is called a **protocol**. Each device in a network must be able to interpret the other device's protocol.

The principal functions of protocols in a telecommunications network are to identify each device in the communication path, to secure the attention of the other device, to verify correct receipt of the transmitted message, to verify that a message requires retransmission because it cannot be correctly interpreted, and to perform recovery when errors occur.

Although business, government, and the computer industry recognize the need for common communications standards, the industry has yet to put a universal standard into effect. Chapter 10 discusses the question of telecommunications standards in greater detail.

TYPES OF SIGNALS: ANALOG AND DIGITAL

Information travels through a telecommunications system in the form of electromagnetic signals. Signals are represented in two ways: There are analog and digital signals. An **analog signal** is represented by a continuous waveform that passes through a communications medium. Analog signals are used to handle voice communications and to reflect variations in pitch.

A **digital signal** is a discrete rather than a continuous waveform. It transmits data coded into two discrete states: 1-bits and 0-bits, which are represented as on–off electrical pulses. Most computers communicate with digital signals, as do many local telephone companies and some larger networks. But if a telecommunications system, such as a traditional telephone network, is set up to process analog signals—the receivers, transmitters, amplifiers, and so forth—a digital signal cannot be processed without some alterations. All digital signals must be translated into analog signals before they can be transmitted in an analog system. The device that performs this translation is called a **modem**. (Modem is an abbreviation for MOdulation/DEModulation.) A modem translates the digital signals of a computer into analog form for transmission over ordinary telephone lines, or it translates analog signals back into digital form for reception by a computer (see Figure 9.2).

TYPES OF COMMUNICATIONS CHANNELS

Communications **channels** are the means by which data are transmitted from one device in a network to another. A channel can utilize different kinds of telecommunications transmission media: twisted wire, coaxial cable, fiber optics, terrestrial microwave, satellite, and wireless transmission. Each has certain advantages and limitations. High-speed transmission media are more expensive in general, but they can handle higher volumes (which reduces the cost per bit). For instance, the cost per bit of data can be lower via satellite link than via leased telephone line if a firm uses the satellite link 100 percent of the time. There is also a wide range of speeds possible for any given medium depending on the software and hardware configuration.

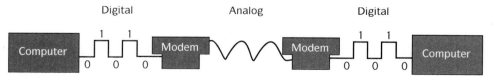

FIGURE 9.2
Functions of the modem. A modem is a device that translates digital signals from a computer into analog form so that they can be transmitted over analog telephone lines. The modem is also used to translate analog signals back into digital form for the receiving computer.

protocol Set of rules and procedures that govern transmission between the components in a network.

analog signal A continuous waveform that passes through a communications medium. Used for voice communications.

digital signal A discrete waveform that transmits data coded into two discrete states as 1-bits and 0-bits, which are represented as on–off electrical pulses. Used for data communications.

modem Device for translating digital signals into analog signals and vice versa.

channels The links by which data or voice are transmitted between sending and receiving devices in a network.

Twisted Wire

Twisted wire consists of strands of copper wire twisted in pairs and is the oldest transmission medium. Most of the telephone system in a building relies on twisted wires installed for analog communication. Most buildings have additional cables installed for future expansion, and so there are usually a number of twisted-pair cables unused in every office of every building. These unused cables can be used for digital communications. Although it is low in cost and is already in place, **twisted wire** is relatively slow for transmitting data, and high-speed transmission causes interference called *crosstalk*. On the other hand, new software and hardware have raised the capacity of existing twisted-wire cables up to 10 megabits per second, which is often adequate for connecting microcomputers and other office devices.

Coaxial Cable

Coaxial cable, like that used for cable television, consists of thickly insulated copper wire, which can transmit a larger volume of data than twisted wire can. It is often used in place of twisted wire for important links in a telecommunications network because it is a faster, more interference-free transmission medium, with speeds of up to 200 megabits per second. However, coaxial cable is thick, is hard to wire in many buildings, and cannot support analog phone conversations. It must be moved when computers and other devices are moved.

Fiber Optics

Fiber optic cable consists of thousands of strands of clear glass fiber, the thickness of a human hair, which are bound into cables. Data are transformed into pulses of light, which are sent through the fiber optic cable by a laser device at a rate of 500 kilobits to several billion bits per second. On the one hand, fiber optic cable is considerably faster, lighter, and more durable than wire media and is well suited to systems requiring transfers of large volumes of data. On the other hand, fiber optic is more difficult to work with, more expensive, and harder to install. It is best used as the backbone of a network and not for connecting isolated devices to a backbone. In most networks, fiber optic cable is used as the high-speed trunk line, while twisted wire and coaxial cable are used to connect the trunk line to individual devices.

Wireless Transmission

Wireless transmission that sends signals through air or space without any physical tether has emerged as an important alternative to tethered transmission channels such as twisted wire, coaxial cable, and fiber optics. Today, common uses of wireless data transmission include pagers, cellular telephones, microwave transmissions, communication satellites, mobile data networks, personal communications services, personal digital assistants, and even television remote controls.

The wireless transmission medium is the *electromagnetic spectrum*, illustrated in Figure 9.3. Some types of wireless transmission, such as microwave or infrared, by nature occupy specific spectrum frequency ranges (measured in megahertz). Other types of wireless transmissions are actually functional uses, such as cellular telephones and paging devices, that have been assigned a specific range of frequencies by national regulatory agencies and international agreements. Each frequency range has its own strengths and limitations, and these have helped determine the specific function or data communications niche assigned to it.

Microwave systems, both terrestrial and celestial, transmit high-frequency radio signals through the atmosphere and are widely used for high-volume, long-distance, point-to-point communication. Because microwave signals follow a straight line and do not bend with the curvature of the earth, long-distance terrestrial transmission systems require that transmission stations be positioned 25 to 30 miles apart, adding to the expense of microwave.

twisted wire Transmission medium consisting of pairs of twisted copper wires. Used to transmit analog phone conversations but can be used for data transmission.

coaxial cable Transmission medium consisting of thickly insulated copper wire. Can transmit large volumes of data quickly.

fiber optic cable Fast, light, and durable transmission medium consisting of thin strands of clear glass fiber bound into cables. Data are transmitted as light pulses.

microwave High-volume, long-distance, point-to-point transmission in which high-frequency radio signals are transmitted through the atmosphere from one terrestrial transmission station to another.

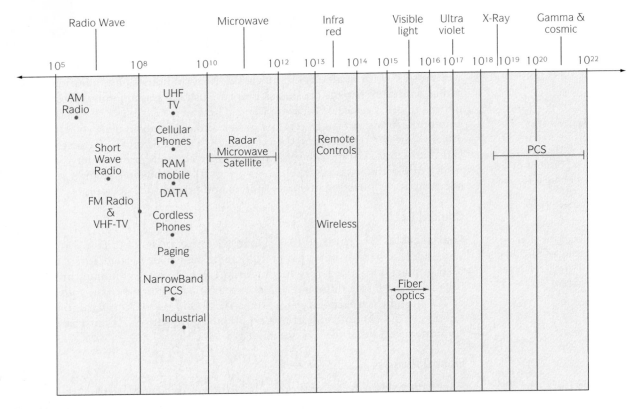

FIGURE 9.3
Frequency ranges for communications media and devices. Each telecommunications transmission medium or device occupies a different frequency range, measured in megahertz, on the electromagnetic spectrum.

satellite Transmission of data using orbiting satellites to serve as relay stations for transmitting microwave signals over very long distances.

This problem can be solved by bouncing microwave signals off **satellites,** enabling them to serve as relay stations for microwave signals transmitted from terrestrial stations. Communication satellites are cost effective for transmitting large quantities of data over long distances. Satellites are typically used for communications in large, geographically dispersed organizations that would be difficult to tie together through cabling media or terrestrial microwave. For instance, the Rite Aid pharmacy chain uses a satellite network to provide instant two-way communications between its stores and its corporate mainframe in Camp Hill, Pennsylvania. Each store has a server (a powerful microcomputer dedicated to storing data and programs—see Section 9.3) which supports cash registers, pharmacy terminals, and the manager's terminal and tracks inventory. The server can communicate with the central mainframe via satellite to post sales and to fill prescriptions stored in the mainframe database (see Figure 9.4).

low-orbit satellites Satellites that travel much closer to the earth than traditional satellites and so are able to pick up signals from weak transmitters while consuming less power.

Conventional communication satellites move in stationary orbits approximately 22,000 miles above the earth. A newer satellite medium, the **low-orbit satellite,** is beginning to be deployed. These satellites travel much closer to the earth and so are able to pick up signals from weak transmitters. They also consume less power and cost less to launch than conventional satellites. McCaw Cellular Communications and Microsoft Corp. have joined together to establish the Teledesic Corp., which is launching 840 low-orbit satellites that will create a high capacity, wireless network capable of transmitting telephone calls, two-way video conferences, and digital images anywhere on earth. With such networks, business persons will be able to travel literally anywhere in the world and have access to full communication capabilities regardless of the adequacy of the telecommunications infrastructure of the country they are in.

More than 3000 Amoco dealers use the ARSTA (Amoco Retail Systems Technology Architecture) satellite communications network to speed communications, transfer data, and reduce costs.

FIGURE 9.4
Satellite transmission at Rite-Aid. Satellites help the Rite Aid pharmacy chain transmit data between its 2960 stores and its corporate mainframe in Camp Hill, Pennsylvania. *Copyright 1994 by Computerworld, Inc., Framingham, MA 01701. Reprinted by permission. Adapted from: Jean S. Bozman, "UNIX PCs Strengthen Pharmacy Chain," Computerworld, August 1, 1994.*

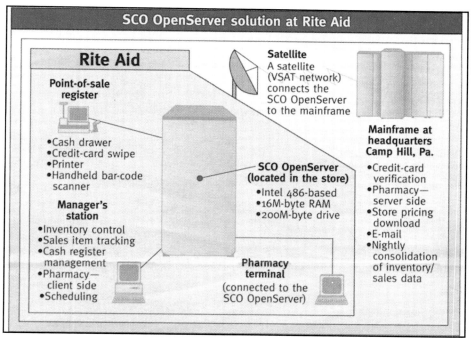

SCO OpenServer solution at Rite Aid

Rite Aid

Point-of-sale register

- Cash drawer
- Credit-card swipe
- Printer
- Handheld bar-code scanner

Manager's station

- Inventory control
- Sales item tracking
- Cash register management
- Pharmacy—client side
- Scheduling

Satellite
A satellite (VSAT network) connects the SCO OpenServer to the mainframe

SCO OpenServer (located in the store)

- Intel 486-based
- 16M-byte RAM
- 200M-byte drive

Pharmacy terminal
(connected to the SCO OpenServer)

Mainframe at headquarters Camp Hill, Pa.

- Credit-card verification
- Pharmacy—server side
- Store pricing download
- E-mail
- Nightly consolidation of inventory/sales data

paging systems A wireless transmission technology in which the pager beeps when the user receives a message; used to transmit short alphanumeric messages.

Other wireless transmission technologies have recently been developed and are being used in situations requiring mobile computing power. **Paging systems** have been in common use for several decades, originally just beeping when the user receives a message and requiring the user to telephone an office to learn what the message is. By the mid-1980s, however, paging devices have been able to receive short alphanumeric messages that the user reads on the pager's screen. Paging is useful for communicating with mobile workers such as repair crews; one-way paging can also provide an inexpensive way of communicating with workers in offices. For example, Ethos Corporation in Boulder, Colorado, markets mortgage-processing software that uses a paging system that can deliver daily changes in mortgage rates to thousands of real estate brokers. The data transmitted through the paging network can be downloaded and manipulated, saving brokers approximately one and a half hours of work each week.

cellular telephone Device that transmits voice or data, using radio waves to communicate with radio antennas placed within adjacent geographic areas called cells.

Cellular telephones (sometimes called mobile telephones) work by using radio waves to communicate with radio antennas (towers) placed within adjacent geographic areas called *cells*. A telephone message is transmitted to the local cell by the cellular telephone and then is handed off from antenna to antenna—cell to cell—until it reaches the cell of its destination, where it is transmitted to the receiving telephone. As a cellular signal travels from one cell into another, a computer that monitors signals from the cells switches the conversation to a radio channel assigned to the next cell. The radio antenna cells normally cover eight-mile hexagonal cells, although their radius is smaller in densely populated localities. While the cellular telephone infrastructure has primarily been used for voice transmission, recent developments have made it capable of two-way digital data transmission. The breakthrough came in the form of a transmission standard called Cellular Digital Packet Data (CDPD), with the support of such telecommunications giants as AT&T, Bell Atlantic, Nynex, Sprint, and McCaw Cellular. CDPD uses the pauses in voice communication, when the transmission channel is idle, filling them with packets of data.

mobile data networks Wireless networks that enable two-way transmission of data files cheaply and efficiently.

Wireless networks explicitly designed for two-way transmission of data files are called **mobile data networks**. These radio-based networks transmit data to and from hand-held computers. Another type of mobile data network is based upon a series of radio towers constructed specifically to transmit text and data. RAM Mobile Data (jointly owned by Ram Broadcasting and Bell South) and Ardis (jointly owned by IBM and Motorola) are two publicly available networks that use such media for national two-way data transmission. Mastercard uses the RAM Mobile Data network for wireless credit-card verification terminals at county fairs or merchants' sidewalk kiosks. Otis Elevators uses the Ardis network to dispatch repair technicians around the country from a single office in Connecticut and to receive their reports. Value-

Pagers are increasingly used for wireless transmission of brief messages in China and throughout the globe.

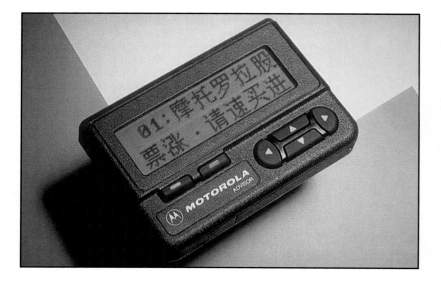

added companies are now beginning to offer services built upon those mobile data networks. For instance, RadioMail has introduced a wireless fax service at only 99 cents per domestic page. The cellular telephone network is also starting to be used for this purpose.

Wireless support is becoming more common in both computer hardware and software. Portable computers, using either internal or external wireless modems, can now be linked to wireless networks. Dell Computer Latitude notebooks, for example, can include the hardware and software for wireless communications, as well as a free trial subscription to RadioMail. IBM's ThinkPads offer similar functionality. Lotus cc:Mail, Microsoft Mail, and WordPerfect Office, among other software packages, all work with wireless services.

One new wireless cellular technology that should begin to be available for both voice and data in 1996 is called **personal communication services (PCS)**. PCS uses lower-power, higher-frequency radio waves than does cellular technology. Because of the lower power, PCS cells are much smaller and so must be more numerous and closer together. The higher-frequency signals enable PCS devices to be used in many places where cellular telephones are not effective, such as in tunnels and inside office buildings. Moreover, because PCS telephones need less power, they can be much smaller (shirt pocket size) and less expensive than cellular telephones. According to some estimates, PCS networks will offer better service and quality than existing cellular telephones while being 20 times more efficient. Also, because they operate at higher, less-crowded frequencies than cellular telephones (see Figure 9.3), they will have the bandwidth to offer video and multimedia communication. The telecommunications industry considers this technology to hold so much potential that in March 1995 about half the PCS licenses being offered within the United States were auctioned off by the United States government for about $7.7 billion. Estimates are that infrastructure expenditures will equal that amount or more before the auction winners can even begin to offer the service to the public, an enormous investment.

Personal digital assistants (PDA) are small, pen-based, hand-held computers capable of entirely digital communications transmission. They have built-in wireless telecommunications capabilities as well as work organization software. A well-known example is the one-pound Apple Newton MessagePad. It can be equipped with a special card that allows it to function as a pager, and when hooked to a cigarette

personal communication services (PCS) A new wireless cellular technology that uses lower-power, higher-frequency radio waves than does cellular technology and so can be used with smaller-sized telephones inside buildings and tunnels.

personal digital assistants (PDA) Small, pen-based, hand-held computers with built-in wireless telecommunications capable of entirely digital communications transmission.

This schematic diagram shows a network overview of the Ardis wireless data transmission system.

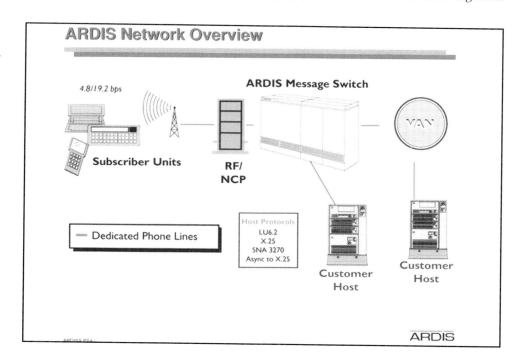

package–sized modem, it will transmit E-mail, faxes, documents for printing, and data to other computers. The Newton also includes an electronic scheduler, calendar and notepad software, and is able to accept handwriting input entered through its special stylus.

JC Penney Co., the fourth-largest retailer in the United States with 1200 retail stores and a large catalog business, provides an example of a mundane but very practical use of wireless technology. The company operates three warehouses nationwide with a combined storage area of 3.3 million square feet. Receiving and storing the goods and later locating, pulling, and shipping them consumes a great deal of time and effort and is very costly. JC Penney has made both processes more efficient, faster, and less expensive through the use of computers and wireless telecommunications, as illustrated in Figure 9.5. As shipments arrive the goods are immediately bar coded. Wireless hand-held scanners then transmit the data on each box to a warehouse computer, which immediately assigns a storage location and wirelessly transmits this data to the forklift operator. The company selected wireless scanners to be used in receiving in order to free the warehouse workers from the inconvenience and potential dangers of strapped-on wired scanners. Later, when goods are to be picked and placed on a conveyor belt that brings them to the shipping dock, the forklift operator is sent a picking list with location data by wireless transmission. Scanners used to read and transmit data on goods on the conveyor belt are wired. (Because these scanners are stationary—the goods pass under them—the designers found no gain in using wireless technology for this task.) JC Penney claims a 23 percent improvement in accuracy as a result of the system, as well as enhanced productivity. The company also expects the system to eliminate the expensive twice-yearly inventory warehouse shutdowns.

While wireless telecommunications holds great potential for the expansion of communication worldwide, the technology does have limitations as well. Wireless transmission is highly error prone because it is susceptible to many kinds of environmental disturbance, from magnetic interference from the sun to automobile ignition emissions. Bandwidth and energy supply in wireless devices require careful management from both hardware and software standpoints (Imielinski and Badrinath, 1994). Security and privacy will be more difficult to maintain because wireless transmission can be easily intercepted (see Chapter 18). Wireless networks require complex error-correcting capabilities that result in repeated transmission of message segments, slowing actual transmission throughput speeds. Moreover, different networks transmit on different radio frequencies and use incompatible protocols so that the modems for different wireless networks are incompatible. Software and hardware technology advances and agreement on standards are all needed before transmission between various wireless networks becomes seamless.

CHARACTERISTICS OF COMMUNICATIONS CHANNELS

The characteristics of the communications channel help determine the efficiency and capabilities of a telecommunications system. These characteristics include the speed of transmission, the direction in which signals may travel, and the mode of transmission.

Transmission Speed

baud A change in signal from positive to negative or vice versa that is used as a measure of transmission speed.

The total amount of information that can be transmitted through any telecommunications channel is measured in bits per second (BPS). Sometimes this is referred to as the *baud rate*. A **baud** is a binary event representing a signal change from positive to negative or vice versa. The baud rate is not always the same as the bit rate. At higher speeds, a single signal change can transmit more than one bit at a time, so the bit rate will generally surpass the baud rate.

Since one signal change, or cycle, is required to transmit one or several bits per second, the transmission capacity of each type of telecommunications medium is a

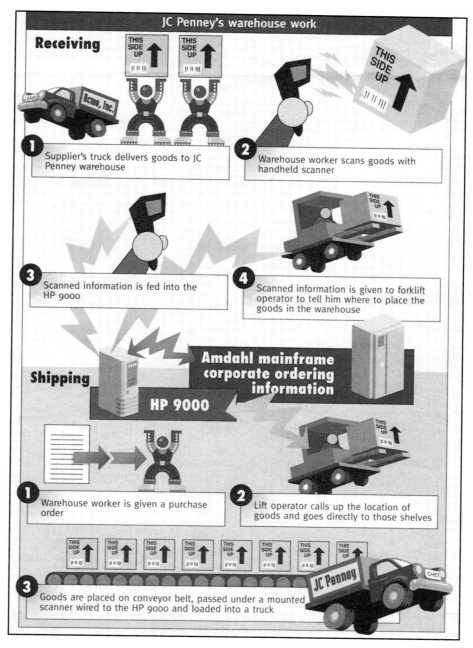

FIGURE 9.5
Wireless transmission at JC Penney's. JC Penney uses wireless hand-held scanners to locate goods for shipping and receiving at its three massive warehouses throughout the U.S. *Adapted from: Mark Halper, "JC Penney Warehouses Do Away with Paper," Computerworld, September 12, 1994.*

bandwidth The capacity of a communications channel as measured by the difference between the highest and lowest frequencies that can be transmitted by that channel.

function of its frequency, the number of cycles per second that can be sent through that medium measured in *hertz* (see Chapter 6). The range of frequencies that can be accommodated on a particular telecommunications channel is called its **bandwidth**. The bandwidth is the difference between the highest and lowest frequencies that can be accommodated on a single channel. The greater the range of frequencies, the greater the bandwidth and the greater the channel's telecommunications transmission capacity. Table 9.3 compares the transmission speed and relative costs of the major types of transmissions media.

Table 9.3	Typical Speeds and Cost of Telecommunications Transmission Media	
Medium	Speed	Cost
Twisted wire	300 BPS–10 MBPS	Low
Microwave	256 KBPS–100 MBPS	
Satellite	256 KBPS–100 MBPS	
Coaxial cable	56 KBPS–200 MBPS	
Fiber optic cable	500 KBPS–10 GBPS	High

BPS = bits per second
KBPS = kilobits per second
MBPS = megabits per second
GBPS = gigabits per second

Transmission Modes

There are several conventions for transmitting signals; these methods are necessary for devices to communicate when a character begins or ends. **Asynchronous transmission** (often referred to as start–stop transmission) transmits one character at a time over a line, each character framed by control bits—a start bit, one or two stop bits, and a parity bit (see Chapter 6). Asynchronous transmission is used for low-speed transmission.

    Synchronous transmission transmits groups of characters simultaneously, with the beginning and ending of a block of characters determined by the timing circuitry of the sending and receiving devices. Synchronous transmission is used for transmitting large volumes of data at high speeds.

Transmission Direction

Transmission must also consider the direction of data flow over a telecommunications network. In **simplex transmission**, data can travel only in one direction at all times. In **half-duplex transmission**, data can flow two ways but can travel in only one direction at a time. In **full-duplex transmission**, data can be sent in both directions simultaneously.

COMMUNICATIONS PROCESSORS

Communications processors, such as front-end processors, concentrators, controllers, multiplexers, and modems, support data transmission and reception in a telecommunications network.

    The **front-end processor** is a small computer (often a programmable minicomputer) dedicated to communications management and is attached to the main, or host, computer in a computer system. The front-end processor performs special processing related to communications such as error control, formatting, editing, controlling, routing, and speed and signal conversion. It takes some of the load off the host computer. The front-end processor is largely responsible for collecting and processing input and output data to and from terminals and grouping characters into complete messages for submission to the CPU of the host computer.

    A **concentrator** is a programmable telecommunications computer that collects and temporarily stores messages from terminals until enough messages are ready to be sent economically. The concentrator then "bursts" signals to the host computer.

    A **controller**, which is often a specialized minicomputer, supervises communications traffic between the CPU and peripheral devices such as terminals and printers. The controller manages messages from these devices and communicates them to the CPU. It also routes output from the CPU to the appropriate peripheral device.

asynchronous transmission Low-speed transmission of one character at a time.

synchronous transmission High-speed simultaneous transmission of large blocks of data.

simplex transmission Transmission in which data can travel in only one direction at all times.

half-duplex transmission Transmission in which data can flow two ways but in only one direction at a time.

full-duplex transmission Transmission in which data can travel in both directions simultaneously.

communications processors Hardware that supports data transmission and reception in a telecommunications network.

front-end processor Small computer managing communications for the host computer in a network.

concentrator Telecommunications computer that collects and temporarily stores messages from terminals for batch transmission to the host computer.

controller Specialized computer that supervises communications traffic between the CPU and the peripheral devices in a telecommunications system.

multiplexer Device that enables a single communications channel to carry data transmissions from multiple sources simultaneously.

A **multiplexer** is a device that enables a single communications channel to carry data transmissions from multiple sources simultaneously. The multiplexer divides the communications channel so that it can be shared by multiple transmission devices. The multiplexer may divide a high-speed channel into multiple channels of slower speed or may assign each transmission source a very small slice of time for using the high-speed channel.

TELECOMMUNICATIONS SOFTWARE

telecommunications software Special software for controlling and supporting the activities of a telecommunications network.

Special **telecommunications software** is required to control and support the activities of a telecommunications network. This software resides in the host computer, front-end processor, and other processors in the network. The principal functions of telecommunications software are network control, access control, transmission control, error detection/correction, and security.

Network control software routes messages, polls network terminals, determines transmission priorities, maintains a log of network activity, and checks for errors. Access control software establishes connections between terminals and computers in the network, establishing transmission speed, mode, and direction. Transmission control software enables computers and terminals to send and receive data, programs, commands, and messages. Error-control software detects and corrects errors, then retransmits the corrected data. Security-control software monitors utilization, log ons, passwords, and various authorization procedures to prevent unauthorized access to a network. More detail on security software can be found in Chapter 18.

9.3 TYPES OF TELECOMMUNICATIONS NETWORKS

topology The shape or configuration of a network.

A number of different ways exist to organize telecommunications components to form a network and hence provide multiple ways of classifying networks. Networks can be classified by their shape or **topology**. Networks can also be classified by their geographic scope and the type of services provided. Wide-area networks, for example, encompass a relatively wide geographic area, from several miles to thousands of miles, whereas local networks link local resources such as computers and terminals in the same department or building of a firm. This section will describe the various ways of looking at networks.

NETWORK TOPOLOGIES

One way of describing networks is by their shape, or topology. As illustrated in Figures 9.6 to 9.8, the three most common topologies are the star, bus, and ring.

The Star Network

star network Network topology in which all computers and other devices are connected to a central host computer. All communications between network devices must pass through the host computer.

The **star network** (see Figure 9.6) consists of a central host computer connected to a number of smaller computers or terminals. This topology is useful for applications where some processing must be centralized and some can be performed locally. One problem with the star network is its vulnerability. All communication between points in the network must pass through the central computer. Because the central computer is the traffic controller for the other computers and terminals in the network, communication in the network will come to a standstill if the host computer stops functioning.

The Bus Network

bus network Network topology linking a number of computers by a single circuit with all messages broadcast to the entire network.

The **bus network** (see Figure 9.7) links a number of computers by a single circuit made of twisted wire, coaxial cable, or fiber optic cable. All of the signals are broadcast in both directions to the entire network, with special software to identify which

FIGURE 9.6
A star network topology. In a star network configuration, a central host computer acts as a traffic controller for all the other components of the network. All communication between the smaller computers, terminals, and printers must first pass through the central computer.

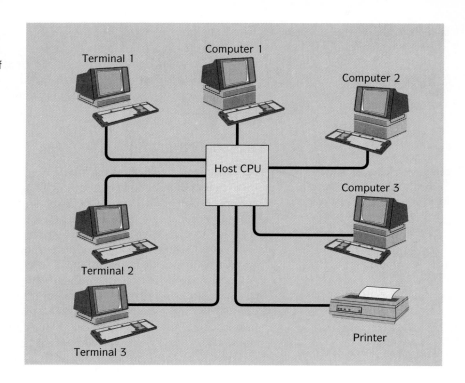

components receive each message (there is no central host computer to control the network). If one of the computers in the network fails, none of the other components in the network is affected. This topology is commonly used for local-area networks (LANs), discussed in the following section.

FIGURE 9.7
A bus network topology. This topology allows for all messages to be broadcast to the entire network through a single circuit. There is no central host, and messages can travel in both directions along the cable.

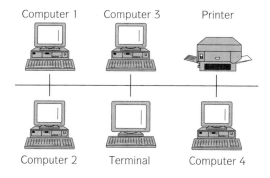

The Ring Network

ring network Network topology in which all computers are linked by a closed loop in a manner that passes data in one direction from one computer to another.

Like the bus network, the **ring network** (see Figure 9.8) does not rely on a central host computer and will not necessarily break down if one of the component computers malfunctions. Each computer in the network can communicate directly with any other computer, and each processes its own applications independently. However, in ring topology, the connecting wire, cable, or optical fiber forms a closed loop. Data are passed along the ring from one computer to another and always flow in one direction.

The token ring network is a variant of the ring network. In the token ring network, all of the devices on the network communicate using a signal or "token." The token is a predefined packet of data, which includes data indicating the sender, receiver, and whether the packet is in use. The tokens may contain a message or be empty.

A token moves from device to device in the network, and each device examines the token as it passes by. If the token contains data and is meant for that device, the

FIGURE 9.8
A ring network topology. In a ring network configuration, messages are transmitted from computer to computer, flowing in a single direction through a closed loop. Each computer operates independently so that if one fails, communication through the network is not interrupted.

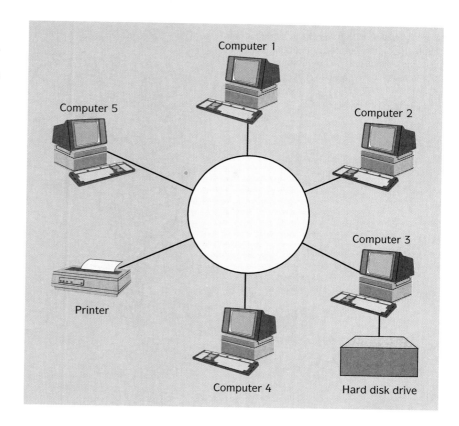

device accepts the data and marks the packet as empty. If a computer wants to send a message, it finds an available token; supplies sender, receiver, and message data; loads the message onto the token; and marks it as used. If no message is pending, the token passes unchanged. The token ring configuration is most useful for transmitting large volumes of data between microcomputers or for transmission between micros and a larger computer.

PRIVATE BRANCH EXCHANGES AND LOCAL-AREA NETWORKS

Networks may be classified by geographic scope into local networks and wide-area networks. Local networks consist of private branch exchanges and local-area networks.

Private Branch Exchanges

private branch exchange (PBX)
Central switching system that handles a firm's voice and digital communications.

A **private branch exchange (PBX)** is a special-purpose computer designed for handling and switching office telephone calls at a company site. Today's PBXs can carry both voice and data to create local networks.

While the first PBXs performed limited switching functions, they can now store, transfer, hold, and redial telephone calls. PBXs can also be used to switch digital information among computers and office devices. For instance, you can write a letter on a microcomputer in your office, send it to the printer, then dial up the local copying machine and have multiple copies of your letter created. All of this activity is possible with a digital PBX connecting "smart" machines in the advanced office. Figure 9.9 illustrates a PBX system.

The advantage of digital PBXs over other local networking options is that they utilize existing telephone lines and do not require special wiring. A phone jack can be found almost anywhere in the office building. Equipment can therefore be moved when necessary with little worry about having to rewire the building. A hard-wired computer terminal or microcomputer connected to a mainframe with coaxial cable

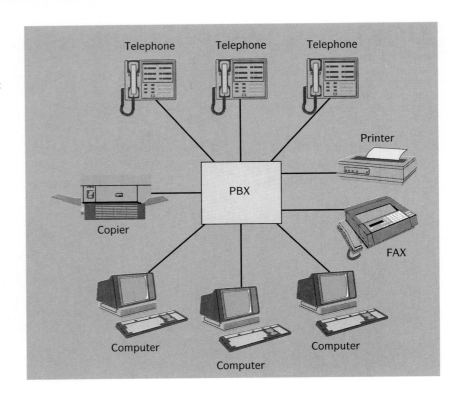

must be rewired at considerable cost each time it is moved. A microcomputer connected to a network by telephone can simply be plugged or unplugged anywhere in the building, utilizing the existing telephone lines. PBXs are also supported by commercial vendors such as the local telephone company, so that the organization does not need special expertise to manage them.

The geographic scope of PBXs is limited, usually to several hundred feet, although the PBX can be connected to other PBX networks or to packet-switched networks (see the discussion of value-added networks in this section) to encompass a larger geographic area. The primary disadvantage of PBXs is that they are limited to telephone lines and that they cannot easily handle very large volumes of data.

Local-Area Networks

A **local-area network (LAN)** encompasses a limited distance, usually one building or several buildings in close proximity. Most LANs connect devices located within a 2000-foot radius and have been widely used to link microcomputers. LANs require their own communications channels.

LANs generally have higher transmission capacities than PBXs, using bus or ring topologies and a high bandwidth. A very fast PBX can have a maximum transmission capacity of over 2 megabits per second. LANs typically transmit at a rate of 256 kilobits per second to over 100 megabits per second. They are recommended for applications requiring high volumes of data and high transmission speeds. For instance, because a picture consumes so many bits of information, an organization might require a LAN for video transmissions and graphics.

LANs are totally controlled, maintained, and operated by end users. This produces the advantage of allowing user control, but it also means that the user must know a great deal about telecommunications applications and networking.

LANs allow organizations to share expensive hardware and software. For instance, several microcomputers can share a single printer by being tied together in a LAN. LANs can promote productivity because users are no longer dependent upon a centralized computer system (which can fail) or upon the availability of a single pe-

FIGURE 9.10

Michelin Milan's LAN. The Milan division of Michelin Italia chose ARCnet as the technology for connecting the devices in its 100-seat local-area network for several reasons, including the floor plan of the Michelin building and the need for a star topology to allow upgrades to the network. *Reproduced with permission of Michelin Italy.*

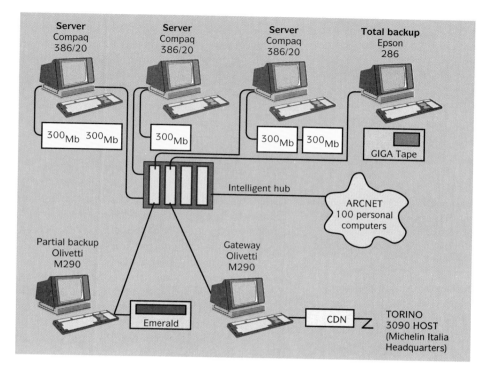

ripheral device such as a printer. Finally, there are many new applications—such as electronic mail, graphics, video teleconferencing, and on-line applications—requiring high-capacity networks.

The most common use of LANs is for linking personal computers within a building or office to share information and expensive peripheral devices such as laser printers. Another popular application of LANs is in factories, where they link computers and computer-controlled machines.

Figure 9.10 illustrates a LAN employed by the Milan division of Michelin Italia, the Italian branch of the Michelin Corporation. The corporation is noted for its tires and guides to hotels and restaurants. Michelin Italia Milan's staff uses the LAN primarily for electronic filing, word processing, and graphics applications. This LAN consists of one hundred personal computer workstations that are attached to three Compaq 386/20 file servers, each equipped with 300-megabyte hard disks. The network also contains an Epson 286 PC and an Olivetti M290 PC for backup and an Olivetti M290 PC serving as a gateway. The entire network and important files are backed up every night using tapes from CigaTape and Emerald Systems Corporation of San Diego, California.

file server Computer in a network that stores various programs and data files for users of the network. Determines access and availability in the network.

The **file server** acts as a librarian, storing various programs and data files for network users. The server determines who gets access to what and in what sequence. Servers may be powerful microcomputers with large hard disk capacity, workstations, minicomputers, or mainframes, although specialized computers are now available for this purpose. The server typically contains the LAN's **network operating system**, which manages the server and routes and manages communications on the network.

network operating system Special software that manages the file server in a LAN and routes and manages communications on the network.

The network **gateway** connects the LAN to public networks, such as the telephone network, or to other corporate networks so that the LAN can exchange information with networks external to it. A gateway is generally a communications processor that can connect dissimilar networks by translating from one set of protocols to another. (A bridge connects two networks of the same type. A router is used to route messages through several connected LANs or to a wide-area network.)

gateway Communications processor that connects dissimilar networks by providing the translation from one set of protocols to another.

The gateway illustrated in Figure 9.10 connects Michelin Italia's Milan division to Michelin Italia's 3090 IBM mainframe host computer in its Torino headquarters.

Application software, such as word processing, works with the network operating system to keep data traffic flowing smoothly.

LAN technology consists of cabling (twisted wire, coaxial, or fiber optic cable) or wireless technology that links individual computer devices, network interface cards (which are special adapters serving as interfaces to the cable), and software to control LAN activities. The LAN network interface card specifies the data transmission rate, the size of message units, the addressing information attached to each message, and network topology (Ethernet utilizes a bus topology, for example).

There are four principal LAN technologies for physically connecting devices—Ethernet, developed by Xerox, Digital Equipment Corporation, and Intel; Appletalk from Apple Computer Incorporated; token ring, developed by IBM and Texas Instruments; and ARCnet, developed by Datapoint. They employ either a baseband or a broadband channel technology. **Baseband** products provide a single path for transmitting text, graphics, voice, or video data, and only one type of data at a time can be transmitted. **Broadband** products provide several paths so that different types of data can be transmitted simultaneously.

LAN capabilities are also defined by the network operating system. The network operating system can reside on every computer in the network, or it can reside on a single designated file server for all the applications on the network. Some of the leading network operating systems include Novell's Netware, Microsoft's LAN Manager, and IBM's PC LAN (Appletalk for networks of Macintosh computers combines technology for physically connecting devices with network operating system functions).

The primary disadvantages of LANs are that they are more expensive to install than PBXs and are more inflexible, requiring new wiring each time the LAN is moved. LANs require specially trained staff to manage and run them.

There are four important criteria for evaluating LANs:

1. How flexible is the system (can new users be added, and how many)?
2. What is the actual performance (as opposed to advertising claims)?
3. What is the true cost of the network, including software, implementation, rewiring, training, network management, and opportunity cost of use?
4. How reliable will the system be in the face of various sorts of disturbances?

These criteria explain why the Milan division of Michelin Italia chose a star network configuration based on ARCnet for its 100-user network. (ARCnet is one of the principal technologies for physically connecting LAN devices described earlier.) The firm wanted a LAN that was easy to install in a squared-off building built in 1949 having several floors. Michelin Italia believed that ARCnet has simple rules, has few instructions, and is more reliable and economical than other alternatives. It can be wired in either twisted-pair wire or fiber optic cable and is easy to modify. While ARCnet's 2.5 megabit-per-second transmission capacity is relatively slow, Michelin Italia felt its actual performance was not much different from other alternatives. Because Michelin needed flexibility in expanding the network, it chose a star topology. When a firm cannot predict how a network will expand, the star configuration allows it to put on another node and create another point in the star.

WIDE-AREA NETWORKS (WANS)

Wide-area networks (WANs) span broad geographical distances, ranging from several miles to across entire continents. Common carriers (companies licensed by the government to provide communications services to the public, such as AT&T or MCI) typically determine transmission rates or interconnections between lines, but the customer is responsible for telecommunications contents and management. It is up to the individual firm to establish the most efficient routing of messages, and to handle error checking, editing, protocols, and telecommunications management.

baseband LAN channel technology that provides a single path for transmitting either text, graphics, voice, or video data at one time.

broadband LAN channel technology that provides several paths for transmitting text, graphics, voice, or video data so that different types of data can be transmitted simultaneously.

wide-area network (WAN) Telecommunications network that spans a large geographical distance. May consist of a variety of cable, satellite, and microwave technologies.

switched lines Telephone lines that a person can access from his or her terminal to transmit data to another computer, the call being routed or switched through paths to the designated destination.

dedicated lines Telephone lines that are continuously available for transmission by a lessee. Typically conditioned to transmit data at high speeds for high-volume applications.

value-added network (VAN) Private, multipath, data-only, third-party-managed networks that are used by multiple organizations on a subscription basis.

WANs may consist of a combination of switched and dedicated lines, microwave, and satellite communications. **Switched lines** are telephone lines that a person can access from his or her terminal to transmit data to another computer, the call being routed or switched through paths to the designated destination. **Dedicated lines**, or nonswitched lines, are continuously available for transmission and the lessee typically pays a flat rate for total access to the line. The lines can be leased or purchased from common carriers or private communications media vendors. Dedicated lines are often conditioned to transmit data at higher speeds than switched lines and are more appropriate for higher-volume transmissions. Switched lines, on the other hand, are less expensive and more appropriate for low-volume applications requiring only occasional transmission.

Individual business firms may maintain their own wide-area networks. Figure 9.11 illustrates a wide-area network used by the Burlington Northern Railroad to help keep its trains moving. The WAN carries traffic controls from dispatch offices to various rail locations, relaying information to make trains stop and start. But private wide-area networks are expensive to maintain, or firms may not have the resources to manage their own wide-area networks. In such instances, companies may choose to use commercial network services to communicate over vast distances.

VALUE-ADDED NETWORKS

Value-added networks are an alternative to firms designing and managing their own networks. **Value-added networks (VANs)** are private, multipath, data-only, third-party-managed networks that can provide economies in the cost of service and in network management because they are used by multiple organizations. The value-added network is set up by a firm that is in charge of managing the network. That firm sells subscriptions to other firms wishing to use the network. Subscribers pay only for the amount of data they transmit plus a subscription fee. The network may utilize twisted-pair lines, satellite links, and other communications channels leased by the value-added carrier.

The term *value added* refers to the extra "value" added to communications by the telecommunications and computing services these networks provide to clients. Customers do not have to invest in network equipment and software or perform their own error checking, editing, routing, and protocol conversion. Subscribers may achieve savings in line charges and transmission costs because the costs of using the

FIGURE 9.11
Burlington Northern's WAN plays a critical role in keeping its trains moving.
Adapted from: Peggy Wallace, "Burlington Northern Puts Down WAN Tracks," illustrator G. Boren, Infoworld, *December 20, 1993.*

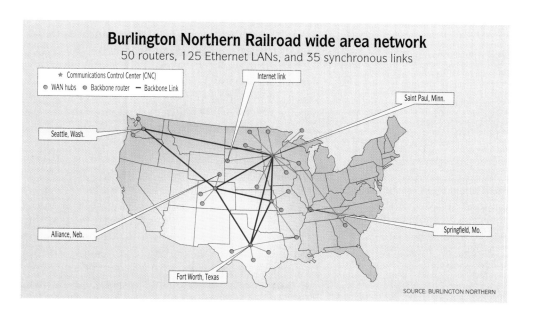

9.3 Types of Telecommunications Networks

Department stores such as Marshall Fields, a unit of Dayton Hudson, use electronic commerce services to track inventory from the warehouses to the truck and into its stores.

network are shared among many users. The resulting costs may be lower than if the clients had leased their own lines or satellite services. VANs are attractive for firms such as Continental Grain because they provide special services such as electronic mail and access to foreign telecommunications systems.

Continental Grain switched from a private network to GE Information Services' (GEIS) value-added network to link its 175 domestic locations with its 45 branch locations in South America, the Far East, and Europe. Continental found that switching to the value-added network reduced costs and reduced operational problems associated with networks. International VANs such as GEIS have representatives with language skills and knowledge of various countries' telecommunications administrations. The VANs have already leased lines from foreign telecommunications authorities or can arrange access to local networks and equipment abroad.

The leading international value-added networks, in addition to GE Information Services Company (GEIS), are Infonet, Telenet, and Tymnet. These networks provide casual or intermittent users international services on a dial-up basis and can provide a private network using dedicated circuits for customers requiring a full-time network. (Maintaining a private network may be most cost effective for organizations with a high communications volume.)

Another way value-added networks provide economies is through **packet switching**. Packet switching breaks up a lengthy block of text into small, fixed bundles of data (often 128 bytes each) called packets (see Figure 9.12). The VAN gathers information from many users, divides it into small packets, and continuously uses various communications channels to send the packets. Each packet travels independently through the network (this contrasts to one firm using a leased line, for example, for one hour and then not using it for three or four hours). Packets of data originating at one source can be routed through different paths in the network, and then may be reassembled into the original message when they reach their destination. Packet switching enables communications facilities to be utilized more fully by more users.

packet switching Technology that breaks blocks of text into small, fixed bundles of data and routes them in the most economical way through any available communications channel.

FIGURE 9.12
Packet switched networks and packet communications. Data are grouped into small packets, framed by identifying information, which are transmitted independently via various communication channels to maximize the potential of the paths in a network.

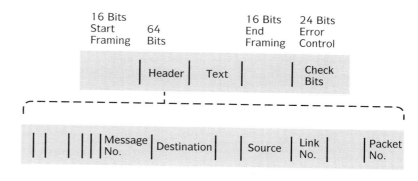

frame relay Shared network service technology that packages data into bundles for transmission but does not use error-correction routines. Cheaper and faster than packet switching.

Frame relay is a faster and less expensive variant of packet switching. Frame relay is a shared network service that packages data into "frames" that are similar to packets. Frame relay, however, does not perform error correction. This is because so many of today's digital lines are cleaner than in the past and networks are more adept at correcting transmission problems. Frame relay can communicate at transmission speeds up to 1.544 megabits per second. Frame relay is essentially used for transmitting data. It is not recommended for any transmissions that are sensitive to varying delay, such as voice or digital video traffic, and it cannot easily control network congestion. Frame relay works successfully only over reliable lines that do not require frequent retransmission because of error.

asynchronous transfer mode (ATM) A networking technology that parcels information into 8-byte "cells," allowing data to be transmitted between computers from different vendors at any speed.

Most corporations today use separate networks for voice, private-line services, and data, each of which is supported by a different technology. An emerging networking technology called **asynchronous transfer mode (ATM)** may overcome some of these problems because it can seamlessly and dynamically switch voice, data, images, and video between users. ATM also promises to tie LANs and wide-area networks together more easily (LANs are generally based on lower-speed protocols, whereas WANs operate at higher speeds). ATM technology parcels information into uniform "cells," each with 53 groups of eight bytes, eliminating the need for protocol conversion. It can pass data between computers from different vendors and permits data to be transmitted at any speed the network handles (Vetter, 1995). ATM currently requires fiber optic cable, but it can transmit up to 2.5 GBPS.

9.4 HOW ORGANIZATIONS USE TELECOMMUNICATIONS FOR COMPETITIVE ADVANTAGE

Baxter International, described in Chapter 2, realized the strategic significance of telecommunications. The company placed its own computer terminals in hospital supply rooms and provided a direct telecommunications link with its central headquarters via a VAN. Customers could dial up a local VAN node and send their orders directly to the company. Since then, many other corporations have realized the strategic potential of networked computer systems.

Telecommunications has helped eliminate barriers of geography and time, enabling organizations to accelerate the pace of production, to speed decision making, to forge new products, to move into new markets, and to create new relationships with customers. Many of the strategic applications described in Chapter 2 would not be possible without telecommunications. Firms that fail to consider telecommunications in their strategic plans will fall behind (Keen, 1986).

FACILITATING APPLICATIONS

Some of the leading telecommunications applications for communication, coordination, and speeding the flow of transactions, messages, and information throughout business firms are electronic mail, voice mail, facsimile machines (FAX), digital information services, teleconferencing, dataconferencing, videoconferencing, and electronic data interchange.

Electronic Mail

electronic mail (E-mail) The computer-to-computer exchange of messages.

Electronic mail, or **E-mail**, is the computer-to-computer exchange of messages. A person can use a microcomputer attached to a modem or a terminal to send notes and even lengthier documents just by typing in the name of the message's recipient. Many organizations operate their own internal electronic mail systems, but communications companies such as GTE, Telenet, MCI, and AT&T offer these services, as do commercial on-line information services such as America Online, CompuServe, and Prodigy and public networks on the Internet (see Chapter 10). E-mail eliminates telephone tag and costly long-distance telephone charges, expediting communication between different parts of the organization. Nestlé SA, the Swiss-based multinational food corporation, installed a new electronic mail system to connect its 60,000 employees in 80 countries. Nestlé's European units can use the electronic mail system to share information about production schedules and inventory levels to ship excess products from one country to another.

E-mail systems present security problems because without adequate protection, electronic eavesdroppers can read the mail as it moves through a network. We discuss such security problems in Chapter 18. The Window on Management looks at the privacy of E-mail messages from a different perspective, examining whether using E-mail and other network facilities to monitor employees is ethical.

Voice Mail

voice mail System for digitizing a spoken message and transmitting it over a network.

A **voice mail** system digitizes the spoken message of the sender, transmits it over a network, and stores the message on disk for later retrieval. When the recipient is ready to listen, the messages are reconverted to audio form. Various "store and forward" capabilities notify recipients that messages are waiting. Recipients have the option of saving these messages for future use, deleting them, or routing them to other parties.

Facsimile Machines (FAX)

facsimile (FAX) Machine that digitizes and transmits documents with both text and graphics over telephone lines.

Facsimile (FAX) machines can transmit documents containing both text and graphics over ordinary telephone lines. A sending FAX machine scans and digitizes the document image. The digitized document is then transmitted over a network and reproduced in hard copy form by a receiving FAX machine. The process results in a duplicate, or facsimile, of the original.

Digital Information Services

Powerful and far-reaching digital electronic services now enable networked microcomputer and workstation users to obtain information from outside the firm instantaneously without leaving their desks. Stock prices, historical references to periodicals, industrial supplies catalogs, legal research, news articles, reference works, weather forecasts, and travel information are just some of the electronic databases that can be accessed on-line. Many of these services have capabilities for electronic mail, electronic bulletin boards, and for on-line discussion groups, shopping, and travel reservations. Table 9.4 describes the leading commercial digital information services. An extension of the Windows 95 operating system will let users use Microsoft Network, Microsoft's on-line information service featuring interactive publishing tools. In the following chapter we describe the capabilities of the Internet, a publicly available network of networks offering access to many thousands of databases throughout the world.

Today, the sheer abundance of networks and on-line information services has created problems of "information overload." Individuals and organizations may be inundated with too much useless information, such as unsolicited E-mail, while valuable information remains hard to find. One solution is to use intelligent agent software. **Intelligent agents** are "smart programs" that can carry out specific, repetitive, and predictable tasks for an individual user, business process, or software applica-

intelligent agents Software programs that can carry out specific, repetitive, and predictable tasks for individuals, organizations, or software applications.

MONITORING WITH NETWORKS: UNETHICAL OR GOOD BUSINESS?

Is the use of networks to monitor employees unethical? Or is it just good business? Employees using networks are vulnerable to electronic supervision in a number of ways. Computers can be programmed to record the total time the employee spends actually working at the computer, the number of keystrokes per minute, even the number of mistakes. Supervisors can sit elsewhere to monitor those numbers or read reports at the end of a work period. Management can also monitor workers using remote network management products that are designed to enable network managers to connect into the network to manage it. For example, Network Sniffer from Network General Corp. of Menlo Park, California, captures and displays network traffic to monitor data for signs of intruders but, by its nature, can also be used to read employees' E-mail. Lanstore from Secure Data, Inc. of Vernon, Connecticut, enables network managers to re-create commands that caused a system "crash" but can also be used to re-create the moment-by-moment computer activities of any person on the network.

Insurance companies, telephone companies, airline reservation sales units, and mail order houses, among others, regularly monitor employees' keystrokes and related data, just as many large corporations use their telephone systems to monitor the destination and length of time of employee telephone calls. For example, Ron Edens, owner of Electronic Banking Systems Inc. of Hagerstown, Maryland, sets a quota of 8500 keystrokes per hour for each employee who opens envelopes and records enclosed payments. Edens also requires that his employees do not talk on the job and do no eating or drinking (the one exception is hard candy) in order to increase their efficiency. Edens' company performs a lockbox function for many companies and charities who choose to outsource

payment receiving and recording rather than performing it in-house. Combining strict monitoring with low wages, Edens' company is able to perform the lockbox function at a lower price than his customers could if they did it themselves. He clearly believes he has a valid business need to monitor his employees closely.

The monitoring of an individual's work in this way has created a great deal of controversy. It is common to see electronic monitoring compared to the "sweatshops" of old, leading even to a recent book titled *The Electronic Sweatshop*. According to the author, "the office of the future will look a lot like the factory of the past." She adds that "modern tools are being used to bring 19th-century working conditions into the white-collar world." Employees of Edens' Electronic Banking Systems complain of monotony and exhaustion as well as of feeling lonely and trapped. Expert studies conclude that workers will feel pressured, paranoid, and even prone to stress-related illnesses from such close surveillance.

Monitoring employee E-mail, which is viewed by many to be an unethical and even an illegal invasion of privacy, is considered legitimate by many companies that claim they need to know that the business facilities they own are being used to further their business goals. Some also argue that they need to be able to search electronic mail messages for evidence of illegal activities, racial discrimination, or sexual harassment. Others argue that the company needs access to business information stored in E-mail files just the same as if it were stored in file cabinets. Privacy of E-mail within a company is not covered by United States federal law. The Electronic Communications Privacy Act of 1986 only prohibits interception or disclosure of E-mail messages by parties outside the company where the messages were sent without a proper warrant. Lawsuits have so far failed to limit the

right of companies to monitor E-mail. For example, when Alana Shoars, a former E-mail administrator at Epson America Inc., discovered her supervisor

> *To Think About:* What management, organization, and technology issues are raised by employee monitoring? Do you believe management should have the right to monitor employees using networks? Why or why not? What legal protections would you recommend for E-mail and why? What elements would you include in a company privacy policy?

was copying and reading employees' E-mail, she sued in the Los Angeles, California, courts, alleging invasion of privacy by the company. Later she filed a class-action suit in the name of 700 Epson employees and 1800 outsiders also charging privacy invasion. Both cases were dismissed on the grounds that E-mail does not fall within the state's wiretapping laws.

Despite the lack of legal restrictions, many observers see the privacy of electronic mail as a serious issue. Michael Godwin, the legal adviser for the Electronic Frontier Foundation, recommends that employers that intend to monitor E-mail establish a stated policy to that effect. Various companies have such policies, including Nordstrom, Eastman Kodak, and Federal Express, all of which claim the right to intercept and read employee E-mail. General Motors and Hallmark Cards have policies that grant employees greater privacy.

Sources: Tony Horwitz, "Mr. Edens Profits from Watching His Workers' Every Move," *The Wall Street Journal,* December 1, 1994; "Does E-Mail Mean Everyone's Mail?" *InformationWEEK,* January 3, 1994; David Bjerklie, "E-Mail: The Boss Is Watching," *Technology Review,* April 1993; and Jim Nash, "Technology Raises Many New Ethics Questions," *Computerworld,* October 14, 1991.

CompuServe gives subscribers access to extensive information, including news reports, travel, weather, education, and financial services—directly from their desktop computers in their homes or offices.

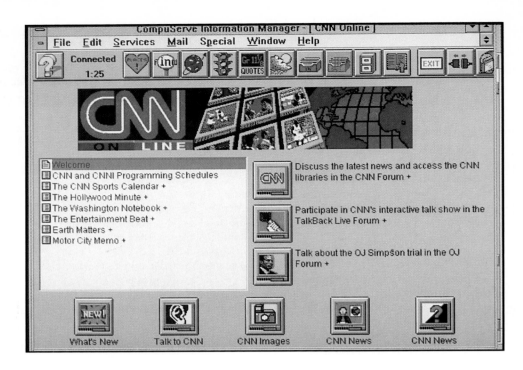

Table 9.4	Commercial Digital Information Services
Provider	**Type of Service**
America Online	General interest/business information
CompuServe	General interest/business information
Prodigy	General interest/business information
Dow Jones News Retrieval	Business/financial information
Quotron	Financial information
Dialog	Business/scientific/technical information
Lexis	Legal research
Nexis	News/business information

tion. They can be programmed to make decisions based on the user's personal preferences—for example, to delete junk E-mail, schedule appointments, or travel over interconnected networks to find the cheapest airfare to California. The agent can be likened to a personal assistant collaborating with the user in the same work environment. It can help the user by performing tasks on the user's behalf; training or teaching the user; hiding the complexity of difficult tasks; helping the user collaborate with other users; or monitoring events and procedures (Maes, 1994). The Window on Technology describes some of the capabilities of intelligent agent software and its implications for networking and electronic commerce.

Teleconferencing, Dataconferencing, and Videoconferencing

teleconferencing Ability to confer with a group of people simultaneously using the telephone or electronic mail group communication software.

People can meet electronically—even though they are hundreds or thousands of miles apart—by using teleconferencing, dataconferencing, or videoconferencing. **Teleconferencing** allows a group of people to "confer" simultaneously via telephone or via electronic mail group communication software (see Chapter 15). Teleconferencing that includes the ability of two or more people at distant locations

dataconferencing
Teleconferencing in which two or more users are able to edit and directly modify data files simultaneously.

videoconferencing Teleconferencing with the capability of participants to see each other over video screens.

to work on the same document or data simultaneously is called **dataconferencing**. With dataconferencing, two or more users at distant locations are able to edit and directly modify data (text, such as word processing documents, numeric, such as spreadsheets, and graphic) files simultaneously. Teleconferencing that also has the capability to let participants see each other "face-to-face" over video screens is termed *video teleconferencing* or **videoconferencing**.

These various forms of electronic conferencing are growing in popularity because they save travel time and cost. Legal firms might use videoconferencing to take depositions and to convene meetings between lawyers in different branch offices. For example, the firm of Howrey & Simon with 300 lawyers in Los Angeles has several expensive teleconferencing rooms that are busy almost constantly, linking them with their staff counterparts in Washington, DC. Designers and engineers use videoconferencing for remote collaboration. The cosmetics manufacturer Estée Lauder is using desktop videoconferencing to enable staff in Manhattan and Melville, Long Island, to view products under design along with the "talking heads" of meeting participants. Johnson Controls uses desktop videoconferencing for training and education partly because instructors can demonstrate an application to a distant user while simultaneously talking about it. Hospitals, universities, and even corporate researchers are using videoconferencing to fill in personnel expertise gaps (Brandel, 1995; Frye, 1995). Electronic conferencing is even useful in supporting telecommuting, enabling home workers to meet with or collaborate with their counterparts working in the office or elsewhere.

Videoconferencing has usually required special video conference rooms and videocameras, microphones, television monitors, and a computer equipped with a codec device that converts video images and analog sound waves into digital signals and compresses them for transfer over communications channels. Another codec on the receiving end reconverts the digital signals back into analog for display on the receiving monitor. These setups used to cost more than $50,000, a daunting price unless value can be demonstrated. By 1995, however, with the availability of technology for using desktop PCs for videoconferencing, the need for special conference rooms had been reduced, although it is still expensive with the cost per seat for videoconferencing at about $2500 (in early 1995). Microcomputer-based desktop videoconferencing systems where users can see each other and simultaneously work on the same document are even lower in cost. Videoconferencing requires a great deal of bandwidth because it is transmitting full motion video.

ELECTRONIC DATA INTERCHANGE

electronic data interchange (EDI)
Direct computer-to-computer exchange between two organizations of standard business transaction documents.

Electronic data interchange (EDI) is the direct computer-to-computer exchange between two organizations of standard business transaction documents such as invoices, bills of lading, or purchase orders. EDI saves money and time because transactions can be transmitted from one information system to another through a telecommunications network, eliminating the printing and handling of paper at one end and the inputting of data at the other. EDI may also provide strategic benefits by helping a firm "lock in" customers, making it easier for customers or distributors to order from them rather than from competitors.

EDI differs from electronic mail in that it transmits an actual structured transaction (with distinct fields such as the transaction date, transaction amount, sender's name and recipient's name) as opposed to an unstructured text message such as a letter.

Figure 9.14 illustrates how EDI operates at the Cummins Engine Company. Cummins implemented EDI to automate purchasing, shipping, and payment transactions with its customers. Cummins transmits price updates and shipping notices directly to its customers' computer system. Customers in turn transmit material releases, reports on receiving discrepancies, and payment and remittance data directly to Cummins' computer system. EDI has replaced paper for these transactions.

INTELLIGENT AGENTS: NETWORK VALETS

What a dream—an electronic intelligent agent that searches your network-based newspaper for the information you need while you, and your computer, are left free to pursue other tasks! That dream recently came true with the release of intelligent agent technology from General Magic of Mountain View, California. Intelligent agents can perform a wide range of tasks for you without your doing anything more than assigning the agent its tasks and sending it off onto the network. For example, you can give a General Magic agent the brand name and model number of a television set you want to purchase and then send the agent off to buy it for you. That intelligent agent would travel through your network, stopping at all the online stores, checking the price and availability, determining which store sells it at the lowest price, returning there, purchasing the TV, and then reporting the results back to you. All the while you are and your computer are free to do other work. Some of the many uses envisioned for these agents include: filtering your E-mail (weeding out the junk mail) and sorting the rest; monitoring a flight you need to meet, notifying you if it is late; monitoring a specific stock for you and entering an order to buy (or sell) when it hits a specific price target; monitoring your customer's computer and launching an order on your computer to produce and ship more product when the customer's stock falls to a certain level.

DHL Worldwide Express, the worldwide express delivery service based in Redwood City, California, and Brussels, uses agent-based package tracking applications to communicate daily with more than 3000 U.S. customers. Using prerecorded phrases, an agent asks touch-tone callers to DHL's toll-free number to punch in their airbill number. If the package has been successfully delivered, the agent re-

sponds with the time, data, and name of the person who signed for it. If not, the agent transfers the caller to a human operator for more assistance.

Intelligent agents can move around interconnected networks, from computer to computer, performing the assigned task, making as many stops as needed until the task is completed. The basic problem that led to the development of the concept of electronic agents is the expensive bandwidth needed at each step as the information is transmitted back and forth. Returning to the television set purchase example, picture the number of data transmissions normally needed for an individual to purchase the TV set online. The buyer logs on to the network and transmits instructions to move to the first electronic store. That store's welcoming message is transmitted back to the shopper's computer, along with instructions on entering data to locate a product for possible purchase. The shopper transmits back the product type, brand, and model number, perhaps after several rounds of menu selection data are transmitted back and forth. The store then transmits the price, availability, and shipping costs back to the potential customer's computer. Next, the shopper transmits instructions to move on to a second store. After visiting another four stores with the equivalent number of transmissions, the buyer transmits instructions to return to the store with the lowest price and goes through the process again, this time adding several transmissions each way in order to enter and confirm the actual purchase. The whole process will result in data being transmitted between the buyer's computer and on-line store computers perhaps 20 or 30 times each way, some of it large quantities of data because of graphics involved in transmitting a store logo or a product picture.

Electronic intelligent agents were developed after the realization that the reason for the flow of so much data

back and forth is that the work is being divided between the shopper's computer and the computers of the stores selling the TVs. With electronic agents,

> **To Think About:** *Suggest problems individuals and organizations can solve using intelligent agents. What organization, management, and technical factors should be considered in determining whether or not to use electronic intelligent agents?*

all computer processing will occur on the computer where the information is stored—in our example, the computers of the merchants. The user (shopper) will not be connected to the network other than to launch the intelligent agent, and, later, to receive its results. The agent moves from computer to computer, doing its work totally on its own. Data are transmitted only once each way, when the buyer launches the intelligent agent and when the agent completes its task and reports back the results, as illustrated in Figure 9.13.

This new technology is a response to another problem as well. Networks now offer too much information, most of it useless to a given individual at any one time. Two examples are all the data an individual has to sort through on-line to find the lowest priced airline flight at the necessary time, and all the "junk mail" people are receiving via their E-mail. Finding that which has value among all the data can be very time-consuming, tedious work. Electronic agents can save the user a great deal of time by removing him or her from the loop.

To program intelligent agents, General Magic developed a proprietary language called Telescript. Telescript code must exist on every node on the network for this to work. As a result intelligent agent technology will work only on a network that supports it. The user must be able to program the agent (with an easy-to-use graphical inter-

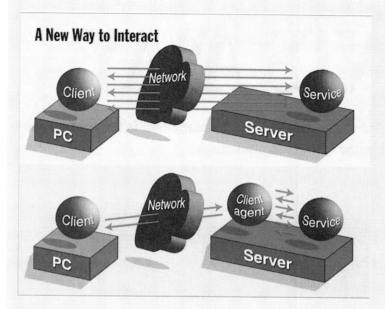

A New Way to Interact

FIGURE 9.13

Intelligent agents. Intelligent agent software cuts down of the number of transmissions that must be sent over a network to complete a transaction between two distant parties such as a purchase or travel reservation. By sending an electronic agent across a network, data are transmitted only once each way, when the buyer launches the intelligent agent and when the agent completes its task and reports back the results. *Adapted from: Peter Wayner, "Agents Away,"* Byte *(May 1994). Reprinted with permission from* BYTE *Magazine, © by McGraw-Hill, Inc., New York, NY. All rights reserved.*

face) to carry the request and the necessary data, while the computer at the other end must have the code necessary to process that request. Intelligent agents are actually quite tiny, requiring very little bandwidth, because they carry only a small amount of information and no processing code.

PersonaLink, a network with Telescript capability, began operating on September 28, 1994. Telecommunications giant AT&T Corp., which established PersonaLink, expects it to become an electronic marketplace. Sony Corporation, on the same day, began shipping the first hand-held communicators that can deploy intelligent agents on the PersonaLink network. Other major companies have shown interest in the

technology as well. For example, Nippon Telephone and Telegraph, Tokyo, Japan, the world's largest telecommunications company, owns a share of General Magic.

While intelligent agent technology can make people more efficient and well informed, it raises some serious technical, social, and legal concerns. Should agents be authorized to execute financial transactions without any human intervention? Should employers be able to create agents that count employees' keystrokes, monitor their telephone calls, or note how often they access important computer files (review the Window on Management)? Can the boss demand to see an employee's agents to check on how well he or she had delegated responsibilities? How

can we be sure that agents won't clog networks or damage another party's agents or computer systems?

Intelligents agents act independently, moving from place to place, collecting information as they go. In some ways this behavior resembles that of computer viruses which can be quite destructive (see Chapter 18 for a discussion of viruses.) Many observers fear that intelligent agents can be used to spy, to gather proprietary information. Others fear that information, such as passwords and credit-card numbers, can be stolen from them. General Magic claims to have designed Telescript and the whole electronic intelligent agent system with these problems in mind. Telescript has a limited vocabulary with many of the potentially dangerous, virus-like functions missing. Moreover, every intelligent agent and every source computer has a secure name and identification, and programmers attempting to create rogue agents will need to know that data before they can successfully invade any computer on a network. Another protection inherent in the design of the system is the limitations set by the host computers. Each computer site is able to limit visiting agents to predesignated functions by simply not coding other functions into their local Telescript software. For example, an airline will enable collection of flight information but will not program any other Telescript function onto its computer. Similarly, each computer will set activity time limits on each intelligent agent, halting all activity by that agent if it exceeds that limit. Finally, the Telescript systems can use encryption to protect the data the agent is carrying.

Sources: Dan Richman, "Let Your Agent Handle It," *InformationWEEK*, April 17, 1995; G. Christian Hill, "Electronic 'Agents' Bring Virtual Shopping a Bit Closer to Reality," *The Wall Street Journal,* September 27, 1994; Peter Wayner, "Agents Away," *Byte,* May 1994.

EDI lowers routine transaction processing costs and turnaround time because there is less need to transfer data from hard copy forms into computer-ready transactions. EDI reduces transcription errors and associated costs that occur when data are entered and printed out many times. Chapter 2 has shown how EDI can also curb inventory costs by minimizing the amount of time components are in inventory. Organizations can most fully benefit from EDI when they integrate the data supplied

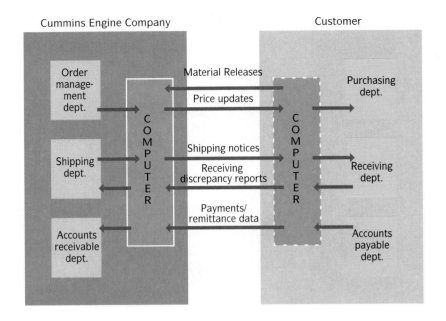

FIGURE 9.14
How EDI works at Cummins Engine Company. Cummins Engine Company uses EDI to automate price, shipping, receiving, and payment transactions with its customers. Cummins' price updates and shipping notices are entered by the appropriate departments directly into Cummins' computer system, which transmits them to its customers' computer systems. Customers' material releases, receiving reports, and payment data are also transmitted directly through the computer systems back to Cummins. *Source: From "EDI Hitting Stride in Data Entry" by Robert Knight,* Software Magazine, *February 1992. Reprinted with the permission of Software* Magazine, *February 1992. Sentry Publishing Company Inc., One Research Drive, Westborough, MA 01581, U.S.A.*

by EDI with applications such as accounts payable, inventory control, shipping, and production planning (Premkumar, Ramamurthy, and Nilakanta, 1994).

For EDI to work properly, four key requirements must be addressed:

1. *Transaction standardization.* Participating companies must agree on the form of the message to be exchanged. Transaction formats and data must be standardized. The American National Standards Institute (ANSI) has developed the X.12 data interchange protocol as a generic, flexible business data interchange standard (see Chapter 10) for EDI, but specific industries have adopted multiple EDI standards. This can raise problems for interorganizational networking, since manufacturing, retail, and banking standards might collide.

2. *Translation software.* Special software must be developed to convert incoming and outgoing messages into a form comprehensible to other companies.

3. *Appropriate "mailbox" facilities.* Companies using EDI must select a third-party, value-added network with mailbox facilities that allows messages to be sent, sorted, and held until they are needed by the receiving computer. For example, the insurance field generally uses Information Network, and office systems tend to use GE Information Services.

4. *Legal restrictions.* To comply with legal requirements, certain transactions require "writing," a "signature," or the "original document" in hard copy form. (EDI messages do not, for example, deal with warranties or limitations of liability and other conditions of doing business typically contained in hard copy business documents.) Parties must agree on the means of verifying that messages are authentic and complete according to the agreed-on protocol, the point in the transaction when the contract between the two parties goes into effect, error-checking procedures, and the level of network security to prevent unauthorized access and use of the system.

As intelligent agent technology and commercial networks open new electronic marketplaces, they will lead to more flexible forms of EDI in which exchange of purchase and sale transactions are not limited to the computer systems of two organizations.

9.5 MANAGEMENT ISSUES AND DECISIONS

The starting point for rational planning of telecommunications is to forget about the "features" of systems and instead to try to understand the requirements of one's organization. A telecommunications plan is more likely to succeed if it advances the key business goals of the company. Cutting costs and installing advanced systems for their own sake is rarely a sufficient reason to justify large telecommunications projects.

THE TELECOMMUNICATIONS PLAN

Telecommunications has enormous potential for enhancing a firm's strategic position, but managers need to determine exactly how the firm's competitive position could be enhanced by telecommunications technology. Managers need to ask how telecommunications can reduce costs by increasing the *scale* and *scope* of operations without additional management costs; they need to determine if telecommunications technology can help them *differentiate* products and services; or if telecommunications technology can improve the firm's *cost structure* by eliminating intermediaries such as distributors or by accelerating business processes.

There are steps to implement a strategic telecommunications plan. First, start with an audit of the communications functions in your firm. What are your voice, data, video, equipment, staffing, and management capabilities? For each of these areas, identify and evaluate your strengths, weaknesses, exposures, and opportunities. Then identify priorities for improvement.

Second, you must know the long-range business plans of your firm. These plans can come from planning documents, interviews with senior management, and annual reports. Your plan should include an analysis of precisely how telecommunications will contribute to the specific five-year goals of the firm and to its longer-range strategies (e.g., cost reduction, distribution enhancement).

Third, identify how telecommunications support the day-to-day operations of the firm. What are the needs of the operating units and their managers? Try to identify critical areas where telecommunications currently does or can have the potential to make a large difference in performance. In insurance, these may be systems that give field representatives quick access to policy and rate information; in retailing, inventory control and market penetration; and in industrial products, rapid, efficient distribution and transportation.

Fourth, develop indicators of how well you are fulfilling your plan for enhancing telecommunications. Try to avoid technical measures (e.g., transmission rates enhanced from 300 to 1200 baud) and focus on business measures (e.g., sales force utilization of high-speed data lines increased from 10 to 40 percent).

IMPLEMENTING THE PLAN

Once an organization has developed a business telecommunications plan, it must determine the initial scope of the telecommunications project. Deciding which telecommunications technology to adopt, and under what circumstances, can prove difficult, given the rapid rate of change in the technology and in the related costs of telecommunications.

Managers should take eight factors into account when choosing a telecommunications network.

The first and most important factor is *distance*. If communication will be largely local and entirely internal to the organization's buildings and social networks, there is little or no need for VANs, leased lines, or long-distance communications.

Along with distance, one must consider the *range of services* the network must support, such as electronic mail, EDI, internally generated transactions, voice mail, videoconferencing, or imaging, and whether these services must be integrated in the same network.

A third factor to consider is *security*. The most secure means of long-distance communications is through lines that are owned by the organization. The next-most secure form of telecommunications is through dedicated leased lines. VANs that slice up corporate information into small packets are among the least secure modes. Finally, ordinary telephone lines, which can be tapped at several locations, are even less secure than VANs.

A fourth factor to consider is whether *multiple access* is required throughout the organization or whether it can be limited to one or two nodes within the organization.

A multiple-access system requirement suggests that there will be perhaps several thousand users throughout the corporation; therefore, a commonly available technology such as installed telephone wire and the related technology of a PBX is recommended. However, if access is restricted to fewer than 100 high-intensity users, a more advanced, higher-speed, more exotic technology like a fiber optic or broadband LAN system may be recommended.

A fifth and most difficult factor to judge is *utilization*. There are two aspects of utilization that must be considered when developing a telecommunications network: the frequency and the volume of communications. Together, these two factors determine the total load on the telecommunications system. On the one hand, high-frequency, high-volume communications suggest the need for high-speed LANs for local communication and leased lines for long-distance communication. On the other hand, low-frequency, low-volume communications suggest dial-up, voice-grade telephone circuits operating through a traditional modem.

It is important to avoid overkill by buying a state-of-the-art, high-capacity, but expensive or unreliable system. A 10-megabit-per-second data exchange rate sounds wonderful, but for many applications it simply is not necessary. In a local office where CRT displays, word processors, and microcomputers are being connected, a broadband LAN with megabit data rates is probably excessive. A PBX working in the kilobit range is totally adequate for this kind of digital communication. Telephone manufacturers have demonstrated that users can build their own inexpensive LANs by using existing telephone wires and plugging their machines into the local telephone network.

A sixth factor is *cost*. How much does each telecommunications option cost? Total costs should include costs for development, operations, maintenance, expansion, and overhead. Which cost components are fixed? Which are variable? Are there any hidden costs to anticipate? It is wise to recall the *thruway effect*. The easier it is to use a communications path, the more people will want to use it. Most telecommunications planners estimate future needs on the high side and still often underestimate the actual need. Underestimating the cost of telecommunications projects or uncontrollable telecommunications costs are principal causes of network failure.

Seventh, you must consider the difficulties of *installing* the telecommunications system. Are the organization's buildings properly constructed to install fiber optics? In some instances, buildings have inadequate wiring channels underneath the floors, which makes installation of fiber optic cable extremely difficult.

Eighth, you must consider how much *connectivity* would be required to make all of the components in a network communicate with each other or to tie together multiple networks. There are so many different standards for hardware, software, and communication systems that it may be very difficult to get all of the components of a network to "talk" to each other or to distribute information from one network to another. Chapter 10 treats connectivity issues in greater detail. Table 9.5 summarizes these implementation factors.

Table 9.5 Implementation Factors in Telecommunications Systems

Distance

Range of services

Security

Multiple access

Utilization

Cost

Installation

Connectivity

Management Challenges

1. Managing LANs. While local-area networks appear to be flexible and inexpensive ways of delivering computing power to new areas of the organization, they must be carefully administered and monitored. LANs are especially vulnerable to network disruption, loss of essential data, access by unauthorized users, and infection from computer viruses (see Chapters 10 and 18). Dealing with these problems or even installing popular applications such as spreadsheets or data management software on a network requires special technical expertise which is not normally available in end-user departments and is in very short supply.

2. Compatibility and standards. There is such a bewildering array of hardware, software, and network standards that managers may have trouble choosing the right telecommunications platform for the firm's information architecture. Telecommunications systems based on one standard may not be able to be linked to telecommunications based on another without additional equipment, expense, and management overhead. Networks that meet today's requirements may lack the connectivity for domestic or global expansion in the future. The compatibility and standards challenge is such a serious management challenge that an entire section of the following chapter is devoted to connectivity issues.

Summary

1. Describe the basic components of a telecommunications system. A telecommunications system is a set of compatible devices that are used to develop a network for communication from one location to another by electronic means. The essential components of a telecommunications system are computers, terminals or other input/output devices, communications channels, communications processors (such as modems, multiplexers, controllers, and front-end processors), and telecommunications software. Different components of a telecommunications network can communicate with each other with a common set of rules termed *protocols*.

Data are transmitted throughout a telecommunications network using either analog signals or digital signals. A modem is a device that translates from analog to digital and vice versa.

2. Measure the capacity of telecommunications channels and evaluate transmission media. The capacity of a telecommunications channel is determined by the range of frequencies it can accommodate. The higher the range of frequencies, called bandwidth, the higher the capacity (measured in bits per second). The principal transmission media are twisted copper telephone wire, coaxial copper cable, fiber optic cable, and wireless transmission utilizing microwave, satellite, low frequency radio, or infrared waves.

Transmission media use either synchronous or asynchronous transmission modes for determining where a character begins or ends and when data are transmitted from one computer to another. Three different transmission modes governing the direction of data flow over a transmission medium are simplex transmission, half-duplex transmission, and full-duplex transmission.

3. Describe the three basic network topologies. The three common network topologies are the star network, the bus network, and the ring network. In a star network, all communications must pass through a central computer. The bus network links a number of devices to a single channel and broadcasts all of the signals to the entire network, with special software to identify which components receive each message. In a ring network, each computer in the network can communicate directly with any other computer but the channel is a closed loop. Data are passed along the ring from one computer to another.

4. Classify the various types of telecommunications networks. Networks can be classified by their shape or configuration or by their geographic scope and type of services provided. Local-area networks (LANs) and private branch exchanges (PBXs) are used to link offices and buildings in close proximity. Wide-area networks (WANs) span a broad geographical distance, ranging from several miles to entire continents and are private networks that are independently managed. Value-added networks (VANs) also encompass a wide geographic area but are managed by a third party, which sells the services of the network to other companies.

5. Identify telecommunications applications that can provide competitive advantages to organizations. Using information systems for strategic advantage increasingly depends on telecommunications technology and applications such as electronic mail, voice mail, FAX, digital information services, teleconferencing, dataconferencing, videoconferencing, and electronic data interchange (EDI). Electronic data interchange (EDI) is the direct computer-to-computer exchange between two organizations of standard business transaction documents such as invoices, bills of lading, and purchase orders.

6. Explain the criteria used in planning for telecommunications systems. Firms should develop strategic telecommunications plans to ensure that their telecommunications systems serve business objectives and operations. Important factors to consider are distance, range of services, security, access, utilization, cost, installation, and connectivity.

Key Terms

Telecommunications
Information superhighway
Telecommunications
   system
Protocol
Analog signal
Digital signal
Modem
Channels
Twisted wire
Coaxial cable
Fiber optic cable
Microwave
Satellite
Low-orbit satellites
Paging systems
Cellular telephone

Mobile data networks
Personal communication
   services (PCS)
Personal digital assistants
   (PDA)
Baud
Bandwidth
Asynchronous transmission
Synchronous transmission
Simplex transmission
Half-duplex transmission
Full-duplex transmission
Communications
   processors
Front-end processor
Concentrator
Controller

Multiplexer
Telecommunications
   software
Topology
Star network
Bus network
Ring network
Private branch exchange
   (PBX)
Local-area network (LAN)
File server
Network operating system
Gateway
Baseband
Broadband
Wide-area network (WAN)
Switched lines

Dedicated lines
Value-added network
   (VAN)
Packet switching
Frame relay
Asynchronous transfer
   mode (ATM)
Electronic mail (E-mail)
Voice mail
Facsimile (FAX)
Intelligent agent
Teleconferencing
Dataconferencing
Videoconferencing
Electronic data inter-
   change (EDI)

Review Questions

1. What is the significance of telecommunications deregulation for managers and organizations?
2. What is a telecommunications system? What are the principal functions of all telecommunications systems?
3. Name and briefly describe each of the components of a telecommunications system.
4. Distinguish between an analog and a digital signal.
5. Name the different types of telecommunications transmission media and compare them in terms of speed and cost.
6. What is the relationship between bandwidth and the transmission capacity of a channel?
7. What is the difference between synchronous and asynchronous transmission? Between half-duplex, duplex, and simplex transmission?
8. Name and briefly describe the different kinds of communications processors.

9. Name and briefly describe the three principal network topologies.
10. Distinguish between a PBX and a LAN.
11. Define a wide-area network (WAN).
12. Define the following:
    - Modem
    - Baud
    - File server
    - Value-added network (VAN)
    - Packet switching
    - Asynchronous transfer mode (ATM)
13. Name and describe the telecommunications applications that can provide strategic benefits to businesses.
14. What are the principal factors to consider when developing a telecommunications plan?

Discussion Questions

1. Your firm has just decided to build a new headquarters building in a suburban setting. You have been assigned to work with an architect on plans for making the new building intelligent—that is, capable of supporting the computing and telecommunications needs of the business. What factors should you consider?
2. Your boss has just read in a leading business magazine that local-area networks are the wave of the future. You are directed to explore how the firm can use these LANs. What words of caution and what factors should the boss consider?

3. You are an electronic parts distributor for television repair shops throughout the country. You would like to edge out regional competitors and improve service. How could you use computers and telecommunications systems to achieve these goals?
4. If a channel has capacity of 1200 bits per second, approximately how long would it take to transmit this book? (Assume that there are 250 words per page and spaces do not count as characters. Do not include graphics.)

Group Project

With a group of two or three of your fellow students, describe in detail the various ways that telecommunications technology can provide a firm with competitive advantage. Use the companies described in Chapter 2 or other chapters you have read about so far to illustrate the points you make, or select examples of other companies using telecommunications from business or computer magazines. Present your findings to the class.

Case Study

GOODYEAR AUTOMATES ITS SALES FORCE

Goodyear Tire & Rubber Co., of Akron, Ohio, manufactures tires and rubber products for automobiles, trucks, and heavy equipment, and sells its products throughout the world. At the end of 1994, it had 16 percent of the world's market for tires. Its sales were growing at an annual rate of 4.2 percent versus an industry average of 2.5 percent. Its 1993 sales had been $11.6 billion while its 1994 profits were estimated to be $568 million. One dark spot on this record, however, is that during 1994 Goodyear's stock dropped 26.5 percent, giving it the dubious distinction of having the worst record that year among the 30 stocks that make up the Dow Jones Industrial Average. Investors feared high interest rates would hurt U.S. auto sales and thus the demand for new tires.

The picture was very different in 1991. At that time the company was heavily debt-laden and was losing money rapidly. It had a 14 percent share of the world's tire market. In June of that year, Stanley C. Gault, became the chief executive officer (CEO) of Goodyear. Gault had previously been the senior vice-president of General Electric followed by a turn as CEO of Rubbermaid. During his stewardship of

Rubbermaid, he led the transformation of the company from a little-known maker of household cleaning items into a $3-billion-a-year maker of 4000 different products. Given this record, he was brought to Goodyear to turn the company around.

Gault accomplished the turnaround through a series of policies. He quickly sold off Goodyear's non-tire businesses, freeing the company to focus its core skills. He engineered a sharp reduction in staff, led the development of a range of new products, and expanded sales by changing its distribution policy. He also issued new stock which helped to reduce its immense debt. By 1993 Goodyear's debt had been drastically reduced. Moreover, not only had the company returned to profitability, but its profit of $388 million that year was more than all other tire makers in the world combined.

The change in distribution channels was a major shift in policy. Historically the company had sold exclusively through independents, many of them selling only Goodyear products. In 1992 Gault initiated a policy to begin selling tires through large retailers in addition to independents, starting with Sears, Roebuck & Co., the largest tire retailer in the United States. The following year, he announced that Goodyear would also begin selling its tires to Wal-Mart Stores, the nation's largest retailer, and to Discount Tire, a major tire discounter.

Not surprisingly, this move to major retailers generated a great deal of antagonism among independent Goodyear dealers. However, in July 1993 four dealers filed a class-action suit alleging that Goodyear's actions had reduced the value of their businesses. Gault refused comment, although in 1994 he did say that the new distribution strategy had not hurt Goodyear dealers as much as dealers thought. He did concede, however, that Goodyear "probably could have communicated and executed [the policy change] more palatably." In early 1995 the company revamped its sales organization. This move was preceded several years earlier by a sales force automation (SFA) development project to automate Goodyear's sales and marketing systems.

Widespread interest in automating sales forces is a 1990s phenomenon. A number of technological developments contributed to the growing popularity of SFA, including lightweight portable computers with multimedia capabilities and graphical user interfaces, the proliferation of LANs and WANs, and integration of databases distributed throughout the enterprise, thus enabling easy access to a wide range of enterprise data. The popularity of such fourth-generation tools as spreadsheets and word processors have made SFA systems easier to use and more productive, as has the spreading use of electronic mail.

Observers believe these systems offer a range of benefits to organizations. Their most basic benefit is that they can increase the productivity of the sales staff. This has been a driving force both because of the intensified competitive environment putting pressure on sales staffs, and because of the business need to keep costs low (in some cases downsized sales forces are expected to increase sales). Traditionally, many salespersons had spent a significant amount of time prior to a sales call collecting information from various computers and via telephone (see Figure 9.15 to obtain a picture of the sales process). For example, a study demonstrated that the sales staff of Deere Power, a maker of diesel engines and other heavy equipment, often spent a full day collecting data before a sales call. Studies indicate that the average sales call now costs about $250, up from only $80 as recently as 1975. Prior to automating its sales

process, Ciba-Geigy Pigments found that its per-call costs were $250, with an average of 11 calls needed before a single sale results.

Efficiencies can be achieved in a variety of ways, as illustrated in Figure 9.16. First, these systems can help salespersons to select the best sales prospects. For instance, an application that Dendrite International Inc. furnishes to nearly 20,000 pharmaceutical company reps contains sales data that helps them target doctors most likely to make use of a new product they are trying to sell. Moreover, with an SFA system, the salesperson can quickly load onto his or her laptop computer all the latest data needed for that day's calls. In addition to customer and product information, the computer will carry production and product availability data, order forms, pricing information, an electronic calendar and a tickler file, word pro-

cessing integrated with mail-merge capabilities and reporting facilities, and even access to E-mail. Studies also show that the average sales rep traditionally spends 9 to 11 minutes per day per account on paperwork, offering immense room for savings through the use of the software on the laptop. For example, with an SFA system, the sales staff will no longer need to write product descriptions, add up orders, call in about production status, or check the order for errors, leaving them more time for selling. Many systems even electronically transmit the orders to the organization.

Automated systems also can result in higher quality sales calls. While the salesperson will actually be in the customer's office, she or he is able to respond as if the customer had come into the salesperson's own office. The salesperson not only will be able to talk about the product and show catalog

FIGURE 9.15

The sales process before and after automation. Laptop computers and corporate networks can radically streamline the sales process and give sales representatives new capabilities. *Adapted from: "Anatomy of the Sales Process,"* Business Week *October 25, 1993.*

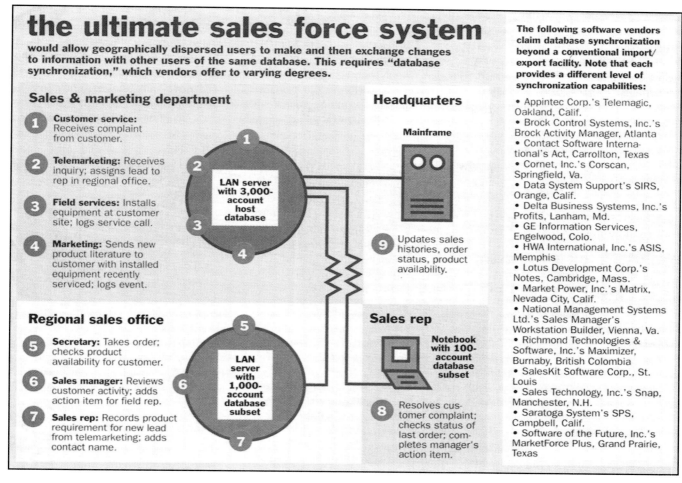

the ultimate sales force system

would allow geographically dispersed users to make and then exchange changes to information with other users of the same database. This requires "database synchronization," which vendors offer to varying degrees.

Sales & marketing department

1 Customer service: Receives complaint from customer.

2 Telemarketing: Receives inquiry; assigns lead to rep in regional office.

3 Field services: Installs equipment at customer site; logs service call.

4 Marketing: Sends new product literature to customer with installed equipment recently serviced; logs event.

Regional sales office

5 Secretary: Takes order; checks product availability for customer.

6 Sales manager: Reviews customer activity; adds action item for field rep.

7 Sales rep: Records product requirement for new lead from telemarketing; adds contact name.

LAN server with 3,000-account host database

LAN server with 1,000-account database subset

Headquarters

Mainframe

9 Updates sales histories, order status, product availability.

Sales rep

Notebook with 100-account database subset

8 Resolves customer complaint; checks status of last order; completes manager's action item.

The following software vendors claim database synchronization beyond a conventional import/export facility. Note that each provides a different level of synchronization capabilities:

• Appintec Corp.'s Telemagic, Oakland, Calif.
• Brock Control Systems, Inc.'s Brock Activity Manager, Atlanta
• Contact Software International's Act, Carrollton, Texas
• Cornet, Inc.'s Corscan, Springfield, Va.
• Data System Support's SIRS, Orange, Calif.
• Delta Business Systems, Inc.'s Profits, Lanham, Md.
• GE Information Services, Engelwood, Colo.
• HWA International, Inc.'s ASIS, Memphis
• Lotus Development Corp.'s Notes, Cambridge, Mass.
• Market Power, Inc.'s Matrix, Nevada City, Calif.
• National Management Systems Ltd.'s Sales Manager's Workstation Builder, Vienna, Va.
• Richmond Technologies & Software, Inc.'s Maximizer, Burnaby, British Colombia
• SalesKit Software Corp., St. Louis
• Sales Technology, Inc.'s Snap, Manchester, N.H.
• Saratoga System's SPS, Campbell, Calif.
• Software of the Future, Inc.'s MarketForce Plus, Grand Prairie, Texas

FIGURE 9.16
The power of sales force automation. If properly designed to take advantage of powerful networks, databases, and desktop computers, automated sales force systems can deliver a wide range of capabilities. *From: "The Hardest Sell,"* Computerworld, *September 20, 1993.*

pictures (stored on the computer) but also might be able to show short video clips. The computer files will include up-to-date production data, allowing the salesperson to respond immediately to a customer's timing requests. Moreover, because the salesperson's computer carries all that data, the salesperson does not need to tie up the client's telephone trying to get cost or production data prior to closing a sale.

While the primary purpose of sales force automation systems is to support the sales force, the data for such a system either come from a number of other functions within the enterprise, including the more directly connected functions of sales management, territory management, customer service, sales forecasting, and marketing but also including such other functions as engineering, pro-

duction, product quality labs, general accounting (including credit and accounts receivable, and executive information systems) (see Chapter 16). SFAs usually offer the ability to forecast sales, to calculate commissions, and to adjust sales quotas, all while in the field. They also support team selling which is particularly valuable for large corporate accounts. They have proven to be valuable in generating new sales. For example, they aid in closing the sale on the spot because of the availability of production data and access to full pricing data so that the sales rep is able to respond immediately to a competitor's price. Companies have also found that after the installation of a sales force system, their current customer attrition rate drops.

Problems do exist with sales force automation systems. First, studies indi-

cate that a new system costs from $7500 to $15,000 per salesperson to develop. Once in place, they usually cost $2500 to $3500 per salesperson per year for maintenance and support. SFAs can be expensive, resulting in multimillion-dollar systems. Moreover, some companies install them without redesigning the sales function and other related functions. Without changing the way the sales staff works and the way the organization both supports the sales staff and makes use of sales data, that company will probably benefit very little from the new, expensive system. Applications that cut down on administrative time for sales reps don't automatically translate into more sales. Another key problem is the failure of top salespersons to use the system. Sales persons' strengths include individualism, a strong memory, and their people skills, and many reject the idea that carrying a laptop computer can help them.

Goodyear's North American tire division, with more than 500 sales staff, covers all the United States, from Maine to Hawaii, from Florida to Alaska. The sales force automation project began in early 1992. The major goal of the project was to boost the efficiency of marketing and sales departments, to make them more effective, and to boost customer relations (especially with the independent dealers). Management believed that the sales staff put in too much "windshield" time (hours spent traveling between home, office, and customers). Document communication was by regular mail, overnight delivery, and fax. The division management seldom was able to talk with the sales staff—after all, the division covered five time zones—and so they felt out of touch. The previous system tracked orders and deliveries on Goodyear's Amdahl mainframe running custom COBOL applications. As with many older mainframe systems, Goodyear's had very poor reporting and analysis features and was difficult to use. Moreover, it had no repository for institutional memory. According to Al Smith, president of Saratoga Systems Inc., of Campbell, California, a producer of the SPS sales automation system that Goodyear adopted, "When salespeople left, they took everything about the customer with them." Goodyear did expect to improve customer service and customer satisfaction. Management wanted the system to support their sales reps in assisting dealers with everything from advertising and sales, to business trends, cutting customer expenses, and running special events and promotions. They planned a system that would replace inadequate or absent technologies with an integrated sales and marketing system that would also work well with Goodyear's suite of financial applications.

Goodyear equipped its sales staff with laptop microcomputers, fax modems, and application and communication software. The core application of Goodyear's sales force automation system, dubbed Samis (Sales And Marketing Information System) is SPS. SPS distributes customer records to sales staffers, engineers, and technicians. The system also uses Metaphor, an IBM data access tool that extracts data from Samis and integrates it with the old COBOL executive information system (EIS). For communications software Goodyear used Advantis Passport.

With the new system, the sales person is able to download data from Goodyear's mainframe DB2 database in the morning into his or her laptop microcomputer, carry all the data needed that day in the laptop so that sales person will not normally need to go on-line during the day, and then upload any new data (orders, customer-contact reports, E-mail) in the evening. Samis also contains software to lighten the paperwork load, causing Dennis Connor, a salesperson who covers 23 dealerships in southern New Jersey and northern Delaware, to remark, "All the paperwork I once had weighing down my trunk now sits in this laptop computer." The sales staff can generate mailings to targeted customers; store small, useful details about the Goodyear dealer; and analyze data on shifts in consumer demand and in buying habits for the customer. The system supports key word searches in the DB2 database, enabling the sales staff in one area to learn about and monitor sales programs and promotions in other areas. Samis also supports the customers directly. For example, according to Jim McDonough, a Goodyear franchisee and owner of the Millburn, New Jersey, Tire & Auto Service, "We go on-line all the time to track my accruals." Finally, the system is much more than a laptop system. Middle management uses the system to communicate with the 26 sales offices and corporation management. In commenting on the overall value of the system to Goodyear, Al Eastwood, the corporate vice-president responsible for replacement sales to franchises and independent dealers, wondered how the company ever got along without Samis and compared it to trying to run the business prior to the invention of the telephone.

Goodyear's marketing department tracks how its staff uses the sales force automation system. According to Al Eastwood, Goodyear's VP responsible for replacement sales to franchisees and independent dealers, the company believes Samis is a worthwhile investment, even though its benefits can't be quantified. "How did you run your business before you could pick up a phone?" he asks.

Sources: Timothy Middleton, "Tire Maker Burns Rubber," *InformationWEEK*, October 31, 1994; Zachary Schiller, "And Fix That Flat Before You Go, Stanley," *Business Week*, January 16, 1995; Jack Falvey, "The Hottest Thing in Sales Since the Electric Fork," *The Wall Street Journal*, January 10, 1994; Michael Fitzgerald, "Users Trying Again with Sales Force Automation," *Computerworld*, November 28, 1994; and John W. Verity, "Taking a Laptop on Call," *Business Week*, October 25, 1993.

Case Study Questions

1. What problems did Goodyear face, and what competitive strategy did the company follow to address these problems?

2. How did sales force automation fit in with and contribute to its strategy? How did the fact that the Samis system was networked support Goodyear's strategy?

3. Evaluate both the benefits and shortcomings of the Samis system. How could it have better supported the company's strategic goals?

4. Evaluate the role of Samis in addressing the disgruntled small dealers and franchisees. Was this a successful move? Was Goodyear's overall strategy successful? Explain your answer.

5. What management, organization and technology issues had to be addressed when Goodyear implemented sales force automation?

References

Brandel, Mary. "Videoconferencing Slowly Goes Desktop." *Computerworld* (February 20, 1995).

Dertouzos, Michael. "Building the Information Marketplace." *Technology Review* (January 1991).

Donovan, John J. "Beyond Chief Information Officer to Network Manager." *Harvard Business Review* (September–October 1988).

Etzioni, Oren, and Daniel Weld. "A Softbot-Based Interface to the Internet." *Communications of the ACM* 37, no. 7 (July 1994).

Frye, Colleen. "Talking Heads: Coming to a Desktop Near You." *Software Magazine* (May 1995).

Gilder, George. "Into the Telecosm." *Harvard Business Review* (March–April 1991).

Grief, Irene. "Desktop Agents in Group-Enabled Projects." *Communications of the ACM* 37, no. 7 (July 1994).

Grover, Varun, and Martin D. Goslar. "Initiation, Adoption, and Implementation of Telecommunications Technologies in U.S. Organizations." *Journal of Management Information Systems* 10, no. 1 (Summer 1993).

Hall, Wayne A., and Robert E. McCauley. "Planning and Managing a Corporate Network Utility." *MIS Quarterly* (December 1987).

Hammer, Michael, and Glenn Mangurian. "The Changing Value of Communications Technology." *Sloan Management Review* (Winter 1987).

Hansen, James V., and Ned C. Hill. "Control and Audit of Electronic Data Interchange." *MIS Quarterly* 13, no. 4 (December 1989).

Imielinski, Tomasz, and B. R. Badrinath. "Mobile Wireless Computing: Challenges in Data Management." *Communications of the ACM* 37, no. 10 (October 1994).

Keen, Peter G. W. *Competing in Time*. Cambridge, MA: Ballinger (1986).

Keen, Peter G. W. *Shaping the Future: Business Design Through Information Technology*. Cambridge, MA: Harvard Business School Press (1991).

Keen, Peter G. W., and J. Michael Cummins. *Networks in Action: Business Choices and Telecommunications Decisions*. Belmont, CA: Wadsworth (1994).

Kim, B. G., and P. Wang. "ATM Network: Goals and Challenges." *Communications of the ACM* 38, no. 2 (February 1995).

Maes, Pattie. "Agents That Reduce Work and Information Overload." *Communications of the ACM* 37, no. 7 (July 1994).

Premkumar, G., K. Ramamurthy, and Sree Nilakanta. "Implementation of Electronic Data Interchange: An Innovation Diffusion Perspective." *Journal of Management Information Systems* 11, no. 2 (Fall 1994).

Railing, Larry, and Tom Housel. "A Network Infrastructure to Contain Costs and Enable Fast Response." *MIS Quarterly* 14, no. 4 (December 1990).

Roche, Edward M. *Telecommunications and Business Strategy*. Chicago: Dryden Press (1991).

Rochester, Jack B. "Networking Management: The Key to Better Customer Service." *I/S Analyzer* 27, no. 12 (December 1989).

Rowe, Stanford H. II. *Business Telecommunications*. New York: Macmillan (1991).

Schultz, Brad. "The Evolution of ARPANET." *Datamation* (August 1, 1988).

Selker, Ted. "Coach: A Teaching Agent That Learns." *Communications of the ACM* 37, no. 7 (July 1994).

Torkzadeh, Gholamreza, and Weidong Xia. "Managing Telecommunications Strategy by Steering Committee." *MIS Quarterly* 16, no. 2 (June 1992).

Vetter, Ronald J. "ATM Concepts, Architectures, and Protocols." *Communications of the ACM* 38, no. 2 (February 1995).

Chapter 10

Enterprise-wide Computing and Networking

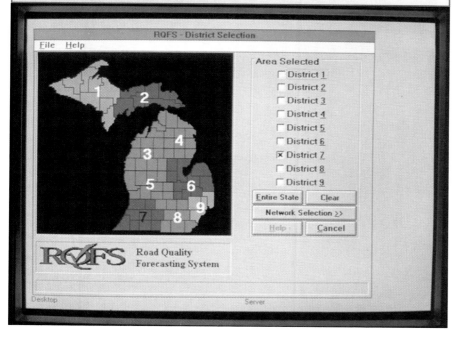

Michigan Transportation Department Reinvents with Networked Computers

Managing all public transportation for the state of Michigan is a big business, with big business challenges. With 3600 employees and an annual budget exceeding $1 billion, the Michigan Department of Transportation (MDOT) had difficulty meeting its customers' needs. When the state legislature, for example, asked how a proposed gasoline tax increase would benefit the transportation system, MDOT had no idea. It just couldn't pull the numbers together using its old mainframe-based information systems.

MDOT management knew it had to reinvent the department. It asked fundamental questions, such as "Why are we in business? What is our mission?" It wanted MDOT to be able to examine all of the state's transportation needs, not just highways. It realized that MDOT had to communicate a lot better within the department in order to communicate better with its customers. So MDOT started moving toward more networked systems based on microcomputers and workstations and unplugging its mainframe. Management began implementing systems based on client/server computing to provide staff members with more immediate access to the data they needed.

Using client/server technology, MDOT developed a strategic Road Quality and Forecasting System that furnishes project managers and pavement engineers with a graphical view of Michigan's roadway infrastructure and upcoming maintenance needs. Engineers using micros can select a geographic area and "try out" various maintenance strategies at their desktops. They can ask the system for the costs and expected life span of various improvements on any number of miles of road. The system instantly shows what Michigan's road network will look like in ten, twenty, or thirty years.

Another client/server application called the Financial Obligation System allows anyone working on a project to access job information using a desktop micro. The network transmits the project manager's funding requests directly to MDOT's program control section. The system checks information automatically before routing it to an accountant, who makes spending decisions directly online. The accountant then routes the requests digitally to the federal highway office in Washington, DC, which has communications links to MDOT. Before this system was implemented, the requisition and approval process used to average four to six weeks. The time lag put MDOT in a financial bind. MDOT had no way of knowing what its federal account balances were. Managers would sometimes have to proceed without approval and pay bills out of the state coffer until the federal funds came in. Now the process can be completed in only 24 hours.

By redesigning its information systems using networks and client/server computing, the Michigan Department of Transportation was able to reduce its work force by 20 percent while increasing the number of programs it handled. ∎

Source: "Michigan Department of Transportation" in "Business Solutions from the New Computer Industry," Intel Corporation, 1994.

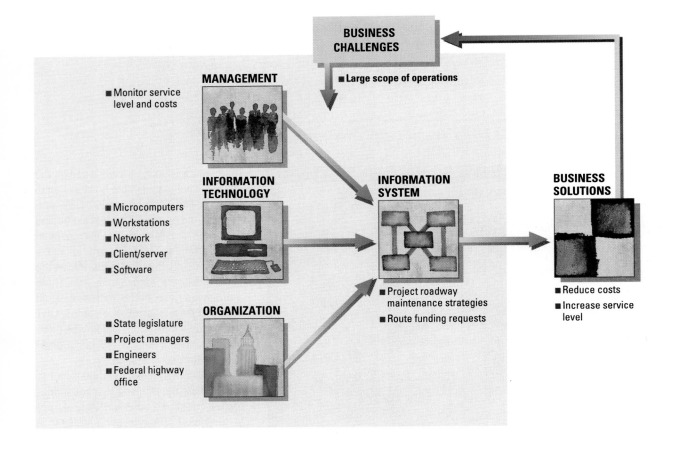

The Michigan Department of Transportation is one of many organizations that has rearranged its hardware, software, and communications capabilities into an enterprise-wide networked architecture. In the process, it transformed itself into a more efficient, effective organization. Instead of relying fundamentally on large centralized mainframe computers for processing, MDOT distributed computing power and information to powerful microcomputers and workstations on the desktop at many different locations. It divided the computer processing for various applications among desktop and larger computers. MDOT tied all of its computers together into a company-wide network and developed communications links to other organizations.

By putting more control of computer processing on the desktop and linking mainframes, minicomputers, and smaller networks into a companywide network, enterprise-wide computing can help organizations achieve new levels of competitiveness and productivity. However, achieving these goals requires an understanding of how to make disparate hardware, software, and communications devices work together.

This chapter examines the components of enterprise-wide computing systems and the technical, economic, and business forces that have shaped them. It also examines the Internet, which links networks from many different organizations so that they can share information with each other. The key to creating networks where users can share data throughout the organization is connectivity. This chapter describes the connectivity models organizations use to link their systems and the standards that make such linkages possible.

Despite the benefits of distributing computing power to the desktop and linking networks, enterprise-wide computing has created new management problems. We describe the problems and their solutions so that organizations can maximize the benefits of client/server architecture.

After completing this chapter, you will be able to:

Learning Objectives

1. Describe the characteristics of enterprise-wide computing.

2. Define the client/server model of computing and explain the roles of clients and servers within this model.

3. Explain why organizations are adopting client/server computing.

4. Define the Internet and describe both the benefits it offers organiza-

tions and the problems it presents to them.

5. Describe important standards used for linking hardware, software, and networks to achieve connectivity.

6. Identify problems posed by enterprise-wide computing and recommend solutions.

10.1   ENTERPRISE-WIDE COMPUTING

enterprise-wide computing An arrangement of the organization's hardware, software, telecommunications, and data resources to put more computing power on the desktop and create a company-wide network linking many smaller networks.

In Chapter 1 we defined information architecture as the particular form that information technology takes in an organization to achieve selected goals. An organization's information architecture consists of its computer hardware and software, telecommunications links, and data files. In **enterprise-wide computing** the components of the information architecture are arranged to place more of the organization's computing power on the desktop and to create networks that link entire enterprises.

ENTERPRISE-WIDE NETWORKING

Figure 10.1 illustrates the implementation of enterprise-wide computing at the Michigan Department of Transportation (MDOT) described in the opening vignette. The systems on the network manage all public transportation within the state. As the diagram shows, the MDOT employees may work at its headquarters, its central campus, or any one of a number of remote campuses or district offices, all of which are networked within their own site. The enterprise-wide network links all of these local sites, their workers, and their information, together into one large network. Operating

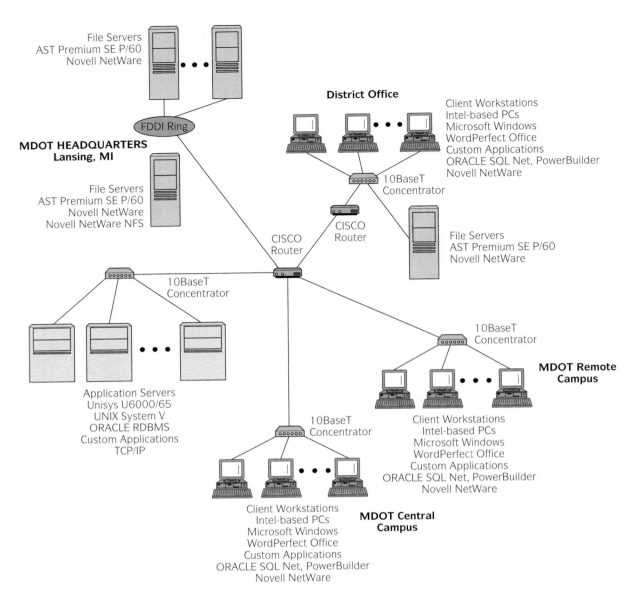

FIGURE 10.1
Enterprise-wide computing at the Michigan Department of Transportation. MDOT's enterprise-wide network links desktop workstations and file servers at remote sites, district offices, and the MDOT headquarters. *Adapted from: "Business Solutions from the New Computer Industry," INTEL 22 a Special Report sponsored by Intel. © Intel Corporation, 1994. Reprinted by permission.*

on these networks are a range of hardware, from Unisys mainframes and various computers acting as servers, to desktop microcomputers and workstations running a wide range of software that employees use to perform their work. With the previous mainframe-centered system, employees had difficulty in both obtaining and using the data they needed to do their jobs. Today, project managers, engineers, regulatory compliance specialists, the purchasing department, in fact virtually all the MDOT employees, are able to access the data they need, regardless of where they are stored, and to manipulate and display them in effective ways using the tools they prefer.

In earlier information systems, mainframes and minicomputers from the same computer manufacturer, using proprietary operating systems, were responsible for most of the firm's information processing. Microcomputers and workstations were used independently by individual users or were linked into small localized networks.

By adopting an enterprise-wide information architecture, Michigan's Department of Transportation now uses a mixture of computer hardware supplied by different hardware vendors. Much of the firms' computer processing takes place on the desktop. The role of the mainframes and minicomputers is diminished and more specialized. Large, complex databases that need central storage are found on mainframes, minis, or specialized file servers, while smaller databases and parts of large databases are loaded on microcomputers and workstations.

Professionals who use a desktop machine are in greater control of the firm's information resources considered as the sum total of the firm's software, hardware, and data. The system is a network. In fact, for all but the smallest organizations the system is composed of multiple networks. A high-capacity backbone network connects many local area networks and devices. The backbone may be connected to many external networks like the Internet. The linking of separate networks, each of which retains its own identity, into an interconnected network is called **internetworking**.

THE CLIENT/SERVER MODEL OF COMPUTING

In enterprise-wide networking, the primary way of delivering computing power to the desktop is known as the client/server model. In the **client/server model** of computing, data and processing power are distributed out into the enterprise rather than being centrally controlled. A client/server system is a user-centric system that emphasizes the user's interaction with the data. Client/server computing splits processing between "clients" and "servers." Both are on the network, but each machine is assigned functions it is best suited to perform. Ideally, the user will experience the network as a single system with all functions, both client and server, integrated and accessible. The **client** is the user point-of-entry for the required function and is normally a desktop computer, a workstation, or a laptop computer. The user generally interacts directly only with the client portion of the application, typically through a graphical user interface. He or she uses it to input data and query a database to retrieve data. Once the data have been retrieved, the user can analyze and report on them, using fourth-generation packages such as spreadsheets, word processors, and graphics applications available on the client machine on his or her own desktop. The **server** satisfies some or all of the user's request for data and/or functionality and might be anything from a supercomputer or mainframe to another desktop computer. Servers store and process shared data and also perform back-end functions not visible to users, such as managing peripheral devices and controlling access to shared databases (see Figure 10.2).

Figure 10.3 illustrates five different ways that the components of an application could be partitioned between the client and the server. The *presentation* component is essentially the application interface—how the application appears visually to the user. The *application logic* component consists of the processing logic, which is shaped by the organization's business rules. (An example might be that a salaried employee is only to be paid monthly.) The *data management* component consists of the storage and management of the data used by the application.

The client/server model requires that application programs be written as two or more separate software components that run on different machines but that appear to operate as a single application. The exact division of tasks depends on the requirements of each application including its processing needs, the number of users, and the available resources. For example, client tasks for a large corporate payroll might include inputting data (such as enrolling new employees and recording hours worked), submitting data queries to the server, analyzing the retrieved data, and displaying results (in character or graphics format) on the screen or on a printer. The server portion will fetch the entered data and process the payroll (weekly and/or monthly). It will also control access so that only users with appropriate security can view or update the data. In the Michigan Department of Transportation network, the

---

internetworking The linking of separate networks, each of which retains its own identity, into an interconnected network.

client/server model A model for computing that splits the processing between "clients" and "servers" on a network, assigning functions to the machine most able to perform the function.

client The user point-of-entry for the required function. Normally a desktop computer, a workstation, or a laptop computer, the user generally interacts directly only with the client, typically through a graphical user interface, using it to input and retrieve data, and to analyze and report on them.

server Satisfies some or all of the user's request for data and/or functionality, such as storing and processing shared data and performing back-end functions not visible to users, such as managing peripheral devices and controlling access to shared databases. It might be anything from a supercomputer or mainframe to another desktop computer.

FIGURE 10.2
The client-server model of computing. In the client/server model, computer processing is split between client machines and server machines, with each machine handling those tasks for which it is best suited. Users interface with the client machines. Client/server machines afford great customization and processing power.

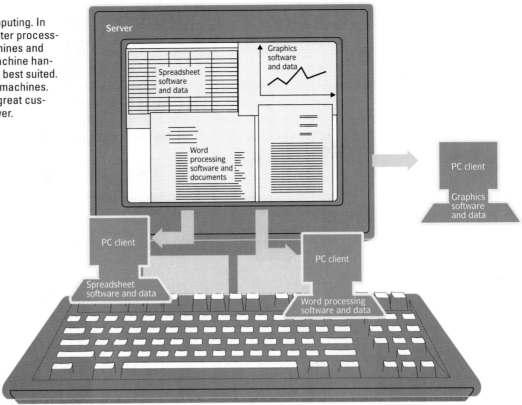

clients are fully functional microcomputers and the servers are specialized mainframes, workstations, and microcomputers.

The client/server model does have limitations. It is difficult to write software that divides processing among clients and servers, although more and more client/server software is commercially available. A specific server can get bogged down quickly when too many users simultaneously want service. In this case, however, only those using that specific server are affected, rather than the whole organization as in the

FIGURE 10.3
Types of client/server computing. There are a variety of ways in which the presentation, application logic, and data management components of an application can be divided among the clients and servers in a network. *Source: "Discover the Fountain of Youth: How to Revitalize Host Systems for Client/Server Computing," "Attachmate" advertising section, DATAMATION Magazine, April 1, 1995. Reprinted by permission of the Gartner Group.*

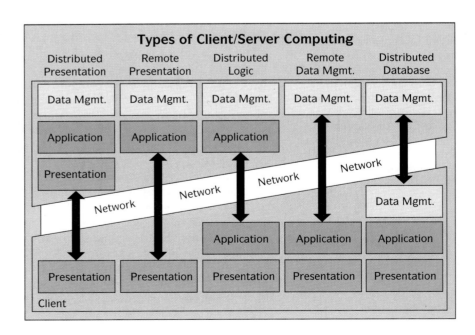

old, centralized architecture. (However, replacing the server or supplementing it by adding another server is far less expensive and much more quickly accomplished than replacing mainframes under the old architecture.) In addition, microcomputers with independent processing power are more difficult to coordinate and administer on a network. As organizations continue to struggle with this problem, their growing experience is combining with improvements in network management software to make networks more manageable.

BUSINESS DRIVERS OF CLIENT/SERVER COMPUTING

Businesses have adopted enterprise-wide networking and client/server computing for many reasons. We describe the major influences that have pushed firms to shift computing capabilities to the desktop and to arrange their resources into information systems that span the entire organization.

Economies of Technology

The enhanced power of microprocessors coupled with falling prices and reliable and accessible communications mechanisms make it both technically and economically feasible to transfer computing power to workers' desktops and to arrange resources into client/server-based information systems. Today's microcomputer machines are as powerful as the mainframe computers of the mid-1980s. Micros and workstations provide desktop computing power and can act as servers in networks, assuming the role formerly filled exclusively by mainframes and minicomputers. Moreover, these desktop machines provide capabilities lacking in traditional mainframes—graphical user interfaces, productivity promoting software such as spreadsheets and word processors, access to commercial on-line information services (see Chapter 9), and interactive audio-visual computing involving multiple media such as sound, moving pictures, and text.

Powerful microprocessors, along with new software and hardware techniques for data transmission and delivery, have also promoted the availability and economy of telecommunications networks for delivering information to desktop machines in businesses and homes. In the 1990s, technology for wireless networks will expand communications capabilities even more through the use of hand-held computers and the exploitation of the cellular telephone network and underutilized radio bandwidths.

Emergence of Knowledge- and Information-based Economies

In knowledge and information-based economies, more workers create or work with information than create or work with their hands. Knowledge and information workers such as engineers, scientists, designers, architects, accountants, or attorneys require easy access to all kinds of information. Client/server systems enhance their productivity and effectiveness by placing that information at their finger tips through their powerful desktop computers and access to the wealth of resources available from digital information services and networks. Chapter 15 describes specific desktop applications used in knowledge work and further explores the role of knowledge work in the organization.

Globalization of the World's Economies

Today companies need seamless communications with their customers, suppliers, and staff, wherever they are, anywhere in the world. Client/server technology is making that communication faster, easier, and less costly. Client/server networks are being used to support coordination between, for example, a product designer in Johannesburg, a component manufacturer in Hong Kong, the product assembler in Mexico, and marketers headquartered in San Francisco and Berlin. More and more companies are also turning to client/server-based on-line systems to offer quick, accurate, low-cost technical customer support (see, for example, our discussions on customer support later in this section and in Section 10.2).

Downsizing for Less Bureaucratic, More Competitive Organizations

The intensely competitive business environment that has emerged in the past decade has resulted in organizations that are flatter—that is, they have fewer levels of management. Lower-level employees, both staff and line, have significantly increased decision-making authority, and workers function more often as members of a team. In addition, the whole business cycle of competition has sped up. A client/server platform intuitively reflects this new business environment better than the old mainframe environment. A client/server infrastructure is more decentralized and able to deliver more information at all organizational levels. The person using a networked desktop computer has more control over his or her own work. Networked computers also allow teams to work closely together, even when members of those teams are hundreds or thousands of miles apart. Moreover, a networked platform is significantly more flexible technology than is a centralized mainframe platform.

In addition, client/server technology is flexible enough to support a nimble organization because it can be transformed rapidly in response to changing competitive needs of the current marketplace. Networks are composed of standardized parts that can quickly be added to connect new team members or even a whole new team. Should the power of an individual's computer prove to be inadequate, it can be replaced or upgraded, normally with no interruption of service and usually at a relatively low cost. Even adding a few hundred or a few thousand staff members to a network can be done in several weeks or months without degradation of service. Adding that many to a mainframe computer might require a major upgrade project that would consume a year or more.

Richmond Savings, the $1.1 billion (Canadian) full service bank of Richmond, British Columbia, has been running all its systems on networked workstations since 1988. The system performs virtually all of the normal banking functions, including automatic payroll deposits, ATMs, even touch-tone balance inquiries. The average measured transaction time is only a quarter of a second using three hundred fifty 386 computers in the bank's 10 branches. According to management, the networked system makes the bank more nimble. For example, it added a touch-tone bill-payment subsystem in 1994 with no degradation of service, although it handles as many as 4000 bills per month. Because of the system, the bank staff was able to change from narrow departmental specialists to full personal bankers who are able to handle all tasks. Bank procedures have changed accordingly (Celko, 1994).

Independent Telecommunications Network Inc. (ITN), an $18 million Overland Park, Kansas, provider of telephone company billing and credit service, installed client/server-based accounting systems because the company is growing fast and needs systems that can grow with it. The systems run on a central server where the data are also stored. The client/server system allows employees to access the data wherever they are and use whichever desktop computer they are already using (including Apples, IBM compatibles, and UNIX workstations). The number of users can easily be expanded as the company grows.

The new business environment requires that employees be more productive, a goal that client/server systems can also help to fulfill. Conversion to a client/server system can support and even stimulate streamlining of business processes (see Chapter 11). Sun Microsystems of Palo Alto, California, a leading producer of workstations, turned to the client/server model when it decided to renovate its financial systems. In designing the new system, Sun realized it had to overhaul its accounting department. Instead of a centralized department relying upon a centralized system with frozen printed reports, 200 users worldwide are able to customize and analyze the data in graphic format. The process of moving to client/server computing also revealed many process bottlenecks. Ultimately Sun cut head count substantially while reducing its time to close its books from 23 days to 8 days.

Customer service is a vital element in a company's ability to compete today. Many companies are moving to client/server systems primarily to improve their ability to service and support their customers. Merrill Lynch, the New York-based financial services giant, allocates to its clients billions of dollars in mortgage forwards every month. To complete its monthly allocations, the company must deliver lists of securities, receive back commitments, and settle the transactions, all within a very short period of time. Previously, two days before the trades, the sales force, traders, and support staff all disrupted their normal work to deliver lists to customers via telephones and faxes. The whole process was error prone with lists being lost and numbers transposed. Today, the new client/server-based system selects the mortgage pool data from the company's trading systems, compiles the lists, and distributes them to clients through direct E-mail and fax links. The system monitors all trades real-time so all involved, including Merrill Lynch customers, get up-to-date information. The system has been so successful that Merrill Lynch is considering installing a similar system for stock trading.

Cost Savings

Perhaps the single most important stimulus to the early spread of client/server technology was the belief that it lowered costs. The cost of MIPS (millions of instructions per second), a popular measure of processing power, is about 100 times greater on mainframes than on microcomputers. Thus, a company needing to increase its processing power can do so at a much lower cost by turning to microcomputers. However, the initial outlay is only one of the costs a company needs to examine, and while many companies claim major cost savings, others are doubtful. Moreover, benefits, such as new sales resulting from easier access to data, are difficult to quantify. We examine the issue of costs in Section 10.4.

10.2   THE INTERNET

An increasingly important way that both public and private organizations are networking internally and with other organizations is through the Internet. The Internet is perhaps the most well-known—and the largest—implementation of internetworking, linking thousands of individual networks all over the world. The Internet has a range of capabilities that can provide many benefits to organizations.

WHAT IS THE INTERNET?

Internet An international network of networks connecting over 20 million people from 100 countries; it is the largest "information superhighway" in the world.

While no generally agreed-upon definition of the **Internet** exists, we can say with certainty that it is an international network of networks, rather than one big network. Estimates indicate over 31,000 different networks from more than 100 countries were connected by the spring 1995, and that it is used by more than 20 million people around the world in education, science, government, and business (Leiner, 1994). The Internet has capabilities that organizations can use to exchange information internally or to communicate externally with other organizations.

For most of its history, the Internet (often referred to simply as the Net) almost exclusively connected scientists and academicians and was used neither by business (except as it related to research) nor by the general public. It began as a United States Department of Defense network to link scientists and university professors around the world. Even today individuals cannot directly connect to the Net, although anyone with a computer and a modem and the willingness to pay a small monthly usage fee can access it through one of the many service providers that are popping up everywhere. Individuals can also access it through such popular on-line services as

CompuServe, Prodigy, and America Online. (Microsoft and IBM are releasing new versions of their microcomputer operating systems with built-in Internet gateways.)

For most people, one of the most puzzling aspects of the Internet is that no one owns it and it has no formal management organization. As a creation of the Defense Department for sharing research data, this lack of centralization was purposeful, to make it less vulnerable to wartime or terrorist attacks. To join the Internet, an existing network need only to pay a small registration fee and agree to certain standards based on TCP/IP (Transmission Control Protocol/Internet Protocol, described in Section 10.3). Costs are low because the Internet owns nothing and so has no real costs to offset. Each organization, of course, pays for its own networks and its own telephone bills, but those costs usually exist independent of the Internet. Networks that join the Internet must agree to move each other's traffic at no charge to the others, much as is the case with mail delivered through the international postal system. This is the reason all the data appear to move at the cost of a local telephone call. The result of all this is that the cost of E-mail and other Internet connections tends to be far lower than equivalent voice, postal, or overnight delivery costs, making the Net a very inexpensive communications medium.

The value of the Internet lies precisely in its ability easily and inexpensively to connect so many diverse people from so many places all over the globe. Anyone who has an Internet address can log on to a computer and reach virtually every other computer on the network, regardless of location, computer type, or operating system. The Internet carries many kinds of traffic and provides users with many functions. We will now briefly describe the most important functions.

Communication, including E-mail, is the most widely used function on the Internet. Many millions of messages are exchanged daily worldwide on E-mail systems, creating a productivity gain that observers have compared to Gutenberg's development of movable type in the fifteenth century. Private individuals typically use the Net E-mail facilities to keep in touch with friends, to gather opinions from other users about a product they are interested in purchasing, to argue political issues, or to talk about anything else people discuss in person, on the telephone, or through the mail. Researchers use this facility to share ideas, information, even documents. The Net has made possible many collaborative research and writing projects using E-mail, even though the participants are thousands of miles apart.

Internet communication functions related to E-mail include on-line forums and chatting. The Internet supports thousands of public forums that operate like electronic bulletin boards on almost any conceivable topic. The Net also supports live, interactive conversations called "chatting" with others anywhere in the world, much as people might do via a telephone conference call, although with the Net the words must be typed in rather than spoken. Anyone interested in chatting can list the names/topics of the hundreds of currently active chat sessions and then join in on one.

Information retrieval is a second basic Internet function. Hundreds of library catalogs are on-line through the Internet, including those of such giants as the Library of Congress, the University of California, and Harvard University. In addition, users are able to search thousands of databases that have been opened to the public by corporations, governments, and nonprofit organizations, databases containing information such as the Central Intelligence Agency's world almanac, the latest satellite weather photos (updated hourly), science fiction reviews, and a molecular biology library. Individuals can gather information on almost any conceivable topic stored in these databases and libraries. For example, teachers interested in finding information on hyperactive children can quickly and easily search computer databases and locate many articles, papers, books, and even conference reports from universities and other organizations all over the world. They can then download the information for their reading and use at their leisure. Other Net users may want to download several years of gold trading statistics from the United States Department of Commerce or see university course offerings in Germany. Many use the Internet

World Wide Web A set of standards for storing, retrieving, formatting, and displaying information using a client/server architecture, graphical user interfaces, and a hypertext language that enables dynamic links to other documents.

to locate and download some of the free, quality computer software that has been made available by developers on computers all over the world.

Easy-to-use offerings of information and products is a third and relatively new function of the Internet. This function, provided by the **World Wide Web** (the Web), is at the heart of the recent explosion in the business use of the Net. The Web is actually a set of standards for storing, retrieving, formatting, and displaying information using a client/server architecture. The Web uses graphical user interfaces for easy viewing. It is based upon a hypertext language called Hypertext Markup Language (HTML) that formats documents and incorporates dynamic links to other documents and pictures stored in the same or remote computers. Using these links, all the user need do is point at a key word, click on it, and immediately be transported to another document, probably on another computer somewhere else in the world. Corporations, for example, offer product technical information, retailers offer goods for sale, public interest groups offer information on issues of concern to the public, and individuals may offer resumés to companies seeking to fill positions.

In the next section we will look a little more closely at specific Internet capabilities that support these functions.

INTERNET CAPABILITIES

One technical aspect of the Net central to understanding its capabilities is its reliance upon client/server technology. Users of the Net control what they do through client applications, using graphical user interfaces or character-based products that control all functions. All the data, including E-mail messages and databases, are stored on servers. Servers dedicated to the Internet or even to specific Internet functions are the heart of the information on the Net.

In addition to communications functions, major Internet capabilities include gophers, Archie, WAIS, Usenet, and the World Wide Web. These are all standards and tools to retrieve and offer information. Table 10.1 lists these capabilities and describes the functions they support.

People-to-People Communications

Internet communication capabilities include E-mail Usenet Newsgroups, Chatting, and Telnet.

ELECTRONIC MAIL (E-MAIL). E-mail is the heart of the Internet because most other functions on the Net rely upon the E-mail and/or the computer address to make

Table 10.1	Major Internet Capabilities
Capability	Functions Supported
E-mail	Person-to-person messaging; document sharing
Usenet newsgroups	Discussion groups on electronic bulletin boards
Chatting	Interactive conversations
Telnet	Log on to one computer system and do work on another
Gophers	Locate textual information using a hierarchy of menus
Archie	Search database of documents, software, and data files available for downloading
WAIS	Locate files in databases using keywords
World Wide Web	Retrieve, format, and display information (including text, audio, graphics, and video) using hyptertext links

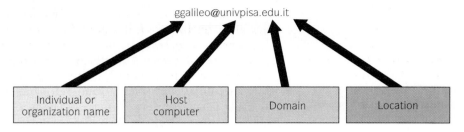

ggalileo@univpisa.edu.it

| Individual or organization name | Host computer | Domain | Location |

FIGURE 10.4

Analysis of an Internet address. The portion of the address to the left of the @ symbol in Net E-mail addresses is the name or identifier of the specific individual or organization. To the right is the computer address. The address may end in either a country indicator (such as 'ja' for Japan), or with a function indicator such as 'com' for a commercial organization or 'edu' for an educational institution. In English, the E-mail address of physicist and astronomer Galileo Galilei would be translated as "G. Galileo @ University of Pisa, educational institution, Italy."

the connections necessary to perform that function. Figure 10.4 illustrates the components of an Internet E-mail address.

The Net has become the most important E-mail system in the world because it connects so many people from all over the world. Writers and scientists use it to collaborate on their work, sales staff use it to keep in touch with their home offices and customers, lawyers use it to communicate with their clients and with each other, and corporations use it to keep in touch with remote sites. Dr. Brendan McKay, a scientist and member of the faculty of the Australian National University in Canberra, carries out his research in collaboration with Dr. Stanislaw Radziszowsky at the Rochester Institute of Technology in Rochester, New York. The two have exchanged over 1000 messages in three years, working together much as they would if they were only a few miles apart. With proper software, the user will find it easy to attach documents and files when sending a message to someone or to broadcast a message to a predefined group. (Broad, 1993; Quarterman, 1993).

Usenet Forums in which people share information and ideas on a defined topic through large electronic bulletin boards where anyone can post messages on the topic for others to see and respond to.

USENET NEWSGROUPS (FORUMS). **Usenet** newsgroups are worldwide discussion groups in which people share information and ideas on a defined topic such as colorimetry or rock bands. Discussion takes place in large electronic bulletin boards where anyone can post messages on the topic for others to see. Over 10,000 such groups exist on almost any conceivable topic. However, each Usenet site is financed independently and controlled by a site administrator, who carries only those groups that he or she chooses. Newsgroups are open so that the discussions sometimes become quite scattered, but many have proven to be very useful. Many of the newsgroups that are seen on the Internet are also available on other networks and information services.

chatting Live, interactive conversations over a public network.

CHATTING. **Chatting** allows people who are on the computer simultaneously to hold live, interactive conversations. The more popular use for this facility today is discussion forums on listed topics, similar to the Usenet forums except far more limited in numbers. Only people who happen to be signed on at the same time are able to talk because messages are not stored. On the other hand, this function can be an effective business tool if people who can benefit from interactive conversations set a specific appointment to meet and talk on a particular topic. The limitation of this is that the topic is open to all without security so that intruders can participate.

Telnet Network tool that allows someone to log on to one computer system while doing work on another.

TELNET. We have included **Telnet** in this section because it allows someone to be on one computer system while doing work on another. Telnet is the protocol that establishes an error-free, rapid link between the two computers, allowing you, for example, to log on to your home computer from a remote computer when you are on the road or working from your home. You can also log on to and use third-party

A computer scientist updates pages on the World Wide Web at CERN, a European particle physics laboratory. By enabling scientists and other professionals to exchange ideas and research instantaneously, the Internet has accelerated the pace of scientific collaboration and the spread of knowledge.

computers that have been made accessible to the public, such as using the catalog of the United States Library of Congress. Telnet will use the computer address you supply to locate the computer you want to reach and connect you to it. You will, of course, have to log in and go through any security procedures you, your company, or the third-party computer owner have in place to protect that computer.

Information Retrieval on the Internet

Because the Internet is a voluntary, decentralized effort with no central listing of participants or sites, much less a listing of the data located at all those sites, its major problem is finding what you need from among the vast storehouses of data found in databases and libraries literally all over the world. Here we will introduce major methods of accessing computers and locating the files you need.

gopher A character-oriented tool for locating data on the Internet that enables the user to locate essentially all textual information stored on Internet servers through a series of easy-to-use, hierarchical menus.

GOPHERS. Gophers are a character-oriented approach to solving that problem (although some now use a graphical interface). A **gopher** is a client/server tool that enables the user to locate essentially all textual information stored on Internet servers through a series of easy-to-use, hierarchical menus. The Internet has thousands of gopher server sites throughout the world. Each gopher site contains its own system of menus listing subject-matter topics, local files, and other relevant gopher sites. One gopher site might have as many as several thousand listings within various levels of its menus. When you, the user, initiate the gopher software in search of a specific topic and select a related item from a menu, the server will automatically transfer you to the appropriate file on that server or to the selected server wherever in the world it is located. Once on the distant server, the process continues—you are presented with more menus of files and other gopher site servers that might interest you. In this way, although you usually cannot go straight to the locale you want (unless you already know where the information is and have the Internet address of that locale), you can move from site to site, locating information that you want anywhere in the world, accomplished via a system of easy-to-understand menus and point-and-click interfaces rather than using a character-based arcane computer language. When you

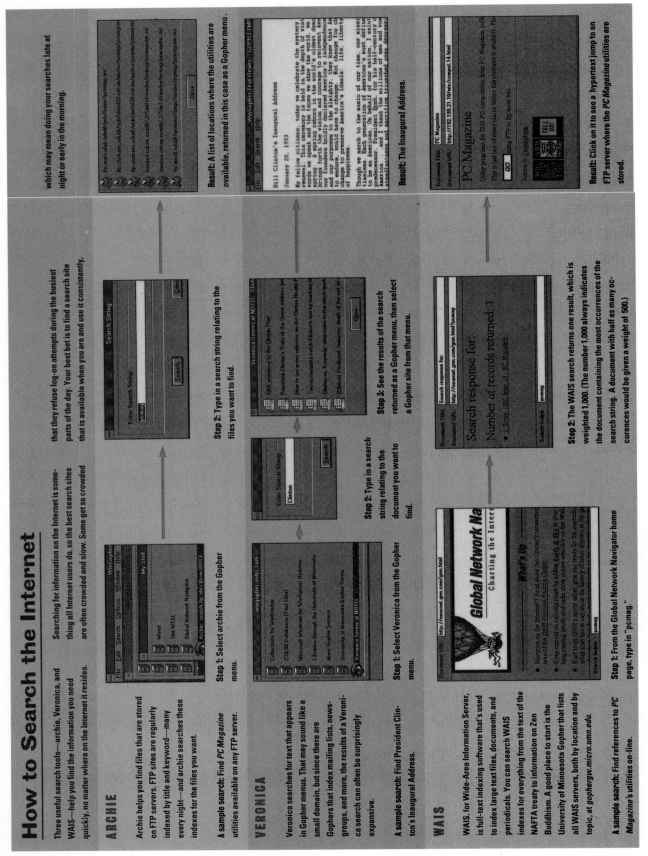

How to Search the Internet

Three useful search tools—archie, Veronica, and WAIS—help you find the information you need quickly, no matter where on the Internet it resides.

Searching for information on the Internet is something all Internet users do, so the best search sites are often crowded and slow. Some get so crowded that they refuse log-on attempts during the busiest parts of the day. Your best bet is to find a search site that is available when you are and use it consistently, which may mean doing your searches late at night or early in the morning.

ARCHIE

Archie helps you find files that are stored on FTP servers. FTP sites are regularly indexed by title and keyword—many every night—and archie searches these indexes for the files you want.

A sample search: Find *PC Magazine* utilities available on any FTP server.

Step 1: Select archie from the Gopher menu.

Step 2: Type in a search string relating to the files you want to find.

Result: A list of locations where the utilities are available, returned in this case as a Gopher menu.

VERONICA

Veronica searches for text that appears in Gopher menus. That may sound like a small domain, but since there are Gophers that index mailing lists, newsgroups, and more, the results of a Veronica search can often be surprisingly expansive.

A sample search: Find President Clinton's Inaugural Address.

Step 1: Select Veronica from the Gopher menu.

Step 2: Type in a search string relating to the document you want to find.

Step 3: See the results of the search returned as a Gopher menu, then select a Gopher site from that menu.

Result: The Inaugural Address.

WAIS

WAIS, for Wide-Area Information Server, is full-text indexing software that's used to index large text files, documents, and periodicals. You can search WAIS indexes for everything from the text of the NAFTA treaty to information on Zen Buddhism. A good place to start is the University of Minnesota Gopher that lists all WAIS servers, both by location and by topic, at *gophergw.micro.umn.edu.*

A sample search: Find references to *PC Magazine*'s utilities on-line.

Step 1: From the Global Network Navigator home page, type in "pcmag."

Step 2: The WAIS search returns one result, which is weighted 1,000. (The number 1,000 always indicates the document containing the most occurrences of the search string. A document with half as many occurrences would be given a weight of 500.)

Result: Click on it to see a hypertext jump to an FTP server where the *PC Magazine* utilities are stored.

Archie, Veronica, and Wide-Area Information Servers (WAIS) are powerful Internet search tools that help users find the information they need wherever it resides. *Adapted from "How to Search the Internet," PC Magazine, October 11, 1994. Reprinted with permission.*

do find information or files you want, you are free to browse, read them on-line, or download them onto your own computer for more leisurely reading or printing. Veronica is an additional capability for searching for text that appears in gopher menus.

ARCHIE. **Archie** addresses the same problem differently through a search of an actual database of documents, software, and data files available for downloading from servers around the world. While no individual Archie database can list more than a very tiny percentage of the files in the world, clicking on a relevant listing from one Archie server will bring you to another computer system where relevant files are stored. There, the Archie server may have yet other relevant references, allowing you to continue your search for pertinent files, moving from database to database, library to library, until you locate what you need. Archie database searches use subject key words you enter, such as "Beijing," "telecommuting," "polymers," or "inflation," resulting in a list of sites that contain files on that topic. Through Archie you are even able to search the catalogs of more than 300 on-line college, university, and government libraries around the world (half of which are outside the United States). Of course, once you find files you want, you may use a file transfer program to download them.

WAIS. **WAIS** (Wide Area Information Servers) is yet a third way to handle the problem of locating files around the world. WAIS is the most thorough way to locate a specific file, but it requires that you know the name of the databases you want searched. Once you specify specific database names and key identifying words, WAIS searches for the key words in all the files in those databases. When the search has been completed, you will be given a menu listing all the files that contain your key words.

The World Wide Web

The World Wide Web—known simply as the Web, or sometimes referred to as WWW or W3—is actually another information retrieval tool similar to gophers, Archie, and WAIS. However, the Web requires special attention in this text because it has had an enormous impact on the commercial use of the Net. The Web is attractive, is easy to use, and lends itself to publishing or providing information to anyone interested. It was originally developed to allow collaborators in remote sites to share their ideas on all aspects of a common project. If the Web were used for two independent projects and later relationships were found between the projects, information could flow smoothly between the projects without making major changes (Berners-Lee et al., 1994).

Those who offer information through the Web must first establish a **home page**—a text and graphical screen display that welcomes the user and explains the organization that has established the page. For most organizations, the home page will lead the user to other pages, with all the pages of a company being known as a *Web site*. For a corporation to establish a presence on the Web, therefore, it must set up a Web site of one or more pages. Figure 10.5 illustrates both the structural and navigational architecture of the Web, showing how it can be used to access information supplied by Datamation magazine.

While the other methods of locating information on the Net are text-based, the Web pages have made such a dramatic impact by combining text, hypermedia, graphics, and sound. Together they can handle all types of digital communication while making it easy to link resources that are half-a-world apart. Graphics allow organizations to communicate more effectively, making their material not only more appealing but also more informative and easier to grasp. Hypermedia (see Chapter 8) provides a point-and-click connection to related information within the same document, between documents on the same computer, or to documents located on another computer anywhere in the world (as long as that computer is also connected

Archie A tool for locating data on the Internet that performs key-word searches of an actual database of documents, software, and data files available for downloading from servers around the world.

WAIS Wide Area Information Servers, a tool for locating data on the Internet that requires the name of the databases to be searched based upon key words.

home page A World Wide Web text and graphical screen display that welcomes the user and explains the organization that has established the page.

FIGURE 10.5

World Wide Web architecture. Organizations such as *Datamation* magazine can store magazine pages or other information on servers that can be accessed through the World Wide Web all over the globe. Through hypertext links, users can easily move from page to page or select the features and topics they want to see. *Adapted from: "The World Wide Web Needs: A Functional Architecture . . . A Structural Architecture . . . and a Navigational Architecture,"* Datamation, *March 1, 1995, p. 41.*

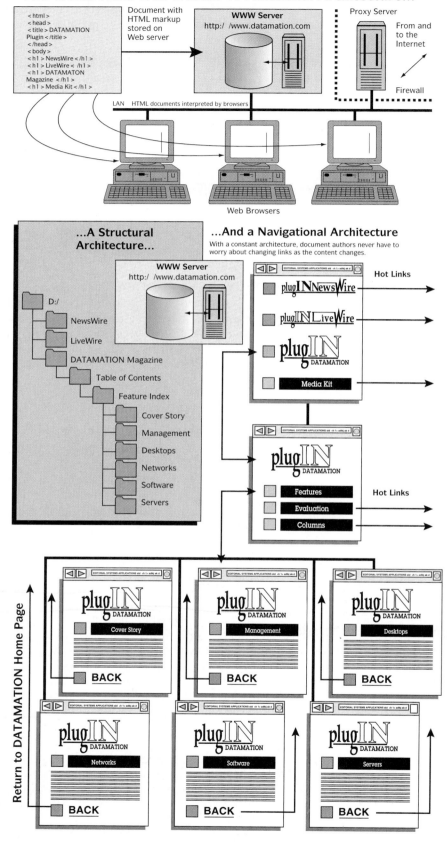

The World Wide Web Needs: A Functional Architecture...

...A Structural Architecture...

...And a Navigational Architecture

to the Net and the hypermedia connection has been programmed in). Sound allows some of the Web displays to talk or play music. Through use of the Web, commercial enterprises are providing information on demand for purposes of customer support, marketing and sales.

The specific hypermedia technology used in the Web is known as hyperlinks. Within any Web document, certain words and/or graphics are highlighted (usually bolded, in a different color, underlined, or some combination thereof). The highlighted objects have hyperlinks embedded within them (not visible to the user) that contain the path to another location, within the same document, a document on the same computer, or a document on another computer. Hyperlinks allow the user to move with ease within complex documents or across the network. If the reader of the document wants more information on the highlighted word, he or she double clicks that word, and quickly that other information will be displayed, even if it is stored halfway around the world. The value of this hyperlink facility, aside from its ease of use, is that the user is free to jump from place to place, following his or her own logic and interest, and does not have to move according to a static, pre-programmed, linear sequence—the user moves around almost as easily as a book reader might follow key words and jump around within an encyclopedia.

Navigating (or *surfing*) the Web requires a graphics computer link to the Internet and a Web browser. (Older links do not allow the transmission of graphics, although a character link remains sufficient for the many users who utilize only the Net's E-mail facility or its ability to share textual documents.) The Web, being a graphical facility, does require that the user have a graphics-capable link. The user must also have a special software tool to navigate the Web known as a Web **browser**. A popular Web browser is Mosaic, which was developed by the National Center for Supercomputing Applications at the University of Illinois, Urbana-Champaign campus. Other commercial browsers have become available that have the same basic capabilities but usually with even more power.

One Web user is Chicago-based Hyatt Hotels Corporation, which has established TravelWeb, a Web site that offers to prospective vacationers pictures and electronic information on 16 resort hotels in the United States and the Caribbean and similar information on 87 non-resort hotels in North America. Travelers will also be able to book reservations with a credit-card number once security problems are overcome. Hyatt management believes the Net is well-suited for the travel and hospitality

browser A software tool that supports graphics and hyperlinks and is needed to navigate the Web.

Prospective travelers can use Travel Web at any time of the day or night to find out information on rooms, rates, reservations, and nearby sightseeing attractions for hotels in the United States and the Caribbean. By analyzing the usage data for this World Wide Web site, participating hotels can learn more about customer preferences.

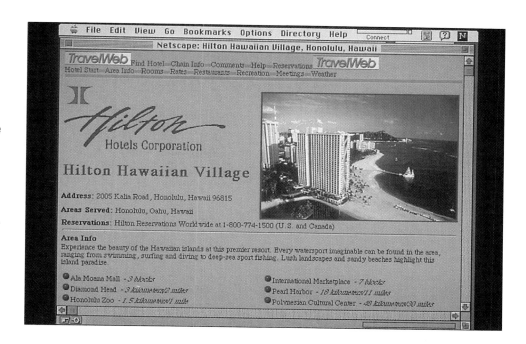

industries because it is easy to keep the Web information up to date compared to printed brochures. The interactive nature of the system helps potential customers feel the information is more relevant to them. The system runs 24 hours per day, whether or not a specific hotel's reservation desk is open. Hyatt is also using the system for market research. It tracks the origin of each user and the screens and hypertext links he or she uses. By analyzing these data, Hyatt learns a great deal about customer preferences. For instance, the hotel chain has found that Japanese users are most interested in the golf facilities of a resort, valuable information in shaping market strategies and for developing hospitality-related products (Wilder, 1995).

INTERNET BENEFITS TO ORGANIZATIONS

Organizations are already benefiting from use of the Internet in many ways, reducing communication costs, enhancing communication and coordination, accelerating the distribution of knowledge, improving customer service and satisfaction, and facilitating marketing and sales. The Internet has enormous potential for helping organizations participate in electronic commerce and for reducing their transaction costs.

Reducing Communication Costs

Prior to the Net, to realize the communications benefits described below, organizations had to build their own wide-area networks or subscribe to a value-added network service. Employing the Internet, while far from cost free, is certainly more cost effective for many organizations than building one's own network or paying VAN subscription fees. Moreover, companies are finding that by using the Net to fulfill a range of their communication needs, they are lowering other communication costs, including their network management expenses and their telephone and fax costs. For instance, one estimate is that a direct mailing or faxing to 1200 customers within the United States will cost $1200 to $1600, whereas the same coverage through the Net will cost only about $10. Adding 600 more recipients who are spread through six other countries would increase the cost only another $10. While all companies can benefit from lower costs, small businesses find reduced communication costs particularly beneficial because it sometimes enables them to compete with larger companies in markets that would otherwise be closed to them.

Enhancing Communication and Coordination

As organizations expand and globalization continues, the need to coordinate activities in far-flung locations is becoming more critical. The Internet has become an important instrument for that coordination. Cygnus Support, a software developer with only 125 employees with offices in both Mountain View, California, and Somerville, Massachusetts, originally turned to the Internet to link their offices inexpensively via E-mail. Recently, Cygnus established an internal Web site to keep employees informed about company developments. Through the Web, employees are able to see a company calendar, the employee policy manual, even the snack food inventory. The company keeps its employees informed on financial and performance issues as well. Employees will even see how much cash the company has in the bank, expressed as the number of months of expenses. Cygnus tracks the number of customer problems and the speed of their resolution and posts this data on the Web also. Finally, the site is important as a tool to help the company manage the large number of telecommuters that work for the company. Computer manufacturer Digital Equipment Corporation (DEC) devotes more than 100 Web servers to internal use. Through these servers they make available to their employees product brochures, organizational charts, policy handbooks, employee databases, interactive training tools, and even stock quotes.

The Internet has made it easier and less expensive for companies to coordinate small staffs when opening new markets or working in isolated places because they do not have to build their own networks. For example, Schlumberger Ltd., the New York and Paris oil drilling equipment and electronics producer, turned to the Net to gain both efficiency and cost savings as it was increasing coordination through communications. The company operates in 85 countries, and in most of them their employees are in remote locations. To install their own network for so few people at each remote location would have been prohibitively expensive. Using the Net, Schlumberger engineers in Dubai (on the Persian Gulf) can check E-mail and effectively stay in close contact with management at a very low cost. In addition, the field staff and personnel in the United States can easily keep track of research projects. Schlumberger has found that since it converted to the Net from its own network, the company's overall communications costs are down 2 percent despite a major increase in network and IT infrastructure spending. The main reason for these savings is the dramatic drop in voice traffic and in overnight delivery service charges (they attach complete documents to their E-mail messages).

Accelerating the Distribution of Knowledge

Because modern economies have become information economies, access to knowledge is critical to the success of many companies (see Chapter 15). To speed product development, to react rapidly to an emerging problem, information gathering must be quick and easy. Yet new knowledge is expanding so swiftly that keeping up is an immense task that requires management's attention. The Internet system helps with this problem. Organizations are using E-mail and the availability of databases all over the world to gain easy access to information resources in such key areas as business, science, law, and government. With blinding speed, the Internet can link a lone researcher sitting at a computer screen to mountains of data (including graphics) all over the world, otherwise too expensive and too difficult to tap. For example, scientists can obtain photographs taken by NASA space probes within an hour. It has become easy and inexpensive for corporations to obtain the latest United States Department of Commerce statistics, current weather data, or laws of legal entities from all over the globe. General Motors claims that Internet library access is vital to its product development research. Entek Manufacturing of Lebanon, Oregon, manufactures equipment to produce plastic sheeting for automobile batteries. The sheeting sometimes develops microscopic holes as a result of the high temperatures of today's automobile motors. Engineer Ron Cordell needed to find a material for

The radiology department of Brigham & Women's Hospital uses the World Wide Web to distribute hypermedia teaching documents with medical images and lists of symptoms from which students can make a diagnosis.

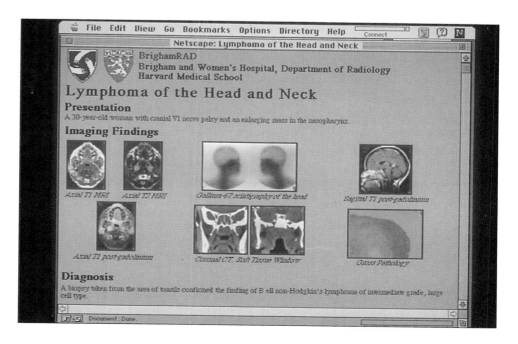

patching these holes and so presented his problem on a polymer forum on the Net. Several hours later an Australian responded via E-mail with the name of an adhesive that did the job. Cordell participates in other forums as well, gathering information that is vital to the running of his business. For example, he is part of a forum on machine vision because Entek uses video cameras to perform detailed microscopic analysis of their manufacturing processes. Access to the Internet costs his company only $8 a month because he uses a gateway offered by Oregon State University. Dell Computer Corporation, the Texas-based PC computer seller, uses the Internet to keep up with its competition, their problems, their hot new ideas through their Usenet news groups. Dell is able, for example, to read about bugs Compaq users are reporting or technical issues that concern Gateway computer users. Dell staff also peruses other related news groups to see, for example, what modem questions are being asked and what mouse products are being recommended or criticized.

Improving Customer Service and Satisfaction

Companies large and small are using the Internet to communicate efficiently to make product information, ordering, and technical support easier and immediately available. For instance, GE Plastics, the $5 billion plastics arm of Pittsfield, Massachusetts, giant General Electric Company, established a Web site with 1500 pages on the Internet in order to distribute hard product information to its customers and product users. Almost immediately it found its home page was being accessed about 12,000 times a month by users searching for technical specifications on Lexan, Cycocla, and other GE resins and polymers. Customers now get information in minutes that in the past took three days using the telephone and mail delivery (Anthes, 1995; Wilder, 1995). Dell Computer has established a Dell news group on the Net and other on-line services to receive and handle customer complaints and questions. They answer about 90 percent of the questions within 24 hours. Dell also does market research for free through these news groups rather than paying a professional for the same information. Recently, for example, the groups gathered customer reaction to a potential change in the color of desktop cases. Their whole Internet presence is important enough to Dell to assign a staff of seven people, who are active 24 hours a day, keeping up with any mention of Dell and the other computer producers in the news groups and answering questions on-line. Synopsis Inc., a Mountain View, California, designer of electronic circuitry, also uses the Internet to give engineering support to its customers. The company spent about $100,000 to establish its Internet presence, which is less than the cost of hiring a single engineer. Synopsis estimates that use of the Net has doubled its capacity to support its customers with the no increase in engineering staff. Synopsis customers can search their on-line product, sales, and technical information database themselves. About 70 percent of customer questions are now answered through this database without the involvement of a Synopsis engineer.

Facilitating Marketing and Sales

Marketing and sales via the Net are new and only now beginning to be viable. The network has traditionally been non-commercial, and a fierce anti-commercial sentiment continues to dominate. Commercial enterprises have had to find ways to market and sell that did not impose upon and offend others. The advent of the Web has made that possible because the Web is a passive instrument—it requires potential customers to seek out offerings by companies rather than having those companies actively reach out to potential customers, as is traditional in most marketing and advertising. Retailers update their Web page offerings virtually as often as needed. Suppliers can also update technical material used by customers just as easily. Even with limitations, the Net helps buyers and sellers make contact. Once the Internet becomes secure enough to transmit on-line purchase transactions, the Net will vastly expand the electronic marketplace, reducing transaction costs (see Chapters 2 and 3).

Sun Microsystems, the Mountain View, California producer of workstations, uses its Web site for marketing. The Web technology allows it, for example, to include its Web address in product ads and provides a place where people can get more information distributed. Cygnus has established an external Web site for marketing and customer support purposes. Visitors to this site can browse customer information, pricing, software documentation, press releases, back copies of its newsletter, and even an employee directory that includes photographs. Browsers can take the customer survey and join the mailing list. Every week Cygnus receives a report listing who has accessed its Web page, giving the firm valuable marketing information and contacts. The site has been attracting several hundred visitors a week. Cygnus also uses its site to strengthen its collaboration with other companies. When Cygnus jointly markets with another company, such as Hitachi, the news release on the Cygnus Web site will highlight the partner's name, allowing the reader to click that name and be transported instantly to the partner's Web site (Ubois, 1995). Digital Equipment Corporation uses the Internet to allow its customers and software developers from all over the world to log on to its DEC Alpha AXP computer and run their own software as a test of the DEC computer. DEC also gives its customers access to more than 3000 documents including sales brochures and technical manuals.

The Window on Organizations presents a few more examples to help stimulate the imagination of students as to the potential uses of this information superhighway.

PROBLEMS ON THE INTERNET

The Internet presents many problems to the business user, largely stemming from the fact that most of the technology and functions are relatively immature.

Security

The Internet is a highway that carries a great deal of personal and organizational information and data, much of it sensitive or proprietary. The types of information that companies may be loathe for outsiders to see include company strategic business plans, profit reports, product development information, pricing data, marketing plans, sales contacts, and scientific research data. Electronic links tend to be exposed to attacks from both thieves and vandals. Internet hackers have found ways to steal passwords as they pass through one site and use them to break into computer systems at other sites all over the world. The lack of security is one reason that the Net, while being widely used to facilitate transactions, is still only in limited use to consummate transactions. We explore this issue in greater detail in Chapter 18.

Technology Problems

A number of technology problems still exist. One issue is the lack of standards. A number of incompatible ways exist to access the Net, allowing specific users to perform certain functions but not others. For example, no single method of E-mailing graphics files exists and so many people cannot mail graphics documents to each other. The lack of standards also affects the ability of organizations to establish a stable link to the Internet. As the traffic on the Net becomes more varied, particularly with the addition of the World Wide Web, links become more complex and can present problems without good technical support. For many companies that support will come from within their own information systems staffs. Others must find that support externally. Figure 10.6 describes the elements of an Internet link that is capable of disseminating information through the Web. We discuss standards in greater detail in section 10.3.

So many people and organizations are sending so much data through the Net, much of it bandwidth-hungry graphics, that telecommunications links are already overloaded. Often users are unable to access the Net, while those who do and use the

EXPLOITING THE INTERNET

How useful is the Internet? Ask New York–based **J. P. Morgan & Co.**, the fifth largest bank in the United States and one of the most prestigious in the world. It became an early Internet user to obtain product support from its vendors. Management felt that their information technology vendors were taking too long to provide technical help. David Spector, the vice-president of corporate technology, decided that the quickest way for his company to report problems to vendors and get back software patches was through the Net. After a tough sell to his management, he was able to sign up for an Internet gateway. Spector claims that problems that used to take days to fix are now remedied in hours, occasionally in minutes. With this success, word of the Net spread, and now Morgan employees all over the world use it to gather information such as corporate financial or government census data. Eventually Morgan began to use it internally, putting on-line a worldwide phone book that is updated at least once a week.

More recently J. P. Morgan decided to become an information provider on the Web, making available risk-measurement data on complex financial derivatives. The company then added government bond, mortgage refinance, and mortgage purchase indices as well as a mortgage-rate survey. Morgan's risk-measurement service, known as RiskMetrics, provides daily risk measurement data on more than 300 bond, currency, and equity instruments. This program has been so successful that the company claims thousands of investors access its site each day to collect these statistics. "The goal is to establish ourselves as a leader in providing information," says Spector, adding that "being positioned as experts is good for our business." J. P. Morgan also has turned to the Web for aid in recruiting college and graduate school graduates. The Net is now used throughout the company.

Seagate Technology Inc., the Scotts Valley, California, disk drive producer, set up a 22-page Web site for $18,000 to recruit potential employees. It calculates the same money would buy only one full-page ad in a local Sunday newspaper. Newspapers have a short shelf life, with the bulk of responses coming within the first three days. On the other hand, the Net page brings responses for three or four weeks each time the company lists a new position. Moreover, the Seagate Web site contains a full description of the company, its goals and culture. The advantage to this, according to corporate employment manager Robert Morquecho is, that "I can spend most of my time [during an interview] selling the position and getting to know more about the individual who's applying."

Trane Co., the LaCrosse, Wisconsin, heating and air-conditioning manufacturer, has re-engineered its business (the Business Transformation Project) so that it could reduce the time needed to manufacture a custom-designed commercial air-conditioning system from 36 days to 6 days. Trane aimed for dramatic improvements in customer service and doubled revenues. Nonetheless, the paperwork still took 46 days using its mainframe-based network. Trane had to find a way to shrink its office cycles. The company then turned to the Net, installing desktop computers at its 120 locations—sales offices, warehouses, corporate offices—and connecting them via the Net. In addition, sales staff were issued laptops. Now Trane staff, their vendors, collaborators, and customers can exchange sales bids and all other documents instantly. Dave Norton, a systems strategist, claims that using the Net, rather than installing its own wide-area network, cut Trane's setup costs by at least 25 percent.

> *To Think About:* How has using the Internet enhanced the performance of the organizations described here? How has it changed these organizations? Using either the organization where you work or one of the companies examined in a chapter-ending case, suggest ways that organization could make effective use of the Internet. What changes to the organization might be necessary for it to use the Net in the ways you suggest?

The *Global Schoolhouse Project* (GSH) is demonstrating the use and value of the Internet to elementary and high schools around the world. Financed by the National Science Foundation and donations from a number of private companies and educational institutions, GSH is demonstrating how classrooms and students can use the Net for research and for interactive, collaborative learning. Schools throughout North America, Europe, and the Pacific rim use live videoconferencing to teach students how to become active learners and information managers and to offer ongoing, on-line training for teachers so that they can use Internet technology effectively in their classrooms.

Sources: Clinton Wilder, "The Internet Pioneers," *InformationWEEK*, January 9, 1995; John R. Vacca, "Mosaic: Beyond Net Surfing," *Byte*, January 1995; "ANS Builds Virtual Private Data Network to Support Business Transformation at Trane," *ANS Update*, November 1994; "Consumer Profile," *ANS Update*, November 1994.

FIGURE 10.6

Distributing information on the World Wide Web. Organizations can distribute information over the World Wide Web if they have the right hardware, software, and telecommunications capabilities. *From: Peter H. Lewis, "Companies Are Rushing to Set Up Shop in Cyberspace,"* The New York Times, *November 2, 1994, p. D6.*

Becoming Web Worthy

What a business needs to set up a computer for disseminating information over the World Wide Web.

•Access to a "server" computer, typically with a lot of processing power and hard-disk storage, connected directly to the Internet. To let remote users reach this server through the Web's "hypertext" navigational software, the computer must contain a set of software commands known as the hypertext transport protocol, or HTTP.

•A fast telephone line for connecting the server to the Internet. Many large businesses use circuits called T-1 lines, which can carry data at the rate of 1.544 million bits a second.

•Any word-processing program that can save files in the form of raw computer text known as ASCII text—the least common denominator among various forms of computer documents.

•The ability to "tag" documents with hypertext markup language, or HTML. Documents tagged with highlighted hypertext links enable a user to click with a mouse on a highlighted passage and be automatically routed to other, related pages—whether elsewhere on the same Web database or to other computers on the World Wide Web.

•"Browser" software for finding one's way around the Web. Mosaic is the most popular browser for pages containing graphics and other images. A program called Lynx is popular for browsing through text-only pages on the Web.

graphics-based Web frequently find connecting to a desired server interminably slow or even virtually impossible during busy times. Moreover, the growing need for bandwidth due to graphics will only expand as the transmission of sound and full motion video expands. All of this is raising the cost of using the Net. Some companies are already finding they need more expensive telecommunications connections, workstations or higher speed computers with improved graphics capability, and even information systems specialists with skills related specifically to the Internet. Individuals and organizations in less developed countries with poor telephone lines, limited hardware and software capacity, or government controls on communications will not be able to take full advantage of Internet resources (Goodman, Press, Ruth, and Rutkowski, 1994).

The availability of so much data has created other technical problems. One not yet satisfactorily solved is how effortlessly to find specific companies, computers, files, information, and services the way we now can with newspapers, magazines, or telephone books. There is no comprehensive method of locating and keeping track of the pages in the World Wide Web; seekers often spend large amounts of time in futile searches. Despite the many new tools and planned indexes to the Web, this problem is far from solved.

Users are suffering psychological burnout as they struggle with their inability to absorb and use all of the Internet's resources. (Some Internet users report receiving 500 E-mail messages a day.) Technology to filter out extraneous information while allowing peole to access the specific information they need will be highly valued.

Legal Issues

Laws governing electronic commerce are mostly nonexistent or are just being written. Precedent often helps little when the technology changes as rapidly as it has been. Legislatures, courts, and international agreements will have to settle such still open questions as the legality and force of E-mail contracts, including the role of electronic signatures, and the application of copyright laws to electronically copied documents. For instance, if a product is offered for sale in Australia via a server in Japan and the purchaser lives in Hungary, whose law applies? Until greater clarity brings stability to these and other critical legal questions, doing business on the Internet will bring a level of unreliability that many will find unacceptable.

The Traditional Internet Culture

The Internet had its origins as a scientific and academic tool. As it grew, a strong anti-commercial culture grew with it. However, as companies began to see selling opportunities using the Net, some are advertising their product or service in the traditional way—broadcasting messages to large groups of people. Net users have shown themselves unwilling to receive electronic "junk mail." One reason for this aversion is very practical—the large number of people who use the Net. For example, a request for help on a specific topic can already bring hundreds of responses from all over the world, more than the requester can possibly handle. Even many commercial users fear that allowing commercial organizations to add hundreds or thousands of unasked-for marketing messages (remember how cheap E-mail is) will make Internet E-mail literally unmanageable. Therefore, while businesses remain free to use the Internet for E-mail, research, and other forms of information exchange, just as anyone else, they will have to learn new ways to market on the Net, ways that do not intrude upon the other users.

All the talk of retail sales on the Web has not produced customers in anywhere near the number the publicity might lead one to expect. For example, Pizza Hut offers pizzas for sale through the Web from 2000 United States outlets, and yet in late 1994 it was receiving only two orders per week that way. Organizations must approach the Internet just as they would any other new and growing technology. Good business practice dictates that the Internet and all it has to offer should be carefully examined but should be adopted only within the framework of clear business and technology plans. Realistic payback targets must be set and plans for the development of business functions on the Net must be established. And, of course, progress must be monitored.

THE FUTURE OF THE INTERNET

The potential for the Internet is enormous. As telecommunications systems with massive bandwidths become common, the capability of the Web, its ease of use and speed, should improve dramatically, making it possible that the uses of the Internet could explode. Coming solutions to security problems that are more available, easier to use, and less expensive will also open the Net to the expansion of transaction consummation, making it, for example, a potentially popular location for more retail trade as well as a preferred vehicle for electronic data interchange.

On the other hand, optimism must be tempered by caution. The Internet is not the only potential vehicle for network information exchange or electronic commerce. The cable, television, telecommunications, and publishing giants are exploring other technologies to accomplish the same tasks as the Internet and one or more such possibilities may rival or even supplant it. Alternative networks are being developed. For example, the United States federal government has established the National Information Infrastructure (NII), a network of networks that is being used across the United States and is growing.

Telecommunications and networks are most likely to increase productivity and competitive advantage when digitized information can move through a seamless web of electronic networks, connecting different kinds of machines, people, sensors, databases, functional divisions, departments, and work groups. Despite all of the advances in desktop processing, user-friendly software, and telecommunications technology, this goal has been difficult to realize because many different kinds of hardware, software, and communications systems still are not able to work together. They lack **connectivity**—the ability of computers and computer-based devices to communicate with one another and "share" information in a meaningful way without human intervention.

connectivity A measure of how well computers and computer-based devices communicate and share information with one another without human intervention.

CONNECTIVITY PROBLEMS

The following are some common examples of the absence of connectivity:

- Desktop microcomputers often cannot use data from the corporate mainframe, often cannot share information among different brands of microcomputers, and many times cannot share information meaningfully even among different pieces of software operating on the same microcomputer.

- Some corporations have multiple E-mail systems within their own firm that cannot communicate with one another.

- IBM, as well as other hardware vendors, sells machines and software that cannot communicate with others even of the same brand because of different hardware designs and operating systems.

- Companies operating overseas have tremendous difficulty building global networks that can seamlessly tie their operations together. Different countries have different telecommunications infrastructures, many owned by national PTTs (Post, Telegraph, and Telephone monopolies) that use disparate networking standards.

There are many reasons why computers and information systems achieved such dizzying heights of incompatibility. Individual computers were designed long before computer networks were built. Before the 1980s, there were no standards for either hardware or software manufacturers; the buyers of equipment lacked market power to demand standards; and hardware and software vendors themselves encouraged product differentiation. Moreover, the process of setting standards is largely political and involves many powerful interest groups, such as private-sector industry associations of equipment, the U.S. federal government, and professional groups such as the Institute of Electrical and Electronic Engineers (IEEE), the American National Standards Institute (ANSI), the International Organization for Standardization (ISO), and the International Telephone and Telegraph Consultative Committee (CCITT).

A GARDEN OF BUZZWORDS: ASPECTS OF CONNECTIVITY

Connectivity encompasses more than just networking. There are many different qualities that an information system with connectivity will have. Let us explore some of the terms used for describing different aspects of connectivity.

Applications portability is the ability to operate the same piece of software on different types of computer hardware. Imagine, for instance, using Lotus 1-2-3 spreadsheet software on a microcomputer at work, saving the results in a file, removing the 1-2-3 program disk, taking it home, and using a Macintosh computer to complete the project.

Migration is the ability to move software from one generation of hardware to another more powerful generation. Most microcomputer software offers upward com-

applications portability The ability to operate the same software on different hardware platforms.

migration The ability to move software from one generation of hardware to another more powerful generation.

patibility. For instance, you can run early versions of Lotus 1-2-3 on later versions of DOS (version 6.0, for example). Downward compatibility is more problematic. Much microcomputer software designed to operate under DOS 6.0 cannot operate on DOS 3.0.

Cooperative processing divides computing tasks among mainframes, minicomputers, microcomputers, or workstations to solve a single common problem. Cooperative processing is a connectivity issue because different machines must be networked and programmed so that they can work together on a single application (see Chapter 6 for a more detailed description of cooperative processing).

Information portability is the sharing of computer files among different types of computer hardware and different software applications. Currently, sharing of files is possible among applications such as word processing that can create a single file standard like ASCII 8 text files (see the discussion of ASCII in Chapter 6). These text files can be transferred into spreadsheet or database applications, but the transfer can take place only on the same hardware platform or machine class. Because different machines and machine classes use different coding schemes (for instance, mainframes often use EBCDIC, and some smaller machines use ASCII 7), even information portability can be difficult.

Interoperability is the ability of a single piece of software to operate on two different kinds of computer hardware, showing users an identical interface, and performing the same tasks. For instance, Microsoft Word word processing software has similar functionality and somewhat similar looks on both the Macintosh and IBM microcomputers, but different versions of the software are required to run on each type of machine.

Interoperability, information and applications portability, and client/server technology require open systems. Open systems promote connectivity because they enable disparate equipment and services to work together. **Open systems** are built upon public, nonproprietary operating systems, user interfaces, application standards, and networking protocols. In open systems, software can operate on different hardware platforms and in that sense can be "portable." Currently, it is prohibitively costly to achieve applications portability without a common shared operating system.

In the microcomputer world, most IBM-compatible microcomputers have used Microsoft/IBM DOS or Microsoft Windows (an operating system shell that runs in conjunction with DOS). Their operating principles are published and they can be used by non-IBM microcomputer makers for a minimal licensing fee. Although DOS has no common user interface, the graphical user interface of Microsoft Windows is a step in this direction. By contrast, most minicomputers and mainframes have proprietary operating systems that cannot be used by different classes of machines and whose operating principles are hidden from public view and vigorously defended with high licensing fees.

Perhaps the key to truly open systems has been the operating system called UNIX. UNIX originated in the research labs of AT&T in the 1970s through engineers who wanted a powerful time-sharing operating system that could operate on many different kinds of computer hardware. Since then, UNIX has come to dominate the engineering market for workstations and is starting to be used by some types of microcomputers. However, there are different versions of UNIX, and no one version has been accepted as an open systems standard. Moreover, today there is slow but genuine progress being made toward more open systems products that are not UNIX-based.

Thus, true connectivity requires a great deal more than simply wiring together different machines or providing limited access to many different computers. Connectivity requires common operating system standards, common telecommunications standards, and even common user interface standards, a similar screen look and feel across different software applications.

---

cooperative processing Dividing computing tasks among networked mainframes, minicomputers, microcomputers, or workstations to solve a single common problem.

information portability The sharing of computer files among different hardware platforms and software applications.

interoperability The ability of a software application to operate on two different machine platforms while maintaining the identical user interface and functionality.

open systems Software systems that can operate on different hardware platforms because they are built on public non-proprietary operating systems, user interfaces, application standards, and networking protocols.

STANDARDS FOR ACHIEVING CONNECTIVITY

Achieving connectivity requires standards for networking, operating systems, and user interfaces. To date, there are no uniform standards that ensure that information systems can achieve the attributes of connectivity described above, but some standards do exist and others are being promoted. This section describes the most important standards that are being used today.

Models of Connectivity for Networks

reference model A generic framework for thinking about a problem.

protocol A statement that explains how a specific task will be performed.

standard Approved reference models and protocols as determined by standard-setting groups for building or developing products or services.

Open Systems Interconnect (OSI) International reference model for linking different types of computers and networks.

Because of the many interests involved in connectivity and standard setting, there are different models for achieving connectivity in telecommunications networks. A **reference model** is a generic framework for thinking about a problem. It is a logical breakdown of some activity (like communications) into a number of distinct steps or parts. Specific protocols are required in order to implement a reference model. A **protocol** is a statement that explains how a specific task, such as transferring data, will be performed. Reference models and protocols become **standards** when they are approved by important standard-setting groups or when industry builds or buys products that support the models and protocols.

Network connectivity can also be achieved without reference models or protocols by using gateways. Firms develop gateways between two disparate networks when it is impossible or too costly to integrate them by complying with reference models or standards. However, gateways are expensive to build and maintain, and they can be slow and inefficient. We now describe the most important models of network connectivity.

The **Open Systems Interconnect (OSI)** model is an international reference model developed by the International Standards Organization for linking different types of computers and networks. It is a framework for defining the functions required in a telecommunications session between two or more computers. It was designed to support global networks with large volumes of transaction processing.

OSI enables a computer connected to a network to communicate with any other computer on the same network or a different network, regardless of the manufacturer by establishing communication rules that permit the exchange of information betwen dissimilar systems. The OSI model divides the telecommunications process into seven layers (see Figure 10.7). Each layer in the OSI model is defined by its communications functions and deals with a specific aspect of the communications process. Each layer has one or several associated protocols. A multi-layer protocol has the advantage of having each layer independent of the others so that it can be changed without affecting the other layers.

Two different computers using OSI standards would each have software and hardware that correspond to each layer of the OSI model. A message sent from one computer to the other would pass downward through all seven layers, starting with the application layer of the sending computer and passing through to the sending computer's physical layer. It would then travel over the communication channel and enter the receiving computer, rising upward through the seven layers in that machine. The process is reversed when the receiving computer responds.

For example, if an officer at a local bank wanted information about a particular client's checking account that was stored in the bank's central host computer, he or she would enter the instructions to retrieve the client's account records into his or her terminal under control of layer 7, the application layer. The presentation layer (layer 6) would change this input data into a format for transmission. Layer 5 (the session layer) initiates the session. Layer 4 (the transport layer) checks the quality of the information traveling from user to host node. Layers 3 and 2 (the network and data link layers) transmit the data through layer 1 (the physical layer). When the message reaches the host computer, control moves up the layers back to the user, reversing the sequence.

HOST A
USER A

HOST B
USER B

OSI LAYERS

7 **Application**
Specialized user functions such as network operating systems, file transfer, electronic mail

6 **Presentation**
Formats data for presentation, provides code conversion

5 **Session**
Establishes a communication between stations on the network

4 **Transport**
Ensures reliable end-to-end data delivery

3 **Network**
Routing and relaying of information packets over a wide area network

2 **Data link**
Packaging and transfer of packets of information, error checking

1 **Physical**
Transmission of raw data over the communications medium

OSI LAYERS

7 **Application**
Specialized user functions such as network operating systems, file transfer, electronic mail

6 **Presentation**
Formats data for presentation, provides code conversion

5 **Session**
Establishes a communication between stations on the network

4 **Transport**
Ensures reliable end-to-end data delivery

3 **Network**
Routing and relaying of information packets over a wide area network

2 **Data link**
Packaging and transfer of packets of information, error checking

1 **Physical**
Transmission of raw data over the communications medium

Information

Transmission Control Protocol/Internet Protocol (TCP/IP) U.S. Department of Defense reference model for linking different types of computers and networks.

The **Transmission Control Protocol/Internet Protocol (TCP/IP)** model was developed by the U.S. Department of Defense and is used in the Internet. Launched in 1972 in conjunction with network research and development done by the Defense Advanced Research Projects Agency (DARPA), its purpose was to help scientists link disparate computers. Because it is one of the oldest communications reference models (and is the model on which the Internet is based), TCP/IP is still widely used, especially in the United States (Europeans tend to favor OSI). Figure 10.8 shows that TCP/IP has a five-layer reference model.

1. *Physical net:* Defines basic electrical transmission characteristic generated during communications.

2. *Network interface:* Handles addressing issues, usually in the operating system, as well as the interface between the initiating computer and the network.

3. *Internet (IP):* Handles system-to-system communication. This layer is a self-contained, connectionless datagram delivery process that does not depend on the network for message receipt acknowledgment. The datagram is a unit of information consisting of a header segment and a text segment. The Internet Protocol receives datagrams from TCP and transmits them through the Internet.

4. *Transmission Control Protocol (TCP):* Performs transport. TCP supports program-to-program communication at the end-user level. The Transmission Control Protocol supports reliable transfer of information independent of the category of computer job at the higher layer (such as E-mail or log-on).

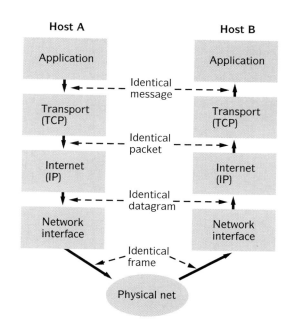

FIGURE 10.8
The Transmission Control Protocol/Internet Protocol (TCP/IP) reference model. This figure illustrates the five layers of the TCP/IP reference model for communications.

5. *Application:* Provides end-user functionality by translating the messages into the user/host software for screen presentation.

Proprietary Approaches: SNA

Systems Network Architecture (SNA) Proprietary telecommunications reference model developed by IBM.

IBM developed the first commercial computer communications model and protocol, called **Systems Network Architecture (SNA)**, in 1974. Over the years, SNA evolved into a full-featured telecommunications model that could support intelligent terminals, communication among terminals, file transfers, on-line transaction processing, and some limited applications portability. SNA networks can even be configured to carry video signals in the unused portion of the bandwidth. Today SNA is the most common communications network model for mainframe and minicomputer networks.

SNA is similar to OSI in that it takes a layered approach to the problem of communications among users and performs similar communications functions (see Figure 10.9). However, the layers do not correspond completely. SNA is not entirely compatible with OSI, even though IBM has sought to make certain aspects of SNA and OSI compatible. SNA is a limited connectivity solution. Applications for one IBM host computer often cannot be operated on other IBM host computers, minicomputers, or micros. These other machines cannot typically even gain access to the larger machines' applications or data. IBM is developing deeper strategies for assuring connectivity in the future.

Other Networking Standards

Integrated Services Digital Network (ISDN) International standard for transmitting voice, data, image, and video to support a wide range of service over the public telephone lines.

Standards have also been developed for transmitting digital data over public switched networks. **Integrated Services Digital Network (ISDN)** is an international digital public switched network standard for transmitting voice, data, image, and video over phone lines. ISDN was developed in the late 1970s by the CCITT (Consultative Committee on International Telegraphy and Telephony), an international standards body representing over 150 countries. Users have access by a limited set of standard multipurpose customer interfaces.

Imagine combining in one single service the following features:

- Complete voice, data, and video connection to anywhere in the world.

- Complete digital connection to any other digital device in the world, from one next door to one halfway around the world.

- Simultaneous use of voice, video, and digital devices.

FIGURE 10.9
The IBM Systems Network Architecture (SNA) reference model. This figure illustrates the seven-layer model that deals with logical units and physical units. SNA can support intelligent terminals, communication among terminals, file transfers, and on-line transaction processing. SNA is the most common communications network model for mainframes and minicomputers in use today.

Layers	SNA	Layers	SNA
7	Application/user	7	Application/user
6	Presentation	6	Presentation
5	Data flow control	5	Data flow control
4	Transmission control	4	Transmission control
3	Path control	3	Path control
2	Data link control	2	Data link control
1	Physical link control	1	Physical link control

Information

- Complete freedom to move devices and people without any rewiring of buildings, or special cables, and with a single physical standard.

- User-controlled definition of video, digital, and data lines. You can use a line for digital personal service this hour, reconfigure the same phone line as an incoming 800 WATS line the next hour, and in the next hour redefine the line as a video line carrying pictures of a group videoconferencing session.

The goal and promise of ISDN is to provide a more functional network to transport all kinds of digital information, regardless of its source or destination. ISDN offers universal data connectivity in direct digital form. Modems are not used with ISDN except when they are needed to link up with a non-ISDN user. ISDN uses standard twisted-pair copper wire to connect desktop devices to building-level concentrators. A central office switching device makes all connections to the outside world. With some simple technology changes, ordinary twisted copper telephone wire can be more fully utilized without expensive recabling.

With Integrated Services Digital Network (ISDN) and videoconferencing systems, Dr. John Champa can share documents and images with other Unisys employees from his home office in suburban Detroit.

There are two levels of ISDN service: Basic Rate ISDN and Primary Rate ISDN. Basic Rate ISDN serves a single desktop with three channels. Two channels are B (bearer) channels with a capacity to transmit 64 kilobits per second of digital data (voice, data, video). A third delta channel (D channel) is a 16-kilobit-per-second channel for signaling and control information (such as the phone number of the calling party). Primary Rate ISDN offers 1.5 MBPS of bandwidth. The bandwidth is divided into 23 B channels and one D channel. This service is intended to meet the telecommunications needs of large users. Plans are underway to increase ISDN transmission capacity.

Local and long-distance telephone companies are trying to stitch together isolated ISDN "islands" into a national network. Currently, implementation of ISDN is restricted by its cost, regional limitations, and the difficulties business firms have experienced in learning how to use the technology.

Operating System Standards: The Open Systems Movement

The battle over operating system standards centers around UNIX. UNIX is the only nonproprietary operating system that can operate on all computers—from microcomputers to mainframes, and irrespective of vendor. However, the effort to make UNIX the operating system standard has encountered considerable opposition. The stakes are high. Briefly, standardized operating systems and communications links between computers would eliminate firms' dependence on one particular hardware vendor, such as IBM or DEC. Moreover, UNIX runs directly counter to the marketing plans of many large vendors. For instance, if UNIX becomes a standard, there is little need for Microsoft Corporation's Windows NT operating system or for IBM's OS/2. UNIX can deliver time-sharing, applications portability, seamless file transfer, and shared user interfaces. Because of the high stakes, vendors have split into two warring camps over the issue of what version of UNIX to support, led by IBM and DEC on one side and AT&T and Sun Corporation on the other.

Table 10.2 summarizes the standards we have described and lists other important standards for graphical user interfaces, electronic mail, packet switching, and electronic data interchange. Any manager wishing to achieve some measure of connectivity in his or her organization should try to use them when designing networks, purchasing hardware and software, or developing information system applications.

Table 10.2 **Standards for Achieving Connectivity**

Area	Standard or Reference Model	Description
Networking	OSI, TCP/IP, SNA	Computer-to-computer communications
Digital public switched network transmission	ISDN	Transmission of voice, video, and data over public telephone lines
Fiber optic transmission	FDDI	100 Mbps data transmission over dual fiber optical ring
Electronic mail	X.400	Permits E-mail systems operating on different hardware to communicate
Packet switching	X.25	Permits different international and national networks to communicate
EDI	X.12 Edifact (Europe)	Standardized transaction format
Graphical user interface	X Windows	High-level graphics description for standardized window management
Operating system	UNIX	Software portable to different hardware platforms

Implementing enterprise-wide computing has created problems as well as opportunities for organizations. Managers need to address these problems as they design and build networks for their organizations.

PROBLEMS POSED BY ENTERPRISE-WIDE COMPUTING

The rapid, often unplanned, development of networks, micros, and workstations has created some of the problems. We have already described the connectivity problems created by incompatible network components and standards. Six additional problems stand out: loss of management control over information systems; the need for organizational change; the complexities of designing an enterprise-wide information technology infrastructure; the difficulty of ensuring network security; the difficulty of ensuring network reliability and management; and the hidden costs of client/server computing (see Table 10.3).

Loss of Management Control over Information Systems

In the 1970s and early 1980s, data and software were confined to the mainframe and the management of the traditional information systems department. Desktop computing and networks have empowered end users to become independent sources of computing power capable of collecting, storing, and disseminating data and software.

The dilemma posed by desktop computing has always been one of central management control versus end-user creativity and productivity. Permitting end users to choose hardware and software can lead to complete chaos and high costs in firms. With desktop computing tools, end users can easily create their own applications and files. It becomes increasingly difficult to determine where data are located and to ensure that the same piece of information, such as a product number, is used consistently throughout the organization. User-developed applications may combine incompatible pieces of hardware and software. Yet observers worry that excess centralization and management of information resources will stifle the independence and creativity of end users and reduce their ability to define their own information needs.

The Need for Organizational Change

Enterprise-wide computing has the potential to change the distribution of power, perquisites, advantages, and resources in organizations. Insofar as information confers power, independence, and advantage, then desktop computing changes existing power arrangements. Decentralization also results in changes in corporate culture and organizational structure. While enterprise-wide computing is an opportunity to

Table 10.3	Problems Posed by Enterprise-wide Networking

Connectivity problems

Loss of management control over systems

Organizational change requirements

Complexity of enterprise-wide technology infrastructure

Network security

Difficulty of ensuring network reliability and management

Hidden costs of client/server computing

re-engineer the organization into a more effective unit, it will only create problems or chaos if the underlying organizational issues are not fully addressed.

Complexities of Designing an Enterprise-wide Information Technology Infrastructure

Designing an enterprise-wide computing infrastructure presents both the business staff and the technical designers with two key related choices: downsizing functions versus keeping them on mainframes; and centralizing functions versus decentralizing them. Mainframes excel at managing and processing large amounts of data but remain poor at making that data easily accessible to end users. On the other hand, desktop computers and workstations are particularly effective with their graphical user interfaces, personal productivity software, and independent processing power. Many companies find it cost effective to process large on-line transaction processing systems on mainframes. Experience also shows that moving a large, working legacy system from a mainframe to smaller computers can be very costly and even risky because no one can guarantee the new system will work as well as the old one. Many companies have concluded that it is best to leave such systems alone, only developing new systems following the client/server model.

As to centralization, experience shows that it is often effective to decentralize data storage if the data are very stable (such as product specifications) whereas it is more effective to centralize the storage of volatile data (such as sales data). Maintaining volatile data at many sites, and protecting their integrity, can be very difficult as well as expensive. When data are replicated and distributed to many different locations, more work is required to ensure that when the data are updated on one computer, they are updated on all other computers.

Difficulty of Ensuring Network Security

Security is of paramount importance in organizations where information systems make extensive use of networks. Networks present end users, hackers, and thieves with many points of access and opportunities to steal or modify data in networks. How can an organization rely on data if one cannot prove where the data came from and who modified them along the way? Moreover, because users may simultaneously access several different computers (their client plus one or more servers) with different security systems, access can become overly complex and seriously interfere with the user's productivity. We discuss these issues in greater detail in Chapter 18.

Complexities of Network Reliability and Management

Managing both information systems technology and corporate data are proving much more difficult in a distributed environment because of the lack of a single central point where the necessary managing can occur. Network technology is still immature and highly complex. The networks themselves have dense layers of interacting technology while the applications too are often intricately layered. In addition, enterprise-wide computing is highly sensitive to different versions of operating systems and network management software, with some applications requiring specific versions of each. It is difficult to make all of the components of large heterogeneous networks work together as smoothly as management envisions (see Figure 10.10).

While most mainframe or minicomputer systems have tools and guidelines to monitor system use, to partition work loads, and to help plan future hardware purchases, these tools normally cannot be adapted to work in the distributed client/server environment. Tools for managing distributed networks are still in their infancy. Adequate, easy-to-use tools are lacking for such vital system functions as system configuration, tuning, system-wide backup and recovery, security, upgrading both system and application software, capacity planning, and the pinpointing of bottlenecks.

FIGURE 10.10
Increasing network complexity and decentralized computing. As more and more new sites are added to a decentralized network, complexity increases because there are so many diverse components to manage and coordinate. *Adapted from "Managing the Costs of Enterprise Computing," Datamation, March 15, 1994, a special report prepared by IBM.*

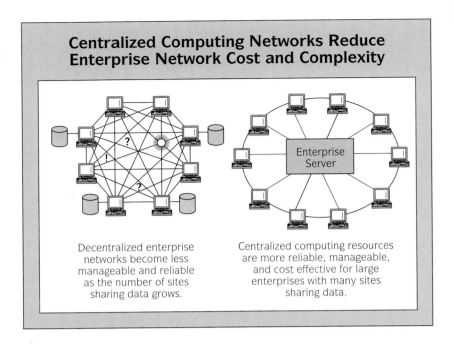

Centralized Computing Networks Reduce Enterprise Network Cost and Complexity

Decentralized enterprise networks become less manageable and reliable as the number of sites sharing data grows.

Centralized computing resources are more reliable, manageable, and cost effective for large enterprises with many sites sharing data.

Performance monitoring tools for client/server networks (for instance, monitoring CPU usage) are also not as well-developed or sophisticated as the tools that are available for mainframes or minis.

downtime Periods of time in which an information system is not operational.

Downtime—periods of time in which the system is not operational—remains much more frequent in client/server systems than in established mainframe systems and should be considered carefully before one takes essential applications off the mainframe. Finally, it is difficult to determine what pieces of an application should be placed on a client and which are suited to the server. Tools for partitioning applications remain immature.

Hidden Costs of Client/Server Computing

While the lure of cost savings has been important in the move to client/server computing, many companies have found that the savings they anticipated did not materialize because of unexpected costs. Hardware acquisition savings resulting from significantly lower costs of MIPS on microcomputers are often offset by high annual operating costs for additional labor and time required for network and system management. The lack of vendor-supplied tools for comprehensive, centralized management of distributed systems with heterogeneous hardware and software components tied together is proving costly indeed.

One-time acquisition costs include planning the network, the original hardware and software, preparation of the physical sites (such as cabling and electrical wiring), hooking up the telecommunications network, installing the hardware and software, and retraining the staff (changing to information systems using client/server processing typically increases training costs for both information systems specialists and end users). Ongoing annual costs include hardware and software maintenance, telecommunications tariff charges, system and network management, and network problem resolution. Forrester Research estimated that the costs of running a large microcomputer network can run 300 percent higher than supporting the same number of users in a mainframe network (Laberis, 1994).

The most difficult to evaluate and control are the hidden costs that accompany a decentralized client/server system. These systems can result in lowered knowledge worker productivity. Professional employees, many being paid $100,000 per year or more, must spend their own time performing such tasks as network maintenance, data backup, technical problem solving, and hardware, software, and software-update installations. The company can find itself paying too high a price for such services. However, potentially even more costly is the fact that the time these knowledge workers spend performing such technical tasks is time not spent performing the valuable functions for which they were hired. As illustrated in Figure 10.11, the Gartner consulting group of Stamford, Connecticut, after a five-year study, concluded that each client/server user cost $40,000 to $50,000 to support over the five-year period, an amount far in excess of the cost of supporting a mainframe terminal user. The largest cost component is labor for development, operations, and support.

While measuring the costs of enterprise-wide computing can be difficult because of the hidden costs, measuring its benefits is even more difficult. How can one put a financial value on easier communication with one's customers, suppliers, or team members? How does one measure the effects of an analyst being able to obtain vital data and analyze it as needed? As we said earlier in this chapter, client/server platforms intuitively reflect the new business environment better than the old mainframe environment because they are more decentralized and flatter, because the person using a networked desktop computer has more control over his or her own work, because networked computers allow teams to work closely together, and because networked organizations appear to be more flexible than those relying strictly on centralized mainframes. Only time and the experience of individual companies can lead to clear answers about the value of the benefits of enterprise-wide computing.

SOME SOLUTIONS

Organizations can counteract problems created by enterprise-wide computing by planning for and managing the associated business and organizational changes, increasing end-user training, asserting data administration disciplines, and considering connectivity and cost controls when planning their information architecture.

Managing the Change

To gain the full benefit of any new technology, organizations must carefully plan for and manage the change. Business processes may need to be re-engineered to insure that the organization fully benefits from the new technology (see Chapter 11). The company's information architecture must be redrawn to shape the new client/server environment (see Chapter 1). Management must address the organizational issues that arise from shifts in staffing, function, power, and organizational culture. Data models must be developed, training be given, network support assigned, and network management tools acquired. The Window on Management describes how one large, multinational corporation managed its downsizing project.

FIGURE 10.11
Cost breakdowns for client/server computing. Labor costs, by far the largest cost component in client/server computing, are frequently underestimated when organizations downsize. *Adapted from: "Client/Server Trimmings," by Julia King and Rosemary Cafasso,* Computerworld, *December 19, 1994. Copyright 1994 by Computerworld, Inc.*

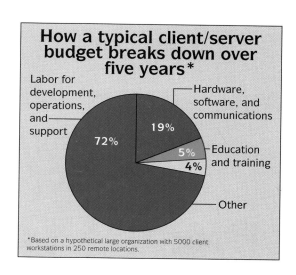

BASS BEER SERVES A CLIENT/SERVER ENVIRONMENT

What is the role of management when a large multinational corporation makes a decision to move from a mainframe environment to a client/server environment? Bass of the United Kingdom recently made such a move, and a close look at the role of management there is instructive.

Bass, which is located in Burton-on-Trent, Staffordshire, England, is the leading brewer in the United Kingdom. But it is also a large and diversified multinational corporation that grossed $6.7 billion in 1993 and includes in its holdings Holiday Inns, soft drink companies, liquor stores, and even betting shops and social clubs. In 1988 Bass management turned to London-based management consultants Nolan Norton (a division of KPMG Peat Marwick, Washington, DC) to do a study of their current systems. At the time, Bass systems were primarily IBM and Unisys Corp. mainframe-based using dumb terminals. The consultants found a company made up of many smaller units, most of which had their own information technology and their own IT policies. The result was many systems that could not communicate with one another, despite the fact that Bass does an unusually large amount of internal trading (such as its Holiday Inns purchasing all their beverages from within the Bass organization). They found that IT skills were spread very unevenly throughout the organization. They also reported that Bass units were purchasing from many different IT suppliers, a costly way to do business. Included in Nolan Norton's report was the conclusion that the current systems were inadequate, that Bass needed to move into client/server technology.

The recommendations came at just the right time. Bass was beginning to feel pressure on its profits stemming both from a beginning recession that was expected to decrease leisure activity spending, and from the cost of conforming to new government regulations. Management accepted the recommendations and decided to try to develop more cost-effective systems.

To launch a project to carry out the recommendations, Bass management created a central IT steering committee with representation from each of the Bass businesses. The project goals included: taking advantage of bulk purchasing of information technology; setting corporate-wide hardware and software standards; creating long-term business partnerships with leading suppliers of information technology; and establishing a system that not only connected the whole corporation, but did so in a seamless way. What did they mean by "seamless"? According to Allan Paterson, director of planning and control in the Bass IT organization, "We are very keen on enterprise-wide transparency. An individual must be able to go to any workstation in a Bass location and with a single password have transparent access to any service on any machine in our network."

The project began by setting some worldwide standards. Bass's management was willing to commit a lot of time to the task of setting standards because once standards have been set up, it is very hard to change. The company must get it right the first time. Included in the standards is a listing of the leading suppliers with whom Bass is establishing long-term partnerships. According to Paterson, those on the list were selected because they were market leaders that had both credibility and stability. Bass now limits their business

units to working with four suppliers: IBM and Unisys for hardware; Novell for networking; and Microsoft Corp. for desktop software. The steering

> *To Think About:* How well did Bass's information systems support its business strategy? How important are standards at Bass? Why? How much connectivity is there at Bass?

committee reserved for itself the job of overseeing information technology purchases for all the Bass units.

Bass has successfully made the move from mainframes to a client/server environment. The company's LANs connect more than 200 IBM AS/400 minicomputers and 4500 PCs, all linked in a client/server environment. Management has also decided they need more internal expertise on the technology they are using. Therefore, they have undertaken a program to get members of their information technology department certified as either Novell NetWare engineers or Microsoft experts.

Personnel was another issue that management had to face. The move to a client/server environment resulted in a drop in information technology staff from 1,300 to 850. In addition, half of the remaining 850 were actually new to the company, having been hired well into the client/server project. Many of the employees who left Bass had mainframe expertise, whereas most of the new employees were skilled in networking and desktop software.

Source: George Black, "Bass Brews Up Hearty Client/Server Strategy," *Software Magazine*, May 1994.

Education and Training

Training to use desktop computers and networked applications is incomplete or entirely absent in many firms. Senior managers have not understood that it takes many hours for employees to learn how to use desktop applications and networks. They have not appreciated the ergonomic problems created by continuous use of computer terminals. (*Ergonomics* refers to the interaction of people and machines in the work environment.) A well-developed training program can help in overcoming problems resulting from the lack of corporate support and understanding (Westin et al., 1985; Bikson et al., 1985). Additionally, technical specialists will need training in client/server development and network support methods. Figure 10.11 shows that firms should expect to spend at least 5 percent of their client/server budgets on training.

Data Administration Disciplines

Chapter 8 described the role of the data administration function in the organization. This role becomes even more important when networks link many different applications and business areas. Organizations must systematically identify where their data are located, which groups are responsible for maintaining each piece of datum, and which individuals and groups are allowed to access and use that data. They need to develop specific policies and procedures to ensure that their data are accurate, available only to authorized users, and properly backed up.

Planning for Connectivity

connectivity audit A method for examining amount of connectivity an organization has by examining the five areas of connectivity: networks, network management and user support, network services, applications, and user interfaces.

Senior management must take a long-term view of the firm's information architecture and must make sure that its systems have the right degree of connectivity for its current and future information needs. Most organizations do not have an idea of how much connectivity they have or how much they lack. The first step is to perform a **connectivity audit**, which examines five areas of connectivity in an organization:

1. *Networks.* How many networks are there? For what class of machines? Who manufactures them? Where are they? How much did they cost?

2. *Network management and user support.* Who is in charge of the networks that have been identified? Are accurate records kept of utilization? What are the authorization procedures? How many staff members maintain and support each network and train its end users? How much does this cost?

3. *Network services.* What services do the existing networks provide? For whom? How are the costs allocated?

4. *Applications.* What kinds of applications are supported by networks? How important are the applications to production and to information interchange?

5. *User interfaces.* What user interfaces are currently used? How do they connect or relate to one another? What applications run under various interfaces?

A connectivity matrix, composed of the major networks along the top axis and the major corporate user groups along the vertical axis, can help identify how networks are used and by whom (Figure 10.12). If documented properly, the connectivity matrix should identify many areas where current networks fail to provide connectivity.

The connectivity audit period is an ideal time to interview key corporate users in order to identify problem areas and potential solutions. Clearly, complete connectivity is usually not needed in most corporations. It is far more sensible to identify classes of connectivity problems and general solutions (however, the solutions should not be so general as to require rewiring the entire company). There is a dilemma here. On the one hand, it is very expensive to develop gateway solutions one at a time, solving brush fires as they flare up. On the other hand, it is usually too expensive to achieve systemic connectivity for older applications.

Managers have serveral connectivity strategies to consider. One strategy tries to identify a class of connectivity problems and provide a general solution. If the connectivity audit identifies large numbers of microcomputer users seeking access to mainframe data, management should try to develop a generic strategy to solve these problems. The strategy might include (1) assuring that a single microcomputer hardware model is the standard, (2) assuring that a single network vendor is chosen, and (3) developing on the mainframe side a coherent long-term strategy for integrating desktop workstations, such as implementing OSI network standards.

A longer-term strategy accepts the reality of today's incompatible systems but maintains a vision of the future, where connectivity is an important goal. Procurement strategy then should focus on new systems and follow the simple rule that, from today, systems will be developed only if (1) they support connectivity standards developed by the firm, and (2) they build upon existing networks and user applications in a seamless fashion.

Once management has identified specific areas where connectivity is needed, it is in a position to measure how much solutions cost. Costs of networks, machines, software, and cable are usually easily measured, whereas benefits are much more difficult to determine. In terms of positions saved or reduced, productivity enhanced, and bottom-line results like more customer orders, connectivity benefits are often elusive to measure, however palpable. One possibility is to measure opportunity costs—how much extra time employees and customers must spend in order to interact with existing systems. These opportunity costs are often much easier to measure.

If we look back to the recent past and consider the promising developments of the future, we can see two lessons emerge. First, seemingly small problems in connectivity should not be solved one at a time, piecemeal, without a larger vision of how to address the connectivity and architecture problems of a business. Pursuit of a piecemeal approach seems to guarantee problems down the road. Second, it is very risky to rely on a single vendor of mainframes or minicomputers to provide connectivity solutions. To follow this approach is to lock one's firm into a particular operating system and very expensive software that can operate only on very costly machines. In the past, this strategy has resulted in enterprise-wide nightmares rather than connectivity.

Controlling Network Costs

Related to connectivity are measures to help firms control enterprise network costs. Some specific strategies that can help control costs include:

- Keeping networks as homogeneous as possible. The fewer protocols and network operating systems from different vendors, the more users can be supported by each network support specialist.
- Limiting the number of hardware and software vendors.

QUAKER OATS COOKS UP A CENTRALIZED CLIENT/SERVER SYSTEM

Can centralization of the management of a corporation's client/server networks be advantageous to the organization? Quaker Oats, the Chicago, Illinois, food and beverage company, thinks the answer is yes. For years Quaker Oats allowed its departments to set up their own networks with their own servers, until the company finally had over 30 such departmental networks. While nobody questioned the business value of departmental networks and servers, the IS department, under the leadership of director of technology planning and support Jon Kozuch, took a hard look at the issue of decentralized network management and concluded that departmental autonomy was detrimental both to the departments and to the company. Over the years the departments had acquired a wide mix of operating systems, networks, and network servers. The very success of these departmental networks was the source of the problems Kozuch addressed. The networks were supported by departmental staff rather than by IS personnel. Every department had its "guru," usually not a technical person, often a clerk or secretary. Problems emerged when gurus began having too much time taken away from their own full-time jobs. The problems became painful when a network would run into problems while the guru was on vacation or at home ill. In those times, users had no place to turn to get technical support, and the network could be down for days.

Seeing these problems, Kozuch formed a team to develop a strategy for managing the diverse collection of net-

works before a real crisis overtook Quaker Oats. The team members first studied the problem themselves, then contracted the services of an external consulting firm, and even discussed their problems with their counterparts from other companies on the Internet. In the end they developed a plan they called Centralized LAN Administration (CLA). The plan was easy to sell to most of the departments because they were the ones facing the problems daily.

The plan transfers technology control and management of all independent departmental networks to the central information systems (IS) department. Both software and hardware are now supported centrally, by IS professionals, under this plan. Their expectation was that the gurus will be able to return to their own work while the networks will be running more consistently. In addition they expected that support and servicing costs should drop dramatically. CLA also includes hardware and software standards to provide consistency throughout the organization. The plan specifies 60 to 100 MHz DEC (Digital Equipment Corporation) servers running Novell NetWare network management software, although existing systems will continue to vary until all upgrades are completed. The plan also settles on Novell's NetWare Management System (NMS) to manage the networks with the expectation that IS professionals will be able to manage all the networks centrally, although they are looking for new software that can do a better job.

Quaker Oats wanted a computing strategy that was flexible so that it could take advantage of new technol-

ogy as it becomes available. The Novell NMS was installed with the understanding that additional capabilities would be needed in the future. NMS

> **To Think About:** What problems can be solved by setting corporate hardware and software standards as Quaker Oats did? By centralized management? What management, organization, and technology issues did Quaker Oats consider? What problems are not addressed by CLA?

will remain a corporate standard as long as it meets future needs, but it was set up to allow other software to be installed with minimal disruption.

In addition to the the Novell NetWare–based file servers, Quaker Oats uses departmental processors to support word processing, Microsoft Mail (an E-mail package), Excel spreadsheets, and scheduling software. It continues to run a mixture of operating systems, including VAX/VMS, OS/400, OSF/1, OS/2, and HP-UX.

The team has been pleased with the results. Quaker Oats has even taken the concept one step further by beginning to install corporate-wide applications on the networks. For example, team members have been searching for an asset management package and have already installed the PeopleSoft human resource system from PeopleSoft Inc., Walnut Creek, California.

Source: Michael Bucken, "Quaker Oats Reins in Departmental Servers," *Software,* January 1995.

- Consolidating servers—keep the number of workgroup and departmental servers to a minimum to simplify network administration (review Figure 10.10).
- Automating the management of the networks, using new network management tools to monitor errors, network traffic, and response times.

The Window on Technology offers a look at Quaker Oats, which addressed many of these problems through centralized standards and client/server network management.

Management Challenges

1. Enterprise-wide computing requires a complete change of mind set. Companies must consider a different organizational structure, a different support structure for information systems, and different procedures of managing employees and desktop processing functions. To implement networked computing successfully, companies must examine and perhaps redesign an entire business process rather than throw new technology at existing business practices and hope it will stick. It is not so much the technology that impedes implementation of the information architecture as it is the careful planning required to implement it.

2. Connectivity and standards are very difficult to enforce, even when a firm's connectivity needs are well understood. Firms are reluctant to abandon their existing, albeit incompatible systems because these systems represented such large investments. Corporate culture and competing interest groups within the firm often resist change. Business practices tend to favor short-term efforts over the long-term planning that is essential for creating an open systems environment.

3. Resolving the centralization versus decentralization debate. Since the growth of minicomputers in the 1970s, a long standing issue among IS managers and CEOs has been the question of centralization. Should processing power and data be distributed to departments and divisions, or should they be concentrated at a central location? The new architecture facilitates decentralization, but this may not always be in the organization's best interest. Managers need to make sure that the commitment to systems centralization or decentralization actually serves organizational objectives.

Summary

1. Describe the characteristics of enterprise-wide computing. Enterprise-wide computing architecture has produced a mixed environment composed mostly of networked desktop workstations and microcomputers. Although it often contains minicomputers and mainframes, computing power tends to take place on the desktop. The organization's hardware, software, and data are much more controlled from the desktop by the professional who uses the desktop machine. The system is a network or multiple networks connecting many local area networks and devices.

2. Define the client/server model of computing and explain the roles of clients and servers within this model. The client/server model is user-centric, with computer processing being split between "clients" and "servers," connected via a network. Each function of an application is assigned to the machine best suited to perform it. Clients are the user point-of-entry to the computer functionality they require and are usually a workstation, a desktop, or a laptop computer with a graphical user interface. The server, which may be anything from a supercomputer to a microcomputer, stores and processes shared data. The user generally interacts only with the client portion of the application. The exact division of tasks between client and server depends on the nature of the application.

3. Explain why organizations are adopting client/server computing. Advances in technology have converged to make client/server computing feasible: Increased computing power at ever lower prices makes the technology affordable. Productive, easy-to-use desktop software has given individuals the tools they need to better perform their assigned functions. A wealth of vital information has increasingly become available to knowledge workers on-line where it can be accessed quickly and easily. In today's advanced knowledge-based and globalized economies, organizations are striving to be more competitive by eliminating layers of bureaucracy and investing lower-level line workers with more responsibility and authority. Client/server computing better supports the organization working in this environment than does the less flexible, more top-down old mainframe system.

4. Define the Internet and describe both the benefits it offers organizations and the problems it presents to them. The Internet is an international network of networks connecting more than 20 million people from over 100 countries and growing very rapidly. The Internet is used for communications, including E-mail, public forums on thousands of topics, and live, interactive conversations. It is also used for information retrieval from hundreds of libraries and thousands of library, corporate, government, and nonprofit databases from around the world. It has developed into an effective way for individuals and organizations to offer information and products through a web of graphical user interfaces and easy-to-use links worldwide. Major Internet capabilities include E-mail, Usenet, chatting, Telnet, gophers, Archie, WAIS, and the World Wide Web.

Organizations benefit from the Internet in a number of ways. Many use the Net to reduce their communications costs when they coordinate organizational activities and communicate with employees. Researchers and knowledge workers are finding the Internet a quick, low-cost way to both gather and disperse knowledge. Customer service units are finding they often are actually able to give customers quicker answers to their product problems while keeping costs controlled. Marketing and sales via the Net is new and requires different approaches than most traditional marketing and sales.

The Internet presents many problems to the business user, largely stemming from the fact that most of the technology is relatively new. Security is difficult because the Net offers spies, thieves, and hackers out to do damage many potential entry points. The rapid growth of Net popularity and the rapid expansion of the transmission of data-intensive graphics, sound, and video applications has created inadequate bandwidth. No adequate system has yet developed to allow individuals to effortlessly search through such immense amounts of data located anywhere in the world. Laws governing electronic commerce are mostly nonexistent or are just being written, making it difficult, for example, to use public networks such as the Net to consummate legal contracts. Traditional Internet culture and the very practical needs of users to avoid being swamped with unwanted messages are causing businesses to find new and creative ways to use the Net for marketing.

5. Describe important standards used for linking hardware, software, and networks to achieve connectivity. Connectivity is a measure of how well computers and computer-based devices can communicate with one another and "share" information in a meaningful way without human intervention. It is essential in enterprise-wide computing where different hardware, software, and network components must work together to transfer information seamlessly from one part of the organization to another. Applications portability, migration, cooperative processing, information portability, interoperability, and open systems are all aspects of connectivity.

There are several different models for achieving connectivity in networks. Public standards like OSI and TCP/IP are recognized as important reference models for network connectivity. Each divides the communications process into layers. TCP/IP is widely used in the United States, whereas OSI is favored in Europe. ISDN is an emerging standard for digital transmission over twisted-pair telephone lines. UNIX is an operating system standard that can be used to create open systems.

6. Identify problems posed by enterprise-wide computing and recommend solutions. Problems posed by enterprise-wide computing include loss of management control over systems; the need to carefully manage organizational change; coping with the complexity of an enterprise-wide technology infrastructure; maintaining network security; difficulty of ensuring network reliablility and management; and controlling the hidden costs of client/server computing.

Solutions include planning for and managing the business and organizational changes associated with enterprise-wide computing, increasing end-user training, asserting data administration disciplines, and considering connectivity and cost controls when planning an information architecture. A connectivity audit identifies existing capabilities and future needs. While many corporations have assumed connectivity as a strategic goal, a more reasonable strategy would move incrementally toward greater connectivity while not giving up the vision of connectivity.

Key Terms

Enterprise-wide computing	Telnet	Cooperative processing	Transmission Control
Internetworking	Gopher	Information portability	Protocol/Internet
Client/server model	Archie	Interoperability	Protocol (TCP/IP)
Client	WAIS	Open systems	Systems Network
Server	Home page	Reference model	Architecture (SNA)
Internet	Browser	Protocol	Integrated Services Digital
World Wide Web	Connectivity	Standard	Network (ISDN)
Usenet	Applications portability	Open Systems Interconnect	Downtime
Chatting	Migration	(OSI)	Connectivity audit

Review Questions

1. Define enterprise-wide computing. List five of its characteristics. How is it related to internetworking?
2. What is client/server computing? What is the difference between the client and the server? What are the different roles each fulfills?
3. What are four major business drivers for client/server computing?
4. What is the Internet? What are its principal functions?
5. Describe at least four basic tools used on the Internet.
6. Describe five ways in which the Internet can benefit many organizations.
7. Describe four basic problems of the Internet.
8. What is connectivity? Why is it a goal for enterprise-wide computing?
9. Give four examples of connectivity problems.
10. Make a list and be able to discuss the meaning of the six different aspects of connectivity.
11. Compare OSI, TCP/IP, and SNA. Why are these limited solutions to network connectivity problems?
12. Describe ISDN and explain why it is important.
13. Why is UNIX important to connectivity?
14. Give five examples of problems posed by enterprise-wide computing architecture.
15. What are some solutions to the problems raised in the previous question?
16. What are the five ingredients of a connectivity audit?

Discussion Questions

1. Should the Internet be used for commercial purposes? Under what circumstances?
2. If computing increasingly moves to the desktop, is there any point in maintaining an information systems department when most of the computing power of the corporation resides on a desktop?
3. What problems result from choosing a single vendor's hardware and software to attain long-term connectivity?
4. Your employer has just announced a new strategic program to achieve complete connectivity of your firm's information systems in five years. What are some of the difficulties and potential dangers of such a policy?

Group Project

Form a group with three or four of your classmates. Perform a connectivity audit of the information systems used by your university or a business with which you are familiar, using the guidelines provided in this chapter. Complete a connectivity matrix. How much connectivity exists at your university? Is this sufficient? If not, recommend a strategy for the university to achieve higher levels of connectivity in the next five years. Present your findings to the class.

Case Study

UNILEVER TRIES TO UNIFY WORLD OPERATIONS

The sun never sets on the worldwide holdings of Unilever, one of the world's largest multinational corporations. The sprawling conglomerate has over 1000 different product brands, 300,000 employees, and more than 300 operating divisions located in 75 countries. Its holdings include T. J. Lipton, Calvin Klein Cosmetics, and Lever Brothers. Unilever's largest core business is food products. Since the 1980s, Unilever has bought more than 100 businesses and sold nearly twice as many. Nevertheless, its cost-conscious management has made sure it has a rich supply of available cash (Unilever's annual cash flow is more than $3 billion) and relatively little debt.

The product of a 1930 merger between a Dutch margarine company and a British soap maker, Unilever maintains two equally powerful co-chairmen—Sir Michael Perry in London and Morris Tabaksblat in Rotterdam. Perry and Tabaksblat are trying to make their octopus-like organization a nimble player in today's hypercompetitive global marketplace. Unilever is constantly mired in battles over soap, ice cream, shampoo, margarine, and sauces with fierce competitors such as Procter & Gamble, Nestlé, Colgate-Palmolive, and Snapple. Unilever needs to fend off these rivals while dealing with slow-growing populations in its mainstay markets and huge increases in its advertising and promotion costs.

As profits in developed markets stagnate, Unilever is shifting its weight to Asia, Latin America, and Central Europe. Perry and Tabaksblat are trying to pare down Unilever's broad array of products into four basic categories: food, personal products, detergents, and specialty chemicals. The food category is focusing on pasta sauces, tea drinks, margarine, and ice cream. The personal products category emphasizes cosmetics, prestige fragrances, and anti-aging skin creams. Management also wants more efficiencies by building plants that serve entire continents instead of just one country. It wants to be able to roll out the best products globally in the shortest period of time.

To balance worldwide headquarters with brand managers and country managers, Perry and Tabaksblat have delegated the job of developing products and marketing strategies for an entire region. This means that Thailand might be the detergent expert for Southeast Asia and the Philippines would handle manufacturing. In Europe, the Frankfurt office would oversee skin care, while the Paris office would be in charge of shampoo. In other words, one country develops new products and creates marketing campaigns for the whole region. In the past, Unilever stressed geographic decentralization. While maintaining a measure of centralized control, it allowed country managers to meet the needs of local markets in different countries.

The firm tries to "Unileverize" its managers with a common organizational culture that transcends national boundaries. Managers are trained at Unilever's international management training college near London and are assigned job positions in various countries throughout their careers.

The senior management of this London- and Rotterdam-based firm be-

---

lieved that with so many companies under one roof, Unilever was "drowning in technology." Unilever had many redundant systems as well as many systems that were poorly conceived and poorly implemented. Management handed Michael Johnson, Unilever's head of information technology, the responsibility of standardizing the behemoth's multitudinous hardware and software systems around an open systems architecture and bringing them together in a global network.

Unilever's old laissez-faire approach toward information systems had left it with a polyglot mix of hardware and software. Despite the official corporate policy of only using IBM, Hewlett-Packard, or DEC hardware, the firm had drastic incompatibility problems. The systems of various operating units had mushroomed out of control. To make his plan work, Johnson had to convince his three designated hardware vendors to cooperate on a cross-vendor software architecture.

According to Norman Weizer, a senior consultant with Big Six accounting firm Arthur D. Little, the challenge for global firms is to provide company-wide information in a consistent, common format while allowing local units to perform effectively. Unilever wanted to pursue this goal by providing a common foundation for disparate far-flung operations without hamstringing its businesses.

Johnson moved quickly. In June 1990 he started focusing on applications portability. He told Unilever's three primary hardware suppliers—IBM, DEC, and Hewlett-Packard—that he wanted to be able to build an application and port it anywhere in the world within ten days. He especially wanted to build "competitive-edge applications" in one place, send them to other Unilever companies, and install them instantly as if the recipients had developed them themselves.

Johnson enlisted Unilever's key hardware and software vendors to agree upon an open systems architecture for the firm that could serve as the foundation for a global network. Unilever chose the suite of standards built around the Open Software Foundation's Applications Environment Specification (AES) for systems and software throughout the corporation. AES is a massive set of standards that includes elements of the OSF/1 operating system, the Motif graphical user interface, OSF's Distributed Computing Environment, SQL (Structured Query Language), and Posix (Posix establishes a standard interface between an applications program and an operating system rather than requiring a specific operating system).

With this base environment, Johnson added important software and database standards. Unilever chose Oracle and Sybase Inc.'s database management systems, Lotus 1-2-3 spreadsheet software, and WordPerfect word processing software. Oracle's SQL Forms and Unify Corporation's Uniface applications environments were selected as front-end software development standards.

Johnson and his team decided to use AES's distributed client/server capabilities as the foundation for Unilever's global data network. Unilever chose Sprint International to manage its pan-European data network. Eventually Unilever hopes its software tools and global network will provide the technology to manage group projects around the world. Perry and Tabaksblat can use a sophisticated E-mail system to help them monitor Unilever's new operating regions.

Unilever believes its move to open systems has not stifled local technology innovation. For instance, Quest International, a Unilever food ingredients and fragrance company based in England and the Netherlands, is using AES standards to develop its critical applications. Quest is relatively small (its 1991 revenue was $842 million) and it could move quickly to new standards.

While Johnson has taken a strong position about standards and open systems, he does not want to disrupt the company's operations during implementation. He realizes that he will not be able to make all of Unilever's operations switch to open systems overnight. Unilever inherited hundreds of proprietary applications that Johnson wants to leave in place until his staff figures out how to make them communicate among computers. While Unilever's company-wide open systems model excludes proprietary systems such as those using IBM's AS/400 minicomputer environment, it is too costly to shut down these machines right away. Johnson is letting companies with AS/400 computers delay the changeover while mandating that all new software purchased or developed for the AS/400 computers must be portable to RISC (reduced instruction set computing) machines that are compatible with AES standards.

Sources: Paula Dwyer et al., "Unilever's Struggle for Growth," *Business Week*, July 4, 1994; Joshua Greenbaum, "Unilever's Unifying Theme," *InformationWEEK*, March 2, 1992; and Floris A. Maljers, "Inside Unilever: The Evolving Transnational Company," *Harvard Business Review*, September–October 1992.

Case Study Questions

1. Analyze Unilever's problems using the competitive forces and value chain models. How well did Unilever's information systems support its business strategy?

2. What problems did Unilever's systems have? How serious were Unilever's connectivity problems? What management, technology, and organization factors were responsible for these problems?

3. How would you characterize Unilever's strategy for dealing with connectivity problems? Do you agree with this strategy?

4. How much connectivity should there be at a firm like Unilever? Would you recommend a five-year systems plan for Unilever to achieve a higher level of connectivity? If so, describe your plan.

References

Anthes, Gary. "Crisis." *Computerworld* (January 2, 1995).

Berg, Lynn. "The SCOOP on Client/Server Costs." *Computerworld* (November 16, 1992).

Berners-Lee, Tim, Robert Cailliau, Ari Luotonen, Henrik Frystyk Nielsen, and Arthur Secret. "The World-Wide Web." *Communications of the ACM 37*, no. 8 (August 1994).

Bikson, Tora K., J. D. Eveland, and Barbara A. Gutek. "Flexible Interactive Technologies for Multi-Person Tasks: Current Problems and Future Prospects." Rand Corporation (December 1988).

Bikson, Tora K., Cathleen Stasz, and Donald A. Mankin. "Computer-Mediated Work: Individual and Organizational Impact on One Corporate Headquarters." Rand Corporation (1985).

Bowman, C. Mic, Peter B. Danzig, Udi Manger, and Michael F. Schwartz. "Scalable Internet Resource Discovery: Research Problems and Approaches." *Communications of the ACM 37*, no. 8 (August 1994.)

Brood, William J. "Doing Science on the Network: A Long Way from Gutenberg." *The New York Times* (May 18, 1993).

Celko, Joe. "Everything You Know Is Wrong." *Datamation* (January 21, 1994).

Chabrow, Eric R. "On-line Employment." *InformationWEEK* (January 23, 1995).

De Pompa, Barbara. "More Power at Your Fingertips." *InformationWEEK* (December 30, 1991).

Dearth, Jeffrey, and Arnold King. "Negotiating the Internet." *InformationWEEK* (January 9, 1995).

Dion, William R. "Client/Server Computing." *Personal Workstation* (May 1990).

Fisher, Sharon. "TCP/IP." *Computerworld* (October 7, 1991).

Flynn, Laurie. "Browsers Make Navigating the World Wide Net a Snap." *The New York Times* (January 29, 1995).

Goldman, Kevin. "Ad Agencies Slowly Set Up Shop at New Address on the Internet." *The Wall Street Journal* (December 29, 1994).

Goodman, S. E., L. I. Press, S. R. Ruth, and A. M. Rutkowski. "The Global Diffusion of the Internet: Patterns and Problems." *Communications of the ACM 37*, no. 8 (August 1994).

Guimaraes, Tom. "Personal Computing Trends and Problems: An Empirical Study." *MIS Quarterly* (June 1986).

Huff, Sid, Malcolm C. Munro, and Barbara H. Martin. "Growth Stages of End User Computing." *Communications of the ACM* (May 1988).

Johnson, Jim. "A Survival Guide for Administrators." *Software Magazine* (December 1992).

Kantor, Andrew. "The Best of the Lot." *Internet World* (January 1995).

King, Julia, and Rosemary Cafasso. "Client/Server Trimmings." *Computerworld* (December 19, 1994).

Laberis, Bill. "Pull the Plug on Computer Hype." *The Wall Street Journal* (April 25, 1994).

Laudon, Kenneth C. "From PCs to Managerial Workstations." In Matthias Jarke, *Managers, Micros, and Mainframes*. New York: John Wiley (1986).

Lee, Denis M. "Usage Pattern and Sources of Assistance for Personal Computer Users." *MIS Quarterly* (December 1986).

Lee, Sunro, and Richard P. Leifer. "A Framework for Linking the Structure of Information Systems with Organizational Requirements for Information Shaving." *Journal of Management Information Systems 8*, no. 4 (Spring 1992).

Leiner, Barry M. "Internet Technology." *Communications of the ACM 37*, no. 8 (August 1994).

Lewis, Peter H. "Getting Down to Business on the Net." *The New York Times* (June 19, 1994).

Maglitta, Joseph, and Ellis Booker. "Seller Beware." *Computerworld* (October 24, 1994).

Markoff, John. "Commerce Comes to the Internet." *The New York Times* (April 13, 1994).

David Morrison. "Business Battles for a Piece of the Net." *Beyond Computing* (January–February 1995).

Mossberg, Walter S. "Before You Cruise the Internet, Get the Right Road Map." *The Wall Street Journal* (January 19, 1995).

"Plans and Policies for Client/Server Technology." *IS Analyzer* 30, no. 4 (April 1992).

Pyburn, Philip J. "Managing Personal Computer Use: The Role of Corporate Management Information Systems." *Journal of Management Information Systems* (Winter 1986–1987).

Quarterman, John S. "To is manager @ bigco.com From: jsq @ tic.com subject: What can businesses get out of the Internet?" *Computerworld* (February 22, 1993).

Richard, Eric. "Anatomy of the World-Wide Web." *Internet World* (April 1995).

Richardson, Gary L., Brad M. Jackson, and Gary W. Dickson. "A Principles-Based Enterprise Architecture: Lessons from Texaco and Star Enterprise." *MIS Quarterly* 14, no. 4 (December 1990).

Semich, J. William. "The World Wide Web: Internet Boomtown?" *Datamation* (January 15, 1995).

Sinha, Alok. "Client-Server Computing." *Communications of the ACM*, 35, no. 7 (July 1992).

Smarr, Larry, and Charles E. Catlett. "Metacomputing." *Communications of the ACM* 35, no. 6 (June 1992).

Tash, Jeffrey B., and Paul Korzeniowski. "Theory Meets Reality for New Breed of APPs." *Software Magazine* (May 1992).

Tetzeli, Rick. "The INTERNET and Your Business." *Fortune* (March 7, 1994).

Ubois, Jeffrey. "CFOs in Cyberspace." *CFO* (February, 1995).

United States General Accounting Office. "FTS 2000: An Overview of the Federal Government's New Telecommunications System." *GAO/IMTEC-90-17FS* (February 1990).

Vacca, John R. "Mosaic: Beyond Net Surfing." *Byte* (January 1995).

Verity, John W., with Robert D. Hof. "The Internet: How It Will Change the Way You Do Business." *Business Week* (November 14, 1994).

Westin, Alan F., Heather A. Schwader, Michael A. Baker, and Sheila Lehman. *The Changing Workplace*. New York: Knowledge Industries (1985).

Wilder, Clinton. "The Internet Pioneers." *InformationWEEK* (January 9, 1995).

Withers, Suzanne. "The Trader and the Internet." *Technical Analysis of Stocks & Commodities* (March 1995).

Xeniakis, John J. "Moving to Mission Critical." *CFO* (September 1994).

Can Client/Server Technology Cure Health Care?

Health care in the United States is in crisis because of both high costs and inadequate health care for millions of people. Various technologies, including client/server, have generated intense interest among health-care professionals in recent years in the hope that they can contribute to lower costs and improved health care. We will examine the question of client/server contributions once we have presented some needed health-care background.

FINANCIAL FACTORS

In 1994 health care constituted about 14 percent of the nation's gross domestic product and was projected to reach 18 percent by the year 2000. Health-care expenditures in 1993 were over $900 billion, making health care one of the largest industries in the United States.

Financially, the industry has done very well but is now coming under intense pressure to change. For-profit health maintenance organizations (HMOs) had been achieving annual profit increases of 20 percent. HMOs charge a flat annual fee for comprehensive health care. Their rapid profit growth can be attributed to a number of factors. They have been able to select mainly healthy, young people from among their corporate customers' employees. Also, they have been able to force hospitals to cut costs in order to get their business. Third, they were able to raise fees without pressure from their main purchasers—large corporations. Their hefty profit growth occurred despite average annual expenditures of over 20 percent of their revenue on administrative costs, advertising, and large executive salaries. Now conditions are changed; HMO

profits are now being squeezed. Their young, healthy population base is aging, requiring more medical care at higher costs. In addition, corporate purchasers of HMO services are closely monitoring their operations and demanding lower premiums, enforcing those demands by opening their HMO selection process to competitive bidding. In addition, many HMO patients are now demanding the option to choose their own doctors, which is more expensive than the more traditional approach of limiting doctor choice to those within the specific HMO medical group.

Similar pressures affect other sectors of the health-care industry. Insurance companies and employers have been pressuring hospitals, clinics, and independent caregivers to focus on efficiency. Traditional medical care has been fee-for-service in a cost-plus market. As a result, doctors, hospitals, and other health-care providers were long able to maintain profits by raising their fees when their costs went up. They experienced no pressure to address cost and efficiency issues. Insurance companies and corporate buyers now scrutinize fee increases very carefully, forcing health caregivers to become more

efficient. Moreover there has been a growth in flat-fee providers—"capitated managed care." These organizations provide total health care for a flat fee and, in the past, also had been able to raise their fees as costs climbed. Now the market has forced them to find ways to cut costs, hopefully while maintaining or improving care quality.

One source of the problem has been administrative costs. Observers agree that doctors and nurses are now spending only 30 to 40 percent of their time giving care to patients. The rest of the time is eaten up by administrative tasks, such as filling out records and paperwork. Similarly, a report from Decision Resources, issued in 1990, concluded that 25 percent of the hospital dollar is spent on administration.

Hospitals present a special problem, partly because they represent a major source of health-care costs and partly because they are so large and have developed their own procedures and standards in health-care financing. Traditionally hospitals have budgeted by costs rather than by revenues or profits. Their budgeting methods have failed to encourage hospital-wide efficiency. For example, each department is traditionally treated as a separate cost center, causing it to be concerned only with its own costs and efficiencies. They have little incentive to cooperate with other departments to reduce overall hospital costs. In a typical example, Georgetown Medical School tells of a hospital where the radiology department saved money by sending out only one copy of a report rather than separate copies to each relevant care provider. This action won that department a hospital efficiency award, but another department, the hospital medical clinic, was forced to hire an additional employee to reproduce and distribute the radiology reports to caregivers who required them.

OTHER FORCES FOR CHANGE

Cost has not been the only force pressuring the health-care industry to change, however. In recent years health care has been decentralizing. Health care has experienced a large rise in specialty services organizations, often new alliances of purchasers and providers who supplement and even replace care traditionally given by hospitals. Many people are going to specialized or general outpatient clinics for much or all of their medical care. Large numbers of patients now incur billing at many institutions, often for a single medical episode. This is taking place partly out of choice, partly to reduce costs, and partly because of the mobility of people.

Another pressure on the industry has been the exploding need for information. Doctors and health-care organizations require hard information on patients and patient problems both to improve treatment and to enable them to cut costs. In addition those who pay for health care (insurance companies and employers) are seeking more information on care-giving procedures, their benefits and limitations. They want to know the cost of specific procedures and their effectiveness. A financial pressure on hospitals has been the decline in inpatient hospital stays. Both the number and length of hospital stays are declining as medical knowledge grows, and as hospitals and insurers

attempt to cut costs. Empty beds lower revenues.

Technology is a potential avenue for health-care change. Central to health care is the patient medical record. The current medical record is mostly paper-based, as doctors and nurses manually record symptoms, diagnoses, and treatment. Actually, patient records include a number of other media as well, including film-based X-rays and scans, strip charts from patient monitoring equipment such as electrocardiograms, voice recordings of clinicians' notes, and video recordings of testing equipment such as MRIs and sonograms. In addition, hospitals and physicians also have some sort of computer record on their patients, even if just for billing purposes. With these types of records, the major files are manually passed from person to person, caregiver to caregiver. During a typical clinic visit, about 30 percent of needed patient information is missing because it is in a different file, usually at a different organization. The lack of a complete file makes it difficult for the caregiver to have needed information concerning the patient. Another problem with mainly paper-based records is that they are generally not accessible for studies on the effectiveness of specific treatments or on causes of illnesses.

Observers agree that health care is traditionally five to ten years behind the rest of United States industry in computerization. Today, health care is the only major industry still relying primarily upon paper records. The lack of computerization is reflected in the low level of health-care expenditures for computer technology. The industry invests between 1 and 3 percent of its budgets in information technology as compared with 4 to 10 percent for such major industries as banking, retailing, manufacturing, and insurance. One study, completed in the spring of 1994, illustrates this lack of computerization with its finding that of the more than 5000 nongovernmental hospitals in the United States, only between 50 and 75 have even some degree of client/server computing. Generally speaking, what hospital computerization does exist has

been instituted by isolated departments using differing technologies and operating systems. These systems tend not to be connected and must also produce paper-based results that then have to be manually forwarded to the physician or nurse.

The availability of low-cost, powerful computers, sophisticated networking (including client/server technology), and videoconferencing is making health-care computerization more practical. In addition, the decentralization of care—and with it the decentralization of the medical record—has made patient information even more difficult for physicians to locate. Combined with the growing demand for more—not less—information on patients, this decentralization is causing health-care providers to find ways to gather that information and make it easily available. To add to the pressure, the United States Medicare system has decreed that all medical claims from providers must be submitted electronically by 1996.

VISIONS OF A NEW HEALTH-CARE INFORMATION SYSTEM

What would an ideal health-care information system be like? Most experts believe it would be centered on a single, lifetime, *computerized patient record (CPR)*. Such a record would contain all expected demographic and medical patient information, including a family history, treatment information, prescriptions, test results, recent X-rays and scans. To encompass all types of current records, the CPR would store video, graphics, and voice as well as documents. It would incorporate automated claims processing and E-mail. Privacy would be guaranteed by using effective computer security. In fact, the privacy of CPRs in a properly controlled system would likely be better than with the current paper-based system. The CPR would be accessed through a community (or even nationwide) network, allowing it to be accessed and updated from different provider locations, including hospitals, clinics, doctors' offices, and often even patients' homes. The system making the record available would be connected to remote clinics and care centers as well and could be used to support and deliver medical services remotely, enabling a specialist at a major hospital to diagnose a patient problem at a remote clinic or even at the patient's home. Figure II.1 is one picture of the uses and users of CPR data. Figure II.2 compares today's paper-based patient record with a CPR.

Such a system will benefit the health-care system in many ways. Institutions are using computer systems to audit the use of a prescribed medication against the patient's CPR, looking for mistakes such as a patient allergy to the medicine or a drug that is counter-indicated due to patient use of another medication. According to one estimate, prescription errors alone add $3 billion a year to national health-care costs. A recent study at Latter-Day Saints Hospital, in Salt Lake City, shows that computers are 60 times more likely to catch such errors than is a manual check of paper records. Computer systems are being used to help doctors make diagnoses and determine cost-effective treatments. For example, CPRs are being connected to expert systems to support disease diagnosis. A two-year study found that an expert system reduced hospital admissions of suspected heart attack victims by 30 percent because it enables physicians to make faster, more accurate diagnoses. Not only does such a system save lives, but it also would save $1 billion a year nationwide in hospitalization expenses. Networked health-care systems can even be used to keep patients away from the hospital altogether. The New England Medical Center in Boston has placed multimedia computers in homes of children with cancer. The systems give parents instructions on changing dressings and administering blood tests, allowing these procedures to be carried out at home. The computer analyzes the blood and automatically notifies the doctor if the blood count has reached a dangerous level.

New CPR-based health-care systems need to meet technical requirements. Bruce Post, the president of the

CPR: Many Users, Many Uses

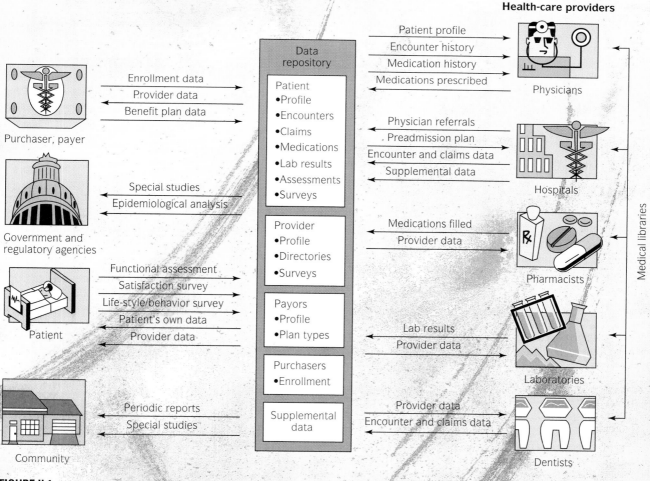

FIGURE II.1

The computerized patient record. A computerized patient record can consolidate data from multiple sources and has many uses. *Adapted from: Scott Wallace, "The Computerized Patient Record," David Jonason illustrator,* Byte, *May 1994.*

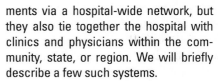

Today's paper-based record:

- Weighs about 4 lbs.
- Incomplete and illegible
- Difficult to spot trends or perform instant analysis
- Not connected to bedside monitors or labs
- Can only be used by one person at a time
- Not connected to billing or other departments
- Only 3 records per hour can be reviewed by staff

Tomorrow's electronic medical record:

- All data accessible from multiple points and at same time by clinicians, administrative, IS departments
- Networked to monitors, labs, other sites
- Easier and quicker than paper record keeping
- More accurate and up-to-date than traditional records
- Automatic calculations and charts; always legible
- Supports federal, state, and regulatory reporting requirements
- Allows faster, accurate analysis of trend data
- Staff can review up to 400 records per hour
- Stronger support for quality assurance/total quality programs

FIGURE II.2
A comparison of paper-based vs. electronic medical records:
Adapted from: Chuck Appleby, "Is Technology the Cure?" InformationWeek, May 10, 1993.

Vermont Health Care Information Consortium, says that such systems must have "effective communications and information sharing." That is, the system must be based upon an integrated database and communications technology that allows all potential users to access it no matter what equipment they have on their desks. The system would also need an easy-to-use, standardized graphical user interface to enable everyone to access it. The interface would include the use of not only the traditional keyboard and mouse but also touch screens and computer pens. The system would also need automated interfaces with laboratory and diagnostic devices both to avoid costly, error-prone data entry activities and to give caregivers the fastest possible access to the data. The system telecommunications policies and standards would have to support

the varied needs of the many institutions it would be serving, including hospitals, clinics, and private practices.

Client/server technology has been recommended for creating health-care applications because it allows information sharing among hospitals, physicians, and insurers, reducing duplication of effort. Desktop workstations deliver information directly to the people who need it. The software tools found in client/server systems help hospitals, HMOs, and other health-care organizations analyze their costs.

EXAMPLES OF CHINS

Client/server systems with computerized patient records, known as community health information networks (CHINs), are already in existence. They are usually hospital-based and link hospital depart-

ments via a hospital-wide network, but they also tie together the hospital with clinics and physicians within the community, state, or region. We will briefly describe a few such systems.

Health Information Network of Tennessee (HINT) uses a client/server system to link doctors with the Memphis Baptist Hospital and with HealthNet Inc., the first insurance provider to link up to the system. One hundred twenty doctors pay $49 per month each to retrieve patient data from their own offices. The data include laboratory test results and results from the radiology department and electrocardiograms, as well as admission and discharge data. Doctors can submit insurance claims directly to HealthNet electronically. In addition they are able to check patient eligibility for specific treatments, and to determine which drugs the company will pay for. HINT includes an E-mail system for the users. Through it, for example, doctors receive electronic confirmation on insurance claim payments.

The Wisconsin Health Information Network (WHIN) originally served nine hospitals owned by Aurora Health Care, Inc. of Milwaukee. Other hospitals have also been joining and it is now becoming statewide. WHIN has links to five insurance companies and 1100 doctors. It provides laboratory test results and medical records. One analyst estimates that each hospital will save between $200,000 and $1 million per year by consolidating test data. Aside from WHIN, Wisconsin currently has 15 proprietary networks that force doctors to have up to five computers and/or terminals on their desks in order to obtain needed data.

CLIENT/SERVER TECHNOLOGY AND COMPUTERIZED HEALTH INFORMATION SYSTEMS

Brigham and Women's Hospital. Boston's Brigham and Women's Hospital is a world-famous 750-bed hospital. It is the teaching arm of Harvard University's Medical School. It employs 7500 people and has an annual revenue of $630 million. The hospital will be merging with the 1000-bed Massachusetts General Hospital.

The hospital had a large legacy of independent support systems running on centralized minicomputers. It recently migrated to a LAN-based client/server environment. In the process all its business and patient applications were converted. The new system has increased on-line patient information availability while also increasing the number of support applications.

The system uses 3900 Intel-based PC clients and has 120 servers running 92 major applications. The servers store the applications and all patient information, process the transactions, and feed information to the clients. The applications are written in MUMPS (Massachusetts General Hospital Utility Multi-Programming System, an application development tool created in the late 1960s and early 1970s for minicomputer systems at Massachusetts General Hospital, which is widely used in health care, engineering, and scientific applications). The network is connected throughout the hospital and to remote clinics as well. It includes not only medical systems but also a connection to patient scheduling and billing systems. The system also has many other features. For example, the system automatically pages the doctor when test results show a patient has a life-threatening condition. It also performs an automatic surveillance to prevent improper or unnecessary use of certain drugs. Figure II.3 gives an overview of the Brigham and Women's Hospital information systems infrastructure.

Hospital management expects the system to save $10 million to $15 million annually. The savings will come from

Brigham and Women's Hospital Information Systems Infrastructure

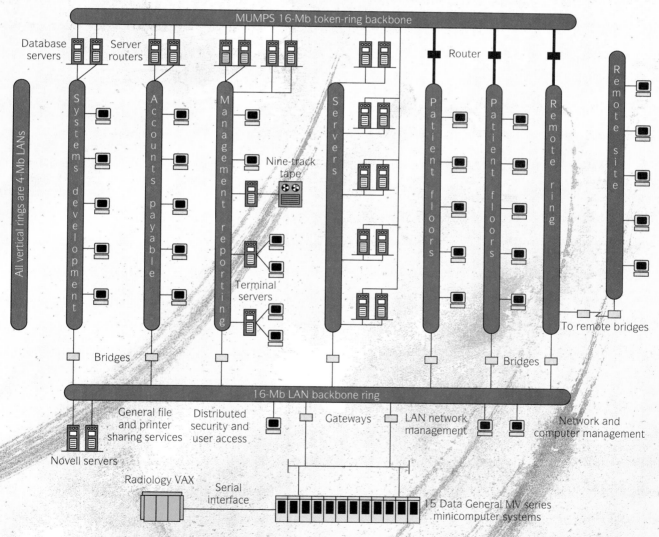

FIGURE II.3
Brigham and Women's Hospital information systems infrastructure. This large urban teaching hospital is making a transition from a minicomputer to a client/server-based architecture. *Adapted from: Scott Wallace, "The Computerized Patient Record," Byte, May 1994.*

many areas. For example, surveillance of patient records should eliminate many redundant laboratory tests and reduce the usage of unneeded drugs. In one case the system has reduced the annual bill for the previously much overused human-growth hormone from $750,000 to $50,000. Administrative savings will come from less paper shuffling and improved coordination of processes—eliminating lots of phone calls and paging, for example.

The hospital faced many problems in developing and installing this system. One was the need to convert to a new system in an institution that works every minute of every day and night. In a hospital, any mistake can have life-and-death consequences. Also, because client/server technology was new to the hospital, the developers and IS staff took a year longer to learn it than the vice-president of systems, John Glaser, had planned. When they did cut over to the new system, the move from several hundred clients to over 3000 produced bottlenecks that actually increased response time twelvefold. Eventually they solved the problem by increasing the number of servers and redirecting some of the clients to different servers.

The hospital still faces a number of obstacles and issues. One of the largest is that of data storage capacity. The daily hospital-wide accumulation of image data from CAT and MRI scans is 3 gigabytes, a staggering amount of storage. The system came on-line with about 10 gigabytes of storage, with plans to expand up to 60. But that still is only 20 days' storage. The challenge for the hospital is to purchase and manage the storage systems needed to keep patient clinical information on-line for 10 years. Another major obstacle is the lack of common definitions for diagnostic medical terms in more than a dozen specialty areas. Once the definitions have been agreed upon, the developers need to establish data definition standards for all these terms. Related to this issue is the need to establish a common CPR identifier so that the record of the patient that comes to the hospital is properly associated with the record

when he or she visits a clinic or a doctor's office. A third major issue is the need for legal clarity on confidentiality issues. With so much confidential data on-line and accessibility at a number of sites within the hospital and the community, questions abound. Who is responsible if private data leaks out or is stolen? Who will be allowed access to the data for the purpose of research? Brigham & Women's Hospital is merging with the 1000-bed Massachusetts General Hospital but the two hospitals' information systems are incompatible. (Massachusetts General has a mix of mainframes, minicomputers, and client/server systems.)

PacifiCare Health Systems, Inc. PacifiCare Health Systems, Inc., of Cyprus, California, is an HMO that feels the same pressures to act as those affecting other HMOs. Management decided they wanted to get ahead of the technology curve by moving to a client/server infrastructure. They decided not to start with medical applications. Instead, they began by replacing the Sales and Marketing (SAM) system with a new client/server SAM system. The $2.2 billion HMO decided that the old system—ten-year-old large VAXclusters and dumb terminals—was inflexible and expensive and could no longer support the needs of the company. The plan was to maintain the VAXclusters as data stores with their 400 gigabytes, but integrate them into the new system. "We have tens of millions of dollars invested in that cluster," explained IS executive Leo Collins. Once this client/server system is running well, the plan is to develop a system to manage enrollment to MediCal/Medicaid (the California version of the federal Medicaid system), and then develop other medical-related systems.

The SAM project ran into many problems. According to Scott Brummett, the director of business operating systems, the biggest problem was the lack of client/server knowledge among the 230-person information systems staff. "A good deal of SAM's costs went to paying for a learning curve that was much steeper than we imagined," he explained. Staff members lacked knowledge not only of client/server technol-

ogy but also of networking. Ultimately the project ran 200 percent over budget, with more than half going for additional costs just to educate developers on using graphical development tools and teaching end users how to use desktop computers.

Another major problem emerged when the development team tested a version of SAM over a TCP/IP network connecting several dozen PCs and a single VAX host. The computer was unable to handle the heavy load of database queries. Collins believes the team did not plan the application well. However, the underlying problem seems to have been that the development tool the team used, Microsoft Corp.'s Visual Basic, offers few guidelines for developing such systems. A third problem was the lack of relevant commercial software for VAX computers, forcing team members to write virtually all of the software. They might have purchased software if they had been able to use a more popular operating system. PacifiCare has not released the final cost of the project, but its annual report indicated that 1993 software development costs alone had risen by 60 percent over 1991 expenditures. Maintenance costs are likely to be high because none of the system is purchased software. Another problem PacifiCare ran into was the limitations in trying to get existing systems to communicate with each other. Properly configuring the middleware—the software gateways that translate between the PC front-end tools and the database servers—was more complex than expected and became a major roadblock.

Ultimately the project fell more than a year behind schedule (as well as way over budget). With all the problems, Brummett and some business managers considered abandoning client/server, but, Brummett said, they decided to continue with it because "we didn't have any alternatives in mind." PacifiCare managers offered a series of lessons they learned when turning to client/server technology for the first time. First, cost overruns might have been avoided with more up-front analysis. One reason for their inadequate analysis, Brummett points out, was that upper management did not require the replacement of SAM to be cost-justified. Other lessons include: Seek out other IS shops that have gone through similar projects and learn as much as you can from them; make sure that outside consultants teach your staff at the same time they are doing their work; realize that middleware can "make or break an application"; and carefully train IS professionals in Windows and other microcomputer technologies.

As of mid-1994, the system was partially in operation but not fully completed. The company has yet to see any measurable payback. However, management does expect payback to start in two or three years, once the system is completed. And they figure they are ahead of the game because they feel they are now well positioned to further

adopt client/servers whereas most other HMOs are only barely sticking their toes in the client/server waters.

Sources: Steve Alexander, "A Healthier Existence," *Computerworld Client/Server Journal,* April 1995; Chuck Appleby, "Client-Server: A Hospital," *InformationWEEK,* October 10, 1994; Stephen Baker, "Hospitals Attack a Crippler: Paper," *Business Week,* February 21, 1994; Milt Freudenheim, "A Bitter Pill for the H.M.O.'s," *The New York Times,* April 28, 1995; Kim S. Nash, "PacificCare Picks Up the Pieces," *Computerworld Client/Server Journal,* May 1994; Scott Wallace, "The Computerized Patient Record," *Byte,* May 1994.

Case Study Questions

1. What management, organization, and technology problems did these medical institutions encounter when trying to build or convert to a client/server system? What other problems did they encounter?

2. Of the problems listed, which ones, if any, do you think will disappear in the next few years? Why?

3. Do you think client/server technology is part of the business strategy for HMOs and hospitals? Why or why not?

4. Do you see this as a part of the solution to the country's medical care problems? Will it be cost effective? Why or why not?

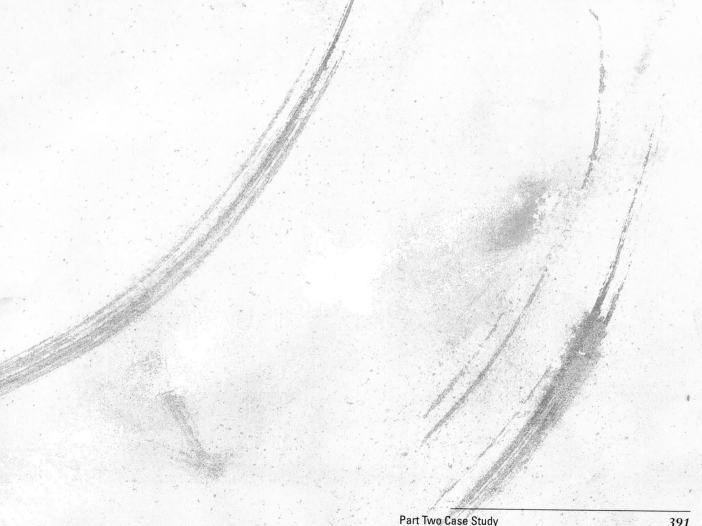

three

Building Information Systems:
Contemporary Approaches

A new information system represents an opportunity for organizational problem-solving and planned organizational change. Alternative approaches for building systems have been devised to minimize the risks in this process. Building an effective information system is both a skill and an art, requiring sensitivity to both technical and organizational concerns. Ensuring information systems quality and managing the implementation process are essential.

Chapter 11
Redesigning the Organization with Information Systems

Chapter 11 is an overview of systems development, showing how building a new information system can redesign and reshape an organization by rationalizing procedures, redesigning business processes, or transforming the nature of the business itself. Plans for new information systems should carefully assess their business value and ensure that they support organizational goals. The chapter describes the basic activities required to design and build any information system. Systems analysis and design combine technical and organizational responsibilities and require participation from both end users and technical specialists.

Chapter 12
Alternative Systems-Building Methods

Chapter 12 describes the major alternative approaches for building information systems: the traditional systems life cycle, prototyping, software packages, end-user development, and outsourcing. Each approach has its own strengths and limitations and is suitable for a particular class of problems. Management issues posed by each approach are carefully analyzed.

Chapter 13
Ensuring Quality with Information Systems

Chapter 13 shows how information systems can contribute to total quality management in the firm, showing the different ways in which systems can help companies improve their products and services. It also describes the principal problems with assuring information systems quality: software reliability and maintainability. The principal methods used for software quality assurance include analysis and design methodologies, metrics, and quality tools. An entire section analyzes the role that Computer-Aided Software Engineering (CASE) can play in the quality assurance process.

Chapter 14
System Success and Failure: Implementation

Chapter 14 looks at the factors responsible for the success and failure of information systems, which are largely organizational in nature. To better understand these factors, one must examine the entire process of implementation and organizational change, with special attention to the role of end users; the level of management support; the dimensions of project risk; and the role of the systems builder as a change agent. While not all aspects of implementation can be controlled, a contingency approach to project management and efforts to secure management and end user support can minimize risks and problems.

In the early 1980s, the Social Security Administration found that its information systems were totally inadequate for its mission and operational needs. To forestall collapse, SSA launched the Systems Modernization Plan, one of the largest information system projects in history. Ten years later, SSA embarked on another ambitious round of technology modernization as it tried to create an information architecture for the twenty-first century. The story of these projects illustrates themes from this section and from the entire text: planning for systems, using systems to redesign organizations, assessing the benefits of information system investments, management of large-scale information systems projects, and organizational obstacles to "strategic transitions."

Redesigning the Organization with Information Systems

New Zealand Designs for Paperless Tax Returns

Since the mid-1980s, New Zealand has been moving away from being one of the most highly regulated economies in the world. Its government agencies now have to be more flexible and responsive. Beset by constant changes in New Zealand's tax collection management, the New Zealand Inland Revenue Department (IRD) could only turn to an inflexible 20-year-old mainframe-oriented system.

So in 1990 IRD decided to modernize its information systems and redesign its business processes. It enlisted Andersen Consulting to help it build a new $300 million information system that would automate tax filing for the country's citizens. The system's objectives were to improve efficiency, generate additional revenue, and reduce the Revenue Department's staff requirements.

The new system, dubbed Future Inland Revenue Systems and Technology (FIRST), allows taxpayers either to mail their income tax forms to a regional tax office or to transmit them electronically to the Revenue Department's computer. Tax forms that previously took three or four months to process by hand can be completed in 14 days. Such service improvements enabled the Revenue Department to cut its staff from 7000 to 5200. By 1997, the Revenue Department hopes to eliminate paper tax forms, queries, and correspondence altogether.

The systems analysis process identified redundant and paper-intensive office functions. Each of the district offices of the Revenue Department was a mirror of the other. The new system design eliminated superfluous tasks. The system building team developed new client/server software programs for functions such as client registration and tax return generation. The Revenue Department decided to implement the new system slowly to leave time for user training and to minimize organizational disruptions.

After a 12-month study, the Revenue Department's Information Technology Group began building the new system. It installed a nationwide network of 240 UNIX file servers, 500 microcomputers, and about 800 terminal devices and developed client/server applications for 40 district offices and 4 regional centers. Individual transactions would be processed on microcomputers or by using terminals in the district offices, while larger applications, such as corporate management systems, remained on the agency's two mainframes. The system handles about 2 million machine transaction inquiries per day.

Although the total cost of FIRST is expected to exceed $300 million, its efficiencies have already produced savings to offset more than 90 percent of this amount. ■

Sources: Randal Jackson, "Inland Revenue Department," *Computerworld: The Global 100*, May 1, 1995, and John McMullen, "Taxation without Vexation," *InformationWEEK*, March 22, 1993.

New Zealand's automated tax filing system illustrates the many factors at work in the development of a new information system. Building the new system entailed analyzing the agency's problems with existing information systems, assessing people's information needs, selecting appropriate technology, and redesigning procedures and jobs. Management had to monitor the system-building effort and to evaluate its benefits and costs. The new information system represented a process of planned organizational change.

This chapter describes how new information systems are conceived, built, and installed, with special at-

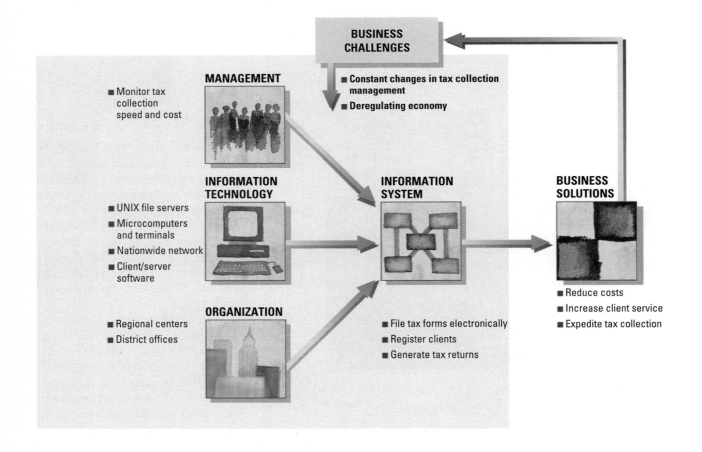

BUSINESS CHALLENGES
- Constant changes in tax collection management
- Deregulating economy

MANAGEMENT
- Monitor tax collection speed and cost

INFORMATION TECHNOLOGY
- UNIX file servers
- Microcomputers and terminals
- Nationwide network
- Client/server software

ORGANIZATION
- Regional centers
- District offices

INFORMATION SYSTEM
- File tax forms electronically
- Register clients
- Generate tax returns

BUSINESS SOLUTIONS
- Reduce costs
- Increase client service
- Expedite tax collection

tention to organizational design issues and business re-engineering. It describes systems analysis and design and other core activities that must be performed to build any information system. The chapter explains how to establish the business value of information systems and how to ensure that new systems are linked to the organization's business plan and information requirements.

After completing this chapter, you will be able to:

Learning Objectives

1. Understand why building new systems is a process of organizational change.

2. Identify the groups who are involved in building systems.

3. Explain how the organization can develop information systems that fit its business plan.

4. Identify the core activities in the systems development process.

5. Describe various models for determining the business value of information systems.

11.1 SYSTEMS AS PLANNED ORGANIZATIONAL CHANGE

This text has emphasized that an information system is a sociotechnical entity, an arrangement of both technical and social elements. The introduction of a new information system involves much more than new hardware and software. It also includes changes in jobs, skills, management, and organization. In the sociotechnical philosophy, one cannot install new technology without considering the people who must work with it (Bostrom and Heinen, 1977). When we design a new information system, we are redesigning the organization.

One of the most important things to know about building a new information system is that this process is one kind of planned organizational change. Frequently, new systems mean new ways of doing business and working together. The nature of tasks, the speed with which they must be completed, the nature of supervision (its frequency and intensity), and who has what information about whom will all be decided in the process of building an information system. This is especially true in contemporary systems, which deeply affect many parts of the organization. System builders must understand how a system will affect the organization as a whole, focusing particularly on organizational conflict and changes in the locus of decision making. Builders must also consider how the nature of work groups will change under the impact of the new system. Builders determine how much change is needed.

Systems can be technical successes but organizational failures because of a failure in the social and political process of building the system. Analysts and designers are responsible for ensuring that key members of the organization participate in the design process and are permitted to influence the ultimate shape of the system. This activity must be carefully orchestrated by information system builders (see Chapter 14).

HOW IS SYSTEMS DEVELOPMENT MANAGED?

The organization must develop a technique for ensuring that the most important systems are built first, that unnecessary systems are not built, and that end users have a full and meaningful role in determining which new systems will be built and how. Figure 11.1 shows the elements of a management structure for developing new

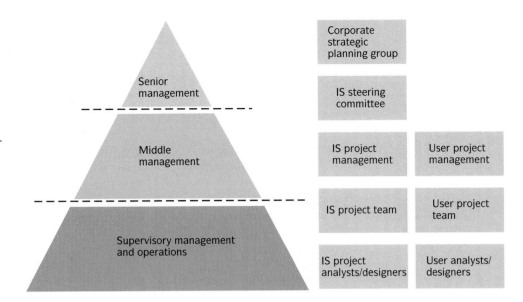

systems. At the apex of this structure is the corporate strategic planning group and the information system steering committee.

The *corporate strategic planning group* is responsible for developing the strategic organization plan. This plan may require the development of new systems. An important function of this committee then is to give overall strategic direction to the information systems area. A second less obvious function is to educate senior management about the systems area so that they understand how dependent the organization is on systems. Senior management provides overall strategic direction (making sure that systems are coordinated with strategic plans) and, equally important, provides funding and strong support. The lack of senior management involvement or senior management's inability to tie information systems to strategic business plans are probably among the most common causes of long-range strategic systems failure in organizations.

The *information systems steering committee* is the senior management group with direct responsibility for systems development and operation. It is composed of division directors from the end-user and information systems areas. The steering committee reviews and approves plans for systems in all divisions; seeks to develop common systems that can be shared; seeks to coordinate and integrate systems; sometimes becomes involved in selecting specific project alternatives; and approves training for new systems. Increasingly, the information systems steering committee is becoming a powerful gatekeeper of systems development.

The next level of management, the *project management team*, is concerned with the management of specific projects. Generally, this is a small group of senior IS managers and end-user managers with responsibility for a single project.

The *project team* is composed of the systems professionals (analysts and programmers) who are directly responsible for building the system. As previously indicated, ultimate end users (e.g., the human resources department) frequently have their own systems professionals who participate directly in the project. Indeed, many large organizations have created a new job title, "business systems analyst," to identify, recruit, and reward systems personnel who work directly for user departments. This is quite a departure from the past, where the data processing department was the sole source of systems professionals.

A typical project team consists of systems analysts, functional analysts (specialists from relevant business areas), application programmers, and perhaps database specialists. This team is responsible for most of the development activities. For certain applications, legal staff representatives and behavioral specialists may be consulted. Discussions with managers from both user areas and information systems will take place at key decision points.

LINKING INFORMATION SYSTEMS TO THE BUSINESS PLAN

information systems plan A road map indicating the direction of systems development, the rationale, the current situation, the management strategy, the implementation plan, and the budget.

Deciding what new systems to build should be an essential component of the organizational planning process. Organizations need to develop an information systems plan that supports their overall business plan. Once specific projects have been selected within the overall context of a strategic plan for the business and the systems area, an **information systems plan** can be developed. The plan serves as a road map indicating the direction of systems development, the rationale, the current situation, the management strategy, the implementation plan, and the budget (see Table 11.1).

The plan contains a statement of corporate goals and specifies how information technology supports the attainment of those goals. The report shows how general goals will be achieved by specific systems projects. It lays out specific target dates and milestones that can be used later to judge the progress of the plan in terms of how many objectives were actually attained in the time frame specified in the plan. An important part of the plan is the management strategy for moving from the current situation to the future. Generally, this will indicate the key decisions made by managers concerning hardware acquisition; telecommunications; centralization/decentralization of authority, data, and hardware; and required organizational change.

The implementation plan generally outlines stages in the development of the plan, defining milestones and specifying dates. In this section, organizational changes are usually described, including management and employee training requirements; recruiting efforts; and changes in authority, structure, or management practice.

ESTABLISHING ORGANIZATIONAL INFORMATION REQUIREMENTS

In order to develop an effective information systems plan, the organization must have a clear understanding of both its long- and short-term information requirements. Two principal methodologies for establishing the essential information requirements of the organization as a whole are enterprise analysis and critical success factors.

Table 11.1 Information Systems Plan	

1. **Purpose of the Plan**
    Overview of plan contents
    Changes in firm's current situation
    Firm's strategic plan
    Current business organization
    Management strategy
 	
2. **Strategic Business Plan**
    Current situation
    Current business organization
    Changing environments
    Major goals of the business plan
 	
3. **Current Systems**
    Major systems supporting business functions
    Major current capabilities
        Hardware
        Software
        Database
        Telecommunications
    Difficulties meeting business requirements
    Anticipated future demands
 	
4. **New Developments**
    New system projects
        Project descriptions
        Business rationale
	New capabilities required
	        Hardware
	        Software
	        Database
	        Telecommunications
	
	5. **Management Strategy**
	    Acquisition plans
	    Milestones and timing
	    Organizational realignment
	    Internal reorganization
	    Management controls
	    Major training initiatives
	    Personnel strategy
	
	6. **Implementation Plan**
	    Detailed implementation plan
	    Anticipated difficulties
	    in implementation
	    Progress reports
	
	7. **Budget Requirements**
	    Requirements
	    Potential savings
	    Financing
	    Acquisition cycle

Enterprise Analysis (Business Systems Planning)

enterprise analysis An analysis of organization-wide information requirements by looking at the entire organization in terms of organizational units, functions, processes, and data elements; helps identify the key entities and attributes in the organization's data.

Enterprise analysis (also called business systems planning) argues that the information requirements of a firm can only be understood by looking at the entire organization in terms of organizational units, functions, processes, and data elements. Enterprise analysis can help identify the key entities and attributes of the organization's data. This method starts with the notion that the information requirements of a firm or a division can be specified only with a thorough understanding of the entire organization. This method was developed by IBM in the 1960s explicitly for establishing the relationship among large system development projects (Zachman, 1982).

The central method used in the enterprise analysis approach is to take a large sample of managers and ask them how they use information, where they get the information, what their environment is like, what their objectives are, how they make decisions, and what their data needs are.

The results of this large survey of managers are aggregated into subunits, functions, processes, and data matrices (see Figure 11.2). Figure 11.2 shows parts of two matrices developed at the Social Security Administration as part of a very-large-scale systems redevelopment effort called the Systems Modernization Plan, which began in 1982.

Figure 11.2A shows a process/organization matrix identifying those persons in the organization who participate in specific processes, such as planning. Figure 11.2B shows a process/data class matrix depicting what information is required to support a particular process, which process creates the data, and which uses it. (*C* in an intersection stands for "creators of data"; *U* stands for "users of data".)

The shaded boxes in Figure 11.2B indicate a *logical application group*—a group of data elements that supports a related set of organizational processes. In this case, actuarial estimates, agency plans, and budget data are created in the planning process. The planning process, in turn, is performed by the commissioner's office, along with deputy commissioners and associate commissioners. This suggests then that an information system focused on actuarial, agency plan, and budget data elements should be built for the commissioners in order to support planning.

One strength of enterprise analysis is that it gives a comprehensive view of the organization and of systems/data uses and gaps. Enterprise analysis is especially suitable for start-up or massive change situations. For instance, it is one of the methods used by the Social Security Administration to bring about a long-term strategic change in its information processing activities. This organization had never before performed a comprehensive analysis of its information requirements. Instead, it had relied on a bottom-up method of responding to whatever users requested, as well as on byproduct approaches where most emphasis was placed on simply performing elementary transaction processing. Enterprise analysis was used to develop a comprehensive view of how the Social Security Administration currently uses information.

Another strength of enterprise analysis is that it helps to produce an organizational consensus by involving a large number of managers and users of data. It helps the organization find out what it should be doing in terms of information processing simply by requiring many managers to think about information (Doll, 1985).

The weakness of enterprise analysis is that it produces an enormous amount of data that is expensive to collect and difficult to analyze. It is a very expensive technique with a bias toward top management and data processing. Most of the interviews are conducted with senior or middle managers, with little effort to collect information from clerical workers and supervisory managers. Moreover, the questions frequently focus not on the critical objectives of management and where information is needed, but rather on what *existing* information is used. The result is a tendency to automate whatever exists. In this manner, manual systems are automated. But in many instances, entirely new approaches to how business is conducted are needed, and these needs are not addressed.

FIGURE 11.2A

Process/organization matrix. This chart indicates who in the organization participates in specific processes and the nature of their involvement.

PROCESS/ORGANIZATION MATRIX — PROCESSES	Commissioner	DC programs and policy	AC disability insurance	AC retirement and survivors ins.	AC supp. security income	AC governmental affairs	AC policy	O actuary	O hearings and appeals	DC management and assessment	AC assessment	O field assessment	O human resources	O material resources	O financial resources	O training	DC systems	AC system integration	AC system requirements	AC system operations	DC operations	AC field operations	Region	District/branch	Teleservice center	AC Central operations	O Program service center	Process center	Module	D International opers.	Module	O Disability opers.	Module	Central records	Module (cert. and coverage)	Data operations centers	Disability determination service
PLANNING																																					
Develop agency plans	M	M	M	M	M		M	M	M	M	S	S	S	S	S	S	S	M	M	M	M	M	M	S		M	S							S		S	
Administer agency budget	M	M	M	S	S	S	S	S	M	M	M	M	S	M	M	M	M	M	S	S	S	M	M	S	S		M	M	M		M		M		M	S	M
Formulate program policies	M	M	M	M	M		M		M	M	S	S		S	S	M	S	M	S	M	M	M				M	M	S			M		S			S	M
Formulate admin. policies	M	M						M				M	M	M	M	M				M																	
Design work processes		M	M	M	M	S	S		M	M	M	S	S	S		S	M	M	M	M	M	M	M	M	S	M	M	M	M	S	M	M	M	M	M	M	M
GENERAL MANAGEMENT																																					
Manage public affairs	M	M	M	S	M	M	S		S	S	S	S		S		S	S	M	M	M	S	S	M	M	M	S	M	S		M	S	M	S		M	S	M
Manage intergovernmental affairs	M	M	M	M	M	M	M		M	M	M	S	M	M	S	S	S	M	M	M	S		M	S	S	S	S	S		M	S	M	S		S		M
Exchange data		M	M	M	M	M	M	S	M	M	S	M	S	M	S	S	S	M	M	M	S	M	M	M	S	M	S		M	M	M		M		M	M	
Maintain administrative accounts		M	S	S	S	S	S	S	M				M	M		S		S			M					S		S						M		S	S
Maintain programmatic accounts		M		M					M					M			S				M		M		M		M							S			
Conduct audits								M	S	S			S					M	S		M	S	S		S		S		S								
Establish organizations		M	M	M	M	M	M	M	M	M	M	M	M	M	M	M	M	M	M	M	M	M	M	M	M	M	M	M	M	M	M	M	M	M	M	M	M
Manage human resources		M	M	M	M	M	M	M	M	M	S	M	M	M	M	M	M	M	M	M	M	M	M	M	M	M	M	M	M	M	M	M	M	M	M	M	M
Provide security							S	M				M			M	M	M	M	M	S	S	S	S	S	S	S	S	S	S	S	S	S	S	S	S	S	S
Manage equipment	S				M				M	M	S	S		M		M	M	M		M	S	M	M	M	M	M	M	S	S	S	S	M	S	M	S	M	
Manage facilities			S						S	M	S	S		M		M	M	S		M	S	M	M	M	M	M	M	M	M		S		M		M		M
Manage supplies	S	S	S	S	S	S	S	S	M	M	S	S		M		M	M	S		M	S	M	M	M	M	M	M	M	S	S	M		S	M	S	M	
Manage data		M	M	M	M		M							M	M	M	M	S	S	S	S	S	S	S	S	S	S	S	S	S	S	S	S	S	S	S	S
Manage workloads	M	M	M	M	M	M	M	M	M	M	M	M	M	M	M	M	M	M	M	M	M	M	M	M	M	M	M	M	M	M	M	M	M	M	M	M	M
PROGRAM ADMIN.																																					
Issue social security numbers									S		S								S				M	M						M							S
Maintain earnings	S								S		S								S				M	M		S		S		S	M	M	M				
Collect claims information																				S			M	M			M		M		M	M	S				
Determine eligibility/entitlement		M	M	M	M		S		M		M	M							S			M	S		M	M		M	M	M	M	M	M	S	M		
Compute payments																			S			M	S	M		M		M		M		M	M				
Administer debt management	S			S			M				M						S	M		M	M	S	M	M	M	M	M	M	M								
SUPPORT																																					
Generate notices																			S				M	M			M		M		M		M				
Respond to programmatic inquiries		M	M	M	M	M	M	M	M	M	M	S							S	M	S	M	M	M	S	M	S	M	M	M	M	M	M	M	M	S	M
Provide quality assessment	M									M	M	M																									

KEY

M = major involvement

S = some involvement

DC = deputy commissioner

AC = associate commissioner

O = office

Strategic Analysis: Critical Success Factors

critical success factors (CSFs) A small number of easily identifiable operational goals shaped by the industry, the firm, the manager, and the broader environment that are believed to assure the success of an organization. Used to determine the information requirements of an organization.

The strategic analysis or critical success factor approach argues that the information requirements of an organization are determined by a small number of **critical success factors (CSFs)** of managers. CSFs are operational goals. If these goals can be attained, the success of the firm or organization is assured (Rockart, 1979; Rockart and Treacy, 1982).

CSFs are shaped by the industry, the firm, the manager, and the broader environment. This broader focus, in comparison to that of previous methods, accounts for the description of this technique as "strategic." An important premise of the strategic analysis approach is that there is a small number of objectives that managers can easily identify and information systems can focus on.

LOGICAL APPLICATION GROUPS	PROCESSES \ DATA CLASSES	Actuarial estimates	Agency plans	Budget	Program regs./policy	Admin. regs./policy	Labor agreements	Data standards	Procedures	Automated systems documentation	Educational media	Public agreements	Intergovernmental agreements	Grants	External	Exchange control	Administrative accounts	Program expenditures	Audit reports	Organization/position	Employee identification	Recruitment/placement	Complaints/grievances	Training resources	Security	Equipment utilization	Space utilization	Supplies utilization	Workload schedules	Work measurement	Enumeration I.D.	Enumeration control	Earnings	Employer I.D.	Earnings control	Claims characteristics	Claims control	Decisions	Payment	Collection/waiver	Notice	Inquiries control	Quality appraisal
PLANNING	Develop agency plans	C	C	C	U	U									U																												
PLANNING	Administer agency budget	C	C	C	U	U						U	U	U		U	U	U		U	U					U	U	U		U		U			U		U			U		U	U
PLANNING	Formulate program policies	U	U		C				U						U				U				U															U					U
PLANNING	Formulate admin. policies		U		U	C	C		U						U				U	U			U																				
PLANNING	Formulate data policies		U	U		U		C	U	U															U	U	U	U															
PLANNING	Design work processes		U		U	U			C	C		U	U						U																			U					U
GENERAL MANAGEMENT	Manage public affairs		U		U	U			U		C	C	C																														
GENERAL MANAGEMENT	Manage intrgovt. affairs	U	U		U	U			U		U		C	C	C															U	U		U	U		U			U				
GENERAL MANAGEMENT	Exchange data				U				U			U	U	U	U	C	U	U												U													
GENERAL MANAGEMENT	Maintain admin. accounts			U		U			U			U	U				C				U					U	U	U								U			U				
GENERAL MANAGEMENT	Maintain prog. accounts			U	U				U			U	U					C														U			U		U	U	U	U		U	
GENERAL MANAGEMENT	Conduct audits				U	U			U	U							U	U	C		U								U														
GENERAL MANAGEMENT	Establish organizations			U		U			U											C	U								U	U													U
GENERAL MANAGEMENT	Manage human resources			U		U	U		U											C	C	C	C	C																			
GENERAL MANAGEMENT	Provide security				U	U		U	U	U															C	C	C	C		U													
GENERAL MANAGEMENT	Manage equipment			U		U		U	U	U															C	C	C	C															
GENERAL MANAGEMENT	Manage facilities			U		U			U																U	U	C																
GENERAL MANAGEMENT	Manage supplies			U		U			U																C	U	U	C															
GENERAL MANAGEMENT	Manage workloads	U		U	U	U			U							U										U	U	U	C	C		U			U		U					U	U
PROGRAM ADMIN.	Issue social security nos.								U				U		U																C	C											
PROGRAM ADMIN.	Maintain earnings								U				U	U	U																U		C	C	C	U							
PROGRAM ADMIN.	Collect claims information				U	U			U						U																U	U				C	C	U	U	U			
PROGRAM ADMIN.	Determine elig/entlmt.								U																						U	U	U			U		C	U	U			
PROGRAM ADMIN.	Compute payments				U				U									U													U		U			U		U	C	C			
PROGRAM ADMIN.	Administer debt mgmt.				U				U									U																					U	C			
SUPPORT	Generate notices								U						U																U		U			U		U	U	U	C		
SUPPORT	Respond to prog. inquiries				U				U		U																				U		U	U		U		U	U	U	U	C	
SUPPORT	Provide quality assessment				U	U			U	U																					U		U			U		U			U		C

KEY
C = creators of data   U = users of data

FIGURE 11.2B
Process/data class matrix. This chart depicts what data classes are required to support particular organizational processes and which processes are the creators and users of data.

The principal method used in CSF analysis is personal interviews—three or four—with a number of top managers to identify their goals and the resulting CSFs. These personal CSFs are aggregated to develop a picture of the firm's CSFs. Then systems are built to deliver information on these CSFs. (See Table 11.2 for examples of CSFs. For the method of developing CSFs in an organization, see Figure 11.3.)

The strength of the CSF method is that it produces a smaller data set to analyze than enterprise analysis. Only top managers are interviewed, and the questions focus on a small number of CSFs rather than a broad inquiry into what information is used or needed. This method can be tailored to the structure of each industry, with different competitive strategies producing different information systems. The CSF method also depends on the industry position and even the geographical location. Therefore, this method produces systems that are more custom-tailored to an organization.

A unique strength of the CSF method is that it takes into account the changing environment with which organizations and managers must deal. This method explicitly

Table 11.2 Critical Success Factors and Organizational Goals

Example	Goals	CSF

Profit concern	Earnings/share
	Return on investment
	Market share
	New product
		Automotive inudstry
		  Styling
		  Quality dealer system
		  Cost control
		  Energy standards

Nonprofit	Excellent health care Meeting government regulations Future health needs	Regional integration with other hospitals Efficient use of resources Improved monitoring of regulations

Source: Rockart (1979).

FIGURE 11.3
Using CSFs to develop systems. The CSF approach relies on interviews with key managers to identify their CSFs. Individual CSFs are aggregated to develop CSFs for the entire firm. Systems can then be built to deliver information on these CSFs.

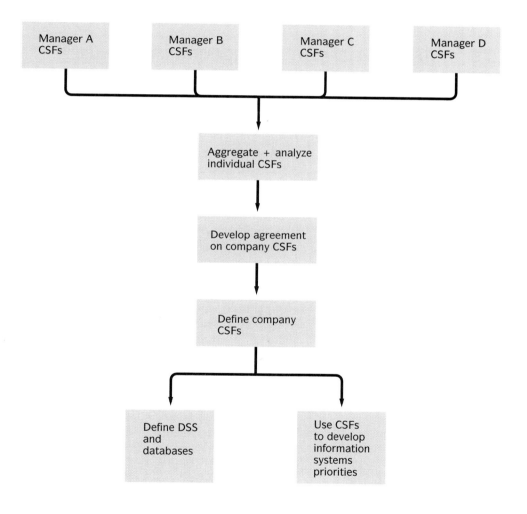

asks managers to look at the environment and consider how their analysis of it shapes their information needs. It is especially suitable for top management and for the development of DSS and ESS. Last, the method produces a consensus among top managers about what is important to measure in order to gauge the organization's success. Like enterprise analysis, the CSF method focuses organizational attention on how information should be handled.

The weakness of this method is that the aggregation process and the analysis of the data are art forms. There is no particularly rigorous way in which individual CSFs can be aggregated into a clear company pattern. Second, there is often confusion among interviewees (and interviewers) between *individual* and *organizational* CSFs. They are not necessarily the same. What can be critical to a manager may not be important for the organization. Moreover, this method is clearly biased toward top managers because they are the ones (generally the only ones) interviewed. Indeed, the method seems to apply only to management reporting systems, DSS, and ESS. It assumes that successful TPSs already exist. Last, it should be noted that this method does not necessarily overcome the impact of a changing environment or changes in managers. Environments and managers change rapidly, and information systems must adjust accordingly. The use of CSFs to develop a system does not mitigate these factors.

11.2 SYSTEMS DEVELOPMENT AND ORGANIZATIONAL CHANGE

automation Using the computer to speed up the performance of existing tasks.

New information systems can be powerful instruments for organizational change. Figure 11.4 shows that there are four kinds of structural organizational change which are enabled by information technology: automation, rationalization, re-engineering, and paradigm shifts. Each carries different rewards and risks.

The most common form of IT-enabled organizational change is **automation**. The first applications of information technology involved assisting employees perform their tasks more efficiently and effectively. Calculating paychecks and payroll registers, giving bank tellers instant access to customer deposit records, and developing a nationwide network of airline reservation terminals for airline reservation agents are all examples of early automation. Automation is akin to putting a larger motor in an existing automobile.

rationalization of procedures The streamlining of standard operating procedures, eliminating obvious bottlenecks, so that automation makes operating procedures more efficient.

A deeper form of organizational change—one that follows quickly from early automation—is **rationalization of procedures**. Automation frequently reveals new bottlenecks in production, and makes the existing arrangement of procedures and structures painfully cumbersome. Rationalization of procedures is the streamlining of standard operating procedures, eliminating obvious bottlenecks, so that automation can make operating procedures more efficient. For example, the New Zealand Inland Revenue Department's system is effective not just because it utilizes state-of-the-art computer technology but because its design allows the IRD to operate more efficiently. The procedures of IRD or of any organization must be rationally structured to achieve this result. Before the IRD could automate its tax filing system, it had to have identification numbers for all taxpayers and standard rules for calculating and submitting tax payments in either paper or electronic form. Without a certain amount of rationalization in the Inland Revenue Department's organization, its computer technology would have been useless.

business re-engineering The radical redesign of business processes, combining steps to cut waste and eliminating repetitive, paper-intensive tasks in order to improve cost, quality or service, and to maximize the benefits of information technology.

A more powerful type of organizational change is **business re-engineering,** in which business processes are analyzed, simplified, and redesigned. Re-engineering involves radically rethinking the flow of work, the business procedures used to produce products and services with a mind to radically reduce the costs of business. A **business process** is a set of logically related tasks performed to achieve a defined business outcome. Some examples of business processes are developing a new product, ordering goods from a supplier, or processing and paying an insurance claim. Table 11.3 describes various ways that information technology can impact these processes. Using information technology, organizations can rethink and streamline their busi-

business process A set of logically related tasks performed to achieve a defined business outcome.

ness processes to improve speed, service, and quality. Business re-engineering reorganizes work flows, combining steps to cut waste and eliminating repetitive, paper-intensive tasks (sometimes the new design eliminates jobs as well). It is much more ambitious than rationalization of procedures, requiring a new vision of how the process is to be organized.

A widely-cited example of business re-engineering is Ford Motor Company's "invoiceless processing." Ford, with over 500 people in its North American Accounts Payable organization alone, discovered that the Mazda Motor Corporation's accounts payable organization employed only 5 people. When Ford management analyzed the company's existing system, it found out that the accounts payable clerks spent most of their time matching purchase orders against receiving documents and invoices and then issuing payments. Mismatches where the purchase order, receiving document, or invoice disagreed were common, forcing the accounts payable clerks to investigate the discrepancies and delay payments. Ford found that re-engineering its entire accounts payable process could prevent mismatches in the first place. The company instituted "invoiceless processing" where the purchasing department enters a purchase order into an on-line database that can be checked by the receiving department when the ordered items arrive. If the received goods match the purchase order, the system automatically generates a check for accounts payable to send to the vendor. There is no need for vendors to send invoices. After re-engineering the accounts payable process, Ford was able to reduce headcount by 75% and produce more accurate financial information (Hammer and Champy, 1993).

Rationalizing procedures and redesigning business processes are limited to specific parts of a business. New information systems can ultimately affect the design of the entire organization by actually transforming how the organization carries out its business or even the nature of the business itself. For instance, Schneider National, described in Chapter 3, used new information systems to create a competitive on-demand shipping service and to develop a new sideline business managing the logistics of other companies. Baxter International's stockless inventory system, described in Chapter 2, transformed Baxter into a working partner with hospitals and into a

Table 11.3	IT Capabilities and Their Organizational Impacts
Capability	Organizational Impact/Benefit
Transactional	IT can transform unstructured processes into routinized transactions
Geographical	IT can transfer information with rapidity and ease across large distances, making processes independent of geography
Automational	IT can replace or reduce human labor in a process
Analytical	IT can bring complex analytical methods to bear on a process
Informational	IT can bring vast amounts of detailed information into a process
Sequential	IT can enable changes in the sequence of tasks in a process, often allowing multiple tasks to be worked on simultaneously
Knowledge Management	IT allows the capture and dissemination of knowledge and expertise to improve the process
Tracking	IT allows the detailed tracking of task status, inputs, and outputs
Disintermediation	IT can be used to connect two parties within a process that would otherwise communicate through an intermediary (internal or external)

Source: Thomas H. Davenport and James E. Short, "The New Industrial Engineering: Information Technology and Business Process Redesign," *Sloan Management Review 11*, Summer 1990.

The Levi Strauss Corporation made organizational changes in order to create an effective system for fulfilling store orders.

paradigm shift Radical reconceptualization of the nature of the business and the nature of the organization.

manager of its customers' supplies. The new system redrew organizational boundaries, allowing Baxter to take over its customers' warehousing functions.

This still more radical form of business change is called a **paradigm shift**. A paradigm shift involves rethinking the nature of the business and the nature of the organization itself. Banks, for instance, may decide not to automate, rationalize, or re-engineer the jobs of tellers. Instead they may decide to eliminate branch banking altogether and seek less expensive sources of funds, like international borrowing. Retail customers may be forced to use the Internet to conduct all their business, or a proprietary network. A paradigm shift is akin to rethinking not just the automobile, but transportation itself.

Of course nothing is free. Paradigm shifts and re-engineering often fail because extensive organizational change is so difficult to orchestrate (see Chapter 14). Some experts believe that 70% of the time they fail. Why then do so many corporations entertain such radical change? Because the rewards are equally high (see Figure 11.4). In many instances firms seeking paradigm shifts and pursuing re-engineering strategies achieve stunning, order-of-magnitude increases in their returns on investment (or productivity). Some of these success stories and some failure stories are included throughout this book.

REDESIGNING BUSINESS PROCESSES

Many companies today are focusing on building new information systems where they can redesign business processes. If the business process is first redesigned before

FIGURE 11.4

Organizational change carries risks and rewards. The most common forms of organizational change are automation and rationalization. These relatively slow-moving and slow-changing strategies present modest returns but little risk. Faster and more comprehensive change—like re-engineering and paradigm shifts—carry high rewards but offer a substantial chance of failure.

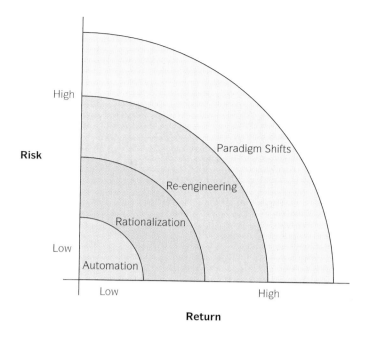

computing power is applied, organizations can potentially obtain very large payoffs from their investments in information technology. Figure 11.5 illustrates how business process redesign worked at Banc One Mortgage, an Indianapolis-based subsidiary of Banc One Corporation in Columbus, Ohio. Banc One, the twelfth-largest bank in the United States, has expanded by aggressively pursuing acquisitions. In 1992, the company expected to move from handling 33,000 loans per year to 300,000 loans per year. To forestall a blizzard of paperwork, Banc One redesigned the mortgage application process so that it required fewer steps and paper forms to complete and reduced the time to process a mortgage to only two days.

In the past, a mortgage applicant filled out a paper loan application. The bank entered the application transaction into its computer system. Specialists such as credit analysts and underwriters from eight different departments accessed and evaluated the application individually. If the loan application was approved, the closing was scheduled. After the closing, bank specialists dealing with insurance or funds in escrow serviced the loan. This "desk-to-desk" assembly-line approach took 17 days.

Banc One Mortgage replaced the sequential desk-to-desk approach with a speedier "work-cell" or team approach. Now, loan originators in the field enter the mortgage application directly into laptop computers. Software checks the application transaction to make sure that all of the information is correct and complete. The loan originators transmit the loan applications using a dial-up network to regional production centers. Instead of working on the application individually, the credit analysts, loan underwriters, and other specialists convene electronically, working as a team to approve the mortgage. After closing, another team of specialists sets up the loan for servicing. The entire loan application process takes only two days. Loan information is also easier to access than before, when the loan application could be in eight or nine different departments. Loan originators can also dial into the bank's network to obtain information on mortgage loan costs or to check the status of a loan for the customer.

By redesigning its entire approach to mortgage processing, Banc One achieved remarkable efficiencies. Instead of automating the way it had always done mortgage processing, it completely rethought the entire mortgage application process. To streamline the paperwork in its mortagage application process, Banc One turned to workflow and document management software, described in the Window on Technology.

FIGURE 11.5
Redesigning mortgage processing at Banc One. By redesigning their mortgage processing system and the mortgage application process, Banc One will be able to handle the increased paperwork as they move from processing 33,000 loans per year to processing 300,000 loans per year. *Adapted from: Mitch Betts, "Banc One Mortgage Melts Paper Blizzard."* Computerworld, *December 14, 1992. Copyright 1992 by CW Publishing, Inc., Framingham, MA 01701. Reprinted from* Computerworld.

Shifting from a traditional approach helped BANC ONE Mortgage slash processing time from 17 days to two

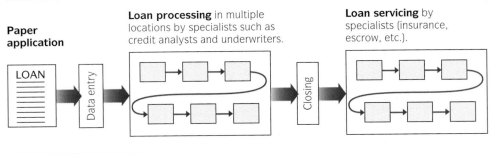

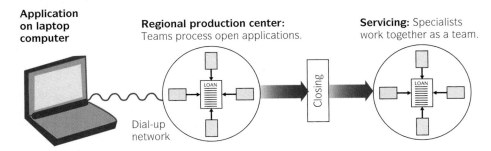

STEPS IN BUSINESS RE-ENGINEERING

Business re-engineering entails developing a business process model of how activities function, analyzing relationships among business units, and implementing changes that would eliminate redundant processes and make business units more effective. Re-engineering experts have outlined five major steps for re-engineering business processes (Davenport and Short, 1990):

1. *Develop the business vision and process objectives.* Senior management needs to develop a broad strategic vision which calls for redesigned business processes. For example, Odense Shipyard's management looked for breakthroughs to lower costs and accelerate product development that would enable the firm to become the market leader in producing double-hulled tanker ships. (See Chapter 1.)

2. *Identify the processes to be redesigned.* Companies should identify a few core business processes to be redesigned, focusing on those with the greatest potential payback. Symptoms of inefficient processes include excessive data redundancy and re-entering information, too much time spent handling exceptions and special cases, or too much time spent on corrections and rework. The analysis should identify what organizational group "owns" the process, what organizational functions or departments are involved in the process, and what changes are required. The methods for identifying organizational information requirements described earlier in this chapter may be useful here.

3. *Understand and measure the performance of existing processes.* If, for example, the objective of process redesign is to reduce time and cost in developing a new product or filling an order, the organization needs to measure the time and cost consumed by the unchanged process. Table 11.4 provides examples of metrics that have been used for the re-engineering analysis.

4. *Identify the opportunities for applying information technology.* The conventional method of designing systems establishes the information requirements of a busi-

CONQUERING THE PAPER MOUNTAIN

Con Edison, the $5 billion utility company, was looking for a way to cut costs, boost efficiency, and improve service to its 3 million gas and electricity customers in New York City and lower Westchester County. Its 1300 customer service representatives were handling 1 million pieces of paper in 20 different offices. When a document was lodged on someone's desktop, no one knew what was happening. The company decided to reconfigure its work processes using workflow software.

Workflow software automates the routing, tracking, and processing of documents and the management of forms. It is often used in conjunction with imaging and document management software, which converts reports, blueprints, file folders, and other paper-based documents into electronic form for storage and access on the computer (see Chapter 15). Both are key tools for streamlining and re-engineering paper-based business processes because they speed the flow of tasks, facilitate document sharing, and reduce paper documents and paperwork decisions.

Con Edison installed Omni-Desk workflow software from Sigma Imaging Systems Inc. of New York. The software runs in a client/server environment. Con Edison's customer service area is using this software on 1350 microcomputers running the OS/2 op-

erating system and 85 Compaq superservers connected to each other in a local area network and linked to a database manager over high-capacity telephone lines. In addition to providing better customer service, Con Edison expects the workflow software to reduce expenses by consolidating jobs. The company expects to save between $2 million and $3 million by eliminating up to 150 clerical positions.

The San Francisco office of Young & Rubicam Inc. turned to workflow software to provide better service to Chevron Corporation, its largest advertising client. The office had used a nine-step paper-based order-tracking and routing system when dealing with Chevron. Managers examining what the office actually did uncovered redundancies, missing steps, and holes in the process. For example, they found that some account coordinators were omitting vital information on forms.

Y & R implemented an application based on Workflow Management System from Action Technologies, Inc. in Alameda, California. Twelve Y&R account coordinators use 486 microcomputers linked via a LAN to an OS/2-compatible file server. With this system, electronic forms can't be passed onto the next stage until all the fields have been filled out. When the system was first introduced as a pilot project, overtime was slashed in half, rework of incorrect papers was down 64%, and the office improved its on-

time record for delivering information to Chevron by 63%.

Douglas Aircraft Company sought better control of its documents to in-

> **To Think About:** How was the use of workflow and document management software related to the business strategies of the companies described here? What management, organization, and technology issues should be addressed when installing workflow and document management software?

crease quality and make distribution more efficient across the company. The company's huge volume of paperwork consumed too much space and prevented employees from quickly locating documents. Management hired external vendors to scan the paper documents and incorporate the electronic files into workflow and distribution software from Interleaf Inc. of Waltham, Massachusetts. Filing documents electronically is expected to save the company about $300,000 each year in paper reproduction costs alone. It will also reduce the time required to write, approve, and distribute manuals when airplanes are designed.

Sources: Paula Klein, "Go with the Flow," and Anne Fischer Lent, "Documenting Change," *InformationWEEK*, March 28, 1994.

ness function or process and then determines how they can be supported by information technology. However, information technology can create new design options for various processes because it can be used to challenge longstanding assumptions about work arrangements that used to inhibit organizations. Table 11.5 provides examples of innovations that have overturned these assumptions using companies discussed in the text. Information technology should be allowed to influence process design from the start.

5. *Build a prototype of the new process.* The organization should design the new process on an experimental basis (see Chapter 12), anticipating a series of revisions and improvements until the redesigned process wins approval. For instance,

Table 11.4   Achieving Operating Excellence: Selected Examples

Example	Activity	Base	Re-engineered	Reference Definitions
Productivity indices Staffing efficiency: PLAINS COTTON COOPERATIVE ASSN. (TELCOT)	Transaction processing	9	450	Base = industry average, thousands of units processed per worker per year, 1991
Staffing levels: PHILLIPS PETROLEUM COMPANY	Corporate staff	36	12	Corporate staff per 100 employees, 1986–1989
Transaction costs: C. R. ENGLAND & SONS, INC.	Invoicing	$5.10	$.15	Cost of sending invoice, 1989–1991
Asset turnover: TOYOTA MOTOR CORP.	Work in process	16	215	Asset turnover, industry average annual turnover, 1990
Velocity PROGRESSIVE INSURANCE	Claims settlement	31 days	4 hours	Base = industry vs. Progressive's Immediate Response service, 1991
Quality FLORIDA POWER & LIGHT CO.	Power delivery	7 hours	32 min.	Base = competitor, power outage per customer per year, 1992
Business precision FARM JOURNAL, INC.	Product variety	1	1,200 +	Number of unique editions per issue, 1985–1990
Customer service L. L. BEAN, INC.	Order fulfillment	61%	93%	Base = industry average, percent of orders filled in 24 hours

Source: Copyright 1993 International Business Machines Corporation. Reprinted with permission from *IBM Systems Journal*, Vol. 32, No. 1.

Mutual Benefit Life implemented a pilot project to redesign its individual life insurance underwriting process. The process involved 40 steps with over 100 people in 12 functional areas. Hoping to raise productivity by 40 percent, MBL centralized all underwriting tasks under a case manager using a workstation application that could draw together data from all over the company. After a brief start-up period, the firm realized that it needed to add specialists such as lawyers or physicians on some underwriting cases ("The Role of IT," 1993).

Following these steps does not automatically guarantee that re-engineering will always be successful. The term *re-engineering* itself is somewhat misleading, suggesting that there are some recognized principles that if followed will always produce predicted outcomes. In fact, the majority of re-engineering projects do not achieve breakthrough gains in business performance. Michael Hammer, one of the leading proponents of re-engineering, states that 70% of re-engineering efforts he has observed have failed (Hammer and Stanton, 1995). Other estimates of unsuccessful engineering projects are equally high (King, 1994; Moad, 1993). Problems with re-engineering are part of the larger problem of orchestrating organizational change, a problem which attends the introduction of all innovations, including information systems. Managing change is neither simple nor intuitive. A re-engineered business process or a new information system inevitably affects jobs, skill requirements, work flows, and reporting relationships. Fear of these changes breeds resistance, confusion, and even conscious efforts to undermine the change effort. The organizational change requirements for new information systems are so important that we devote an entire chapter (Chapter 14) to this topic.

Table 11.5   New Process Design Options with Information Technology

Assumption	Technology	Option	Examples
Field personnel need offices to receive, store, and transmit information	Wireless communications	Personnel can send and receive information wherever they are	IBM Sales Ernst & Young
Information can appear in only one place at one time	Shared databases	People can collaborate on the same project from scattered locations; information can be used simultaneously wherever it is needed	Odense Shipyards Banc One
People are needed to ascertain where things are located	Automatic identification and tracking technology	Things can tell people where they are	United Parcel Service Schneider National
Businesses need reserve inventory to prevent stockouts	Telecommunications networks and EDI	Just-in-time delivery and stockless supply	Wal-Mart Baxter International

11.3   OVERVIEW OF SYSTEMS DEVELOPMENT

Whatever their scope and objectives, new information systems are an outgrowth of a process of organizational problem solving. A new information system is built as a solution to some type of problem or set of problems the organization perceives it is facing. The problem may be one where managers and employees realize that the organization is not performing as well as expected, or it may come from the realization that the organization should take advantage of new opportunities to perform more successfully.

Review the diagrams at the beginning of each chapter of this text. They show an information system that is a solution to a particular set of business challenges or problems. The resulting information system is an outgrowth of a series of events called systems development. **Systems development** refers to all the activities that go into producing an information systems solution to an organizational problem or opportunity. Systems development is a structured kind of problem solving with distinct activities. These activities consist of systems analysis, systems design, programming, testing, conversion, and production and maintenance.

Figure 11.6 illustrates the systems development process. The systems development activities depicted here usually take place in sequential order. But some of the activities may need to be repeated or some may be taking place simultaneously, depending on the approach to system building that is being employed (see Chapter 12). Note also that each activity involves interaction with the organization. Members of the organization participate in these activities and the systems development process creates organizational changes. Chapter 14 describes the challenge of managing these organizational changes surrounding system building.

systems development The activities that go into producing an information systems solution to an organizational problem or opportunity.

SYSTEMS ANALYSIS

Systems analysis is the analysis of the problem that the organization will try to solve with an information system. It consists of defining the problem, identifying its causes, specifying the solution, and identifying the information requirements that must be met by a system solution.

The key to building any large information system is a thorough understanding of the existing organization and system. Thus, the systems analyst creates a road map of the existing organization and systems, identifying the primary owners and users of data in the organization. These stakeholders have a direct interest in the information affected by the new system. In addition to these organizational aspects, the analyst also briefly describes the existing hardware and software that serve the organization.

systems analysis The analysis of a problem that the organization will try to solve with an information system.

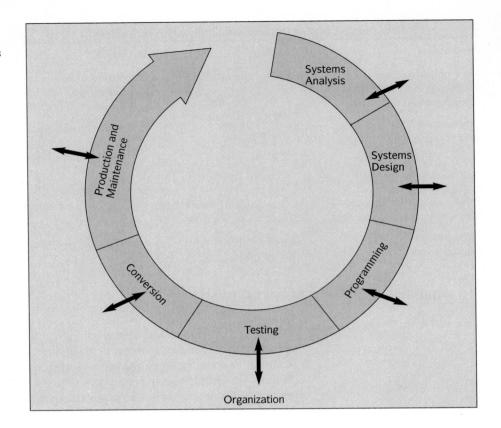

From this organizational analysis, the systems analyst details the problems of existing systems. By examining documents, work papers, and procedures; observing system operations; and interviewing key users of the systems, the analyst can identify the problem areas and objectives to be achieved by a solution. Often the solution requires building a new information system or improving an existing one.

Feasibility

feasibility study As part of the systems analysis process, a way to determine whether the solution is achievable, given the organization's resources and constraints.

In addition to suggesting a solution, systems analysis involves a **feasibility study** to determine whether that solution is feasible, or achievable, given the organization's resources and constraints. Three major areas of feasibility must be addressed:

1. **Technical feasibility:** whether the proposed solution can be implemented with the available hardware, software, and technical resources.

technical feasibility Determines whether a proposed solution can be implemented with the available hardware, software, and technical resources.

2. **Economic feasibility:** whether the benefits of the proposed solution outweigh the costs. We explore this topic in greater detail in Section 11.4, Understanding the Business Value of Information Systems.

economic feasibility Determines whether the benefits of a proposed solution outweigh the costs.

3. **Operational feasibility:** whether the proposed solution is desirable within the existing managerial and organizational framework.

Normally the systems analysis process will identify several alternative solutions that can be pursued by the organization. The process will then assess the feasibility of each. Three basic solution alternatives exist for every systems problem:

operational feasibility Determines whether a proposed solution is desirable within the existing managerial and organizational framework.

1. To do nothing, leaving the existing situation unchanged
2. To modify or enhance existing systems
3. To develop a new system

There may be several solution design options within the second and third solution alternatives. A written systems proposal report will describe the costs and benefits, advantages and disadvantages of each alternative. It is then up to management to determine which mix of costs, benefits, technical features, and organizational impacts represents the most desirable alternative.

Establishing Information Requirements

information requirements A detailed statement of the information needs that a new system must satisfy; identifies who needs what information, and when, where, and how the information is needed.

Perhaps the most difficult task of the systems analyst is to define the specific information requirements that must be met by the system solution selected. This is the area where many large system efforts go wrong and the one that poses the greatest difficulty for the analyst. At the most basic level, the **information requirements** of a new system involve identifying who needs what information, where, when, and how. Requirements analysis carefully defines the objectives of the new or modified system and develops a detailed description of the functions that the new system must perform. Requirements must consider economic, technical, and time constraints, as well as the goals, procedures, and decision processes of the organization. Faulty requirements analysis is a leading cause of systems failure and high systems development costs (see Chapter 14). A system designed around the wrong set of requirements either will have to be discarded because of poor performance or will need to be heavily revised. Therefore, the importance of requirements analysis must not be underestimated.

Developing requirements specifications may involve considerable research and revision. A business function may be very complex or poorly defined. A manual system or routine set of inputs and outputs may not exist. Procedures may vary from individual to individual. Such situations will be more difficult to analyze, especially if the users are unsure of what they want or need (this problem is extremely common). To derive information systems requirements, analysts may be forced to work and rework requirements statements in cooperation with users. Although this process is laborious, it is far superior to and less costly than redoing and undoing an entire system. There are also alternative approaches to eliciting requirements that help minimize these problems (see Chapter 12).

In many instances, business procedures are unclear or users disagree about how things are done and should be done. Systems analysis often makes an unintended contribution to the organization by clarifying procedures and building organizational consensus about how things should be done. In many instances, building a new system creates an opportunity to redefine how the organization conducts its daily business.

Some problems do not require an information system solution, but instead need an adjustment in management, additional training, or refinement of existing organizational procedures. If the problem is information-related, systems analysis may still be required to diagnose the problem and arrive at the proper solution.

SYSTEMS DESIGN

systems design Details how a system will meet the information requirements as determined by the systems analysis.

While systems analysis describes what a system should do to meet information requirements, **systems design** shows how the system will fulfill this objective. The design of an information system is the overall plan or model for that system. Like the blueprint of a building or house, it consists of all the specifications that give the system its form and structure. Information systems design is an exacting and creative task demanding imagination, sensitivity to detail, and expert skills.

Systems design has three objectives. First, the systems designer is responsible for considering alternative technology configurations for carrying out and developing the system as described by the analyst. This may involve analyses of the performance of different pieces of hardware and software, security capabilities of systems, network alternatives, and the portability or changeability of systems hardware.

Second, designers are responsible for the management and control of the technical realization of systems. Detailed programming specifications, coding of data, documentation, testing, and training are all the responsibility of the design staff. In addition, designers are responsible for the actual procurement of the hardware, consultants, and software needed by the system.

Third, the systems designer details the system specifications that will deliver the functions identified during systems analysis. These specifications should address all of the managerial, organizational, and technological components of the system solution. Table 11.6 lists the types of specifications that would be produced during systems design.

Logical and Physical Design

The design for an information system can be broken down into logical and physical design specifications. **Logical design** lays out the components of the system and their relationship to each other as they would appear to users. It shows what the system solution will do as opposed to how it is actually implemented physically. It describes inputs and outputs, processing functions to be performed, business procedures, data models, and controls. (Controls specify standards for acceptable performance and methods for measuring actual performance in relation to these standards. They are described in detail in Chapter 18.)

Physical design is the process of translating the abstract logical model into the specific technical design for the new system. It produces the actual specifications for hardware, software, physical databases, input/output media, manual procedures, and specific controls. Physical design provides the remaining specifications that transform the abstract logical design plan into a functioning system of people and machines.

logical design Lays out the components of the information system and their relationship to each other as they would appear to users.

physical design The process of translating the abstract logical model into the specific technical design for the new system.

Table 11.6	Design Specifications

Output
  Medium
  Content
  Timing
	Controls
	  Input controls (characters, limit, reasonableness)
	  Processing controls (consistency, record counts)
	  Output controls (totals, samples of output)
	  Procedural controls (passwords, special forms)

Input
  Origins
  Flow
  Data entry	

User interface
  Simplicity
  Efficiency
  Logic
  Feedback
  Errors
	Security
	  Access controls
	  Catastrophe plans
	  Audit trails

Database design
  Logical data relations
  Volume and speed requirements
  File organization and design
  Record specifications
	Documentation
	  Operations documentation
	  Systems documents
	  User documentation

Processing
  Computations
  Program modules
  Required reports
  Timing of outputs
	Conversion
	  Transfer files
	  Initiate new procedures
	  Select testing method
	  Cut over to new system

Manual procedures
  What activities
  Who performs them
  When
  How
  Where
	Training
	  Select training techniques
	  Develop training modules
	  Identify training facilities

	Organizational changes
	  Task redesign
	  Job design
	  Process design
	  Office and organization structure design
	  Reporting relationships

Design Alternatives

Like houses or buildings, information systems may have many possible designs. They may be centralized or distributed, on-line or batch, partially manual, or heavily automated. Each design represents a unique blend of all of the technical and organizational factors that shape an information system. What makes one design superior to others is the ease and efficiency with which it fulfills user requirements within a specific set of technical, organizational, financial, and time constraints.

Before the design of an information system is finalized, analysts will evaluate various design alternatives. Based on the requirements definition and systems analysis, analysts construct high-level logical design models. They then examine the costs, benefits, strengths, and weaknesses of each alternative.

Figures 11.7A and 11.7B illustrate design alternatives for a corporate cost system, which maintains data on the costs of various products produced by the corporation's operating units in various locations. The first alternative is a batch system that maximizes the efficiency and economy of computer processing but requires extensive manual preparation of data. The batch system requires the following steps:

1. Operating units prepare cost sheets with product cost data by plant. Sheets are mailed to corporate cost accounting at corporate headquarters.

2. Corporate cost accounting reviews cost sheets and prepares transaction forms, which are entered into the system.

3. The corporate product database is updated twice weekly via batch processing. The database maintains standard product cost data by plant and links local product numbers to corporate product numbers. The update also produces standard cost sheets.

4. Copies of the standard cost sheets are mailed back to the operating units.

There is also a time lag between the preparation of operating unit cost sheets and the point when this information is reflected on the product database.

FIGURE 11.7A

First conceptual design alternative for the corporate cost system. This design entails relatively inexpensive and efficient computer processing but extensive manual preparation of data. There is also a time lag between the preparation of operating unit cost sheets and the point when this information is reflected on the product database.

FIGURE 11.7B

Second conceptual design alternative for the corporate cost system. This design is relatively expensive in terms of hardware and software, as well as the security and recovery procedures required to maintain the integrity of the database. On-line processing is also more expensive than batch processing. However, the design considerably streamlines manual activities and provides up-to-the-minute information to both corporate cost accounting and the operating units.

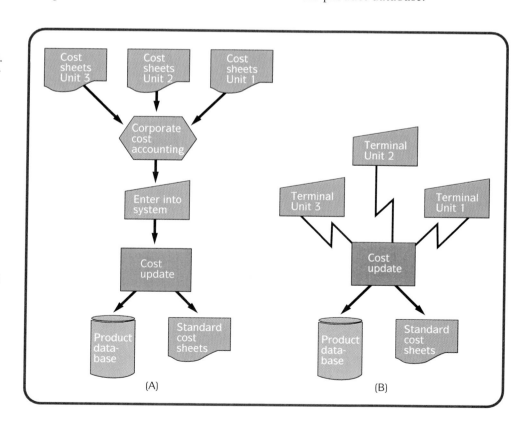

The second design alternative is an on-line system featuring more timely information and reduced manual effort, but at greater cost for computer processing, software, and security and recovery procedures required to maintain the integrity of the product database. The steps for the on-line system are as follows:

1. Operating units enter their own product cost data on-line via local CRT terminals with telecommunications links to the central corporate mainframe.

2. Through extensive on-line editing, the operating unit product data are edited. Errors are corrected and the data immediately update the corporate product database.

3. Up-to-date product cost information is available immediately after update. The system produces hard copy standard cost sheets or allows the operating units to perform on-line inquiries about product cost information.

This alternative reduces manual activities and provides up-to-the-minute information both to corporate cost accounting and to the operating units.

The Role of End Users

Information systems design cannot be directed by technical specialists alone. It demands a very high level of participation and control by end users. User information requirements drive the entire systems-building effort. Users must have sufficient control over the design process to ensure that the system reflects their business priorities and information needs, not the biases of the technical staff.

Working on design increases users' understanding and acceptance of the system, reducing problems caused by power transfers, intergroup conflict, and unfamiliarity with new system functions and procedures. As Chapter 14 points out, insufficient user involvement in the design effort is a major cause of system failure.

Some MIS researchers have suggested that design should be "user led." However, other researchers point out that systems development is not an entirely rational process. Users leading design activities have used their position to further private interests and gain power rather than to enhance organizational objectives. Users controlling design can sabotage or seriously impede the systems-building effort (Franz and Robey, 1984).

The nature and level of user participation in design vary from system to system. There is less need for user involvement in systems with simple or straightforward requirements than in those with requirements that are elaborate, complex, or vaguely defined. Transaction processing or operational control systems have traditionally required less user involvement than strategic planning, information reporting, and decision-support systems. Less structured systems need more user participation to define requirements and may necessitate many versions of design before specifications can be finalized.

Different levels of user involvement in design are reflected in different systems development methods. Chapter 12 describes how user involvement varies with each development approach.

COMPLETING THE SYSTEMS DEVELOPMENT PROCESS

The remaining steps in the systems development process translate the solution specifications established during systems analysis and design into a fully operational information system. These concluding steps consist of programming, testing, conversion, and production and maintenance.

Programming

The process of translating design specifications into software for the computer constitutes a smaller portion of the systems development cycle than design and perhaps

programming The process of translating the system specifications prepared during the design stage into program code.

the testing activities. But it is here, in providing the actual instructions for the machine, that the heart of the system takes shape. During the **programming** stage, system specifications that were prepared during the design stage are translated into program code. On the basis of detailed design documents for files, transaction and report layouts, and other design details, specifications for each program in the system are prepared.

Some systems development projects assign programming tasks to specialists whose work consists exclusively of coding programs. Other projects prefer programmer/analysts who both design and program functions. Since large systems entail many programs with thousands—even hundreds of thousands—of lines of code, programming teams are frequently used. Moreover, even if an entire system can be programmed by a single individual, the quality of the software will be higher if it is subject to group review (see Chapter 13).

Testing

testing The exhaustive and thorough process that determines whether the system produces the desired results under known conditions.

Exhaustive and thorough **testing** must be conducted to ascertain whether the system produces the right results. Testing answers the question, "Will the system produce the desired results under known conditions?"

The amount of time needed to answer this question has been traditionally underrated in systems project planning (see Chapter 13). As much as 50 percent of the entire software development budget can be expended in testing. Testing is also time-consuming: Test data must be carefully prepared, results reviewed, and corrections made in the system. In some instances, parts of the system may have to be redesigned. Yet the risks of glossing over this step are enormous.

Testing an information system can be broken down into three types of activities:

unit testing The process of testing each program separately in the system. Sometimes called program testing.

Unit testing, or program testing, consists of testing each program separately in the system. While it is widely believed that the purpose of such testing is to guarantee that programs are error free, this goal is realistically impossible. Testing should be viewed instead as a means of locating errors in programs, focusing on finding all the ways to make a program fail. Once pinpointed, problems can be corrected.

system testing Tests the functioning of the information system as a whole in order to determine if discrete modules will function together as planned.

System testing tests the functioning of the information system as a whole. It tries to determine if discrete modules will function together as planned and whether discrepancies exist between the way the system actually works and the way it was conceived. Among the areas examined are performance time, capacity for file storage and handling peak loads, recovery and restart capabilities, and manual procedures.

acceptance testing Provides the final certification that the system is ready to be used in a production setting.

Acceptance testing provides the final certification that the system is ready to be used in a production setting. Systems tests are evaluated by users and reviewed by management. When all parties are satisfied that the new system meets their standards, the system is formally accepted for installation.

It is essential that all aspects of testing be carefully thought out and that they be as comprehensive as possible. To ensure this, the development team works with users to devise a systematic test plan. The **test plan** includes all of the preparations for the series of tests previously described.

test plan Prepared by the development team in conjunction with the users; it includes all of the preparations for the series of tests to be performed on the system.

Figure 11.8 shows an example of a test plan. The general condition being tested here is a record change. The documentation consists of a series of test-plan screens maintained on a database (perhaps a microcomputer database) that is ideally suited to this kind of application.

Users play a critical role in the testing process. They understand the full range of data and processing conditions that might occur within their system. Moreover, programmers tend to be aware only of the conditions treated in their programs; the test data they devise are usually too limited. Therefore, input from other team members and users will help ensure that the range of conditions included in the test data is complete. Users can identify frequent and less common transactions, unusual conditions to anticipate, and most of the common types of errors that might occur when

FIGURE 11.8
A sample test plan to test a record change. When developing a test plan, it is imperative to include the various conditions to be tested, the requirements for each condition tested, and the expected results. Test plans require input from both end users and information system specialists.

Procedure	Address and Maintenance "Record Change Series"		Test Series 2		
	Prepared By:	Date:	Version:		
Test Ref.	Condition Tested	Special Requirements	Expected Results	Output On	Next Screen
2	Change records				
2.1	Change existing record	Key field	Not allowed		
2.2	Change nonexistent record	Other fields	"Invalid key" message		
2.3	Change deleted record	Deleted record must be available	"Deleted" message		
2.4	Make second record	Change 2.1 above	OK if valid	Transaction file	V45
2.5	Insert record		OK if valid	Transaction file	V45
2.6	Abort during change	Abort 2.5	No change	Transaction file	V45

the system is in use. User input is also decisive in verifying the manual procedures for the system.

Conversion

Conversion is the process of changing from the old system to the new system. It answers the question, "Will the new system work under real conditions?" Four main conversion strategies can be employed: the parallel strategy, the direct cutover strategy, the pilot study strategy, and the phased approach strategy.

In a **parallel strategy,** both the old system and its potential replacement are run together for a time until everyone is assured that the new one functions correctly. This is the safest conversion approach because, in the event of errors or processing disruptions, the old system can still be used as a backup. However, this approach is very expensive, and additional staff or resources may be required to run the extra system.

The **direct cutover** strategy replaces the old system entirely with the new system on an appointed day. At first glance, this strategy seems less costly than parallel conversion strategy. However, it is a very risky approach that can potentially be more costly than parallel activities if serious problems with the new system are found. There is no other system to fall back on. Dislocations, disruptions, and the cost of corrections may be enormous.

The **pilot study** strategy introduces the new system only to a limited area of the organization, such as a single department or operating unit. When this pilot version is complete and working smoothly, it is installed throughout the rest of the organization, either simultaneously or in stages.

The **phased approach** strategy introduces the new system in stages, either by functions or by organizational units. If, for example, the system is introduced by functions, a new payroll system might begin with hourly workers who are paid weekly, followed six months later by adding salaried employees who are paid monthly to the system. If the system is introduced by organizational units, corporate headquarters might be converted first, followed by outlying operating units four months later.

A formal **conversion plan** provides a schedule of all the activities required to install the new system. The most time-consuming activity is usually the conversion

conversion The process of changing from the old system to the new system.

parallel strategy A safe and conservative conversion approach where both the old system and its potential replacement are run together for a time until everyone is assured that the new one functions correctly.

direct cutover A risky conversion approach where the new system completely replaces the old one on an appointed day.

pilot study A strategy to introduce the new system to a limited area of the organization until it is proven to be fully functional; only then can the conversion to the new system across the entire organization take place.

phased approach Introduces the new system in stages either by functions or by organizational units.

conversion plan Provides a schedule of all activities required to install a new system.

of data (see the Window on Organizations). Data from the old system must be transferred to the new system, either manually or through special conversion software programs. The converted data then must be carefully verified for accuracy and completeness.

Moving from an old system to a new one requires that end users be trained to use the new system. Detailed **documentation** showing how the system works from both a technical and end-user standpoint is finalized during conversion time for use in training and everyday operations. Lack of proper training and documentation contributes to system failure (see Chapter 14), so this portion of the systems development process is very important.

documentation Descriptions of how an information system works from both a technical and end-user standpoint.

Production and Maintenance

After the new system is installed and conversion is complete, the system is said to be in **production.** During this stage, the system will be reviewed by both users and technical specialists to determine how well it has met its original objectives and to decide whether any revisions or modifications are in order. Changes in hardware, software, documentation, or procedures to a production system to correct errors, meet new requirements, or improve processing efficiency are termed **maintenance.**

production The stage after the new system is installed and the conversion is complete; during this time the system is reviewed by users and technical specialists to determine how well it has met its original goals.

Studies of maintenance have examined the amount of time required for various maintenance tasks (Lientz and Swanson, 1980). Approximately 20 percent of the time is devoted to debugging or correcting emergency production problems; another 20 percent is concerned with changes in data, files, reports, hardware, or system software. But 60 percent of all maintenance work consists of making user enhancements, improving documentation, and recoding system components for greater processing efficiency. The amount of work in the third category of maintenance problems could be reduced significantly through better system analysis and design practices. Table 11.7 summarizes the systems development activities.

maintenance Changes in hardware, software, documentation, or procedures to a production system to correct errors, meet new requirements, or improve processing efficiency.

Chapter 3 has described the many ways in which organizations can differ. Systems likewise differ in terms of their size, technological complexity, and the organizational problems they are meant to solve. Because there are different kinds of systems and situations in which each is conceived or built, a number of methods have been developed to build systems. We describe these various methods in the next chapter.

Table 11.7	**Systems Development**
Core Activity	**Description**
Systems analysis	Identify problem(s) Specify solution Establish information requirements
Systems design	Create logical design specifications Create physical design specifications Manage technical realization of system
Programming	Translate design specifications into program code
Testing	Unit test Systems test Acceptance test
Conversion	Plan conversion Prepare documentation Train users and technical staff
Production and Maintenance	Operate the system Evaluate the system Modify the system

EUROPCAR STRUGGLES TO MIGRATE ITS SYSTEMS

How does a corporation that is actually a patchwork of almost independent local companies all over Europe with the same name face the European economic integration that has already begun? That is exactly the question Europcar began thinking about in the late 1980s. Paris-based Europcar Interrent, Europe's number one European-based auto rental agency, had grown over the years partly by acquiring local companies. As with many companies that have expanded by purchasing existing, independent local companies, Europcar did not fully integrate the newly acquired units. Instead, the firm allowed them mostly to continue business operations as they had done in the past, only under the new corporate name. This approach to expansion is often followed by banks in the United States, leaving them with disparate business practices and isolated computer systems inherited from the acquired companies. For Europcar these inheritance problems were magnified by the mass of differing laws, cultures, and languages resulting from the many countries in which they operate. Management determined it had no choice but to make changes if Europcar were to continue to be competitive once the economic integration accelerated beginning in 1993. When Europcar purchased the giant German-based Interrent in 1989, management began to move.

The problem Europcar faced was the many different computer systems in nine countries residing on 55 different mainframe and minicomputers, each with its own software and data sets. Robert Verasdonck, Europcar's corporate director of information systems, decided to convert these systems into a single client/server-based platform with data residing in a relational database to service all the local Europcar units. The new system would consolidate reservations, billing, and fleet management for the company's business across Europe.

Because he knew this was a daunting technical task, Verasdonck decided to outsource both the conversion job and the operation of the new system once it was completed. He turned to the Windsor, England, office of Perot Systems to do both jobs.

While Perot Systems account manager Rod Thompson and his team knew that the task they faced was difficult, the real problems emerged only as they began to work. "It sort of crept up on us," Thompson recalled. Some of the problems were technical. For example, according to Thompson, "There were too many data sources for a single migration tool to handle. Automatic conversion just wasn't going to do the trick." Ultimately Perot Systems was forced to assign up to 40 engineers to the task of manually converting and migrating the data.

The technical problems proved to be secondary, however. As is usually the case, the technical problems only reflected the underlying business problems, which in this case were organizational—Europcar had not standardized its business policies and practices across the company as it acquired new organizations. Each of the 55 systems reflected the information needs, business practices, customer preferences, and corporate cultures of the local unit it was serving. The systems also represented disparate local business operations such as local rates, local products, local contracts (Austria levies a tax on mileage on cars driven within the country but does not tax driving outside the country), and local accounting practices. Because information systems can only reflect the business environment, Verasdonck and Thompson quickly realized that creating a single unified system was impossible without first addressing the business issue of organizational unity. Before they could convert the data and programs, the company would first need to develop corporate standards and operating procedures. The new, unified system

had to blend a wide range of languages, currencies, and corporate cultures into a single business entity.

Even establishing corporate standards is usually not adequate, however.

> **To Think About:** It has been said that the significance of conversion in systems development has been underestimated. Do you agree? What management, organization, and technology issues did Europcar have to address when converting its systems?

In the complex environment of Europcar, standard data formats will not work if they are not accepted and supported locally. Building that support and educating the users became a key task of Verasdonck. In December 1993, at a meeting of local management, he discovered that local managers wanted to undertake the educational process as quickly as possible. The new system was to be used by some 3000 employees at 800 offices across Europe. Verasdonck launched a crash training program, establishing 37 training centers throughout Europe that together were capable of training 225 users each week.

The new system, dubbed Greenway, went fully operational in February 1995 and can handle up to 4000 users simultaneously. It incorporates five Sequent 2000/790 computers running Oracle databases which can be accessed throughout Europe from 960 Europcar offices equipped with microcomputers. The new system gave the local office staffs an added bonus they have found very helpful—the reservation clerks are now also connected to the various major airline reservation systems in addition to their own system.

The job is not over, however. Europcar has franchises in more than 80 countries in Africa, Asia, Australia, South America, and the Caribbean. Verasdonck and Thompson now plan to convert all these franchises to the new system, adding even more local customs, laws, languages, and operating procedure problems.

Sources: Pierre Berger and Cara A. Cunningham, "Europcar Drives Rocky Road to Unix," *Computerworld,* March 6, 1995; Joshua Greenbaum, "Under Repair,"

InformationWEEK, October 3, 1994, and "A Bumpy Road for Europcar," *InformationWEEK,* February 7, 1994.

11.4   UNDERSTANDING THE BUSINESS VALUE OF INFORMATION SYSTEMS

Information systems can have several different values for business firms. As we have pointed out in earlier chapters, information systems can provide a temporary competitive advantage to firms. A consistently strong information technology infrastructure can, over the longer term, play an important strategic role in the life of the firm. Looked at less grandly, information systems can permit firms simply to survive. In many cases, survival even at a mediocre level will dictate investment in systems. In addition, government regulations may require these survival investments.

Strategy cannot be pursued when a firm is financially unsound. The worth of systems from a financial perspective essentially revolves around the question of return on invested capital. The value of systems from a financial view comes down to one question: Does a particular IS investment produce sufficient returns to justify its costs? There are many problems with this approach, not the least of which is how to estimate benefits and count the costs.

CAPITAL BUDGETING MODELS

Capital budgeting models are one of several techniques used to measure the value of investing in long-term capital investment projects. The process of analyzing and selecting various proposals for capital expenditures is called **capital budgeting.** Firms invest in capital projects in order to expand production to meet anticipated demand, or to modernize production equipment in order to reduce costs. Firms also invest in capital projects for many noneconomic reasons, such as to install pollution control equipment, or to convert to a human resources database in order to meet some government regulations, or to satisfy nonmarket public demands. Information systems are considered long-term capital investment projects.

capital budgeting The process of analyzing and selecting various proposals for capital expenditures.

Six capital budgeting models are used to evaluate capital projects:

- The payback method
- The accounting rate of return on investment (ROI)
- The cost-benefit ratio
- The net present value
- The profitability index
- The internal rate of return (IRR)

Cash Flows

All capital budgeting methods rely on measures of cash flows into and out of the firm. Capital projects generate cash flows into and out of the firm. The investment cost is an immediate cash outflow caused by the purchase of the capital equipment. In subsequent years, the investment may cause additional cash outflows that will be balanced by cash inflows resulting from the investment. Cash inflows take the form of increased sales of more products (for reasons including new products, higher quality, or increasing market share), or reduction in costs of production and operation. The difference between cash outflows and cash inflows is used for calculating the financial worth of an investment. Once the cash flows have been established, several alternative methods are available to compare different projects with one another, and to make a decision about the investment.

Limitations of Financial Models

Financial models are used in many situations: to justify new systems, explain old systems post hoc, and to develop quantitative support for a political position. Political decisions made for organizational reasons have nothing to do with the cost and benefits of a system.

Financial models assume that all relevant alternatives have been examined, that all costs and benefits are known, and that these costs and benefits can be expressed in a common metric, specifically, money. When one has to choose among many complex alternatives, these assumptions are rarely met in the real world, although they may be approximated. Table 11.8 lists some of the more common costs and benefits of systems. **Tangible benefits** can be quantified and assigned a monetary value. **Intangible benefits,** such as more efficient customer service or enhanced decision making, cannot be immediately quantified but may lead to quantifiable gains in the long run.

Information Systems as a Capital Project

Many well-known problems emerge when financial analysis is applied to information systems (Dos Santos, 1991). Financial models do not express the risks and uncertainty of their own cost and benefit estimates. Costs and benefits do not occur in the same time frame—costs tend to be up front and tangible, while benefits tend to be back-loaded and intangible. Inflation may affect costs and benefits differently. Technology—especially information technology—can change during the course of the project, causing estimates to vary greatly. Intangible benefits are difficult to quantify. These factors play havoc with financial models.

The difficulties of measuring intangible benefits give financial models an "application bias": Transaction and clerical systems that displace labor and save space always produce more measurable, tangible benefits than management information sys-

tangible benefits Benefits that can be quantified and assigned monetary value; they include lower operational costs and increased cash flows.

intangible benefits Benefits that are not easily quantified; they include more efficient customer service or enhanced decision making.

Table 11.8	Costs and Benefits of Information Systems
Costs	Benefits
Hardware	**Tangible**
	Cost savings
Telecommunications	Increased productivity
	Low operational costs
Software	Reduced work force
	Lower computer expenses
Services	Lower outside vendor costs
	Lower clerical and professional costs
Personnel	Reduced rate of growth in expenses
	Reduced facility costs
	Intangible
	Improved asset utilization
	Improved resource control
	Improved organizational planning
	Increased organizational flexibility
	More timely information
	More information
	Increased organizational learning
	Legal requirements attained
	Enhanced employee good will
	Increased job satisfaction
	Improved decision making
	Improved operations
	Higher client satisfaction
	Better corporate image

tems, decision-support systems, or computer-supported collaborative work systems (see Chapter 15).

There is some reason to believe that investment in information technology requires special consideration in financial modeling. Capital budgeting historically concerned itself with manufacturing equipment and other very long-term investments like electrical generating facilities, telephone networks, and the like. These investments had expected lives of more than one year and up to twenty-five years. Computer-based information systems are similar to other capital investments in that they produce an immediate investment cost, and are expected to produce cash benefits over a term greater than one year.

Information systems differ from manufacturing systems in that their expected life is shorter. The very high rate of technological change in computer-based information systems means that most systems are seriously out of date in five to eight years. Although parts of old systems survive as code segments in large programs—some programs have code that is fifteen years old—most large-scale systems after five years require significant investment to redesign or rebuild them.

The high rate of technological obsolescence in budgeting for systems means simply that the payback period must be shorter, and the rates of return higher, than typical capital projects with much longer useful lives.

The bottom line with financial models is to use them cautiously and to put the results into a broader context of business analysis. Let us look at an example to see how these problems arise and can be worked out. The following case study is based on a real-world scenario, but the names have been changed.

CASE EXAMPLE: PRIMROSE, MENDELSON, AND HANSEN

Primrose, Mendelson, and Hansen is a 250-person law partnership on Manhattan's West Side. Founded in 1923, Primrose has excelled in corporate, taxation, environmental, and health law. Its litigation department is also well known.

The Problem

Spread out over three floors of a new building, each of the hundred partners has a secretary. Many partners have a 386 PC on their desktops but rarely use them except to read the E-mail. Virtually all business is conducted face-to-face in the office, or when partners meet directly with clients on the clients' premises. Most of the law business involves marking up (editing), creating, filing, storing, and sending documents. In addition, the tax, pension, and real estate groups do a considerable amount of spreadsheet work.

These attorneys access legal files through a sophisticated information system to expedite their research and recording processes.

With overall business off 30 percent since 1987, the chairman, Edward W. Hansen III, is hoping to use information systems to cut costs, enhance service to clients, and bring partner profits back up.

First, the firm's income depends on billable hours, and every lawyer is supposed to keep a diary of his or her work for specific clients in 30-minute intervals. Generally, senior lawyers at this firm charge about $500 an hour for their time. Unfortunately, lawyers are not good record keepers, often forget what they have been working on, and must go back to reconstruct their time diaries. The firm hopes that there will be some automated way of tracking billable hours.

Second, a great deal of time is spent communicating with clients around the world, with other law firms both in the United States and overseas, and especially with Primrose's branches in Los Angeles, Tokyo, London, and Paris. The FAX has become the communication medium of choice, generating huge bills and developing lengthy queues.

Third, Primrose has no client database! A law firm is a collection of fiefdoms—each lawyer has his or her own clients and keeps the information about them private. This, however, makes it impossible for management to find out who is a client of the firm, who is working on a deal with whom, and so forth. The firm maintains a billing system, but the information is too difficult to search. What Primrose needs is an integrated client management system that would take care of billing, hourly charges, and make client information available to others in the firm. Even overseas offices want to have information on who is taking care of a particular client in the United States.

Fourth, there is no system to track costs. The head of the firm and the department heads who compose the executive committee cannot identify what the costs are, where the money is being spent, who is spending it, and how the firm's resources are being allocated. Perhaps, for instance, health law is declining and the firm should trim associates (nonpartnered lawyers). A decent accounting system that could identify the cash flows and the costs a bit more clearly than the existing journal does would be a big help.

The Solution

There are many problems at Primrose; information systems could obviously have some survival value and perhaps could grant a strategic advantage to Primrose if a system were correctly built and implemented. We will not go through a detailed systems analysis and design here. Instead, we will sketch the solution that in fact was adopted, showing the detailed costs and estimated benefits. These will prove useful for estimating the overall business value of the new system—both financial and nonfinancial.

The technical solution adopted was to create a local-area network composed of 100 fully configured 486SX microcomputers, three OS/2 file servers, and an Ethernet 10 MBS (megabit per second) local-area network using coaxial cable. This network connects most of the lawyers and their secretaries into a single integrated system, yet permits each lawyer to configure his or her desktop with specialized software and hardware. The older 386 machines were passed down to the secretaries.

All machines were configured with DOS running Windows as the basic operating system, while the file servers ran OS/2. A networked relational database was installed, running under network software. Lotus Notes for Windows was chosen as the internal mail system because it provided an easy-to-use interface and good links to external telecommunications networks and mail systems. It could be used to develop simple client management and billing applications. Notes can also incorporate spreadsheets. The Primrose network is linked to external networks so that the firm can obtain information on-line from Lexis (a legal database) and several financial database services.

The new system required Primrose to hire a chief information officer and director of systems—a new position for most law firms. Four systems personnel were required to operate the system and train lawyers. Outside trainers were hired as well for a short period.

Figure 11.9 shows the estimated costs and benefits of the system. The system had an actual investment cost of $1,170,700 in the first year (Year 0) and total cost over six years of $4,068,466. The estimated benefits total $5,760,000 after six years. Was the investment worth it? If so, in what sense was it worth it? There are financial and nonfinancial answers to this question. Let us look at the financial models first. They are depicted in Figure 11.10.

The Payback Method

payback method A measure of the time required to pay back the initial investment of a project.

The **payback method** is quite simple: It is a measure of time required to pay back the initial investment of a project. The payback period is computed as

$$\frac{\text{Original investment}}{\text{Annual net cash inflow}} = \text{Number of years to pay back}$$

In the case of Primrose, it will take 5.06 years to pay back the initial investment. On the surface, this seems like a moderate time to return the investment—not too

Primrose, Mendelson, and Hansen
Intellex Legal Information System (ILIS)
Estimated Costs and Benefits 1993–1998

		Year:	0 1993	1 1994	2 1995	3 1996	4 1997	5 1998	
Costs									
Hardware									
	File Servers	3@50000	$150,000	$10,000	$10,000	$10,000	$10,000	$10,000	
	PCs	100@3000	$300,000	$10,000	$10,000	$10,000	$10,000	$10,000	
	Network cds	100@500	$50,000	$0	$0	$0	$0	$0	
	Scanners	6@1200	$7,200	$1,200	$1,200	$1,200	$1,200	$1,200	
	Fax Boards	100@250	$25,000	$0	$0	$0	$0	$0	
Telecommunications									
	Gateways	2@8000	$16,000	$400	$400	$400	$400	$400	
	Cabling	100000	$100,000	$0	$0	$0	$0	$0	
Software									
	Database	10000	$10,000	$10,000	$10,000	$10,000	$10,000	$10,000	
	Network	10000	$10,000	$2,500	$2,500	$2,500	$2,500	$2,500	
	Groupware	100@500	$50,000	$1,000	$1,000	$1,000	$1,000	$1,000	
	Windows	100@125	$12,500	$5,000	$5,000	$5,000	$5,000	$5,000	
Services									
	Nexis/Lexis	50000	$50,000	$50,000	$50,000	$50,000	$50,000	$50,000	
	Training	300@200	$30,000	$30,000	$30,000	$30,000	$30,000	$30,000	
Personnel									
	CIO	100000	$100,000	$110,000	$121,000	$133,100	$146,410	$161,051	
	Systems Pers	4@50000	$200,000	$216,000	$233,280	$251,942	$272,098	$293,866	
	Trainer	2@30000	$60,000	$63,600	$67,416	$71,461	$75,749	$80,294	
Total			$1,170,700	$509,700	$541,796	$576,603	$614,356	$655,310	$4,068,466
Benefits									
1. Billing enhancements			$300,000	$400,000	$500,000	$600,000	$600,000	$600,000	
2. Reduced paralegals			$25,000	$25,000	$25,000	$25,000	$25,000	$25,000	
3. Reduced clerical			$25,000	$25,000	$25,000	$25,000	$25,000	$25,000	
4. Reduced messenger			$0	$0	$0	$0	$0	$0	
5. Reduced telecommunications			$10,000	$10,000	$10,000	$10,000	$10,000	$10,000	
6. Lawyer efficiencies			$120,000	$240,000	$360,000	$480,000	$600,000	$600,000	
Total Benefits			$480,000	$700,000	$920,000	$1,140,000	$1,260,000	$1,260,000	$5,760,000

FIGURE 11.9
Costs and Benefits of the Intellex Legal Information System (ILIS). This spreadsheet analyzes the costs and the benefits of implementing an information system for the law firm. The costs for hardware, telecommunications, software, services, and personnel are analyzed over a six-year period.

Year:		0	1	2	3	4	5
Net Cash Flow		($690,700)	$190,300	$378,204	$563,397	$645,644	$604,690

(1) Payback Period   = 5.06 years

      With uneven cash flows, sum inflows until
      they equal the initial investment (1,170,700)

Year 2 = 190,300	$190,300
Year 3 = 378,204	$568,504
Year 3 = 122,196	$690,700
Year 4 = 563,397	$1,131,901
Year 5 = 38,799	

(2) Accounting Rate of Return (ROI)

(Total Benefits-Total Costs-Depreciation) /Useful Life
$$\frac{\text{(Total Benefits-Total Costs-Depreciation) /Useful Life}}{\text{Total initial investment}} = \frac{(5,760,000-2,897,766-1,170,700)\ /6}{1,170,700} = \frac{281,922}{1,170,700} = 24\%$$

      With uneven cash flows, use total benefits
      less total depreciation, divided by useful life
      to establish the numerator

(3) Cost-Benefit Ratio $\dfrac{\text{Total Benefits}}{\text{Total Costs}} = \dfrac{5,760,000}{4,068,466} = 1.42$

(4) Net Present Value   @NPV(.05,D50..I50) = $1,262,120-1,170,700 = $91,420

(5) Profitability Index   NPV/Investment $1,262,120/1,170,700   1.07

(6) Internal rate of return (IRR)   @IRR(.05,D50..I50) =   48%

FIGURE 11.10
Financial models. In order to determine the financial basis for a project, a series of financial models help determine the return on invested capital. These calculations include the payback period, the accounting rate of return (ROI), the cost-benefit ratio, the net present value, the profitability index, and the internal rate of return (IRR).

long and not very short either. The payback method is a popular method because of its simplicity and power as an initial screening method. It is especially good for high-risk projects where the useful life is difficult to know. If a project pays for itself in two years, then it matters less how long after two years the system lasts.

The weakness of this measure is its virtues: The method ignores the time value of money, the amount of cash flow after the payback period, the disposal value (usually zero with computer systems), and the profitability of the investment.

Accounting Rate of Return on Investment (ROI)

Firms make capital investments in order to earn a satisfactory rate of return. Determining a satisfactory rate of return depends on the cost of borrowing money, but other factors can enter into the equation. Such factors include the historic rates of return expected by the firm. In the long run, the desired rate of return must equal or exceed the cost of capital in the marketplace. Otherwise, no one will lend the firm money.

The **accounting rate of return on investment (ROI)** calculates the rate of return from an investment by adjusting the cash inflows produced by the investment for depreciation. It gives an approximation of the accounting income earned by the project.

To find the ROI, one first calculates the average net benefit. The formula for the average net benefit is as follows:

$$\frac{(\text{Total benefits} - \text{Total cost} - \text{Depreciation})}{\text{Useful life}} = \text{Net benefit}$$

accounting rate of return on investment (ROI) Calculation of the rate of return from an investment by adjusting cash inflows produced by the investment for depreciation. Approximates the accounting income earned by the investment.

This net benefit is divided by the total initial investment to arrive at ROI (Rate of Return on Investment). The formula is

$$\frac{\text{Net benefit}}{\text{Total initial investment}} = \text{ROI}$$

In the case of Primrose, the average rate of return on the investment is 24 percent. The cost of capital (the prime rate) has been hovering around 6 to 8 percent, and returns on invested capital in corporate bonds are at about 10 percent. On the surface, this investment returns more than other financial investments.

The weakness of ROI is that it can ignore the time value of money. Future savings are simply not worth as much in today's dollars as are current savings. On the other hand, ROI can be modified (and usually is) so that future benefits and costs are calculated in today's dollars. (The present value function on most spreadsheets will perform this conversion.)

Net Present Value

Evaluating a capital project requires that the cost of an investment (a cash outflow usually in year 0) be compared with the net cash inflows that occur many years later. But these two kinds of inflows are not directly comparable because of the time value of money. Money you have been promised to receive three, four, and five years from now is not worth as much as money received today. Money received in the future has to be discounted by some appropriate percentage rate—usually the prevailing interest rate, or sometimes the cost of capital. **Present value** is the value in current dollars of a payment or stream of payments to be received in the future. It can be calculated by using the formula

present value The value in current dollars of a payment or stream of payments to be received in the future.

$$\text{Payment} \times \frac{1 - (1 + \text{interest})^{-n}}{\text{Interest}} = \text{Present value}$$

Thus, in order to compare the investment (made in today's dollars) with future savings or earnings, you need to discount the earnings to their present value and then calculate the net present value of the investment. The **net present value** is the amount of money an investment is worth, taking into account its cost, earnings, and the time value of money. The formula for net present value is

net present value The amount of money an investment is worth, taking into account its cost, earnings, and the time value of money.

Present value of expected cash flows − Initial investment cost = Net present value

In the case of Primrose, the present value of the benefits is $1,262,120 and the cost (in today's dollars) is $1,170,700, giving a net present value of $91,420. In other words, the net present value of the investment is $91,420 over a six-year period.

Cost-Benefit Ratio

A simple method for calculating the returns from a capital expenditure is to calculate the **cost-benefit ratio,** which is the ratio of benefits to costs. The formula is

cost-benefit ratio A method for calculating the returns from a capital expenditure by dividing total benefits by total costs.

$$\frac{\text{Total benefits}}{\text{Total costs}} = \text{Cost-benefit ratio}$$

In the case of Primrose, the cost-benefit ratio is 1.42, meaning that the benefits are 1.42 times greater than the costs. The cost-benefit ratio can be used to rank several projects for comparison. Some firms establish a minimum cost-benefit ratio that must be attained by capital projects. The cost-benefit ratio can of course be calculated using present values to account for the time value of money.

Profitability Index

One limitation of net present value is that it provides no measure of profitability. Neither does it provide a way to rank order different possible investments. One sim-

profitability index Used to compare the profitability of alternative investments; it is calculated by dividing the present value of the total cash inflow from an investment by the initial cost of the investment.

ple solution is provided by the profitability index. The **profitability index** is calculated by dividing the present value of the total cash inflow from an investment by the initial cost of the investment. The result can be used to compare the profitability of alternative investments.

$$\frac{\text{Present value of cash inflows}}{\text{Investment}} = \text{Profitability index}$$

In the case of Primrose, the profitability index is equal to 1.07. The project barely returns more than its cost. Projects can be rank ordered on this index, permitting firms to focus on only the most profitable projects.

Internal Rate of Return (IRR)

internal rate of return (IRR) The rate of return or profit that an investment is expected to earn.

Internal rate of return (IRR) is a variation of the net present value method. It takes into account the time value of money. **Internal rate of return (IRR)** is defined as the rate of return or profit that an investment is expected to earn. IRR is the discount (interest) rate that will equate the present value of the project's future cash flows to the initial cost of the project (defined here as a negative cash flow in year 0 of $690,700). In other words, the value of R (discount rate) is such that Present value − Initial cost = 0. In the case of Primrose, the IRR is 48 percent. This seems to be a healthy rate of return.

Results of the Capital Budgeting Analysis

Using methods that take into account the time value of money, the Primrose project is cash-flow positive over the time period and does return more benefits than it cost. However, the returns are not stellar. Against this analysis, one might ask what other investments would be better from an efficiency and effectiveness point of view. Also, one must ask if all the benefits have been calculated. It may be that this investment is necessary for the survival of the firm, or necessary to provide a level of service demanded by its clients. What are other competitors doing? In other words, there may be other intangible and strategic business factors to take into account (see the Window on Management). Let's look at these other intangible possibilities.

NONFINANCIAL AND STRATEGIC CONSIDERATIONS

Other methods of selecting and evaluating information system investments involve nonfinancial and strategic considerations. When the firm has several alternative investments to select from, it can employ portfolio analysis and scoring models. Several of these methods can be used in combination.

Portfolio Analysis

Rather than using capital budgeting, a second way of selecting among alternative projects is to consider the firm as having a portfolio of potential applications. Each application carries risks and benefits. The portfolio can be described as having a certain profile of risk and benefit to the firm (see Figure 11.11). While there is no ideal profile for all firms, information-intensive industries (e.g., finance) should have a few high-risk–high-benefit projects to ensure that they stay current with technology. Firms in non-information-intensive industries should focus on high-benefit–low-risk projects.

The general risks are as follows:

- Benefits may not be obtained.
- Costs of implementation may exceed budgets.
- Implementation time frames are exceeded.
- Technical performance is less than expected.
- The system is incompatible with existing software/hardware.

FIGURE 11.11
A system portfolio. Companies should examine their portfolio of projects in terms of potential benefits and likely risks. Certain kinds of projects should be avoided altogether and others developed rapidly. There is no ideal mix. Companies in different industries have different profiles.

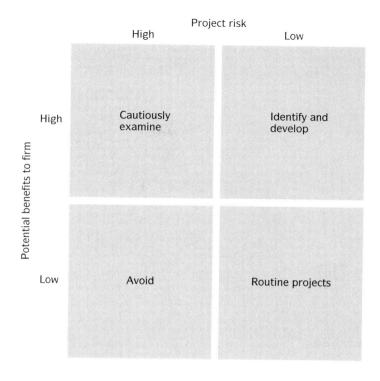

Risks are not necessarily bad. They are tolerable as long as the benefits are commensurate. In general, there are three factors that increase the risks of a project: project size, organizational experience, and project task complexity (Ein-Dor and Segev, 1978; McFarlan, 1981; Laudon, 1989). These are described in Chapter 14.

Once strategic analyses have determined the overall direction of systems development, a **portfolio analysis** can be used to select alternatives. Obviously, one can begin by focusing on systems of high benefit and low risk. These promise early returns and low risks. Second, high-benefit–high-risk systems should be examined. Low-benefit–high-risk systems should be totally avoided, and low-benefit–low-risk systems should be re-examined for the possibility of rebuilding and replacing them with more desirable systems having higher benefits.

portfolio analysis An analysis of the portfolio of potential applications within a firm to determine the risks and benefits and select among alternatives for information systems.

Scoring Models

A quick, and sometimes compelling, method for arriving at a decision on alternative systems is a **scoring model**. Scoring models give alternative systems a single score based on the extent to which they meet selected objectives (the method is similar to the *objective attained* model) (Matlin, 1989; Buss, 1983).

In Table 11.9 the firm must decide among three alternative office automation systems (a mainframe system, a minicomputer system, and a microcomputer-based system). Column 1 lists the criteria that decision makers may apply to the systems. These criteria are usually the result of lengthy discussions among the decision-making group. Often the most important outcome of a scoring model is not the score but simply agreement on the criteria used to judge a system (Ginzberg, 1979; Nolan, 1982).

Column 2 lists the weights that decision makers attach to the decision criterion. The scoring model helps to bring about agreement among participants concerning the rank of the criteria.

Columns 3 to 5 use a 1-to-5 scale (lowest to highest) to express the judgments of participants on the *relative* merits of each system. For example, concerning the percentage of user needs that each system meets, a score of 1 for a system argues that this system when compared to others being considered will be low in meeting user needs.

scoring model A quick method for deciding among alternative systems based on a system of ratings for selected objectives.

WEIGHING INTANGIBLES

"Will this new IS project will be worth its price? Should I fund it?" These are the traditional questions faced by corporate executives everywhere. "Sure, I know how to use a return on investment (ROI) or a cost-benefit analysis (CBA), but is that sufficient for me to make a decision?" The answer to this question is a clear and resounding "No!" These traditional financial measures were developed for a manufacturing economy where the value of an investment was judged by the money it saved the company—primarily reduced labor costs. Today, the problem with these measures as tools to judge the value of a new information system is not that they do not help, because they do. Rather, it is that they do not tell the whole story. Information systems usually have other benefits, intangible benefits that are not susceptible to narrow financial measurements—benefits that improve customer relations or boost competitiveness. Another drawback of traditional financial measures such as ROI and net present value is that they assume a static business strategy and a single business scenario. The most dynamic companies are looking to change their business strategies and scenarios.

The question that executives must be able to answer is, "How can I measure the intangible benefits before I make a decision on whether to build the system?" This dilemma is shared by virtually any organization that uses computers, and it has been wrestled with repeatedly. Every solution includes continuing to use traditional ROI and CBA measures. But they go beyond. JC Penney Co. has established a capital appropriations committee for all technology investments that exceed $150,000. The committee includes JC Penney CEO W. R. Howell and six other top managers. Proposals to this committee must include a traditional ROI based on costs and benefits. In addition, the proposers are required to include a sec-

tion devoted to examining competitive considerations. The proposals describe both quantifiable and nonquantifiable benefits. Some projects come in with no quantifiable benefits yet are considered competitive necessities. After a project is completed, the company evaluates whether the anticipated costs and benefits were realized. At Conoco, Inc., the Houston, Texas, energy company, developers use an interview form to hold numerous in-depth interviews on potential benefits prior to applying for project funding. In all affected departments, the department head and frequent users are interviewed for 30 to 60 minutes each. Summaries of the interviews are included in the management report on costs and benefits.

One of the most interesting approaches, developed by Oracle Corp., the Redwood Shores, California, software giant, attempts to quantify intangible benefits to make a final decision more clear-cut. Oracle's approach is a model it calls CB-90, which relies upon ideas from the emerging field of information economic analysis. CB-90 requires the team to identify and analyze both tangible and intangible elements relevant to the project decision through the use of three factors. The process begins with the appointment of a committee of managers who will be impacted by the proposed system, including one or two from IS. For example, when management at Watkins-Johnson Co., the $250 million Palo Alto, California, electronics firm, used CB-90 to help them make decisions concerning a new financials application, the team included a combination of managers and staffers from credit, collections and cost accounting, as well as other financial experts. They began with the first factor, the traditional tangible *cost-benefit analysis*, identifying benefits one at a time, in business terms (readable English). This required that the team discuss each one and reach agreement on its value. In the area of tangible benefits, CB-90 pushes its

users further than normal, requiring them to search out tangible benefits that have traditionally been overlooked. For example, Watkin-Johnson's

> **To Think About:** Some say that business managers who demand traditional financial analysis to justify an information systems investment might miss out on valuable business opportunities. Do you agree? Do you think attempts to quantify intangible benefits and risks, such as CB-90, are helpful to management to make better decisions on systems investments? Explain your responses. What management, organization, and technology factors should be addressed when making information systems investment decisions?

tangible benefits included not only a reduced head count, but also an accounts receivable cycle that is shortened by two days. This reduced cycle is a tangible benefit because by sending out invoices two days earlier, the company's cash flow is improved by two days. This, in turn, causes short-term borrowing costs to decline.

Once agreement on tangible benefits has been achieved, the committee assigns a percentage weight to each according to its perceived importance. Each item is then judged according to the likelihood of that benefit being achieved. Both of these numbers require the approval of the whole team and so cause the team members to look deeply at the value of the anticipated benefits. Next, multiplying the weight by the likelihood produces a numerical rating for each tangible benefit. Next, the committee must tackle the more difficult second and third factors of the CB-90 model, *intangible benefit analysis* and *intangible risks*. Watkins-Johnson's intangible benefits included better control of departmental budgets and improved financial reporting to executives. Its intangible risks included the system's inability to respond to quick changes in the manufacturing climate and possible employee resistance to any sort of change.

The final step in the CB-90 model is putting these weighted factors into a score sheet that totals the rate and score and concludes with a recommendation. Edward Abell, manager of information planning at Watkins-Johnson, believes CB-90 is quite valuable. His back-ground is IS, not finance. In the past, a lot of this kind of decision making was seat of the pants. Perhaps the greatest value of CB-90 is that it forces management to build consensus prior to the system being developed. When the work begins, top management and IS professionals already agree upon the goals and expectations of the new system, and even upon the weight and value of the specific benefits and risks.

Sources: Jeff Moad, "Time for a Fresh Approach to ROI," *Datamation*, February 15, 1995; Alice LaPlante, "No Doubt About IT," *Computerworld*, August 15, 1994; J. William Semich, "Here's How to Quantify IT Investment Benefits," *Datamation*, January 7, 1994.

Table 11.9 Scoring Model Used to Choose Among Alternative Office Automation Systems*

Criterion	Weight	Central Mainframe		Department Minicomputer		Individual PCs	
Percentage of user needs met	0.40	2	0.8	3	1.2	4	1.6
Cost of the initial purchase	0.20	1	0.2	3	0.6	4	0.8
Financing	0.10	1	0.1	3	0.3	4	0.4
Ease of maintenance	0.10	2	0.2	3	0.3	4	0.4
Chances of success	0.20	3	0.6	4	0.8	4	0.8
Final score			1.9		3.2		4.0

Scale: 1 = low, 5 = high.

One of the major uses of scoring models is in identifying the criteria of selection and their relative weights. In this instance, an office automation system based on PCs appears preferable.

As with all "objective" techniques, there are many qualitative judgments involved in using the scoring model. This model requires experts who understand the issues and the technology. It is appropriate to cycle through the scoring model several times, changing the criteria and weights, to see how sensitive the outcome is to reasonable changes in criteria. Scoring models are used most commonly to confirm, to rationalize, and to support decisions, rather than being the final arbiters of system selection.

If Primrose had other alternative systems projects to select from, it could have used the portfolio and scoring models as well as financial models to establish the business value of its systems solution.

Management Challenges

1. Major risks and uncertainties in systems development. Information systems development has major risks and uncertainties that make it difficult for the systems to achieve their goals. Sometimes, the cost of achieving them is too high. One problem is the difficulty of establishing information requirements, both for individual end users and for the organization as a whole. The requirements may be too complex or subject to change. Another problem is that the time and cost factors to develop an information system are very difficult to analyze, especially in large projects. Chapters 12 and 14 describe some ways of dealing with these risks and uncertainties, but the issues remain major management challenges.

2. Determining benefits of a system when they are largely intangible. As the sophistication of systems grows, they produce fewer tangible and more intangible benefits. By definition, there is no solid method for pricing intangible benefits. Organizations could lose important opportunities if they only use strict financial criteria for determining information systems benefits. On the other hand, organizations could make very poor investment decisions if they overestimate intangible benefits.

3. Developing an effective information systems plan. The greatest difficulty with plans in general is choosing the right plan, implementing it effectively, and adjusting the plan as conditions merit. Simply developing an information systems plan and a strategic plan is no guarantee of success or survival.

4. Managing change. Although building a new information system is a process of planned organizational change, this does not mean that change can always be planned or controlled. Individuals and groups in organizations have varying interests, and may resist changes in procedures, job relationships, and technologies. Chapter 14, on implementation, describes the problems of change management in greater detail.

Summary

1. Understand why building new systems is a process of organizational change. Building a new information system is a form of planned organizational change that involves many different people in the organization. Because information systems are sociotechnical entities, a change in information systems involves changes in work, management, and the organization. There are four levels of change that can result from the introduction of information technology: automation, rationalization of procedures, business process redesign (business re-engineering) and paradigm shift. Business re-engineering has the potential to dramatically improve productivity by streamlining work flows and redundant processes.

2. Identify the groups who are involved in building systems. Most organizations today have a well-established management structure for controlling the development of systems. All medium-sized and large systems involve senior, middle, and supervisory management, along with information systems professionals. Large and medium-sized organizations usually have a corporate information system steering committee to allocate resources to system projects. The project team is directly responsible for building the system.

3. Explain how the organization can develop information systems that fit its business plan. Organizations should develop an information systems plan that describes how information technology supports the attainment of their goals. The plan indicates the direction of systems development, the rationale, implementation strategy, and budget. Enterprise analysis and critical success factors (CSFs) can be used to elicit organization-wide information requirements that must be addressed by the plan.

4. Identify the core activities in the systems development process. The core activities in systems development are systems analysis, systems design, programming, testing, conversion, and production and maintenance. Systems analysis is the study and analysis of problems of existing systems and the identification of requirements for their solution. Systems design provides the specifications for an information system solution, showing how its technical and organizational components fit together.

5. Describe various models for determining the business value of information systems. Capital budgeting models such as the payback method, accounting rate of return on investment (ROI), cost-benefit ratio, net present value, profitability index, and internal rate of return (IRR) are the primary financial models for determining the business value of information systems. Portfolio analysis and scoring models include nonfinancial considerations and can be used to evaluate alternative information systems projects.

Key Terms

Information systems plan	Feasibility study	Acceptance testing	Tangible benefits
Enterprise analysis	Technical feasibility	Test plan	Intangible benefits
Critical success factors (CSFs)	Economic feasibility	Conversion	Payback method
Automation	Operational feasibility	Parallel strategy	Accounting rate of return on investment (ROI)
Rationalization of procedures	Information requirements	Direct cutover	Present value
Business re-engineering	Systems design	Pilot study	Net present value
Business process	Logical design	Phased approach	Cost-benefit ratio
Paradigm shift	Physical design	Conversion plan	Profitability index
Systems development	Programming	Documentation	Internal rate of return (IRR)
Systems analysis	Testing	Production	Portfolio analysis
	Unit testing	Maintenance	Scoring model
	System testing	Capital budgeting	

Review Questions

1. Why can a new information system be considered planned organizational change? Describe the four kinds of organizational change that are enabled by information technology.

2. Name the groups responsible for the management of systems development. What are the responsibilities of each?
3. What are the major categories of an information systems plan?
4. How can enterprise analysis and critical success factors be used to establish organization-wide information system requirements?
5. What is business process redesign (business re-engineering)? How does it differ from automation and rationalization of procedures?
6. List and describe the five steps suggested for business re-engineering.
7. What is the difference between systems analysis and systems design?
8. What is feasibility? Name and describe each of the three major areas of feasibility for information systems.
9. What are information requirements? Why are they difficult to determine correctly?
10. What is the difference between the logical design and the physical design of an information system?
11. Why is the testing stage of systems development so important? Name and describe the three stages of testing for an information system.
12. What is conversion? Why is it important to have a detailed conversion plan?
13. What role do programming, production, and maintenance play in systems development?
14. Name and describe the capital budgeting methods used to evaluate information systems projects.
15. What are the limitations of financial models for establishing the value of information systems?
16. Describe how portfolio analysis and scoring models can be used to establish the worth of systems.

Discussion Questions

1. It has been said that information systems design cannot be directed by technical specialists alone. Discuss.
2. Information systems often have to be redesigned after testing. Discuss.
3. Which conversion strategy would you use for the following? Why?
   - A system to track stock purchase and sale transactions
   - A process control system at a chemical plant
   - A system to record student attendance at a 2000-student high school
   - A corporate accounting system that will consolidate general ledger data from ten different operating units
4. Discuss the roles of users and information processing specialists in the following systems development activities:
   - Systems analysis
   - Determination of information requirements
   - Assessment of feasibility
   - Design
   - Testing
   - Conversion
5. The only way to understand what information is needed by the organization is to do a comprehensive study of how various organizational groups actually use information. Discuss.

Group Project

With three or four of your classmates, read the following case or a description of another system in this text. Prepare a report describing (on the basis of the information provided) some of the design specifications that might be appropriate for the Information Exchange Platform or the system you select. Present your findings to the class.

CURING CHAOS AT METHODIST HOSPITAL

Methodist Hospital is a large teaching hospital in Indianapolis, Indiana. In 1990 it had about 43,000 patient admissions, served 250,000 outpatients, and handled 80,000 emergency room visits. During the 1970s, the hospital had purchased a mainframe-based turnkey billing and patient records system. A turnkey system is delivered to a customer as a complete hardware and software configuration. The client simply has to "turn the key" to begin the system. Since then, the hospital's information systems department has spent most of its time maintaining the old system and working on a five- to seven-year application backlog. User departments such as the hospital laboratory and emergency room became frustrated because their computing needs could not be satisfied. So they bought their own systems, none of which communicated with the others.

When Walter Zerrenner took over as Methodist Hospital's chief information officer in 1989, he found three strategic information systems plans sitting on a shelf. There was never any time to implement them. The plans were developed without any user input, so no one outside the information systems department was committed to them.

Zerrenner brought in a team from Andersen Consulting in Chicago to assess the state of the hospital's information systems department as well as user attitudes toward the department. The assessment turned up three incompatible wide area networks, more than twenty incompatible local area networks, and more than one hundred different information systems throughout the hospital.

Information systems in different departments in Methodist Hospital use different identification codes for the same patients. Patients had to register separately in each department, often answering the same questions over and over again. The mainframe patient management system showed that lab tests were scheduled but did not display the results. The results of the tests were stored on a separate departmental system in the lab. The only place to find complete information on a patient was in a paper file.

The mainframe patient management system could only be acessed from terminals located within the hospital. Physicians complained that they could not use microcomputers in their offices to dial into the system for patient information. The system kept information only on patients who were formally admitted to the hospital. Even that information was available on-line for only five days after a patient's discharge. If a discharged patient had unforeseen complications, his or her medical records could only be found in manual paper files. Additionally, the mainframe patient management system did not handle outpatients or people who merely came in for tests. Yet most users liked the way the mainframe system worked. Dr. Chris Steffy, a resident in internal medicine, believed it was more efficient and rich in functions than other systems he had used.

Zerrenner formed a 25-member information systems planning committee with representatives from all of the hospital's major departments, including a contingent of physicians and nurses. Zerrenner and the planning committee identified three options for an improved patient information system: (1) scrap the existing systems; (2) try to make all of the existing systems communicate with each other; and (3) establish a centralized data-base for the data collected by individual departments.

The first solution meant walking away from the hospital's enormous investment in existing systems, which did work well for individual departments. The second solution appeared to be a logistical nightmare, because the information systems department would have had to create a separate interface for every departmental system. Physicians would have had to sit at terminals and sign on and off each individual system. The third solution seemed the only reasonable choice. The database could obtain information from each departmental system and make it commonly available.

Zerrenner built a working model of the new system, called the Information Exchange Platform (IXP), for users to evaluate. People were encouraged to sit down at a workstation, sign on with a password, and use a mouse to move around sample windows, viewing patient data, graphing the results, or sending the data via E-mail to another physician for consultation. The system uses the Sybase relational database management system running on an IBM RS/6000 file server. From the prototype, the development team created a pilot system. The pilot features a patient care application that provides physicians with patient information generated by hospital procedures and an application that allows a person to access the laboratory computer system, the radiology computer system, and the physician office system on IXP microcomputer workstations.

The Information Exchange Platform was never designed to capture all of the data from individual departments. A second committee, a broad-based information systems steering committee formed by Zerrenner, is determining what information is needed by multiple departments. The project has adopted an 80/20 rule, focusing on the most important information that is used 80 percent of the time. Most of that information consists of lab, radiology, patient demographics, and electrocardiogram interpretations.

Sources: Scott D. Palmer, "A Plan That Cured Chaos," *Datamation*, January 1, 1993; and E. W. Martin, "Methodist Hospital of Indiana, Inc.," in E. Wainwright Martin, Daniel W. De Hayes, Jeffrey A. Hoffer, and William C. Perkins, *Managing Information Technology*, eds. (New York: Macmillan, 1994).

Case Study Questions

1. Prepare a report analyzing the problems with Methodist Hospital's systems. Describe the problems and their causes. What management, organization, and technology factors were responsible?

2. If you were the systems analyst for this project, list five questions you would ask during interviews to elicit the information needed for your systems analysis report.

3. Do you agree that the Information Exchange Platform was the best solution for Methodist Hospital? Why or why not? What would you recommend? Why?

4. Evaluate the approach to systems building that was used for the IXP project.

5. Describe the role of end users and technical specialists in analyzing the problem and in developing the solution.

6. What conversion strategy would you use when the Information Exchange Platform is completed?

7. Why could it be said that the Information Exchange Platform is only one part of the solution for Methodist Hospital?

References

Ahituv, Niv, and Seev Neumann. "A Flexible Approach to Information System Development." *MIS Quarterly* (June 1984).

Alter, Steven, and Michael Ginzberg. "Managing Uncertainty in MIS Implementation." *Sloan Management Review* 20 (Fall 1978).

Bacon, C. James. "The Uses of Decision Criteria in Selecting Information Systems/Technology Investments." *MIS Quarterly* 16, no. 3 (September 1992).

Banker, Rajiv D., Robert J. Kauffman, and M. Adam Mahmood. *Strategic Information Technology Management: Perspectives on Organizational Growth and Competitive Advantage* Harrisburg, PA: Idea Group Publishing (1993).

Barki, Henri, and Jon Hartwick. "User Participation, Conflict and Conflict Resolution: The Mediating Roles of Influence." *Information Systems Research* 5, no. 4 (December 1994).

Beath, Cynthia Mathis, and Wanda J. Orlikowski. "The Contradictory Structure of Systems Development Methodologies: Deconstructing the IS-User Relationship in Information Engineering." *Information Systems Research* 5, no. 4 (December 1994).

Bostrum, R. P., and J. S. Heinen. "MIS Problems and Failures: A Socio-Technical Perspective; Part I: The Causes." *MIS Quarterly* 1 (September 1977); "Part II: The Application of Socio-Technical Theory." *MIS Quarterly* 1 (December 1977).

Bullen, Christine, and John F. Rockart. "A Primer on Critical Success Factors." Cambridge, MA: Center for Information Systems Research, Sloan School of Management (1981).

Buss, Martin D. J. "How to Rank Computer Projects." *Harvard Business Review* (January 1983).

Cerveny, Robert P., Edward J. Garrity, and G. Lawrence Sanders. "A Problem-Solving Perspective on Systems Development." *Journal of Management Information Systems* 6, no. 4 (Spring 1990).

Davenport, Thomas H., and James E. Short. "The New Industrial Engineering: Information Technology and Business Process Redesign." *Sloan Management Review* 31, no. 4 (Summer 1990).

Davidson, W. H. "Beyond Engineering: The Three Phases of Business Transformation." *IBM Systems Journal* 32, no. 1 (1993).

Davis, Gordon B. "Determining Management Information Needs: A Comparison of Methods." *MIS Quarterly* 1 (June 1977).

Davis, Gordon B. "Information Analysis for Information System Development." In *Systems Analysis and Design: A Foundation for the 1980's*, eds. W. W. Cotterman, J. D. Cougar, N. L. Enger, and F. Harold. New York: John Wiley (1981).

Davis, Gordon B. "Strategies for Information Requirements Determination." *IBM Systems Journal* 1 (1982).

Dennis, Alan R., Robert M. Daniels, Jr., Glenda Hayes, and Jay F. Nunamaker, Jr. "Methodology-Driven Use of Automated Support in Business Process Re-Engineering." *Journal of Management Information Systems* 10, no. 3 (Winter 1993–1994).

Doll, William J. "Avenues for Top Management Involvement in Successful MIS Development." *MIS Quarterly* (March 1985).

Dos Santos, Brian. "Justifying Investments in New Information Technologies." *Journal of Management Information Systems* 7, no. 4 (Spring 1991).

Ein-Dor, Philip, and Eli Segev. "Strategic Planning for Management Information Systems." *Management Science* 24, no. 15 (1978).

El Sawy, Omar, and Burt Nanus. "Toward the Design of Robust Information Systems." *Journal of Management Information Systems* 5, no. 4 (Spring 1989).

Emery, James C. "Cost/Benefit Analysis of Information Systems." Chicago: Society for Management Information Systems Workshop Report No. 1 (1971).

Flatten, Per O., Donald J. McCubbrey, P. Declan O'Riordan, and Keith Burgess. *Foundations of Business Systems*, 2nd ed. Fort Worth, TX: Dryden Press (1992).

Franz, Charles, and Daniel Robey. "An Investigation of User-Led System Design: Rational and Political Perspectives." *Communications of the ACM* 27 (December 1984).

Gerlach, James H., and Feng-Yang Kuo. "Understanding Human-Computer Interaction for Information Systems Design." *MIS Quarterly* 15, no. 4 (December 1991).

Ginzberg, Michael J. "Improving MIS Project Selection." *Omega, Internal Journal of Management Science* 6, no. 1 (1979).

Ginzberg, Michael J. "The Impact of Organizational Characteristics on MIS Design and Implementation." Working paper CRIS 10, GBA 80-110. New York University Center for Research on Information Systems, Computer Applications and Information Systems Area (1980).

Goodhue, Dale L., Laurie J. Kirsch, Judith A. Quillard, and Michael D. Wybo. "Strategic Data Planning: Lessons from the Field." *MIS Quarterly* 16, no. 1 (March 1992).

Gould, John D., and Clayton Lewis. "Designing for Usability: Key Principles and What Designers Think." *Communications of the ACM* 28 (March 1985).

Grudnitski, Gary. "Eliciting Decision Makers' Information Requirements." *Journal of Management Information Systems* (Summer 1984).

Hammer, Michael. "Reengineering Work: Don't Automate, Obliterate." *Harvard Business Review* (July–August 1990).

Hammer, Michael, and James Champy. *Reengineering the Corporation.* New York: HarperCollins (1993).

Hammer, Michael, and Steven A. Stanton. *The Reengineering Revolution.* New York: HarperCollins (1995).

Keil, Mark and Erran Carmel. "Customer-Developer Links in Software Development." *Communications of the ACM* 38, no. 5 (May 1995).

Kendall, Kenneth E., and Julie E. Kendall. *Systems Analysis and Design,* 3rd ed. Englewood Cliffs, NJ: Prentice Hall (1994).

Kim, Chai, and Stu Westin. "Software Maintainability: Perceptions of EDP Professionals." *MIS Quarterly* (June 1988).

King, Julia. "Re-engineering Slammed." *Computerworld* (June 13, 1994).

King, William R. "Alternative Designs in Information System Development." *MIS Quarterly* (December 1982).

Konsynski, Benn R. "Advances in Information System Design." *Journal of Management Information Systems* 1 (Winter 1984–1985).

Laudon, Kenneth C. "CIOs Beware: Very Large Scale Systems." New York: Center for Research on Information Systems, New York University Stern School of Business, working paper (1989).

Lientz, Bennett P., and E. Burton Swanson. *Software Maintenance Management.* Reading, MA: Addison-Wesley (1980).

McFarlan, F. Warren. "Portfolio Approach to Information Systems." *Harvard Business Review* (September–October 1981).

Mahmood, Mo Adam, and Gary J. Mann. "Measuring the Organizational Impact of Information Technology Investment." *Journal of Management Information Systems* 10, no. 1 (Summer 1993).

Matlin, Gerald. "What Is the Value of Investment in Information Systems?" *MIS Quarterly* 13, no. 3 (September 1989).

Moad, Jeff. "Does Reengineering Really Work?" *Datamation* (August 1, 1993).

Nolan, Richard L. "Managing Information Systems by Committee." *Harvard Business Review* (July–August 1982).

Parker, M. M. "Enterprise Information Analysis: Cost-Benefit Analysis and the Data-Managed System." *IBM Systems Journal* 21 (1982), 108–123.

Premkumar, G., and William R. King. "Organizational Characteristics and Information Systems Planning: An Empirical Study." *Information Systems Research* 5, no. 2 (June 1994).

Raghunathan, Bhanu, and T. S. Raghunathan. "Adaptation of a Planning System Success Model to Information Systems Planning." *Information Systems Research* 5, no. 3 (September 1994).

Rockart, John F. "Chief Executives Define Their Own Data Needs." *Harvard Business Review* (March–April 1979).

Rockart, John F., and Michael E. Treacy. "The CEO Goes on Line." *Harvard Business Review* (January–February 1982).

"The Role of IT in Business Reengineering." *I/S Analyzer* 31, no. 8 (August 1993).

Shank, Michael E., Andrew C. Boynton, and Robert W. Zmud. "Critical Success Factor Analysis as a Methodology for MIS Planning." *MIS Quarterly* (June 1985).

Short, James E. and N. Venkatranan. "Beyond Business Process Redesign: Redefining Baxter's Business Network." *Sloan Management Review* (Fall 1992).

Vessey, Iris, and Sue Conger. "Learning to Specify Information Requirements: The Relationship between Application and Methodology." *Journal of Management Information Systems* 10, no. 2 (Fall 1993).

Vitalari, Nicholas P. "Knowledge as a Basis for Expertise in Systems Analysis: Empirical Study." *MIS Quarterly* (September 1985).

Wagner, Ina. "A Web of Fuzzy Problems: Confronting the Ethical Issues." *Communications of the ACM* 36, no. 4 (June 1993).

Wetherbe, James. "Executive Information Requirements: Getting It Right." *MIS Quarterly,* 15, no. 1 (March 1991).

Zachman, J. A. "Business Systems Planning and Business Information Control Study: A Comparison." *IBM Systems Journal* 21 (1982).

Zmud, Robert W., William P. Anthony, and Ralph M. Stair, Jr. "The Use of Mental Imagery to Facilitate Information Identification in Requirements Analysis." *Journal of Management Information Systems* 9, no. 4 (Spring 1993).

Alternative Systems-Building Methods

ClubCorp Serves Its Members with a Rapid Method of Developing Applications

Competition for members is fierce amongst private clubs. With average annual membership fees nearing $3000, the elimination by the United States federal government of most individual federal income tax deductions for club dues, and growing competition from luxury hotels, club membership actually declined slightly during the early 1990s. The problem faced by $1.2 billion ClubCorp International Inc.—how to keep its members and attract new ones—was summarized by Jerry Gelinas, ClubCorp's marketing director—"Our members decide whether to stay with us every month when they pay their dues." The competitive strategy ClubCorp chose to follow was that of product differentiation, setting itself apart with a higher level of service than other hospitality providers. Kathy McDonald, manager of the Ft. Lauderdale, Florida, Tower Club, one of ClubCorp's 250 dining, athletic, and country clubs, believes that "The main reason people join private clubs is for recognition."

To better serve their members, ClubCorp developed a new information system that would track member interests and link that information to reservations, allowing the clubs to offer more personal service based upon recognition of their members. For example, when Tower Club member and investment banker Paul Sallarulo called and made a luncheon reservation for himself and his secretary, Linda Nobilski, the computer system indicated that Nobilski likes flowers and candy. When the pair arrived for lunch, the club had peach-colored roses and chocolate-covered cherries waiting.

The new system also carries a digitized photograph of each member, so that the staff can view the pictures of members with reservations and so be able to greet each one personally. The system is used by the receptionists, food and beverage managers, chefs, and maitre d's to personalize all service. In addition, when a member from a club travels to another ClubCorp club in a different city, that member's computer file is transmitted to the other club so that it too can provide this same kind of personalized service.

When ClubCorp decided to develop its new system, it needed to create the system as quickly as possible while controlling its cost. The company chose to use a rapid applications development method that took only 15 weeks to complete, as opposed to an estimated one year using more traditional methods. Cost was held to $167,000, partly as a result of the shorter time needed for development. The higher speed and lower

cost were achieved by a combination of factors. ClubCorp used an object-oriented development tool and built the system through prototyping. Also, ClubCorp went to an outside development consulting group, IBM Consulting Group's Southwest Rapid Solutions Services in Dallas, Texas, who are experts in this type of development. Finally, one key feature of the company's approach was the emphasis upon the central role of the prospective business users of the new system. Dan Barth, ClubCorp's CIO, likes to tell the story of the "sexy, glitzy, and Star Wars-like" reservation screen the information systems developers created, which they presented to the prospective users with great pride. When the users tried it, one user asked a simple question— "Why can't the reservation screen look just like the reservation sheets we are already used to using?" The glitzy screen was, of course, abandoned in favor of the more familiar and appropriate

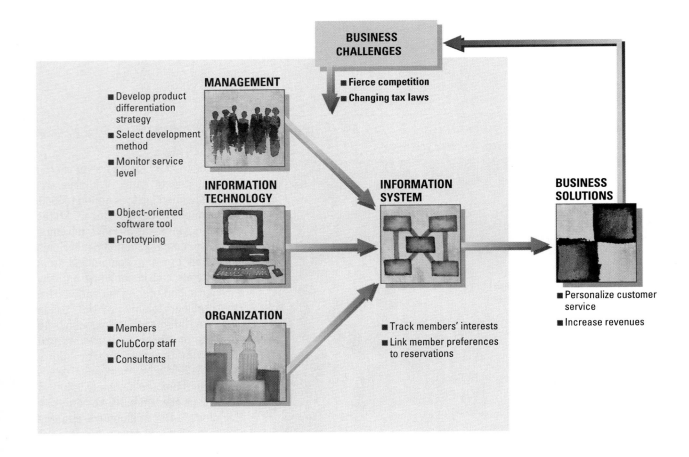

design suggested by the user. In the final system, users are presented with 11 file folder tabs (with functional labels such as "Reservations") as a main menu. Each tabbed file folder will bring up a familiar-looking screen to allow the specific user to retrieve and enter needed information.

Similar rapid development methods are being used by others as well. In 1994 Ontario, Canada's Workers Compensation Board developed a fraudulent-claims management system in less than nine months. The staff "requires easy and immediate access to shared data from various applications and databases while maintaining strict data integrity," according to Kerry Long, the VP of information services of the Compensation Board. The system has reduced the time investigators required on a fraud case from up to four weeks to less than half a day.

As for ClubCorp, the rapidly developed system has apparently been a success. Its employees appear happy with the system and are providing club members with improved service. Members are responding to the higher level of service as can be seen in membership applications—the Tower Club list of prospective members has doubled in size in the year since the system has been in place. ∎

Sources: Eric R. Chabrow, "Member of the RAD Club," *Information Week*, November 21, 1994; and David S. Linthicum, RADical Development," *PC Magazine*, November 8, 1994.

Like ClubCorp, many organizations are examining alternative methods of building new information systems. While they are designing and building some applications entirely on their own, they are also turning to software packages, external consultants, and other strategies to reduce time, cost, and inefficiency. This chapter examines the use of prototyping, application software packages, end-user development, and outsourcing as systems-building alternatives to the traditional systems life cycle method of building an entire information system from scratch.

There is no one approach that can be used for all situations and types of systems. Each of these approaches has advantages and disadvantages, and each provides managers with a range of choices. This chapter describes and compares the various approaches so that managers know how to choose among them.

After completing this chapter, you will be able to:

Learning Objectives

1. Distinguish between the various systems-building alternatives: the traditional systems life cycle, prototyping, application software packages, end-user development, and outsourcing.

2. Understand the strengths and limitations of each approach.

3. Describe the types of problems for which each approach is best suited.

4. Describe the solutions to the management problems created by these approaches.

12.1 THE TRADITIONAL SYSTEMS LIFE CYCLE

systems life cycle Traditional methodology for developing an information system that partitions the systems development process into six formal stages that must be completed sequentially with a very formal division of labor between end users and information systems specialists.

The **systems life cycle** is the oldest method for building information systems and is still used today for complex medium or large systems projects. This methodology assumes that an information system has a life cycle similar to that of any living organism, with a beginning, a middle, and an end. The life cycle for an information system has six stages: project definition, systems study, design, programming, installation, and post-implementation. Figure 12.1 illustrates these stages. Each stage consists of basic activities that must be performed before the next stage can begin.

The life cycle methodology is a very formal approach to building systems. It partitions the systems development process into distinct stages and develops an information system sequentially, stage by stage. The life cycle methodology also has a very formal division of labor between end users and information systems specialists. Technical specialists such as systems analysts and programmers are responsible for much of the systems analysis, design, and implementation work; end users are limited to providing information requirements and reviewing the work of the technical

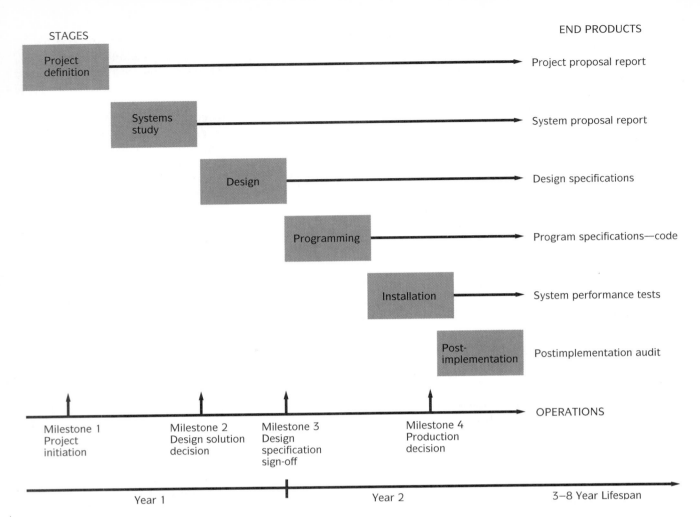

FIGURE 12.1
The life cycle methodology for system development. The life cycle methodology divides systems development into six formal stages with specifics for milestones and end products at each stage. A typical medium-sized development project requires two years to deliver and has an expected life span of three to eight years.

staff. Formal sign-offs or agreements between end users and technical specialists are required as each stage is completed.

Figure 12.1 also shows the product or output of each stage of the life cycle that is the basis for such sign-offs. The project definition stage results in a proposal for the development of a new system. The systems study stage provides a detailed systems proposal report outlining alternative solutions and establishing the feasibility of proposed solutions. The design stage results in a report on the design specifications for the system solution that is selected. The programming stage results in actual software code for the system. The installation stage outputs the results of tests to assess the performance of the system. The post-implementation stage concludes with a post-implementation audit to measure the extent to which the new system has met its original objectives. We now describe the stages of the life cycle in detail.

STAGES OF THE SYSTEMS LIFE CYCLE

project definition Stage in the systems life cycle that determines whether or not the organization has a problem and whether or not the problem can be solved by launching a system project.

The **project definition** stage tries to answer the questions, "Why do we need a new system project?" and "What do we want to accomplish?" This stage determines whether the organization has a problem and whether that problem can be solved by building a new information system or by modifying an existing one. If a system pro-

systems study Stage in the systems life cycle that analyzes the problems of existing systems, defines the objectives to be attained by a solution, and evaluates various solution alternatives.

ject is called for, this stage identifies its general objectives, specifies the scope of the project, and develops a project plan that can be shown to management.

The **systems study** stage analyzes the problems of existing systems (manual or automated) in detail, identifies objectives to be attained by a solution to these problems, and describes alternative solutions. The systems study stage examines the feasibility of each solution alternative for review by management. This stage tries to answer the questions, "What do the existing systems do?" "What are their strengths, weaknesses, trouble spots, and problems?" "What should a new or modified system do to solve these problems?" "What user information requirements must be met by the solution?" "What alternative solution options are feasible?" "What are their costs and benefits?"

Answering these questions requires extensive information gathering and research; sifting through documents, reports, and work papers produced by existing systems; observing how these systems work; polling users with questionnaires; and conducting interviews. All of the information gathered during the systems study phase will be used to determine information system requirements. Finally, the systems study stage describes in detail the remaining life cycle activities and the tasks for each phase.

design Stage in the systems life cycle that produces the logical and physical design specifications for the systems solution.

The **design** stage produces the logical and physical design specifications for the solution. Because the life cycle emphasizes formal specifications and paperwork, many of the design and documentation tools described in Chapter 13, such as data flow diagrams, structure charts, or system flowcharts are likely to be utilized.

programming Stage in the systems life cycle that translates the design specifications produced during the design stage into software program code.

The **programming** stage translates the design specifications produced during the design stage into software program code. Systems analysts work with programmers to prepare specifications for each program in the system. These program specifications describe what each program will do, the type of programming language to be used, inputs and outputs, processing logic, processing schedules, and control statements such as those for sequencing input data. Programmers write customized program code typically using a conventional third-generation programming language such as COBOL or FORTRAN or a high-productivity fourth-generation language. Since large systems have many programs with hundreds of thousands of lines of program code, entire teams of programmers may be required.

installation Systems life cycle stage consisting of testing, training, and conversion; the final steps required to put a system into operation.

The **installation** stage consists of the final steps to put the new or modified system into operation: testing, training, and conversion. The software is tested to make sure it performs properly from both a technical and a functional business standpoint. (More detail on testing can be found in Chapter 13.) Business and technical specialists are trained to use the new system. A formal conversion plan provides a detailed schedule of all of the activities required to install the new system, and the old system is converted to the new one.

post-implementation The final stage of the systems life cycle in which the system is used and evaluated while in production and is modified to make improvements or meet new requirements.

The **post-implementation** stage consists of using and evaluating the system after it is installed and is in production. It also includes updating the system to make improvements. Users and technical specialists will go through a formal post-implementation audit that determines how well the new system has met its original objectives and whether any revisions or modifications are required. After the system has been fine-tuned it will need to be maintained while it is in production to correct errors, meet requirements, or improve processing efficiency. Over time, the system may require so much maintenance to remain efficient and meet user objectives that it will come to the end of its useful life span. Once the system's life cycle comes to an end, a completely new system is called for and the cycle may begin again.

LIMITATIONS OF THE LIFE CYCLE APPROACH

The systems life cycle is still used for building large transaction processing systems (TPS) and management information systems (MIS) where requirements are highly structured and well-defined. It will also remain appropriate for complex technical systems such as space launches, air traffic control, and refinery operations. Such applications need a rigorous and formal requirements analysis, predefined specifications, and tight controls over the systems-building process. However, the systems life cycle methodology has serious limitations and is not well suited for most of the small desktop systems that will predominate during the 1990s and beyond.

The Life Cycle Approach Is Very Resource Intensive. A tremendous amount of time must be spent gathering information and preparing voluminous specification and sign-off documents. It may take years before a system is finally installed. If development time is too prolonged, the information requirements may change before the system is operational. The system that takes many years and dollars to build may be obsolete while it is still on the drawing board.

The Life Cycle Approach Is Inflexible and Inhibits Change. The life cycle approach does allow for revisions to the system to ensure that requirements are met. Whenever requirements are incorrect or an error is encountered, the sequence of life cycle activities can be repeated. But volumes of additional documents must be generated, substantially increasing development time and costs. Because of the time and cost to repeat the sequence of life cycle activities, the methodology encourages freezing of specifications early in the development process. This means that changes cannot be made. Once users approve specification documents, the specifications are frozen. However, users traditionally have had trouble visualizing a final system from specification documents. In reality, they may need to see or use a system to make sure they know what it is they need or want. Because this is not possible with the life cycle approach, it is common for users to sign off on specification documents without fully comprehending their contents, only to learn during programming and testing that the specifications are incomplete or not what they had in mind. Proper specifications cannot always be captured the first time around, early enough in the life cycle when they are easy to change.

The Life Cycle Method Is Ill-Suited to Decision-Oriented Applications. Decision making can be rather unstructured and fluid. Requirements constantly change or decisions may have no well-defined models or procedures. Decision makers often cannot specify their information needs in advance. They may need to experiment with concrete systems to clarify the kinds of decisions they wish to make. Formal specification of requirements may inhibit systems builders from exploring and discovering the problem structure (Fraser et al., 1994). This high level of uncertainty cannot be easily accommodated by the life cycle approach.

Some of these problems can be solved by the alternative strategies for building systems that are described in the remainder of this chapter.

12.2 PROTOTYPING

prototyping Process of building an experimental system quickly and inexpensively for demonstration and evaluation so that end users can better determine information requirements.

prototype Preliminary working version of an information system for demonstration and evaluation purposes.

iterative Process of repeating the steps to build a system over and over again.

Prototyping consists of building an experimental system rapidly and inexpensively for end users to evaluate. By interacting with the prototype, users can get a better idea of their information requirements. The prototype endorsed by the users can be used as a template to create the final system.

The **prototype** is a working version of an information system or part of the system, but it is meant to be only a preliminary model. Once operational, the prototype will be further refined until it conforms precisely to users' requirements. For many applications, a prototype will be extended and enhanced over and over again before a final design is accepted. Once the design has been finalized, the prototype can be converted to a polished production system.

The process of building a preliminary design, trying it out, refining it, and trying again has been called an **iterative** process of systems development because the steps required to build a system can be repeated over and over again. We noted earlier that the traditional life cycle approach involved some measure of reworking and refinement. However, prototyping is more explicitly iterative than the conventional life cycle, and it actively promotes system design changes. It has been said that prototyping replaces unplanned rework with planned iteration, with each version more accurately reflecting users' requirements.

The prototype version will not have all the final touches of the complete system. Reports, sections of files, and input transactions may not be complete; processing may not be very efficient, but a working version of the system or part of the system will be available for users to evaluate. They can start interacting with the system, deciding what they like and dislike, what they want or do not want. Since most users cannot describe their requirements fully on paper, prototyping allows them to work with a system in order to determine exactly what they need. The methodology anticipates that they will change their minds; these changes can be incorporated easily and inexpensively during an early stage of development.

Prototyping is less formal than the life cycle method. Instead of generating detailed specifications and sign-off documents, prototyping quickly generates a working model of a system. Requirements are determined dynamically as the prototype is constructed. Systems analysis, design, and implementation all take place at the same time.

STEPS IN PROTOTYPING

Figure 12.2 shows a four-step model of the prototyping process. The steps consist of the following:

Step 1. Identify the user's basic requirements. The system designer (usually an information systems specialist) works with the user only long enough to capture his or her basic information needs.

Step 2. Develop a working prototype. The system designer creates a working prototype quickly, most likely using the fourth-generation software tools described in Chapter 7 that speed application development. Some features of computer-aided software engineering (CASE) tools described in Chapter 13 can be used for prototyping, as can multimedia software tools that present users with interactive storyboards that sketch out the tasks of the proposed system for evaluation and modification (Madsen and Aiken, 1993). The prototype may only perform the most important functions of the proposed system, or it may consist of the entire system with a restricted file.

Step 3. Use the prototype. The user is encouraged to work with the system in order to determine how well the prototype meets his or her needs and to make suggestions for improving the prototype.

Step 4. Revise and enhance the prototype. The system builder notes all changes requested by the user and refines the prototype accordingly. After the prototype has been revised, the cycle returns to step 3. Steps 3 and 4 are repeated until the user is satisfied.

When no more iterations are required, the approved prototype then becomes an operational prototype that furnishes the final specifications for the application. Sometimes the prototype itself is adopted as the production version of the system. Prototyping is more rapid, iterative, and informal than the systems life cycle method has proven to be.

ADVANTAGES AND DISADVANTAGES OF PROTOTYPING

Certain types of information systems can be developed more efficiently and effectively using prototyping than using the traditional systems life cycle. For instance, when the Du Pont Company used prototyping along with heavy user involvement to build its systems, it produced more than 400 new programs with no failures and reduced maintenance by 70 to 90 percent (Arthur, 1992).

FIGURE 12.2
The prototyping process. The process of developing a prototype can be broken down into four steps. Because a prototype can be developed quickly and inexpensively, the developers can go through several iterations, repeating steps 3 and 4, in order to refine and enhance the prototype before arriving at the final operational one.

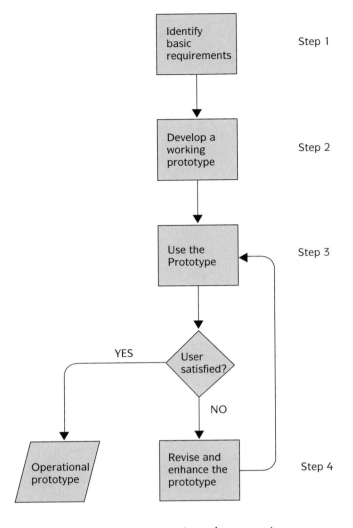

Prototyping is most useful when there is some uncertainty about requirements or design solutions. Requirements may be difficult to specify in advance or they may change substantially as implementation progresses. This is particularly true of decision-oriented applications, where requirements tend to be very vague. Management realizes that better information is needed but is unsure of what this entails. For example, a major securities firm requests consolidated information to analyze the performance of its account executives. But what should the measures of performance be? Can the information be extracted from the personnel system alone, or must data from client billings be incorporated as well? What items should be compared on reports? Will intermediate processing based on some form of statistical analysis be involved? For many decision-support applications such as this one, it is unlikely that requirements can be fully captured on the initial written specifications. The final system cannot be clearly visualized because managers cannot foresee how the system will work.

Prototyping is especially valuable for the design of the **end-user interface** of an information system (the part of the system that end users interact with, such as on-line display and data entry screens or reports). User needs and behavior are not entirely predictable (Gould and Lewis, 1985) and are strongly dependent on the context of the situation. The prototype enables users to react immediately to the parts of the system they will be dealing with. Figure 12.3 illustrates the prototyping process for an on-line calendar for retail securities brokers. The first version of the screen was built according to user-supplied specifications for a calendar to track appointments and activities. But when users actually worked with the calendar screen, they suggested adding labels for month and year to the screen and a box to indicate whether

end-user interface The part of an information system through which the end user interacts with the system, such as on-line screens and commands.

FIGURE 12.3

Prototyping a portfolio management application. This figure illustrates the process of prototyping one screen for the Financial Manager, a client and portfolio management application for securities brokers. Figure 12.3A shows an early version of the on-line appointment screen. Based on the special needs of a client, Figure 12.3B has two enhancements: a "done" indicator to show whether the task has been completed and a "link" to reference information maintained by the system on the client with whom the broker has an appointment.

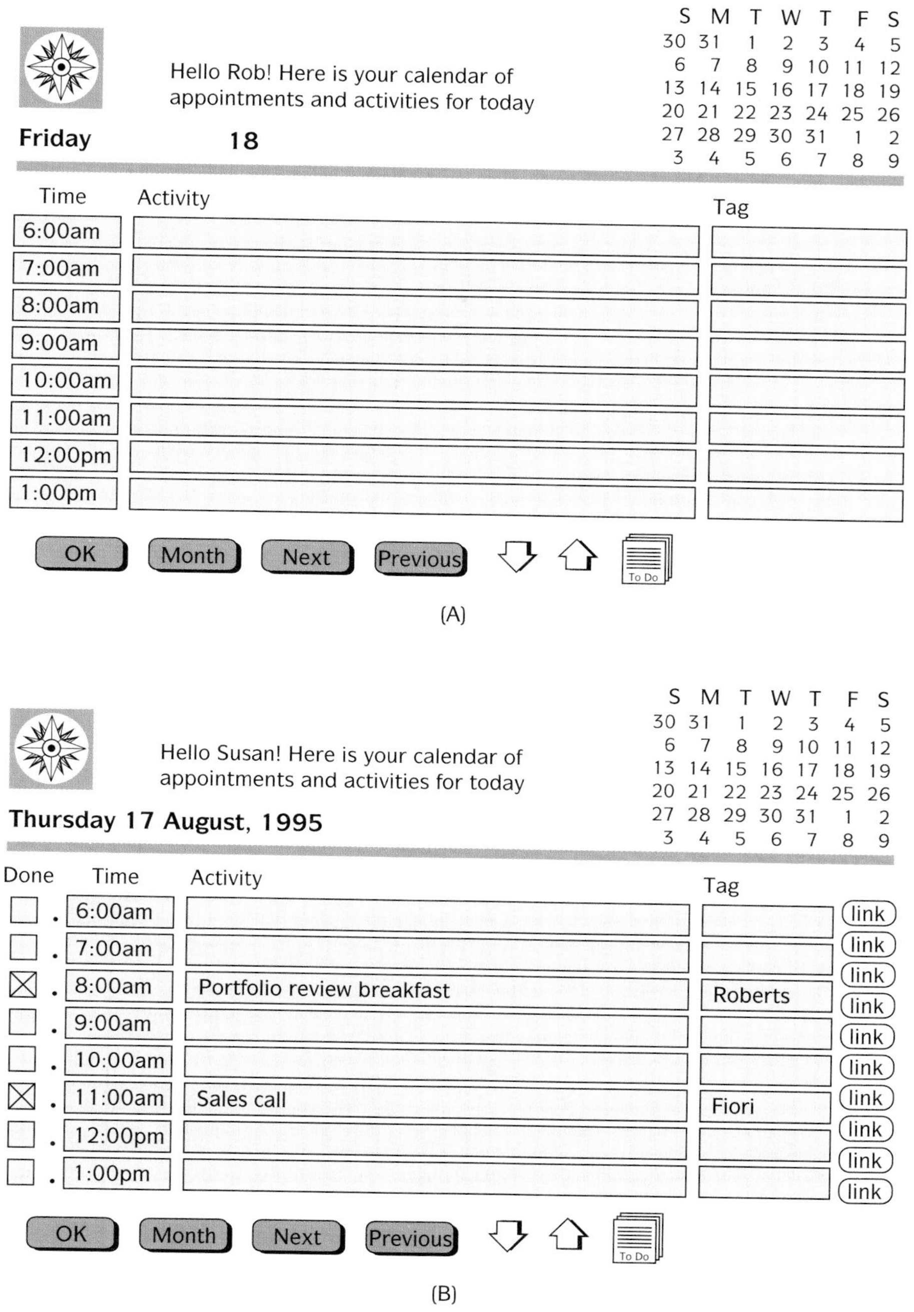

(A)

(B)

the appointment had been met or an activity completed. The brokers also found that they wanted to access information that was maintained in the system about clients with whom they had appointments. The system designer added a link enabling brokers to move directly from the calendar screen to the clients' records.

In other instances, end-user requirements may be clear enough, but systems builders may be unsure of certain technical features of the design solution. For example, a major supermarket chain contemplates revamping its inventory control system. It wants easy on-line access to its master files from multiple locations. The application will require numerous screens for on-line data entry and for retrieval of key pieces of information. But the systems team is unsure of how the screens should flow from one to the other on-line and needs to fine-tune screen formats as well. So the team decides to prototype many of the screens, using a tool for generating interactive applications. The screens are quickly developed, showing users how they will flow and how they will appear on-line.

Prototyping has been widely hailed as a panacea for the problems inherent in traditional systems development process. It encourages intense end-user involvement throughout the systems development life cycle. Users interact with a working system much earlier in the design process. As they react to and refine each version of the prototype, users become more intimately involved in the design effort (Cerveny et al., 1986). Prototyping is more likely to produce systems that fulfill user requirements, especially when it is used for decision-support applications. It promises to eliminate excess development costs and design flaws that occur when requirements are not fully captured the first time around. User satisfaction and morale are usually heightened because users can be presented with an actual working system, preliminary though it may be, in a very short period of time.

However, prototyping may not be appropriate for all applications. It should neither substitute for careful requirements analysis, structured design methodology, or thorough documentation, nor totally replace traditional development methods and tools. Both the method and the development tools currently used for prototyping have very real limitations.

Applications that are oriented to simple data manipulation and records management are considered good candidates for prototyping. However, systems that are based on batch processing or that rely on heavy calculations and complex procedural logic are generally unsuitable for the prototyping process. Prototyping is better suited for smaller applications. Large systems must be subdivided so that prototypes can be built one part at a time (Alavi, 1984). Subdividing a large system may not be possible without a thorough requirements analysis using the conventional approach, since it may be hard to see at the outset how the different parts will affect each other.

Rapid prototyping can gloss over essential steps in systems development. Basic systems analysis and requirements analysis cannot be short-circuited. The appeal of an easily and rapidly developed prototype may encourage the development team to move too quickly toward a working model without capturing even a basic set of requirements. This may be especially problematic when a large system is under development. It may not be clear how prototypes can be created for a big system or parts of the system unless prototyping is preceded by a comprehensive and thorough requirements analysis.

The final steps to convert the prototype into a polished production system may not be carried out. Once finished, the prototype often becomes part of the final production system. If the prototype works reasonably well, management may not see the need for reprogramming and redesign. Some of these hastily constructed systems may be difficult to maintain and support in a regular production environment. Since prototypes are not carefully constructed, their technical performance may be very inefficient. They may not easily accommodate large quantities of data or a large number of users in a production environment.

Prototyped systems still need to be fully documented and tested, but often these steps are shortchanged. Because prototypes are constructed so effortlessly, managers may assume that testing can be handled by users on their own; any oversights in testing can be corrected later. Because the system is so easily changed, documentation may not be kept up to date.

12.3 DEVELOPING SYSTEMS WITH APPLICATION SOFTWARE PACKAGES

application software package Set of prewritten, precoded application software programs that are commercially available for sale or lease.

Another alternative strategy is to develop an information system by purchasing an application software package. As introduced in Chapter 7, an **application software package** is a set of prewritten, precoded application software programs that are commercially available for sale or lease. Application software packages may range from a simple task (e.g., printing address labels from a database on a microcomputer) to over 400 program modules with 500,000 lines of code for a complex mainframe system. When an appropriate software package is available, it eliminates the need for writing software programs when an information system is developed and reduces the amount of design, testing, installation, and maintenance work as well. Table 12.1 provides examples of applications for which packages are commercially available.

Packages have flourished because organizations have many common information requirements for functions such as payroll, accounts receivable, general ledger, or inventory control. For such universal functions with standard accounting practices, a generalized system will fulfill the requirements of many organizations. Therefore, it is not necessary for a company to write its own programs; the prewritten, predesigned, pretested software package can fulfill the requirements and can be substituted instead. Since the package vendor has already done most of the design, programming, and testing, the time frame and costs for developing a new system should be considerably reduced.

Packages are likely to be chosen as a development strategy under the following circumstances:

1. *Where functions are common to many companies.* For example, every company has a payroll system. Payroll systems typically perform the same functions: They calculate gross pay, net pay, deductions, and taxes. They also print paychecks and reports. Consequently, application software packages have been widely used for developing payroll systems.

2. *Where information systems resources for in-house development are in short supply.* With trained and experienced systems professionals in limited supply, many

Table 12.1	Examples of Applications for Which Application Packages Are Available	
Accounts payable	Human resources
Accounts receivable	Installment loans
Architectural design	Inventory control
Banking systems	Job accounting
Bond and stock management	Job costing
Check processing	Library systems
Computer-aided design	Life insurance
Construction costing	Mailing labels
Data management systems	Mathematical/statistical modeling
Document imaging	Order entry
Electrical engineering	Payroll
Education	Performance measurement
E-mail	Process control
Financial control	Real estate management
Forecasting and modeling	Route scheduling
Forms design	Sales and distribution
General ledger	Savings systems
Government purchasing	Stock management
Graphics	Tax accounting
Health care	Utilities control
Health insurance	Word processing
Hotel management	Work scheduling

companies do not have staff that is either available or qualified to undertake extensive in-house development projects. Under such circumstances, packages may be the only way to enable a new system to be developed. Most companies also lack the budget to develop all of their systems in-house. Consequently, the most cost-effective development strategy is likely to involve an application software package.

3. *When desktop microcomputer applications are being developed for end users.* Numerous easy-to-use application packages have been developed for microcomputers and are the primary source of applications for desktop systems.

ADVANTAGES AND DISADVANTAGES OF SOFTWARE PACKAGES

It is tempting to view software packages as the long-awaited antidote to escalating software and development costs. Application software packages can facilitate system design, testing, installation, maintenance support, and organizational acceptance of a new system. Packages also have serious limitations.

Advantages of Packages

Design activities may easily consume up to 50 percent or more of the development effort. Since design specifications, file structure, processing relationships, transactions, and reports have already been worked out by the package vendor, most of the design work has been accomplished in advance. Software package programs are extensively pretested before they are marketed so that major technical problems have been eliminated. Testing the installed package can be accomplished in a relatively shorter period. Many vendors supply sample test data and assist with the testing effort. Vendors also supply tools and assistance in installing major mainframe or minicomputer systems and provide much of the ongoing maintenance and support for the system. For systems such as human resources or payroll, the vendor is responsible for making changes to keep the system in compliance with changing government regulations. The vendor supplies periodic enhancements or updates; these are relatively easy for the client's in-house staff to apply.

Fewer internal information systems resources are necessary to support a package-based system. Since 50 to 80 percent of information systems budgets can be consumed by maintenance costs, the package solution is one way to cut these costs and free up internal staff for other applications. The package vendor maintains a permanent support staff with expert knowledge of the specific application package. If a client's information systems personnel terminate or change jobs, the vendor remains a permanent source of expertise and help. System and user documentation are prewritten and are kept up to date by the vendor.

An added benefit of packages is the way they can reduce some of the organizational bottlenecks in the systems development process. The need to work and rework design specifications is reduced because the package specifications are already fixed; users must accept them as is. External design work is often perceived as being superior to an in-house effort. The package offers a fresh start by a third party who is in a stronger position to take advantage of other companies' experiences and state-of-the-art technology. Management can be more easily convinced to support a new information system based on packaged software because major software costs appear to be fixed. Problems with the system can be attributed to the limitations of the package rather than to internal sources. Thus, the major contribution of packages may be their capacity to end major sources of organizational resistance to the systems development effort.

Disadvantages of Packages

Rarely noted are the disadvantages of packages, which can be considerable, and even overwhelming, for a complex system. Commercial software has not yet achieved the level of sophistication and technical quality needed to produce multipurpose packages that can do everything well that users want in a specific application. It is much easier to design and code software that performs one function very well than to create a system with numerous complex processing functions. For example, many human resources package vendors had to develop specialized packages for processing employee retirement benefits or applicant tracking because these functions were not handled well by the more comprehensive, multipurpose human resources packages.

In some circumstances, packages may actually hamper the development effort by raising conversion costs. Although package vendors often provide conversion software and consulting help, a package may actually prolong the conversion process, especially if conversion to the package is from a sophisticated automated system. In such cases, conversion costs have been known to be so astronomical as to render the entire development effort unfeasible. Conversion to a package is easiest from simple manual applications or from automated applications that are not very sophisticated.

Packages may not meet all of an organization's requirements. To maximize market appeal, packages are geared to the most common requirements of all organizations. But what happens if an organization has unique requirements that the package does not address? To varying degrees, package software developers anticipate this problem by providing features for customization that do not alter the basic software. **Customization** features allow a software package to be modified to meet an organization's unique requirements without destroying the integrity of the package software. For instance, the package may allocate parts of its files or databases to maintain an organization's own unique pieces of data. Some packages have a modular design that allows clients to select only the software functions with the processing they need from an array of options. Packages can also be customized with user

customization The modification of a software package to meet an organization's unique requirements without destroying the integrity of the package software.

SAP's R/3 software package runs in client/server environments and can be customized to accommodate different languages, currencies, tax laws, and accounting practices.

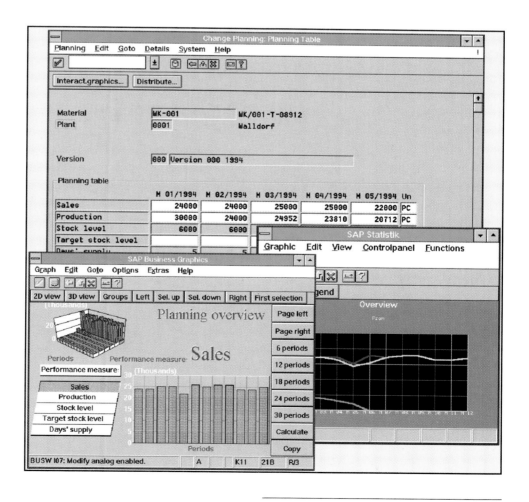

exits, places in the package program code where clients can exit from the processing performed by package programs to call software modules they write themselves for their own unique processing functions.

It is standard policy among vendors to refuse to support their products if changes have been made that altered the package's source code. Some packages have been so heavily modified with user source code changes that they are virtually unrecognizable and unmaintainable. In addition to making maximum use of the package's customization tools, one way to prevent this situation is to add front- or back-end programs that run before or after the package and do not interfere with the package software. These front or back ends may be much more extensive than the package software itself. For example, one corporation we observed developed its payroll system using a leading mainframe payroll package. The package left so many important requirements unmet that the company had to use its own programmers to write huge front- and back-end programs to supplement the package. The final structure of the system with front and back ends added looked like Figure 12.4.

So much modification and additional programming may be required to customize a package that implementation is seriously prolonged. Customization that is allowed within the package framework may be so expensive and time-consuming that it eliminates many advantages of the package. Figure 12.5 shows how package costs in relation to total implementation costs rise with the degree of customization.

The initial purchase price of the package can be deceptive because of these hidden implementation costs. An internal study by one company of the cost and time required to install six major application packages (including manufacturing resources planning, the general ledger, accounts receivable, and fixed assets) showed that total implementation costs ranged from 1.5 times to 11 times the purchase price of the package. The ratio was highest for packages with many interfaces to other systems. The same study showed that management and support costs for the first year following installation averaged twice the original package purchase price.

SELECTING SOFTWARE PACKAGES

Application software packages must be thoroughly evaluated before they can be used as the foundation of a new information system. The most important evaluation criteria are the functions provided by the package, flexibility, user-friendliness, hardware, software resources, database requirements, installation and maintenance ef-

FIGURE 12.4
A substantially customized package. To customize some packages to meet the specific requirements of an organization may require so much modification that large front-end and back-end programs must be written to handle processing requirements not met by the original package. If extensive customization is required, the extra programs often are more elaborate than the package and the features of the original package are practically lost in the final system.

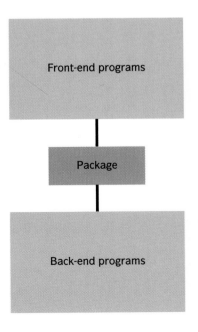

FIGURE 12.5
The effects of customizing a software package on total implementation costs. As the modifications to a software package rise, so does the cost of implementing the package. Sometimes the savings promised by the package are whittled away by excessive changes. As the number of lines of program code changed approaches 5 percent of the total lines in the package, the costs of implementation rise fivefold.

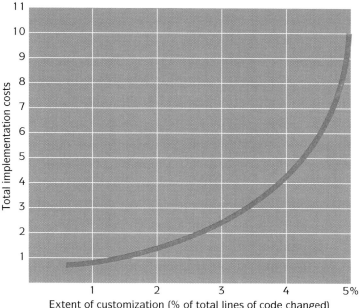

Extent of customization (% of total lines of code changed)

fort, documentation, vendor quality, and cost. The Window on Technology examines one small company's business and technical requirements for a software package.

The package evaluation process is often based on a **Request for Proposal (RFP)**, which is a detailed list of questions submitted to vendors of packaged software. The RFP is likely to include questions such as the following.

Request for Proposal (RFP) Detailed list of questions submitted to vendors of packaged software or other computer services to determine if the vendor's product can meet the organization's specific requirements.

Package Evaluation Criteria

Functions Included   The functions included vary by application. But for the specific application, the following considerations are important:

- How many of the functional requirements will the package meet?
- Which functions can be supported only by modifying the package code?
- How extensive are the modifications required?
- Which functions cannot be supported at all by the package?
- How well will the package support future as well as current needs?

Flexibility

- How easy is the package to modify?
- What customization features are included?
- Is the vendor willing to modify the software for the client?

User-Friendliness

- How easy is the package to use from a nontechnical standpoint?
- How much training is required to understand the package system?
- How much user control does the package allow?

Hardware and Software Resources

- What model computer can the package run on?
- What operating system is required?
- How much CPU and storage resources does the package take up?
- How much computer time is needed to run the package?

TRAMMEL CROW UPGRADES ITS HUMAN RESOURCES SYSTEMS

In the early 1990s, a spotlight shone on human resources systems throughout the business community like no time in the past. The business environment was changing rapidly—companies were expanding geographically, globalizing, downsizing, or re-engineering. Management needed to be able to exploit more fully their employees' skills and talents. Managers also needed to be able to redeploy their staffs nimbly in response to rapidly changing competitive factors and new business opportunities. Flattened organizations were pushing responsibility and authority out and down, and the new centers of responsibility demanded control over their own human resources functions. Jeff Comport, a consultant with the Gartner Group, of Stamford, Connecticut, explains that the human resources (HR) departments are "No longer charged with being the gatekeepers of HR information—line management is saying 'get out of the way' and give us access to the planning information we need as the actual users of human resources."

The human resources function itself had become excessively complex. Over the years many companies had developed separate systems to cover such human resources functions as payroll, compensation planning, Equal Employment Opportunity Compliance (EEOC), recruitment, COBRA, retirement, pensions, education and training, health insurance, life insurance, and so on. Many of these systems were isolated from one another. With the advances in computer technology, business managers began to demand systems that would allow them to get their hands on their data when and where they wanted, in the format they needed, and using the combinations of data that their business planning required. They also were no longer willing to accept systems with character-based interfaces that required information systems professionals to

use them. To put it simply, the human resources function had gone from being a recordkeeping function to being a strategic function, and the HR information systems were not yet reflecting that transition.

Trammel Crow Co., a small Dallas real estate services company, faced a similar human resources problem—its business was demanding more from its human resources function, but existing systems were unable to effectively deliver the services demanded. For example, its payroll system was handled by an outside service bureau, Automatic Data Processing (ADP), of Roseland, New Jersey. Payroll data were first keyed in by Trammel Crow's data entry staff, then transmitted to ADP for processing. Later, the updated data were brought back in-house into the employee master file so they could be accessed by Trammel Crow employees. This data was always outdated. According to Doug Klein, a Trammel Crow systems analyst, "The payroll information was two weeks old."

In addition to payroll, Trammel Crow also had EEOC, recruiting, and pension planning systems. All were in-house, DOS-based systems that used Paradox database management software from Borland International Inc. of Scotts Valley, California. Not only did these three in-house systems not communicate with the ADP payroll system, they did not even communicate with each other. Data had to be transferred manually from one system to another. During the real estate downturn of late 1980s, Trammel Crow began to realize that its system was not able to respond quickly enough to requests. The systems could not support the company as it began to downsize and cut expenses.

As the problems became more clear, Trammel Crow began to think about a new human resources system. Managers articulated a number of requirements any new system must meet. First, they decided that payroll must be brought back in-house so that it could

be easily integrated with other functions, and so the data would be available on a more timely basis. They decided the new system had to be strong

To Think About: Review the advantages and disadvantages of software packages presented in this text and in class. Do you think Trammel Crow was correct in turning to a software package rather than developing the system in-house? How was the selection of a software package related to the firm's business strategy?

in payroll, which meant not only that it had the function Trammel Crow required but also that it was able to perform the payroll calculations rapidly without tying up the whole computer system. The system also had to be strong in human resources, meaning that it must encompass the functionality Trammel Crow required. Moreover, the various functions had to be integrated—no more manual transferring of data or duplicate storage of data. Managers also wanted the new system to be able to talk with Paradox because so many of the users were already familiar with the Paradox query and reporting facilities and wanted to continue to use them.

Technically, managers decided the system had to be client/server-based, while the data must be stored in a relational database. In addition they decided they would not look at any system unless the vendor could demonstrate both features on a currently running system—they would accept no promises for future functionality. Once they made the client/server decision, it logically followed that payroll calculations had to occur in the server if they were to achieve their twin goals of fast calculations without tying up the network. They also demanded a user-friendly interface, although, interestingly, the payroll department staff wanted to retain a character-based interface because of their comfort with the old ways. This meant that any new system would need to be flexible enough to allow users to choose between a character-based and a graphics-based interface.

Finally, Trammel Crow decided it would be best served by purchasing a software package that met its requirements rather than trying to develop a system in-house. Many human resources systems are available on client/server platforms. In fact, HR is the most common first client/server application within many companies. Experience shows that the biggest obstacles to moving into client/server technology are the complexities of setting up and mastering a network at the same time a new HR application is installed. The learning curve needed for each was steep enough without having to learn both simultaneously. In addition, when things go wrong (as they surely will in systems as complex as these), it is difficult to isolate the problems when the infrastructure and the application are both brand-new. However, in this area Trammel Crow did have a major advantage. It already had an operational network that connected two hundred 486 PCs and included servers that stored some HR data. Thus, said Klein, "We weren't going in completely blind."

The new system Trammel Crow selected was Human Resources CS Series from Ross Systems Inc. of Redwood City, California. It met all of the company's criteria better than any other package. For example, it was client/server-based and was running on a relational database. A competitive system claimed both of these features but when it turned out the relational database feature was in development and so could not be demonstrated, Trammel Crow dropped the system from consideration. Klein says the company liked the fact that the Ross software came with application development tools, enabling Trammel Crow to do some customization. Klein was additionally impressed because those development tools were from a third-party company—Omnis 7, from Blyth Software Inc. of Foster City, California. This meant that Ross would be focusing its technical staff on enhancing its HR and payroll systems, and not on upgrading its development tools. The system included connections to financial applications such as general ledger and accounts payable, and Klein found they could even link the Ross software to their current financial applications running on their IBM AS/400 minicomputer. They were also able to have Trammel Crow's various remote sites

enter their weekly time sheet data online locally rather than filling out paper time sheets to be transmitted to the central office for data entry as occurred in the past.

The system did have weaknesses, however. First, it searched data too slowly to make drilling down for details practical. Moreover, the reports generated through the system are old-fashioned and character-based in style, thus making it impossible for Klein and others to create reports that are of real presentation quality.

The development project was primarily a conversion from an old system, and Klein found it went well. The company was able to transfer 3000 employee records from its eight offices into the new system within three months. One problem was that the company was unable to save money by converting over to the new system (although this was not one of the original goals). Because the Trammel Crow contract with ADP had been very favorable, it was difficult to reduce costs further.

Sources: Kym Gilhooly, "HR Bellies Up to Boardroom via Client/Server Offerings," *Software Magazine*, January 1995; and Connie Winkler, "The New Line On Managing People," *InformationWeek*, May 23, 1994.

Database/File Characteristics

- What kind of database/file structure does the package use?
- Do the standard fields in the package file correspond to the data elements specified by the application requirements?
- Does the database or file design support the client's processing and retrieval requirements?
- Are there provisions to add customized user fields for data elements that are not standard with the package?

Installation Effort

- How much change in procedures would the package necessitate?
- How difficult would it be to convert from the current system to the package system?

Maintenance

- Does the vendor supply updates or enhancements to the system?
- How easy are these changes to apply?
- What is the minimum internal staff necessary for ongoing maintenance and support (applications programmers, analysts, database specialists)?
- Is the source code clear, structured, and easy to maintain?

Documentation

- What kind of documentation (system and user) is provided with the package?
- Is it easy to understand and use?
- Is the documentation complete, or must the client write additional instructions in order to use the package?

Vendor Quality

- Is the vendor experienced in this application area?
- Does the vendor have a strong sales and financial record?
- Will the vendor continue to remain in business and support the package?
- What kinds of support facilities does the vendor provide for installation and maintenance (support staff, hotlines, training facilities, research and development staff)?
- Is the vendor responsive to clients' suggestions for improvements?
- Does the vendor have an active user group that meets regularly to exchange information on experiences with the package?

Cost

- What is the purchase or lease price of the basic software?
- What does the purchase price include (add-on modules; on-line, retrieval, or screen generator facilities; consulting time; training; installation support)?
- Is there a yearly maintenance fee and contract?
- What are the annual operating costs for the estimated volume of processing expected from the package?
- How much would it cost to tailor the package to the user's requirements and install it?

The Window on Management examines the issue of vendor quality when other requirements lead the potential purchaser of the package to a small, unknown company.

PACKAGED SOFTWARE AND THE SYSTEMS DEVELOPMENT PROCESS

Table 12.2 illustrates how the use of an application software package affects the systems development process. Systems analysis will include a package evaluation effort that is usually accomplished by sending out requests for proposals (RFPs) to various package vendors. The responses to the RFP will be compared to the system requirements generated during this phase, and the software package that best meets these requirements will be selected. Design activities will focus on matching requirements to package features. Instead of tailoring the systems design specifications directly to user requirements, the design effort will consist of trying to mold user requirements to conform to the features of the package.

One of the principal themes of this book has been the need to design systems that fit well with the organizations they serve. But when a package solution is selected, such a fit may be much harder to attain. The organization no longer has total control over the systems design process. Even with the most flexible and easily customized package, there are limits to the amount of tailoring allowed. Firms that are experienced in using packaged software for major business applications have noted that even the best packages cannot be expected to meet more than 70 percent of most organizations' requirements. But what about the remaining 30 percent? They will have to go unmet by the package or be satisfied by other means. If the package cannot adapt to the organization, the organization would have to adapt to the package and change its procedures. One of the most far-reaching impacts of software packages is their potential effect on organizational procedures. The kind of information a company can store for an application such as accounts receivable, for example, and

Table 12.2 Application Package Development Cycle

Systems Analysis

    Identify problem

    Identify user requirements

    Identify solution alternatives

    Identify package vendors

    Evaluate package versus in-house development

    Evaluate packages

    Select package

Systems Design

    Tailor user requirements to package features

    Train technical staff on package

    Prepare physical design

    Customize package design

    Redesign organizational procedures

Programming, Testing, and Conversion

    Install package

    Implement package modifications

    Design program interfaces

    Produce documentation

    Convert to package system

    Test the system

    Train users on package

Production and Maintenance

    Correct problems

    Install updates or enhancements to package

the way in which the company organizes, classifies, inputs, and retrieves this information could be largely determined by the package it is using.

12.4 END-USER DEVELOPMENT

end-user development The development of information systems by end users with little or no formal assistance from technical specialists.

In many organizations, end users are developing a growing percentage of information systems with little or no formal assistance from technical specialists. This phenomenon is called **end-user development**. End-user development has been made possible by the special fourth-generation software tools introduced in Chapter 7. Even though these tools are less computer-efficient than conventional programming languages, decreasing hardware costs have made them technically and economically feasible. With fourth-generation languages, graphics languages, and microcomputer tools, end users can access data, create reports, and develop entire information systems on their own, without professional systems analysts or programmers. Alternatively, end users may rely on information systems specialists for technical support but may perform many systems development activities themselves that had previously been undertaken by

CAN SAAB FIND HAPPINESS WITH A MANUFACTURING PACKAGE FROM A TINY, UNKNOWN VENDOR?

Can a company select a critical application package from a small, unknown vendor and be satisfied? While conventional wisdom says no, after much searching Saab-Scania trucks came to the opposite conclusion, and ultimately found their judgment to be justified.

Saab-Scania, known simply as Scania, is the truck manufacturing arm of the Swedish automobile company Saab. With headquarters in Sodertalje, Sweden, and production plants in Sweden, France, the Netherlands, and Brazil, Scania produces 140 trucks per day, making it the second largest truck manufacturer in the world (Volvo is the first). Truck components come to the factories from many places, including two Scania plants located in Sweden. Scania has long used computers to help keep the production lines moving fast while maintaining the lowest possible parts inventory. In the late 1980s Scania management began realizing that the company's computer systems were becoming outdated. They decided to take action.

Hans Lundmark, a Scania production computer engineer, said that the problem was that Scania was becoming locked in to outdated, proprietary systems. Scania's computer system was a Sperry Univac using a proprietary operating system and running a manufacturing application designed for that hardware and operating system. With this technology platform, Scania could not continue to build new programs on to the system. Management decided they needed to move into a relational database environment to get the flexibility to add new tables or fields as their production needs changed. The decision required two levels of decisions. First, they would need to decide on the platform on which to run the new software, and then they would need to select the application software

package and its underlying RDBMS vendor.

The platform decision was relatively easy. Scania already had a large commitment to Digital Equipment Corporation (DEC) VAX/VMS hardware and operating systems for use in its commercial systems. A great deal of new software and technology were being developed for the VAX and its VMS operating system. In addition, the DEC VAX is a popular platform for running the UNIX operating system and the many applications being developed for UNIX. Finding the correct application software was another issue.

In addition to deciding on the DEC VAX platform, on RDBMS technology, and on the business functions they needed the manufacturing package to perform, Scania determined its other main requirement was for a package that is flexible enough to be adapted to its well-established production methods and not the other way around. Scania was not interested in using a package that required too much modification to fit its environment. Management examined about seven well-known packages and found all of them unacceptable due to their lack of flexibility. The company would have had to adapt its work practices to accommodate such software or to make very detailed complex changes to the way the software worked, an approach that the software vendors would not support. Ultimately Scania turned to Computer-Integrated Interactive Manufacturing (Ciim) from unknown Avalon Software Inc. of Tucson, Arizona.

Why Ciim? First, although it would require some modification, it was far more flexible than other packages. Based on the experience of others using Ciim, Scania would be able to use about 80 percent of the package without modification. Second, its broad functionality includes production planning, shop floor control, production engineering, transport data

monitoring, handling of bills of material and order processing, determining manpower requirements, monitoring production efficiency and quality con-

To Think About: Why might Scania management be concerned about abstract ideas such as "outdated" and "proprietary" if the plants were producing well and the company was the number two worldwide in its very competitive field? Was the selection of Ciim a wise management decision? Why or why not? Explain your answer. What management, organization and technology issues should be addressed when selecting a software package?

trol, essentially all of the functions Scania was seeking. Third, Ciim was based on Oracle RDBMS, the largest independent vendor of relational database management systems. Fourth, the software would run on the VAX under either VMS or UNIX. Fifth, Ciim was written using Oracle's computer-aided software engineering (CASE) tools (see the discussion of CASE in Chapter 13). According to Lundmark, the Oracle CASE tools made it easier for Scania to work with Ciim and fit it into its environment. In addition, Scania promised a lot of support through its Swedish distributor, IFS Industrial Systems. Avalon demonstrated its commitment to Scania by flying its chairman and chief technical officer, Tim Sheridan, to Sweden to demonstrate its product (by Scania having the demonstration hosted by DEC in Sweden emphasized the close relationship between Avalon and DEC).

Avalon and Ciim did present several problems to Scania. Despite its position in 1993 as the largest value-added reseller in the manufacturing sector for Oracle (as well as for Sybase Inc.), its 1993 revenues were only $9 million. In addition, at the time Scania

the information systems department. Many of these end-user-developed systems can be created much more rapidly than those using the traditional systems life cycle. Figure 12.6 illustrates the concept of end-user development.

END-USER COMPUTING TOOLS: STRENGTHS AND LIMITATIONS

End-user computing tools have increased the speed and ease with which certain kinds of applications can be created. Many fourth-generation tools have application design knowledge built in. For instance, when fourth-generation languages are linked to a database, the database has already been organized and defined. Many fourth-generation tools can easily access data, produce reports or graphics, or even generate simple data entry transactions.

FIGURE 12.6
End user versus system life cycle development. End users can access computerized information directly or develop information systems with little or no formal technical assistance. On the whole, end-user developed systems can be completed more rapidly than those developed through the conventional systems life cycle. *Source: Adapted from James Martin,* Applications Development without Programmers, © *1982, p. 119. Adapted by permission of Prentice Hall, Englewood Cliffs, NJ.*

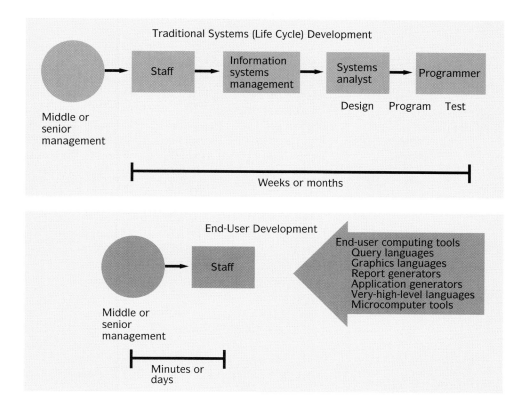

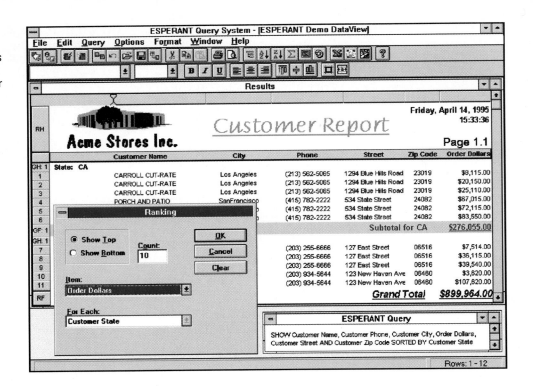

Features such as the easy-to-use graphical interface and natural language capabilities of Esperant's query software allow end users to develop some applications on their own.

Many organizations have reported appreciable gains in application development productivity by using fourth-generation tools. Productivity enhancements based on conventional programming languages, such as structured programming (see Chapter 13), have resulted in a maximum productivity improvement of only 25 percent (Jones, 1979). In contrast, some studies of organizations developing applications with fourth-generation tools have reported productivity gains of 300 to 500 percent (Green, 1984–1985; Harel, 1985). While these gains are not on the order of the magnitude of ten times initially claimed for fourth-generation methods, they are still very impressive.

Finally, fourth-generation tools have new capabilities, such as graphics, spreadsheets, modeling, and ad-hoc information retrieval, that meet important business needs.

Unfortunately, fourth-generation tools still cannot replace conventional tools for some business applications because their capabilities remain limited. Most of these tools were designed for simple systems manipulating small files. Fourth-generation processing is relatively inefficient, and the languages consume large amounts of computer resources. Most fourth-generation languages process individual transactions too slowly and at too high a cost to make these systems suitable for large transaction processing systems. Slow response time and computer performance degradation often result when large files are used. For instance, the New Jersey State Division of Motor Vehicles had a backlog of 1.4 million vehicle registration and ownership records that could not be processed quickly because the department had built its new vehicle registration system using Ideal, a fourth-generation tool. Part of the system had to be reprogrammed in COBOL to accommodate the high transaction volume.

Most fourth-generation tools are more nonprocedural than conventional programming languages. They thus cannot easily handle applications with extensive procedural logic and updating requirements. For example, applications such as those used for the design of nuclear reactors, optimal production scheduling, or tracking daily trades of stocks, bonds, and other securities require complex processing and often the matching of multiple files. Procedural logic must be used to specify processing functions, utility functions, error-handling conditions, specialized interfaces, and highly customized reporting. The logic for such functions is more easily expressed and controlled by conventional procedural code. The specification of procedural logic with fourth-generation languages is slow compared to the specification of non-procedural functions, such as the generation of screens, reports, or graphics. For applications based on a large amount of specialized procedural logic, the overall productivity advantage of fourth-generation tools may be lost (Martin, 1982).

Fourth-generation tools make their greatest contribution to the programming and detail design aspects of the systems development process but have little impact on other systems-building activities. Productivity in systems analysis, procedural changes, conversion, and other aspects of design are largely independent of the choice of programming tool. Fourth-generation languages alone cannot overcome traditional organizational and infrastructural problems such as the lack of well-defined and well-integrated databases, standardized data management techniques, and integrated communications networks that typically hamper information system implementations (Grant, 1985).

MANAGEMENT BENEFITS AND PROBLEMS

Since end users can create many applications entirely on their own or with minimal assistance from information systems specialists, end-user-developed information systems can be created much more rapidly and informally than traditional systems. This situation has created both benefits and problems for organizations because these systems are outside the constraints of the formal information systems environment. Without question, end-user development provides many benefits to organizations. These include the following:

- *Improved requirements determination.* With users developing their own systems, there is less need to rely on information systems specialists for requirements analysis and less chance that user requirements will be misinterpreted by technical specialists.

- *User involvement and satisfaction.* Users are more likely to use and approve of systems they design and develop themselves.

- *Control of the systems development process by users.* Fourth-generation tools enable end users to take a more active role in the systems development process. Users can create entire applications themselves or with minimal assistance from information systems professionals. The tools often support prototyping, allowing end users to create experimental systems that can be revised quickly and inexpensively to meet changing requirements. With end users playing a much larger role in application creation, fourth-generation tools have helped break down the barrier between users and programmers that has hampered conventional systems development.

- *Reduced application backlog.* User-developed systems can help relieve the application backlog by transferring the responsibility for development from the information systems staff to end users. The productivity of professional information systems specialists can also be boosted by the use of fourth-generation languages.

At the same time, end-user computing poses organizational risks because it occurs outside of traditional mechanisms for information systems management and control. Most organizations have not yet developed strategies to ensure that end-user-developed applications meet organizational objectives or meet quality assurance standards appropriate to their function. The most critical challenges posed by end-user computing are the following:

- *Insufficient review and analysis when user and analyst functions are no longer separate.* Without formal information systems analysts, user-developed applications have no independent outside review. There are no independent sources of problem analysis or alternative solutions. It may also be difficult for users to specify complete and comprehensive requirements.

- *Lack of proper quality assurance standards and controls.* User-developed systems are often created rapidly, without a formal development methodology.

While there are productivity and design advantages to be gained by avoiding conventional development methodologies, user-developed systems often lack appropriate standards, controls, and quality assurance procedures. There may not be adequate disciplines for testing and documentation. User-developed systems may lack controls for the completeness and validity of input and updating, audit trails, operating controls, project controls, and standards for stable interfaces among subsystems (Chapter 18 provides more detail on these controls).

- *Uncontrolled data.* With end-user computing tools, end-user groups outside the traditional information systems department can easily create their own applications and files. Many of these end-user-created files will contain the identical pieces of information, but each user application may update and define these data in a different way. Without formal data administration disciplines, it will become increasingly difficult to determine where data are located and to ensure that the same piece of information (such as product number or annual earnings) is used consistently throughout the organization (more details on the problem of uncontrolled data can be found in Chapters 8 and 10).

- *Proliferation of "private" information systems.* Users can use fourth-generation tools to create their own "private" information systems that are hidden from the rest of the organization. Such systems can conceal information from other groups. An undocumented private system cannot be easily turned over to another individual when the creator of that system leaves his or her job (Davis and Olson, 1985).

MANAGING END-USER DEVELOPMENT

How can organizations maximize the benefits of end-user applications development while keeping it under management control? A number of strategies have been suggested. Some have already been described in Chapter 10. Additional measures include using information centers and other training and support facilities for end-user development, establishing application development priorities, and establishing well-defined controls for end-user-developed applications.

Information Centers

information center A special facility within an organization that provides training and support for end-user computing.

One way both to facilitate and to manage end-user application development is to set up an information center. The **information center** is a special facility that provides training and support for end-user computing. Information centers feature hardware,

Retail staff receive instruction in this New Jersey computer management class. An important function of information centers is to make end users feel proficient with computers.

software, and technical specialists that supply end users with tools, training, and expert advice so that they can create information system applications on their own. With information-center tools, users can create their own computer reports, spreadsheets, or graphics, or extract data for decision making and analysis with minimal technical assistance. Information-center consultants are available to instruct users and to assist in the development of more complex applications.

Information-center staff members combine expert knowledge of the hardware, software, and databases for end-user applications with strong interpersonal communications skills. They function primarily as teachers and consultants to users, but they may also take part in the analysis, design, and programming of more complex applications. Typical services provided by information-center staff include the following:

- Training in high-level languages and development tools
- Assistance in accessing and transferring data
- Assistance in debugging programs
- Assistance with applications, queries, and reports requiring high-level programming languages
- Consultation on appropriate tools and methodologies for developing applications
- Assistance in establishing quality assurance standards and controls
- Generation and modification of prototypes
- Providing reference materials on information center resources
- Providing liaison with other information processing groups (such as database specialists) that support information center resources
- Maintaining a catalog of existing applications and databases
- Evaluating new hardware and software

Information-center hardware may consist of mainframes, minicomputers, microcomputers, workstations, or a combination of these machines. Typical software tools in information centers include word processing software, modeling or planning software, desktop database software, graphics software, report generators, user-friendly fourth-generation languages for queries or simple applications, and high-level programming languages for fourth-generation applications development.

Information centers provide many management benefits:

- They can help end users find tools and applications that will make them more productive.
- They prevent the creation of redundant applications.
- They promote data sharing and minimize integrity problems (see Chapter 8).
- They ensure that the applications developed by end users meet audit, data quality, and security standards.

Another important benefit of information centers is that they can help establish and enforce standards for hardware and software so that end users do not introduce many disparate and incompatible technologies into the firm (Fuller and Swanson, 1992; see Chapter 10). The information center generally works with the firm's information systems department to establish standards and guidelines for hardware and software acquisition. The information center will assist users only with hardware and software that have been approved by management.

Policies and Procedures to Manage End-User Computing

In addition to using information centers, managers can pursue other strategies to ensure that end-user computing serves larger organizational goals (see Alavi, Nelson, and Weiss, 1987–1988; Rockart and Flannery, 1983).

Managers can supplement central information centers with smaller distributed centers that provide training and computing tools tailored to the needs of different operating units and business functional areas. Managers can also make sure that the support provided is attuned to the needs of different types of end-user application developers. For instance, end users who use only high-level commands or simple query languages to access data will require different training and tools than end users who can actually write software programs and applications using fourth-generation tools (Rockart and Flannery, 1983). Training and support should also consider individual users' attitudes toward computers, educational levels, cognitive styles, and receptiveness to change (Harrison and Rainer, 1992).

Management should not allow end-user applications to be developed randomly. The organization should incorporate end-user systems into its strategic systems plans. The methodologies for establishing organization-wide information requirements that were described in Chapter 11 can help identify end-user applications with organization-wide benefits.

Management should also develop controls on end-user computing. These could include the following:

- Cost justification of end-user information system projects
- Hardware and software standards for user-developed applications
- Companywide standards for microcomputers, word processing software, database management systems, graphics software, and query and reporting tools
- Quality assurance reviews, specifying whether only individual end users or whether specialists from the information systems or internal audit departments should review end-user-developed information systems
- Controls for end-user-developed applications covering testing, documentation, accuracy, and completeness of input and update, backup, recovery, and supervision

These controls are described in detail in Chapter 18. The control process should flag critical applications that supply data to other important systems. Such systems warrant more rigorous standards. For instance, Northwest Airlines, Inc. established policies and guidelines for end-user development that ask users to classify the applications they develop according to critical nature so that the firm can take special steps to ensure data integrity and security (McMullen, 1992).

12.5 OUTSOURCING INFORMATION SYSTEMS

outsourcing The practice of contracting computer center operations, telecommunications networks, or applications development to external vendors.

If a firm does not want to use its own internal resources to build and operate information systems, it can hire an external organization that specializes in providing these services to do the work. The process of turning over an organization's computer center operations, telecommunications networks, or applications development to external vendors of these services is called **outsourcing**.

Because information systems play such a large role in contemporary organizations, information technology now accounts for about half of most large firms' capital expenditures. In firms where the cost of information systems function has risen rapidly, managers are seeking ways to control those costs and are treating information technology as a capital investment instead of an operating cost of the firm. One option for controlling these costs is to outsource.

ADVANTAGES AND DISADVANTAGES OF OUTSOURCING

Outsourcing is becoming popular because some organizations perceive it as being more cost effective than it would be to maintain their own computer center and information systems staff. The provider of outsourcing services can benefit from economies of scale (the same knowledge, skills, and capacity can be shared with many different customers) and is likely to charge competitive prices for information systems services. Outsourcing allows a company with fluctuating needs for computer processing to pay for only what it uses rather than to build its own computer center to stand underutilized when there is no peak load. Some firms outsource because their internal information systems staff cannot keep pace with technological change. But not all organizations benefit from outsourcing, and the disadvantages of outsourcing can create serious problems for organizations if they are not well understood and managed.

Advantages of Outsourcing

The most popular explanations for outsourcing are the following:

ECONOMY.   Outsourcing vendors are specialists in the information systems services and technologies they provide. Through specialization and economies of scale, they can deliver the same service and value for less money than the cost of an internal organization. For instance, American Standard reported saving $2 million annually from outsourcing its financial and payroll operations. Wabco and American Ultramar slashed annual information systems processing costs approximately in half. While some outsourcing vendors have promised annual reductions of 50 percent in information technology costs, savings of 15 to 30 percent are more common (Loh and Venkatraman, 1992).

SERVICE QUALITY.   Because outsourcing vendors will lose their clients if the service is unsatisfactory, companies often have more leverage over external vendors than over their own employees. The firm that outsources may be able to obtain a higher level of service from vendors for the same or lower costs.

PREDICTABILITY.   An outsourcing contract with a fixed price for a specified level of service reduces uncertainty of costs.

FLEXIBILITY.   Business growth can be accommodated without making major changes in the organization's information systems infrastructure. As information technology permeates the entire value chain of a business, outsourcing may provide superior control of the business because its costs and capabilities can be adjusted to meet changing needs (Loh and Venkatraman, 1992).

MAKING FIXED COSTS VARIABLE.   Some outsourcing agreements, such as running payroll, are based on the price per unit of work done (such as the cost to process each check). Many outsourcers will take into account variations in transaction processing volumes likely to occur during the year or over the course of the outsourcing agreement. Clients only need to pay for the amount of services they consume, as opposed to paying a fixed cost to maintain internal systems that are not fully utilized.

FREEING UP HUMAN RESOURCES FOR OTHER PROJECTS.   Scarce and costly talent within an organization can refocus on activities with higher value and payback than they would find in running a technology factory.

FREEING UP FINANCIAL CAPITAL.   Some agreements with outsourcers include the sale for cash of the outsourced firm's technology capital assets to the vendor. For instance, when Blue Cross and Blue Shield of Massachusetts outsourced its computer operations and systems development to Electronic Data Systems (EDS), EDS paid Blue Cross with cash and a promissory note for its computer center and other computer equipment (Caldwell, 1992).

Disadvantages of Outsourcing

Not all organizations obtain these benefits from outsourcing. There are dangers in placing the information systems functions outside the organization. Outsourcing can create serious problems such as loss of control, vulnerability of strategic information, and dependence on the fortunes of an external firm.

Loss of Control.   When a firm farms out the responsibility for developing and operating its information systems to another organization, it can lose control over its information systems function. Outsourcing places the vendor in an advantageous position where the client has to accept whatever the vendor does and whatever fees the vendor charges. If a vendor becomes the firm's only alternative for running and developing its information systems, the client must accept whatever technologies the vendor provides. This dependency could eventually result in higher costs or loss of control over technological direction.

Vulnerability of Strategic Information. Trade secrets or proprietary information may leak out to competitors because a firm's information systems are being run or developed by outsiders. This could be especially harmful if a firm allows an outsourcer to develop or to operate applications that give it some type of competitive advantage.

Dependency. The firm becomes dependent on the viability of the vendor. A vendor with financial problems or deteriorating services may create severe problems for its clients.

WHEN TO USE OUTSOURCING

Since outsourcing has both benefits and liabilities and is not meant for all organizations or all situations, managers should assess the role of information systems in their organization before making an outsourcing decision. There are a number of circumstances under which outsourcing makes a great deal of sense:

■ *When there is limited opportunity for the firm to distinguish itself competitively through a particular information systems application or series of applications.* For instance, both the development and operation of payroll systems are frequently outsourced to free the information systems staff to concentrate on activities with a higher potential payoff, such as customer service or manufacturing systems. Figure 12.7 illustrates a matrix that could help firms determine appropriate applications for outsourcing. Applications such as payroll or cafeteria accounting, for which the firm obtains little competitive advantage from excellence, are strong candidates for outsourcing. If carefully developed, applications such as airline reservations or plant scheduling could provide a firm with a distinct advantage over competitors. The firm could lose profits, customers, or market share if such systems have problems. Applications where the rewards for excellence are high and where the penalties for failure are high should probably be developed and operated internally.

FIGURE 12.7
Rewards and penalties of outsourcing. This reward/penalty matrix shows that those applications with low reward for excellence and low penalty for problems are good candidates for outsourcing. *Source: Paul Clermont. "Outsourcing Without Guilt," Computerworld (September 9, 1991). Copyright 1991 by CW Publishing, Inc., Framingham, MA 01701. Reprinted from Computerworld.*

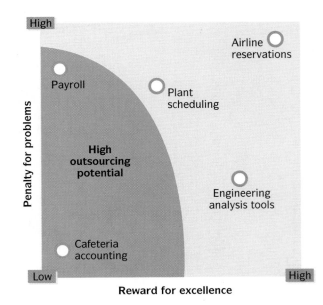

CHAPTER 12   *Alternative Systems-Building Methods*

Companies may also continue to develop applications internally while outsourcing their computer center operations when they do not need to distinguish themselves competitively by performing their computer processing onsite. For instance, the Eastman Kodak Co., a pioneer in outsourcing, initially farmed out its information systems operations—including mainframe processing, telecommunications, and personal computer support—to IBM and DEC. It kept application development and support in-house because it felt that these activities had competitive value (Clermont 1991).

- *When the predictability of uninterrupted information systems service is not very important.* For instance, airline reservations or catalog shopping systems are too "critical" to be trusted outside. If these systems failed to operate for a few days or even a few hours, they could close down the business (see Chapter 2). On the other hand, a system to process employee insurance claims could be more easily outsourced because uninterrupted processing of claims is not critical to the survival of the firm.

- *When outsourcing does not strip the company of the technical know-how required for future information systems innovation.* If a firm outsources some of its systems but maintains its own internal information systems staff, it should ensure that its staff remains technically up to date and has the expertise to develop future applications.

- *When the firm's existing information systems capabilities are limited, ineffective, or technically inferior.* Some organizations use outsourcers as an easy way to revamp their information systems technology. For instance, they might use an outsourcer to help them make the transition from traditional mainframe-based computing to a new information architecture—distributed computing environment.

Despite the conventional wisdom on when to outsource, companies sometimes do outsource strategic functions, as we see with Ford of Europe in the Window on Organizations. In any case, if systems development and the information systems function are well managed and productive, there may not be much immediate benefit that can be provided by an external vendor.

MANAGING OUTSOURCING

To obtain value from outsourcing, organizations need to make sure the process is properly managed. With sound business analysis and an understanding of outsourcing's strengths and limitations, managers can identify the most appropriate applications to outsource and develop a workable outsourcing plan.

Segmenting the firm's range of information systems activities into pieces that potentially can be outsourced makes the problem more manageable and also helps companies match an outsourcer with the appropriate job. Noncritical applications are usually the most appropriate candidates for outsourcing. Firms should identify mission-critical applications and mission-critical human resources required to develop and manage these applications. This would allow the firm to retain its most highly skilled people and focus all of its efforts on the most mission-critical applications development (Roche, 1992). Setting technology strategy is one area that companies should not abdicate to outsourcers. This strategic task is best kept in-house.

Ideally, the firm should have a working relationship of trust with an outsourcing vendor. The vendor should understand the client's business and work with the client as a partner, adapting agreements to meet the client's changing needs. For instance, defense contractor General Dynamics Corporation in Falls Church, Virginia, chose Computer Sciences Corp. (CSC) of El Segundo, California, to take over its data center management, network operations, applications development, and other information services. General Dynamics signed a 10-year contract worth $3 billion with CSC because CSC knew the defense business; it understood the regulations and the critical

FORD OF EUROPE MAKES ITS OUTSOURCING CONTRACTORS PART OF THE ORGANIZATIONAL TEAM

When Ford of Europe recently outsourced its computer functions that support its giant Parts and Services Operations, it went against all conventional wisdom. That wisdom says that companies should not outsource critical, strategic functions. Organizations normally want critical functions to be in the hands of people whose loyalty is clearly to their own organization. Ford views its parts and services unit function as strategic, one in which it intends to distinguish itself, and one in which continuity of computer service is central. Why then did Ford do it, and, perhaps more basic, how did Ford deal with the need to make the outsourcing contractor committed to and part of the Ford team?

Ford of Europe is a $2.4 billion Ford division based in Cologne, Germany. It has major data centers in Cologne, Daventry, England, and Valencia, Spain. In February 1994, Ford signed a five-year outsourcing contract with Computer Sciences Corp. (CSC) of El Segundo, California, to run these three data centers and to develop new applications for Ford. Ford's aim is to improve the efficiency of its parts and services operations. The total contract is worth about $100 million over the five years, although the final value will depend both upon how much development work Ford wants to be done and how quickly it wants it done (tighter deadlines will cost Ford more to be achieved). The computing power CSC will be managing is huge—72 MIPS of mainframes alone.

Ford officials believe they need to improve service throughout Europe. Their first target was to give service centers access to an up-to-the-minute picture of what parts are in stock locally, and, if out of stock, which other service centers will have the needed parts in stock and available. A new system, the Dealer Computer Architecture Strategy, has reduced the average time needed to

locate a part from 20 minutes to about 2 seconds. Ford intends to make similar improvements in other functions within the parts and service area.

In order for CSC to do this work for Ford, CSC employees will be given access to Ford's privileged, proprietary information, and they will have to work as if they are full members of the Ford organization and team. The questions Ford faced were: How could officials structure the agreement so that they could trust this outside organization with their proprietary information; and how could they set up their relationship with CSC so that CSC employees would act with the same loyalty and care for Ford's future that Ford's own employees have? Bartolini's solution was to make it "very clear right from the outset: If you're going to do business with Ford's Parts and Services Operations, it's us and only us in terms of the automotive industry." Ford would regard it as an unfriendly action if CSC were to work with the parts and services function of another automobile manufacturer. Language establishing the requirement of exclusivity was inserted into the agreement. According to CSC's European outsourcing director, Phil Watkins, many information technology shops raise the question of exclusivity during negotiations, but the issue is not usually made part of the legal agreement.

How does this help Ford to address the issues of proprietary information and organizational loyalty? By putting teeth in the contract, Ford management has made it clear to CSC how serious they are. How serious is CSC about this aspect of its relationship with Ford? Watkins says that although his organization does remain free to seek automotive contracts with Ford competitors in areas other than parts and service, "Before doing that, we would check with Ford to see if it was an issue with them." Outsourcing vendors usually claim they will be the partner of their

clients, but in this case, CSC has given up the very real possibility of other business in the automotive industry in order to gain and hold this lucrative

> **To Think About:** Did outsourcing Ford's parts and services function support its business strategy? Why or why not? Do you believe Ford faced any risks by doing this? If so, do you think the company has successfully dealt with those risks? Again, why or why not?

contract with Ford. They have put their "eggs" in the same basket as Ford's—giving up other potential business for this contract instills in CSC a vested interest in the success of this contract and in the success of Ford. The very size of the contract is another inducement to draw CSC even further into partnership with Ford. And holding out the carrot of possible other business, which Ford has done, cements the relationship between the two even tighter.

Ford has other factors in its favor. As a further enticement to draw CSC in as a partner, Ford has agreed to allow CSC to use the immense processing power of its three data centers to process work of CSC's other customers (as long as they are not part of the automotive industry). Moreover, CSC has been rather successful in garnering outsourcing business in Europe. CSC signed a contract with British aerospace in November 1993, and one with the Dutch service company RAET in the same month. CSC also signed a contract with Belgacom (the Belgian state-owned telephone company) in February 1994. As successful as it has become, it seems likely that CSC will not be tempted by potential business in areas that conflict with its Ford contract.

Source: Mark Halper, "Ford Drives Exclusive Outsourcing Deal," *Computerworld*, February 21, 1994.

success factors for the industry. General Dynamics would have had to teach other contractors the rules of the defense environment before they could do the work (Livingston, 1992).

Firms should clearly understand the advantages provided by the vendor and what they will have to give up to obtain these advantages. For lower operating costs, can the client live with a five-second response time during peak hours or next-day repair of microcomputers in remote offices?

Organizations should not abdicate management responsibility by outsourcing. They need to manage the outsourcer as they would manage their own internal information systems department by setting priorities, ensuring that the right people are brought in, and guaranteeing that information systems are running smoothly. They should establish criteria for evaluating the outsourcing vendor that include performance expectations and measurement methods for response time, transaction volumes, security, disaster recovery, backup in the event of a catastrophe (see Chapter 18), processing requirements of new applications, and distributed processing on microcomputers, workstations, and LANs.

Firms should design outsourcing contracts carefully so that the outsourcing services can be adjusted if the nature of the business changes. For instance, Meritor Savings Bank in Philadelphia was a $12 billion colossus when it signed a one-year outsourcing contract with Electronic Data Systems. Three years later, Meritor had closed two thirds of its branches and shrunk to $4 billion in assets. Its slimmed-down

Table 12.3	Comparison of Systems Development Approaches		
Approach	Features	Advantages	Disadvantages
Systems life cycle	Sequential step-by-step formal process Written specifications and approvals Limited role of users	Necessary for large complex systems and projects	Slow and expensive Discourages changes Massive paperwork to manage
Prototyping	Requirements specified dynamically with experimental system Rapid, informal, and iterative process Users continually interact with the prototype	Rapid and inexpensive Useful when requirements uncertain or when end-user interface is important Promotes user participation	Inappropriate for large, complex systems Can gloss over steps in analysis, documentation, and testing
Application software package	Commercial software eliminates need for internally developed software programs	Design, programming, installation, and maintenance work reduced Can save time and cost when developing common business applications Reduces need for internal information systems resources	May not meet organization's unique requirements May not perform many business functions well Customization raises development costs
End-user development	Systems created by end users using fourth-generation software tools Rapid and informal Minimal role of information systems specialists	Users control systems building Saves development time and cost Reduces application backlog	Can lead to proliferation of uncontrolled information systems Systems do not always meet quality assurance standards
Outsourcing	Systems built and sometimes operated by external vendor	Can reduce or control costs Can produce systems when internal resources not available or technically deficient	Loss of control over the information systems function Dependence on the technical direction and prosperity of external vendors

state of affairs required far fewer processing services. Meritor fortunately had placed a provision into the original contract so that EDS services could be adjusted to the size of the bank (Schatz, 1993). Organizations should constantly re-evaluate their vendors and decisions to outsource in light of changing business conditions and the growing pool of available outsourcing services (Lacity, Willcocks, and Feeny, 1995).

Table 12.3 compares the advantages and disadvantages of each of the systems-building alternatives described in this chapter.

Management Challenges

1. Determining the right systems development strategy to use. Sometimes organizations encounter problems that cannot be addressed by any of the systems development strategies described in this chapter. For instance, a large complex system may have some unstructured features. The ultimate configuration of the system cannot be decided beforehand because information requirements or the appropriate technology are uncertain. Alternatively, a proposed system calls for major organizational as well as technical changes. In such instances, a firm may need to pursue a strategy of phased commitment in which systems projects are broken down into smaller portions and developed piece by piece in phases, or a firm may need to postpone the project altogether.

2. Controlling information systems development outside the information systems department. There may not be a way to establish standards and controls for end-user development that are appropriate. Standards and controls that are too restrictive not only may generate user resistance but also may stifle end-user innovation. If controls are too weak, the firm may encounter serious problems with data integrity and connectivity. It is not always possible to find the right balance.

3. Selecting a systems development strategy that fits into the firm's information architecture and strategic plan. End-user development, application software packages, or outsourcing may be appropriate short-term solutions, but they may not be in the firm's best long-term interests. These solutions may result in disparate applications that cannot be easily integrated into the firm's overall information architecture. Organizations need to evaluate carefully the long-term impact of their applications development strategies.

Summary

1. Distinguish between the various systems-building alternatives: the traditional systems life cycle, prototyping, application software packages, end-user development, and outsourcing. The traditional systems life cycle—the oldest method for building systems—breaks the development of an information system into six formal stages: project definition, systems study, design, programming, installation, and post-implementation. The stages must proceed sequentially, have defined outputs, and require formal approval before the next stage can commence.

Prototyping consists of building an experimental system rapidly and inexpensively for end users to interact with and evaluate. The prototype is refined and enhanced until users are satisfied that it captures all of their requirements and can be used as a template to create the final system.

Developing an information system using an application software package eliminates the need for writing software programs when developing an information system. Using a software package cuts down on the amount of design, testing, installation, and maintenance work required to build a system.

End-user development is the development of information systems by end users, either alone or with mini-mal assistance from information systems specialists. End-user developed systems can be created rapidly and informally using fourth-generation software tools.

Outsourcing consists of using an external vendor to build (or operate) a firm's information systems. The system may be custom-built or may use a software package. In either case, the work is done by the vendor rather than by the organization's internal information systems staff.

2. Understand the strengths and limitations of each approach. The traditional systems life cycle is still useful for large projects that need formal specifications and tight management control over each stage of systems building. However, the traditional method is very rigid and costly for developing a system, and is not well suited for unstructured, decision-oriented applications where requirements cannot be immediately visualized.

Prototyping encourages end-user involvement in systems development and iteration of design until specifications are captured accurately. The rapid creation of prototypes can result in systems that have not been completely tested or documented or that are technically inadequate for a production environment.

Application software packages are helpful if a firm does not have the internal information systems staff or financial resources to custom-develop a system. To meet an organization's unique requirements, packages may require extensive modifications that can substantially raise development costs. A package may not be a feasible solution if implementation necessitates extensive customization and changes in the organization's procedures.

The primary benefits of end-user development are improved requirements determination, reduced application backlog, and increased end-user participation in and control of the systems development process. However, end-user development, in conjunction with distributed computing, has introduced new organizational risks by propagating information systems and data resources that do not necessarily meet quality assurance standards and that are not easily controlled by traditional means.

Outsourcing can save application development costs or allow firms to develop applications without an internal information systems staff, but it can also make firms lose control over their information systems and make them too dependent on external vendors.

3. Describe the types of problems for which each approach is best suited. The traditional systems life cycle is appropriate for large transaction processing systems (TPS) and management information systems (MIS) with complex processing and requirements that need rigorous and formal requirements analyses, predefined specifications, and tight controls over the systems-building process.

Prototyping is useful for simple applications where requirements are vague or unstructured or for designing the end-user interface portions of large complex systems. Prototyping is not suitable for designing all aspects of large systems that require batch processing or complex processing logic.

Software packages are best suited for applications with requirements common to many organizations and a limited number of functions that can be supported by commercial software.

The best candidates for end-user development are applications with relatively simple processing logic and small files that can be developed easily with fourth-generation tools.

Outsourcing is appropriate for applications that are not sources of competitive advantage or that require technical expertise not provided by the firm.

4. Describe the solutions to the management problems created by these approaches. Organizations can overcome some of the limitations of using software packages by performing a thorough requirements analysis and using rigorous package selection procedures to determine the extent to which a package will satisfy its requirements. The organization can customize the package or modify its procedures to ensure a better fit with the package.

Information centers help promote and control end-user development. They provide end users with appropriate hardware, software, and technical expertise to create their own applications and encourage adherence to application development standards. Organizations can also develop new policies and procedures concerning systems development standards, training, data administration, and controls to manage end-user computing effectively.

Organizations can benefit from outsourcing by outsourcing only part of their information systems, by thoroughly understanding what information systems functions are appropriate to outsource, by designing outsourcing contracts carefully, and by trying to build a working partnership with the outsourcing vendor.

Key Terms

Systems life cycle	Installation	End-user interface	End-user development
Project definition	Post-implementation	Application software	Information center
Systems study	Prototyping	package	Outsourcing
Design	Prototype	Customization	
Programming	Iterative	Request for Proposal (RFP)	

Review Questions

1. What is the traditional systems life cycle? What are its characteristics?
2. Describe each of the steps in the systems life cycle.
3. What are the advantages and disadvantages of building an information system using the traditional systems life cycle?
4. What do we mean by information system prototyping?
5. Under what conditions is prototyping a useful systems development approach? What kinds of problems can it help solve?
6. Describe five ways in which prototyping differs from the traditional systems life cycle.
7. List and describe the steps in the prototyping process.
8. List and describe four limitations of prototyping.
9. What is an application software package? Under what circumstances should packages be used to build information systems?
10. What are the principal advantages of using application software packages to develop an information system? Why do packages have a strong appeal to management?

11. List and describe several disadvantages of software packages.
12. What is package customization? Under what circumstances can it become a problem when implementing an application software package?
13. List the main criteria for evaluating an application software package.
14. How is the systems development process altered when an application software package is being considered and selected?
15. What do we mean by end-user development?
16. What are the advantages and disadvantages of end-user development? What kinds of problems is it suited for?

17. What is an information center? How can information centers solve some of the management problems created by end-user development?
18. Name some policies and procedures for managing end-user development.
19. What is outsourcing? Under what circumstances should it be used for building information systems?
20. What are the advantages and disadvantages of outsourcing?
21. Describe some solutions to the management problems created by outsourcing.

Discussion Questions

1. A widely cited research report found that prototyping facilitated communication between users and information systems designers but that designers who used prototyping had difficulty controlling and managing the design process. Discuss.
2. It has been observed that successful prototyping depends less on the selection of software tools than on the corporate culture. Discuss.
3. Some have said that the best way to avoid using professional programmers is to install an application software package. Discuss.

4. One information systems publication stated that, at best, in-house development of a system that is already available in package form is apt to cost fifteen times as much as the package version and take three to four times as long to recover the out-of-pocket investment. Discuss.
5. What theories describing the impact of information systems on organizations could be applied to describe outsourcing?

Group Project

With a group of your classmates, obtain product information or attend a demonstration for a microcomputer application software package such as DacEasy Accounting/Payroll, Quicken, Managing Your Money, or Microsoft Profit for Windows. Write an analysis of the strengths and limitations of the package you select. Present your findings to the class.

Case Study

CAN A GERMAN SOFTWARE GIANT PROVIDE CLIENT/SERVER SOLUTIONS?

SAP A.G., based in Walldorf, Germany, is Europe's largest vendor of software running on IBM mainframe computers and is an emerging leader in software packages for client/server environments. Its worldwide revenue in 1993 amounted to $665 million. Among its clients are the Dow Chemical Company, E. I. du Pont de Nemours & Company, Chevron Corporation, Apple Computer, IBM, Intel, and the Exxon Corporation.

SAP sells integrated software applications for a wide range of business functions, including human resources, plant management, and manufacturing. The software modules are integrated, so that they can automatically share data between them and they have their own common database management system. The programs come in 12 foreign languages. Specific versions are tailored to accommodate different currencies, tax laws, and accounting practices. Managers can generate reports in their own local languages and currencies yet have the same reports generated in the language and currency that are used as the corporate standard by top management. SAP's R/2 System runs on IBM-compatible mainframes and its R/3 system runs in a client/server environment.

Businesses appreciate the multinational flavor of the software, especially its ability to overcome language and currency barriers fluently and to connect divisions and operating units spread around the world. Marion Merrel Dow Inc. is using SAP software for its financial and sales-and-service departments because it believes that no other available packages can handle its global business needs. More than 2100 firms use the R/2 system and more than 1800 firms use the R/3 system.

Despite being a standard software package, SAP software can be customized by approximately 10 percent. The software can be customized to multinational currencies and accounting practices. SAP makes this flexibility one of its key selling points. SAP has also benefited from two strategic moves. It developed R/3 to take advantage of open systems with client/server architecture, and it began promoting the package as a platform for business re-engineering. While R/2 appeals mainly to large Fortune 1000 companies seeking to tie together far-flung global operations, R/3 appeals to medium and smaller businesses with annual sales of less than $5 billion.

R/3 is an integrated, client/server, distributed system with a graphical user interface that runs on smaller and cheaper hardware than R/2. (R/2 runs on Siemens, IBM, and IBM-compatible mainframes; R/3 operates on a wide range of computers, including Unix-based machines, PowerPC-enabled IBM AS/400 minicomputers, and other file servers.) The back-end server and front-end client portions of R/3 can run on a number of different operating systems, including five variations of UNIX, Digital Equipment Corporation's VAX/VMS operating system, and Hewlett-Packard's MPE operating system. Versions for OS/2, Windows NT, and other operating systems are being developed as well. R/3 offers a number of options for its graphical user interface: Presentation Manager under OS/2, Motif under UNIX, and Microsoft Windows under DOS.

The R/3 package includes integrated financial accounting, production planning, sales and distribution, cost-center accounting, order costing, materials management, human resources, quality assurance, fixed assets management, plant maintenance, and project planning applications. Users do not have to shut down one application to move to another; they can just click on a menu choice. R/3 also provides word processing, filing systems, E-mail, and other office support functions.

R/3 can be configured to run on a single hardware platform, or it can be partitioned to run on separate machines (in whatever combination users choose in order to minimize network traffic and place data where users need it the most. For instance, a firm could put the data used most frequently by its accounting department on a file server located close to the accounting department to minimize network traffic. A central data dictionary keeps track of data and their location to maintain the integrity of distributed data. SAP will sell clients a blueprint of R/3's information, data, and function models and software tools to facilitate custom development and integration of existing applications into R/3. Royal LePage Real Estate Service Ltd., a $450 million commercial and residential real estate services company headquartered in Toronto, with branch offices across Canada, selected R/3 in 1991. It initially used R/3 to run a general ledger application on its IBM RS/6000 UNIX workstation. The general ledger application had to tie into an existing mainframe financial application that used a package from Dun & Bradstreet Software, a rival vendor. Royal LePage then started using R/3 for fixed assets and accounts payable applications and is adding accounts receivable, purchasing, payroll, and human resources components to the R/3 system.

Royal LePage liked R/3 because it supported the company's goal of creating a distributed computing environment that gives each branch more data and processing power and integrates its applications and branches to a greater extent than before. Don Logan, the vice president and controller, believes R/3 initially saved the firm over $2 million in systems development and support costs and perhaps $1 million more over time. Over half the savings came from reducing programming time through the use of R/3. Klaus Besier, head of SAP America, Inc. (the Lester, Pennsylvania, subsidiary of SAP A.G.), thinks that the most important feature of R/3 may be the way it helps organizations automate their business processes. By adopting the system design offered by the package, companies can evaluate and streamline their business processes. The promise of re-engineering was what initially attracted the Eastman Kodak Company to SAP software. Kodak launched a pilot project in 1991 that installed SAP programs to redefine the job of order taking. The SAP package lets order takers make immediate decisions about granting customers credit and lets them access production data on-line so that they can tell customers exactly when their orders will be available for shipment. The project resulted in a 70 percent reduction in the amount of time it took to deliver products; response time to customers was also cut in half. These results prompted Kodak to use SAP software as the global architecture for all of its core systems.

The intricate and sophisticated features of SAP software deeply affect the infrastructure of a corporation. Installing SAP's fully integrated suite of software modules with all the business alterations required is a complex process with many interdependent options which can overwhelm smaller firms lacking the resources of top-tier large corporations. Even corporations experienced in using R/2 need additional help when switching to R/3 because SAP has not yet developed a structured conversion process. R/3 requires companies to reconfigure their business processes to fit the software. The total cost of implementation can run three times the price of the software alone. Installing the software package, reengineering business functions, training information systems and business staff, and hiring outside consultants typically runs $1 million to $10 million.

Unfortunately, SAP has lagged in product support. SAP has a large internal staff to support its software packages, but it also uses legions of consultants from consulting firms such as Price Waterhouse, Andersen Consulting, EDS Corporation, and Coopers & Lybrand. These external consultants work with SAP clients to install the SAP packages. Because SAP is growing so fast, there is a worldwide shortage of SAP experts with experience implementing R/3.

Louis Dingerdissen, vice president of MIS for Kodak's health group, observed that experts in SAP software are in short supply, and that it can take 16 weeks of training to get end users up to speed on SAP software—far too long. With SAP quickly signing up new clients, the support situation could worsen before it gets better, or SAP may have to slow down its growth a bit.

One reason for the shortage of SAP consultants is that it can take years for even experienced technologists to understand all of the complexities and methodologies of SAP software. SAP vice chairman and co-founder Hasso Plattner admitted that it takes about three years, or two or three installations of the package, before a consultant becomes an expert in the software. (R/3 was built with SAP's own internally developed programming language called ABAP. Users need to work with Abap to modify or extend the SAP software

package.) SAP pairs one or more of its seasoned eight- to ten-year German veterans with less experienced U.S. consultants at each installation. But according to Greg Staszko, a partner at the Cincinnati branch of Deloitte & Touche (a leading accounting and consulting firm), the SAP experts tend to be trouble-shooters or product experts rather than business consultants, so clients do not necessarily get the best advice on how to integrate the software into their business operations most efficiently and painlessly. The perception remains among some U.S. companies that even an on-site SAP expert who knows the financial accounting module cannot correct a bug in the sales and distribution module.

To augment the ranks of qualified consultants, SAP built a world training headquarters in Walldorf, costing an estimated $50 million to $60 million. It recruited more consultants by signing agreements with new consulting firms such as Cap Gemini America and Coopers & Lybrand, and de-emphasized its relationship with firms such as Computer Sciences Corporation and KPMG Peat Marwick, which it felt did not work out well.

Other product support include using Intel Corporation's ProShare video-conferencing software to provide customers with face-to-face advice and inviting customers to send project teams to SAP for training prior to implementation. To facilitate installation by small companies, SAP started shipping Special Delivery, a bundled system that comes with hardware, software, and consulting services for a fixed price of $500,000.

Jim Bensman, the former president of SAP America Inc. (SAP's U.S.

subsidiary) believes that the arrangement with KPMG Peat Marwick in the United States floundered because Peat Marwick did not train consultants sufficiently. SAP continues to work with Peat Marwick in Europe, however. Sources reported that Computer Sciences Corporation spent a lot of money on training but did not bring any clients to SAP.

Sources: John J. Xenakis, "In Search of a System," *CFO*, January 1995; Rosemary Cafasso, "Success Strains SAP Support," *Computerworld*, September 5, 1994, and "SAP American Plans Improvements for R/3 Package," *Computerworld*, June 6, 1994; Doug Bartholomew, "SAPs Trojan Horse," *InformationWeek*, April 24, 1995, "SAP Goes One Further," *InformationWeek*, October 31, 1994, "SAP America: R/2 + R/3 = ?" *InformationWeek*, January 10, 1994, and "An American Beachhead," *InformationWeek*, March 9, 1992; and Mike Ricciuti and J. William Semich, "SAP's Client/Server Battle Plan," *Datamation*, March 15, 1993.

Case Study Questions

1. What advantages and disadvantages of application software packages are illustrated by SAP?

2. Analyze the specific strengths and weaknesses of SAP software packages.

3. If you were the manager of a corporation looking for new business application software, would you choose SAP? Would you choose another package? Why or why not? What management, organization, and technology factors would you consider?

References

Alavi, Maryam. "An Assessment of the Prototyping Approach to Information System Development." *Communications of the ACM* 27 (June 1984).

Alavi, Maryam, R. Ryan Nelson, and Ira R. Weiss. "Strategies for End-User Computing: An Integrative Framework." *Journal of Management Information Systems* 4, no. 3 (Winter 1987–1988).

Anderson, Evan A. "Choice Models for the Evaluation and Selection of Software Packages." *Journal of Management Information Systems* 6, no. 4 (Spring 1990).

Arthur, Lowell Jay. "Quick and Dirty." *Computerworld* (December 14, 1992).

Bersoff, Edward H., and Alan M. Davis. "Impacts of Life Cycle Models on Software Configuration Management." *Communications of the ACM* 34, no. 8 (August 1991).

Caldwell, Bruce. "Blue Cross, in Intensive Care, Beeps EDS." *InformationWeek* (January 27, 1992).

Carr, Houston H. "Information Centers: The IBM Model vs. Practice." *MIS Quarterly* (September 1987).

Cerveny, Robert P., Edward J. Garrity, and G. Lawrence Sanders. "The Application of Prototyping to Systems Development: A Rationale and Model." *Journal of Management Information Systems* 3 (Fall 1986).

Christoff, Kurt A. "Building a Fourth Generation Environment." *Datamation* (September 1985).

Clermont, Paul. "Outsourcing Without Guilt." *Computerworld* (September 9, 1991).

Cotterman, William W., and Kuldeep Kumar. "User Cube: A Taxonomy of End Users." *Communications of the ACM* 32, no. 11 (November 1989).

Cross, John. "IT Outsourcing: British Petroleum's Competitive Approach." *Harvard Business Review* (May-June 1995).

Davis, Gordon B. and Margrethe H. Olson. *Management Information Systems*, 2nd ed. New York: McGraw-Hill (1985).

Davis, Sid A., and Robert P. Bostrum. "Training End Users: An Experimental Investigation of the Role of the Computer Interface and Training Methods." *MIS Quarterly* 17, no. 1 (March 1993).

Fraser, Martin D., Kuldeep Kumar, and Vijay K. Vaishnavi. "Strategies for Incorporating Formal Specifications in Software Development." *Communications of the ACM* 37 no. 10 (October 1994).

Fuller, Mary K., and E. Burton Swanson. "Information Centers as Organizational Innovation." *Journal of Management Information Systems* 9, no. 1 (Summer 1992).

Gould, John D., and Clayton Lewis. "Designing for Usability: Key Principles and What Designers Think." *Communications of the ACM* 28 (March 1985).

Grant, F. J. "The Downside of 4GLs." *Datamation* (July 1985).

Green, Jesse. "Productivity in the Fourth Generation." *Journal of Management Information Systems* 1 (Winter 1984–1985).

Harel, Elie C., and Ephraim R. McLean. "The Effects of Using a Nonprocedural Computer Language on Programmer Productivity." *MIS Quarterly* (June 1985).

Harrison, Allison W., and R. Kelly Rainer, Jr. "The Influence of Individual Differences on Skill in End-User Computing." *Journal of Management Information Systems* 9, no. 1 (Summer 1992).

Holtzblatt, Laren, and Hugh Beyer. "Making Customer-Centered Design Work for Teams." *Communications of the ACM* 36, no. 10 (October 1993).

Huff, Sid L., Malcolm C. Munro, and Barbara H. Martin. "Growth Stages of End User Computing." *Communications of the ACM* 31, no. 5 (May 1988).

Janson, Marius, and L. Douglas Smith. "Prototyping for Systems Development: A Critical Appraisal." *MIS Quarterly* 9 (December 1985).

Jenkins, A. Milton. "Prototyping: A Methodology for the Design and Development of Application Systems." *Spectrum* 2 (April 1985).

Johnson, Richard T. "The Infocenter Experience." *Datamation* (January 1984).

Jones, T. C. "The Limits of Programming Productivity." Guide and Share Application Development Symposium, Proceedings. New York: Share (1979).

Kozar, Kenneth A., and John M. Mahlum. "A User-Generated Information System: An Innovative Development Approach." *MIS Quarterly* (June 1987).

Kraushaar, James M., and Larry E. Shirland. "A Prototyping Method for Applications Development by End Users and Information Systems Specialists." *MIS Quarterly* (September 1985).

Lacity, Mary C., Leslie P. Willcocks, and David F. Feeny." IT Outsourcing: Maximize Flexibility and Control." *Harvard Business Review* (May-June 1995).

Livingston, Dennis. "Outsourcing: Look Beyond the Price Tag." *Datamation* (November 15, 1992).

Loh, Lawrence, and N. Venkatraman. "Determinants of Information Technology Outsourcing." *Journal of Management Information Systems* 9, no. 1 (Summer 1992).

Loh, Lawrence, and N. Venkatraman. "Diffusion of Information Technology Outsourcing: Influence Sources and the Kodak Effect." *Information Systems Research* 3, no. 4 (December 1992).

Lucas, Henry C., Eric J. Walton, and Michael J. Ginzberg. "Implementing Packaged Software." *MIS Quarterly* (December 1988).

McMullen, John. "Developing a Role for End Users." *InformationWeek* (June 15, 1992).

Madsen, Kim Halskov, and Peter H. Aiken. "Experience Using Cooperative Interative Storyboard Prototyping." *Communications of the ACM* 36, no. 4 (June 1993).

Martin, James. *Application Development without Programmers*. Englewood Cliffs, NJ: Prentice Hall (1982).

Martin, J., and C. McClure. "Buying Software Off the Rack." *Harvard Business Review* (November–December 1983).

Mason, R. E. A., and T. T. Carey. "Prototyping Interactive Information Systems." *Communications of the ACM* 26 (May 1983).

Matos, Victor M, and Paul J. Jalics. "An Experimental Analysis of the Performance of Fourth-Generation Tools on PCs." *Communications of the ACM* 32, no. 11 (November 1989).

McLean, Ephraim, Leon A. Kappelman and John P. Thompson. "Converging End-User and Corporate Computing." *Communications of the ACM* 36, no. 12 (December 1993).

Ponko, Raymond. *End-User Computing*. New York: Wiley and Sons (1988).

Rivard, Suzanne, and Sid L. Huff. "Factors of Success for End-User Computing." *Communications of the ACM* 31, no. 5 (May 1988).

Roche, Edward M. *Managing Information Technology in Multinational Corporations*. New York: Macmillan (1992).

Rockart, John F., and Lauren S. Flannery. "The Management of End-User Computing." *Communications of the ACM* 26, no. 10 (October 1983).

Schatz, Willie. "Bailoutsourcing." *Computerworld* (January 25, 1993).

Timmreck, Eric M. "Performance Measurement: Vendor Specifications and Benchmarks." In *The Information Systems Handbook*, eds. F. Warren McFarlan and Richard C. Nolan. Homewood, IL: Dow-Jones-Richard D. Irwin (1975).

Trauth, Eileen M., and Elliot Cole. "The Organizational Interface: A Method for Supporting End Users of Packaged Software." *MIS Quarterly* 16, no. 1 (March 1992).

White, Clinton E., and David P. Christy. "The Information Center Concept: A Normative Model and a Study of Six Installations." *MIS Quarterly* (December 1987).

Willis, T. Hillman, and Debbie B. Tesch. "An Assessment of Systems Development Methodologies." *Journal of Information Technology Management* 2, no. 2 (1991).

Zahniser, Richard A. "Design by Walking Around." *Communications of the ACM* 36, no. 10 (October 1993).

Chapter *13*

Ensuring Quality with Information Systems

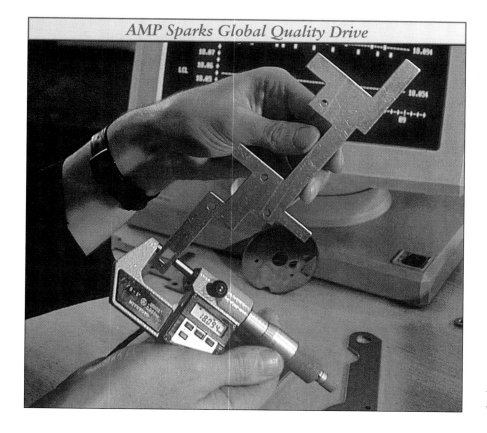

AMP Sparks Global Quality Drive

AMP, a world leader in electrical and electronic connectors and interconnection systems, faces a growing problem in the 1990s—how to globalize quality. One of president and CEO William J. Hudson's goals for his company is "to have every manufacturing facility be a quality certifiable site regardless of location, capable of delivering acceptable products to any customer, anywhere in the world." For a company with 1994 sales of nearly $4 billion and with 28,000 employees at 180 facilities in 36 countries, this would appear to be a tall order. Hudson sees the effort to achieve quality as an integral part of a broader drive toward much higher productivity, growth, and profitability. AMP reflects that drive by spending 12 percent of its sales annually on R&D in a search for new products. The company has also demonstrated its commitment through ongoing quality programs that were begun in the early 1980s.

More recently, AMP's quality drive has been exemplified by its Journey to Excellence program, first established in 1990. The program has five components, each stressing a different aspect of the quality issue. Self-Assessment/Gap Analysis focuses upon making improvements and then measuring the company against the Baldridge and European Quality Award criteria. The goal is to achieve world-class quality status. Benchmarking, on the other hand, is used to measure AMP's practices against the best practices of other companies. Manufacturing resource planning is used as a formal methodology to aid in achieving day-by-day operational quality. Value-adding management is a tool to eliminate wasteful activities by re-engineering both individual tasks and larger work processes. Global standardization of quality management specifically addresses the global side of the company. Within this com-

ponent, AMP's leadership addressed directly the two major issues they believe all multinational companies face: globalizing quality so that products and services are of the same high quality, wherever they are created; and integrating quality improvement into the drive to achieve growth and productivity targets internationally.

Information systems are making a significant contribution to global standardization of quality management. To support their quality program, AMP uses its worldwide on-line network to run a system known as the Quality Scoreboard. This system makes available daily quality information, including key performance indicators relating to customers, distributors, internal operations, suppliers, and even competitors. A total of 2500 managers, at all company levels and from sites all over the world, have access to this system. They use it to monitor company performance, and when they spot problems, they can also

use the system to initiate corrective action. A second system, dubbed the Delivery Scorecard, enables managers to keep in touch with actual daily operations by making available to them daily reports on shipping and scheduling for the entire company. ■

Source: Jerry Bowles, "Quality 2000: The Next Decade of Progress," *Fortune*, September 19, 1994.

The experience of AMP illustrates some of the ways in which information systems and the information systems function can be used to improve quality throughout the firm. Yet few organizations have used information systems in this manner, and information systems have special quality problems of their own.

We have explored various facets of quality in information systems throughout this text, but quality is the special focus of this chapter. Here

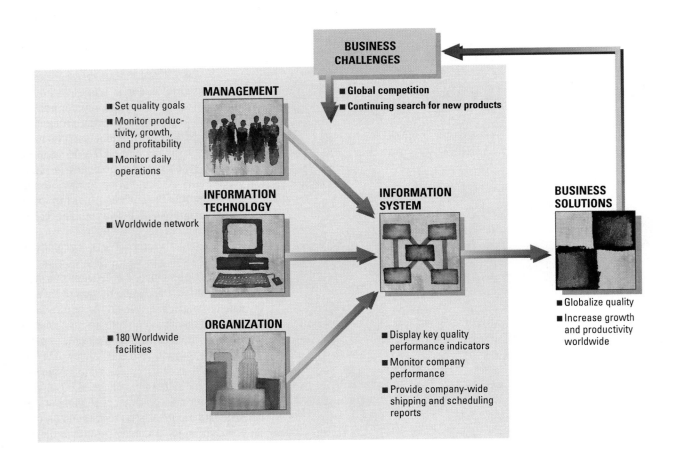

we will examine the ways in which information systems can contribute to improving quality throughout the organization. We will then outline the quality problems peculiar to information systems, focusing on the need for quality assurance in the development of software. Finally we will describe traditional and new methodologies and tools for improving software quality and overall system effectiveness.

After completing this chapter, you will be able to:

Learning Objectives

1. Describe how information systems can contribute to total quality management in an organization.

2. Explain why information systems must pay special attention to software quality assurance.

3. Identify the principal solutions to information systems quality problems.

4. Describe the traditional tools and methodologies for promoting information systems quality.

5. Describe new approaches for promoting information systems quality.

13.1 HOW CAN INFORMATION SYSTEMS PROMOTE QUALITY?

quality Conformance to producer specifications and satisfaction of customer criteria such as quality of physical product, quality of service, and psychological aspects.

The emergence of a global economy has stimulated worldwide interest in achieving quality. Companies can no longer be satisfied with producing goods and services that compete only with goods produced within their own country—consumers can now select from a broad range of products and services produced anywhere in the world. Before examining how information systems can contribute to quality throughout the organization, we must first define the term **quality**.

Traditional definitions for quality have focused upon the conformance to specifications (or the absence of variation from those specifications). With this definition, a producer can easily measure the quality of its products. Achieving quality under this definition requires three steps from the manufacturer: First, establish product specifications. Second, measure products as they are produced to determine whether or not they achieve the standards established in the specifications. Third, alter the manufacturing process whenever necessary to bring the products up to standard. A wristwatch manufacturer, for example, might include a specification for reliability that requires that 99.995 percent of the watches will neither gain nor lose more than one second per month. Another requirement might be that 99.995 percent of the watches are sturdy enough to withstand being dropped 25 times onto a carpet or a linoleum floor from a height of seven feet. Simple tests will enable the manufacturer to measure precisely against these specifications.

However, achieving quality is not quite that simple and direct. The definition of quality has been changing and broadening in recent years. Defining quality as conformance to specifications views it from a producer's perspective only. Customers have a different perspective, being more concerned with value for their dollar. They normally apply three criteria. First, customers are concerned with the quality of the physical product. They want to know if the product is durable, how safe it is, its reliability, its ease of use and installation, its stylishness, and how well the producer supports the product. Second, customers are concerned with the quality of service, by which they mean the accuracy and truthfulness of the advertising, the timeliness and accuracy of the billing process, responsiveness to warranties (implied as well as specified), and ongoing product support. Finally, customer concepts of quality include the psychological aspects: how well do the sales and support staff know their products, the courtesy and sensitivity of the staff, and even their neatness, the reputation of the product. For companies to compete globally, they need to include a customer perspective in any definition of quality.

Management has been questioning the idea that quality costs more. Today many senior executives have come to the conclusion that the lack of quality is actually a significant expense. While we all understand that product returns and repairs result in added costs for repair (labor, parts replacement, and additional shipping), only recently has management focused on the many previously hidden costs that arise from producing products that are not high quality. Assume, for example, that nine of every 100 watches the wristwatch manufacturer produces are defective. Some of the previously unnoticed costs in producing those nine watches include:

- Materials used to manufacture nine defective watches
- Labor needed to manufacture nine defective watches
- A 9 percent increase in the wear and tear on production machinery, resulting in a 9 percent increase in maintenance, parts replacement, and eventual equipment replacement
- A 9 percent increase in inventory cost for raw material, work-in-process, and finished products
- A 9 percent increase in the cost of storage space to store the raw materials, work-in-process, and finished products
- A 9 percent increase in the inspection staff needed to inspect the nine defective watches
- An increase in liability insurance and legal defense costs in order to protect and defend the manufacturer from lawsuits.

Today more and more businesses are turning to an idea known as total quality management. **Total quality management (TQM)** is a concept that makes quality the responsibility of all people within an organization. TQM holds that the achievement of quality control is an end in itself. Everyone is expected to contribute to the overall improvement of quality—the engineer who avoids design errors, the production worker who spots defects, the sales representative who presents the product properly to potential customers, and even the secretary who avoids typing mistakes. Total quality management encompasses all of the functions within an organization.

TQM is based on quality management concepts developed by American quality experts such as W. Edwards Deming and Joseph Juran, but was popularized by the Japanese. Japanese management adopted the goal of zero defects, focusing on improving their products or services prior to shipment rather than correcting them after they have been delivered. Japanese companies often give the responsibility for quality consistency to the workers who actually make the product or service, as opposed to a quality control department. Studies have repeatedly shown that the earlier in the business cycle a problem is eliminated, the less it costs for the company to eliminate it. Thus the Japanese quality approach not only brought a shift in focus to the workers and an increased respect for product and service quality but also lowered costs.

As the quality movement has spread to Europe and the United States, both quality within information systems departments and the role of information systems in corporatewide quality programs have come under intense scrutiny. How can information systems contribute to overall quality in the organization? How can quality be promoted in information systems themselves?

total quality management (TQM) A concept that makes quality control a responsibility to be shared by all people in an organization.

HOW INFORMATION SYSTEMS CONTRIBUTE TO TOTAL QUALITY MANAGEMENT

Quality programs differ greatly from company to company. Some are merely generalized "sales" campaigns intended to sensitize employees to the need to strive for more quality in their daily work. At the opposite extreme, quality programs can result in fundamental changes in the way a company does its business. Companies also follow different routes in achieving quality, as we shall describe below. Whatever route a company selects, the more it tries to achieve with its quality programs, the more information systems can contribute to the success of those programs.

Information systems can fill a special role in corporate quality programs for a number of reasons. First, IS is deeply involved with the daily work of other departments throughout the organization. IS analysts usually have taken a leading role in designing, developing, and supporting such varied departmental systems as corporate payrolls, patent research systems, chemical process control systems, logistics systems, and sales support systems. IS professionals also maintain their knowledge of these departments through their participation in departmental information planning. In addition, IS personnel are usually key to the sharing of data between departments because they have unique knowledge of the relationships between various departments. Often, only IS personnel know where certain data originate, how other departments use and store them, and which other functions would benefit from having access to them. With this broad understanding of the functional integration of the corporation, IS personnel can be valuable members of any quality project team.

The IS staff in effective information systems departments have three skills that are critical to the success of a quality program. First, they are specialists in analyzing and redesigning business processes. Second, many IS technicians are experienced in quantifying and measuring procedures and critical activities in any process. Typically, IS departments have long been involved with measurements of their own service. Third, IS project managers are skilled in managing tasks and projects. Project manager training has long been a staple of better IS departments; such training includes the use of project management software. These skills can contribute a great deal to any serious quality program, which will normally be organized as a project and will usually be heavily task-oriented.

The information systems staff is the source of ideas on the application of technology to quality issues; often they are also the people who can make that technology available to the quality project. For example, with the help of IS departments, statistical analysis software is becoming more widely used in the drive for quality. Goodmark Foods, Inc., the leading U.S. producer of snack meats, received support from its information systems group to apply such software to their manufacturing. The software helps workers see when and by how much each piece of snack meat deviates from the specified weight (Mandell, 1992).

Let us discuss some of the more significant approaches companies follow in their quality programs and illustrate contributions IS can make.

SIMPLIFYING THE PRODUCT, THE PRODUCTION PROCESS, OR BOTH.
Quality programs usually have a "fewer-is-better" philosophy —the fewer steps in a process, the less time and opportunity for an error to occur. A few years ago Carrier Corporation, the Syracuse, New York manufacturing giant, was faced with an eroding market share. It believed it was not communicating effectively with customers. One reason: a 70 percent error rate in using their manual order entry system to match customers and products when ordering Carrier's commercial air-conditioning units. The system required so many steps to process an order that mistakes were all but inevitable. Errors sometimes went undetected until the end of the manufacturing line, where workers might discover a wrong coil or some other similar problem. Big mistakes occasionally affected customers. In 1988, the company finally instituted a TQM program in which information technology played a large role. Carrier now coordinates everything from sales to manufacturing by using an expert system (LaPlante, 1992). When IS professionals were able to reduce the number of steps, the number of errors dropped dramatically, manufacturing costs dropped, and Carrier found itself with happier customers.

BENCHMARK. Many companies have been effective in achieving quality by setting strict standards for products, services, and other activities, and then measuring performance against those standards. Companies may use external industry standards, standards set by other companies, internally developed high standards, or some combination of the three. The chapter-opening vignette described how AMP uses information systems to measure its current practices against "best" practices and to meet quality criteria that would qualify the company for the Baldridge and European Quality Awards. AMP's management requires that all production systems be certified under ISO 9000 and MRP II Class A standards for quality assessment.

MRP II Class A quality certification goes to manufacturing companies that use MRP II to boost quality and productivity and to cut costs. To be certified Class A, manufacturers must reduce inventories by 30 percent or more, improve customer service by 15 percent, show an overall productivity gain of at least 15 percent, and reduce costs by a minimum of 20 percent. Du Pont Merck Pharmaceutical Company, a $900 million pharmaceutical manufacturer based in Wilmington, Delaware, aimed for Class A certification by enhancing user training, system interfaces, and operations support. Its information systems department created new software interfaces between existing corporate systems and manufacturing resources planning software and trained employees on how to use the integrated system in accordance with MRP II techniques and procedures (King, 1993).

PHH FleetAmerica, the $1 billion fleet leasing unit of Hunt Valley, Maryland's PHH Corporation, recently turned to benchmarking in order to add value to its services for its customers. The firm analyzed every process and defined the 16 key ones that run its business. Then, for each of these 16 processes, the company developed a set of benchmark standards that is based upon two external sets, the standards its competitors meet and its customer expectations. Having established these new standards, the company re-engineered many of the processes. Now it is benchmarking all of them.

L. L. Bean Inc., the Freeport, Maine mail order clothing company, uses benchmarking to achieve an order shipping accuracy of 99.9 percent. In fact, during one period in the spring of 1994, the company shipped 500,000 packages in a row without a single error. L. L. Bean has been so successful that copier giant Xerox Corporation of Rochester, New York, turned to it to learn how to use benchmarking for its copier parts shipping function.

IS contributes to these efforts in many ways. IS staff participates in re-engineering projects and helps to design and build the systems that make the quality processes possible. Any study of quality programs shows that information is a top concern to those involved, and IS is often central to the collection of that information. To improve production or sales, for example, management needs data to determine both what is being done right and what is being done wrong. IS is usually the key to making that information available in a timely fashion and in a format useful to those who need it for quality purposes. For instance, manufacturing data have traditionally been supplied to management in summary form at the end of the manufacturing process. In effect it is historical data that at best can be used to reduce future problems. Real-time data are needed to correct problems as they occur, as the quality team at Continental General Tire, in Charlotte, North Carolina, realized. It installed a local area network that gives plant floor operators real-time data on raw materials as those materials arrive at the plant. In this way, flawed raw material batches are discovered very quickly, before the plant uses them to produce substandard tires.

To provide better information for benchmarking, information systems specialists can work with business specialists either to design new systems or to analyze quality-related data found in existing systems. For instance, credit memo transactions stored in accounting systems contain a wealth of detail on customer returns. Mail order firms such as L. L. Bean typically ask customers returning merchandise to select "reason codes" explaining why each item was returned (see Figures 13.1(A) and 13.1(B)). They and other mail order companies have designed their information systems to analyze these return transactions. A report from these systems showing return transaction frequency and dollar value summarized by week or month and broken down by the reason for the returns will help management target areas where mistakes are being made.

The quality assurance technician at Continental General Tire in Charlotte, North Carolina, is gathering real-time data for the manufacturing production process.

Inventory systems may contain data showing that customers are not being shipped their products in a timely manner or that other problems are occurring. Relevant metrics include

- Vendor promises versus actual delivery dates
- Frequency of rejected shipments at the receiving department
- Credit approval turnaround time for new customers
- Inventory value over time
- Work orders for scrap and rework

USE CUSTOMER DEMANDS AS A GUIDE TO IMPROVING PRODUCTS AND SERVICES.   Improving customer service, making customer service the number one priority, will improve the quality of the product itself, as is clear from the Carrier example described above. The Window on Organizations shows how one small business, 800-FLOWERS, addressed the question of customer satisfaction in a quality program. It also shows the contribution of information systems in building a system and making needed information available when required. The chapter-ending case study shows how Corning Asahi Video (CAV) relied primarily upon customer needs to address the quality issue, with information systems playing a central role in the project to improve quality.

Figure 13.2 shows how Pizza Hut designed its information systems to reflect its new emphasis on quality in its business strategy. Facing falling profits, Pizza Hut's management decided to focus less on minimizing costs and more on keeping its customers happy. It launched a customer satisfaction measurement system in January 1995 that monitors customer satisfaction on a weekly basis. The system uses the company's customer database which tracks the buying patterns of more than 25 million delivery customers. These customer sales data are captured by a point-of-sale system when a customer buys a pizza. Each week, the customer satisfaction measurement system downloads 50,000 customer names and telephone numbers to The Gallup Organization. Gallup calls those customers and polls them about speed of service, quality of food, and willingness to repurchase food at Pizza Hut. The results are analyzed by management to help identify and correct problems. The data are also used to construct a "loyalty index" for calculating management bonuses. Although this system costs approximately $5 million annually to operate, Pizza Hut research

Do you need to return something? Please follow these 6 simple steps.

❶ Please tell us what you want us to do (check one):

☐ **Provide a reimbursement.** (Your refund will be made by original method of payment, unless otherwise requested.)
☐ **Exchange the item.** (Use the exchange section at the bottom of this form.
☐ **Other** (please specify)_____

❷ Circle the item listed below that you are returning.
❸ Choose a reason code from the back and enter it in the box below.
❹ Please circle the name and address above we should use in mailing your refund or exchange. If different, please note on the back of this form.
❺ Please provide your telephone number in case we have any questions.
( ) - / Daytime/Evening
Circle one

❻ Detach and enclose this form, place it with your return in a securely wrapped package, and send it to:

L.L.Bean Returns Dept.,
Desert Road Campus
Freeport, Maine 04033

Questions call 1-800-341-4341.*

Choose reason from options on back.

Mdse Value.   Tax   Shipping   Total Amount   Payment

How to make an exchange. Please use the space below to tell us which items you wish to exchange for the merchandise you are returning. On U.S. and Canadian exchanges, L.L. Bean will waive its regular shipping charges on exchange orders.

FIGURE 13.1(A)
Quality indicators in information systems. A company's information systems can be mined for data that might indicate quality problems. Companies such as L. L. Bean carefully analyze the codes indicating the reasons why customers return their purchases to identify items with quality problems. *Reprinted with permission of L. L. Bean Inc., Freeport, Maine.*

shows that a customer is worth $7200 over his or her lifetime, making the system worth more than any marketing program the company has devised to date (McWilliams, 1995).

REDUCE CYCLE TIME. Experience indicates that the single best way to address quality problems is to reduce the amount of time from the beginning of a process to its end (cycle time). Reducing cycle time usually results in fewer steps, an improvement right there. But reducing cycle time has other advantages. With less time passing between beginning and end, workers will be better aware of what came just before, and so are less likely to make mistakes. Shorter cycles means that errors are often caught earlier in production (or logistics or design or whatever the function), often before the product is complete, eliminating many of the hidden costs listed above. Fred Wenninger, CEO of disk drive producer Iomega Corporation in Roy, Utah, explains that "When your cycle is 28 days and you spot a defect at the end of the line, you can imagine how hard it is to isolate the problem." Iomega was spending $20 million a year to fix defective drives at the end of its 28-day production cycle. Re-engineering the production process allowed them to reduce cycle time to a day and a half, eliminating this problem and winning the prestigious Shingo Prize for Excellence in American Manufacturing. The Continental General example cited above also demonstrates the value of reducing cycle time.

Reasons for return.

Letting us know why you are returning an item will help us speed your refund or exchange, and provide even better products in the future. Find the reason that best matches why you are making the return. Then write the code number in the left hand column of the return area on the other side of this form.

FIT & SIZING

TOO SMALL	TOO LARGE
21 Chest/bust	31 Chest/bust
22 Waist	32 Waist
23 Hip	33 Hip
24 Rise	34 Rise
25 Too narrow	35 Too wide
26 Too short	36 Too long
28 Overall	38 Overall

DURABILITY/PERFORMANCE
41 Excessive shrinkage
42 Color faded or bled
46 Does not work
47 Didn't last or hold up
48 Did not perform as intended
49 Not waterproof

SERVICE
51 Arrived too late
52 Wrong item shipped
53 Damaged in transit
55 Coordinate not received

SATISFACTION
61 Returning a gift
62 Changed my mind
66 Didn't like styling
67 Didn't like material
68 Didn't like color
69 Priced too high for item received

QUALITY
71 Faulty zipper
72 Material defect
73 Seam defective
74 Marked or soiled
75 Not well made
76 Components differ in shade
77 Finish unacceptable
78 Difficult to assemble
79 Part missing*

CATALOG
81 Item not as described
82 Item not as pictured
83 Color not as shown
84 Fit not as shown

*Have any questions? Part missing? Please call one of our Customer Service Representatives at 1-800-341-4341. (If outside U.S. or Canada call 207-865-3161), and let them know so that we can straighten it all out. We carry most replacement parts in stock, and we'll try to ship the part out right away.

New or different address?

If you are making a return, and want your refund or exchange sent to a new or different address, please write the new shipping information here and mark the appropriate box below:

Name
_____

Address _____ Apt. no. _____

City _____ State _____ Zip Code _____

☐ Gift? ☐ Address for this shipment only ☐ Permanent change of address

We'd enjoy hearing from you.

We welcome your comments and suggestions. Use the space below, and mail it to:

L.L.Bean®
Freeport, Maine 04033

FIGURE 13.1(B)
Bean provides a detailed list of codes describing reasons why customers might return merchandise. *Reprinted with permission of L.L. Bean, Inc.*

IMPROVE THE QUALITY AND PRECISION OF THE DESIGN. Quality and precision in design will eliminate many production problems. Computer-aided design (CAD) software has made dramatic quality improvements possible in a wide range of businesses from aircraft manufacturing to production of razor blades. Alan R. Burns, a mining engineer from Perth, Australia, was able to use CAD to invent and design a new product that promises to have a major impact upon the tire industry. His concept was a modular tire made up of a series of replaceable modules or segments so that when one segment is damaged, only that segment would need replacing rather than replacing the whole tire. The modules are not pneumatic and so cannot deflate. Moreover they can be changed quickly and easily by one person. Burns researched the tire field and discovered that his new tire would likely find a ready market in the heavy equipment vehicle market (such as the backhoes and earth movers used in construction). He established a company, Airboss, and proceeded to design his product. He first established quality performance measurements for such key tire characteristics as load, temperature, speed, wear life, and traction. He then entered this data into a CAD software package to design the modules. Using the software he was able iteratively to design and test until he was satisfied with the results. He did not need to develop an actual working model until the iterative design process was almost complete. The product he produced was of much higher quality than would have been possible through manual design and testing because of the speed and accuracy of the CAD software.

BUILDING AN ORGANIZATION TO SELL FLOWERS

Why would someone pay $2 million to buy a four-year-old company that was already $7 million in debt and losing another $400,00 each month? Certainly it appeared that Jim McCann was taking quite a risk when he bought 800-FLOWERS under those circumstances in 1987. However, McCann had a vision, one that was becoming reality even prior to his purchase of 800-FLOWERS. Having set up his first flower shop in Manhattan in 1976, McCann already owned a chain of 14 floral shops in the New York City metropolitan region and had established a successful, 24-hour flowers-by-telephone business operating out of Bayside, New York. He bought 800-FLOWERS because "it was the best marketing idea I'd seen in our sleepy little industry."

McCann realized that the problem with 800-FLOWERS was that it had few if any repeat customers due to poor service and inconsistent quality. To get customers, the business was relying on a large and costly telemarketing center and expensive national advertising. McCann recognized that selling flowers is a "nickel-and-dime business." Each sale cannot be generated by expensive advertising if the company is to be profitable. To be successful, he would have to rely on repeat customers. The underlying problem, the reason few customers came back, was poor service and poor quality. To solve the problem, McCann rebuilt his organization to give customers quality service, service that would bring them back repeatedly.

800-FLOWERS had a network of 8000 florists around the country to design and deliver all orders. McCann decided that he needed fewer florists, but florists that could be held to standards for design, flower freshness, and delivery. He replaced the existing network with 2500 florists who agreed to his standards, including a guarantee of

same-day delivery for all orders received by 1 P.M. McCann then hired a staff of 15 quality control experts who spot-checked the florists to make certain they kept their flowers fresh and sold only fresh flowers. They also examined the quality of the arrangements. Next, he moved the 800-FLOWERS telemarketing center from its 55,000 square foot facility in Dallas, Texas, to much smaller facilities in Bayside. He sold the $15 million Dallas telephone center to help finance the move and changes. He added 30 more telereps to his staff in Bayside and trained them in customer service. His telerep philosophy? "I want them to infuse their personality in each conversation so that customers feel they've made a personal connection," he said, adding that he never criticizes them for staying on the phone too long as many other telemarketing operations do. 800-FLOWERS offered customer guarantees that wilted floral arrangements could be returned within seven days; arrangements the customer didn't like could be returned when they arrived.

McCann had one other critical area to address to complete the building of the new organization and achieve the quality he desired—sales processing. Making a sale requires a number of steps by the telerep: writing the order; obtaining credit-card approval; determining which 800-FLOWERS florist is closest to the delivery location; describing and deciding on a floral arrangement; forwarding the order to the florist. Each step in the manual process increased the chance of human error, and thus the possibility of a wrong delivery. McCann purchased a $4 million NCR midrange computer, including network and terminals to centrally process orders more efficiently. The system reduces processing time from ten minutes to less than five. The computer system includes computer images of floral arrangements that the telereps can use to aid them as they talk with customers. The organi-

zation of 2500 florists was brought into the whole process by being connected to the network. A computer, a modem (to connect them to the net-

> **To Think About:**   How did technology promote quality at 800-FLOWERS? Could technology alone have solved 800-FLOWERS' quality problems? What was the relationship between quality, technology, and 800-FLOWERS' business strategy?

work), and a printer were installed in each florist shop. McCann found that the data from the computer system had other uses as well. For example, by tracking the orders, he has been able to anticipate the volume on any given day, allowing both 800-FLOWERS and the 2500 florists to have available added staff and product on days of predicted high volume.

In hindsight, McCann's $2 million investment was indeed visionary. Today he has four telemarketing centers, one each in New York, Massachusetts, Georgia, and Texas. On Valentine's Day alone 800-FLOWERS processed 250,000 orders. The company generated $200 million in gross sales (and net profits of $10 million) in 1994. It is now selling through CompuServe, America Online, In-Flight Phones on American Airlines, and kiosks on highways. Approximately 50 percent of sales come from the 800 number, 10 percent from the on-line computer services, and 40 percent from flower shops, with the on-line sales growing the most dramatically. The company has even expanded into new services, including 800-CANDIES, 800-BASKETS, and 800 GROWERS (for buying fruit gifts).

Sources: Richard D. Smith, "From One Little Shop, an 800-Flowers Garden Grows," *The New York Times,* January 8, 1995, and Leah Ingram, "One Blooming Business," *Profit,* May–June 1994.

FIGURE 13.2

Pizza Hut's customer satisfaction measurement system. Pizza Hut designed an information system that uses point-of-sale data to identify customers to survey each week about their impressions of Pizza Hut's food and service. *Adapted from: "The Measure of Loyalty," Computerworld, February 13, 1995.*

THE MEASURE OF LOYALTY

Last month, Pizza Hut launched a new program to monitor customer satisfaction on a weekly basis. The program uses the company's impressive customer database system, which Pizza Hut has used to track the buying patterns of more than 25 million delivery customers.

1 Customer buys pizza (delivery or dine-in)

2 POS information (name, address, phone, order details) is added to 25 million customer database in Wichita, Kan., headquarters

3 50,000 customer records are downloaded to Gallup each week for a three-minute phone survey with each customer

4 Survey data is uploaded and tabulated by system; repurchase willingness ("loyalty index") calculated for each customer

5 Survey results available for on-line management decision support; company can make operational adjustments quickly to correct problems

6 Annual bonuses for management tied to improvement in loyalty index (target: 10% improvement annually)

With the assistance of computer-aided design, Airboss developed, manufactured and marketed this revolutionary segmented tire. The tires are ideally suited for heavy equipment such as earth movers because of their superior handling traction and maneuverability.

INCREASE THE PRECISION OF PRODUCTION. For many products, one key way to achieve quality is to tighten production tolerances. CAD software has also made this possible. Most CAD software packages include a facility to translate design specifications into specifications both for production tooling and for the production process itself. In this way, products with more precise designs can also be produced more efficiently. Once his tire segment design was completed, Burns used the CAD software to design his manufacturing process, testing via computer just as he had done with product design. In his testing he discovered, for example, that the segment would cool unevenly. He was able to correct the problem even before developing the production equipment. He was also able to design a shorter production cycle, improving quality while increasing his ability to meet customer demand more quickly.

B-Line Systems, Inc., a producer of electrical support products for commercial, industrial, and institutional construction projects, increased precision in its overall manufacturing operations by implementing MAC-PAC® OPEN, an integrated manufacturing, distribution, and financial software system from Andersen Consulting. The system integrates the flow of information from one process to another, one department to another, and one site to another, enabling businesses to employ "Quick Response" strategies to meet customer needs, improve product quality, and increase productivity. The software runs on UNIX hardware or IBM AS/400 minicomputers. MAC-PAC® OPEN helped B-Line manage its overall operations more tightly. The firm lowered the number of late customer shipments and raised the percentage of line items shipped without backorder from 94 to 98 percent. Orders that were previously delivered in six weeks can now be fulfilled in less than two weeks ("B-Line Systems," 1994).

Komag of Milpitas, California, the world's largest supplier of 5 1/4-inch and smaller sputtered thin-film disks for disk drives in all types of computers, must control hundreds of variables in its manufacturing process. Through carefully controlled application of materials, machines, robotics, instrumentation, and skilled production professionals, the process transforms uncoated aluminum disks into highly technical precision products. Komag also needed more precision in its production process. It implemented MESA, from Camstar Systems Inc., a Manufacturing Execution System (MES). MESA is designed to meet information requirements of manufacturing shop floor management in complex batch/log process manufacturing environments. This system allows Komag to monitor hundreds of process manufacturing execution steps to analyze yield, productivity, and machine utilization. System capabilities include real-time lot movement and inventory tracking, generation of process control charts, lot history and process data, application of process parameters per operation step, and immediate response to out-of-control process variances and yield problems. Managers can obtain data on key production variables by product, process, machine, and shift. Within six months after implementing the new system, Komag doubled output (Komag, 1994).

INCLUDE LINE WORKERS IN ANY QUALITY PROCESS. Experience has shown that involvement of the people who perform the function is critical to achieving quality in that function. One reason L. L. Bean was able to attain nearly error-free picking was the involvement of warehouse workers in the design of the picking process. These workers suggested, for example, that high-volume items be stored close to packing stations. They also plotted their own picking movements on flowcharts in order to identify other inefficient movements.

Although the information systems area could potentially make many more contributions like these, its involvement in corporate quality programs has provoked a great deal of controversy. IS has been criticized for a reluctance to become involved in organization-wide quality programs. Often IS focuses exclusively upon technological capabilities while not reaching out to aid the rest of the company in the ways described above. For example, many IS departments are criticized for failure to use

Companies can improve the quality of products and services by including line workers in their quality management processes.

customer demands as a guide to improving their products and services. On the other hand, non-IS departments often fail to consider contributions the IS staff might make to their quality project and so do not reach out to involve them. It is not uncommon for IS to be viewed only as technical support with little to contribute to the planning or content of the quality program.

THE NEED FOR SOFTWARE QUALITY ASSURANCE

Another reason that information systems fall short of helping the organization meet its quality goals is that the systems themselves do not perform as required. The underlying quality issue for information systems departments is software quality assurance.

Producing software of high quality is critical to most large organizations because of software's central function in so many departments—payroll, accounts receivable, manufacturing, sales, research, management. An undiscovered error in a company's credit software or process control software can result in millions of dollars of losses. For more and more companies, software has even become an integral part of the products sold. Computer software is now part of automobile fuel consumption systems, dishwasher and VCR controls, and fax machines. Several years ago, a hidden software problem in AT&T's long distance system brought down that system, bringing the New York–based financial exchanges to a halt and interfering with billions of dollars of business around the country for a number of hours. Modern passenger and commercial vehicles are increasingly dependent upon computer programs for critical functions. A hidden software defect in a braking system could result in the loss of lives.

Like other types of production, software production is unique and presents its own set of problems. One special characteristic of software development is that its usual goal is to build only one copy of the final product (except for companies developing software for public sale). For most manufactured products—aircraft, automobiles, paper clips, socks—once development begins, hundreds, thousands or even millions of copies of the product are manufactured. With software, quality problems must be solved the first time; the design must be of high quality on the first try.

Meeting user needs can be difficult in a process where the end user commits to the product before that product has been built. In effect, the final system is "purchased" in advance, bought "sight unseen." Defining user needs and judging the quality of the completed system have proven to be major challenges. Most systems development projects begin by defining user information requirements and specifications in the form of systems analysis and design documents.

The problem is that meeting specifications does not necessarily guarantee quality. The completed system may in fact meet the specifications but not satisfy the user's needs. This occurs because of inaccurate, incomplete, or improperly detailed specifications, omitting functions in the specifications, or changing user needs during the development period. Specifications often fail to consider the system from the perspective of the users. While designers will concentrate on functionality, they frequently overlook ease of learning and use, unquestioned accuracy and reliability, or speed of response. All of these factors are important to the success of a system.

System response time is a common example of a detailed specification that is omitted or inadequately defined. A customer service representative, who is the end user in a customer service function, may need a query response time of no more than five seconds, but the specifications may contain no reference to response time. If at delivery the response time were ten seconds, the system would meet specifications but would not meet user needs. Perhaps a five-second response time was specified and was achieved during testing with one or two simultaneous users. Would the system satisfy this specification if response time deteriorates to twenty seconds when 100 users are on the system simultaneously? Does such a system serve user needs? If the system does respond within five seconds 80 percent of the time when 100 people are on the system, has the system met its specifications when it fails to meet that specification 20 percent of the time? Can a system be expected to meet such a requirement 100 percent of the time? The lack of agreed-upon measurable standards in specifications leads to dissatisfied users and systems that do not meet user needs. Often quality is not quantified in the specifications so that judgments about system quality become subjective, making it difficult to determine if the system actually meets the users' needs. We treat the issue of user satisfaction again in Chapter 14.

The Maintenance Nightmare

Computer software has traditionally been a nightmare to maintain. Maintenance, the process of modifying a system in production use, is the most expensive phase of the systems development process. Table 13.1 indicates the size of the maintenance problem. In one fifth of information systems departments, 85 percent of personnel hours are allocated to maintenance, leaving little time for new systems development. In most organizations, nearly half of information systems staff time is spent in the maintenance of existing systems. One estimate attributes 60 percent of all business expenditures on computing to maintenance of COBOL software (Freedman, 1986).

Why are maintenance costs so high? One major reason is organizational change. The firm may experience large internal changes in structure or leadership, or change

Table 13.1	The Maintenance Problem	
Annual personnel hours		
Maintain and enhance current systems		48.0%
Develop new systems		46.1%
Other		5.9%
20% of the survey allocated 85% of its efforts to maintenance and enhancements		
Frequency of activity		
Errors—emergency		17.4%
Change—data, inputs, files, hardware		18.2%
Improve—user enhancements, efficiency, documentation, etc.		60.3%
Other		4.1%

Sources: Bennett P. Lientz and E. Burton Swanson, *Software Maintenance Management* (Reading, MA: Addison-Wesley, 1980); and L. H. Putnam and A. Fitzsimmons, "Estimating Software Costs," *Datamation*, September 1979, October 1979, and November 1979.

may come from its surrounding environment. These organizational changes affect information requirements. Another reason appears to be software complexity, as measured by the number and size of interrelated software programs and sub-programs and the complexity of the flow of program logic between them (Banker, Datar, Kemerer, and Zweig, 1993). A third common cause of long-term maintenance problems is faulty systems analysis and design, especially information requirements analysis. Some studies of large TPS systems by TRW, Inc., have found that a majority of system errors—64 percent—result from early analysis errors (Mazzucchelli, 1985).

Figure 13.3 illustrates the cost of correcting errors. Part (A) is based on the experience of consultants reported in the literature. Part (B) shows the results of a quality assurance study of large national defense software projects.

If errors are detected early, during analysis and design, the cost to the systems development effort is small. But if they are not discovered until after programming, testing, or conversion has been completed, the costs can soar astronomically. A minor logic error, for example, that could take one hour to correct during the analysis and design stage could take 10, 40, or 90 times as long to correct during programming, conversion, or postimplementation, respectively.

To be able to handle maintenance quickly and inexpensively, a software system must be flexible. A flexible system can more quickly and easily be modified when problems occur or business requirements change over the years—which they most certainly will. For example a sales system must be able to accommodate new

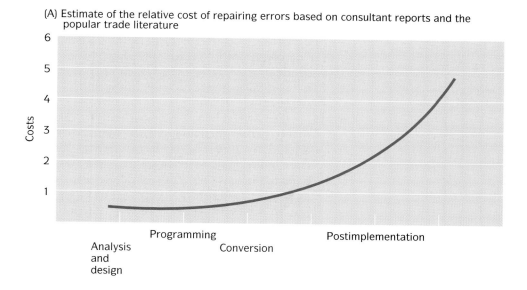

(A) Estimate of the relative cost of repairing errors based on consultant reports and the popular trade literature

(B) Origin, frequency, and severity of errors in large national defense and space programs

Error Type	% of Total Errors	Relative Severity	% of Total Cost of Errors
Design	66%	2.5	83 + %
Logic	17%	1.0	8 + %
Syntax	17%	1.0	8 + %

FIGURE 13.3

The cost of errors over the systems development cycle. The most common, most severe, and most expensive system errors develop in the early design stages. They involve faulty requirements analysis. Errors in program logic or syntax are much less common, less severe, and less costly to repair than design errors. *Source: Alberts, 1976.*

products, new sales staff, and even new offices with little or no problems. Otherwise, a system that may be successful in the short run becomes a long-run failure. Many designers do not consider the aspect of change as they design new systems. However, even if they do design a flexible system, flexibility can seem to be expensive and time-consuming. Its benefits are not always understood or appreciated by the users. Target dates and cost limitations often force developers to sacrifice flexibility in order to complete a project as promised or as wanted. Unfortunately, the corporation may pay a much heavier price at a later time.

Bugs and Defects

bugs Program code defects or errors.

A major problem with software is the presence of hidden **bugs** or program code defects. Studies have shown that it is virtually impossible to eliminate all bugs from large programs. The main source of bugs is the complexity of decision-making code. Even a relatively small program of several hundred lines will contain tens of decisions leading to hundreds or even thousands of different paths. Important programs within most corporations are usually much larger, containing tens of thousands or even millions of lines of code, each with many times the choices and paths of the smaller programs. Such complexity is difficult to document and design—designers document some reactions wrongly or fail to consider some possibilities.

Zero defects, a goal of the total quality management movement, cannot be achieved in larger programs. Complete testing is simply not possible. Fully testing programs that contain thousands of choices and millions of paths would require thousands of years. Eliminating software bugs is an exercise in diminishing returns, because it would take proportionately longer testing to detect and eliminate obscure residual bugs (Littlewood and Strigini, 1993). Even with rigorous testing, one could not know for sure that a piece of software was dependable until the product proved itself after much operational use. The message? We cannot eliminate all bugs, and we cannot know with certainty the seriousness of the bugs that do remain.

Even when bugs are found, they are difficult to remove. Experience has shown that bug fixes often do not work. In many cases, the effort to fix a bug will introduce an entirely new bug or series of bugs. Studies by the Predictably Dependable Computing Systems research project have shown that once a bug has been "repaired," there is only a 50–50 chance that the program will function without failure as long as it did before the attempt to fix the bug (Littlewood and Strigini, 1992).

To achieve quality in software development, an organization must first reach agreement as to what quality is. Some developers view quality as the absence of programming defects. Clearly the presence of too many bugs will lower the quality of a system, but we have just learned that while zero defects may be an appropriate goal, such a situation can never be achieved in software development. Even if a system had no bugs, if it were slow, difficult to use, missing critical functions or inflexible, it certainly would not be a quality system. Any definition of quality must be viewed from the user perspective. It must be broad in scope and specific enough to encompass the satisfaction of user needs. A quality system must do the following:

- Achieve the business goals articulated by the user department
- Operate at an acceptable cost, commensurate with the value produced for the firm
- Meet carefully defined performance standards (such as response time and system availability)
- Produce accurate, reliable output with assurance that its dependability is "good enough" for the purpose intended
- Be easy to learn and use
- Be flexible

SOME SOLUTIONS TO INFORMATION SYSTEM QUALITY PROBLEMS

Information systems are complex, and solutions to quality problems are equally complex. They include the use of an appropriate systems development methodology, proper resource allocation during systems development, the use of metrics, attention to testing, and the use of quality tools.

The Role of Methodologies

To limit problems and increase quality when building systems, developers must begin with a disciplined methodology that sets standards for all phases of the project. Good systems development methodologies (historically often referred to as structured development methodologies) will normally include the following:

- Proven methods for determining and documenting both system specifications and system design

- Programming standards that result in understandable, maintainable code that is not overly complex

- Guidelines for developing quality measurements to be agreed upon by all interested parties prior to development

- Standards and methods for testing the system

- Software tools to be used at every phase to standardize the work in the project and to improve the quality of the output

- Project control methods, including numerous project milestones at which user approval will be required (see Chapter 14)

development methodology A collection of methods, one or more for every activity within every phase of a development project.

A **development methodology** is actually just a collection of methods, one or more for every activity within every phase of a development project. The user of a methodology seldom uses every method within it because most projects do not require every possible activity. Numerous useful development methodologies exist, some suited to specific technologies, others reflecting differing development philosophies. Information systems departments, in conjunction with management of other departments, select the methodology they believe best fits the needs of their company. Larger corporations, employing multiple technologies, may select multiple methodologies to be used with differing technologies. However, the key to quality development is to select an appropriate methodology and then enforce its use. We will discuss several specific methodologies in sections 13.2 and 13.3.

Since a quality system must achieve the business goals established by the user, it stands to reason that system quality begins with complete, detailed, accurate specifications documented in a form that users can understand. Some methodologies document specifications using flowcharts and diagrams, others use verbal descriptions. One popular method, prototyping, is discussed in Chapter 12. Specifications must also include agreed-upon measures of system quality so that the system can be evaluated objectively while it is being developed and once it is completed. We cannot overemphasize that quality specifications—clear, precise representations of user needs—are critical to the development of a quality system.

Resource Allocation During Systems Development

resource allocation Determination of how costs, time, and personnel are assigned to different activities of a systems development project.

Views on **resource allocation** during systems development have changed significantly over the years. Resource allocation determines the way the costs, time, and personnel are assigned to different phases of the project. In earlier times, developers focused on programming, with only about 1 percent of the time and costs of a project being devoted to systems analysis (determining specifications). As the information systems professionals have moved closer to a business or user perspective on quality, they have come to understand the central role of specifications. Moreover, technology that is now being used for systems development forces expenditures in analysis and design work to expand. Consequently, project resources are being shifted to earlier stages in the project cycle. More time is being spent in specifications and systems analysis, decreasing the proportion of programming time, and reducing the need for so much maintenance time. Figure 13.4 demonstrates the shift, although the ideal allocation of time represented in the figure is now considered to be outdated. Current literature suggests that about one quarter of a project's time and cost should be expended in specifications and analysis, with perhaps 50 percent of its resources being allocated to design and programming. Installation and postimplementation ideally should require only one quarter of the project's resources.

Software Metrics

software metrics Objective assessments of the software used in a system in the form of quantified measurements.

Software metrics can play a vital role in increasing the quality of a project. **Software metrics** are objective assessments of the system in the form of quantified measurements. Ongoing use of metrics allows the IS department and the user jointly to measure the performance of the system and identify problems as they occur. Software metrics include input metrics, output metrics, capacity metrics, performance/quality metrics, and value metrics.

The educational and experience level of system developers is an example of an input metric. The number of transactions that can be processed in a specified unit of time is an example of a capacity metric. Response time is a performance metric in an on-line system. The number of checks printed per hour is a system output metric for a payroll system. One metric for programming quality is the number of bugs per hundred lines of code. The business value of a transaction is an example of a value metric.

function point analysis Software output metric that measures the number of inputs, outputs, inquiries, files, and external interfaces used in an application. Used to assess developer productivity and software efficiency.

A widely used output metric is function points, which can help measure the productivity of software developers and the efficiency of the software itself regardless of the programming language employed. **Function point analysis** measures the number of inputs, outputs, inquiries, files, and external interfaces to other software used in an application. The results can be used to calculate the cost per function point of writing a piece of software and the number of function points written per programmer in a specified unit of time.

Unfortunately, most manifestations of quality are not so easy to define in metric terms. In those cases the developers must find indirect measurements. For example, an objective measurement of the ease of use of a newly developed system might be

FIGURE 13.4
Ideal and actual software development costs. Ideally, relatively balanced amounts of time are allowed for analysis, design, programming, and installation. About 8% of costs are allocated ideally to analysis and design, 60% to programming and installation, and 32% to long-term maintenance. Actually, however, the early stages of analysis and design receive far fewer resources than is desirable. Programming and installation (including all important testing) also receive less time and fewer resources than is desirable, reflecting pressure to deliver a workable system as soon as possible. As a result, systems maintenance is far more expensive than is desirable—about 50% of the total software costs over the expected life span of the system. *Source: Alberts, 1976.*

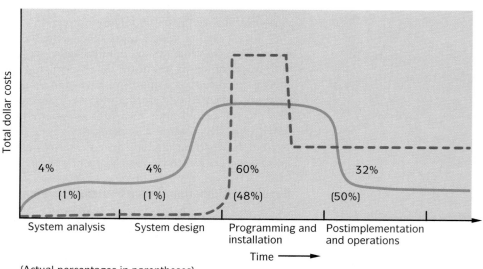

(Actual percentages in parentheses)

Legend: - - - actual
———— ideal

the average amount of time operators take to learn it. Throughout the life of the system, ease of use might be measured by the number of calls for help the IS staff receives per month from system operators. For metrics to be successful, they must be carefully designed, formal, and objective. They must measure significant aspects of the system. One warning, however: Software metrics will be effective in judging the quality of the system only if the users agree to the measurements in advance. Finally, metrics are of no value unless they are used consistently. Few IS departments make wide use of formal, objective metrics today even though studies show they can significantly improve quality.

Testing

Early, regular, and thorough testing will contribute significantly to system quality. In general, software testing is often misunderstood. Many view testing as a way to prove the correctness of work they have done. In fact, we know that all sizable software is riddled with errors. The reason we test must be to uncover these errors. Any other motivation will result in a less than thorough testing process.

walkthrough A review of a specification or design document by a small group of people carefully selected based on the skills needed for the particular objectives being tested.

Testing begins at the design phase. Because no coding yet exists, the test normally used is a **walkthrough**—a review of a specification or design document by a small group of people carefully selected based on the skills needed for the particular objectives being tested. Once coding begins, coding walkthroughs also can be used to review program code. However, code must be tested by computer runs. When errors are discovered, the source is found and eliminated through a process called **debugging**.

debugging The process of discovering and eliminating the errors and defects—the bugs—in program code.

Chapter 11 describes the various stages of testing required to put an information system in operation—program testing, system testing, and acceptance testing. Testing will be successful only if planned properly. Early in the project, before any testing begins, a test plan must be prepared. The plan must include test cases so that the developers can be certain that they have tested an appropriate range of valid and invalid input. Invalid input must be tested to be certain the system handles errors appropriately. Tests must also be tailored to the needs of the technology used in the system, as the Window on Technology describes.

Quality Tools

Finally, system quality can be significantly enhanced by the use of quality tools. Today, many tools have been developed to address every aspect of the systems development process. Information systems professionals are using project management software to manage their projects. Products exist to document specifications and system design in text and graphic forms. Programming tools include data dictionaries, libraries to manage program modules, and tools that actually produce program code (see Chapters 7, 8, and 12). Many types of tools exist to aid in the debugging process. The most recent set of tools automates much of the preparation for comprehensive testing. Tool technology is still relatively new and in many cases the value is still unproven. Nonetheless, tools are having a significant impact on system quality and on development costs. We will discuss various types of tools in sections 13.2 and 13.3.

13.2 TRADITIONAL TOOLS AND METHODOLOGIES FOR QUALITY ASSURANCE

spaghetti code Unstructured, confusing program code with tangled logic that metaphorically resembles a pot of cooked spaghetti.

In the early days of programming, few methodologies existed. User specifications were gathered in informal conversations that were written up in hard-to-follow narratives. Programs were written in complex and confusing code. When such code was so undecipherable that the logic flow appeared to be as entangled as a cooked pot of spaghetti, it was referred to as **spaghetti code**. Systems were inflexible, maintenance all but impossible.

TESTING CLIENT/SERVER SYSTEMS

A consultant war story describes two financial services firms, one in New York and one in London that installed similar client/server systems. Both used microcomputer and Sun Microsystems workstation clients operating through Sun servers and both ran the Sybase relational database management system. The New York system worked from the moment it went into production; the London system still functions poorly, even though it serves far fewer users than the New York system. Why? The answer, experts believe, lies in how thoroughly each system was tested prior to deployment. The New York system underwent rigorous testing; the London system did not.

Many people believe that client/server systems don't need to be tested as rigorously as mainframe systems because they are small and because the programs they run may be small. To end users, client/server systems appear to be small, even if they are not, because they normally are not built around giant-sized programs as many mainframe systems are and because they are run on desktop microcomputers. Nonetheless, Hyatt Hotels found out the hard way that client/server systems need testing as much as any other systems, if not more. Hyatt recently developed a sales application based on Gupta SQLBase relational database management system technology, running within a client/server environment. Hyatt did not thoroughly test the system prior to rolling it out, not because it did not believe testing to be important—Hyatt has long been committed to rigorous testing of larger systems. In this case, however, Hyatt did not have the necessary facilities installed to test client/server systems. The result? The system met with serious performance problems due to inappropriate electrical wiring in some of the Hyatt sites. Hyatt now tests all systems, small as

well as large, client/server as well as mainframe-based, throughout the application development cycle.

Client/server specialists have come to realize that testing is just as critical for client/server systems as for others, perhaps even more critical. Ken Dec, the research director for IT at the highly respected Gartner Group consulting organization located in Stamford, Connecticut, explains "you've got the equivalent of a mainframe sitting on the desktop. Testing becomes absolutely essential." Capers Jones, the chairman of Software Productivity Research, Inc. of Burlington, Massachusetts, and a long-time leader in the field of software testing, is concerned about the effects of less testing. He believes that client/server applications are built with much less rigor and formality than mainframe systems, leading to higher maintenance costs and lower quality levels.

Many in the field have come to believe that it is important to test client/server systems more thoroughly and frequently than what would be required for mainframe systems. The reason is that client/server technology has more variables than does mainframe technology. With a client/server system, in addition to all the other elements that need to be tested in a mainframe system, developers also must test the graphical user interface (GUI), network protocols, gateways, and the distribution of the application functions geographically and by client/server tier. The Hyatt failure described above highlights one of the issues, namely that every client/server environment is unique and so each needs to be tested in the actual production environment. (Many client/server failures occur when systems are tested in environments that don't mimic real-world applications.) Jones points out that whereas legacy systems normally achieve a rating of 95 percent bug free, client/server systems reach only 75 percent bug free (as measured by the bugs that appear after the systems are put into production).

Dan Amedro, a vice president of Hyatt's technology arm, Regency Systems Solutions of Oakbrook Terrace, Illinois, emphasizes another

> **To Think About:** What other technical, organizational, and management issues does the testing of client/server systems present?

aspect of the issue, pointing out that "When there are problems, narrowing down the cause is more complex with client-server."

One reason companies do less testing of client/server systems is that too few tools exist to test all the different components. Each of the functions we listed above, and all the many other functional aspects of a client/server system, need to be tested separately with specialized tools. For example, specialized tools are needed to test balance processing loads (making certain no client or server has been assigned more functionality than it can efficiently handle). Developers need to test applications once they have been distributed to the desktop computers and the servers in order to determine that the various parts in fact do work properly together (such testing would have avoided Hyatt's problem). GUIs need their own testing tools.

No standardized client/server testing method has emerged. Nonetheless, we do know certain elements any client/server testing plan must include. A major IBM testing center, known as the Open Systems Center, located outside Dallas, emphasizes the testing of connectivity, networking, databases, gateways, systems management tools, stresses of a production environment, and on-site replication of the tested solution. One list of test types, in the order of their use, is shown in Table 13.2.

Experts disagree on the cost of client/server testing. Hyatt estimated that testing added 15 percent to the cost of a new, nationwide sales system (not the one referred to in the first paragraph of this Window). Mike Manks, the technical director for the national client/server consulting practice of Coopers & Lybrand, advocates that a project manager budget 20 to 30 percent of the cost for testing, debugging, and redeveloping the software. Bill Christie, a client/server specialist for IBM in New York, believes that the numbers should be even higher—up to half the cost in client/server develop- ment. When thorough testing is not done, he claims, projects see large cost overruns.

Source: Jacqueline Henry, "Is Your System Really Ready?" *Information Week*, October 17, 1994.

Table 13.2	Twelve Types of Tests

Unit: Checks every line of code

Component: Examines functions developed by multiple developers

Integration: Determines whether multiple business functions work together

System: Verifies that an application will work using live data

Performance: Evaluates the performance of memory, disk, network bandwidth, and software applications

Stress and availability: Ensures the application can hold up in a production environment

Destructive: Emphasizes error detection and recovery procedures

Documentation: Verifies that documentation is helpful to users and analysts

Usability: Ensures that the application's interface actually assists the user

Build regression: Tests an application as developers add chunks of code or whole new software

User acceptance: Final verification prior to testing the application

Pilot: Provides end-to-end system analysis to ensure smooth migration

Note: Presented in common testing methodology order
Source: Table, "Twelve Types of Tests" from "Is Your System Really Ready?" by Jacqueline Henry from *Information Week*, October 17, 1994, p. 44.

structured Refers to the fact that techniques are instructions that are carefully drawn up, often step-by-step, with each step building upon a previous one.

top-down An approach that progresses from the highest, most abstract level to the lowest level of detail.

In reaction to these early problems, new methodologies emerged in the 1970s. These methodologies incorporated a range of methods or techniques to carry out the major functions of a development project. The methodologies, and the methods they included, usually are described by the terms *structured* and *top-down*. **Structured** refers to the fact that the techniques are instructions that are carefully drawn up, often step-by-step, with each step building upon the previous step. **Top-down** refers to an approach that progresses from the highest, most abstract level to the lowest level of detail—from the general to the specific. For example, the highest level of a top-down depiction of a human resources system would show the main human resources functions, such as personnel, benefits, employment, and Equal Economic Opportunity (EEO). Each of these would then be exploded or decomposed down to the next layer. Benefits, for example, might include pension, employee savings, health care, and insurance. Each path is broken down, layer by layer, until the material at the lowest level is easily graphed and documented. Top-down is used for analysis, design, and programming.

The traditional structured methodologies are process-oriented rather than data-oriented. While data descriptions are part of the methods, the process-oriented methodologies focus on how the data are transformed rather than on the data themselves. These methodologies are largely linear—each phase must be completed before the next one can begin. Top-down structured methodologies have been used to develop large numbers of systems for two decades, so that a great many existing systems have been developed in this way. Despite growing interest in other methodologies, they remain an important methodological approach today.

The methodologies discussed in this section include structured analysis, structured design, structured programming, and flowcharts. Using these methodologies can promote quality by improving communication, reducing errors caused by faulty program logic or unclear specifications, and creating software that is easier to understand and to maintain.

STRUCTURED ANALYSIS

structured analysis Top-down method for defining system inputs, processes, and outputs and for partitioning systems into subsystems or modules that show a logical graphic model of information flow.

Structured analysis is a widely used top-down method for defining system inputs, processes, and outputs. It offers a logical graphic model of information flow, partitioning a system into tiers of modules that show manageable levels of detail. It rigorously specifies the processes or transformations that occur within each module and the interfaces that exist between them. Its primary tool is the **data flow diagram (DFD)**, a graphic representation of a system's component processes and the flow of data between them.

data flow diagram (DFD) Primary tool in structured analysis that graphically illustrates a system's component processes and the flow of data between them.

Data Flow Diagrams

Data flow diagrams show how data flow to, from, and within an information system and the processes that transform the data. DFDs are constructed using four basic symbols, illustrated in Figure 13.5. These symbols consist of the following:

1. The data flow symbol, an arrow showing the flow of data.

2. The process symbol, rounded boxes or bubbles depicting processes that transform the data.

3. The data store symbol, an open rectangle indicating where data are stored.

4. The external entity symbol, either a rectangle or a square indicating the sources or destinations of data.

data flows The movement of data between processes, external entities, and data stores in a data flow diagram.

Data flows show the movement of data between processes, external entities, and data stores. They always contain packets of data, with the name or content of each data flow listed beside the arrow. The flows are of known composition and represent data that are manual or automated. Data flows are labelled with the name of the data flow, which could be reports, documents, or data from a computer file.

processes Portray the transformation of input data flows to output data flows in a data flow diagram. Each has a unique reference number and is named with a verb–object phrase.

Processes portray the transformation of input data flows to output data flows. An example is a process that transforms a sales order into an invoice or that calculates an employee's gross pay from his or her time card. The convention for naming a process consists of combining a strong verb with an object. For example, we could call the process that calculates gross pay Calculate gross pay. Each process has a

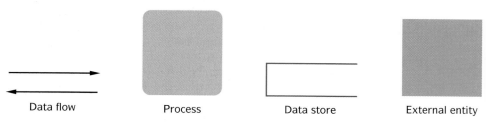

| Data flow | Process | Data store | External entity |

FIGURE 13.5
Data flow diagram symbols. Data flow diagrams can be constructed by using four symbols: *Arrows* represent the flow of data; *processes* transform input data flows into output data flows; *data stores* represent collections of data used or maintained by the system; and *external entities* represent sources or destinations of data and help to define the boundary of a system.

data stores Manual or automated inventories of data.

external entities Originators or receivers of information outside the scope of the system portrayed in the data flow diagram. Sometimes called *outside interfaces*.

unique reference number (such as 1.0, 2.0, etc.) so that it can be easily distinguished from other processes in the data flow diagram.

Data stores are either manual or automated inventories of data. They consist of computer files or databases, file cabinets, card files, microfiche, or a binder of paper reports. The name of the data store is written inside the data store symbol.

External entities are originators or receivers of information. They consist of customers, suppliers, or government agencies external to the organization, or employees or departments within the organization but outside the current system. External entities are sometimes called outside interfaces because they are outside the boundary or scope of the system treated by the data flow diagram.

Figure 13.6 shows a simple data flow diagram for a mail-in university course registration system. Students submit registration forms with their name, identification number, and the numbers of the courses they wish to take. In process 1.0, the system verifies that each course selected is still open by referencing the university's course file. The file distinguishes courses that are still open from those that have been canceled or filled. Process 1.0 then determines which of the student's selections can be accepted or rejected. Process 2.0 enrolls the student in the courses for which he or she has been accepted. It updates the university's course file with the student's name and identification number and recalculates the class size. If maximum enrollment has been reached, the course number is flagged as closed. Process 2.0 also updates the university's student master file with information about new students or changes in address. Process 3.0 then sends each student applicant a confirmation-of-registration letter listing the courses for which he or she is registered and noting the course selections that could not be fulfilled.

The diagrams can be used to depict higher-level processes as well as lower-level details. Through leveled data flow diagrams, a complex process can be broken down into successive levels of detail. An entire system can be divided into subsystems with

FIGURE 13.6

Data flow diagram for mail-in university registration system. The system has three processes. Verify availability (1.0), Enroll student (2.0), and Confirm registration (3.0). The name and content of each of the data flows appear adjacent to each arrow. There is one external entity in this system, the student. There are two data stores: the student master file and the course file.

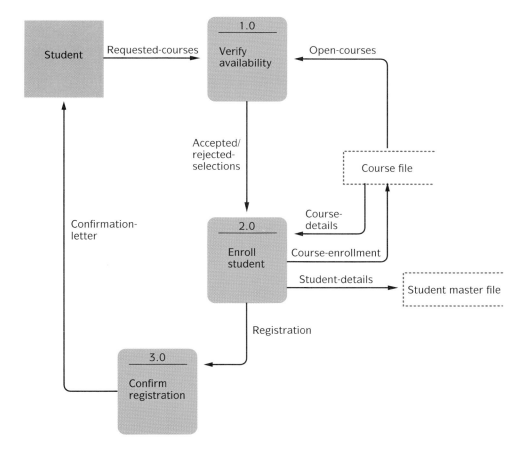

a high-level data flow diagram. Each subsystem, in turn, can be divided into additional subsystems with second-level data flow diagrams, and the lower-level subsystems can be broken down again until the lowest level of detail has been reached.

Figures 13.7(A), 13.7(B), and 13.7(C) show leveled data flow diagrams for a pension recordkeeping and accounting system. Figure 13.7(A) is the most general picture of the system. It is called a context diagram. The **context diagram** always depicts an entire system as a single process with its major inputs and outputs. Subsequent diagrams can then break the system down into greater levels of detail.

The next level of detail, Figure 13.7(B), shows that the system is comprised of five major processes: tracking participation in the pension plan (1.0); tracking service that can be credited to pension benefits (2.0); capturing employee earnings data (3.0); maintaining actuarial tables (4.0); and calculating pension benefits (5.0). Figure 13.7(C) explodes process 5.0, Calculate benefit, into greater detail. It shows that this process can be further decomposed into processes to calculate final average earnings (5.1); the normal retirement benefit (5.2); the early retirement benefit (5.3); the survivor's benefit (5.4); and a process to generate benefits statements (5.5).

context diagram Overview data flow diagram depicting an entire system as a single process with its major inputs and outputs.

Other Structured Analysis Tools

Other tools for structured analysis include a data dictionary, which we first described in Chapter 8. In structured analysis, the data dictionary contains information about individual pieces of data and data groupings within a system. The data dictionary defines the contents of data flows and data stores so that system builders understand exactly what pieces of data they contain. The dictionary also provides information on the meaning and format of each data item and the data flows and data stores where it is used. **Process specifications** describe the transformations occurring within the lowest-level processes of the data flow diagrams. They express the logic for each process.

process specifications Describe the logic of the transformations occurring within the lowest-level processes of the data flow diagrams.

The output of structured analysis is a structured specification document that includes data flow diagrams for system functions, data dictionary descriptions of data flows and data stores, process specifications, input and output documents, and security, control, performance, and conversion requirements.

STRUCTURED DESIGN

Structured design is primarily a software design discipline, but it is often associated with structured analysis and other structured approaches. **Structured design** encompasses a set of design rules and techniques that promotes program clarity and simplicity, thereby reducing the time and effort required for coding, debugging, and maintenance. Sometimes structured design is also referred to as top-down design or composite design. The main principle of structured design is that a system should be designed from the top down in hierarchical fashion and refined to greater levels of detail. The design should first consider the main function of a program or system, then break this function into subfunctions and decompose each subfunction until the lowest level of detail has been reached. In this manner, all high-level logic and the design model are developed before detailed program code is written. If structured analysis has been performed, the structured specification document can serve as input to the design process.

structured design Software design discipline, encompassing a set of design rules and techniques for designing a system from the top down in a hierarchical fashion.

As the design is formulated, it is documented in a structure chart. The **structure chart** is a top-down chart, showing each level of design, its relationship to other levels, and its place in the overall design structure. Figure 13.8 shows a structure chart that can be used for a payroll system. If a design has too many levels to fit onto one structure chart, it can be broken down further on more detailed structure charts. A structure chart may document one program, one system (a set of programs), or part of one program.

structure chart System documentation showing each level of design, the relationship among the levels, and the overall place in the design structure; can document one program, one system, or part of one program.

FIGURE 13.7A
Context diagram for a pension benefits recordkeeping and accounting
system. This diagram provides an
overview of the entire pension benefits recordkeeping and accounting
system, showing its major inputs and
outputs. The context diagram depicts
the entire system as a single process
that can be exploded into more detailed data flow diagrams at lower
levels. Data flow to and from this pension benefits recordkeeping and accounting system. The external entities are the payroll department, the
actuary, and the employee.

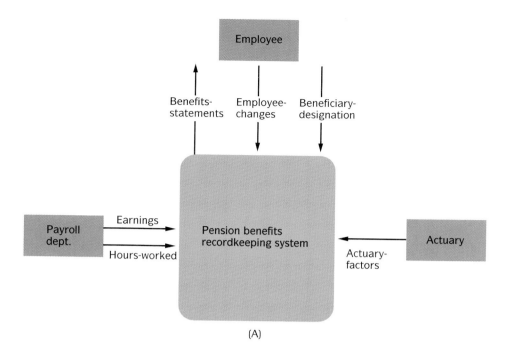

(A)

FIGURE 13.7B
Zero-level data flow diagram for a pension
benefits recordkeeping and accounting system. This data flow diagram explodes the
context diagram into a more detailed picture
of the pension benefits recordkeeping and
accounting system. It shows that the system
consists of five major processes that can, in
turn, be broken down into more detailed
data flow diagrams.

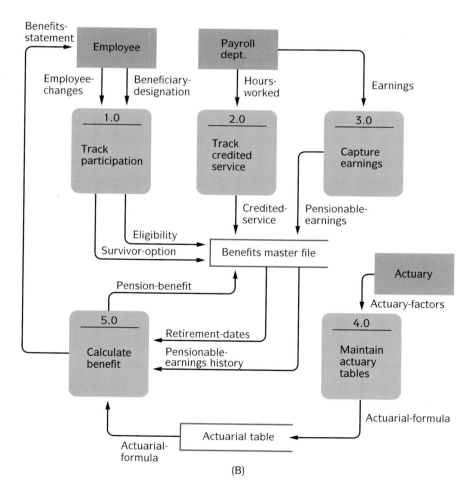

(B)

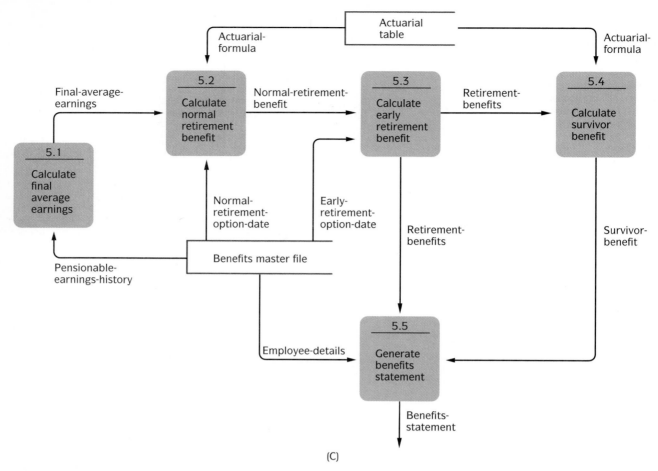

FIGURE 13.7C
First-level data flow diagram for a pension benefits recordkeeping and accounting system. This data flow diagram breaks down the process *Calculate benefit* (5.0) into further detail. It illustrates that calculating pension benefits entails processes to calculate final average earnings (5.1), normal retirement benefit (5.2), early retirement benefit (5.3), survivor benefit (5.4), and a process to generate a benefits statement (5.5).

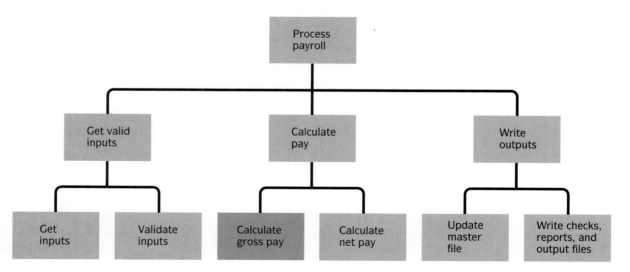

FIGURE 13.8
High-level structure chart for a payroll system. This structure chart shows the highest or most abstract level of design for a payroll system, providing an overview of the entire system.

STRUCTURED PROGRAMMING

structured programming
Discipline for organizing and coding programs that simplifies the control paths so that the programs can be easily understood and modified. Uses the basic control structures and modules that have only one entry point and one exit point.

module A logical unit of a program that performs one or a small number of functions.

Structured programming extends the principles governing structured design to the writing of programs. It also is based upon the principle of modularization, which follows from top-down development.

Structured programming is a method of organizing and coding programs that simplifies control paths so that the programs can be easily understood and modified. Structured programming reduces the complexity created when program instructions jump forward and backward to other parts of the program, obscuring the logic and flow of the program.

Each of the boxes in the structure chart represents a component **module**. Programs can be partitioned into modules, each of which constitutes a logical unit that performs one or a small number of functions. Ideally, modules should be independent of each other. They should be interconnected so that they have only one entry to and exit from their parent modules. They should share data with as few other modules as possible.

There should be no obscure connections with other modules that would create a "ripple effect," whereby a change to module A creates unanticipated changes in modules B, D, and F. Minimizing connections among modules minimizes paths by which errors can be spread to other parts of the system.

Each module should also be kept to a manageable size. An individual should be able to read the program code for the module and easily keep track of its functions. Within each module, program instructions should not wander and should be executed in top-down fashion.

Proponents of structured programming have shown that any program can be written using three basic control constructs, or instruction patterns: (1) simple sequence, (2) selection, and (3) iteration. These control constructs are illustrated in Figure 13.9.

sequence construct The sequential single steps or actions in the logic of a program that do not depend on the existence of any condition.

selection construct The logic pattern in programming where a stated condition determines which of two or more actions can be taken depending on which satisfies the stated condition.

iteration construct The logic pattern in programming where certain actions are repeated while a specified condition occurs or until a certain condition is met.

system flowchart Graphic design tool that depicts the physical media and sequence of processing steps used in an entire information system.

The **sequence construct** executes statements in the order in which they appear, with control passing unconditionally from one statement to the next. The program will execute statement A and then statement B.

The **selection construct** tests a condition and executes one of the two alternative instructions based on the results of the test. Condition R is tested. If R is true, statement C is executed. If R is false, statement D is executed. Control then passes to the next statement.

The **iteration construct** repeats an instruction as long as the results of a conditional test remain true. Condition S is tested. If S is true, statement E is executed and control returns to the test of S. If S is false, E is skipped and control passes to the next statement.

Any one or any combination of these control structures can accommodate any kind of processing logic required by a program. There is a single entry and exit point for each structure so that the path of the program logic remains clear.

FLOWCHARTS

Flowcharting is an old design tool that is still in use. **System flowcharts** detail the flow of data throughout an entire information system. Program flowcharts describe the processes taking place within an individual program in the system and the sequence in which they must be executed. Flowcharting is no longer recommended for program design because it does not provide top-down modular structure as effectively as other techniques. However, system flowcharts may still be used to document physical design specifications because they can show all inputs, major files, processing, and outputs for a system and they can document manual procedures.

Using specialized symbols and flow lines, the system flowchart traces the flow of information and work in a system, the sequence of processing steps, and the physical media on which data are input, output, and stored. Figure 13.10 contains the

FIGURE 13.9
Basic control constructs. The
three basic control constructs
used in structured programming are sequence, selection,
and iteration.

Sequence
    Action A
    Action B

Selection
    IF Condition R
        Action C
    ELSE
        Action D
    ENDIF

Iteration
    DO WHILE Condition S
        Action E
    ENDDO

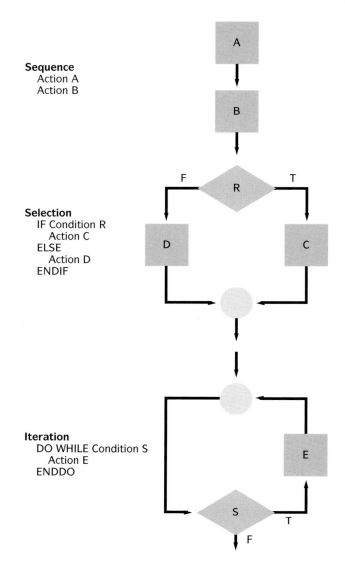

basic symbols for system flowcharting. The plain rectangle is a general symbol for a major computer processing function. Flow lines show the sequence of steps and the direction of information flow. Arrows are employed to show direction if it is not apparent in the diagram.

Figure 13.11 illustrates a high-level system flowchart of a payroll system.

LIMITATIONS OF TRADITIONAL METHODS

The traditional structured approach has served the information systems professionals and their user communities well. Nonetheless, it has its shortcomings. Most critics consider structured methodologies to be slow and unresponsive to the fast-changing business world of the 1990s. The process is very linear. Completion of structured analysis is required before structured design can begin, and structured programming must await the completed deliverables from structured design. The slowness translates into increased cost.

Because a large system development project will last one to two years, specifications drawn up at the beginning are bound to change as business needs change. However, a change in specifications requires that the analysis documents and then the design documents must be modified before the programs can be changed to reflect the new requirement.

FIGURE 13.10
Basic system flowchart symbols. Use these symbols and interconnecting lines to show the sequence of processing taking place within a system and the physical media used in each step.

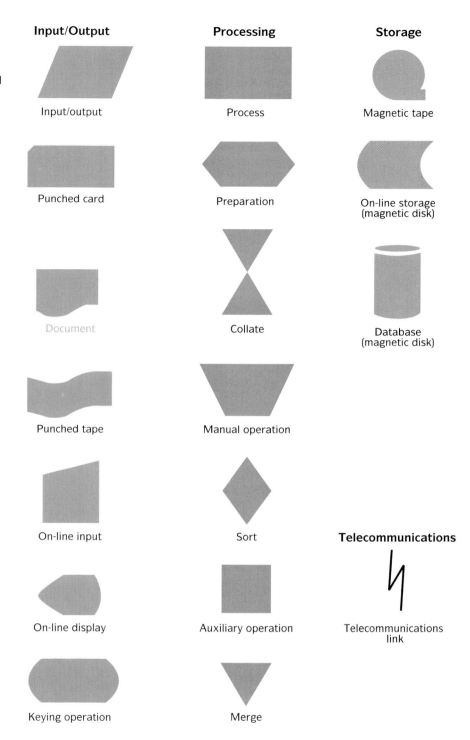

Structured methodologies are function-oriented. They focus on the processes that transform the data. The storage of the data is described as an appendage to those processes. Yet, business management has come to understand that the most valuable portion of information systems is the data. Data generated by one department may be used by many other departments, each of which will process them differently. For example, production quality data might be used by the production department, research labs, marketing and sales staffs, corporate management, and even customers. In addition, for most systems even the department that generates the data will use them in many ways and will continually change the ways the data are

FIGURE 13.11
System flowchart for a payroll system. This is a high-level system flowchart for a batch payroll system. Only the most important processes and files are illustrated. Data are input from two sources: time cards and payroll-related data (such as salary increases) passed from the human resources system. The data are first edited and validated against the existing payroll master file before the payroll master is updated. The update process produces an updated payroll master file, various payroll reports (such as the payroll register and hours register), checks, a direct deposit tape, and a file of payment data that must be passed to the organization's general ledger system. The direct deposit tape is sent to the automated clearinghouse that serves the banks offering direct deposit services to employees.

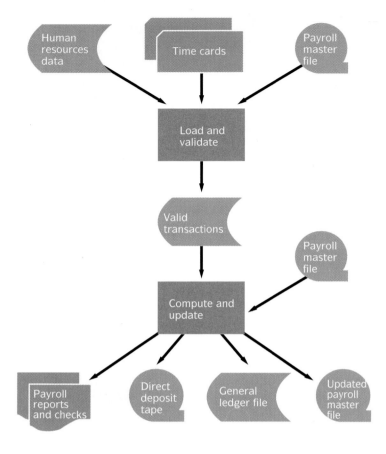

used. It has become clear that the data are more permanent than the processes that use or transform them. Systems that focus on data can be smaller and more flexible, making them easier to modify and more responsive to changing business needs.

The IS profession has long wanted to find ways to reuse code as a way to reduce costs. Despite the fact that specific groups of data are usually processed the same way in different programs, a separate programming procedure must be written every time someone wants to take an action on a particular piece of data. Why take the time and pay the cost to rewrite the code each time a tax calculation needs to be done or a specific chemical needs to be analyzed? Hopes that program modularization would solve this problem of reusability have not been fulfilled. Critics believe we must look beyond structured approaches to find solutions to this critical productivity issue.

New techniques have been developed to address many of these problems. For example, **joint application design (JAD)** is a design method that brings users and IS professionals into a room together for an interactive design of the system. Properly prepared and facilitated, JAD sessions can significantly speed up the design phase while involving users in the design at a level previously not possible. (Traditional methods of system specification may still be used with JAD.) Prototyping (discussed in Chapter 12) also speeds up design while involving users more and increases the flexibility of the whole process. Nonetheless, the IS profession has been trying to develop other methodologies in an attempt to replace structured methodologies.

joint application design (JAD) A design method which brings users and IS professionals into a room together for an interactive design of the system.

13.3   NEW APPROACHES TO QUALITY

In addition to the traditional methodologies and tools, system builders are turning to object-oriented development, computer-aided software engineering (CASE), and software re-engineering to help cope with information systems quality problems.

OBJECT-ORIENTED SOFTWARE DEVELOPMENT

object-oriented software development Approach to software development that de-emphasizes procedures and shifts the focus from modeling business processes and data to combining data and procedures to create objects.

We have already introduced object-oriented programming in Chapter 7. Object-oriented programming is part of a larger approach to systems development called object-oriented development. **Object-oriented software development** differs from traditional methodologies in the way it handles the issue of process versus data. Traditional structured analysis and design put procedures first. They first view a system in terms of what it is intended to *do* and then develop models of procedures and data. Object-oriented software development de-emphasizes procedures. The focus shifts from modeling business processes and data to combining data and procedures into objects. The system is viewed as a collection of classes and objects and the relationships among them. The objects are defined, programmed, documented, and saved for use with future applications.

Proponents of object-oriented development claim that objects can be more easily understood by users than traditional representations of a system. For example, accounts receivable personnel tend to think of entities such as customers, credit limits, and invoices—the same level at which objects are built. Object-oriented analysis (OOA) and object-oriented design (OOD) are based upon these objects and are believed to more closely model the real world than previous methods, which describe a system in terms of inputs, outputs, and data flows. However, some research shows that object-oriented software development methods may be more difficult to use for specifying information requirements than traditional structured methods (Vessey and Conger, 1994). Only more experience will tell if object-oriented software development is an improvement.

Benefits of an Object-Oriented Approach

Because objects are reusable, object-oriented software development directly addresses the issue of reusability and is expected to reduce the time and cost of writing software. Of course, no organization will see savings from reusability until it builds up a library of classes and objects to draw upon. Object-oriented software development experience is still very limited, so it is too early to evaluate the approach. Nonetheless, early studies have been promising. Experience has shown that programming productivity gains of better than 10:1 are possible. Electronic Data Systems Corp. (EDS) studied the benefits by building a maintenance management system twice, once using structured techniques and once using object-oriented programming. EDS equalized the skill level of the two project teams and had them work from the same specifications. They found a productivity improvement of 14:1 using object-oriented programming (International Data Corporation, 1992). Maintenance costs are also lowered by reducing multiple maintenance changes. For example, when the U.S. postal system changed the ZIP code from five to nine digits, each program within a company had to be changed. If a company's programs were object-oriented, the programmer would only have had to modify the code within the object, and the change would be reflected in all the programs using that object.

Object-oriented software development is leading to other changes in methods. Once a library of objects exists, design and programming often can begin without waiting for analysis documents (see Figure 13.12). Rather, in theory, design and programming can be carried out together, beginning as soon as requirements are completed. Developers—users and IS professionals—use iterations of rapid prototyping to design the system. The prototype, when completed, will encompass a great deal of the programming needed for the completion of the system.

Object-oriented methods should increase the involvement of users. Users may find objects easier to understand and more natural to work with than structured tools such as design charts. In addition, iterative prototyping relies heavily on users, placing them at the center of design and even of programming.

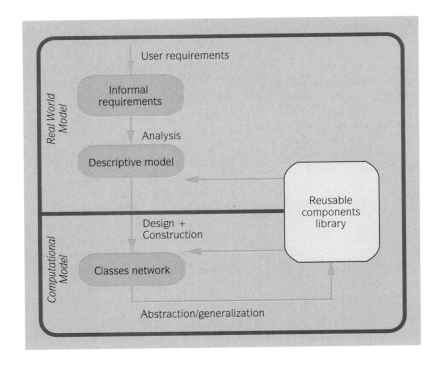

Obstacles to Using Object-Oriented Techniques

Although the demand for training in object-oriented techniques and programming tools is exploding, object-oriented software development is still in its infancy and is too unproven for most companies to adopt it. No agreed-upon object-oriented methodology yet exists, although several have been proposed. Moreover, many companies are hesitant to try it because it requires extensive staff training and a major methodological reorientation. Management is also aware that a complete switch to object-oriented development will take a long time. Most companies have a major investment in existing structured systems that would have to be maintained until the time came that they needed replacement. Until then, the IS departments would have to retain expertise in both structured and object-oriented methods.

New technology needs to be developed for the use of object-oriented methods. Data dictionaries for storing structured data definitions and program code are not appropriate for object-oriented programming. New object-oriented dictionaries need to be developed. CASE tools (discussed below) have been developed to support structured methodologies and are just starting to be redesigned for use with object-oriented development. Even new metrics need to be developed, as many of the metrics now used to evaluate system quality cannot be applied to object-oriented coding.

COMPUTER-AIDED SOFTWARE ENGINEERING (CASE)

computer-aided software engineering (CASE) The automation of step-by-step methodologies for software and systems development to reduce the amount of repetitive work the developer needs to do.

Computer-aided software engineering (CASE)—sometimes called computer-aided systems engineering—is the automation of step-by-step methodologies for software and systems development to reduce the amount of repetitive work the developer needs to do. By automating many routine software development tasks and enforcing adherence to design rules, CASE can free the developer for more creative problem-solving tasks. CASE tools can facilitate creation of clear documentation and coordination of team development efforts (Forte and Norman, 1992). Team members can share their work more easily by accessing each other's files to review or modify what has been done. Systems developed with CASE and the newer methodologies have been found to be more reliable and require maintenance less often (Dekleva, 1992). Many CASE tools are microcomputer based, with powerful graphical capabilities.

CASE tools provide automated graphics facilities for producing charts and diagrams, screen and report generators, data dictionaries, extensive reporting facilities, analysis and checking tools, code generators, and documentation generators. Most CASE tools are based on one or more of the popular structured methodologies. Some are starting to support object-oriented development and support for building client/server applications. In general, CASE tools try to increase productivity and quality by doing the following:

- Supporting a standard development methodology and design discipline. The design and overall development effort will have more integrity.

- Improving communication between users and technical specialists. Large teams and software projects can be coordinated more effectively.

- Organizing and correlating design components and providing rapid access to them via a design repository.

- Automating tedious and error-prone portions of analysis and design.

- Automating testing and controlling rollout.

Key elements of CASE are described in Table 13.3.

Examples of CASE Tools

CASE tools have been classified in terms of whether they support activities at the front end or the back end of the systems development process. Front-end CASE tools focus on capturing analysis and design information in the early stages of systems development. They automate the process of creating data flow diagrams, structure charts, entity-relationship diagrams, and other specifications so that they can be easily revised to improve design before coding begins. Table 13.4 describes the strengths and limitations of CASE tools.

Back-end CASE tools address coding, testing, and maintenance activities and include text editors, formatters, syntax checkers, compilers, cross-reference generators, linkers, symbolic debuggers, execution profilers, code generators, and application generators. Back-end tools help convert specifications automatically into program code.

CASE products such as Andersen Consulting's Foundation and Knowledge Ware's Application Development Workbench represent more fully integrated tools that are starting to support the entire systems development process, including

Table 13.3	Elements of CASE

Diagramming tools: Graphics tools for drawing symbols for data flow diagrams, structure charts, entity-relationship diagrams, or other types of diagrams associated with a particular methodology.

Syntax verifier: Verifies the accuracy and completeness of information entered into a system in conformance with the rules of a particular structured methodology.

Prototyping tools: Screen, report, and menu generators allow the analyst to paint desired screen and report layouts or menu paths through a system without complex formatting specifications or programming.

Information repository: A central information database which serves as a mechanism for storing all types of software assets—screen and report layouts, diagrams, data definitions, program code, project schedules, and other documentation. The repository coordinates, integrates, and standardizes the different pieces of information so they can be easily accessed, shared by analysts, and reused in future software work.

Code generators: These can generate modules of executable code from higher-level specifications. Some CASE tools use icons to indicate various program functions and translate these symbols into programs.

Development methodology: Some CASE products contain checklists or narratives detailing an entire development methodology that help monitor and control the entire systems development project.

Project management tools: Some CASE tools integrate their components with popular stand-alone tools for project scheduling and resource estimation, while others incorporate project management software into the CASE tool kit.

Table 13.4	What CASE Tools Can and Cannot Do

CASE Tools Can:

1. Automate many manual tasks of systems development.
2. Promote standardization based on a single methodology.
3. Promote greater consistency and coordination during a development project.
4. Generate a large portion of the documentation for a system, such as data flow diagrams, data models, structure charts, or other specifications.

CASE Tools Cannot:

1. Automatically provide a functional, relevant system. It is just as easy to produce a bad system as to produce a good system using CASE tools.
2. Interface easily with databases and fourth-generation languages.
3. Automatically force analysts to use a prescribed methodology or create a methodology when one does not exist.
4. Radically transform the systems analysis and design process.

project management and automatic generation of program code for routine parts of an application.

Analysts use CASE tools to help capture requirements and specifications by storing the information in a CASE database, where it can be easily retrieved and revised. The CASE tools facilitate up-front design and analysis work, so that there are fewer errors to correct later on. CASE text and graphics editors help the analyst create technically correct diagrams, process descriptions, and data dictionary entries. The analyst can draw diagrams by choosing from a set of standard symbols and positioning the symbols on the screen. Text information can be added to the diagram or used to describe processes and data flows using the CASE tool's text editor.

Many CASE tools automatically tie data elements to the processes where they are used. If a data flow diagram is changed from one process to another, the elements in the data dictionary would be altered automatically to reflect the change in the diagram (see Figure 13.13). CASE tools also contain features for validating design; included in these features are automatic balancing of data flow diagrams and checking diagrams and specifications for completeness and consistency. Some tool kits contain prototyping features such as screen and report painters, which allow analysts to draw screen or report formats for users to review. CASE tools thus support iterative design by automating revisions and changes and providing prototyping facilities.

A central element in the CASE tool kit is the information repository, which stores all the information defined by the analysts during the project. The repository includes data flow diagrams, structure charts, entity-relationship diagrams (see Figure 13.14), data definitions, process specifications, screen and report formats, notes and comments, test results and evaluations, source code, status and audit information, and time and cost estimates. The CASE database can be shared by members of a project team and contains features to restrict changes to only specified analysts.

The Challenge of Using CASE

To be used effectively, CASE tools require more organizational discipline than the manual approach. Every member of a development project must adhere to a common set of naming conventions, standards, and development methodologies. Without this discipline, analysts and designers will cling to their old ways of developing systems and will attempt to incorporate the CASE tool in the process. This can actually be counterproductive because of the incompatibility between the old approach and new tools. The best CASE tools enforce common methods and standards, which may discourage their use in situations where organizational discipline is lacking.

Actual productivity gains from CASE remain difficult to define. A few firms have reported tangible cost savings from using CASE, while others note more rapid gen-

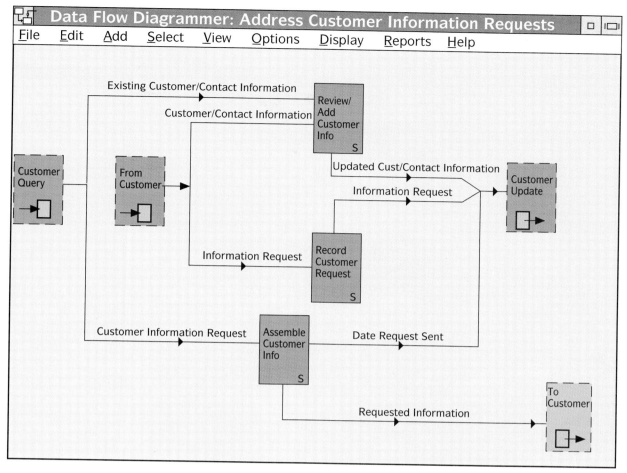

FIGURE 13.13

The data flow diagrammer in Knowledge Ware's Application Development Workbench can produce a multi-level process model that ensures that the movement of data is consistent from one level to the next. The CASE tool ensures that the data flows entering or leaving a process are included in the level below. *Diagram provided courtesy of Sterling Software, Application Development Division.*

eration of systems or higher-quality software once developers have learned to use CASE tools (Banker, Kauffman and Kumar, 1991–1992). Some studies have found that CASE tools improve productivity while others have found that CASE tools have no significant impact on productivity and a relatively weak effect on the quality of specifications (Vessey, Jarvenpaa, and Tractinsky, 1992). The issue remains clouded because productivity gains in software development have traditionally been difficult to measure and to quantify.

While it facilitates some aspects of systems development, CASE is not a magic cure-all. It can accelerate analysis and design and promote iterative design, but it does not enable systems to be designed automatically or ensure that business requirements are met. Systems designers still have to understand what a firm's business needs are and how the business works. (See the Window on Management to learn how one large corporation selected its CASE tools to serve the needs of the business.) Systems analysis and design are still dependent upon the analytical skills of the analyst/designer. Some of the productivity gains attributed to CASE may actually be the result of systems developers improving communication, coordination, and software integrity by agreeing on a standard methodology rather than from the use of automated CASE tools themselves.

CASE provides a set of labor-saving tools that automate software development work. But the actual software development process to be automated is defined by a

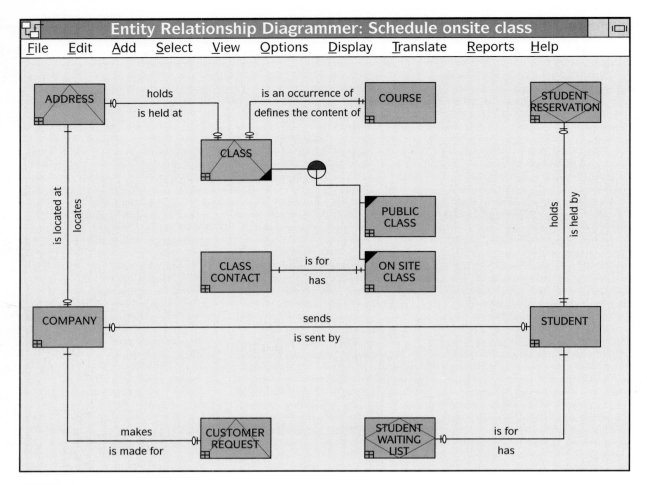

FIGURE 13.14
The entity-relationship diagrammer in Knowledge Ware's Application Development Workbench helps systems designers build a logical data model by documenting the types of entities found in an organization and how they relate. This CASE tool can display an entity-relationship diagram for the entire entity model or for a context-sensitive view. This figure, for example, displays only the entities and relationships relevant to the process of scheduling a class. *Diagram provided courtesy of Sterling Software, Application Development Division.*

methodology. If a firm lacks a methodology, CASE tools may be used to automate disparate, and often incompatible, practices rather than integrating or standardizing a firm's systems development approach.

SOFTWARE RE-ENGINEERING

software re-engineering Methodology that addresses the problem of aging software by salvaging and upgrading it so that the users can avoid a long and expensive replacement project.

reverse engineering The process of taking existing programs' code, file, and database descriptions and converting them into corresponding design-level components that can then be used to create new applications.

Software re-engineering is a methodology that addresses the problem of aging software. A great deal of the software that organizations use was written without the benefit of structured analysis, design, and programming. Such software is difficult to maintain or update. However, the software serves the organization well enough to continue to be used, if only it could be more easily maintained. The purpose of re-engineering is to salvage such software by upgrading it so that the users can avoid a long and expensive replacement project. In essence, developers use re-engineering to extract intelligence from existing systems, thereby creating new systems without starting from scratch. Re-engineering involves three steps: reverse engineering, revision of design and program specifications, and forward engineering.

    Reverse engineering entails extracting the underlying business specifications from existing systems. Older, nonstructured systems do not have structured documentation to clarify the business functions the system is intended to support. Nor do they have

FEDERATED SELECTS AN APPLICATION DEVELOPMENT INFRASTRUCTURE

How does a company select an application development infrastructure? Retailing giant Federated Department Stores recently went through the process, and its experience will be instructive to us all.

Step One. Determining Business Requirements. Federated information systems established a project with a goal of installing a new environment in which to build applications. The project began with a study of application development technology, and to aid the project team members, it hired the consulting firm, of Deloitte & Touche. The consultants quickly advised Federated to step back from examining technology so early and instead to begin the process with a business requirements study. Their rationale? Technology decisions must be business driven so they will serve the goals of the business. First make business decisions, and then use those decisions as the foundation for selecting the appropriate technology. Federated agreed. As David Guzmán, a Federated director of information technology based in Norcross, Georgia, explained it, "We figured out that we needed to make a decision about how our business processes should be structured; then our future technical architecture would come out of that decision." They also realized that this process would take some time and, in the meantime, all development could not stop while waiting for this project to be completed. Therefore, they decided to allow development to continue using interim tools until final technology decisions were made.

Step Two. Adopting a Technology Paradigm. The team doing the business requirements study found that Federated management described it company's future business structure as "central direction and local execution." This decentralized business vision led the project team members to conclude

that they needed to follow a client/server paradigm. In a distributed client/server model, the data, business process, presentation, and the application itself could all be partitioned based on business needs. Federated's decision to improve customer service and to decentralize decision making was driving its move to client/server.

Step Three. An Overview of the Technology Infrastructure. Once Federated made the decision to go to client/server technology, the team then decided to move off the mainframe completely, to move all applications and databases into a client/server environment. Team members also concluded that they needed to tightly couple application development to the business process so that as business processes change, the systems that support those processes would also change. For example, a change in point-of-sale procedures should be able to be quickly reflected in an enabling application.

Step Four. Determining the Type of Development Tools. Having made the most fundamental decision, team members then turned back to reviewing technology. They quickly decided that they did not want to use a series of small client/server development tools because that environment would be too difficult to manage. Instead they agreed to search for an all-encompassing CASE tool.

Step Five. Narrowing the List. Many CASE tools are available, too many for an in-depth examination of each. Therefore, the next task was to winnow down the list to only a few candidates. Federated began by drawing up a list of minimum requirements for CASE tool functionality. The list included such obvious items as support for client/server infrastructure and the ability to manage centrally a client/server development environment. Because the team members planned to move all applications into a client/

server environment, the final candidate tools needed to be able to run from a client/server environment also (some client/server development tools actually

> **To Think About:** As an information systems director at Federated, how would you have attempted to sell Federated's management team on a project to examine and possibly change the company's information systems development infrastructure? If you were a member of that management team, what problems might you have with the project? What management, organization, and technology factors should be considered when selecting CASE tools?

run only on a mainframe). Ultimately they reduced the list to two candidates, Seer Technology's Seer/HPS and Texas Instrument's IEF 5.2.

Step Six. Evaluating the Remaining Candidates. The remaining candidates needed to be examined far more thoroughly in order to determine which one (if either) would meet Federated's needs. First, the team made a more specific list of requirements, including re-engineering support; distributed systems support; an integrated, full-life-cycle, repository-based system; rapid prototyping capability; and reasonable cost. Federated also wanted a tool that would support location analysis, a key function in developing client/server applications. Location analysis helps a development project team determine the location of an application's presentation (interface), data, and business application (process). Location refers both to the geographic location and to the client versus the server: where to locate servers, how many clients to allocate per site, the data flow needs across the entire system. Guzmán explained that Federated "needed a development architecture that would help to decide,

'What is the most appropriate tier to put an app[lication] on based on these things? On the client? On the server?' We needed a total system that could help us decide who does what, when, where, and how often for deciding how to slice the client/server partitions."

Step Seven. Making the Final Selection. The team ultimately selected Seer/HPS. Although neither candidate offered location analysis, HPS did offer part of the job with a single tool to partition the presentation, data, and process elements across the client/server tiers. Federated considered its data repository superior because it was able to support multiple workgroups on disparate servers, and even do it in real-time. Also, the repository is object-oriented, thus supporting both the reuse of code for new development and more efficient maintenance of existing applications (see Chapter 12).

HPS also included a change management function, a key function that is particularly difficult to manage in a complex client/server environment. The Federated team also was impressed with the ease of management of the HPS tools. The tools are centralized on the network so they can be centrally managed. Many other tools are loaded on to the desktop computers of individual developers (over 600 in the case of Federated), making management nearly impossible. The team also concluded that the overall functionality of IEF is contained in a set of related but not integrated tools, tools which the users must make work together. On the other hand, HPS functionality is contained in a single, integrated tool. Another factor that was important to the project team, although not one of the basic requirements, was the team members' desire to replace their high-quality IBM main-

frame system with a very impressive new system, impressive enough to win the users over. In their mind that meant a Windows interface, which Seer supports. It also meant to them the use of an Oracle database, and Peer was just about to release a new version of its repository in Oracle. Finally, the team was concerned about the cost. While the price tag for Seer/HPS appears to be high at over $1 million, it was actually cheap compared to most alternatives. For example, if Federated had decided to select a set of CASE tools that is loaded on individual developer computers one at a time, the cost would be about $3500 each, which for a large company like Federated would total over $2 million.

Source: J. William Semich, "Big Development Jobs Need CASE," *Datamation,* September 1, 1994.

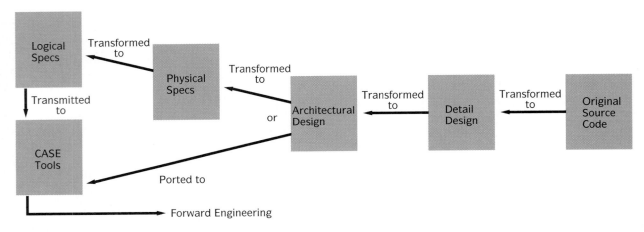

FIGURE 13.15
Steps in the reverse engineering process. The primary function of reverse engineering is to capture the functional capabilities—the process logic—of the existing system in a simplified form that can be revised and updated for the basis of the new replacement system. *Source: Thomas J. McCabe and Eldonna S. Williamson, "Tips on Reengineering Redundant Software,"* Datamation, *April 15, 1992. Reproduced with permission from DATAMATION©.*

forward engineering The final step in re-engineering when the revised specifications are used to generate new, structured program code for a structured and maintainable system.

adequate documentation of either the system design or the programs. Reverse engineering tools, such as those supplied by Bachman Information Systems of Cambridge, Massachusetts, read and analyze the program's existing code, file, and database descriptions and produce structured documentation of the system. The output will show design-level components, such as entities, attributes, and processes. With structured documentation to work from, the project team can then revise the design and specifications to meet current business requirements. In the final step, **forward engineering,** the revised specifications are used to generate new, structured code for a structured and maintainable system. In Figure 13.15, you can follow the re-engineering process. Note that CASE tools can be used in the forward engineering step.

Re-engineering can have significant benefits. It allows a company to develop a modern system at a much lower cost than would be the case if it had to develop an entirely new system. The newly re-engineered system will reflect current business requirements, and it will be capable of being modified as those requirements change. During the revision phase of the project, the technology of the system can also be upgraded, so that, for example, the new system can be networked or the code can be generated using relational database technology. Finally, unstructured programs contain a large amount of redundant code. Re-engineering allows the developers to eliminate redundancy, thus reducing the size and complexity of the programs, resulting in fewer opportunities for current and future bugs.

It should be pointed out that software re-engineering is a very complex undertaking, requiring much more than just running old code through a CASE tool to produce a new system. Additional research and analysis are usually required to determine all of the business rules and data requirements for the new system (Aiken, Muntz, and Richards, 1994).

Management Challenges

1. Applying quality assurance standards in large system projects. We have explained why the goal of zero defects in large, complex pieces of software is impossible to achieve. If the seriousness of remaining bugs cannot be ascertained, what constitutes an acceptable if not perfect performance? And even if meticulous design and exhaustive testing could eliminate all defects, software projects have time and budget constraints that often prevent management from devoting as much time to thorough testing as it should. Under these circumstances it will be difficult for managers either to define a standard for software quality or to enforce it.

2. Enforcing a standard methodology. Although structured methodologies have been available for 25 years, very few organizations have been able to enforce them. One survey found that only 15 to 20 percent of all organizations it studied used structured analysis and design in a consistent manner. It is impossible to use CASE or newer object-oriented methods effectively unless all participants in system building adopt a common development methodology as well as common development tools. Methodologies are organizational disciplines.

3. Agreeing on what constitutes quality in information systems. Many information systems professionals tend to view system problems as primarily technical issues. Yet many quality problems related to information systems, including software quality assurance, are not merely technical issues. Information systems specialists need to work in partnership with other areas of the organization to develop a shared sense of quality linked to larger business goals.

Summary

1. Describe how information systems can contribute to total quality management in an organization. Information systems can contribute to total quality management by helping other business functions perform their work more effectively, by helping to analyze and redesign business processes, by suggesting new ways to apply technology to enhance quality, and by sharing their experience in quantifying and measuring procedures with other areas of the organization. Information systems can help organizations simplify their products and production processes, meet benchmarking standards, improve customer service, reduce production cycle time, and improve the quality and precision of design and production.

2. Explain why information systems must pay special attention to software quality assurance. Software plays a central role in most organizations and is an integral part of daily operations, products, and services. However, it presents quality problems because of the difficulty in developing software that captures user specifications accurately, because of the high costs of maintaining software and correcting errors, and because software bugs may be impossible to eliminate.

3. Identify the principal solutions to information systems quality problems. Information systems quality problems can be minimized by using structured systems development methodologies, software metrics, thorough testing procedures, quality tools, and by reallocating resources to put more emphasis on the early stages of the systems development cycle.

4. Describe the traditional tools and methodologies for promoting information systems quality. Structured analysis highlights the flow of data and the processes through which data are transformed. Its principal tool is the data flow diagram. Structured design and programming are software design disciplines that produce reliable, well-documented software with a simple, clear structure that is easy for others to understand and maintain. System flowcharts are useful for documenting the physical aspects of system design.

5. **Describe new approaches for promoting information systems quality.** Object-oriented software development is expected to reduce the time and cost of writing software and of making maintenance changes because it models a system as a series of reusable objects that combine both data and procedures. Computer-aided software engineering (CASE) automates step-by-step methodologies for systems development. It promotes standards and improves coordination and consistency during systems development. CASE tools help system builders build a better model of a system and facilitate revision of design specifications to correct errors. Software re-engineering helps system builders reconfigure aging software to conform to structured design principles, making it easier to maintain.

Key Terms

Quality	Debugging	Context diagram	Joint application design
Total quality management	Spaghetti code	Process specifications	(JAD)
(TQM)	Structured	Structured design	Object-oriented software
Bugs	Top-down	Structure chart	development
Development	Structured analysis	Structured programming	Computer-aided software
methodology	Data flow diagram (DFD)	Module	engineering (CASE)
Resource allocation	Data flows	Sequence construct	Software re-engineering
Software metrics	Processes	Selection construct	Reverse engineering
Function point analysis	Data stores	Iteration construct	Forward engineering
Walkthrough	External entities	System flowchart	

Review Questions

1. What is total quality management? How can information systems contribute to it?
2. Describe some approaches that companies follow in their quality programs and the way that they can be supported by information systems.
3. Why can software become such an important quality problem for information systems? Describe two software quality problems.
4. Name and describe four solutions to software quality problems.
5. What is structured analysis? What is the role of the following in structured analysis: data flow diagrams, data dictionaries, process specifications?
6. What are the principles of structured design? How can it promote software quality?
7. What is the relationship of structured programming to structured design?
8. Describe the use of system flowcharts.
9. What is the difference between object-oriented software development and traditional structured methodologies?
10. What is CASE? How can it promote quality in information systems?
11. What are some of the key elements of CASE tools?
12. What are software re-engineering and reverse engineering? How can they promote quality in information systems?

Discussion Questions

1. If it is impossible to eliminate all of the errors in a complex piece of software, how much time should be spent in testing?
2. How can information system quality benefit from using some of the system-building approaches described in Chapter 12 (systems life cycle, prototyping, software packages, fourth-generation development, outsourcing)? What quality problems are created by each of these approaches?

Group Project

Systems Analysis and Design Project: Healthlite Yogurt Company

Healthlite Yogurt Company is a market leader in the expanding U.S. market for yogurt and related health products. Healthlite is experiencing some sharp growing pains. With the growing interest in low-fat, low-cholesterol health foods, spurred on by the aging of the baby boomers, Healthlite's sales have tripled over the past five years. At the same time, however, new local competitors, offering fast delivery from local production centers and lower prices, are challenging Healthlite for retail shelf space with a bevy of new products. Without shelf space, products cannot be retailed in the United States, and new products are needed to expand shelf space. Healthlite needs to justify its share of shelf space to grocers and is seeking additional shelf space for its new yogurt-based products such as frozen desserts and low-fat salad dressings.

Healthlite's biggest challenge, however, has not been competitors, but the sweep of the second hand. Yogurt is a very short shelf-life commodity. With a shelf life measured in days, yogurt must be moved very quickly.

Healthlite maintains its U.S. corporate headquarters in Danbury, Connecticut. Corporate headquarters has a central mainframe computer that maintains most of the major business databases. All production takes place in local processing plants, which are located in New Jersey, Massachusetts, Tennessee, Illinois, Colorado, Washington, and California. Each processing plant has its own minicomputer, which is connected to the corporate mainframe. Customer credit verification is maintained at the central corporate site where customer master files are maintained and order verification or rejection is determined. Once processed centrally, order data are then fed to the appropriate local processing plant minicomputer.

Healthlite has 20 sales regions, each with approximately 30 sales representatives and a regional sales manager. Healthlite has a 12-person marketing group in corporate headquarters and a corporate director of sales and marketing. Each salesperson is able to store and retrieve data for assigned customer accounts using a terminal in each regional office linked to the corporate mainframe. Reports for individual salespeople (printouts of orders, rejection notices, customer account inquiries) and for sales offices are printed in the regional offices and mailed to them.

Sometimes, the only way to obtain up-to-date sales data is for managers to make telephone calls to subordinates and then piece the information together. Data about sales and advertising expenses and customer shelf space devoted to Healthlite products is maintained manually at the regional offices. Each regional office maintains its own manual records of customer shelf space and promotional campaigns. The central computer contains only consolidated, company-wide files for customer account data and order and billing data.

The existing order processing system requires sales representatives to write up hard copy tickets to place orders through the mail. Approximately 100 workers at Healthlite corporate headquarters open, sort, keypunch, and process 100,000 order tickets per week. This order information is transmitted each evening from the mainframe to a minicomputer at each of Healthlite's processing sites. This daily order specifies the total yogurt and yogurt product demand for each processing center. Each processing center then produces the amount and type of yogurt and

yogurt-related products ordered and then ships the orders out. Shipping managers at the processing centers assign the shipments to various transportation carriers.

Rapid growth, fueled by Healthlite's "health" image and by branching into new yogurt-based products, has put pressures on Healthlite's existing information systems. By mid-1994, growth in new products and sales had reached a point where Healthlite was printing new tickets for the sales force every week. The firm was choking on paper. For each order, a salesperson filled out at least two forms per account. Some sales representatives have more than 80 customers.

As it became bogged down in paper, Healthlite saw increased delays in the processing of its orders. Since yogurt is a fresh food product, it could not be held long in inventory. Yet Healthlite had trouble shipping the right goods to the right places in time. It was taking between four days and two weeks to process and ship out an order, depending on mail delivery rates. Healthlite also found accounting discrepancies of $1.5 million annually between the sales force and headquarters.

Communication between sales managers and the sales representatives has been primarily through the mail or by telephone. For example, regional sales managers have to send representatives letters with announcements of promotional campaigns or pricing discounts. Sales representatives have to write up their monthly reports of sales calls and then mail this information to regional headquarters.

Healthlite is considering new information system solutions. First of all, the firm would like a system that expedites order processing. Management would also like to make better use of information systems to support sales and marketing activities and to take advantage of leading-edge information technology.

Sales and Marketing Information Systems: Background

Sales and marketing are vital to the operation of any business. Orders must be processed and related to production and inventory. Sales of products in existing markets must be monitored and new products must be developed for new markets. The firm must be able to respond to rapidly changing market demands, proliferation of new products and competing firms, shortened product life spans, changing consumer tastes, and new government regulations.

Firms need sales and marketing information for product planning, pricing decisions, devising advertising and other promotional campaigns, forecasting market potential for new and existing products, and determining channels of distribution. They must also monitor the efficiency and effectiveness of the distribution of their products and services.

The sales function of a typical business captures and processes customer orders and produces invoices for customers and data for inventory and production. A typical invoice is illustrated here.

```
┌─────────────────────────────────────────────────┐
│ Customer:                                          │
│ Highview Supermarket                               │
│ 223 Highland Boulevard                             │
│ Ossining, NY 10562                                 │
│ Customer Number 00395                              │
│                                                    │
│                        Order Number 598422         │
│                        Order Date: 03/07/96        │
│ QTY ITEM NO.  DESCRIPTION   UNIT PRICE  AMOUNT      │
│ 100 V3392     8 oz. Vanilla    $.44      $44.00     │
│ 50 S4456      8 oz. Strawberry $.44      $22.00     │
│ 65 L4492      8 oz. Lemon      $.44      $28.60     │
│ SHIPPING: $6.50                                    │
│ TOTAL INVOICE: $101.10                             │
└─────────────────────────────────────────────────┘
```

Data from order entry are also used by a firm's accounts receivable system and by the firm's inventory and production systems. The production planning system, for instance, builds its daily production plans based on the prior day's sales. The number and type of product sold will determine how many units to produce and when.

Sales managers need information to plan and monitor the performance of the sales force. Management also needs information on the performance of specific products, product lines, or brands. Price, revenue, cost, and growth information can be used for pricing decisions, for evaluating the performance of current products, and for predicting the performance of future products.

From basic sales and invoice data, a firm can produce a variety of reports with valuable information to guide sales and marketing work. For weekly, monthly, or annual time periods, information can be gathered on which outlets order the most, on the average order amount, on which products move slowest and fastest, on which sales-persons sell the most and least, on which geographic areas purchase the most of a given product, and on how current sales of a product compare to last year's product.

With a group of three or four of your classmates design a new system for Healthlite. Prepare a systems analysis and design report and present your results to the class. In your report you should do the following:

- Describe Healthlite's problems and their relationship to existing systems.
- List the principal goals and objectives of the system.
- Consider what pieces of information the new system or systems should contain, how this information should be organized and stored, and how it should be captured.
- Consider what new business procedures must be designed and how you will implement them without alienating major constituencies.
- Consider the human interface issues, if new software is envisioned.

Your systems design report should contain the following:

1. Management summary—relation to corporate strategy, benefits, and implementation schedule
2. Data flow diagram or system flowchart for the system
3. Sample data entry screen design
4. Description of the functions of the system
5. Report specifications
6. File design
7. Conversion procedures
8. Quality assurance measures

It is important to establish the scope of the system. It should be limited to order processing and related sales and marketing activities. You do not have to redesign Healthlite's manufacturing, accounts receivable, distribution, or inventory control systems for this exercise.

Case Study

RE-ENGINEERING PROJECT POLISHES CORNING ORDER PROCESSING FUNCTION

Can re-engineering save a company in trouble? That is precisely the problem Corning Asahi Video (CAV) faced in 1991 after four straight losing years and losses amounting to millions. CAV, with 1200 employees, is one of only two United States suppliers of television glass. The TV glass business is changing, with a growing emphasis upon larger tubes. Switching over to the production of larger tubes would require large capital investment, a step its parent is not ready to take at this time. CAV's main facilities are located in State College, Pennsylvania. Corning, Inc. is the parent company and the majority owner, with the rest of the company owned by Asahi. Fifty percent of CAV's business is with one company, Philips Display Components Co. In early 1991, Corning issued an ultimatum—restore the unit to profitability, and do it quickly!

CAV had many problems, but the one management chose to focus on first in its effort to return to profitability was order taking. In 1991 the existing system was 20 years old, paper and telephone based. Orders were taken by telephone and then entered into the antiquated system at corporate headquarters. Paper reports were split out for the State College facility and then faxed and confirmed by telephone. Processing an average order required 20 to 25 people to spend a total of 45 staff hours and 180 elapsed days before completion. Analysts found it involved performing about 250 separate tasks and cost about $2200. The whole computer system, including accounts payable and billing, was antiquated. The workflow included a manual inventory and many manual document hand-offs. The customer service department was also poorly organized. The customer service staff was small and was split between Corning's New York headquarters and CAV's Pennsylvania production facility. One customer service representative could be responsible for over $100 million in business and yet would be the only one who knew that customer and that customer's business. This left CAV quite vulnerable in the case of that person becoming ill or leaving the company.

Service of customers suffered heavily under this system. As a result of the split customer service department, customers could receive two different answers to the same question. Because the system was paper-based, customer inventory and order status queries could not be answered immediately. Instead they were told, "I'll get back to you as soon as I can." When the CAV representative did call back with

an answer, the customer often had better information than the customer service representative. Orders were regularly mixed up, wrong items shipped, too many trucks dispatched, some of them empty, goods were lost in the warehouse. Margaret Coffey, the CAV customer service manager said that "our customers at times feel like victims." An internal study found that all of these problems cost CAV over $2 million annually, mainly in overtime, telephone bills, accidental discounts, and extra trucking costs. Adding to the losses was a $1.8 million federal fine assessed against Corning, Asahi Glass America, and CAV for emitting illegal levels of arsenic into the air in 1989 at two manufacturing facilities.

The project to fix these problems began in June and July 1991, with CAV issuing the employees a challenge to turn it around. All 1200 employees attended three-day meetings during which they talked about the business and listened to customer complaints. That autumn, a twelve-person cross-functional team was established. Eight members were full-time, three were from information systems, including Walt Surdak, the IS director. The team was given a deadline of the end of 1992 to complete the whole project. They met off-site three days a week for a total of fifteen days to discuss improvements needed. The customer service members of the team worked extra long hours because they were not relieved of their regular duties while participating in the project. The team met with customers, discussed CAV and customer problems, and drew up plans for solving the problems. They virtually redesigned the order processing system, completing the task in late 1991.

One decision they made was to purchase software rather than to build it. Traditionally, CAV built most of its own systems because, according to Corning senior vice president for information systems, Harvey Shrednick, "in the past, we always said 'We're different, we need to grow our own.' " This time, however, they had no time to write their own application—to meet the end-of-1992 deadline, they had to begin

testing the new system by mid-summer. In addition, they estimated that the cost of writing their own system would be over $1 million.

The team also decided that those who designed the system should implement it. The team's proposal was endorsed by senior management in January 1992, and they established a steering committee to oversee the progress of the project. Coffey was appointed project leader, along with Scott Patterson, the IS business manager and the IS liaison to customer service. The team decided to use Innovation, Corning's own in-house methodology for handling new technology, as the framework for the project. The methodology organizes the work into five stages: Gain knowledge; determine feasibility; test practicality; prove profitability; and commercialize. One reason for selecting this approach is that it made communicating with upper management easier because they already understood it. The team also set as a goal to "Minimize risk and investment."

Several forces impacted their selection of the technology. Selection had to be one of the first steps, being completed in late winter or early spring of 1992. The system needed to be inexpensive—the company was trying to save money and return the company to profitability, and had no intention of financing a new technology project at any price. The team had to install it quickly. If it were to be up-and-running by year's end, they had to set a mid-summer deadline for testing to begin. Patterson also set as a key goal, the need to keep the technology from being a risk factor because "there were enough risks already." The team also wanted to be able to select a software package that would meet their needs while running on DEC VAX computers, the computer technology they were currently using in CAV.

In selecting a commercial software package, the team began by evaluating the package being used elsewhere in Corning, but they rejected it because it did not include certain key functions they felt CAV needed. Ultimately, they selected the only package they believed did meet their needs, DCS Logistics from Andersen Consulting. A DEC VAX version was available, although it was not being used anywhere on a VAX, making the VAX version unproved and therefore risky. They could not afford the loss of time if the package did not work because they could miss management's tight deadline. Shrednick was leery because he had been burnt before by two other software vendors who had unsuccessfully pioneered VAX platform packages with his firm. Ultimately he agreed to try it, however, when the DEC vice-president of distribution called and persuaded Shrednick that the package actually was stable. The early cost estimate was $119,000 to purchase the software plus an additional $400,000 for personnel and consulting expenses.

The next step was to test the practicality of the selected solution. The team set up an on-site, seven-week prototype system in April–May 1992, known as the "Conference Room Pilot." The pilot team was led by consultants from Arthur Andersen, the vendor. The pilot used actual customer data so that the CAV team could realistically evaluate the software to determine if it actually would do the job. The pilot was successful.

During the prove-the-profitability phase, July–October, 1992, the customer service function was redesigned and the affected organizations with it. The customer service function was consolidated at State College, and four jobs were eliminated—including Coffey's! Not surprisingly, problems materialized. The sales staff felt threatened because of the increased customer service role in the new workflow. Passive resistance emerged as department heads often were simply unavailable for meetings. The team addressed these problems squarely, according to Patterson, by sitting "down and helping them understand why we are dealing with this."

The project placed particularly heavy burdens on the customer service representatives who had to work on the project while maintaining the current customer service level (it was already too low to be allowed to drop further). Many had to work ten to twelve hours per day, six and often seven days per week. They had to participate in the tests, which meant learning the new system at the same time. One way the project kept the morale of the team high and kept the company supporting them was through consistent communications. Everyone in CAV received weekly E-mail and voice mail updates. More specialized periodic reports were sent to specific groups, such as team members. That interest was high became evident when the team opened its redesign meetings and found that they drew 50 to 60 people.

During November 1992, the team began to deploy the system. CAV actually converted over to the system immediately after New Year's Day. Last-minute bugs did appear, but the team had good support over the New Year's weekend. In January 1993, the deployment was completed and the project came in on schedule and within budget. Work did continue, however. In February, a new re-engineering consultancy group was established within the corporate IS group. That spring CAV began to enhance the order processing system, expanding its reporting capabilities, and creating a friendlier user interface. Enhancements are continuing.

What was the cost of the project? The research, feasibility, and testing phases each cost $30,000, all for internal personnel time. The prove-the-profitability phase cost $670,000, including $180,000 for internal personnel, $323,000 for external personnel, and $167,000 for hardware and software. Deployment cost $190,000, split evenly between internal and external personnel. The total cost was $950,000.

Was the project a success? Clearly in some ways it was. Currently, to process an average order still requires 20 to 25 people, but they spend a total of 5 staff hours and 90 elapsed days before completion. Separate tasks to be performed were reduced to 9 and cost about $500. (See Figure 13.16.) The company estimates it saves more than $1.6 million in errors and cost overruns, while annual personnel savings amount to $400,000. Customer service has been greatly improved. The new order system is linked to CAV's warehouse, inventory, and distribution systems so that now fast and accurate information is available (see Figure 13.17). CAV even plans to give its customers direct access to the system. Eventually customers will be able to enter orders, review status, release products and bill upon receipt. Don Babiez, the purchasing agent for Philips Display, says that as a customer "the redesign has freed me, the account managers and others to work on things that have more value. It has worked fairly well."

The project has become an important model for major re-engineering projects throughout CAV and also for Corning Glassware and Steuben Crystal (a Corning company). The project even won *Computerworld* magazine's Re-engineering Team of the Year Award. The project did contribute to turning around CAV's profit problems.

In 1994 CAV announced a reorganization, including some reduction in sales and other staff. Coffey now heads the new corporate re-engineering consultancy group. Kenneth Freeman, the chief executive officer of CAV who led the turnaround of that unit, has been named Corning vice president of human resources and administration, where he is championing re-engineering projects. Ruth Reisbeck, who was the CAV quality control coordinator, now is the quality and purchasing manager at Corning Engineering.

As of this writing, the parent company, Corning, is still not sure it wants to invest further in the business because the emphasis in the business has switched to larger television tubes. Management has not made the investment into the new equipment required to retool a new family of tubes. In fact, since the project ended, Corning sold more of its share of the company to Asahi, reducing its ownership to 51 percent.

Sources: Joseph Maglitta, "Glass Act," *Computerworld*, January 17, 1994; and Harvey R. Shrednick, "A Decade of Improvements," *Information Week*, January 30, 1995.

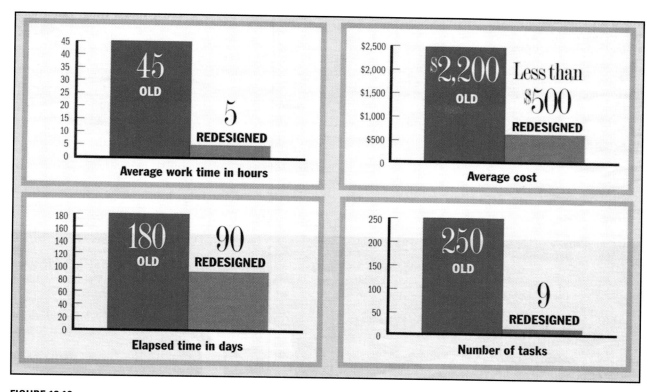

FIGURE 13.16
Corning's order fulfillment process before and after re-engineering. Corning drastically simplified its order process, significantly decreasing errors and the time and cost to place an order. *Source: Joseph Maglitta, "Glass Act,"* Computerworld, January 17, 1994.

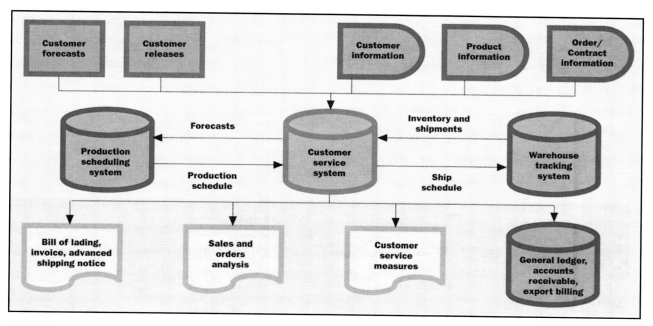

FIGURE 13.17
Corning's new order fulfillment system. Corning streamlined and simplified its order fulfillment system so that customer information is only entered once into a centralized database. *Source: Joseph Maglitta, "Glass Act,"* Computerworld *January 17, 1994.*

Case Study Questions

1. Define and describe the problems faced by Corning Asahi Video. How were these problems related to quality issues?

2. What management, organization, and technology factors contributed to those problems?

3. What was Corning Asahi's solution to these problems? What aspects of quality were addressed by the solution?

4. What were the key factors in the successful development and installation of the new order processing system?

5. What technology, organization, and management issues were raised by this project?

6. Would you judge the project as being successful? Why or why not?

References

Abdel-Hamid, Tarek K. "The Economics of Software Quality Assurance: A Simulation-Based Case Study." *MIS Quarterly* (September 1988).

Aiken, Peter, Alice Muntz, and Russ Richards. "DOD Legacy Systems: Reverse Engineering Data Requirements." *Communications of the ACM* 37, no. 5 (May 1994).

Alberts, David S. "The Economics of Software Quality Assurance." Washington DC: National Computer Conference, 1976 Proceedings.

Banker, Rajiv D., Srikant M. Datar, Chris F. Kemerer, and Dani Zweig. "Software Complexity and Maintenance Costs." *Communications of the ACM* 36, no. 11 (November 1993).

Banker, Rajiv D., Robert J. Kaufmann, and Rachna Kumar. "An Empirical Test of Object-Based Output Measurement Metrics in a Computer-Aided Software Engineering (CASE) Environment." *Journal of Management Information Systems* 8, no. 3 (Winter 1991–1992).

Banker, Rajiv D., and Chris F. Kemerer. "Performance Evaluation Metrics in Information Systems Development: A Principal-Agent Model." *Information Systems Research* 3, no. 4 (December 1992).

"B-Line Systems: From Chaos to Coordination." *Datamation* (September 15, 1994).

Blum, Bruce I. "A Taxonomy of Software Development Methods." *Communications of the ACM* 37, no. 11 (November 1994).

Boehm, Barry W. "Understanding and Controlling Software Costs." *IEEE Transactions on Software Engineering* 14, no. 10 (October 1988).

Booch, Grady. *Object Oriented Design with Applications.* Redwood City, CA: Benjamin Cummings (1991).

Bouldin, Barbara M. "What Are You Measuring? Why Are You Measuring It?" *Software Magazine* (August 1989).

Coad, Peter, with Edward Yourdon. *Object-Oriented Analysis.* Englewood Cliffs, NJ: Prentice Hall (1989).

Dekleva, Sasa M. "The Influence of Information Systems Development Approach on Maintenance." *MIS Quarterly* 16, no. 3 (September 1992).

DeMarco, Tom. *Structured Analysis and System Specification.* New York: Yourdon Press (1978).

Dijkstra, E. "Structured Programming" in *Classics in Software Engineering,* ed. Edward Nash Yourdon. New York: Yourdon Press (1979).

Flatten, Per O., Donald J. McCubbrey, P. Declan O'Riordan, and Keith Burgess. *Foundations of Business Systems,* 2nd ed. Fort Worth, TX: Dryden Press (1992).

Forte, Gene, and Ronald J. Norman. "Self-Assessment by the Software Engineering Community." *Communications of the ACM* 35, no. 4 (April 1992).

Freedman, David H. "Programming Without Tears." *High Technology* 6 no. 4 (April 1986).

Gane, Chris, and Trish Sarson. *Structured Systems Analysis: Tools and Techniques.* Englewood Cliffs, NJ: Prentice Hall (1979).

Henderson-Sellers, Brian, and Julian M. Edwards. "The Object-Oriented Systems Life Cycle." *Communications of the ACM* 33, no. 9 (September 1990).

International Data Corporation. "Object Technology: A Key Software Technology for the '90s." *Computerworld* (May 11, 1992).

Keyes, Jessica. "New Metrics Needed for New Generation." *Software Magazine* (May 1992).

King, Julia. "Quality Conscious," *Computerworld* (July 19, 1993).

"Komag Chooses MES for Production Control." *Datamation* (September 15, 1994).

Korson, Tim, and McGregor, John D. "Understanding Object Oriented: A Unifying Paradigm." *Communications of the ACM* 33, no. 9 (September 1990).

Krajewski, Lee J. and Larry P. Ritzman. *Operations Management,* 3 ed. Reading, MA: Addison-Wesley, 1993.

LaPlante, Alice. "For IS, Quality is 'Job None,' " *Computerworld* (January 6, 1992).

Lientz, Bennett P., and E. Burton Swanson. *Software Maintenance Management.* Reading, MA: Addison-Wesley (1980).

Littlewood, Bev, and Lorenzo Strigini. "The Risks of Software." *Scientific American* (November 1992).

Littlewood, Bev, and Lorenzo Strigini. "Validation of Ultra-high Dependability for Software-Based Systems." *Communications of the ACM* 36, no. 11 (November 1993).

McIntyre, Scott C., and Higgins, Lexis F. "Object-Oriented Analysis and Design: Methodology and Application." *Journal of Management Information Systems* 5, no. 1 (Summer 1988).

McWilliams, Brian. "Coming Back for More." *Computerworld* (Feburary 13, 1995).

Maletz, Mark C. "KBS Circles: A Technology Transfer Initiative that Leverages Xerox's Leadership through Quality Program." *MIS Quarterly* 14, no. 3 (September 1990).

Mandell, Mel. "Statistical Software Rings in Quality." *Computerworld* (January 6, 1992).

Martin, James, and Carma McClure. *Structured Techniques: The Basis of CASE.* Englewood Cliffs, NJ: Prentice Hall (1988).

Mazzucchelli, Louis. "Structured Analysis Can Streamline Software Design." *Computerworld* (December 9, 1985).

Moran, Robert. "The Case against CASE." *InformationWEEK* (February 17, 1992).

Nerson, Jean-Marc. "Applying Object-Oriented Analysis and Design." *Communications of the ACM* 35, no. 9 (September 1992).

Norman, Ronald J., and Jay F. Nunamaker, Jr. "CASE Productivity Perceptions of Software Engineering Professionals." *Communications of the ACM* 32, no. 9 (September 1989).

Palley, Michael A. and Sue Conger. "Health Care Information Systems and Formula-Based Reimbursement: An Empirical Study of Diagnosis Related Groups, Patient Account Systems, and Hospital Compliance Costs." *Health Care Management Review* 20, no. 2 (1995).

Putnam, L. H., and A. Fitzsimmons. "Estimating Software Costs." *Datamation* (September 1979, October 1979, and November 1979).

Radding, Alan. "Quality is Job No. 1." *Datamation* (October 1, 1992).

Rettig, Marc. "Software Teams." *Communications of the ACM* 33, no. 10 (October 1990).

Rigdon, Joan E. "Frequent Glitches in New Software Bug Users." *The Wall Street Journal* (January 18, 1995).

Swanson, Kent, Dave McComb, Jill Smith, and Don McCubbrey. "The Application Software Factory: Applying Total Quality Techniques to Systems Development." *MIS Quarterly*, 15, no. 4 (December 1991).

Vessey, Iris, and Sue A. Conger. "Requirements Specification: Learning Object, Process, and Data Methodologies." *Communications of the ACM* 37, no. 5 (May 1994).

Vessey, Iris, Sirkka I. Jarvenpaa, and Noam Tractinsky. "Evaluation of Vendor Products: CASE Tools as Methodology Companions." *Communications of the ACM* 35, no. 4 (April 1992).

Yourdon, Edward, and L. L. Constantine. *Structured Design.* New York: Yourdon Press (1978).

Zultner, Richard E. "TQM for Technical Teams." *Communications of the ACM* 36, no. 10 (October 1993).

Chapter 14

System Success and Failure: Implementation

California DMV's Drive to Nowhere

Around 1965, when the Beach Boys were the rage, the on-line system for California's Department of Motor Vehicles was hot technology. Twenty-five years later, the DMV, which tracks 50 million driver's licenses and vehicle registrations and collects $5.2 billion in taxes annually, was still using this system. Although it could run on upgraded hardware (a powerful IBM ES/9000 mainframe) and handle 1 million transactions per day, the software couldn't change with the times. It was still based on assembly language, which was extremely difficult to maintain. Adding a social security number to the driver's license file and vehicle registration file took 18 person-years of programming time. Retrieval of data in the system's old-style flat files was quick, but the system could not perform "what-if" searches. Regional DMV offices used decade-old IBM Series/1 minicomputers and dumb terminals to communicate with the mainframe.

In 1987, the DMV embarked on an ambitious new project to convert to a NonStop Cyclone SQL relational database running on 24 Tandem Cyclone computers. The following year, DMV hired the consulting firm of Ernst & Young to develop applications in COBOL and fourth-generation languages for the new technology platform. The project stalled. Ernst & Young withdrew in 1990 and was replaced by a team of DMV staffers, who tried to develop applications using Texas Instruments' Information Engineering Facility (IEF) CASE tools. But the team could not surmount the steep learning curve for the new tools.

Seven years and $44 million later, the DMV finally pulled the funding plug on the project. Not a single application had been written. DMV director Frank Zolin had learned that it would take an additional $100 million and four years to make the system work. After an internal investigation, a DMV spokesman said the agency had adopted untested relational database technology that could not handle the agency's daily transaction demand from more than 30,000 users. Tandem Computers Inc. said it had fulfilled its responsibility in the project and blamed the failure on poor project management after the withdrawal of Ernst & Young. Ernst & Young said it had only been involved with the project for less than a year. With no replacement in sight, the DMV is making do with its strained outdated technology and $44 million of updated but unusable data.

According to Craig Cornett, director of state administration for the California state legislative analyst's office, incompatible statewide computer systems, poor access to departmental databases, and a lack of standards plagued other state projects. The DMV project wasn't the only megaproject that was poorly managed. ∎

Sources: Jean S. Bozman, "DMV Disaster," *Computerworld*, May 9, 1994, and "California IS Projects Mismanaged," *Computerworld*, May 23, 1994; and Chuck Appleby, "Agency's Drive to Nowhere," *InformationWEEK*, June 13, 1994.

The California DMV is hardly alone. In nearly every organization, information systems projects take much more time and money to implement than originally anticipated, or the completed system does not work properly. When this occurs, companies may not realize any benefits from their information system investment and the system may not be able to solve the problem for which it was intended. Because so many information systems are trouble-ridden, designers, builders, and users of information systems should

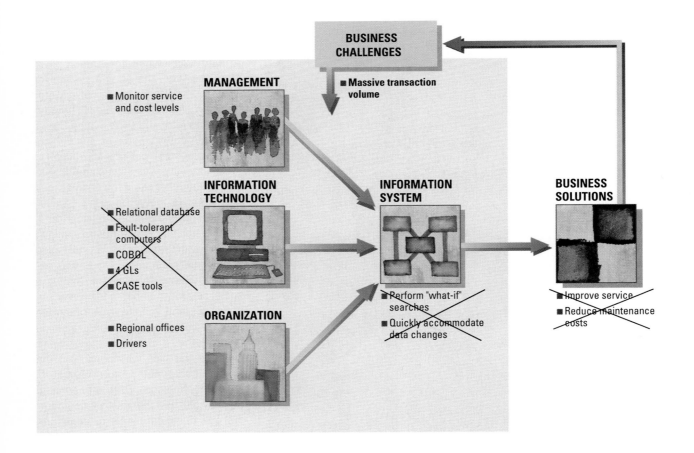

understand how and why they succeed or fail.

Problems with information system technology are only one reason why information systems succeed or fail. Managerial and organizational factors also play a powerful role in system outcome because implementing an information system is a process of organizational change. This chapter explores the managerial, organizational, and technological factors responsible for information system success and failure and examines the process of implementation.

After completing this chapter, you will be able to:

Learning Objectives

1. Identify major problem areas in information systems.

2. Determine whether a system is successful.

3. Describe the principal causes of information system failure.

4. Describe the relationship between the implementation process and system outcome.

5. Describe appropriate strategies to manage the implementation process.

14.1 INFORMATION SYSTEM FAILURE

system failure An information system that either does not perform as expected, is not operational at a specified time, or cannot be used in the way it was intended.

As many as 75 percent of all large systems may be considered to be operating failures. Although these systems are in production, they take so much extra time and money to implement or are so functionally deficient that businesses can't reap the expected benefits. Studies of federal government projects have found that a large number were poorly designed, full of inaccurate or incomplete data, delivered but not used, delivered late and over budget, reworked, or abandoned (Anthes, 1992).

Many information **system "failures"** are not necessarily falling apart, but either they clearly are not used in the way they were intended, or they are not used at all. Users have to develop parallel manual procedures to make these systems work properly. For example, the employee benefits department of a multi-unit manufacturing concern continues to maintain all of the benefits data for the company's 20,000 employees manually, despite the presence of an automated, on-line system for pension and life insurance benefits. Users complain that the data in the system are unreliable because they do not capture the prior benefits plan data for employees from acquisitions and because payroll earnings figures are out of date. All pension calculations, pre-retirement estimates, and benefits analysis must be handled manually.

In some systems, nearly all of the reports put out for management are never read. They are considered worthless and full of figures of no consequence for decision making or analysis (Lucas, 1981). For instance, managers in a prominent commercial bank with branches throughout the United States and Europe found its batch loan account system virtually useless. Pages of reports were filled with zeros, making it practically impossible to assess the status of a client's loan. The amount of the loan, the outstanding balance, and the repayment schedule had to be tracked manually. The bank was also highly dissatisfied with its on-line client reporting system. Although the bank maintained files on all areas for client accounts (loans, savings, Individual Retirement Accounts, checking), only checking and savings account data were available on-line. Therefore, managers and analysts could not obtain complete client profiles when they needed them.

Other automated systems go untouched because they are either too difficult to use or because their data cannot be trusted. Users continue to maintain their records manually. For instance, a nationally known executive recruiting firm found that essential reports on search activity are routinely three months out of date. The firm has to develop statistics manually on the number of executive searches initiated in a given month. Recruiters have no way of tracking and coordinating searches among the company's branch offices in New York, Chicago, Houston, and Los Angeles.

Still other systems flounder because of processing delays, excessive operational costs, or chronic production problems. For instance, the batch accounts receivable system of a medium-sized consumer products manufacturer was constantly breaking down. Production runs were aborting several times a month, and major month-end runs were close to three weeks behind schedule. Because of excessive reruns, schedule delays, and time devoted to fixing antiquated programs, the information systems staff had no time to work out long-term solutions or convert to an on-line system.

In all of these cases, the information systems in question must be judged failures. Why do system failures occur?

INFORMATION SYSTEM PROBLEM AREAS

The problems causing information system failure fall into multiple categories, as illustrated by Figure 14.1. The major problem areas are design, data, cost, and operations. These problems can be attributed not only to technical features of information systems but to nontechnical sources as well. In fact, most of these problems stem from organizational factors.

Design

The actual design of the system fails to capture essential business requirements or improve organizational performance. Information may not be provided quickly enough to be helpful; it may be in a format that is impossible to digest and use; or it may represent the wrong pieces of data.

The way in which nontechnical business users must interact with the system may be excessively complicated and discouraging. A system may be designed with a poor **user interface**. The user interface is the part of the system that end users interact with. For example, an input form or an on-line screen may be so poorly arranged that no one wants to submit data. The procedures to request on-line information retrieval may be so unintelligible that users are too frustrated to make requests. A graphical user interface that is supposed to be intuitively easy to learn may discourage use because display screens are cluttered and poorly arranged or because users don't understand the meaning and function of the icons. For example, most users of

user interface The part of the information system through which the end user interacts with the system; type of hardware and the series of on-screen commands and responses required for a user to work with the system.

FIGURE 14.1
Information system problem areas. Problems with an information system's design, data, cost, or operations can be evidence of a system failure.

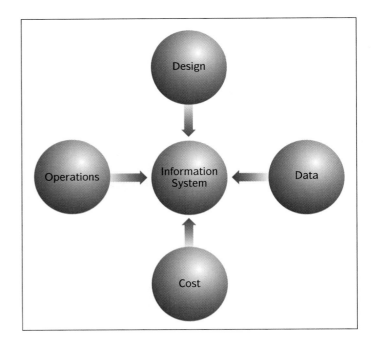

A well designed GUI, such as the top illustration, can make a system easy to use, whereas one that is cluttered, over featured, and poorly designed will add to users' frustrations. *Adapted from William Brandel and Lynda Radosovich, "GUIs Still a Sticky Issue,"* Computerworld, *August 1. 1994. Copyright 1994 by CW Publishing, Inc. Framingham, MA 01701. Reprinted from Computerworld.*

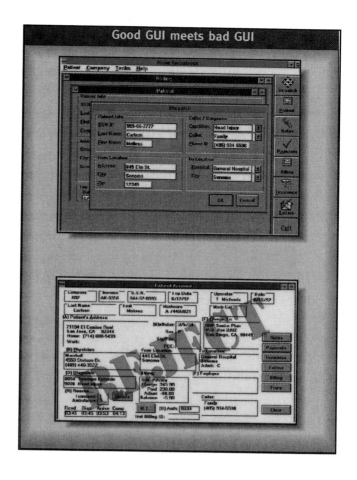

Good GUI meets bad GUI

Microsoft Publisher did not understand an icon with arrows pointing in all four directions that was meant to designate that they could move boxes in any direction around the screen. The problem was solved when programmers embedded a moving truck with the word *move* on it within the four arrows (Bulkeley, 1992). A high percentage of business software developed or purchased by companies goes unused or underused because it lacks an appropriate user interface.

An information system will be judged a failure if its design is not compatible with the structure, culture, and goals of the organization as a whole. As pointed out in Chapter 3, management and organization theorists have viewed information system technology as closely interrelated with all of the other components of organizations—tasks, structure, people, and culture. Since all of these components are interdependent, a change in one will affect all of the others. Therefore, the organization's tasks, participants, structure, and culture are bound to be affected when an information system is changed. Designing a system redesigns the organization.

Historically, information system design has been preoccupied with technical issues at the expense of organizational concerns. The result has often been information systems that are technically excellent but incompatible with their organization's structure, culture, and goals. Without a close organizational fit, such systems have created tensions, instability, and conflict.

Data

The data in the system have a high level of inaccuracy or inconsistency. The information in certain fields may be erroneous or ambiguous; or they may not be broken out properly for business purposes. Information required for a specific business function may be inaccessible because the data are incomplete.

Cost

Some systems operate quite smoothly, but their cost to implement and run on a production basis is way over budget. Other systems, such as the California Department of Motor Vehicles project described in the chapter-opening vignette, may be too costly to complete. In both cases, the excessive expenditures cannot be justified by the demonstrated business value of the information they provide.

Operations

The system does not run well. Information is not provided in a timely and efficient manner because the computer operations that handle information processing break down. Jobs that abort too often lead to excessive reruns and delayed or missed schedules for delivery of information. An on-line system may be operationally inadequate because the response time is too long.

MEASURING SYSTEM SUCCESS

How can we tell whether or not a system is successful? This is not always an easy question to answer. Not everyone may agree about the value or effectiveness of a particular information system. Individuals with different decision-making styles or ways of approaching a problem may have totally different opinions about the same system. A system valued highly by an analytical, quantitatively oriented user may be totally dismissed by an intuitive thinker who is more concerned with feelings and overall impressions. Likewise, a junior sales manager with a new MBA in marketing may be more appreciative of information system reports on the demographic characteristics of his territory than a veteran representative who has worked the same territory for 15 years and knows it by heart. The perception and use of information systems can be heavily conditioned by personal and situational variables (Lucas, 1981). To further complicate the picture, what users say they like or want in a new information system may not necessarily produce any meaningful improvements in organizational performance (Markus and Keil, 1994).

Nevertheless, MIS researchers have looked for a formal set of measures for rating systems. Various criteria have been developed, but the following measures of system success, illustrated in Figure 14.2, are considered the most important.

1. *High levels of system use,* as measured by polling users, employing questionnaires, or monitoring parameters such as the volume of on-line transactions.

2. *User satisfaction with the system,* as measured by questionnaires or interviews. This might include users' opinions on the accuracy, timeliness, and relevance of information; on the quality of service; and perhaps on the schedule of operations. Especially critical are managers' attitudes on how well their information needs were satisfied (Ives et al., 1983; Wescott, 1985) and users' opinions about how well the system enhanced their job performance (Davis, 1989).

FIGURE 14.2
Measures of information system success. MIS researchers have different criteria for measuring the success of an information system. They consider the five measures in the figure to be the most important.

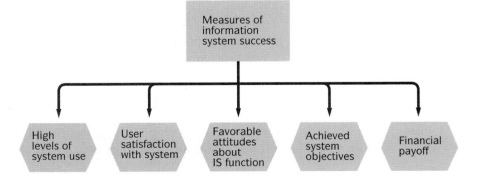

CHAPTER **1 4**   System Success and Failure: Implementation

3. *Favorable attitudes* of users about information systems and the information systems staff.

4. *Achieved objectives,* the extent to which the system meets its specified goals, as reflected by improved organizational performance and decision making resulting from use of the system.

5. *Financial payoff* to the organization, either by reducing costs or by increasing sales or profits.

The fifth measure is considered to be of limited value even though cost/benefit analysis may have figured heavily in the decision to build a particular system. The benefits of an information system may not be totally quantifiable. Moreover, tangible benefits cannot be easily demonstrated for the more advanced decision-support system applications. And even though cost/benefit methodology has been rigorously pursued, the history of many systems development projects has shown that realistic estimates have always been difficult to formulate. MIS researchers have preferred to concentrate instead on the human and organizational measures of system success such as information quality, system quality, and the impact of systems on organizational performance (Lucas, 1981; DeLone and McLean, 1992).

14.2 CAUSES OF INFORMATION SYSTEM SUCCESS AND FAILURE

As described in Chapter 4, systems are developed in the first place because of powerful external environmental forces and equally powerful internal or institutional forces. Many systems fail because of the opposition of either the environment or the internal setting.

As many MIS researchers have pointed out, the introduction or alteration of an information system has a powerful behavioral and organizational impact. It transforms the way various individuals and groups perform and interact. Changes in the way information is defined, accessed, and used to manage the resources of the organization often lead to new distributions of authority and power (Lucas, 1975). This internal organizational change breeds resistance and opposition and can lead to the demise of an otherwise good system. An important characteristic of most information systems is that individuals are asked or required to change their behavior in order to make the system function.

But there are other reasons why a system may fail. Several studies have found that in organizations with similar environments and institutional features, the same innovation will be successful in some organizations but fail in others. Why? One explanation focuses on different patterns of implementation.

THE CONCEPT OF IMPLEMENTATION

implementation All of the organizational activities working toward the adoption, management, and routinization of an innovation.

Implementation refers to all of the organizational activities working toward the adoption, management, and routinization of an innovation. Figure 14.3 illustrates the major stages of implementation described in research literature and the major approaches to the subject (see also Tornatsky et al., 1983).

Some of the implementation research focuses on actors and roles. The belief is that organizations should select actors with appropriate social characteristics and systematically develop organizational roles, such as "product champions," in order to innovate successfully (see Figure 14.4). Generally, this literature focuses on early adoption and management of innovations.

A second school of thought in the implementation literature focuses on strategies of innovation. The two extremes are top-down innovation and grass-roots innovation. There are many examples of organizations in which the absence of senior management support for innovation dooms the project from the start. At the same

FIGURE 14.3
Approaches and implementation stages in the implementation literature. The Xs indicate the stages of implementation on which the different approaches tend to focus. For instance, literature that uses an actor/role approach to implementation tends to focus on the early stages of adoption and management.

APPROACHES	IMPLEMENTATION STAGES		
	Adoption	Management	Routinization
Actors' roles	XXXX	XXXX	
Strategy		XXXX	
Organizational factors		XXXX	XXXX

FIGURE 14.4
Actors in the innovation process. During implementation, the roles of actors include being product champions, bureaucratic entrepreneurs, and gatekeepers. In order to be successful in their roles as innovators and sponsors of change, actors should have certain demographic characteristics including social status in the organization, higher education, and social, technical, and organizational sophistication.

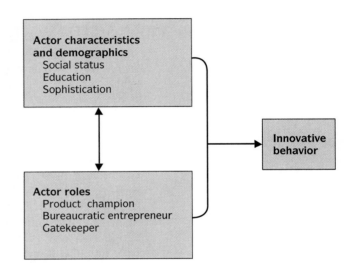

time, without strong grass-roots, end-user participation, information system projects can also fail.

A third approach to implementation focuses on general organizational change factors as being decisive to the long-term routinization of innovations. Table 14.1 illustrates some of the key organizational actions required for long-term, successful implementation, and indicators of success (Yin, 1981).

change agent In the context of implementation, the individual acting as the catalyst during the change process to ensure successful organizational adaptation to a new system or innovation.

In the context of implementation, the systems analyst is a **change agent**. The analyst not only develops technical solutions but also redefines the configurations, interactions, job activities, and power relationships of various organizational groups. The analyst is the catalyst for the entire change process and is responsible for ensuring that the changes created by a new system are accepted by all parties involved. The change agent communicates with users, mediates between competing interest groups, and ensures that the organizational adjustment to such changes is complete.

One model of the implementation process is the Kolb/Frohman model of organizational change. This model divides the process of organizational change into a seven-stage relationship between an organizational *consultant* and his or her *client*. (The consultant corresponds to the information system designer and the client to the user.) The success of the change effort is determined by how well the consultant and client deal with the key issues at each stage (Kolb and Frohman, 1970). Other mod-

| **Table 14.1** | **Actions and Indicators for Successful System Implementation** |

Support by local funds

New organizational arrangements

Stable supply and maintenance

New personnel classifications

Changes in organizational authority

Internalization of the training program

Continual updating of the system

Promotion of key personnel

Survival of the system after turnover of its originators

Attainment of widespread use

Source: Yin (1981).

els of implementation describe the relationship as one between designers, clients, and decision makers, who are responsible for managing the implementation effort to bridge the gap between design and utilization (Swanson, 1988).

Studies of the implementation process have examined the relationship between information system designers and users at different stages of systems development. Studies have focused on issues such as the following:

- Conflicts between the technical or machine orientation of information systems specialists and the organizational or business orientation of users
- The impact of information systems on organizational structures, work groups, and behavior
- The planning and management of systems development activities
- The degree of user participation in the design and development process

CAUSES OF IMPLEMENTATION SUCCESS AND FAILURE

Implementation research to date has found no single explanation for system success or failure. Nor does it suggest a single formula for system success. However, it has found that implementation outcome can be largely determined by the following factors:

- The role of users in the implementation process
- The degree of management support for the implementation effort
- The level of complexity and risk of the implementation project
- The quality of management of the implementation process

These are largely behavioral and organizational issues and are illustrated in Figure 14.5.

User Involvement and Influence

User involvement in the design and operation of information systems has several positive results. First, if users are heavily involved in systems design, they have more opportunities to mold the system according to their priorities and business requirements and more opportunities to control the outcome. Second, they are more likely to react positively to the system because they have been active participants in the change process itself (Lucas, 1974).

Incorporating the user's knowledge and expertise leads to better solutions. However users often take a very narrow and limited view of the problem to be solved and may overlook important opportunities for improving business processes

FIGURE 14.5
Factors in information system success or failure. The implementation outcome can be largely determined by the role of users; the degree of management support; the level of risk and complexity in the implementation project; and the quality of management of the implementation process. Evidence of success or failure can be found in the areas of design, cost, operations, or data of the information system.

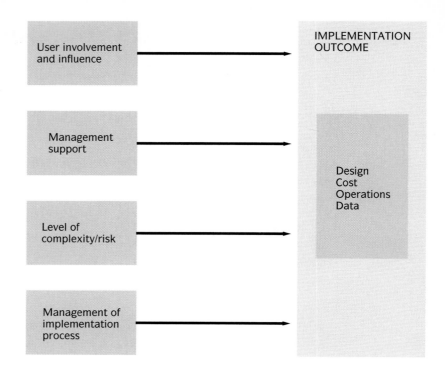

or innovative ways to apply information technology. The skills and vision of professional system designers are still required much in the same way that the services of an architect are required when building a new house. The outcome would most likely be inferior if people tried to design their houses entirely on their own (Markus and Keil, 1994).

The User–Designer Communications Gap   The relationship between consultant and client has traditionally been a problem area for information system implementation efforts. Users and information systems specialists tend to have different backgrounds, interests, and priorities. This is referred to as the **user–designer communications gap**. These differences lead to divergent organizational loyalties, approaches to problem solving, and vocabularies. Information systems specialists, for example, often have a highly technical or machine orientation to problem solving. They look for elegant and sophisticated technical solutions in which hardware and software efficiency is optimized at the expense of ease of use or organizational effectiveness. Users, on the other hand, prefer systems that are oriented to solving business problems or facilitating organizational tasks. Often the orientations of both groups are so at odds that they appear to speak in different tongues. These differences are illustrated in Table 14.2, which depicts the typical concerns of end users and technical specialists (information system designers) regarding the development of a new information system. Communication problems between end users and designers are a major reason why user requirements are not properly incorporated into information systems and why users are driven out of the implementation process.

Systems development projects run a very high risk of failure when there is a pronounced gap between users and technicians and when these groups continue to pursue different goals. Under such conditions, users are often driven out of the implementation process. Participation in the implementation effort is extremely time-consuming and takes them away from their daily activities and responsibilities. Since they cannot comprehend what the technicians are saying, they conclude that the entire project is best left in the hands of the information specialists alone. With so many implementation efforts guided by purely technical considerations, it is no wonder that many systems fail to serve organizational needs.

user–designer communications gap The difference in backgrounds, interests, and priorities that impede communication and problem solving among end users and information systems specialists.

Table 14.2	The User–Designer Communications Gap	
User Concerns	**Designer Concerns**
Will the system deliver the information I need for my work?	How much disk storage space will the master file consume?
How quickly can I access the data?	How many lines of program code will it take to perform this function?
How easily can I retrieve the data?	How can we cut down on CPU time when we run the system?
How much clerical support will I need to enter data into the system?	What is the most efficient way of storing this piece of data?
How will the operation of the system fit into my daily business schedule?	What database management system should we use?

Management Support

If an information systems project has the backing and approval of management at various levels, it is more likely to be perceived positively by both users and the technical information services staff. Both groups will feel that their participation in the development process will receive higher-level attention and priority. They will be recognized and rewarded for the time and effort they devote to implementation. Management backing also ensures that a systems project will receive sufficient funding and resources to be successful. Furthermore, all of the changes in work habits and procedures and any organizational realignments associated with a new system depend on management backing to be enforced effectively. If a manager considers a new system to be a priority, the system will more likely be treated that way by his or her subordinates (Doll, 1985; Ein-Dor and Segev, 1978).

Level of Complexity and Risk

Systems differ dramatically in their size, scope, level of complexity, and organizational and technical components. Some systems development projects, such as the CONFIRM project described in the Window on Technology, are more likely to fail because they carry a much higher level of risk than others.

Researchers have identified three key dimensions that influence the level of project risk (McFarlan, 1981).

Project Size.   The larger the project—as indicated by the dollars spent, the size of the implementation staff, the time allocated to implementation, and the number of organizational units affected—the greater the risk. Therefore, a $5 million project lasting for four years and affecting five departments in 20 operating units and 120 users will be much riskier than a $30,000 project for two users that can be completed in two months. Another risk factor is the company's experience with projects of given sizes. If a company is accustomed to implementing large, costly systems, the risk of implementing the $5 million project will be lowered. The risk may even be lower than that of another concern attempting a $200,000 project when the firm's average project cost has been around $50,000.

Project Structure.   Some projects are more highly structured than others. Their requirements are clear and straightforward, so that the outputs and processes can be easily defined. Users know exactly what they want and what the system should do; there is almost no possibility of their changing their minds. Such projects run a much lower risk than those whose requirements are relatively undefined, fluid, and constantly changing; where outputs cannot be easily fixed because they are subject to users' changing ideas; or because users cannot agree on what they want.

THE COLLAPSE OF CONFIRM: WHAT WENT WRONG?

In March 1988, the Hilton Hotels Corporation, Marriott Corporation, and Budget Rent-A-Car Corporation contracted to a large-scale information systems project with AMR Information Services, Inc., a subsidiary of American Airlines Corporation. The new information system, called CONFIRM, was to be the first system to fully integrate hotel, rental car, and airline reservations. By enabling consumers to make airlines, hotel, and car reservations through a single computerized system, CONFIRM would be superior to any existing reservation system in the travel industry. AMR had built the highly successful SABRE airline reservation system that provided strategic benefits for American Airlines. Hilton, Marriott, and Budget hoped that AMR's expertise would create a strategic reservation system for them.

CONFIRM was supposed to be completed in June 1992 at a cost of $125 million. Five hundred technical personnel worked on the project. But after more than three years of work, it was delayed another 18 months. The International Reservations and Information Consortium (Intrico) overseeing the project discovered major problems when the system was tested on site by the Hilton Hotels Corporation. Hilton users found that the system's user interface, mainframe transaction processing, and mainframe database did not adequately communicate with one another.

CONFIRM runs on two IBM 3090 mainframes. One houses the central reservations system, which runs under Transaction Processing Facility (a special operating system environment for processing heavy volumes of

transactions). The other mainframe houses a DB2 relational database in a MVS (an IBM mainframe operating system) environment. The database contains decision-support information such as customer histories and pricing data. The system requires application-to-application bridging between the two CPUs for some 60 applications. When processing the internal transactions, the operating systems and application software on both computers must be closely coordinated.

Intrico used Information Engineering Facility (IEF), Texas Instrument's CASE product to automatically generate the software code that ran on the MVS operating system. However, IEF could not generate the right code to make the software that allows the two machines to communicate with the outside world work properly. This software front end, called Transaction Management Function, served as a gateway to the various airline, hotel, and rental car airport reservation systems and would direct incoming data from each center to the appropriate mainframe. The software running on the mainframe using Transaction Processing Facility was written in the C programming language.

When it came time to connect the two separately developed system modules, Intrico found that they did not communicate very well. The program sending information from one processor could not coordinate with the program receiving information in the other processor. In the event of a system crash, CONFIRM's DB2 database could be recovered only in pieces, not in its entirety. The problems were not insurmountable, but they would require another two years to fix. Intrico disbanded in July 1992 after spending three and one-half years and $125 million on the faltering project.

In September 1992, AMR sued Marriott, Hilton, and Budget, alleging they caused CONFIRM's failure by withholding funds, making poor

To Think About: Evaluate the level of complexity and risk in this project. What management, organization, and technology issues had to be addressed by the CONFIRM system? What problems did the project encounter? Why do you think the project had these problems? How might they have been avoided? Were ethical considerations involved?

staffing assignments, and withdrawing prematurely. The three partners in turn countersued AMR. Budget's suit cited AMR for mismanagement, incompetence, and poor choice of development tools and methodologies, noting that AMR used a large group of outsiders instead of its seasoned SABRE staff to staff the project. The lawsuits cited letters written by Max Hopper, AMR's senior vice president of information systems, to Intrico partners and AMR employees stating that some individuals responsible for managing CONFIRM were inept and that some members of the CONFIRM management team "did not disclose the true status of the project in a timely manner." AMR reached out-of-court settlements with all of its partners for undisclosed amounts by January 1994.

Sources: Effy Oz, "When Professional Standards Are Lax: The CONFIRM Failure and Its Lessons," *Communications of the ACM* 37, no. 10 (October 1994); Mark Halper, "AMR Back in Hot Seat," *Computerworld*, April 5, 1993; and " John P. McPartlin, "The Collapse of CONFIRM," *InformationWEEK*, October 19, 1992.

Experience With Technology. The project risk will rise if the project team and the information system staff lack the required technical expertise. If the team is unfamiliar with the hardware, system software, application software, or database management system proposed for the project, it is highly likely that one or all of the following will occur:

- Unanticipated time slippage because of the need to master new skills
- A variety of technical problems if tools have not been thoroughly mastered
- Excessive expenditures and extra time because of inexperience with the undocumented idiosyncrasies of each new piece of hardware or software

These dimensions of project risk will be present in different combinations for each implementation effort. Table 14.3 shows that eight different combinations are possible, each with a different degree of risk. The higher the level of risk, the more likely it is that the implementation effort will fail.

Management of the Implementation Process

The development of a new system must be carefully managed and orchestrated. Each project involves research and development. Requirements are hard to define at the level of detail for automation. The same piece of information may be interpreted and defined differently by different individuals. Multiple users have different sets of requirements and needs. Costs, benefits, and project schedules must be assessed. The final design may not be easy to visualize. Since complex information systems involve so many interest groups, actors, and details, it is sometimes uncertain whether the initial plans for a system are truly feasible.

Often basic elements of success are forgotten. Training to ensure that end users are comfortable with the new system and fully understand its potential uses is often sacrificed or forgotten in systems development projects. In part this is because the budget is strained toward the end of a project, and at the very point of startup there are insufficient funds for training (Bikson et al., 1985).

The conflicts and uncertainties inherent in any implementation effort will be magnified when an implementation project is poorly managed and organized. As illustrated in Figure 14.6, a systems development project without proper management will most likely suffer these consequences:

- Cost overruns that vastly exceed budgets
- Time slippage that is much greater than expected
- Technical shortfalls resulting in performance that is significantly below the estimated level
- Failure to obtain anticipated benefits

Table 14.3   **Dimensions of Project Risk**

Project Structure	Project Technology Level	Project Size	Degree of Risk
High	Low	Large	Low
High	Low	Small	Very low
High	High	Large	Medium
High	High	Small	Medium-low
Low	Low	Large	Low
Low	Low	Small	Very low
Low	High	Large	Very high
Low	High	Small	High

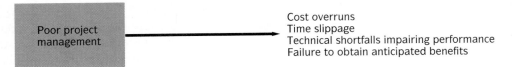

Poor project management → Cost overruns
Time slippage
Technical shortfalls impairing performance
Failure to obtain anticipated benefits

FIGURE 14.6
Consequences of poor project management. Without proper management, a systems development project will take longer to complete and most often will exceed the budgeted cost. The resulting information system will most likely be technically inferior and may not be able to demonstrate any benefits to the organization.

How badly are projects managed? On average, private sector projects are underestimated by one half in terms of budget and time required to deliver the complete system promised in the system plan. A very large number of projects are delivered with missing functionality (promised for delivery in later versions). Government projects suffer about the same failure level, perhaps worse (Laudon, 1989; Helms and Weiss, 1986).

Why are projects managed so poorly and what can be done about it? Here we discuss some possibilities.

Ignorance and Optimism. The techniques for estimating the length of time required to analyze and design systems are poorly developed. There are no standards; there is little sharing of data within and across organizations; and most applications are "first time" (i.e., there is no prior experience in the application area). Academics generally do not study large-scale commercial systems but instead focus on small-scale, easily taught or learned software projects. The larger the scale of systems, the greater the role of ignorance and optimism. Very large-scale systems (VLSS)—sometimes called Grand Design systems—suffer extraordinary rates of failure (Laudon, 1989; United States General Services Administration, 1988). The net result of all these factors is that estimates tend to be optimistic, "best case," and wrong. It is assumed that all will go well when in fact it rarely does.

The Mythical Man-Month. The traditional unit of measurement used by systems designers to project costs is the **man-month**. Projects are estimated in terms of how many man-months will be required. However, while costs may vary as a product of people and months, the progress of the project does not, as pointed out by Frederick P. Brooks (Brooks, 1974). As it turns out, people and months are not interchangeable in the short run on systems projects. (They may be interchangeable in the long run, but we live in the short run.) In other words, adding more workers to projects does not necessarily reduce the time needed to complete a systems project.

man-month The traditional unit of measurement used by systems designers to estimate the length of time to complete a project. Refers to the amount of work a person can be expected to complete in a month.

Unlike cotton picking—where tasks can be rigidly partitioned, communication between participants is not required, and training is unnecessary—systems analysis and design involves *tasks that are sequentially linked, cannot be performed in isolation, and require extensive communications and training.* Software development is inherently a group effort, and hence communication costs rise exponentially as the number of participants increases. Moreover, when personnel turnover approaches 20 to 30 percent, many of the participants in software projects require a great deal of learning and communication.

Given these characteristics, adding labor to projects can often slow down delivery, as the communication, learning, and coordination costs rise very fast and detract from the output of participants. For comparison, imagine what would happen if five amateur spectators were added to one team in a championship professional basketball game. Chances are quite good that the team composed of five professional basketball players would do much better in the short run than the team with five professionals and five amateurs.

Falling Behind: Bad News Travels Slowly Upward. Slippage in projects, failure, and doubts are often not reported to senior management until it is too late. To some extent, this is characteristic of projects in all fields. The CONFIRM project described in the Window on Technology is a classic example. Members of the CONFIRM project management team did not immediately come forward with accurate information when the project started encountering problems. Clients continued to invest in a project that was faltering because they were not informed of its problems with database, decision-support, and integration technologies (Oz, 1994).

Another example of this problem is the crash of the space shuttle *Challenger* in January 1986. The information that O-ring seals on the space shuttle might not perform well in the cold January weather and that engineers strongly objected to launching the shuttle in cold weather did not reach the top National Aeronautics and Space Administration (NASA) management team, which ultimately decided to launch. The reasons, while not entirely clear, in part involve the well-understood principle that bearers of bad news are often not appreciated and that senior management wants schedules to be met.

Organizational hierarchy has a pathological and deadly side: Senior management is often kept in the dark (see Chapters 3 and 4). For systems projects, this seems to be especially true. Systems workers know that management has promised a delivery date to important user groups, that millions of dollars have been spent, and that careers depend on timely delivery of the whole system. As the project falls behind, one day at a time, no one wants to bother senior management with minor slippage details. Eventually, days add up to months and then to years. By then it is too late to save the project, no matter how many people are added to the team.

THE CHALLENGE OF BUSINESS RE-ENGINEERING

Given the challenges of innovation and implementation, it is not surprising to find a very high failure rate among business re-engineering projects, which typically require extensive organizational change. A series of studies back up Michael Hammer's observation that 70 percent of all re-engineering projects fail to deliver promised benefits. Many information systems to support business re-engineering take too long to develop and don't deliver what the company wants. The Cambridge, Massachusetts, consulting firm of Arthur D. Little, Inc. found that only 16 percent of the 350 business executives they surveyed were "fully satisfied" with their business re-engineering efforts. Moreover, 68 percent of the executives reported that their re-engineering projects had unintended side effects, creating new problems instead of solving old ones (Caldwell, 1994).

In some cases, these problems stemmed from management's inability to identify the critical problems to be solved by re-engineering or to distinguish between radical revamping of core business processes and incremental changes. In such instances, companies wound up only making incremental improvements in ongoing operations instead of radically redesigning their business processes. But in many cases, major hurdles to re-engineering were caused by poor implementation and change management practices that failed to address widespread fears of change. Figure 14.7 summarizes Deloitte & Touche's findings about the greatest obstacles to successful business re-engineering. Studies by CSC Index Inc. and others report similar results. Dealing with fear and anxiety throughout the organization, overcoming resistance by key managers, changing job functions, career paths, recruitment, and training pose even greater threats to re-engineering than companies' difficulties with visualizing and designing breakthrough changes to their business processes (Maglitta, 1994). Re-engineering problems are part of the larger problem of organizational implementation and change management.

THE IMPLEMENTATION PROCESS: WHAT CAN GO WRONG

The following problems are considered typical for each stage of systems development when the implementation process is poorly managed.

FIGURE 14.7
Obstacles to business re-engineering. Resistance to organizational change poses the greatest obstacle to business re-engineering efforts. *Adapted from: Bruce Caldwell, "Missteps, Miscues," InformationWEEK, June 20, 1994.*

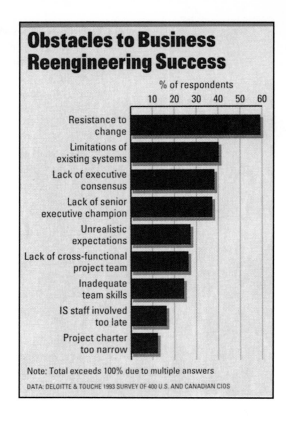

Obstacles to Business Reengineering Success

% of respondents

Note: Total exceeds 100% due to multiple answers

DATA: DELOITTE & TOUCHE 1993 SURVEY OF 400 U.S. AND CANADIAN CIOS

Analysis

- Time, money, and resources have not been allocated to researching the problem. The problem remains poorly defined. Objectives of the implementation project will be vague and ambiguous; benefits will be difficult to measure.

- Little or no time is spent in preliminary planning. There are no standards to use in estimating preliminary costs or the duration of the project.

- The project team is not properly staffed. Personnel are assigned on an as available basis and cannot dedicate themselves to the project. User groups to be served by the system are not represented on the team.

- The information services staff promises results that are impossible to deliver.

- Requirements are derived from inadequate documentation of existing systems or incomplete findings from systems study activities.

- Users refuse to spend any time helping the project team gather the requisite information.

- Project analysts cannot interview users properly. They do not know how to ask the right questions. They cannot carry on an extended conversation with users because they lack good communications skills.

Design

- Users have no responsibility for or input to design activities. The design, therefore, reflects the biases of the technical staff. It does not mesh well with the structure, activities, and culture of the organization or the priorities of management.

- The system is designed only to serve current needs. No flexibility has been built in to anticipate the future needs of the organization.

- Drastic changes in clerical procedures or staffing are planned without any organizational impact analysis.
- Functional specifications are inadequately documented.

Programming

- The amount of time and money required for software development is underestimated.
- Programmers are supplied with incomplete specifications.
- Not enough time is devoted to the development of program logic; too much time is wasted on writing code.
- Programmers do not take full advantage of structured design or object-oriented techniques. They write programs that are difficult to modify and maintain.
- Programs are not adequately documented.
- Requisite resources (such as computer time) are not scheduled.

Testing

- The amount of time and money required for proper testing is underestimated.
- The project team does not develop an organized test plan.
- Users are not sufficiently involved in testing. They do not help to create sample test data or review test results. They refuse to devote much time to the testing effort.
- The implementation team does not develop appropriate acceptance tests for management review. Management does not review and sign off on test results.

Conversion

- Insufficient time and money are budgeted for conversion activities, especially for data conversion.
- Not all of the individuals who will use the system are involved until conversion begins. Training begins only when the system is about to be installed.
- To compensate for cost overruns and delays, the system is made operational before it is fully ready.
- System and user documentation is inadequate.
- Performance evaluations are not conducted. No performance standards are established, and the results of the system are not weighed against the original objectives.
- Provisions for system maintenance are inadequate. Insufficient information systems personnel are trained to support the system and to make maintenance changes.

14.3 MANAGING IMPLEMENTATION

Not all aspects of the implementation process can be easily controlled or planned (Alter and Ginzberg, 1978). However, the chances for system success can be increased by anticipating potential implementation problems and applying appropriate corrective strategies. Various project management, requirements gathering, and planning methodologies have been developed for specific categories of problems. Strategies have also been devised for ensuring that users play an appropriate role throughout the implementation period and for managing the organizational change process.

CONTROLLING RISK FACTORS

One way implementation can be improved is by adjusting the project management strategy to the level of risk inherent in each project. If a systems development project is placed in the proper risk category, levels of risk can be predicted in advance and strategies developed to counteract high-risk factors (McFarlan, 1981).

Implementers must adopt a contingency approach to project management, handling each project with the tools, project management methodologies, and organizational linkages geared to its level of risk. There are four basic project management techniques:

1. External integration tools link the work of the implementation team to that of users at all organizational levels.

2. Internal integration tools ensure that the implementation team operates as a cohesive unit.

3. Formal planning tools structure and sequence tasks, providing advance estimates of the time, money, and technical resources required to execute them.

4. Formal control tools help monitor the progress toward goals.

The risk profile of each project will determine the appropriate project management technique to apply, as illustrated in Table 14.4.

External Integration Tools

external integration tools Project management technique that links the work of the implementation team to that of users at all organizational levels.

Projects with relatively *little structure* must involve users fully at all stages. Users must be mobilized to support one of many possible design options and to remain committed to a single design. Therefore, **external integration tools** must be applied.

- Users can be selected as project leaders or as the second-in-command on a project team.
- User steering committees can be created to evaluate the system's design.
- Users can become active members of the project team.
- The project can require formal user review and approval of specifications.
- Minutes of all key design meetings can be distributed widely among users.
- Users can prepare the status reports for higher management.
- Users can be put in charge of training and installation.
- Users can be responsible for change control, putting a brake on all nonessential changes to the system once final design specifications have been completed.

Internal Integration Tools

internal integration tools Project management technique that ensures that the implementation team operates as a cohesive unit.

Projects with *high levels of technology* benefit from **internal integration tools**. The success of such projects depends on how well their technical complexity can be managed. Project leaders need both heavy technical and administrative experience. They must be able to anticipate problems and develop smooth working relationships among a predominantly technical team.

- Team members should be highly experienced.
- The team should be under the leadership of a manager with a strong technical and project management background.
- Team meetings should take place frequently, with routine distribution of meeting minutes concerning key design decisions.
- The team should hold regular technical status reviews.
- A high percentage of the team should have a history of good working relationships with each other.
- Team members should participate in setting goals and establishing target dates.
- Essential technical skills or expertise not available internally should be secured from outside the organization.

Table 14.4 **Strategies to Manage Projects by Controlling Risks**

Project Structure	Project Technology Level	Project Size	Degree of Risk	Project Management Tool
1. High	Low	Large	Low	High use of formal planning High use of formal control
2. High	Low	Small	Very low	High use of formal control Medium use of formal planning
3. High	High	Large	Medium	Medium use of formal control Medium use of formal planning
4. High	High	Small	Medium-low	High internal integration
5. Low	Low	Large	Low	High external integration High use of formal planning High use of formal control
6. Low	Low	Small	Very low	High external integration High use of formal control
7. Low	High	Large	Very high	High external integration High internal integration
8. Low	High	Small	High	High external integration High internal integration

This project team of professionals is using portable computing tools and documents to enhance communication, analysis and decision making.

formal planning tools Project management technique that structures and sequences tasks; budgeting time, money, and technical resources required to complete the tasks.

formal control tools Project management technique that helps monitor the progress toward completion of a task and fulfillment of goals.

Formal Planning and Control Tools

Projects with *high structure* and *low technology* present the lowest risk. The design is fixed and stable and the project does not pose any technical challenges. If such projects are large, they can be successfully managed by **formal planning and control tools**. With project management techniques such as PERT (Program Evaluation and Review Technique) or Gantt charts, a detailed plan can be developed. (PERT lists the specific activities that make up a project, their duration, and the activities that must be completed before a specific activity can start. A Gantt chart such as that illustrated in Figure 14.8 visually represents the sequence and timing of different tasks in a development project, as well as their resource requirements.) Tasks can be defined and resources budgeted. These project management techniques can help managers identify bottlenecks and determine the impact that problems will have on project completion times.

- Milestone phases can be selected.
- Specifications can be developed from the feasibility study.

HRIS COMBINED PLAN-HR (Gantt chart, timeline 1994 Oct – 1996 Apr)

Task	Da	Who
DATA ADMINISTRATION SECURITY		
QMF security review/setup	20	EF TP
Security orientation	2	EF JV
QMF security maintenance	35	TP GL
Data entry sec. profiles	4	EF TP
Data entry sec. views est.	12	EF TP
Data entry security profiles	65	EF TP
DATA DICTIONARY		
Orientation sessions	1	EF
Data dictionary design	32	EF WV
DD prod, coordn-query	20	GL
DD prod. coord-live	40	EF GL
Data dictionary cleanup	35	EF GL
Data dictionary maint.	35	EF GL
PROCEDURES REVISION DESIGN PREP		
Work flows (old)	10	PK JL
Payroll data flows	31	JL PK
HRIS P/R model	11	PK JL
P/R interface orient. mtg.	6	PK JL
P/R interface coordn. I	15	PK
P/R interface coordn.	8	PK
Benefits interfaces (old)	5	JL
Ben. interfaces new flow	8	JL
Ben. communication strategy	3	PK JL
New work flow model	15	PK JL
Posn. data entry flows	14	WV JL

RESOURCE SUMMARY

Name	Da	Who	Oct '94	Nov	Dec	Jan '95	Feb	Mar	Apr	May	Jun	Jul	Aug	Sep	Oct	Nov	Dec	Jan '96	Feb	Mar	Apr
Edith Farrell	5.0	EF	2	21	24	24	23	22	22	27	34	34	29	26	28	19	14	4	3		
Woody Holand	5.0	WH	5	17	20	19	12	10	14	10	2										
Charles Pierce	5.0	CP		5	11	20	13	9	10	7	6	8	4	4	4	4	4				
Ted Leurs	5.0	TL		12	17	17	19	17	14	12	15	16	2	1	1	1	1				9
Toni Cox	5.0	TC	1	11	10	11	11	12	19	19	21	21	21	17	17	12	9	3	2		
Patricia Clark	5.0	PC	7	23	30	34	27	25	15	24	25	16	11	13	17	10	3				
Jane Lawton	5.0	JL	1	9	16	21	19	21	21	20	17	15	14	12	14	8	5				
David Holloway	5.0	DH	4	4	5	5	5	2	7	5	4	16	2								6
Diane O'Neill	5.0	DO	6	14	17	16	13	11	9	4											
Joan Albert	5.0	JA	5	6			7	6	2	1				5	5	1					
Marie Marcus	5.0	MM	15	7	2	1	1														
Don Stevens	5.0	DS	4	4	5	4	5	1													
Casual	5.0	CASL		3	4	3			4	7	9	5	3	2							
Kathy Manley	5.0	KM		1	5	16	20	19	22	19	20	18	20	11	2						
Anna Borden	5.0	AB				9	10	16	15	11	12	19	10	7	1						
Gail Loring	5.0	GL		3	6	5	9	10	17	18	17	10	13	10	10	7	17	14	13	3	1
UNASSIGNED	0.0	X												9	236	225	230	216	178	9	7
Co-op	5.0	CO		6	4				2	3	4	4	2	4	16						
casual	5.0	CAUL								3	3	3									
TOTAL DAYS			49	147	176	196	194	174	193	195	190	181	140	125	358	288	284	237	196	12	23

FIGURE 14.8
Formal planning and control tools help to manage information systems projects successfully. The Gantt chart in this figure was produced by a commercially available project management software package. It shows the task, man-days, and initials of each responsible person, as well as the start and finish dates for each task. The resource summary provides a good manager with the total man-days for each month and for each person working on the project to successfully manage the project. The project described here is a data administration project.

- Specification standards can be established.
- Processes for project approval can be developed.

Standard control techniques will successfully chart the progress of the project against budgets and target dates, so that the implementation team can make adjustments to meet their original schedule.

- Disciplines to control or freeze the design can be maintained.
- Deviations from the plan can be spotted.
- Periodic formal status reports against the plan will show the extent of progress.

Overcoming User Resistance

In addition to fine-tuning project management strategies, implementation risks can be reduced by securing management and user support of the implementation effort. Section 14.2 has shown how user participation in the design process builds commitment to the system. The final product is more likely to reflect users' requirements. Users are more likely to feel that they control and own the system. Users are also more likely to feel satisfied with an information system if they have been trained to use it properly (Cronan and Douglas, 1990).

However, MIS researchers have also noted that systems development is not an entirely rational process. Users leading design activities have used their position to further private interests and to gain power rather than to promote organizational objectives (Franz and Robey, 1984).

Participation in implementation activities may not be enough to overcome the problem of user resistance. The implementation process demands organizational change. Such change may be resisted because different users may be affected by the system in different ways. While some users may welcome a new system because it brings changes they perceive as beneficial to them, others may resist these changes because they believe the shifts are detrimental to their interests (Joshi, 1991).

If the use of a system is voluntary, users may choose to avoid it; if use is mandatory, resistance will take the form of increased error rates, disruptions, turnover, and even sabotage. Therefore, the implementation strategy must not only encourage user participation and involvement; it must also address the issue of counterimplementation (Keen, 1981). **Counterimplementation** is a deliberate strategy to thwart the implementation of an information system or an innovation in an organization.

Researchers have explained user resistance with one of three theories (Markus, 1983; Davis and Olson, 1985):

1. **People-oriented theory.** Factors internal to users as individuals or as a group produce resistance. For instance, users may resist a new system or any change at all because they are lazy and do not wish to learn new ways of doing things.

2. **System-oriented theory.** Factors inherent in the design create user resistance to a system. For instance, users may resist a system because its user interface is confusing and they have trouble learning how to make the system work.

3. **Interaction theory.** Resistance is caused by the interaction of people and systems factors. For instance, the system may be well designed and welcomed by some users but resisted by others who fear it will take away some of their power or stature in the organization.

Strategies have been suggested to overcome each form of user resistance:

People oriented:	User education (training)
	Coercion (edicts, policies)
	Persuasion
	User participation (to elicit commitment)
System oriented:	User education
	Improve human factors (user/system interface)

counterimplementation A deliberate strategy to thwart the implementation of an information system or an innovation in an organization.

people-oriented theory User-resistance theory focusing on factors internal to users.

system-oriented theory User-resistance theory focusing on factors inherent in the design of the system.

interaction theory User-resistance theory stating that resistance is caused by the interaction of people and systems factors.

User participation (for improved design)

Package modification to conform to organization
    when appropriate

Interaction: Solve organizational problems before introducing
                         new systems

Restructure incentives for users

Restructure the user–designer relationship

Promote user participation when appropriate

Strategies appropriate for the interaction theory incorporate elements of people-oriented and system-oriented strategies. There may be situations in which user participation is not appropriate. For example, some users may react negatively to a new design even though its overall benefits outweigh its drawbacks. Some individuals may stand to lose power as a result of design decisions (Robey and Markus, 1984). In this instance, participation in design may actually exacerbate resentment and resistance.

The Window on Management illustrates how some of the implementation strategies described here were applied to head off a potential re-engineering diaster.

DESIGNING FOR THE ORGANIZATION

The entire systems development process can be viewed as planned organizational change, since the purpose of a new system is to improve the organization's performance. Therefore, the development process must explicitly address the ways in which the organization will change when the new system is installed. In addition to procedural changes, transformations in job functions, organizational structure, power relationships, and behavior will all have to be carefully planned. For example, Figure 14.9 illustrates the organizational dimensions that would need to be addressed for planning and implementing office automation systems.

Although systems analysis and design activities are supposed to include an organizational impact analysis, this area has traditionally been neglected. An **organizational impact analysis** explains how a proposed system will affect organizational structure, attitudes, decision making, and operations. To integrate information systems successfully with the organization, thorough and fully documented organizational impact assessments must be given more attention in the development effort.

Allowing for the Human Factor

The quality of information systems should be evaluated in terms of user criteria rather than the criteria of the information systems staff. In addition to targets such as memory size, access rates, and calculation times, systems objectives should include standards for user performance. For example, an objective might be that data entry clerks learn the procedures and codes for four new on-line data entry screens in a half-day training session.

Areas where users interface with the system should be carefully designed, with sensitivity to ergonomic issues. **Ergonomics** refers to the interaction of people and machines in the work environment. It considers the design of jobs, health issues, and the end-user interface of information systems. The impact of the application system on the work environment and job dimensions must be carefully assessed. One noteworthy study of 620 Social Security Administration claims representatives showed that the representatives with on-line access to claims data experienced greater stress than those with serial access to the data via teletype. Even though the on-line interface was more rapid and direct than teletype, it created much more frustration. Representatives with on-line access could interface with a larger number of clients per day. This changed the dimensions of the job for claims representatives. The restructuring of work—involving tasks, quality of working life, and performance—had a more profound impact than the nature of the technology itself (Turner, 1984).

The Window on Organizations describes some of the ways that companies can address user interface issues.

organizational impact analysis Study of the way a proposed system will affect organizational structure, attitudes, decision making, and operations.

ergonomics The interaction of people and machines in the work environment, including the design of jobs, health issues, and the end-user interface of information systems.

HOECHST HEADS OFF A RE-ENGINEERING DISASTER

Hoechst Celanese Corporation of Somerville, New Jersey, desperately needed a new order system. Its German parent corporation, Hoechst International, had suffered heavy losses in 1993. As part of a widespread corporate reorganization to slash costs and boost competitiveness in an increasingly competitive global marketplace, management wanted to expedite orders, reduce errors, and reduce huge inventory overstock caused by sales forecasts that were only 60 percent accurate.

Hoechst Celanese makes 45,000 pound bales of material for clothing, carpets, home furnishings, and auto parts. In December 1994, it proudly rolled out a new order commitment system for faster and more accurate bulk deliveries to its manufacturing plants in the United States, Mexico, and Canada. The system integrates all customer information, including order placement, inventory, and shipping, using EDI and client/server technology. It provides a real-time view of production scheduling along with just-in-time manufacturing and automatic replenishment of customer inventories. This highly acclaimed achievement was the culmination of a two-year re-engineering effort that almost failed.

In early 1994, Jen Helke, the fulfillment manager at Hoecht's polyester unit, was assigned to make the new order commitment process operational at the company's Spartanburg, South Carolina, factory. She had to fight to get involved in the re-engineering project. By the time she arrived, the system was in final testing. Helke had trouble getting answers to simple questions such as why certain display screens were created the way they were. The re-engineering team appeared too busy or uninterested to explain.

Re-engineering team leader Tolly Pruitt acknowledged that management had focused so much on building the re-engineering team that it forgot to build ways to let newcomers in. The team was designed to oversee the order entry reorganization and then disband. When the team was hand-picked by Unit Vice President Tony White and other top executives in July 1992, it included a Dutch-born manufacturing analyst, a chemical engineer turned sales person, a female financial analyst, and a minority quality manager with a biology degree. Pruitt, a group engineering manager in Hoescht's fibers and film operation, described himself as "a high-strung pioneer." Information systems manager Dwight Earl later joined the effort. No customer service representative was included. Management worried that members were too diverse to work together.

To build team spirit, the team members climbed mountains with ropes together on several off-site, Outward Bound–style retreats. The group discussed ethnic differences, mission statements, and thinking styles. In January 1993, after interviewing more than one hundred workers in order processing, manufacturing, credit, warehousing, and sales, the group emerged with an information systems road map, ready to begin implementation. Cambridge Technology Partners of Cambridge, Massachusetts, created the software for the system, which runs on a DEC VAXcluster in Charlotte, Hewlett-Packard 9000 workstations, and Windows-based microcomputers.

At that point Helke joined the team and started asking questions. She didn't understand how the team made its decisions yet had no documentation. Team members had trouble going back to justify what they had done. Helke discovered that people did not feel any ownership of the system; they felt it had been handed to them without their input. The order entry workers, stressed by having to learn a difficult

> **To Think About:** Describe the management problems that occurred during the re-engineering effort. What were the causes of these problems? What strategies were used to solve these problems? How successful were they?

new system, complained about the re-engineering effort.

In February 1994, fifteen people, including the entire order fulfillment group, key customer service representatives, Helke, and the re-engineering team, left work early for a half-day site retreat with Tim Irwin, a consultant from Atlanta-based Irwin-Browning Associates, who had been hired to do team building. As people laid their issues on the table, there were tears, accusations, anger, and lack of trust. The customer service representatives took matters very personally. "Why did you let them do this to us?" they asked Helke.

Eventually the meeting worked out a mutually agreeable rollout plan. Workers started inputting increasing numbers of orders into the system in March, and by early April, the conversion was complete. Teams from the re-engineering, corporate information systems, and business groups fine-tuned the system the rest of the year, eliminating data communications bugs and speeding database access. Although the system is running smoothly, personality conflicts remain.

Source: Joseph Maglitta, "Too Darn Tight," *Computerworld*, January 16, 1995.

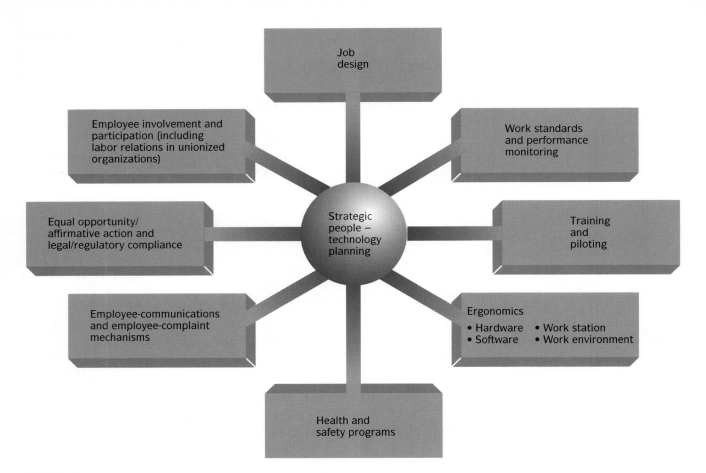

FIGURE 14.9
Key human organizational factors for office automation planning and implementation. For successful implementation, the planner must consider ergonomics, job design, work standards, health and safety, training, employee communications, employee participation, and legal/regulatory factors. *Reprinted with permission of G.K. Hall & Co., an imprint of Macmillan Publishing Company, from* The Changing Workplace *by Alan F. Westin et al. Copyright © 1985 by G.K. Hall & Co.*

SOCIOTECHNICAL DESIGN

Most contemporary systems-building approaches tend to treat end users as essential to the systems-building process but playing a largely passive role relative to other forces shaping the system such as the specialist system designers and management. A different tradition rooted in the European social democratic labor movement assigns users a more active role, one that empowers them to codetermine the role of information systems in their workplace (Clement and Van den Besselaar, 1993).

sociotechnical design Design to produce information systems that blend technical efficiency with sensitivity to organizational and human needs.

This tradition of participatory design emphasizes participation by the individuals most affected by the new system. It is closely associated with the concept of sociotechnical design. A **sociotechnical design** plan establishes human objectives for the system that lead to increased job satisfaction. Designers set forth separate sets of technical and social design solutions. The social design plans explore different work group structures, allocation of tasks, and the design of individual jobs. The proposed technical solutions are compared with the proposed social solutions. Social and technical solutions that can be combined are proposed as sociotechnical solutions. The alternative that best meets both social and technical objectives is selected for the final design. The resulting sociotechnical design is expected to produce an information system that blends technical efficiency with sensitivity to organizational and human needs, leading to high job satisfaction (Mumford and Weir, 1979). Systems with compatible technical and organizational elements are expected to raise productivity without sacrificing human and social goals.

REUTERS DESIGNS FOR USABILITY

Greg Garrison heads one of the highest priority projects for Reuters, the London-based international news and financial information organization. His mission: Establish a mechanism to improve the usability of Reuters' market data displays for all of its information-based products.

Housed in a set of laboratories behind Reuters' Fleet Street headquarters, the project is tightly guarded because of its potential impact on every future Reuters product. Reuters' core product is information, accounting for 70 percent of its revenues. If Reuters can make the display systems delivering that information easier to use, it will sell more information and increase profits.

The project is creating a mechanism whereby Reuters can improve the usability of its data display products that short-circuits its traditional design loop, in which users ask their sales representatives for design changes and the sales reps pass those requests to developers who might or might not incorporate them in future releases of the product.

Formally, the unit in charge of the project is known as a customer performance support group, but most people in Reuters and beyond like to call it the usability group. It is described as a "virtual team" made up of Garrison and three other Reuters staff members, plus representatives from companies such as Interaction Graphics, Human Factors International Inc., Microsoft Corporation, and Logica UK Ltd. The team has access to more than 500 experts in fields ranging from ergonomics to computer metrics. One of the virtual team members is dubbed the "semiotician savant"

and is responsible for translating computer actions into symbols such as Windows icons. (Semiotics is the study of symbols and their origins.)

Instead of performing market research and asking users what they think, Reuters' usability group actually observes users as they work with Reuters' information system products in "usability laboratories." The usability laboratory consists of two rooms. One is for the user, accompanied by a Reuters assistant, to try out the application under investigation. The second room, separated by a glass panel, contains monitors. The monitors can see a duplicate of the user screen and can communicate with the user either visually or via intercom.

To test an application, Reuters asks each user to perform a set of tasks described in a script. For instance, the user might be asked to look up the current price of a specified stock, create a chart of that stock's performance for a given period, find any relevant news about the company and locate fundamental financial data about the company. As the user performs the tasks, the usability group's monitors can see which bits of the tasks cause problems. One monitor follows the script, timing the user's efforts to complete each task and noting pauses that interrupt the flow of work. A film of the user's experience is used for more accurate timings, measuring events on tape down to the video frame. When fully operational, the usability labs can conduct three or four major tests of 100 users each per month.

The usability group is working closely with Reuters' help desks to find out even more about users' problems and concerns. Reuters created a data-

base that classifies the content of incoming calls to its help desk so that it can analyze the problems encountered across its entire product line. It made

---

To Think About: How was system usability related to Reuters' business strategy? What problems do usability labs solve for Reuters? What kinds of problems can't be solved this way? If you were a manager, what steps would you take to eliminate user interface problems?

---

improvements when it found, for example, that 34 percent of all help desk calls in April 1994 concerned its RT workstation and that 20 percent of the calls about the RT workstation reflected usability problems. When Reuters further analyzed the calls concerning usability issues, it found that 28 percent of the calls concerned problems with quote lists (see Figure 14.10). So Reuters simplified the mechanisms for setting up quote lists in a new version of the RT.

The usability team developed a set of guidelines called the Reuter Customer Centered Design Process (CCDP) that must be used by all Reuters' development teams. The CCDP specifies that all products must be reviewed by the usability group before they are released and that graphical user interface icons have the same meaning and function in all Reuters systems. CCDP provides a library of standardized Windows icons, which designers can access on-line from their desktop computers.

Source: David Bannister, "NO GUT, No Glory?" *Waters*, Winter 1994.

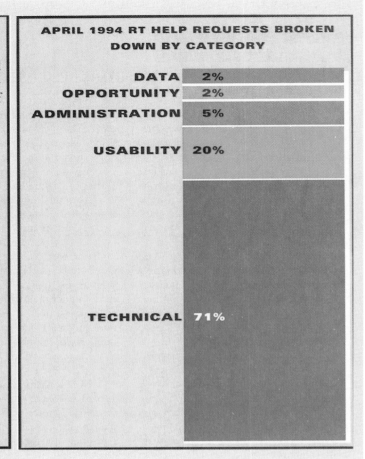

WHY RT USERS CALL REUTERS' TECHNICAL HELP LINE	
TICKERS	6
QUOTES	68
ERROR MESSAGES	10
FORMATS	12
GENERAL WINDOWS QUERIES	100
GRAPHS	25
HOT WINDOWS	5
LIMITS	6
QUOTE LISTS	120
SAVE/RESTORE	30
SCREEN	8
SETTINGS	38
TERMINOLOGY	7
USER ERROR	31
NEWS	13
PRINTING	17
UNCLASSIFIED	30
TOTAL	526

Reuters received a total of 2,588 phone calls on its technical help line last April. Roughly 20 percent of those calls concerned the Reuter Terminal. Following is a breakdown of the subjects of the RT inquiries provided by the CPS group.

APRIL 1994 RT HELP REQUESTS BROKEN DOWN BY CATEGORY

Category	Percent
DATA	2%
OPPORTUNITY	2%
ADMINISTRATION	5%
USABILITY	20%
TECHNICAL	71%

FIGURE 14.10
Reuters analysis of help desk calls. By analyzing statistics gathered from users phoning its help desk for assistance, Reuters identified problems with its products and made improvements to enhance their usability. *Adapted from: David Bannister, "No GUT, No Glory?"* Waters, *Winter 1994.*

Management Challenges

1. Organizational inertia. In the absence of an organizational crisis, it is difficult to focus organizational attention and resources on developing new systems because organizations are so resistant to change. Much large-scale system development is initiated in periods of organizational crisis and is not planned. These periods are not well suited to rational planning and implementation.

2. Dealing with the complexity of large-scale systems projects. Large-scale systems that affect large numbers of organizational units and staff members and that have extensive information requirements are difficult to oversee, coordinate, and plan for. Implementing such systems, which have multi-year development periods, is especially problem-ridden because the systems are so complex.

3. Estimating the time and cost to implement a successful large information system. There are few reliable techniques for estimating the time and cost to develop medium- to large-scale information systems. Few projects take into account the long-term maintenance costs of systems. Guidelines presented in this chapter are helpful but cannot guarantee that a large information system project can be precisely planned and given a projected budget.

Summary

1. Identify major problem areas in information systems. A high percentage of systems are considered failures because they are not used in the way they were intended. Some are not used at all. System failure is evidenced by problems with design, data, cost, or operations. The sources of system success or failure are primarily behavioral and organizational.

2. Determine whether a system is successful. Criteria for evaluating the success of an information system include (1) level of system use, (2) user satisfaction, (3) favorable user attitudes about the information system and its staff, (4) achieved objectives, and (5) financial payoff to the organization.

3. Describe the principal causes of information system failure. The principal causes of information system failure are (1) insufficient or improper user participation in the systems development process, (2) lack of management support, (3) high levels of complexity and risk in systems development process, and (4) poor management of the implementation process. There is a very high failure rate among business re-engineering projects because they require extensive organizational change.

4. Describe the relationship between the implementation process and system outcome. Implementation is the entire process of organizational change surrounding the introduction of a new information system. One can better understand system success and failure by examining different patterns of implementation. Especially important is the relationship between participants in the implementation process, notably the interactions between system designers and users. Conflicts between the technical orientation of system designers and the business orientation of end users must be resolved. The success of organizational change can be determined by how well information systems specialists, end users, and decision makers deal with key issues at various stages in implementation.

5. Describe appropriate strategies to manage the implementation process. Management support and control of the implementation process are essential, as are mechanisms for dealing with the level of risk in each new systems project. Some companies experience organizational resistance to change. Project risk factors can be brought under some control by a contingency approach to project management. The level of risk in a systems development project is determined by three key dimensions: (1) project size, (2) project structure, and (3) experience with technology. The risk level of each project will determine the appropriate mix of external integration tools, internal integration tools, formal planning tools, and formal control tools to be applied.

Appropriate strategies can be applied to ensure the correct level of user participation in the systems development process and to minimize user resistance. Information system design and the entire implementation process should be managed as planned organizational change. Participatory design emphasizes the participation of the individuals most affected by a new system. Sociotechnical design aims for an optimal blend of social and technical design solutions.

Key Terms

System failure	Man-month	People-oriented theory	Sociotechnical design
User interface	External integration tools	System-oriented theory	
Implementation	Internal integration tools	Interaction theory	
Change agent	Formal planning tools	Organizational impact	
User–designer	Formal control tools	analysis	
communications gap	Counterimplementation	Ergonomics	

Review Questions

1. What do we mean by information system failure?
2. What kinds of problems are evidence of information system failure?
3. How can we measure system success? Which measures of system success are the most important?
4. Define implementation. What are the major approaches to implementation?
5. Why is it necessary to understand the concept of implementation when examining system success and failure?
6. What are the major causes of implementation success or failure? How are they related to the failure of business re-engineering projects?
7. What is the user–designer communications gap? What kinds of implementation problems can it create?
8. List some of the implementation problems that might occur at each stage of the systems development process.
9. What dimensions influence the level of risk in each systems development project?
10. What project management techniques can be used to control project risk?
11. What strategies can be used to overcome user resistance to systems development projects?
12. What organizational considerations should be addressed by information system design?

Discussion Questions

1. You are a member of your corporation's management committee, which oversees and approves systems development projects. What criteria would you consider in evaluating new project proposals? What

would you look for to determine whether the project was proceeding successfully?

2. A prominent MIS researcher has observed that "The reason most information systems have failed is that we have ignored organizational behavior problems in the design and operation of computer-based information systems" (Lucas, 1974). Discuss.

Group Project

Form a group with two or three other students. Write a description of the implementation problems you might expect to encounter for the information system you designed for your systems analysis and design project. Write an analysis of the steps you would take to solve or prevent these problems. Alternatively, you could describe the implementation problems that might be expected for one of the systems described in the Window boxes or chapter-ending cases in this text. Present your findings to the class.

Case Study

THE SPECTACULAR COLLAPSE OF THE LONDON STOCK EXCHANGE PROJECT

Perhaps the most costly information system project failure in history occurred in London, England, in early 1993. On March 12 London Stock Exchange (LSE) chief executive Peter Rawlins made the stunning public announcement that the LSE Taurus project was being abandoned. The estimated cost (that is, "loss") to the LSE was $100 million. An additional $500 million was lost by the exchange's customers, a number that was later reduced to $400 million, giving a total loss of half a billion dollars for the London financial community. However, these numbers reflect only the monetary cost. The real cost of the nearly decade-long project was far greater than that. More than 350 employees and consultants immediately lost their jobs. The exchange lost nearly 10 years in its attempt to modernize. The opportunity costs—other ways that time, resources, and money could have been spent to benefit the London financial community, and the gains that could have resulted—cannot even be estimated.

Perhaps the largest cost of all (and the one that is most difficult to measure) may have been the harm done to the LSE's reputation. The strategic aim of the Taurus project was to strengthen the exchange's reputation as a world financial network leader in the face of increasing competition from the Frankfurt and Milan financial markets. The failed project did just the opposite, severely damaging the exchange's reputation both domestically and internationally. No less a person than the LSE head of public policy and external relations, Martin Hall, was quoted as saying, "Clearly it has had an effect . . . on confidence in us." According to some reports, it even became common for the London Stock Exchange to be the butt of jokes in London's pubs.

Rawlins made his announcement only after repeated delays in the project. When the project target date slipped from October 1989, to October 1992, to the spring of 1994, the LSE turned to Andersen Consulting for a project review. Its assessment was damning. In a follow-up but equally damning assessment commissioned by the LSE's chief finance officer, Jane Barker, Coopers & Lybrand consultant Stuart Senior concluded that costs were mounting, that more delays were certain, and that the problems were so great that it would take another 15 months just to sort them out. When the LSE board of directors heard this report from Barker, they ordered the project terminated immediately. Not surprisingly, Rawlins announced his resignation the same day he announced the end of Taurus.

The origins of Taurus go back to the 1986 event known as the "Big Bang," during which the LSE was turned into a self-regulating organization, with the Bank of England having oversight responsibility. Many regulations were lifted, brokers were freed to set their own commissions, and ultimately the open-outcry market was replaced by electronic trading. One result of the Big Bang was a virtual explosion of trading volume on the London Stock Exchange, fed partly by the increased broker competition that resulted from the deregulation. Contrary to popular opinion, the Big Bang did not include a technological revolution. At that time, using Talisman, the existing LSE batch trading system, settling a trade required three to six weeks. In the United States trades were settled in three to five days and only two days in Japan. Part of London's problem was that the inefficient and inflexible system was primarily paper-based. The new system, dubbed Taurus, was intended to automate this process, including registering, transferring, and settling all United Kingdom equity shares. The system was to be based upon a high-speed, high-security network throughout London's financial center that would link the databases of the various brokers, bankers, investors, and registrars (clearing banks that keep the registers of shareholder transactions) who together would be the users of the system. The system would electronically move the transaction and ownership data as needed, cutting trade settlement time down to three days. The concept also included replacing paper share certificates with electronically generated statements and enabling instantaneous money transfer to occur simultaneously with the change in share ownership.

With the failure of the project, of course, none of this occurred. Trades still can take weeks to be settled. What went wrong? In attempting to understand why a project of this size fails, one can say two things with certainty, even if you know nothing about the project except its size and that it failed: First, the causes of failure are complex; and second, sharp disagreements will exist as to what those causes are. With these caveats in mind, however, let us examine some of the explanations that have been given for the project failure.

According to Mike Jones, head of development at Capel Cure Myers, a leading London security broker, the choice of a database proved to be a technical disaster. The project selected Vista from Vista Concepts Inc., New York, which Jones says "is a fine database." The problem was that it was the wrong database for this project because it was structured only for on-line real-time processing. While the heart of Taurus was to be on-line real-time, the LSE planned to use Vista also to support batch processing and to coordinate distributed databases, two functions for which it was not designed. The LSE also planned to augment the system with several high-security communica-

tions packages. As a result, when the LSE settled on Vista, it planned to do a little "tinkering at the edges," says Jones, but in the end it did a 60 percent rewrite. The inevitable result of a major rewrite of such a complex system is that it became a bug-ridden database that did not work well.

Despite the poor choice for a DBMS, project failures of this magnitude are seldom the result of technical problems. Sir Andrew Hugh Smith, the chairman of the exchange, believes that the planned system was too complex, trying to accomplish too much. He points out that it was originally intended only as a settlement system. As time passed, however, it grew until it had become a full "share registration and transfer system" as well. Specifications were driven by a number of forces, including complex legislation and changing needs of investors. For example, according to chairman Smith in his post-cancellation remarks, "the needs of investors have changed since Taurus was designed." But an even greater cause for the expansion of the system's functions may have been the many conflicting, powerful vested interests, and the LSE's unwillingness to choose among them. In a speech before about one hundred members of the Securities Industry Management Association, Sherwood Computer Services director John N. Everett expressed his opinion that "Taurus tried to jump too far, too quickly and with too many vested interests." According to Lynton Jones, chief executive of OM London Ltd., London's automated options and futures exchange, "registrars were most bothered [by Taurus,] because they stood to lose their business." The registrars are dominated by three giant companies, Lloyds, National Westminster, and Barclays banks, and one Anderson consultant concluded that the project "became a cocktail of all of the needs of the steering committee," largely dominated by the major banks. Some people laid the blame at the feet of the Bank of England, the overseer of the LSE, for failing to control these many and conflicting vested interests.

On the other hand, there are those who also believe that the project was too narrowly focused. Jones says that Taurus was to be used for settling United Kingdom domestic stock trades only, but he points out that "a number of British stocks are international stocks." There were more than 600 international securities listed on the LSE in 1991 and 1992.

One explanation for the failure, and for the attempt to satisfy all the vested interests in the specifications, is the longstanding culture of the LSE—its long history of "trying to be all things to all people," according to Chairman Smith. For example, in 1973, when the LSE formed the International Stock Exchange of Great Britain and Ireland, the LSE chose to become a federation of all the stock exchanges in the United Kingdom and Ireland, rather than allowing a string of independent exchanges much as exist in the United States. It then accepted regulatory and other responsibilities for the full cycle of equity trading, from order taking to settlement. The exchange also has become the vendor of trade data to all the exchange members, rather than following the model of many other exchanges, such as those in the United States, where the exchanges simply feed the data to such third-party vendors as Automatic Data Processing (ADP) and Reuters, who in turn widely distribute them. As trading became more complex following the Big Bang, the LSE was unable to let go of any of these functions.

Some blame the failure of the project on the fact that it was outsourced. Project development was awarded to Coopers & Lybrand. James Rowley, director of the equity division of Warburg, says that the project was outsourced to "dodge the responsibility for Taurus." OM's Lynton Jones says that because total responsibility was shifted outside the LSE, no one from the exchange's technical staff was around to offer objective opinions or otherwise monitor the project. After the project was canceled, one project consultant supported this view, saying, "It's always good to have an external monitor to watch what's going on, but that was maybe an affront to Rawlins' masculinity. He fired monitors some time ago." The LSE also outsourced the running of its computer systems, to begin once Taurus was completed. This contract was awarded to Andersen Consulting, an international leader in information systems consulting. One project consultant said that this resulted in a lack of incentives to complete the implementation work because the contract workers knew they had no job when the project was finished. Critics further note that Andersen was selected without competitive bidding. The reason given for not opening that contract up to bidding was that it was too complex with too many areas to allow for such a process. Nonetheless, the critics emphasize that prior to his stint as LSE chief executive, Rawlins had been an Andersen partner.

Where does the London Stock Exchange go from here? During May 1994, the LSE's overseer, the Bank of England, announced a new project known as Crest. This project will address settlements only, and so is simpler in design than Taurus. The system is projected to be able to handle 150,000 trades per day, compared with the daily volume of 40,000 trades handled by London in 1994. Its response time for end users will be less than five seconds. A string of top-of-the-line Tandem fault-tolerant computers will serve as the host computer and will be linked in a network to users' microcomputers or Unix systems. Crest client software will be installed and integrated into existing systems at user sites, comprised of stock exchange members, some one hundred institutional members, and registrars. The project is scheduled to be completed in 1996 and is budgeted for $50 million, with about $7.5 million of that amount earmarked for the actual system construction. The project is scheduled to complete construction and begin testing with users in 15 months, although detailed specifications are not due until the end of 1994. Use of the system will not be mandatory. Alison MacKenzie, finance sector analyst with International Data Corp., finds a great deal of caution about this project in the London financial community following the Taurus debacle. Many do believe that the LSE simply cannot afford to fail this time. However, the target date of Crest is seven years after the Taurus target date, and the project goals are much more narrowly defined. Taurus' goal had been to maintain the LSE's position as an international leader. But now, by automating and speeding up trade settlement, the LSE would only be playing catch up.

Sources: Paul Tate, "City of London Tries Again," *InformationWEEK*, May 30, 1994; Paul Tate, with Philip Hunter and John P. McPartlin, "Taurus: Born Under a Bad Sign," *InformationWEEK*, March 22, 1993; and Maureen Duffy, "London's Embarrassing Mistake," *Wall Street & Technology*, May 1993.

Case Study Questions

1. Classify and describe the problems with the Taurus project using the categories described in the section in this chapter on causes of information systems success and failure. What management, organization, and technology factors caused these problems?

2. Was Rawlins' resignation, thereby taking personal responsibility for the failure of the project, appropriate? Why or why not?

3. What do you think could and should have been done differently at the beginning of the project to prevent its failure?

4. From the little you know of the new Crest project, what lessons have and have not been learned from Taurus? Describe changes to Crest or steps that need to be taken to make it more likely to succeed.

References

Alter, Steven, and Michael Ginzberg. "Managing Uncertainty in MIS Implementation." *Sloan Management Review* 20 (Fall 1978).

Anthes, Gary H. "Why Uncle Sam Can't Compute." *Computerworld* (May 18, 1992).

Barki, Henri, and Jon Hartwick. "Rethinking the Concept of User Involvement." *MIS Quarterly* 13, no. 1 (March 1989).

Baroudi, Jack, Margrethe H. Olson, and Blake Ives. "An Empirical Study of the Impact of User Involvement on System Usage and Information Satisfaction." *Communications of the ACM* 29, no. 3 (March 1986).

Baroudi, Jack, and Wanda Orlikowski. "A Short Form Measure of User Information Satisfaction: A Psychometric Evaluation and Notes on Use." *Journal of Management Information Systems* 4, no. 4 (Spring 1988).

Batiste, John L. "The Application Profile." *MIS Quarterly* (September 1986).

Best, James D. "The MIS Executive as Change Agent." *Journal of Information Systems Management* (Fall 1985).

Bikson, Tora K., Cathleen Stasz, and D. A. Mankin. "Computer Mediated Work. Individual and Organizational Impact in One Corporate Headquarters." Santa Monica, CA: Rand Corporation (1985).

Brooks, Frederick P. "The Mythical Man-Month." *Datamation* (December 1974).

Bulkeley, William. "Programmers Need to Keep It Simple." *The Wall Street Journal* (June 30, 1992).

Cafasso, Rosemary. "Few IS Projects Come in on Time, on Budget." *Computerworld* (September 12, 1994).

Caldwell, Bruce. "Missteps, Miscues." *InformationWEEK* (June 20, 1994).

Clement, Andrew, and Peter Van den Besselaar. "A Retrospective Look at PD Projects." *Communications of the ACM* 36, no. 4 (June 1993).

Cooper, Randolph B., and Robert W. Zmud. "Information Technology Implementation Research: A Technological Diffusion Approach." *Management Science* 36, no. 2 (February 1990).

Corbato, Fernando J. "On Building Systems That Will Fail." *Communications of the ACM* 34, no. 9 (September 1991).

Cronan, Timothy Paul, and David E. Douglas. "End-user Training and Computing Effectiveness in Public Agencies: An Empirical Study." *Journal of Management Information Systems* 6, no. 4 (Spring 1990).

Davis, Fred R., "Perceived Usefulness, Ease of Use, and User Acceptance of Information Technology." *MIS Quarterly* 13, no. 3 (September 1989).

Davis, Gordon B., and Margrethe H. Olson. *Management Information Systems,* 2nd ed. New York: McGraw-Hill (1985).

DeLone, William H., and Ephrain R. McLean. "Information System Success: The Quest for the Dependent Variable." *Information Systems Research* 3, no. 1 (March 1992).

Delong, William H. "Determinants of Success for Computer Usage in Small Business." *MIS Quarterly* (March 1988).

Doll, William J. "Avenues for Top Management Involvement in Successful MIS Development." *MIS Quarterly* (March 1985).

Ein-Dor, Philip, and Eli Segev. "Organizational Context and the Success of Management Information Systems." *Management Science* 24 (June 1978).

Franz, Charles, and Daniel Robey. "An Investigation of User-Led System Design: Rational and Political Perspectives." *Communications of the ACM* 27 (December 1984).

Ginzberg, M. J. "The Impact of Organizational Characteristics on MIS Design and Implementation." Working paper CRIS 10, GBA 80-110. New York University Center for Research on Information Systems, Area Computer Applications and Information Systems Area (1980).

Ginzberg, Michael J. "Early Diagnosis of MIS Implementation Failure: Promising Results and Unanswered Questions." *Management Science* 27 (April 1981).

Gould, John D., and Clayton Lewis. "Designing for Usability: Key Principles and What Designers Think." *Communications of the ACM* 28 (March 1985).

Gullo, Karen. "Stopping Runaways in Their Tracks." *InformationWEEK* (November 13, 1989).

Hammer, Michael, and Steven A. Stanton. *The Reengineering Revolution.* New York: HarperCollins (1995).

Helms, Glenn L., and Ira R. Weiss. "The Cost of Internally Developed Applications: Analysis of Problems and Cost Control Methods." *Journal of Management Information Systems* (Fall 1986).

Hirscheim, R. A. "User Experience with and Assessment of Participative Systems Design." *MIS Quarterly* (December 1985).

Ives, Blake, Margrethe H. Olson, and Jack J. Baroudi. "The Measurement of User Information Satisfaction." *Communications of the ACM* 26 (October 1983).

Joshi, Kailash. "A Model of Users' Perspective on Change: The Case of Information Systems Technology Implementation." *MIS Quarterly* 15, no. 2 (June 1991).

Keil, Mark, Richard Mixon, Timo Saarinen, and Virpi Tuunairen. "Understanding Runaway IT Projects." Journal of Management Information Systems 11, no. 3 (Winter 1994-95).

Keen, Peter W. "Information Systems and Organizational Change." *Communications of the ACM* 24 (January 1981).

Kolb, D. A., and A. L. Frohman. "An Organization Development Approach to Consulting." *Sloan Management Review* 12 (Fall 1970).

Laudon, Kenneth C. "CIOs Beware: Very Large Scale Systems." Center for Research on Information Systems, New York University Stern School of Business, working paper (1989).

Lederer, Albert L., Rajesh Mirani, Boon Siong Neo, Carol Pollard, Jayesh Prasad, and K. Ramamurthy. "Information System Cost Estimating: A Management Perspective." *MIS Quarterly* 14, no. 2 (June 1990).

Lederer, Albert, and Jayesh Prasad. "Nine Management Guidelines for Better Cost Estimating." *Communications of the ACM* 35, no. 2 (February 1992).

Lucas, Henry C., Jr. *Toward Creative Systems Design.* New York: Columbia University Press (1974).

Lucas, Henry C., Jr. *Why Information Systems Fail.* New York: Columbia University Press (1975).

Lucas, Henry C., Jr. *Implementation: The Key to Successful Information Systems.* New York: Columbia University Press (1981).

McFarlan, F. Warren. "Portfolio Approach to Information Systems." *Harvard Business Review* (September–October 1981).

McPartlin, John P. "Uncle Sam Calls in the Reserves." *InformationWEEK* (April 27, 1992).

Maglitta, Joseph. "Rocks in the Gears." *Computerworld* (October 3, 1994).

Marcus, Aaron. "Human Communication Issues in Advanced UIS." *Communications of the ACM* 36, no. 4 (April 1993).

Markus, M. L. "Power, Politics and MIS Implementation." *Communications of the ACM* 26 (June 1983).

Markus, M. Lynne, and Mark Keil. "If We Build It, They Will Come: Designing Information Systems That People Want to Use." *Sloan Management Review* (Summer 1994).

Miller, Steven E. "From System Design to Democracy." *Communications of the ACM* 36, no. 4 (June 1993).

Moore, Gary C., and Izak Benbasat. "Development of an Instrument to Measure the Perceptions of Adopting an Information Technology Innovation." *Information Systems Research* 2, no. 3 (September 1991).

Mumford, Enid, and Mary Weir. *Computer Systems in Work Design: The ETHICS Method.* New York: John Wiley (1979).

Oz, Effy. "When Professional Standards Are Lax: The CONFIRM Failure and Its Lessons." *Communications of the ACM* 37, no. 10 (October 1994).

Raymond, Louis. "Organizational Context and Information System Success: A Contingency Approach." *Journal of Management Information Systems* 6, no. 4 (Spring 1990).

Robey, Daniel, and M. Lynne Markus. "Rituals in Information System Design." *MIS Quarterly* (March 1984).

Singleton, John P., Ephraim R. McLean, and Edward N. Altman. "Measuring Information Systems Performance." *MIS Quarterly* 12, no. 2 (June 1988).

Swanson, E. Burton. *Information System Implementation.* Homewood, IL: Richard D. Irwin (1988).

Tait, Peter, and Iris Vessey. "The Effect of User Involvement on System Success: A Contingency Approach." *MIS Quarterly* 12, no. 1 (March 1988).

Tornatsky, Louis G., J. D. Eveland, M. G. Boylan, W. A. Hetzner, E. C. Johnson, D. Roitman, and J. Schneider. *The Process of Technological Innovation: Reviewing the Literature.* Washington, DC: National Science Foundation (1983).

Turner, Jon A. "Computer Mediated Work: The Interplay Between Technology and Structured Jobs." *Communications of the ACM* 27 (December 1984).

United States General Services Administration. "An Evaluation of the Grand Design Approach to Developing Computer-Based Application Systems." Washington, DC: General Services Administration (September 1988).

Westcott, Russ. "Client Satisfaction: The Yardstick for Measuring MIS Success." *Journal of Information Systems Management* (Fall 1985).

Westin, Alan F., Heather A. Schweder, Michael A. Baker, and Sheila Lehman. *The Changing Workplace*. White Plains, NY, and London: Knowledge Industry Publications, Inc. (1985).

White, Kathy Brittain, and Richard Leifer. "Information Systems Development Success: Perspectives from Project Team Participants." *MIS Quarterly* (September 1986).

Yin, Robert K. "Life Histories of Innovations: How New Practices Become Routinized." *Public Administration Review* (January–February 1981).

System Modernization at the Social Security Administration: 1982–1995

The Social Security Administration (SSA) consists of approximately 63,000 employees located in 1300 field offices, 10 regional offices, 37 teleservice centers, 7 processing centers, 4 data operations centers, and the Baltimore headquarters. SSA administers the major social insurance programs of the United States and several other related programs, which include:

- *Retirement and Survivors Insurance (RSI)*
- *Disability Insurance (DI)*
- *Supplemental Security Income (SSI)*

In order to administer these programs, SSA maintains 260 million names in its account number file (enumeration file), 240 million earnings records, and 50 million names on its master beneficiary file. In addition to keeping these files current, SSA annually issues 10 million new Social Security cards, pays out $170 billion, posts 380 million wage items reported by employers, receives 7.5 million new claims, recomputes (because of changes in beneficiary status) 19 million accounts, and handles 120 million bills and queries from private health insurance companies, carriers, and intermediaries. Virtually every living American has some relationship with SSA.

In the early 1980s, the long-term funding for Social Security payments in the United States was in serious jeopardy, and SSA's computerized administrative systems were nearing collapse. This was an unusual state of affairs for SSA. As the flagship institution of the New Deal, SSA had developed broad bipartisan support, and there was never any serious question about its long-term financial viability until the late 1970s. In addition, since its incep-

tion in 1935, SSA had been one of the leading innovators and implementors of advanced information technology in the United States. With a special long-term relationship with IBM from the mid-1930s to the late 1960s, SSA was a test site for many of the leading commercial hardware and software innovations of this period.

In 1982, SSA announced its Systems Modernization Plan (SMP), a $500 million five-year effort to completely rebuild its information systems and administrative processes. Since then, the SMP has been expanded to $1 billion and ten years. The SMP was one of the largest civilian information system rebuilding efforts in history. Ten years later, SSA embarked on another ambitious round of technology modernization as it tried to create an information architecture for the twenty-first century.

SSA illustrates many central problems of management, information technology, and organization faced by private and public organizations in a period of rapid technical and social change. Although SSA operates in a unique federal government environment, many

large private organizations have exhibited similar problems in this time period. The problems and solutions illustrated in this case are generic.

The case is organized into three sections. Section I describes the overall situation at SSA in the period before SMP, roughly 1972–1982. Section II describes the experience of SMP. Section III considers the long-term prospects of SSA.

SECTION I: ORGANIZATION, MANAGEMENT, AND SYSTEMS, 1972–1982

The overall system environment at SSA in 1982 could best be described as a hodge-podge of software programs developed over a twenty-year period in four different machine environments. In the history of the agency, no one had ever conducted an information system requirements study to understand the overall requirements of the agency or the specific requirements of its subunits. There had been no planning of the information systems function for more than 20 years. Instead, as in many private organizations, systems drifted along from year to year, with only incremental changes.

Software

SSA software resulted from decades of programming techniques. The enumeration system, which supports the issuance of Social Security numbers, was designed in the late 1950s and had never been changed. The earning system was designed in 1975, the claims processing system was unchanged from the early 1960s, and other systems were also inherited from the late 1960s and 1970s. The software was a product of unplanned patchwork, with no regard given to its deterioration over time.

From the 1950s to the 1980s, there was four major equipment transitions. However, the software was not improved or redesigned at any of these transitions. All of SSA's files and programs were maintained on over 500,000 reels of magnetic tape, which was susceptible to aging, cracking, and deterioration. Because tape was the storage medium, all data processing was batch sequential.

In summary, there were 76 different software systems making up SSA's basic computer operations. These software systems were themselves congeries of programs that performed the primary business functions of SSA. There were more than 1300 computer programs encompassing over 12 million lines of COBOL and other code.

Most of the 12 million lines of code were undocumented. They worked, but few people in the organization knew how or why, which made maintenance extremely complex. In the 1960s and 1970s, Congress and the President made continual changes in the benefit formulas, each of which required extensive maintenance and changes in the underlying software. A change in cost-of-living rates, for instance, required sorting through several large interwoven programs, which took months of work.

Because of the labor-intensive work needed to change undocumented software and the growing operations crisis, software development staff were commonly shifted to manage the operations crisis. The result was little development of new programs.

It did not help matters that few people in Congress, the Office of the President, the Office of Management and Budget, or other responsible parties understood the deleterious impact of program changes on SSA systems capabilities. Unfortunately, SSA did not inform Congress of its own limitation.

What is unusual about SSA is that in the late 1970s it had not begun to make the transition to newer storage technology, file management and database technology, or more modern software techniques. In this respect, SSA was about five years behind private industry in making important technological transitions.

Hardware

By 1982, SSA was operating outdated, unreliable, and inadequate hardware, given its mission. Many of the computers had not been manufactured or marketed for ten years or more. Eleven IBM 360/65 systems were no longer manufactured or supported. Although more modern equipment might have required $1 million annually for maintenance and operations expenses, SSA was spending more than $4 million to keep these antiquated machines in service.

The antiquated hardware forced SSA to rely on third-party maintenance services. Because of frequent breakdowns, over 25 percent of the production jobs ended before completion (abended jobs), and 30 percent of the available computer processing power was idle. As a result of hardware deficiencies, a number of specific program impacts became apparent in 1982:

- Earnings enforcement operations, which help detect overpayments, were more than three years behind schedule.

- The computation of benefit amounts to give credit for additional earnings after retirement was three years behind schedule.

- SSI claims and post-eligibility redeterminations could be processed only three times a week rather than five times a week. This meant delays of several days or weeks for SSI beneficiaries.

- In order to process cost-of-living increases in 1982 for 42 million individuals, SSA had to suspend all other data processing for one week.

- In 1982, there was a three-month backlog of data needed to notify employers about incorrectly reported employee earnings. This created a suspense file with more than 2 million entries of unposted earnings and required additional manual work to handle employer correspondence.

SSA estimated that its gross computing capacity was deficient by more than 2000 CPU hours per month. SSA estimated that it needed 5000 central processing hours per month, but its capacity was only 3000 CPU hours per month.

Telecommunications

SSA depends heavily on telecommunications to perform its mission. Its 1300 field offices need timely access to data stored at the central computer facility in Baltimore. In 1982, however, SSA's telecommunications was the result of an evolving system dating back to 1966. The primary telecommunications system was called the Social Security Administration Data Acquisition and Response System (SSADARS), designed to handle 100,000 transactions per day. One year after it was built in 1975, the system was totally saturated. Each year teleprocessing grew by 100 percent. By 1982 the SSADARS network was frequently breaking down and was obsolete and highly inefficient.

One result of the saturated communications system was that senior SSA local executives working in field offices were forced to come in on the weekends in order to key in data to the SSADARS system, which was overloaded during the week. By 1982, there was little remaining CPU telecommunications capacity in the off-peak periods to handle the normal growth of current workloads. Entire streams of communications were frequently lost. At peak times, when most people wanted to use the system, it was simply unavailable. The result was telecommunications backlogs ranging from 10,000 to 100,000 messages at a time.

Database

The word *database* can be used only in a very loose sense to refer to SSA's 500,000 reels of magnetic tape on which it stored information on clients in major program areas. Each month SSA performed 30,000 production jobs, requiring more than 150,000 tapes to be loaded onto and off of machines. The tapes themselves were disintegrating, and errors in the tapes, along with their physical breakdown, caused very high error rates and forced a number of re-runs. More than one third of the operations staff (200 people) was required simply to handle the tapes.

As in many private sector organizations, data were organized at SSA by programs, and many of the data elements were repeated from one program to the next. SSA estimates that there were more than 1300 separate programs, each with its own data set. Because there was no data administration function, it was difficult to determine the total number of data elements, or the level of redundancy within the agency as a whole or even within program areas.

Management Information Systems

In 1982, SSA had a woefully inadequate capability in the MIS area. Because the data were stored on magnetic tape and were generally not available to end-user managers throughout the organization, all requests for reports had to be funneled through the information systems operations area.

But there was a crisis in operations, and this meant delays of up to several years in the production of reports crucial for management decision making. As long as all of the data were stored in a format that required professional computer and information systems experts to gain access to them, general management always had to deal with the Information Systems Department. This group had a stranglehold over the organization. Their attitude, as one commentator noted, was summed up in the statement "Don't bother us or the checks won't go out."

How Could This Happen?

There are two explanations for SSA's fall from a leading-edge systems position to near collapse in the early 1980s. First, there were internal institutional factors involving middle and senior management. Second, a sometimes hostile and rapidly changing environment in the 1970s added to SSA's woes.

In the 1970s, Congress had made more than 15 major changes in the RSI program alone. These changes increasingly taxed SSA's systems to the point where systems personnel were working on weekends to make required program changes.

In 1972 Congress passed the Supplemental Security Income (SSI) program, which converted certain state-funded and -administered income maintenance programs into federal programs. SSA suddenly found itself in the welfare arena, which was far removed from that of a social insurance agency. Unprepared local staffs suddenly faced thousands of angry applicants standing in line. Riots occurred in some cities. Other programs, such as Medicaid and changes in disability insurance, as well as cost-of-living (COLA) escalators, all severely taxed SSA's systems and personnel capacity. The 1978 COLA required changes in over 800 SSA computer programs.

The number of clients served by SSA doubled in the 1970s. But because of a growing economic crisis combining low growth and high inflation (stagflation), Congress was unwilling to expand SSA's work force to meet the demands of new programs. There was growing public and political resistance to expanding federal government employment at the very time when new programs were coming on line and expectations of service were rising.

SSA management in this period consistently overstated its administrative capacity to Congress and failed to communicate the nature of the growing systems crisis. SSA pleas for additional manpower were consistently turned down or reduced by Congress and the White House. Workloads of employees dramatically increased, and morale and job satisfaction declined. Training was reduced, especially in the systems area, as all resources were diverted to the operations crisis.

Toward the end of the 1970s, the political environment changed as well. A growing conservative movement among Republicans and Democrats interested in reducing the size of all federal programs led to increasing pressure on SSA to reduce employment levels. In the long actuarial funding debate at the beginning of the 1980s, there was talk about "privatizing" Social Security and abolishing the agency altogether.

Complicating SSA's environment was the Brooks Act of 1965, which mandated competitive procurement of computing equipment and services. Up to 1965, SSA had had a longstanding and beneficial relationship with IBM. Virtually all of SSA's equipment was manufactured by IBM and purchased on a noncompetitive basis. IBM provided planning, technical support, software support, and consulting services to SSA as part of this relationship.

By the 1970s this close relationship had ended. IBM shifted its support and marketing efforts away from the federal arena because of the Brooks Act. SSA found itself in a new competitive environment, forced to do all of its own planning, development, and procurement work. As the workload rapidly expanded at SSA in the 1970s, the agency needed a well-planned, closely managed transition to new computing equipment and software. This transition never occurred.

A challenging environment might have been overcome by a focused and dedicated management group. Perhaps the most critical weakness of all in SSA's operation in the 1970s was its inability to gain management control over the information systems function and over the information resource on which the organization itself was based.

Senior management turnover was a critical problem. In its first 38 years, SSA had six commissioners with an average tenure of 6.5 years. Two men led the agency for 27 of its 38 years. But from 1971 to 1981, SSA had seven commissioners or acting commissioners with an average tenure of 1.1 years. None of these commissioners had any experience at SSA. The senior staff of the agency was also repeatedly shaken up in this period. Compared to earlier senior managers, those of the 1970s failed to realize the critical importance of information systems to SSA's operation. Long-range planning of the agency or systems became impossible. Authority slowly but inevitably devolved to operations-level groups, the only ones that knew what was going on.

With new senior management came four major reorganizations of the agency. Major SSA programs were broken down into functional parts and redistributed to new functional divisions. Program coherence was lost. Performance measures and management control disappeared as managers and employees struggled to adapt to their new functions.

Efforts at Reform

SSA made several efforts in this period to regain control and direction in the systems area on which its entire operation critically depended. In 1975, SSA created the Office of Advanced Systems (OAS) within the Office of the Commissioner. SSA hoped that this advanced, high-level planning group with direct access to senior management would develop a strategy for change. Unfortunately, this effort failed to reform SSA's manual and batch processes and was opposed by systems operations management and the union. There was no White House support for it and no suggestion from Congress or the White House that needed funding would be forthcoming. In 1979 the OAS was abolished by a new management team.

A second effort at reform began in 1979. This time the idea originated with new senior management. Called *partitioning,* the new reform effort sought to break SSA's internal operations into major program lines—like product lines—so that each program could develop its own systems. This plan was quickly rejected by the White House, Congress, and outside professionals.

A third reform effort also began in 1979. Here SSA sought to replace the aging SSADARS telecommunications network with new, high-speed communications terminals in the district offices and new telecommunications computers in the Baltimore headquarters. After a competitive procurement process, SSA contracted with the Paradyne Corporation for 2000 such terminals. Unfortunately, the first 16 systems failed all operational tests on delivery in 1981. Investigations produced charges of bidding fraud (selling systems to SSA that did not exist, "black boxes with blinking lights"), securities fraud, bribery, bid rigging, perjury, and an inadequate SSA systems requirements definition. By 1983 SSA took delivery of all of the terminals, and they did perform for their expected life of eight years. But the procurement scandal further reduced SSA's credibility in Congress and the White House.

Senior management turnover, lack of concern, and failed efforts at reform took a severe toll in the systems area. Planning of information systems was either not done or was done at such a low operational level that no major changes in operations could be accomplished.

SECTION II: THE SYSTEMS MODERNIZATION PLAN

As the crisis at SSA became increasingly apparent to Congress, the General Accounting Office, and the President's Office, pressure was placed on SSA to develop a new strategy. In 1981 a new commissioner, John Svahn, a recently appointed former insurance executive with systems experience, began work on a strategic plan to try to move SSA data processing from collapse to a modern system. The result was a five-year plan called the Systems Modernization Plan (SMP). SMP was intended to bring about long-range, tightly integrated changes in software, hardware, telecommunications, and management systems. At $500 million, the original cost estimate in 1982, the SMP was one of the single most expensive information systems projects in history. The goals of the SMP were as follows:

- Restore excellence to SSA systems and return the agency to its state-of-the-art position.
- Avoid disruption of service.
- Improve service immediately by purchasing modern hardware.
- Improve staff effectiveness and productivity.
- Restore public confidence by enhancing accountability, auditability, and detection of fraud.

SMP Strategy

As a bold effort to secure a total change at SSA, the SMP adopted a conservative strategy. This strategy called for SSA to do the following:

- Achieve modernization through incremental, evolutionary change, given the unacceptable risks of failure.
- Build on the existing systems, selecting short-term, feasible approaches that minimize risks.
- Separate the modernization program from the operations and maintenance programs.
- Use an external system integration contractor to provide continuity to the five-year project.
- Utilize industry-proven, state-of-the-art systems engineering technology.
- Establish a single organizational body to plan, manage, and control SMP.
- Elevate systems development and operations to the highest levels of the agency.

SMP Implementation

The original plan foresaw a five-year effort broken into three stages: survival, transition, and state of the art. In the survival stage (18 months), SSA would focus on new hardware acquisition to solve immediate problems of capacity shortage. In the transition stage (18 months), SSA would begin rebuilding software, data files, and telecommunications systems. In the final state-of-the-art stage, SSA would finalize and integrate projects to achieve a contemporary level of systems. The SMP involved six interrelated programs.

1. The Capacity Upgrade Program (CUP). CUP was developed to reconfigure and consolidate the physical computing sites around central headquarters in Baltimore; to acquire much higher-capacity and more modern computers; to eliminate sequentially organized magnetic tape files and switch over to direct access devices; and to develop a local computing network for high-speed data transfers.

2. The System Operation and Management Program (SOMP). SOMP was intended to provide modern automated tools and procedures for managing and controlling SSA's main computer center operations in Baltimore. Included were automated job scheduling tools, job station monitoring and submission systems, operational job procedures, training, and a central integrated control facility to ensure that SSA would make a smooth transition to a modern data center environment.

3. The Data Communications Utility Program (DCUP). DCUP was designed to re-engineer SSA's major telecommunications system (SSADARS). What SSA wanted was a transparent conduit for the transmission of data between and among processing units of different manufacture using a single integrated network. More than 40,000 on-line terminals were to be used in the 1300 field offices.

4. Software Engineering Program (SEP). SEP was designed to upgrade the existing software and retain as much of it as possible so that entirely new code did not have to be written. A critical part of the SEP was a top-down, functional analysis (using the enterprise system planning method) of the Social Security process—all of the business and organizational functions of SSA. Hopefully, this top-down planning effort would

provide the framework for the redesign of SSA's total system by establishing the requirements for improvements in existing software. A second key aspect of the software engineering effort was the implementation of new software engineering technology. This involved developing and enforcing programming standards, developing quality controls, and using modern computer-aided software development tools. Special emphasis was placed on the development of modern program documentation, standardization of programs, and conversion to higher-level languages whenever possible.

5. Database Integration. The database integration project involved four objectives. As a survival tactic, SSA wanted to reduce the current labor-intensive, error-prone magnetic tape operation by converting all records to high-speed disk, direct access storage devices (DASD). A second goal was to establish a data administration function to control the definition of data elements and files. A third goal was to eliminate the data errors by establishing data controls, validating files, and developing modern storage disk technology. A fourth objective was to integrate the variety of databases, making communication among them transparent.

6. Administrative Management Information Engineering Program (AMIE). SSA was fundamentally dependent on manual activities to conduct most of its administration. Requests for personnel actions, purchase requisitions, telephone service, travel orders, building modifications, training requests—all of these administrative matters were processed manually. The AMIE program was designed to integrate MIS with other programmatic modernization activities: to automate and modernize labor-intensive administrative processes and to develop management MIS to improve the planning and administrative process.

The End of SMP: Success and Failure

SMP had become increasingly controversial: Critics claimed failure while the

agency's leaders claimed success. By 1988 Dorcas Hardy, the new SSA commissioner, quietly ended SMP and announced a new plan called the "2000: A Strategic Plan." What had the SMP accomplished in five years?

For much of the earlier years of SMP the environment was supportive and sympathetic to the modernization program. By 1986, however, criticism was beginning to develop over the rising costs and seeming endless time frame. In large part the critics drew strength from the fact that the SMP project had been extended by SSA for an additional five years (to 1992) and had doubled in expected cost to $1 billion; no major software breakthroughs were apparent to the public or Congress; and the effort to modernize SSA's "back-end" or database appeared to stall.

The White House increasingly pressed SSA to make plans for reducing its staff by one quarter, or 20,000 positions. By the end of 1988, the SSA staff had been reduced by 17,000 workers, from 83,000 down to 66,000, mostly by attrition. These reductions were made in anticipation of sharp increases in productivity brought about by the SMP modernization efforts. There was little systematic effort to examine this hope.

Under pressure from the White House, the new commissioner abandoned the pact with the union. The union began a long, drawn-out battle with the management for control over the implementation process. This battle frequently resulted in public congressional testimony challenging management claims of enhanced service, quality, and productivity. In labor's view, SSA management put excessive pressure on employees to work faster in order to "make the modernization program look good." "The Unions and the employees looked forward to system modernization," according to Rose Seaman, an SSA claims representative and SMP oversight person for the American Federation of Government Employees (AFGE), but "systems modernization never delivered. Instead there is great pressure on claims reps to perform clerical functions the system cannot perform, and to alter records so that processing times are reduced."[1]

The General Accounting Office (GAO), responding to requests from the House Government Operations Committee (Rep. Jack Brooks, Democrat of Texas, chairman), issued many highly critical reports of SSA's procurement policies. In one report issued in 1986, GAO charged that SSA failed to redevelop software or to develop a true database architecture. In another 1987 report, GAO claimed that SSA's new Claims Modernization Software would handle only 2 percent of the workload (merely initial applications for retirement and not the application processing or post-entitlement changes)! The report chided SSA for dropping modernization of the post-entitlement process which accounts for 94 percent of daily SSA transactions. SSA management heatedly denied GAO's allegations, but the backsliding in software became a major weapon of SMP opponents. GAO called for a halt in procurements. Hardy refused and began purchasing 40,000 full-color desktop terminals.

A review of SMP by the Office of Technology Assessment (OTA, a Congressional research agency) concluded that the White House, Congress, and SSA were all to blame for SSA's failure. The White House was blamed for prematurely seeking huge work-force reductions before the new systems were in place. It was also blamed for continuing political interference in the agency and for failure to support senior management. Congress was blamed for failing to understand the complexity of SSA programs and the long-term nature of total systems change. In addition, OTA blamed new procurement laws for slowing down and complicating the purchase of new hardware.

OTA pointed to a number of faults at SSA. From the very beginning of SMP, SSA failed to rethink its method of doing business. SMP basically sought to automate an organizational structure and way of doing business established in the 1930s. SSA failed, for instance, to question the role of 1300 field offices—are they really needed in a day of wide-area networks and microcomputers? Should SSA's major data files be centralized in Baltimore? SSA failed to re-

think its basic architecture of a centralized mainframe operation in Baltimore serving the entire country. Why not a more decentralized structure? Why not minicomputers in every District Office? OTA also pointed to SSA's failure to develop new software on a timely basis and a new database architecture. It was felt these shortcomings, especially in software and database, would ultimately come to haunt SSA thereafter. In general, SMP lacked a vision for the future around which it could build a powerful new information architecture.[2]

GAO, OTA, and labor critics believed that whatever increases in productivity occurred from 1982 to 1988 resulted largely from work-force reduction, deterioration in service, and asking the remaining employees to work harder, rather than any result of technology per se. Although public surveys published by SSA showed the general public thought SSA did a fine job, surveys of field office employees and managers with direct knowledge of the situation showed declining service quality, employee performance, and morale.

As employee levels dropped, managers complained in interviews that the "work load is oppressive," recalling days in the 1960s when lines of clients surrounded SSA offices. While managers praised the new claims modernization software, teleservice centers, and pre-interviewing techniques which permit clericals to answer questions of clients using on-line queries, the overall reduction in labor force put a "crushing load on District Office personnel." Employees and managers reported many of the most capable managers and claims representatives were leaving SSA for the private sector or other government jobs as working conditions deteriorated.[3]

For the critics SSA had made some improvements in service and processing, but these resulted early in the SMP plan and were largely the result of hardware purchases and running the old software faster. Whatever progress in productivity occurred did so at the expense of employees and service to clients.

By 1988, SSA management conceded that SMP had indeed doubled in

size to a projected $1 billion, but by 1988 the SMP plan had actually spent slightly less ($444 million) than the original estimate of $500 million. Management conceded that the time required to reach state-of-the-art processing had been extended to 1992; that "there was an excessive emphasis on hardware, that software development was slow, and that the agency carried over large balances of unbudgeted funds from year to year (indicating difficulty in managing projects and allocated funds).[4] In fact, software development was four years behind schedule, and the database redesign (the so-called "backend" of the system) was still being considered after five years. Nevertheless, SSA had documented steady improvement in a number of measures of services to beneficiaries, many of which are due to the SMP:

- A 25 percent decrease in RSI claims processing time.
- A small decrease in DI claims processing time (2.2 days).
- A high and improving rate of RSI claims accuracy (95.7 to 97.2 percent).
- A 41 percent decrease in SSI processing time.
- A 7 percent decrease in SSI blind/disabled processing time.
- A 47 percent decrease in RSDI (Retired Survivors Disability Insurance) change of status processing time.
- Stable administrative costs in RSI since 1980 (1.1 percent of benefits).

Management pointed to the following key changes brought about by the SMP:

Management claimed that overall SMP brought about a 25 percent increase in productivity. The agency was now doing slightly more "work" in 1988 than it was in 1982 but with 17,000 fewer employees. SSA created a new deputy commissioner for systems development and raised the status of systems in the organization to the senior management level. Management noted that SMP had made great progress in its specific specific program areas:

Hardware Capacity Upgrade. Between 1982 and 1988 SSA increased process-

1982	Today
6 weeks to receive a Social Security card	Takes 10 working days
4 years to post annual wage reports	Done in 5 months
Over a month to process an RSI claim	Done in about 20 days
4 years to do annual recomputations for those entitled to higher benefits	Done in 6 months
3 weeks of computer processing for annual cost-of-living increases	Done in 25 hours
15 days for payments in emergency situations	Received in 5 days

ing capacity twentyfold, from 20 MIPS to a total of 400 MIPS, replacing outdated computers purchased without competitive bids with hardware supplied by three manufacturers on a competitive basis.

System Operation and Management Program (SOMP). The central processing facility in Baltimore developed efficient job scheduling standards and procedures for handling tapes and documents so that 95 percent of its processing is completed on time.

Data Communications Utility Program (DCUP). Under SMP a network of more than 50,000 devices was installed nationwide, with the objective of putting a terminal on every claims representative's desktop. Network capacity increased from 1200 characters per second in 1982 to 7000 characters per second in 1988.

Software Engineering. SSA made major progress redesigning the software for the retirement program. Now millions of retired persons can initiate the claims process or inquire about their accounts using an 800 number teleservice or have a claims representative initiate the claim on-line from a district office. In 1982 this capability was not even dreamed of. Developing such interactive systems to deliver services required entirely new code; the old software could not be salvaged.

Database Integration. SAA converted 500,000 reels of tape to more modern DASDs. All master files were converted to disk, making it possible to handle more than 2 million inquiries per day directly on-line. SSA developed its own in-house data management system called the Master Data Access Method (MADAM) to handle all on-line and batch access to SSA master files.

However, the data are still organized according to major program areas. SSA has yet to develop an integrated database for all or even some of its major programs that could provide a "whole person" view of SSA clients. A major difficulty is deciding on an overall database architecture that could integrate information from the major program areas.

SECTION III: SSA'S STRATEGIC PLAN AND INFORMATION SYSTEMS PLAN

SSA issued a new Agency Strategic Plan (ASP) in 1988. The plan was updated in 1991 to incorporate a wider vision of the agency's future. The new ASP strategic priorities called for improvements in client access to SSA, the appeals process, and the disability process; movement toward a "paperless agency"; and establishment of a decentralized data processing structure.

In August 1990 Renato A. DiPentima took over as deputy commissioner of systems. DiPentima initiated a seven-year Information Systems Plan (ISP) in September 1991 to support the Agency Strategic Plan. The ISP was updated in 1992 and late 1993.

The Information Systems Plan is SSA's long-range plan for managing information systems as the agency moves into the 1990s and beyond. Its primary goal is to support the Agency Strategic Plan by building a systems environment that improves service to the public and SSA users. Long-term strategic priorities include improving the disability process, the appeals process, and the public's access to SSA by turning SSA into a paperless agency with electronic claims folders and establishing a coop-

erative processing architecture. The Information Systems Plan was designed to be a continuous plan that could always be upgraded.

Both plans address the challenges faced by SSA as it moves into the twenty-first century. SSA's total workload is expected to increase by 26 percent between 1990 and 2005. There will be limited funding for new initiatives, coupled with increased demands for higher level of service to the public. In the past, most SSA clients preferred to visit SSA field offices. Today, they prefer to conduct their business over the telephone and they expect the same fast, efficient service they receive in the private sector. SSA must enhance systems to handle increasing workloads without hiring more employees, keeping costs low because of scarce budgetary resources. The number of field and operational employees has already decreased substantially since the 1980s and the remaining employees require new technologies to handle the increased workload.

SSA still maintains a centralized mainframe system at its Baltimore headquarters linked to 39,000 dumb terminals in its field offices and teleservice centers via SSANet, the main SSA Network (the former Data Communications and Utility Program described earlier). The Information Systems Plan calls for moving SSA toward a distributed architecture, ending its total reliance on centralized mainframe computers for its programmatic applications that deliver services to SSA clients. Selected business functions will be distributed between headquarters and local processors. Most SSA employees will use LAN-based intelligent workstations with multiple levels of software running on platforms ranging from mainframes to microcomputers. Databases will be distributed. Greater efficiency will result from having processing close to the data source and information user. Figure III.1 illustrates SSA's target systems environment.

The SSA's next round of technology modernization calls for $1.125 billion to be spent between 1994 and 1998 on an IWS/LAN (intelligent workstation and

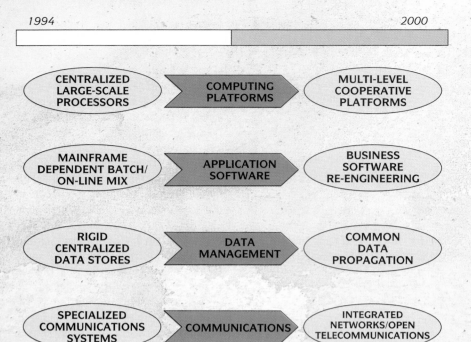

FIGURE III.1

SSA's Target Systems Environment. *Source: Social Security Administration, "Information Systems Plan." Baltimore, Maryland: Department of Health and Human Services, September 1994.*

local-area network) Technology Program. IWS/LAN is intended to move SSA to a more decentralized computing environment by replacing SSA's "dumb terminals" with 95,000 486 microcomputers arranged in token ring LANs. The LANs will give SSA field staff more autonomous computing power and the ability to perform word processing, to share data, and to exchange E-mail messages. They will be linked to the agency's main network, SSANet (see Figure III.2).

By distributing processing and storing data at the level where the work is done, the number of data accesses and the volume of network traffic should be minimized, increasing the response time for many workloads. This arrangement will allow the automation of many functions that are presently not cost effective to do on a mainframe or practical to do on a standalone microcomputer, giving SSA the computer capacity to handle increasing workloads.

The SSA's computer center in Baltimore will continue to supply mainframe processing power. SSA expects to use its existing mainframe software

for programs such as retirement and supplemental security that are already automated, with the microcomputers emulating the old terminals. But as applications are rewritten, the microcomputers will perform more of the processing and the mainframe will gradually evolve into a database server role. SSA has argued that implementation of IWS/LAN is essential to provide an infrastructure for future electronic delivery and re-engineering initiatives and to avoid problems and expenditures resulting from breakdowns in existing dumb terminals.

By the end of the 1990s, SSA will have replaced many batch applications with on-line interactive systems, starting with the Title II Claims process. Eventually the Title XVI, disability, and Title II post-entitlement processes will be handled on-line. By the year 2000, SSA expects to convert most of its major systems to an interactive environment using an "appearance of update" technique, which from the user perspective appears to update master records on-line. Expert systems, such as an application to pro-

vide answers to telephone inquiries, will help reduce manual processing.

Although databases will be distributed over SSA's multi-level telecommunications system, commercial DBMS are still not capable of handling SSA's specific requirements under a distributed processing environment. SSA plans to monitor the performance improvements of commercial DBMS as they mature for future consideration. The decision to distribute SSA's large databases will be based on cost/benefit and service improvement considerations.

SSA is reducing transmission costs by using telephone switching systems to integrate network access whenever possible, relying on FTS-2000 to provide a common connection to be shared by voice services, video teleconferencing, FAX, LAN interconnections, and SSANet. SSA communications planning will use OSI standards, specifying appropriate protocols, interfaces, and network technologies to obtain required intercommunication and interoperability.

SSA points to many service improvements that resulted from these systems initiatives. An 800 phone number now receives 300,000 calls a day. Seventy percent of babies in the United States are enumerated at birth, eliminating the need to make separate applications for Social Security numbers. Kiosks installed in some locations provide public information.

Is Distributed Technology Enough?

In the spring of 1994, the Office of Technology Assessment released a report stating that the SSA's $1.1 billion five-year migration from mainframe to client/server computing was technically sound, but ahead of the agency's understanding of how to use intelligent workstations and LANs to improve service delivery. The OTA report reiterated concerns raised by the GAO that SSA was unlikely to realize significant benefits because it had not linked its proposed technology strategy to specific service delivery improvements. GAO questioned SSA's plans to implement IWS/LAN be-

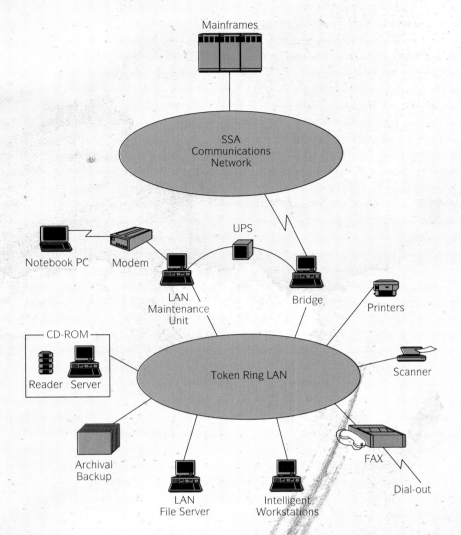

Mainframes

SSA
Communications
Network

Notebook PC   Modem

UPS

LAN
Maintenance
Unit

Bridge

Printers

CD-ROM

Reader   Server

Token Ring LAN

Scanner

Archival
Backup

LAN
File Server

Intelligent
Workstations

FAX

Dial-out

FIGURE III.2
SSA"s Target Distributed Processing System. *Source: Social Security Administration,*
"Information Systems Plan." Baltimore, Maryland: Department of Health and Human Services,
September 1994.

fore determining the service delivery improvements that could result from this technology. OTA noted that SSA had made a "good-faith effort" to restructure its service delivery but that the agency had "prioritized . . . installation according to current SSA operational and service delivery needs—essentially automating marginal improvements in the status quo." OTA believed that SSA needed to include its clients, labor representatives, and individuals with experience in electronic service delivery into its planning process and it needed to re-engineer its business processes to dramatically improve service. OTA also believed SSA had not done enough

analysis of the costs and benefits of automation, including IWS/LAN, and of the impact of automation against specific performance goals.

OTA pointed out that SSA's ever-increasing workload, coupled with staff reductions from further government downsizing, could again threaten SSA's ability to deliver the level of service expected by Congress and the public. The use of 800 telephone numbers, a key component of SSA's current service delivery strategy, is overloaded during peak periods. (Most callers receive a busy signal on their first attempt to call.)

OTA also questioned the feasibility of managing a massive distributed com-

puting environment from a single facility in Baltimore. Deputy Commissioner DiPentima responded by noting that it was a big challenge to maintain such a large network and monitor it centrally. If SSA were to monitor the network locally, it would require 2000 LAN managers. The centrally managed network has been able to process 20 million transactions per day with 99.9 percent uptime.

OTA recommended that SSA receive funding for re-engineering and service delivery planning and that the agency participate in governmentwide electronic delivery pilots and projects such as:

- The use of toll-free 800 telephone numbers for service delivery.

- Electronic data interchange for filing earnings reports by business.

- Direct electronic deposit of benefits payments.

- Electronic bulletin boards and networks to provide the public with information about SSA.

- Multiprogram electronic benefits delivery in which a single card could be used to obtain payment for Social Security benefits, Medicaid, and food stamps.

- Integrated electronic records for SSA recipients, providing a single "electronic folder" instead of separate electronic and paper files.

- Automated disability determination to streamline determination of initial and ongoing medical qualifications for disability insurance benefits.

Determining eligibility for disability benefits is considered the most troubled SSA service. SSA must continually assure that recipients are eligible based on their medical and financial condition. Candidates for disability benefits are currently evaluated by State Disability Determination Service (DDS) offices, which are funded by SSA but are run by the states. Initial disability determinations can take up to several months, with a backlog of 750,000 cases. The backlog of continuing reviews is even larger. The error rate for Disability

Insurance (DI), resulting in overpayments to eligible recipients, payments to ineligible recipients, or denial of benefits to qualified people, is estimated to be around 3.5 percent, similar to the error rate for Supplemental Security Income (SSI) programs. SSA-sponsored studies have suggested that automation will play a small role in improving the disability process in comparison to radically changing the organization and the flow of disability work. SSA set up a re-engineering task force in mid-1993, with the full support of top management, to focus on ways to radically improve the disability benefit determination process. The staff has conducted over 1000 interviews and visited SSA offices and Disability Determination Service offices in a majority of states.

Much has been learned by SSA about the difficulties of building systems that can meet ever-changing business needs. Management has learned that deploying new information technology does not automatically translate into fewer employees, especially when transaction volumes are increasing. How successful will SSA be in moving toward a more decentralized architecture? Will SSA's information systems infrastructure be able to provide the level of service the public and Congress expects? These are just some of the difficult questions facing SSA as it moves into the twenty-first century.

Sources: Kenneth C. Laudon (with Alan F. Westin), *Information Technology at SSA, 1935–1995*, forthcoming; Social Security Administration, "Information Systems Plan" (Baltimore: MD, Department of Health and Human Services, September 1994); Office of Technology Assessement, "The Social Security Administration's Decentralized Computer Strategy: Issues and Options" (Washington, DC: U.S. Government Printing Office, April 1994); Gary H. Anthes, "SSA Needs to Improve Business Planning," *Computerworld*, May 16, 1994; and Office of Technology Assessment, "The Social Security Administration and Information Technology, a Case Study" (Washington DC: U.S. Congress, 1986).

Case Study Questions

1. What were the major factors in SSA's past that made it a leading innovator in information systems technology? How did these supportive factors change in the 1970s?

2. Describe briefly the problems with SSA's hardware, software, data storage, and telecommunications systems prior to SMP.

3. What were the major environmental and institutional factors that created the crisis at SSA?

4. Why did SSA's reform efforts in the late 1970s fail?

5. What were the major elements of SSA's implementation strategy for SMP? Describe its major proejcts.

6. What successful changes in management and organizational structure have been brought about by SMP? How secure are these changes (what environmental factors could destroy them)?

7. In what areas has SMP had the greatest success? In what areas has SMP not succeeded? Why?

8. Evaluate SSA's IWS/LAN Technology Program in light of SSA's history of information system projects.

9. How successful has SSA been in creating an appropriate information system architecture for the year 2000? Justify your explanation.

[1] "Union Faults SSA Modernization Plan," *Federal Computer Week*, October 9, 1989.

[2] Office of Technology Assessment, "The Social Security Administration and Information Technology, a Case Study" (Washington DC: U.S. Congress, 1986).

[3] Based on interviews in northeastern U.S. metropolitan area District Offices by the authors and Alan F. Westin.

[4] Social Security Administration, "Report on Social Security Administration Computer Modernization and Related Expenditures," prepared for the Senate Appropriations Committee, February 1989, p. ii.

Management and Organizational Support Systems

Today's information economy and society puts a special premium on the management of information in the organization. Capturing and distributing intelligence and knowledge, leadership, collaboration, and group decision making have become vital to organizational innovation and survival. This section describes how information systems can foster these objectives and support new kinds of management decision making by individuals and groups.

Chapter 15
Information and Knowledge Work Systems

Chapter 15 examines the principal types of information systems supporting knowledge and information work in the organization. Technologies for document management, collaborative work, and project management facilitate communication, collaboration, and coordination among groups in the organization. Knowledge work systems are explicitly customized to meet the unique information requirements of skilled professionals and knowledge workers.

Chapter 16
Enhancing Management Decision Making

Chapter 16 focuses on decision support systems (DSS), group decision support systems (GDSS) and executive support systems (ESS). These systems are more helpful to managers faced with unstructured and semi-structured decisions than traditional information systems. Examples of individual, group, and organizational decision support systems and of leading-edge executive support applications show how these systems enhance the management decision-making process.

Chapter 17
Artificial Intelligence

Chapter 17 traces developments in artificial intelligence and shows how they can create information systems that capture knowledge and intelligence for organizations. Businesses can benefit from expert systems, which automate selected aspects of the decision-making process and from neural network applications, which imitate the thought processes of the biological brain. Numerous examples of expert systems, neural networks, fuzzy logic, genetic algorithms, and other intelligent techniques illuminate the capabilities and limitations of artificial intelligence applications in business.

Part Four Case Study:
EPRINET: A Strategic Network for the Utility Industry

This case illustrates how information technology was used to enhance the effectiveness of the Electronic Power Research Institute EPRI, an organization whose principal product was new knowledge. It illustrates some of the benefits and problems of implementing ambitious knowledge work systems. EPRINET was part of a larger strategic transition that EPRI had to undergo.

Chapter 15

Information and Knowledge Work Systems

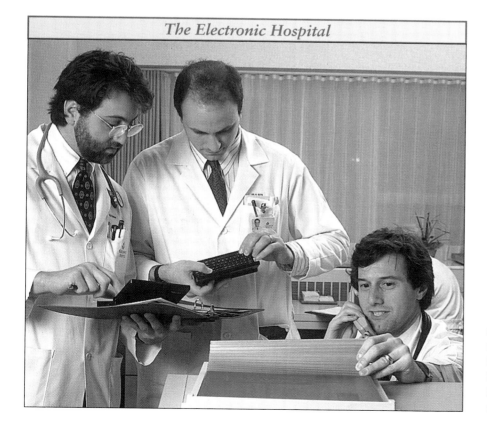

The Electronic Hospital

Computer technology is joining the battle to improve medical care while reducing cost. Hospitals such as New York University Hospital and St. Luke's—Roosevelt Hospital Center, both in New York City, have long stored such hospital records as patient records, medical test orders and results, operating room schedules, and medical supplies on internal networks. Now, on-line medical research is playing a growing role in the constant need for medical research and information.

A massive amount of new medical information is continuously being generated, and doctors need access to this information to provide quality medical care. More and more, medical professionals are turning to on-line medical databases to diagnose unusual and unfamiliar symptoms. Collins Kellogg, an internist in Watertown, New York, was baffled when one of his patients turned deep red on one side of his body and chalk white on the other whenever the patient exercised. Using an on-line medical database, Kellogg quickly identified the problem as Harlequin's syndrome, a rare nervous disorder that can be cured by a neurosurgeon.

These databases enable doctors to keep up with the enormous amount of new medical research that is being published daily. William Tierney, professor of medicine at Indiana University School of Medicine, consulted the popular Medline database when a woman was admitted to the school hospital with an inflamed and severely painful pancreas but showing none of the normal causes for this condition. Triggering a search with key words that included *pancreas* as well as the name of a new arthritis drug she was taking, English language abstracts of two Japanese and two French medical journal articles were identified that reported a link between the drug and the inflammation. Dr. Tierney removed the woman from the drug and she quickly improved. Not only did the search take only a few minutes, but Dr. Tierney would not have been able to find these articles in any other way because of both the language problem and the impossibility of an individual keeping up with the 3700 journals that are stored in the Medline database. Aside from identifying rare conditions, the use of these databases has resulted in a reduction of unnecessary procedures and so a lowering of hospital costs and a shortening of hospital stays. In addition to general medical databases like Medline, a number of databases now exist that focus on such specialties as cancer, AIDS, and medical ethics.

Television and telecommunications technologies have combined to improve medical care while reducing costs by bringing medical expertise back into the home and into other places where medical knowledge is required. Through the growth of telemedicine, doctors are able to see patients in their home without ever leaving the hospital. The Emory University Health Communications Project has developed a point-to-point video system known as Picasso that enables doctors to examine patients remotely. The system uses a television camera, computer software, and telecommunications transmission to send pictures from the patient to a doctor waiting in the hospital. Picasso systems cost only $5000 although a portable system in an oversized briefcase runs about $11,000. With such equipment, paramedics can actually do house calls rather than just rushing the patient to the hospital for treatment. Not only does this save the time of the doctor but studies have shown that 85 percent of patients transported to a hospital by paramedics do not actually need hospitalization at that time, so that Picasso is reducing unneeded hospitalization and patient inconvenience as well. Emory University

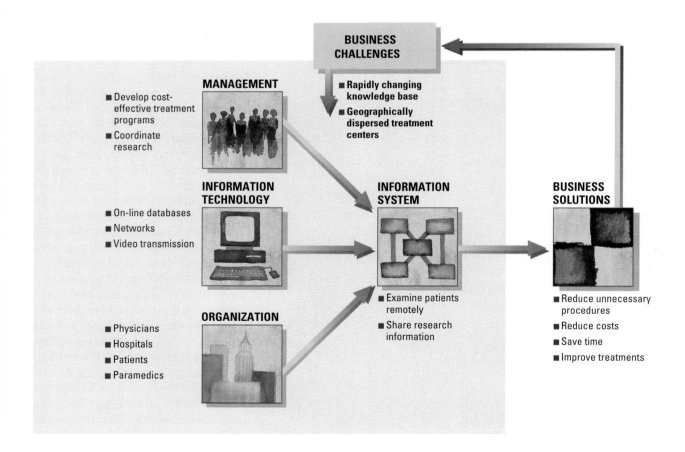

plans to use it to enable on-the-spot diagnosis at the 1996 Summer Olympics being held in Atlanta, and also expects to try it out with mountain rescue teams and police SWAT squads. ∎

Sources: Michael Fitzgerald, "Pictures Tell the Story to Atlanta Doctors," *Computerworld*, September 26, 1994; Fred Guterl, "The Doctor Will See You Now—Just Not in Person," *Business Week*, October 3, 1994; and Ron Winslow, "More Doctors Are Adding On-Line Tools to Their Kits," *The Wall Street Journal*, October 7, 1994.

Collaborating and communicating with other experts and sharing ideas and information are essential requirements not only for medical institutions but for businesses today as well. Advanced industrial societies have shifted from a manufacturing to an information economy in which the basis of wealth is the production of information and knowledge. The shift calls for new kinds of information systems to help organizations create, coordinate, and distribute information to achieve their goals. Such systems are called information and knowledge work systems, and they are the focus of this chapter.

This chapter describes the emergence of information and knowledge work and the unique information requirements of information and knowledge workers. Because offices play such a pivotal role in contemporary organizations, information systems designed to support major office activities and to promote collaborative work have become increasingly critical. We describe the major types of information systems used for disseminating and coordinating the flow of information in the organization and for supporting the activities of highly skilled knowledge workers and professionals.

After completing this chapter, you will be able to:

Learning Objectives

1. Define information work and the information economy.

2. Describe the roles of knowledge workers and data workers in the organization.

3. Describe the roles and principal activities of the office in contemporary business.

4. Explain the contributions of the principal types of office automation technologies.

5. Understand unique requirements of knowledge work systems.

6. Describe the major types of knowledge work systems.

15.1 KNOWLEDGE AND INFORMATION WORK

Chapter 1 introduced the emergence of the information economy as one of the key challenges of information systems today. The shift to an economy where the major source of wealth and prosperity is the production and distribution of information and knowledge has profound implications for the kinds of information systems found in contemporary organizations and the way they are used.

TRANSFORMATION OF THE ECONOMY

Since the turn of the century, the United States, Canada, and Western Europe have been moving toward a service and information economy and away from an agricultural and manufacturing economy. The percentage of people who work in offices using information to produce economic value has been rising and the percentage of workers who work with their hands in factories or on farms has been declining. (In the United States, the percentage of jobs in manufacturing has fallen from 27 percent in 1920 to 17 percent today and is expected to be 12 percent by 2005.) Among white-collar workers, the fastest growing occupations have been clerical, professional, and technical workers, and managers and administrators.

Four factors are involved in this shift. First, there has been a worldwide shift in the production of manufactured goods in which third world and developing societies have become centers of manufacturing. At the same time, the so-called advanced societies have shifted toward services. Textile products and steel ingots are more economically produced in Asian countries, while North American and European countries are the primary sources for bioengineering services and products or computer software.

Second, there has been a rapid growth in knowledge and information-intense products and services. **Knowledge- and information-intense products** are products that require a great deal of learning and knowledge to produce. Intensification of knowledge utilization in the production of traditional products has increased as well. This trend is readily seen throughout the automobile industry where both design and production now rely heavily upon knowledge-intensive information technology. Over the past decade, the automobile producers have sharply increased their hiring of computer specialists, engineers, and designers while reducing the number of blue-collar production workers. Entire new information services have sprung up, such as CompuServe, Dow Jones News Service, and Lexis. These fields are now employing millions of people.

Third, there has been a substitution of knowledge and information workers for manual production workers within the goods sectors. Machine tool operators, for instance, have often been replaced by technicians who monitor computer-controlled machine tools. Fourth, new kinds of knowledge- and information-intense organizations have emerged that are devoted entirely to the production, processing, and distribution of information. For instance, environmental engineering firms, which specialize in preparing environmental impact statements for municipalities and private contractors, simply did not exist prior to the 1960s. These new kinds of organizations also employ millions of people.

With these changes, there were conservatively 63 million information workers in the U.S. economy (around 52 percent of the labor force) by 1980. As early as 1976, the value of information sector products and services had already exceeded that of the manufacturing or goods sector (see Figure 15.1). By 1990, the information sector (including services) accounted for $3 out of every $4 of GNP (gross national product) in the United States. The shift toward information work and workers has had profound implications for the kinds of information technologies and systems found at the heart of business enterprises. Because so much of the U.S. and other advanced economies depends on knowledge and information work, any overall advance in productivity and wealth critically depends on increasing the productivity of knowledge and information workers.

WHAT IS KNOWLEDGE AND INFORMATION WORK?

To describe how information systems can increase the productivity of information and knowledge workers, we need to understand what kinds of jobs these workers

knowledge- and information-intense products Products that require a great deal of learning and knowledge to produce.

FIGURE 15.1
Emergence of the information economy. The value of the information sector in the U.S. economy began to exceed the value of the manufacturing or goods sector by 1976 and has continued to surpass it into the 1990s. *Reprinted by permission of the publisher from "Technology and the Service Sector." by Stephen S. Roach,* Technological Forecasting and Social Change, *Vol. 34, No. 4, December 1988. Copyright 1988 by Elsevier Science Publishing Co., Inc.*

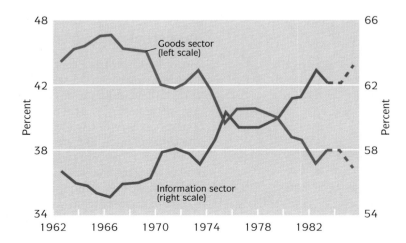

Table 15.1 Examples of Information, Service, and Goods Industries

Information	Goods	Service
Telephone	Agriculture	Hotels
Trade	Logging	Business service
Finance	Chemicals	Auto repair
Insurance	Steel	Medical service
Education	Farm machines	Amusements

Sources: Wolff and Baumol, 1987; U.S. Census 1990.

perform. First, we have to establish some basic definitions. Table 15.1 gives some examples of information, service, and goods industries.

Distinguishing Knowledge and Data Workers

information workers People in the labor force who primarily create, work with, or disseminate information.

information work Work that primarily consists of creating or processing information.

knowledge workers People such as engineers, scientists, or architects who design products or services or create new knowledge for the organization.

data workers People such as secretaries or bookkeepers who primarily use, process, and disseminate the organization's paperwork.

The U.S. Department of Labor defines as **information workers** all those people in the labor force who primarily create, work with, or disseminate information. **Information work** is work that consists primarily of creating or processing information. There are two commonly accepted types of information workers: **knowledge workers** (those who primarily create new information and knowledge) and **data workers** (who primarily use, process, or disseminate information). Thus, knowledge work refers to work that primarily creates new information or knowledge. Data work is work that involves the use, manipulation, or dissemination of information.

In contrast, service workers are those people who primarily deliver a service, and goods workers are those who primarily work with physical objects or transform physical materials. Examples of each of these four kinds of workers are given in Table 15.2.

These distinctions are not always easy to apply, and some occupations like managers both create new information and distribute data. Scholars handle this ambiguity by classifying half the managers as knowledge workers and half as data workers.

Knowledge and data workers can be distinguished by the amount of formal education required for them to be qualified to work in the field. Knowledge workers—like engineers, judges, scientists, writers, and architects—all must exercise independent

Table 15.2 Examples of Occupations for Knowledge, Data, Service, and Goods Workers

Knowledge	Data	Service	Goods
Architect	Salesperson	Waiter	Teamster
Engineer	Accountant	Sanitary engineer	Welder
Judge	Lawyer	Cook	Machine operator
Scientist	Pharmacist	Nurse	Lumberman
Reporter	R.R. conductor	Hairdresser	Fisherman
Researcher	Foreman	Child care worker	Farmer
Writer	Draftsman	Gardener	Construction worker
Actuary	Real estate salesperson	Cleaner	Miner
Programmer	Secretary	Barber	Glazier
Manager*	Manager	Clergy*	Factory operative

*Many occupations—like managers and clergy—cannot be easily classified. Managers, for instance, sometimes create new knowledge and information when they write reports and hence often act like knowledge workers. At other times, they read and disseminate reports like data workers. Scholars handle this situation by classifying half of the managers as knowledge workers and half as data workers. A similar situation exists with clergy: They both provide a service and disseminate information. In the future we will need better data on specific occupations.
Source: Wolff and Baumol, 1987; Porat, 1977.

judgment and creativity based on their mastery of a large body of specialized knowledge. Therefore, they usually must obtain an advanced degree and/or a professional certification before beginning their work careers. Data workers, such as sales personnel, accountants, real estate agents, and secretaries, on the other hand, primarily process information and do not create it. Typically, this type of work does not require advanced educational degrees, although some college or even an undergraduate degree is often required.

Not surprisingly, these two groups of workers tend to have different information systems needs. While data and knowledge workers both use office automation systems, data workers rely upon them as their primary or only system. However, to do their work, knowledge workers often require specific knowledge work systems based on powerful professional workstations and highly specialized software.

Where are knowledge and data workers concentrated? All information workers work in offices (even if that office is at home or the work is being done on a plane) or rely directly on offices for support (such as salespeople or laboratory researchers). However, knowledge workers and data workers are distributed differently in the economy. Knowledge workers are rather equitably distributed across all industries, whereas data workers are concentrated in service industries, finance, government, and trade (see Figure 15.2). This stands to reason; data workers are predominantly the clerical and sales workers, who dominate in the service sector.

FIGURE 15.2
The distribution of knowledge and data workers in the U.S. economy. Where are the knowledge and data workers? Knowledge workers are distributed equally across all industries whereas data workers are concentrated in service industries, finance, government, and trade. *Source: Wolff and Baumol, 1987.*

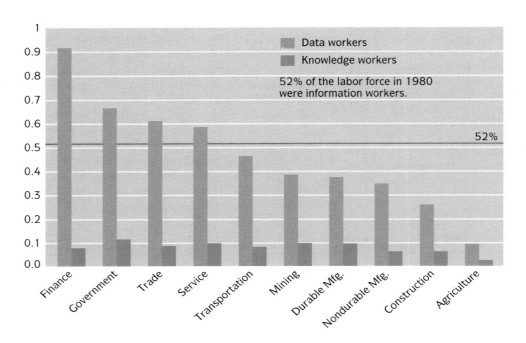

INFORMATION WORK AND PRODUCTIVITY

As we have indicated, knowledge- and information-intense industries have become the fastest-growing industries in the United States, while the fastest-growing segment of the American labor force is the information workers. The country has also experienced a dramatic shift in capital investment patterns in recent years—in the early 1980s, for the first time, capital investment per information worker began to surpass capital investment per factory worker. In 1989, over 70 percent of all capital investment was in the area of information technology, with most of that 70 percent going directly into offices.

While information technology has increased productivity in manufacturing, the extent to which computers have enhanced the productivity of information workers is under debate. Some studies show that investment in information technology has not led to any appreciable growth in productivity among office workers and that the average white-collar productivity gain from 1980 to 1990 has been only 0.28 percent an-

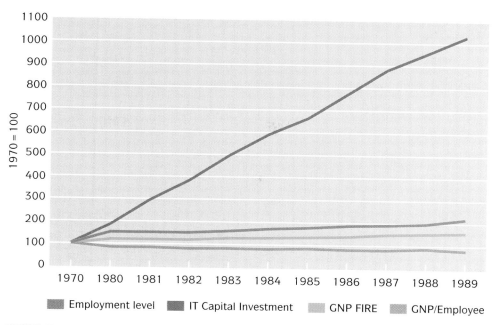

FIGURE 15.3

Productivity in three knowledge and information-intense industries—finance, insurance, and real estate. This chart compares employment levels, investment in information technology, gross national product, and the amount of gross national product per employee in the finance, insurance, and real estate sectors of the U.S. economy. It shows that the amount of gross national product produced per employee in this sector remained stagnant and even slightly declined between 1970 and 1989 while the capital investment in information technology increased tenfold. Employment levels and the amount of GNP produced by this sector only rose slightly during this period. (The amounts are in 1982 dollars.)
Source: Azimuth Corporation, 1993. Copyright 1993 by Azimuth Corporation. Reprinted by permission.

nually (Roach, 1988). Figure 15.3 shows that the amount of gross national product (the total value of goods and services produced per employee) in the finance, insurance, and real estate industries remained stagnant and even declined slightly between 1970 and 1989, while the capital investment in information technology increased tenfold.

Other studies suggest that information technology investments are starting to generate a productivity payback. Brynjolfsson and Hitt's detailed examination of information systems spending at 380 large firms over a five-year period found that return on investment (ROI) averaged over 50 percent per year for computers of all sizes (Brynjolfsson and Hitt, 1993). Morgan Stanley economist Steven Roach observed that after stagnating in the 1980s, productivity in service industries grew at an annual rate of 3 percent in the early 1990s (Roach, 1993). It is too early to tell whether these gains are short term or represent a genuine turnaround in service sector productivity.

Productivity changes among information workers are difficult to measure because of the problems of identifying suitable units of output for information work (Panko, 1991). How does one measure the output of a law office? Should one measure productivity by examining the number of forms completed per employee (a measure of physical unit productivity), or by examining the amount of revenue produced per employee (a measure of financial unit productivity) in an information- and knowledge-intense industry?

Even if one agrees on a suitable measure of productivity, different organizations can produce different results. Figure 15.4 compares the productivity of two major U.S. government agencies, the Internal Revenue Service (IRS) and the Social Security Administration (SSA). Both were early users of computers and both invested heavily in new information system technology between 1970 and 1990. If we measure IRS productivity by looking at the number of forms completed per employee, and SSA productivity by the number of clients handled per employee, the productivity of the Internal Revenue Service remained stagnant between 1970 and 1990, while Social Security

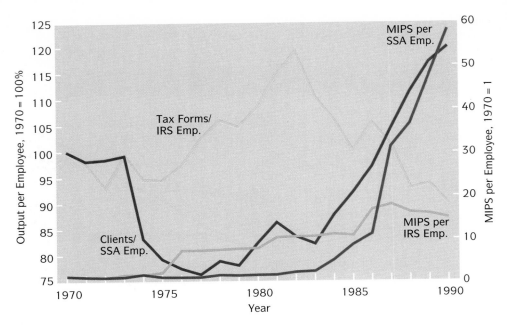

FIGURE 15.4
Productivity and investment in information technology in the U.S. Internal Revenue Service (IRS) and the Social Security Administration (SSA). Between 1970 and 1990 both organizations invested heavily in information technology. The amount of investment in information technology is indicated by MIPS per employee. IRS productivity is measured by the number of forms completed per employee, and SSA productivity is measured by the number of clients handled per employee. The left and right axes are indexes. The chart shows that between 1970 and 1990 the number of tax forms completed per IRS employee at first rose but then declined 10%, while the number of MIPS per employee rose fifteen-fold. During the same period the number of clients handled per SSA employee increased 20% with a sixty-fold increase in MIPS per employee. These findings suggest that investing in information technology does not necessarily increase productivity.

Administration productivity grew during the same period. The reasons for these differences are not only technological. During the 1980s, Congress demanded that SSA cut its work force by one third in exchange for providing $1 billion in new information system technology. The Social Security Administration had to make procedural and job design changes to accommodate a growing number of clients with fewer staff members. These organizational changes were enhanced by new information systems technology, but without these changes, gains in SSA productivity would probably not have been possible. Introduction of information technology alone does not necessarily guarantee productivity. Firms are more likely to produce high returns on information technology investments if they rethink their procedures, processes, and business goals.

15.2 INFORMATION WORK AND OFFICE AUTOMATION

Information work is concentrated in offices, and office automation systems have been developed to facilitate the processing, distribution, and coordination of information in the firm. Here we describe the role of offices in contemporary organizations and show how this role can be supported by various types of office automation technologies.

THREE ROLES OF THE OFFICE WITHIN THE ORGANIZATION

No longer a mundane clerical typing pool or simply a "bureaucratic nightmare," by the 1980s, scholars and computer vendors alike came to see the office as one of the most important work sites for professional knowledge and data workers. Offices to-

FIGURE 15.5
The three major roles of offices. Offices perform three major roles. [1] They coordinate the work of local professionals and information workers. [2] They coordinate work in the organization across levels and functions. [3] They couple the organization to the external environment.

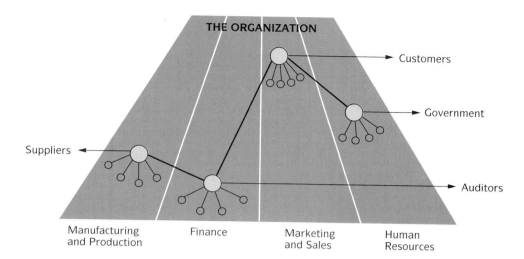

day involve an incredibly diverse array of professional, managerial, sales, and clerical employees. Offices are groups composed of people who work together toward shared goals. In this sense, office work is complex and cooperative, and yet highly individualistic. It represents not a factory of collaborating workers so much as an orchestra of highly trained individuals. Offices perform three critical organizational roles (see Figure 15.5):

- They coordinate and manage the work of local professional and information workers within the organization.

- They link the work being performed across all levels and functions throughout the organization.

- They couple the organization to the external environment, including to its clients and suppliers; when you call an organization, you call an office.

OFFICE ACTIVITIES AND TECHNOLOGIES

office activities The principal activities performed at offices; these include managing documents, scheduling and communicating with people, managing data, and managing projects.

To fulfill the roles that we have described, offices usually perform the five major **office activities** illustrated in Table 15.3: managing documents, scheduling individuals and groups, communicating with individuals and groups, managing data on individuals and groups, and managing projects. Table 15.3 also contains the authors' estimate, on average, of percentage of effort (capital investment and time) the office invests in each activity. For example, we estimate that document management characteristically consumes about 40 percent of the total office effort in time expended and capital investment. Information technology which has been developed to support each of these activities, is listed in the far right column of the table. Some of these technologies, such as groupware, actually support more than one of these activities.

office automation systems (OAS) Computer systems, such as word processing, voice mail systems, and video conferencing systems, that are designed to increase the productivity of information workers in the office.

Office automation systems (OAS) can be defined as any application of information technology that intends to increase productivity of information workers in the office. Fifteen years ago, office automation meant only the creation, processing, and management of documents. Today, although professional knowledge and information work remains highly document-centered, office work requires a great deal more from its office automation systems. Digital image processing—word and document—is also at the core of today's systems, as are high-speed digital communications services. Because office work involves many people jointly engaged in projects, contemporary office automation systems have powerful project management tools and group assistance tools like networked digital calendars. An ideal contemporary office automation system would involve a seamless network of digital machines linking professional, clerical, and managerial work groups and running a variety of types of software (see again Table 15.3).

Table 15.3 Office Automation: Roles, Activities, and Systems in the Modern Office

General Roles of Offices	Activities in an Office	Percentage of Effort	Information Technology Assistance
1. Coordination and management of people and work	1. Managing documents Creating, storing/retrieving, and communicating image (analog) and digital documents	40%	Document management Word processing hardware and software Desktop publishing Digital image processing
2. Linking organizational units and projects	2. Scheduling individuals and groups Creating, managing, and communicating documents, plans, and calendars	10%	Digital calendars Electronic calendars and schedules Electronic mail Groupware
3. Coupling the organization to outside groups and people	3. Communicating with individuals and groups Initiating, receiving, and managing voice and digital communications with diverse groups and individuals	30%	Communications PBX and digital phone equipment Voice mail Groupware
	4. Managing data on individuals and groups Entering and managing data to track external customers, clients, and vendors and internal individuals and groups	10%	Data management Desktop database for client/customer tracking, project tracking, and calendar information (personal information manager)
	5. Managing projects Planning, initiating, evaluating, monitoring projects Resource allocation Personnel decisions	10%	Project management Desktop project management tools CPM and PERT methods

Source: © 1990 Azimuth Corporation

While the first wave of office automation systems established technologies designed to support such obvious clerical activities as word processing and simple task coordination, today's office applications are based on an array of technologies: document management technologies, technologies for collaborative work, desktop data management technologies, and project management technologies (see Table 15.4).

Table 15.4	Contemporary Office Technologies
Office Activity	Technology
Managing documents	Document imaging/workflow management
Collaborative work	Groupware, E-mail, electronic calendars
Managing information	Desktop data management (personal information managers)
Managing projects	Desktop project managers

Managing Documents

Technologies that are used to create, process, and manage documents are known as document management technologies. These technologies include word processing, desktop publishing, document imaging, and workflow management. Word processing is the most widely used technology in today's offices, a result of the dramatic increase in productivity it has brought to all information workers—clerks, managers, and knowledge workers alike. Desktop publishing allows the user to produce professional publishing-quality output using documents created with word processing software. A skilled user of a desktop publisher can produce brochures, newsletters, and reports that approach the quality of a professional typesetter and graphics designer. Desktop publishing packages, such as PageMaker by Aldus, offer enhanced text handling and page layout capabilities. They allow the user to resize, rotate, and modify graphics images. This technology also includes a computer language, often Adobe System's Postscript, to define the page, type fonts, and graphics for high-quality laser printers and other output devices.

Document Imaging and Workflow Management Systems

While word processing and desktop publishing address the creation and presentation of documents, they only exacerbate the existing paper avalanche problem. Hundreds of billions of pieces of paper are produced by businesses each year. The U.S. banking industry handled 50 billion checks in 1990 at an average handling cost of five cents, or a total handling cost of $2.5 billion. Ultramar Oil, a Long Beach, California, oil refinery, maintains about 20,000 material safety data sheets in huge notebooks; if an emergency chemical spill occurs, employees must manually search these notebooks for the appropriate sheet or sheets that contain the life-saving and damage control information they urgently need.

The issue concerns far more than sheer quantity, however. Workflow problems arising from paper handling are enormous. According to International Data Corporation (IDC, 1990), processing an insurance underwriting application submitted on paper would typically require about 11 clerical steps and 6 professional steps, and could take 33 days (see Figure 15.6). Customer calls often require the customer service staff to locate paper documents and then call the customer back. Locating documents that are lost or mis-sorted adds to the time and cost. A major New York bank estimated that if it eliminated the return calls, it could save millions of dollars every year just in the phone bill (not to mention staff time costs and customer relations problems).

document imaging systems
Systems that convert documents and images into digital form so that they can be stored and accessed by the computer.

One way to reduce problems stemming from paper-based workflow is to employ document imaging systems. **Document imaging systems** are systems that convert documents and images into digital form so that they can be stored and accessed by the

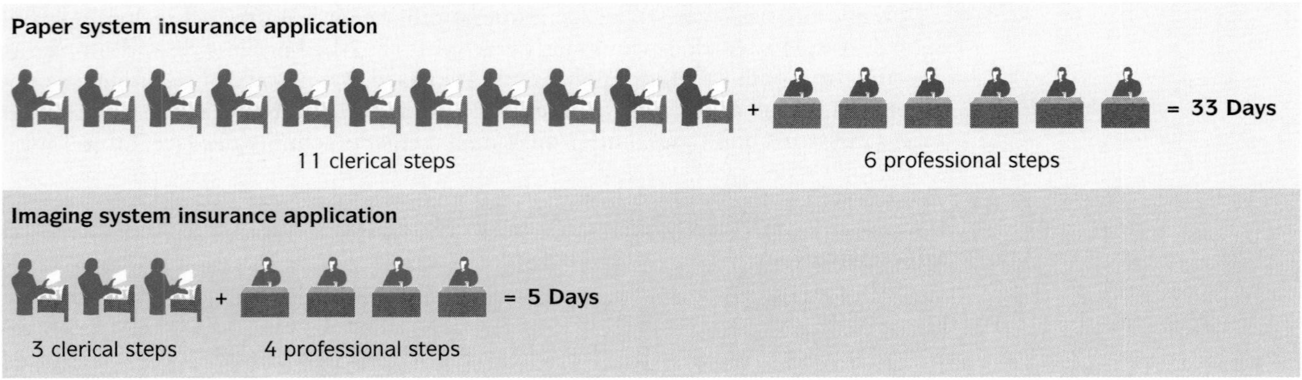

= 33 Days

11 clerical steps

6 professional steps

Imaging system insurance application

+ = 5 Days

3 clerical steps

4 professional steps

FIGURE 15.6
Insurance underwriting application enhanced by imaging and workflow automation. The improved efficiency and reduced workflow justify the expense of an image management system. The application requiring 33 days in a paper system would take only 5 days with image management and workflow redesign, resulting in tremendous savings to the insurance company. *Source: "Image Management Systems," IDC White Paper, Computerworld, September 24, 1990. Copyright 1990 by CW Publishing, Inc., Framingham, MA 01701. Reprinted from* Computerworld.

jukebox A device for storing and retrieving many optical disks.

index server In imaging systems, a device that stores the indexes that allow a user to identify and retrieve a specific document.

workflow management The process of streamlining business procedures so that documents can be moved easily and efficiently from one location to another.

computer. Such systems store, retrieve, and manipulate a digitized image of a document, allowing the document itself to be discarded. The system must contain a scanner that converts the document image into a bit-mapped image, storing that image as a graphic. This technology is different from optical character recognition (OCR) which "reads" a printed optical character, identifies the character by determining its pattern, and then stores it in the computer in its digital form. With OCR, a document is character-based and can be edited like any document created in a word processor. However, with imaging systems, a picture of the document is stored. With imaging systems, the document will originally be stored on a magnetic disk, where it can be retrieved instantly. When it ceases to be active, it will be transferred to an optical disk where it will be stored for as many months or years as is needed. Optical disks, kept on-line in a **jukebox** (a device for storing and retrieving many optical disks), require up to a minute to retrieve the document automatically. A typical large jukebox will store over 10 million pages (an 8 1/2″ by 11″ document usually requires about 50 kilobytes of storage after data compression).

An imaging system also requires an **index server** to contain the indexes that will allow users to identify and retrieve the document when needed. Once the document has been scanned, index data are entered so that the document can be retrieved in a variety of ways, depending upon the application. For example, the index may contain the document scan date, the customer name and number, the document type, and some subject information. Finally, the system must include retrieval equipment, primarily workstations capable of handling graphics, although printers are usually included.

To achieve the large productivity gains promised by imaging technology, organizations must redesign their workflow. In the past, the existence of only one copy of the document largely shaped workflow. Work had to be performed serially; two people could not work on the same document at the same time. Documents needed to be protected so they would not be lost or destroyed. Documents containing confidential data had to be locked up. Significant staff time had to be devoted to filing and retrieving documents. Critical analytical work could not be done because files could not be found—either because they were out (in use) or because they were not filed according to the kind of data the individual needs to analyze (an insurance company cannot study breast cancer claim costs if the documents are filed by the name of the insured rather than by the type of illness).

Once a document has been stored electronically, workflow management can change the traditional methods of working with documents. **Workflow management** is the process of streamlining business procedures so that documents can be moved more easily and efficiently from one location to another. Imaging technology automates processes such as routing documents to different locations, securing approvals, scheduling, and generating reports. Document integrity—protection against loss, destruction or prying eyes—can be handled through data backup, and through terminal and/or log in ID security, just as with other computer data. Two or more people can work simultaneously on the same document, allowing a much quicker completion date. Work need not ever be delayed because a file is "out" or a document is "in transit." And with a properly designed indexing system, users will be able to retrieve files in many different ways, based upon the content of the document.

Let us look at two actual success stories. The United Services Automobile Association, with 13,600 employees, is the largest direct writer of property and casualty insurance in the United States. Selling directly to members via mail or telephone, it is the largest mail order firm in the United States as well. USAA receives over 100,000 letters and mails over 250,000 items daily. USAA has developed the largest imaging system in the world, storing 1.5 billion pages. All incoming mail received each day by the policy department is scanned and stored on optical disk. The original documents are thrown away. Six of USAA's major regional offices across the country are hooked up to its imaging network, illustrated in Figure 15.7. The network consists of image scanners, optical storage units, a mainframe computer, and a local area network to link service representatives' workstations and the scanner workstations located in the firm's mail room. Mail clerks feed documents into a scanner, which digitizes them and transmits the data to USAA's Management Folder Software for storage on optical disk. Service representatives can retrieve a client's file on-line and view documents from personal computers on their desktops. About 2000 people use the network.

FIGURE 15.7
United States Automobile Association's (USAA) imaging network. Scanners enter mail received by USAA's policy department into the imaging system, which stores and distributes the digitally processed image of the document electronically. Service representatives have immediate on-line access to clients' data.

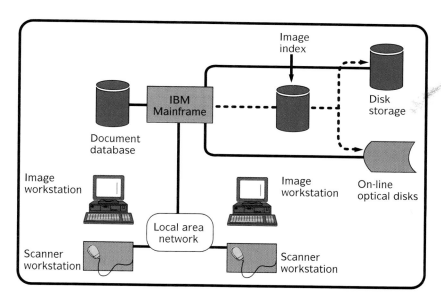

Users believe that the imaging system reduces the amount of time their work would take with a paper-based system by one third, saving paper and storage costs. Before this system was introduced, 200 clerks had to search for files in a 39,000 square-foot warehouse, a process that might take one day or up to two weeks if the files were lying on a policy reviewer's desk. Customer service has been improved because electronic documents can be accessed more rapidly. Three-week-old files can be accessed in less than one second; six-month-old letters in 15 to 20 seconds; mail up to two years old in less than two minutes (Lasher, Ives, and Jarvenpaa, 1991; "USAA Insuring Progress," 1992).

The San Jose Medical Center is a 315-bed community trauma facility in San Jose, California. In the fall of 1991, it began installing an imaging system based upon a Banyan Systems, Vines network, and 21 Wang and IBM-compatible 80386 workstations. The system cost about $450,000. The center expects full payback in less than 18 months ($380,000 payback the first year), partially through staff reductions and partially through elimination of the estimated $13 cost for retrieving each file manually. In addition, the center will use the system to generate an additional $150,000 annual income through making document copies. In the past, it met requests for copies by sending the documents to a copying service, with the copy requester paying the copying service. The hospital estimates it did 70 percent of the copying work without any compensation. Now it will be paid for the service without an accompanying increase in work. Most important to the mission of the center, document retrieval time is reduced from about 20 minutes to almost instantaneously, a critical improvement when a medical emergency occurs (Nash, 1992).

Imaging systems, combined with workflow management, can bring many benefits to an organization:

- *Cost savings, as we have documented, can be significant.* According to the International Data Corporation, such corporations as American Express, Citicorp, and Federal Express believe they are realizing annual savings of 20 percent.

- *Paper reduction is clear.* Most people will be working from electronic copies, not paper copies.

- *Linked closely to paper reduction is floor space.* One major U.S. law firm estimates that turning to document imaging freed up 80 percent of its office space.

- *Time saving is another benefit.* The same law firm claims a 50 percent reduction in time spent filing, copying, storing, and retrieving documents. This benefit can be very significant for organizations that currently archive paper documents and then require two or more days to locate these documents.

- *Work management is enhanced.* One bank mortgage department has automated the work queues so that no mortgage operator has more than five mortgages in his or her queue at a time.

- *Customer service can be dramatically improved.* Customer service staff can answer questions instantly. Customers are not placed on hold while the staff member searches for the file. Customers do not have to be called back because the file is not available. Customer satisfaction can be enhanced by a company's ability to complete its work more quickly; for example, a company can respond to a medical claim in days instead of weeks.

Image technology is also a source of genuine competitive advantage. American Express Travel Related Services (TRS), one of the subsidiaries of the American Express Corporation, depends heavily on its imaging system to provide its "country club billing" service and aura of high status and quality. Many customers expect copies of their charge-card transactions returned to them to substantiate tax deductions or business expenses. The huge amount of paper that must be processed to include customers' receipts with their credit-card bill had become prohibitively expensive and difficult to manage. In 1984, TRS adopted a digital imaging system that provides reduced images of the receipts on neat laser-printed pages. By using imaging in creative ways, American Express claims to have reduced its billing costs by 25 percent while offering its customers a unique service (Markoff, 1988).

The Window on Management illustrates how imaging can provide benefits to small businesses as well as large ones.

However, installing new, far-reaching technology is usually expensive and risky. Imaging technology is no exception:

- *Imaging can be very expensive.* The average significant imaging project starts out in the $1 million to $2 million range. To succeed, the project must commence after careful planning, including a thorough up-front feasibility study.

- *Hardware and software compatibility is a major stumbling block.* While every vendor professes to have open systems, many imaging systems have connectivity problems. Even if a firm purchases a complete system from one vendor so

DOCUMENT IMAGING COMES TO SMALL BUSINESS

Document imaging is so expensive and specialized that it has been useful only for large corporations in such document-centered industries as insurance, law, and banking. But not any more. The price of document imaging has come down, while new, creative applications are continually being developed. Moreover, smaller businesses in other industries are now adopting the technology. Not everyone should jump aboard, however. As with many technologies, a company considering the use of document imaging must be ready for it. This means that, management must first know its business well and understand how documents fit in with the business. It must also have a business strategy that includes a role for document imaging, whether that role be traditional cost containment or something more unusual such as a new service. Moreover, as with any other new technology, planning is essential. Finally, a move into document imaging will be successful only if management pays close attention to costs and to acquiring and installing technology that works.

JBS & Associates of Chicago, Illinois, made such a move in 1993 and has shown that it can be done. It is a small company of 17 employees and fiscal 1993 sales of $7 million. JBS is in the business of auctioning nonperforming real estate loans. The way the process has traditionally worked, a series of loans are brought together to be auctioned. Potential investors gather in rooms where documents relating to the loans to be auctioned are displayed. The documents might include credit reports, plot plans, and promissory notes. The auctions usually lasted two days. Because the documents were physically present, they were sometimes stolen by potential buyers who did not want their competition to have access to all available information.

Joel D. Zegart, president of JBS, understood his business well and developed a business strategy involving document imaging. He reasoned that if documents were visible on a computer screen rather than actually being there, no thefts could occur. More fundamentally, he believed that if potential buyers could have access to the documents a month in advance, it would be easier for bidders to learn critical details about the delinquent properties for sale. More potential buyers would participate, increasing the competition while leveling the playing field. Finally, he also realized that once documents were available as computer images, they can be viewed anywhere, not just at the site of the auction. "We wanted to change the landscape of how real estate auctions work," Zegart commented.

The JBS plan included a tight deadline in order to be ready for a particular auction it would handle. Managers gave themselves 90 days to design and assemble the system and then only six weeks to scan 2.7 million documents. Karen Kamphausen, a JBS vice president, knew that the system had to work because the bidders are all wealthy financiers who will not wait around patiently for a slow or down computer. They also will demand images of high quality. Furthermore, to be useful, the system had to be fast during the auction itself. JBS also needed to be able to scan with complete accuracy at a very high speed—JBS would have to scan nearly 70,000 documents per day (including weekends) to meet the deadline.

The system JBS purchased included large magnetic disks rather than optical storage, which was rejected as too slow for it's needs. JBS also purchased three high-quality scanners. The whole system cost the company $1 million. During implementation, JBS ran into several problems. Imaging required 18 hours per day (2.7 million

documents involves truckloads of paper). Managers encountered technical installation difficulties, a common occurrence with new technology. JBS had

> **To Think About:** *How was document imaging related to JBS's business strategy? What management, organization, and technology factors did Zegart have to consider when installing JBS's imaging system? Suggest other ways small businesses will find less expensive document imaging systems useful.*

to spend time training its employees. The company did receive a significant amount of help from its vendor, Optika Imaging Systems, Inc., of Colorado Springs, Colorado. Optika reasoned, with Zegart's urging, that this installation would be publicity for Optika—good or bad, and therefore it had a lot more at stake than just a sale. Ultimately, the system and the auction were a success.

Zegart's million-dollar bet paid off—getting rid of paper transformed his small auctioneering firm into a nationwide powerhouse. JBS can match the big industry players in selling off billions of dollars of delinquent loans. JBS now handles some of the largest sales of loans by the U.S. government's Resolution Trust Corporation.

Zegart is still upgrading the system, spending $400,000 in 1994 for hardware, software, and training. He reasons that the technology is changing fast and his continuing investment is actually R&D. His perspective is, "If you don't put your money into R&D, you're going to go out of business." He also finds himself in a new business, having established a document imaging consultancy practice.

Source: Amy Bermar, "Picture Your Business Paper-Free," *Profit,* May–June 1994.

that all parts work well together, the system may not work with the firm's existing technology. It is not uncommon for a purchaser to discover that its new imaging system is not compatible with the network already in use throughout the company. To avoid this problem, the purchaser should demand on-site testing of all components before signing an agreement with the vendor.

- *Power demands for an imaging system can be very large.* The firm should include power usage costs and any upgrading costs in its plan and estimates.

- *Major benefits will not accrue if the imaging system is installed only to increase automation of the current workflow.* Organizations must use the opportunity to make workflow changes that will provide the large productivity gains this technology promises.

- *Major workflow changes can result in organizational disruption and worker distress.* Because jobs and patterns of work are affected by imaging technology and workflow redesign, organizations should plan carefully to include a great deal of training in their imaging projects.

Reports of major productivity gains have come from both businesses and the government. However, such gains will come only if the application is chosen carefully. The following areas are considered very promising for imaging:

- *Banks*—check processing, loan (including mortgage) processing, credit cards, international funds transfer, finance, trust and stock ownership transfer

- *Insurance companies*—underwriting, claims processing, investment management

- *Pharmaceutical industry*—applications, regulatory affairs, medical libraries

GROUPWARE: NEW TECHNOLOGY FOR COLLABORATIVE WORK

Almost all office automation software has been designed for the individual who is working alone. Yet our definition of an office earlier in this chapter states that offices are work groups composed of people who work together toward shared goals. **Groupware** is a new kind of software that recognizes the significance of groups in offices by providing functions and services that support the collaborative activities of work groups. The goal of groupware is to improve the effectiveness of the work group by providing electronic links between its members.

What happens in groups? Members of the group perform the following activities:

- Schedule meetings
- Hold meetings
- Communicate with one another
- Collaborate to develop ideas
- Share the preparation of documents
- Share knowledge
- Share information on the work each member is doing

Groupware is a growing field of software meant to support all of these activities. No precise definition of groupware has emerged, but terms like *cooperative* and *collaborative* are commonly used when discussing it. Groupware usually includes such functions as information sharing, electronic meetings, scheduling, and E-mail. This technology requires the use of a network to connect the members of the group as they work on their own desktop computers, often in widely scattered locations. The groupware definition of groups is fluid, allowing users to define the work groups, with multiple group definitions allowed. For example, a manager may define a group of only those people who work for him. A group may be established for all employees dealing with a specific customer. A company-wide group may be established. Of course, an individual will belong to as many of those groups as is appropriate.

groupware Software that recognizes the significance of groups in offices by providing functions and services that support the collaborative activities of work groups.

electronic calendaring Software that tracks appointments and schedules in an office.

electronic mail (E-mail) Software that allows the electronic exchange of messages between users in remote locations.

electronic meeting software Software designed to enhance the productivity of face-to-face group meetings or of meetings among participants in scattered locations.

Electronic calendaring is a broadly accepted technology. Although its software has been typically used to keep track of appointments for individuals, groupware calendaring software adds a focus on group schedules, allowing individuals to view the calendars of other members of their own group. One popular function is the ability of the software automatically to search the calendars of members of the group for an acceptable meeting time and then to schedule that meeting for each individual in the group.

Electronic mail (E-mail) is software that allows the electronic exchange of messages. Electronic mail can enhance productivity by speeding up information flow and lessening the need for placing telephone calls or paper-based messaging systems. E-mail thus reduces group coordination costs. It also creates new patterns of social interaction so that people can share new data and ideas (Sproull and Kiesler, 1991). Some E-mail systems are limited to message exchanges between users of a single computer. More commonly, however, E-mail systems also pass messages from computer to computer, sometimes within the same location, sometimes halfway round the world. Many UNIX systems accomplish this by a dial-up telephone link. However, in recent years E-mail has come more and more to reside on networks. Because groupware, by definition, must connect workers on separate computers, groupware software often includes an E-mail function, even though many purchasers of groupware already have one or more E-mail systems installed. For E-mail to be fully effective within an organization that uses multiple E-mail systems, that organization must make those systems "talk" to each other so that an individual on one system can communicate with someone on a different E-mail system.

Electronic meeting software packages are designed to increase the productivity of a face-to-face group meeting or to make possible a meeting of participants in scattered locations. Some such software will do both, and some electronic meeting software utilizes videoconferencing. We discuss the way in which this software enhances the decision-support function in Chapter 16. We will discuss the remainder of the workgroup functions together, as they all involve shared messages and documents. Groupware enhances collaboration by allowing the exchange of ideas (in the form of electronic messages) on a given topic. All the messages on that topic will be saved in a group, stamped with the date, time, and author. Any group member can review the ideas of others at any time and add ideas of his or her own. Similarly, individuals can post a document for other members of the group to comment upon and/or edit. Members of a group can post requests for help from the group, and any member of the group can respond and can view the responses of other members of the group. Finally, if a group so chooses, the members of that group can store their work notes on the groupware so that all others in the group can see what progress is being made, what problems occur, and what activities are planned.

Lotus Notes

The leading groupware software has been Lotus Notes from Lotus Software, in Cambridge, Massachusetts. Lotus Notes is essentially a way to share a database over a network to create information-sharing applications. The databases are collections of documents stored in a group and can contain free-form text, graphics, file attachments, and—with additional software and hardware—sound, image, and video data. However, Lotus databases are very different from more traditional databases. A traditional customer database, for example, will have a number of fixed fields, such as customer name, number, address, telephone, comments, and so on. The user can search each of these fields, by field, except probably the comments field. With a Notes database the user can search the whole database as a group, so that the user does not have to know database organization or be concerned about such issues as numeric versus alphanumeric. Moreover, Lotus Notes can operate on a wide range of systems, including IBM-compatible microcomputer workstations running OS/2 or Windows, Macintosh computers, or workstations running UNIX. The data are stored in a distributed database, with servers at key locations wherever needed. Lotus Notes runs on both LANs and WANs, using several popular network operating systems, such as Novell, Banyan, and IBM. The user interface is Windows-like and icon-based. The result of all this flexibility is a database system that allows information to be shared and accessed throughout a large organization, and that is precisely the value of Lotus Notes. And, of course, the database the user accesses will look the same whether it is stored in Atlanta, Bangkok, or Lucerne.

The software supports **compound documents,** which are documents that consist of differing types of information from separate sources; for example, a single document combining graphics, spreadsheet data, and character-based text is a compound document. Figure 15.8 illustrates a compound document displayed through Lotus Notes. In Notes the whole document—graphics, spreadsheet data, and text—is stored as a single record, whereas with normal office software the various elements are stored as separate files that are combined at print time. Lotus Notes is compatible with a wide range of popular desktop word processors, spreadsheets, and graphics packages.

In Notes, each application is a separate database. The system is delivered with predefined template applications that can be used as is or modified. The user can also create customized applications from scratch. Each application has its own icon on the main menu (see Figure 15.9). Each Notes database logs all pertinent communications among members of a workgroup so that the notes can be kept for future reference and shared. Members of the team can access each member's contribution and comment on it, or they can use Notes to distribute reference information to other team members. Figure 15.10 shows how Notes was used to distribute information and to pool ideas in a sales discussion database. Members of the entire organization involved in sales and marketing could access documents, comment on them, or add new information.

The Emergency Operations Center of Pacific Gas and Electric (PG&E) uses Lotus Notes to receive damage reports and repair requests from 150 offices throughout the 93,000 square miles in Northern California. While management in San Francisco may use the database to view a chronological list of outages, the local offices will use it to produce a listing of outages that still need repairing. When the San Francisco earthquake hit in October 1989, PG&E found the system to be quite effective in facilitating the management of the many repairs urgently needed. The database was also the

compound document Electronic document that consists of differing types of information acquired from separate sources such as graphics, database, spreadsheet data, and text-based programs.

FIGURE 15.8
Compound document on Lotus Notes. In this example, a compound document incorporates scanned images and text data. *Courtesy of Lotus Development Corporation.*

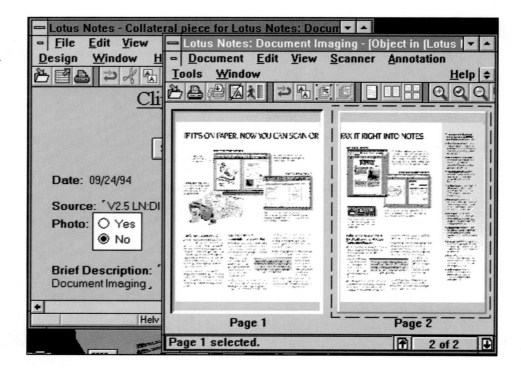

FIGURE 15.9
Lotus Notes desktop. Each icon represents
a different Notes applications. By clicking
on the icon, this user can work with people
all over the world. *Courtesy of Lotus
Development Corporation.*

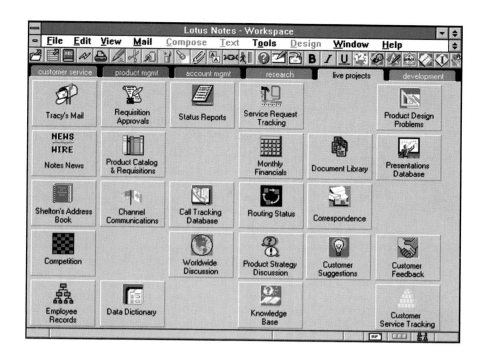

source for information supplied to the press on the types of outages that had occurred (Lotus Notes Application Profile).

Manufacturers Hanover Trust (MHT), which merged with Chemical Bank in 1992, also turned to Notes originally to improve the effectiveness of its sales operation. MHT found itself with vast quantities of data that were neither well integrated nor easily accessible. Using Lotus Notes, the account officers and corporate trust sales staff can maintain their records in a way that is organized and widely accessible. They set up a company profiles database that centralizes client and prospect information. The communications profiles database is used to keep track of day-to-day communications between bank staff and its customers. Account officers can bring up a one-page summary of information on the customer, view contacts for a specific

FIGURE 15.10
Activities, events, and issues can be readily
discussed and shared with various team
members. *Courtesy of Lotus Development
Corporation.*

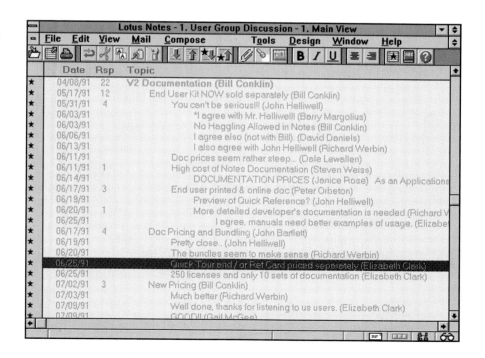

product, or examine all contacts for the past six months. The bank's staff is now able to be far more knowledgeable as it deals with customers—from knowing the nickname of the client or contact to knowing which banks that customer uses in Norway. Before Notes, sharing of information was time-consuming and was not successful if one did not know whom to ask, or if that person was on vacation. Of course, in the past when a staff member left MHT, he or she took valuable information. Now all of that information is stored on Notes and is easily retrieved when needed, using a range of flexible views. The applications also help managers track staff activities, analyze the effectiveness of their time use, and plan future work (Lotus Notes Application Profile).

Ernst & Young, one of the Big Six accounting firms, hopes to improve its worldwide competitiveness by using Lotus Notes to create a communications infrastructure. In the past, Ernst & Young could not respond quickly to worldwide business opportunities because its international offices were often unaware of activities in the other branches and even branches in the same country. The company's offices in the United States, the United Kingdom, Canada, the Netherlands, and Australia are linking Lotus Notes to Oracle relational databases, eliminating the need for multiple copies of files. Employees' desktop computers are tied into local area networks, which are connected regionally into a private wide-area network (WAN). Figure 15.11 illustrates the infrastructure created for the company's offices in the United Kingdom, so that staff can work together on projects that require regional teamwork. The Eastern regional offices share an Oracle database containing staff demographic data that helps Ernst & Young put together the best team for a specific job. Managers from these offices are building a shared client and prospect database to

FIGURE 15.11
Ernst & Young's knowledge work infrastructure. Ernst & Young is developing a network linking its offices in the United Kingdom to speed up the pace of collaboration using groupware and other communications tools.
Adapted from: George Black, "Taking Notes, Big Sixer Aims for Head of the Class," Software Magazine, March 1995, Sentry Publishing Company, Inc.

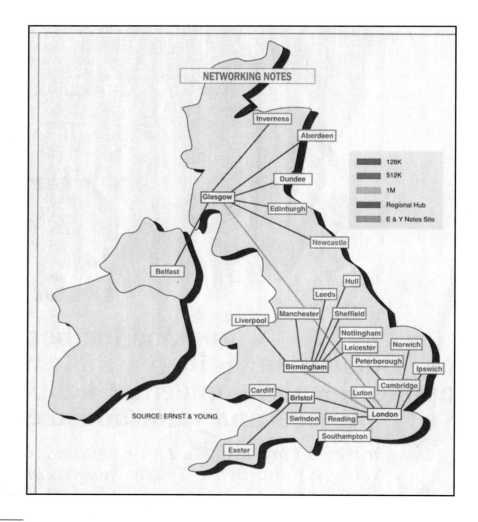

help employees stay abreast of developments in other offices. Using Notes, employees can share a diary, which may be more effective than posting notices on bulletin boards (Black, 1995).

Not satisfied with sharing information only within an organization, however, in early 1994 Lotus announced that in 1995 Lotus and AT&T will jointly offer a new service known as Network Notes, which supports sharing of information between organizations. With AT&T offering the network facilities throughout the world, organizations will be able to open their Notes databases not only to their own people in remote locations but also to customers and suppliers where appropriate. Bullivant, Houser, Bailey, Pendergrass & Hoffman, a Portland, Oregon, law firm, has already begun to open its databases to its clients. Traditionally, perhaps 20 percent of a lawyer's time has been spent reporting to a client. Now at Bullivant a client is able to examine the working files of his or her case and see progress without disrupting the work or generating costs, thus lowering the client's bill significantly. However, Bullivant's chief operating officer, Don Evans, believes the greatest value of opening its files to its clients lies in the increased involvement of the clients in their own cases. Johnson & Higgins, a large New York City insurance broker, is already sharing its Notes databases with a dozen of its clients and expects most of its big customers to be doing the same before long. James River Corporation, the $4.6 billion paper and packaging company in Richmond, Virginia, and a Johnson & Higgins client, finds that it is in constant electronic dialogue with Johnson & Higgins. The result, from James River's side, is that it works with more information and Johnson & Higgins is more responsive (Kirkpatrick, 1994). Many observers believe the ability to create such close ties between organizations, their customers, and their suppliers will transform the way companies do business.

Group Collaboration via the Internet

Chapter 10 has described the multiple ways in which organizations can use the Internet for group collaboration and coordination, especially the Internet capabilities for E-mail, discussion groups, and information sharing on the World Wide Web. (The Web allows collaborators in remote sites to display and exchange information that includes text, graphics, and sound about a common project or related projects using hypermedia links.) The Internet is much less expensive to use than proprietary products such as Lotus Notes and provides many groupware-like functions. Because the World Wide Web is so powerful and easy to use, some analysts predict that the Web will supplant Lotus Notes for some groupware functions. Table 15.5 compares the capabilities for group collaboration of Lotus Notes and the World Wide Web.

Groupware has not been well accepted everywhere it has been installed. The Window on Organizations provides insight into the serious controversies that groupware has engendered in a number of companies.

Table 15.5   **Groupware Capabilities of Lotus Notes and the World Wide Web**

	Strengths	Weaknesses
Lotus Notes	All-in-one system Mature technology Powerful model for organizing information Integrated security	Proprietary technology Weak user interface
World Wide Web	Open architecture Easy to distribute Administrative independence of organizations using it	Immature hypertext markup language Undeveloped security Limited document management (backward links between documents not yet available)

Source: Marc Donner, "Lotus Notes and the World Wide Web," Morgan Stanley, April 27, 1995.

THE GROUPWARE CONTROVERSY

Groupware focuses on technology needed to support small groups as they work together. As a result, it incorporates a broad range of office functions—the creation, editing, storage, and management of documents; electronic mail; calendaring; and even electronic videoconferencing. Individual employees who have been accustomed to working independently are now experiencing both the benefits and the problems of working more closely as a team. Most groupware users see benefits to its use. For example, Fred Bonner, director of computer systems for the Discovery Channel, believes that meeting room vacancies have risen by 40 percent since his company has begun using groupware. Similarly, Barry Barron, who is manager of information systems for the Port of Oakland (California), states that "We hold fewer meetings now, and those that we do hold involve fewer people." He attributes the reduction in numbers of meetings to the ability of groupware to keep each department informed about other departments' activities. Nonetheless, the shift in work methods, made possible by groupware, has engendered a surprising amount of contention.

Some of the controversy arises from the functions and controls built into the software. For example, Action Technologies, Inc.'s Coordinator Workgroup Productivity System includes "voucher routing" in its groupware. To circulate a memo electronically, the software requires that the memo be classified prior to being sent. The user classifies the memo (request, consultation, order, etc.) and establishes action deadlines. The software updates the schedules of both the recipients and their groups, which includes the recipients' managers. The recipient need not have been consulted about these deadlines.

Ray Howell, who is assistant vice-president for information management in NCR's commercial insurance division, believes that many employees "might be afraid of a product that automatically schedules people, puts priorities on things, and possibly sends messages to management when they fail." He says that employees "might feel Big Brother is watching." Bob Sickles, a systems manager at the White Plains, New York, headquarters of General Foods, believes the key to installing scheduling software is changing the organizational culture. Before actually installing the software, which was to be used by 4000 employees, he produced a humorous 20-minute video titled "Nightmare on North Street: The Scheduling Monster," detailing the frustration and inefficiency of the system everyone was using. He also built support among staff and secretaries first so that line managers and personnel would hear good things about the software both from above and below. He introduced the product in a phased rollout, delivering it first to several groups who had particularly wide and frequent contact with the rest of the organization. In this way, the news of the software's success spread before most people had to start to use it. His efforts worked, and his own studies showed that the average time devoted to the scheduling process per meeting declined from 19.5 minutes to 5.6 minutes.

Another common cultural problem organizations often face when they are installing groupware is the fear many employees have of sharing their information. There is some information that people want to keep to themselves or share with just a few colleagues. Groupware changes both the formal and informal ways that people communicate. The boundaries and rules of communication change. People might know what to do in public and what to do in private but they don't necessarily know what to do in "cyberspace."

Diagraph Corp., a St. Louis, Missouri, bar code and ink-jet equipment manufacturer, approached the issue carefully when it decided to centralize its sales program on a groupware centralized database. Sales representatives are often fiercely competitive and hesitate to share prospect information in a common database if it helps another person win the customer.

To Think About: Assume your manager has asked you to make a recommendation as to whether or not your work group should install groupware. From what you know about groupware, would you recommend this technology? Why or why not? What management, organization, and technology factors would you consider in making your recommendation? What steps would you take to reduce the problems and maximize the value of the software?

Diagraph "had a hard time getting sales reps to let their data be centrally deposited," according to IS director Susan Ittner. The solution was to change the company incentives. Although every department in Diagraph has access to the notes the sales staff is required to file after a customer contact, the sales rep who initiates the contact is now given credit if the sale is closed. Moreover, the company now includes the number of customer leads ("handoffs") they provide coworkers in their performance rating. Hewlett-Packard's PC division has modified its compensation system to give monetary reward to salespersons who work in teams rather than individually.

Group editing of documents has also generated controversy. Using Instant Update from On Technology, Inc., in Cambridge, Massachusetts, an author can use the network to make a document available to a selected list of employees for updating. Matthew Ghourdjian, IS director of Hennigan & Mercer (a Los Angeles law firm), finds that this function allows his firm to create needed legal documents rapidly. However, Greg O'Hara, a system supervisor at Wright-Patterson Air Force Base, believes that software which allows someone other than the author to update a document threatens the integrity of that document. Moreover, groupware often does not manage document update timing adequately. If two people are simultaneously editing the same document, the changes made and saved by the first person might be wiped out when the second person saves later changes.

Groupware E-mail raises additional problems. Employees comfortable with their E-mail systems may actively resist joining group discussions. The privacy of traditional E-mail systems has a different "look and feel" from the much more public space of workgroup computing. Moreover, many large organizations have E-mail systems that were installed by local business units, resulting in numerous, noncompatible systems being installed. A typical example is US West Commu-

nications of Denver, which has about 38,000 employees in 15 states running 14 different E-mail systems—DEC's All-In-1, IBM's PROFS, Wang's WangOffice, and a number of UNIX-based local-area network systems. Most of these systems do not "talk" with each other, effectively preventing most employees from communicating through E-mail. Groupware not only does not solve this problem, but it can only contribute to the confusion by bringing in yet another E-mail system. Obviously, what many corporations need is either standardization on a single corporatewide E-mail system, or at least a limited, approved list of systems that can communicate with each other.

Finally, groupware systems can generate opposition from managers be-

cause they can erode the traditional hierarchy. Seeing the name of the person posting on a Lotus Notes database matters little unless the reader personally knows the person and his or her position. The ideas of a secretary could conceivably carry the same weight as those of a senior manager.

Sources: Colleen Frye, "Groupware Means Change," *Software Magazine*, May 1995; David Coleman, "Groupware: Changing Business for the '90s," *Computerworld*, February 2, 1994; Stephanie Stahl, "Groupware's Culture Problem," *InformationWEEK*, May 23, 1994; and John J. Xenakis, "Documents by Committee," *InformationWEEK*, December 9, 1991, and "Shared Interests," *InformationWEEK*, December 30, 1991.

Other problems are emerging. One concern is that groupware allows too much data to be collected. When this occurs, it becomes easy for the trivial to flood out the significant. Chase Manhattan Bank, NA, found its Lotus Notes forum so flooded with messages that it appointed expert editors to delete insignificant, inaccurate, or misleading entries. Electronic scheduling can have the same result. Metropolitan Life Insurance Co. found that meetings that used to take hours to arrange took only 30 seconds when scheduled electronically. People found that it was so easy to schedule meetings that they started scheduling unnecessary meetings. E-mail can also swamp staff with an overabundance of information (Sheng et al., 1989–1990). Heavy users of multiple E-mail facilities might have to check Microsoft Mail, Vax Notes, CompuServe, and MCI Mail for messages. Groupware alone is not able to promote information sharing if team members do not feel it is in their interest to share, especially in organizations that encourage competition among employees, an issue also explored in the Window on Organizations. Groupware requires more careful implementation than many other applications to ensure its productivity in the marketplace (Grudin, 1994).

Nonetheless, it seems clear from our examples (and many others) that the use of this technology can enhance the work of a group if the applications are properly designed to fit the organization's needs and work practices. Groupware today may be compared to the situation surrounding spreadsheets ten years ago—its use is new and we can only dimly see its long-range value.

MANAGING INFORMATION: DESKTOP DATABASES

While business firms have traditionally stored basic transaction data in huge corporate databases on mainframes, desktop microcomputers provide many office workers with the opportunity to develop their own individual client tracking systems, customer lists, and supplier and vendor databases. However, most office workers do not create these databases on their own because microcomputer database languages are still too difficult for nonprogrammers to use. Instead, a new kind of software that is customized for specific data management needs of salespersons, managers, real estate agents, stockbrokers, and the like is now beginning to appear. This new software is often called **personal information managers;** it consists of packaged database tools designed to support specific office data management tasks.

personal information manager
Packaged database tool designed to support specific office data management tasks for an information worker.

One example of a personal information manager is The Financial Manager (Azimuth Corporation), designed to serve the desktop information needs of account executives and portfolio managers in the financial services industry. Financial managers typically have from 500 to 1000 clients; each client has one or more accounts or portfolios of investments. Financial managers also have a full calendar of events, activities, and planned actions. In addition, each manager has several routine projects; these include sending letters to clients, telephoning clients, and prospecting for business. The Financial Manager keeps track of a manager's clients, portfolios, calendars, appointments, and projects.

MANAGING PROJECTS: DESKTOP PROJECT MANAGERS

project management software
Software that facilitates the development, scheduling, and management of a project by breaking the complex project into simpler subtasks, each with its own completion time and resource requirements.

Offices are the organization's control points that coordinate the flow of resources to projects and evaluate results. **Project management software** breaks a complex project down into simpler subtasks, each with its own completion time and resource requirements. Once a user knows what is needed by each subtask, delivery schedules can be written and resources allocated. Two traditional project management techniques (see Chapter 14) are CPM (Critical Path Method) and PERT (Program Evaluation and Review Technique).

Contemporary project managers have begun to use graphical user interfaces, permitting managers to operate the programs with a mouse. Project managers also have access to high-quality presentation graphics, permitting photographic slide and overhead transparency output. Whereas project management software initially focused on a single user, contemporary packages can be accessed by many members of a work group.

15.3 KNOWLEDGE WORK SYSTEMS

Because knowledge work and data work are both information work, both use many of the same information systems (particularly office automation systems). However, knowledge work is also specialized; thus it requires specialized information systems. This section describes the features of knowledge work that can be supported by specific knowledge work systems.

THE ROLE OF KNOWLEDGE WORK IN THE ORGANIZATION

The Bureau of Labor Statistics defines knowledge work as having four characteristics. This definition has generally been accepted by sociologists and economists as well. First, knowledge work is supported by a codified body of knowledge that is generally and widely accepted as valid. The body of knowledge is usually found in books stored in a library. Second, this body of knowledge must be capable of being taught at universities. It differs from a skill that can only be learned through experience and apprenticeship. Third, practitioners of the body of knowledge normally must prove their mastery of that knowledge by being certified, usually either by the state or by a university. Fourth, the profession must maintain standards of admission for the practitioner through regulation by independent professional organizations. The professional bodies must also maintain professional and educational standards and guidelines and a statement of ethics. Thus the knowledge worker must have more than technique and skill. These characteristics are summarized in Table 15.6.

Knowledge- and information-intense products and services have been expanding rapidly. Knowledge work remains critical to the development of new products in more traditional industries, including pharmaceuticals, electronics, and automobiles. It has also become central to a range of newer services such as environmental analysis and financial and investment advice. To understand knowledge work systems thoroughly, we first must explore the ways knowledge workers contribute to business firms.

Table 15.6	Characteristics of Knowledge Work

1. Based on codified body of knowledge
2. Body of knowledge taught at schools or universities
3. Practitioners usually require certification by the state or a school
4. Practitioners regulated by independent professional organizations

Three roles stand out. Perhaps the most distinctive role of knowledge workers is to interpret the ever-expanding external knowledge bases for the organization. A central purpose for hiring knowledge workers is to keep the firm abreast of developments in science, technology, the arts, and social thought. Developments in these areas often contain business opportunities or risks. As more and more value in the economy depends on knowledge and information products, the only way a firm can keep up is to invest heavily in knowledge workers. Indeed, the fastest-growing industries are those that produce information- and knowledge-intensive products.

A second role that knowledge workers are uniquely qualified to perform is as internal consultants to their firms. They can advise managers about changes in technology and science, and can bring formal models to bear on problems. They can also perform research, write reports, and provide professional expertise. While most corporations hire external consultants from time to time to supplement their work, it is the internal knowledge worker who is the main source of consulting information.

Third, knowledge workers are organizational change agents. Based on external developments in science and the arts, they are expected to evaluate and initiate change projects and to promote them.

Knowledge workers exhibit two other relevant characteristics that are unique among information workers. Their knowledge base and their understanding of what

Using data drawn from NASA satellites, Texaco scientists can pinpoint changes in the condition of vegetation and water in areas of operations so that the company can determine the cause and take appropriate environmental protection actions.

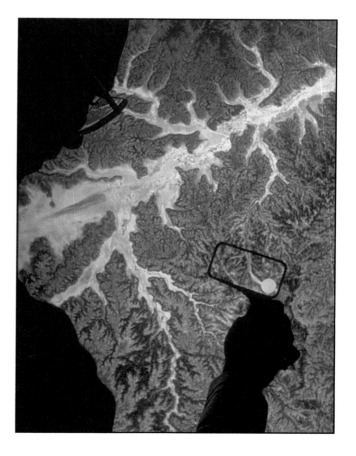

to do with that knowledge prevent them from being subjected to the same kind of supervision and authority that other information workers will be subjected to. They often know more than their boss. Therefore, they are usually autonomous. In addition, knowledge workers often are physically segregated into research areas.

These unique roles and conditions of knowledge workers produce special requirements for the information systems they use and provide the rationale for the development of those systems. **Knowledge work systems (KWS)** are specifically designed to promote the creation of new knowledge and ensure that new knowledge and technical expertise are properly integrated into the business.

REQUIREMENTS OF KNOWLEDGE WORK SYSTEMS

Knowledge workers are focused on the expanding knowledge base external to their work group and to the organization that employs them. They need easy access to electronically stored external knowledge bases. The knowledge they must access might be in journal articles stored in libraries or in collections of scientific research or legal findings. They usually need mail links to other professionals working in universities or in other businesses. They also often need mail links to other knowledge workers working within their own organization, whether at another site within the country or abroad. Consequently, one characteristic of knowledge work systems is that they incorporate more links to external data and information than is customary with other corporate systems. (See Figure 15.12.)

A second characteristic of knowledge work systems is the software they require. Typically their software contains far more powerful graphic, analytic, document management, and communications capabilities than other corporate systems.

Third, knowledge work systems require considerably more computing power than is true for other information work. Engineers may need to run thousands of complex calculations to determine the strength and safety of a specific part they are designing. Lawyers may need to scan through thousands of documents and legal findings before recommending a strategy. Graphics applications are particularly greedy for computing power. To understand the greater power needs of graphics, remember that a one-page document stored in character format (an ordinary word processing document) requires perhaps 8 K of disk space to store, while that document stored in a bit-mapped graphic format requires about 50 K, a ratio of maybe 6:1. The computer requires a commensurate increase in power to manipulate the larger, bit-mapped file rather than the smaller character-based file. Graphic simulations have become common and even necessary to much of the work of knowledge workers, from architects to pharmaceutical research chemists. Designers and drafts-

FIGURE 15.12
Requirements of knowledge work systems. Knowledge work systems require strong links to external knowledge bases in addition to specialized hardware and software.

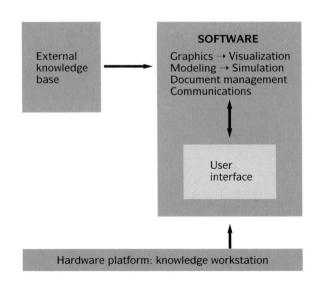

men, using computer-aided design (CAD) systems to design such products as automobile bodies, need three-dimensional graphics software to visualize and model the product on screen before producing a physical model. Even more intensive simulations, called virtual reality, can be so large as to require very large and fast supercomputers.

A user-friendly interface is very important to a knowledge worker's system. User-friendly interfaces save a lot of time by allowing the user to perform the needed tasks and get to the required information without having to spend a lot of time learning how to use the computer. While saving time is important to any worker, it is more important for knowledge workers than for most other employees because a knowledge worker's time is so costly—wasting a knowledge worker's time is simply too expensive.

Finally, knowledge work systems usually require the use of workstations. As described in Chapter 6, a **workstation** is a desktop computer that is far more powerful than a conventional microcomputer. The workstation has powerful graphics, analytic, document management, and communications capabilities, and the ability to perform several complicated tasks at one time. Knowledge workstations are often designed and optimized for the specific tasks to be performed so that a design engineer will require a different workstation than does a lawyer.

workstation Desktop computer with powerful graphics, mathematical processing, and communications capabilities as well as the ability to perform several complicated tasks at one time. Often used in scientific or design work.

EXAMPLES OF KNOWLEDGE WORK SYSTEMS

Knowledge work systems will vary greatly, depending upon the profession and the specific application being supported. Design engineers need graphics with enough power to handle three-dimensional computer-aided design (CAD) systems. On the other hand, financial analysts are more interested in having access to a myriad of external databases and in optical disk technology so that they can access massive amounts of financial data very quickly. In this text we cannot describe all of the many types of knowledge work systems. What we have done, instead, is to select three very different types of such systems as examples that will help you to understand the breadth and power of knowledge work systems. We now examine conventional computer-aided design systems, "virtual reality" systems for simulation and modeling, and investment workstations.

Computer-Aided Design: Developing a New Product

computer-aided design (CAD) Information system that automates the creation and revision of designs using sophisticated graphics software.

Computer-aided design (CAD) automates the creation and revision of designs, using computers and sophisticated graphics software. With a CAD system, the designer is usually able to produce a more sophisticated and functional design than with manual methods. The design is done on the computer before production begins, significantly reducing both design time and expensive engineering changes once production has begun. Equally large savings come during the modeling function. Using a more traditional design methodology, each new design modification requires a mold to be made and a prototype to be physically tested. That process has to be repeated many times over, which is very expensive and time-consuming. Using a CAD workstation, the designer needs only to make a physical prototype toward the end of the design process. The ability of the CAD software to design the tooling and the manufacturing process also saves a great deal of time and money while producing a manufacturing process with far fewer problems.

CAD workstations are starting to be used in many areas. For example, the development of new automobiles, from idea to the first delivery, traditionally required about five years. Using CAD software, Japanese auto makers have taken about a year out of that cycle, and American manufacturers are now rapidly moving to achieve similar results. Faster development not only lowers the cost significantly but also allows the producer to respond more quickly to changing market demands. The chapter-ending case explores the benefits of CAD in more detail.

The new Hong Kong airport is being designed with CAD software. The Window on Technology describes this project, illustrating the wide range of specialized CAD systems that exist.

Virtual Reality: Immersion in Fantasy

virtual reality systems Interactive graphics software and hardware that create computer-generated simulations that provide sensations that emulate real-world activities.

Virtual reality systems have visualization, rendering, and simulation capabilities that go far beyond those of conventional CAD systems. They use interactive graphics software to create computer-generated simulations that are so close to reality that users believe they are participating in a "real-world" situation. Virtual reality is a relatively new technology that is just starting to provide benefits in educational, scientific, and business work.

Virtual reality is interactive in such a way that the user actually feels immersed in the "world" the computer creates. Imagine, for example, a computer version of an architectural design for a house. The house will be built for you, but for now it is still only a design in a computer. Now imagine that with the aid of the computer, you walk through that house, checking out its features and making changes on the spot until you are satisfied with the design. Perhaps the door to the bathroom opens the wrong way, or the living room is too narrow and its north window is not high enough for its width, or the light switch in the front hall is on the wrong side, or you want the linen closet in the kitchen instead of in the hallway. Once construction begins, these changes would be very expensive. Even worse, you might not even realize you wanted these changes until after the house is complete and you move in. At the design stage, however, such changes are quick and inexpensive to make. This is the very real fantasy world of virtual reality—software of this type actually exists and is being used today.

How does it work? The virtual world is an implicit world, one that exists only in the computer. To enter that world, the user dons special clothing, headgear, and equipment, depending upon the application. The clothing contains sensors that record the user's movements and immediately transmit that information back to the computer. For instance, to walk through the house, you will need garb that monitors the movement of your feet, hands, and head. You will also need goggles that contain video screens and sometimes audio attachments and feeling gloves so that you can be immersed in the computer feedback. As you walk straight ahead through the house, the images in front of you come closer. If you turn to the right (or turn your head to the right), the image will shift to your left. If you open the door, you will see the door opening and the next room will appear through the doorway. Walk through that doorway and look around, and you will find you are in the next room. Turn around and you can see the previous room through the doorway (unless you already closed the door behind you).

As you might imagine, this is new and very expensive technology. It may take years for the price to come down. For that reason, it may also take many years for large numbers of applications to be developed. In the meantime, however, some commercial applications have been developed and are in use.

Matsushita Electric Works in Japan has put virtual reality to work in its department stores; it has developed an application very similar to the house example we used above. The stores sell kitchen appliances and cabinets. To promote these products Matsushita has created an application it calls Virtual Kitchen. The prospective buyers bring their kitchen layouts to the department store where trained staff enters a copy of the design into the computer. The customers then don the appropriate equipment and suddenly find themselves in their own kitchen. Now they can try out the appliances in various sizes, colors, and locations. They can test new cabinets, opening and closing the cabinet doors and drawers. They can place their existing table and chairs into the picture so the scene will be very realistic. They can walk around and discover the feel and ambiance of the new kitchen. With this technology, the customer is able to buy with a great deal more confidence. Matsushita is able to make many more on-the-spot sales.

FLYING HIGH WITH CAD

Hong Kong's Kai Tak Airport is the third busiest international airport in the world for passengers and the second busiest for freight. With only one runway, it reached its absolute capacity in 1994. It cannot be enlarged because it sits in the middle of densely populated Kowloon, the section of Hong Kong on the Kowloon Peninsula. To meet predicted traffic through the year 2040, the Chep Lap Kok Airport is being built at a cost of $16 billion on land that will be reclaimed on a nearby island.

The new airport, with two runways, will be connected to Hong Kong by a 1500-yard bridge, the second largest suspension bridge in the world. It will include both a highway and a rail link. Finally, a complete town for 20,000 employees will be built, including housing, shopping and commercial centers, recreation facilities, and sewage and refuse systems. When completed in 1997, Chep Lap Kok Airport will be able to service 87 million passengers and 9.9 million tons of cargo a year. It is one of the largest infrastructure projects in the world.

The design of the airport is a massive undertaking involving a number of design firms and an astonishing array of computer-aided design (CAD) software packages and other sophisticated technology. It also involves sophisticated, creative ways to link the designers and their designs.

The runway design had to take into account local topology, the urban surroundings, prevalent wind patterns, and criteria from the International Civil Aviation Authority. The designers had to assume the airport would be able to accommodate 900-passenger jets that are now only on the drawing boards.

The architecture firm of Foster Asia won the contract for the overall design coordination role and the design of the ¾-mile-long, 60-dock airport terminal building. It was given only two years to complete its work. Foster Asia teamed up with the Australian engineering firm Mott Connell and formed the Mott Consortium. The consortium had to keep track of a multidisciplinary team of more than 200 professionals handling architectural design, structural design, civil engineering, and production of specialized airport systems.

The client, Hong Kong's Provisional Airport Authority, requires that all 10,000 design and construction drawings be produced using CAD software. To integrate the work, the consortium purchased UNIX workstations and microcomputers for each technician and linked them into a LAN. The consortium decided to use CAD software from Intergraph Corp. because it was especially well suited for large projects. When run on a UNIX workstation, Intergraph can process large amounts of data very quickly. It also has file reference capabilities to coordinate the work of various design groups.

The size and scope of the terminal building project and the large number of design professionals involved required project managers to divide up the design in a logical way. Since architects need to work on different aspects of designs, such as vertical structure, horizontal structure, signage, and interior planning, the team defined 15 aspects to store in separate files. For each of the nine building levels, architects wanted to work on different aspects of the design and see what changes had been made. With the file reference capability, they can overlay files to create composite drawings.

The CAD software integrates "protection surfaces" into the design—complex 3-D pictures of heights and patterns that airplanes will be able to fly. All the data had to be related to the basic Hong Kong survey grid maps so that the output could be used by other disciplines designing more detailed plans of portions of the airport. The final master plan allows a user to overlay the basic plan without having to combine plans.

The network allows any designer to easily call up his or her own work at any workstation or PC. To visualize the terminal from the view of the passenger by simulating walkthroughs, they are using Intergraph's Design Review. This software is also useful for obtaining client approval on details. The roof design is being done by Ove Arup &

To Think About: Do you think this project could be attempted without CAD technology? Why or why not? How would the lack of CAD technology affect the cost and timing of such a project? What benefits to the clients might have caused them to require the designers to produce all documents on CAD software?

Partners, who are using a structural analysis package, Oasys, on a PC-LAN. Numerous other packages are being used for design of terminal details.

Other facets of the project, including land reclamation, the bridge, the highway, the railway systems, and an analysis of the town and its infrastructure, are being designed by other companies. All are using a wide array of specialized CAD programs. Each team is very dependent upon the output of work by other teams. To integrate the work, the Mott Consortium uses an optical jukebox holding 54 read-only optical disks of 650 megabytes each. Finished drawings are archived to the optical disks, where they are immediately available to all via a network. Each drawing has a version number so that it can be updated later if needed. When updates that might affect the work of other teams do occur, earlier versions of the same document are marked with a warning.

The airport project is the largest such project in the history of Hong Kong. It is difficult to imagine how this project could take place without the technology the designers have available.

Sources: Anna Foley, "Design Firm Flies Through the Airport Project with CAD," *Computerworld,* September 5, 1994; "New Airport to Serve as Region's Gateway," *The Wall Street Journal,* October 12, 1994; and Ross Milburn, "Flying High," *Computer Graphics World,* February 1993.

Other architectural applications have been developed. Hewlett-Packard is designing a new European office using virtual reality equipment from VPL Research of Redwood City, California. The city of Berlin, Germany, is using the same equipment to design a new subway system to link the formerly separated East and West sections of the city. The University of North Carolina at Chapel Hill has its own virtual reality system that it is using to design its new computer sciences building, Sitterson Hall (Newquist, 1992).

Caterpillar Inc. in Peoria, Illinois, is using virtual reality mock-ups for new wheel loader and back hoe loader designs. Operators wearing special helmets "see" a simulated task and maneuver "virtual" machines to determine flexibility in tight spaces or visibility from the cab. The simulations help Caterpillar reduce the time required for evaluating design changes on new models from nine months to one. Caterpillar wants to let customers use virtual reality to field-test new designs before they are built (Richards, 1994).

Many major pharmaceutical firms have research centers in the Chapel Hill area. Using the University of North Carolina's virtual reality system, they create computer-generated molecular worlds. In recent years they have been using a mouse and CAD software to move structures around as they search for workable compounds. However, using Chapel Hill's virtual reality system, they simply reach in, seize the structures, and break them, move them, or bind them as they wish.

At General Electric's Research and Development Center in Schenectady, New York, GE scientists are working with a group of surgeons from Boston's Brigham and

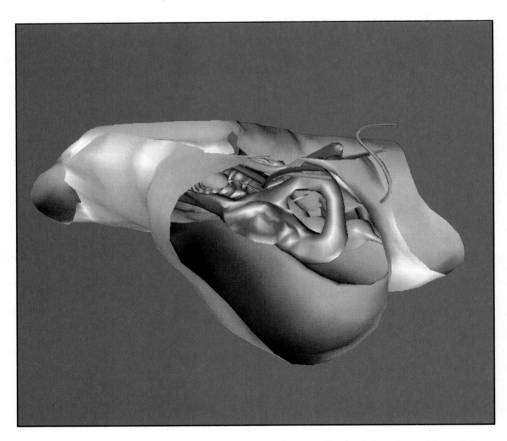

Virtual reality helps medical schools teach anatomy and surgery by simulating the workings of the human body, allowing students the options of 3-D viewing and unlimited removal and repositioning of tissues.

Women's Hospital to develop a virtual reality system to be used in surgery. One of their stated goals is to be able to superimpose a 3-D image of the patient onto the patient and then to operate on the image and the patient at the same time. Further in the future, they want to be able to create an image of the patient and then "walk through" that image, moving between various organs. They hope they will then be able to perform surgery on the image, surgery with such precision that no damage to surrounding tissue will occur. The surgeon's actions on the large virtual image would be duplicated by computer-controlled instruments on the patient.

While these are futuristic hopes, the GE research team is making progress. Currently, for example, they are able to use a magnetic resonance imaging machine (MRI) to make two-dimensional slice pictures of a volunteer's brain. Using virtual reality goggles, and with those MRI images as input, they are able to view the virtual brain with superb, three-dimensional reality. They are able not only to rotate the brain but also to peel off layers of the image to reveal the parts below. They have used these images to put a special cap on a volunteer, project the image of his own brain on that cap, and then sketch onto the cap the surgical pathway through the brain's furrows to a spot where they might need to perform surgery. While the process of operating on the image itself is still a long way away, the team does hope that within the next several years they will be able to create a "virtual" image that surgeons can have beside the operating table so that they can consult it during the operation (Naj, 1993).

Investment Workstations Leveraging Knowledge Workers in the Financial Industry

The key assets of knowledge workers are their knowledge and their time. While some knowledge workers use workstations that are on the cutting edge of technologies, others use more established technologies to leverage those two key assets. New York–based Chancellor Capital Management, Inc. developed its own investment workstations to help it manage $25 billion in assets for 300 clients. The workstations integrate the wide range of data required by portfolio managers from the firm's investment management systems and its portfolio accounting systems and make them available with the touch of a button. By providing one-stop information faster and with fewer errors, the workstations streamline Chancellor's entire investment process, from stock selection to updating accounting records.

The workstations were developed in-house; the computers are Intel-based microcomputers built within Chancellor. The software was either written within Chancellor or purchased by Chancellor to integrate into software its workers had written. Their goals? First, Chancellor wanted to eliminate much of the drudgery that goes with computers to give its traders and asset managers more time to concentrate on making decisions and developing strategies. Second, the company wanted to integrate its front and back offices so that data integrity issues would disappear and all systems would report identical data. Third, Chancellor wanted a more open, flexible system environment, one that could be tailored to an individual's needs while also being able to integrate new software when needed.

Previously Chancellor's data were stored separately in its accounting, trading, research, and analytical systems. That not only meant a loss of data integrity but also an increase in the difficulty the professional staff had in locating and accessing data. The professional staff had to use separate systems to access data on differing areas of investment.

Chancellor built software bridges between these systems with one feeding the other, thus reducing data integrity problems while making access easy. It installed a new user interface so that users have one very friendly screen with a number of windows on it. Different users have different windows, depending upon their own needs. The user can move from one window to another with ease, noting a market trend in one window, checking a second window to determine the state of his or her assets, then to a third window to check analysts' reports on stocks he or she is interested in, and finally moving to a fourth window to execute the trades he or she has decided upon. In the past, each of these moves would have required the user to log off one system and on to another, a process that is not only time-wasting but frustrating as well. These windows represent a tremendous enhancement in speed and efficiency.

Integrating the software used in the front office and the back office enabled trading within the firm to become paperless. Moreover, Chancellor was able to automate its share allocation function. In the past, when it had an order to buy 100,000 shares of *x*, *y*, or *z* stock, Chancellor had to figure out manually what percentage was allocated to each account. The process was very time-consuming. Aside from the time saved and the errors reduced, this change brought another benefit: Chancellor can now handle any trade volume it needs to. For example, in September 1992 Chancellor officially turned bullish on stocks. In a few days it went from a significant cash position down to near zero, executing 1200 to 1500 trades per day—double or triple its normal volume. No problems were encountered.

Next, Chancellor added electronic mail to its workstation network. Then the firm began to add electronic interfaces to its brokers so that even the orders to the brokers and the trade-execution confirmations became electronic. To keep the system open and give Chancellor the freedom to change brokers, if desired, Chancellor's staff wrote these interfaces themselves, formatting the data to meet the specific broker's needs. Chancellor also finds that because of its open systems environment, new programs can be integrated with little problem. For example, at the time of this writing, the users of Telerate, one of Chancellor's fixed income services, must access the software through dedicated terminals supplied by Telerate's vendors. With its new, open system, however, Chancellor is planning to distribute Telerate through its own workstation network, making it as easy to access as other Chancellor systems (Michaels, 1993).

Management Challenges

1. Increased demands for employee learning and change. Because the knowledge base and the technologies used in information and knowledge work change rapidly, people are under a great deal of pressure to continue learning and training to maintain their jobs and may need to learn new and different jobs in a short time. Organizations must identify and recruit employees who have the capacity and desire to learn, and they must devote more resources to training. If retraining fails, they may need to retire older workers earlier than in the past. This may both raise costs and create an ethical dilemma for the firm (see Chapter 5).

2. Integration of knowledge work into the organization. It is difficult to integrate knowledge workers into a traditional, hierarchical organization. Knowledge workers tend to be very self-directed and autonomous and are somewhat set off from the rest of the organization. They cannot be told what to do. Changes in authority structure and work arrangements are necessary if companies are to utilize their talents without alienating them.

3. Designing information systems that truly enhance the productivity of knowledge workers. Information systems that truly enhance the productivity of knowledge workers may be difficult to build because the manner in which information technology can enhance higher-level tasks such as those performed by managers and professionals (i.e., scientists or engineers) is not always clearly understood (Sheng et al. 1989–1990). High-level knowledge workers may resist the introduction of any new technology, or they may resist knowledge work systems because such systems diminish personal control and creativity. For instance, some architects may resist using computer-aided architectural rendering systems because they fear the computer-generated representations of buildings cannot convey the individual artistry and imagination of hand-drawn renderings.

Summary

1. Define information work and the information economy. Advanced economies in the United States, Canada, and Western Europe have been transformed from industrial economies where most wealth came from manufacturing to information economies where most wealth originates in information and knowledge production. Today, the majority of workers perform information work. Information work consists primarily of creating or processing information.

2. Describe the roles of knowledge workers and data workers in the organization. There are two kinds of information workers. Knowledge workers are employees such as engineers, architects, scientists, or attorneys whose primary job is to create new information for the organization. Knowledge workers interpret the external knowledge base for the organization, advise management, and act as change agents to bring new knowledge into the firm. Data workers are employees such as secretaries, accountants, or salespersons, whose primary job is to use, process, and disseminate information for the organization. Managers perform both knowledge and data work.

3. Describe the roles and principal activities of the office in contemporary business. Offices coordinate information work in the organization, link the work of diverse groups in the organization, and couple the organization to its external environment. Offices and office work are therefore central to the success of any contemporary organization. The major office activities are document management, scheduling, communications, data management, and project management.

4. Explain the contributions of the principal types of office automation technologies. Word processing, desktop publishing, and digital imaging systems support the document management activities of the office. Electronic calendar and groupware systems support scheduling activities. Electronic mail systems and groupware support its communications activities. Desktop data management systems and customized personal information managers support data management activities. Project management systems break down complex projects into simpler subtasks, producing delivery schedules, allocating resources, and supporting the project management activities of the office.

5. Understand unique requirements of knowledge work systems. Knowledge work systems require easy access to an external knowledge base; powerful computer hardware that can support software with intensive graphics, analysis, document management, and communications capabilities; and a friendly user interface. Knowledge work systems often run on workstations.

6. Describe the major types of knowledge work systems. Knowledge work systems must be customized for the particular type of knowledge work being performed. Computer-aided design systems and virtual reality systems that create interactive simulations that behave like the real world require graphics and powerful modeling capabilities. Knowledge work systems for financial professionals provide access to external databases and the ability to access massive amounts of financial data very quickly.

Key Terms

Knowledge- and information-intense products	Office automation systems (OAS)	Electronic mail (E-mail)	Knowledge work systems (KWS)
Information workers	Document imaging systems	Electronic meeting software	Workstation
Information work	Jukebox	Compound document	Computer-aided design (CAD)
Knowledge workers	Index server	Personal information manager	Virtual reality systems
Data workers	Workflow management	Project management software	
Office activities	Groupware		
	Electronic calendaring		

Review Questions

1. What are the characteristics of an information economy?
2. Describe the differences between information workers, knowledge workers, data workers, and service workers.
3. What is the relationship between information work and productivity in contemporary organizations?
4. Describe the roles of the office in organizations.
5. What are the five major activities that take place in offices?
6. What is office automation? How has it changed over time?
7. What are the principal types of information systems technology that support the roles and activities of the office? Relate each technology to the role(s) it supports.
8. List and describe the uses for document imaging systems in the modern office.
9. What is groupware? How does it support information work? Describe its capabilities.
10. What are the four distinguishing characteristics of knowledge work?
11. What role do knowledge workers play in the organization?
12. What are the generic requirements of knowledge work systems? Why?
13. What is CAD? Describe its role and significance in business today.
14. What is virtual reality? How does it differ from CAD?

Discussion Questions

1. Knowledge workers tend to be treated differently than other workers within businesses today. Define the nontechnical problems these differences might create within the organization. Do you think the problems are significant? Discuss how you would deal with these problems.

2. Perhaps the largest challenge corporate management faces today is finding ways to keep up with the explosion of new information. In what ways is this critical to the future of a knowledge-intensive high-tech company? What long-range strategies do you think such companies need to institute to meet this challenge? Discuss them, their cost, and their potential effectiveness.

Group Project

With three or four of your classmates, investigate a high-tech business nearby and observe the role played by knowledge workers in this business. Describe the kinds of knowledge work systems that would be valuable for that business. Define the hardware, software, data, and procedural components for each system, and design a knowledge workstation for one of these systems. Your workstation description could consist of a written report, a diagram, or both. Present your findings to the class. Alternatively, your group could select a professional occupation such as a scientist, an engineer, an architect, or an attorney, and design a professional workstation for that occupation.

Case Study

DESIGNING THE PAPERLESS AIRPLANE

The Boeing Company had 1994 sales of $21.9 billion and net earnings of $856 million, a giant company by any measure. The largest business of this Seattle, Washington–based firm is in commercial aircraft, with 1994 sales of $16.9 billion. The company is the single largest exporter in the United States and the number one commercial aircraft producer in the world with 55 to 60 percent of the world market since the 1970s. Since its introduction in 1966, the Boeing 747 had been the company's cash cow. Boeing made an operating profit of around $30 million per 747 for years. Boeing currently has sole possession of the long-range widebody jet airliner market with its 747-400 that seats 420 passengers and sells for $150 million. The 747-400 is no longer Boeing's most profitable aircraft (the distinction currently belongs to Boeing's 218-seat $100 million 767-300 long-range twin). But large planes are

still big business. The company is now entering the mid- to long-range twin-engine widebody market just after European competitor Airbus Industrie opened the market in late 1994. Boeing is also coming under new leadership with 53-year-old Philip M. Condit as president. Condit is expected to succeed Frank Shrontz first as chief executive and then as chairman by the time Shrontz retires in 1997.

Despite Boeing's enviable position, the company is facing serious problems. First, its 1994 sales represent a drop of $3.5 billion from 1993, a reduction of 13.8 percent, while company earnings fell by 31 percent from $1.244 billion in 1993. Commercial jet transport deliveries fell to only 270 in 1994 versus 330 in 1993. The company projects deliveries to be only 230 for 1995 despite the introduction of a new commercial line (the 777). In March 1995, Boeing offered retirement incentives to about

13,000 workers as part of its announced plan to cut its work force to 110,000 by the end of 1995, down from 166,000 at its height in 1989.

Second, Boeing is facing a very serious challenge to its world domination of the commercial airline market, primarily from Airbus Industrie. In 1985, when Airbus had 15 percent of the world commercial aircraft market, its management announced a goal of 33 percent, a target it reached in 1994. Amazingly, Airbus accomplished this without any offerings in the large two- and four-engine widebody niche, a situation the company is correcting rapidly. Airbus's new A330 widebody twinjet plane went into service in November 1994, giving it a six-month head start over Boeing's competing 777 family (described in detail below). In late 1994 Airbus announced a new four-engine double-decker plane, the A3XX, priced at about $200 million. This plane will carry 570 passengers (in a three-class configuration) up to 8400 miles, with operating costs projected to be 20 percent lower than Boeing's competing 747-400. Airbus estimates that it will sell 1000 A3XX aircraft within 20 years and also estimates development cost to be about $8 billion. Industry analysts suggest development will probably cost at least $10 billion and could easily reach $15 billion. The major question facing Airbus is whether it can raise the money needed to develop the A3XX. Airbus is owned by several European governments that have traditionally financed Airbus development projects. However, a recent international agreement now limits all government subsidies for large civilian aircraft development. In 1994, Jean Pierson, head of Airbus, announced a new goal of 50 percent of the world market in less than a decade, and with its record, few analysts doubt its resolve or the seriousness of this threat to Boeing.

Boeing does face two other challengers also. McDonnell Douglas has recently begun supplying its new tri-engine widebody MD-11 aircraft, designed to compete in the less-than-four-engine widebody market, although sales of this aircraft are badly lagging. In addition, Japanese companies are closely watching the market, ready to jump in if they see Boeing or Airbus weakening. The Japanese have targeted the commercial airline market as one of the industries they want to penetrate.

Third, the market for new commercial aircraft is softening. The main reasons are half a decade of large airline industry losses and major price wars. Boeing's main competition may actually be its own old aircraft that are still in use. Previously, airlines commonly replaced 20-year-old aircraft. Their replacement timetables ordinarily would be swelling orders for aircraft to be delivered in the late 1990s. Boeing CEO Frank Shrontz believes that the "Replacement business means the difference between slow growth and the strong sales needed to finance future models." However, the cost of new planes has risen so dramatically that airlines are often choosing to refurbish older ones to

make them last longer, rather than placing orders for new aircraft.

Fourth, Boeing's aircraft manufacturing process has been labeled as "shockingly primitive, cumbersome, and slow" by *Fortune* magazine, which also described what it views as a "mulish resistance to change" by veteran production managers. Boeing is also faced with great uncertainty relating to its new 777 entry. *The New York Times* calls the process of designing and developing a new aircraft a "crapshoot." Designing and developing a new line takes years, and in the interim, the situation (or even the existence) of individual airline companies can change dramatically, as can overall airline market conditions. Moreover, such development is immensely expensive (as we have already seen), and the high cost of development means that it will take many years of solid sales once delivery has begun before the company will earn back its original investment and finally begin to experience any profit at all.

Boeing has developed a multifaceted strategy to respond to these problems. The fundamental component of this strategy is to cut costs and prices. As we indicated above, the company has already reduced its work force by one third in six years. Management is also working to cut development and production costs. At the same time the company is making design changes so that new planes will be significantly cheaper to operate than are existing planes. Boeing's plan is to use the lowered costs to drop new plane prices so dramatically that it becomes cheaper for an airline to purchase and operate a new plane than to refurbish and operate an aging one. Management established a goal of reducing production costs by 25 percent between 1992 and 1998. They also intend to radically reduce the time needed to build a plane; for example, lowering the production time of 747s and 767s from 18 months in 1992 down to 8 months in 1996. Reducing production time would result in major cost savings, for example, by reducing inventory expenses. It would also benefit Boeing customers by reducing market uncertainties they face

during the time between placing an order and delivery of the aircraft. Oftentimes in the past an airline would place an order during a high point in the business cycle but 18 months later would find itself taking delivery well after a downturn in the cycle.

A second strategic decision was to hold tight and not attempt to compete directly with the Airbus A3XX by developing a new line. Condit does not believe there is enough of a market to warrant even one company investing up to $15 billion to develop such a large, four-engine widebody plane. He reasons that with the advent of smaller twin-engine planes such as the Boeing 767 and the Airbus A330, there has been a reduction in the use of the large 747s. He points out that many airlines that used to fly overseas passengers to hubs and then fly them out on large 747s now prefer to fly the passengers direct from point of departure to destination, such as Cincinnati to Zurich or Detroit to Amsterdam. By using smaller planes and avoiding hubs, the airlines avoid both slot congestion and the high cost of flying into and out of such major hubs as New York's Kennedy Airport and London's Heathrow Airport. Condit also claims that only two airlines, British Airways and Singapore Air Lines, are openly lobbying for the production of these giant planes. He concludes that, "If there isn't enough market to justify one [superjumbo] program, then I wonder why [Airbus] would do it. And certainly you would not want to do two programs in these circumstances." Condit also wonders about the accuracy of Airbus's projection of 1000 sales in 20 years. He points out that it took 30 years for Boeing to sell 1100 of the immensely popular 747s.

A third element of Boeing's strategy is to upgrade its existing aircraft lines. Boeing has invested $2.5 billion to upgrade its 737 short-haul line, and management is considering extensive redesign of the 747 in order to make it a reasonable competitor of the A3XX. The 747 upgrade would cost about $3 billion and would include a new, more efficient wing and some redesign to allow it to carry 520 passengers nearly 9000 miles.

The project would include applying digital technology (CAD) learned in the production of the new 777 in order to reduce the updated plane's selling price. Speculation is that the new 747 will be a double-decker, making it particularly useful for Asian routes where limited landing slots make a high passengers-per-landing ratio an imperative.

Finally, the company is in the process of introducing a new aircraft line, the 777, to compete in and hopefully to dominate the twin-engine widebody market that is just opening. Actually, Boeing first began to assess market preferences for such a plane in late 1986 and on October 15, 1990, United Airlines placed the first order for 34 of the new 777s. Two weeks later, on October 29, the project was approved by Boeing's board of directors and work began in earnest. In April 1994, Boeing publicly unveiled the new aircraft, and on June 12, 1994, the 777 made its first flight. The first delivery, to United Airlines, was announced for the spring of 1995.

The 777 class are medium-sized, widebody, twinjet commercial passenger aircraft. They are designed to fly with only two pilots, thus reducing the cost of operations. They use the largest, most powerful aircraft engines ever built, achieving from 74,000 to 100,000 pounds of thrust each. The engine size is necessary if only two engines are lifting the large airplane and its passenger load. Using only two engines reduces operating costs by saving on fuel, maintenance, and spare parts. Boeing claims that altogether the 777 will cost 25 percent less to operate than older Boeing models. The planes are 209 feet long with wingspans of 199 feet. They use a number of new, lightweight, cost-effective structural materials such as a new composite material for the floors and a new aluminum alloy in the wing skin that also improves corrosion and fatigue resistance. As a result of the lighter materials and fewer engines, the 777s weigh about 500,000 pounds versus 800,000 for the four-engine 747s. The planes will use a "fly-by-wire" flight control system in which aircraft control and maneuver commands are transmitted to the elevators, rudder ailerons, and flaps as electrical signals flowing through electrical wires rather than by mechanical steel cables. Fly-by-wire control systems are easier to construct, lighter weight, and require fewer spare parts and less maintenance.

The 777s are priced at between $116 million and $140 million. Gordon A. McKinzie, United Airline's liaison with Boeing for the 777 project, stated "This is what we wanted: the minimum number of engines, the minimum number of crew." He added that the per-seat cost will be 20 percent less than that of the DC-10s which United will be replacing. Industry analysts estimate that it will take about 300 aircraft and four years for Boeing to break even. However, they warn that if sales are slow, if this process is stretched out over 20 years, Boeing will never make a profit on the planes.

The first 777s to be built are known as A-Market aircraft. They have a range of 4520 to 5500 miles, enabling them to serve such runs as New York to San Francisco, London to New York, Tokyo to San Francisco, and Chicago to Honolulu. The planes weigh from 506,000 to 535,000 pounds and seat between 305 and 440 passengers, depending upon the seating configuration (they will seat up to 10 across), carrying about as many passengers as some of the older 747s. As of the spring of 1995 Boeing had orders for 147 planes and options for 108 more from 16 airlines including Thai Airways, British Airways, Japan Airlines, Emirates Air, Continental Airlines, and the International Lease Finance Corporation.

The B-Market planes will be longer-range, capable of a higher take-off weight despite using the same body as the A-Market planes. They will carry between 305 and 328 passengers up to 8435 miles, making them able to be used on such routes as London to Los Angeles, Tokyo to Sydney, and Chicago to Seoul. Their range matches that of the 747s. Boeing released 25 percent of the B-Market design specifications on March 2, 1995, and at that time had 45 orders in hand.

Boeing management saw the development and production of the new 777 line as an opportunity to move toward their goals of lowering aircraft cost while speeding up production. They also wanted to produce a better product than ever before. To achieve these goals, they made many changes in their design and production methods. Management of the 777 project decided that tweaking the existing processes would bring only minor improvements. Instead, they opted to re-engineer the whole process. One major innovation was their decision to involve customers in design and testing. Four buyers—United, ANA, British Airways, and Japan Airlines—each kept a team of two to four engineers on site to work with the Boeing project team during the design, building, and testing phases. During design, Boeing designers had what a company representative called an "intensive customer dialogue" to define and develop the new plane's configuration. One of the results was that 80 items that had been optional equipment in past lines were made standard in response to users' requests, including satellite communications and global position systems.

Because during fabrication each airplane has to be individually configured to match customer specifications, making optional equipment standard reduces variability during design and production of an order. The results are a lower cost of production and redesign and ultimately a lower sale price. In addition, other vital changes were made in response to customer requests. For example, the length of the wingspan of the 777 is far greater than that of previous Boeing planes. The users wanted the wingspan to be no greater than those of DC-10s and 767s so that the 777s would fit into existing airport gate and taxiway spaces. To accommodate this request, Boeing changed the wing design to incorporate a hinge to allow the wing tip to fold once the plane is on the runway, a feature that has long been common on military aircraft. Another issue raised by the customers involved the wing fuel intake panel. The 777 wing has a sharp upward sweep, resulting in the fuel intake panel being 31 inches higher than it is on 747s. At that location it was too high for current airport fuel trucks. Boeing agreed to move the intake panels closer to the aircraft body where they would be at an appropriate height for existing fuel trucks.

One key change involves the move to paperless design—the "paperless airplane." Boeing has had to fight a paper war to design its airplanes. The final design of the Boeing 747 consisted of 75,000 engineering drawings, a typical example of the job. But the original design is only the opening battle of the paper war. The specific problem that propelled Boeing to move to paperless design is the need to repeatedly copy and reuse these designs. Every order for a plane or group of planes is customized according to the customer's requirement so that, for example, the seating arrangements and the electronic equipment will differ from order to order. In such situations, Boeing designers long ago realized they would save a great deal of time and work if they reused existing designs rather than designing the customized configuration from scratch. However, the process of design customization was manual and took more than 1000 engineers a year of full-time work to complete. To reuse old stored paper aircraft configurations and parts designs, the engineers first needed to laboriously search through immense amounts of paper drawings to find appropriate designs to reuse for the configuration ordered. They then laboriously copied the old designs to use as a starting point for the new ones. Inevitably, errors crept in to the new designs, large numbers of errors given the large numbers of design sheets, because of unavoidable copying mistakes.

The thousands of engineers who manually worked on these designs rarely compared notes. If production engineers at Boeing's factory in Auburn, Washington, built a mock-up of a new jet and found a part that didn't fit, they sent a complaint to the designers back in Renton. The designers pulled out their drawings, reconfigured the part, made sure it matched drawings of surrounding parts, and sent the new design back to Auburn. Planes were built in fits and starts, filling warehouses with piles of paper and years of wasted byproducts.

Another problem with manual design was that the staff needed to create life-size mock-ups in plywood and plastic in order to make sure the pipes and wires that run through the plane are placed properly and do not interfere with other necessary equipment. They also needed to verify the accuracy of part specifications. This was a slow, expensive, laborious process. A third substantial problem occurred at production time. Errors would again occur when part numbers or specifications were manually copied and at times incorrectly copied onto order sheets, resulting in many wrong or mis-sized parts arriving. This not only was costly but also held up production. All of these obstacles caused Boeing to decide to turn to a computer-aided design (CAD) system and to a team approach to designing and building the 777.

In addition to involving customers in the design process, Boeing established "design-build teams" that bring designers and fabricators from a range of specialties together throughout the whole process. In this way changes that used to have to be made after production began are now made during design because of the presence of production staff on the design team, saving a great deal of time and cost. Boeing's primary aim in turning to a CAD system was to reduce the possibility of human error.

Boeing's CAD system is gigantic, employing nine IBM mainframes, a Cray supercomputer, and 2200 workstations, and ultimately storing 3500 billion bits of information. The hardware alone cost hundreds of millions of dollars. It is one of the world's largest networks. Fiber-optic links connect Boeing's Seattle-area plants with a plant in Wichita, Kansas, which is constructing the flight deck for the 777, and with plants in Japan that are building most of the 777's fuselage. Boeing engineers calculate that their system has exchanged more than 1.5 trillion bytes of production data with Japan alone.

The amount of data on the network is so vast—more than 600 databases in different software languages—that information is sometimes hard for users to find. Some engineers need four kinds of computers on their desks to obtain the information they need. Analysts have likened the network to the Tower of Babel.

Boeing purchased 3-dimensional graphics software called Catia developed by France's Dassault Systems, a unit of Dassault Aviation SA. Catia stands for "computer-aided three-dimensional interactive application." The system enables engineers to call up any of the 777's 3 million parts, modify them, fit them into the surrounding structure, and put them back into the plane's "electronic box" so that other engineers can make their own adjustments.

For instance, an engineer designing the rib of the aircraft's wing might find that the wing spar abutting the rib overlaps it by 11/100ths of an inch. He or she could move the computer icon to the intruding spar, and the system would call up the name and telephone number of the designer for that piece. In the past, the clash would trigger a new pile of paperwork. With the new CAD system, engineers can alter the rib's design to fit snugly against the spar in 30 minutes. Boeing officials claim they could use the system to redesign large pieces of an airplane's fuselage in a matter of weeks. Without computers, the task would take years and be much less accurate. The system has cut the time spent reworking 777 parts by over 90 percent, compared to the paper-based approach for earlier models.

The team set a specific goal of reducing engineering changes and ill-fitting components by 50 percent as compared to the last major Boeing design project (767s). CAD software enables engineers to test how all parts fit together without having to build models and without having to solve most problems during the assembly of the first aircraft at which time extensive redesign of the aircraft and of individual parts is very costly and time-consuming. CAD software also enables a great deal of testing to be done electronically. Moreover, the designs stored in the CAD software system can be used to generate parts orders and fabrication specifications automatically without all the errors that result from copying by hand. Finally, by electronically storing aircraft configurations and parts designs, those designs can be quickly and easily located, copied, and used as the basis for designing new plane orders.

Boeing put in more engineering time on the project than originally planned because the software proved somewhat slow and complicated to manipulate. Some engineers had trouble making the transition from working two-dimensionally on paper to working three-dimensionally on the computer screen. Boeing is working with IBM and Dassault to improve the CAD system for advanced versions of the 777. Boeing management believes the ease with which the parts are going together will make up for the increased front-end costs.

Another major production change Boeing made was to break from the traditional method of building the whole plane sequentially. Instead, workers moved to parallel production, building selected sections of the plane simultaneously. They also developed a range of new fabrication methods. One such new method came out of the Boeing Sheet Metal Center. Previously doors were sent to the assembly floor in large batches of parts, requiring assembly personnel to spend a great deal of time locating and picking the required door parts before actual door assembly could begin. Instead, door parts now arrive in ready-to-assemble kits.

The preliminary results have certainly been promising. The Sheet Metal Center, with its door kits and other innovations, reduced parts inventory awaiting assembly from $270 million in 1993 to $130 million in 1994. Other departments made equivalent gains. The airplane was designed entirely on the computer screen, and it was assembled without first building mock-ups. Using electronic pre-assembly, many of the space conflicts were solved before any physical production took place. The

value of electronic design software was proven, for example, when the wing flaps were designed and electronically tested in mid-1992 wholly on the computer. Later, in 1994, the actual tests on a live aircraft showed that the wing flaps worked perfectly. The accuracy of the CAD design system is clear. In the past, the typical horizontal or vertical variances of any part was three-eighths to one-half inch. Using the CAD system to design the parts, the average variance was reduced to 23 one thousandths of an inch vertically and 11 one thousandths of an inch horizontally. The company reports that it exceeded its goal of cutting overall engineering design errors by 50 percent. Boeing has announced that the time to design and build a 777 order has already been reduced to 10 months compared to the 18 months required for 747 and 767 orders. Total cost to design and bring the 777 to production was $4 billion.

One final issue Boeing faced was that of testing and receiving governmental approval for operation from the U.S. Federal Aviation Administration (FAA). Boeing established a giant testing program that at various times included nine planes using three different engines. Standard certification testing has not been a problem. In addition to the standard tests, however, Boeing has scheduled a special set of 1000 cycles (takeoffs and landings) on each airframe/engine combination to simulate day-to-day flight operations and maintenance procedures. The planes are operating in a wide range of environments, flying all types of trip lengths in all types of weather and climate under all types of airport conditions. Flight and maintenance teams from three buyers are participating fully in these tests. These special tests began on December 29, 1994, and were scheduled to be completed in four months although in the past this cycle of testing would have taken a full year. Ninety tests totaling 430 flight hours were on actual United runs with United personnel to help United prepare for the introduction of its new 777 fleet.

The main testing hurdle Boeing faces is the need to achieve ETOPS

certification. ETOPS stands for Extended-range Twinjet Operations, and ETOPS approval is granted by the FAA. It is needed before commercial long-range flights over water can occur. It is required for two-engine planes (four-engine planes are less vulnerable to problems from engine failure since the failure of one or two engines will leave two or three still operating). In the past ETOPS approval has come only after the plane has been in service two years so its performance can be evaluated under actual operational conditions. However, Airbus expects to receive ETOPS approval for A330 flights of up to 90 minutes over water in late 1995, after only one year in service. Boeing considers approval for the 777 earlier than that to be crucial if it is to prevent Airbus from garnering too large a portion of the twin-engine widebody market. Boeing's goal is to obtain ETOPS approval at the same time the 777 aircraft goes into service in the spring of 1995. That is part of the reason for the far-more-extensive-than-normal testing program. Boeing is working closely with the FAA to achieve early ETOPS certification, but it is still a gamble. The FAA has given no commitment in advance although FAA officials do admit they are negotiating with Boeing on the scope of the tests. Boeing management believes that the computerized design of the airplane, along with the heavy testing regimen, should justify an early award. Analysts believe the failure to achieve quick ETOPS certification will not impact current orders due to financial penalties associated with cancellation. United's McKinzie agrees, saying United will take delivery anyway but would use the planes for overland routes rather than the Hawaii routes they had hoped to use them for. However, it is likely future sales will be impacted, causing some orders to go to Airbus and even perhaps giving new life to McDonnell Douglas' MD-11.

In early 1995, Ronald Woodard, president of Boeing's airplane group, announced new major cost-cutting initiatives, including a further reduction of managerial and administrative jobs. On April 1, 1995, Boeing began a series of

80 tests designed for ETOPS certification and won FAA approval for transoceanic flights without two years of testing. Boeing made its first delivery of 777s, to United Airlines, on May 15, 1995. The 777 entered commercial service in June 1995.

Sources: Matthew L. Wald, "FAA Allows Boeing 777 to Skip a Test Period," *The New York Times* (May 31, 1995); Jeff Cole, "Boeing's Retirement Incentive Plan Stirs Concern About Number of Jobs to Be Cut," *The Wall Street Journal,* March 23, 1995; John Holusha, "Can Boeing's New Baby Fly Financially?" *The New York Times,* March 27, 1994; Bill Richards, "The Future Is Now," *The Wall Street Journal,* November 14, 1994; Howard Banks, "Superjumbo," *Forbes,* October 24, 1994; Shawn Tully, "Why to Go for Stretch Targets," *Fortune,* November 4, 1994; Boeing News Release, "Boeing 777 Designers Take B-Market to New Level," Boeing Commercial Airplane Group, March 2, 1995; "Boeing 777 Sets New Standards in Aircraft Design," Boeing Commercial Airplane Group (no date); The Boeing Company, "News Release Summary of the Annual Report, 1994."

Case Study Questions

1. Analyze Boeing's competitive position using the competitive forces and value chain models.

2. What is Boeing's competitive business strategy? In what ways do you consider this strategy sound? Risky? Explain your answers.

3. Describe how the Boeing 777 line fits in with this strategy.

4. What role do knowledge work systems play in Boeing's business strategy? Evaluate the significance of that role.

5. How well does the knowledge work system function as a factor in Boeing's business strategy?

6. What management, organization, and technology problems do you think the use of the knowledge work software presented to Boeing? What steps do you think they did take or should have taken to deal with these problems?

References

Amaravadi, Chandra S., Olivia R. Liu Sheng, Joey F. George, and Jay F. Nunamaker, Jr. "AEI: A Knowledge-Based Approach to Integrated Office Systems." *Journal of Management Information Systems* 9, no. 1 (Summer 1992).

Applegate, Linda. "Technology Support for Cooperative Work: A Framework for Studying Introduction and Assimilation in Organizations." *Journal of Organizational Computing* 1, no. 1 (January–March 1991).

Bair, James H. "A Layered Model of Organizations: Communication Processes and Performance." *Journal of Organizational Computing* 1, no. 2 (April–June 1991).

Berst, Jesse. "Deciphering Lotus' Notes." *Computerworld* (May 18, 1992).

Bikson, Tora K., J. D. Eveland, and Barbara A. Gutek. "Flexible Interactive Technologies for Multi-Person Tasks: Current Problems and Future Prospects." Rand Corporation (December 1988).

Black, George. "Taking Notes, Big Sixer Aims for Head of the Class." *Software Magazine* (March 1995).

Bohn, Roger E. "Measuring and Managing Technological Knowledge." *Sloan Management Review* (Fall 1994).

Brynjolffson, Erik. "The Productivity Paradox of Information Technology." *Communications of the ACM* 36, no. 12 (December 1993).

Brynjolfsson, Erik and Lorin Hitt. "New Evidence on the Returns to Information Systems." MIT Sloan School of Management (October 1993).

Busch, Elizabeth, Matti Hamalainen, Clyde W. Holsapple, Yongmoo Suh, and Andrew B. Whinston. "Issues and Obstacles in the Development of Team Support Systems." *Journal of Organizational Computing* 1, no. 2 (April–June 1991).

Daly, James. "Insurer Sees Future in Imaging Strategy." *Computerworld* (January 6, 1992).

Davis, Gordon B., Roseann Webb Collins, Michael A. Eirman, and William D. Nance. "Productivity from Information Technology Investment in Knowledge Work," in Rajiv D. Banker, Robert J. Kauffman and Mo Adam Mahmood, eds. *Strategic Information Technology Management.* Harrisburg, PA: Idea Group Publishing (1993).

Edelstein, Herbert A. "Imaging Shifts Emphasis to Workflow Management." *Software Magazine* (November 1991).

Giuliao, Vincent E. "The Mechanization of Office Work." *Scientific American* (September 1982).

Grudin, Jonathan. "Groupware and Social Dynamics: Eight Challenges for Developers." *Communications of the ACM* 37, no. 1 (January 1994).

Horton, Marjorie, Priscilla Rogers, Laurel Austin, and Michael McCormick. "Exploring the Impact of Face-to-Face Collaborative Technology on Group Writing." *Journal of Management Information Systems* 8, no. 3 (Winter 1991–1992).

International Data Corporation White Paper. "Image Management Systems." *Computerworld* (September 24, 1990).

Johansen, Robert. "Groupware: Future Directions and Wild Cards." *Journal of Organizational Computing* 1, no. 2 (April–June 1991).

Kirkpatrick, David. "Why Microsoft Can't Stop Lotus Notes." *Fortune* (December 12, 1994).

Kling, Rob, and Charles Dunlop. "Controversies about Computerization and the Character of White Collar Worklife." *The Information Society* 9, no. 1 (January–March 1993).

Korzeniowski, Paul. "Building New APPS on E-mail." *Software Magazine* (March 1992).

Kusekoski, Gene. "Corporate Videotex: A Strategic Business Information System." *MIS Quarterly* 13, no. 4 (December 1989).

LaPlante, Alice. "Group(ware) Therapy." *Computerworld* (July 27, 1992).

Lasher, Donald R., Blake Ives, and Sirkka L. Jarvenpaa. "USAA-IBM Partnerships in Information Technology: Managing the Image Project." *MIS Quarterly* 15, no. 4 (December 1991).

Lee, Soonchul. "The Impact of Office Information Systems on Power and Influence." *Journal of Management Information Systems* 8, no. 2 (Fall 1991).

Liker, Jeffrey K., Mitchell Fleischer, Mitsuo Nagamachi, and Michael S. Zonnevylle. "Designers & Their Machines: CAD Use and Support in the U.S. and Japan." *Communications of the ACM* 35, no. 2 (February 1992).

Lotus Development Corporation. "Lotus Notes Application Profile" (1991).

Mann, Marina M., Richard L. Rudman, Thomas A. Jenckes, and Barbara C. McNurlin. "EPRINET: Leveraging Knowledge in the Electronic Industry." *MIS Quarterly* 15, no. 3 (September 1991).

Margolis, Nell. "Imaging: It's a Jungle in There." *Computerworld* (July 6, 1992).

Markoff, John. "American Express Goes High-Tech." *The New York Times* (July 31, 1988).

Michaels, Jenna. "Managing Technology." *Wall Street & Technology* (February 1993).

Naj, Amal Kumar. "Virtual Reality Isn't a Fantasy for Surgeons." *The Wall Street Journal* (March 3, 1993).

Nash, Jim. "Imaging Heals Hospital's Sick File System." *Computerworld* (March 2, 1992).

Newquist, Harvey P. "Virtual Reality's Commercial Reality." *Computerworld* (March 30, 1992).

Olson, Gary M., and Judith S. "User-Centered Design of Collaboration Technology." *Journal of Organizational Computing* 1, no. 1 (January–March 1991).

Orlikowski, Wanda J. "Learning from Notes: Organizational Issues in Groupware Implementation." Sloan Working Paper no. 3428, Cambridge, MA: Sloan School of Management, Massachusetts Institute of Technology 1992.

Panko, Raymond R. "Is Office Productivity Stagnant?" *MIS Quarterly* 15, no. 2 (June 1991).

Porat, Marc. *The Information Economy: Definition and Measurement.* Washington, DC: U.S. Department of Commerce, Office of Telecommunications (May 1977).

Press, Lawrence. "Systems for Finding People." *Journal of Organizational Computing* 2, nos. 3 and 4 (1992a).

Press, Lawrence. "Lotus Notes (Groupware) in Context." *Journal of Organizational Computing* 2, nos. 3 and 4 (1992b).

Ramanathan, Srinivas, P. Venkat Rangan, and Harrick M. Vin. "Designing Communication Architectures for Inter-Organizational Multimedia Collaboration." *Journal of Organizational Computing* 2, nos. 3 and 4 (1992).

Richards, Bill. "The Future Is Now." *The Wall Street Journal* (November 14, 1994).

Roach, Stephen S. "Industrialization of the Information Economy." New York: Morgan Stanley and Co. (1984).

Roach, Stephen S. "Technology and the Service Sector." *Technological Forecasting and Social Change* 34, no. 4 (December 1988).

Roach, Stephen S. "Services Under Siege—The Restructuring Imperative." *Harvard Business Review* (September–October 1991).

Roach, Stephen S. "Making Technology Work." New York: Morgan Stanley and Co. (1993).

Ruhleder, Karen, and John Leslie King. "Computer Support for Work Across Space, Time, and Social Worlds." *Journal of Organizational Computing* 1, no. 4 (1991).

Schatz, Bruce R. "Building an Electronic Community System." *Journal of Management Information Systems* 8, no. 3 (Winter 1991–1992).

Sheng, Olivia, R. Liu, Luvai F. Motiwalla, Jay F. Nunamaker, Jr., and Douglas R. Vogel. "A Framework to Support Managerial Activities Using Office Information Systems." *Journal of Management Information Systems* 6, no. 3 (Winter 1989–1990).

Smarr, Larry, and Charles E. Catlett. "Metacomputing." *Communications of the ACM* 35, no. 6 (June 1992).

Sproull, Lee, and Sara Kiesler. "A Two-Level Perspective on Electronic Mail in Organizations." *Journal of Organizational Computing* 1, no. 2 (April–June 1991).

Sproull, Lee, and Sara Kiesler. *Connections: New Ways of Working in the Networked Organization.* Cambridge, MA: MIT Press (1992).

Starbuck, William H. "Learning by Knowledge-Intensive Firms." *Journal of Management Studies* 29, no. 6 (November 1992).

Sterling, Theodor D., and James J. Weinkam. "Sharing Scientific Data." *Communications of the ACM* 33, no. 8 (August 1990).

"USSAA Insuring Progress." *InformationWEEK* (May 25, 1992).

Westin, Alan F., Heather A. Schwader, Michael A. Baker, and Sheila Lehman. *The Changing Workplace.* New York: Knowledge Industries (1985).

Wolff, Edward N., and William J. Baumol. "Sources of Postwar Growth of Information Activity in the U.S." C. V. Starr Center for Applied Economics, New York University, no. 87-14 (June 1987).

Chapter 16

Enhancing Management Decision Making

The Ideal Investment Portfolio: What Does the System Say?

Redstone Advisors is a $550-million money management firm specializing in taxable and tax-exempt fixed income investments. It must track and analyze complex financial instruments under rapidly changing market conditions. Redstone has monthly policy meetings to determine how its investment portfolios will be constructed. The meetings establish general guidelines for the portfolios, such as the percentage of cash, the weight of each sector, and the average duration of the portfolios (that is, the average number of years for the underlying bonds to reach maturity). The firm then makes trades to bring its portfolios into line with the established guidelines.

To help its traders make buy and sell decisions, Redstone uses a LAN-based portfolio management system called PORTIA supplied by Thomson Financial Services in Boston and

London. Redstone analysts enter proposed trades into PORTIA. The system has a "what-if" capability; when they enter the proposed trades PORTIA tells them what the portfolio will look like. The traders can keep experimenting with different trades until the simulated portfolio matches the investment guidelines. They can even examine the portfolio from many angles using multiple currencies—their system's base currency, the currency of a particular security, or a currency for the selected portfolio. The system allows users to examine the impact of various currencies on investment performance. With this information, they then make the trades. Once the actual trades have been entered into PORTIA, the change is instantly reflected in a portfolio's cash balances and holdings. According to Marc Vincent, Redstone's management director, the ability to perform what-if analysis and to know exact portfolio holdings and cash balances improves productivity and decision making. ∎

Sources: "Fixed Income Money Manager Boosts Efficiency with Flexible, Comprehensive System," *Wall Street and Technology* 12, no. 6 (May 1994), and Sheila O'Henry, "The Portfolio Management and Accounting Supermarket," *Wall Street and Technology* 11, no. 5 (November 1993).

With the ability to perform complex calculations and to create what-if scenarios, Redstone's portfolio management system is a classic example of a decision-support system. Decision-support systems (DSS) provide powerful analytic capabilities for supporting managers during the process of arriving at a decision.

Most of the information systems described throughout this text help people make decisions in one way or another, but DSS are part of a special category of information systems that are explicitly designed to enhance managerial decision making. Other systems in this category are group decision-support systems (GDSS), which support decision making in groups, and executive support systems (ESS), which provide information for making strategic-level decisions. This chapter describes the characteristics of each of these types of information systems and shows how each actually enhances the managerial decision-making process.

After completing this chapter, you will be able to:

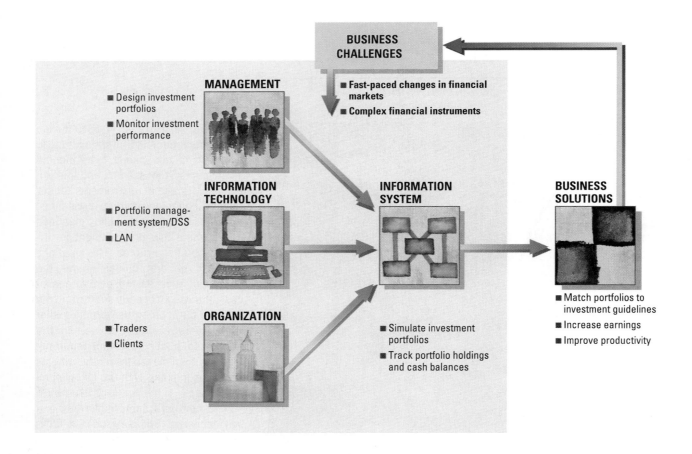

BUSINESS CHALLENGES
- Fast-paced changes in financial markets
- Complex financial instruments

MANAGEMENT
- Design investment portfolios
- Monitor investment performance

INFORMATION TECHNOLOGY
- Portfolio management system/DSS
- LAN

ORGANIZATION
- Traders
- Clients

INFORMATION SYSTEM
- Simulate investment portfolios
- Track portfolio holdings and cash balances

BUSINESS SOLUTIONS
- Match portfolios to investment guidelines
- Increase earnings
- Improve productivity

16.1   DECISION-SUPPORT SYSTEMS (DSS)

In the 1970s, a number of companies began developing information systems that were quite different from traditional MIS systems. These new systems were smaller (in terms of labor and cost). They were interactive (unusual at the time) and were designed to help end users utilize data and models to discuss and decide (not solve) semistructured and unstructured problems (Henderson and Schilling, 1985). By the late 1980s, these early efforts to assist individual decision making were extended to groups and entire organizations.

WHAT ARE DECISION-SUPPORT SYSTEMS?

decision-support system (DSS)

Computer system at the management level of an organization that combines data, sophisticated analytical models, and user-friendly software to support semistructured and unstructured decision making.

These systems are called decision-support systems (DSS). As we noted in Chapter 1, **decision-support systems (DSS)** assist management decision making by combining data, sophisticated analytical models, and user-friendly software into a single powerful system that can support semistructured or unstructured decision making. The DSS is under user control from early inception to final implementation and daily use. Figure 16.1 is a schematic diagram of a DSS.

In Figure 16.1, the relationships between DSS and the organization's existing TPS, KWS, and MIS are left deliberately vague. In some cases, DSS are linked closely to existing corporate information flows. Often, however, DSS are isolated from major organizational information systems. DSS tend to be stand-alone systems, developed by end-user divisions or groups not under central IS control, although it is obviously better if they are integrated into organizational systems when this is a functional requirement (Hogue, 1985).

DSS as a Philosophy

Stated simply, the philosophy of DSS is to give users the tools necessary to analyze important blocks of data, using easily controlled sophisticated models in a flexible manner. DSS are designed to deliver capabilities, not simply to respond to information needs (Keen and Morton, 1982; Sprague and Carlson, 1982).

DSS are more targeted than MIS systems. MIS systems provide managers with routine flows of data and assist in the general control of the organization. In contrast, DSS are tightly focused on a specific decision or classes of decisions such as routing, queuing, evaluating, and so forth. Table 16.1 summarizes the differences between DSS and MIS. In philosophy, DSS promises end-user control of data, tools, and sessions. MIS is still largely dominated by professionals: Users receive information from a professional staff of analysts, designers, and programmers. In terms of objectives, MIS focuses on structured information flows to middle managers. DSS is aimed at top managers and middle managers, with emphasis on change, flexibility, and a quick

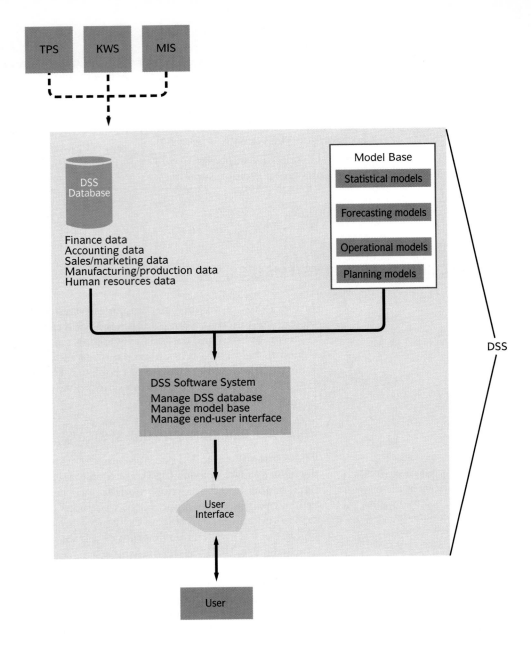

response; with DSS there is less of an effort to link users to structured information flows and a correspondingly greater emphasis on models, assumptions, and display graphics. Both DSS and MIS rely on professional analysis and design. However, whereas MIS usually follows a traditional systems development methodology, freez-

Table 16.1	Differences between DSS and MIS	
Dimension	**DSS**	**MIS**
Philosophy	Provide integrated tools, data, models, and language to users	Provide structured information to end users
Systems analysis	Establish what tools are used in the decision process	Identify information requirements
Design	Iterative process	Deliver system based on frozen requirements

ing information requirements before design and throughout the life cycle, DSS systems are consciously iterative, are never frozen, and in a sense are never finished.

Figure 16.2 shows how a DSS would support stock investment decisions. In this figure, a DSS is portrayed as a set of capabilities that would be useful in a number of decision processes used in making investment decisions. Making such decisions requires reviewing portfolios, individual company research data, and stock data (the databases).

Four core DSS capabilities are portrayed in Figure 16.2, and all DSS can be characterized in this manner (Sprague and Carlson, 1982):

- **Representations:** Conceptualizations of information used in making decisions, such as graphs, charts, lists, reports, and symbols to control operations.
- **Operations:** Logical and mathematical manipulations of data, such as gathering information, generating lists, preparing reports, assigning risks and values, generating statistics, and simulating alternatives.
- **Memory aids:** Databases, views of data, work spaces, libraries, links among work spaces and libraries, and other capabilities to refresh and update memory.
- **Control aids:** Capabilities that allow the user to control the activities of the DSS. They include a software language permitting user control of representations, operations, and memory which features menus, function keys, conventions, training, "help" commands, and tutorials.

In essence, a DSS is a decision-making scratch pad, backed up by databases, that decision makers can use to support many decision-making processes. It can be applied to problems with quantifiable dimensions that provide criteria for the evaluation of alternative solutions. The DSS helps the decision maker identify the best alternative. This approach to DSS as a set of core capabilities goes to the heart of the DSS philosophy and provides a benchmark against which we can compare and critique any DSS in the marketplace.

Characteristics of DSS: What It Means to Support Decisions

With this understanding of the components and philosophy of DSS, it is possible to discuss more precisely what is meant by decision support. (Here it may be helpful to review Chapter 4, which discusses management decision making from several perspectives.) Chapter 4 introduces the distinction between structured, unstructured, and semistructured decisions. Structured problems are repetitive and routine, for which known algorithms provide solutions. Unstructured problems are novel and nonroutine, for which there are no algorithms for solution. One can discuss, decide,

representations In DSS, conceptualizations of information in the form of graphs, charts, lists, reports, and symbols to control operations.

operations In DSS, logical and mathematical manipulations of data.

memory aids In DSS, capabilities to update and refresh memory, including databases, views of data, work spaces, and libraries.

control aids Capabilities that allow the user to control the activities and functions of the DSS.

FIGURE 16.2
DSS approach to investment decisions. In a DSS approach to systems, the emphasis is on providing capabilities to answer questions and reach decisions. The four core capabilities are representations, operations, memory aids, and control aids. *Source: Adapted from Sprague, R. H. and E. D. Carlson, Building Effective Decision Support Systems, Englewood Cliffs, NJ: Prentice-Hall, 1982.*

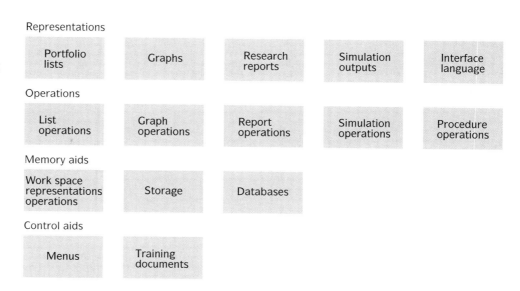

and ruminate about unstructured problems, but they are not solved in the sense that one finds an answer to an equation (Henderson and Schilling, 1985). Semistructured problems fall between structured and unstructured problems. DSS are designed to support semistructured and unstructured problem analysis.

Chapter 4 also introduces Simon's description of decision making, which consists of four stages: intelligence, design, choice, and implementation. Traditionally, TPS and MIS have provided managers with information on day-to-day operations, whereas operations research (OR) has provided management with models for making choices. DSS is designed to incorporate the data of TPS/MIS and the models of OR. It is intended to help design and evaluate alternatives and monitor the adoption or implementation process.

A well-designed DSS can be used at many levels of the organization. Senior management can use a financial DSS to forecast the availability of corporate funds for investment by division. Middle managers within divisions can use these estimates and the same system and data to make decisions about allocating division funds to projects. Capital project managers within divisions, in turn, can use this system to begin their projects, reporting to the system (and ultimately to senior managers) on a regular basis about how much money has been spent.

As noted in Chapter 4, it is a mistake to think that decisions are made only by individuals in large organizations. In fact, most decisions are made collectively. Chapter 4 describes the rational, bureaucratic, political, and "garbage-can" models of organizational decision making. Frequently, decisions must be coordinated with several groups before being finalized. In large organizations, decision making is inherently a group process, and DSS can be designed to facilitate group decision making. The next section of this chapter deals with this issue.

Finally, DSS should provide session control for end users. That is, end users should be able to find relevant data, choose and operate relevant models, and control operations without professional intervention. Professionals are, of course, needed to build the databases, model bases, and control language. Experts should be available for consultation, training, advice, and support, but sessions should be end-user driven.

EXAMPLES OF DSS APPLICATIONS

There are many ways in which DSS can be used to support decision making. Table 16.2 lists examples of DSS in well-known American organizations. To illustrate the range of capabilities of DSS, we will now describe some recent DSS applications.

Table 16.2 Examples of DSS Systems	
American Airlines	Price and route selection
Champlin Petroleum	Corporate planning and forecasting
Equico Capital Corporation	Investment evaluation
Frito-Lay, Inc.	Price, advertising, and promotion section
General Dynamics	Price evaluation
Juniper Lumber	Production optimization
Kmart	Price evaluation
National Gypsum	Corporate planning and forecasting
Southern Railway	Train dispatching and routing
Texas Oil and Gas Corporation	Evaluation of potential drilling sites
United Airlines	Flight scheduling
U.S. Department of Defense	Defense contract analysis

The Advanced Planning System—A Manufacturing DSS

To support most kinds of manufacturing, companies use a type of software known as manufacturing resources planning (MRPII). The typical MRPII system includes such applications as master production scheduling, purchasing, material requirements planning, and even general ledger. Many thousands of these packages have been installed around the world. While they are useful as far as they go, these packages usually run on a mainframe so that they can process massive amounts of data. As a result, they are too large and slow to be used for what-if simulations and too procedural to be modified into decision-support software. A Canadian company, Carp Systems International of Kanata, Ontario, sells the Advanced Planning System (APS) to give the user DSS functionality using the data from existing MRPII systems.

APS allows a range of "what-if" processing by pulling the relevant data from the manufacturing software and performing calculations based upon user-defined variables. After Hurricane Andrew hit south Florida in 1992, Trane's Unitary Productions division in Fort Smith, Arkansas, was asked to quickly ship 114 five-ton air-conditioning systems to small businesses in the affected area. Using APS, within minutes Trane's could determine not only how long it would take to build the units but also how the added production would affect its existing customer commitments. The company found that it was able to fit the added production in without disrupting existing orders. It delivered the units weeks before the competition did.

Pitney Bowes, the $3.3 billion business equipment manufacturer, uses the software to simulate supply changes. Pitney Bowes carries enough manufacturing inventory to satisfy demand for 30 days. Using APS, the firm asked to see the impact if it would reduce the inventory to 15 days. APS responded with an answer within five minutes, including an estimate of what Pitney Bowes would save. Similarly, Sikorsky Aircraft of Stratford, Connecticut, claims that over a three-year period, the company has been able to use this software to help halve its inventory even while its sales doubled.

APS is a complex piece of software costing from $150,000 to $1 million and requiring intensive computing power. It runs on an IBM RS/6000 workstation. As with any other software, users caution that APS (and similar packages) are only as good as the data. If the data are out of date or wrong, APS only allows the user to do wrong things more quickly (Rifkin, 1992).

Yasuda Models Financial Investment Decisions

Yasuda Fire and Marine Insurance Co. of Tokyo found itself evolving ever more into a financial services firm as it was issuing an increasing number of savings-oriented insurance policies. These policies have a wide range of maturities and fluctuating interest rates. Yasuda had been using a computer model to help guide its managers in financial investment decisions, but it was no longer adequate for management decision making. It could not handle the many and complex factors involved with financial markets, nor could it address the numerous government regulations regarding these investments. Management decided to develop a new decision-support system that would more effectively guide Yasuda's investment managers as they invest their portfolios of assets.

Yasuda turned to Frank Russell Co., a Tacoma, Washington, investment consulting firm, to help its managers develop the new DSS. Together they produced the Russell/Yasuda model, a more complex and realistic description of the financial markets that also took into consideration government regulations for minimum capital reserves. Previous models were unrealistic because they had been developed at a time when assumptions had to be simplified to work with limited computing power. Now, however, the two firms were able to combine highly advanced stochastic mathematical models, lightening-fast C and Fortran programming languages, and very powerful workstations based on IBM RISC chips to achieve the result they needed. Older models could search for only a single answer; they had no ability to optimize their response. With the vast increase in power, the new Russell/Yasuda model searches for the best possible results before issuing an optimized investment strategy. Depending on the number of scenarios, the system can arrive at a solution in one to three hours.

The DSS tells Yasuda investment managers how to invest their portfolio of assets in order to meet multiple and conflicting objectives. The firm can thus produce a high income to pay the annual interest on savings-type policies while still maximizing profits. The outcome has been very positive. After one year of using the model, Yasuda's income was up $26 million over what the old model would have produced, according to Yasuda deputy president Kunihiko Sasamoto. Yasuda is now able to pay bonuses on its savings-oriented policies that are larger than those its competitors can pay without sacrificing the longer-term goal of maximizing profits. As a result Yasuda has for now gained a real competitive advantage in its ability not only to retain existing customers but also to attract new ones (Betts, 1993).

The Egyptian Cabinet DSS

The Egyptian Cabinet is composed of the Prime Minister, thirty-two other ministers, and four ministerial-level committees with their staffs. Decision making here is, by its very nature, strategic because it involves questions of survival: balance of payments, deficit management, public sector performance, economic growth, and national defense.

Decision making at these high levels of governments, or corporations, is often portrayed as a rational decision process. But in fact, decision making involves managing issues that are forced on decision makers with varying and shifting priorities. Issues circulate continuously; they enter and exit through participants and are resolved in the sense that they dissolve or go away or are overtaken by other issues. The issues are themselves complex, poorly defined, interdependent, and related to many features of society. Information is voluminous but unreliable and qualitative.

In 1985, the Egyptian Cabinet developed a three-person Information and Decision Support Center (IDSC) to assist its own decision-making process (Figure 16.3). Today, 150 people work full time providing DSS services to the Cabinet on critical issues. The IDSC system is based upon a network of 110 microcomputers connected to a mainframe. Software includes standard desktop packages such as dBASE III for database management, Lotus 1-2-3 spreadsheet software, and FOCUS, a fourth-generation language and application generator, all of which have been fully converted to Arabic form. The electronic mail system is bilingual (Arabic/English).

One of the first uses of IDSC was to develop a new tariff structure to replace an inconsistent and complex structure that was thought to be impeding economic growth. The goal of the policy set forth by the Cabinet was to create a consistent, simple tariff structure; increase revenues to the treasury; and promote economic growth without harming poor citizens. A microcomputer-based DSS model was built of the proposed new tariff structure, using a prototyping methodology.

The new policy activated many opposing groups. The Ministry of Industry, hoping to increase local production of auto parts, supported new tariffs on imported auto parts. This was supported as well by the Ministry of Economy, which supported local production. But the policy was opposed by the Ministry of Finance because it would reduce customs revenue.

The DSS was walked around, back and forth, from one ministry to another, making adjustments to the proposed tariffs, playing "what-if" games to see the impact of tariff changes on revenue and local employment. After one month of intensive effort, agreement was reached on the new tariff policy. Builders of the DSS felt the system reduced conflict by clarifying the trade-offs and potential impacts of tariff changes. While early estimates of higher tariffs claimed $250 million in increased revenues would result, the DSS predicted $25 million. By 1987, the actual increased revenue was $28 million (El Sherif and El Sawy, 1988).

FIGURE 16.3
The cabinet decision-making process with IDSC. *Source: Figure 2. The Cabinet Decision-Making Process After IDSC (El Sherif and El Sawy. Reprinted with permission from* MIS Quarterly, *Volume 12, Number 4, December 1988).*

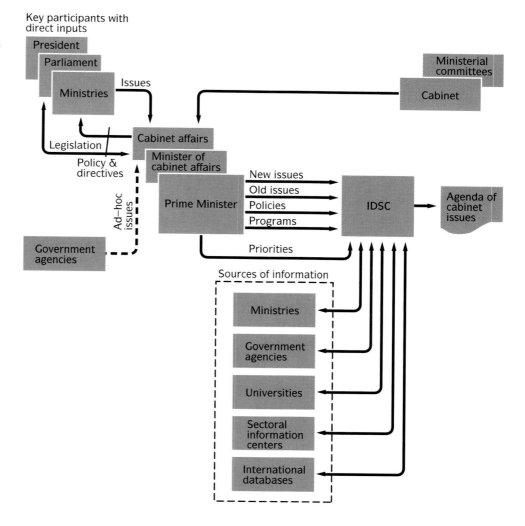

The Egyptian Cabinet's DSS illustrates the idea that a DSS is not just an application, but a generalized capability for addressing decision makers' needs. Unlike an MIS system, DSS do not simply involve a routine, steady flow of data, but instead can be flexibly responsive to new situations by using data and analytic models (even spreadsheets) to work through the consequences of decisions and assumptions.

DSS can also be used as training instruments to teach managers how to make better decisions. Ford Motor Company and Pacific Telesis are among the companies using simulation software that lets managers practice making decisions before they are faced with real-world decision making on the job (see the Window on Management).

COMPONENTS OF DSS

DSS database A collection of current or historical data from a number of applications or groups.

Review Figure 16.1 again. It shows that a decision-support system has three basic components—a database, a model base, and the DSS software system. The **DSS database** is a collection of current or historical data from a number of applications or groups, organized for easy access by a range of applications. The DSS database management system protects the integrity of the data while controlling the processing that keeps the data current; it also saves historical data. DSS do not create or update data, for that is not their purpose. Rather, they use live organizational data (from such systems as production and sales) so that individuals and groups are able to make decisions based upon actual conditions.

PRACTICING DECISION MAKING

"All great teams do something we don't do in business—they practice." The quote is from Nick Zeniuk, business planning and launch manager for Ford Motor Co. Lincoln Continentals in Dearborn, Michigan. Lincoln Continental has decided to do something about the lack of decision-making practice, and so is now using a simulator for this purpose. Designing, building and marketing a new automobile model requires thousands of decisions made by hundreds of employees, and Ford wants to improve their decision-making skills. During the early years of the 1990s, more than 100 engineers, planners, and marketing and financial experts who are members of Ford's new product development team have attended a two-day seminar during which they use a business simulator for practice in decision making. The goal for the seminar is to integrate decision-making learning into ongoing education at Ford. Zeniuk says Ford and other companies need permanent learn-

ing of decision-making skills rather than teaching them on a crisis basis only, as has been the common practice in the past. The overall strategic goal for Ford is to re-architect its core business processes so that employees will be able to do more with less while doing it faster. Managers involved in product development who know how to make the very best choices each and every time would bring the company closer to this objective.

The simulator was developed by the Center for Organizational Learning at the Sloan School of Management at M.I.T. in Cambridge, Massachusetts, using the Strategy Support Simulation System from MicroWorlds, Inc., also in Cambridge. It is actually a game with a number of interacting variables of time, cost, and quality. It is intended to help managers understand the dynamic complexities of the issues they confront and the long-term implications of their decisions. Using the simulator, managers are able to make decisions they might avoid making in the real world, experimenting with new ways to solve

problems. "With a simulated world, its OK to try, and more is sometimes learned by screwing up than by doing well," says Sloan Center graduate stu-

> *To Think About:* *Do you think decision-making skills can be taught, and why? Suggest other possible methods for teaching decision making. How can using simulation systems such as those described help promote a firm's business strategy?*

dent and simulator co-author Don Seville. The game is always played by a team of two or three managers or engineers, never by individuals alone.

The simulator resembles a what-if tool such as those found in popular spreadsheets. However, the simulator is much more complex, with more dynamic relationships among the many elements of the simulation model. Currently it uses generic automobile design and production process data rather than live Ford data. The student might choose a function in which to invest capital, such as marketing or training. The software will then simulate its financial performance impact over a ten-year period. The student can then play with various elements, simulating marketplace interventions, such as speeding up development time or reducing expenditures on production tooling. The data has been generic because "If the world looks too much like the real thing, people get wrapped up in the details and miss the dynamic relationships," says Seville. However, Ford does plan to use some actual Ford data in the next release so that it will more accurately reflect the real world and Ford's historical experience.

Pacific Telesis in San Francisco and Nynex Corp. in New York have also begun developing simulation software, in this case to teach their informa-

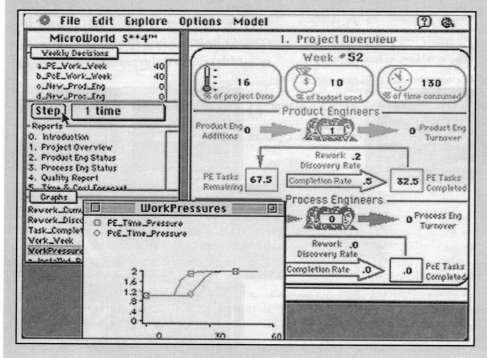

tion systems managers about the dynamic telecommunications marketplace. Their intention is to get the information systems managers "to think differently: to focus on customers and the marketplace and to take a holistically integrated view of business," according to William Nusbaum, vice president of organizational architecture design at San Francisco's Pacific Bell.

The simulator, dubbed Telesim, simulates the telecommunications market in three modules. The first is an *interior* view—the world as seen from inside the offices of a telecommunications company (showing the manager's office, a hallway, meeting rooms, and activities around the water cooler). The second is a *landscape* view—a physical representation of a telephone company's sales and service region (showing facilities and networks in both cities and rural areas). The third is *marketscape*—a representation of market demand and company/product response. This simulator was developed by Coopers & Lybrand Consulting's Information/Communications Group using software from ThinkingTools, Monterey, California. Players use strategies such as pricing network services, preannouncing services, or acquiring new technologies to counter competition or to capture new markets and revenue.

Most DSS do not have direct access to organizational data for two reasons. First, the organization will want to protect the data from accidental or inappropriate changes. In addition, it is a slow and expensive process for the DSS to search through large corporate databases. The process affects not only the performance of the DSS but also all the other systems using the database. Instead, DSS usually use data that have been extracted from relevant databases (internal and external) and stored specifically for use by the DSS.

A **model base** is a collection of mathematical and analytical models that can easily be made accessible to the DSS user. A **model** is an abstract representation that illustrates the components or relationships of a phenomenon. A model can be a physical model (such as a model airplane), a mathematical model (such as an equation), or a verbal model (such as a description of a procedure to write up an order). Each decision-support system is built for a specific set of purposes and will make different collections of models available depending upon those purposes.

Perhaps the most common models available in model bases are libraries of statistical models. Such libraries usually contain the full range of expected statistical functions including means, medians, deviations, and scatter plots. The software has the ability to project future outcomes by analyzing a series of data. Statistical modeling software can be used to help establish relationships, such as relating product sales to differences in age, income, or other factors between communities. Optimization models, often using linear programming, determine optimal resource allocation to maximize or minimize specified variables such as cost or time. The Advanced Planning System (discussed above) uses such software to determine the effect that filling a new order will have upon meeting target dates for existing orders. A classic use of optimization models is to determine the proper mix of products within a given market to maximize profits.

Forecasting models are often used to forecast sales. The user of this type of model might supply a range of historical data to project future conditions and the sales that might result from those conditions. The decision maker could then vary those future conditions (entering, for example, a rise in raw materials costs or the entry of a new, low-priced competitor in the market) to determine how these new conditions might affect sales. Companies often use this software to attempt to predict the actions of competitors. Model libraries exist for specific functions, such as financial and risk analysis models.

Among the most widely used models are **sensitivity analysis** models that ask "what-if" questions repeatedly to determine the impact of changes in one or more factors on outcomes. "What-if" analysis—working forward from known or assumed conditions—allows the user to vary certain values to test results in order to better predict outcomes if changes occur in those values. "What happens if" we raise the price by 5 percent or increase the advertising budget by $100,000? What happens if we keep the price and advertising budget the same? Desktop spreadsheet software,

model base A collection of mathematical and analytical models that can easily be made accessible to the DSS user.

model An abstract representation that illustrates the components or relationships of a phenomenon.

sensitivity analysis Models that ask "what-if" questions repeatedly to determine the impact of changes in one or more factors on outcomes.

such as Lotus 1-2-3 or Microsoft Excel, is often used for this purpose. Backwards sensitivity analysis software is used for goal seeking: If I want to sell one million product units next year, how much must I reduce the price of the product?

The third component of DSS is the **DSS software system**. The DSS software system permits easy interaction between the users of the system and the DSS database and model base. The DSS software system manages the creation, storage, and retrieval of models in the model base and integrates them with the data in the DSS database. The DSS software system also provides a graphic, easy to use, flexible user interface that supports the dialogue between the user and the DSS. DSS users are usually corporate executives or managers, persons with well-developed working styles and individual preferences. Often they have little or no computer experience and no patience for learning to use a complex tool, so the interface must be relatively intuitive. In addition, what works for one may not work for another. Many executives, offered only one way of working (a way not to their liking) will simply not use the system. In order to mimic a typical way of working, a good user interface should allow the manager to move back and forth between activities at will.

BUILDING DSS

Building a DSS is different from building a TPS or MIS system. Developing TPS or MIS results in systems that represent a response to a specific set of information needs. Development of DSS systems focuses on identifying a problem and a set of capabilities that users consider helpful in arriving at decisions about that problem. DSS generally use smaller amounts of data, do not need on-line transaction data, involve a smaller number of important users, and tend to employ more sophisticated analytic models than other systems. Because DSS are customized to specific users and specific classes of decisions, they require much greater user participation to develop. In addition, they must be flexible and must evolve as the sophistication of users grows. Building DSS must therefore use a changing, evolving method that is iterative. Iterative development utilizing prototyping is recommended (see Chapter 12).

Factors in DSS Success and Failure

As experience with DSS has grown, a number of factors have been identified as important to their success and failure. The success factors are not very different from those of MIS and other systems. These factors are described in detail in Chapter 14. Several studies have noted that user training, involvement, and experience; top management's support; length of use; and novelty of the application were the most important factors in DSS success. Success is defined as perceived improvements in decision making and overall satisfaction with the DSS (Alavi and Joachimsthaler, 1992; Sanders and Courtney, 1985).

A smaller study of 34 DSS found that DSS orientation toward top management (assistance with making important decisions) and return on investment are the most important factors in the approval process for DSS (Meador and Keen, 1984; King, 1983). This important finding highlights what organizations are looking for when they develop DSS. Organizations need support for upper management decision making, which requires custom-built, flexible, and easy-to-use systems that address important organizational problems.

16.2 GROUP DECISION-SUPPORT SYSTEMS (GDSS)

The early work in DSS focused largely on supporting individual decision making. However, because so much work is accomplished in groups within organizations, during the late 1980s system developers and scholars began to focus on how computers can support group and organizational decision making. This work followed

---

DSS software system DSS component that permits easy interaction between the users of the system and the DSS database and model base.

even earlier efforts to develop electronic aids to community and societal decision making in the 1970s, based largely on mainframes (see Laudon, 1977). As a result of the focus on computer support of group decision making, a new category of systems developed, known as group decision-support systems (GDSS).

WHAT IS A GDSS?

group decision-support system (GDSS) An interactive computer-based system to facilitate the solution to unstructured problems by a set of decision makers working together as a group.

A **group decision-support system (GDSS)** is an interactive computer-based system to facilitate the solution of unstructured problems by a set of decision makers working together as a group (DeSanctis and Gallupe, 1987). GDSS were developed in response to growing concern over the quality and effectiveness of meetings. The underlying problems in group decision making have been the explosion of decision-maker meetings, the growing length of those meetings, and the increased number of attendees. Estimates on the amount of a manager's time spent in meetings range from 35 to 70 percent.

Meeting facilitators, organizational development professionals, and information systems scholars have been focusing on this issue and have identified a number of discrete meeting elements that need to be addressed (Grobowski et al., 1990; Kraemer and King, 1988; Nunamaker et al., 1991). Among these elements are the following:

1. *Improved pre-planning,* to make meetings more effective and efficient.

2. *Increased participation,* so that all attendees will be able to contribute fully even if the number of attendees is large. Free riding (attending the meeting but not contributing) must also be addressed.

3. *Open, collaborative meeting atmosphere,* in which attendees from various organizational levels feel able to contribute freely. The lower-level attendees must be able to participate without fear of being judged by their management; higher-status participants must be able to participate without having their presence or ideas dominate the meeting and result in unwanted conformity.

4. *Criticism-free idea generation,* enabling attendees to contribute without undue fear of feeling personally criticized.

5. *Evaluation objectivity,* creating an atmosphere where an idea will be evaluated on its merits rather than on the basis of the source of the idea.

6. *Idea organization and evaluation,* which require keeping the focus on the meeting objectives, finding efficient ways to organize the many ideas that can be generated in a brainstorming session, and evaluating those ideas not only on their merits but also within appropriate time constraints.

7. *Setting priorities and making decisions,* which require finding ways to encompass the thinking of all the attendees in making these judgments.

8. *Documentation of meetings* so that attendees will have as complete and organized a record of the meeting as may be needed to continue the work of the project.

9. *Access to external information,* which will allow significant, factual disagreements to be settled in a timely fashion, thus enabling the meeting to continue and be productive.

10. *Preservation of "organizational memory,"* so that those who do not attend the meeting can also work on the project. Often a project will include teams at different locations who will need to understand the content of a meeting at only one of the affected sites.

One response to the problems of group decision making has been the adoption of new methods of organizing and running meetings. Techniques such as facilitated meetings, brainstorming, and criticism-free idea generation have become popular and are now accepted as standard. Another response has been the application of technology to the problems resulting in the emergence of group decision-support systems.

THE HOHENHEIM CATEAM ROOM

How does the physical environment of a group decision-support system meeting room affect the work of a GDSS-supported group? How do ergonomics affect the decision-making process? These are some of the questions that were explored by information systems researchers at the University of Hohenheim, in Stuttgart, Germany. Their methodology? Do the research and design their own GDSS room—the Computer Aided Team Room, known as the CATeam Room.

The information systems specialists worked with interior and furniture design architects from the State Academy of the Arts in Stuttgart. Realizing that people's sense of privacy and their social interactions can be affected by their level of physical comfort and the design of their meeting environment, the team looked into alternative designs for meeting rooms. In their quest for a meeting room design that would enhance group work, the team

consulted specialists in psychology and ergonomics and visited GDSS research laboratories in the United States.

One of the principal questions addressed by the project was the relationship of seating arrangements in the GDSS meeting room to meeting interactions. The team started with a set of basic rules that demanded a maximum of 12 participants in a meeting (a limitation set because of the small size of the room they had available). The table they endorsed at the end included built-in computer equipment that could automatically be stored inside the table at the push of a button so that the room could be used for traditional non-GDSS meetings. The table also is modular, allowing flexibility. For example, the room could be rearranged into a U-shape for a teaching situation. The team also wanted seating arrangements that would create a friendly teamwork atmosphere. While their principles did not include a specification for participant equality, that proved, in the end, to be the deciding factor for the table setup. This issue

is particularly important because meeting attendees often come from a range of different organizational levels, creating an initial atmosphere of inequality.

To Think About: 1. *This chapter listed ten specific meeting elements that need to be addressed to improve decision-making meetings. Which of these elements are addressed by the CATeam ergonomic design, and in what ways might the design improve meetings?*
2. *Do you believe that the physical placement of the computer is adequate for guaranteeing the privacy of an attendee's work? Can you think of ways that privacy could be further protected?*

The final decision for table shape called for a round table called a Roundabout (see Figure 16.4). With a round table, everyone is equal, and the arrangement is democratic. Face-to-face contact is equally possible with anyone at the table. A GDSS requires a

FIGURE 16.4
The Roundabout Table Model. The system that the CATeam researchers at the University of Hohenheim settled upon as the final design for a GDSS room table was the Roundabout table. With this design, everybody is equal, and face-to-face contact is equally possible with all participants at the table.

computer projection screen so that all can view the common screens together (as well as independently on their own PCs). To support the Roundabout solution, the CATeam project decided to use two common screens opposite each other. That way everyone would be able to view a screen easily and comfortably without attendees having to turn around or otherwise disturb the symmetry of the arrangement.

The placement of the computer equipment within the table also con-tributed to an environment of equality. When in use, the computer screen is placed slightly below table level. The team saw two advantages to this arrangement. First, no computer equipment would interfere with the attendees' eye-to-eye contact with other attendees. Second, an attendee's monitor can only be viewed by the closest neighbor, if at all. They believe that privacy, and therefore anonymity, are protected.

The Roundabout design was selected for display by the jury of the 1989 "Anno 2000 Office Design Competition" in Milan.

Source: Henrik Lewe and Helmut Krcmar, "The Design Process for a Computer-Supported Cooperative Work Research Laboratory: The Hohenheim CATeam Room," *Journal of Management Information Systems*, Winter 1991–1992. Helmut Krcmar, Henrik Lewe, and Gerhard Schwabe: *Empirical CATeam Research of Meetings*. Working Paper no. 38 of the Information Systems Department, University of Hohenheim, Germany, 1993.

CHARACTERISTICS OF GDSS

How can information technology help groups to arrive at decisions? Scholars have identified at least three basic elements of GDSS: hardware, software, and people. *Hardware* refers first to the conference facility itself, including the room, the tables, and the chairs. Such a facility must be physically laid out in a manner that supports group collaboration. It must also include some electronic hardware, such as electronic display boards, as well as audiovisual and computer equipment. The Window on Organizations examines one important aspect to the physical setup—the ergonomics of the meeting room design.

A wide range of *software tools,* including tools for organizing ideas, gathering information, ranking and setting priorities, and other aspects of collaborative work are now being used to support decision-making meetings. We describe these tools below. *People* refers not only to the participants but also to a trained facilitator and often to a staff that supports the hardware and software. Together these elements have led to the creation of a range of different kinds of GDSS, from simple electronic boardrooms to elaborate collaboration laboratories. In a collaboration laboratory, individuals work on their own desktop microcomputers. Their input is integrated on a file server and is viewable on a common screen at the front of the room; in most systems the integrated input is also viewable on the individual participant's screen. See Figure 16.5 for an illustration of an actual GDSS collaborative meeting room.

One can appreciate the potential value of GDSS by examining their software tools. We describe the functions of several types of tools central to a full-blown collaboration laboratory. We then give an overview of a GDSS meeting so that you can understand its potential to support collaborative meetings. Finally, we examine how GDSS affect the problems we have described, and their power to enhance group decision making.

GDSS SOFTWARE TOOLS

Some of the features of the groupware tools for collaborative work described in Chapter 15 can be used to support group decision making. But GDSS are considered more explicitly decision-oriented and task-oriented than groupware, as they focus on helping a group solve a problem or reach a decision (Dennis et al., 1988). Groupware is considered more communication-oriented. Specific GDSS software tools include the following:

- *Electronic questionnaires* aid the organizers in pre-meeting planning by identifying issues of concern and by helping to insure that key planning information is not overlooked.

- *Electronic brainstorming tools* allow individuals simultaneously and anonymously to contribute ideas on the topics of the meeting.

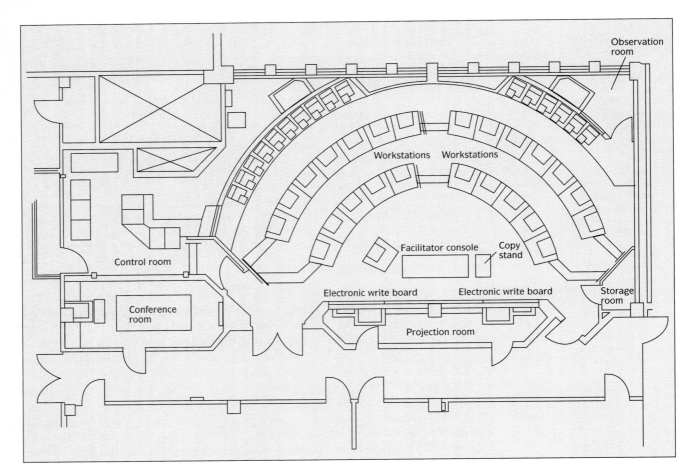

FIGURE 16.5
Illustration of PLEXSYS decision room. The large group room was opened in 1987, with 24 IBM PS/2 workstations. A gallery holds 18 observers. The room has 38 audio pick-up microphones and 6 video cameras with stereo audio. Two large-screen electronic displays and projectors permit playing of videotapes, discs, 35 mm slides, and computer graphics presentations. *Source: Figure 2b. Decision Room for Larger Groups (Dennis, George, Jessup, Nunamaker, and Vogel. Reprinted with permission from the MIS Quarterly, Volume 12, Number 4, December 1988).*

- *Idea organizers* facilitate the organized integration and synthesis of ideas generated during brainstorming.
- *Questionnaire tools* support the facilitators and group leaders as they gather information before and during the process of setting priorities.
- *Tools for voting or setting priorities* make available a range of methods from simple voting, to ranking in order, to a range of weighted techniques for setting priorities or voting.
- *Stakeholder identification and analysis tools* use structured approaches to evaluate the impact of an emerging proposal upon the organization, and to identify stakeholders and evaluate the potential impact of those stakeholders upon the proposed project.
- *Policy formation tools* provide structured support for developing agreement on the wording of policy statements.
- *Group dictionaries* document group agreement on definitions of words and terms central to the project.

Additional tools are available, such as group outlining and writing tools, software that stores and reads project files, and software that allows the attendees to view internal operational data stored by the organization's production computer systems.

The Ventana Corporation demonstrates the features of its GroupSystems for Windows electronic meeting software, which helps people create, share, record, organize, and evaluate ideas in meetings, between offices, or around the world.

Overview of a GDSS Meeting

electronic meeting system (EMS)
Collaborative GDSS that uses information technology to make group meetings more productive by facilitating communication as well as decision making. Supports meetings at the same place and time or in different places and times.

An **electronic meeting system (EMS)** is a type of collaborative GDSS that uses information technology to make group meetings more productive by facilitating communication as well as decision making. It supports any activity where people come together, whether at the same place at the same time or in different places at different times (Dennis et al., 1988; Nunamaker et al., 1991). IBM has a number of EMS installed at various sites. Each attendee has a workstation. The workstations are networked and are connected to the facilitator's console that serves as both the facilitator's workstation and control panel and the meeting's file server. All data that the attendees forward from their workstations to the group are collected and saved on the file server. The facilitator is able to project computer images onto the projection screen at the front center of the room. The facilitator also has an overhead projector available. Whiteboards are visible on either side of the projection screen. Many electronic meeting rooms are arranged in a semicircle and are tiered in legislative style to accommodate a larger number of attendees.

The facilitator controls the use of tools during the meeting, often selecting from a large tool box that is part of the organization's GDSS. Tool selection is part of the pre-meeting planning process. Which tools are selected depends upon the subject matter, the goals of the meeting, and the facilitation methodology the facilitator will use.

Each attendee has full control over his or her own microcomputer. An attendee is able to view the agenda (and other planning documents), look at the integrated screen (or screens as the session moves on), use ordinary desktop microcomputer tools (such as a word processor or a spreadsheet), tap into production data that have been made available, or work on the screen associated with the current meeting step and tool (such as a brainstorming screen). However, no one can view anyone else's screens so that an individual's work is confidential until he or she releases it to the file server for integration with the work of others. All input to the file server is anonymous—at each step everyone's input to the file server (brainstorming ideas, idea evaluation and criticism, comments, voting, etc.) can be seen by all attendees on the integrated screens, but no information is available to identify the source of specific inputs. Attendees enter their data simultaneously

FIGURE 16.6
Group system tools. The sequence of activities and collaborative support tools used in an electronic meeting system (EMS) facilitates communication among attendees and generates a full record of the meeting. *Adapted from "Electronic Meeting Systems to Support Group Work," by Nunamaker, Dennis, Valacich, Vogel, and George, printed in* Communications of the ACM, *July 1991.*

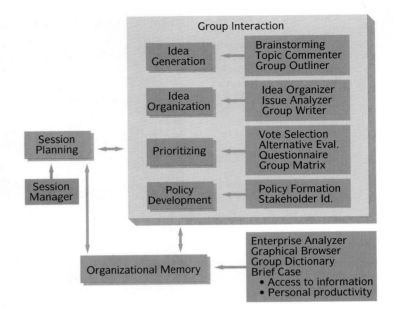

rather than in round-robin fashion as is done in meetings that have little or no electronic systems support.

Figure 16.6 shows the sequence of activities at a typical EMS meeting. For each activity it also indicates the type of tools used and the output of those tools. During the meeting all input to the integrated screens is saved on the file server. As a result, when the meeting is completed, a full record of the meeting (both raw material and resultant output) is available to the attendees and can be made available to anyone else with a need for access.

HOW GDSS CAN ENHANCE GROUP DECISION MAKING

GDSS are still relatively new, so firm conclusions are not yet possible. Nonetheless, scholars and business specialists have studied these systems, and the systems are now being used more widely, so that we are able at least to understand their potential benefits and even evaluate some of the tools. We look again at how GDSS affect the ten group meeting issues raised earlier.

1. *Improved pre-planning.* Electronic questionnaires, supplemented by word processors, outlining software, and other desktop PC software, can structure planning, thereby improving it. The availability of the planning information at the actual meeting also can serve to enhance the quality of the meeting. Experts seem to feel that these tools add significance and emphasis to meeting pre-planning.

2. *Increased participation.* Studies show that in traditional decision making meetings without GDSS support the optimal meeting size is three to five attendees. Beyond that size, the meeting process begins to break down. Using GDSS software, studies show the meeting size can increase while productivity also increases. One reason for this is that attendees contribute simultaneously rather than one at a time, and can thus make more efficient use of the meeting time. Free riding is apparently decreased too, perhaps because the one or two individuals who are not working will stand out when everyone else in the room is busy at workstations. Interviews of GDSS meeting attendees indicate that the quality of participation is higher than in traditional meetings.

3. *Open, collaborative meeting atmosphere.* GDSS contribute to a more collaborative atmosphere in several ways. First, anonymity of input is essentially guaranteed. An individual need not be afraid of being judged by his or her boss for con-

tributing a possibly offbeat idea. Anonymity also reduces or eliminates the deadening effect that often occurs when high-status individuals contribute. Even the numbing pressures of social cues are reduced or eliminated.

4. *Criticism-free idea generation.* Anonymity ensures that attendees can contribute without fear of personally being criticized or of having their ideas rejected because of the identity of the contributor. Several studies show that interactive GDSS meetings generate more ideas and more satisfaction with those ideas than verbally interactive meetings (Nunamaker et al., 1991). GDSS can help reduce unproductive interpersonal conflict (Miranda and Bostrum, 1993–1994).

5. *Evaluation objectivity.* Anonymity prevents criticism of the source of the ideas, thus supporting an atmosphere in which attendees focus on evaluating the ideas themselves. The same anonymity allows participants to detach themselves from their own ideas and so are able to view them from a critical perspective. Evidence suggests that evaluation in an anonymous atmosphere increases the free flow of critical feedback and even stimulates the generation of new ideas during the evaluation process.

6. *Idea organization and evaluation.* GDSS software tools used for this purpose are structured and are based on methodology. They usually allow individuals each to organize and then submit their results to the group (still anonymously). The group then iteratively modifies and develops the organized ideas until a document is completed. Attendees have generally viewed this approach as productive.

7. *Setting priorities and making decisions.* Anonymity helps lower-level participants have their positions taken into consideration along with the higher-level attendees.

8. *Documentation of meetings.* Evidence at IBM indicates that post-meeting use of the data is crucial. Attendees use the data to continue their dialogues after the meetings, to discuss the ideas with those who did not attend, and even to make presentations (Grobowski et al., 1990). Some tools even enable the user to zoom in to more detail on specific information.

9. *Access to external information.* Often a great deal of meeting time is devoted to factual disagreements. More experience with GDSS will indicate whether or not GDSS technology reduces this problem.

10. *Preservation of "organizational memory."* Specific tools have been developed to facilitate access to the data generated during a GDSS meeting, allowing nonattendees to locate needed information after the meeting. The documentation of a meeting by one group at one site has also successfully been used as input to another meeting on the same project at another site.

Experience to date suggests that GDSS meetings can be more productive, make more efficient use of time, and produce the desired results in fewer meetings. One problem with understanding the value of GDSS is their complexity. A GDSS can be configured in an almost infinite variety of ways. In addition, the effectiveness of the tools will partially depend upon the effectiveness of the facilitator, the quality of the planning, the cooperation of the attendees, and the appropriateness of tools for different types of meetings. These systems are also rather expensive, so that much of the usage to date has been by corporations holding meetings at university GDSS research facilities. Because of their high price, GDSS integration into daily corporate life must await further evidence of their effectiveness.

Researchers have noted that the design of an electronic meeting system is only one of a number of contingencies that affect the outcome of group meetings. Other factors, including the nature of the group, the task, the cultural setting, and the context also affect the process of group meetings and meeting outcomes (Dennis et al., 1988; Nunamaker et al., 1991; Watson, Ho and Raman, 1994). Figure 16.7 graphically illustrates these relationships.

FIGURE 16.7
The research model for electronic meetings. For effective group meetings, include the nature of the group, the task to be accomplished, and the context of the meeting in the design of the EMS. *Source: Figure 3. A Research Model (Dennis, George, Jessup, Nunamaker, and Vogel. Reprinted with permission from the MIS Quarterly, Volume 12, Number 4, December 1988.)*

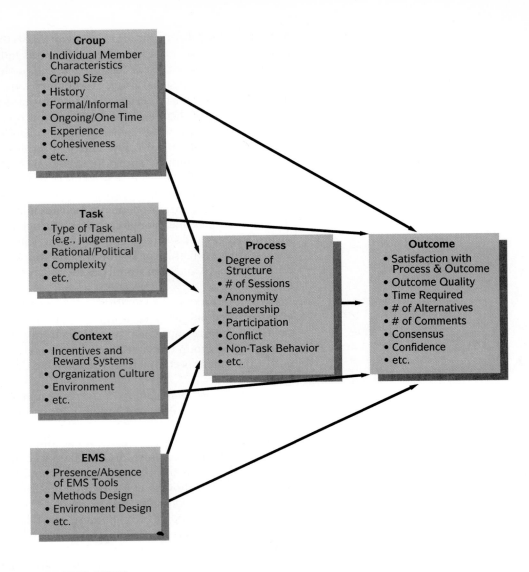

16.3 EXECUTIVE SUPPORT SYSTEMS (ESS)

executive support system (ESS) Information system at the strategic level of an organization designed to address unstructured decision making through advanced graphics and communications.

We have described how DSS and GDSS help managers make unstructured and semi-structured decisions. **Executive support systems (ESS)** also help managers with unstructured problems, focusing on the information needs of senior management. Combining data from both internal and external sources, ESS create a generalized computing and communications environment that can be focused and applied to a changing array of problems. ESS help senior executives monitor organizational performance, track activities of competitors, spot problems, identify opportunities, and forecast trends.

THE ROLE OF ESS IN THE ORGANIZATION

briefing books On-line data in the form of fixed-format reports for executives; part of early ESS.

drill down The ability to move from summary data down to lower and lower levels of detail.

Prior to ESS, it was common for executives to receive numerous fixed-format reports, often hundreds of pages every month (or even every week). The first systems developed specifically for executives in the early 1980s were mainframe systems designed to replace that paper, delivering the same data to the executive in days rather than in weeks. Executives had access to the same data, only it was on-line in the form of reports. Such systems were known as senior management **briefing books**. Using a briefing book, executives usually could **drill down** (move from a piece of summary data down to lower and lower levels of detail). Briefing books did not spread widely through the executive suites. The data that could be provided by briefing books were limited and the briefing books were too inflexible.

By the late 1980s, ways were found to bring together data from throughout the organization and allow the manager to select, access, and tailor them easily as needed. Today, an ESS is apt to include a range of easy-to-use desktop analytical tools. Use of the systems has migrated down several organizational levels so that the executive and his or her subordinates are able to look at the same data in the same way.

Today's systems try to avoid the problem of data overload so common in paper reports because the data can be filtered or viewed in graphic format (if the user so chooses). Systems have maintained the ability to drill down (even starting from a graph). However, with access to so much critical data, designers must be certain that any ESS protects against altered data finding their way back to the originating system.

One limitation in ESS is that they use data from systems designed for very different purposes. Often data that are critical to the senior executive are simply not there. For example, sales data coming from an order entry transaction processing system are not linked to marketing information, a linkage the executive would find useful. External data are now much more available in many ESS systems. Executives need a wide range of external data, from current stock market news to competitor information, industry trends, and even projected legislative action. Through their ESS, many managers have access to news services, financial market databases, economic information, and whatever other public data they may require.

ESS today include tools for modeling and analysis. For example, many ESS use Lotus 1-2-3, Excel, or other spreadsheets as the heart of their analytical tool base. With only a minimum of experience, most managers find they can use these common software packages to create graphic comparisons of data by time, region, product, price range, and so on. Costlier systems include more sophisticated specialty analytical software. (While DSS use such tools primarily for modeling and analysis in a fairly narrow range of decision situations, ESS use them primarily to provide status information about organizational performance.)

ESS are increasingly being used by employees several levels below the senior executives. This has solved the problem of members of executives' staffs working from different data than the executive, and this is one of the reasons use of these systems is spreading. Middle management will use the same data in a somewhat different manner, focusing on their own area of responsibility and emphasizing plan-versus-actual analysis (variances between forecasts and actual results).

DEVELOPING ESS

ESS are executive systems, and executives create special development problems (we introduced this topic in Section 16.1). Because executives' needs change so rapidly, most executive support systems are developed through prototyping. A major difficulty for developers is that high-level executives expect success the first time. Developers must be certain that the system will work before they demonstrate it to the user. In addition, the initial system prototype must be one that the executive can learn very rapidly. Finally, if the executive finds that the ESS offers no added value, he or she will reject it.

One area that merits special attention is the determination of executive information requirements. ESS need to have some facility for environmental scanning. A key information requirement of managers at the strategic level is the capability to detect signals of problems in the organizational environment that indicate strategic threats and opportunities (Walls et al., 1992). The ESS needs to be designed so that both external and internal sources of information can be used for environmental scanning purposes. The Critical Success Factor methodology for determining information requirements (see Chapter 11) is recommended for this purpose. Table 16.3 suggests steps for eliciting such requirements.

Table 16.3 **Steps for Determining ESS Requirements**

1. Identify a set of issue-generating critical events.

2. Elicit from the executive his assessment of the impact of the critical events on his goals and derive a set of critical issues.

3. Elicit from the executive three to five indicators which can be used to track each critical issue.

4. Elicit from the executive a list of potential information sources for the indicators.

5. Elicit from the executive exception heuristics for each indicator.

Reprinted by permission of Joseph G. Walls, George R. Widmeyer, and Omar A. El Sawy, "Building an Information System Design Theory for Vigilant EIS," *Information Systems Research*: Vol. 3, No. 1 (March 1992), p. 56, The Institute of Management Sciences.

Another area of concern is providing the data required by ESS from many areas of the organization without disrupting important operational systems. The Window on Technology explores this issue.

Because ESS could potentially give top executives the capability of examining other managers' work without their knowledge, there may be some resistance to ESS at lower levels of the organization. Implementation of ESS should be carefully managed to neutralize such opposition (see Chapter 14).

Cost justification presents a different type of problem with ESS. Since much of an executive's work is unstructured, how does one quantify benefits for a system that primarily supports such unstructured work? An ESS is often justified in advance by the intuitive feeling that it will pay for itself (Watson et al., 1991). If ESS benefits can ever be quantified, it is only after the system is operational.

BENEFITS OF ESS

How do executive support systems benefit managers? As we stated earlier, it is difficult at best to cost-justify an executive support system. Nonetheless, interest in these systems is growing, so it is essential to examine some of the potential benefits scholars have identified.

Commander EIS provides executives with easy-to-use graphics, communications, and financial analysis tools for scanning the external environment and for analyzing the performance of their firm.

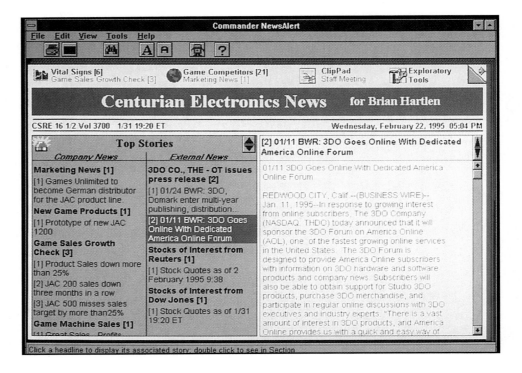

Much of the value of ESS is found in their flexibility. These systems put data and tools in the hands of executives without addressing specific problems or imposing solutions. Executives are free to shape the problems as they need, using the system as an extension of their own thinking processes. These are not decision-making systems; they are tools to aid executives in making decisions.

The most visible benefit of ESS is their ability to analyze, compare, and highlight trends. The easy use of graphics allows the user to look at more data in less time with greater clarity and insight than paper-based systems can provide. In the past, executives obtained the same information by taking up days and weeks of their staffs' valuable time. By using ESS, those staffs and the executives themselves are freed up for the more creative analysis and decision making in their jobs. ESS capabilities for drilling down and highlighting trends may also enhance the quality of such analysis and decision making (Leidner and Elam, 1993–1994).

Executives are using ESS to monitor performance more successfully in their own areas of responsibility. Some are also using these systems to monitor key performance indicators. The timeliness and availability of the data result in needed actions being identified and taken earlier. Problems can be handled before they become too damaging; opportunities can also be identified earlier as well.

ESS can and do change the workings of organizations. Immediate access to so much data allows executives to better monitor activities of lower units reporting to them. That very monitoring ability often allows decision making to be decentralized and to take place at lower operating levels. Executives are often willing to push decision making further down into the organization as long as they can be assured that all is going well. ESS can enable them to get that assurance. A well-designed ESS could dramatically improve management performance and increase upper management's span of control.

We will close our examination of ESS by looking at actual examples of ESS in use.

EXAMPLES OF ESS

To illustrate the various ways in which ESS can enhance management decision making, we now describe three executive support systems, one for private industry and two for the public sector. These systems were developed for very different reasons and serve their organizations in different ways.

Pratt & Whitney

Pratt & Whitney is a multibillion-dollar corporation located in East Hartford, Connecticut, whose Commercial Engine Business (CEB) produces jet engines. The firm's executives view customer service and product performance as the heart of their business and therefore the heart of their strategic plan to expand their market share. Walt Dempsey, a member of the company's business management and planning department, launched a study to assess the information needs that would support their strategic plan. The study led to the purchase of Commander EIS, a leading ESS package from Comshare. Commander EIS features colorful presentations and a pictorial menu that can be learned intuitively, with variances and exceptions highlighted in color. Users can access data with a touch screen, a mouse, or a keyboard and they can zoom in for deeper levels of detail either by navigating on their own or by following predefined paths.

Implementation began with a prototype built for the president of CEB, Selwyn Berson. Commander EIS allows Berson to track key quality and reliability measures for each jet engine model by customer. The data are shown from existing production systems and provide information on reliability, spare engine and parts availability, and deliveries. Using this system, CEB is able to answer customers' questions regarding repair status and can project how long repairs will take. Berson and others are able to drill down to determine reasons for repairs on specific engines. They also are capable of drilling down to specific data on service to an individual customer. Thus, CEB executives are able to determine where quality improvements need to be

WAREHOUSING DATA

Why are many companies embracing data warehousing? A *data warehouse* is a collection of current and historical operational data stored for use in executive support systems (ESS) and decision support systems (DSS). The data are usually extracted from a number of sources, and collected, integrated, and then stored and managed in a relational database (RDBMS) for quick and easy access without affecting the data of the underlying transaction processing systems. The data in the warehouse might be updated daily, weekly, biweekly or monthly, depending upon the type of data and the needs of the data users.

Data warehouses have become popular for many reasons. The most fundamental reason is the growing demand that executives and management have rapid, easy access to operational data for purposes of planning and decision making. The downsizing movement and the accompanying trend toward flatter organizations have distributed decision making, making it even more urgent that a broad range of data be made more widely available.

A second major reason relates to the historical form and location of data. Over the years application systems have appeared on a wide range of disparate computers within a single company—on mainframes, minicomputers, network servers, desktop micros, workstations, and even laptops. They have been stored in flat files, hierarchical databases, and relational databases. Individuals who are not information systems professionals yet needed access to such scattered data found it impossible to gather them together. Traditionally, executives or managers who wanted access to such data would request a special program or report from the IS department, work that normally required weeks to complete. Yet when managers are operating within today's business pressure cooker, they need that information to-

day, not next week or the week after. By next week, business conditions and even the problems will often have changed and the data requested last week will no longer be relevant. The old ways then available of getting data to decision makers could no longer be tolerated—new ways had to be found.

In making such data available to management, the IS department had several major problems. First, it had to find ways to do so without slowing down or interfering with operational systems and without corrupting operational data. The solution was to give the decision makers access to copies of the data rather than the original, live data themselves. In this way it would establish data-platform independence—gathering the data from all sources, mainframes to laptops, sales to production, into a single database or set of databases. Second, the IS staff realized they had to satisfy many different application data needs. Whereas the order processing department needed the data in a specific, set format, for example, the sales staff needed it in different formats, the marketing department needed to massage the data in a range of ways, the corporate management team needed to combine some of the sales data with external economic data today and with manufacturing data tomorrow. The solution was data-application independence, giving the ESS and DSS systems of these managers access to copies of the data they needed in an independent data warehouse. None could touch production data directly, and none could change the data in the data warehouse, but each could access it for use in his or her own way. Users from various business functions could then also be presented with a single, consistent interface.

Other factors have contributed to the move to data warehousing as well. Client/server systems and graphical user interfaces have both contributed to making it easier to give users access to the data they need. While companies traditionally built separate applications

for each ESS or DSS need, most find it cheaper and easier to bring the data together and then build a single, generic application that allows all the decision

> *To Think About:*   *From management, organization, and technology standpoints, what are the advantages of the data warehouse approach to making data available for ESS and DSS? What are the disadvantages of using such software? What management, organization, and technology issues need to be addressed when contructing a data warehouse?*

makers and planners to meet most of their data retrieval and analysis needs. The trend to downsizing has been helped because these data warehouse systems have made it easier for companies to replace people with technology. A company can have fewer layers of people, but those people will have better access to data. Finally, these systems have become very fast, with companies using RDBMS for easy data access while data warehousing systems have turned to parallel processing to obtain great speed.

The National Association of Securities Dealers Inc. (NASD) moved to data warehousing because they had 3000 employees working on PCs, Macintoshes, and UNIX workstations. This Washington, DC, organization owns and operates the NASDAQ stock exchange and monitors the performance of security dealers. They began looking for ways to collect and present data in a uniform manner in 1990, and ultimately purchased and installed Commander from Comshare Inc. of Ann Arbor, Michigan. The original system was developed to serve the president and 14 others of the company's top management, but what assistant manager of management support Sam Ireland found at first was that few of them were willing to use it. He undertook a major campaign to sell them on the system, and after a year, they were relying on it for daily performance analysis. As the word spread, others wanted access to the system, and by the end of 1994 about 200 in middle and senior management were using it.

Because the retail grocery business generates massive amounts of data, data access can be slow, causing H. E. Butt Grocery Co., a grocery store chain in San Antonio, Texas, to look for a faster way to access its data. Eventually the company turned to data warehouse software. It looked for a system that could handle very complex queries, and ultimately selected Warehouse VPT from Red Brick Systems of Los Gatos, California, because of its high query response speeds. It achieves these speeds for several reasons: It uses parallel processing where needed, and it uses an algorithm to evaluate each query to determine the fastest way to execute the query (optimization). In addition it uses many indexes, a major help when databases top 10 gigabytes.

Reno Air, an airline headquartered in Reno, Nevada, faced a data problem because it was too small to operate its own reservation system and so outsourced it to EDS Corporation. EDS ran it on an IBM 3090 and supplied Reno with weekly and monthly printed reports on the airline's routes, traffic, and revenue. This information was simply too old—managers had to find a more timely way to access the data. In 1994 they purchased Express/EIS from Information Resources Inc. of

Waltham, Massachusetts, because they believed it was capable of handling massive amounts of data. EDS now extracts and downloads data daily into Reno Air's Oracle relational database, which users access via Express/EIS.

HCIA Inc., a $40 million health-care information company in Baltimore, Maryland, also faced a data bottleneck. Their product is data—they sell clinical data to health-care providers, insurers, financial institutions, and drug companies. In 1991 all of their data was stored on 30,000 magnetic tapes processed through a large mainframe computer. When a customer requested information, the response could take HCIA days to weeks, an unacceptable response time in the 1990s. The company decided to install a distributed client/server system running Informix OnLine RDBMS as a data warehouse. The result was a 90 percent faster response time in answering customer queries.

Lawn mower and snow blower giant Toro Co. of Minneapolis, Minnesota, decided it was having trouble tracking its $750 million in annual sales. "Managers were working with a series of printouts generated at different periods," claims Randy Jones, the corporate controller. At first they tried to build a traditional one-size-fits-all information retrieval application but discovered that it would be very expensive and complex. Instead they turned to the data warehouse concept and also purchased Commander to run in

client/server-mode over a local area network. Now, according to Jones, the 77,000 monthly sales records are constantly accessed and analyzed, while the company has cut 20 percent off of its billing cycle. Jones claims that "The CEO, president and chief financial officer use the system all day long."

Of course, problems do exist with the data warehouse approach. For example, systems can take a long time and a great deal of effort to develop because the data can be so widely scattered. Many companies even have a lot of their important data stored on isolated desktop computers that are not integrated into the corporate IS department. Another problem is that some companies do not want to take on a new way to access their data because they do not want to acquire, learn, and maintain yet another user interface. Instead they want to give their employees access to their data through software they already know and are using, such as through Microsoft's Excel spreadsheet. Nonetheless, data warehousing has become an important method of speeding data to managers and decision makers.

Sources: Katherine Bull, "The Ideal File Cabinet," *InformationWeek*, January 16, 1995; and Paul Korzeniowski, "Are You Tired of Drilling for Data?" and "Wanted: Built-In Data Analysis," *InformationWeek*, September 19, 1994.

made in terms of both customer service and engine quality. CEB's ESS is helping them to meet their strategic plan objectives. The system was originally used by about 25 senior executives, although Pratt & Whitney expects the number of users to grow to over 200 ("The New Role," January 1992).

The United States General Services Administration

The General Services Administration (GSA) manages the vast real estate holdings of the United States government. In a period of tight federal budget restraints and as part of Vice President Gore's "reinventing government" initiatives, the organization needed to find ways to optimize the use of the government's multibillion-dollar inventory of 16,000 properties worldwide. Yet GSA managers facing this challenge had no system that would support them by making easily available to them the 4 gigabytes of data stored in their computers. The data were available only in old-fashioned printed reports and through slow, expensive custom programming. Analysis of the data was nearly impossible. GSA's response was GAMIS (Glenn Asset Management Information System), an executive support system based primarily on Lotus Notes that literally puts the needed data and analysis at the finger tips of the GSA's nontechnical managers.

The main purpose of the system was to give management quick and easy views of the organization's assets. Managers now can easily use ad hoc queries and perform "what-if" analysis, receiving the results on screen, in graphics format when desired. After indicating a specific office building, for example, the user will be offered 13 choices of data on that building, such as who occupies it, its financials, information on the congressional district it is in (if it is in the United States), and even a scanned photograph of the building. The data can be accessed via geographic information system (GIS) software from MapInfo Corp. (see Chapter 7). Through this software interface, the user begins with a national map and drills down into regional and city maps that show detail on location and type of property. Another click of the mouse and the user will pull up all the data on that piece of property. Users can limit the data at the outset, specifying, for example, that they want to look only at Justice Department properties with more than 50,000 square feet of floor space. All of the data are available to about 100 GSA employees in Washington, while about 50 employees in each of the ten regions have access to all of the data for their own region. Washington employees also have available a database of commercial properties with rental space available.

With GAMIS, nontechnical managers can access and analyze gigabytes of information that were formerly available only via printouts and custom programming. The system has received high marks from many officials, including John Glenn, Democratic Senator from Ohio and long a vocal critic of the GSA's antiquated computer system. When Glenn first saw the system demonstrated, he was reported to have been so impressed that the GSA named the system after him. Observers have also praised the system because it was built from off-the-shelf software, making it quick and inexpensive to develop, providing high returns with minimum investments (Anthes, 1994).

New York State Office of General Services

The New York State Office of General Services (OGS) is responsible for servicing other state agencies throughout New York. Its services include (but are not limited to) design and construction, maintenance of state buildings, food and laundry services to both correctional facilities and health-related institutions, statewide vehicle management, and centralized printing. With this diversity of services, an annual budget well over $500 million, and more than 4000 employees, executive oversight was a nightmare. Until 1986, OGS automatically received annual budget increases in line with inflation rates. Budget deficits were made up through supplemental allocations by the legislature. OGS felt no pressures to improve efficiency or stay within its budget. That changed in 1986 when a new administrative head of the agency was appointed. He decided that the organization had to operate in a more efficient, effective, and responsive manner. He also wanted to avoid year-end deficits. These objectives required better management at the top.

The first module of a new OGS ESS was implemented in 1988. The system allows the executives to monitor status by program, comparing budget to actual expenditures and showing estimated expenditures through the remainder of the fiscal year. Management can drill down to see specific details in any category. The system contains only raw data, allowing the users great flexibility in aggregating and analyzing it to meet their needs. For example, users are able to view a single expense category by month across organizations, or view several months of expenses for a given unit. Because the raw data are there, the executives can drill down to the source. The system includes exception reporting so that budget problems are highlighted and detected early. Executives are also using the system to compare budgetary control by units to spot personnel performance problems.

Since the system was developed for a government agency, the cost was of more than normal concern—the system had to be built inexpensively. The system uses ordinary microcomputers networked with the agency's mainframe and off-the-shelf, standard, inexpensive software tools. The total cost was less than $100,000. The system is menu-driven and very easy to use. New users are trained through a 30-minute demonstration, and experience has shown that this is all that they need. No user manual is available.

One interesting byproduct of the system has been the need to develop productivity measures. Future development will focus on the area of performance analysis, attempting to answer such questions as how many people are required to work in specific units. The ESS called for OGS to measure something that it had never measured before. The work of developing these measures should in itself contribute to the drive for more efficiency (Mohan et al., 1990). This ESS is helping the Office of General Services enhance management control.

Management Challenges

1. Building information systems that can actually fulfill executive information requirements. Even with the use of Critical Success Factors and other information requirements determination methods, it may still be difficult to establish information requirements for ESS and DSS serving senior management. Chapter 4 has already described why certain aspects of senior management decision making cannot be supported by information systems because the decisions are too unstructured and fluid. Even if a problem can be addressed by an information system, senior management may not understand its true information needs. For instance, senior managers may not agree on the firm's critical success factors, or the critical success factors

they describe may be inappropriate or outdated if the firm is confronting a crisis requiring a major strategic change.

2. Integrating DSS and ESS with existing systems in the business. Even if system builders know the information requirements for DSS or ESS and use data warehousing tools, it may be extremely difficult to fulfill them using data from the firm's existing information systems. Various MIS or TPS may define important pieces of data, such as the time period covered by fiscal year, in different ways. It may not be possible to reconcile data from incompatible internal systems for analysis by managers. A significant amount of organizational change may be required before the firm can build and install effective DSS and ESS.

Summary

1. Define a decision-support system (DSS) and a group decision-support system (GDSS). A decision-support system (DSS) is an interactive system under user control that combines data, sophisticated analytical models, and user-friendly software into a single powerful system that can support semistructured or unstructured decision making. A group decision-support system (GDSS) is an interactive computer-based system to facilitate the solution of unstructured problems by a set of decision makers working together as a group rather than individually.

2. Describe the components of decision-support systems and group decision-support systems. The components of a DSS are the DSS database, the model base, and the DSS software system. The DSS database is a collection of current or historical data from a number of applications or groups that can be used for analysis. The model base is a collection of mathematical and analytical models that are used for analyzing the data in the database. The DSS software system allows users to interact with the DSS database and model base directly.

Group decision-support systems (GDSS) have hardware, software, and people components. Hardware components consist of the conference room facilities, including seating arrangements and computer and other electronic hardware. Software components in-

clude tools for organizing ideas, gathering information, ranking and setting priorities, and documenting meeting sessions. People components include participants, a trained facilitator, and staff to support the hardware and software.

3. Explain how decision-support systems and group decision-support systems can enhance decision making. Both DSS and GDSS support steps in the process of arriving at decisions. DSS provide results of model-based analysis that help managers design and evaluate alternatives and monitor the progress of the solution that was adopted. GDSS help decision makers meeting together to arrive at a decision more efficiently and are especially useful for increasing the productivity of meetings larger than four or five people. However, the effectiveness of GDSS is contingent upon the nature of the group, the task, and the context of the meeting.

4. Describe the capabilities of executive support systems (ESS). Executive support systems (ESS) help managers with unstructured problems that occur at the strategic level of management. ESS provide data from both internal and external sources and provide a generalized computing and communications environment that can be focused and applied to a changing array of problems. ESS help senior executives spot problems, identify opportunities, and forecast trends. They can filter out extraneous details for high-level overviews, or they can drill down to provide senior managers with detailed transaction data if required.

5. **Describe the benefits of executive support systems.** ESS help senior managers analyze, compare, and high-light trends so that they more easily may monitor organizational performance or identify strategic problems and opportunities. ESS may increase the span of control of senior management and allow decision making to be decentralized and to take place at lower operating levels.

Key Terms

Decision-support system (DSS)	**Control aids**	**DSS software system**	**Executive support system (ESS)**
Representations	**DSS database**	**Group decision-support system (GDSS)**	**Briefing books**
Operations	**Model base**	**Electronic meeting system (EMS)**	**Drill down**
Memory aids	**Model**		
	Sensitivity analysis		

Review Questions

1. What is a decision-support system (DSS)? How does it differ from a management information system (MIS)?
2. What are the four capabilities of a DSS?
3. How can DSS support unstructured or semistructured decision making?
4. What are the three basic components of a DSS? Briefly describe each.
5. In what ways is building decision-support systems different from building traditional MIS systems?
6. What is a group decision-support system (GDSS)? How does it differ from a DSS?
7. What are the three underlying problems in group decision making that have led to the development of GDSS?

8. Describe the three elements of a GDSS.
9. Name five GDSS software tools.
10. What is an electronic meeting system (EMS)?
11. For each of the three underlying problems in group decision making referred to in question 7, describe one or two ways GDSS can contribute to a solution.
12. Define and describe the capabilites of an executive support system.
13. Define *briefing books*. Explain why they were not adequate to support executive decision making.
14. In what ways is building executive support systems different from building traditional MIS systems?
15. What are the benefits of ESS? How do they enhance managerial decision making?

Discussion Questions

1. Some have argued that all information systems support decision making. The argument holds that conceptually, a DSS is just a good MIS. Discuss.
2. What kinds of skills must you, as an end user of systems, have in order to participate in the design and use of a DSS?

3. Identify an organization with which you are familiar. Identify specific areas where DSS could help decision making and describe the DSS you would recommend.

Group Project

With three or four of your classmates, identify several groups in your university that could benefit from a GDSS. Design a GDSS for one of those groups, describing its hardware, software, and people elements. Present your findings to the class.

SETTING A STRATEGY FOR EXECUTIVE INFORMATION SYSTEMS

This case is based on a real-world company with a real-world dilemma, although the names have been changed to enable the circumstances to be made public. The names and positions of the experts whose recommendations we will examine are real. These four experts bring four different perspectives to the case.

The company, Thor Industries, is a U.S.-based areospace/defense company operating in a highly competitive and cost-conscious government market. Thor recently went through a major reorganization that has left the IS department severely overburdened. The company has a high-level ESS Planning Committee made up of the vice presidents of information systems, production, finance, engineering, and sales/marketing. That committee has just launched its first ESS project.

The ESS Planning Committee informed David Saunders, vice president of MIS, that it wants an ESS to span several Thor operating groups, using data from a number of current mainframe, midrange, and server-based databases and applications. The purpose of the ESS is to facilitate joint development of budgets, schedules, and measures of progress and to monitor the ongoing performance of major projects. The ESS has to be easy to use. The system will be based on a network of desktop equipment and will heavily emphasize graphics.

Saunders sees the project as a real opportunity for his staff to become more closely involved with the company while they build their own skills and reputations. But he has a number of concerns. First, the project has high profile inside the company because it is beamed toward senior management—*he* must succeed. Second, the chairman of the ESS Planning Committee, Howard Leaderman, has informed Saunders that

there will be a budget large enough to allow software and hardware purchases but that IS will be "evaluated on its ability to manage costs over the long term." Third, Saunders' senior staff members are apprehensive because they do not know desktop technology and are concerned that they will lose their value to the company. They also fear that the project will result in their being moved into line units as ongoing support where, they believe, their careers will be damaged. Some of the lower-level staff are also concerned because their experience is primarily with technology that could now become out-of-date. Saunders does have one advantage in his staff—some of his lower-level employees have gained extensive experience at Thor over the past several years installing desktop systems. Saunders has also already prepared some of his management for the coming changes in IS technology—for example, Leaderman has just attended a client/server conference on Saunders' recommendation.

What follows are the recommendations to Saunders made by four people with real experience in planning such projects.

Phil Carpenter, marketing manager of Mozart Systems, proposes a strategy that preserves Thor's investment in its current systems. He recommends that the system be built on top of the existing mainframe, midrange, and server-based data, leaving that data and the systems that produce it in place. Thor should develop a graphical microcomputer-based executive information system that will act as a bridge to data stored in disparate locations. The system would provide an easy, intuitive way to view and manipulate data from multiple sources without changing the software code of the company's underlying business applications.

To do so requires a careful selection of a development tool. The tool not only must create an easy-to-use graphical interface (which many tools do) but also must have some capabilities for accessing databases using SQL (Structured Query Language) and for linking up to mainframes and minicomputer systems (which few tools do).

Advantages of this approach are many. Investment in current systems will indeed be protected—they will not be touched. Staff fears should be allayed because the company will continue to need the same staff as before. Little additional training will be needed, so costs will be kept down. Costs will be minimized in another way also. The approach will require the purchase of only a modest amount of hardware and software, and will mainly use Thor's existing stock. Development time will also be minimal, with the use of the appropriate user-friendly tool (he does not recommend a specific tool).

Saj-Nicole A. Joni, regional practice manager for Microsoft Consulting, also sees leaving current production systems in place for now. She would build a client/server-based ESS on top of the existing systems. However, she raises a whole set of different issues, most of which are nontechnical.

Successful executive information systems require a strong sense of ownership and support from top management. Joni wonders if the project has the necessary charter to go forward and to make the key decisions that will affect the involved divisions. She wants to know where the clear executive project ownership is that must exist if the project is to avoid failure. Thor's executives appear enthusiastic, but the specifications for the ESS do not answer questions such as the following: What are the critical short-term business issues to be addressed by the system?

What are the long-term issues? Who will use the system and how will they use it? How will this ESS actually improve the way Thor's executives manage the business?

This project will result in a major change in how critical data are used at high levels and how the data are shared. Thor's management needs to define the information that will be used, and it needs to ensure that the ESS will provide a fair and consistent view of that information across divisions. The system designers should develop a clear data model based on the executives' information needs for meeting business objectives. Joni does not believe that modifying Thor's existing applications will provide the unified information that top management needs on its desktop.

Joni wonders if the project is addressing such major information systems issues as restructuring the department, reducing headcount, or retraining workers. She believes that with such a high visibility and high impact project, IS should form a special project team made up of smart, eager volunteers. The team should be supplemented by outside expertise in building GUI-based ESS client/server systems.

Joni believes that client/server technology is the direction of the future. Thor does not yet have a centralized client/server infrastructure. She suggests that Thor start to construct such an infrastructure with an open architecture using appropriate standards. She recommends that the graphical user interface for the ESS be built with off-the-shelf tools to standardize application interfaces and to provide flexibility for the future.

Ronald Sella is manager of emerging technology services for Information Builders, Inc. Sella believes that the most difficult issues for Thor are the human ones—retraining Saunders' staff and redefining job descriptions. He recommends that Saunders solve his problem by purchasing a third-party, 4GL-based ESS package.

Sella sees several "human factor" advantages to using a purchased ESS package. First, the IS staff would remain in their traditional positions, thus

eliminating their fears over their future. They would, however, have to provide some technical support to the project and its resulting system. Second, training is minimal and easy. The ESS software vendor will train Thor's staff to use the software and will provide technical support for that software. System development using the 4GL software will, he believes, be relatively easy; for this reason he suggests purchasing such a package.

Sella also recommends that Saunders base the new system on client/server technology, suggesting that the database software be SQL-based and relational to facilitate multi-vendor cross-platform connectivity. The software used by the new ESS system must support access to a wide variety of databases so that it can access Thor's current data. Costs would be limited because Thor would have to purchase little new software or hardware and would avoid large training or reorganization costs.

Jim Powell, distributed information services manager for Texas Instruments, brings a focus on changing technology to the discussion. He believes that the emergence of client/server technology has been an information systems watershed, bringing changes as significant as the development of microcomputers did in the beginning of the 1980s. Powell concludes that Thor must pursue the change to client/server technology—the risks of doing so are less than in staying with technology that is becoming outdated.

A technology transition of such fundamental importance cannot simply happen. Powell recommends that Saunders make a reformulation of Thor IS strategy his first priority. He then urges the setting of very clear architectural standards to push new development toward the emerging environment. He also warns Saunders not to "manually hard code each [client/server] application." He believes that Thor will be developing hundreds of such applications over the coming five to ten years. Such a large amount of work must be done in a standardized way, using a software development tool.

Powell raises yet another issue, one he believes Saunders has not ad-

dressed. The growth of microcomputers and now the change to client/server technology means that data will no longer be centralized. They will be "spread out across thousands of workstations and hundreds of servers." Controlling and even just keeping track of data is a massive problem that Saunders must address.

Finally, Powell believes the staff issues are also critical—but he has a very different slant. He notes that IS professionals keep close track of changes in their industry. Regardless of what they are saying, Powell asserts, Saunders' IS staff will ultimately be more troubled by working in a company where technology is falling behind than by working in one that is moving to leading-edge technology. To help the staff make the transition, he emphasizes the need for an organized training program to teach new skills. He also urges the company to map out new career paths for the staff. As he says, "It will not happen by osmosis."

Which strategy for building ESS should Saunders follow?

Source: Damian Rinaldi and John Desmond, "Preserve Investment or Move On?" *Software Magazine,* March 1992.

Case Study Questions

1. If you were in David Saunders' position, what would you recommend? Why? Develop the pros and cons of your decision. What management, organization, and technology issues would you consider?

2. None of the four consultants lays out the risks of his or her recommendations. Add a paragraph to each description delineating those risks.

3. Joni raises the issue of effective executive sponsorship. Why do you think she stresses this issue? Why will this particular project need such strong, high-level leadership?

4. All the recommendations dealt with staff issues, with several of them stressing these issues above all others. From what you know,

do you believe the staff problem will be as significant as they indicate? Why? How would you handle the staff issue? Why?

5. Two of the experts (Joni and Powell) urge Saunders to use this project to make a transition to client/server technology, indicating this as a fundamental shift in IS strategic direction. Assuming they are correct about the direction of technology, do you think Saunders should make this technology shift? Why? What are the risks of making that shift through the ESS high-visibility project? Would you accept Joni and Powell's client/server recommendations? Why?

References

Alavi, Maryam, and Erich A. Joachimsthaler. "Revisiting DSS Implementation Research: A Meta-Analysis of the Literature and Suggestions for Researchers." *MIS Quarterly* 16, no. 1 (March 1992).

Anthes, Gary H. "Notes System Sends Federal Property Data Nationwide." *Computerworld* (August 8, 1994).

Betts, Mitch. "Insurer's Financial Model Spawns Profits." *Computerworld* (July 5, 1993).

Bonzcek, R. H., C. W. Holsapple, and A. B. Whinston. "Representing Modeling Knowledge with First Order Predicate Calculus." *Operations Research* 1 (1982).

Chidambaram, Laku, Robert P. Bostrom, and Bayard E. Wynne. "A Longitudinal Study of the Impact of Group Decision Support Systems on Group Development." *Journal of Management Information Systems* 7, no. 3 (Winter 1990–1991).

Dennis, Alan R., Joey F. George, Len M. Jessup, Jay F. Nunamaker, and Douglas R. Vogel. "Information Technology to Support Electronic Meetings." *MIS Quarterly* 12, no. 4 (December 1988).

Dennis, Alan R., Jay F. Nunamaker, Jr., and Douglas R. Vogel. "A Comparison of Laboratory and Field Research in the Study of Electronic Meeting Systems." *Journal of Management Information Systems* 7, no. 3 (Winter 1990–1991).

DeSanctis, Geraldine, and R. Brent Gallupe. "A Foundation for the Study of Group Decision Support Systems." *Management Science* 33, no. 5 (May 1987).

DeSanctis, Geraldine, Marshall Scott Poole, Howard Lewis, and George Desharnias. "Computing in Quality Team Meetings." *Journal of Management Information Systems* 8, no. 3 (Winter 1991–1992).

Easton, George K., Joey F. George, Jay F. Nunamaker, Jr., and Mark O. Pendergast. "Two Different Electronic Meeting Systems." *Journal of Management Information Systems* 7, no. 3 (Winter 1990–1991).

El Sawy, Omar. "Personal Information Systems for Strategic Scanning in Turbulent Environments." *MIS Quarterly* 9, no. 1 (March 1985).

El Sherif, Hisham, and Omar A. El Sawy. "Issue-Based Decision Support Systems for the Egyptian Cabinet." *MIS Quarterly* 12, no. 4 (December 1988).

Gallupe, R. Brent, Geraldine DeSanctis, and Gary W. Dickson. "Computer-Based Support for Group Problem-Finding: An Experimental Investigation." *MIS Quarterly* 12, no. 2 (June 1988).

Ginzberg, Michael J., W. R. Reitman, and E. A. Stohr, eds. *Decision Support Systems.* New York: North Holland (1982).

Gopal, Abhijit, Robert P. Bostrum, and Wynne W. Chin. "Applying Adaptive Structuration Theory to Investigate the Process of Group Support Systems Use." *Journal of Management Information Systems* 9, no. 3 (Winter 1992–1993).

Grobowski, Ron, Chris McGoff, Doug Vogel, Ben Martz, and Jay Nunamaker. "Implementing Electronic Meeting Systems at IBM: Lessons Learned and Success Factors." *MIS Quarterly* 14, no. 4 (December 1990).

Henderson, John C., and David A. Schilling. "Design and Implementation of Decision Support Systems in the Public Sector." *MIS Quarterly* (June 1985).

Hiltz, Starr Roxanne, Kenneth Johnson, and Murray Turoff. "Group Decision Support: Designated Human Leaders and Statistical Feedback." *Journal of Management Information Systems* 8, no. 2 (Fall 1991).

Ho, T. H., and K. S. Raman. "The Effect of GDSS on Small Group Meetings." *Journal of Management Information Systems* 8, no. 2 (Fall 1991).

Hogue, Jack T. "Decision Support Systems and the Traditional Computer Information System Function: An Examination of Relationships During DSS Application Development." *Journal of Management Information Systems* (Summer 1985).

Hogue, Jack T. "A Framework for the Examination of Management Involvement in Decision Support Systems." *Journal of Management Information Systems* 4, no. 1 (Summer 1987).

Houdeshel, George, and Hugh J. Watson. "The Management Information and Decision Support (MIDS) System at Lockheed, Georgia." *MIS Quarterly* 11, no. 2 (March 1987).

Jessup, Leonard M., Terry Connolly, and Jolene Galegher. "The Effects of Anonymity on GDSS Group Process with an Idea-Generating Task." *MIS Quarterly* 14, no. 3 (September 1990).

Jones, Jack William, Carol Saunders, and Raymond McLeod, Jr. "Media Usage and Velocity in Executive Information Acquisition: An Exploratory Study." *European Journal of Information Systems* 2 (1993).

Keen, Peter G. W., and M. S. Scott Morton. *Decision Support Systems: An Organizational Perspective.* Reading, MA: Addison-Wesley (1982).

King, John. "Successful Implementation of Large Scale Decision Support Systems: Computerized Models in U.S. Economic Policy Making." *Systems Objectives Solutions* (November 1983).

Kraemer, Kenneth L., and John Leslie King. "Computer-Based Systems for Cooperative Work and Group Decision Making." *ACM Computing Surveys* 20, no. 2 (June 1988).

Laudon, Kenneth C. *Communications Technology and Democratic Participation.* New York: Praeger (1977).

Le Blanc, Louis A., and Kenneth A. Kozar. "An Empirical Investigation of the Relationship Between DSS Usage and System Performance." *MIS Quarterly* 14, no. 3 (September 1990).

Leidner, Dorothy E., and Joyce L. Elam, "Executive Information Systems: Their Impact on Executive Decision Making." *Journal of Management Information Systems* 10, no. 3 (Winter 1993–1994).

Lewe, Henrik, and Helmut Krcmar. "A Computer-Supported Cooperative Work Research Laboratory." *Journal of Management Information Systems* 8, no. 3 (Winter 1991–1992).

McLeod, Poppy Lauretta, and Jeffry R. Liker. "Electronic Meeting Systems: Evidence from a Low Structure Environment." *Information Systems Research* 3, no. 3 (September 1992).

Meador, Charles L., and Peter G. W. Keen. "Setting Priorities for DSS Development." *MIS Quarterly* (June 1984).

Miranda, Shaila M., and Robert P. Bostrum. "The Impact of Group Support Systems on Group Conflict and Conflict Management." *Journal of Management Information Systems* 10, no. 3 (Winter 1993–1994).

Mohan, Lakshmi, William K. Holstein, and Robert B. Adams. "EIS: It Can Work in the Public Sector." *MIS Quarterly* 14, no. 4 (December 1990).

"The New Role for 'Executive Information Systems.'" *I/S Analyzer* (January 1992).

Nunamaker, J. F., Alan R. Dennis, Joseph S. Valacich, Douglas R. Vogel, and Joey F. George. "Electronic Meeting Systems to Support Group Work." *Communications of the ACM* 34, no. 7 (July 1991).

Panko, Raymond R. "Managerial Communication Patterns." *Journal of Organizational Computing* 2, no. 1 (1992).

Post, Brad Quinn. "A Business Case Framework for Group Support Technology." *Journal of Management Information Systems* 9, no. 3 (Winter 1992–1993).

Rifkin, Glenn. "'What-If' Software for Manufacturers." *The New York Times* (October 18, 1992).

Rockart, John F., and David W. DeLong. "Executive Support Systems and the Nature of Work." Working Paper: Management in the 1990s, Sloan School of Management (April 1986).

Rockart, John F., and David W. DeLong, *Executive Support Systems: The Emergence of Top Management Computer Use.* Homewood, IL: Dow-Jones Irwin (1988).

Sambamurthy, V., and Marshall Scott Poole. "The Effects of Variations in Capabilities of GDSS Designs on Management of Cognitive Conflict in Groups." *Information Systems Research* 3, no. 3 (September 1992).

Sanders, G. Lawrence, and James F. Courtney. "A Field Study of Organizational Factors Influencing DSS Success." *MIS Quarterly* (March 1985).

Silver, Mark S. "Decision Support Systems: Directed and Nondirected Change." *Information Systems Research* 1, no. 1 (March 1990).

Sprague, R. H., and E. D. Carlson. *Building Effective Decision Support Systems.* Englewood Cliffs, NJ: Prentice Hall (1982).

Stefik, Mark, Gregg Foster, Daniel C. Bobrow, Kenneth Kahn, Stan Lanning, and Luch Suchman. "Beyond the Chalkboard: Computer Support for Collaboration and Problem Solving in Meetings." *Communications of the ACM* (January 1987).

Turban, Efraim. *Decision Support and Expert Systems: Management Support Systems.* New York: Macmillan (1993).

Turoff, Murray. "Computer-Mediated Communication Requirements for Group Support." *Journal of Organizational Computing* 1, no. 1 (January–March 1991).

Tyran, Craig K., Alan R. Dennis, Douglas R. Vogel, and J. F. Nunamaker, Jr. "The Application of Electronic Meeting Technology to Support Senior Management." *MIS Quarterly* 16, no. 3 (September 1992).

Vogel, Douglas R., Jay F. Nunamaker, William Benjamin Martz, Jr., Ronald Grobowski, and Christopher McGoff. "Electronic Meeting System Experience at IBM." *Journal of Management Information Systems* 6, no. 3 (Winter 1989–1990).

Volonino, Linda, and Hugh J. Watson. "The Strategic Business Objectives Method for EIS Development." *Journal of Management Information Systems* 7, no. 3 (Winter 1990–1991).

Walls, Joseph G., George R. Widmeyer, and Omar A. El Sawy. "Building an Information System Design Theory for Vigilant EIS." *Information Systems Research* 3 no. 1 (March 1992).

Watson, Richard T., Geraldine DeSanctis, and Marshall Scott Poole. "Using a GDSS to Facilitate Group Consensus: Some Intended and Unintended Consequences." *MIS Quarterly* 12, no. 3 (September 1988).

Watson, Richard T., Teck Hua Ho, and K. S. Raman. "Culture: A Fourth Dimension of Group Support Systems. *Communications of the ACM* 37, no. 10 (October 1994).

Watson, Hugh J., Astrid Lipp, Pamela Z. Jackson, Abdelhafid Dahmani, and William B. Fredenberger. "Organizational Support for Decision Support Systems." *Journal of Management Information Systems* 5, no. 4 (Spring 1989).

Watson, Hugh J., R. Kelly Rainer, Jr., and Chang E. Koh. "Executive Information Systems: A Framework for Development and a Survey of Current Practices." *MIS Quarterly* 15, no. 1 (March 1991).

Chapter 17

Artificial Intelligence

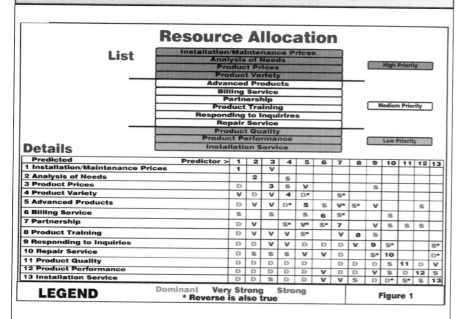

Artificial Intelligence Uncovers Customer Preference Patterns

Management is often able to pinpoint the level of customer satisfaction, but how can it know why customers react as they do? Whereas satisfaction and preference can often be determined by analyzing sales data and customer satisfaction surveys, management would also like to know why—why customers feel as they do, what the specific factors are that determine customer reaction. To fulfill this need, Stephen Hokanson left his job as manager of an artificial intelligence program with Boeing Computer Services and established a small Philadelphia-based company called Pattern Discovery, Inc. His company's specialty is finding hidden relationships in customer survey data, thereby uncovering answers to the client question of "why." For example, for Public Service Gas & Electric Co. of

Newark, New Jersey, he discovered that if customer billing is accurate, customers view their electric service as reliable. For a large fast food chain, he found that restroom cleanliness leads to a better customer perception of the quality of the food. The ultimate goal is to find those few issues that drive fundamental perceptions, giving the client specific targets to address in order to improve customer satisfaction.

To discover these hidden relationships, Hokanson begins with a customer survey, one that varies from customer to customer. He uses nonlinear mathematical techniques to identify relationships that would otherwise not be found. The software he has developed to do the nonlinear analysis is based upon an artificial intelligence technique known as fuzzy logic. For hardware he uses a Pentium desktop computer. The processing of the data is very computation-intensive and can take from 10 to 300 hours to complete, depending upon the number of survey questions and of survey respondents.

Pattern Discovery's approach has worked for a number of other clients during the company's first two years, including Roadway Express in Akron, Ohio, and Volvo Cars of North America, Inc. of Rockleigh, New Jersey. Hokanson has decided to expand beyond being only a service provider. He is now developing custom software for his clients by combining his fuzzy logic analysis with their decision-support systems. ■

Source: Julia King, "AI Determines Customer Preference," *Computerworld*, November 14, 1994.

By using artificial intelligence techniques, Pattern Discovery was able to develop sophisticated methods to find cause-and-effect relationships in data that would otherwise be impossible for human beings to discern. Although Pattern Discovery is a small business, artificial intelligence techniques are being used by organizations of all sizes. We will examine fuzzy logic techniques in this chapter. Other artificial intelligence applications capture the knowledge of recognized experts and make that knowledge available to other workers in the organization. Organi-

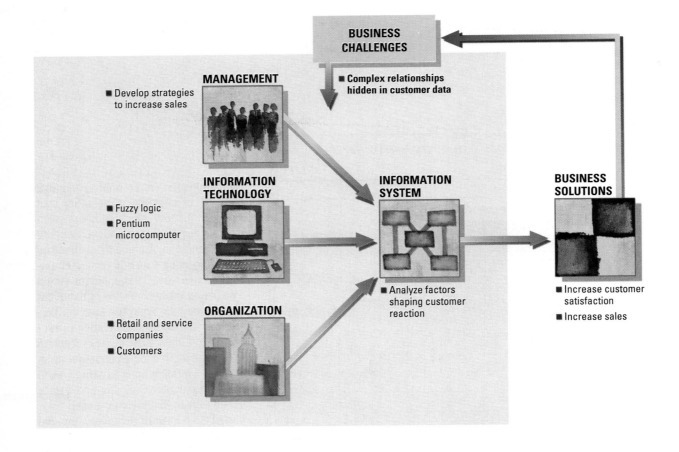

zations can benefit from a variety of software and hardware techniques for acquiring, retaining, and leveraging knowledge, provided they understand both the potential and pitfalls of this technology.

This chapter explains what artificial intelligence is and what artificial intelligence systems can and cannot do. It shows how expert systems, neural networks, fuzzy logic, and other artificial intelligence techniques capture knowledge and intelligence, while pointing out their limitations. The chapter then describes how these techniques can create information systems that capture knowledge and intelligence for organizations; the chapter also identifies the requirements of successful artificial intelligence applications.

After completing this chapter, you will be able to:

Learning Objectives

1. Define artificial intelligence.

2. Describe how artificial intelligent techniques evolved.

3. Define an expert system and explain how it works.

4. Define neural networks and show how they are used in business.

5. Identify other intelligent techniques.

17.1   WHAT IS ARTIFICIAL INTELLIGENCE?

The effort to use computers to understand or imitate aspects of human intelligence began in the 1950s. In 1956, Marvin Minsky (now at M.I.T.), Claude Shannon of Bell Laboratories, and other innovators in the early study of computers and intelligence met at a conference at Dartmouth College. John McCarthy, then an assistant professor of mathematics at Dartmouth, coined the term *artificial intelligence* for the theme of the conference. The conference's high point was the unveiling of what some people thought was the first expert system, Logic Theorist. The system processed nonnumerical symbols instead of crunching numbers, and it proved several theorems in the *Principia Mathematica* of Alfred North Whitehead and Bertrand Russell. No magazine would publish the proof of the theorems because the results had been produced by a machine. This was the first software to claim properties of artificial intelligence. Ever since that time, skeptics, pundits, journalists, and serious scholars have argued over what artificial intelligence means.

WHAT ARTIFICIAL INTELLIGENCE IS AND IS NOT

artificial intelligence The effort to develop computer-based systems that can behave like humans, with the ability to learn languages, accomplish physical tasks, use a perceptual apparatus, and emulate human expertise and decision making.

Artificial intelligence is commonly defined as the effort to develop computer-based systems (both hardware and software) that behave as humans. Such systems would be able to learn natural languages, accomplish coordinated physical tasks (robotics), utilize a perceptual apparatus that informs their physical behavior and language (visual and oral perception systems), and emulate human expertise and decision making (expert systems). Such systems would also exhibit logic, reasoning, intuition, and the just plain common-sense qualities that we associate with human beings. Figure 17.1 illustrates the elements of the artificial intelligence family. In addition to these areas, "intelligent" machines, the physical hardware that performs these tasks is another important aspect of AI.

No existing system comes close to possessing any of these human qualities, but what has been developed is nevertheless of profound interest. Artificial intelligence has become, without a doubt, the most controversial subject in computer science and information systems circles, as well as in the broader community of scholars and decision makers. Since the Renaissance, men and women in their physical form and mental accomplishments have been at the center of the cultural universe, the measure of

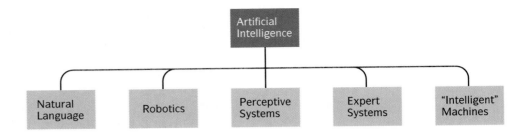

all things. Now to be joined by a lowly machine, an artificial, inanimate object, represents a challenging cultural revolution that most people resist. Critics of the study of artificial intelligence argue that it is a waste of time and resources, a study dotted with significant failures and few accomplishments that succeeds only insofar as it denigrates the power and elegance of human thought processes. The most militant critics argue that artificial intelligence insults the very nature and role of human beings.

Supporters of the study of artificial intelligence point to the noble goal of using it as a way of understanding human intelligence and as a vehicle for distributing expertise. Artificial intelligence systems, if they could be developed, might lead to a quantum leap in social wealth and well-being. The new technology, supporters argue, will increase individual and social potential by distributing knowledge more widely.

In this chapter, we will try to avoid making judgments about whether artificial intelligence is a worthwhile pursuit. Instead, we will give the views of both critics and supporters, as well as some real-world examples. You can decide for yourself whether artificial intelligence is a worthwhile pursuit with potential real-world benefits.

HUMAN AND ARTIFICIAL INTELLIGENCE

Before describing artificial intelligence, it is worthwhile to distinguish more fully between *artificial* and human intelligence because successful artificial intelligence systems are neither artificial nor intelligent. A thermostat and an autopilot are the best examples of systems that solve problems in a goal-oriented, machinelike, artificial way. Yet no one calls thermostats or autopilots intelligent.

This raises the question: What would a truly *artificial intelligent* system look like? Successful artificial intelligence systems are based on human expertise, knowledge, and selected reasoning patterns. Existing artificial intelligence systems do not come up with new and novel solutions to problems. Existing, practical artificial intelligence systems that try to reproduce the expertise of humans do not behave like human experts at all, but rather are limited to mundane (albeit important) tasks. Existing systems extend the powers of experts, but in no way substitute for them or "capture" much of their intelligence. Briefly, existing systems lack the common sense and generality of naturally intelligent machines like human beings.

For instance, John McCarthy, one of the early founders of the study of artificial intelligence, noted in 1987 that "no one knows how to make a general database of common-sense knowledge that could be used by any program that needed the knowledge. Along with other information, such a database would contain what a robot would need to know about the effects of moving objects around, what a person can be expected to know about his family, and the facts about buying and selling. This does not depend on whether the knowledge is to be expressed in a logical language or in some other formalism. When we take the logic approach to AI, lack of generality shows up in that the axioms we devise to express common-sense knowledge are too restricted in their applicability for a general common-sense database." McCarthy believed that "getting a language for expressing general common sense knowledge for inclusion in a general database is the key problem of generality in AI" (McCarthy, 1987), although he expected intelligent computer programs to be developed eventually.

Now let us examine *human* intelligence. As it turns out, human intelligence is vastly complex and much broader than computer or information systems. Philosophers, psychologists, and other students of human cognition have all recognized that key aspects of human intelligence are beyond description and therefore are not easily imitated by a consciously designed machine—if a problem cannot be described, it cannot be programmed.

At least four important capabilities are involved in human intelligence: reasoning, behavior, the use of metaphor and analogy, and the creation and use of concepts.

- *Human intelligence is a way of reasoning.* One part of human intelligence can be described as the application of rules based on human experience and genetics. (Whether this rule-governed behavior takes the form *"if x, then y"* is not known.) These rules, although not always consciously invoked, are an important part of the knowledge carried by all human beings as an inheritance from the broader culture and the human gene pool.

- *Human intelligence is a way of behaving.* Even if humans do not actually invoke rules, they are obligated to act as if they did by a culture and a society that values reasonable, intelligent behavior. Human intelligence, at the very least, consists of acting in a way that can be described as intelligent.

- *Human intelligence includes the development and use of metaphors and analogies.* What distinguishes human beings from other animals is their ability to develop associations and to use metaphors and analogies such as "like" and "as." Using metaphor and analogy, humans create new rules, apply old rules to new situations, and at times act intuitively and/or instinctively without rules. Much of what we call "common sense" or "generality" in humans resides in the ability to create metaphor and analogy.

- *Human intelligence includes the creation and use of concepts.* It has long been recognized that humans have a unique ability to impose a conceptual apparatus on the world around them. Meta-concepts such as cause and effect and time, and concepts of a lower order such as breakfast, dinner, and lunch, are all imposed by human beings on the world around them. Thinking in terms of these concepts and acting on them are central characteristics of intelligent human behavior.

Artificial intelligence refers to an effort to develop machines that can reason, behave, compare, and conceptualize. While this may be a noble effort, clearly none of the successful systems described in this chapter comes close to achieving this form of human intelligence. However, what has been developed using artificial intelligence is of interest and is starting to provide some benefits to organizations.

THE DEVELOPMENT OF ARTIFICIAL INTELLIGENCE

bottom-up approach In the history of artificial intelligence, the effort to build a physical analog to the human brain.

The story of artificial intelligence, or AI, is really two stories[1] (see Figure 17.2). One is the history of efforts to develop physical machines that mimic what people think is the way an animal or human physical brain works. This is called the **bottom-up approach**, the effort to build a physical analog to the human brain. A second story

---

[1] Actually, the story of AI is much deeper and more controversial than can be presented here in such a brief introduction. Involved in this larger debate are questions about the nature of human beings and knowledge, the proper relationship between responsible human beings and machines, and the difference between promise and reality. For a positive view of AI, see Edward A. Feigenbaum and Pamela McCorduck, *The Fifth Generation: Artificial Intelligence and Japan's Computer Challenge to the World* (Reading, MA: Addison-Wesley, 1985), and Paul M. Churchland and Patricia Smith Churchland, "Could A Machine Think?" *Scientific American*, January 1990. For a counter view of AI, see Hubert L. Dreyfus and Stuart E. Dreyfus, *Mind Over Machine: The Power of Human Intuition and Expertise in the Era of the Computer* (New York: Free Press, 1986), and John R. Searle, "Is the Brain's Mind a Computer Program?" *Scientific American*, January 1990.

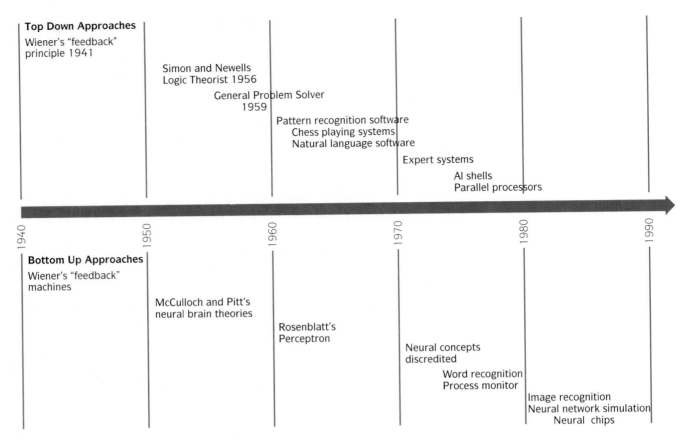

FIGURE 17.2
The evolution of artificial intelligence. The parallel development of the top-down and bottom-up approaches can be traced through the various milestones supporting each approach.

focuses on the effort to develop a logical analog to how the brain works. This approach is called the **top-down approach**.

The Bottom-Up Approach

The beginnings of contemporary AI started in World War II with the concept of "feedback." Norbert Weiner, a scientist and mathematician at M.I.T. in the 1940s, developed a method of radar control of anti-aircraft guns for the U.S. army that required calculating the expected location of an aircraft based on new information—"feedback"—from radar. This early period of self-correcting artillery machines started the physical or bottom-up approach to artificial intelligence. Weiner went on to propose in several books that feedback could explain how humans think. He believed that the principle could be applied to make machines think like humans.

Warren McCulloch, a biologist interested in brain function, and Walter Pitts, a mathematician, used Weiner's idea of feedback to develop a theory of how brains work. In their theory, a brain was composed of millions of neuron cells, which processed binary numbers (they were either "on" or "off") that were connected into a network that took in feedback or information from the environment. Learning was simply a matter of teaching the neurons in a brain how to respond to the environment. In 1960 these ideas were taken further by Cornell scientist Frank Rosenblatt. Rosenblatt demonstrated a machine called a Perceptron, which was composed of 400 photoelectric cells that could perceive letters or shapes. It could recognize letters (as long as they were all the same size and type) and could be taught: Operators would increase or decrease voltages in certain areas of the machine when mistakes were made.

Interest in the bottom-up approach then lagged for years, but by the 1980s interest was growing, and work began on word, pattern, and image recognition and on neural network machines that attempt to emulate the physical thought processes of the human brain. In Section 17.3 we describe neural networks in greater detail.

The Top-Down Approach

The logical or top-down school of AI has gone through three stages. In its earliest stage, the goal was to develop a general model of human intelligence. This was followed by a period in which the extraordinary power of third-generation computers—the machines of the 1960s—was applied to more limited problems like playing chess games or to special areas like machine tool control. Last, beginning in the 1970s, expert systems emerged in which the goals of AI were more limited to understanding knowledge in specific and highly limited areas.

One of the first top-down efforts was the Logic Theorist, introduced in 1956 at the Dartmouth Summer Research Project on Artificial Intelligence. Its developers, Herbert Simon (a Carnegie-Mellon psychologist and scientist) and Alan Newell (a RAND corporation scientist) used software that mimicked deductive logic: selecting the correct rules and postulates so as to create a coherent logical chain of "if x then y" statements from premises to conclusion. The problem with this approach was that for even simple real-world problems, hundreds of thousands, or millions, of such rules are required.

In the 1960s, newly developed third-generation computers made it possible to consider thousands of computations per second to test out millions of rules, one at a time. But even a simple game like chess contained 10^{120} possible moves. Faster computers was not a total solution. Ways had to be found to pare down the search tree in order to avoid a **combinatorial explosion**. A combinatorial explosion arises when a problem requires a computer to test more rules than it has the capacity to examine in order to reach a solution. An exhaustive search through all possibilities on a chessboard would quickly swamp all the computers known to exist in the 1980s. Newell and Simon responded by developing a model of human problem solving called the *General Problem Solver*. The objective was to use simple rules to pare down the search tree. But this solution did not work because no one could come up with sensible general rules of problem solving that were useful in all situations.

However some success could be achieved in restricted domains such as chess using sufficient processing power. New search strategies and decision trees were developed to reduce the need for an exhaustive search. Figure 17.3 shows several decision trees and some possible search strategies (random, exhaustive, and rule-guided).

Figure 17.3 illustrates the search strategies that could be used to solve a simple problem: finding the goal at *J*. One possibility *(A)* is to search the tree randomly until the goal at *J* is found. Without recording failed paths, a random search will repeat errors and attain the goal only by chance. Another possibility *(B)* is exhaustive searching of the tree, recording all choices and not taking the same path twice. A simple set of rules is to start always on the far left, take every path to its end, retrace one, two, or three steps if you do not attain the goal, and try again. Eventually you will find the goal at *J*. A much more economical method is a rule-guided search *(C)*. Here the rule is to evaluate all paths and to take the first path that reduces the distance between the origin and the goal. If the distance to the goal is not reduced, backtrack one step and try again.

From these developments emerged expert systems, which consist of a limited number of rules for a very specific and limited domain of human expertise (such as making a mortgage decision). A major effort of AI systems today is to develop simple rules that can pare down the search tree and make searching efficient. In limited areas of expertise, from diagnosing a car's ignition system to classifying biological specimens, the rules of thumb used by real-world experts can be understood, codified, and placed in a machine. In the following section we explain what expert systems are and how they work.

combinatorial explosion In computer processing, the overload that results when trying to test more rules to reach a solution than the computer is capable of handling.

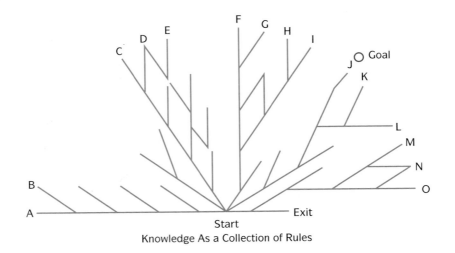

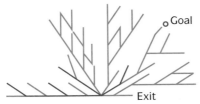

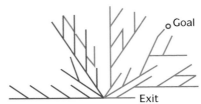

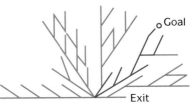

(A) Random searching of a tree of rules   (B) Exhaustive searching of tree   (C) Rule-guided searching of tree

FIGURE 17.3
Decision making in AI systems. Some kinds of knowledge can be represented as a decision tree, a collection of paths from an origin to a goal. The various techniques for searching from the origin to the goal illustrated are (A) random searching that will repeat errors and attain the goal only by chance; (B) exhaustive searching that will record all searches and not take the same path twice, eventually reaching the goal; and (C) rule-guided searching that evaluates the paths and takes the first path to reduce the distance between the origin and the goal until the goal is reached.

17.2 EXPERT SYSTEMS

expert system Knowledge-intensive computer program that captures the expertise of a human in limited domains of knowledge.

An **expert system** is a knowledge-intensive program that solves a problem by capturing the expertise of a human in limited domains of knowledge and experience. An expert system can assist decision making by asking relevant questions and explaining the reasons for adopting certain actions. Some of the common characteristics of expert systems are the following:

- They perform some of the problem-solving work of humans.
- They represent knowledge in forms such as rules or frames.
- They interact with humans.
- They can consider multiple hypotheses simultaneously.

Today, expert systems are quite narrow, shallow, and brittle. They lack the breadth of knowledge and the understanding of fundamental principles of a human expert. Expert systems today do not "think" as a human being does. A human being perceives significance, works with abstract models of causality, and can jump to conclusions. Expert systems do not resort to reasoning from first principles, do not draw analogies, and lack common sense.

Above all, expert systems are not a generalized expert or problem solver. They typically perform very limited tasks that can be performed by professionals in a few minutes or hours. Problems that cannot be solved by human experts in the same short period of time are far too difficult for an expert system. But by capturing human expertise in limited areas, expert systems can provide organizational benefits.

HOW EXPERT SYSTEMS WORK

Four major elements compose an expert system: the knowledge domain or base, the development team, the AI shell, and the user (see Figure 17.4). Subsequently, we will describe each of these parts.

The Knowledge Base

knowledge base Model of human knowledge that is used by expert systems.

What is human knowledge? AI developers sidestep this thorny issue by asking a slightly different question: How can human knowledge be modeled or represented in a way that a computer can deal with it? This model of human knowledge used by expert systems is called the **knowledge base**. Three ways have been devised to represent human knowledge and expertise: rules, semantic nets, and frames.

A standard structured programming construct (see Chapter 13) is the IF–THEN construct, in which a *condition* is evaluated. If the condition is true, an *action* is taken. For instance:

> IF
> INCOME > $45,000 (condition)
> PRINT NAME AND ADDRESS (action)

rule-based expert system An AI program that has a large number of interconnected and nested IF–THEN statements or "rules" that are the basis for the knowledge in the system.

A series of these rules can be a knowledge base. Any reader who has written computer programs knows that virtually all traditional computer programs contain IF–THEN statements. The difference between a traditional program and a **rule-based expert system** program is primarily one of degree and magnitude. AI programs can easily have 200 to 10,000 rules, far more than traditional programs, which may have 50 to 100 IF–THEN statements. Moreover, in an AI program the rules tend to be interconnected and nested to a far larger degree than in traditional programs, as shown in Figure 17.5. The order in which the rules are searched depends in part on what information the system is given. Multiple paths lead to the same result, and the rules themselves can be interconnected. Hence the complexity of the rules in a rule-based expert system is considerable.

rule base The collection of knowledge in an AI system that is represented in the form of IF–THEN rules.

Could you represent the knowledge in the *Encyclopedia Britannica* this way? Probably not, because the **rule base** would be too large, and not all the knowledge in the encyclopedia can be represented in the form of IF–THEN rules. In general, expert

FIGURE 17.4
Components of an expert system. The four basic elements of an expert system are the knowledge base, the development team, the AI shell, and the user.

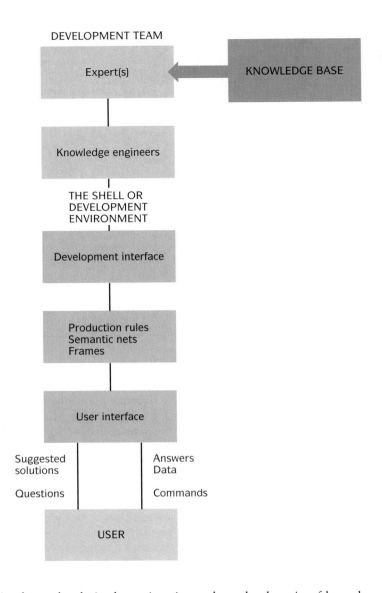

systems can be efficiently used only in those situations where the domain of knowledge is highly restricted (such as in granting credit) and involves no more than a few thousand rules.

semantic nets Expert systems that use the property of inheritance to organize and classify knowledge when the knowledge base is composed of easily identifiable chunks or objects of interrelated characteristics.

frames Method of organizing expert system knowledge into chunks, but the relationships are based on shared characteristics determined by the user rather than a hierarchy.

Semantic nets can be used to represent knowledge when the knowledge base is composed of easily identified chunks or objects of interrelated characteristics. Semantic nets can be much more efficient than rules. They use the property of inheritance to organize and classify objects. A condition like "Is-A" ties objects together—"Is-A" is a pointer to all objects of a specific class. For instance, Figure 17.6 shows a semantic net that is used to classify kinds of automobiles. All specific automobiles in the lower part of the diagram inherit characteristics of the general categories of the automobiles above them. Insurance companies can use such a semantic net to classify cars into rating classes.

Frames also organize knowledge into chunks, but the relationships are based on shared characteristics rather than a hierarchy. This approach is grounded in the belief that humans use "frames" or concepts to make rapid sense out of perceptions. For instance, when a person is told to "look for a tank and shoot when you see one," experts believe humans invoke a concept or frame of what a tank should look like. Anything that does not fit this concept of a tank is ignored. In a similar fashion, AI researchers can organize a vast array of information into frames. The computer is then instructed to search the database of frames and list connections to other frames of interest. The user can then follow the various pathways pointed to by the system.

FIGURE 17.5
Rules in an AI program. An expert system contains a number of rules to be followed when utilized. The rules themselves are interconnected; the number of outcomes is known in advance and is limited; there are multiple paths to the same outcome; and the system can consider multiple rules at a single time. The rules illustrated are for simple credit-granting expert systems.

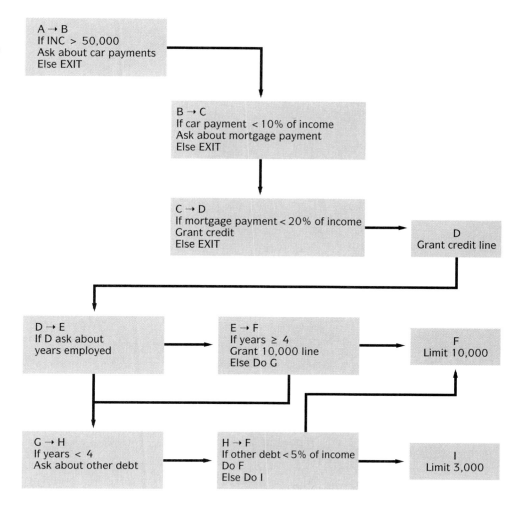

Figure 17.7 shows a part of a knowledge base organized by frames. A "CAR" is defined by characteristics or slots in a frame as a vehicle, with four wheels, a gas or diesel motor, and an action like rolling or moving. This frame could be related to just about any other object in the database that shares any of these characteristics, such as the tank frame.

FIGURE 17.6
Semantic nets to model knowledge. Knowledge can be organized into semantic nets with inheritance. All lower levels inherit the characteristics of those objects above. For example, a Dodge Caravan inherits the characteristics of "family car" as well as "automobile." The link among levels is crucial; in this case, the link is "is-a." In other instances it could be "produces," "looks like," and so forth.

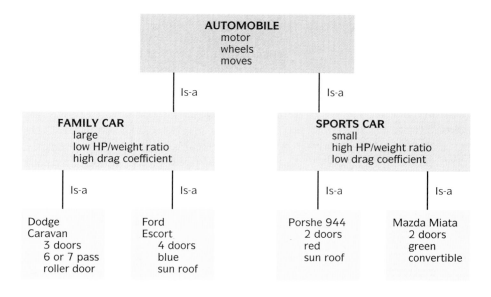

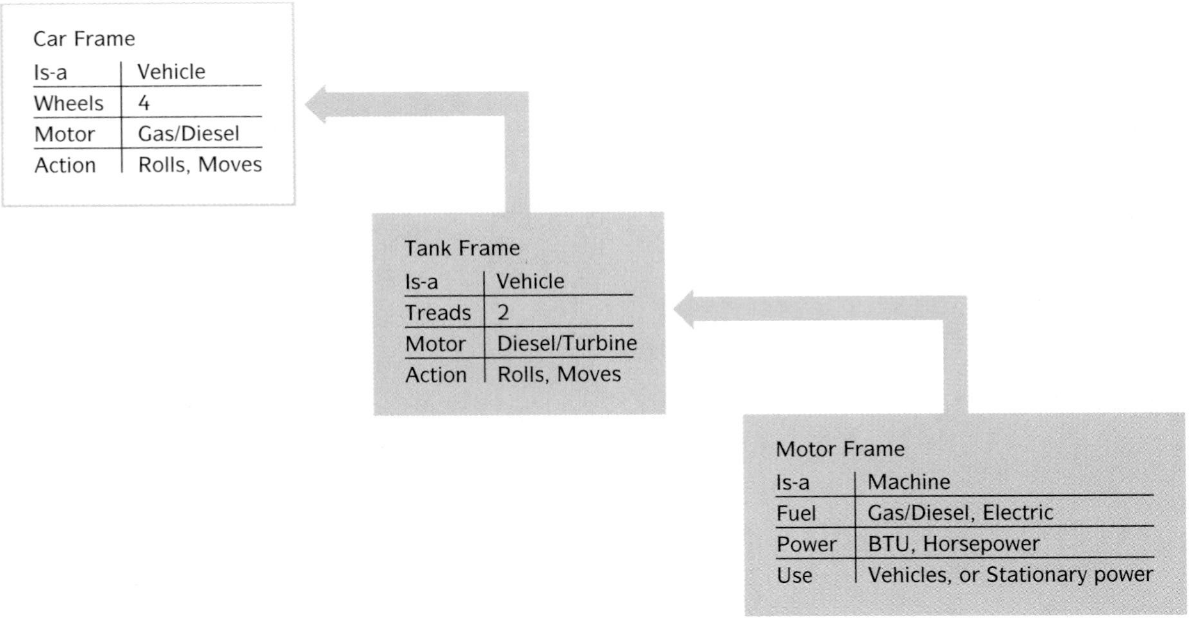

FIGURE 17.7
Frames to model knowledge. Knowledge and information can be organized into frames in a manner similar to semantic nets. Frames capture the relevant characteristics of the objects of interest. This approach is based on the belief that humans use "frames" or concepts to narrow the range of possibilities when scanning incoming information in order to make rapid sense out of perceptions.

The Development Team

An AI development team is composed of one or several "experts" who have a thorough command over the knowledge base and one or more **knowledge engineers** who can translate the knowledge (as described by the expert) into a set of rules, frames, or semantic nets. A knowledge engineer is similar to a traditional systems analyst but has special expertise in eliciting information and expertise from other professionals. The knowledge engineer interviews the expert or experts and specifies the decision rules and knowledge that must be captured by the system.

knowledge engineer Specialist who elicits information and expertise from other professionals and translates it into a set of rules, frames, or semantic nets for an expert system.

The Shell

The **AI shell** is the programming environment of an expert system. AI systems can be developed in just about any programming language, such as BASIC or Pascal. In the early years of expert systems, computer scientists used specialized programming languages such as LISP or Prolog that could process lists of rules efficiently. Today a growing number of expert systems use either the C language or, more commonly, AI shells that are user-friendly development environments. AI shells can quickly generate user interface screens, capture the knowledge base, and manage the strategies for searching the rule base. The best of these AI shells generate C code, which can then be integrated into existing programs or tied into existing data streams and databases.

AI shell The programming environment of an expert system.

One of the most interesting parts of expert systems is the **inference engine**. The inference engine is simply the strategy used to search through the rule base. Two strategies are commonly used: forward chaining and backward chaining (see Figure 17.8).

In **forward chaining**, the inference engine begins with the information entered by the user and searches the rule base to arrive at a conclusion. The strategy is to "fire," or carry out, the action of the rule when a condition is true. In Figure 17.8, beginning on the left, if the user enters a client with income greater than $100,000, the engine will fire all rules in sequence from left to right. If the user then enters information indicating that the same client owns real estate, another pass of the rule base will

inference engine The strategy used to search through the rule base in an expert system: can be forward or backward chaining.

forward chaining Strategy for searching the rule base in an expert system that begins with the information entered by the user and searches the rule base to arrive at a conclusion.

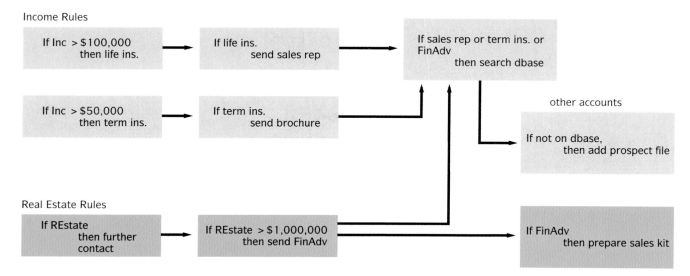

Income Rules

| If Inc > $100,000 then life ins. | → | If life ins. send sales rep | → | If sales rep or term ins. or FinAdv then search dbase |

| If Inc > $50,000 then term ins. | → | If term ins. send brochure |

other accounts

If not on dbase, then add prospect file

Real Estate Rules

| If REstate then further contact | → | If REstate > $1,000,000 then send FinAdv |

If FinAdv then prepare sales kit

FIGURE 17.8
Inference engines in expert systems. An inference engine works by searching through the rules and "firing" those rules that are triggered by facts gathered and entered by the user. Basically, a collection of rules is similar to a series of nested "IF" statements in a traditional software program; however, the magnitude of the statements and degree of nesting are much greater in an expert system.

occur and more rules will fire. The rule base can be searched each time the user enters new information. Processing continues until no more rules can be fired.

In **backward chaining**, an expert system acts more like a problem solver who begins with a question and seeks out more information to evaluate the question. The strategy for searching the rule base starts with a hypothesis and proceeds by asking the user questions about selected facts until the hypothesis is either confirmed or disproved. In our example in Figure 17.8, ask the question, "Should we add this person to the prospect database?" Begin on the right of the diagram and work toward the left. You can see that the person should be added to the database if a sales rep is sent, term insurance is granted, or a financial adviser will be sent to visit the client.

backward chaining Strategy for searching the rule base in an expert system that acts like a problem solver by beginning with a hypothesis and seeking out more information until the hypothesis is either proved or disproved.

The User

The role of the user is both to pose questions of the system and to enter relevant data to guide the system along. The user may employ the expert system as a source of advice or to perform tedious and routine analysis tasks.

EXAMPLES OF SUCCESSFUL EXPERT SYSTEMS

There are many successful expert systems. However, there is no accepted definition of *successful*. What is successful to an academic ("It works!") may not be successful to a corporation ("It cost a million dollars!"). While some of the better-known expert systems are quite large and cost millions of dollars, others are less expensive and tackle interesting but smaller problems. Some of the most celebrated systems are not used to facilitate routine decision making. Finding out which successful systems are used on a daily basis is difficult because corporations regard this information as proprietary. Nevertheless, we can briefly describe some of the better-known commercial success stories.

Whirlpool uses the *Consumer Appliance Diagnostic System* (CADS) to help its customer service representatives handle its 3 million annual telephone inquiries. The system expedites customer service by directing customers to a single source of help without delay. Previously, customers who had a problem or question about Whirlpool products might have to be put on hold or directed to two or three different representatives before their questions could be answered. Whirlpool developed CADS using

Aion's Development System for OS/2 as its expert system shell. Two knowledge engineers worked with one programmer and three of the company's customer service experts to capture 1000 rules for 12 product lines. By 1999, Whirlpool expects to use CADS to respond to 9 million calls annually.

The National Aeronautic and Space Administration (NASA) developed MARVEL, its Multimission Automation for Real-Time Verification of Spacecraft Engineering Link to monitor its *Voyager* missions without burning out analyst after analyst. Spacecraft flights on long missions generate voluminous and critical information that must be carefully analyzed. MARVEL monitors NASA's computer-command subsystem, which receives and executes commands from the ground and also analyzes power, propulsion flight-data subsystems, and telecommunications functions. NASA developed MARVEL with the assistance of the equivalent of 1.5 full-time computer scientists and two mission experts. MARVEL is based on Software Architecture and Engineering's Knowledge Engineering System expert system shell and runs on Sun workstations.

Countrywide Funding Corp. in Pasadena, California, loan underwriters with about 400 underwriters in 150 offices around the country, developed a microcomputer-based expert system in 1992 to make preliminary creditworthiness decisions on loan requests. The company had experienced rapid, continuing growth and used the system to help ensure consistent and high-quality loan decisions.

CLUES (Countrywide's Loan Underwriting Expert System) has about 400 rules. Countrywide tested the system by having every loan application handled by a human underwriter fed to CLUES. The system was refined until it agreed with the underwriter in 95 percent of the cases. However, Countrywide will not rely on CLUES to reject loans because the expert system cannot be programmed to handle exceptional situations such as those involving a self-employed person or complex financial schemes. An underwriter will review all rejected loans and will make the final decision. CLUES has other benefits. Traditionally an underwriter could handle six or seven applications a day. Using CLUES, the same underwriter can evaluate at least sixteen per day (Nash, 1993).

The Digital Equipment Corporation (DEC) and Carnegie-Mellon University developed XCON in the late 1970s to configure VAX computers on a daily basis. The system configures customer orders and guides the assembly of those orders at the customer site. XCON has been used for major functions such as sales and marketing, manufacturing and production, and field service, and played a strategic role at DEC (Sviokla, June 1990; Barker and O'Conner, 1989). It is estimated that XCON and related systems saved DEC approximately $40 million per year.

Table 17.1 describes other well-known expert systems in terms of their size and programming languages. As can be seen, these systems generally have a minimum of several hundred rules. Note Digital Equipment Corporation's XCON, which started out with 250 rules but expanded to about 10,000.

These examples show that expert systems can provide organizations with an array of benefits, including reduced errors, reduced cost, reduced training time, improved decisions, and improved quality and service. The Window on Organizations shows how expert systems can be applied to solve some problems in medicine and health care.

BUILDING AN EXPERT SYSTEM

Building an expert system is similar to building other information systems, although building expert systems is an iterative process with each phase possibly requiring several iterations before a full system is developed. While no agreed-upon development cycle yet exists, we describe here typical steps.

The team members must first select a problem appropriate for an expert system. The project will balance the potential savings produced by the proposed system against the cost. Table 17.2 shows an estimate of tentative costs related to system

EXPERT SYSTEMS ARE GOOD MEDICINE FOR HEALTH-CARE PROBLEMS

How can the medical field make use of expert systems? Two examples will help us to understand the variety of beneficial applications. When Kaiser Foundation Health Plan, Inc. of Oakland, California, manually processed individual applications for membership, it is not surprising that the whole operation took weeks to complete. Information on applicants was recorded on scratch pads and then transferred to index cards. The process included about 15 steps that required these cards to be passed from processor to processor in a linear fashion. All applicants had to have their applications reviewed by a member of the medical staff. Processing applications often took from four to six weeks. Once management realized the need for a better way, they turned to expert systems to solve the problem.

Developing an expert system application could not have changed the situation significantly if Kaiser had not first re-engineered the business process. Joe Yuson, a Kaiser project manager, used a CASE tool, Information Engineering Facility (IEF) from Texas Instruments, to analyze the business area. Yuson found Kaiser was facing one primary issue with two facets—customer satisfaction and turnaround time. The company had to find ways to complete the process more quickly. The analysts redesigned the process to significantly reduce the number of steps. Criteria were then established for determining which applications required review by the medical staff and which ones did not. The analysts collected the rules used by both the enrollment and the medical staffs to evaluate applications. In building the system, they included adequate flexibility to give local system users the ability to maintain their own rules in certain areas so that, for example, the number of cigarette packs allowed in one year or height/weight limits could be estab-

lished locally rather than nationally.

Kaiser purchased a rule-based expert system development tool, Aion Development System from Trinzie Corporation, and used it to code the rules medical staff members use when reviewing membership applications. The result, an expert system dubbed SIMR (System for Individual Marketing and Review), has been very rewarding. The medical staff now has to review only 60 percent of the membership applications because SIMR accepts 28 percent outright and rejects another 12 percent of the applications outright without medical review. The applications of the 40 percent that do not need medical review are now completed in two days while those of the other 60 percent are completed within two to three weeks.

LDS Hospital in Salt Lake City, Utah, has developed an expert system for a very different use. Dr. David C. Classen, a clinical epidemiologist there, calls it "the most complex artificial intelligence system ever created for clinical decision-making." This expert system, the "antibiotic computer consultant" (AIC), is but one part of HELP (Health Evaluation Through Logical Processing), LDS's hospital-wide information system. The AIC helps a doctor to determine proper antibiotic treatment for specific patients, an exceedingly complex task. When a patient comes to a doctor with an infection, the doctor turns to the system with information on the infection site and type and also identifies the patient to the computer. The system determines the pathogens that are the most likely to have caused the infection. The software examines the patient's medical records (which have been collected by HELP), looks for similar cases nationwide over the past ten years, and then displays the five antibiotic regimens most likely to be effective against all of the pathogens, as well as the cost of the prescription for each regimen.

The system has been so successful that it has been expanded to include all cases involving antibiotics, even those when antibiotics are prescribed to pre-

> *To Think About:* What are the benefits of using expert systems in health care? How did expert system technology change the delivery of health care in both organizations? What management, organization, and technology issues should be considered before implementing expert systems for health care?

vent infection during surgery. One of the great criticisms of artificial intelligence systems in medicine was that they were so unwieldy and required physicians to enter so much information that they were never used. However, with AIC, the information is already available, including patient information from the HELP patient database. The system is so easy to use that 88 percent of the physicians say they would recommend the program to others. Eighty-five percent of them say that the program improved their selection of antibiotics, and 81 percent agreed that it improves patient care. Further evidence of its usability is the fact that physicians access the system on average three times per day. As to its efficacy, a study reported in the medical journal *Archives of Internal Medicine,* reports that physicians using the system make better decisions and make them faster. Whereas physicians selected the best treatment in 77 percent of the cases, the computer achieved a 94 percent correct rating.

Sources: Melinda Carol Ballou, "Expert System Modernized Kaiser," *Computerworld,* November 14, 1994; Mitch Betts, "Doctors Get HELP to Fight Infections," *Computerworld,* June 6, 1994.

Table 17.1 Some Well-Known Expert Systems

Name of System or Project	Brief System Description	Method of Verification	Number of Rules	Programming Language
Authorizer's Assistant (American Express)	Authorize credit transactions	Field test	1000	ART
Hub Slaashing (American Airlines)	Recommend flight schedule changes when airports disrupted	Field test	39	C
CLUES (Countrywide Funding Corp.)	Authorize loans	Field test	400	Inference Corp. ART—IM (AI shell)
Robot (Ford Motor)	Diagnose sick robots	Field test	200	Texas Instruments Personal Consultant
Mail Prospector (R. R. Donnelly)	Test mailing lists	Field test	NA	More/2
Heuristic Dendral	Identify organic compounds by analysis of mass spectrograms	Field use	400	Interlisp
MYCIN	Diagnose certain infectious diseases and recommend appropriate drugs	Scientific (BV)	400	Interlisp
Prospector	Aid geologists in evaluating mineral sites for potential deposits	Field use	Largest knowledge base, 212 assertions, and 133 inference rules	DEC 10
XCON (DEC)	Configure VAX computer systems	Field use	10,000	OPS4 (implemented in MACLISP)

NA = *Not available*

size. As expert system technology and computer hardware grow more efficient, these costs should become lower. The team members will then develop a prototype system to test assumptions about how to encode the knowledge of experts. Next they will develop a full-scale system, focusing mainly on the addition of a very large number of rules. Since the complexity of the entire system grows with the number of rules, the integrity of the system may be threatened. A fundamental conflict develops be-

Table 17.2 Resources Required to Develop an Expert System

Resources	TYPE OF SYSTEM		
	Small	Large	Very Large
Rules	50–450	500–3000	3000–10,000
Person-years needed for development	0.25–0.50	1–3	3–25
Project cost (including design and development staff, knowledge engineers, computing, and overhead)	$50,000–$80,000	$300,000–$1.5 million	$2 million–$30 million

tween faithfulness to the complexity of the real world and the comprehensibility of the system. Generally the system will be pruned to achieve simplicity and power.

When the experts and the knowledge engineers are satisfied that the system is complete, it can be tested by a range of experts within the organization against the performance criteria established in earlier stages. Once tested, the system will then be integrated into the data flow and work patterns of the organization. (This is considered one of the more challenging aspects of expert-system building.) Finally, as with other systems, the expert system must be maintained. Typically the environment in which an expert system operates is continually changing so that the expert system must also continually change. Some expert systems, especially large ones, are so complex that in a few years the maintenance costs equal the development costs. In the case of XCON (see Table 17.1), about 30 to 50 percent of the approximately 10,000 rules had to be changed each year.

Expert systems can be built by purchasing fully developed, off-the-shelf systems, by purchasing artificial intelligence shells, or by creating a custom system from scratch. Off-the-shelf expert systems have already incorporated the knowledge of experts into a full-function application. An example would be the Financial Advisor system, produced by Palladian Software, Inc., of Cambridge, Massachusetts. Financial Advisor helps executives analyze a proposed investment in a new plant, warehouse, or product, or examine the acquisition of another company. The system has captured the expertise of financial analysts in many corporations and made this knowledge base (set of rules) available to other corporations.

A second approach to expert systems is to build a new one using an artificial intelligence shell. A shell is a piece of software that uses a predetermined strategy and a limited, reasonably user-friendly language to develop small expert systems. With artificial intelligence shells, the user has to supply the knowledge to the system. This is very different from buying a fully developed off-the-shelf expert system. A good example of an expert system shell is M.1, manufactured by Teknowledge, Inc., of Palo Alto, California. This system operates on large microcomputers and is priced considerably less than the $100,000 to multimillion-dollar systems that operate on mainframes.

M.1, according to the manufacturer, is best suited to structured selection applications. Teknowledge defines such problems as those that a human expert can solve in less than 30 minutes, that do not involve extensive calculations, that can be solved through a telephone discussion with an expert, and that have only a few dozen conclusions to choose from.

In general, M.1 can be used to create "intelligent manuals" that clients can consult in a question-and-answer fashion. The demonstration disk of M.1's capabilities includes a wine adviser (which recommends what type of wine to serve with meals), a bank services adviser (which matches banking requirements with bank services), and a photography adviser (which uses information about environmental conditions to recommend which shutter speed and film type to use). Figure 17.9 illustrates how M.1 was used to diagnose a problem with a microcomputer monitor.

A third approach is to have a knowledge engineer custom-build an expert system. The knowledge engineer interviews the expert (or experts), develops the decision rules and knowledge frames, and builds the expert system. In building the system, the knowledge engineer may use a development tool such as an artificial intelligence shell or a programming language such as LISP, Prolog, or C. Only the largest corporations have the resources and internal expertise to build extensive custom-developed systems.

In the past, expert systems were primarily custom-built, running on expensive and specialized workstations that were optimized for executing LISP instructions. Today, most expert systems are developed using commercial AI shells, which typically are written in C or C++, so that they can run efficiently using inexpensive microcomputers or workstations and be compatible with the organization's existing systems (Hayes-Roth and Jacobstein, 1994).

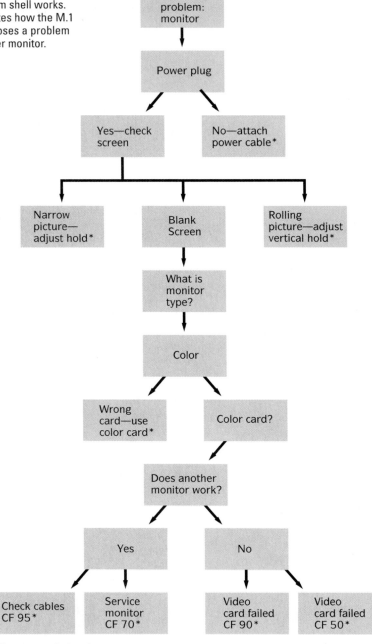

FIGURE 17.9
How an expert system shell works. This diagram illustrates how the M.1 expert system diagnoses a problem with a microcomputer monitor.

*Recommended action

PROBLEMS WITH EXPERT SYSTEMS

A thorough understanding of expert systems also requires awareness of their current limitations and problems.

Expert Systems Are Limited to Certain Problems

In answer to the question, "Why do some expert systems work?" critics point out that virtually all successful expert systems deal with problems of classification in which there are relatively few alternative outcomes and in which these possible outcomes are all known in advance. Contrary to early promises, expert systems do best

in automating lower-level clerical functions. Even in th
uations, however, expert systems require large, lengthy
efforts. For these kinds of problems, hiring or training i
pensive than building an expert system.

Important Theoretical Problems Exist

There are significant theoretical problems in knowledge
knowledge exists primarily in textbooks. There are no ad
deep causal models or temporal trends. No expert system,
textbook on information systems or engage in other creati
foreseen by system designers. Many experts cannot express t
IF–THEN format. Expert systems cannot yet replicate kno ...uge that is intuitive,
based on analogy and on a "sense of things."

Expert Systems Are Not Applicable to Complex Managerial Problems

The applicability of expert systems to complex managerial problems is currently highly limited. Many managerial problems generally involve drawing facts and interpretations from divergent sources, evaluating the facts, and comparing one interpretation of the facts with another, and do not involve analysis or simple classification. Expert systems cannot address complex problems requiring intuition to solve. Expert systems based on the prior knowledge of a few known alternatives are unsuitable for the problems managers face on a daily basis.

Expertise Is Collective

For many problems there are no single experts. Expertise may be distributed throughout an organization. Coordinating this expertise to formulate policies and actions is a key focus of management efforts. Expert systems cannot help here because they cannot synthesize knowledge from several different experts any better than ordinary systems analysis and design can.

Expert Systems Are Expensive to Maintain

The knowledge base of expert systems is fragile and brittle; they cannot learn or change over time. In fast-moving fields like medicine or the computer sciences, keeping the knowledge base up to date is a critical problem. For applications of even modest complexity, expert system code is generally hard to understand, debug, and maintain. Adding new rules to a large rule-based program nearly always requires revision of the control variables and conditions of earlier rules. Which of these entries to change to make the next rule work is often far from obvious.

A More Limited Role For Expert Systems

Although expert systems lack the robust and general intelligence of human beings, they can provide benefits to organizations if their limitations are well-understood. Expert systems have proved especially useful for certain types of diagnostic problems. They can provide electronic checklists for lower-level employees in service bureaucracies like banking, insurance, sales, and welfare agencies. Elements of expert system technology have been incorporated into a wide variety of products and services (Hayes-Roth and Jacobstein, 1994). (An example would be expert tax advice provided in popular financial planning and tax calculation software packages.) In limited areas, expert systems can help organizations make higher-quality decisions using fewer people.

CASE-BASED REASONING

Most expert systems work by applying a set of IF–THEN–ELSE rules against a knowledge base, both of which are extracted from human experts. For certain problems, such as service and product support for customers, systems employing case-based reasoning can be more useful. In **case-based reasoning (CBR)**, descriptions of past experiences of human specialists, represented as "cases," are stored in a database for later retrieval when the user encounters a new case with similar parameters. The system searches for stored cases similar to the new one, finds the closest fit, and applies the solutions of the old case to the new case. Successful solutions are tagged to the new case and both are stored together with the other cases in the knowledge base. Unsuccessful solutions are also appended to the case database along with explanations as to why the solutions didn't work (see Figure 17.10). Thus, in contrast to rule-based expert systems, the knowledge base for the case-based reasoning system is continuously expanded and refined by users.

For example, let us examine Compaq Computer of Houston, Texas, a company that operates in a highly competitive, customer service–oriented business environment and is flooded daily with customer phone calls crying for help. Keeping those customers satisfied requires Compaq to spend millions of dollars annually to maintain large, technically skilled, customer-support staffs. When customers call with problems, they first must describe the problem to the customer service staff, and then wait on hold while customer service transfers the call to an appropriate technician. The customer then describes the problem all over again while the technician tries to come up with an answer—all in all a most frustrating experience. To improve cus-

FIGURE 17.10
How case-based reasoning works. Case-based reasoning represents knowledge as a database of past cases and their solutions. The system uses a 6-step process to generate solutions to new problems encountered by the user.

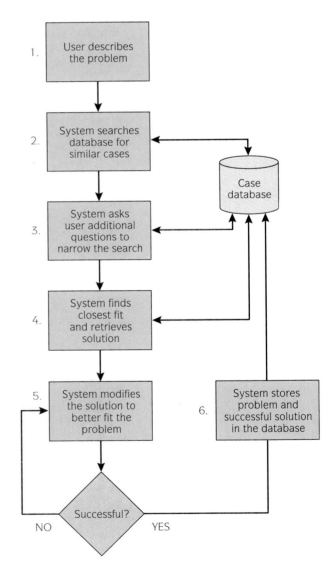

tomer service while at the same time reining in costs, Compaq began giving away case-based reasoning software to customers purchasing its Pagemarq printer and cut its customer-support staff. The software knowledge base is a series of several hundred actual cases of Pagemarq printer problems—actual war stories about smudged copies, printer memory problems, jammed printers, all the typical problems people face with laser printers. This knowledge base was developed by having trained CBR staff enter case descriptions in textual format into the CBR system. They entered certain key words necessary to categorize the problem (*smudge, smear, lines, streaks, paper jam*). They also entered a series of questions that might need to be asked to allow the software to further narrow the problem. Finally, solutions were attached to each case.

With the Compaq-supplied CBR system running on their computer, owners no longer need to call Compaq's service department. Instead they run the software and describe the problem to the software. The system swiftly searches actual cases, discarding unrelated ones, selecting related ones. If necessary to further narrow the search results, the software will ask the user for more information. In the end one or a few cases relevant to the specific problem are displayed, along with their solutions. Now, customers can solve most of their own problems quickly without even a telephone call while Compaq saves $10 million to $20 million annually in customer-support costs. For example, a woman with smudged output can bypass Compaq and instead run the software (stored on her own computer). It searches its knowledge base, usually identifying one or more relevant cases that suggest solutions (in this instance perhaps a specific part needs cleaning). The software then displays detailed pictures of the printer and the relevant printer parts so the user can fix the problem herself.

The Window on Management shows how another company, Loma Engineering, used CBR to cut its product development time while also reducing development costs.

17.3 OTHER INTELLIGENT TECHNIQUES

Clearly the pursuit of artificial intelligence will remain a persistent theme in the years ahead. While some considerable progress will be made in expert systems, the development of parallel processing at the hardware level—the idea of breaking up a problem into many small components and then processing each component simultaneously using hundreds or even thousands of computers operating in parallel—is likely to unleash a host of new possibilities. Subsequently, we review briefly the development of three intelligent computing techniques that are developing into major fields of business applications: neural networks, fuzzy logic, and genetic algorithms.

NEURAL NETWORKS

There has been an exciting resurgence of interest in bottom-up approaches to artificial intelligence in which machines are designed to imitate the physical thought process of the biological brain. Figure 17.11 shows two neurons from a leech's brain. The soma or nerve cell is at the center, and it acts like a switch, stimulating other neurons and being stimulated in turn. Emanating from the neuron is an axon, which is an electrically active link to the dendrites of other neurons. Axons and dendrites are the "wires" that electrically connect neurons to one another. The junction of the two is called a synapse. This simple biological model is the metaphor for the development of neural networks. **Neural networks** consist of hardware or software that attempts to emulate the processing patterns of the biological brain.

neural network Hardware or software that attempts to emulate the processing patterns of the biological brain.

The human brain has about 100 billion (10^{11}) neurons, each having about 1000 dendrites, which form 100,000 billion (10^{14}) synapses. The brain operates at about 100 hertz (each neuron can fire off a pulse 100 times per second)—very slow by computer standards where, for example, an Intel 80486 chip operates at up to 100 megahertz, or

ENABLING REUSE OF DESIGNS THROUGH ARTIFICIAL ENGINEERING

Inability of engineers to draw upon and reuse previous designs can be very costly and time-consuming, as the management of Loma Engineering realized in 1990. Loma Engineering Ltd. of Farnsborough, England, produces customized equipment used by pharmaceutical and food manufacturing companies to inspect their products during the production cycle. Loma's in-line inspection systems verify the quality, weight, count, and purity of food and drug products as they move along production lines. Such systems include metal detectors; check-weighers, which can weigh individual items or verify quantity in bulk packaging; and camera-based inspection equipment. These inspection machines cost from $10,000 to $20,000. Loma's systems can continuously assess product packages as they move through a production run and can reject a faulty product without stopping a line. Loma produces approximately $22.5 million in annual revenues for its parent company, Loma Group Plc., and employs 200 workers in factories in Germany, France, and the Netherlands.

The problem Loma management faced was the cost and time needed to customize and individualize every piece of equipment the company sold. Every piece must be designed to the individual customer's specifications. Not only does each food and drug product require individual approaches to testing, but the equipment also needs to be customized according to the product safety laws and electrical requirements of the country of purchase. Despite the fact that most machines were very similar to previously produced pieces of equipment, Loma engineers were custom-designing each item essentially from scratch.

Management knew that the engineers could save a great deal of time, and thereby reduce costs, if they were able to reuse previous designs by modifying them to fit the newly ordered products rather than to design each item from scratch. The issue was the engineers' ability to locate existing designs of similar products. As Mark

Rawet, Loma's Engineering group marketing manager, put it, "The only way we could reuse designs would be if an engineer could remember and trace a similar job—quite a task given that thousands of units are produced in our Farnsborough factory each year." Engineers needed to find a way to store past designs on the computer and then be guided through those designs to find one that had identical or very similar specifications to the current order. Management believed that such a computer program would result in a major reduction in engineering time and costs.

Rawet says that Loma began by looking at traditional databases in order to store the designs. However, none existed that would allow the engineers to input new product requirements and find the related, existing designs. With traditional databases, the engineers would still need to know which designs to look at. Ultimately, Loma turned to CBR Express, case-based reasoning software from Inference Corp. of El Segundo, California. Loma's database consists of experiences of product configurations over time. The engineer can then enter parameters for the new Loma product being ordered (a new case) and the system will seek out similar cases, locating the closest fits by asking questions as needed to help it in its task. At each stage of questioning, the system lists a number of likely configurations and the probability of the configuration being the right one. As more specifications are fed in, the list changes. When a match or matches (identical or very similar designs) are located, the engineer can use it (them) as the basis for the design of the newly ordered product. New cases (designs) are appended to the database for future use. Loma put about 1000 cases, representing all of its core products, onto the system during the first year of system operation.

The case-based reasoning application, which cost $15,000 to $20,000, has been a success for Loma. For example, Loma used to require 12 to 14 weeks to produce a Loma 6000 check-weigher product. Using the case-based reasoning software, Loma has cut two

to three weeks from that time. It combined this savings with factory automation improvements to reduce overall production time to four to six weeks.

> **To Think About:** How did using case-based reasoning technology support Loma's business strategy? How did it change the way Loma conducted its business? What organizational and management problems would Loma likely have faced when it adapted CBR Express for such a central function?

Before CBR Express was installed and populated with cases, 100 percent of new Loma orders had to go through the engineering department, but now only 25 percent of new orders require an engineer to design it. Loma engineers expect that number to drop even further over time, as more cases are added to the system.

The system has pleased Loma management in other ways also. While it took a year to get the system fully operative, the company actually began benefiting from it after only three months. The system was cost-justified based on a 12-month payback period, but payback came much quicker than that. One reason for the rapid payback is that by reducing design time, CBR Express has allowed Loma to speed up production without increasing the number of workers, thus significantly enhancing worker productivity. One word of warning from Loma, however. Inference Corp. has also proven to be a good partner for Loma because Inference does about one third of its business in Europe and so has a strong presence there. Nicki Davis, a Loma support engineer, says that "Before embarking on building the system, you have to very carefully think through what you are trying to achieve and make sure the questions [the software asks] are structured in the right way."

Source: Connie Winkler, "Redrawing Design Process Cuts Repetition at Loma," *Software Magazine,* April 1994.

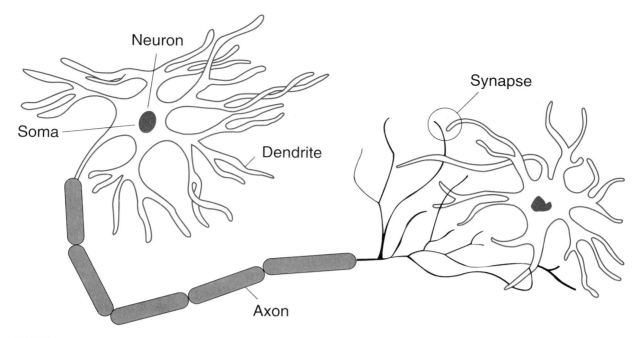

FIGURE 17.11
Biological neurons of a leech. Simple biological models, like the neurons of a leech, have influenced the development of artificial or computational neural networks in which the biological cells are replaced by transistors or entire processors. *Source: Defense Advance Research Projects Agency (DARPA), 1988. Unclassified. Hereinafter "DARPA, 1988."*

millions of cycles per second, executing one instruction at a time. But the brain's neurons operate in parallel, and the human brain can accomplish about 10^{16} or 10 million billion interconnections per second. This far exceeds the capacity of any known machine, or any machine now planned or ever likely to be built with current technology. The human brain weighs three pounds and occupies about .15 square meters. You can think of the brain as several score supercomputers on your shoulder and then some.

No technology known now can come close to these capabilities. But elementary neuron circuits can be built and studied, and far more complex networks of neurons have been simulated on computers. Figure 17.12 shows an artificial neural network with two neurons. The resistors in the circuits are variable and can be used to "teach" the network. When the network makes a mistake (i.e., chooses the wrong pathway through the network and arrives at a false conclusion), resistance can be raised on some circuits, forcing other neurons to fire. If this learning process continues for

FIGURE 17.12
Artificial neural network with two neurons. In artificial neurons, the biological neurons become processing elements (switches), the axons and dendrites become wires, and the synapses become variable resistors that carry weighted inputs (currents) that represent data. *Source: DARPA, 1988.*

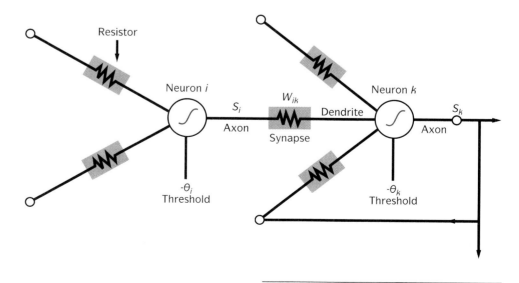

thousands of cycles, the machine "learns" the correct response. Neural networks can be "taught" by finding a pattern of connections which allows the network to carry out a desired computation.

One feature that distinguishes neural networks from digital computers is the inherent parallelism: The simple neurons or switches are highly interconnected and operate in parallel. Instead of a single personal computer executing a single instruction at a time, imagine 64,000 personal computers all connected to one another and all working simultaneously on parts of the same problem. A neural network computer can be defined, then, as an interconnected set of parallel switches or processors for which the network can be controlled by intervention. Neural networks are very different from expert systems, where human expertise has to be modeled with rules and frames. In neural networks, the physical machine emulates a human brain and can be taught from experience.

The Difference between Neural Networks and Expert Systems

What is different about neural networks? Several answers can now be given. First, expert systems, like most traditional systems, seek to emulate or model a human expert's way of solving a set of problems. The knowledge engineer observes humans, builds a model of their expertise, and then writes a computer program or algorithm that implements the model. The program incorporates specific rules which are derived from human experts and their experiences in a limited problem domain. The resulting expert system is optimized to perform a single task for which it was designed.

Neural networks, so their builders claim, do not model human intelligence, do not program solutions, do not use knowledge engineers, and do not aim to solve specific problems per se. Instead of putting intelligence into programs, neural network designers seek to put the intelligence into the hardware in the form of a generalized capability to learn. The idea is to build machines that solve entire classes of problems.

Take a simple problem like identifying a cat. An expert system approach (Figure 17.13A) would interview many people to understand how humans recognize cats. This would result in a large set of rules, or frames, programmed into an expert system. A television camera connected to the system would scan shapes in the environment, and the system would analyze the signals against the rule base of the system. After scanning a few thousand rules, one at a time, the system would label each perceived object as either a cat or not a cat.

In contrast, a trainable neural network (Figure 17.13B) would be brought to the test site, connected to the television, and started out on the process of learning. Every time a cat was not correctly perceived, the system's interconnections would be adjusted. When cats were correctly perceived, the system would be left alone and another object scanned.

Although the most powerful neural network machine today can only approximate the thinking ability of a bee or a cockroach, useful neural network applications are being developed. Because of the way neural nets "learn," they can identify complex relationships and patterns, and are appropriate for making classifications, generalizations, or decisions in cases where less than 100 percent accuracy can be tolerated.

Neural network applications are emerging in medicine, science, and business to address problems in pattern classification, prediction and financial analysis, and control and optimization (Widrow, Rumelhart, and Lehr, 1994). Neural networks are now being used to analyze the results of pap smear tests that detect cervical cancer. Until recently, pap smear analysis relied solely on a visual examination of every smear to find abnormal cells. The technician uses a microscope to search each smear for the telltale abnormal cells that indicate cancer or a precancerous condition. Most smears will be negative (contain only healthy cells), indicating the absence of cancer. However, each smear might contain up to 500,000 cells, and only a tiny percentage of the cells might be abnormal, making it very difficult to locate them. Manually searching the cells is a slow, tedious, and inexact process. Estimates are that 30 to 50

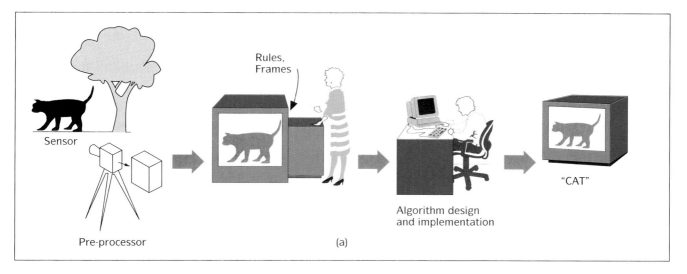

FIGURE 17.13A
An expert system approach. The expert system would rely upon a large set of rules or frames as the knowledge base for identifying a cat. Using the rules, the system would analyze the information gathered or data supplied by a television camera scanning signals to determine the classification of the scanned image.

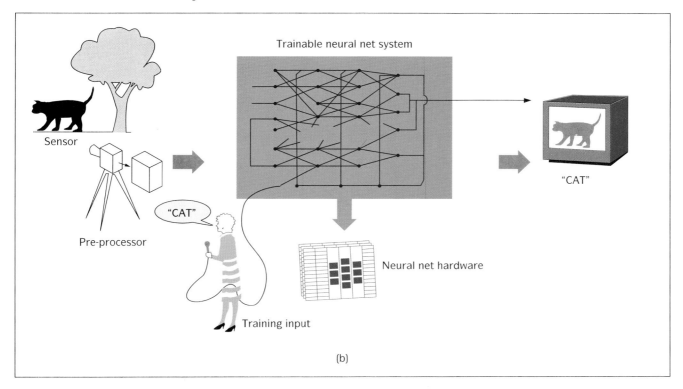

FIGURE 17.13B
A neural network approach. Without an established rule base to rely on, the trainable neural network will start out on the process of learning based on the scanned images provided. Interconnections are adjusted when the images are correctly perceived, resulting in a "learning process."

percent of all positive smears (those containing abnormal cells) are falsely rated negative—that is, the cancerous condition is not identified and treated in 30 to 50 percent of the cases.

Neural network technology has been used to develop a system that reduces the error rate to about 3 percent. Papnet by Neuromedical Systems Inc. of Suffern, New York, examines all the cells in the smear and selects the 128 most abnormal cells for display on the monitor. The technician then reviews the selected cells and has the software mark and record any that are deemed to be truly abnormal. Using this system, the technician requires less than one-fifth the time to examine a smear while achieving perhaps ten times the accuracy of the existing manual methods. Papnet was shown thousands of both normal and abnormal cells, in many different positions, even touching and over-lapping, as they would be in real life. Many different color stains were used. When Papnet improperly identified a cell, the system was corrected, and in this way it slowly

Because they can identify complex relation-ships and patterns in vast quantities of data, neural networks are starting to be used for eval-uating certain cancer screening tests and for stock picking.

learned to distinguish between normal and abnormal. Papnet's accuracy has been verified through studies done at Montefiore Medical Center in the Bronx, New York.

The Window on Technology illustrates that neural network applications are also now being used by the financial investment industry to discern patterns in vast pools of data that might help investment firms predict the performance of equities, corporate bond ratings, or corporate bankruptcies (Lin, 1993). In another example, Mellon Bank in Pittsburgh, Pennsylvania, is using a neural network to help detect credit-card fraud. The network was taught to recognize irregular patterns in charge-card purchases and to evaluate potentially fraudulent transactions.

Japanese firms are using neural networks in prediction of securities ratings, timing of stock buying and selling, prediction of future yield of securities, inspection of flaws in steel plate, classification of welding defects, sound analysis, and identification of parts on a lens production line (Asakawa and Takagi, 1994). Eastman Kodak Corporation and other companies are using Process Insights, a neural network process control software package, to reduce waste, improve product quality, and increase plant throughput. Neural networks are being used to perform sensitivity studies, determine process set points, detect faults, and predict process performance. Plants owned by Fujitsu Ltd. and Nippon Steel Corporation are using a neural control system to detect "breakout" (when imperfect control allows spillage of molten steel) before it occurs, so that corrective measures can be taken. The system has reduced costs by several million dollars a year.

Unlike expert systems, which typically can provide explanations for their solutions, neural networks cannot always explain why they arrived at a particular solution. Moreover, neural nets cannot always guarantee a completely certain solution, always arrive at the same solution again with the same input data, or always guarantee the "best" solution (Trippi and Turban, 1989–1990). However, these examples suggest that in most current applications, neural networks are best used as aids to human decision makers instead of substitutes for them.

Building Neural Networks

While neural networks now promise a great deal, the available tools are quite primitive by biological standards. Basically, there are two approaches to building neural networks. In one approach, specialized machines are hardwired in the form of neural network computing machines. The resulting systems are expensive, experimental, and largely confined to laboratories, although some are just now appearing commercially. A second and much less expensive approach is to use special software to simulate a neural network on a traditional computer. While a traditional computer will not have a parallel machine capability, and processing will be slower, to some extent this can be compensated for by using high-speed machines.

The power of neural network machines is measured differently from standard machines, where storage is measured in bytes of RAM memory and speed is measured in MIPS (millions of instructions per second). In neural machines, storage is measured in terms of capacity, which is measured in terms of the total number of interconnects between neurons. Speed is measured in terms of the total number of interconnects that can take place per second. Figure 17.14 compares the power of some available neural network simulators to the power of common biological brains.

There remains a considerable gap between available machine power and, say, the processing capabilities of higher-order animals like dogs and cats, or even humans. Special-purpose neural network chips specifically designed to operate as neural nets (as opposed to simulating neural nets with software) will rapidly advance the state of the art. Despite these advances, the most powerful dedicated neural network machines today equal the thinking ability of a fly or at best a cockroach. Several orders of magnitude of enhancements in neural network technology are required to produce high levels of intelligence. Nevertheless, even at this level, the pattern-recognition power of neural networks is starting to provide benefits to organizations.

THE NEURAL NETWORK APPROACH TO STOCK PICKING

How effective are neural networks in picking stocks for investment? This is a question that those who work in the field of financial investments can no longer avoid. Neural networks are starting to be used to select stocks, and their promoters claim great success.

A leading proponent of neural networks for stock selection is Arthur Lipper III, the founder of Arthur Lipper Corporation and the weekly Lipper Mutual Fund Performance Analysis (MFPA). He has long been a Wall Street innovator. MFPA, which measures and compares the performance of mutual funds for the professional investment community, was founded in 1967, well before any other such service. Lipper's latest innovation is ATHENA, a neural network system that he says predicts the "year-ahead, total return performance of individual stocks with great accuracy, using only known financial data." While no public, real-life performance data has yet been made available, Lipper claims that in tests of ATHENA, it has produced returns that are 200 percent over the average performance of common stocks in the stock market, as measured by Standard & Poor's 500 Index (a collection of 500 stocks chosen to represent the entire stock market). This performance is far beyond the gains of any existing mutual fund. The Fidelity Disciplined Equity described below, for example, has only outperformed the same index by about 3.5 percent over the seven years of its existence.

ATHENA examines the financial and market data of only about 2000 stocks because Lipper has not used any stocks with market capitalization of less than $1 billion. His rationale is that these typically are higher-than-average-quality companies, making his stock selection less risky. He is attempting to develop a neural network system for smaller companies as well and also one

for international stock management. Asked to explain how his system works, he merely says that it "correlates vast amounts of data in search of answers." He says the system processes each stock through "more than 30,000 combinations and calculations each month to produce the year-ahead total return performance rankings." He adds that "No human being can cope with the vast quantities of data a neural network processes." He points out that whereas expert systems can only examine data in ways defined in rules by human experts, neural networks are nonlinear. They will test all possible combinations of the data elements to determine which combinations have had predictive significance in the past. Therefore, he says, "In the case of a neural network, we have no way of knowing precisely which combinations of data items were indicative of a specific result. In other words, he does not know how the stocks are selected. As an example he offers the fact that the system ranked IBM highly in October 1993 but not in September 1993 or February 1994. But, he says, "An 82% probability exists, based on the system's record, that by October 1994, IBM will be in the top 20% of the stocks in the 700-company universe of October 1993." The stock did rise in that period, from 45 1/2 to 65 1/4, a gain of 43 percent. The S&P 500 in the same period was up less than one percent. The investment industry is waiting with real interest to see if ATHENA can actually produce returns of this type in real-time use rather than through back testing.

Another user of neural networks allows us to see just how one manager selects stocks with the help of a neural network. In the five years ending in 1993, only 13 mutual funds had outperformed the stock market as a whole for five years in a row. And, as of October 1994, only two of those were outperforming the market through three-fourths of the sixth year. One of

those two very elite funds, Fidelity Disciplined Equity, is managed by Brad Lewis, who uses a neural network to help him pick his stocks. Lewis is a

> **To Think About:** What do you consider to be the strengths of using neural networks for investment? The weaknesses? How would you go about using this technology to aid you in making investment decisions, and why? How much can neural network technology change the business of mutual funds?

graduate of the U.S. Naval Academy and a helicopter pilot who became what he himself calls a computer nerd. Now he manages three Fidelity mutual funds, including Small Cap and Stock Selector, spending nearly half his time programming his computer to select stocks.

Lewis' system, which runs on a 90-megahertz desktop computer, also uses massive amounts of data to select stocks. Disciplined Equity attempts to mirror the S&P 500 stock index in terms of the industry weightings of that index, but Lewis' goal is to outperform the index every year and hopefully every quarter. Lewis is very clear that his neural network is only part of his system for stock selection. The selection process starts every Friday afternoon when his desktop starts processing the data on 2800 stocks. It works the whole weekend in order to produce the expected return of those stocks over the following nine months. The data it examines includes a wide range of data, such as the stocks' price-earnings ratio for the next twelve months, the price-to-book ratio, insider buys and sells, and economic environment factors such as the yield curve and industrial production rates-of-change. He offers as an example the possibility that the neural network system might find that over the past ten years General Electric is "a buy when the yield curve is accelerating upward." The analyst may not have thought of this relationship and so would not be looking for it using any other system. However, the neural network will find it if it is there. "The neural net learns very fast how a lot of variables combine to affect a stock's price," he points out. Once the system determines the complex set of factors that has affected a stock's price during the past ten years, the analyst can assume that these factors remain relevant for the next year or two. He adds, however, that one key issue is how far back one can go in the data and still be valid. For example, the factors that moved IBM stock in 1958 don't apply now because IBM has become an entirely different company.

When the weekend run is completed, Lewis has a recommendation as to what stocks to buy and what to sell. He does not know why the computer makes specific recommendations, only that they work in most environments. Lewis does not just follow the recommendation of the neural network. He first must go through several other steps. The data is run through an optimizer he also developed to create an optimum portfolio. He must manage his industry risk carefully. If he let the

computer run amok, it would pick 50 tiny small-company stocks, which carry more risk than a portfolio that also includes large companies. The optimizer actually places constraints on stock selection that Lewis builds in order to make certain his portfolio approximately reflects the industry balance of the S&P 500 itself. He has programmed in other rules as well. For example, he does not want to hold more than one day's average trading volume of a stock so that he can get out quickly without affecting the market. A third program then takes the list put out by the optimizer and compares it to the current holdings of his portfolio. It makes sure, for example, that he does not end up with more shares of a specific stock than planned because he already holds so many shares of that stock. It also checks other factors such as the volatility of the stocks.

Asked if he countermands the computer and makes subjective decisions about buying and selling, Lewis answers that he used to do so a lot. But as he has gained experience with the system and became more confident about its results, he has come to trust it and so makes subjective decisions only rarely. Lewis also points out that he

uses the same neural network to select stocks for the other two funds he manages. The differences between the three funds are in their stated goals. To accommodate these differences, he has written separate optimizers for each of the three funds.

Lewis also notes that there are factors that affect stock performance that the computer can't identify. The price of certain types of stocks can be driven up when investing themes or fads sweep into the market. For instance, in the fall of 1993 the hype surrounding the information superhighway drove up prices of telecommunications stocks. Lewis' neural network shunned many fast-rising telecommunications stocks because their prices were high relative to other measures such as their earnings and Lewis had programmed the computer to discard stocks that were too expensive. The performance of the fund at that time suffered relative to many of its peers by not owning them.

Sources: Fred W. Frailey, "Brad Lewis," *Kiplinger's Personal Finance Magazine,* October 1994; Arthur Lipper III, "Using Science to Manage Investments," *AI in Finance,* Premier Issue 1994; and *Fidelity Disciplined Equity Fund Semiannual Report,* April 30, 1994.

FIGURE 17.14
Computational capabilities of neural and biological networks. The shaded area shows the range of speeds and storage capacities of neural networks in relation to those of biological networks. Neural networks, although powerful, only have the computational power of a fly's brain.

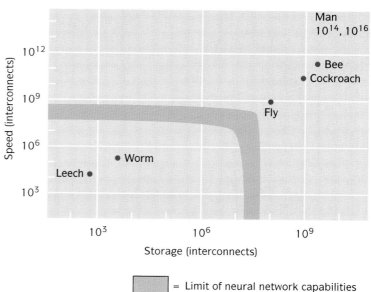

FUZZY LOGIC

Traditional computer programs require precision—on/off, yes/no, right/wrong. However, we human beings do not experience the world this way. We might all agree that 120° is hot, and 40° is cold, but is 75° hot, warm, comfortable, or cool? The answer depends on many factors—the wind, the humidity, the individual experiencing the temperature, one's clothing, one's expectations. Many of our activities are also inexact. Tractor-trailer drivers would find it nearly impossible to back their rig into a space precisely specified to less than an inch on all sides. Fuzzy logic, a relatively new, rule-based development in AI, tolerates imprecision and even uses it to solve problems we could not have solved before. **Fuzzy logic** consists of a variety of concepts and techniques for representing and inferring knowledge that is imprecise, uncertain, or unreliable. Fuzzy logic can create rules that use approximate or subjective values and incomplete or ambiguous data. By expressing logic with some carefully defined imprecision, fuzzy logic is closer to the way people actually think than traditional IF—THEN rules.

Ford Motor Co. has developed a fuzzy logic application that backs a simulated tractor-trailer into a parking space. The application uses the following three rules:

IF the truck is *near* jackknifing, THEN *reduce* the steering angle;

IF the truck is *far away* from the dock, THEN steer *toward* the dock;

IF the truck is *near* the dock, THEN point the trailer *directly at* the dock.

The following set of fuzzy logic rules control interest rates; they were developed by Lotfi Zadeh of the University of California at Berkeley (widely regarded as the founder of fuzzy logic programming):

Increase interest rates *slightly* IF unemployment is *low* AND inflation is *moderate;*

Increase interest rates *sharply* IF unemployment is *low* AND inflation is *moderate* BUT rising *sharply;*

Decrease interest rates *slightly* IF unemployment is *low* BUT increasing AND inflation rate is *low* and *stable.*

This logic makes sense to us as human beings, for it represents how we think as we back that truck into its berth or make economic decisions.

How does the computer make sense of this programming? The answer is relatively simple. The terms (known as *membership functions*) are imprecisely defined so that, for example, in Figure 17.15 *cool* is between 50° and 70°, although the temperature is most clearly cool between about 60° and 67°. Note that cool is overlapped by *cold* and *norm.* To control the room environment using this logic, the programmer would develop similarly imprecise definitions for humidity and other factors such as outdoor wind and temperature. The rules might include one that says *If the temperature is cool or cold and the humidity is low while the outdoor wind is high and the outdoor temperature is low, raise the heat and humidity in the room.* The computer would combine the membership function readings in a weighted manner and, using all the rules, raise and lower the temperature and humidity.

Fuzzy logic is widely used in Japan for home applicances such as refrigerators, vacuum cleaners, washers, dryers, rice cookers, and air conditioners, and is gaining popularity in the United States. Its popularity has occurred partially because managers find they can use it to reduce costs and shorten development time. Fuzzy logic code requires few IF–THEN rules, making it simpler than traditional code. The control rules required in the trucking example above, plus its term definitions, might require hundreds of IF–THEN statements to implement in traditional logic. Rockwell International uses fuzzy logic to control motor idling because the logic is able to reduce system implementation time by a factor of ten. Compact code requires less computer capacity, allowing Sanyo Fisher USA to implement camcorder controls for auto focusing and image stabilization without adding expensive memory to its product.

fuzzy logic Rule-based AI that tolerates imprecision by using nonspecific terms called membership functions to solve problems.

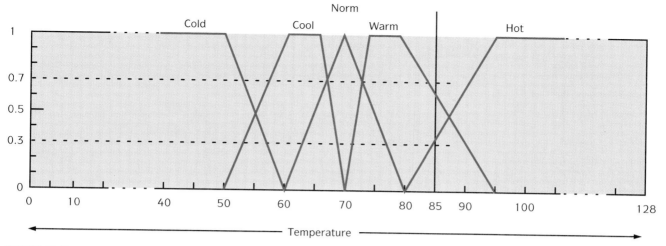

FIGURE 17.15
Implementing fuzzy logic rules in hardware. The membership functions for the input called temperature are in the logic of the thermostat to control the room temperature. Membership functions help translate linguistic expressions such as "warm" into numbers that can be manipulated by the computer. *Source: James M. Sibigtroth, "Implementing Fuzzy Expert Rules in Hardware," AI Expert, April 1992. © 1992 Miller Freeman., Inc.*

Fuzzy logic is especially suitable for complex problems or applications that involve descriptive or intuitive thinking.

Fuzzy logic also allows us to solve problems not previously solvable, thus improving product quality. In Japan, Sendai's subway system uses fuzzy logic controls to accelerate so smoothly that standing passengers need not hold on. Mitsubishi Heavy Industries in Tokyo has been able to reduce the power consumption of its air-conditioners by 20 percent through implementing control programs in fuzzy logic. NASA space shuttle flights in 1992 and 1993 used fuzzy logic–based temperature control devices. Table 17.3 lists some of the major application areas for fuzzy systems.

Auto-focusing camcorders employ a focus algorithm based on fuzzy logic. The camera examines three focus points and then uses fuzzy logic to determine the one spot that has the highest probability of being the main subject.

Table 17.3	A Partial List of Application Areas of Fuzzy Systems

Transportation
(subways, helicopters, elevators, traffic control, and air control for highway tunnels)

Automobiles
(engines, brakes, transmissions, cruise control systems)

Consumer electronics
(washing machines, driers, refrigerators, vacuum cleaners, rice cookers, televisions, VCRs, air conditioners, kerosene fan heaters, microwave ovens, shower systems, video cameras)

Robotics

Computers

Telecommunications

Other Industries
(steel, chemical, power generation, construction, nuclear, aerospace)

Engineering
(electrical, mechanical, civil, environmental, geophysics)

Safety/Maintenance

Agriculture

Medicine

Management
(credit evaluation, damage/risk assessment, stock picking, marketing analysis, production management, scheduling, decision-support systems)

Education (CAI)

Source: From "Fuzzy Systems: An Overview by Toshinori Munakata and Yashvant Jani, *Communications of the ACM*, March 1994, Vol. 37, No. 3, p. 71. Reprinted by permission.

Management has also found fuzzy logic useful for decision making and organizational control. A Wall Street firm had a system developed that selects companies for potential acquisition, using the language stock traders understand. (According to financial analysts, the rules for trading are "fuzzy.") Along similar lines, Japanese experts developed the Yamaichi Fuzzy Fund, a trading system that handles 65 industries and a majority of stocks listed on the Nikkei index (Munakata and Jani, 1994). Recently a fuzzy logic system has been developed to detect possible fraud in medical claims submitted by health-care providers anywhere in the United States.

Fuzzy logic applications have their own limitations. They cannot "learn." It is not always easy to define good membership functions and fuzzy rules. (To overcome these limitations, Japanese developers are starting to create hybrid systems that meld fuzzy logic and neural network technology.) Questions such as why a particular fuzzy system needs so many rules or when a fuzzy systems builder should stop adding rules are not easily answered. Validation and verification of fuzzy systems require extensive testing (Munakata and Jani, 1994). Nevertheless, fuzzy logic technology is making important contributions in artificial intelligence applications.

GENETIC ALGORITHMS

genetic algorithms Problem-solving methods that promote the evolution of solutions to specified problems using the model of living organisms adapting to their environment.

Genetic algorithms (also referred to as adaptive computation) refer to a variety of problem-solving methods that are conceptually based on the method that living organisms use to adapt to their environment—the process of evolution. Genetic algorithms promote the "evolution" of solutions to particular problems. The genetic algorithm itself controls the generation, variation, adaptation, and selection of possible problem solutions using genetically based processes such as reproduction of solutions based on fitness, crossover of "genes," and mutation for random change of "genes." As solutions alter and combine, the worst ones are discarded and the better ones survive to go on and produce even better solutions. The genetic algorithms "breed" programs that solve problems even when no person can fully understand their structure (Holland, 1992).

Genetic algorithms originated in the work of John H. Holland, a professor of psychology and computer science at the University of Michigan. Holland was impressed by the adaptive capabilities of living organisms to solve problems posed by their environment. He developed a programming technique that worked the way populations solve problems by changing and reorganizing their component parts using processes such as reproduction, mutation, and natural selection. Holland devised a "genetic code" of binary digits that could be used to represent any type of computer program with a one representing true and a zero representing false. Each of the binary digits is tied to the triggering of a specific action in the computer program that the string is meant to represent, just as bits of genetic material trigger certain actions in the organisms they represent. With a long enough string of digits, any object can be represented by the right combination of digits and thus any computer program which performs the combination of actions needed to arrive at a desired solution can be represented in this manner.

The genetic algorithm provides methods for searching all possible combinations of digits to identify the right string representing the best possible structure for the problem. In one method, one first randomly generates a population of strings consisting of combinations of binary digits. Each string corresponds to one of the variables in the problem. One then applies a test for fitness, ranking the strings in the population according to their level of desirability as possible solutions. Once the initial population is evaluated for fitness, the algorithm then produces the next generation of strings (consisting of strings that survived the fitness test plus offspring strings produced from mating pairs of strings) and tests their fitness. The process continues until a solution is reached (see Figure 17.16).

Solutions to certain types of problems in areas of optimization, product design, and the monitoring of industrial systems are especially appropriate for genetic algorithms. Many business problems require optimization because they deal with issues such as minimization of costs, maximization of profits, most efficient scheduling, and use of resources. Proven algorithms have already been developed for such problems when there are only a few variables to consider. But many situations are a great deal more dynamic and complex, involving hundreds of variables or hundreds of formulas. Genetic algorithms are suitable for solving such problems because they can attack a solution from many directions at once.

Like neural networks, genetic algorithms are ideal applications for massively parallel computers. Each processor can be assigned a single string, with the algorithm focusing on a single string when performing a fitness test or on a pair of strings when generating a crossover. The entire population of a genetic algorithm can be processed in parallel, offering growing potential for solving problems of enormous complexity.

Commercial applications of genetic algorithms are emerging. Engineers at General Electric use a genetic algorithm to help them design jet turbine aircraft engines, a complex problem involving about 100 variables and 50 constraint equations. The engineers evaluate design changes on a workstation that runs a simulation of the engine in operation. Because each design change requires a new simulation to test its effectiveness, the designers can spend weeks on solutions that may or may not be optimal. Using an expert system reduced the time to produce a satisfactory design from several weeks to several days. However, the expert system would produce solutions only up to a point. Further improvements then required simultaneous changes in large numbers of variables. At that point GE introduced a genetic algorithm. The genetic algorithm took an initial population of designs produced by the expert system and generated a design that contained three times the number of improvements over the best previous version in a period of only two days.

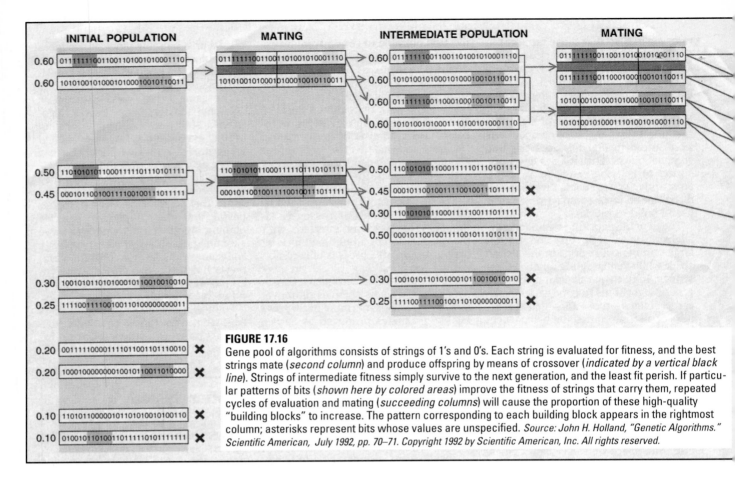

FIGURE 17.16
Gene pool of algorithms consists of strings of 1's and 0's. Each string is evaluated for fitness, and the best strings mate (*second column*) and produce offspring by means of crossover (*indicated by a vertical black line*). Strings of intermediate fitness simply survive to the next generation, and the least fit perish. If particular patterns of bits (*shown here by colored areas*) improve the fitness of strings that carry them, repeated cycles of evaluation and mating (*succeeding columns*) will cause the proportion of these high-quality "building blocks" to increase. The pattern corresponding to each building block appears in the rightmost column; asterisks represent bits whose values are unspecified. *Source: John H. Holland, "Genetic Algorithms." Scientific American, July 1992, pp. 70–71. Copyright 1992 by Scientific American, Inc. All rights reserved.*

Researcher David Goldberg at the University of Illinois developed a genetic algorithm that learned how to control a gas pipeline system modeled on the system that carries natural gas from the Southwest to the Northeast United States. This system features a network of pipelines with many branches, compressors to adjust the pressure in individual branches, and valves to regulate gas flow into storage tanks. Goldberg's genetic algorithm produced a system that was more cost efficient in delivering gas to meet demand in all appropriate areas than the system that was in use. Other organizations using genetic algorithms include the Coors Brewing Company, which uses genetic algorithms for scheduling the fulfillment and shipment of orders, and the U.S. Navy, which uses genetic algorithms for scheduling F-16 tryouts (Burtka, 1993).

WHY ARE THESE TECHNOLOGIES INTELLIGENT?

Assessing the intelligence of machines is no different than assessing the intelligence of people. Intelligence is in the eye of the beholder and reflects the culture and *Zeitgeist,* or spirit, of every age. Artificial intelligence applications can exhibit so much power, in the sense of mastery over an environment, that they assume in the eyes of many the quality of "intelligence," a quality normally reserved for humans.

But we must remember always that we use this word *intelligence* only metaphorically. These machines are not human. There is a difference between a "model" of human knowledge and human knowledge itself. Economists who "model" the economy never claim that their models "are" the economy. While the human brain is "just a machine" and potentially understandable, as is any machine, the human brain nevertheless is a very special kind of machine, and not much progress has been made in understanding it.

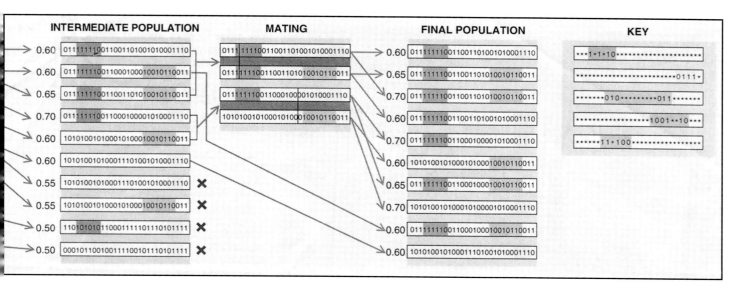

| INTERMEDIATE POPULATION | MATING | FINAL POPULATION | KEY |

In this light, artificial intelligence applications are programmed reflections of human intelligence, artifacts of humans, presumably under our control. And it is well to remember their limitations.

WHY BUSINESS SHOULD BE INTERESTED IN ARTIFICIAL INTELLIGENCE

Given the experimental nature and high costs of artificial intelligence systems, why should businesses be interested in them at this point? The most important reasons are the following:

- To capture and preserve expertise that might be lost through the retirement, resignation, or death of an acknowledged expert.

- To enhance the distribution of knowledge in an organization. Storing information in an active form creates an organizational knowledge base that many employees can examine, much like an electronic textbook or manual, so that others may learn rules of thumb not found in textbooks.

- To create a mechanism that is not subject to human feelings like fatigue and worry. This may be especially useful when jobs may be environmentally, physically, or mentally dangerous to humans. These systems may also be useful advisers in times of crisis.

- To eliminate routine and unsatisfying jobs that are currently held by human beings.

- To provide solutions to problems that are too complex to be handled by humans.

- To maintain the strategic position of a company in an industry. Expert systems, like other systems, can be used as a marketing device, to reduce the cost of production or to improve existing product lines.

All of these contributions of artificial intelligence have potential strategic importance. Clearly, most progress in artificial intelligence of direct relevance to general business has been made in expert systems, but neural systems are rapidly developing more powerful applications than expert systems.

Management Challenges

1. Creating robust expert systems. Expert systems must be changed every time there is a change in the organizational environment. Every time there is a change in the rules used by experts, they have to be reprogrammed. It is difficult to provide expert systems with the flexibility of human experts.

2. Creating cost-effective expert systems. Many thousands of businesses have undertaken experimental projects in expert systems, but only a small percentage have created expert systems that are actually used on a production basis. We have already described the problems of building and maintaining expert systems and the limitations of expert system applications. In many cases, expert systems that would be genuinely useful in business settings cannot be cost-justified.

3. Determining appropriate applications for artificial intelligence. Finding suitable applications for artificial intelligence techniques is not so easy. Some parts of business processes are rule based, others based on patterns, and still others based on exhaustive searching of manual files for the "needle in the haystack." Identifying the business process, identifying the right technique, and determining how to build the system require a focused effort.

Summary

1. Define artificial intelligence. Artificial intelligence is the development of computer-based systems that behave like humans. There are five members of the artificial intelligence family: natural language, robotics, perceptive systems, expert systems, and "intelligent" machines. The field of artificial intelligence is controversial because of disagreements about theory, practical worth, and social consequences.

2. Describe how artificial intelligent techniques evolved. Artificial intelligence has two main thrusts. The bottom-up approach attempts to mimic the physical human brain at the machine level. Norbert Weiner's "feedback" machines, Frank Rosenblatt's Perceptron, and contemporary neural network computers are based on this approach. The top-down approach attempts to represent human knowledge through logic. Newell and Simon's Logic Theorist and General Problem Solver and contemporary expert systems are the leading examples of this school of thought.

3. Define an expert system and explain how it works. Expert systems are knowledge-intensive computer programs that solve problems that heretofore required human expertise. The systems embody human knowledge using rules, frames, or concepts. Expert systems have four components: the knowledge base, the development team, the AI shell, and the user. The knowledge base can be represented using rules, semantic nets, or frames. The

strategy to search through the knowledge base, called the inference engine, can use either forward or backward chaining. Developing expert systems requires the use of prototyping and special knowledge engineers to elicit knowledge from the organization's experts.

4. Define neural networks and show how they are used in business. Neural networks consist of hardware and software that attempt to mimic the thought processes of the human physical brain. Neural networks are notable for their ability to "learn" without programming and to recognize patterns that cannot be easily described by humans. They are being used in science, medicine, and business primarily to discriminate patterns in massive amounts of data.

5. Identify other intelligent techniques. Other examples of machine intelligence include fuzzy logic and genetic algorithms. Fuzzy logic is a software technology that expresses logic with some carefully defined imprecision so that it is closer to the way people actually think than traditional IF–THEN rules. Fuzzy logic has been used for controlling physical devices and is starting to be used for limited decision-making applications. Genetic algorithms develop solutions to particular problems using genetically based processes such as fitness, crossover, and mutation to "breed" solutions. Genetic algorithms are starting to be applied to problems involving optimization, product design, and monitoring industrial systems.

Key Terms

Artificial intelligence	Knowledge base	Knowledge engineer	Case-based reasoning
Bottom-up approach	Rule-based expert system	AI shell	(CBR)
Top-down approach	Rule base	Inference engine	Neural network
Combinatorial explosion	Semantic nets	Forward chaining	Fuzzy logic
Expert system	Frames	Backward chaining	Genetic algorithms

Review Questions

1. What is artificial intelligence?
2. What are the five elements of artificial intelligence research?
3. What is the difference between artificial intelligence and natural or human intelligence?
4. What are the two major lines of development in artificial intelligence research? Describe the key aspects of each.
5. State a good working definition of an expert system.

6. Describe each of the elements of an expert system.
7. What are frames and semantic nets?
8. What is meant by forward- and backward-chaining expert systems?
9. Cite three examples of successful expert systems. How many rules does each possess?
10. What is case-based reasoning?
11. What is the difference between knowledge engineering and conventional systems analysis?
12. Describe five problems and limitations of expert systems.

13. Describe a neural network.
14. What kinds of tasks would a neural network be good at?
15. Define and describe fuzzy logic.
16. What are genetic algorithms? How can they help organizations solve problems? What kinds of problems are they suited for?
17. State four reasons why business should be interested in artificial intelligence.

Discussion Questions

1. A famous person has declared that artificial intelligence will lead to a fundamental redistribution of knowledge because all persons will be able to have their own knowledge-based system, giving them access to knowledge that heretofore only experts have possessed. Discuss.
2. The CEO, in an effort to cut middle-management costs, has just announced a major effort to use artificial intelligence and expert systems to assist managers and, if possible, through attrition, to reduce the total cost of management. Discuss.
3. Describe some information systems applications that would benefit from using fuzzy logic.

Group Project

With a group of your classmates, find a task in an organization (near your college or university) that requires some intelligence to perform and that might be suitable for an expert system. Describe as many of the rules required to perform this task as possible. Interview and observe the person performing this task. Consider changing the task in order to simplify the system. Report your findings to the class.

Case Study

AMERICAN EXPRESS CHANGES ITS CREDIT-CARD STRATEGY

American Express, the New York City–based travel and financial services giant, has been going through a crisis during which its market share has been dropping and its profits declining. A key question for American Express is the role of technology, including artificial intelligence applications, in this crisis, and the ability of American Express to execute the strategies devised to bring the company back to a hoped-for robust and rosy future.

Background American Express has had three major divisions: IDS Financial

Services, which is a mutual fund and insurance company; TRS (Travel Related Services), which includes both American Express travel services and its credit-card businesses; and Shearson Lehman Brothers (which was sold in 1994, as we shall see below), the Wall Street stock brokerage giant. The heart of the company is TRS, particularly its credit-card business. Traditionally, American Express offered only a *credit card* which cost the holder a hefty annual fee while requiring the user to pay the credits in full each month—no continuing balance and paying over time is allowed. In theory this

card was not in competition with the bank *charge cards* such as Visa and MasterCard, which had smaller or no annual fees but allowed card holders to pay off only a small portion of their debt each month. These bank charge cards made most of their profit from the interest on the unpaid debt, a source of income traditionally lacking for American Express. The value of the American Express card lay in its services and its prestige—a kind of snob appeal. Among the services is that card holders had no specific spending limits. Rather the amount a specific card holder could charge was based upon an individual's ability to pay monthly. While card holders never know in advance if something will be approved, if their payment record is good and income is sound, purchases will be approved that might be refused with a bank charge card. American Express charged merchants an average fee of 3.2 percent for each purchase, as compared with a fee of approximately 2 percent charged by Visa and MasterCard.

Technology Policy American Express has long had a reputation for being on the technological leading edge. The firm is willing, even eager, to be one of the first to attempt to use a new technology, even if the attempt carries a high risk of failure. One reason for this policy was the support of James Robinson, the chairman of American Express in the late 1980s and early 1990s. He became a corporate champion of a program to develop leading-edge technologies because he saw this as a strategic issue for his company. He believed that a few successes will more than offset cost of the failures, particularly if those trying the new technology can spot the failures soon enough and halt them. His support became a key reason for the success of the policy.

The company first began to attempt to harness artificial intelligence in 1984 when Louis Gerstner, then the chief executive officer of American Express' TRS division, concluded that his company had been negligent in exploring new technology. Gerstner, who later went on to become the CEO of IBM, pushed a program to take more technology risks and to spend more money on those risks. Under his leadership, the company attempted to develop a system that would handle fluctuations in foreign exchange rates to obtain top value for funds transferred internationally (foreign exchange rates are a key issue for American Express). The project failed and was abandoned both because it was too broad in scope and because the developers had problems with the technology. However, Gerstner was undeterred, and in early 1986 the company jumped right into a project to develop an application that came to be called the Authorizer's

Assistant. This system automated elements of the credit authorizers' function and proved to be a major success.

The new technology development policy was refined over the years. The foreign exchange rate and Authorizer's Assistant projects were 100 percent financed by corporate money, an inducement for the operating units to take a risk on new technology. When Gerstner first asked operating units to submit applications for corporate funds for leading-edge technology projects, he received 80 applications. He financed five of them, including Authorizer's Assistant. However, Gerstner soon realized that because the business units making the applications would contribute nothing, their managements mostly viewed the funds as play money and did not really buy into the projects they were submitting. Gerstner therefore changed the rules so that corporate and the applying unit would each pay half the cost, still a major inducement to try something new, but only if the project made real business sense to the business unit. Management later realized that the whole corporation would be better served by a technology transfer program so that the new technology could spread more quickly to other units if the first projects with it were successful. Therefore the funding formula was changed again. "Now we have 40-40-20 sharing, with corporate and one business unit putting up most of the cost and another business unit committing 20% of the development budget as an incentive for further technology transfer," explained Neal Goldsmith, one of American Express' six directors of technology strategy, with responsibility for AI technology.

American Express has established criteria for funding projects, including:

- The technology should be 18 to 36 months from deployment in order to keep American Express on the leading edge.
- The project must be either a feasibility study at $25,000 or less to evaluate new technology, or it must be a prototype in the six-fig-

ure range that can be developed in 12 to 24 months.

- Value to the business unit must be measured in dollars.
- The applicant must show that the product will be in strategic alignment with existing business goals.
- The technology must have cross-business unit value.

On the issue of the risk of failure, American Express management expected a 50 percent failure rate with the projects it funds. Goldsmith figured that a 50 percent failure rate also meant a 50 percent success rate, and that would benefit American Express in the long run. Goldsmith said he didn't mind "failing forward, where you learn a valuable lesson about the limits of the technology." However, the one type of failure he would not accept is when a research and development project is successful, but the application doesn't get implemented. Goldsmith treats it like a personal failure.

The results have been gratifying. About one fifth of the proposal submissions are actually funded. The projects have been in many areas, including but not limited to artificial intelligence, telecommunications, and parallel computer systems. The technology transfer policy has also been working. Authorizer's Assistant, for example, became the foundation first for Credit Assistant and then for New Accounts Assistant.

The Artificial Intelligence "Assistant" Applications Authorizer's Assistant was the first rule-based system to be put into production at American Express. Credit authorization is a fundamental business function for American Express to reduce the use of stolen cards and the accumulation of high charge-card bills by people who cannot afford to pay. At the same time, credit authorizers do not want to deny credit to legitimate card holders, which may result in losing business.

When card holders purchase products using the American Express card, they see the merchant obtain approval by "swiping" the card through the little American Express machine usually kept right near the cash register. The little swipe machine is actually connected to American Express' authorization system. Thousands of transactions using the American Express card actually occur every minute of every day. They all use credit information on the card holder taken from the millions of card-holder data files being stored and processed by American Express' computer in Phoenix, Arizona.

Prior to installation of the Authorizer's Assistant rule-based system, more than 700 credit authorizers worked at computer terminals, examining the data on each card holder as requests for approval came in. The authorizer might need to look at as many as 16 screens of data per customer, a cumbersome process that resulted in too many wrong authorization decisions. The authorizer quickly decided whether to accept or reject the credit request and immediately transmitted that response back to the merchant through the swipe machine. Decisions were made based upon a range of variables, including the card holder's spending patterns, recent purchases, and requests that are very much out of the pattern of the individual (such as an unusually large purchase or purchases made in far-distant cities on consecutive days for a card holder that does not normally travel that way).

The Authorizer's Assistant project had a series of stated goals, including:

- It had to work quickly in real time.
- It had to make authorizations more frequently and quickly than the current method while still achieving a higher rate of accuracy.
- It had to rely upon the card holder data that are already stored in their Phoenix computers.
- It had to minimize fraud and credit losses from improper or incorrect authorizations.
- Necessary training time and costs for authorizers had to be reduced.
- The system had to stabilize the authorization staffing levels by transferring some of the authorization responsibilities to the computer.
- System users had to be able, upon request, to see the line of reasoning of any "decision" made by the computer system—the human authorizer must be able to know why the system arrived at the conclusion it did.
- It had to spot too rapid a movement from place to place, such as different cities each day (when not part of normal pattern of that card holder).
- It had to spot and respond to a sudden increase in spending amounts.
- The system had to be easy to maintain—rule additions, deletions, and changes must be able to be made within a minimum amount of time.

Authorizer's Assistant distills the knowledge of American Express' best authorizers into a rule-based expert system and works with human authorizers. The system requires only two screens and recommends credit approval, disapproval, or further search. The software used to develop the system came from Inference Corp. of Los Angeles. The first prototype took six months to complete and had 520 rules (today it contains more than 1000 rules). The system was instituted without the retailers even realizing a change had been made. The system considerably reduced the cost of the human authorizers, according to Goldsmith, resulting in dollar savings estimated at tens of millions of dollars annually.

With financial support from corporate, Authorizer's Assistant became a centerpiece of American Express' drive to transfer technology. The shell of the system was first moved from the authorization unit into the TRS credit department where it was used to develop Credit Assistant. While the shell was similar to Authorizer's Assistant, the knowledge base was different. The system helps the credit department staff to determine whether and when to turn overdue accounts over to collection. It

searches for both credit risk and potential fraud. With the help of the system, management review of transactions have been reduced from an average of 22 per case to one. Management calculates that the system has resulted in a 20 percent improvement in productivity, saving the company a minimum of $1.4 million annually. Next the shell was transferred into the new accounts processing group where it became the foundation of New Accounts Assistant. This system evaluates the eligibility of new credit account applicants against a set of criteria embedded into the rule base of the system. Figure 17.17 illustrates the transfer of this technology. American Express plans to develop a "knowledge highway" of the knowledge base of all three "Assistant" systems so that the company can do more sophisticated evaluation of credit data.

Changing Business Strategies at American Express American Express has undergone significant changes in its business strategies over the past decade as the credit/charge-card business has developed. In the mid-1980s management decided that American Express needed to compete in the charge-card business and so in 1987 launched its new Optima card. The launch was slow but apparently successful at first. In 1990 profits from all its cards reached $956 million. However, in 1991, after ten years of growth at breakneck speeds, the credit-card operation began to crumble. Tens of thousands of card holders were canceling their cards each week—card holders fell from 14 million to 13 million in that year and the alarming drop continued over the next several years. There appeared to be several reasons for the decline. First, snob appeal was no longer an effective marketing strategy for the American Express card. Related to that was the increased choice card users were being offered as the number and type of charge cards multiplied. A fierce price war took place between various charge-card issuers. Interest rates were lowered significantly (although they remained high compared to other interest rates). Card issuers

FIGURE 17.17
Technology transfer at American Express. American Express pays careful attention to its technology transfer programs because information drives its business.
Adapted from: Steve Ditlea, "How AMEX Leverages Technology Assets," Datamation, *December 1, 1992, p. 95.*

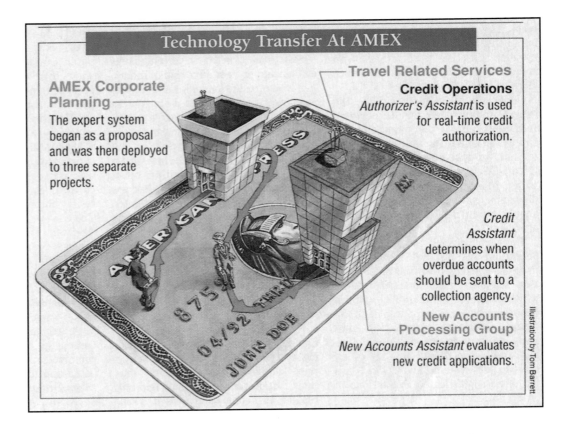

Technology Transfer At AMEX

AMEX Corporate Planning
The expert system began as a proposal and was then deployed to three separate projects.

Travel Related Services
Credit Operations
Authorizer's Assistant is used for real-time credit authorization.

Credit Assistant determines when overdue accounts should be sent to a collection agency.

New Accounts Processing Group
New Accounts Assistant evaluates new credit applications.

Illustration by Tom Barrett

began offering a wide range of tailor-made premiums—cash back, airline travel frequent flier mileage credits, credits toward the purchase of an automobile, free gasoline, and so forth.

In July 1991, American Express placed Harvey Golub in charge of its credit-card business. Golub, a former consultant for management consultant firm McKinsey and Co., was also named president of American Express. One of his first acts was to commission Bain & Company to study the reasons why American Express card customers were canceling their cards. The study indicated that many wanted a charge card rather than a credit card. However, many others did want a credit card, but they also wanted to be able to shop at places that did not take the American Express card. Golub and his staff decided that it was useless to try to hold on to those card holders who had signed up in the 1980s for reasons of prestige. Instead, their new strategy became to concentrate on keeping the loyalty of business travelers—their core group.

Earlier in 1991, Kenneth Chenault was placed in charge of the U.S. card business. He played a key role in successfully convincing senior management that American Express had to deal with the highly effective incentives from charge-card issuers such as the Citicorp AAdvantage card which offers users one mile of American Airlines frequent flier credit for every dollar charged to the card. The American Express card launched a membership mileage program in late spring 1991. Chenault also convinced senior management to consider lowering retailer fees in order to attract more merchants to use its card because American Express lagged badly in the number of retail outlets where its card was accepted. Studies indicated that card holders could use their cards for only 70 percent of their purchases because of the limited number of merchants who accepted it.

In 1992 profits from cards fell to $243 million. By that time Optima card holders had accumulated $1.5 billion in unpaid charges since the card's inception, indicating problems either in accepting applications for charge-card customers or in authorizing charge-

card purchases. During the same year, a widespread rebellion against American Express' higher merchant fees became evident when a group of Boston restaurateurs together publicly dropped the card. Golub, with Chenault, moved quickly to cut overall operating costs, and they began a program to cut the fees charged to merchants. Golub commissioned McKinsey to study the worth of the American Express card to merchants—that is, to determine how much the merchants' sales rise if they offer the American Express card. They found that they could demonstrate that the card is so effective in raising sales that American Express did not need to cut fees much for travel-oriented merchants such as rent-a-car companies and airlines. However, they would need to cut sharply the mass-market retailer fees because those merchants gained less from accepting the prestigious American Express card. As a result management created a tailored fee cut that on average only lowered fees by 0.3 percent instead of the much higher cut that would have been necessary if all merchants had been treated the same. The company then began a major campaign to have its sales force call on one million key merchants to get them to sign up. As these programs progressed, spending per card began to increase, indicating that both the new air mileage program and the effort to sign up more merchants were succeeding.

By the beginning of 1993 the Optima card crisis appeared to be receding. Management began to consider issuing a souped-up version of Optima. According to Phillip Riese, who took over credit-cards operation in 1993, "The original quest was for one great credit card." However, he adds, "when we did our research and showed customers a broad array of products, different customers went for different products. There was no silver bullet."

In July 1993, Chenault was given charge of all of TRS. He instituted a cost-cutting effort that planned to cut a minimum of $500 million over the next few years. He expected to eliminate as many as 6000 jobs. However, when he took over, card holders were down to 11 million. *The Wall Street Journal* described TRS when Chenault took over as "in shambles." Thomas Facciola, a Salomon Brothers analyst, said that "TRS looked like the U.S. auto companies at the time when the Japanese started exporting cars to the U.S. There were a lot of things that had to happen." The size of the problem managers faced was summed up by Peter Dimsey, president of MasterCard International for the United States, who said, "The strength of the hand they have is to be a real force in the travel and entertainment market. Now they are trying to be all things to all people and make themselves look like a bank card, where they have a disadvantage." He further explained that "In the past, they have been revolving-credit bashers. Now, all of a sudden, they come in with a revolving-credit product. It creates confusion in the minds of consumers. At the same time, merchants may say this is no different from MasterCard or Visa, so why should we pay a premium for it." Facciola summarized their situation from the perspective of merchants accepting their card. "A lot of merchants still don't accept American Express' cards relative to MasterCard and Visa," he said. "They [American Express] really have to focus on maintaining their market share overseas and that they need to continue to roll out new products that are meaningfully differentiated from existing products."

Later in 1993 American Express announced that it would launch a series of charge and credit cards. Why the new cards? Golub had concluded that more than half of American Express charge-card holders would be better off with a less expensive credit card. Affluent business travelers like the charge card, but American Express took a product that was very upscale, added frills to it, and sold it to an increasing number of people who didn't need it in a utilitarian sense. He noted that an ideal product meets actual needs. Golub hopes to increase charge-card balances from $7 billion to $30 billion before the year 2000, which would add an additional $450 million to $600 million in earnings annually. Based upon their studies, he came to the conclusion that American Express needed 10 to 15 different cards, each meant to attract about one million card holders. One new credit card he envisioned, for example, would include enough extra services to warrant a $100 annual fee. He also said that American Express needed to be much more savvy in avoiding bad credit risks with charge cards than it had been with Optima. Finally, he said that American Express needed to be accepted by more merchants and he proposed trying to sign up virtually every place American Express card holders might go to spend their money.

During 1994, American Express sold its Shearson Lehman Brothers unit in order to concentrate more on its main businesses. The sale placed even more pressure on TRS to succeed because it was left in the position of needing to produce 70 percent of American Express' profit. The only possible areas of growth in the credit/charge-card business are new customers (new card holders), more spending from existing customers, and a growth in interest charges from the unpaid balance of charge cards.

The first new card to be issued used the Optima name and came out in the autumn of 1994. It was meant to appeal to people who borrow a lot, and so it features low interest rates. Chenault took personal control of the development of the new card, including overseeing its basic concept and its marketing. By the end of 1994, about 900,000 of these cards had been issued. In the near future the company plans to introduce a card with no annual fee and to include other benefits that will make it appeal to various groups who are not business travelers. Frank Skillern, a long-time associate of Golub's who had been put in charge of Optima rescue, was given charge of American Express' traditional green, gold, and platinum credit cards. He plans to revive this business by breaking the customers up into a half-dozen smaller customer groups. He plans to pay special attention to the frequent business travelers, who make up 45 percent of their card holders because this is the largest group and most loyal group and the group from whom the company makes the most money. Skillern said he plans, for example, to allow the frequent business travelers to be able to make unusually large purchases. He also plans to create a special version of the credit card for senior citizens. The card will have an annual fee of only $35, and it will include special services for this group such as a free "ask the pharmacist" information line. He also plans a *debit* card which will automatically deduct the cost of a purchase from the card holder's bank account. The plan to sign up new merchants is in full swing—they have already signed up Sears and Kmart, for example, and are working on Wal-Mart.

In January 1995 the company announced a joint venture with America Online to offer a range of electronic financial services to American Express card holders. Through America Online, the estimated 1.6 million card holders who belong to that on-line service will be able to take care of their travel needs and manage their personal banking. The new service, known as ExpressNet, will allow users to pay bills, see billing histories, list recent transactions, and download all of this data onto their own personal computers. Users will also be able to "chat" on-line with personal-finance experts from American Express' new Financial Advisors unit. As for travel, customers will be able not only to make hotel, auto, and airline reservations on-line but also to do extensive research about possible destinations. Similar services have already been announced by Visa, teamed with Microsoft Corporation, and MasterCard, teamed with Netscape Communications (a maker of Internet software).

Competition for the on-line business will be fierce. While American Express was the last of the three to announce such plans, ExpressNet is already available while the others are still in the planning stage. Moreover, all companies offering this type of service will have to overcome user fears about security when doing one's banking through a public network.

The Future of American Express

The new strategy clearly has major risks. The plan is highly complex—the sheer range of proposed card programs increases chances of massive

mistakes such as were made with the Optima charge debt. Moreover, many fear the range of cards will diffuse the American Express image. The new ExpressNet venture carries its own risks. While the company is showing clear progress, *The New York Times* characterizes its future as "uncertain." Travel Related Services earnings for 1994 are way up and are expected to reach $1 billion when finally announced, a rise of 10 percent from 1993. The Optima problems seem to have been solved, as Figure 17.18 indicates. The same figure demonstrates that spending per card by existing card

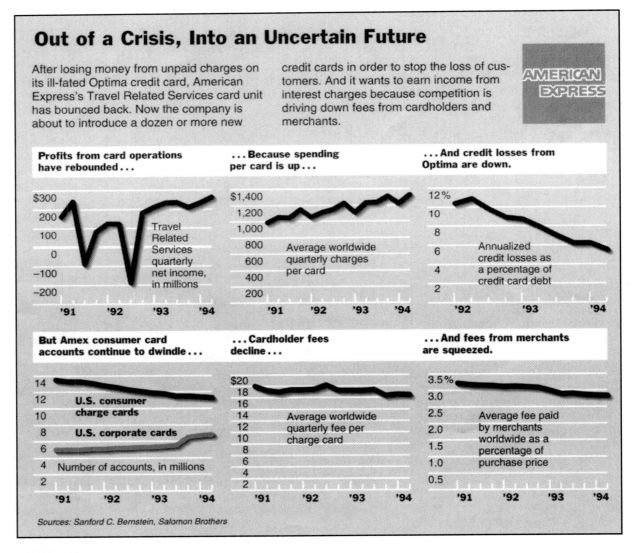

FIGURE 17.18
American Express Travel Related Services' credit-card business. Credit cards are a key source of revenue for American Express. *Adapted from: Saul Hansell, "The New Deal at American Express," The New York Times (July 31, 1994).*

holders is up. Fees from merchants are about $4 billion, having fallen to about 2.8 percent of purchases.

Golub was promoted to chairman and CEO in February 1993, while Chenault was promoted to vice chairman of American Express in January 1995.

Sources: G. Bruce Knecht, "American Express Elevates Chenault," *The Wall Street Journal*, January 26, 1995; James Sandburg, "American Express Goes On-line for Card Holders," *The Wall Street Journal*, January 30, 1995; Harvey P. Newquist, *The Brain Makers* (Indianapolis, IN: SAMS Publishing, 1994), and "AI at American Express," *AI Expert*, January 1993; Steve Ditlea, "How American Express Leverages Technology Assets," *Datamation*, December 1, 1992; and Saul Hansell, "The New Deal at American Express," *The New York Times*, July 31, 1994.

Case Study Questions

1. From a management perspective, describe the causes of the business crisis that American Express found itself facing. What management, organization, and technology factors were at work? Evaluate the American Express business response to that crisis.

2. Describe the Optima Card problems. Assuming TRS used the artificial intelligence Assistant systems for the Optima Card, what might account for the problems that occurred with that card?

3. Evaluate American Express' credit-card strategies using the competitive forces and value chain models. How do artificial intelligence systems support those strategies? In what ways can they be helpful? What are the risks in using them?

4. How did the use of artificial intelligence systems change the way American Express conducted its business?

5. In what ways are the American Express policies on technology risk taking and technology transfer appropriate for the company? Inappropriate? Explain your answer.

References

Allen, Bradley P. "Case-Based Reasoning: Business Applications." *Communications of the ACM* 37, no. 3 (March 1994).

Asakawa, Kazuo, and Hideyuki Takagi. "Neural Networks in Japan." *Communications of the ACM* 37, no. 3 (March 1994).

Bansal, Arun, Robert J. Kauffman, and Rob R. Weitz. "The Modeling Performance of Regression and Neural Networks." *Journal of Management Information Systems* 10, no. 1 (Summer 1993).

Barker, Virginia E., and Dennis E. O'Connor. "Expert Systems for Configuration at Digital: XCON and Beyond." *Communications of the ACM* (March 1989).

Basu, Amit, and Alan R. Heyner. "Embedded Knowledge-based Systems and Box Structure Methods." *Journal of Management Information Systems* 8, no. 4 (Spring 1992).

Blanning, Robert W., David R. King, James R. Marsden, and Ann C. Seror. "Intelligent Models of Human Organizations: The State of the Art." *Journal of Organizational Computing* 2, no. 2 (1992).

Bobrow, D. G., S. Mittal, and M. J. Stefik. "Expert Systems: Perils and Promise." *Communications of the ACM* 29 (September 1986).

Braden, Barbara, Jerome Kanter, and David Kopcso. "Developing an Expert Systems Strategy." *MIS Quarterly* 13, no. 4 (December 1989).

Brody, Herb. "The Neural Computer." *Technology Review* (August–September 1990).

Burtka, Michael. "Genetic Algorithms." *The Stern Information Systems Review* 1, no. 1 (Spring 1993).

Byrd, Terry Anthony. "Implementation and Use of Expert Systems in Organizations: Perceptions of Knowledge Engineers." *Journal of Management Information Systems* 8, no. 4 (Spring 1992).

Carlson, David A., and Sudha Ram. "A Knowledge Representation for Modeling Organizational Productivity." *Journal of Organizational Computing* 2, no. 2 (1992).

Churchland, Paul M., and Patricia Smith Churchland. "Could a Machine Think?" *Scientific American* (January 1990).

Clifford, James, Henry C. Lucas, Jr., and Rajan Srikanth. "Integrating Mathematical and Symbolic Models through AESOP: An Expert for Stock Options Pricing." *Information Systems Research* 3, no. 4 (December 1992).

Cox, Earl. "Solving Problems with Fuzzy Logic." *AI Expert* (March 1992).

Cox, Earl. "Applications of Fuzzy System Models." *AI Expert* (October 1992).

Creecy, Robert H., Brij M. Masand, Stephen J. Smith, and Davis L. Waltz. "Trading MIPS and Memory for Knowledge Engineering." *Communications of the ACM* 35, no. 8 (August 1992).

Dhar, Vasant. "Plausibility and Scope of Expert Systems in Management." *Journal of Management Information Systems* (Summer 1987).

El Najdawi, M. K., and Anthony C. Stylianou. "Expert Support Systems: Integrating AI Technologies." *Communications of the ACM* 36, no. 12 (December 1993).

Feigenbaum, Edward A. "The Art of Artificial Intelligence: Themes and Case Studies in Knowledge Engineering." *Proceedings of the IJCAI* 5 (1977).

Feigenbaum, Edward A., and J. A. Feigenbaum, eds. *Computers and Thought*. New York: McGraw-Hill (1963).

Feigenbaum, Edward A., and Pamela McCorduck. *The Fifth Generation: Artificial Intelligence and Japan's Computer Challenge to the World*. Reading, MA: Addison-Wesley (1985).

Gelernter, David. "The Metamorphosis of Information Management." *Scientific American*, (August 1989).

Goldberg, David E. "Genetic and Evolutionary Algorithms Come of Age." *Communications of the ACM* 37, no. 3 (March 1994).

Griggs, Kenneth. "Visual Aids That Model Organizations." *Journal of Organizational Computing* 2, no. 2 (1992).

Hayes-Roth, Frederick. "Knowledge-Based Expert Systems." *Spectrum IEEE* (October 1987).

Hayes-Roth, Frederick, and Neil Jacobstein. "The State of Knowledge-Based Systems." *Communications of the ACM* 37, no. 3 (March 1994).

Hinton, Gregory. "How Neural Networks Learn from Experience." *Scientific American* (September 1992).

Holland, John H. "Genetic Algorithms." *Scientific American*, (July 1992).

Jacobs, Paul S., and Lisa F. Rau. "SCISOR: Extracting Information from On-line News." *Communications of the ACM* 33, no. 11 (November 1990).

Kanade, Takeo, Michael L. Reed, and Lee E. Weiss. "New Technologies and Applications in Robotics." *Communications of the ACM* 37, no. 3 (March 1994).

Leonard-Barton, Dorothy, and John J. Sviokla. "Putting Expert Systems to Work." *Harvard Business Review*, (March–April 1988).

Lin, Frank C., and Mei Lin. "Neural Networks in the Financial Industry." *AI Expert* (February 1993).

McCarthy, John. "Generality in Artificial Intelligence." *Communications of the ACM* (December 1987).

Marsden, James R., David E. Pingry, and Ming-Chian Ken Wang. "Intelligent Information and Organization Structures: An Integrated Design Approach." *Journal of Organizational Computing* 2, no. 2 (1992).

Meador, C. Lawrence, and Ed G. Mahler. "Choosing an Expert System Game Plan," *Datamation* (August 1, 1990).

Meyer, Marc H., and Kathleen Foley Curley. "An Applied Framework for Classifying the Complexity of Knowledge-Based Systems." *MIS Quarterly* 15, no. 4 (December 1991).

Michaelson, Robert, and Donald Michie. "Expert Systems in Business." *Datamation* (November 1983).

"M.1 Makes a Direct Hit." *PC Magazine* (April 16, 1985).

Motiwalla, Luvai, and Jay F. Nunamaker, Jr. "Mail-Man: A Knowledge-Based MAIL Assistant for Managers." *Journal of Organizational Computing* 2, no. 2 (1992).

Munakata, Toshinori, and Yashvant Jani. "Fuzzy Systems: An Overview." *Communications of the ACM* 37, no. 3 (March 1994).

Mykytyn, Kathleen, Peter P. Mykytyn, Jr., and Craig W. Stinkman. "Expert Systems: A Question of Liability." *MIS Quarterly* 14, no. 1 (March 1990).

Nash, Jim. "Expert Systems: A New Partnership." *AI Expert* (December 1992).

Nash, Jim. "State of the Market, Art, Union, and Technology," *AI Expert* (January 1993).

Newquist, Harvey P. "AI at American Express." *AI Expert* (January 1993).

Newquist, Harvey P. *The Brain Makers*. Indianapolis, IN: SAMS Publishing (1994).

Rumelhart, David E., Bernard Widrow, and Michael A. Lehr. "The Basic Ideas in Neural Networks." *Communications of the ACM* 37, no. 3 (March 1994).

Searle, John R. "Is the Brain's Mind a Computer Program?" *Scientific American* (January 1990).

Self, Kevin. "Designing with Fuzzy Logic." *Spectrum IEEE* (November 1990).

Sibigtroth, James M. "Implementing Fuzzy Expert Rules in Hardware." *AI Expert* (April 1992).

Simon, H. A., and A. Newell. "Heuristic Problem Solving: The Next Advance in Operations Research." *Operations Research* 6 (January–February 1958).

Stein, Eric W. "A Method to Identify Candidates for Knowledge Acquisition." *Journal of Management Information Systems* 9, no. 2 (Fall 1992).

Storey, Veda C., and Robert C. Goldstein, "Knowledge-Based Approaches to Database Design," *MIS Quarterly,* 17, no. 1 (March 1993).

Stylianou, Anthony C., Gregory R. Madey, and Robert D. Smith. "Selection Criteria for Expert System Shells: A Socio-Technical Framework." *Communications of the ACM* 35, no. 10 (October 1992).

Sviokla, John J. "Expert Systems and Their Impact on the Firm: The Effects of PlanPower Use on the Information Processing Capacity of the Financial Collaborative." *Journal of Management Information Systems* 6, no. 3 (Winter 1989–1990).

Sviokla, John J. "An Examination of the Impact of Expert Systems on the Firm: The Case of XCON." *MIS Quarterly* 14, no. 5 (June 1990).

Tam, Kar Yan. "Automated Construction of Knowledge-Bases from Examples." *Information Systems Research* 1, no. 2 (June 1990).

Tank, David W., and John J. Hopfield. "Collective Computation in Neuronlike Circuits." *Scientific American* (October 1987).

Trippi, Robert, and Efraim Turban. "The Impact of Parallel and Neural Computing on Managerial Decision Making." *Journal of Management Information Systems* 6, no. 3 (Winter 1989–1990).

Turban, Efraim, and Paul R. Watkins. "Integrating Expert Systems and Decision Support Systems." *MIS Quarterly* (June 1986).

Wallich, Paul. "Silicon Babies." *Scientific American* (December 1991).

Waltz, David L. "Artificial Intelligence." *Scientific American* (December 1982).

Weitzel, John R., and Kenneth R. Andrews. "A Company/University Joint Venture to Build a Knowledge-Based System." *MIS Quarterly* 12, no. 1 (March 1988).

Weitzel, John R., and Larry Kerschberg. "Developing Knowledge Based Systems: Reorganizing the System Development Life Cycle." *Communications of the ACM* (April 1989).

Weizenbaum, Joseph. *Computer Power and Human Reason—From Judgment to Calculation*. San Francisco: W. H. Freeman (1976).

Weizenbaum, Joseph. "ELIZA—A Computer Program for the Study of Natural Language Communication Between Man and Machine." *Communications of the ACM* (January 1983).

White, George M. "Natural Language Understanding and Speech Recognition." *Communications of the ACM* 33, no. 8 (August 1990).

Widrow, Bernard, David E. Rumelhart, and Michael A. Lehr. "Neural Networks: Applications in Industry, Business and Science." *Communications of the ACM* 37, no. 3 (March 1994).

Zadeh, Lotfi A. "The Calculus of Fuzzy If/Then Rules." *AI Expert* (March 1992).

Zadeh, Lotfi A. "Fuzzy Logic, Neural Networks, and Soft Computing." *Communications of the ACM* 37, no. 3 (March 1994).

EPRINET: A Strategic Network for the Utility Industry

The Electric Power Research Institute (EPRI) is the research and development consortium for the U.S. electric utility industry. It is one of the largest private research firms in the United States, with headquarters in Palo Alto, California and search sites around the country. EPRI has six technical research divisions: Generation and Storage, Nuclear Power, Environment, Electrical Systems, Customer Systems, and Exploratory Research. EPRI's business is information and its product is knowledge. EPRI contracts with energy experts in 36 countries to research subjects of interest to its members.

EPRI is funded by its member firms and since its founding in 1972 has invested $4.3 billion in various research projects. The funds for these projects have come from the contributions of 700 member electrical utilities, representing 70% of total electricity sales in the United States. EPRI recently added its first international affiliate, the British utility PowerGen.

EPRI's internal research and development staff of 450 scientists and engineers manage 1600 projects, which are conducted by over 400 utility, university, commercial, government, and other R & D contractors in 36 countries. The projects span many technologies, from electricity generation at the power station to electricity use in the home. Many of the issues they deal with are global, such as the greenhouse effect, acid rain, and superconductivity.

EPRI is a very information-intensive organization. Spanning 19 years of research, EPRI's databases contain over eight gigabytes of information, equivalent to 2.7 million pages of technical documents with diagrams and formulas. Each year EPRI distributes millions of copies of reports, report summaries, and software. Each year EPRI also holds several hundred seminars and workshops and handles over 13,000 hotline telephone inquiries.

Originally EPRI's mission extended only to the management of its research and development program. This changed after 1978. Because of deregulation, the electric utility industry experienced intense change. In the past, federal regulations defined and protected individual utility service territories. Since deregulation, electric utilities compete for large customers against gas utilities, independent power producers, other utilities, and sometimes the large customers themselves. They must also contend with rising public pressure to protect the environment. For instance, Pacific Gas & Electric (PG&E) is working with the environmental groups on renewable energy sources.

Competitive pressures in the utility industry required EPRI to find more efficient ways to deliver the results of its research and expertise to its clients. EPRI and its members wanted to compress the "information float," the time from the findings of R & D to the analysis of their results and to the application of those results in industry. The sheer volume and complexity of its scientific information made it difficult to distribute this information. Research results were unavailable for one to 24 months while detailed reports were being produced. When the technical reports finally made it out the door, members were expected to wade through massive volumes of documents to find the nuggets of documents they needed.

EPRI tried to solve these problems in 1984 by launching the development of a state-of-the-art electronic information and communications network called EPRINET. EPRINET provides four anchor services and various specialty services. The anchor services are electronic mail, a natural language retrieval system, electronic directories and catalogues, and videoconferencing.

The natural language retrieval system allows users to retrieve information from EPRI's databases by entering a few keywords in English. Users can use this facility to search on-line directories, abstracts, catalogues, and papers.

EPRINET's principal directory describes its technical staff, listing their names, positions, relevant publications, and recent projects by area of expertise. The directory also catalogues EPRI research work, including status reports, papers, articles, videotapes, and speeches. EPRI wants to put Technical Interest Profiles on-line. The profiles identify the kind of information members want to obtain from EPRI.

EPRI introduced videoconferencing in April 1991. Some members prefer to videoconference rather than to scan research papers on a specific topic. They can use EPRINET to identify the EPRI experts and arrange a videoconference with those experts. The network posts an announcement telling members the date and time of the videoconference.

The specialty services are special products and services that help people deal with information overload and locate colleagues with similar interests. These services are tailored to a particular use. An example might be an on-line forum that allows engineers to discuss and evaluate various options for keeping biological organisms out of hydropower plant machinery. Each forum can have its own news briefs, announcements, report database, software models, and directory of participants. The specialty services even provide up-to-date industy news, electronic bulletin boards, and an "ask the EPRI expert" facility for answering questions on-line. If a requestor does not know the name of the appropriate expert, the system will route the request to be reviewed by an EPRI staff member, who forwards it to the appropriate expert.

EPRIGEMS are interactive expert system modules that use expert system technology to capture EPRI research findings and the knowledge of EPRI staff. Each module works on a particular utility problem, such as boiler maintenance or nuclear plant life extension. Some EPRIGEMS provide users with appropriate experts whom they can contact through EPRINET's electronic mail system.

ElectriGuide is a research catalog on CD-ROM that contains three major databases, with abstracts of 7000 EPRI technical reports, plus descriptions of 1000 EPRI products and 23,000 research projects. It contains color slide presentations for selected topics such as end-user forecasting. After using the CD-ROM catalog, users can order published and audiovisual items on-line through EPRINET.

EPRI's management launched EPRINET by initiating a period of intense automation from 1984 to 1987. EPRI's information technology division focused on raising the level of computer literacy of EPRI staff members, establishing connectivity among EPRI's internal computer environments and to external computer networks, and building a core of strategic databases. Management realized that some of EPRI's suppliers and customers might become their competitors unless EPRI retained its position as the hub of research in the industry.

EPRI installed microcomputers on virtually every desk in 1985 and established a lending library of laptop microcomputers. A series of user-friendly programs was written to help project managers use computers to administer research projects. EPRINET's E-mail facility was introduced in 1985, but persuading staff to use it required active use by EPRI's president, senior executives, and project managers. EPRI installed a telephone help line and software lending library and began training its members in the most commonly used software programs. EPRI developed a facility to transfer documents in revisable format between IBM mainframes, IBM microcomputers and clones, Macintosh microcomputers, and NBI word processors, using PROFS and a translation program among word processing packages. Management selected the IBM Information Network, supplemented by Tymnet for high-speed global transmission of data (about 40% of U.S. electric utilities use that network) and customized PROFS to send and receive messages from two other international networks, BITNET and MCI Mail.

EPRI established an EPRINET Utility Advisory Group (UAG) to involve its member utilities from the start in its information technology planning. UAG represented the full range of utility responsibilities, including technology transfer, power plant operations, R & D engineering, and design. One of UAG's first assignments was to describe the utility engineer of the future and what information technologies the engineer would need.

The first production version of EPRINET was released in May 1990. Soon after management began a marketing campaign to promote use of the network internally among EPRI project and program managers and externally among member utilities and research contractors. Since that time, the number of EPRINET users has climbed steadily. By April 1991, virtually every EPRINET employee was connected.

Management originally believed that the implementation of EPRINET and cultural changes associated with the organization's strategic transition could be undertaken separately. The average age of the EPRI scientific staff was over 45 years and the staff was unaccustomed to working with computers. EPRI's new mission required that staff members change their roles and accept responsibility for delivering the results of their research to EPRI's members. They had to learn to travel with laptop computers, retrieve information electronically, and use electronic mail to "talk" with colleagues and contractors instead of the telephone. EPRI won some immediate converts, but many staff members changed reluctantly. Some instability resulted from trying to undertake intense automation without readying the organization for new ways of working. EPRI's management could not resolve these problems all at once.

The EPRINET project needed a top-level executive from outside the information systems department to serve as its sponsor to the rest of the organization. Initially, it could not find a corporate champion from the R & D staff because the organization was in such transition. The project "sponsor" wound up being a coalition of three executives. Although not ideal, the coalition worked.

At first the EPRINET project team avoided corporate naysayers, who worried about licensing agreements, information overload, and whether money to sustain the new databases would be taken away from advanced research projects. The project team feared they would undermine the project. As time went on, the team realized that these opponents identified some real problems and that they made valuable suggestions, so the teams started drawing them out. The team tried to win over opponents by demonstrating EPRINET's value in saving staff and member time to communicate research findings, experimenting with pilot systems, and launching a program to orient member utilities to EPRINET's services and benefits.

How successful is EPRINET? Heavy users of the system believe EPRINET provides a collaborative environment where people feel more informed and task forces and businesses can operate more efficiently. A number of users have reported finding, in minutes, pieces of information that might have taken several weeks in the past. Member utilities have reported that EPRINET allows them to make better use of EPRI's knowledge, saving time, developing new products, and increasing revenue. For instance, Common-

wealth Edison estimated that the market-targeting capabilities of EPRI's industrial market information system software helped it make new sales in the industrial sector which increased its revenues by $2 million a year.

EPRI is continuing to refine the network and incorporate new technologies. It has licensed Mosaic, a graphical user interface to the Internet, and is adding enhanced security and order processing features to make it an interface for EPRINET (EPRI members can currently access EPRINET through AlterNet data network connections to the Internet, IBM's Advantis network, or MCI's Tymnet network.) Mosaic will consolidate EPRINET's numerous user interfaces into a few viewing paradigms and help EPRI display its charts, diagrams, and pictures.

Sources: Clinton Wilder, "Mosaic Means Business," *InformationWEEK*, July 11, 1994 and Marina M. Mann, Richard L. Rudman, Thomas A. Jenckes, and Barbara C. McNurlin, "EPRINET: Leveraging Knowledge in the Electric Utility Industry," *MIS Quarterly* 15, no. 3 (September 1991).

Case Study Questions

1. What is EPRI's goal as an organization? Why did that goal change?

2. What are the strategic implications of EPRINET for EPRI and for its subscribing members?

3. What are EPRI's critical success factors? How well did EPRINET address those factors?

4. What kinds of problems did EPRI encounter during implementation of EPRINET? What management, organization, and technology factors were responsible for those problems? Would you have managed the EPRINET project differently?

5. How important is EPRINET for solving the problems faced by the electric utlity industry? What are some of the problems it cannot address?

6. Can you suggest some other information system applications that would benefit EPRI? How could EPRI benefit from the expanding capabilities of the Internet?

five

Managing Contemporary Information Systems

The pervasiveness and power of contemporary information systems have made security, control and developing global systems key management problems. Part Five concludes the text by examining the management, organization, and technology dimensions of these problems and by describing strategies, procedures, and technologies for meeting these challenges.

Chapter 18
Controlling Information Systems

Chapter 18 demonstrates why management must take special measures to ensure that information systems are secure and effectively controlled. Without proper safeguards, information systems are highly vulnerable to destruction, abuse, error, and loss, especially in networked environments. Both general and application-specific controls can be applied to ensure that information systems are accurate, reliable, and secure. An appropriate control structure for information systems will consider costs and benefits. This chapter highlights the importance of information system security and auditing.

Chapter 19
Managing International Information Systems

Chapter 19 analyzes the principal challenges confronting organizations that want to use information systems on an international scale. Organizations need to design appropriate business strategies and information systems infrastructures for this purpose and they need to overcome significant management, organization, and technology obstacles to systems that transcend national boundaries.

Part Five Case Study:
Phantom Profits Haunt Kidder Peabody

On April 17, 1994, the Wall Street securities firm of Kidder Peabody sent shock waves throughout the financial community by firing Joseph Jett, its most successful bond trader. By posting phantom bond trades as profits, Jett had actually lost $90 million for the company. This case study examines the circumstances surrounding Jett's dismissal and asks students to assess the role played by information systems and the management control environment in Kidder's bond trading fiasco.

Chapter *18*

Controlling Information Systems

Flooding Brings Midwest Systems to a Standstill

On July 11, 1993, the computers for the city of Des Moines, Iowa, expired. Eight feet of water had filled the sub-basement of one of the city's two main administrative centers, disrupting electrical power. Des Moines had to shut down an IBM mainframe, the terminal network, and the private branch exchange located on the second floor. With the city's mainframe and telephone switches knocked out, Des Moines' police department had trouble communicating the information commanders needed to make decisions during the flood crisis.

Des Moines businesses were likewise crippled because the city lost its drinking water supply, which was also used to cool the mainframes of many computer centers. The same plight befell many companies throughout the flood-stricken Midwest, as unrelenting rains caused the Missouri and Mississippi rivers to overflow their banks.

The flooding created the worst disruption to companies' computer centers since the Chicago flood of 1992, when more than 250 million gallons of water poured into the tunnels below Chicago's business district. The ensuing flood caused power failures and water damage that forced Chicago's businesses to a standstill. The flood hit the headquarters of the Chicago Board of Trade (CBOT), which contains the computers that run Chicago's commodity trading systems and offices of 80 member brokerages. All trading stopped. Major banks, retail stores, and government centers were crippled. Billions of dollars reportedly were lost.

During both floods, the firms that had contingency plans for such disasters recovered more quickly. A Des Moines financial services firm, a bank, an insurance company, and a manufacturer of wheels and tires switched their information system operations to "hot site" computer centers provided by Comdisco, Inc., Sungard Recover Services, Inc., and IBM Business Recovery Services, three disaster recovery services firms. These companies resumed normal operations within a day or two. But on July 15, four days later, the city's mainframe and the computer centers of other firms that failed to anticipate such contingencies were still down because these organizations did not have a disaster recovery plan. No one could have predicted that a river could swallow a Des Moines city building. ■

Sources: Ellis Booker, "Data Dowsed in Midwest Floods," *Computerworld*, July 19, 1993; and Ellis Booker and Jim Nash, "Great Chicago Flood of '92: IS Groups Stay High and Dry," *Computerworld*, April 20, 1992.

Vulnerability to floods and other natural disasters is but one of many problems that organizations relying on computer-based information systems may face. Hardware and software failures, communications disruptions, employee errors, and use by unauthorized people may prevent information systems from running properly or running at all.

Computer systems play such a critical role in business, government, and daily life that organizations must take special steps to protect their information systems and ensure their accuracy and reliability. The Des Moines and Chicago organizations with disaster recovery plans took these steps; others did not. This chapter describes how information systems can be *controlled* so that they serve the purposes for which they are intended.

After completing this chapter you will be able to:

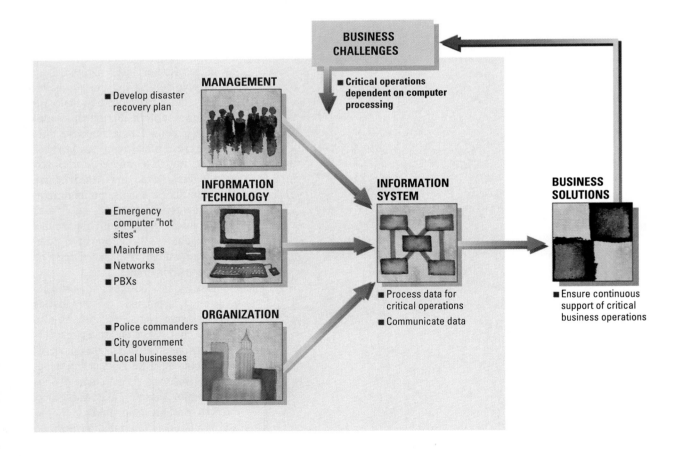

18.1 SYSTEM VULNERABILITY AND ABUSE

Before computer automation, data about individuals or organizations were maintained and secured as paper records dispersed in separate business or organizational units. Information systems concentrate data in computer files that can potentially be accessed more easily by large numbers of people and by groups outside the organization. Consequently, automated data are more susceptible to destruction, fraud, error, and misuse.

When computer systems fail to run or work as required, firms that depend heavily on computers experience a serious loss of business function. A 1992 survey of 450 Fortune 1000 firms found that unplanned disruptions in computer service occur nine times per year, on average, and result in an average of four hours of downtime each time. The study concluded that the ensuing lost productivity and customer dissatisfaction cost U.S. businesses $4 billion a year and resulted in at least 37 million hours of lost worker productivity (McPartlin, 1992). The longer computer systems are "down," the more serious the consequences for the firm. Some firms relying on computers to process their critical business transactions might experience a total loss of business function if they lost computer capability for more than a few days.

WHY SYSTEMS ARE VULNERABLE

There are many advantages to information systems when they are properly safeguarded. But when large amounts of data are stored in electronic form, they are vulnerable to many more kinds of threats than when they exist in manual form. For example, an organization's entire recordkeeping system can be destroyed by a computer hardware malfunction. Table 18.1 lists the most common threats to computerized information systems. They can stem from technical, organizational, and environmental factors compounded by poor management decisions.

Table 18.1 Threats to Computerized Information Systems	
Hardware failure	Fire
Software failure	Electrical problems
Personnel actions	User errors
Terminal access penetration	Program changes
Theft of data, services, equipment	Telecommunications problems

Computerized systems are especially vulnerable to such threats for the following reasons:

- A complex information system cannot be replicated manually. Most information cannot be printed or is too voluminous to be handled manually.

- There is usually no visible trace of changes in computerized systems because computer records can be read only by the computer.

- Computerized procedures appear to be invisible and are not easily understood or audited.

- The development and operation of automated systems require specialized technical expertise, which cannot be easily communicated to end users. Systems are open to abuse by highly technical staff members who are not well integrated into the organization. (Programmers and computer operators can make unauthorized changes in software while information is being processed or can use computer facilities for unauthorized purposes. Employees may make unauthorized copies of data files for illegal purposes.)

- Although the chances of disaster in automated systems are no greater than in manual systems, the effect of a disaster can be much more extensive. In some cases, all of the system's records can be destroyed and lost forever.

- Most automated systems are accessible by many individuals. Information is easier to gather but more difficult to control.

- On-line information systems are even more difficult to control because data files can be accessed immediately and directly through computer terminals. Legitimate users may gain easy access to computer data that were previously not available to them. They may be able to scan records or entire files that they are not authorized to view. By obtaining valid users' log ons and passwords, unauthorized individuals can also gain access to such systems. The chances of unauthorized access to or manipulation of data in on-line systems are considerably higher than in the batch environment.

NEW VULNERABILITIES

Advances in telecommunications and computer software have magnified these vulnerabilities. Through telecommunications networks, information systems in different locations can be interconnected. The potential for unauthorized access, abuse, or fraud is not limited to a single location but can occur at any access point in the network.

Additionally, more complex and diverse hardware, software, organizational, and personnel arrangements are required for telecommunications networks, creating new areas and opportunities for penetration and manipulation. Wireless networks using radio-based technology are even more vulnerable to penetration because radio frequency bands are easy to scan. The vulnerabilities of telecommunications networks are illustrated in Figure 18.1. Developing a workable system of controls for telecommunications networks is a complex and troubling problem.

The efforts of "hackers" to penetrate computer networks have been widely publicized. A **hacker** is a person who gains unauthorized access to a computer network for profit, criminal mischief, or personal pleasure. The potential damage from intruders is frightening. The Window on Organizations describes problems created by hackers for organizations that use the Internet.

Most recently, alarm has risen over hackers propagating **computer viruses,** rogue software programs that spread rampantly from system to system, clogging computer memory or destroying programs or data. More than 2100 viruses are known to exist, with 50 or more new viruses created each month. (Figure 18.2 describes the characteristics of the most common viruses found to date.) The most notorious virus outbreak occurred in November 1988, when Robert Morris, a brilliant computer science student, introduced a program through a Cornell University terminal that spread uncontrollably throughout the Internet network, which ties together numerous other networks, including National Science Foundation Network (NSF Net) linking universities, research labs, and other institutions. Morris intended his program to reside quietly on Internet computers, but it echoed throughout the network

hacker A person who gains unauthorized access to a computer network for profit, criminal mischief, or personal pleasure.

computer virus Rogue software programs that are difficult to detect and spread rapidly through computer systems, destroying data or disrupting processing and memory systems.

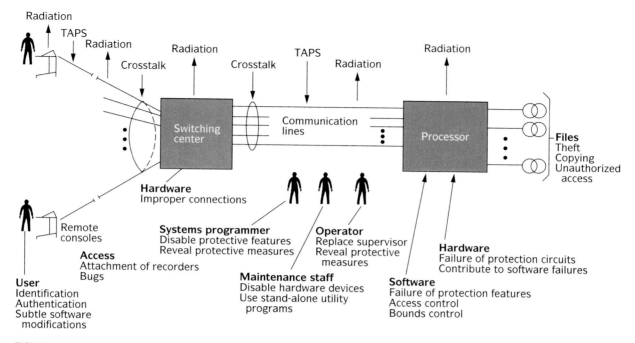

FIGURE 18.1

Telecommunication network vulnerabilities. Telecommunications networks are highly vulnerable to natural failure of hardware and software and to misuse by programmers, computer operators, maintenance staff, and end users. It is possible to "tap" communications lines and illegally intercept data. High-speed transmission over twisted wire communications channels causes interference called crosstalk. Radiation can disrupt a network at various points as well.

FIGURE 18.2

Frequently Occurring Computer Viruses *From "Viruses Continue to Wreak Havoc at Many U.S. Companies" by Gary H. Anthes,* Computerworld, *June 28, 1993. Copyright 1993 by Computerworld, Inc., Framingham, MA 01701. Reprinted from* Computerworld *by permission.*

COMPUTERS

Frequently Occuring Computer Viruses

VIRUS NAME	FREQUENCY AS % OF ALL INCIDENTS	WHAT IT DOES
FORM	34.7%	Makes a clicking sound with each keystroke, but only on the 18th of the month. Has a hidden, obscene reference to someone named Corinne.
JOSHI	6.4	Freezes your PC once a year, on Jan. 5, until the phrase 'Happy Birthday Joshi' is typed on the keyboard.
STONED	4.0	Once the most common virus, it sometimes displays on-screen 'Your PC is now Stoned.'
CANSU	3.4	One out of every eight times the PC is switched on, it displays a V-shaped symbol on the screen.
MICHELANGELO	3.3	Very nasty. It wipes out most of your data on March 6, the artist's birthday.
MONKEY-2	2.7	Mysterious. Hides in memory and infects every disk it contacts, making some unusable.
GREEN CATERPILLAR	1.6	Most effective in color, it unleashes a little worm that crawls around the screen rearranging characters, changing their color.

Source, IBM

UPROOTING THE INTERNET HACKERS

Business use of the Internet has been growing rapidly over the past few years. Nonetheless, many businesses are hesitant to use it for more than E-mail, if that. Distrust of Internet security is a major cause of the hesitation. About four Internet break-ins occur every day, according to the Computer Emergency Response Team at the Software Engineering Institute of Carnegie-Mellon University in Pittsburgh (see below). The Internet Society in Reston, Virginia, estimates that about 30,000 organizations that would link up to the Internet have not done so due to security concerns. The Internet has no central authority or management and therefore no one to install the technology or establish network-wide security policies. Meanwhile, a number of Internet security breaches have received wide publicity, calling into question the ability of any company to secure its data when using the Internet.

The main concern comes from unwanted intruders, hackers, who use the latest technology and their skill to break into supposedly secure computers. In October 1993, the magnitude of the problem first became clear when a group of hackers broke into the computer of Panix (Public Access Network Corp.), a commercial seller of access to the Internet. The hackers had embedded a program in the Panix computer which collected passwords from users of the Panix system. With those passwords, they then were able to access other computers connected to the Internet to steal both data and more passwords. The security of the whole system had been compromised. Other break-ins have increased the concern.

The breaching in November 1993 of the National Weather Service computers brought more publicity and put a spotlight on the risks of hackers. While the hackers apparently had other prey in mind and used the weather service network only to break into other computers on the Internet, they could have done great damage. John Ward, a com-

puter manager for the U.S. Weather Bureau, points out that damage to its systems could result in the grounding of all commercial airplane flights, resulting in hundreds of millions of dollars of economic loss. The hackers were traced and eventually caught. That they were Danish and operating in Denmark highlighted the international magnitude of the problem. In October 1994, newspapers revealed that a group of hackers had stolen valuable copies of new software from such companies as Microsoft Corp. and IBM. The thieves quietly made the software available for free to people through the Internet. This time the break-in occurred at Florida State University where the stolen software had been kept. Most of the "recipients" of the free software were not from the United States, again highlighting the worldwide nature of the problem. James P. Lennane, president of DeScribe Inc. of Naples, Florida, whose word processor was among the stolen products being given away, summed up one perspective by charging that "The Internet is a conduit of criminal activity."

Another worry surfaced in September 1994, when it was revealed that the underlying software formula for a data encryption system belonging to RSA Data Security Inc. of Redwood City, California, was being distributed on the Internet. Data encryption is viewed as one effective protection against data thieves. Even if hackers could steal encrypted data as it travels through the Internet (or any other network), it would be meaningless gibberish if the thieves did not have the encryption key to unscramble it. RSA's encryption software has become a kind of encryption standard. It is used by IBM, Apple, Sun Microsystems, Microsoft, and Lotus Development Corporation, among many others. It is the only encryption system with the legal approval of the U.S. federal government to be exported. Now that its coding has been circulated on the Internet, data transmitted using RSA software is no longer secure—it can be unscrambled.

The question most businesses are asking is what can their organization do? A number of answers exist, but whether they are used or not and how

> **To Think About:** In light of these security problems, under what circumstances might you recommend that your organization use the Internet? What management, organization, and technology issues would you consider?

effective they will be can only be known over time. The U.S. Weather Bureau discovered that its computer system still contained active passwords for people who were no longer employed there, an obvious breach of security. Aside from the obvious need to remove all passwords when employees leave, one rule of good security is to require system users to change their passwords often, perhaps monthly, perhaps more often, depending upon the risk. Computers can be and often are programmed to force password changing as often as the organization requires. This will not stop password stealing altogether—many other ways exist to obtain someone's password. But it would tighten one of the key loopholes.

Technology is another possibility. Some companies are achieving a measure of security by installing firewalls. *Firewall* is a general term for a range of devices that operate between networks, such as routers and gateways. While their primary purposes include directing network traffic and making possible the flow of data between different networks, they have also been pressed into service in the security battle. Some of these firewalls are being used to route all communications through a third-party computer, allowing no one directly into the home computer. In that way, potential hackers cannot get in to wander through the directories and to implant secret programs where they wish. Other devices allow the user of the firewall to list all applications and computer user log ons that are allowed to send messages to the computer being protected. If a message arrives from a source not on the firewall table, it is simply rejected.

Many companies are working on robust data encryption systems for the Net. Others are developing secure ways to process transactions. For example, Netscape Communications Corporation, Mountain View, California, and Bank of America are jointly offering a new service that enables consumers, making purchases over the Net, to pay using any of the more popular credit cards without risk. This service will encrypt the data, will work in real time, and will be free to the consumer. However, such systems are new and untested. Achieving full security on the Net will likely take some time.

One organization exists for the purpose of addressing security on the Internet. CERT (the Computer Emergency Response Team referred to above) helps both to determine who is breaking in to the Internet and to devise solutions to the method used for the break-in. When an Internet user reports a new break-in, CERT does not publicize it until a solution has been found. "We don't want to create mass hysteria if there's no way to address a new, isolated problem," says Moira West, manager of CERT's incident-response team. "We also don't want to alert the entire intruder community about it," she adds. With the increase in break-ins, the U.S. Defense Department's Advanced Research Projects Agency (ARPA) is planning to add funding to CERT in order to dou-

ble its staff. The Federal Bureau of Investigation (FBI) also investigates computer crimes reported to it, 80 percent of which are on the Internet.

Sources: Catherine Jones, "Castle Internet Under Attack," *Client/Server Computing*, April 1995; David Bernstein, "Insulate Against Internet Intruders," *Datamation*, October 1, 1994; John J. Fialka, "The Latest Flurries at Weather Bureau: Scattered Hacking," *The Wall Street Journal*, October 10, 1994; John Markoff, "Computer Code Is Out," *The New York Times*, September 17, 1994 and "A Dose of Computer Insecurity," *The New York Times*, October 30, 1993; Joseph C. Panettiere, "Guardian of the Net," *InformationWeek*, May 23, 1994; Jared Sandberg, "Hackers Put Pirated Software on Internet," *The Wall Street Journal*, October 31, 1994; Joshua Zecher, "Commerce with Caution on the Internet," *Wall Street & Technology*, July 1994.

in minutes, tying up computer memory and storage space as it copied and recopied itself hundreds of thousands of times.

The virus was quickly detected, but hundreds of computer centers in research institutions, universities, and military bases had to shut down. Estimates of the number of systems actually infected ranged from 6000 to 250,000. A virus that was not intended to harm caused upward of $100 million in lost machine time, lost access, and direct labor costs for recovery and cleanup.

In addition to spreading via computer networks, viruses can invade computerized information systems from "infected" diskettes from an outside source, through infected machines, or even from on-line electronic bulletin boards. The potential for massive damage and loss from future computer viruses remains (see Figure 18.3). A survey conducted by the National Computer Security Association (NCSA) and Dataquest, Inc. found that the average virus attack affected 142 PCs and took 2.4 days to eradicate, with many taking more than 5 days to correct. The study predicted that viruses would cost U.S. businesses $2 million in 1994 alone (Anthes, 1993).

Fears mounted about predictions of a Michelangelo virus that was scheduled to erupt on March 6, 1992, to destroy computer data on hard disks around the globe. The virus was so named because its creator programmed it to come alive on Michelangelo's 517th birthday. Alarmists worried that hundreds of thousands of systems could be affected. Fortunately, when the dreaded day arrived, only a few hundred systems reported damage. Organizations were able to use antivirus software and screening procedures to reduce the chances of infection. **Antivirus software** is special software designed to check computer systems and disks for the presence of various computer viruses. Often the software can eliminate the virus from the infected area. However, most antivirus software is effective only against viruses already known when the software is written—to protect their systems, management must continually update their antivirus software.

antivirus software Software designed to detect and often eliminate computer viruses from an information system.

Advances in computer software have also increased the chances of information system misuse and abuse. Using fourth-generation languages, end users can now perform programming functions that were formerly reserved for technical specialists. They can produce programs that inadvertently create errors, and they can manipulate the organization's data for illegitimate purposes. Chapter 5 contains a more detailed discussion of computer crime and abuse.

FIGURE 18.3

From "Viruses Continue to Wreak Havoc at Many U.S.Companies" by Gary H. Anthes, Computerworld, June 28, 1993. *Copyright 1993 by Computerworld, Inc., Framingham, MA 01701. Reprinted from Computerworld by permission.*

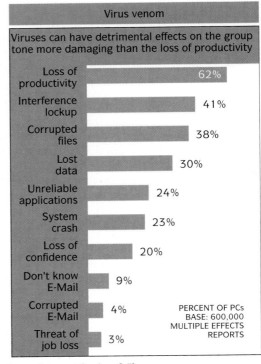

Source: Dataquest, San Jose, Calif.

Companies can detect and eliminate computer viruses in their systems by regularly using anti-virus software.

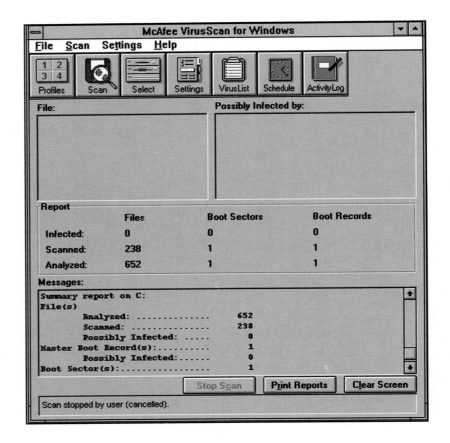

The growth of database systems, where data are shared by multiple application areas, has also created new vulnerabilities. All data are stored in one common location, but many users may have the right to access and modify them. It may not be easy to identify who is using or possibly misusing the data in such circumstances. Since the data are used by more than one organizational unit, the effect of an error may reverberate throughout the organization. There may also be less chance of discovering errors. Each functional unit has less individual control over the data and has fewer grounds for knowing whether the computer is right.

CONCERNS FOR SYSTEM BUILDERS AND USERS

The heightened vulnerability of automated data has created special concerns for the builders and users of information systems. These concerns include disaster, security, and administrative error.

Disaster

Computer hardware, programs, data files, and other equipment can be destroyed by fires, power failures, or other disasters. Such disasters can disrupt normal operations and even bring an entire organization to a standstill. It may take many years and millions of dollars to reconstruct destroyed data files and computer programs. If an organization needs them to function on a day-to-day basis, it will no longer be able to operate. This is why companies such as Visa USA Inc. and National Trust, for example, employ elaborate emergency backup facilities.

Visa USA Inc. has duplicate mainframes, duplicate network pathways, duplicate terminals, and duplicate power supplies. Visa even uses a duplicate data center in McLean, Virginia, to handle half of its transactions and to serve as an emergency backup to its primary data center in San Mateo, California. National Trust, a large bank in Ontario, Canada, uses uninterruptable power supply technology provided by International Power Machines (IPM), a provider of power protection technology. The electrical power at National Trust's Mississauga location fluctuates frequently during the normal business day, largely due to a nearby shopping mall.

fault-tolerant computer systems
Systems that contain extra hardware, software, and power supply components that can back the system up and keep it running to prevent system failure.

Fault-tolerant computer systems contain extra hardware, software, and power supply components that can back the system up and keep it running to prevent system failure. Fault-tolerant computers contain extra memory chips, processors, and disk storage devices. They can use special software routines or self-checking logic built into their circuitry to detect hardware failures and automatically switch to backup devices. Parts from these computers can be removed and repaired without disruption to the computer system. Their increased reliability is the reason the European Community banks are using fault-tolerant computer systems to clear cross-border transaction trading in the new unified European currency, the European Currency Unit (ECU). Eventually the European Community countries expect to make the ECU their single currency for international trade, making the stability of this clearing function critical to the stability of the world economy. In 1992 European banks were already processing 40 billion ECUs a day, and its users cannot afford a failure of the computer system.

on-line transaction processing
Transaction processing mode in which transactions entered on-line are immediately processed by the computer.

Fault-tolerant technology is used by firms for critical applications with heavy on-line transaction processing requirements. In **on-line transaction processing**, transactions entered on-line are immediately processed by the computer. Multitudinous changes to databases, reporting, or requests for information occur each instant.

Rather than build their own backup facilities, many firms contract with disaster recovery firms, such as Comdisco Disaster Recovery Services in Rosemont, Illinois, and Sungard Recovery Services headquartered in Wayne, Pennsylvania. The chapter-opening vignette shows how these disaster recovery firms provide "hot sites" housing spare computers at various locations around the country where subscribing firms can run their critical applications in an emergency. Disaster recovery services now offer

CLIENT/SERVER DISASTER PLANNING

Is it less important to back up client/server systems than to back up mainframe-based systems? Apparently many managers do seem to think so. A recent survey of 200 large U.S. corporations relying upon client/server systems found that two thirds have no disaster recovery plan for data stored away from their central computers. However, disasters do not discriminate based upon infrastructure type—fires and earthquakes play no favorites. Cedar Sinai Medical Center in Los Angeles found that out when the Northridge earthquake of January 1994 knocked out half of its network.

Cedar Sinai's Dennis Martin, manager of computer resource administration, indicated after the earthquake that they had anchored most of their systems at their central location but not at the remote locations. They now plan to tie them down and to install uninterruptible power supplies at the outlying sites also. In contrast, the network of ITT Gilfillan, a radar manufacturer located in Van Nuys—the town right next to Northridge—survived with few problems, partly because it was already backing up its off-site server data. Backup of client/server systems has become important enough that all three of the leading mainframe disaster recovery services (Sungard, Comdisco, and IBM) are now offering client/server recovery options as part of their service.

If your organization relies upon a client/server infrastructure, your management needs to address the problem or risk a disaster with no way to recover from it quickly, if at all. The questions your management has to face are How do we go about instituting a disaster program for our client/server infrastructure? Should our management rely upon an outside service for disaster recovery or do it internally?

Instituting a client/server disaster recovery program. Most experts agree that client/server disaster recovery is much more complex than it is in a mainframe environment. Planning and testing, which are critical to a main-

frame disaster recovery program, become even more critical within a distributed environment. Vashdev Vangani, the manager of computing

> *To Think About:* *What management, technology, and organization reasons do you think led Vashdev Vangani to conclude that backing up all nodes of a 500-user network is impossible? What management, technology, and organization issues should be addressed in a disaster recovery plan?*

and telecommunications at Mazda Motors, located in Irvine, California, points out that recovering all data from a network with 500 users is impossible. Therefore, he began the process at Mazda by carefully evaluating what network data must be backed up. ITT Gilfillan took another approach, deciding to bring all of its key network servers back into the corporate data center where they can more easily be backed up along with the mainframe data. Whichever approach is used, the disaster recovery service firms strongly recommend that an organization begin with a business analysis, using the results of the study to determine what must be backed up. The organization needs to identify how much data there is and what data need to be backed up in the event of disaster. The analysis will also need to identify which managers and technical employees are critical to a rapid recovery from a disaster and what they will need (in programs, data, and equipment) to bring the system back. Critical business employees who will need to be brought back online very quickly must also be identified so the plan can include the equipment and steps needed to hook them up after a disaster. Experts do point out, however, that it is important to keep to a minimum the number of people identified as critical, partly because a flood or earthquake can make it physically

difficult to get to many of the people. Testing also is key. Testing will build team skills so that disaster recovery will actually work if a disaster occurs. It also will allow the organization to find and solve problems.

Determining whether to rely on an outside, third-party service or to do it themselves internally can be a complex issue. Many companies do not use outside services because they are viewed as expensive. For many they may be. However, Chuck Littleton, director of information services at Dallas-based Bluebonnet Savings Bank BSF (with branches throughout the Southwest United States), urges companies to look

at the issue carefully. He found that it was actually cheaper for his firm to go outside. "We could have set up our own network recovery operations for about the same price—$200,000 for the first year," he points out. However, he explains, costs fell by 70 percent the second year because of backup and recovery improvements that resulted from testing. Moreover, technology keeps changing very rapidly, and smaller companies will find it very expensive if not impossible to keep up with such changes. Disaster service companies will keep up for them.

A final point. As with mainframe disaster planning, procedures must be

established for client/server backup and disaster recovery, and they must be enforced, which requires the backing of management. When Bluebonnet Savings turned to IBM for disaster recovery services, senior management accompanied the other Bluebonnet employees who participated in recovery testing. This surely gave the whole company a message as to the importance of the function.

Source: Monica Snell, "A Case of Do . . . Or Die," *Client/Server Computing*, February 1995; and Barbara DePompa, "Date with Disaster," *InformationWEEK*, May 2, 1994.

backup for client/server systems as well as traditional mainframe applications (see the Window on Management). Disaster recovery firms also offer "cold sites," special buildings designed to house computer equipment; they do not contain computers, but they can be made operational in one week.

Security

security Policies, procedures, and technical measures used to prevent unauthorized access, alteration, theft, or physical damage to information systems.

Security refers to the policies, procedures, and technical measures used to prevent unauthorized access or alteration, theft, and physical damage to information systems. Security can be promoted with an array of techniques and tools to safeguard computer hardware, software, communications networks, and data. We have already discussed disaster protection measures. Other tools and techniques for promoting security will be described in subsequent sections.

Errors

Computers can also serve as instruments of error, severely disrupting or destroying an organization's recordkeeping and operations. Errors in automated systems can occur at many points in the processing cycle: through data entry, program error, computer operations, and hardware. Figure 18.4 illustrates all of the points in a typical processing cycle where errors can occur. Even minor mistakes in automated systems can have disastrous financial or operational repercussions. For instance, on February 25, 1991, during Operation Desert Storm, a Patriot missile defense system operating at Dharan, Saudi Arabia, failed to track and intercept an incoming Scud missile launched by Iraq. The failure was traced to a software error in the system's weapons control computer. The Scud hit an Army barracks, killing 28 Americans.

18.2   CREATING A CONTROL ENVIRONMENT

controls All the methods, policies, and procedures that ensure protection of the organization's assets, accuracy and reliability of its records, and operational adherence to management standards.

To minimize errors, disaster, computer crime, and breaches of security, special policies and procedures must be incorporated into the design and implementation of information systems. The combination of manual and automated measures that safeguard information systems and ensure that they perform according to management standards is termed *controls*. **Controls** consist of all the methods, policies, and organizational procedures that ensure the safety of the organization's assets, the accuracy

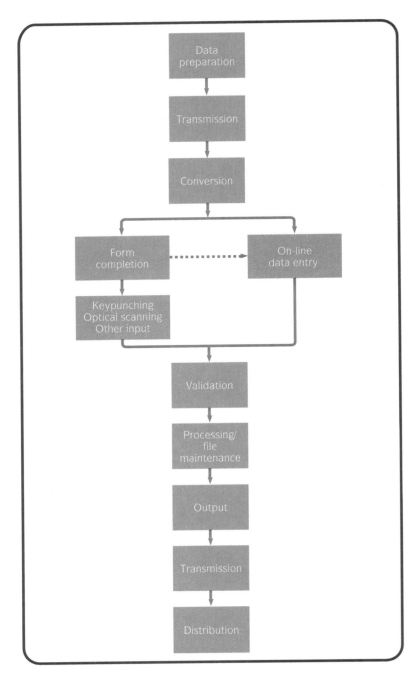

and reliability of its accounting records, and operational adherence to management standards.

In the past, the control of information systems was treated as an afterthought, addressed only toward the end of implementation, just before the system was installed. Today, however, organizations are so critically dependent on information systems that vulnerabilities and control issues must be identified as early as possible. The control of an information system must be an integral part of its design. Users and builders of systems must pay close attention to controls throughout the system's life span.

Computer systems are controlled by a combination of general controls and application controls.

General controls are those that control the design, security, and use of computer programs and the security of data files in general throughout the organization. On

general controls Overall controls that establish a framework for controlling the design, security, and use of computer programs throughout an organization.

the whole, general controls apply to all computerized applications and consist of a combination of system software and manual procedures that create an overall control environment.

Application controls are specific controls unique to each computerized application, such as payroll, accounts receivable, and order processing. They consist of both controls applied from the user functional area of a particular system and from programmed procedures.

application controls Specific controls unique to each computerized application

GENERAL CONTROLS

General controls are overall controls that ensure the effective operation of programmed procedures. They apply to all application areas. General controls include the following:

- Controls over the system implementation process
- Software controls
- Physical hardware controls
- Computer operations controls
- Data security controls
- Administrative controls

Implementation Controls

implementation controls Audit of the systems development process at various points to make sure that it is properly controlled and managed.

Implementation controls audit the systems development process at various points to ensure that the process is properly controlled and managed. The systems development audit should look for the presence of formal review points at various stages of development that enable users and management to approve or disapprove the implementation. (Examples of such review points are user and management sign-offs on the initial systems proposal, design specifications, conversion, testing, and the post-implementation audit described in Chapter 12.)

The systems development audit should also examine the level of user involvement at each stage of implementation and check for the use of a formal cost/benefit methodology in establishing system feasibility. The audit should also look for the use of controls and quality assurance techniques for program development, conversion, and testing. (These issues are discussed in Chapters 11–13).

An important though frequently neglected requirement of systems building is appropriate documentation. Without good documentation that shows how a system operates from both a technical and a user standpoint, an information system may be difficult, if not impossible, to operate, maintain, or use. Table 18.2 lists the various pieces of documentation that are normally required to run and maintain an information system. The systems development audit should look for system, user, and operations documentation that conforms to formal standards.

Software Controls

software controls Controls to ensure the security and reliability of software.

Controls are essential for the various categories of software used in computer systems. **Software controls** monitor the use of system software and prevent unauthorized access of software programs, system software, and computer programs.

System software controls govern the software for the operating system, which regulates and manages computer resources to facilitate execution of application programs. System software controls are also used for compilers, utility programs, reporting of operations, file setup and handling, and library recordkeeping. System software is an important control area because it performs overall control functions for the programs that directly process data and data files. **Program security controls** are designed to prevent unauthorized changes to programs in systems that are already in production.

program security controls Controls designed to prevent unauthorized changes to programs in systems that are already in production.

Table 18.2	Essential User and Technical Documentation for an Information System
Technical Documentation	**User Documentation**
System flowchart	Sample reports/output layouts
File layouts	Sample input forms/screens
Record layouts	Data preparation instructions
List of programs/modules	Data input instructions
Program structure charts	Instructions for using reports
Narrative program/module descriptions	Security profiles
Source program listings	Functional description of system
Module cross references	Work flows
Error conditions/actions	Error correction procedures
Abnormal termination	Accountabilities
Job setup requirements	Processing procedure narrative
Job run schedules	List/description of controls
Report-output distribution	Responsible user contact
Responsible programmer contact	
Job control language listings	
Backup/recovery procedures	
Run control procedures	
File access procedures	
Hardware/operating system requirements	

Hardware Controls

hardware controls Controls to ensure the physical security and correct performance of computer hardware.

Hardware controls ensure that computer hardware is physically secure and check for equipment malfunction. Computer hardware should be physically secured so that it can be accessed only by authorized individuals. Access to rooms where computers operate should be restricted to computer operations personnel. Computer terminals in other areas or microcomputers can be kept in locked rooms. Computer equipment should be specially protected against fires and extremes of temperature and humidity. Organizations that are critically dependent on their computers must also make provisions for emergency backup in case of power failure.

Many kinds of computer hardware also contain mechanisms that check for equipment malfunction. Parity checks detect equipment malfunctions responsible for altering bits within bytes during processing. Validity checks monitor the structure of on-off bits within bytes to make sure that it is valid for the character set of a particular computer machine. Echo checks verify that a hardware device is performance ready. Chapter 6 discusses computer hardware in detail.

Computer Operations Controls

computer operations controls Procedures to ensure that programmed procedures are consistently and correctly applied to data storage and processing.

Computer operations controls apply to the work of the computer department and help ensure that programmed procedures are consistently and correctly applied to the storage and processing of data. They include controls over the setup of computer processing jobs, operations software and computer operations, and backup and recovery procedures for processing that ends abnormally.

Instructions for running computer jobs should be fully documented, reviewed, and approved by a responsible official. Controls over operations software include manual procedures designed to both prevent and detect error. These are comprised of specified operating instructions for system software, restart and recovery procedures, procedures for the labeling and disposition of input and output magnetic tapes, and procedures for specific applications.

Human-operator error at a computer system at the Shell Pipeline Corporation caused the firm to ship 93,000 barrels of crude oil to the wrong trader. This one error cost Shell $2 million. A computer operator at Exxon Corporation headquarters inadvertently erased valuable records about the 1989 grounding of the Exxon *Valdez* and the Alaskan oil spill that were stored on magnetic tape. Such errors could have been avoided had the companies incorporated tighter operational safeguards.

System software can maintain a system log detailing all activity during processing. This log can be printed for review so that hardware malfunction, abnormal endings, and operator actions can be investigated. Specific instructions for backup and recovery can be developed so that in the event of a hardware or software failure, the recovery process for production programs, system software, and data files does not create erroneous changes in the system.

Data Security Controls

data security controls Controls to ensure that data files on either disk or tape are not subject to unauthorized access, change, or destruction.

Data security controls ensure that valuable business data files on either disk or tape are not subject to unauthorized access, change, or destruction. Such controls are required for data files when they are in use and when they are being held for storage. It is easier to control data files in batch systems, since access is limited to operators who run the batch jobs. However, on-line and real-time systems are vulnerable at several points. They can be accessed through terminals as well as by operators during production runs.

When data can be input on-line through a terminal, entry of unauthorized input must be prevented. For example, a credit note could be altered to match a sales invoice on file. In such situations, security can be developed on several levels:

- Terminals can be physically restricted so that they are available only to authorized individuals.

- System software can include the use of passwords assigned only to authorized individuals. No one can log on to the system without a valid password.

- Additional sets of passwords and security restrictions can be developed for specific systems and applications. For example, data security software can limit access to specific files, such as the files for the accounts receivable system. It can restrict the type of access so that only individuals authorized to update these specific files will have the ability to do so. All others will only be able to read the files or will be denied access altogether.

Systems that allow on-line inquiry and reporting must have data files secured. Figure 18.5 illustrates the security allowed for two sets of users of an on-line personnel database with sensitive information such as employees' salaries, benefits, and medical histories. One set of users consists of all employees who perform clerical functions such as inputting employee data into the system. All individuals with this type of profile can update the system but can neither read nor update sensitive fields such as salary, medical history, or earnings data. Another profile applies to a divisional manager, who cannot update the system but can read all employee data fields for his or her division, including medical history and salary. These profiles would be established and maintained by a data security system. A multilayered data security system is essential for ensuring that this information can be accessed only by authorized persons. The data security system illustrated in Figure 18.5 provides very fine-grained security restrictions, such as allowing authorized personnel users to inquire about all employee information except in confidential fields such as salary or medical history.

FIGURE 18.5
Security profiles for a personnel system. These two examples represent two security profiles or data security patterns that might be found in a personnel system. Depending upon the security profile, a user would have certain restrictions on access to various systems, locations, or data in an organization.

SECURITY PROFILE 1

User: Personnel Dept. Clerk

Location: Division 1

Employee Identification
Codes with This Profile: 00753, 27834, 37665, 44116

Data Field Restrictions	Type of Access
All employee data for Division 1 only	Read and Update
• Medical history data	None
• Salary	None
• Pensionable earnings	None

SECURITY PROFILE 2

User: Divisional Personnel Manager

Location: Division 1

Employee Identification
Codes with This Profile: 27321

Data Field Restrictions	Type of Access
All employee data for Division 1 only	Read Only

Although the security risk of files maintained off-line is smaller, such data files on disk or tape can be removed for unauthorized purposes. These can be secured in lockable storage areas, with tight procedures so that they are released only for authorized processing. Usage logs and library records can be maintained for each removable storage device if it is labeled and assigned a unique identity number.

Administrative Controls

administrative controls
Formalized standards, rules, procedures, and disciplines to ensure that the organization's controls are properly executed and enforced.

segregation of functions Principle of internal control to divide responsibilities and assign tasks among people so that job functions do not overlap to minimize the risk of errors and fraudulent manipulation of the organization's assets.

Administrative controls are formalized standards, rules, procedures, and control disciplines to ensure that the organization's general and application controls are properly executed and enforced. The most important administrative controls are (1) segregation of functions, (2) written policies and procedures, and (3) supervision.

Segregation of functions is a fundamental principle of internal control in any organization. In essence, it means that job functions should be designed to minimize the risk of errors or fraudulent manipulation of the organization's assets. The individuals responsible for operating systems should not be the same ones who can initiate transactions that change the assets held in these systems. Responsibilities for input, processing, and output are usually divided among different people to restrict what each one can do with the system. For example, the individuals who operate the system should not have the authority to initiate payments or to sign checks. A typical arrangement is to have the organization's information systems department responsible for data and program files and end users responsible for initiating input transactions or correcting errors. Within the information systems department, the duties of programmers and analysts are segregated from those of computer equipment operators. (The organization of the information systems department is discussed in Chapter 3.)

Table 18.3 Effect of Weakness in General Controls

Weakness Area	Impact
Implementation controls	New systems or systems that have been modified will have errors or fail to function as required.
Software controls (program security)	Unauthorized changes can be made in processing. The organization may not be sure of which programs or systems have been changed.
Software controls (system software)	These controls may not have a direct effect on individual applications. Since other general controls depend heavily on system software, a weakness in this area impairs the other general controls.
Physical hardware controls	Hardware may have serious malfunctions or may break down altogether, introducing numerous errors or destroying computerized records.
Computer operations controls	Random errors may occur in a system. (Most processing will be correct but occasionally it may not be.)
Data file security controls	Unauthorized changes can be made in data stored in computer systems or unauthorized individuals can access sensitive information.
Administrative controls	All of the other controls may not be properly executed or enforced.

Written policies and procedures establish formal standards for controlling information system operations. Procedures must be formalized in writing and authorized by the appropriate level of management. Accountabilities and responsibilities must be clearly specified.

Supervision of personnel involved in control procedures ensures that the controls for an information system are performing as intended. With supervision, weaknesses can be spotted, errors corrected, and deviations from standard procedures identified. Without adequate supervision, the best-designed set of controls may be bypassed, short-circuited, or neglected.

Weakness in each of these general controls can have a widespread effect on programmed procedures and data throughout the organization. Table 18.3 summarizes the effect of weaknesses in major general control areas.

APPLICATION CONTROLS

Application controls are specific controls within each separate computer application, such as payroll or order processing. They include both automated and manual procedures that ensure that only authorized data are completely and accurately processed by that application. The controls for each application should take account of the whole sequence of processing, manual and computer, from the first steps taken to prepare transactions to the production and use of final output.

Not all of the application controls discussed here are used in every information system. Some systems require more of these controls than others, depending on the importance of the data and the nature of the application.

Application controls focus on the following objectives:

1. *Completeness of input and update.* All current transactions must reach the computer and be recorded on computer files.
2. *Accuracy of input and update.* Data must be accurately captured by the computer and correctly recorded on computer files.
3. *Validity.* Data must be authorized or otherwise checked with regard to the appropriateness of the transaction. (In other words, the transaction must reflect the right event in the external world. The validity of an address change, for example, refers to whether a transaction actually captured the right address for a specific individual.)
4. *Maintenance.* Data on computer files must continue to remain correct and current.

Application controls can be classified as (1) input controls, (2) processing controls, and (3) output controls.

Input Controls

Input controls check data for accuracy and completeness when they enter the system. There are specific input controls for input authorization, data conversion, data editing, and error handling.

Input authorization.   Input must be properly authorized, recorded, and monitored as source documents flow to the computer. For example, formal procedures can be set up to authorize only selected members of the sales department to prepare sales transactions for an order entry system. Sales input forms might be serially numbered, grouped into *batches,* and logged so that they can be tracked as they pass from sales units to the unit responsible for inputting them into the computer. The batches may require authorization signatures before they can be entered into the computer.

Data conversion.   Input must be properly converted into computer transactions, with no errors as it is transcribed from one form to another. Transcription errors can be eliminated or reduced by keying input transactions directly into computer terminals from their source documents. (Point-of-sale systems can capture sales and inventory transactions directly by scanning product bar codes.)

   Batch control totals can be established beforehand for transactions grouped in batches. These totals can range from a simple document count to totals for quantity fields such as total sales amount (for the batch). Computer programs count the batch totals from transactions input. Batches that do not balance are rejected. On-line, real-time systems can also utilize batch controls by creating control totals to reconcile with hard copy documents that feed input.

Edit checks.   Various routines can be performed to edit input data for errors before they are processed. Transactions that do not meet edit criteria will be rejected. The edit routines can produce lists of errors to be corrected later. The most important types of edit techniques are summarized in Table 18.4.

   An advantage of on-line, real-time systems is that editing can be performed up front. As each transaction is input and entered it can be edited, and the terminal operator can be notified immediately if an error is found. Alternatively, the operator may fail to correct the error on purpose or by accident. The system can be designed to reject additional input until the error is corrected or to print a hard copy error list that can be reviewed by others.

Processing Controls

Processing controls establish that data are complete and accurate during updating. The major processing controls are run control totals, computer matching, and programmed edit checks.

   Run control totals reconcile the input control totals with the totals of items that have updated the file. Updating can be controlled by generating control totals dur-

Table 18.4 Important Edit Techniques

Edit Technique	Description	Example
Reasonableness checks	To be accepted, data must fall within certain limits set in advance, or they will be rejected.	If an order transaction is for 20,000 units and the largest order on record was 50 units, the transaction will be rejected.
Format checks	Characteristics of the contents (letter/digit), length, and sign of individual data fields are checked by the system.	A nine-position Social Security number should not contain any alphabetic characters.
Existence checks	The computer compares input reference data to tables or master files to make sure that valid codes are being used.	An employee can have a Fair Labor Standards Act code of only 1, 2, 3, 4, or 5. All other values for this field will be rejected.
Dependency checks	The computer checks whether a *logical* relationship is maintained between data for the *same* transaction. When it is not, the transaction is rejected.	A car loan initiation transaction should show a logical relationship between the size of the loan, the number of loan repayments, and the size of each installment.
Check digit	An extra reference number called a *check digit* follows an identification code and bears a mathematical relationship to the other digits. This extra digit is input with the data, recomputed by the computer, and the result compared with the one input.	See the check digit in Figure 18.6 for a product code using the Modulus 11 check digit system.

FIGURE 18.6

Check digit for a product code. This is a product code with the last position as a check digit, as developed by the Modulus 11 check digit system, the most common check digit method. The check digit is 7 and is derived by the steps listed in this figure. Errors in the transcription or transposition of this product code can be detected by a computer program that replicates the same procedure for deriving the check digit. If a data entry person mistakenly keys in the product number as 29753, the program will read the first five digits and carry out the Modulus 11 process. It will derive a check digit of 4. When this is compared to the original check digit on the last position of the product code, the program will find that the check digits do not match and that an error has occurred.

Product Code:	2 9 7 4 3
Weight:	6 5 4 3 2
Multiply each product code number by weight:	12 45 28 12 6
Sum results:	12 + 45 + 28 + 12 + 6 = 103
Divide the sum by modulus:	103/11 = 9 with remainder of 4
Subtract remainder from modulus number to obtain check digit:	11 − 4 = 7
Add check digit to original product code to obtain new code:	297437

ing processing. The totals, such as total transactions processed or totals for critical quantities, can be compared manually or by computer. Discrepancies are noted for investigation.

computer matching Processing control that matches input data with information held on master files.

Computer matching matches the input data with information held on master or suspense files, with unmatched items noted for investigation. Most matching occurs during input, but under some circumstances it may be required to ensure completeness of updating. For example, a matching program might match employee time cards with a payroll master file and report missing or duplicate time cards.

Edit checks verify reasonableness or consistency of data. Most edit checking occurs at the time data are input. However, certain applications require some type of reasonableness or dependency check during updating as well. For example, consistency checks might be utilized by a utility company to compare a customer's electric bill with previous bills. If the bill were 500 percent higher this month compared to last month, the bill would not be processed until the meter was rechecked.

Output Controls

output controls Ensure that the results of computer processing are accurate, complete, and properly distributed.

Output controls ensure that the results of computer processing are accurate, complete, and properly distributed. Typical output controls include the following:

- Balancing output totals with input and processing totals
- Reviews of the computer processing logs to determine that all of the correct computer jobs were executed properly for processing
- Audits of output reports to make sure that totals, formats, and critical details are correct and reconcilable with input
- Formal procedures and documentation specifying authorized recipients of output reports, checks, or other critical documents

DEVELOPING A CONTROL STRUCTURE: COSTS AND BENEFITS

Information systems can make exhaustive use of all of the control mechanisms previously discussed. But they may be so expensive to build and so complicated to use that the system is economically or operationally unfeasible. Some cost/benefit analysis must be performed to determine which control mechanisms provide the most effective safeguards without sacrificing operational efficiency or cost.

One of the criteria that determine how much control is built into a system is the *importance of its data*. Major financial and accounting systems, for example, such as a payroll system or one that tracks purchases and sales on the stock exchange, must have higher standards of controls than a system to inventory employee training and skills or a "tickler" system to track dental patients and remind them that their six-month checkup is due. For instance, Swiss Bank invested in additional hardware and software to increase its network reliability because it was running critical financial trading and banking applications (see the Window on Technology).

standing data Data that are permanent and affect transactions flowing into and out of a system.

Standing data, the data that are permanent and that affect transactions flowing into and out of a system (e.g., codes for existing products or cost centers) require closer monitoring than individual transactions. A single error in transaction data will affect only that transaction, while a standing data error may affect many or all transactions each time the file is processed.

The cost effectiveness of controls will also be influenced by the efficiency, complexity, and expense of each control technique. For example, complete one-for-one checking may be time-consuming and operationally impossible for a system that processes hundreds of thousands of utilities payments daily. But it might be possible to use this technique to verify only critical data such as dollar amounts and account numbers, while ignoring names and addresses.

risk assessment Determining the potential frequency of occurrence of a problem and the potential damage if the problem were to occur. Used to determine the cost/benefit of a control.

A third consideration is the *level of risk* if a specific activity or process is not properly controlled. System builders can undertake a **risk assessment,** determining

INCREASING THE RELIABILITY OF SWISS BANK'S NETWORK

Swiss Bank Corp. understands how vital the control of its network operations is to the success of its network and its business. When in late 1972 Swiss Bank merged with trading firm O'Conner Partnership, the bank had to find a way to merge its worldwide T1 network with O'Conner's domestic network. The main issue in merging the two systems, in addition to cost, was reliability, a key factor in the financial trading and banking industries. To merge the two, Swiss Bank at first determined it would have to invest heavily in new telecommunications bandwidth, an expensive approach. To avoid this expenditure, the bank turned instead to multiplexing technology and data compression to greatly increase the data the current system could handle. The bank chose technology that also would increase the reliability and security of the newly merged network.

The compression equipment the bank purchased was Datamizer IV from Symplex Communications Corp. Datamizer includes an error detection facility as well as load balancing and congestion control. It compresses the voice traffic from the new organization's PBXs separately from the data traffic and sends them both out over the T1 line. According to Swiss Bank network engineer Mike Raffety, Datamizer continuously monitors the T1 trunks, and if the traffic gets too heavy, the voice traffic is bumped to public networks, giving the data priority for uninterrupted transmission.

Swiss Bank also determined that it could improve reliability through redundancy. The bank installed dual network devices such as the Datamizers and also employed backup telecommunications circuits to give the needed redundancy. The Datamizer monitors the primary network for outages, and when it detects an outage, it automatically routes traffic to the backup.

Other steps the bank has taken to further increase network security include installing encryption devices between the multiplexers and the trans-

> **To Think About:** What was the relationship between network reliability and Swiss Bank's business strategy? What other technology factors did Swiss Bank have to address as a result of merging the two networks described here?

mission lines. The whole approach was relatively inexpensive—16 Datamizers cost the bank $16,000 each. The bank calculates that the increased compression facility of this technology saved it the purchase cost in the first month.

Source: Joanie M. Wexler, "Swiss Bank Blends Nets," *Computerworld,* May 10, 1993.

the likely frequency of a problem and the potential damage if it were to occur. For example, if an event is likely to occur no more than once a year, with a maximum of a $1000 loss to the organization, it would not be feasible to spend $20,000 on the design and maintenance of a control to protect against that event. However, if that same event could occur at least once a day, with a potential loss of over $300,000 a year, $100,000 spent on a control might be entirely appropriate.

Table 18.5 illustrates sample results of a risk assessment for an on-line order processing system that processes 30,000 orders per day. The probability of a power failure occurring in a one-year period is 30 percent. Loss of order transactions while power is down could range from $5000 to $200,000 for each occurrence, depending on how long processing was halted. The probability of embezzlement occurring over a yearly period is about 5 percent, with potential losses ranging from $1000 to $50,000 for each occurrence. User errors have a 98 percent chance of occurring over a yearly period, with losses ranging from $200 to $40,000 for each occurrence. The average loss for each event can be weighted by multiplying it by the probability of its occurrence annually to determine the expected annual loss. Once the risks have been assessed, system builders can concentrate on the control points with the greatest vulnerability and potential loss. In this case, controls should focus on ways to minimize the risk of power failures and user errors.

In some situations, organizations may not know the precise probability of threats occurring to their information systems, and they may not be able to quantify the impact of events that disrupt their information systems. In these instances, management

---

Table 18.5	On-Line Order Processing Risk Assessment		
Exposure	Probability of Occurrence (%)	Loss Range/ Average ($)	Expected Annual Loss ($)
Power failure	30	5000–200,000 (102,500)	30,750
Embezzlement	5	1000–50,000 (25,500)	1,275
User error	98	200–40,000 (20,100)	19,698

This chart shows the results of a risk assessment of three selected areas of an on-line order processing system. The likelihood of each exposure occurring over a one-year period is expressed as a percentage. The next column shows the highest and lowest possible loss that could be expected each time the exposure occurred and an "average" loss calculated by adding the highest and lowest figures together and dividing by 2. The expected annual loss for each exposure can be determined by multiplying the "average" loss by its probability of occurrence.

may choose to describe risks and their likely impact in a qualitative manner (Rainer, Snyder, and Carr, 1991).

To decide which controls to use, information system builders must examine various control techniques in relation to each other and to their relative cost effectiveness. A control weakness at one point may be offset by a strong control at another. It may not be cost effective to build tight controls at every point in the processing cycle if the areas of greatest risk are secure or if compensating controls exist elsewhere. The combination of all of the controls developed for a particular application will determine its overall control structure.

18.3 AUDITING INFORMATION SYSTEMS

Once controls have been established for an information system, how do we know that they are effective? To answer this question, organizations must conduct comprehensive and systematic *audits*. Large organizations have their own internal auditing group charged with this responsibility.

THE ROLE OF AUDITING IN THE CONTROL PROCESS

MIS audit Identifies all the controls that govern individual information systems and assesses their effectiveness.

An **MIS audit** identifies all of the controls that govern individual information systems and assesses their effectiveness. To accomplish this, the auditor must acquire a thorough understanding of operations, physical facilities, telecommunications, control systems, data security objectives, organizational structure, personnel, manual procedures, and individual applications.

The auditor should collect and analyze all of the material about a specific information system, such as user and system documentation, sample inputs and outputs, and relevant documentation about integrity controls. The auditor usually interviews key individuals who use and operate the system concerning their activities and procedures. Application controls, overall integrity controls, and control disciplines are examined. The auditor should trace the flow of sample transactions through the system and perform tests, using, if appropriate, automated audit software.

The audit lists and ranks all control weaknesses and estimates the probability of their occurrence. It then assesses the financial and organizational impact of each threat. Figure 18.7 is a sample auditor's listing of control weaknesses for a loan system. It includes a section for notifying management of such weaknesses and for management's response. Management is expected to devise a plan for countering significant weaknesses in controls.

Nature of Weakness and Impact	Chance for Substantial Error		Effect on Audit Procedures	Notification to Management	
	Yes/ No	Justification	Required Amendment	Date of Report	Mangement Response
Loan repayment records are not reconciled to borrower's records during processing.	Yes	Without a detection control, errors in individual client balances may remain undetected.	Confirm a sample of loans.	5/10/95	Interest Rate Compare Report provides this control.
There are no regular audits of computer-generated data (interest charges).	Yes	Without a regular audit or reasonableness check, widespread miscalculations could result before errors are detected.		5/10/95	Periodic audits of loans will be instituted.
Programs can be put into production libraries to meet target deadlines without final approval from the Standards and Controls group.	No	All programs require management authorization. The Standards and Controls group controls access to all production systems, and assigns such cases to a temporary production status.			

FIGURE 18.7

Sample auditor's list of control weaknesses. This chart is a sample page from a list of control weaknesses that an auditor might find in a loan system in a local commercial bank. This form helps auditors record and evaluate control weaknesses and shows the result of discussing those weaknesses with management, as well as any corrective actions taken by management.

DATA QUALITY AUDITS

data quality audit Surveys of end users, files, and samples of files for accuracy and completeness of data in an information system.

An important aspect of information system auditing is an analysis of data quality. **Data quality audits** are accomplished by the following methods:

- Surveying end users for their perceptions of data quality
- Surveying entire data files
- Surveying samples from data files

This data quality auditor is analyzing the quality of data for a client by conducting a survey of data files for accuracy in the information system.

Unless regular data quality audits are undertaken, organizations have no way of knowing to what extent their information systems contain inaccurate, incomplete, or ambiguous information. Some organizations, such as the Social Security Administration, have established data quality audit procedures. These procedures control payment and process quality by auditing a 20,000-case sample of beneficiary records each month. The FBI, on the other hand, did not conduct a comprehensive audit of its record systems until 1984. With few data quality controls, the FBI criminal record systems were found to have serious problems.

A study of the FBI's computerized criminal record systems found a total of 54.1 percent of the records in the National Crime Information Center System to be inaccurate, ambiguous, or incomplete, and 74.3 percent of the records in the FBI's semi-automated Identification Division system exhibited significant quality problems. A summary analysis of the FBI's automated Wanted Persons File also found that 11.2 percent of the warrants were invalid. A study by the FBI itself found that 6 percent of the warrants in state files were invalid and that 12,000 invalid warrants are sent out nationally each day. The FBI has taken some steps to correct these problems, but low levels of data quality in these systems have disturbing implications.

- More than 14,000 persons could be at risk of being falsely detained and perhaps arrested because of invalid warrants.

- In addition to their use in law enforcement, computerized criminal history records are increasingly being used to screen employees in both the public and private sectors. This is the fastest growing use of these records in some states. Many of these records are incomplete and show arrests but no court disposition; that is, they show charges without proof of conviction or guilt. Many individuals may be denied employment unjustifiably because these records overstate their criminality.

- These criminal record systems are not limited to violent felons. They contain the records of 36 million people, about one third of the labor force. Inaccurate and potentially damaging information is being maintained on many law-abiding citizens.

The level of data quality in these systems threatens citizens' constitutional right to due process and impairs the efficiency and effectiveness of any law enforcement programs in which these records are used (Laudon, 1986a).

Data that are inaccurate, untimely, or inconsistent with other sources of information can also create serious operational and financial problems for businesses. When bad data go unnoticed, they can lead to bad decisions, product recalls, and even financial losses. For instance, Geer DuBois, a New York advertising agency, lost a $2.5-million-a-year account after the agency's billing system failed to credit the client for a six-figure payment. Even though Geer DuBois repaid the client with interest, the client decided to use another advertising firm. First Financial Management Corporation of Atlanta had to restate its earnings for the first nine months of the year because a subsidiary had lost track of some records after changing its accounting system (Wilson 1992). A 1992 study by the University of California at Los Angeles (UCLA) found an error rate of 9% in purchases made using laser scanners at checkout counters. Overcharges outnumbered undercharges by 2 to 1 because many merchandise items had higher prices in the scanner's database than on the shelf (Betts, 1994).

Management Challenges

1. Controlling large distributed multi-user networks. No system is totally secure, but large distributed multi-user networks are especially difficult to secure. Security becomes more problematic when networks are no longer confined to individual departments or groups or to centralized mainframe systems. It is very difficult to assert company-wide control over networks using heterogeneous hardware, software, and communications components when thousands of workers can access networks from many remote locations.

2. Subjectivity of risk analysis. Risk analysis depends on assumptions. For instance, the flawed Patriot missile system described earlier in this chapter was originally designed to work under a much less stringent environment than that in which it was actually used during Operation Desert Storm. Subsequent analyses of its effectiveness were downgraded from 95 percent to 13 percent (Neumann, 1993). Since risks are only potential events, not certainties, they are often overestimated or underestimated. Measures to avoid risk can also be used to stifle innovation or change.

3. Designing systems that are neither overcontrolled or undercontrolled. The biggest threat to information systems is posed by authorized users, not outside intruders. Most security breaches and damage to information systems come from organizational insiders. If there are too many passwords and authorizations required to access an information system, the system will go unused. Controls that are effective but that do not prevent authorized individuals from using a system are difficult to design.

Summary

1. **Show why automated information systems are so vulnerable to destruction, error, and abuse.** Organizations have become so dependent on computerized information systems that they must take special measures to ensure that these systems are properly controlled. With data easily concentrated into electronic form and many procedures invisible through automation, systems are vulnerable to destruction, misuse, error, fraud, and hardware or software failures. The effect of disaster in a computerized system can be greater than in manual systems because all of the records for a particular function or organization can be destroyed or lost. On-line systems and those utilizing telecommunications are especially vulnerable because data files can be immediately and directly accessed through computer terminals or at many points in the telecommunications network. Computer "viruses" can spread rampantly from system to system, clogging computer memory or destroying programs and data.

2. **Describe the role of controls in safeguarding information systems.** Controls consist of all the methods, policies, and organizational procedures that ensure the safety of the organization's assets, the accuracy and reliability of its accounting records, and adherence to management standards. For computerized information systems, controls consist of both manual and programmed procedures. Controls that safeguard information system security are especially important in today's on-line networked environment.

3. **Distinguish between general controls and application controls.** There are two main categories of controls: general controls and application controls. General controls control the overall design, security, and use of computer programs and files for the organization as a whole. They include physical hardware controls; system software controls; data file security controls; computer operations controls; controls over the system implementation process; and administrative controls.

Application controls are controls unique to specific computerized applications. They focus on the completeness and accuracy of input, updating and maintenance, and the validity of the information in the system. Application controls consist of (1) input controls, (2) processing controls, and (3) output controls.

4. **Describe the most important techniques for controlling information systems.** Some of the principal application control techniques are programmed routines to edit data before they are input or updated; run control totals; and reconciliation of input source documents with output reports.

5. **Identify the factors that must be considered when developing the controls for information systems.** To determine what controls are required, designers and users of systems must identify all of the control points and control weaknesses and perform risk assessment. They must also perform a cost/benefit analysis of controls and design controls that can effectively safeguard systems without making them unusable.

6. **Explain the importance of auditing information systems.** Comprehensive and systematic MIS auditing can help organizations to determine the effectiveness of the controls in their information systems. Regular data quality audits should be conducted to help organizations ensure a high level of completeness and accuracy of the data stored in their systems.

Key Terms

Hacker	Security	Hardware controls	Input authorization
Computer virus	Controls	Computer operations controls	Data conversion
Antivirus software	General controls	Data security controls	Batch control totals
Fault-tolerant computer systems	Application controls	Administrative controls	Edit checks
On-line transaction processing	Implementation controls	Segregation of functions	Processing controls
	Software controls	Input controls	Run control totals
	Program security controls		Computer matching

Review Questions

1. Why are computer systems more vulnerable than manual systems to destruction, fraud, error, and misuse? Name some of the key areas where systems are most vulnerable.
2. Name some features of on-line information systems that make them difficult to control.
3. What are fault-tolerant computer systems? When should they be used?
4. What are controls? What distinguishes controls in computerized systems from controls in manual systems?
5. What is the difference between general controls and application controls?
6. Name and describe the principal general controls for computerized systems.
7. Describe how each of the following serve as application controls: batching, edits, computer matching, run control totals.
8. What kinds of edit techniques can be built into computer programs?
9. How does MIS auditing enhance the control process?
10. What is the function of risk assessment?
11. Why are data quality audits essential?
12. What is security? List and describe controls that promote security for computer hardware, computer networks, computer software, and computerized data.

Discussion Questions

1. It has been said that controls and security should be one of the first areas to be addressed by information system designers. Discuss.
2. The Young Professional Quarterly magazine publishing company receives thousands of subscription orders by mail each day. A document is created for each order. The order documents are batched in groups of 30 to 50, and a header form is completed showing the total number of documents per batch. The documents are then keyed and verified by separate data entry clerks and processed each night. An edit/validation program rechecks the number of units in each batch. It prints valid and invalid batch reports and posts valid batches to a valid transaction file. The valid transaction file is fed to a series of programs that updates Young Professional Quarterly's inventory, produces sales invoices, and feeds the accounts receivable system. The Valid Batch Report is reconciled to the totals on the batch headers. Batches listed in the Invalid Batch Report are reviewed, corrected, and resubmitted. List and discuss the control weaknesses in this system and their impact. What corrective measures would you suggest?
3. Suppose you were asked to help design the controls for an information system. What pieces of information would you need?
4. Many organizations, such as Visa USA, cited earlier in this chapter, take elaborate precautions for backing up their computer systems. Why is this essential? What considerations must be addressed by a backup plan?

Group Project

Form a group with two or three other students. Select a system described in one of the Window boxes or chapter-ending cases. Write a description of the system, its functions, and its value to the organization. Then write a description of both the general and application controls that should be used to protect the organization. Present your findings to the class.

CAN WE TRUST MUTUAL FUND PRICING?

Few if any industries handle as much data as quickly as do the financial markets. With well over 10,000 financial instruments (stocks, bonds, mutual funds, futures, and others) trading daily and trading volume in the many hundreds of millions of shares, keeping up with values is a Herculean task. The problem is compounded for the huge mutual fund industry because traders not only need current information on the value of all the stocks, bonds, and other instruments they hold, but they must also calculate the value of their funds at the end of each trading day. Public confidence is fundamental to the survival of the mutual fund—after all, the investing public has placed over $2 trillion of its money into the care of mutual funds. Imagine, then, the shock of investors worldwide when they found out that Fidelity Investments, the largest and one of the most respected mutual fund companies in the world, had deliberately released false data on the value of its funds at the close of trading on June 17, 1994.

Fidelity's problem arose from the need of mutual fund managers to report their funds' net asset value (NAV) to the National Association of Securities Dealers (NASD) by 5:30 P.M. of the trading day (all times cited are New York time). The NASD then passes the data to Lipper Analytical Services, which checks for extreme price movements (a simple form of data validation) and calculates each fund's total returns. By 6:15 P.M. Lipper forwards this data to the various news services which in turn distribute them to subscribing newspapers. According to Ken Marlin, president of Telekurs NA Inc., a New York supplier of financial markets data, the deadline was set many years ago by the Associated Press (AP) and was necessary to give the newspapers enough lead time to get their type set for the morning editions. Given that the stock markets close at 4:00 P.M., and financial data suppliers such as Telekurs can't get closing price data to the funds until 4:20 P.M., the funds have only about 70 minutes to calculate their NAV and report it. (The basic calculation is the sum of the price of each financial instrument the fund owns multiplied by the number of shares.) It is truly a daily race against time with no spare room for unexpected problems.

A fund's alternative, if it cannot make the deadline, is to report NA (not available), something funds take great pains to avoid. When NA appears as a fund's price in the newspapers, many market observers claim, investor confidence in that fund is eroded. Enough NAs and the whole industry could be hurt. Moreover, the next morning when investors fail to find their fund valuations, they call the fund in large numbers, swamping the fund's customer service lines.

In the case of Fidelity on that Friday, when the 5:30 P.M. deadline arrived, the firm did not have the NAV for 166 of its 208 funds. A low-level employee, not wanting to report NA, decided to transmit the prior day's prices as that day's closing prices. The employee apparently intended to correct the inaccurate numbers when accurate numbers became available. The inaccurate prices were only caught because that Friday was "triple-witching day," the one day each quarter when three sets of market futures and options were expiring simultaneously. The markets are usually quite volatile on such days, and static fund prices would be surprising.

Fidelity was not punished. Although it is illegal for funds to report incorrect prices, funds are not normally penalized. In fact inaccurate fund prices are reported every day, although usually not knowingly. According to a Lipper Analytical spokesperson, 30 to 40 fund prices, out of the total of about 3800 funds, will have to be repriced daily. On average another 20 to 25 do report NA daily. The requirement for speed is only one of the problems.

Another is that the many new, exotic financial instruments, such as mortgage-backed bonds, are difficult to price. In addition, closing prices can be more difficult to determine in this age of global markets—many securities are still being traded someplace else in the world when the New York markets close. Furthermore, many instruments, such as corporate bonds, are illiquid and may not have traded at the end of a particular day. In this case, the actual value may have changed because bond prices in general may have risen or fallen, but the particular bond the fund owns will not have traded. One reason funds are seldom penalized for inaccuracies is the difficulties of calculating NAV. In addition, however, they also are not penalized because no apparatus exists for the NASD to verify the accuracy of NAV prices (aside from the one simple check Lipper does to identify extreme price movement).

In Fidelity's case, the problem that day resulted from an information systems software bug. Fidelity's closing stock prices are obtained from five different financial data suppliers, using their state-of-the-art portfolio accounting software. On that day one of Fidelity's outside providers made a change in its software. It transmitted the correct data but changed the format, adding a couple of fields that had never been there before. Fidelity's programs, unable to handle the new data format, filled the data fields instead with all nines. At 5:00 P.M. when Fidelity employees discovered the problem, they had only a half hour to correct it, too little time to modify their own programs.

Many observers believe that investors normally are not hurt by these pricing errors. After all, the daily NAV feed to NASD is only for reporting to newspapers. Mutual funds do use their own internal numbers, which can be calculated at a somewhat more leisurely pace, to calculate actual buy and sell prices. However, others point out that the numbers reported in the newspapers are used by many mutual fund investors to help them make buy and sell decisions. Moreover, some stockbrokers often use them to report on customer account values. Industry experts point out that NAV pricing problems are growing worse. Fund pricing errors are increasing as the number of funds multiply and also because fund holdings are a lot more complex than they used to be.

Sources: Leslie Eaton, "Errors Seem on Rise in Figuring Fund Prices," *The New York Times*, June 14, 1994; Robert McGough, John R. Emshwiller, and Sara Calian, "Deliberate Mispricing at Fidelity Highlights Lax Controls on Quotes," *The Wall Street Journal*, June 23, 1994; Carrie R. Smith, "The Price Is Right . . . or Is IT?" *Wall Street & Technology*, September 1994.

Case Study Questions

1. Evaluate the importance of the mutual fund pricing problems described here to a firm such as Fidelity. Do they need to be addressed? Why?

2. Identify control weaknesses in the mutual fund NAV price reporting process that allow for inaccurate prices to be reported in the newspapers. What management, organization, and technology factors were responsible for those weaknesses?

3. Design controls for the pricing process to deal with these problems.

4. What other changes to the overall pricing and reporting system might you make to help solve the problem of inaccurate pricing?

References

Anderson, Ross J. "Why Cryptosystems Fail." *Communications of the ACM* 37, no. 11 (November 1994).

Anthes, Gary H. "Viruses Continue to Wreak Havoc at Many U.S. Companies." *Computerworld* (June 28, 1993).

Betts, Mitch. "Human Error Trips Up Laser Scanner Accuracy." *Computerworld* (June 27, 1994).

Boockholdt, J. L. "Implementing Security and Integrity in Micro-Mainframe Networks." *MIS Quarterly* 13, no. 2 (June 1989).

Borning, Alan. "Computer System Reliability and Nuclear War." *Communications of the ACM* 30, no. 2 (February 1987).

Buss, Martin D. J., and Lynn M. Salerno. "Common Sense and Computer Security." *Harvard Business Review* (March–April 1984).

Charette, Ron. "Inside RISKS: Risks with Risk Analysis." *Communications of the ACM* 34, no. 5 (June 1991).

Chaum, David. "Security Without Identification: Transaction Systems to Make Big Brother Obsolete." *Communications of the ACM* 28 (October 1985).

Fithen, Katherine, and Barbara Fraser. "CERT Incident Response and the Internet." *Communications of the ACM* 37, no. 8 (August 1994).

Halper, Stanley D., Glenn C. Davis, Jarlath P. O'Neill-Dunne, and Pamela R. Pfau. *Handbook of EDP Auditing.* Boston: Warren, Gorham and Lamont (1985).

Hoffman, Lance. *Rogue Programs.* New York: Van Nostrand Reinhold (1990).

"Information Security and Privacy." *EDP Analyzer* (February 1986).

Kahane, Yehuda, Seev Neumann, and Charles S. Tapiero. "Computer Backup Pools, Disaster Recovery, and Default Risk." *Communications of the ACM* 31, no. 1 (January 1988).

King, Julia. "It's C.Y.A. Time." *Computerworld* (March 30, 1992).

Laudon, Kenneth C. "Data Quality and Due Process in Large Interorganizational Record Systems." *Communications of the ACM* 29 (January 1986a).

Laudon, Kenneth C. *Dossier Society: Value Choices in the Design of National Information Systems.* New York: Columbia University Press (1986b).

Littlewood, Bev, and Lorenzo Strigini. "The Risks of Software." *Scientific American* 267, no. 5 (November 1992).

Loch, Karen D., Houston H. Carr, and Merrill E. Warkentin. "Threats to Information Systems: Today's Reality, Yesterday's Understanding." *MIS Quarterly* 16, no. 2 (June 1992).

McPartlin, John P. "The True Cost of Downtime." *InformationWEEK* (August 3, 1992).

Maglitta, Joe, and John P. Mello, Jr. "The Enemy Within." *Computerworld* (December 7, 1992).

Needham, Roger M. "Denial of Service: An Example." *Communications of the ACM* 37, no. 11 (November 1994).

Neumann, Peter G. "Risks Considered Global(ly)." *Communications of the ACM* 35, no. 1 (January 1993).

Perrow, Charles. *Normal Accidents.* New York: Basic Books (1984).

Post, Gerald V., and J. David Diltz. "A Stochastic Dominance Approach to Risk Analysis of Computer Systems." *MIS Quarterly* (December 1986).

Rainer, Rex Kelley, Jr., Charles A. Snyder, and Houston H. Carr. "Risk Analysis for Information Technology." *Journal of Management Information Systems* 8, no. 1 (Summer 1991).

Straub, Detmar W. "Controlling Computer Abuse: An Empirical Study of Effective Security Countermeasures."

Curtis L. Carlson School of Management, University of Minnesota (July 20, 1987).

Tate, Paul. "Risk! The Third Factor." *Datamation* (April 15, 1988).

Thyfault, Mary E., and Stephanie Stahl. "Weak Links." *InformationWEEK* (August 10, 1992).

United States General Accounting Office. "Computer Security: Virus Highlights Need for Improved Internet Management." *GAO/IMTEC-89-57* (June 1989).

United States General Accounting Office. "Computer Security: DEA Is Not Adequately Protecting National Security Information." *GAO/IMTEC-92-31* (February 1992).

United States General Accounting Office. "Patriot Missile Defense: Software Problem Led to System Failure at Dharan, Saudi Arabia." *GAO/IMTEC-92-26* (February 1992).

Weber, Ron. *EDP Auditing: Conceptual Foundations and Practice*, 2nd ed. New York: McGraw-Hill (1988).

Wilson, Linda. "Devil in Your Data." *InformationWEEK* (August 31, 1992).

Chapter 19

Managing International Information Systems

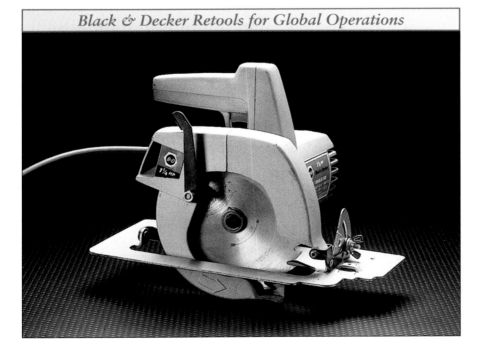

Black & Decker Retools for Global Operations

Black & Decker had worked its way out of a market share slump and decline in the early 1980s to become the world's largest manufacturer and distributor of power tools for the do-it-yourself market in the 1990s. Fifty percent of Black & Decker's sales come from overseas. One way Black & Decker retains its worldwide leadership is through the development of global information systems. Black & Decker is revamping its information systems to enhance its global operational capability, bringing the global IS plan into the global business plan. The firm wants to push development resources and computing power down as close to the end user as possible while at the same time pulling together computer hardware and software resources on a global basis. The objective is to improve management of information flow worldwide without sacrificing local flexibility and initiative.

Black & Decker can point to many specific accomplishments: It linked acquired business operations via standard financial reporting systems. It implemented EDI and bar coding selectively at major retailers in the United States and initiated pilot projects in Europe. It initiated development of a strategic IS plan to support global business operations. It shifted some information systems development to business units. It consolidated multiple mainframe data centers, initiated migrations from mainframes to PCs, LANS, and midrange platforms, and consolidated telecommunications networks. Additionally, Black & Decker implemented a total quality process in information systems.

Black & Decker encountered difficulties trying to consolidate data centers and introduce common information systems in Europe. Data definition is a real problem because Black & Decker operates in 15 European countries. In the United States, Black & Decker was much more centralized, but in Europe, Black & Decker, like most multinationals, was organized on a country basis with each country running its own show. This meant that there was no standard coding structure for products, customers, spare parts, invoices, or bills of lading. In short, the entire paper processing enterprise was tailored to local needs. Business has certain inefficiencies if each country produces all its own parts manuals, each with different numbers. On the other hand, a company cannot force common systems or data definitions that are contrary to local practices.

Black & Decker's European MIS director started the long process toward common systems by focusing on those countries where Black & Decker has large manufacturing facilities (Italy, Germany, and the United Kingdom). From 1986 to 1989, Black & Decker standardized the manufacturing countries on IBM mainframes and adopted the same CAD/CAM software standards for engineering and design as used in the United States.

It used to take several weeks to roll up the year-end figures from 40 different financial reports produced by 120 Black & Decker offices around the world. The reports were delivered by courier, fax, and E-mail, causing cumbersome administration. In 1993, Black & Decker rolled out a new common financial software package called Micro Control to all offices throughout the globe. Budgets are produced on Micro Control templates and then reported automatically to corporate headquar-

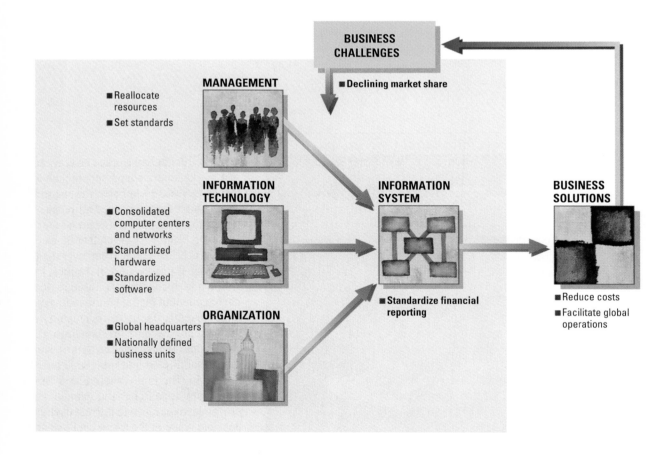

ters. Now, year-end results are available in a couple of days (not weeks). Monthly budgets can be done in days.

Even with common software many problems remain. The most significant are data definitions, and behind this problem, the questions of what are best: global or regional definitions and systems, and business. For instance, it may be best to develop regional suppliers, closer to the factories, and closer to ultimate customers. If this is true, it may be best to develop regional data definitions rather than imposing some grand worldwide standard that does not satisfy anyone in Europe, the United States, or Asia. If regional is better, this means parts, customer numbers, and vendors should be defined regionally. ∎

Sources: Susan Caminiti, "A Star Is Born," *Fortune: The Tough New Consumer*, Autumn/Winter 1993, and Bruce Caldwell, "Black & Decker Retools," *Information Week*, September 23, 1991.

Black & Decker is one of many business firms that are moving toward global forms of organization that transcend national boundaries. But Black & Decker could not make this move unless it reorganized its information systems. Black & Decker consolidated its computer centers and standardized some of its information systems so that the same system could be used by disparate business units in different countries.

The changes Black & Decker made are some of the changes in international information infrastructures—the basic systems needed to coordinate worldwide trade and other activities—that organizations need to consider if they want to operate across the globe. As Black and Decker's experience illustrates, such changes are not always easy to make. Information technology is both a powerful driver of the movement toward international business and a powerful servant. This chapter explores how to organize, manage, and control the development of international information systems.

After completing this chapter, you will be able to:

Learning Objectives

1. Identify the major factors behind the growing internationalization of business.

2. Choose among several global strategies for developing business.

3. Understand how information systems support different global strategies.

4. Manage the development of international systems.

5. Understand the main technical alternatives in developing global systems.

19.1   THE GROWTH OF INTERNATIONAL INFORMATION SYSTEMS

We have already described two powerful worldwide changes driven by advances in information technology that have transformed the business environment and posed new challenges for management. One is the transformation of industrial economies and societies into knowledge- and information-based economies. The other is the emergence of a global economy and global world order.

The precise outlines of the new global world order are unclear but the general dimensions and features are unmistakable. The goal from the American point of view is to become the world's leading supplier of sophisticated products, high value-added services, and new useful knowledge, designs, and ideas. In this pursuit, the United States is in direct competition with Western Europe and Japan, to be joined by China, and a resurgent middle Europe in the middle of the twenty-first century. The new world order will sweep away national corporations, national industries, national economies controlled by domestic politicians. Much of the Fortune 500, the 500 largest U.S. corporations, will disappear in the next 50 years, mirroring past behavior of large firms since 1900. Except for a few nimble survivors, most of these dinosaurs will be replaced by fast-moving networked corporations that transcend national boundaries. It is vital that you as future managers understand the forces moving us toward this new world order and learn how to control this new empire.

In 1970 only 5 percent of the manufactured goods sold in the United States were imported and 30 percent of the labor force worked in manufacturing. Today, about 21 percent of the manufactured goods sold in the country are imported and only about 17 percent of the labor force works in manufacturing.[1] A similar story can be told about Europe and Japan: The growth of international trade has radically altered domestic economies around the globe. About $1 trillion worth of goods, services, and financial instruments—one fifth of the annual U.S. gross national product—changes hands each day in global trade.

Consider the laptop computer as an example. The CPU is likely to have been designed and built in the United States; the DRAM (or dynamic random access memory, which makes up the majority of primary storage in a computer) was designed in the United States but built in Malaysia; the screen was designed and assembled in Japan using American patents, the keyboard was from Taiwan, and finally assembly was in Japan where the case was also made. Management of the project was located in Silicon Valley along with marketing, sales, and finance that coordinated all the myriad activities from financing and production to shipping and sales efforts. None of this would be possible without powerful international information and telecommunication systems, an international information systems infrastructure.

In order to be effective, managers need a global perspective on business and an understanding of the support systems needed to conduct business on an international scale.

DEVELOPING THE INTERNATIONAL INFORMATION SYSTEMS INFRASTRUCTURE

International information systems infrastructure: The basic information systems required by organizations to coordinate worldwide trade and other activities.

This chapter describes how to go about building an international information systems infrastructure suitable for your international strategy. An infrastructure is the constellation of facilities and services, such as highways or telecommunications networks, required for organizations to function and prosper. An **international information systems infrastructure** consists of the basic information systems required by organizations to

Arrow International, an international supplier of innovative medical devices, has international distributors as well as direct sales, manufacturing, and warehouse units throughout the globe. Businesses need an international information systems infrastructure to coordinate their worldwide activities.

- WORLD HEADQUARTERS
- ARROW DIRECT SALES
- INTERNATIONAL DISTRIBUTORS
- MANUFACTURING
- WAREHOUSE

[1]See *Statistical Abstract of the United States,* Tables No. 1409 and 1301.

coordinate worldwide trade and other activities. As we noted in Chapter 1, a firm will not be able to achieve its goals and strategies without appropriate information systems. Figure 19.1 illustrates the reasoning we will follow throughout the chapter and depicts the major dimensions of an international information systems infrastructure.

The basic strategy to follow when building an international system is first to understand the global environment in which your firm is operating. This means understanding the overall market forces or *business drivers* that are pushing your industry toward global competition. A **business driver** is a force in the environment to which businesses must respond and that influences the direction of the business. Likewise, examine carefully the inhibitors or negative factors that create *management challenges*—factors that could scuttle the development of a global business. Once you have examined the global environment, you will need to consider a *corporate strategy for competing in that environment*. How will your firm respond? You could ignore the global market and focus on domestic competition only, sell to the globe from a domestic base, or organize production and distribution around the globe. There are many in-between choices.

Once you have developed a strategy, it is time to consider *how to structure your organization* so it can pursue the strategy. How will you accomplish a division of labor across a global environment? Where will production, administration, accounting, marketing, and human resource functions be located? Who will handle the systems function?

Once you have designed an international organization, you will have to consider the management issues in implementing your strategy and making the organization design come alive. Key here will be the design of business procedures. How can you

Business driver A force in the environment to which businesses must respond and that influences the direction of business.

FIGURE 19.1
International information systems infrastructure. The major dimensions for developing an international information systems infrastructure are the global environment, the corporate global strategies, the structure of the organization, the management and business procedures, and the technology platform.

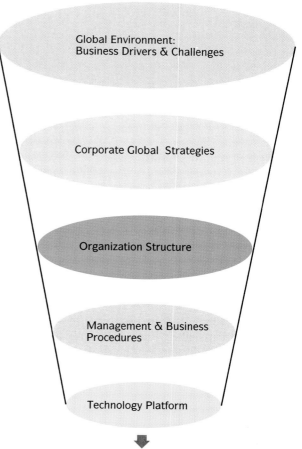

Global Environment:
Business Drivers & Challenges

Corporate Global Strategies

Organization Structure

Management & Business Procedures

Technology Platform

International Information Systems Infrastructure

discover and manage user requirements? How can you induce change in local units to conform to international requirements? How can you re-engineer on a global scale, and how can you coordinate systems development?

The last issue to consider is the technology platform. Although changing technology is a key driving factor leading toward global markets, you need to have a corporate strategy and structure before you can rationally choose the right technology.

Once you have completed this process of reasoning, you will be well on your way toward an appropriate international information infrastructure capable of achieving your corporate goals. Let us begin by looking at the overall global environment.

THE GLOBAL ENVIRONMENT: BUSINESS DRIVERS AND CHALLENGES

Table 19.1 illustrates the business drivers in the global environment that are leading all industries toward global markets and competition.

The global business drivers can be divided into two groups: general cultural factors and specific business factors. There are five easily recognized general cultural factors driving internationalization since World War II. Information, communication, and transportation technologies have created a *global village* in which communication (by telephone, television, radio, or computer network) around the globe is no more difficult and not much more expensive than communication down the block. Moving goods and services to and from geographically dispersed locations has fallen dramatically in cost.

Global culture The development of common expectations, shared artifacts, and social norms among different cultures and peoples.

The development of global communications has created a global village in a second sense: There is now a **global culture** created by television and other globally shared media like movies which permits different cultures and peoples to develop common expectations about right and wrong, desirable and undesirable, heroic and cowardly. A shared culture, with shared cultural artifacts like news programs and movies, permits the emergence of shared societal norms concerning proper attire, proper consumption, good and bad government. These cultural and societal sentiments are bolstered by a prolonged period of political stability on a global scale not seen in the modern age. The collapse of the Eastern bloc has speeded up the growth of a world culture enormously, increased support for capitalism and business, and reduced the level of cultural conflict considerably.

A last factor to consider is the growth of a global knowledge base. At the end of World War II, knowledge, education, science, and industrial skills were highly concentrated in North America, Europe, and Japan, with the rest of the world euphemistically called the "Third World." This is no longer true. Latin America, China, Southern Asia, and Eastern Europe have developed powerful educational, industrial, and scientific centers, resulting in a much more democratically and widely dispersed knowledge base.

Table 19.1	The Global Business Drivers

General Cultural Factors
    Global communication and transportation technologies
    Development of "global culture"
    Emergence of global social norms
    Political stability
    Global knowledge base

Specific Business Factors
    Global markets
    Global production and operations
    Global coordination
    Global workforce
    Global economies of scale

These general cultural factors leading toward internationalization result in four specific business globalization factors that affect most industries. The growth of powerful communications technologies and the emergence of world cultures creates the condition for *global markets*—global consumers interested in consuming similar products that are "culturally" approved. Coca-Cola, American tennis shoes (made in Korea but designed in Los Angeles), and *Dallas* (a TV show) can now be sold in Latin America, Africa, and Asia.

Responding to this demand, *global production and operations* have emerged with precise on-line coordination between far-flung production facilities and central headquarters thousands of miles away. At Sealand Transportation, a major global shipping company based in Newark, New Jersey, shipping managers in Newark can watch the loading of ships in Rotterdam on-line, check trim and ballast, and trace packages to specific ship locations as the activity proceeds. This is all possible through an international satellite link.

The new global markets and pressure toward global production and operation have called forth whole new capabilities for *global coordination* of all factors of production. Not just production but also accounting, marketing and sales, human resources, and systems development (all the major business functions) can now be coordinated on a global scale. Frito Lay, for instance, can develop a marketing sales force automation system in the United States, and once provided, may try the same techniques and technologies in Spain. Micro marketing—marketing to very small geographic and social units—no longer means marketing to neighborhoods in the United States, but to neighborhoods throughout the world! In our laptop computer example above, design has become internationalized and coordinated through shared culture (defining what is good design) and dense communications networks. These new levels of global coordination permit for the first time in history the location of business activity according to comparative advantage. Design should be located where it is best accomplished, as should marketing, production, and finance.

Finally, global markets, production, and administration create the conditions for powerful, *sustained global economies of scale*. Production driven by worldwide global demand can be concentrated where it can be best accomplished, fixed resources can be allocated over larger production runs, and production runs in larger plants can be scheduled more efficiently and precisely estimated. Lower cost factors of production can be exploited wherever they emerge. The result is a powerful strategic advantage to firms that can organize globally. These general and specific business drivers have greatly enlarged world trade and commerce.

Not all industries are similarly affected by these trends. Clearly, manufacturing has been much more affected than services that still tend to be domestic—and highly inefficient. However, the localism of services is breaking down in telecommunications, entertainment, transportation, financial services, and general business services including law. Clearly those firms within an industry who can understand the internationalization of their industry and respond appropriately will reap enormous gains in productivity and stability.

Business Challenges

While the possibilities of globalization for business success are enormous, it would be a mistake to think that the path toward a truly global economy is free of fundamental obstacles or that your company can simply coast to international glory. Far from it. Fundamental forces are operating to inhibit a global economy and to disrupt international business. Table 19.2 lists the most common and powerful challenges to the development of global systems.

At a cultural level, **particularism**, making judgments and taking action on the basis of narrow or personal characteristics, in all its forms (religious, nationalistic, ethnic, regionalism, geopolitical position) rejects the very concept of a shared global culture, and rejects the penetration of domestic markets by "foreign" goods and

particularism Making judgments and taking actions on the basis of narrow or personal characteristics.

| Table 19.2 | **Challenges and Obstacles to Global Business Systems** |

General
    Cultural particularism: regionalism, nationalism
    Social expectations: "brand name" expectations; work hours
    Political laws: transborder data and privacy laws

Specific
    Standards: different EDI, E-mail, telecommunications standards
    Reliability: phone networks not reliable
    Speed: data transfer speeds differ, slower than U.S.
    Personnel: shortages of skilled consultants

services. Differences among cultures produce differences in social expectations, politics, and ultimately legal rules. In certain countries, like the United States, consumers expect "domestic" name brand products to be built domestically and are disappointed to learn that much of what they thought of as domestically produced is in fact foreign made.

Different cultures produce different political regimes. Among the many different countries of the world there are different laws governing the movement of information, information privacy of their citizens, origins of software and hardware in systems, radio and satellite telecommunications. Even the hours of business and the terms of business trade vary greatly across political cultures. These different legal regimes complicate global business and must be taken into account when building global systems.

transborder data flow The movement of information across international boundaries in any form.

For instance, European countries have very strict laws concerning transborder data flow and privacy. **Transborder data flow** is defined as the movement of information across international boundaries in any form. Some European countries prohibit the processing of financial information outside their boundaries or the movement of employee information to foreign countries. The European Commission (the highest planning body for the integration of Europe) is considering a Digital Services Data Protection Directive that would restrict the flow of any information to countries (like the United States) that do not meet strict European information laws on personal information. That means, for instance, that a French marketing manager may not be able to use his or her credit card in New York because the credit information cannot be forwarded to the United States given its privacy laws. In response, most multinational firms develop information systems within each European country to avoid the cost and uncertainty of moving information across national boundaries.

Cultural and political differences profoundly affect organizations' standard operating procedures. A host of specific barriers arise from the general cultural differences, everything from different reliability of phone networks to the shortage of skilled consultants (see Steinbart and Nath, 1992). The Window on Organizations illustrates how such differences have affected attempts by corporations to spread information systems technology advances across international borders.

National laws and traditions have created disparate accounting practices in various countries, which impact the way profits and losses are analyzed. German companies generally do not recognize the profit from a venture until the project is completely finished and they have been paid. British firms, on the other hand, begin posting profits before a project is completed when they are reasonably certain they will get the money. Many European companies do not report per-share earnings, which is considered essential for U.S. and British firms.

These accounting practices are tightly intertwined with each country's legal system, business philosophy, and tax code. British, U.S., and Dutch firms share a predominantly Anglo-Saxon outlook that separates tax calculations from reports to shareholders to focus on showing shareholders how fast profits are growing. Continental European accounting practices are less oriented toward impressing investors, focusing on demonstrating compliance with strict rules, and minimizing tax liabilities. These diverging accounting practices make it difficult for large international companies with units in different countries to evaluate their performance.

Cultural differences can also affect the way organizations use information technology. For example, Japanese firms utilize FAX extensively but are reluctant to take advantage of the capabilities of E-mail. One explanation is that the Japanese view E-mail as poorly suited for much intragroup communication and depiction of the complex symbols used in the Japanese written language (Straub, 1994).

Language remains a significant barrier. Although English has become a kind of standard business language, this is truer at higher levels of companies and not throughout the middle and lower ranks. Software may have to be built with local language interfaces before a new information system can be successfully implemented.

Currency fluctuations can play havoc with planning models and projections. Although a great deal of progress has been made in developing a common currency for the European Economic Community, occasionally this regime breaks down, evidenced by the British pound fluctuation in 1992 and 1993, or the American dollar fluctuating against the Japanese yen and stronger European currencies. A product that appears profitable in Mexico or Japan may actually produce a loss due to changes in foreign exchange rates.

These inhibiting factors must be taken into account when you are designing and building an international infrastructure for your business.

STATE OF THE ART

Where do firms now have international applications and where do they plan expansion in the future? Figure 19.2 indicates the state of the art in terms of current applications and likely future growth areas of international systems infrastructure.

One might think given the opportunities for achieving competitive advantages outlined above, and the interest in future applications, that most international companies have rationally developed marvelous international systems architectures. Nothing could be further from the truth. Most companies have inherited patchwork international systems from the distant past, often based on concepts of information processing developed in the 1960s—batch-oriented reporting from independent foreign divisions to corporate headquarters, with little on-line control and communication. At some point, corporations in this situation will face powerful competitive

FIGURE 19.2
Frequency and type of business entities supported by global systems and databases. Most current IT applications are relatively simple office systems involving budgeting, communications, and general ledger financial coordination. Most corporations have local human resource and equipment/facilities systems. In the future, global firms plan to expand product support, customer service, and supplier systems to global stature. *Source: Adapted from Blake Ives and Sirkka Jarvenpaa, "Wiring the Stateless Corporation: Empowering the Drivers and Overcoming the Barriers," SIM Network, September/October 1991, p. 4C. Reprinted courtesy of Society for Information Management.*

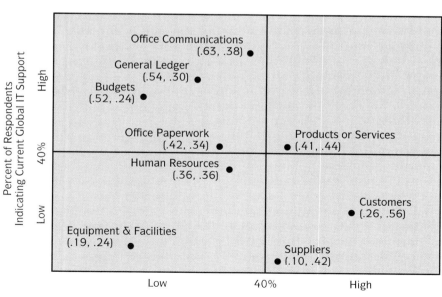

THE 800-POUND GORILLA OF TRANSNATIONAL TECHNOLOGICAL CHANGE

How do you handle a major change in information technology in a multinational corporation? The answer is the same as the old vaudeville routine on how to handle an 800-pound gorilla. "Very carefully!" Organizational and technological changes that might be relatively easily accepted within one country may be very difficult to institute across national boundaries due to the peculiar characteristics of the national cultures involved. Transnational cultural change is a virtual mine field that a manager must navigate with great care, as American Eric Singleton recently discovered as he traveled through Europe.

Singleton, who is the information systems director for the Orange County (Florida) property appraiser's office, located in Orlando, recently led his organization through a downsizing into client/server technology. In the first year after implementation, his organization's technology operating costs dropped a whopping 45 percent. The following year, those costs held steady, proving that the savings were genuine. Singleton was able to apply some of those savings to hiring more staff, acquiring more new technology, and increasing training division-wide. Flushed with success and a great deal of enthusiasm, he embarked upon a European speaking tour to share his experiences with his European counterparts. He spoke in Geneva, Switzerland; Birmingham, England; Paris, France; and Copenhagen, Denmark, where his audience came from an even wider range of European countries. He returned home quite discouraged about the future of client/server technology in most of these countries. The problems were seldom technological, however. Instead, they were rooted in attitude and culture.

The most widespread attitude he encountered was one of an unwillingness to overcome tradition. One Dutch government information systems director with 15 years' experience in the United States, E. F. Tolberg, proposed a downsizing project which he believed would dramatically improve the way the organization functioned. He was surprised to learn that if he were allowed to downsize the technology, he still could not improve the functioning of the business because he would not be allowed to do any business re-engineering. The current way of doing business, he was told, is over 400 years old. It simply cannot be changed.

One source of this unwillingness may be a different level of management knowledge of technology. William Brant, IS director at Grand Metropolitan Plc., believes that "In the U.S., upper management is more comfortable with technology [than in Europe]." Cedric Thomas, joint director general of consultants at Pierre Audoin Conseil in Paris, believes Europeans are much more concerned with planning and control than are their American counterparts. "They'll implement the technology if they control it," he says. "It's a risk-free approach, [whereas] people in the U.S. might just say, 'Go for it.' "

Another cultural difference Singleton met was the European tendency to show much more concern about the loss of employee jobs upon downsizing than do their American counterparts. Andrew Carlsson, chief executive officer of a large Swedish bank, explained that in Sweden the businesses will not even consider laying off employees as a result of technological change. The lack of job reduction savings dramatically changes return-on-investment (ROI) calculations that affect a decision on a project. The issue becomes an economic one: How can a company achieve a positive return if its payroll costs do not decrease? In some countries, Sweden included, government unemployment policy is actually a disincentive to a company laying off employees.

Both language and culture can erect major hurdles. Kumiyo Nakakoji,

> **To Think About:** Can you suggest other ways multinational corporate management might engender acceptance of technological change in dubious units abroad? In making the suggestions, discuss the potential risks of such strategies.

a research fellow at the University of Colorado, offers the case of a major United States groupware software vendor that wanted to market its product in Japan. The vendor hired a professional translator to translate the application help messages and user's manual. Problems occurred because professional translators were unfamiliar with the vocabulary of a very specialized field like computer groupware. In the Japanese translation, the term *groupware* became "a device for a crowd" where, in fact, the Japanese normally just translated as "groupware" (written phonetically in Japanese phonetic kana characters). The result, Nakakoji points out, is Japanese that is as awkward and ridiculous sounding to the Japanese as were the English versions of Japanese manuals that Americans laughed at for years.

However, Nakakoji explains that the cultural problems can be even greater than the language problems. Using the same example of groupware, she points out that a major function of that software is to record the events of a meeting and to support the decision-making process during that meeting. The problem is, this function is irrelevant in Japan where formal meetings merely ratify decisions already made before the meeting. Japanese workers, she says, would never challenge their managers in formal meetings. Nakakoji claims that brainstorming is done after work, often in social settings, and that negotiations take place privately, prior to any "meeting." Hence that key function of a groupware application is not relevant to the Japanese business environment.

Ethical differences can present major problems also. Americans, for example, are usually offended when customs officials in some other countries "lose" the papers necessary to import the equipment needed to set up a new corporate network. While Americans may rise up in indignation and say, "I refuse to pay a bribe," Thomas Donaldson, a Georgetown School of Business professor in Washington, DC, believes that one must bend to local customs if doing so does not violate human rights and if it is impossible to do business otherwise. He points out that in many countries these "gratuities" are commonplace and that, in fact, salaries of such officials are set low in anticipation of such income (as is often true of cab drivers and waiters and waitresses). The IS manager from the United States will have to make that decision if she or he intends to complete the company's project. Legal issues may be involved here also. The U.S. Foreign Corrupt Practices Act prohibits bribes to foreign officials in order to influence a buying decision on behalf of one's firm. However, it does not prohibit the payments such as to a low-level customs official to smooth the handling of one's goods. Donaldson does say, however, that if the action

conflicts with one's ethical code and violates human rights, a company should not bend. The prime recent example was South Africa, where many foreign companies withdrew as internal opposition to apartheid grew.

Singleton did find that some of the differences he discovered were very much business- and economic-based. For instance, he traveled to Europe just as a recession was spreading, while the United States was already starting to recover from its recent recession. In the recovery cycle, management in most companies is much more likely to invest in new technology than they are as an economy is entering into a recession. Another very real business problem he met was explained to him by Fredrique Cantemerle, president of a French document imaging company. Cantemerle believes that the best software is produced in the United States. However, that software is also usually marketed first in the United States and does not reach Europe until much later. Therefore, he explains, even if a company wanted to install client/server hardware, it very likely would not yet have enough software available to make the project worthwhile.

While the general lesson from these experiences and issues is that each national unit within a multinational organization needs to be understood and dealt with individually, management should not conclude that multinational change is all but impossible. Singleton,

for example, suggested to Carlsson that he find productive ways—ways which would have a positive effect on his bank's bottom line—to use the "excess" staff that was no longer needed due to the downsizing. One use he suggested was to turn some of them into trainers to help his users become "superusers." Singleton claims that very few users make use of any more than a small fraction of the functionality of a network, and teaching them other uses will raise the company's efficiency and so boost its return on investment. If lack of access to the newest and most effective software is a problem, a multinational organization can make use of its U.S. unit to make that software available. As to the effects of the recession, the policy of many companies in Japan is to increase investment in technology during a business downturn so that they will be better positioned when the recovery comes. The conclusion is that management of information technology change within a multinational organization requires creativity, but effective ways can often be found.

Sources: Kumiyo Nakakoji, "Crossing the Cultural Boundary," *Byte*, June 1994; Eric Singleton, "The Accidental IS Tourist," *Computerworld Client/Server Journal*; Dr. H. Jefferson Smith and Dr. Ernest A. Kallman, "Dealing with Ethics on a Global Basis," *Beyond Computing*, September/October 1994; Paul Tate, "Hands Across the Borders," *Information Week*, October 10, 1994.

challenges in the marketplace from firms that have rationally designed truly international systems. Still other companies have recently built technology platforms for an international infrastructure but have nowhere to go with it because they lack global strategy. For instance, one survey of 100 global firms found that 52 percent never or rarely considered information systems when devising global strategies (Cox, 1991).

As it turns out, there are significant difficulties in building appropriate international infrastructures. The difficulties involve planning a system appropriate to the firm's global strategy, structuring the organization of systems and business units, solving implementation issues, and choosing the right technical platform. Let us examine these problems in greater detail.

19.2 ORGANIZING INTERNATIONAL INFORMATION SYSTEMS

There are three organizational issues facing corporations seeking a global position: choosing a strategy, organizing the business, and organizing the systems management area. The first two are closely connected, so we will discuss them together.

GLOBAL STRATEGIES AND BUSINESS ORGANIZATION

There are four main global strategies that form the basis for global firms' organizational structure. These are domestic exporter, multinational, franchiser, and transnational. Each of these strategies is pursued with a specific business organizational structure (see Table 19.3). For simplicity's sake, we describe three kinds of organizational structure or governance: centralized (in the home country), decentralized (to local foreign units), and coordinated (all units participate as equals). There are other types of governance patterns observed in specific companies (e.g., authoritarian dominance by one unit, a confederacy of equals, a federal structure balancing power among strategic units, and so forth; see Keen, 1991).

domestic exporter Strategy characterized by heavy centralization of corporate activities in the home country of origin.

The **domestic exporter** strategy is characterized by heavy centralization of corporate activities in the home country of origin. Nearly all international companies begin this way, and some move on to other forms. Production, finance/accounting, sales/marketing, human resources, and strategic management are set up to optimize resources in the home country. International sales are sometimes dispersed using agency agreements or subsidiaries, but even here foreign marketing is totally reliant on the domestic home base for marketing themes and strategies. Caterpillar Corporation and other heavy capital equipment manufacturers fall into this category of firm.

multinational Global strategy that concentrates financial management and control out of a central home base while decentralizing production, sales, and marketing operations to units in other countries.

The **multinational** strategy concentrates financial management and control out of a central home base while decentralizing production, sales, and marketing operations to units in other countries. The products and services on sale in different countries are adopted to suit local market conditions. The organization becomes a far-flung confederation of production and marketing facilities in different countries. Many financial service firms, along with a host of manufacturers like General Motors, Chrysler, and Intel, fit this pattern.

franchiser Firm where product is created, designed, financed, and initially produced in the home country, but for product-specific reasons must rely heavily on foreign personnel for further production, marketing, and human resources.

Franchisers are an interesting mix of old and new. On the one hand the product is created, designed, financed, and initially produced in the home country, but for product-specific reasons must rely heavily on foreign personnel for further production, marketing, and human resources. Food franchisers like McDonald's, Mrs. Fields Cookies, and Kentucky Fried Chicken fit this pattern. McDonald's created a new form of fast-food chain in the United States and continues to rely largely on the United States for inspiration of new products, strategic management, and financing. Nevertheless, because the product must be produced locally—it is perishable—extensive coordination and dispersal of production, local marketing, and local recruitment of personnel are required. Generally, foreign franchisees are clones of the mother country units, yet fully coordinated worldwide production that could optimize factors of production is not possible. For instance, potatoes and beef can generally not be bought where they are cheapest on world markets but must be produced reasonably close to the area of consumption.

Transnational firms are the stateless, truly globally managed firms which may represent a larger part of international business in the future. Transnational firms have no single national headquarters but instead have many regional headquarters

Table 19.3	**Global Business Strategy and Structure**			
	STRATEGY			
BUSINESS FUNCTION	Domestic Exporter	Multinational	Franchiser	Transnational
Production	Centralized	Dispersed	Coordinated	Coordinated
Finance/Accounting	Centralized	Centralized	Centralized	Coordinated
Sales/Marketing	Mixed	Dispersed	Coordinated	Coordinated
Human Resources	Centralized	Centralized	Coordinated	Coordinated
Strategic Management	Centralized	Centralized	Centralized	Coordinated

MacDonald's offers Chinese diners a full selection of burgers, fries, and drinks. MacDonald's patrons in other countries will find the same choices available to them.

transnational Truly globally managed firms which have no national headquarters; value-added activities are managed from a global perspective without reference to national borders, optimizing sources of supply and demand and taking advantage of any local competitive advantage.

and perhaps a world headquarters. In a **transnational** strategy, nearly all of the value-adding activities are managed from a global perspective without reference to national borders, optimizing sources of supply and demand wherever they appear, and taking advantage of any local competitive advantages. Transnational firms take the globe, not the home country as their management frame of reference. The governance of these firms has been likened to a federal structure in which there is a strong central management core of decision making, but considerable dispersal of power and financial muscle throughout the global divisions. Few companies have actually attained transnational status, but Citicorp, Sony, Ford, and others are attempting this transition.

Information technology and improvements in global telecommunications are giving international firms more flexibility to shape their global strategies. Protectionism and a need to serve local markets better encourage companies to disperse production facilities and at least become multinational. At the same time, the drive to achieve economies of scale and take advantage of short-term local advantages moves transnationals toward a global management perspective and a concentration of power and authority. Hence, there are forces of decentralization and dispersal, as well as forces of centralization and global coordination (Ives and Jarvenpaa, 1991).

GLOBAL SYSTEMS TO FIT THE STRATEGY

The configuration, management, and development of systems tend to follow the global strategy chosen (Roche, 1992; Ives and Jarvenpaa, 1991). Figure 19.3 depicts the typical arrangements. By "systems" we mean the full range of activities involved in building information systems: conception and alignment with the strategic business plan, systems development, and ongoing operation. For the sake of simplicity, we consider four types of systems configuration. *Centralized systems* are those where systems development and operation occur totally at the domestic home base. *Duplicated systems* are those where development occurs totally at the home base, but operations are handed over to autonomous units in foreign locations. *Decentralized systems* are those where each foreign unit designs its own, totally unique solutions and systems. Last, *networked* systems are those in which systems development and operations occur in an integrated and coordinated fashion across all units. As can be seen in Figure

FIGURE 19.3
Global strategy and systems configurations. The large X's show the
dominant pattern, and the small x's
show the emerging patterns. For
instance, domestic exporters rely
predominantly on centralized systems, but there is continual pressure and some development of decentralized systems in local
marketing regions.

SYSTEM CONFIGURATION	STRATEGY			
	Domestic Exporter	Multi National	Franchiser	Transnational
Centralized	X			
Duplicated			X	
Decentralized	x	X	x	
Networked		x		X

19.3, domestic exporters tend to have highly centralized systems in which a single domestic systems development staff develops worldwide applications. Multinationals
offer a direct and striking contrast: Here foreign units devise their own systems solutions based on local needs with few if any applications in common with headquarters
(the exceptions being financial reporting and some telecommunications applications).
Franchisers have the simplest systems structure: Like the products they sell, franchisers develop a single system usually at the home base and then replicate it around the
world. Each unit—no matter where it is located—has the same identical applications.
Last, the most ambitious form of systems development is found in the transnational:
Networked systems are those in which there is a solid, singular global environment
for developing and operating systems. This usually presupposes a powerful telecommunications backbone, a culture of shared applications development, and a shared
management culture that crosses cultural barriers. The networked systems structure
is most visible in financial services where the homogeneity of the product, money, and
money instruments seems to overcome cultural barriers.

REORGANIZING THE BUSINESS

How should a firm organize itself for doing business on an international scale?
Developing a global company and an information systems support structure requires
following these principles:

1. Organize value-adding activities along lines of comparative advantage. For instance, marketing/sales functions should be located where they can best be performed, for least cost and maximum impact; likewise with production, finance,
human resources, and information systems.

2. Develop and operate systems units at each level of corporate activity—national,
regional, and international. In order to serve local needs, there should be *host
country systems units* of some magnitude. *Regional systems* units should handle
telecommunications and systems development across national boundaries that
take place within major geographic regions (European, Asian, American).
Transnational systems units should be established to create the linkages across
major regional areas and coordinate the development and operation of international telecommunications and systems development (Roche, 1992).

3. Establish at world headquarters a single office responsible for development of international systems, a global chief information officer (CIO) position.

Many successful companies have devised organizational systems structures along these principles. The success of these companies relies not just on the proper organization of activities. A key ingredient is a management team that can understand the risks and benefits of international systems and that can devise strategies for overcoming the risks. We turn to these management topics next.

19.3 MANAGING GLOBAL SYSTEMS

The survey of 100 large global corporations described earlier found that CIOs believed the development and implementation of international systems were the most difficult problems they faced. Table 19.4 lists what these CIOs believed were the principal management problems posed by developing international systems.

It is interesting to note that these problems are the chief difficulties managers experience in developing ordinary domestic systems as well! But these are enormously complicated in the international environment.

A TYPICAL SCENARIO: DISORGANIZATION ON A GLOBAL SCALE

Let us look at a common scenario. A traditional multinational consumer goods company based in the United States and operating in Europe would like to expand into Asian markets and knows that it must develop a transnational strategy and a supportive information systems structure. Like most multinationals it has dispersed production and marketing to regional and national centers while maintaining a world headquarters and strategic management in the United States. Historically, it has allowed each of the subsidiary foreign divisions to develop its own systems. The only centrally coordinated system is financial controls and reporting. The central systems group in the United States focuses only on domestic functions and production. The result is a hodgepodge of hardware, software, and telecommunications. The mail systems between Europe and the United States are incompatible. Each production facility uses a different manufacturing resources planning system (or different version with local variations), and different marketing, sales, and human resource systems. The technology platforms are wildly different: Europe is using mostly UNIX-based file servers and PC clones on desktops. Communications between different sites are poor, given the high cost and low quality of European intercountry communications. The U.S. group is moving from an IBM mainframe environment centralized at headquarters to a highly distributed network architecture based on a national value-added network, with local sites developing their own local area networks. The central systems group at headquarters was recently decimated and dispersed to the U.S. local sites in the hope of serving local needs better and reducing costs.

Table 19.4 Management Issues in Developing International Systems	
Agreeing on common user requirements	88%
Inducing procedural business changes	79
Coordinating applications development	77
Coordinating software releases	69
Encouraging local users to take on ownership	58

Source: Adapted from Butler Cox, *Globalization: The IT Challenge* (Sunnyvale, CA: Amdahl Executive Institute, 1991).

What do you recommend to the senior management leaders of this company who now want to pursue a transnational strategy and develop an information systems infrastructure to support a highly coordinated global systems environment? Consider the problems you face by re-examining Table 19.4. The foreign divisions will resist efforts to agree on common user requirements—they have never thought about much other than their own units' needs. The systems groups in American local sites, which have been recently enlarged and told to focus on local needs, will not easily accept guidance from anyone recommending a transnational strategy. It will be difficult to convince local managers anywhere in the world that they should change their business procedures to align with other units in the world, especially if this might interfere with their local performance. After all, local managers are rewarded in this company for meeting local objectives of their division or plant. Finally, it will be difficult to coordinate development of projects around the world in the absence of a powerful telecommunications network, or therefore difficult to encourage local users to take on ownership in the systems developed. What should you recommend given these typical obstacles?

STRATEGY: DIVIDE, CONQUER, APPEASE

core systems Systems that support functions that are absolutely critical to the organization.

Figure 19.4 lays out the main dimensions of a solution. First, consider that not all systems should be coordinated on a transnational basis—only some "core" systems are truly worth sharing from a cost and feasibility point of view. **Core systems** are systems that support functions that are absolutely critical to the organization. Other systems should only be partially coordinated because they share key elements, but they do not have to be totally common across national boundaries. For such systems, a good deal of local variation is possible and desirable. A last group of systems are peripheral, truly provincial, and are needed to suit local requirements only.

FIGURE 19.4
Agency and other coordination costs increase as the firm moves from local option systems toward regional and global systems. On the other hand, transaction costs of participating in global markets probably decrease as firms develop global systems. A sensible strategy is to reduce agency costs by developing only a few "core" global systems which are vital for global operations, leaving other systems in the hands of regional and local units.
Adapted from Edward M. Roche, Managing Information Technology in Multinational Corporations. *New York: Macmillan, 1992.*

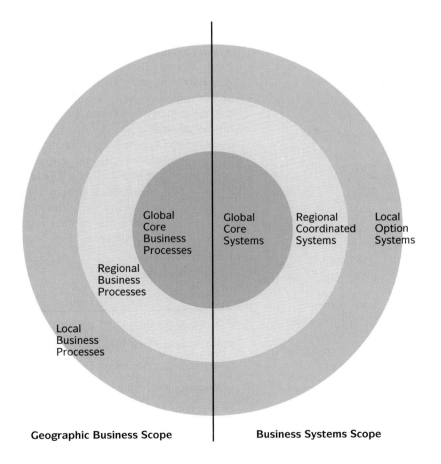

Global Core Business Processes

Global Core Systems

Regional Coordinated Systems

Local Option Systems

Regional Business Processes

Local Business Processes

Geographic Business Scope

Business Systems Scope

Define Core Business Processes

How do you identify "core systems"? The first step is to define a short list of truly critical core business processes. Business processes have been defined before in Chapter 11, which you should review. Briefly, **business processes** are sets of logically related tasks performed to achieve a defined business outcome, such as shipping out correct orders to customers or delivering innovative products to the market. Each business process typically involves many functional areas working together, effectively communicating and coordinating.

The way to identify these core business processes is to conduct a workflow analysis. How are customer orders taken, what happens to them once they are taken, who fills the order, how is it shipped to the customer? What about suppliers? Do they have access to manufacturing resource planning systems so that supply is automatic? You should be able to identify and set priorities in a short list of ten business processes that are absolutely critical for the firm.

Next, can you identify centers of excellence for these processes? Is the customer order fulfillment superior in the United States, manufacturing process control superior in Germany, and human resources superior in Asia? You should be able to identify some areas of the company, for some lines of business, where a division or unit stands out in the performance of one or several business functions.

When you understand the business processes of a firm, you can rank order them. You can then decide which processes should be core applications, centrally coordinated, designed, and implemented around the globe, which should be regional and local. At the same time, identifying the critical business processes, the really important ones, you have gone a long way to defining a vision of the future that you should be working toward.

Identify Core Systems to Coordinate Centrally

By identifying the critical core business processes, you begin to see opportunities for transnational systems. The second strategic step is to conquer the core systems and define these systems as truly transnational. The financial and political costs of defining and implementing transnational systems are extremely high. Therefore, keep the list to an absolute minimum, letting experience be the guide and erring on the side of minimalism. By dividing off a small group of systems as absolutely critical, you divide opposition to a transnational strategy. At the same time, you can appease those who oppose the central worldwide coordination implied by transnational systems by permitting peripheral systems development to go on unabated, with the exception of some technical platform requirements.

Choose an Approach: Incremental, Grand Design, Evolutionary

A third step is to choose an approach. Avoid piecemeal approaches. These will surely fail for lack of visibility, opposition from all who stand to lose from transnational development, and lack of power to convince senior management that the transnational systems are worth it. Likewise, avoid *grand design* approaches that try to do everything at once. These also tend to fail due to an inability to focus resources. Nothing gets done properly, and opposition to organizational change is needlessly strengthened because the effort requires huge resources. An alternative approach is to evolve transnational applications from existing applications with a precise and clear vision of the transnational capabilities the organization should have in five years.

Make the Benefits Clear

What is in it for the company? One of the worst situations to avoid is to build global systems for the sake of building global systems. From the beginning, it is crucial that senior management at headquarters and foreign division managers clearly understand the benefits that will come to the company as well as to individual units. While each

---

business processes Sets of logically related tasks performed to achieve a defined business outcome; each business process typically involves many functional areas working together.

system offers unique benefits to a particular budget, the overall contribution of global systems lies in four areas.

Global systems—truly integrated, distributed, and transnational systems—contribute to superior management and coordination. A simple price tag cannot be put on the value of this contribution, and the benefit will not show up in any capital budgeting model. It is the ability to switch suppliers on a moment's notice from one region to another in a crisis, the ability to move production in response to natural disasters, and the ability to use excess capacity in one region to meet raging demand in another.

A second major contribution is vast improvement in production, operation, and supply and distribution. Imagine a global value chain, with global suppliers and a global distribution network. For the first time, senior managers can locate value-adding activities in regions where they are most economically performed.

Third, global systems mean global customers and global marketing. Fixed costs around the world can now be amortized over a much larger customer base. This will unleash new economies of scale at production facilities.

Last, global systems mean the ability to optimize the use of corporate funds over a much larger capital base. This means, for instance, that capital in a surplus region can be moved efficiently to expand production of capital-starved regions; that cash can be managed more effectively within the company and put to use more effectively.

These strategies will not by themselves create global systems. You will have to implement what you strategize and this is a whole new challenge.

IMPLEMENTATION TACTICS: COOPTATION

cooptation Bringing the opposition into the process of designing and implementing the solution without giving up control over the direction and nature of the change.

The overall tactic for dealing with resistant local units in a transnational company is cooptation. **Cooptation** is defined as bringing the opposition into the process of designing and implementing the solution without giving up control over the direction and nature of the change. As much as possible, raw power should be avoided. Minimally, however, local units must agree on a short list of transnational systems and raw power may be required to solidify the idea that transnational systems of some sort are truly required.

How should cooptation proceed? Several alternatives are possible. One alternative is to permit each country unit the opportunity to develop one transnational application first in its home territory, and then throughout the world. In this manner, each major country systems group is given a piece of the action in developing a transnational system, and local units feel a sense of ownership in the transnational effort. On the down side, this assumes the ability to develop high-quality systems is widely distributed, and that, say, the German team can successfully implement systems in France and Italy. This will not always be the case. Also, the transnational effort will have low visibility.

A second tactic is to develop new transnational centers of excellence, or a single center of excellence. There may be several centers around the globe that focus on specific business processes. These centers draw heavily from local national units, are based on multinational teams, and must report to worldwide management—their first line of responsibility is to the core applications. Centers of excellence perform the initial identification and specification of the business process, define the information requirements, perform the business and systems analysis, and accomplish all design and testing. Implementation, however, and pilot testing occur in World Pilot Regions where new applications are installed and tested first. Later, they are rolled out to other parts of the globe. This phased roll-out strategy is precisely how national applications are successfully developed.

WRAPPING UP: THE MANAGEMENT SOLUTION

We can now reconsider how to handle the most vexing problems facing managers developing the transnational information system infrastructures that were described in Table 19.4.

legitimacy The extent to which one's authority is accepted on grounds of competence, vision, or other qualities.

- *Agreeing on common user requirements:* Establishing a short list of the core business processes and core support systems will begin a process of rational comparison across the many divisions of the company, develop a common language for discussing the business, and naturally lead to an understanding of common elements (as well as the unique qualities that must remain local).

- *Inducing procedural business changes:* Your success as a change agent will depend on your legitimacy, your actual raw power, and your ability to involve users in the change design process. **Legitimacy** is defined as the extent to which your authority is accepted on grounds of competence, vision, or other qualities. The selection of a viable change strategy, which we have defined as evolutionary but with a vision, should assist you in convincing others that change is feasible and desirable. Involving people in change, assuring them that change is in the best interests of the company and their local units is a key tactic.

- *Coordinating applications development:* Choice of change strategy is critical for this problem. At the global level there is simply far too much complexity to attempt a grand design strategy of change. It is far easier to coordinate change by making small incremental steps toward a larger vision. Imagine a five-year plan of action rather than a two-year plan of action, and reduce the set of transnational systems to a bare minimum in order to reduce coordination costs.

- *Coordinating software releases:* Firms can institute procedures to ensure that all operating units convert to new software updates at the same time so that everyone's software is compatible.

- *Encouraging local users to take on ownership:* The key to this problem is to involve users in the creation of the design without giving up control over the development of the project to parochial interests. Recruiting a wide range of local individuals to transnational centers of excellence helps send the message that all significant groups are involved in the design and will have an influence.

Even with the proper organizational structure and appropriate management choices, it is still possible to stumble over technological issues. Choices of technology, platforms, networks, hardware, and software are the final elements in building transnational information system infrastructures. The Window on Management describes how two large multinational corporations are grappling with these problems as they merge their companies.

19.4 TECHNOLOGY ISSUES AND OPPORTUNITIES

Information technology is itself a powerful business driver encouraging the development of global systems, but it creates significant challenges for managers. Global systems presuppose that business firms develop a solid technical foundation and are willing to continually upgrade facilities.

MAIN TECHNICAL ISSUES

Hardware, software, and telecommunications pose special technical challenges in an international setting. The major hardware challenge is finding some way to standardize the firm's computer hardware platform when there is so much variation from operating unit to operating unit and from country to country. Figure 19.5 illustrates the diverse hardware platforms used by Citibank Asia-Pacific in various countries. (Citibank Asia-Pacific is starting to centralize some back-office applications such as check and savings account processing, loan processing, and general ledger and to consolidate computer centers.) Managers will need to think carefully about where to locate the firm's computer centers and about how to select hardware suppliers. The

TRAVELING DOWN THE ROAD OF INTERNATIONAL TECHNOLOGY INFRASTRUCTURE MERGERS

How can two giants in the travel agency field, one American and one European, merge their information technology infrastructure? Carlson Travel Group, with a 1993 revenue of $7.1 billion, is headquartered in Minnetonka, Minnesota, and does its main business primarily in the United States. Wagonlit Travel, a giant subsidiary of Accor Group of Paris, France, is strong mainly in Europe. They have been competitors, however, and shared 30 major clients, such as Munich-based Siemens A.G.

The merger occurred because each wanted to add strength in the other's main territory and because both wanted to expand into other parts of the world, particularly Asia. The drive to merge came from their large clients who wanted to be able to have all of their travel business handled by one agency, an agency that could service them anywhere in the world. "The big push [to internationalize travel agencies] is to provide seamless transactions and integrated global data," explains Scott Guerrero, vice president of IS at Fenton, Missouri-based Maritz Travel Co. Robert Bardoux, an international vice president at Wagonlit, explains, "We had U.S. clients who wanted to consolidate their business with one agency. If we didn't have a large enough presence in the U.S., we would risk losing bids." One reason the big multinational corporations want to concentrate all their travel business with one agent is so that they can better control their own travel costs through access to all of their travel records. With appropriate data, they not only can stay on top of the travel expenditure habits of their employees but also will be able to negotiate special rates with hotels, auto rental companies, and airlines. Hanna Murphy, travel manager in Siemens' San Jose, California, office, values the new

merger because he can easily obtain worldwide information and go into global trend analysis.

The product of the merger, London-based Carlson Wagonlit Travel, laid out a five-year consolidation plan that began to take effect in July 1994. The reason the company will take so long to complete the merger is because of the difficulties of amalgamating two very different corporate cultures and technology infrastructures. "We didn't want to do too much too fast and have it blow up," explained Matt Manley, Carlson's chief information officer. After all, the new company will have 4000 locations in 125 countries. Carlson has a highly centralized, IBM mainframe technology infrastructure, an infrastructure made possible by the fact that its primary business is within one country. Wagonlit's technology infrastructure is more decentralized and operates over a wide range of disparate platforms, including IBM's AS/400 and Digital Equipment Corporation's (DEC) VAX. This decentralized infrastucture stems from their need to have a strong presence in a number of European countries each of which has different laws and procedures as well as individualized computerized reservation systems (CRSs).

The business plan gives Carlson control of all operations within the United States for the time being while Wagonlit has been given control over all European operations. A new company, Carlson Wagonlit Development, is based in London and is taking charge of developing business in Asia and Australia where the two companies currently have very little presence.

Merging the two technology infrastructures has been made more difficult because of the lofty goals the new company has set—it expects to have a fully integrated company with standardized systems at the end of those five years. The new company must first select a worldwide architecture. It has already

made certain architecture decisions. Eventually the new company will operate on a single open, distributed client/server architecture. The telecom-

> *To Think About:* What organization, management, and technology problems do you think the two companies are likely to experience as they merge and develop a common technology infrastructure?

munications choices made will have to supply fast, frame-relay service between all locations. The standard programming language will be either C or C++. The servers will use a variant of UNIX or Windows NT. Carlson and Wagonlit are also establishing a single central repository of object-oriented code (Carlson already has some object-oriented applications).

Data will be made available in a uniform way to both customers and employees. "The peculiarity of business travel is the huge amount of detailed information we need to keep accessible," explains Alain Le Doaré, Wagonlit's vice-president of international information technology. From a business perspective, all offices will share a single CRS. Customer information needs will be addressed through a single information support system that customers will be able to access in order to monitor their own data. The new company also is building a company-wide point-of-sale system as part of the CRS that automates many of the repetitive tasks that today are normally done manually. For example, travel agents will no longer need to manually search through schedules and fare options seeking the lowest possible fare options. A new system will automate that search and will include in the search criteria information on the client company's travel policies.

The initial version of this application was so complicated that low-fare

---

major global software challenge is finding applications that are user friendly and that truly enhance the productivity of international work teams. The major telecommunications challenge is making data flow seamlessly across networks shaped by disparate national standards. Overcoming these challenges requires systems integration and connectivity on a global basis.

Hardware and Systems Integration

The development of transnational information system infrastructures based on the concept of "core" systems raises questions about how the new core systems will fit in with the existing suite of applications developed around the globe by different divisions, different people, and for different kinds of computing hardware. The goal is to develop global, distributed, and integrated systems. Briefly, these are the same

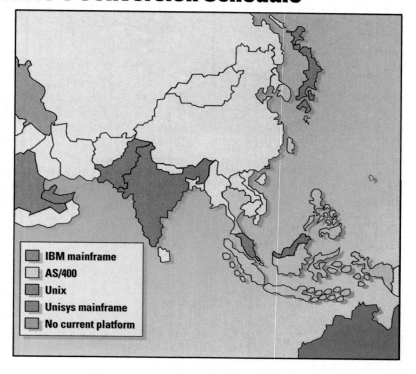

Citibank Asia-Pacific's Conversion Schedule

Country	Conversion date
Australia	December '94
Guam	March '96
Hong Kong	April '95
India	October '97
Indonesia	November '96
Japan	No conversion
Malaysia	May '95
Pakistan	August '98
Philippines	June '96
Saudi Arabia	October '97
Singapore	March '95
South Korea	October '97
Taiwan	August '97
Thailand	August '96
Turkey	September '95
United Arab Emirates	January '97

- IBM mainframe
- AS/400
- Unix
- Unisys mainframe
- No current platform

FIGURE 19.5

Citibank Asia-Pacific's hardware platforms. Citibank Asia-Pacific uses different hardware platforms in the various countries where it operates. It is consolidating its computer centers and standardizing core back-office applications to run on software at its Singapore IBM mainframe. *Adapted from: Clinton Wilder, "Making Borders Disappear," InformationWEEK (February 27, 1995). Copyright © 1995 by CMP Publications Inc., 600 Community Drive, Manhasset, NY 11030. Reprinted from InformationWEEK with permission.*

problems faced by any large domestic systems development effort. However, the problems are more complex because of the international environment. For instance, in the United States, IBM Corp. and IBM operating systems have played the predominant role in building core systems for large organizations, whereas in Europe UNIX was much more commonly used for large systems. How can the two be integrated in a common transnational system?

There are two choices to solve integration problems: Remain with a proprietary architecture (generally IBM) or move new core systems to an open architecture. Generally, an open architecture means a UNIX foundation, a client/server architecture, and reliance on PC DOS/Windows machines or UNIX machines on the desktop.

The correct choice will often depend on the history of the company's systems and the extent of commitment to proprietary systems. For instance, finance and insurance firms have typically relied almost exclusively on IBM proprietary equipment and architectures in the 1980s, and it would be extremely difficult and cost ineffective to abandon that equipment and software. Newer firms and manufacturing firms generally find it much easier to adopt open UNIX systems for international systems. As we pointed out in previous chapters, open UNIX-based systems are far more cost effective in the long run, provide more power at a cheaper price, and preserve options for future expansion.

Once a hardware platform is chosen, the question of standards has to be addressed. Just because all sites use the same hardware does not guarantee common, integrated systems. Some central authority in the firm has to establish data, as well as other technical standards, for sites to comply with. For instance, technical accounting terms such as the beginning and end of the fiscal year must be standardized (review our earlier discussion of the cultural challenges to building global businesses), as well as the acceptable interfaces between systems, communications speeds and architectures, and network software.

Connectivity

The heart of the international systems problem is telecommunications—linking together the systems and people of a global firm into a single integrated network just like the phone system but capable of voice, data, and image transmissions. However, integrated global networks are extremely difficult to create (see Figure 19.6). For example, many countries cannot even fulfill basic business telecommunications needs such as obtaining reliable circuits, coordinating among different carriers and the regional telecommunications authority, obtaining bills in a common currency standard, and obtaining standard agreements for the level of telecommunications service provided.

Despite moves toward economic unity, Europe remains a hodgepodge of disparate national technical standards and service levels. The problem is especially critical for banks or airlines that must move massive volumes of data around the world. Although most circuits leased by multinational corporations are fault-free more than 99.8 percent of the time, line quality and service vary widely from the north to the south of Europe. Network service is much more unreliable in southern Europe (Stahl, 1992).

Although the European Economic Community has endorsed EDIfact as the European electronic data interchange (EDI) standard, existing European standards for networking and EDI are very industry-specific and country-specific. Most European banks use the SWIFT (Society for Worldwide Interbank Financial Telecommunications) protocol for international funds transfer, while automobile companies and food producers often use industry-specific or country-specific versions of standard protocols for EDI. Complicating matters further, the United States standard for EDI is ANSI (American National Standards Institute) X.12. Although the Open Standards Interconnect (OSI) reference model for linking networks is more popular in Europe than it is in the United States, it is not universally accepted. Various industry groups have standardized on other networking architectures, such

FIGURE 19.6

Problems of international networks. There are numerous hurdles to overcome before companies can successfully run networked systems that span many countries. *Adapted from: Mary E. Thyfault, "Virtual Europe," InformationWEEK (November 14, 1994). Copyright © 1994 by CMP Publications Inc., 600 Community Drive, Manhasset, NY 11030. Reprinted from InformationWEEK with permission.*

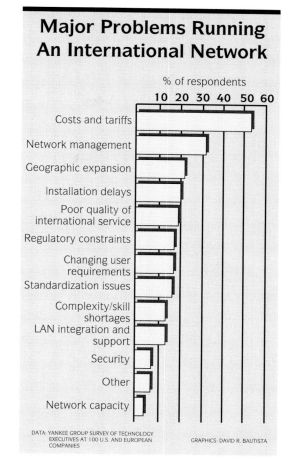

Major Problems Running An International Network

% of respondents

- Costs and tariffs
- Network management
- Geographic expansion
- Installation delays
- Poor quality of international service
- Regulatory constraints
- Changing user requirements
- Standardization issues
- Complexity/skill shortages
- LAN integration and support
- Security
- Other
- Network capacity

DATA: YANKEE GROUP SURVEY OF TECHNOLOGY EXECUTIVES AT 100 U.S. AND EUROPEAN COMPANIES

GRAPHICS: DAVID R. BAUTISTA

as Transmission Control Protocol/Internet Protocol (TCP/IP); IBM's proprietary Systems Network Architecture (SNA); and Digital Equipment's proprietary network architecture, Decnet. Even standards such as ISDN (Integrated Services Digital Network) vary from country to country.

Firms have had two basic options for providing international connectivity: Build their own international private network, or rely on a network service based on the public switched networks throughout the world.

One possibility is for the firm to put together its own private network based on leased lines from each country's PTT (Post, Telegraph, and Telephone authorities). Each country however has different restrictions on data exchange, technical standards, and acceptable vendors of equipment. These problems magnify in certain parts of the world. In Europe, and the United States, reliance on PTTs makes more sense while these public networks expand services to compete with private providers.

The second major alternative to building one's own network is to use one of several expanding network services. With deregulation of telecommunications around the globe, private providers have sprung up to service business customers' data needs, along with some voice and image communications.

Although common in the United States, IVANs (International Value-Added Network Services) are expanding in both Europe and Asia. These private firms offer valued-added telecommunications capacity usually rented from local PTTs or international satellite authorities, and then resell it to corporate users. IVANs add value by providing protocol conversion, operating mailboxes and mail systems, and offering integrated billing that permits a firm to track its data communications costs. Currently these systems are limited to data transmissions, but in the future they will expand to voice and image.

With limited information technology resources, Frank Russell Co., a financial firm, created a powerful global network to link its headquarters in Tacoma, Washington with offices in New York City, Toronto, London, Sydney, Tokyo, and Zurich.

A third possibility, virtual private networks (VPN), is beginning to emerge in the international market, as described in the Window on Technology.

Software

Compatible hardware and communications provide a platform but not the total solution. Also critical to global core infrastructure is software. The development of core systems poses unique challenges for software: How will the old systems interface with the new? Entirely new interfaces must be built and tested if old systems are kept in local areas (which is common). These interfaces can be costly and messy to build. If new software must be created, another challenge is to build software that can be realistically used by multiple business units from different countries when these business units are accustomed to their unique procedures and definitions of data.

Aside from integrating the new with the old systems, there are problems of human interface design and functionality of systems. For instance, in order to be truly useful for enhancing productivity of a global workforce, software interfaces must be easily understood and mastered quickly. Graphical user interfaces are ideal for this but presuppose a common language—often English. When international systems involve knowledge workers only, English may be the assumed international standard. But as international systems penetrate deeper into management and clerical groups, a common language may not be assumed and human interfaces must be built to accommodate different languages and even conventions.

What are the most important software applications? While most international systems focus on basic transaction and MIS systems, there is an increasing emphasis on international collaborative work groups. *EDI*—electronic data interchange—is a

NETWORKING EUROPE

European companies are discovering that they have a third choice for long-distance networks. They no longer must choose only between private networks and public networks. With private networks, the company must lease (or own) and manage its own lines and equipment—an expensive, high fixed-cost approach to telecommunications that is viable only for very large companies with a high volume of calls. Public networks are cheaper and entail little in fixed costs but are not as reliable and are far less secure. Virtual private networks (VPN) create the illusion of a private network and have their strengths while actually using regular public network equipment and charging users only for actual services rendered, thus resulting in a lower cost than a private network. Virtual private networks have seen growing popularity in the United States for more than half a decade, coming into existence soon after the telecommunications deregulation in 1984. Until recently, they have not been available in Europe.

The change in Europe may be a technological revolution, but it is driven by competitive market forces. European telecommunications remains much more highly regulated than it is within the United States. Philip Barton, network manager at London drug conglomerate ICI Zeneca Ltd., believes that what he calls "Europe's regulatory nonsense" needs to be eliminated. He claims that companies pay ten times the true cost of a call in Europe because the call crosses national boundaries and competition is regulated within each country.

The drive to change European telecommunications has been led by an organization known as European VPN Users Association (EVUA), a group of about 40 multinational corporations. EVUA members have 6000 sites in Europe, and each company spends about $50 million annually on telecommunications, giving them together the market power to force changes. The European regulatory and business environment was changing prior to the EVUA—the European Community is committed to a more competitive environment in 1998. Nevertheless, EVUA companies were not satisfied and would not wait. They are looking not only for lower costs but also for more standardization. Bard Haerland, vice-president of worldwide telecommunications at Unisys Corp. of Blue Bell, Pennsylvania, sees the arrival of virtual networks in Europe as the beginning of global services in a global marketplace. Corporate customers will now get one bill (single-billing) for the whole company in the currency the customer designates. Stan Welland, manager of corporate telecommunications at General Electric Co., Fairfield, Connecticut, points out that companies that don't have single-billing can't effectively manage their customer base. Julie MoDrak, director of communications and information center services for Allied Van Lines, Inc. of Naperville, Illinois, adds, "We don't even know how much we're spending in our smaller office in Europe. Each office gets a bill and just pays it. Here in the U.S. we'd never expect to pay it without a detailed breakdown." Thanks to single-billing, these corporations will also be able to receive volume discounts, something not possible when each locality was billed individually.

VPNs are now being offered in Europe by all three major United States long-distance carriers—AT&T, MCI, and Sprint. MCI has established a joint venture with the United Kingdom long-distance carrier, and the new company,

> **To Think About:** *Analyze the differing roles of technology, government, and business in the recent availability of VPNs in Europe. What management, organization, and technology issues have to be addressed when deciding on whether to use a virtual private network?*

BT/MCI, made VPN available in eight European countries before the end of 1994. AT&T's WorldPartner consortium offered VPN services in 23 European countries during the first quarter of 1995, and Sprint's service, already available in the United Kingdom, will be available through Eunetcom in other European countries as soon as regulatory approval has been received. EVUA has already negotiated very aggressive discounts for its members. Included in their pacts with the VPN providers is an agreement that pan-European dialing (using only seven digits to dial each other), single-billing, and calling-card services will be available in 1995. Problems exist, as Figure 19.5 indicates. Changing the regulatory environment is a major hurdle because so many countries are involved. Nonetheless, VPN are now available to larger companies in Europe, and surely competition will see to it that the technology will soon be offered to smaller companies as well.

Source: Mary E. Thyfault, "Virtual Europe," *InformationWeek,* November 14, 1994.

Lotus 1-2-3 screen displays and menu options in the user interface have been translated into Japanese to accommodate end users in East Asia.

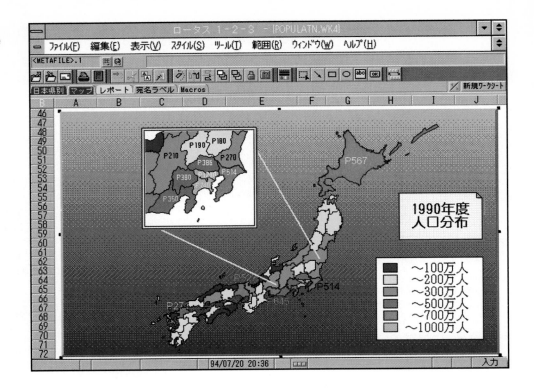

common global transaction processing application used by manufacturing and distribution firms to connect units of the same company, as well as customers and suppliers on a global basis. *Groupware systems* like electronic mail, videoconferencing, Lotus Notes, and other products supporting shared data files, notes, and electronic mail are much more important to knowledge- and data-based firms like advertising firms, research-based firms in medicine and engineering, and graphics and publishing firms. The Internet will be increasingly employed for such purposes.

NEW TECHNICAL OPPORTUNITIES

There are four major technical advances that should fall in price and gain in power over the next few years that have importance to global networking and systems. After many years of stagnant development, PTTs in Europe and local Bell operating companies in the United States are finally moving ISDN (Integrated Services Digital Network) into the marketplace. Chapter 10 has described the benefits of using ISDN as an international standard for transmitting voice, images, and data over the public telephone network. ISDN will make networking services of all kinds as readily available as a phone jack in the wall. International ISDN services are just now becoming available as the United States and other countries extend their geographic coverage.

virtual private networks (VPN)
The ability to custom configure a network using a portion of the public switched network to create the illusion of a private network for a company.

Virtual private networks (VPN) add features to the basic public telephone system that are usually available only to private networks. The basic idea of these services is that the local phone company provides each corporate user the ability to custom configure a network and use whatever portion of the public switched net is needed to do the job while charging only for services used. In a sense, the phone company becomes a digital network company, providing many features of a private network (including abbreviated dialing) for firms operating internationally. Firms using virtual private networks avoid the expense of leasing entire lines and many of the technical and maintenance problems of private networks. The Window on Technology explores the forces that have spread virtual private networks from the United States to Europe.

Finally, the variety of satellite systems described in Chapter 9 will revolutionize communications because they bypass existing ground-based systems. Thus, a salesperson in China could send an order confirmation request to the home office in London effortlessly and expect a reply instantly. The evolution of digital cellular phone and personal communications services will greatly increase the number of cellular communications units and wireless networks. These kinds of "communicate and compute anytime, anywhere" networks will be built throughout the 1990s.

Management Challenges

1. **The social and political role of "stateless" firms.** It is one thing to talk about a stateless transnational firm, but the people who work in these firms do have states, cultures, and loyalties; the operating divisions of these firms do in fact reside in various nation-states with their own laws, politics, and cultures. It is unclear precisely how these stateless firms fit into the national cultures they must serve. In reality, so-called stateless firms have had to be very careful to show local populations that they do serve the interests of the state and broader culture.

2. **The difficulties of managing change in a multicultural firm.** While engineering change in a single corporation in a single nation can be difficult, costly, and long term, bringing about significant change in very large scale global corporations can be daunting. Agreeing on "core

business processes" in a transnational context, and then deciding on common systems requires either extraordinary insight, a lengthy process of consensus building, or the exercise of sheer power.

3. **Lines of business and global strategy.** Firms will have to decide whether some or all of their lines of business should be managed on a global basis. There are some lines of business in which locale variations are slight, and the possibility exists to reap large rewards by organizing globally. Microcomputers and power tools may fit this pattern, as well as industrial raw materials. Other consumer goods may be quite different by country or region. It is likely that firms with many lines of business will have to maintain a very mixed organizational structure.

Summary

1. **Identify the major factors behind the growing internationalization of business.** There are both general culture factors as well as specific business factors to consider. The growth of cheap international communication and transportation has created a "world culture" with stable expectations or norms. Political stability and a growing global knowledge base that is widely shared contribute also to the world culture. These general factors create the conditions for global markets, global production, coordination, distribution, and global economies of scale.

2. **Choose among several global strategies for developing business.** There are four basic international strategies: domestic exporter, multinational, franchiser, and transnational. In a transnational strategy, all factors of production are coordinated on a global scale. However, the choice of strategy is a function of the type of business and product.

3. **Understand how information systems support different global strategies.** There is a connection between firm strategy and information system design. Transnational firms must develop networked system configurations and permit considerable decentralization of development and operations. Franchisers almost always duplicate systems across many countries and use centralized financial controls. Multinationals typically rely on decentralized independence among foreign units with some movement toward development of networks. Domestic

exporters are typically centralized in domestic headquarters with some decentralized operations permitted.

4. **Manage the development of international systems.** Implementing a global system requires an implementation strategy. Typically, global systems have evolved without conscious plan. The remedy is to define a small subset of core business processes and focus on building systems which could support these processes. Tactically, you will have to coopt widely dispersed foreign units to participate in the development and operation of these systems, being careful not to lose overall control.

5. **Understand the main technical alternatives in developing global systems.** The main hardware and telecommunications issues are systems integration and connectivity. The choices for integration are to go either with a proprietary architecture or with an open systems technology like UNIX. Global networks are extremely difficult to build and operate. Some measure of connectivity may be achieved either by relying on local PTT authorities to provide connections, building a system oneself, or relying on private providers to supply communications capacity. The trend appears toward growing reliance on private providers, although public authorities and PTTs are moving forward rapidly with ISDN and other digital services to compete with private companies. The main software issue concerns building interfaces to existing systems and providing much-needed group support software.

Key Terms

International information systems infrastructure	Particularism	Franchiser	Cooptation
Business driver	Transborder data flow	Transnational	Legitimacy
Global culture	Domestic exporter	Core systems	Virtual private networks (VPN)
	Multinational	Business processes	

Review Questions

1. What are the five major factors to consider when building an international information systems infrastructure?
2. Describe the five general cultural factors leading toward growth in global business and the four specific business factors. Describe the interconnection among these factors.
3. What is meant by a global culture?
4. What are the major challenges to the development of global systems?
5. Why have firms not planned for the development of international systems?
6. Describe the four main strategies for global business and organizational structure.
7. Describe the four different system configurations that can be used to support different global strategies.
8. What are the major management issues in developing international systems?
9. What are three principles to follow when organizing the firm for global business?
10. What are three steps of a management strategy for developing and implementing global systems?
11. What is meant by cooptation, and how can it be used to build global systems?
12. Describe the main technical issues facing global systems.
13. Describe three new technologies that can help firms develop global systems.

Discussion Questions

1. As a member of your company's global information systems group that oversees development of global core systems, what criteria would you use to determine if an application should be developed as a global application or as a peripheral local application?
2. As the CEO of a domestic exporter with large production facilities in the United States, you are considering moving toward a multinational model by creating production facilities in Europe and Asia. What strategy would you follow in building an international information infrastructure? What applications would you recommend be shared and global or common, and how would you implement the strategy?

Group Project

With a group of students, identify an area of emerging information technology and explore how this technology might be useful for supporting global business strategies. For instance, you might choose an area like digital telecommunications (e.g., electronic mail, wireless communications, value-added networks) or collaborative work group software or new standards in operating systems or EDI. It will be helpful to choose a business scenario to discuss the technology. You might choose, for instance, an automobile parts franchiser or a clothing franchise like the Limited Express as example businesses. What applications would you make global, what core business processes would you choose, and how would the technology be helpful?

GLOBAL INFORMATION SYSTEMS TO SUPPORT
NESTLÉ'S GLOBAL BUSINESS STRATEGY

Can a multinational corporation's information systems strategy be designed to support its global business strategy? In the case of good and pharmaceutical giant Nestlé, we will first examine its business strategy for the food side of its business, and then we will describe its information systems approach in order that you may evaluate how well its information systems actually support its global business strategy.

Nestlé SA, headquartered in Vesey, Switzerland, is a $43 billion (1993) food and pharmaceutical company that operates virtually all over the world. The corporation has close to 300 operating companies and includes 80 information technology units to service its approximately 200,000 employees worldwide. This large diverse company even has three official languages— English, French, and Spanish. In the food area, while it is best known for its coffee, chocolate, and milk products, it actually is the manufacturer and/or purveyor of thousands of products virtually all over the world. It has been an enormously successful company, increasing sales in 1993 by 5.5 percent, resulting in a 7 percent increase in earnings, reaching $2.2 billion in 1993.

In recent years Nestlé's global business strategy has changed in response to changing market conditions in Europe and the United States. These two giant markets have long accounted for a majority of Nestlé's sales and profits, and they continue to do so. Nonetheless, they are mature markets, and as is often the case in such markets, Nestlé management is watching their profit margins sink as fierce competition cuts into either Nestlé's market share or its profit margin (lowered profits in order to maintain market share). For example, in the United States in the first three years of the 1990s manage-

ment watched their coffee business lose a total of $100 million due to fierce price competition from Folgers Coffee (a Procter & Gamble brand). They have had to restructure their coffee operations in the United States and close down four of their seven plants. This is a general trend in the mature markets, causing Salomon Brothers financial analyst Les Pugh to comment that "The days of the 15 percent operating margin for the U.S. food industry are dead and buried." In Europe Nestlé's operating margin has fallen to 10.7 percent, below such major competitors as Kellogg, Heinz, and Hershey.

The question facing Nestlé management was what business strategy should they follow to compensate for the lower profit margins in the very countries where their major sales and profits have traditionally occurred? In the so-called mature markets, undaunted—or perhaps actually spurred on—by the increasingly tough competition, Nestlé management has continued to move ahead with their strategy of acquisitions. In recent years, for example, they have acquired Carnation, Stouffer's, Perrier, Hills Brothers, and Buitoni. Their goal in continued expansion has been to improve their margin of profit through economies of scale. Nonetheless, their major strategy to counteract reduced profits and other market problems in Europe and the United States has been to emphasize accelerating the growth of both sales and profit in the less developed countries.

Nestlé has long and vigorously pursued a globalization policy. Behind that policy is its strong commitment to a strategy of localization and regionalization. This localization and regionalization strategy involves at least five principles. First, Nestlé leadership does not believe in trying to sell the same product world-

wide. Rather, they buy or develop products that fit well in the local market and culture. The proof of their commitment to this type of strategy can be seen in several startling statistics. Nestlé owns about 8000 different brands worldwide, but of these, about 7250 (over 90 percent) are registered in only one country, and only 80 (one percent) are registered in ten or more countries. Second, Nestlé is committed to reliance upon local and regional staff to manage its interests. Thus, many national and regional managers in the Nestlé organization—at present about 100—spend their whole careers in their own country and region. Their career paths never require them to do a stint in the home office or in a more "advanced" country to gain experience, as is the custom for so many managers in most American and European firms. Even the exception sometimes proves the case. Austrian-born Alfred Senhauser has risen to become the general manager of Nestlé Thailand. However, he has spent 30 years working for Nestlé in Thailand and has become a naturalized Thai citizen. He even changed his name to Att Senasarn.

The third principle in the strategy of localization is Nestlé's patience and long-term perspective as it builds its presence in a specific national market. For example, in talks with Chinese officials, management persevered for 13 years before they were invited in to actually do business. The fourth principle is Nestlé's willingness to evaluate market possibilities on a regional basis. For example, the company looks at Thailand, Vietnam, Laos, Cambodia, and the neighboring Chinese province of Yunnan as a single geographic and cultural region. Since the population of this region is as large as Europe, Nestlé is moving geographically and fast. Fifth, Nestlé is committed to developing products from the less developed countries made from ingredients native to those countries, thereby supporting the local economies while keeping costs low.

Has Nestlé's globalization strategy been successful? By the end of 1993 at least 25 percent of its sales was coming from East and Southeast Asia and Latin America. That 25 percent totals to more than all of General Mills' worldwide sales in the same year. Watinee Khutrakul, a director of Deemar Survey Research in Thailand and the person considered to be the leading market tracker in Asia, says, "As long as big competitors remain tentative about this part of the world, Nestlé can sweep up the market in any product category it chooses." To better understand and appreciate how Nestlé executes its policies, we need to look at some examples of this globalization strategy in practice.

Nestlé is a market leader worldwide in coffee sales. However, coffee is overwhelmingly sold as a hot beverage, which presents special marketing problems in steamy, tropical Thailand. In 1987, Nestlé's Nescafé coffee sales in Thailand were climbing at a rate of between 7 and 10 percent annually, a solid growth in such a sultry country after being on the market for only 10 years. Nonetheless, the Thai economy was expanding at an extremely rapid rate, and local Nestlé management felt they could do better. While coffee has traditionally been advertised on the basis of its aroma and its stimulation power, Senasarn and his staff decided to shift this advertising emphasis. They mapped an advertising campaign they thought would better fit the local culture and climate, selling Nescafé as a way to relax from the tensions of the office, from the noisy city traffic and even from romance. Rudolf Tschan, Nestlé zone manager for Asia, viewed the first TV ad and angrily rejected the whole approach, but he did not have the authority to overrule the local team's decision—and they remained committed to their new marketing approach. They then strayed even further from the traditional coffee marketing when they began to produce and market a cold coffee-based product called Nescafé

Shake. They even designed special plastic containers in which to mix the drink. They then invented a dance, which they called the Shake, to help sell the product. Senasarn even decided to run an annual "talent" contest for "the Shake girl." The result of all this localization? By 1993, the Shake girl contest had become as big as the Miss Thailand event, and Nestlé coffee sales have jumped to $100 million, four times its 1987 level. As Khutrakul explained it, Nestlé "made coffee into a Thai drink."

Nestlé's successful entrance into China is an example of the Nestlé management tenacity and their willingness to invest for the long run. It is also another example of their localization policies. While they began talks with China in 1973, it was not until 1987 that they were given their first business opportunity there. The government of Heilongjiang Province (in northeastern China, formerly known as Manchuria) asked Nestlé to help them boost their powdered milk production. Heilongjiang had neither adequate milk supplies, nor a dependable transportation infrastructure, nor factories to produce the powdered milk. Intent upon success in China, Nestlé viewed this as an opportunity and moved ahead vigorously. In 1990 Nestlé opened a powdered milk and a baby cereal plant in China. In order to get the milk management needed to their factories, they decided to establish their own, more dependable milk collection network. They established "milk roads" from 27 villages in the region to their collection points (known as chilling centers) where the milk was weighed and analyzed. The farmers used traditional Chinese methods to take their milk down the gravel milk roads—wheelbarrows, bicycles, and feet. As an incentive to increasing production, Nestlé decided to pay the farmers promptly for their milk. Within 18 months the number of milk cows in the district climbed from 6000 to 9000. To further aid the farmers, Nestlé decided to hire retired government workers and teachers as farm agents, bringing in Swiss experts to train them in animal health and hygiene. These new farm agents were given a commission based on sales to add further incentives for in-

creasing the quantity and quality of the milk.

This approach is beginning to pay off financially for Nestlé. Whereas the powdered milk factory produced only 316 tons of powdered milk and infant formula its first year, it turned out 10,000 tons in 1994, an increase of over 3000 percent in four years, and Nestlé is tripling the capacity of the factory and initiating construction of other factories. It has the exclusive right to sell its products throughout China for 15 years. To improve their sales capacity, the area managers have established a van delivery system exclusively for Nestlé products. According to David Sheridan of James Cappel in London, Nestlé sales were about $200 million in 1994 and had become profitable. He expects sales to reach $700 million by the end of the decade, and he thinks Nestlé will be all alone in this field. "I haven't found another company willing to pour resources into China like this. The big payoff is still to come, but you can bet it will be solid and long-lasting," he says.

In Malaysia, Nestlé faced a very different kind of problem. Malaysia exports large quantities of cocoa beans, but Malay beans are of lower quality than many others due to their being less rich in flavor. Nestlé wanted to start selling chocolate bars in Malaysia, but the national market was not large enough to justify a Malaysian chocolate candy bar plant using higher-quality imported cocoa beans. The solution came from Johnny Santos, the Filipino head of Nestlé Singapore. He suggested developing a lower-quality but lower-priced candy bar in Malaysia and exporting it to the Asean countries—Malaysia, Singapore, the Philippines, Indonesia, and Thailand. Asea is a trade group, and the high tariffs of its member countries are significantly reduced if the item is produced within one of its member nations. Nestlé decided to develop new versions of two popular Nestlé chocolate candy brands, KitKat and Smarties (an M&Ms competitor). Management worked with farmers to increase cocoa bean quality while also developing new formulas for the two candies. The candy, while being less tasty than the imported competition, sells for a 30 percent lower price, while still giving Nestlé a 20 percent profit margin. Now, according to Low Ming Siong, a directory of Kuala Lumpur's Crosby Research office, because of its lower price, "KitKat is one of the fastest-growing products in Malaysia in its category."

Even in some of the less developed Asian countries, Nestlé is beginning to see some of the market maturation that has taken place in Europe and the United States, and Nestlé's response is an indication of its flexibility in working with local conditions. American-style supermarkets are appearing in large numbers in Taiwan, Malaysia, and Thailand. In Taiwan, for example, the sales of one supermarket chain, Makro, reached about $1 billion in 1994. In Thailand supermarkets accounted for 8 percent of Nestlé's urban business five years ago; today [1994] it's 45 percent of the business. The problem for Nestlé is that supermarkets mean a serious reduction in profit margin. Nestlé Thailand's response? It overhauled its sales team. It nicknamed the new team the "Red Hot Sales Force," staffed it with college graduates who were fluent in English, and gave the team members a great deal of training in increasing supermarket product sales and in techniques in building partnerships with supermarket managers.

What about Nestlé's information systems infrastructure? With 80 different information technology units, its information technology infrastructure has been described as a virtual "Tower of Babel," with all types of hardware and software being used, including equipment from IBM, Hewlett-Packard, and Digital Equipment Corporation (DEC) running both proprietary and open systems. Some of these systems are redundant. There has been no way for developers to communicate with each other. Every time Nestlé makes another acquisition, this condition is only made worse.

Therefore, Nestlé has embarked upon a program to standardize and coordinate its information systems. The word *standardize* does not mean that everyone will do everything the same way. Rather, to Nestlé IS, standardization has several goals: First, standard-

ization should promote communication between various units of the company, if for no other reason than that Vesey management needs to be able to communicate with its many units and to monitor and control their activities. Second, Nestlé's annual technology budget is more than 500 million Swiss francs or about $340 million, and Manfred Kruger, assistant vice president of management services in Vesey, believes that IT standards will prove to be cost effective by eliminating redundancies and building more effective systems. The company has decided to move to a client/server environment internationally, and to that effect has already established some standards, including UNIX; Oracle RDBMS; R/3 integrated material, distribution, and accounting applications from SAP (see the case at the end of Chapter 12); Powersoft's Powerbuilder application development tools; and Ernst & Young's Navigator for development methodology and CASE tools. However, the work of standardization has barely begun. Nestlé still needs to establish standards in many other areas.

According to Jean-Claude Dispaux, Nestlé senior vice president and Kruger's boss, headquarters does have the power to enforce any standards they institute for all units of this global giant. All Nestlé really needs to do is block the IT budget of the noncomplying unit until it accepts the standards. However, this is rarely done. Nestlé prefers to push responsibility out to the countries. What Kruger does instead is to recommend standards. This approach reflects Kruger's personal philosophy that "nothing works if you don't get key players to agree." In addition, Kruger's experience has shown him that the staff in Vesey, Switzerland, is just too far away from most of the Nestlé locations to understand their problems. Previously, for example, when his organization had standardized on a specific microcomputer vendor, he heard a large outcry from the operating units. Ultimately his organization listened and replaced the recommended vendor with a list of recommended PCs from which the local units could select.

The heart of Kruger's technology strategy is "a culture of working together" that reflects his belief that key players must agree. To develop a core application (whether in Vesey or elsewhere), IS gathers together a team representing a number of different organizations and the appropriate hardware and software technologies. The team will work to reach consensus on application requirements and development strategies. Once the application has been developed, it is sent to field organizations for adaptation. After modification to meet local needs, the appropriate version is deployed in various countries. For example, when corporate IS wanted to develop a life cycle for corporate microcomputer development, Nestle brought in 20 developers from eight countries. The result was a set of standards that have blended smoothly into different Nestlé units.

Sources: Joshua Greenbaum, "Nestlé's Global Mix," *Information Week*, April 25, 1994, and "Nestle Makes the Very Best...Standard?" *Information Week*, August 23, 1993; and Carla Rappaport, "Nestlé's Brand Building Machine," *Fortune*, September 19, 1994.

Case Study Questions

1. What kind of global business strategy is Nestlé pursuing?

2. Do you think Nestlé's information systems strategy supports its global business strategy? How is it supportive? In what ways is it not supportive? What changes would you make to this strategy?

3. Do you think Kruger's approach to establishing and enforcing standards fits in well with Nestlé's global business strategy? Explain.

4. What management problems do you envision for Kruger's approach?

5. How do you think Nestlé should determine which new systems must conform to corporate information systems standards, and which ones need not conform?

References

Cash, James I., F. Warren McFarlan, James L. McKenney, and Lynda M. Applegate. *Corporate Information Systems Management*, 3rd ed. Homewood, IL: Irwin (1992).

Chismar, William G., and Laku Chidambaram. "Telecommunications and the Structuring of U.S. Multinational Corporations." *International Information Systems* 1, no. 4 (October 1992).

Cox, Butler. *Globalization: The IT Challenge*. Sunnyvale, California: Amdahl Executive Institute (1991).

Deans, Candace P., and Michael J. Kane. *International Dimensions of Information Systems and Technology*. Boston, MA: PWS-Kent (1992).

Deans, Candace P., Kirk R. Karwan, Martin D. Goslar, David A. Ricks, and Brian Toyne. "Key International Issues in U.S.-Based Multinational Corporations." *Journal of Management Information Systems* 7, no. 4 (Spring 1991).

Dutta, Amitava. "Telecommunications Infrastructure in Developing Nations." *International Information Systems* 1, no. 3 (July 1992).

Holland, Christopher, Geoff Lockett, and Ian Blackman. "Electronic Data Interchange Implementation: A Comparison of U.S. and European Cases." *International Information Systems* 1, no. 4 (October 1992).

Ives, Blake, and Sirkka Jarvenpaa. "Applications of Global Information Technology: Key Issues for Management." *MIS Quarterly* 15, no. 1 (March 1991).

Ives, Blake, and Sirkka Jarvenpaa. "Global Business Drivers: Aligning Information Technology to Global Business Strategy." *IBM Systems Journal* 32, no. 1 (1993).

Ives, Blake, and Sirkka Jarvenpaa. "Global Information Technology: Some Lessons from Practice." *International Information Systems* 1, no. 3 (July 1992).

Karin, Jahangir, and Benn R. Konsynski. "Globalization and Information Management Strategies." *Journal of Management Information Systems* 7 (Spring 1991).

Keen, Peter. *Shaping the Future*. Cambridge, MA: Harvard Business School Press (1991).

King, William R., and Vikram Sethi. "An Analysis of International Information Regimes." *International Information Systems* 1, no. 1 (January 1992).

Mannheim, Marvin L. "Global Information Technology: Issues and Strategic Opportunities." *International Information Systems* 1, no. 1 (January 1992).

Nelson, R. Ryan, Ira R. Weiss, and Kazumi Yamazaki. "Information Resource Management within Multinational Corporations: A Cross-Cultural Comparison of the U.S. and Japan." *International Information Systems* 1, no. 4 (October 1992).

Neumann, Seev. "Issues and Opportunities in International Information Systems." *International Information Systems* 1, no. 4 (October 1992).

Palvia, Shailendra, Prashant Palvia, and Ronald Zigli, eds. *The Global Issues of Information Technology Management*. Harrisburg, PA: Idea Group Publishing (1992).

Roche, Edward M. *Managing Information Technology in Multinational Corporations*. New York: Macmillan (1992).

Sadowsky, George. "Network Connectivity for Developing Countries" *Communications of the ACM* 36, no. 8 (August 1993).

Stahl, Stephanie. "Global Networks: The Headache Continues." *InformationWeek* (October 12, 1992).

Steinbart, Paul John, and Ravinder Nath. "Problems and Issues in the Management of International Data Networks." *MIS Quarterly* 16, no. 1(March 1992).

Straub, Detmar W. "The Effect of Culture on IT Diffusion: E-Mail and FAX in Japan and the U.S." *Information Systems Research* 5, no. 1 (March 1994).

Phantom Profits Haunt Kidder Peabody

On the morning of April 18, 1994, the Wall Street financial community awoke to headlines revealing that Joseph Jett, one of the most successful traders on Wall Street, had been fired. Jett, who at age 36 was the head of zero-coupon bond trading at Kidder, Peabody Group Inc., had earned $210 million for Kidder in 1993, nearly half of the firm's total profit of $439 million. He personally had earned $9 million in salary, commissions, and bonus and had been honored as Kidder's trader of the year for 1993.

Jett made his huge profits by trading government bond strips. Strips are created when the interest and principal portions of bonds are split into two separately traded instruments. The bond strips represent the bonds' interest payments—owners of strips have the right to the bonds' interest payments. Profits are made from buying strips in the open market and then reselling them at a higher price. The price of the strips will normally rise as the due date of the underlying bond approaches. The bonds, stripped of their interest portion, are known as zero-coupon bonds. Both the strips and the bonds are widely traded. Strips produce a very narrow profit on each trade, requiring a huge number of trades to make a large profit. However, many traders do consider them to be risk free.

Once Jett had taken over the zero-coupon bond desk, in early 1993, he reported to Edward Cerullo, age 44, who was an executive managing director of Kidder and the head of its 750-person fixed-income securities group. Cerullo was widely considered to be Kidder's number two executive, after CEO Michael Carpenter. He was the person who had built Kidder's bond trading business, the foundation of Kidder's recent successes. Insiders report Cerullo made

as much as $20 million in 1993, double his 1992 income. Much of that was a bonus based upon the profits of Jett.

THE SCHEME UNCOVERED

In late March 1994, David Bernstein, who also reported to Cerullo, noticed that Jett's trading volume had been exploding, and he became suspicious. He began an intensive review of those trades and, at home over the weekend, he discovered that Jett had not been closing his trades. Jett had not actually booked any real profits. His profits were really fakes. Bernstein called in the Kidder accountants, and in early April they determined that Jett's legitimate trades had actually lost $90 million, whereas his fake trades had resulted in about $350 million in phantom profits. Bernstein took all of this to Cerullo, and on Sunday evening, April 17, Jett received a hand-delivered letter at his home informing him that he had been dismissed. Jett's scheme had apparently unraveled.

The next day Kidder notified the Securities and Exchange Commission (SEC) and the New York Stock Exchange (NYSE). The firm also reassigned six other bond traders and

trade-processing staff because they had not reported the scheme to management. Later, when asked why they were not fired, Carpenter explained, "Are they bad people? No. They just didn't catch it."

Jett's scheme was relatively simple. He would buy interest strips for forward delivery (delivery at a later date). However, when the contracts came due, he did not actually settle them. Instead he rolled them forward, closing the current strips and opening new ones due at a later date. Every time he rolled a position over, he booked a profit, but it was a fictitious profit, fictitious because nothing was ever settled, no cash ever changed hands, and Kidder never received any cash. Nor could Kidder ever collect accrued interest for strips it no longer owned. The so-called "profits" were actually only an agreement that Kidder would sell the strips back to the government in the future, and when Jett rolled the position over, the commitment was rolled over with it. Once the contracts were rolled over, Kidder no longer owned the earlier ones. In order to keep the scheme going, Jett had to keep writing the strips farther out in time and for larger amounts so the computerized accounting system would be fooled. The quantities became so large that Jett claimed to control more than twice the total amount of some bonds that had been stripped.

Jett told Kidder he had made trades involving $1.76 trillion in principal value in the first three months of 1994. Only $79 billion of those trades were real. The remaining $1.6 trillion, representing 95 percent, was never traded. Since Kidder officials apparently focused on the net profit of the department, not on individual types of trades, the phony trades obscured the losses. No one noticed the implausibility of what Jett was doing until the spring of 1994. It turned out that Jett never made any legitimate

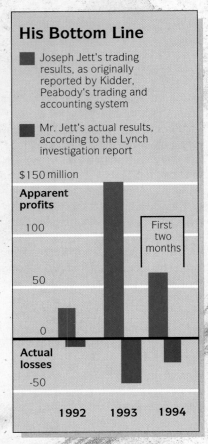

His Bottom Line

■ Joseph Jett's trading results, as originally reported by Kidder, Peabody's trading and accounting system

■ Mr. Jett's actual results, according to the Lynch investigation report

$150 million

Apparent profits

First two months

100

50

0

Actual losses

-50

1992   1993   1994

THE NEW YORK TIMES

FIGURE V.1
Apparent profits vs. actual losses at Kidder Peabody. Kidder Peabody's trading and accounting system recorded Joseph Jett's phantom trade as profits, when they actually produced losses for the firm. *Adapted from: Sylvia Nasar, "Kidder Scandal Tied to Failure of Supervision," The New York Times (August 5, 1994).*

profits for Kidder—his trading actually lost $85,415,000 for the company (see Figure V.1).

Jett was able to take a bogus profit on the price of the strip, the interest portion of the bond, before it was "reconstituted," or turned back into the original bond because Kidder's trading system recognized a profit on the date that a forward "recon" was entered into the system. In other words, the system allowed Jett to report as "trades" what were really only a stated intention to make transactions in the future. The "profits" Jett reported reflected accrued interest that would never be received. Jett was rewarded with huge bonuses for the profits he claimed, when his trading was actually producing losses.

This accounting loophole, which allowed Jett to book a nonrealized profit at the time a trade was opened, resembled a giant ponzi scheme. According to Robert Dickey, a former Kidder trader, "You can make a temporary profit, but it's not real." He said the computer system defect was known by Jett's predecessors. In fact, it later came to light that in May 1993 Kidder accountant Charles Fiumefreddo noticed the critical flaw in the accounting system and suggested that it be fixed. His request was ignored. See Figure V.2 for a further explanation of the strips and Jett's scheme.

Kidder CEO Carpenter's public response was to claim that the trades were essentially harmless because they did not involve the mortgage or derivative markets and "involved no customers." He was correct that no customer was directly harmed because all these trades were for Kidder's own account. Carpenter also said that the scheme was "an isolated incident that happened despite the diligent efforts" to make Kidder's compliance control and risk management "state of the art." He announced that Kidder would take legal action against Jett. Giant conglomerate General Electric was also involved as the parent of Kidder Peabody.

GE CEO Jack Welch stated that the scheme "violates everything we believe in and stand for." Welch also an-

nounced that Kidder had hired Gary Lynch to "lead a comprehensive investigation into what went wrong and to recommend steps to prevent a recurrence." Lynch was a partner at Kidder's outside law firm, Davis, Polk & Wardwell. He had an impeccable reputation for honesty and tenacity, and his background was perfect for the job. He had spent thirteen years at the SEC, the last four years as its enforcement chief. He was the lawyer who led the investigation and prosecution of the notorious insider trading case against Drexel Burnham Lambert and traders Ivan Boesky, Dennis Levine, Michael Milken, and Martin Siegel in the late 1980s.

Cerullo, Jett's boss, had not personally unearthed the problem. His public response was that Kidder's internal controls met industry standards. He added that he could not possibly have immersed himself in the financial records of the 750 traders that report to him. He further contended that Jett's profits had grown over an extended period of time, and at an appropriate growth rate, leaving no reason for him to be suspicious. Finally, he claimed that Jett's positions (holdings) were never as large as the reported $10 billion and were certainly within normal bounds. According to Alan Cohen, a New York defense lawyer who is a former head of the securities fraud unit of the Manhattan United States Attorney's office, "Traders have enormous discretion in what they buy and sell, and the more senior they are, the more discretion they have," meaning that large, successful traders are normally not closely monitored at Wall Street firms.

The size of the Kidder loss was difficult to determine at first. Despite Cerullo's claim, experienced traders estimated that Jett had to have been holding more than $10 billion in bonds in order to be able to record $350 million in profits, whether or not the profits were phony. Later, former government-bond desk traders estimated Jett's holdings to have been about $18 billion. The financial result of the discovery was that Kidder's income had been inflated by about $350 million over the previous 15 months. The investigation later found

FIGURE V.2

How Joseph Jett could fool Kidder Peabody's accounting system. *Adapted from: Floyd Norris, "Kidder, Peabody, Where Trading Went Awry,"* The New York Times, *April 19, 1994.*

Conjuring Phantom Profits: A Scenario

Here is how Joseph Jett, who was dismissed as chief of Kidder Peabody's Government bond trading department, was said to be using quirks of the firm's accounting system to take credit for profits that existed only on paper.

STRIPPED AND RECONSTITUTED BONDS

A Treasury bond is a promise by the Treasury to make two kinds of payments: interest twice a year before the bond matures, and the principal (the face value of the bond) upon maturity.

When the Treasury issues the bond it is all in one piece, but the two components are often traded separately later: as a "strip" of coupons and the principal payment. The pieces can also be put back together, in a move called a recon.

Sometimes the bonds trade for slightly more in pieces than together, or vice versa; brokers routinely strip or reconstitute bonds to make arbitrage profits out of the small price differences.

30-year Treasury bond due in May 2007

Face value: **$1,000**
Interest rate: **12%**

+

Interest coupons
$60 every six months

Principal payment
$1,000 on maturity

FORWARD TRADES AND EPHEMERAL PROFITS

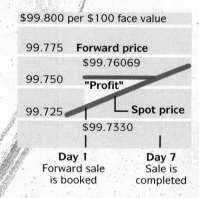

$99.800 per $100 face value

99.775   **Forward price**
         $99.76069
99.750
         "Profit"
99.725   **Spot price**
         $99.7330

Day 1   **Day 7**
Forward sale   Sale is
is booked   completed

This forward sale of $8 million in strips was booked by Kidder Peabody as yielding $2,215 "profit" on the first day, falling to zero six days later.

A strip's principal payment component trades at a discount to face value that gradually shrinks in a predictable way as maturity approaches. Kidder Peabody's accounting system allows for this when assessing the value of forward trades.

When a broker records a forward sale—a deal struck today to sell a strip for a set price on a date in the future—the system notes that the forward price is higher than today's spot price, and books the difference as a profit. That profit is reduced each day as the spot price rises closer to the forward price, disappearing entirely the day the deal is completed.

If the deal were reversed and the broker was buying rather than selling, this temporary paper profit would be a paper loss instead.

OFFSETS THAT DIDN'T OFFSET

Apparently, Kidder's accounting system used different formulas to calculate the temporary gain or loss for different kinds of transactions.

Mr. Jett is said to have booked forward recon transactions with the Federal Reserve that offset each other exactly, leaving his net position in the market neutral and risk-free. The "trades" with the Fed were accounting fictions, since no money changed hands. But the complexities of the Kidder accounting system had the effect of crediting him with temporary paper profits on some of the trades that were larger than the paper losses on the offsetting trades. That made it appear the Mr. Jett was making profits for the firm without running any risk.

The paper profits on any one set of forward trades soon diminished to zero, but by then Mr. Jett booked yet more phantom profits on new trades.

The New York Times

that Jett held $600 billion in phony strip positions at the end and had "booked" 60,000 trades that were actually never closed. Kidder's 1993 profits had to be reduced from $439 million to $89 million. Observers say the total loss, including the "profits" earned, made the scheme one of the biggest ever recorded on Wall Street.

BACKGROUND

The story of the loss goes back a number of years. General Electric purchased an 80 percent share of Kidder, Peabody Group Inc., the 120-year-old New York–based investment banking firm, in April 1986 for $602 million. General Electric Co. (GE) is a Stamford, Connecticut–based conglomerate with 220,000 employees. Jack Welch, the chairman of GE since 1981, has been called "one of the most respected managers in corporate America" by The New York Times. He has the reputation of being nearly obsessive about internal controls and says that the key to his management style is the avoidance of surprises. Under his guidance, GE became a highly profitable cash-rich company. For example, in 1993 the company reported record gross earnings of $4 billion and net earnings of $1 billion, or $2.03 per share, this even after taking a one-time charge of $.24 per share for the Kidder fiasco.

Financial analysts believe that one reason Welch was so successful was that he cut GE's bureaucracy and decentralized the company. In order to counterbalance the decentralization and remain consistent with his strong emphasis upon control, he established a formidable team of internal auditors to keep tab on the various semi-independent units. Welch also is reputed to be very "results-oriented," another oft-cited reason for GE's success over the last few years.

GE purchased Kidder near the end of the era when junk bonds were hot. The insider trading scandal was about to break. The scandal led to the most famous Wall Street legal case of the 1980s, and to the collapse of Drexel Burnham Lambert and the conviction of two billionaire traders, Ivan Boesky and Michael Milken. One key figure in the junk bond scandal was Martin Siegel, a successful Kidder trader who had been secretly cooperating with Boesky in insider trading. In 1987, now under the spotlight of the insider trading investigation, Kidder and its parent GE settled civil insider trading charges and instituted a compliance system designed to help management detect the most complex trading crimes. Kidder placed compliance supervisors in every one of Kidder's departments and business units. The compliance officers and auditors were directed to analyze trading positions and transactions for different types of risks, including liquidity and interest rate moves.

Because Jett's transactions were risk free, they went undetected by the firm's compliance officers for a long time. And since securities firms execute thousands of trades each day, compliance officers may be able to check only a small sample of transactions. There's an assumption that most senior people are honest. Unless one has reason to believe that trades are bogus, the chances of catching fraudulent trades are very low. Traders have been able to outsmart lawyers and auditors because financial instruments are changing so rapidly that few compliance supervisors and auditors understand how they are traded.

In 1989 Welch appointed his friend and trusted employee Michael A. Carpenter as chief executive officer (CEO) of Kidder Peabody. Carpenter was a British-born, former management consultant who had spent the previous several years consulting to GE's strategic planning function, particularly in the GE Credit Corporation area.

In the 1990s Kidder's biggest success was in the field of repackaging mortgage-backed securities into complex bundles known as collateralized mortgage obligations (CMOs). Mortgage-backed bonds are securities created by pooling home mortgages. CMOs are derivatives; that is, they are trading instruments that change value according to the change in the value of underlying financial instruments, in this case mortgage bonds. Bonds, in turn, are dependent upon interest rates, rising in value when interest rates fall and falling when interest rates rise. In 1993 Kidder underwrote a total of $81 billion in home mortgage–backed securities, more than any other investment bank and fully 85 percent of Kidder's total underwriting that year. In other words, the company had all its eggs in one basket, a basket totally dependent upon the behavior of interest rates.

During the early 1990s, interest rates in the United States fell sharply as the country struggled to come out of a recession. Profits in fixed incomes were easy—all one had to do was to hold bonds and related instruments. However, by the end of 1993, an economic recovery was in full swing and the United States Federal Reserve Bank began to raise interest rates. During the first months of 1994, interest rates were rising at a fairly rapid rate. As rates rose, applications for new mortgages declined. Mortgage bond underwriting for the second quarter was down by 72 percent. This was particularly harmful at Kidder because it was far more dependent than other Wall Street firms upon mortgage-backed securities.

Joseph Jett, the central figure in the success of Kidder in those years, came from the small midwestern town of Wickliffe, Ohio. On a scholarship to the Massachusetts Institute of Technology, Jett earned a bachelor's degree in chemistry in 1980 and a masters in 1982. He began his working career at GE as a senior process engineer in the plastics division and advanced to production engineer in 1985. Apparently unhappy with his choice of careers, he quit his job and enrolled in Harvard University, completing requirements for an MBA degree in 1987 (the degree was not awarded, apparently because he did not pay all of his university bills). He then turned to Wall Street where he was hired as a junior trader in mortgage-backed securities at Morgan Stanley & Co. He quickly graduated to a position of arbitrage trader. In 1989 when Morgan's structured-finance group was reorganized, he was laid off. He then moved to CS First Boston as a junior mortgage-backed securities trader. When the position was eliminated in 1991, he was hired by Kidder as a government bond trader, an area in which he had no trading experience. At the age of 33, his meteoric rise began.

Jett began contributing significantly to Kidder's profits almost immediately. In 1993 he was so successful that he was promoted to the position of chief of government bond trading (the zero-coupon bond desk) where he oversaw 16 traders plus a support staff. In 1993, because his trading had apparently contributed $210 million, or nearly half of the total published Kidder profits, he earned $9 million. In January 1994 he was honored with the Kidder "Chairman's Award" as the star 1993 Kidder employee. In accepting the honor at the annual Kidder retreat at Boca Raton, Florida, his speech focused upon the importance of making money, preaching profit at all costs. "This is war," he was quoted as saying. "You do anything to win. You make money at all costs."

Signs of trouble at Kidder began in 1991 when Linda LaPrade sued Kidder claiming Cerullo pressured her to inflate bids on government securities in order to amass a larger share of the securities for later resale. She further alleged he told her "profits and performance were most important," threatening to fire her if she did not comply. Cerullo denied the charges, calling her a disgruntled former employee. The same year Cerullo was fined $5000 and censured by the National Association of Securities Dealers (NASD) for improperly supervising a bond trader named Ira Saferstein. Saferstein had created fake mortgage-backed bond trades. NASD said that Cerullo "did not object to Saferstein's execution of these transactions and failed to take steps to reverse or adjust" them. Cerullo's explanation was that "The guy did something we told him not to do. He did it again and we fired him on the spot."

In 1992, according to several Kidder traders, Hugh Bush, a trader who worked next to Jett, was fired immediately after raising questions with Cerullo about what he considered to be improper trades by Jett. Bush apparently accused Jett of "mismarking"—mis-recording—trading positions, which is

illegal. According to reports, Bush was promptly fired and Cerullo never investigated the allegation. Later Cerullo would not say why Bush was fired but he did say that Bush "never came to me and made any accusations about Jett or anyone." Also in 1992 Scott Newquist raised questions about Jett's trades. Newquist was a Kidder investment-banking chief and a member of the inventory committee, a group responsible for tracking the firm's trading positions. Newquist later claimed he brought allegations of problems with Jett's positions to Carpenter, telling him that the inventory committee was relying on "vague assertions" about Jett's huge trading positions. But, Newquist contends, Carpenter did nothing because of his (Carpenter's) narrow focus on profit. Carpenter denied that Newquist ever asked him to take any action and further denied being only concerned with the bottom line.

During the Lynch investigation of the Jett affair, it came out that Michael Carpenter, the CEO, had no securities license and had been running the company illegally. Carpenter later claimed he did not need a license because he was not really running the firm, although he did not deny that he was CEO. In March 1993, Carpenter did finally take and pass the required examinations and obtain a license to manage a broker-dealer firm.

The Jett affair was actually the second major bond-related calamity involving Kidder in 1994. Kidder Peabody, along with several other major Wall Street firms such as Bear, Stearns, had invested large amounts of money into several hedge funds run by Askin Capital Management. As bond prices fell sharply in late 1993 and early 1994, Askin took large losses. By early 1994 the company was forced into bankruptcy and the investors' entire $600 million was lost. Kidder was the largest single investor in the fund.

TURMOIL AND INSTABILITY AT KIDDER

In the weeks and months that followed the firing of Jett, both the business press

and Lynch investigated Kidder Peabody, and a great deal of speculation ensued. A search of the various regulatory records found that there were no prior complaints about Jett; he had had no major disciplinary problems. In late April, word leaked out that GE had invested another $200 million into Kidder, making up 95 percent of the $210 million loss. On April 22 Kidder discharged Neil Margolin for concealing losses ("improperly valuing inventory positions") of about $10 million. Margolin was a 29-year-old, relatively green trader, who also reported to Cerullo. Mismarking positions is a fairly common problem on Wall Street and often leads to dismissal. A check of Margolin's record showed no history of disciplinary action. Kidder once again announced that the hidden losses did not result in losses for any Kidder customer or any other Wall Street firm, that Margolin's trades were all for Kidder's own account.

On May 10 at a preliminary court hearing, Kidder formally accused Jett of fraud. At that same hearing, Jett asked Kidder to release to him a $5-million account that he claimed was his. The account contained part of Jett's 1993 earnings. Jett claimed he was unable to pay rent and his legal fees without access to his funds. While denying Jett his funds, Kidder was paying the legal fees of Cerullo and other employees under investigation. Kidder did offer to release enough funds for Jett's living expenses and "reasonable" legal fees, which would leave Kidder in the position of being able to determine the size of Jett's defense. At the same hearing, Lynch complained that Jett had not responded to his repeated requests for an interview.

As soon as the scandal was uncovered, a question arose as to the real value of the mortgage-based securities held by Kidder. Most investment banks value the price of their securities at the close of every trading day. However, because interest rates were rising fast in the spring of 1994, turbulence in the government bond market resulted, making pricing more difficult. Also, few trades of these securities were occurring with the number of new mortgages dropping precipitously, making legitimate daily prices impossible to obtain. Several former Kidder traders claimed that the value of Kidder mortgage-related positions were calculated far less often than at most firms, although Carpenter denied the assertion. On May 12, KPGM Peat Marwick, the third largest accounting firm in the United States, completed a review of Kidder's mortgage bond inventory and turned it over to Carpenter. According to Carpenter the report concluded that "No adjustments [in pricing] have been suggested as a result." On the same day, Kidder also claimed its mortgage department had made money so far in 1994, despite having incurred losses since mid-March. Carpenter denied the rumors of large losses.

Throughout May and June, Kidder experienced the departure of a number of experienced traders. On June 22, GE CEO Welch announced that he had replaced Carpenter as Kidder CEO. Welch said that Carpenter's removal was not the result of any findings in the continuing investigation, and he reiterated that Mr. Carpenter is "a close personal friend." Rather, he said, his purpose was to restore the confidence of Kidder's clients.

Carpenter was replaced by two GE executives. Dennis D. Dammerman, GE's chief financial officer, became Kidder's temporary CEO. Like Carpenter before him, he had no background in the securities business, although he did have extensive financial markets experience. *The Wall Street Journal* called him "Mr. Welch's most trusted lieutenant." Dennis J. Nayden, age 40, was named Kidder's chief operating officer and the person to replace Dammerman when he returns to his GE post. Nayden had been the executive vice president of GE Capital Services. He too had no background in the securities business. *The Wall Street Journal* called him "GE's top financial trouble-shooter."

Another leading figure in this drama was Melvin Mullin, age 46, a former professor of mathematics who came to Kidder in 1988. By 1993 he was considered the number three person in the firm, having made $58 million for

Kidder. He was the person who hired Jett in 1991 and was his supervisor for several years. When Mullin moved on, Jett replaced him at the zero-coupon bonds desk. At one point Mullin hired his wife, Denise Mullin, as a bond trader. She was a very experienced, successful trader, and the controversy that surrounded her was only related to the propriety of her being supervised by her husband. Mullin also earned commission on all her sales, as he did on all his reportees. In 1993 Denise Mullin resigned after a great deal of pressure from executives at both GE and Kidder. When she left, auditors found errors in her account and had to reduce the value of her holdings by $2 million.

On July 11, Kidder announced it had fired Peter Bryant, a London-based Kidder options trader who also reported to Mullin. Hired in 1986 from Lazard Brothers & Co., he was considered a leading futures and options salesman and Kidder's top producer in the London office. Earlier in 1994 he had been promoted to senior vice-president. The firm claimed he had hidden losses totaling $6 million on about a dozen option trades on French and Spanish government treasury bonds. Kidder announced that it would take a $10 million pretax write down in the second quarter. The write down was higher than the stated loss because of questions about how to price the options, the same problem Kidder was facing with other mortgage-based securities. Bryant denied all charges. A search turned up no disciplinary cases on his regulatory record.

On July 23 Cerullo announced that he had resigned from Kidder. Cerullo's position supervising 750 traders was split, and he was replaced by two traders. Steven Baum had been the head of Kidder's commercial mortgages group. He came to Kidder from Salomon Brothers. Baum had been censured by the NASD (National Association of Securities Dealers) in 1991 for improperly supervising a bond trader who created fake mortgage-backed bond trades. William Watt was based in London where he had been responsible for Eurobond trading and

sales. He had also been a supervisor of Bryant's. With Cerullo's departure, the newspapers speculated that many more traders would leave Kidder. Traders had liked working for Cerullo both because he gave his traders great freedom in their work and he rewarded them with large bonuses. For example, in 1993, Kidder had one of the highest compensation ratios on Wall Street, paying its traders and staff $882 million, more than half its net revenue. Kidder paid its sales force mainly on commission instead of salary plus bonuses.

On the same day, July 23, Kidder also announced that Gregory Fiske Wilbur had been forcibly retired. Wilbur worked out of the Palo Alto, California, office (near Silicon Valley) where he specialized in high-technology stocks. He was reputed to be one of the top Kidder brokers. The company had forced him to take early retirement after 33 years because he was the subject of numerous client complaints and lawsuits. Clients claimed that Wilbur's speculative, sometimes unauthorized, trading had cost them millions of dollars. Wall Street rumors indicated that GE had paid more than $3 million to settle these suits.

Jett spoke to federal prosecutors again on July 25 and told them that he had been ordered to reduce his trading positions in early April, two weeks before he was fired. He stated that David Bernstein, acting for Cerullo, had told him that Kidder was in violation of net capital rules. The SEC requires brokerage houses to maintain a minimum ratio of net capital (cash plus other easily convertible assets) to debt. If accurate, this revelation suggested that Kidder's financial condition was worse than had been previously suspected. Kidder denied Jett's charges. In early August, Kidder revealed that for the month of July the company had a pre-tax loss of $56 million.

Mullin was the next to go. The announcement that he was fired was made on August 3. Mullin had earned $2.7 million in 1993, partly based on Jett's trades. During the Lynch inquiry, he had told the investigators that there was no way he could have reviewed

1500 to 2000 trade tickets per day. Reasons given for his firing included his allowing a trader to work without a securities license (Kaplan) and hiring and supervising his own wife despite objections from both Kidder and GE officials.

CHARGES AND COUNTERCHARGES

Finally, on August 4, the long-awaited Lynch report on the Jett case was released. At first read it seemed a scathing report. Its findings included the following conclusions:

- Jett, acting on his own, "knowingly manipulated Kidder's trading and accounting systems to generate" about $350 million in false profits. Although Kidder's internal auditors had conducted two reviews of Jett's trading desk in 1993, they never caught on because they were inexperienced and had been given "misrepresentations" by Jett.

- Jett's scheme started much earlier and went on much longer than had previously been thought. It actually began in 1991.

- The scheme had actually generated $349.7 million in phony profits and $85.4 million in actual losses.

- The investigators calculated that, if settled, the total trades by Jett in bonds and strips would have been over $34 billion. It also pointed out that Jett had actually reported $1.7 trillion in phony trades.

- Kidder's 750-team bond trading group, under Cerullo's supervision, had operated as an independent fiefdom, uncontrolled by senior management, it said, the group ran amok.

- Richard O'Donnell, Kidder's senior vice-president and chief financial officer (CFO), was exonerated from any blame. As CFO O'Donnell's responsibilities included overseeing the firm's accounting and control (audit) functions. In an interview, Lynch excused O'Donnell, saying "the accounting people got involved so late in the game." The report did say that there were "a string of misjudgments and missed opportunities." It also noted that O'Donnell did learn about anomalies in Jett's ledger but did not investigate them.

- Mullin was criticized for not reviewing trade tickets and other documents and for failing to respond to objections about Jett's trading from another trader (Bush). The report also noted that Mullin had championed Jett without understanding his trading activities.

- Much of the blame was directed at Cerullo. The report said he did not examine Jett's trading, not even by sampling, for information about settlement dates and counterparties, information that would have disclosed Jett's deceptions. The report concludes that Cerullo's supervision of Jett was "seriously deficient." However, the report did support Cerullo's denial that he had of any knowledge of the scheme.

- The investigators firmly rejected Carpenter's oft repeated contention that the Jett problem could have happened at any firm, that a clever crook will beat the system every time. Nonetheless, it concluded that Carpenter bore no direct responsibility for the affair, except that it happened on his watch.

- The report urged Kidder to institute new policies and procedures for trader supervision, including a manual or computer review of trade tickets.

The report concluded that the ultimate problem was the emphasis throughout Kidder on profits and greed. Although "Jett was provided the opportunity to generate false profits by trading and accounting systems," it was his supervisors who allowed Jett to use that opportunity for over two years because they never understood what Jett was doing in his day-to-day trading activity or the reason for his apparent profitabilty. "The door to Jett's abuses was opened as much by human failings as by inadequate formal systems," it concluded. It also said of Jett's supervisors that "Their focus was on profit and loss, and risk-management data provided no insight into the mechanics of Jett's trading."

Over the next few days, strong criticisms of the report emerged. Those criticisms included:

- It is hard to believe that Jett could have acted alone. Even an anonymous GE financial officer who did not work at Kidder was quoted as asking, "How could $350 million in profits go into the books when no money changed hands?" The implication is that Jett must have had help, even if that help was just purposeful inattention.

- The report did not address the issue of why questions were not raised earlier, given that the trading pattern persisted over a long period of time and involved such enormous sums of money. Where were the GE and Kidder auditors in 1991 and 1992?

- The report fails to deal with Jett's accusation that Cerullo was aware of his trading activities. In fact, a statement by Brian Finkelstein cited in the report seemed to indicate that Cerullo was aware of the trades, and yet this statement was never addressed.

- Many wondered how O'Donnell could be exonerated from responsibility. John Coffee, a Columbia University professor in securities law, asked, "How could the accountants not have insisted that whole time on being able to identify assets?" Others pointed to the fact that three of those transferred when the discovery was first made were from O'Donnell's office, indicating some responsibility from within his department. Many wanted to know why the report did not address the question of where the cash was. Not a penny had come into Kidder through Jett's trades, yet the auditors and accountants never examined the issue. In fact, critics point out, the word "cash" is never even mentioned in the report. Others point out that $1.7 trillion in trades in 1993, an amount equaling nearly half of all U.S. treasury securities in private hands, should have triggered the interest of the auditors.

- Many questioned how Carpenter could possibly be exonerated when Jett's profits constituted more than 20 percent of his company's profits—Jett was his biggest profit producer. Moreover, Carpenter awarded Jett the annual "Chairman's Award." Did Carpenter ever look into what Jett was doing, and if not, why not? Didn't this constitute a failure to supervise?

- The report fails to ask why Jett's superiors who had been fired or forced to retire were allowed to keep millions of bonus dollars based upon the phantom "profit" of their supervisee. Even more, why had Cerullo been given a $10 million severance package?

However, the strongest criticism was reserved for Lynch himself. Lynch was filling multiple, conflicting roles for Kidder. First, he was hired by Kidder to investigate the whole affair in order to aid Kidder in improving its own procedures. In addition, he was representing the company in an arbitration claim against Jett. In a third role, Lynch was also representing Kidder with the Securities and Exchange Commission, the New York Stock Exchange, and the Manhattan United States attorney's office as they investigated Kidder in relation to the Jett affair. The question critics raised is, how could Lynch "zealously" represent his client in front of these legal entities while also fully revealing in his investigations the depth of the responsibility borne by Kidder and its management? In his report, Lynch's primary responsibility had to be to protect his client, Kidder Peabody. Critics also concluded that it would be difficult to find other Kidder executives culpable without having interviewed Jett, the key figure in the scandal.

The conclusion of many observers was that the main purpose of the report was to be a bargaining chip with the SEC, NYSE regulators, and the government attorneys. Lynch would be dealing with William McLucas, the SEC chief of the enforcement division. Lynch had held that same office until 1989. When he left, he had handpicked McLucas as his successor. Kidder must have felt it had reason to expect good relations with the SEC and to believe the Lynch report would be taken seriously.

THE INEVITABLE END

The losses at Kidder continued. Losses for August amounted to about $30 million, with losses for year-to-date reaching nearly $250 million after taxes, already the worst in Kidder's 129-year history. On December 15, with 1994 net losses estimated at nearly $1 billion, GE sold most of Kidder's remaining assets to PaineWebber. The sale occurred at the worst possible time because Wall Street was undergoing its worst slump in years. A total of 2250 Kidder employees lost their jobs and Kidder ceased to exist. At the end of 1994, GE announced that it expected to report record profits for that year.

Consultants have pointed out that there are ways for companies to avoid the risks and losses suffered by Kidder Peabody. Merrill Lynch, for example, puts limits on the size of trades and trading positions. Merrill traders don't have the opportunity to reap record profits, but they also don't have the chance to generate huge losses as Jett did.

Sources: William M. Carley, Michael Siconolfi, and Amal Kumaar Naj, "How Will Welch Deal with Kidder Scandal? Problems Keep Coming," *The Wall Street Journal*, May 3, 1994; Laurie P. Cohen, "Wall Street's Compliance Problem Spotlighted by Kidder's Case," *The Wall Street Journal*, April 19, 1994; Kurt Eichenwald, "Learning the Hard Way How to Monitor Traders," *The New York Times*, March 9, 1995; Douglas Frantz with Sylvia Nasar, "The Ghost in Kidder's Money-Making Machine," *The New York Times*, April 29, 1994;

Douglas Frantz, "Ousted Kidder Trader Seeks Release of Assets," *The New York Times*, May 6, 1994; Saul Hansell, "Kidder, Peabody Jolted by Phantom Bond Trades," *The Wall Street Journal*, April 19, 1994; Linda Himelstein, "They Said, He Said, at Kidder Peabody," *Business Week*, August 8, 1994; Laura Jereski and Michael Siconolfi, "GE's Kidder Investment Brings a Sorrowful Return Thus Far," *The Wall Street Journal*, July 12, 1994, "High Leverage at Kidder Could Lead to Headaches," *The Wall Street Journal*, June 7, 1994, and "Kidder Peabody Gets Infusion from GE, but Problems Mount," *The Wall Street Journal*, June 15, 1994; Steve Lohr, "Kidder Dismisses 2nd Trader, Saying He Concealed Loss," *The New York Times*, April 23, 1994; Sylvia Nasar, "Kidder Scandal Tied to Failure of Supervision," *The New York Times*, August 5, 1994, "Kidder Trader Wants Funds Freed," *The New York Times*, May 30, 1994, "Kidder's No. 2 Executive Resigns," *The New York Times*, July 23, 1994, and "Multiple Motives for Kidder's Self-Examination," *The New York Times*, August 8, 1994; Sylvia Nasar and Douglas Frantz, "A Dramatic Rise, and a Nasty Fall," *The New York Times*, April 22, 1994; Floyd Norris, "Fool's Profits: Just How Dumb Was Kidder," *The New York Times*, August 7, 1994, and "Kidder, Peabody, Where Trading Went Awry," *The New York Times*, April 19, 1994; Terence P. Pare, "Jack Welch's Nightmare on Wall Street," *Fortune*, September 5, 1994; Joe Queenan, "A Sure Tip-Off," *Barrons*, May 2, 1994; Michael Quint, "G.E. Ousts Kidder, Peabody Chief," *The New York Times*, June 23, 1994; Michael Siconolfi, "Fired Kidder Aide Tells U.S. He Acted on Orders, Firm Violated Capital Rules," *The Wall Street Journal*, July 26, 1994, "Jett Fires Back, Says Kidder Refuses Data," *The Wall Street Journal*, September 7, 1994, "Kidder Says Review Approves the Way It Values Mortgage-backed Bonds," *The Wall Street Journal*, May 13, 1994, "Kidder Trader in Bond Options Dismissed," *The Wall Street Journal*, July 12, 1994, "Lynch's Dual Role in Inquiry Prompts Question," *The Wall Street Journal*, August 5, 1995, "Report Faults Kidder for Laxness in Jett Case," *The Wall Street Journal*, August 5, 1995, "Saga of Kidder's Jett: Sudden Downfall of an Aggressive Wall Street

Trader," *The Wall Street Journal,* April 19, 1994, and "Kidder Discloses Phony Trades, Fires a Trader," *The Wall Street Journal,* April 18, 1994; Michael Siconolfi, Laura Jereski, and Steven Lipin, "GE's Mr. Welch Ousts Kidder's Chairman, Names Financial Aides," *The Wall Street Journal,* June 23, 1994; Gary Weiss, "What Lynch Left Out," *Business Week,* August 22, 1994.

Case Study Questions

1. Describe the problem or problems that eventually caused the collapse of Kidder Peabody. What management, organization, and technology factors contributed to or caused the problems?

2. What was Cerullo's responsibility, if any, for these problems, and particularly for the Jett affair? Answer the same questions for O'Donnell, Carpenter, and Welch.

3. Why do you think Jett was not caught earlier?

4. Do you think computer information systems could have prevented the problems and prevented the collapse of Kidder? Why or why not?

5. Assume you have been assigned the task of designing a new computerized accounting information system that would address the underlying problems. Define your goals for such a system, the kind of data it should capture, where and how that data should be captured, the types of reporting it should include, who would receive those reports, and what other computer systems should make use of the data.

International Case Studies

From Geelong & District Water Board to Barwon Water:
An Integrated IT Infrastructure
Joel B. Barolsky and Peter Weill
University of Melbourne (Australia)

Ginormous Life Insurance Company
Len Fertuck
University of Toronto (Canada)

Kone Elevators
Tapio Reponen
Turku School of Economics and
Business Administration (Finland)

Festo Pneumatic
Helmut Krcmar and Bettina Schwarzer
University of Hohenheim (Germany)

Corning Telecommunications Division
Andrew Boynton, University of North Carolina at Chapel Hill
and the International Institute for Management Development (Switzerland) and
Michael E. Shank, Renaissance Vision

From Geelong & District Water Board to Barwon Water: An Integrated IT Infrastructure[1]

Joel B. Barolsky and Peter Weill, University of Melbourne (Australia)

Joe Adamski, the Geelong and District Water Board's (GDWB) Executive Manager Information Systems, clicked his mouse on the phone messages menu option. Two messages had been left. The first was from an IT manager from a large Sydney-based insurance company confirming an appointment to "visit the GDWB and to assess what the insurance company could learn from the GDWB's IT experience." The second was from the general manager of another large water board asking whether Adamski and his team could assist, on a consultancy basis, in their IT strategy formulation and implementation.

The site visit from the insurance company was the 35th such request the Board had received since the completion of the first stage of their IT infrastructure investment strategy in January 1992. These requests were a pleasant diversion but the major focus of the GDWB's IT staff was to nurture and satisfy the increasing demands from the operational areas for building applications utilizing the newly installed IT infrastructure. The Water Board also faced the problem of balancing further in-house developments with external requests for consulting and demands from the GDWB's IT staff for new challenges and additional rewards.

ORGANIZATION BACKGROUND

The GDWB was constituted as a public utility of the Australian State of Victoria in July 1984 following an amalgamation of the Geelong Waterworks and Sewerage Trust and a number of other smaller regional water boards. The Board has the responsibility for the collection and distribution of water and the treatment and disposal of wastewater within a 1,600 square mile region in the southwest part of the State. In 1991, the permanent population serviced by the Board exceeded 200,000 people, this number growing significantly in the holiday periods with an influx of tourists.

The GDWB financed all its capital expenditure and operational expenditure through revenue received from its customers and through additional loan borrowings. Any profits generated were reinvested in the organization or used to pay off long-term debt. For the financial year 1990/91 the Board invested over $35.3 million in capital works and spent over $25 million in operating expenditure. Operating profit for the year 1990–91 exceeded $62.4 million on total assets of $292.5 million.

In 1992, the GDWB was headed by a Governing Board with a State Government-appointed chairperson and eight members, elected by the residents of

the community, who each sat for a three-year term. Managerial and administrative responsibilities were delegated to the GDWB's Executive Group which consists of the CEO and Executive Managers from each of the five operating divisions, namely Information Systems, Finance, Corporate Services, Engineering Development and Engineering Operations. From 1981 to 1992, the number of GDWB employees across all divisions rose from 304 to 454.

The GDWB's head office, situated in the regional capital city of Geelong, housed most of the Board's customer service, administrative, engineering, IT and other managerial staff. Complementing these activities, the GDWB operated five regional offices and a specialized 24-hour emergency contact service.

Commenting on the Board's competitive environment at the time, the GDWB's CEO, Geoff Vines, stated, "Although the organization operated in a monopolistic situation there still were considerable pressures on us to perform efficiently. Firstly, and most importantly, our objective was to be self funding—our customers wouldn't tolerate indiscriminate rate increases as a result of our inefficiencies and we could not go cap in hand to the State Government. Secondly, the amalgamation trend of water boards was continuing and the stronger the Board was the less likely it would be a target of a takeover. And thirdly, we did in a sense compare ourselves with private sector organizations and in some ways with other water boards. We had limited resources and we have to make the most of them."

KEY PROBLEM AREAS

Relating the situation up until the mid-1980's, Vines said that the Board faced a major problem in collectively identifying its largest assets—the underground pipes, drains, pumps, sewers and other facilities. He explained that most of these facilities were installed at least two or three meters below the surface and therefore it was almost impossible to gain immediate physical access to them. The exact specifications of each particular asset could only be ascertained through a thorough analysis of the original installation documentation and other geophysical surveys and maps of the area.

The limitations on identifying these underground facilities impacted operational performance in a number of key areas:

- most of the maintenance work conducted by the Board was based on reactive responses to leaks and other faults in the systems. It was difficult to introduce a coordinated preventative maintenance program because it was not possible to accurately predict when a particular pipe or piece of equipment was nearing the end of its expected life span.

- only a limited number of hard copies of this facility information could be kept. This significantly reduced the productivity of the engineering and operations staff, especially in remote areas where they had to request this information from the central record-keeping systems. Backlogs and inaccuracies in filing also impacted

efforts to repair, upgrade or install new piping, pumps and other equipment. On numerous occasions changes would be made to one set of plans without the same changes being recorded on the other copies of the same plans. Engineers designing improvements to existing facilities were often confronted with the problem of not being sure whether they were using the most up-to-date information of the facilities currently installed in the area concerned.

- the Board could not place realistic replacement values and depreciation charges on these underground assets.

With over 100,000 rateable properties in its area of responsibility, the GDWB maintained a centralized paper filing system containing more than a billion pages of related property information. The documents, most of which were of different sizes, quality, and age, were divided into 95,000 different files and sorted chronologically within each file. Access to the documents was made difficult as larger documents were cumbersome to copy and older documents were beginning to disintegrate. Having just one physical storage area significantly increased the potential exposure to fire and other risks and limited the wider distribution and sharing of the information. In the early 1980s, it was commonplace for a customer request for a statement of encumbrances placed at one of the GDWB's regional offices to take in excess of four weeks. The delays usually centered on finding the appropriate documents at the Property Services' central files, making the necessary copies, and transferring the documents back to the regional offices.

THE INFORMATION SYSTEMS DIVISION

In 1985, PA Consulting was commissioned to conduct a comprehensive

review of the Board's strategy, management, operations structures and systems. One of the recommendations made by the consultants was that the Board should institute a more systematic approach to strategic planning. A major outcome of the planning process that followed was to create a new division for computing services and to recruit a new manager for this new area who reported directly to the CEO. The EDP Division was created with the objectives of "satisfying the Board's Information System needs through the provision of integrated and secure corporate computer systems and communication network." Vines said that the Board needed a stand-alone information services group that could be used as a resource center for all users and that could add value to the work conducted by each functional group within the Board.

In April 1987, Joe Adamski was employed to fill the new position of EDP Manager (later changed to Executive Manager Information Systems). At the time of his arrival, only a small part of the GDWB's work systems were computerized, the main components of which included:

- a "low-end" IBM System 38, primarily to run financial and other accounting software and some word processing applications. The System ran an in-house developed rate collection system which kept basic information on ratepayers including property details and consumption records;

- 19 "dumb" terminals—none of the Board's regional offices had terminal access to the central computer systems;

- a terminal link to the local university's DEC 20 computer to support the technical and laboratory services; and

- four stand-alone PCs, running some individual word processing packages as well as spreadsheet (Lotus 1–2–3), basic CAD and database applications.

Computer maintenance, support and development was allocated to the Finance Division and delegated to an EDP supervisor (and three staff) who reported to the Finance Manager. Adamski noted, "The computer set-up when I joined was pretty outdated and inefficient. For example, the secretarial staff at Head Office were using the System 38's word processing facility and had to collect their dot matrix printouts from the computer room situated on the ground floor of the five-story building. In the technical area, some water supply network analysis data was available through the use of the DEC 20 system; however, hard copy output had to be collected from the University which was over five kilometers away. Most of the design engineers were using old drafting tables with rulers, erasers and pencils as their only drafting tools."

Recognizing that some users required immediate solutions to problems they were facing, the Board purchased additional terminals, peripherals and stand-alone microcomputers for the various areas thought to be in greatest need. Adamski said that these additional purchases further compounded some of the Board's computer-related problems. "We had a situation where we had at least four different CAD packages in use in different departments and we couldn't transfer data between them. There was a duplication of peripheral equipment with no sharing of printers, plotters and other output devices. In addition, various managers began to complain that system expertise was too localized and that there was little compatibility between the various applications."

PLANNING THE NEW ROLE FOR IT

In July 1988, Adamski initiated a long-term computing strategy planning process with the establishment of a special planning project team with both IT and user representatives. The team embarked on a major program of interviews and discussion with all user areas within the Board. They investigated other similar public utilities across Australia to assess their IT strategies and infrastructures and made contact with various computer hardware and software vendors to determine the latest available technologies and indicative costs.

The Project Team developed a comprehensive corporate computing strategy that would provide, as Adamski put it, the "quantum leap forward in the Board's IT portfolio." Adamski said that central to the computing strategy that was devised was that there should be as much integration and flexibility as possible in all the Board's technical and administrative systems. "Linked to this strategy was the notion that we should strive for an 'open systems' approach with all our applications. This meant that each system had to have publicly specifiable interfaces or 'hooks' so that each system could talk to each other. From the users' perspective an open systems approach meant that all the different applications looked pretty much the same and it was simple and easy to cross over from one to the other. It also meant that if we weren't happy with one particular product within the portfolio or we wanted to add a new one we could do it without too much disruption to the whole system."

He continued, "A key decision was made that we should build on our existing IT investments. With this in mind we had to make sure that the new systems were able to use the data and communicate with the System 38. We wanted only one hardware platform using only one operating system and only one relational data base management system (RDBMS). We also wanted only one homogenous network that was able to cater to a number of protocols and interfaces such as the network system for the microcomputers, workstations and the Internet connection. There also had to be a high degree of compatibility and interaction with all the data files and applications that were proposed. In view of this, we chose a UNIX platform with a client/server architecture."

In addition to specifying the software components of the system, the Project Team outlined the hardware that was necessary to run the new systems and the additional staff that needed to be hired. To achieve the stated computing strategies and benefits, the Team also recommended that implementation take place over three key stages, with a formal progress review instituted at the end of each stage.

APPROVAL

In February 1989, the corporate computing strategy planning process was completed and Adamski presented the key recommendations to the Governing Board. In his presentation, Adamski stated that the infrastructure cost of implementing the strategy was estimated to be about $5 million for the entire project (excluding data capture costs) and that the project would take up to the end of 1995 for full commissioning.

Vines stated, "From my perspective, the proposed IT strategy took into account the critical functions in the organization that needed to be supported, such as customer services, asset management and asset creation. These were fundamental components of the Board's corporate objectives and the computer strategy provided a means to realize these objectives and provide both short- and long-term benefits. There were some immediate short-term benefits, such as securing property services data that had no backup, and productivity gains in design and electronic mail. From a long-term perspective, I believe you can never really do an accurate rate-of-return calculation and base your decision solely on that. If you did you probably would never make such a large capital investment in IT. We did try to cost-justify all the new systems as best we could but we stressed that implementing IT strategy should be seen as providing long-term benefits for the entire organization that were not immediately measurable and would come to fruition many years later. Until all the information was captured and loaded on the IT facilities from the manual systems, the full benefits could not be realized."

Following an extensive and rigorous tendering process, it was decided that the Board should follow a multi-vendor solution as no one vendor could provide a total solution. Sun Microsystems was selected as the major hardware vendor and was asked to act as "prime contractors" in implementation. As prime contractors Sun was paid one project fee and then negotiated separate contracts with all other suppliers.

IMPLEMENTATION

In April 1990, the implementation of the IT strategy commenced with the delivery of the Sun file servers and workstations and installation of a homogenous network throughout the Board. Adamski said that the implementation stage went surprisingly smoothly. "We didn't fire anybody as a direct result of the new systems, but jobs were changed. There was some resistance to the new technology—most of it was born out of unfamiliarity and fear of not having the appropriate skills. Some people were very committed in doing things 'their way.' When some of these people started to

perceive tangible productivity benefits, their perspectives started to change. We tried to counsel people as best we could and encourage them to experiment with the new systems. Most people eventually converted but there were still some objectors."

Adamski added that while they were implementing the new systems it was important for the IS Division not to lose sight of its key objectives and role within the organization. "We had to make sure that we didn't get carried away with the new whiz-bang technology and reduce our support and maintenance of the older, more conventional systems. For example, the Board went onto a new tariff system and we had to make significant changes to our rating system to accommodate this. Having an application generator in place significantly improved the systems upgrade time."

In May 1992, the Board's computer facilities included 4 Sun file servers, 80 Sun workstations, 100 microcomputers,

40 terminals, and the IBM System 38 Model 700. By this time, the IS Division had implemented the following components of the systems (see Figure 1 for a schematic of the systems):

1. A **Document Imaging Processing System (DIPS)** used for scanning, storing and managing all documents on each property within the GDWB region which were being kept in the 95,000 separate paper files. This system was also used for the storage, backup and retrieval of 25,000 engineering plans and drawings. DIPS gave designated Head Office departments and regional offices real-time access to all property documentation and allowed them to print out scanned images when required. The system had a sophisticated indexing system that facilitated easy retrieval of stored images by users and access by other programs. Figure 2 presents a copy of a scanned property plan from DIPS.

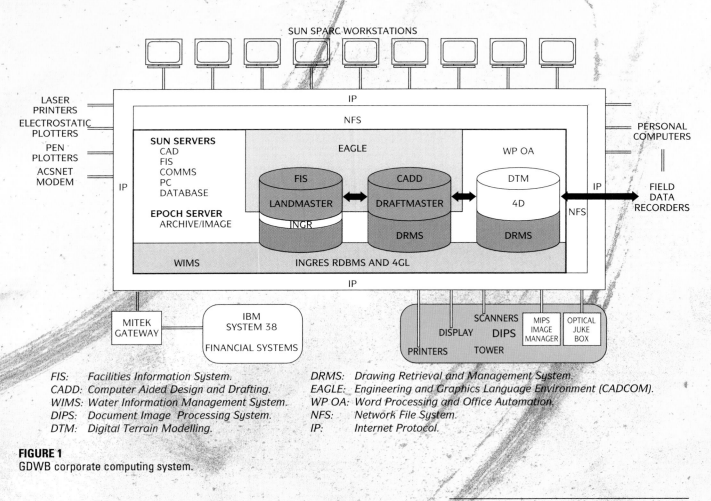

FIS: Facilities Information System.
CADD: Computer Aided Design and Drafting.
WIMS: Water Information Management System.
DIPS: Document Image Processing System.
DTM: Digital Terrain Modelling.

DRMS: Drawing Retrieval and Management System.
EAGLE: Engineering and Graphics Language Environment (CADCOM).
WP OA: Word Processing and Office Automation.
NFS: Network File System.
IP: Internet Protocol.

FIGURE 1
GDWB corporate computing system.

FIGURE 2
Example of a building plan kept for each rateable property.

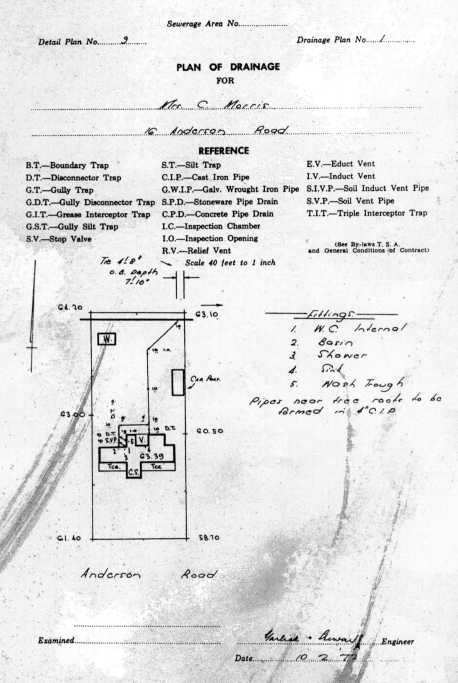

TORQUAY SEWERAGE AUTHORITY

Sewerage Area No.......................

Detail Plan No.........*9*......

Drainage Plan No....*1*........

PLAN OF DRAINAGE
FOR

........................*Mrs. C. Morris*........................

........................*16 Anderson Road*........................

REFERENCE

B.T.—Boundary Trap	S.T.—Silt Trap	E.V.—Educt Vent
D.T.—Disconnector Trap	C.I.P.—Cast Iron Pipe	I.V.—Induct Vent
G.T.—Gully Trap	G.W.I.P.—Galv. Wrought Iron Pipe	S.I.V.P.—Soil Induct Vent Pipe
G.D.T.—Gully Disconnector Trap	S.P.D.—Stoneware Pipe Drain	S.V.P.—Soil Vent Pipe
G.I.T.—Grease Interceptor Trap	C.P.D.—Concrete Pipe Drain	T.I.T.—Triple Interceptor Trap
G.S.T.—Gully Silt Trap	I.C.—Inspection Chamber	
S.V.—Stop Valve	I.O.—Inspection Opening	
	R.V.—Relief Vent	(See By-laws T. S. A. and General Conditions of Contract)

Scale 40 feet to 1 inch

Examined..

........................*Garlick & Stewart*........................ Engineer

Date......*10. 2. '77*......

2. A digital mapping **Facilities Information System (FIS)** that provided for the storage, management and on-going maintenance of all graphic (map related) and nongraphic information relating to water and wastewater services, property information, property boundaries, and easements throughout the Board's region. The FIS system provided a computerized "seamless" geographic map covering the entire GDWB region. The system encompassed the storing of all maps in digital form and attaching map coordinates to each digital point. Every point on a digital map was linked to a unique X and Y coordinate, based on the standard Australian Mapping Grid system, and had a specific address linked to it. Once each point on a map was precisely addressed and identified, specific attributes were attached to it. These attributes were then used as methods of recording information or used as indexes for access to/by other programs, for example, sewer pipe details, property details, water consumption, vertical heights above sea level, etc. The selected map area

FIGURE 3
Illustration of the type of
information available on
the Facilities Information
System.

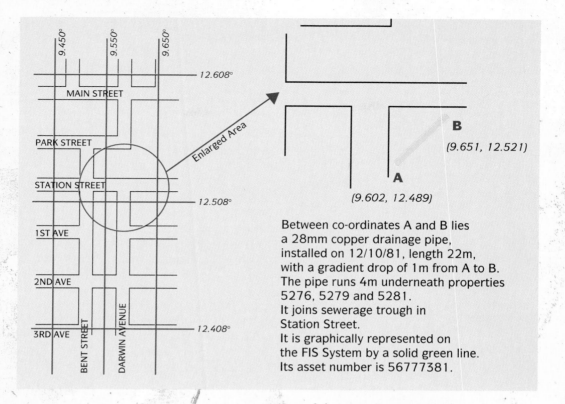

Between co-ordinates A and B lies
a 28mm copper drainage pipe,
installed on 12/10/81, length 22m,
with a gradient drop of 1m from A to B.
The pipe runs 4m underneath properties
5276, 5279 and 5281.
It joins sewerage trough in
Station Street.
It is graphically represented on
the FIS System by a solid green line.
Its asset number is 56777381.

with all the related attributes and information was then displayed graphically in full color on a high resolution workstation monitor (see Figure 3).

The FIS allowed cross referencing to financial, rating and consumption data (through indexing) held on the System 38. It also enabled each underground facility to be numbered, catalogued and identified as an asset with their associated data being integrated into other asset management systems. The FIS enabled data stored on a particular map to be "layered," with water pipes at one layer, sewer pipes at another, property boundaries at a third, future plans at another, and so on. This gave users the ability to recall maps in layers and to select the level and amount of detail they required. The system was centered around a mouse-driven graphic interface where the user zoomed in and out and/or panned around particular areas—at the broadest level, showing the whole of southern Victoria, and at the most detailed, the individual plumbing and drainage plan of one particular property (through cross-referencing to the DIPS system).

3. A **Computer Aided Design and Drafting (CADD)** system that provided an integrated programmable 3-D environment for a range of civil, mechanical, electrical, surveying and general engineering design and drafting applications. It offered the following features:

  ■ Display manipulation, including multiple angle views, zooms and pans;

  ■ Geometric analysis, including automatic calculation of areas, perimeters, moments of inertia and centroids; and

  ■ Various customization features such as user-defined menus and prompts and a user-friendly macro language.

4. **Word Processing and Office Automation (WP/OA)** systems providing users the ability to prepare quality documentation integrating graphics, spreadsheets, mail merge and data bases, as well as other utilities such as electronic mail and phone message handling.

5. **A Relational Database Management System and a 4th Generation Language** as a base foundation for the development of new applications. Some of the RDBMS applications included:

  ■ A Drawing and Retrieval Management System (DRMS) to control the development, release and revision of all CADD projects and files; and

  ■ A Water Information Management System (WIMS) used for the storage and management of hydrographic engineering and laboratory data, both current and historical.

OUTCOMES

Vines said that one of the most important strategic outcomes of the changes introduced had been the way in which decision-making at all levels with the organization had been enhanced. "This improvement is largely due to the fact that people have now got ready access to information they have never had before. This information is especially useful in enhancing our ability to forward plan. The flow and reporting of financial information has also speeded up and we now complete our final accounts up to two months earlier than we used to. In the areas that have come on-line there has been a definite improvement in productivity and in customer service. The CADD system, for example, is greatly enhancing our ability to design and plan new facilities. The turnaround time, the accuracy of the plans and the creativity of the designers has been improved dramatically. In many departments there has been a change in work practices—some of the mundane activities are handled by the computer, allowing more productive work to be carried out, like spending more time with customers. Our asset management and control also started to improve. There was greater integrity in the information kept, and having just one central shared record meant that updating with new data or changes to existing data was far more efficient."

Adamski added that the initial reaction by Board staff to the whole corporate computing strategy "ranged from scepticism to outright hostility." He continued, "By the end of 1991, I would say that there had been a general reversal in attitude. Managers started to queue outside my office asking if we could develop specific business applications for them. They had begun to appreciate what the technology could do and most often they suddenly perceived a whole range of opportunities and different ways in which they could operate. One manager asked me, for example, if we could use document imaging technology to eliminate the need for any physical paper flows within his office. Technically this was possible but it was not really cost justifiable and the corporate culture would not really have supported it. Putting together the IS Division budget is now a difficult balancing act with a whole range of options and demands from users. I now ask the users to justify the benefits to be derived from new application proposals and I help out with the cost side. Cost/benefit justification usually drives the decisions as well as the "fit" with the existing IT and other corporate objectives. What also must be considered is that these objectives are not written in stone. They are flexible and can and should adjust to changes in both the internal and external environment."

A number of GDWB staff indicated that the new systems had enhanced their ability to fulfill their work responsibilities:

- A customer service officer at one of the Board's regional offices stated that the DIPS had enabled her to respond to customer requests for encumbrance statements within a matter of minutes instead of weeks. She added that a number of customers had sent letters to their office complimenting them on the improvements in the service they received. She said that new DIPS system had "flow on" benefits that weren't fully recognized. She cited the case where local architects were able to charge their clients less because they had more ready access to information from the GDWB.

- A maintenance manager declared that the FIS system had enabled his department to predict when pipes and drains should be replaced before they actually ruptured or broke down, by examining their installation dates and the types of materials used. He said this process over time started to shift the emphasis of his department's maintenance work from being reactive to being more preventative. He added that the system also enabled him to easily identify and contact the residents that would be affected by the work that the Board was going to do in a particular area. He said that the FIS enabled him to plot out with his mouse a particular area of a map on his screen. It would then "pick up" all the relevant properties in the area and identify the names and addresses of the current ratepayers residing in those properties.

- A secretary to a senior head office manager said that despite being a little daunted at first by the new wordprocessing system, she felt the system had helped her consid-erably. She said that besides the obvious benefits in being able to prepare and edit documents on a WYSIWYG screen, she also had the ability of viewing as well as integrating scanned property plans, correspondence, and other documents from the DIPS System.

Adamski said that one of the flow-on benefits from the FIS system in particular was that the Board had the potential of selling the information stored on the system to authorities such as municipal councils and other public utilities such as Telecom, the State Electricity Commission and the Gas and Fuel Corporation. He added that they had also considered marketing the information to private organizations such as building managers, architects and property developers, and that the return from these sales could significantly reduce the overall costs in developing the FIS system.

THE FUTURE

Commenting on the future prospects for the Board's IS Division, Adamski said, "There are some very complex applications that we are developing but we now have the skills, the tools, and the infrastructure to develop them cost-effectively and to ensure that they deliver results. I think one of the main reasons why we are in this fortuitous position is that we chose a UNIX platform with client/server processing and a strong networking backbone. It gives us the flexibility and integration that we set out to achieve and we will need in the future to realize both our long- and short-term objectives. It's a lot easier now to cost-justify requests for new applications. The challenges ahead lie in three areas. Firstly, it's going to be difficult to consistently satisfy all our users' needs in that their expectations will be increasing all the time and they will become more demanding. We have to recognize these demands and at the same time keep investing in and maintaining our infrastructure. Secondly, we still have some way to go in developing a total corporate management information system. There are still some "islands of data" floating around and the challenge is to get it all integrated. And thirdly, as the most senior IT manager at the Board I have to make sure that we retain our key IT staff and we compensate them adequately, both monetarily and in providing them stimulating and demanding work."

The Geelong and District Water Board changed its name to Barwon Water in February 1994. The name change reflected the change in the organisation's governance structure with the appointment by the State Government of a professional, "skills-based" Governing Board to replace the community-elected members. This initiative was part of a broader Government strategy to commercialise state-owned utilities and to strive for greater efficiencies and productivity across the whole public service.

Four months after the name change, Geoff Vines retired and was replaced by Dennis Brockenshire as Barwon Water's Chief Executive. Brockenshire, formerly a senior manager with the State Electricity Commission, had considerable business and engineering experience relating to large-scale supply systems serving a large customer base. Commenting on Barwon Water's Information Technology (IT) infrastructure, Brockenshire stated, *"Barwon Water has made and continues to make a significant investment in IT. The organisation has spent something in the region of $7 to $10 million in building its IT infrastructure and has recurrent costs of 3% of total expenditure. I want to make sure we get an appropriate return for this investment. It is critical that IT delivers real business benefits. Since I've come into this role, I have insisted that my line managers justify any new IT investment on the grounds of the business value it will create."*

From the period 1992 to 1995, Barwon Water's Information Systems (IS) department had focused most of its efforts in capturing all the relevant mapping, customer and facilities data for its key systems. Significant resources were allocated to utilize the existing IT infrastructure to improve customer service and to streamline workflows. Improvements in security were also a major priority given the confidential and private nature of information stored on the various databases and the listing of Barwon Water's home page on the World Wide Web. In terms of hardware and software, the IBM System 38 was replaced by a Sun SPARCstation server running the Prophecy accounting package in a UNIX operating environment. The IS department had commenced work on an executive information system to assist with cost and performance measurement, particularly at the business unit level. This system would provide the core information to support a major benchmarking exercise in which Barwon Water compared its performance on key processes to other organisations, both within and external to the water industry.

Business processes were mapped and examined where steps could be eliminated or substituted by new IT applications. An interesting example of this was the introduction of a paperless encumbrance certificating system. In this system a solicitor handling a property matter could interact with Barwon Water via the fax machine without the need to actually visit an office. All documents sent to and from Barwon Water and those transferred within the organisation were accomplished entirely on the system with no need to print a hardcopy. Processing times for these applications were reduced from an average of 10 days to a few hours.

A number of other efficiency gains were realised with the utilization of the IT infrastructure. The productivity of the engineering design staff increased by 20 to 50% for most drawings and by 90% for re-drawings. The systems distributed computing design also reduced design cycles by enabling staff to share files and work on a common file to avoid duplicated effort. Overall staff numbers with Barwon Water had dropped to 400 by July 1995. Adamski said that while the total reduction in staff numbers could not be directly attributed to the new systems, there were several areas where staff had been made redundant or redeployed. He said that in many cases the systems "freed-up" front-line service personnel to spend more time listening and being responsive to customer concerns.

Barwon Water continued to receive acclaim for its innovative IT systems. In 1994 it was awarded the Geelong Business Excellence Award in the Innovation Systems/Development of Technology category. It also received a nomination for the award for innovation by the Washington-based Smithsonian Institute.

A major organisational restructure in early 1995 saw Joe Adamski take over the responsibility for strategic planning as well as information systems. Adamski said that this restructure ensured that IT developments would be closely aligned with broader business objectives and strategies. He added that having the senior IT executive responsible for business planning symbolised how essential IT had become to the organisation's operations and its management and control systems. As part of the restructure new business units were formed with the managers of these units made accountable for both revenue and cost items.

Commenting on future challenges, Adamski outlined his vision for Barwon Water as the computing centre for the Greater Geelong region. *"Geelong and district covers 5,000 square kilometers. Within this region, there has recently been an amalgamation of councils into two supercouncils—the City of Greater Geelong and the Surf Coast Council. These two organisations serve the same customers as ourselves. We have articulated what we see as benefits of using common databases, mapping and other information to serve these customers. Suggested benefits include a service shopfront where customers could pay rates, water tariffs and apply for property approvals at the same place. These systems we now have in place at Barwon Water would be a good starting point in building this regional concept. Data is our most valuable asset and there is no point in duplicating it."*

[1]A summarized version of a case study written by Joel B. Barolsky and Peter Weill of the Graduate School of Management, University of Melbourne, Australia. It was written as the basis of discussion rather than to illustrate either effective or ineffective handling of a managerial situation. Copyright © by Joel B. Barolsky and Peter Weill. Funding for this research was provided by IBM Consulting (USA).

Case Study Questions

1. Describe the Geelong and District Water Board and the environment in which they operate. What problems did GDWB have before 1988? What were the management, organization, and technology factors that contributed to those problems?

2. Describe the role of information systems at GDWB and the GDWB's information system portfolio before July 1988.

3. Describe and critique the process of upgrading GDWB's information systems portfolio.

4. How did the water board justify its investments in new information system technology? What were the benefits? How were they justified?

Ginormous Life Insurance Company

Len Fertuck, University of Toronto (Canada)

Ginormous Life is an insurance company with a long tradition. The company has four divisions. Each operates its own computers. The IS group provides analysis, design and programming services to all the divisions. The divisions are actuarial, marketing, operations, and investment, all located at the corporate headquarters building. Marketing also has field offices in twenty cities across the country.

The Actuarial Division is responsible for the design and pricing of new kinds of policies. They use purchased industry data and weekly summaries of data obtained from the Operations Division. They have their own DEC minicomputer, running the UNIX operating system, to store data files. They do most of their analysis on microcomputers and Sun workstations, either on spreadsheets or with a specialized interactive language called APL.

The Marketing Division is responsible for selling policies to new customers and for follow-up of existing customers in case they need changes to their current insurance. All sales orders are sent to the Operations Division for data entry and billing. They use purchased external data for market research and weekly copies of data from operations for follow-ups. They have their own DEC VAX minicomputer with dumb terminals for clerks to enter sales data. There are also many microcomputers used to analyze market data using statistical packages like SAS.

The Operations Division is responsible for processing all mission-critical financial transactions, including pay-roll. They record all new policies, send regular bills to customers, evaluate and pay all claims, and cancel lapsed policies. They have all their data and programs on a large IBM ES/9000 mainframe. The programs are often large and complex because they must service not only the fifteen products currently being sold, but also the 75 old kinds of policies that are no longer being sold, but still have existing policy holders. Clerks use dumb terminals to enter and update data. Application programs are almost always written in COBOL. Some recent applications have used a SQL relational database to store data, but most use COBOL flat files. The average age of the transaction processing programs is about ten years.

The Investment Division is responsible for investing premiums until they are needed to pay claims. Their data consists primarily of internal portfolio data and research data obtained by direct links to financial data services. They have a DEC minicomputer to store their data. The internal data are received by a weekly download of cash flows from the Operations Division. External data are obtained as needed. They use microcomputers to analyze data obtained from the mini or from commercial data services.

A controlling interest in Ginormous Life has recently been purchased by Financial Behemoth Corp. The management of Financial Behemoth has decided that the firm's efficiency and profitability must be improved. Their first move has been to put Dan D. Mann, a hotshot information systems specialist from Financial Behemoth, in charge of the Information Systems Division. He has been given the objective of modernizing and streamlining the computer facilities without any increase in budget.

In the first week on the job, Dan discovered that none of the staff of 200 information systems specialists know anything about CASE tools, End-User Computing or LANs. All microcomputer applications have been purchased, so no one has experience in implementing microcomputer systems. There is no evidence of any formal Decision Support Systems or Executive Information Systems in the organization. There have been a few tentative experiments with DB2, a relational database product, purchased from IBM, their mainframe vendor. Most managers say that "they do not need all those fancy Executive Information Systems." They would be happy if Information Systems would just provide basic reports on the financial performance of each product line and customer group.

There have been some problems with these systems. Maintenance is difficult and costly because almost every change to the data structure of applications in operations requires corresponding changes to applications in the other divisions. There has been a growing demand in other divisions for faster access to operations data. For instance, the Investment Division claims that they could make more profitable investments if they had continuous access to the cash position in operations. Marketing complains that they get calls from clients about claims and cannot answer them because they do not have current access to the status of the claim. Management wants current access to a wide variety of data in summary form so they can get a better understanding of the business. The IS group says that it would be difficult to provide access to data in operations because of security considerations. It is difficult to ensure that users do not make unauthorized changes to the COBOL files.

The IS group complains that they cannot deliver all the applications the users want because they are short-staffed. They spend 90 percent of their time maintaining the existing systems, most of which are in the COBOL language. The programmers are mostly old and experienced and employee turnover is unusually low, so there is not likely to be much room for improvement by further training in programming. Morale is generally good despite the perception of overwork. Employees often remark that the company is a very pleasant and benevolent place to work. At least they did until rumors of deregulation and foreign competition started to sweep the industry.

Dan began to look for ways to solve the many problems of the Information Systems Division. He solicited proposals from various vendors and consultants in the computer industry. After a preliminary review of the proposals, Dan was left with three broad options suggested by IBM, Oracle Corp., and Systemotion, a local consulting firm. The proposals are briefly described below.

IBM proposed an integrated solution using IBM hardware and software. The main elements of their proposal are:

- **Data and applications will remain on a mainframe.** The IBM ES/9000 series of hardware running their proprietary operating system will provide mainframe services. Mainframe hardware capacity will have to be approximately doubled. AS/400 minicomputers running under the OS/400 operating system will replace DEC minicomputers. RS/6000 workstations running AIX, a flavor of the UNIX operating sys-

tem, can be used for actuarial computations. All hardware will be interconnected with IBM's proprietary SNA network architecture. Microcomputers will run under the OS/2 operating system and the IBM LAN Server to support both Microsoft Windows applications and locally designed applications that communicate with mainframe databases.

- **A DB2 relational database will store all data on line.** Users will be able to access any data they need through their terminals or through microcomputers that communicate with the mainframe.

- **Legacy systems will be converted using re-engineering tools,** like Design Recovery and Maintenance Workbench from Intersolve, Inc. These will have the advantage that they will continue to use the COBOL code that the existing programmers are familiar with. New work will be done using CASE tools with code generators that produce COBOL code.

- **Proven technology.** The IBM systems are widely used by many customers and vendors. Many mission-critical application programs are available on the market that address a wide variety of business needs.

Oracle Corp. proposed that all systems be converted to use their Oracle database product and its associated screen and report generators. They said that such a conversion would have the following advantages:

- **Over 75 hardware platforms are supported.** This means that the company is no longer bound to stay with a single vendor. Oracle databases and application programs can be easily moved from one manufacturer's machine to another manufacturer's machine by a relatively simple export and import operation as long as applications are created with Oracle tools. Thus the most economical hardware platform can be used

for the application. Oracle will also access data stored in an IBM DB2 database.

- **Integrated CASE tools and application generators.** Oracle has its own CASE tool and its own form and report generators. Databases designed with the Oracle CASE tool can be automatically created in an Oracle database using CASE*Generator. SQL*Forms, one of their application generation tools, can design and generate screens for a wide variety of terminals. The same design can be implemented on dumb terminals, a Macintosh, X-Windows in UNIX, or Systems Application Architecture (SAA) in an IBM environment. Applications are created using graphic tools that eliminate the need for a language like COBOL. In fact, the programmer cannot see the underlying language that is being used for implementation. The designer works entirely with visual prototyping specifications. SQL*ReportWriter can generate reports in the same way.

- **Vertically integrated applications.** Oracle sells a number of common applications, like accounting programs, that can be used as building blocks in developing a complete system. These applications could eliminate the need to redevelop some applications.

- **Distributed network support.** A wide variety of common network protocols like SNA, DecNet, Novell, and TCP/IP are supported. Different parts of the database can be distributed to different machines on the network and accessed or updated by any application. Access can be controlled at the file, record, or field level for each user on the system. All data is stored on line for instant access. The data can be stored on one machine and the applications can be run on a different machine, including a microcomputer or workstation, to provide a client/server environment. The ability to distribute a database allows a large database on an expensive mainframe to be distributed to a number of cheaper minicomputers.

Systemotion proposed a state-of-the-art system using the Sybase Object Oriented Relational Data Base Management System (OORDBMS) with applications implemented in a Microsoft Windows environment. This proposal offers the following advantages:

- *A modern object-oriented database.* Sybase is a relatively new entrant in the database field so it is able to exploit the benefits of an object-oriented approach without having to worry about a large number of legacy applications already coded in an older non-object-oriented version. This means that it is possible to include complex validation rules in the database rather than having to code them in the application code. This reduces application testing and speeds development as well as improving data integrity.

- *Client/server systems.* Since Sybase is object-oriented, it is a natural product for a client/server environment. It becomes particularly easy to install the database on a server (commonly one or more Hewlett-Packard or DEC minicomputers) and place the applications and entry screens on microcomputers or workstations like those from Sun Microsystems. Object-oriented applications can be easily built using graphic languages like Power Builder or Visual Basic. The database can be easily extended to store graphics like photos or scanned documents. This could allow business re-engineering to reduce the paper burden that is common in insurance firms. The client applications would run on a LAN with

Microsoft SQL Server, a networked relational DBMS server.

- *Open UNIX environment.* Many programs have been written for the UNIX operating system. UNIX can be run on many different hardware platforms and network communication systems. This openness will make it possible to integrate applications on a number of platforms while obtaining the cost benefits of downsizing to smaller platforms.

- *Easy integration with purchased Windows applications.* The object-oriented approach meshes well with the Windows environment that has a feature called Object Linking and Embedding (OLE), which permits direct reference from one Windows software product to another. Thus it is quite easy to write a program that obtains data from a central database and brings it into a spreadsheet, like Excel, where it can be analyzed, manipulated, or graphed. The graph, in turn, can be embedded in a word processor report. If new data are downloaded into the spreadsheet, the graph will automatically be updated whenever the report is opened in the word processor. This makes it easy to satisfy management needs for information within the word-processing or spreadsheet environment they are familiar with. It also makes it relatively easy to create customized management and executive information systems. In addition, many functions can be performed directly by purchased Windows programs to eliminate the need to design, build, and maintain many applications.

Dan is not sure which approach to take for the future of Ginormous Life. He appreciates that whichever route he follows, the technology will have an enormous impact on the kinds of applications

his staff will be able to produce in the future and the way in which they will produce them. He is concerned about industry trends toward downsizing and distribution of systems. While this trend may eventually prove to be more efficient, his staff does not have much experience with the new technologies that would be required. He is uncertain about whether there will be a sufficient payoff to justify the organizational turmoil that will result from a major change in direction.

Dan must prepare a strategy for the renewal of the Information Systems Division over the next three years. As his assistant, he has asked you to address the following questions:

Case Study Questions

1. Prepare a list of factors or issues that must be considered in developing a strategy and selecting a technology platform for Ginormous.

2. Analyze how each of the three proposals performs on each factor or issue. If you find issues that a proposal fails to address, advise Dan as to the significance of the omission and how you think the proposal might be modified to address that issue.

3. Advise Dan on special criteria, if any, he might need to apply when evaluating a proposal for a company-wide information strategy coming from a technology vendor. Explain your reasoning.

4. Assuming Dan were to make his decision without seeking further information from the proposers, recommend to him which proposal he should accept and your reason for selecting that proposal.

5. Based upon your advice in the previous question, state the order in which each component of the new technology should be introduced and the reason for selecting the order.

Kone Elevators

Tapio Reponen, Turku School of Economics and Business
Administration (Finland)

Elevators are products that are made according to customer specification. Each building is different, and the products have to fit the building's structure and framework. However, the elevator components can often be selected from a range of standard components either in predefined sets (pre-engineered, standard elevators) or in custom-made combinations (nonstandard elevators). The following description illustrates how information systems can support the process of elevator sales, order, and delivery at Kone Elevators, an international elevator manufacturer with headquarters in Helsinki, Finland.

"*Kone Lifts, good morning. Larry Liftagain speaking. How can I help you?*"

"*Good morning. This is Mr. Beaver from Bayswater Builders. I would like to have a quotation for a lift for our new project, please.*"

The pre-engineered elevator sale is usually handled by the salesman himself, using tools, materials, and procedures provided by sales support, engineering, and manufacturing. If the salesman needs additional information or if the equipment is outside the pre-engineered range, he contacts the Engineering department for further calculations and specifications.

Larry's sales tool kit consists of his PC with its tendering system, traffic analysis and simulation programs, price and material lists, and his sales guide and technical information binders. He also needs tools to communicate with his own back-up in sales support and in engineering. This is pos-

sible either by electronic mail and messaging systems or by conventional phone and fax. Finally, he will enter the order received in the Order book and project management system, where the elevator will be managed and followed up from the specification throughout material order, installation and testing to final hand-over to the customer. After customer hand-over the data is transferred to the maintenance and call-out system for the guarantee period and often beyond.

Tender Enquiry

"*Yes, Mr. Beaver, we will be pleased to provide you with a quotation, but I'll need some information from you to specify the type of the lift. What type of building are we dealing with?*

"*A small office building, with six floors.*"

"*How many occupants will there be on each floor? Have you reserved any space for the lift shaft and the machine room? Is the machine room on top or at the bottom of the building?*"

Tender Preparation

Larry has obtained all the data that he needs: the customer details, building drawings, and the specification request from the architect or consultant. He inputs these to the tendering system. The elevator type, load, travel height and number of stops provide the basic range and specification. The further

items to be specified are the door type, width, height, control features, elevator car interior, signals and push buttons on car and landings. The specification is made by selecting from a predefined list of items. If the item combinations are restricted or not allowed, a message will be displayed. If the customer requests a feature that does not appear on the standard list, it can either be added as a local item, which will be purchased from a subcontractor, or the salesman can ask for a specification from the Kone factory.

Based on the items selected, the basic tender price is calculated. The price includes the value of materials, which can be partly from a Kone factory and partly from local subcontractors; the installation and labor cost; elevator service during the guarantee period; any adjustable items for market area or building customer type, possibly indexing and discounts included.

The tender documents will be produced by combining the selected values and parameters to predefined letter and text blocks in word-processing. The tender letters and technical description of the items tendered can be modified by the salesman, if required to suit this particular customer and project.

Tender Follow-up and Negotiation

"*Good morning, Larry! Nice Monday, the sun is shining and the sky is blue! What's up this week?*"

"Good morning, boss! I just printed out my action list for this week. The first thing I'll do is to follow up a tender I sent to Bayswater Builders last week. Then I have another three outstanding tenders which I need to track. The project we tendered in Brighton is due to be decided this week and I'm 90 percent sure we're going to get it."

When the tenders are registered in the salesman's system, the follow-up and updating of data can take place in an organized way. During the negotiations the elevator specifications often change, alternative options are submitted to the customer, the price is negotiated, and the schedules and installation programs are agreed on. All changes and modifications are done by changing parameters in the original tender. Different versions are saved and the full tender history is available for sales managers and salesmen themselves, if required.

Order Booking

"Good afternoon, Mr. Liftagain, this is Mr. Beaver from Bayswater Builders. At our meeting this morning we decided to give the lift order to Kone, for the price and specifications agreed in your revised quotation on Friday. I will send you the letter of instruction confirming this. When can you give me the detailed schedule and the final drawings?"

The order was received, but this is just the start for the next phase of the job: the implementation. The order is transferred from the tendering system to the order book, job numbers are opened, the customer details, commercial details, cost budget estimate, elevator specification, and project schedule are entered.

Interface to Other Systems

Information about the new order is sent automatically to the financial department, who will open job numbers in the accounting systems. The new elevators will appear in order book reports for the sales and branch managers and other authorized users.

The factory will be informed about the new order received. This can take place at order booking, or in cases where the drawings and completion of specification is handled locally by the salesman, the complete order is sent to the factory at no-return point—just in time for the manufacture.

Drawings

After the tender and specification have been agreed, the production of layout and design drawings starts. These drawings are produced either by the salesman or by the engineering department when technical expertise and advanced CAD systems are required. The salesman's drawing system can be a parameter driven PC CAD, which fills the building and elevator dimensions into pre-defined layout sheets. This enables the salesman to submit standard drawings to the architect and builder in a few minutes or hours, sometimes even in their office.

Installation Planning and Scheduling

"Hi Larry, this is Bob! Listen, I noticed on my capacity plan that you've booked a new order with Bayswater Builders—well done! When you're ready with the specs (= technical specifications), can you arrange the handover to Peter, who I've appointed as supervisor. He will also make the detailed installation plan and coordinate the deliveries from the factory, as usual. I can see in his labor plan that he has two men available in September for the installation work. The estimated hours proposed by the computer say we will take 3 weeks to complete, so we can achieve the handover to customer on 1st October, as planned."

Factory Order

When the drawings have been approved, the remaining items of the specification have been agreed on, and the car interior and landing features designed, the salesman fills in the order

form and specification for the factory. When the order form is in electronic format, the system checks whether the components, options and the combinations are allowed, the dimensions are within acceptable limits, and all mandatory items have been specified. The completed order is sent electronically to the supplying factory. The order consists of the material list, order header and customer details, contact person, delivery groups and required schedule.

The order confirmation is received, including confirmed transfer price, delivery groups and schedules.

Any items that are purchased locally from sub-contractors are specified. Prices and schedules are agreed and monitored.

Site and Installation Activities

"Good morning, gentlemen, welcome to our Monday site meeting. The building works are progressing on schedule and the lift installation is due to start next week. We have the Installation Supervisor Peter Jones from Kone Lifts here to agree on the next steps. Peter, can you tell us about your program?"

"Good morning, all. The lift installation is due to start next Monday and to continue for 3 weeks. I have two men working on site and I will be visiting twice a week. The materials will arrive in two shipments. The first one, consisting of the shaft and machine room equipment, will arrive next Monday. The doors, car finishes and signal equipment will arrive the following Monday. I have spoken to your transport manager and he has arranged for your truck driver to assist in moving the equipment from the lorry to the area assigned by the site manager. The installation work will progress in 11 steps—here is the step-by-step plan—starting from unloading and distributing the material, installing the machine room equipment, and ending at commissioning and testing. The time allowed for each activity, you can see in this schedule. My guys will be filling in time sheets and progress reports every week which will be used for the payroll and monitoring of site progress. . . ."

Handover

"Hello Mr. Beaver, how are you? You have a nice group of lifts in here, completed all on time, as planned. Let's take a closer look. . . . So, everything is in order, we have received your interim payments, the final invoice will be sent to you today. I would like to introduce you to our Maintenance Manager Paul Simon. He and his guys will be looking after your lifts for the next 12 months, as per our contract. If you have any further projects, please don't hesitate to contact us."

This is a typical successful elevator order-delivery process, which demonstrates all parts of the process. Selling is not always so easy and becomes more complicated and harder all the time.

KONE ELEVATORS

Kone Elevators is the third largest elevator manufacturer in the world, the market share being around 15 percent, compared to Otis Elevators' (in the U.S.) 25 percent and Shindler's (in Switzerland) 19 percent. The company employs more than 17,000 people worldwide, fewer than one in ten of whom are Finnish. The primary strategic objective, since the late 1960s, has been the creation of a multinational elevator and escalator company via the acquisition of national elevator companies in various countries.

Kone Oy was founded in 1910, and the first elevator was delivered eight years later. In 1968 Kone expanded from the Finnish domestic market into Scandinavia by acquiring the Swedish company ASEA, tripling elevator deliveries in the process. The second step in intensive acquisition took place in 1975 when Kone acquired the Westinghouse elevator and escalator business in Europe, thus doubling sales.

The 1980s saw Kone's breakthrough in North America, and in Europe expansion continued when two leading Italian elevator companies, Sabiem and Fiam, joined the organization in 1985 and 1986 respectively. During 1987, joint-venture operations for elevator production were started in Australia, India and Turkey.

On two occasions the company has absorbed nonprofitable operations as large or even larger than itself and turned them into profitable ones. Profitability has been restored through using the same business concept in all units.

Each acquisition constitutes a separate case. Kone has tried to handle them very flexibly with their own schedules, measures and models. Following acquisition the role of each new unit has been thought over, and some of its operations have been standardized with other units of the corporation. Sometimes the changes have taken several years, and there have been some cultural differences. Although Kone has a similar business concept in each unit, it's been realized in different ways in different countries. On occasions tough measures have had to be used in order to remove obstacles to company reorganization.

Kone has learned several cultural lessons. For instance, in Italy you have to agree on everything with top management. Direct contacts with different functions such as accounting failed to work, if the decisions had not been made first at the top level. Implementing new models and systems therefore took more time than expected. In Germany the thinking was quite functional; users thought that it was the task of the systems specialists from Finland to implement new systems without bothering them.

Kone is now a global company whose operations have been organized into five areas: Europe North, Central, and South, Asia-Pacific, and the Americas. Each area is headed by a full-time Area Director. The sales of new elevators and installations are organized by local companies in each country. Within each area, there is one Engineering Center for product engineering and design and tailoring to customer orders. The Engineering Center compiles and delivers market specific elevators from Kone standard components to local customers.

Component manufacturing is organized globally so that in Europe, for example, there are over ten component factories in different countries. The elevator components are transported to the Logistics Center, which is located with the Engineering Center. The Engineering and Logistics Centers are the area service centers of the elevator delivery process. On site elevator installation is carried out in each country by the local organization. A locally competitive product, an elevator that meets customer requirements, is developed in each area, but Kone's standard components are used in all areas.

Kone Elevators is now organized in the following way:

- Sales and Installations, separate companies in each country.
- Engineering and logistics, one unit within each geographical area.
- Components production, a global operation.

COMPETITION IN THE ELEVATOR BUSINESS

The elevator business is a highly competitive one, with overcapacity in production. The demand for new elevators and industrial cranes is on the decline in all markets except the Far East. The downturn in the construction industry seems set to last, since in many countries there is overproduction of both office space and flats. In such a situation the competition for market shares is fierce, and there is a great deal of pressure on price levels.

The business in elevator modernization, maintenance, and repair continues to grow and form an increasingly significant proportion of the sales industry. In this line of business there is a structural, permanent-looking change happening to which companies must adapt. The focus in building new elevators must be shifted toward maintenance. In this competitive situation the maintenance of customer service is extremely important.

Kone Elevators aims at competitive success through a decentralized business concept, the aim of which is to combine economies of scale and local flexibility. The key element in Kone strategy is the global logistics system, which is based on common basic system modules that can be modified and localized to suit local users' needs. The global logistics system informs every person involved in the process of the tasks they need to perform in order to get the elevator delivered and installed on time. The system makes it possible to schedule and record major activities, such as orders to the Engineering Center, component orders released, installations programmed, elevators shipped, and installations completed. Each elevator order can be tracked down on screens or reports at the main points of the process. With this system, Kone salesmen can give more reliable and quicker responses to customer requirements.

With this global mode of operation Kone has been successful in a very difficult competitive situation. A combination of good customer service and cost effectiveness has been achieved. However, the structural change in competition offers new challenges to Kone's management, in terms of how to adapt the company to the changing environment.

Director of Information Systems Markku Rajaniemi stated from his Helsinki headquarters that:

"During the 80's many medium-sized elevator companies disappeared from the market, mostly through acquisition. Small companies survived by flexibility and low cost, big companies developed their products and activities and utilized economies of scale, while mid-sized companies were caught in between and got eaten up by the big ones. Kone has also grown by acquiring typically medium-sized companies with small resources for developing activities and low economies of scale. We organized the activities so that local companies can benefit from Kone development activities and scale advantages.

Our competitiveness is very much based on our systems to manage the global logistics where orders, components and products are moving between countries. We try to combine global scale and local flexibility with our three level management (global, area, and country)."

INFORMATION TECHNOLOGY IN KONE ELEVATORS

Kone Elevators has a decentralized data processing set-up, with around 200 medium-size computers (HP9000, AS400) and with around 200 Local Area Networks (NOVELL). The main operating systems are UNIX, OS400, OSF-UX and DOS. In international data transmission different services from multiple network operators are used. The transmission protocols are TCP/IP and SNA Routers.

Kone's information technology strategy is roughly as follows:

The main corporate activities are research and testing of new technologies, updating Elevators Headquarters IT on corporate technical standards, and negotiating and managing frame agreements with corporate-wide hardware and software suppliers. Development, management and support of Kone's international telecommunications network is an important task.

Elevator Headquarters concentrates on developing and updating technical standards and the application architecture, developing the Kone Elevators application portfolio in line with business needs and priorities, and organizing support and maintenance of portfolio applications. Providing Kone units with adequate support in general and specific IT issues is also important.

Company IT activities involve defining business requirements and analyzing business benefits, procuring hardware and software in line with Kone's technical standards, and managing implementation projects. They also include running local computer operations and the development and maintenance of local applications and adaptations. Managing the migration of the local infrastructure towards harmonization constitutes an important task.

Kone Elevators has a common applications architecture, which maps out the main applications in a unit, describes their functionality and defines their interfaces. It also describes the underlying common data structure and how the various applications access data. The applications architecture is a vital communication vehicle in developing, implementing and maintaining systems applications.

The technical standard defines the hardware, software and telecommunications solutions applicable in the units. Deviations from these standards are allowed only after consultation with headquarters' IT function.

Altogether this is a very coordinated decentralized solution. Units have to work within a given frame, but they take care of their own operations. Within the framework there is some flexibility for individual solutions.

In the units, coordination has been experienced as mainly positive, although some complaints have been made about the fact that matters had been defined in too great detail. Personnel in the information systems function are, however, of the opinion that the input of coordination has even been limited, so that the function's resources would just suffice to provide sufficient support to the local unit.

At Kone Elevators there are around one hundred IS professionals who are mainly decentralized in different units. The objective of the IS function is to obtain software that is as complete as possible, in order for its own software production to be as limited as possible. Total IS costs are around 2 percent of sales, an average level in manufacturing.

The applications are divided into three different areas:

- Management systems, e.g. management accounting and budgeting
- Operations support, e.g. logistic systems
- Resource management, e.g. personnel administration, supplier control and customer service.

Kone has concentrated on internal systems. It has not invested much on external links. They have thought that it is enough to have information less frequently, but in a reliable and consistent form. Recently, however, there has been discussion on how to improve the quality of market information, but there are no ongoing projects.

References

Annual Report, Kone 1992.

Hurskainen Jorma, Business Process Approach to Global Logistics Case: Kone Elevators, in Joining the Global Roll, Jahnukainen and Vepsäläinen (eds), Helsinki 1992, pp. 86–102.

Rajaniemi Markku, Process Development in Perspective, ibid, pp. 132–138.

Interviews, Ulla Mäkelä and Markku Rajaniemi, Kone Elevators.

Case Study Questions

1. What kind of global strategy is Kone Elevators pursuing?

2. Evaluate Kone's information systems in light of this strategy. How well do they support it?

3. Evaluate Kone's strategy for managing its international information systems infrastructure.

4. How easy would it have been for Kone to implement the order-delivery system described at the beginning of this case on an international basis? What management, organization, and technology issues had to be addressed?

5. How strategic is the order-delivery system described here for a firm such as Kone? Why?

Festo Pneumatic

Helmut Krcmar and Bettina Schwarzer, University of Hohenheim (Germany)

Festo, a medium-sized German company headquartered in Esslingen, with 3500 employees around the world, is one of the world market leaders in the field of pneumatics and device control. The company was founded in 1925 and opened its first subsidiary, in Italy, in 1956. By now Festo has branches in 187 countries, offering full service for its products around the world (See Figure 1). Festo has four major product groups: Festo Electronic, which offers products and services for electronic device control; Festo Tooltechnic, offering electronic and air-pressure tools for crafts and industry; Festo Didactic, which provides courses for all kinds of device control; and finally Festo Pneumatic, which manufactures valves and cylinders and provides complete solutions for device control.

The major group is Festo Pneumatic, which specializes in the design and manufacturing of valves and cylinders, offering 35,000 components and 4,000 products by catalogue. It also provides custom-made solutions for device control in which cylinders are combined with other Festo components according to specific customer requirements. This combined approach of manufacturing components and offering complete solutions distinguishes Festo from most of its competitors in the pneumatic business. All products are designed and produced in Germany. Only in the case of special made-to-order cylinders does production take place in the subsidiaries to meet customer requirements. Of the products manufactured in Germany, 55% are exported.

Festo Pneumatic has 35 subsidiaries and more than 100 branch offices selling its products. In general, all pneumatic products are designed and manufactured in Germany; therefore the same product is available around the world. As parts are shipped all over the world from the German production site and warehouse, all orders have to be processed centrally. Processing a workload of about 200–300 orders with an average of 4 items per order from each of the major subsidiaries daily, Festo Pneumatic is dependent on a global computer system.

Even though Festo is a fairly small company with only 1000 employees abroad, it is highly internationalized and continuously expanding its international engagements, now turning to Eastern Europe. The subsidiaries are independent companies, but are dependent on the German headquarters because they neither design nor manufacture products. Festo Pneumatic Germany views its subsidiaries as "shops" for selling the company's products in foreign markets. Not only in the business area but also in the field of information systems Festo pursues a centralized approach. Hardware and software are selected in the corporate headquarters, which also provides systems support. The major advantage of this approach is cost savings; detailed knowledge of the systems can be centralized in one place. Any changes in the system only have to be made in one place and are then taken to all subsidiaries. This not only reduces costs but also guarantees that the system is the same everywhere.

In 1976, confronted with continuing international growth and an increasing workload, Festo Pneumatic decided to implement a common system in the headquarters and the subsidiaries to be able to handle and improve order processing, logistics, and production on an international basis. The goals pursued with the system were "high quality of customer service" and "minimized stock levels." To match the structure of their international operations Festo decided to implement one common system for all subsidiaries, as they had exactly the same information processing requirements in their data exchange with the headquarters. As there was no standardized software package available at that time, a system was developed in-house starting in 1976. Development took place in the headquarters and beginning in 1978 the system was introduced in the subsidiaries.

Due to the lack of standardized software packages at that time and the high costs of in-house development, most competitors did not have sophisticated systems in place when Festo introduced its first integrated system. At that time the rationale for systems development was not strategic advantage—the idea of strategic information systems was not yet known—but simply to make order processing on an international basis more efficient. Still, Festo realized that the new system helped them to gain competitive advantage; the time for order processing was shortened and Festo was able to respond quicker to customer requests.

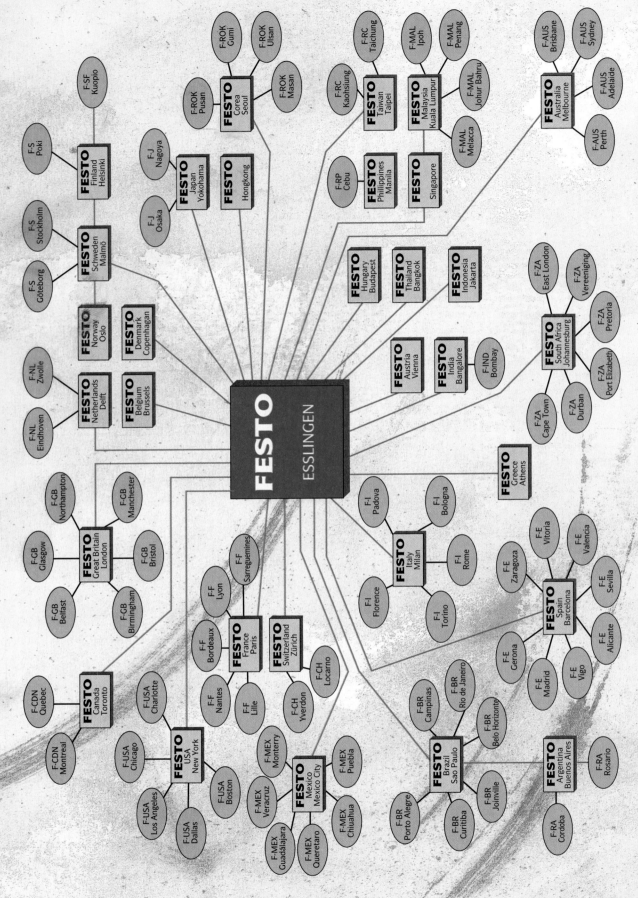

FIGURE 1
Festo corporate organization.

Over the years the system has been continuously improved to meet changing requirements. Festo's current FIP-2 system, used for order processing, logistics, and manufacturing, was developed based on its experiences with the first system. All components of the old system that worked well are also used in the new system, with new technology replacing the components that were no longer appropriate. The FIP-2 system is based on the Cobol 85, RPG, and High Level RPG programming languages and uses TurboImage for database management.

Before systems development took place, the hardware platform was carefully chosen by experts after a one-year study of different vendors. The main criterion for hardware selection was scalability, to make sure that the same hardware could be used in subsidiaries of different sizes. Festo headquarters always used IBM computers but it selected Hewlett Packard computers for its subsidiaries. Today Festo's 24 subsidiary headquarters run the system on HP 3000 computers with the RISC-technology based operating system MPE/iX. No matter whether four or 2000 people are using the system at the same time, all users can work in the same systems environment.

Customers order in the subsidiaries' branches by either telephone or FAX (in some cases there are shops for over-the-counter sales). Festo's branch offices in various countries use microcomputers linked directly to an HP 3000 in each subsidiary's headquarters for order entry. An order is entered into the FIP-2 system on a microcomputer and then transmitted to subsidiary headquarters either immediately or once a day, depending on the type of connection between the branch office and subsidiary headquarters. There the order is checked for availability of components in the country's own warehouse. If the components are available, the order is processed in the country. Otherwise, the orders are collected and transmitted every hour or once a day (depending on the size and importance of the subsidiary) via an X.25 packet-switched network to an HP 3000 in

Festo headquarters in Germany. The HP 3000 at German headquarters in turn transforms the data to make processing on an IBM 3090 mainframe possible. The IBM mainframe is linked to Festo's German branches, so German orders are entered directly into this system. The IBM combines orders from abroad with the German orders and processes them. The system checks the stocks in the German warehouse and the production schedule and returns with a confirmation of the order to the subsidiaries, stating the expected date of delivery. Data are then transmitted to an AEG 80–30 computer which is used to manage the warehouse. Festo reports no problems with these linkages on either a national or international level, although some problems may arise when transmitting data to and from technologically underdeveloped countries such as Brazil.

If the components are in stock, the AEG 80-30 in the warehouse handles the request. A warehouse note is printed, giving information on where the components are to be found in the warehouse and how many components are needed for the order. The parts are removed from the warehouse and commissioned. The worker enters the "finished" status into the system and a delivery note, the bill and a confirmation of the order are printed by the system. These papers are put into the packet and sent to the subsidiary either on the road or by air. The subsidiary either puts the components in its own warehouse or puts together the required parts for the individual orders.

Apart from the orders processed together, customer-specific orders can be transmitted to the German headquarters. In this case, all components for the order are packed together and marked in the German warehouse. They are delivered to the subsidiary together with the other parts. After checking them in the subsidiary they can be delivered directly to the customer without putting them into the warehouse.

Designing one common system for use in different countries was not as easy as it sounds and caused a number

of problems. Apart from the different languages that are required, for example in printed material for the use of the customer, country-specific features have to be implemented. For example, in Italy the revenue authorities require that bills sent to the same customer have to be numbered in the correct order of issue, whereas in other countries the revenue authorities have their own numbering system and are not interested in the number on the bill. If special features are only needed in one country Festo allows the subsidiary to make the changes itself, providing support for the systems support people in the subsidiaries if needed. If several countries have the same requirements, the changes are made at headquarters and then implemented abroad. In making the changes at headquarters, so far only headquarters systems personnel has been involved. This policy is being changed in order to gain advantage of the knowledge available in the subsidiaries.

Whereas in former times, the system provided Festo with a competitive advantage as the system allowed faster processing of orders, the competitive situation has changed over the years due to the increasing availability of standard software. Today, software is readily available, and in order to be able to compete all companies use integrated systems. Festo has adapted to the new situation and is focusing on improving customer service. One potential area for benefits that has been identified is incorporating expert systems into the system. Expert systems can support the sales people in their meetings by suggesting system configurations. Thereby the ordering process can be speeded up and qualitatively improved.

Case Study Questions

1. What kind of global strategy is Festo Pneumatic pursuing?

2. Evaluate Festo's FIP-2 system in light of this strategy. How well does this system support it?

3. Evaluate Festo Pneumatic's strategy for managing its international information systems infrastructure.

4. How much competitive advantage does Festo's FIP-2 system provide?

5. What problems did Festo have implementing its order processing, logistics and production system?

tem? What management, organization, and technology issues had to be addressed?

6. Festo's order processing, logistics, and production system is custom-developed. In this partic-

ular instance, is it an advantage or disadvantage to have custom-built software?

Corning Telecommunications Division (A): The Flexible Manufacturing Systems Project

Andrew Boynton, University of North Carolina at Chapel Hill and the International Institute for Management Development (Switzerland)
Michael E. Shank, Renaissance Vision

Driving across the Gibson Bridge toward his office in July 1990, Bob McAdoo, senior vice president and head of manufacturing for the Telecommunications division of Corning, Inc., thought about the appropriations request he would be discussing with his staff on Friday morning. The division was requesting $5 million for a new planning and scheduling system plus a reconfigured information system to cope with manufacturing changes at its Wilmington, NC, plant, where Corning made optical waveguides. Such a sum was not an incidental capital investment. Moreover, exactly what they would be getting for the money was hard to say. The budget for hardware and packaged software was dwarfed by the costs of design work and consultants. The consultants would be designing a system that had never been built before, and after problems with the last systems-development project, ATLAS, the idea of breaking new ground in software was troubling. (ATLAS, even though it was a well-understood business data system, had been two years late and millions over budget.) In addition, no one could tell McAdoo if the proposed Flexible Manufacturing System (FMS) would work once it was designed, written, and implemented. All they would say

is that they "didn't think the plant could continue to work without it."

OPTICAL WAVEGUIDES

Optical waveguides are glass fibers that allow communication by light rather than electricity. One fifth thinner than a human hair, the core of these fibers can carry more than 16,000 simultaneous phone conversations (compared with 24 for copper wire). Unlike copper, optical fiber can also carry information in both directions (sending and receiving) simultaneously. Fibers can transmit light more than 100 miles without regeneration and operate 20,000 feet under water with a 40-year life. Despite their close resemblance to fishing line when coated, fibers can withstand 1 million pounds per square inch of tensile stress. Optical fiber can also carry more information much faster than copper wire. Fiber's carrying capacity of 1.8 billion bits per second can transmit the Encyclopedia Britannica and the Bible around the earth together in less than 2 seconds.

Optical fibers behave like "light pipes." Because of their differences in composition, the refractive index of the core is higher than that of the outer coat (cladding). As a result, light rays

traveling through the core will be reflected back into the core if they stray from a straight line and bounce into the core/cladding interface. Consequently, light stays in the core even when the fiber is bent.

The two types of fiber were multimode and single mode. Multimode was primarily used for local building-to-building and intrabuilding wiring, where its comparatively large core size contributed to reduced installation costs. Multimode was available in several glass and coating designs, which when combined with various optical performance levels, resulted in a wide and increasing variety of stock-keeping units (SKUs).

Single-mode fiber was used primarily by telephone companies. Initial applications were for long-distance telecommunication applications by companies like MCI, AT&T, and Sprint. New types of fiber and coatings, and declining systems costs after 1983, led to many new applications by regional telephone companies (e.g., Bell South), cable television companies, and long distance communication companies. Given the efforts by telephone companies to emphasize product standardization and compatibility of competing vendors' products, fewer single-mode than multimode fiber SKUs existed. Single-mode fiber represented approximately 90% of the market volume.

Corning sold almost all of its fiber to optical-fiber cablers. A few cablers accounted for approximately 80% of Corning's sales, with 200 customers making up the remaining 20%. Essentially, cablers packaged the optical fiber in a variety of materials to protect it during installation and to limit the effects of its installed environments. From a materials point of view, cablers added little to the value of the fiber, and the fiber itself was a large portion of the cost of fiber cabling. Excess capacity plagued the cabling industry, and barriers to entry were low. Telephone companies' purchases comprised 70% of the optical-cable market, and these companies were adept at creating a level playing field through specification standards and purchasing strategies. Product quality and service were important to the phone companies, but these parameters were viewed largely as requirements for entry. Bidding to attract the phone companies' business was fierce. Overall, profits for optical cablers tended to be low, which was consistent with the financial performance they achieved when these same cablers had been copper-wire cablers.

As the costs of fiber optic systems declined, phone-company fiber-cable installation migrated from long-haul telecommunications trunks (e.g., MCI) through regional telecommunications (e.g., Bell South) interoffice trunks joining central-office switching systems to feeder cables connecting central-office switches directly to large businesses or to residential neighborhoods (see Figure 1). Phone companies were betting that optical systems' costs would decline to the degree that they would be no different than the costs of a copper wire system for final telephone line connections to residences (distribution and drop cables). When the fiber could be installed to the home, the phone companies would be able to take advantage of fiber's unlimited capacity to provide a raft of new information services such as video entertainment on demand, home shopping, and home education. This development would allow the phone companies to become the aggressive, high-growth information firms they had envisioned at the time of divestiture.

The cable television market also used single mode fiber, to improve picture quality and channel capacity and as a defensive posture against the phone companies, who were interested in entering the home entertainment video market. Cable TV's mass deployment of fiber had lagged the phone companies by five years, but growth since 1988 had been strong.

Beyond the phone companies and cable TV markets, another large and growing segment was premises wiring—banks, corporate offices, universities, hospitals, industrial complexes, and brokerage houses. These customers made up the market for mul-

TELEPHONE OUTSIDE PLANT NETWORK

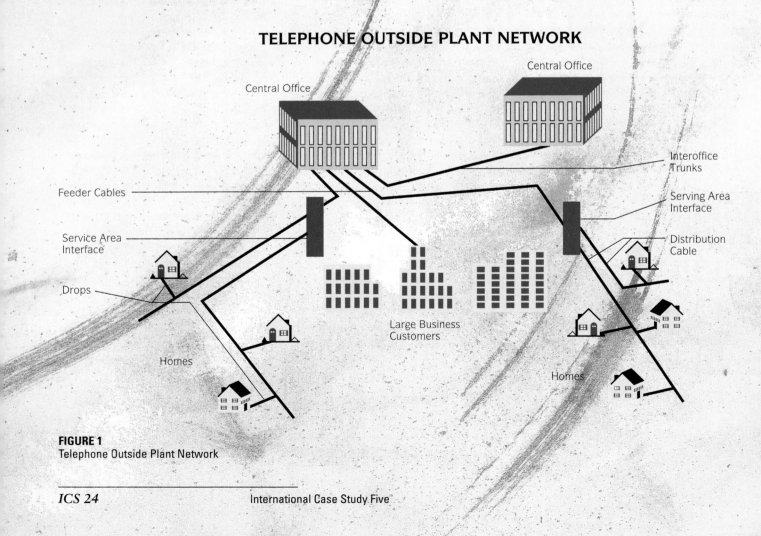

FIGURE 1
Telephone Outside Plant Network

timode fiber. Standards had not progressed as far in this segment, and several different multimode glass and fiber designs serviced the market. Given the lack of concentrated purchasing observed in the phone company segment, the buying patterns were not as orderly. Many fiber cablers and systems integrators would often bid on the same premises job, and quote turnaround times and cable lead times were key determinants in establishing the winning bidder.

Cablers passed these segment pressures directly to Corning and other suppliers—AT&T and Spectran. While Corning and AT&T devoted a large percentage of their fiber capabilities to single mode, Spectran owed its existence to the multimode market. Spectran used attractive pricing, rapid quote turnaround, and competitive lead times to attract business.

Another interesting segment was the undersea telecommunications market. Transoceanic cables had been developed and installed linking the U.S. with Europe and Japan. Undersea cables were installed around the perimeter of Italy in time to be used for transmitting the recent World Cup Soccer matches. In these applications long length, low loss, high strength fibers were used to reduce the installed system cost. Increased interest was developing in an altered single mode fiber design, which optimized optical performance at longer wavelengths, thus resulting in lower loss fibers and further reductions in installed system cost.

Beyond these current markets, new segments were on the horizon for fiber, including fiber for tethered weapons, navigation, and sensor applications. Product designs were still being finalized, but it was clear that new glass and coating designs beyond today's product lines would be required to meet these segments' requirements.

Waveguides at Corning Incorporated

Corning, Inc., in 1990 was composed of four primary sectors, Specialty Glass and Ceramics, Communications, Laboratory Services, and Consumer Housewares. Specialty Glass and Ceramics marketed over 40,000 specialty materials, including eyeglass materials, and auto-emission filters. The Communications sector produced optical fiber, opto-electrical components for fiber networks, video display glass, and liquid crystal displays. Laboratory Services provided clinical testing, life-science research, and environmental testing services. Consumer Housewares produced such well-known products as Corning Ware®, Revere Ware®, and Corelle® dinnerware.

In 1989-90, the Communications sector contributed approximately 21% to Corning's revenues and 37% to its profits, increases of over 35% in both categories. A significant contribution to corporate profits came from optical waveguides. Corning's quality and delivery had consistently provided a significant profit margin on this product.

Corning developed the first technically feasible optical fiber in 1970. The company then worked for eight years refining the technology and developing a proprietary low-cost manufacturing method. Despite years of only moderate interest from telephone companies and cablers, Corning funded the research and, in 1979, built a manufacturing plant in Wilmington. The plant operated for three years producing only samples and small orders for pilot projects before its first major order was received, which followed the deregulation of the telecommunications industry in 1982.

At that time, MCI announced plans to build a nationwide fiber-optic network and ordered one hundred thousand kilometers of fiber from Corning. The order, ten times larger than any prior one, was for a new type of single-mode fiber that was still experimental at the company. To meet MCI's requirements, therefore, Corning moved a new generation of fiber technology from the lab to the plant floor, installed new production equipment, and embarked on one of the largest plant expansions in Corning's history. By 1986, sixteen years after proving the commercial feasibility of optical fiber, Corning's fiber-optics operations were running twenty-four hours a day and turning a profit.

The MCI order was quickly followed by others as competition in the telecommunications industry developed. In 1983, Corning funded the largest expenditure request in its history, $100 million, to expand the Wilmington plant to meet rapidly increasing demand and install Corning's fifth generation of fiber-optic manufacturing technology. Corning's dedication to its new technology and its willingness to invest allowed the company to compete with larger rivals such as AT&T and "Japan, Inc.," to become a world leader in waveguide manufacturing. In 1991 Corning Communications, having initiated a "total quality" effort to measure the performance of all business and manufacturing processes to determine competitive capabilities, was pursuing the Baldrige Award.

The initial growth phase, fueled by the needs of long-distance companies, had appeared endless, and to remain an industry's technological leader, Corning had averaged changes in production machinery every 12–24 months. In the second half of 1986, however, as Corning continued to increase its production capacity, the initial growth stopped. The market for long-distance lines was saturated, and increasingly customized fiber-optic, especially multimode, orders from the cable industry changed the demands on Corning's waveguide plant. By 1990, these new demands were not optimally satisfied by the manufacturing and information systems at the plant. By early 1991, construction to again increase the size and capacity of the plant substantially had begun, and this effort required the attention of everyone in the factory to maintain existing production levels.

Current Manufacturing and Information Systems

In the Laydown stage, a machine called a "lathe" systematically coated a ceramic rod with a precise chemical deposit buildup to make a "blank" (Figure 2). During the process, the inner chemical buildup formed what would be the core of the optical fiber. The chemicals were then changed to build what would become the outer coat (clad) of the fiber. The completed blank (or "preform") looked like a large cigar.

In the Consolidation stage, the blank was heated in a furnace to remove water and impurities, and to consolidate the porous blank into pure glass. The blank purified in the Consolidation stage next moved on to the Draw stage. In Draw, the blanks ("glass cigars") were placed in holders, and a small furnace heated the extreme tip of each blank, causing the melted tip to drop down a tower. The tip pulled along a small strand of optical fiber from the blank, which was threaded through a machine that applied different chemical coatings to the outside of the fiber and measured its width. At the bottom of the tower, a tractor pulled the fiber at a preset rate, and the fiber was collected on a take-up reel.

From Draw, the bulk reel of optical fiber moved to Off Line Screening (OLS), where tensile strength was measured. The reel then traveled to Measurement for a large battery of optical tests. The fiber was measured and cut to standard lengths and, in the Wind stage, taken off the special measurement spools and rewound on shipping spools.

Mike Jordan, planning and scheduling supervisor, had briefed Bob McAdoo on the complexity of production scheduling at the Wilmington plant: "In making waveguides, the process is different from standard production like making automobiles. With cars, ten Chevy engines and ten Chevy bodies make ten Chevy cars, with some quality reworking. Here, in optical waveguides, we can mix ten batches of the same chemicals under the same conditions with the same computer-controlled processes. Sometimes we'll get seven batches that can be sold; sometimes we'll get ten. Each batch will differ slightly from the other batches. For ex-

DESCRIPTION OF FIBER-OPTIC MANUFACTURING PROCESS

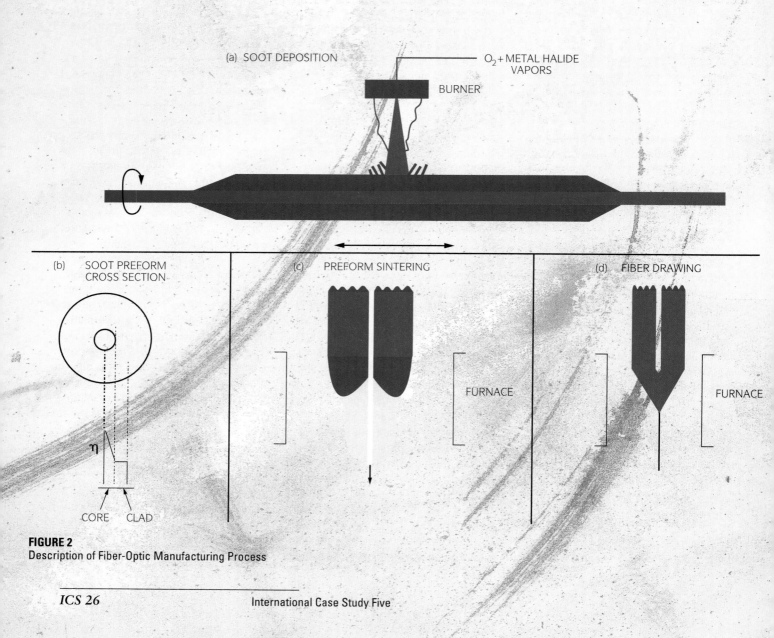

FIGURE 2
Description of Fiber-Optic Manufacturing Process

ample, the maximum length of optical fibers will vary as bad sections are cut out. Glass-geometry precision will differ slightly from batch to batch. So we don't know how many saleable end products we'll get because of differences in selection yield. We also don't know how many end products will be Oldsmobiles and many will be Chevys due to the distribution of characteristics. Luckily, we can substitute Oldsmobiles for Chevys here. Customers will take a higher quality cable for the same price. But this substitution costs us money. Selection, distribution, and substitution complicate the planning process."

Manufacturing waveguides required highly exact, computer-controlled systems, but the early emphasis on standard fiber products with few modifications for the long-distance companies had resulted in a system limited to keeping costs low while maintaining efficiency and high quality. The system was designed to control manufacturing at each step of the production process (Laydown, Consolidation, etc.). The primary function of the information system was to identify equipment and process problems in each individual production stage.

The tight controls coded into the system allowed few modifications in the product or production process. To get around the product and process controls, a small percentage of the plant's production was run as "experimental" products. Each production process had to be individually "tricked" into letting new products move through the system. The products were moved manually through the entire production process with computer overrides at each step. For example, new or customized products with diameters or lengths that were different from standard fibers required engineers to override set specifications in the Draw and Measurement systems. Since all fibers looked essentially identical to the naked eye, special fiber reels were identified with colored dots and batch numbers to flag them as requiring special processing. The manual intervention was not only time consuming and labor intensive, but also prone to human error.

Computer overrides often conflicted with standard costing information and with constants in production algorithms. Thus costs could not be accumulated on special orders and new products. Inappropriate algorithm constants resulted in incorrect production information, and reported yields exceeded actual process inputs.

Information was captured by the system on each of the individual processes but was used to control only that process. No information was passed along by the system to the next production stage. Operators even keyed in reel identification numbers manually at each stage. This division of production information resulted in a vertically oriented information system that employees called, along with the associated computers, "stovepipes" of information. Each stovepipe was monitored and controlled by a separate staff (the stovepipe's "feudal lord"). Computers stored highly summarized information on products completed and in inventory.

The stovepipe infrastructure of the current system did not allow potentially useful information to be shared across production stages. The different systems had dramatically different field definitions and sizes, which offered little opportunity to integrate the data across the stovepipes. For example, measurement information from the OLS stage could not be used to eliminate later quality checks or to determine sampling strategies in the Measurement stage. The systems provided no means of feeding information forward or backward in the production process. Information on fiber defects discovered in later process steps required manual intervention, communication, and correction. Information gathered in prior stages, such as diameter measurements and usable fiber lengths determined in Draw, was unavailable to Measurement technicians, who might spend hours searching reels for a long usable fiber. Consolidating information from the different systems resulted in unacceptable delays in providing production information. In short, the stovepipe systems did not allow the plant to maximize the use of its capital-intensive equipment.

Designed to meet high demand for a few products, the system did not track work in process. All orders were matched to inventory. However, when a relatively stable supply of a few products had moved through the system, supervisors had been able to coordinate production based on inventory levels.

As the number of products multiplied and became more customized, and as customers demanded shorter lead times, a "Sneaker Patrol," the plant's production and scheduling staff, had become responsible for determining what was in the plant and adjusting production schedules in an attempt to meet customer orders. The 4-week production plan listed the number of blanks of each product type to start. As orders came in or were canceled and as the yields changed in the production process, the Sneaker Patrol made schedule revisions. Currently, numerous daily schedule changes and comprehensive changes were made weekly to the 4-week plan.

Pressure to increase responsiveness can be seen in the fact that, in 1988, Corning fiber salespeople put pressure on Wilmington to respond in less than one day with delivery and cost information for customers; in 1991, they were pressuring Wilmington to respond in less than four hours. In 1991, Wilmington had a several-hour goal and monitored performance to meet that goal.

All changes which were based on information that was often two days old, were projected by hand. Most information was gathered and transmitted by the production staff, the Sneaker Patrol, walking through the plant with clipboards and changing the colored and numbered dots on different carts of fiber reels. This process was being stretched to the limit as the Wilmington plant continued to add new fiber products and prepared to add additional capacity.

Mike Jordan, who as planning and scheduling supervisor, was also head of the Sneaker Patrol, explained how the process was being stretched: "A customer was buying multimode product of long length. This is not a standard product, so we have to begin a 'yellow-dot experiment,' where the particular yellow dot indicates 'produce long-length multimode.' The customer calls back in a few days and says he doesn't want the long-length. Because we can't waste good in-process fiber, I have to go out and take off the yellow dot from this particular experiment and produce this in-process fiber for stock. The next day, the same customer calls and says he wants a different bandwidth multimode. I then have to run out again and find some in-process fiber of that band width by looking around the plant and then put a yellow dot on that to indicate the length the customer wants. Can you imagine this happening many times each day? It does!"

The same information gathered for scheduling was used to quote order lead times to customers. Quoting a lead time one or two days longer than a competitor could lose an order. Missing a deadline or shipping incorrect product violated one of Corning's top cultural values. Currently, a significant percentage of customer orders were for shipment in less than 5 days, but the plant took over 6 days to complete most of the orders, even though the production process required significantly less time. All other delays were caused by the logistics of moving between operations (a minimal amount of time) and scheduling conflicts and inefficiencies.

Mike O'Koren, the Wilmington plant manager, described the plant as computer intensive but reliant on "people intervention" and "customized people processes": "The customers are wanting more one-of-a-kind orders with shorter lead times. Our record of error-free shipments and past turn-around time has made customer service a competitive advantage. Maintaining this advantage is crucial to our success. Right now we don't have a system in place that allows us to shrink lead times. The only way we do it now is with what people do in their heads. We promise orders based on what we think is on the shop floor. We've been stretched pretty thin. As our volume increases and the number of product choices multiplies the people system is going to break down."

Reliance on customized people processes and mutual production adjustments between feudal lords and the Sneaker Patrol had created a large informal communications network in the plant. Production processes had evolved to conform to this network.

Jordan estimated that the plant could accept orders for 10% more fiber a month if quote times could be reduced through the scheduling of a "made-to-order" manufacturing system. He explained that, in the information environment he envisioned, he could be much more effective: "I want to be able to sit at home or in the office and, on the PC, identify what fiber is in stock or anywhere on the floor. Now I have to check what is in the inventory or on the floor to see what is there. Today we have almost zero visibility about ware in process."

Jordan hoped, however, that any new systems wouldn't be as difficult to implement as the last systems project with which he had been involved: "Although this is my vision for fast response to our customer requests, the last information system project I was involved with, ATLAS, left me with a healthy dose of skepticism. ATLAS has worked out great, but not without some pain. Now we can see all orders, which customers place through the sales force at corporate, in 5 minutes. Before ATLAS, it took over 24 hours for us to get an order. I felt the project was badly undersourced. The system was being designed for multiple uses in multiple divisions. Coordination between all parties was difficult. Senior management in our sector didn't buy in initially, and without that pressure brought to bear, the project stagnated. It didn't work until we at Wilmington held our ground, insisted on getting the resources required, and fought for the project to be completed—the right way. After we at Wilmington started kicking, the guys at corporate got involved and insured that corporate IS [Information Systems] put the resources on the project for our sector. We learned a great deal during ATLAS, and it is a real lifesaver now. I just wonder if new systems will be as difficult to implement."

On a recent visit to the Wilmington plant, McAdoo had spoken with O'Koren about the effect of the proposed new information system on the people who composed the informal communications network. O'Koren thought the new system would provide tremendous benefits to customers, but he was less enthusiastic about the effect on plant personnel: "Many people have done nothing but act as information transmitters in this network since the business was started. They feel very threatened. I think they're going to have to learn new jobs."

McAdoo noted that, as O'Koren was speaking, a large fish on his PC's aquarium display had turned and eaten several smaller fish.

The Appropriations Request

The decision to request $5 million to revamp waveguide manufacturing (see Figure 3) had not been straightforward. On the one hand, the waveguide project had always been a high-risk, high-return project. Historically, large appropriations requests had been granted, and they had paid off. On the other hand, the configuration and timing of the local-loop market appeared as uncertain as the long-distance market had in 1970.

Tom LaGarde, manager of IS at the Wilmington factory, had been heavily involved with the preparation of the request. He discussed with McAdoo how the implementation effort would be managed: "At the highest level, we have a review board consisting of senior managers at corporate that meet twice a year to make sure the project is not out of sync with the company. We have been asked to submit appropriation requests twice a year after the initial request is approved. As we present each request, we have to establish where we've been and where we are going and establish how much money has been spent and what will be needed. We brought in Global Analysis, a Big Five consulting firm, because we felt our corporate IS group, though talented, did not have the experience for this type of project. We're using a computer-based tool to plan, track, test, and man-

FIGURE 3
Flexible Manufacturing Systems

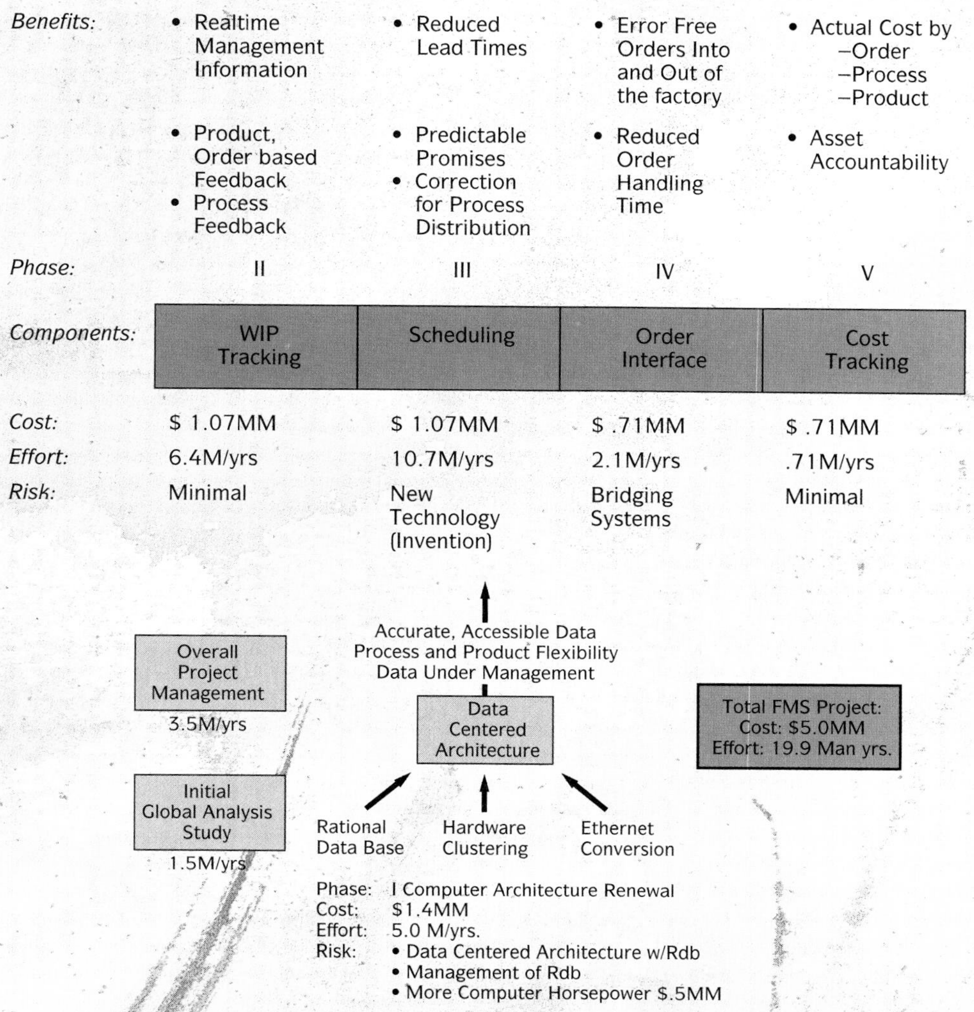

Benefits:	• Realtime Management Information	• Reduced Lead Times	• Error Free Orders Into and Out of the factory	• Actual Cost by −Order −Process −Product
	• Product, Order based Feedback • Process Feedback	• Predictable Promises • Correction for Process Distribution	• Reduced Order Handling Time	• Asset Accountability

Phase:	II	III	IV	V
Components:	WIP Tracking	Scheduling	Order Interface	Cost Tracking
Cost:	$ 1.07MM	$ 1.07MM	$ .71MM	$ .71MM
Effort:	6.4M/yrs	10.7M/yrs	2.1M/yrs	.71M/yrs
Risk:	Minimal	New Technology (Invention)	Bridging Systems	Minimal

Overall Project Management
3.5M/yrs

Initial Global Analysis Study
1.5M/yrs

Accurate, Accessible Data
Process and Product Flexibility
Data Under Management

Data Centered Architecture

Rational Data Base   Hardware Clustering   Ethernet Conversion

Total FMS Project:
Cost: $5.0MM
Effort: 19.9 Man yrs.

Phase: I Computer Architecture Renewal
Cost: $1.4MM
Effort: 5.0 M/yrs.
Risk: • Data Centered Architecture w/Rdb
• Management of Rdb
• More Computer Horsepower $.5MM

age the project—a tool that connects each project person. There is a great deal of technical risk beyond the sheer size and complexity of the project. We have no experience with the relational database technology, which has to provide rapid and flexible access to great quantities of information. The other dimension of technical risk is the finite-forward-scheduling component—which has never been developed before. We will break the project into seven teams of 5–7 people from about five organizations—contract programming houses, Global Analysis, corporate Engineering and IS, Digital, and the Wilmington factory. As for my organization, I'll have to provide support for the project. At the same time, the plant must have other information needs met. Combine this with a major plant expansion and the plant at

capacity, and the difficulties inherent in the implementation become clear."

McAdoo picked up the appropriations request sitting on his desk to read through the body of the proposal. He knew he had to make a case to William Cunningham, manager of the entire Communications sector, to invest this much money on an information system. Furthermore, $5 million would require approval at the chairman level. Would changing the way information was managed at Wilmington convert a factory designed to produce standard products into a flexible manufacturing facility? Were there other, better, alternatives to FMS? McAdoo and his staff had considered the option that Corning not put any more money into waveguides. They had also looked for, but not found, some other way to fix the current problem. The

staff believed in FMS; after all, they had spent the last year in intensive analysis and design. But did they understand the industry forces, and did these forces require the type of strategy suggested by FMS? Finally, would the system work? How, given the ATLAS project delay and cost, could he recommend an information-systems project of this magnitude of this strategic importance?

McAdoo wanted to make sure his staff had thought through the issues carefully before he made a decision. Did his staff have answers to the myriad of important questions? Sighing, McAdoo got up and started the long walk to the meeting with his staff. He would then have the weekend to think things over, but on Monday he had to meet with Cunningham and make a recommendation on FMS.

FIGURE 4
Abstract from Appropriation Request

Background

This is the first information systems project of this scope and scale undertaken by the Communications sector. Extensive outside assistance is planned to conduct the project because of its size and technical complexity. After several months of review and negotiations, we selected the consulting firm of Global Analysis for their expertise in building manufacturing support systems and methodology for conducting Business Area Analysis. We are extremely satisfied with that decision.

Corning began the analysis with Global Analysis on October 4, 1989. The objectives of the study were to develop a data architecture to serve as the foundation for FMS and to define a planning and factory scheduling system for the manufacture of optical waveguides. This study was completed on plan, March 23, 1990, and serves as the basis for defining the requirements of the systems that are planned for construction under this Appropriation Request.

Request

The vision for Flexible Manufacturing Systems is that every product made on the factory floor can be traced to a customer requirement, production forecast, or specific order (inventory or customer). This contrasts with our present system, which does not have this capability. In the current system, products are not tracked until they reach inventory. All current production is made for inventory, not for customer orders. Tracking production and linking specific product with customer orders is currently done manually. The FMS project constructed to automate and enhance that capability consists of two major components:

1. Information systems for planning, scheduling, tracking, and fulfilling customer order requirements in the factory.
2. A major renewal of the plant information infrastructure to include the plant computer network, the computer architecture, and plant databases.

The project will run from the 1989 planning stage through completion in 1993. Personnel from Corning, Global Analysis, DEC, and other outside contractors will be engaged in all phases of the project. Global Analysis will receive between 30–40% of the funds. The project will take approximately 19.9 man years to complete.

Project Structure

The FMS project can be partitioned into five major phases:
I.   Computer Architecture Renewal
II.   Ware-in-Process Tracking
III.   Scheduling
IV.   Order Interface
V.   Cost Tracking

Each of the FMS phases consists of several projects that complete the implementation.

Phase I. Computer Architecture Renewal

To describe the computer architecture renewal, we have coined the term "Data Centered Architecture." This means an architecture for information management that is founded on the relationships between the fundamental elements of information that the business uses to operate (e.g., orders, products, processes, and equipment). These are key assets of the business and critical to operations. The Wilmington computer architecture is designed to serve the accessibility and accuracy of that asset. The new computer architecture will result in a data system that is highly accessible and places the key data assets under management to the benefit of all information-system users. The Data Centered Architecture will serve as a flexible information resource through an access structure that is known to all and accessible from any computer system in the Division.

In addition to a new design for the information system, there are three major technology components in the new architecture: (1) Digital Equipment Corporation's *RDB* database, which will manage the data, (2) Hardware Clustering, which allows direct access to the database by the plant manufacturing computers, and (3) Ethernet, which allows network access to the database by all business, process-control, and personal computers.

Phase II. Ware-in-Process Tracking

This phase consists of a system that links factory-floor machine events to the central database and provides user programs for data reporting and analysis. Individual orders, products, blanks, and fibers can be tracked in manufacturing, and process results can be analyzed quickly. The WIP Tracking phase will introduce the "Shop Order" into the factory as a tracking mechanism to link all products on the factory floor to a customer requirement. This information is not currently available. WIP Tracking also provides the shop-floor information required for the Scheduling and Cost Tracking phases of FMS.

Phase III. Scheduling

The scheduling system being developed for FMS takes into consideration three key attributes of the process of manufacturing optical waveguides. The manufacturing process produces a *distribution* of saleable optical fiber in terms of the performance capabilities of the product as opposed to discrete end products. In Waveguide manufacture, there is the capability to *substitute* fiber of one characteristic for another. A characteristic of fiber-optical performance is that a fiber of higher performance can be sold against a lesser requirement. Finally, the manufacturing process itself provides *variable* output.

The scheduling system is a finite-capacity-planning system. In conjunction with process results from the WIP Tracking system, it will characterize the process distribution using actual historical data and allow the planner to predict with a set degree of certainty what the process output will be. The historical record will be used as the basis of the capacity plan, and this will yield a daily schedule for manufacturing. The Shop Orders specified in the schedule will be checked regularly to compensate for any unexpected process variability. This systematic approach to scheduling will result in reduced lead times for orders and a method for creating reliable and predictable promises for fiber to the customer, which in turn can result in shorter quoted lead times.

Phase IV. Order Interface

The plant has an interface to the corporate business data system (ATLAS) for both the initiation of orders and the fulfillment of orders for shipping. The FMS Order Interface will allow the plant to act on an order requested by the customer by delivering the order to the planning and scheduling systems established by the Scheduling Phase. In addition to glass and coating, information on optical, strength, and length requirements plus any other special labeling, invoicing, packing, or handling requirements will be communicated and checked for each order. The Order Interface is a systematic method to insure the plant's ability to fill orders in an error-free manner. There is a risk associated with bridging the two systems together, but this is recognized and will be a major focus of systems maintenance.

Phase V. Cost Tracking

The Cost Tracking phase is primarily a reporting function that takes advantage of the Shop Order tracking mechanism and its linkage to actual machine hours recorded in the database by the WIP Tracking phase. Cost Tracking will allow cost information to be automatically loaded into the FACTS corporate financial system. Also, it is essential in determining the cost of developmental products and the cost of all products generated for government contracts.

Flexible Manufacturing Systems Diagram

Figure 3 identifies the Benefits, Cost, Time, Effort, Risk, and Technology of each phase of the project and the time, cost, and effort for the total project. It also portrays the fundamental nature of the Data Centered Architecture to all components of FMS.

Alternatives

There are alternatives to FMS. One is to maintain the status quo. However, the manual nature of our current planning and scheduling systems in the face of increasing product complexity does not meet the quality requirements that we have set for ourselves as an organization. Failure to select the correct fibers on a major order in 1989 made this clear. Another option is to build the new planning and scheduling systems without the information-systems renewal. This would result in a degree of benefit in plant scheduling but would not deliver the Lead-Time Reduction, Cost Tracking, or Accountability for Flexibility in adapting to new products and processes critical to the "make-to-order" business environment. Other options include increasing inventory or putting products on consignment at customer sites. Both of the options may significantly shorten lead times.

The business strategy that the Communications sector has put in place requires the Total Quality information systems that FMS delivers. A customer-order-based focus throughout the organization is fundamental to the ability to detect and exploit opportunities that are strategically targeted. FMS delivers the manufacturing practices and information systems that will enable that focus.

Energy, Impact, Environmental Control, and Raw-Material Statements

This project will result in no significant additional energy consumption, will not result in the need for any environmental control, and will not result in any additional raw-material requirements.

Corning Telecommunications Division (B): FMS Executive Summary

Background

As a world leader in the optical-fiber industry, the Corning Optical Waveguide Business has grown in recent years, both in volume and in the number of different products manufactured. Despite the technical complexity of fiber manufacturing, competitive pressure continues to require shorter lead times for product delivery.

The business computer systems in place at the Wilmington Plant have been developed over the past decade and, as in many high-growth industries, have generally been incrementally improved (as opposed to redesigned) in an attempt to keep pace with changes in the business. These systems are no longer capable of optimally providing the level and kind of support needed to facilitate Corning's continual plant expansions in the industry; therefore, a new systems capability is required. This capability has been named Flexible Manufacturing System (FMS).

The need for a new systems capability to support optical-fiber manufacturing at Wilmington is being driven by several factors, particularly:

- Market Demand for Shorter Lead Times
- Product Proliferation
- Current System Inflexibility
- Renewal of the Computer Architecture

The FMS project is a multi-year effort to provide enabling manufacturing systems for a high-volume, high-product-count, short-lead-time, "Make-to-Order" business environment. It involves the reconfiguration and integration of our plantwide computer network and data architecture and the implementation of new information systems. The FMS project goal is to allow the plant to manufacture directly to customer requirements. The intent is to provide the Optical Waveguide Business with the proper information support system for planning, scheduling, operations management, and control and to create a business system that is flexible enough to handle the rapidly changing aspects of the optical-fiber business.

Through FMS, the demand for shorter lead times will be fulfilled by a real-time order-promising capability at the factory and increased efficiency in manufacturing scheduling. The impact of product proliferation will be reduced by building information systems that utilize a common database to eliminate the redundant and complex data structure of the existing systems. The current system inflexibility is the motivation to implement a new integrated information system for the manufacturing operation.

Benefits

The functional requirements of FMS have been developed by building a comprehensive description of the business needs identified by members of the Communications sector in Business Management, Sales and Customer Service, Production Supervision, Process and Product Engineering, Advanced Fiber Products, Computer Services, Quality Engineering, and others. The benefits that FMS will deliver are based on the requirements of the overall organization.

The goal of FMS is to allow the plant to manufacture directly to customer requirements. When a customer orders a product through ATLAS, it will be promised using a real-time capacity model, scheduled in the factory by Planning and Production, visible to the Operator on the floor, and checked before it leaves the plant to the exact specification it received at order entry into the ATLAS system.

The primary benefits of the FMS system are listed in Exhibit 1. These benefits highlight the system's potential contribution to our:

- Flexibility to adapt to new products and production processes.
- On-demand information on orders, production and inventory.
- Cost tracking for orders, experiments and custom products.

FMS will address several areas of responsiveness that are imperative to the survival of the business. Our Sales/Customer Service organizations have seen that reduced lead time can be a competitive edge. Customers know our price and quality. Many orders are now sold on the ship-date commitment. The requirement to compete in this environment is unavoidable. FMS will increase responsiveness in quoting, promising and filling orders, decrease manufacturing processing time and allow more rapid new product and process introductions. Through FMS and new technology in processes and products, we can continue to expand the business by addressing niche markets and finding new fiber applications.

Our business strategy is to provide unparalleled value to our customers through Customer Service, Total Quality, and Low Cost. FMS's ability to reduce lead time is a Customer Service advantage that will prevent the loss of market share and potentially result in increased market share. FMS will enable Total Quality efforts to provide the organization with the data required to measure all aspects of manufacturing. Making the right product at the right time will result in manufacturing efficiency and reduced cost.

It is envisioned that portions of FMS could be installed in other manufacturing facilities. FMS has been designed to facilitate that opportunity. It views the output of each process step as an end product, so that it could be applied to a smaller manufacturing organization as well.

Corning Telecommunications Division (C): FMS Progress Report

Jim Reid, in charge of managing Corning's Flexible Manufacturing Systems Project, assessed the status of the project: "We now have 4 project teams instead of the original 7. With production at capacity and construction for expansion starting, we haven't been able to test modules as we've developed them. We are now focusing on some critical technical issues and the relational database is proving to be a real bear. It is supposed to function for 24 hours a day, 7 days a week. It is taking us longer to get the system to run efficiently from the database than we had thought. The relational technology takes too much time to do all the joins. With the CPU cranking away, it takes up to 20 minutes for screens to appear for ware-flow tracking. Our goal is a 10-second response time. Now we are looking at ways to recreate the database structure—to have less reliance on tables and logical joins and simply create permanent fields for information we know we will want. This isn't a show-stopper or even close, we just have to learn the technology and manage it better.

To our relief, we have a simulation completed for the finite-forward-scheduling module. We designed the module on a PC and then tested it with a month of real factory information. The calculations only took 40 minutes on the PC to schedule the entire factory, and it did it well. This was a new-invention area, and we're sailing through.

We also have developed a central repository on the Mac using database technology. This repository contains standards for screens, data definitions, code definitions, etc. As we develop a module, we put information about the module in the repository. All project teams have access to the repository, and we've been able to use about 80% of the modules we've designed for different parts of the overall system. Each project team gets all the information about naming files, fields, and designing screens from the repository. Our ability to coordinate and share knowledge is a real strong point.

Another problem had arisen when we discovered we couldn't buy a package for process manufacturing. It didn't work. We aren't tracking large batches in small numbers; we have thousands and thousands of batches of fiber running through. No package could handle it. Now we have to develop it from scratch. Most packages want to treat each fiber blank as a batch, but each fiber blank for us turns into many different fiber products for our customers. Our custom system will have to take into account this complexity, but we think we can handle it."

Tom LaGarde, manager of Information Systems at the Wilmington factory, commented on the progress thus far: "Jim [Reid] has been shorted some resources from my staff due to other expectations. Despite these difficulties, he has done a masterful job. Jim's development teams are moving at a pace faster than the organization can assimilate the new FMS technology. The plant is slowing Jim down. His resources are very expensive, so he has decided to spread the resources out over a longer period of time to better time his technical development efforts with our organizational learning capacity. There is also more and more attention being given to the plant expansion, and this slows Jim down. Jim is competing for resources with all these activities going on and has decided to develop FMS in a serial fashion rather than a parallel fashion—saving money for Corning and keeping pace with what parts of FMS can be adopted at the plant."

This case was prepared by Assistant Professor Andrew C. Boynton, Darden School, University of Virginia, and Ph.D. candidate Michael E. Shank, University of North Carolina, Chapel Hill. Copyright ©1991 by the Darden Graduate Business School Foundation, Charlottesville, Virginia.

Case Study Questions

1. Use the competitive forces and value chain models to analyze the Corning Telecommunications Division. What competitive forces did Corning have to deal with? What were the strategic advantages of switching to a flexible manufacturing system for optical waveguides?

2. What were the problems with Corning's existing manufacturing system for optical waveguides? How serious were they? What management, organization, and technology factors contributed to these problems?

3. What management, organization, and technology issues had to be addressed to implement a flexible manufacturing system successfully?

4. What were the dangers and risks of this project?

5. What criteria would you have used to determine whether Corning should invest in this project?

6. Should Corning have made the $5 million investment in the new flexible manufacturing system? Explain your answer. Analyze the status of the project.

Appendix A: Functional Information Systems

This appendix provides more detail on how organizations use information systems from a functional perspective. Information systems can be classified by the specific organizational function they serve as well as by organizational level. The major organizational functions consist of sales and marketing, manufacturing, finance, accounting, and human resources. We now describe typical information systems that support each of these functions, showing functional applications for each organizational level.

SALES AND MARKETING SYSTEMS

The sales and marketing function is responsible for selling the organization's product or service. Marketing is concerned with identifying the customers for the firm's products or services, determining what they need or want, planning and developing products and services to meet their needs, and advertising and promoting these products and services. Sales is concerned with contacting customers, selling the products and services, taking orders, and following up on sales.

Table A.1 shows that information systems are used in sales and marketing in a number of ways. At the strategic level, sales and marketing systems monitor trends affecting new products and sales opportunities, support planning for new products and services and monitor the performance of competitors. At the management level, sales and marketing systems support market research, advertising and promotional campaigns, and pricing decisions. They analyze sales performance and the performance of the sales staff. Knowledge-level sales and marketing systems support marketing analysis workstations. At the operational level, sales and marketing systems assist in locating and contacting prospective customers, tracking sales, processing orders, and providing customer service support.

A typical sales information system is one for recording sales using a point-of-sale device, which is illustrated in Figure A.1. A point-of-sale device captures data about

Table A.1   Examples of Sales and Marketing Information Systems

System	Description	Organization Level
Order Processing	Enter, process, and track orders	Operational
Point-of-Sale System	Record sales data	Operational
Sales Region Analysis	Analyze performance of sales territories	Management
Market Analysis	Identify customers and markets using data on demographics, markets, consumer behavior, and trends	Knowledge
Pricing Analysis	Determine prices for products and services	Management
Sales Trend Forecasting	Prepare 5-year sales forecasts	Strategic

each item sold at the time the sale takes place. For example, when a purchase is made at a Wal-Mart store, described in Chapter 2, point-of-sale terminals record the bar code of each item passing the checkout counter and send a purchase transaction directly to a central computer at Wal-Mart headquarters. The computer collects the sales data (which identify each item sold and the amount of the sale) and consolidates them for further management analysis. Wal-Mart managers examine these sales data to monitor sales activity and buying trends. The data are also used for placing orders to suppliers to replenish inventory of fast-selling goods. Figure A.1 illustrates how this point-of-sale system works.

MANUFACTURING AND PRODUCTION SYSTEMS

The manufacturing and production function is responsible for actually producing the firm's goods and services. Manufacturing and production systems deal with the planning, development, and maintenance of production facilities; the establishment of production goals; the acquisition, storage, and availability of production materials; and the scheduling of equipment, facilities, materials, and labor required to fashion finished products.

Table A.2 shows some typical manufacturing and production information systems arranged by organizational level. Strategic-level manufacturing systems deal with the firm's long-term manufacturing goals, such as where to locate new plants or whether to invest in new manufacturing technology. At the management level, manufacturing and production systems analyze and monitor manufacturing and production costs and resources. Knowledge manufacturing and production systems create and distribute design knowledge or expertise to drive the production process, and operational manufacturing and production systems deal with the status of production tasks.

Most manufacturing and production systems use some sort of inventory control system, illustrated in Figure A.2. Data about each item in inventory, such as the num-

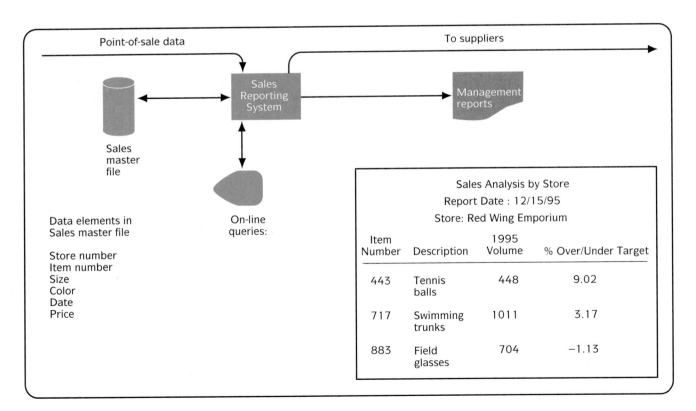

FIGURE A.1

Table A.2	Examples of Manufacturing and Production Information Systems	
System	Description	Organization Level
Plant Scheduling	Schedule the production of a product by coordinating jobs, labor, supplies, and finances	Operational
Material Movement Control	Track purchases, receipts, and shipments	Operational
Machine Control	Control the actions of machines and equipment	Operational
Computer-Aided Design (CAD)	Design new products	Knowledge
Production Planning	Decide when and how much products should be produced	Management
Inventory Control	Determine and maintain optimal level of stock for goods in process and finished goods	Management
Facilities Location	Decide where to locate new production facilities	Strategic

ber of units depleted because of a shipment or purchase or the number of units replenished by reordering or returns are either scanned or keyed into the system. The inventory master file contains basic data about each item—the unique identification code for each item, the description of the item, the number of units on hand, the number of units on order, and the reorder point—the number of units in inventory that triggers a decision to reorder in order to prevent a stockout. (Companies can estimate

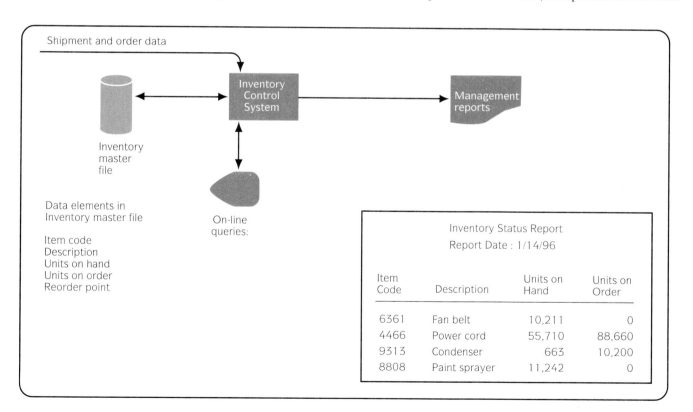

FIGURE A.2

the number of items to reorder or they can use a formula for calculating the least expensive quantity to order called the *economic order quantity*.) The system produces reports such as the number of each item available in inventory, the number of units of each item to reorder, or items in inventory that must be replenished.

Many firms are trying to create a seamless manufacturing process by integrating the various types of automated manufacturing systems using computers and communication technology. The data produced in one system are immediately available to be used by other systems. Leading-edge applications such as the computer-aided design/computer-aided manufacturing (CAD/CAM) system used by Odense Shipyards, which is described in the Window on Management in Chapter 1, are even using the data from computer-generated designs to drive the actual fabrication and assembly of products. Before computer-integrated manufacturing, design engineers had to draft plans on paper and then hand them over to experts in manufacturing. The product development cycle was prolonged because the process required so many manual steps and handoffs.

FINANCE AND ACCOUNTING SYSTEMS

The finance function is responsible for managing the firm's financial assets, such as cash, stocks, bonds, and other investments in order to maximize the return on these financial assets. The finance function is also in charge of managing the capitalization of the firm (finding new financial assets in stocks, bonds, or other forms of debt). In order to determine whether the firm is getting the best return on its investments, the finance function must obtain a considerable amount of information from sources external to the firm.

The accounting function is responsible for maintaining and managing the firm's financial records—receipts, disbursements, depreciation, payroll—to "account" for the flow of funds in a firm. Finance and accounting share related problems— how to keep track of a firm's financial assets and fund flows. They provide answers to questions such as: What is the current inventory of financial assets? What records exist for disbursements, receipts, payroll, and other fund flows?

Table A.3 shows some of the typical finance and accounting systems found in a typical large organization. Strategic-level systems for the finance and accounting function establish long-term investment goals for the firm and provide long-range forecasts of the firm's financial performance. At the management level, information systems help managers oversee and control the firm's financial resources. Knowledge systems

Table A.3	Examples of Finance and Accounting Information Systems	
System	**Description**	**Organization Level**
Payroll	Produce paychecks and maintain payroll records	Operational
Accounts Receivable	Track money owed the firm	Operational
Cash Management	Track firm's receipts and disbursements to determine funds available for investment	Operational
Portfolio Analysis	Design the firm's portfolio of investments	Knowledge
Budgeting	Prepare short-term budgets	Management
Capital Investment Analysis	Evaluate the profitability of long-term capital expenditures	Management
Profit Planning	Plan long-term profits	Strategic

support finance and accounting by providing analytical tools and workstations for designing the right mix of investments to maximize returns for the firm. Operational systems in finance and accounting track the flow of funds in the firm through transactions such as paychecks, payments to vendors, securities reports, and receipts.

A typical finance and accounting system found in all businesses is an accounts receivable system (see Figure A.3). An accounts receivable system keeps track of the money owed to the firm by its customers. Every customer purchase generates an "account receivable"—that is, the customer owes the firm money. Some customers pay immediately in cash, and others are granted credit. The accounts receivable system records the data from every invoice in a master file that also contains information on each customer, including credit rating. As the business goes on day after day, the system also keeps track of all the bills outstanding and can produce a variety of reports, both on paper and on computer screens, to help the business collect bills. The system also answers queries regarding a customer's payment history and credit rating. This system supplies information to the general ledger system, which tracks all cash flows of the firm.

HUMAN RESOURCES SYSTEMS

The human resources function is responsible for attracting, developing, and maintaining the firm's work force. Human resources identifies potential employees, maintains complete records on existing employees, and creates programs to develop employees' talents and skills.

Strategic-level human resources systems identify the manpower requirements (skills, educational level, types of positions, number of positions, and cost) for meeting the firm's long-term business plans. At the management level, human resources

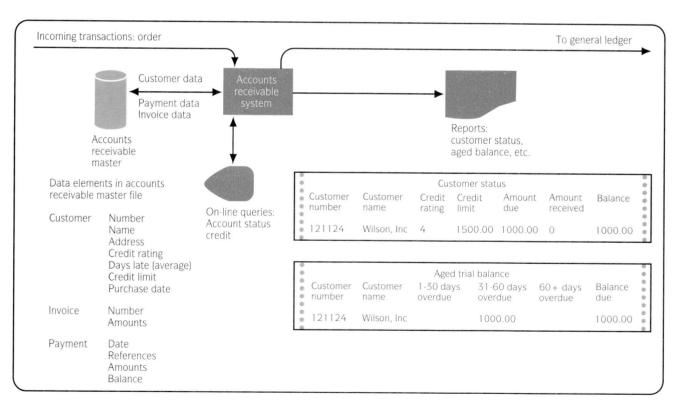

FIGURE A.3

Table A.4	Examples of Human Resources Information Systems	
System	Description	Organization Level
Employee Record keeping	Maintain records of employees	Operational
Training and Development	Track employee training, skills, and performance appraisals	Operational
Career Pathing	Design career paths for employees	Knowledge
Compensation Analysis	Analyze the range and distribution of employee wages, salaries, and benefits	Management
Contract Cost Analysis	Analyze the impact of projected changes in labor union contracts to the company's human resources costs	Management
Manpower Planning	Plan the long-term labor force needs of the organization	Strategic

systems help managers monitor and analyze the recruitment, allocation, and compensation of employees. Knowledge systems for human resources support analysis activities related to job design, training, and the modeling of employee career paths and reporting relationships. Human resources operational systems track the recruitment and placement of the firm's employees (see Table A.4).

Figure A. 4 illustrates a typical human resources system for employee record keeping. It maintains basic employee data, such as the employee's name, age, sex, marital status, address, educational background, salary, job title, date of hire, and date of termination. The system can produce a variety of reports, such as lists of newly hired employees, employees who are terminated or on leaves of absence, employees classified

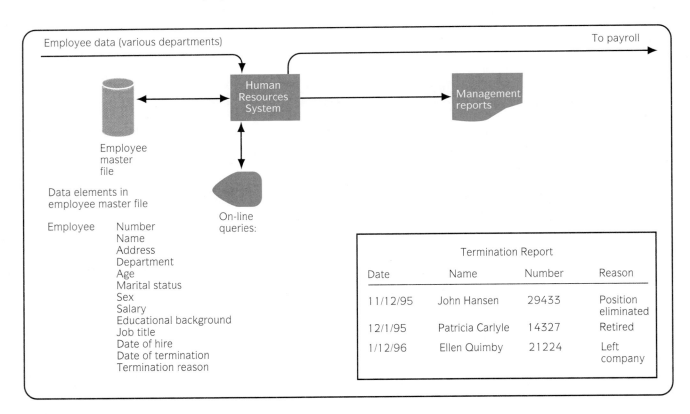

FIGURE A.4

by job type or educational level, or employee job performance evaluations. Such systems are typically designed to provide data that can satisfy federal and state record keeping requirements for Equal Employment Opportunity (EEO) and other purposes.

Glossary

Acceptance testing: Provides the final certification that the system is ready to be used in a production setting.

Accountability: The mechanisms for assessing responsibility for decisions made and actions taken.

Accounting rate of return on investment (ROI): Calculation of the rate of return from an investment by adjusting cash inflows produced by the investment for depreciation. Approximates the accounting income earned by the investment.

Ada: Programming language that is portable across different brands of hardware; is used for both military and nonmilitary applications.

Adhocracy: Task force organization, such as a research organization, designed to respond to a rapidly changing environment and characterized by large groups of specialists organized into short lived multi-disciplinary task forces.

Administrative controls: Formalized standards, rules, procedures, and disciplines to ensure that the organization's controls are properly executed and enforced.

Agency theory: Economic theory that views the firm as a nexus of contracts among self-interested individuals rather than a unified, profit-maximizing entity.

AI shell: The programming environment of an expert system.

Analog signal: A continuous wave form that passes through a communications medium. Used for voice communications.

Anti-virus software: Software designed to detect and often eliminate computer viruses from an information system.

Application controls: Specific controls unique to each computerized application.

Application generator: Software that can generate entire information system applications; the user needs only to specify what needs to be done and the application generator creates the appropriate program code.

Application software: Programs written for a specific business application in order to perform functions specified by end users.

Application software package: Set of prewritten, precoded, application software programs that are commercially available for sale or lease.

Applications portability: The ability to operate the same software on different hardware platforms.

Applications Portability Profile (APP): Standards for operating systems, database management, data interchange, programming languages, user interfaces, and networking to be enforced by U.S. federal government procurements in order to achieve connectivity.

Archie: A tool for locating data on the Internet that performs key word searches of an actual database of documents, software and data files available for downloading from servers around the world.

Arithmetic-logic unit (ALU): Component of the CPU that performs the principal logical and arithmetic operations of the computer.

Artificial intelligence: The effort to develop computer-based systems that can behave like humans, with the ability to learn languages, accomplish physical tasks, use a perceptual apparatus, and emulate human expertise and decision making.

ASCII: American Standard Code for Information Interchange. A 7- or 8-bit binary code used in data transmission, microcomputers, and some large computers.

Assembly language: A programming language developed in the 1950s that resembles machine language but substitutes mnemonics for numeric codes.

Asynchronous transfer mode (ATM): Networking technology that parcels information into 8-byte "cells," allowing data to be transmitted between computers of different vendors at any speed.

Asynchronous transmission: Low-speed transmission of one character at a time.

Attribute: Piece of information describing a particular entity.

Backward chaining: Strategy for searching the rule base in an expert system that acts like a problem solver by beginning with a hypothesis and seeking out more information until the hypothesis is either proved or disproved.

Bandwidth: The capacity of a communications channel as measured by the difference between the highest and lowest frequencies that can be transmitted by that channel.

Bar code: Form of OCR technology widely used in supermarkets and retail stores in which identification data are coded into a series of bars.

Baseband: LAN channel technology that provides a single path for transmitting text, graphics, voice, or video data at one time.

BASIC (Beginners All-purpose Symbolic Instruction Code): General-purpose programming language used with microcomputers and for teaching programming.

Batch control totals: A type of input control that requires counting transactions or any quantity field in a batch of transactions prior to processing for comparison and reconciliation after processing.

Batch processing: A method of processing information in which transactions are accumulated and stored until a specified time when it is convenient and/or necessary to process them as a group.

Baud: A change in signal from positive to negative or vice-versa that is used as a measure of transmission speed.

Behavioral models: Descriptions of management based on behavioral scientists' observations of what managers actually do in their jobs.

Bit: A binary digit representing the smallest unit of data in a computer system. It can only have one of two states, representing 0 or 1.

Bit mapping: The technology that allows each pixel on the screen to be addressed and manipulated by the computer.

Bottom-up approach: In the history of artificial intelligence, the effort to build a physical analog to the human brain.

Bounded rationality: Idea that people will avoid new uncertain alternatives and stick with tried-and-true rules and procedures.

Briefing books: On-line data in the form of fixed-format reports for executives.

Broadband: LAN channel technology that provides several paths for transmitting text, graphics, voice, or video data so that different types of data can be transmitted simultaneously.

Browser: A software tool that supports graphics and hyperlinks and is needed to navigate the Web.

Bugs: Program code defects or errors.

Bureaucracy: Formal organization with a clear-cut division of labor, abstract rules and procedures, and impartial decision making that uses technical qualifications and professionalism as a basis for promoting employees.

Bureaucratic models: Models of decision making where decisions are shaped by the organization's standard operating procedures (SOPs).

Business driver: A force in the environment to which businesses must respond and that influences the direction of business.

Business process: A set of logically related tasks performed to achieve a defined business outcome.

Business reengineering: The radical redesign of business processes, combining steps to cut waste and eliminating repetitive, paper-intensive tasks in order to improve cost, quality, and service, and to maximize the benefits of information technology.

Bus network: Network topology linking a number of computers by a single circuit with all messages broadcast to the entire network.

Byte: A string of bits, usually eight, used to store one number or character stored in a computer system.

C: Powerful programming language with tight control and efficiency of execution; is portable across different microprocessors and is used primarily with microcomputers.

Cache: High speed storage of frequently used instructions and data.

Capital budgeting: The process of analyzing and selecting various proposals for capital expenditures.

Carpal tunnel syndrome (CTS): Type of RSI in which pressure on the median nerve through the wrist's bony carpal tunnel produces pain.

Case-based reasoning (CBR): Artificial intelligence technology that represents knowledge as a database of cases.

CD-ROM: Compact disk read-only memory. Read-only optical disk storage used for imaging, reference, and database applications with massive amounts of data and for multimedia.

Cellular telephone: Device that transmits voice or data, using radio waves to communicate with radio antennas placed within adjacent geographic areas called cells.

Centralized processing: Processing that is accomplished by one large central computer.

Central processing unit (CPU): Area of the computer system that manipulates symbols, numbers, and letters and controls the other parts of the computer system.

Change agent: In the context of implementation, the individual acting as the catalyst during the change process to ensure successful organizational adaptation to a new system or innovation.

Channels: The links by which data or voice are transmitted between sending and receiving devices in a network.

Chatting: Live, interactive conversations over a public network.

Choice: Simon's third stage of decision making, when the individual selects among the various solution alternatives.

Class: Feature of object-oriented programming so that all objects belonging to a certain class have all of the features of that class.

Classical model of management: Traditional descriptions of management that focused on its formal functions of planning, organizing, coordinating, deciding, and controlling.

Client: The user point-of-entry for the required function. Normally a desktop computer, workstation, or laptop computer, the user generally interacts directly only with the client, typically through a graphical user interface, using it to input and retrieve data, and to analyze and report on them.

Client/server model: A model for computing that splits the processing between "clients" and "servers" on a network, assigning functions to the machine most able to perform the function.

Coaxial cable: Transmission medium consisting of thickly insulated copper wire. Can transmit large volumes of data quickly.

COBOL (COmmon Business Oriented Language): Predominant programming language for business applications because it can process large data files with alphanumeric characters.

Cognitive style: Underlying personality disposition toward the treatment of information, selection of alternatives, and evaluation of consequences.

Combinatorial explosion: In computer processing, the overload that results when trying to test more rules to reach a solution than the computer is capable of handling.

Competitive forces model: Model used to describe the interaction of external threats and opportunities that affect an organization's strategy and ability to compete.

Compiler: Special system software that translates a higher-level language into machine language for execution by the computer.

Compound document: Electronic document that consists of differing types of information acquired from separate sources such as graphics, database, spreadsheet, and text-based programs.

Computer abuse: The commission of acts involving a computer which may not be illegal but are considered unethical.

Computer-aided design (CAD): Information system that automates the creation and revision of designs using sophisticated graphics software.

Computer-aided software engineering (CASE): The automation of step-by-step methodologies for software and systems development to reduce the amount of repetitive work the developer needs to do.

Computer-based information systems (CBIS): Information systems that rely on computer hardware and software for processing and disseminating information.

Computer crime: The commission of illegal acts through the use of a computer or against a computer system.

Computer generations: Major transitions in computer hardware; each generation is distinguished by a different technology for the components that do the processing.

Computer hardware: Physical equipment used for input, processing, and output work in an information system.

Computer matching: Processing control that matches input data to information held on master files.

Computer mouse: Hand-held input device whose movement on the desktop controls the position of the cursor on the computer display screen.

Computer operations controls: Procedures to ensure that programmed procedures are consistently and correctly applied to data storage and processing.

Computer software: Detailed preprogrammed instructions that coordinate computer hardware components in an information system.

Computer virus: Rogue software programs that are difficult to detect and spread rapidly through computer systems, destroying data or disrupting processing and memory systems.

Computer vision syndrome (CVS): Eye strain condition related to cathode ray tube (CRT) use, with symptoms including headaches, blurred vision, and dry, irritated eyes.

Concentrator: Telecommunications computer that collects and temporarily stores messages from terminals for batch transmission to the host computer.

Connectivity: A measure of how well computers and computer-based devices communicate and share information with one another without human intervention.

Connectivity audit: A method for examining amount of connectivity an organization has by examining five areas of connectivity such as network standards, user interfaces and applications.

Context diagram: Overview data flow diagram depicting an entire system as a single process with its major inputs and outputs.

Control aids: Capabilities that allow the user to control the activities and functions of the DSS.

Controller: Specialized computer that supervises communications traffic between the CPU and the peripheral devices in a telecommunications system.

Controls: All of the methods, policies, and procedures that ensure protection of the organization's assets, accuracy and reliability of its records, and operational adherence to management standards.

Control unit: Component of the CPU that controls and coordinates the other parts of the computer system.

Conversion: The process of changing from the old system to the new system.

Conversion plan: Provides a schedule of all activities required to install a new system.

Cooptation: Bringing the opposition into the process of designing and implementing the solution without giving up control over the direction and nature of the change.

Copyright: A statutory grant which protects creators of intellectual property against copying by others for any purpose for a period of 28 years.

Core systems: Systems that support functions that are absolutely critical to the organization.

Cost-benefit ratio: A method for calculating the returns from a capital expenditure by dividing the total benefits by total costs.

Counterimplementation: A deliberate strategy to thwart the implementation of an information system or an innovation in an organization.

Critical success factors (CSFs): A small number of easily identifiable operational goals shaped by the industry, the firm, the manager, and the broader environment that are believed to assure the success of an organization. Used to determine the information requirements of an organization.

Cultural theory: Behavioral theory stating that information technology must fit into an organization's culture or the technology won't be adopted.

Customization: The modification of a software package to meet an organization's unique requirements without destroying the integrity of the package software.

Cylinder: Represents circular tracks on the same vertical line within a disk pack.

Data: Streams of raw facts representing events occurring in organizations or the physical environment before they have been organized and arranged into a form that people can understand and use.

Data administration: A special organizational function for managing the organization's data resources, concerned with data planning, information policy, maintenance of data dictionaries, and data quality standards.

Database: Collection of data organized to service many applications at the same time by organizing data so that they appear to be in one location.

Database administration: Refers to the more technical and operational aspects of managing data, including physical database design and operation.

Database management system (DBMS): Special software to create and maintain a database and enable individual business applications to extract the data they need without having to create separate files or data definitions in their computer programs.

Data bus width: The number of bits that can be moved at one time between the CPU, primary storage, and the other devices of a computer.

Dataconferencing: Teleconferencing in which two or more users are able to edit and directly modify data files simultaneously.

Data conversion: Process of properly transcribing data from one form into another form for computer transactions.

Data definition language: The component of a database management system that defines each data element as it appears in the database.

Data dictionary: An automated or manual tool for storing and organizing information about the data maintained in a database.

Data element: A field.

Data flow diagram (DFD): Primary tool in structured analysis that graphically illustrates the system's component processes and the flow of data between them.

Data flows: The movement of data between processes, external entities, and data stores in a data flow diagram.

Data management software: Software used for creating and manipulating lists, creating files and databases to store data, and combining information for reports.

Data manipulation language: A language associated with a database management system that is employed by end users and programmers to manipulate data in the database.

Data quality audit: Survey of files and samples of files for accuracy and completeness of data in an information system.

Data redundancy: The presence of duplicate data in multiple data files.

Data security controls: Controls to ensure that data files on either disk or tape are not subject to unauthorized access, change, or destruction.

Data stores: Manual or automated inventories of data.

Data workers: People such as secretaries or bookkeepers who process and disseminate the organization's paperwork.

Debugging: The process of discovering and eliminating the errors and defects— the bugs— in program code.

Decisional roles: Mintzberg's classification for managerial roles where managers initiate activities, handle disturbances, allocate resources, and negotiate conflicts.

Decision and control theory: Behavioral theory stating that the function of the organization is to make decisions under conditions of uncertainty and risk and that organizations centralize decision making and create a hierarchy of decision making to reduce uncertainty and to ensure survival.

Decision-support systems (DSS): Computer systems at the management level of an organization that combine data and sophisticated analytical models to support semistructured and unstructured decision making.

Decision table: A graphic in the form of a table that portrays the conditions that affect a decision; used for documenting situations in which the decision process is highly structured.

Decision trees: Sequential tree-like diagrams that present the conditions affecting a decision and the actions that can be taken. The branches represent the paths that may be taken in the decision-making process.

Dedicated lines: Telephone lines that are continuously available for transmission by a lessee. Typically conditioned to transmit data at high speeds for high-volume applications.

Descartes' rule of change: A principle that states that if an action cannot be taken repeatedly, then it is not right to be taken at any time.

Design: Simon's second stage of decision making, when the individual conceives of possible alternative solutions to a problem.

Design: Stage in the systems life cycle that produces the logical and physical design specifications for the systems solution.

Desktop publishing: Technology that produces professional-quality documents combining output from word processors with design, graphics, and special layout features.

Development methodology: A collection of methods, one or more for every activity within every phase of a development project.

Digital image processing: Technology that converts documents and graphic images into computerized form so that they can be stored, processed, and accessed by computer systems.

Digital scanners: Input devices that translate images such as pictures or documents into digital form for processing.

Digital signal: A discrete wave form that transmits data coded into two discrete states as 1-bits and 0-bits, which are represented as on-off electrical impulses. Used for data communications.

Direct access storage device (DASD): Refers to magnetic disk technology which permits the CPU to locate a record directly, in contrast to sequential tape storage that must search the entire file.

Direct cutover: A risky conversion approach where the new system completely replaces the old one on an appointed day.

Direct file access method: Method of accessing records by mathematically transforming the key fields into the specific address for the records.

Direct file organization: Method of storing records so that they can be accessed in any sequence without regard to their actual physical order on storage media.

Distributed database: A database that is stored in more than one physical location. Parts or copies of the database are physically stored in one location and other parts are stored and maintained in other locations.

Distributed processing: The distribution of computer processing work among multiple computers linked by a communication network.

Divisionalized bureaucracy: Combination of many machine bureaucracies, each producing a different product or service, under one central headquarters.

Documentation: Descriptions of how an information system works from either a technical or end-user standpoint.

Document imaging systems: Systems that employ digital image processing to store, retrieve, and manipulate a digitized image of a document, allowing the document itself to be discarded.

Domestic exporter: Global strategy characterized by heavy centralization of corporate activities in the home country of origin.

DOS: Operating system for 16-bit microcomputers based on the IBM Personal Computer standard.

Downsizing: The process of transferring applications from large computers to smaller ones.

Downtime: Periods of time in which an information system is not operational.

Drill down: The ability to move from summary data down to lower and lower levels of detail.

DSS database: A collection of current or historical data from a number of applications or groups.

DSS software system: DSS component that permits easy interaction between the users of the system and the DSS database and model base.

EBCDIC: Extended Binary Coded Decimal Interchange Code. Binary code representing every number, alphabetic character, or special character with 8 bits, used primarily in IBM and other mainframe computers.

Economic feasibility: Determines whether the benefits of the proposed solution outweigh the costs.

Edit checks: Routines performed to verify input data and correct errors prior to processing.

Electronic calendaring: Software that tracks appointments and schedules in an office.

Electronic data interchange (EDI): Direct computer-to-computer exchange between two organizations of standard business transaction documents.

Electronic mail: The computer-to-computer exchange of messages.

Electronic market: A marketplace that is created by computer and communication technologies which link many buyers and sellers via interorganizational systems.

Electronic meeting software: Software designed to enhance the productivity of face-to-face meetings or of meetings among participants in scattered locations.

Electronic meeting system (EMS): Collaborative GDSS that uses information technology to make group meetings more productive by facilitating communication as well as decision making. Supports meetings at the same place and time or in different places and times.

End user: Representative of a department outside of the information systems group for whom information systems applications are developed.

End-user development: The development of information systems by end users with little or no formal assistance from technical specialists.

End-user interface: The part of the information system through which the end user interacts with the system, such as on-line screens and commands.

End-user software: Software tools that permit the development of applications by end users with little or no professional programmer intervention or that enhance the productivity of professional programmers.

Enterprise analysis: An analysis of organization-wide information requirements by looking at the entire organization in terms of organizational units, functions, processes, and data elements; helps identify the key entities and attributes in the organization's data.

Enterprise-wide computing: An arrangement of the organization's hardware, software, telecommunications, and data resources to put more computing power on the desktop and create a companywide network linking many smaller networks.

Entity: A person, place, or thing about which information must be kept.

Entity-relationship diagram: Methodology for documenting databases illustrating the relationship between various entities in the database.

Entrepreneurial structure: Young, small firm in a fast-changing environment dominated by a single entrepreneur and managed by a single chief executive officer.

Environmental factors: Factors external to the organization that influence the adoption and design of information systems.

EPROM: Erasable programmable read-only memory. Subclass of ROM chip that can be erased and reprogrammed many times.

Ergonomics: The interaction of people and machines in the work environment, including the design of jobs, health issues, and the end-user interface of information systems.

Ethical no free lunch rule: Assumption that all tangible and intangible objects are owned by someone else unless there is a specific declaration otherwise and that the creator wants compensation for his work.

Ethics: Principles of right and wrong that can be used by individuals acting as free moral agents to make choices to guide their behavior.

Executive support systems (ESS): Information systems at the strategic level of an organization designed to address unstructured decision making through advanced graphics and communications.

Expert system: Knowledge-intensive computer program that captures the expertise of a human in limited domains of knowledge.

External entities: Originators or receivers of information outside the scope of the system portrayed in the data flow diagram. Sometimes called *outside interfaces*.

External integration tools: Project management technique that links the work of the implementation team to that of users at all organizational levels.

Facsimile (FAX): Machine that digitizes and transmits documents with both text and graphics over telephone lines.

Fair Information Practices (FIP): A set of principles originally set forth in 1973 that governs the collection and use of information about individuals and forms the basis of most U.S. and European privacy law.

Fault-tolerant computer systems: Systems that contain extra hardware, software and power supply components that can back the system up and keep it running to prevent system failure.

Feasibility study: A way to determine whether a solution is achievable, given the organization's resources and constraints.

Feedback: Output that is returned to the appropriate members of the organization to help them evaluate or correct input.

Fiber optic cable: Fast, light, and durable transmission medium consisting of thin strands of clear glass fiber bound into cables. Data are transmitted as light pulses.

Field: A grouping of characters into a word, group of words, or complete number.

File: A group of records of the same type.

File server: Computer in a network that stores various programs and data files for users of the network. Determines access and availability in the network.

Floppy disk: Removable magnetic disk primarily used with microcomputers. The two most common standard sizes are 3.5-inch and 5.25-inch disks that are made up of polyester film with magnetic coating.

Focused differentiation: Competitive strategy for developing new market niches where a business can compete in the target area better than its competitors.

Formal control tools: Project management technique that helps monitor the progress toward completion of a task and fulfillment of goals.

Formal planning tools: Project management technique that structures and sequences tasks, budgeting time, money, and technical resources required to complete the tasks.

FORTRAN (FORmula TRANslator): Programming language developed in 1956 for scientific and mathematical applications.

Forward chaining: Strategy for searching the rule base in an expert system that begins with the information entered by the user and searches the rule base to arrive at a conclusion.

Forward engineering: The final step in re-engineering when the revised specifications are used to generate new, structured program code for a structured and maintainable system.

Fourth-generation language: A programming language that can be employed directly by end users or less skilled programmers to develop computer applications more rapidly than conventional programming languages.

Frame relay: Shared network service technology that packages data into bundles for transmission but does not use error correction routines. Cheaper and faster than packet switching.

Frames: Method of organizing expert system knowledge into chunks, but the relationships are based on shared characteristics determined by the user rather than a hierarchy.

Franchiser: Firm where the product is created, designed, financed, and initially produced in the home country, but must rely heavily on foreign personnel for further production, marketing, and human resources.

Front-end processor: Small computer managing communications for the host computer in a network.

Fuzzy logic: Rule-based AI that tolerates imprecision by using non-specific terms called membership functions to solve problems.

Garbage can model: Model of decision making that states that organizations are not rational and that decisions are

solutions that become attached to problems for accidental reasons.

Gateway: Communications processor that connects dissimilar networks by providing the translation from one protocol to another.

General controls: Overall controls that establish a framework for controlling the design, security, and use of computer systems throughout an organization.

Genetic algorithms: Problem-solving methods that promote the evolution of solutions to specified problems using the model of living organizisms adapting to their environment.

Gigabyte: Approximately one billion bytes. Unit of computer storage capacity.

Global culture: The development of common expectations, shared artifacts, and social norms among different cultures and peoples.

Gopher: A character-oriented tool for locating data on the Internet that enables the user to locate essentially all textual information stored on Internet servers through a series of easy-to-use, hierarchical menus.

Graphical user interface: The part of an operating system that users interact with that uses graphic icons and the computer mouse to issue commands and make selections.

Graphics language: A computer language that displays data from files or databases in graphic format.

Group decision-support system (GDSS): An interactive computer-based system to facilitate the solutions to unstructured problems by a set of decision makers working together as a group.

Groupware: Software that recognizes the significance of groups in offices by providing functions and services that support the collaborative activities of work groups.

Hacker: A person who gains unauthorized access to a computer network for profit, criminal mischief, or personal pleasure.

Hard disk: Magnetic disk resembling a thin steel platter with an iron oxide coating; used in large computer systems and in many microcomputers.

Hardware controls: Controls to ensure the physical security and correct performance of computer hardware.

Hierarchical data model: One type of logical database model that organizes data in a treelike structure. A record is subdivided into segments that are connected to each other in one-to-many parent-child relationships.

High-level language: Programming languages where each source code statement generates multiple statements at the machine-language level.

Home page: A World Wide Web text and graphical screen display that welcomes the user and explains the organization that has established the page.

Hypermedia database: Approach to data management that organizes data as a network of nodes linked in any pattern established by the user.

Immanuel Kant's Categorical Imperative: A principle that states that if an action is not right for everyone to take it is not right for anyone.

Implementation: Simon's final stage of decision making, when the individual puts the decision into effect and reports on the progress of the solution.

Implementation: All of the organizational activities working toward the adoption, management, and routinization of an innovation.

Implementation controls: Audit of the systems development process at various points to make sure that it is properly controlled and managed.

Incremental decision making: Choosing policies most like the previous policy.

Index: A table or list that relates record keys to physical locations on direct access files.

Indexed sequential access method (ISAM): File access method to directly access records organized sequentially using an index of key fields.

Index server: In imaging systems, a device that stores the indexes that allow a user to identify and retrieve a specific document.

Inference engine: The strategy used to search through the rule base in an expert system: can be forward or backward chaining.

Information: Data that have been shaped into a form that is meaningful and useful to human beings.

Informational roles: Mintzberg's classification for managerial roles where managers act as the nerve centers of their organizations, receiving and disseminating critical information.

Information architecture: The particular form that information technology takes in a specific organization to achieve selected goals or functions.

Information center: A special facility within an organization that provides training and support for end-user computing.

Information partnership: Cooperative alliance formed between two corporations for the purpose of sharing information to gain strategic advantage.

Information policy: Formal rules governing the maintenance, distribution, and use of information in an organization.

Information portability: The sharing of computer files among different hardware platforms and software applications.

Information requirements: A detailed statement of the information needs that a new system must satisfy; identifies who needs what information, and when, where, and how the information is needed.

Information rights: The rights that individuals and organizations have with respect to information which pertains to themselves.

Information superhighway: High-speed digital telecommunications networks that are national or worldwide in scope and accessible by the general public rather than restricted to use by members of a specific organization or set of organizations such as a corporation.

Information system: Interrelated components that collect, process, store, and disseminate information to support decision making, control, analysis, and visualization in an organization.

Information systems department: The formal organizational unit that is responsible for the information systems function in the organization.

Information systems managers: Leaders of the various specialists in the information systems department.

Information systems plan: A road map indicating the direction of systems development, the rationale, the current situation, the management strategy, the implementation plan, and the budget.

Information work: Work that primarily consists of creating or processing information.

Information workers: People in the labor force who primarily create, work with, or disseminate information.

Inheritance: Feature of object-oriented programming in which a specific class of objects receives the features of a more general class.

Input: The capture or collection of raw data from within the organization or from its external environment for processing in an information system.

Input authorization: Proper authorization, recording, and monitoring of source documents as they enter the computer system.

Input controls: Procedures to check data for accuracy and completeness when they enter the system, including input authorization, batch control totals, and edits.

Installation: Systems life cycle stage consisting of testing, training, and conversion; the final steps required to put a system into operation.

Institutional factors: Factors internal to the organization that influence the adoption and design of information systems.

Intangible benefits: Benefits that are not easily quantified; they include more efficient customer service or enhanced decision making.

Integrated Services Digital Network (ISDN): International standard for transmitting voice, video, and data to support a wide range of service over the public telephone lines.

Integrated software package: A software package that provides two or more applications, such as spreadsheets and word processing, providing for easy transfer of data between them.

Intellectual property: Intangible property created by individuals or corporations which is subject to protections under trade secret, copyright, and patent law.

Intelligence: The first of Simon's four stages of decision making, when the individual collects information to identify problems occurring in the organization.

Interaction theory: User-resistance theory stating that resistance is caused by the interaction of people and systems factors.

Internal integration tools: Project management technique that ensures that the implementation team operates as a cohesive unit.

Internal rate of return (IRR): The rate of return or profit that an investment is expected to earn.

International information systems infrastructure: The basic information systems required by organizations to coordinate world-wide trade and other activities.

Internet: An international network of networks connecting over 20 million people from 100 countries; it is the largest "information superhighway" in the world.

Internetworking: The linking of separate networks, each of which retains its own identity, into an interconnected network.

Interoperability: The ability of a software application to operate on two different machine platforms while maintaining the identical user interface and functionality.

Interorganizational systems: Information systems that automate the flow of information across organizational boundaries and link a company to its customers, distributors, or suppliers.

Interpersonal roles: Mintzberg's classification for managerial roles where managers act as figureheads and leaders for the organization.

Interpreter: A special language translator that translates each source code statement into machine code and executes it one at a time.

Intuitive decision makers: Cognitive style that describes people who approach a problem with multiple methods in an unstructured manner, using trial and error to find a solution.

Iteration construct: The logic pattern in programming where certain actions are repeated while a specified condition occurs or until a certain condition is met.

Iterative: Process of repeating the steps to build a system over and over again.

Joint application design (JAD): A design method which brings users and IS professionals into a room together for an interactive design of the system.

Jukebox: A device for storing and retrieving many optical disks.

Key field: A field in a record that uniquely identifies instances of that record so that it can be retrieved or updated.

Kilobyte: One thousand bytes (actually 1024 storage positions). Used as a measure of microcomputer storage capacity.

Knowledge and information-intense products: Products that require a great deal of learning and knowledge to produce.

Knowledge base: Model of human knowledge that is used by expert systems.

Knowledge engineer: Specialist who elicits information and expertise from other professionals and translates it into a set of rules, frames, or semantic nets for an expert system.

Knowledge-level decision making: Evaluating new ideas for products and services, ways to communicate new knowledge and distribute information.

Knowledge-level systems: Information systems that support knowledge and data workers in an organization.

Knowledge workers: People such as engineers, scientists, or architects who design products or services or create new knowledge for the organization.

Knowledge work systems (KWS): Information systems that aid knowledge workers in the creation and integration of new knowledge in the organization.

Legitimacy: The extent to which one's authority is accepted on grounds of competence, vision, or other qualities.

Liability: The existence of laws that permit individuals to recover the damages done to them by other actors, systems, or organizations.

Local area network (LAN): Tele-communications network that requires its own dedicated channels and that encompasses a limited distance, usually one building or several buildings in close proximity.

Logical design: Lays out the components of the information system and their relationship to each other as they would appear to users.

Logical view: Representation of data as they would appear to an application programmer or end user.

Low-orbit satellites: Satellites that travel much closer to the earth than traditional satellites and so are able to pick up signals from weak transmitters while consuming less power.

Machine bureaucracy: Large bureaucracy organized into functional divisions that centralizes decision making, produces standard products, and exists in a slow-changing environment.

Machine cycle: Series of operations required to process a single machine instruction.

Machine language: Programming language consisting of the 1s and 0s of binary code.

Magnetic disk: A secondary storage medium in which data are stored by means of magnetized spots on a hard or floppy disk.

Magnetic ink character recognition (MICR): Input technology that translates characters written in magnetic ink into digital codes for processing.

Magnetic tape: Inexpensive and relatively stable secondary storage medium in which large volumes of information are stored sequentially by means of magnetized and nonmagnetized spots on tape.

Magneto-optical disk: Optical disk system that is erasable. Data are recorded by a high-powered laser beam that heats tiny spots in the magnetic media.

Mainframe: Largest category of computer, classified as having 50 megabytes to over 1 gigabyte of RAM.

Maintenance: Changes in hardware, software, documentation, or procedures to a production system to correct errors, meet new requirements, or improve processing efficiency.

Management control: Monitors how efficiently or effectively resources are utilized and how well operational units are performing.

Management information systems (MIS): Computer systems at the management level of an organization that serve the functions of planning, controlling, and decision making by providing routine summary and exception reports.

Management-level systems: Information systems that support the monitoring, controlling, decision-making, and administrative activities of middle managers.

Managerial roles: Expectations of the activities that managers should perform in an organization.

Man-month: The traditional unit of measurement used by systems designers to estimate the length of time to complete a project. Refers to the amount of work a person can be expected to complete in a month.

Master file: Contains all permanent information and is updated during processing by transaction data.

Megabyte: Approximately one million bytes. Unit of computer storage capacity.

Megahertz: A measure of cycle speed, or the pacing of events in a computer; one megahertz equals one million cycles per second.

Memory aids: In DSS, capabilities to update and refresh memory, including databases, views of data, work spaces, and libraries.

Microcomputer: Desktop or portable computer with 640 kilobytes to 64 megabytes of RAM.

Microeconomic model: Model of the firm that views information technology as a factor of production that can be freely substituted for capital and labor.

Microprocessor: Very large-scale integrated circuit technology that integrates the computer's memory, logic, and control on a single chip.

Microsecond: One millionth of a second.

Microwave: High-volume, long-distance, point-to-point transmission in which high-frequency radio signals are transmitted through the atmosphere from one terrestrial transmission station to another.

Middle managers: People in the middle of the organizational hierarchy who are responsible for carrying out the plans and goals of senior management.

Migration: The ability to move software from one generation of hardware to another more powerful generation.

Millisecond: One thousandth of a second.

Minicomputer: Middle-range computer with about 10 megabytes to over 1 gigabyte of RAM.

MIS audit: Identifies all the controls that govern individual information systems and assesses their effectiveness.

Mobile data networks: Wireless networks that enable two-way transmission of data files cheaply and efficiently.

Model: An abstract representation that illustrates the components or relationships of a phenomenon.

Model base: A collection of mathematical and analytical models that can easily be made accessible to the DSS user.

Modem: Device for translating digital signals into analog signals and vice-versa.

Module: A logical unit of a program that performs one or a small number of functions.

Muddling through: Method of decision making involving successive limited comparisons where the test of a good decision is whether people agree on it.

Multimedia: Technologies that facilitate the integration of two or more types of media such as text, graphics, sound, voice, full-motion video, or animation into a computer-based application.

Multinational: Global strategy that concentrates financial management and control out of a central home base while decentralizing production, sales, and marketing operations to units in other countries.

Multiplexer: Device that enables a single communications channel to carry data transmissions from multiple sources simultaneously.

Multiprocessing: An operating system feature for executing two or more instructions simultaneously in a single computer system by using more than one central processing unit.

Multiprogramming: A method of executing two or more programs concurrently using the same computer. The CPU only executes one program but can service the input/output needs of others at the same time.

Multitasking: The multiprogramming capability of primarily single-user operating systems such as those for microcomputers.

Nanosecond: One billionth of a second.

Negligence: Finding of fault when a producer's product causes physical or economic harm to individuals that could and should have been prevented.

Net present value: The amount of money an investment is worth, taking into account its cost, earnings, and the time value of money.

Network data model: A logical database model that is useful for depicting many-to-many relationships.

Network operating system: Special software that manages the file server in a LAN and routes and manages communications on the network.

Network topology: The shape or arrangement of a network.

Neural network: Hardware or software that attempts to emulate the processing patterns of the biological brain.

New information architecture: An arrangement of the organization's hardware, software, telecommunications, and data resources to put more computing power on the desktop and create a companywide network linking many smaller networks.

Node: Each of the devices in a network.

Normalization: The process of creating small stable data structures from complex groups of data when designing a relational database.

Object code: Program instructions that have been translated into machine language so that they can be executed by the computer.

Object-oriented database: Approach to data management that stores both data and the procedures acting on the data as objects that can be automatically retrieved and shared.

Object-oriented programming: Approach to software development that combines data and procedures into a single object.

Object-oriented software development: Approach to software development that de-emphasizes procedures and shifts the focus from modeling business processes and data to combining data and procedures to create objects.

Office activities: The principal activities performed at offices; these include managing documents, scheduling and communicating with people, managing data, and managing projects.

Office automation systems (OAS): Computer systems, such as word processing, voice-mail systems, and video-conferencing systems, that are designed to increase the productivity of information workers in the office.

On-line processing: A method of processing information in which transactions are entered directly into the computer system and processed immediately.

On-line transaction processing: Transaction processing mode in which transactions entered on-line are immediately processed by the computer.

Open systems: Software systems that can operate on different hardware platforms because they are built on public non-proprietary operating systems, user interfaces, application standards, and networking protocols.

Open Systems Interconnect (OSI): International reference model for linking different types of computers and networks.

Operating system: The system software that manages and controls the activities of the computer.

Operational control: Deciding how to carry out tasks specified by upper and middle management and establishing criteria for completion and resource utilization.

Operational feasibility: Determines whether the proposed solution is desirable within the existing managerial and organizational framework.

Operational-level systems: Information systems that monitor the elementary activities and transactions of the organization.

Operational managers: People who monitor the day-to-day activities of the organization.

Operations: In DSS, logical and mathematical manipulations of data.

Optical character recognition (OCR): Form of source data automation in which optical scanning devices read specially designed data and translate the data into digital form for the computer.

Optical disk: Secondary storage device on which data are recorded and read by laser beams rather than by magnetic means.

Organization (behavioral definition): A collection of rights, privileges, obligations, and responsibilities that are delicately balanced over a period of time through conflict and conflict resolution.

Organization (technical definition): A stable formal social structure that takes resources from the environment and processes them to produce outputs.

Organizational culture: The set of fundamental assumptions about what products the organization should produce, how and where it should produce them, and for whom they should be produced.

Organizational impact analysis: Study of the way a proposed system will affect organizational structure, attitudes, decision making, and operations.

Organizational models: Models of decision making that take into account the structural and political characteristics of an organization.

OS/2: Powerful operating system used with the 32-bit IBM/Personal System/2 microcomputer workstations that supports multitasking, networking, and more memory-intensive applications than DOS.

Output controls: Ensure that the results of computer processing are accurate, complete, and properly distributed.

Outsourcing: The practice of contracting computer center operations, telecommunications networks, or applications development to external vendors.

Packet switching: Technology that breaks blocks of text into small fixed bundles of data and routes them in the most economical way through any available communications channel.

Page: Small section of a program, which can be easily stored in primary storage and quickly accessed from secondary storage.

Paging system: A wireless transmission technology in which the pager beeps when the user receives a message; used to transmit short alphanumeric messages.

Parallel processing: Type of processing in which more than one instruction can be processed at a time by breaking down a problem into smaller parts and processing them simultaneously with multiple processors.

Parallel sensor system: A machine consisting of many nodes that each act as a processor feeding information to a hierarchy of higher-level nodes.

Parallel strategy: Conservative conversion approach where both the old system and its replacement are run together until everyone is assured that the new one functions correctly.

Parity: An extra bit built into the EBCDIC and ASCII codes used as a check bit to ensure accuracy.

Particularism: Making judgements and taking actions on the basis of narrow or personal characteristics.

Pascal: Programming language used on microcomputers and to teach sound programming practices in computer science courses.

Patent: A legal document that grants the owner an exclusive monopoly on the ideas behind an invention for 17 years; designed to ensure that the inventors of new machines or methods are rewarded for their labor while making widespread use of their inventions.

Payback method: A measure of the time required to pay back the initial investment of a project.

Pen-based input: Input devices such as tablets, notebooks, and notepads consisting of a flat-screen display tablet and a pen-like stylus that digitizes handwriting.

People-oriented theory: User-resistance theory focusing on factors internal to users.

Personal communication services (PCS): A new wireless cellular technology that uses lower-power, higher-frequency radio waves than does cellular technology and so can be used with smaller-sized telephones inside buildings and tunnels.

Personal digital assistants: Small, pen-based, hand-held computers with built-in wireless telecommunications capable of entirely digital transmission.

Personal information manager: Packaged database tool designed to support specific office data management tasks for an information worker.

Phased approach: Introduces the new system in stages either by functions or by organizational units.

Physical design: The process of translating the abstract logical model into the specific technical design for the new system.

Physical view: The representation of data as they would be actually organized on physical storage media.

Pilot study: A strategy to introduce the new system to a limited area of the organization until it is proven to be fully functional.

Pixel: The smallest unit of data for defining an image in the computer. The computer reduces a picture to a grid of pixels. The term *pixel* comes from picture element.

PL/1 (Programming Language 1): Programming language developed by IBM in 1964 for business and scientific applications.

Pointer: A special type of data element attached to a record that shows the absolute or relative address of another record.

Political models: Models of decision making where decisions result from competition and bargaining among an organization's interest groups and key leaders.

Political theory: Behavioral theory that describes information systems as the outcome of political competition between organizational subgroups for influence over the policies, procedures, and resources of the organization.

Portfolio analysis: An analysis of the portfolio of potential applications within a firm to determine the risks and benefits and select among alternatives for information systems.

Post implementation: Final stage of the systems life cycle in which the system is used and evaluated while in production and is modified to make improvements or meet new requirements.

Post-industrial theory: Behavioral theory stating that the transformation of advanced industrial countries into post-industrial societies creates flatter organizations dominated by knowledge workers where decision making is more decentralized.

Present value: The value, in current dollars, of a payment or stream of payments to be received in the future.

Primary activities: Activities most directly related to the production and distribution of a firm's products or services.

Primary storage: Part of the computer that temporarily stores program instructions and data for use by the CPU.

Printer: A computer output device that provides paper "hard-copy" output in the form of text or graphics.

Privacy: The claim of individuals to be left alone, free from surveillance or interference from other individuals, organizations, or the state.

Private branch exchange (PBX): Central switching system that handles a firm's voice and digital communications.

Processing: The conversion of raw input into a form that is more meaningful to humans.

Processing controls: Routines for establishing that data are complete and accurate during processing.

Process specification: Describes the logic of the transformations occurring within the lowest-level processes of the data flow diagrams.

Product differentiation: Competitive strategy for creating brand loyalty by developing new and unique products and services that are not easily duplicated by competitors.

Production: The stage after the new system is installed and the conversion is complete; during this time the system is reviewed by users and technical specialists to determine how well it has met its original goals.

Production or service workers: People who actually produce the products or services of the organization.

Professional bureaucracy: Knowledge-based organization such as a law firm or hospital that is dominated by department heads with weak centralized authority; operates in a slowly changing environment.

Profitability index: Used to compare the profitability of alternative investments; it is calculated by dividing the present value of the total cash inflow from an investment by the initial cost of the investment.

Program: A series of statements or instructions to the computer.

Program-data dependence: The close relationship between data stored in files and the software programs that update and maintain those files. Any change in data organization or format requires a change in all the programs associated with those files.

Programmers: Highly trained technical specialists who write computer software instructions.

Programming: The process of translating the system specifications prepared during the design stage into program code.

Program security controls: Controls designed to prevent unauthorized changes to programs in systems that are already in production.

Project definition: Stage in the systems life cycle that determines whether or not the organization has a problem and whether or not the problem can be solved by launching a system project.

Project management software: Software that facilitates the development, scheduling, and management of a project by breaking the complex project into simpler subtasks, each with its own completion time and resource requirements.

PROM: Programmable read-only memory. Subclass of ROM chip used in control devices because it can be programmed once.

Protocol: Set of rules and procedures that govern transmission between the components in a network.

Prototype: Preliminary working version of an information system for demonstration and evaluation purposes.

Prototyping: Process of building an experimental system quickly and inexpensively for demonstration and evaluation so that users can better determine information requirements.

Pseudocode: Method for expressing program logic that uses plain English statements rather than graphic symbols, trees, tables, or programming languages to describe a procedure.

Query language: A high-level computer language used to retrieve specific information from databases or files.

RAM: Random access memory. Primary storage of data or program instructions that can directly access any randomly chosen location in the same amount of time.

Rationalization of procedures: The streamlining of standard operating procedures, eliminiating obvious bottlenecks, so that automation makes operating procedures more efficient.

Rational model: Model of human behavior believing that people, organizations, and nations make consistent, value-maximizing calculations within certain constraints.

Record: A group of related fields.

Reduced instruction set computing (RISC): Technology used to enhance the speed of microprocessors by embedding only the most frequently used instructions on a chip.

Reference model: A generic framework for thinking about a problem.

Register: Temporary storage location in the ALU or control unit where small amounts of data and instructions reside for thousandths of a second just before use.

Relational data model: A type of logical database model that treats data as if they were stored in two-dimensional tables. It can relate data stored in one table to data in another as long as the two tables share a common data element.

Repetitive stress injury (RSI): Occupational disease that occurs when muscle groups are forced through the same, repetitive actions often with high impact loads or thousands of repetitions of low impact loads.

Report generator: Software that creates customized reports in a wide range of formats that are not routinely produced by an information system.

Representations: In DSS, conceptualization of information in the form of graphs, charts, lists, reports, and symbols to control operations.

Request for Proposal (RFP): Detailed list of questions submitted to vendors of packaged software or other computer services to determine if the vendor's product can meet the organization's specific requirements.

Resource allocation: Determination of how costs, time, and personnel are assigned to different activities of a systems development project.

Responsibility: Accepting the potential costs, duties, and obligations of one's decisions.

Reverse engineering: The process of taking existing programs, file and database descriptions and converting them into corresponding design-level components that can then be used to create new applications.

Ring network: Network topology in which all computers are linked by a closed loop in a manner that passes data in one direction from one computer to another.

Risk assessment: Determining the potential frequency of occurrence of a problem and the potential damage if the problem were to occur. Used to determine the cost/benefit of a control.

Risk Aversion Principle: Principle that one should take the action which produces the least harm or incurs the least cost.

ROM: Read-only memory. Semi-conductor memory chips that contain program instructions. These chips can only be read from; they cannot be written to.

Rule base: The collection of knowledge in an AI system that is represented in the form of IF-THEN rules.

Rule-based expert system: An AI program that has a large number of interconnected and nested IF-THEN statements or "rules" that are the basis for the knowledge in the system.

Run control totals: Procedures for controlling completeness of computer updating by generating control totals that reconcile totals before and after processing.

Satellite: Transmission of data using orbiting satellites to serve as relay stations for transmitting microwave signals over very long distances.

Satisficing: Choosing the first available alternative in order to move closer toward the ultimate goal instead of searching for all alternatives and consequences.

Schema: The logical description of an entire database, listing all the data elements in the database and the relationships among them.

Scoring model: A quick method for deciding among alternative systems based on a system of ratings for selected objectives.

Secondary storage: Relatively long-term, non-volatile storage of data outside the CPU and primary storage.

Sector: Method of storing data on a floppy disk in which the disk is divided into pie-shaped pieces or sectors. Disk storage location can be identified by sector and data record number.

Security: Policies, procedures, and technical measures used to prevent unauthorized access, alteration, theft, or physical damage to information systems.

Segregation of functions: Principle of internal control to divide responsibilities and assign tasks among people so that job functions do not overlap to minimize the risk of errors and fraudulent manipulation of the organization's assets.

Selection construct: The logic pattern in programming where a stated condition determines which of two or more actions can be taken depending on which satisfies the stated condition.

Semantic nets: Expert systems that use the property of inheritance to organize and classify knowledge when the knowledge base is composed of easily identifiable chunks or objects of interrelated characteristics.

Semiconductor: An integrated circuit made by printing thousands and even millions of tiny transistors on a small silicon chip.

Senior managers: People at the highest organizational level who are responsible for making long-range decisions.

Sensitivity analysis: Models that ask "what-if" questions repeatedly to determine the impact of changes in one or more factors on outcomes.

Sequence construct: The sequential single steps or actions in the logic of a program that do not depend on the existence of any condition.

Sequential file organization: A method of storing records in which records must be retrieved in the same physical sequence in which they are stored.

Server: Satisfies some or all of the user's request for data and/or functionality, such as storing and processing shared data and performing back-end functions not visible to users, such as managing peripheral devices and controlling access to shared databases. It might be anything from a supercomputer or mainframe to another desktop computer.

Sociological theory: Behavioral theory stating that organizations develop hierarchical bureaucratic structures and standard operating procedures to cope in unstable environments and that organizations can't change routines when environments change.

Sociotechnical design: Design to produce information systems that blend technical efficiency with sensitivity to organizational and human needs.

Software: The detailed instructions that control the operation of a computer system.

Software controls: Controls to ensure the security and reliability of software.

Software metrics: Objective assessments of the software used in a system in the form of quantified measurements.

Software package: A prewritten, precoded, commercially available set of programs that eliminates the need to write software programs for certain functions.

Software re-engineering: Methodology that addresses the problem of aging software by salvaging and upgrading it so that the users can avoid a long and expensive replacement project.

Source code: Program instructions written in a high-level language before translation into machine language.

Source data automation: Input technology that captures data in computer-readable form at the time and place the data are created.

Spaghetti code: Unstructured, confusing program code with tangled logic that metaphorically resembles a pot of cooked spaghetti.

Spreadsheet: Software displaying data in a grid of columns and rows, with the capability of easily recalculating numerical data.

Standard: Approved reference models and protocols as determined by standard-setting groups for building or developing products or services.

Standard operating procedures (SOPs): Precise, defined rules for accomplishing tasks that have been developed to cope with expected situations.

Standing data: Data that are permanent and affect transactions flowing into and out of a system.

Star network: Network topology in which all computers and other devices are connected to a central host computer. All communications between network devices must pass through the host computer.

Storage technology: Physical media and software governing the storage and organization of data for use in an information system.

Stored program concept: The idea that a program cannot be executed unless it is stored in a computer's primary storage along with required data.

Strategic decision making: Determining the long-term objectives, resources, and policies of an organization.

Strategic information systems: Computer systems at any level of the organization that change the goals, operations, products, services, or environmental relationships to help the organization gain a competitive advantage.

Strategic-level systems: Information systems that support the long-range planning activities of senior management.

Strategic transition: A movement from one level of sociotechnical system to another. Often required when adopting strategic systems that demand changes in the social and technical elements of an organization.

Strict liability in tort: Class of liability whenever a defective product causes injury and the manufacturer can be held liable regardless of whether or not the defect could have or should have been prevented.

Structure chart: System documentation showing each level of design, the relationship among the levels, and the overall place in the design structure; can document one program, one system, or part of one program.

Structured: Refers to the fact that techniques are instructions that are carefully drawn up, often step-by-step, with each step building upon a previous one.

Structured analysis: Method for defining system inputs, processes, and outputs and for partitioning systems into subsystems or modules that show a logical graphic model of information flow.

Structured decisions: Decisions that are repetitive, routine, and have a definite procedure for handling them.

Structured design: Software design discipline, encompassing a set of design rules and techniques for designing a system from the top down in a hierarchical fashion.

Structured programming: Discipline for organizing and coding programs that simplifies the control paths so that the programs can be easily understood and modified. Uses the basic control structures and modules that have only one entry point and one exit point.

Structured Query Language (SQL): The emerging standard data manipulation language for relational database management systems.

Subschema: The logical description of the part of a database required by a particular function or application program.

Supercomputer: Very sophisticated and powerful computer that can perform very complex computations extremely rapidly.

Support activities: Activities that make the delivery of the primary activities of a firm possible.

Switched lines: Telephone lines that a person can access from his or her terminal to transmit data to another computer, the call being routed or switched through paths to the designated destination.

Switching costs: The expense a customer or company incurs in lost time and resources when changing from one supplier or system to a competing supplier or system.

Synchronous transmission: High-speed simultaneous transmission of large blocks of data.

System failure: An information system that either does not perform as expected, is not operational at a specified time, or cannot be used in the way it was intended.

System flowchart: Graphic design tool that depicts the physical media and sequence of processing steps used in an entire information system.

System-oriented theory: User-resistance theory focusing on factors inherent in the design of the system.

System residence device: The secondary storage device on which a complete operating system is stored.

System 7: Operating system for the Macintosh computer which supports multitasking and has powerful graphics and multimedia capabilities.

Systems analysis: The analysis of a problem which the organization will try to solve with an information system.

Systems analysts: Specialists who translate business problems and requirements into information requirements and systems.

Systems design: Details how a system will meet the information requirements as determined by the systems analysis.

Systems development: The activities that go into producing an information systems solution to an organizational problem or opportunity.

Systems life cycle: Traditional methodology for developing an information system that partitions the systems development process into six formal stages that must be completed sequentially with a very formal division of labor between end users and information systems specialists.

Systems Network Architecture (SNA): Proprietary telecommunications reference model developed by IBM.

System software: Generalized programs that manage the resources of the computer.

Systems study: Stage in the systems life cycle that analyzes the problems of existing systems, defines the objectives to be attained by a solution, and evaluates various solution alternatives.

System testing: Tests the functioning of the information system as a whole in order to determine if discrete modules will function together as planned.

Tangible benefits: Benefits that can be quantified and assigned monetary value; they include lower operational costs and increased cash flows.

Technical feasibility: Determines whether a proposed solution can be implemented with the available hardware, software, and technical resources.

Technostress: Stress induced by computer use whose symptoms include aggravation, hostility towards humans, impatience, and enervation.

Telecommunications: Communication of information by electronic means, usually over some distance.

Telecommunications software: Special software for controlling and supporting the activities of a telecommunications network.

Telecommunications system: Collection of compatible hardware and software arranged to communicate information from one location to another.

Telecommunications technology: Physical devices and software that link various hardware components and transfer data from one physical location to another.

Teleconferencing: Ability to confer with a group of people simultaneously using the telephone or electronic mail group communication software.

Telnet: Network tool that allows someone log onto one computer system while doing work on another.

Terabyte: Approximately 1 trillion bytes; unit of computer storage capacity.

Testing: The exhaustive and thorough process that determines whether the system produces the desired results under known conditions.

Test plan: Prepared by the development team in conjunction with the users; it includes all of the preparations for the series of tests to be performed on the system.

Time sharing: The sharing of computer resources by many users simultaneously by having the CPU spend a fixed amount of time on each user's program before proceeding to the next.

Top-down: An approach that progresses from the highest most abstract level to the lowest level of detail.

Top-down approach: In the history of artificial intelligence, the effort to develop a logical analog to how the brain works.

Total quality management (TQM): A concept that makes quality control a responsibility to be shared by all people in an organization.

Touch screen: Input technology that permits the entering or selecting of commands and data by touching the surface of a sensitized video display monitor with a finger or pointer.

Track: Concentric circle on the surface area of a disk on which data are stored as magnetized spots; each track can store thousands of bytes.

Trade secret: Any intellectual work or product used for a business purpose that can be classified as belonging to that business provided it is not based on information in the public domain.

Traditional file environment: A way of collecting and maintaining data in an organization that leads to each functional area or division creating and maintaining its own data files and programs.

Transaction cost theory: Economic theory that states that firms exist because they can conduct marketplace transactions internally more cheaply than they can with external firms in the marketplace.

Transaction file: In batch systems, the file in which all transactions are accumulated to await processing.

Transaction processing systems (TPS): Computerized systems that perform and record the daily routine transactions necessary to the conduct of the business; they serve the operational level of the organization.

Transborder data flow: The movement of information across international boundaries in any form.

Transform algorithm: Mathematical formula used to translate a record's key field directly into the record's physical storage location.

Transmission Control Protocol/Internet Protocol (TCP/IP): U.S. Department of Defense reference model for linking different types of computers and networks.

Transnational: Truly globally managed firms which have no national headquarters; value-added activities are managed from a global perspective without reference to national borders, optimizing sources of supply and demand and taking advantage of any local competitive advantage.

Tuple: A row or record in a relational database.

Twisted wire: Transmission medium consisting of pairs of twisted copper wires. Used to transmit analog phone conversations but can be used for data transmission.

Unit testing: The process of testing each program separately in the system. Sometimes called program testing.

UNIX: Operating system for microcomputers, minicomputers, and mainframes that is machine-independent and supports multiuser processing, multitasking, and networking.

Unstructured decisions: Nonroutine decisions in which the decision maker must provide judgment, evaluation, and insights into the problem definition; there is no agreed-upon procedure for making such decisions.

Usenet: Forums in which people share information and ideas on a defined topic through large electronic bulletin boards where anyone can post messages on the topic for others to see and respond to.

User-designer communications gap: The differences in backgrounds, interests, and priorities that impede communication and problem-solving among end users and information systems specialists.

User interface: The part of the information system through which the end user interacts with the system; type of hardware and the series of on-screen commands and responses required for a user to work with the system.

Utilitarian Principle: Principle that one should take the action that achieves the higher or greater value.

Utility program: System software consisting of programs for routine, repetitive tasks, which can be shared by many users.

Value-added network (VAN): Private, multipath, data-only third party managed networks that are used by multiple organizations on a subscription basis.

Value chain model: Model that highlights the activities that add a margin of value to a firm's products or services where information systems can best be applied to achieve a competitive advantage.

Vendor-managed inventory: Approach to inventory management that assigns the supplier the responsibility to make inventory replenishment decisions based on order, point-of-sale data or warehouse data supplied by the customer.

Very-high-level programming language: Programming language using fewer instructions than conventional languages. Used primarily as a professional programmer productivity tool.

Videoconferencing: Teleconferencing with the capability of participants to see each other over video screens.

Video display terminal (VDT): A screen, also referred to as a cathode ray tube (CRT). Provides a visual image of both user input and computer output.

Videotex: Multimedia delivery of information to remote terminals typically used for consumer or commercial delivery systems such as electronic shopping, banking, news, and financial database services.

Virtual private networks (VPNs): The ability to custom configure a network and use whatever portion of the public switched network is needed to do the job while only charging for the services used; provided by the local phone company to each corporate user.

Virtual reality systems: Interactive graphics software and hardware that create computer-generated simulations that provide sensations that emulate real-world activities.

Virtual storage: A way of handling programs more efficiently by the computer by dividing the programs into small fixed or variable-length portions with only a small portion stored in primary memory at one time.

Voice input device: Technology that converts the spoken word into digital form for processing.

Voice mail: System for digitizing a spoken message and transmitting it over a network.

Voice output device: Converts digital output data into spoken words.

WAIS (Wide Area Information Servers): A tool for locating data on the Internet that requires the name of the databases to be searched based upon key words.

Walkthrough: A review of a specification or design document by a small group of people carefully selected based on the skills needed for the particular objectives being tested.

Warranty: A representation expressed by the seller of goods representing that the goods are fit for purchase and use.

Wide area network (WAN): Telecommunications network that spans a large geographical distance. May consist of a variety of cable, satellite, and microwave technologies.

Windows: A graphical user interface shell that runs in conjunction with the DOS microcomputer operating system. Supports multitasking and some forms of networking.

Windows 95: A 32-bit operating system with a streamlined graphical user interface that can support software written for DOS and Windows but can also run programs that take up more than 640 K of memory. Features multitasking, multithreading, and powerful networking capabilities.

Windows NT: Powerful operating system developed by Microsoft for use with 32-bit microcomputers and workstations based on Intel and other microprocessors. Supports networking, multitasking, and multiprocessing.

Word length: The number of bits that can be processed at one time by a computer. The larger the word length, the greater the speed of the computer.

Word processing: Office automation technology that facilitates the creation of documents through computerized text editing, formatting, storing, and printing.

Word processing software: Software that handles electronic storage, editing, formatting, and printing of documents.

Workflow management: The process of streamlining business procedures so that documents can be moved easily and efficiently from one location to another.

Workstation: Desktop computer with powerful graphics, mathematical processing, and communications capabilities as well as the ability to perform several complicated tasks at one time. Often used in scientific or design work.

World Wide Web: A set of standards for storing, retrieving, formatting and displaying information using a client/server architecture, graphical user interfaces, and a hypertext language that enables dynamic links to other documents.

WORM: Write once, read many. Optical disk system that allows users to record data only once; data cannot be erased but can be read indefinitely.

X Windows: Standard for high-level graphics description used for standardized window management and construction of graphical user interfaces.

Name Index

Charles, Robert B., 157
Chaum, David, 716
Cheney, Paul H., 68
Chidanbaram, Laku, 637, 750
Chin, Wynne W., 637
Chismar, William G., 750
Christoff, Kurt A., 473
Christy, David P., 473
Churchland, Pamela Smith, 643
Churchland, Paul M., 643, 681
Clark, Thomas D. Jr., 39
Clement, Andrew, 108, 546, 552
Clemons, Eric K., 49, 58, 61, 68
Clermont, Paul, 464, 465, 473
Clifford, James, 681
Coad, Peter, 520
Cohen, Michael, 135
Cohen, Yeshayahu, 297
Cole, Elliot, 473
Coleman, David, 589
Collins, Roseanne Webb, 605
Collins, W. Robert, 158, 176
Cone, Edward, 169, 182
Conger, Sue A., 436, 505, 521
Conner, Dennis, 338
Connolly, James, 68
Connolly, Terri, 135, 637
Constantine, L. L., 521
Cooper, Randolph B., 553
Copeland, Duncan G., 61, 68
Corbato, Fernando J., 553
Cotterman, William W., 473
Cougar, J. Daniel, 176
Courtney, James F., 618, 638
Cox, Butler, 729, 733, 750
Cox, Earl, 681
Coy, Peter, 95
Creecy, Robert H., 681
Cronan, Timothy Paul, 543, 553
Cross, John, 473
Cross, W. Bruce, 297
Culnan, Mary J., 21, 39
Cummins, J. Michael, 339
Cunningham, Cara A., 421
Curley, Kathleen Foley, 682
Cushman, John H., 68

D

Dahmani, Abdelhafid, 638
Daly, James, 605
Daniels, Robert M. Jr., 435
Datar, Srikant M., 489, 520
Date, C. J., 297
Davenport, Thomas H., 405, 408, 435
Davidson, W. H., 435
Davis, Alan M., 473
Davis, Fred R., 553
Davis, Glenn C., 716
Davis, Gordon B., 25, 39, 435, 460,
    473, 529, 543, 553, 605
Davis, Sid A., 473
Deans, Candace P., 750
DeGeorge, Gail, 51
De Hayes, Daniel W., 435
Dejoie, Roy, 176
Dekleva, Sasa M., 507, 520
DeLone, William H., 529, 553
DeLong, David W., 638
DeMarco, Tom, 520
Demasco, Patrick W., 226
Denning, Dorothy E., 149, 176
Dennis, Alan R., 435, 621, 622, 623,
    624, 625, 626, 637, 638

DePompa, Barbara, 217, 226, 699
Dertouzos, Michael, 339
DeSanctis, Geraldine, 619, 637, 638
Desharnias, George, 637
Desmond, John, 636
Dhar, Vasant, 681
Dickson, Gary W., 637
Dickson, W. J., 109
Dijkstra, E., 520
Diltz, J. David, 716
DiMaggio, Paul J., 97, 108
Ditlea, Steve, 678, 681
Doll, William J., 400, 435, 533, 553
Donner, Marc, 587
Donovan, John J., 339
Dos Santos, Brian, 422, 435
Douglas, David E., 543, 553
Dreyfus, Hubert L., 643
Dreyfus, Stuart E., 643
Drucker, Peter, 97, 98, 101, 108
du Bois, Martin, 112
Duffy, Maureen, 552
Dunkle, Debora, 91, 109
Dunlop, Charles, 605
Dutta, Amitava, 750
Dutton, William H., 15, 40, 88, 108
Dwyer, Paula, 303

E

Easton, George K., 637
Eaton, Leslie, 716
Edelstein, Herbert A., 605
Edens, Ron, 325
Edwards, Julian M., 520
Ein-Dor, Philip, 429, 435, 533, 553
Eirman, Michael A., 605
Eisenstat, Russell A., 108
Elam, Joyce L., 629, 637
El Najdawi, M. K., 681
El Sawy, Omar A., 108, 435, 628, 637,
    638
El Sharif, Hisham, 637
Emery, James C., 435
Emmett, Arielle, 68, 226
Emshwiller, John R., 716
Etzioni, Amitai, 78, 108
Etzioni, Oren, 339
Eveland, J. D., 16, 40, 77, 108, 529,
    553, 605
Everest, G. C., 297

F

Fallows, James, 262
Falvey, Jack, 338
Fayol, Henri, 108, 113
Feder, Barnaby J., 110, 176
Fedorowicz, Jane, 39
Feeny, David F., 68, 468, 473
Feibus, Michael, 226
Feigenbaum, Edward A., 643, 681
Feigenbaum, J. A., 681
Fertuck, Len, IC11
Fialka, John J., 695
Fithen, Katherine, 716
Fitzgerald, Michael, 338, 569
Fitzmaurice, George W., 226
Fitzsimmons, A., 488, 521
Flannery, Lauren S., 461, 462, 473
Flatten, Per O., 435, 520
Fleischer, Mitchell, 606

Foley, Anna, 595
Ford, Henry, 76
Forrest, David, 262
Forte, Gene, 507, 520
Foster, Gregg, 638
Fowler, George, 176
Frailey, Fred W., 667
Franz, Charles, 416, 435, 543, 553
Fraser, Barbara, 716
Fraser, Martin D., 442, 473
Fredenberger, William B., 638
Freedman, David H., 23, 71, 262,
    489, 520
Freeman, John, 73, 82, 108
Frohman, A. L., 102, 109, 531, 553
Frye, Colleen, 327, 339, 589
Fuller, Mary K., 461, 473
Furger, Roberta, 166, 176

G

Gabriel, Trip, 162, 176
Galegher, Jolene, 135, 637
Gallupe, R. Brent, 619, 637
Gane, Chris, 520
Garceau, Linda, 297
Garrity, Edward J., 435, 446, 473
Gaulet, Stanley C., 335
Gelernter, David E., 681
George, Joey F., 135, 605, 622, 624,
    626, 637, 638
Gerhart, Mark, 263
Gerlach, James H., 435
Geyelin, Milo, 175
Gilder, George, 339
Gilhooly, Kym, 453
Ginzberg, Michael J., 102, 108, 429,
    435, 473, 539, 552, 553, 637
Giuliao, Vincent E., 605
Glenn, John, 632
Goldberg, David E., 681
Goldstein, Robert C., 297, 682
Goleman, Daniel, 127
Goodhue, Dale L., 297, 436
Gopal, Abhijit, 637
Gorry, G. Anthony, 39, 108, 120, 135
Goslar, Martin D., 339, 750
Gotterbarn, Donald, 176
Gould, John D., 436, 444, 473, 553
Gouldner, Alvin, 78, 108
Graham, Robert L., 150, 176
Grant, F. J., 459, 473
Green, Jesse, 458, 473
Greenbaum, Joshua M., 47, 238, 241,
    262, 421, 739, 749
Greenwald, John, 182
Grief, Irene, 339
Griggs, Kenneth, 682
Grobowski, Ronald, 135, 619, 625, 638
Gronert, Elke, 297
Grover, Varun, 297, 339
Grudin, Jonathan, 589, 605
Grudnitski, Gary, 436
Gullo, Karen, 553
Gurbaxani, V., 91, 93, 108
Gutek, Barbara A., 605
Guterl, Fred, 569

H

Haavind, Robert, 262
Hall, Gene, 68

Thakur, Meru, 262
Thearling, Kurt H., 226
Thomborson, Clark D., 203, 226
Thompson, James, 78, 109
Thompson, John P., 473
Thompson, Tom, 226
Thyfault, Mary E., 717, 741, 743
Timmreck, Eric M., 473
Toffler, Alvin, 98, 109
Tomsho, Robert, 67
Torkzadeh, Gholamreza, 339
Tornatsky, Louis G., 16, 40, 529, 553
Toyne, Brian, 750
Tractinsky, Noam, 509, 521
Trauth, Eileen M., 473
Treacy, Michael E., 28, 40, 67, 401, 436
Trippi, Robert, 665, 682
Tucker, Lewis W., 226
Tuer, David, 70
Tuerkheimer, Frank M., 177
Tully, Shawn, 605
Turban, Efraim, 638, 665, 682
Turner, Joel E., 262
Turner, Jon A., 109, 544, 554
Turoff, Murray, 637, 638
Tushman, Michael L., 82, 109
Tuunairen, Uirpi, 553
Tversky, A., 125, 135
Tweed, Vera, 262
Tyran, Craig K., 638

U

Ullah, Nasr, 226
Ullman, Jeff, 298
Ullrich, Walter A., 68

V

Vaishnavi, Vijay K., 262, 442, 473
Valacich, Joseph S., 624, 638
Van den Besselaar, Peter, 546, 552
Van Overen, Peter, 226
Vassilou, Yannis, 246, 263
Venkatraman, N., 59, 68, 436, 463, 473
Verity, John W., 51, 338
Vessey, Iris, 436, 505, 509, 521, 553
Vetter, Ronald J., 323, 339
Vicinanza, Stephen S., 263
Vincent, Mark, 608
Vin, Harrick M., 606
Vitalari, Nicholas P., 436
Vitale, Michael R., 53, 59, 68
Vogel, Douglas R., 135, 589, 598, 606,
    622, 624, 626, 637, 638
Volonino, Linda, 638
von Daehne, Niklas, 5

W

Wagner, Ina, 436
Wald, Matthew L., 605
Wallace, Peggy, 321
Wallich, Paul, 682
Walls, Joseph G., 627, 628, 638
Walton, Eric J., 473
Waltz, David L., 681, 682
Wang, Ming-Chian Ken, 682
Wang, P., 339
Wang, Richard Y., 297
Warkenpin, Merrill E., 716
Watkins, Paul R., 682
Watson, Hugh J., 40, 625, 628, 637, 638
Watson, Richard T., 638
Wayne, Leslie, 68
Wayner, Peter, 325, 329
Weber, Bruce W., 49, 58, 68
Weber, Max, 75, 97, 109
Weber, Ron, 717
Wegner, Peter, 263
Weill, Peter, IC2–IC10
Weiner, Norbert, 644, 674
Weinkam, James J., 606
Weir, Mary, 546, 553
Weiser, Mark, 216, 226
Weiss, Ira R., 461, 472, 536, 553, 750
Weiss, Lee E., 682
Weiss, Stephen F., 298
Weitz, Rob R., 681
Weitzel, John L., 682
Weizenbaum, Joseph, 682
Weld, Daniel, 339
Wescott, Russ, 529, 554
Westin, Alan F., 546, 554, 606
Westin, Stu, 262, 436
Wetherbe, James C., 40, 109, 436
Wexler, Joanie M., 709
Whang, S., 91, 108
Wherry, Phillip, 158, 176
Whinston, A. B., 605, 637
Whistler, Thomas L., 97, 109
White, Clinton E., 473
White, George M., 263, 682
Whitehead, Alfred North, 641
White, Kathy Brittain, 554
Widmeyer, George R., 628, 638
Widrow, Bernard, 662, 682
Wiederhold, Gio, 263
Wilder, Clinton, 739
Wiley, John, 96
Wilkes, Maurice V., 263
Willcocks, Leslie P., 468, 473
Williams, Lena, 165, 177
Williamson, Eldonna S., 511
Williamson, Miday, 218, 226
Williamson, Oliver E., 93, 109
Willis, T. Hillman, 473

Wilson, Linda, 11, 158, 176, 717, 739
Winkler, Connie, 249, 453, 660
Winslow, Ron, 569
Wiseman, Charles, 68
Wolff Edward N., 571, 572, 606
Wolfram, Stephen, 226
Wolinksy, Carol, 177
Wood, Elizabeth, 226
Wood, Lamont, 255
Woodruff, David, 182
Woodward, Joan, 78, 109
Wrapp, H. Edward, 116, 117, 135
Wybo, Michael D., 297, 436
Wynne, Bayard E., 637

X

Xenakis, John J., 472, 589
Xia, Weidong, 339

Y

Yamazaki, Kazumi, 750
Yap, C. S., 91
Yates, JoAnne, 53, 68
Yin, Robert K., 530, 554
Young, Luke T., 226
Yourdon, Edward, 520, 521

Z

Zachman, J. A., 400, 436
Zadeh, Lofti A., 682
Zahniser, Richard A., 473
Zecher, Joshua, 695
Zellner, Wendy, 67
Zeniuk, Nick, 616
Zigli, Ronald, 750
Zmud, Robert W., 436, 553
Zonnevylle, Michael S., 606
Zultner, Richard E., 521
Zweig, Dani, 489, 520

Organizations Index

Morgan Stanley, 573
Motorola, 85, 95, 198, 199
Mott Consortium, 595
Mrs. Fields Cookies, 58, 730
Mutual Benefit Life, 410
Muze Inc., 212

N

National Aeronautic and Space
    Administration (NASA), 266,
    537, 652, 669
National Association of Securities
    Dealers Inc. (NASD), 630
National Car Rental, 54
National Center for Health Statistics,
    166
National Computer Security Assocation
    (NCSA), 695
National Counsel on Compensation
    Insurance, 166–67
National Gypsum, 612
National Institute of Science and
    Technology (NIST), 159
National Library of Congress, 170
National Science Foundation, 692
National Trust, 697
National Weather Service, 694
NationsBank-CRT, 254–55
NCR, 174–75, 588
Nestle SA, 324
Netscape Communications
    Corporation, 695
Network General Corp., 325
Neuromedical Systems Inc., 663–64
News Corp., 303
Newspaper Association, 143
New York State Office of General
    Services, 632–33
New York Telephone, 162
Nordstrom, 325
Northern Telecom Ltd., 169
Northwest Airlines, 58
Novell, 320
NuSkin, 3–6, 9–10
Nynex, 303, 310

O

Occupational Safety and Health
    Administration (OSHA), 168
Odense Shipyards, 22–23, 411
Office Ergonomics, Inc., 169
On Technology, Inc., 588
Optika Systems, Inc., 581
Oracle Corporation, 430–31
Otis Elevators, 310

P

Pacific Bell (PacBell), 162, 164, 257
Pacific Gas and Electric (PG&E),
    584–85
Pacific Telesis, 164, 303, 615–16
Paine-Webber, 51
Palladian Software Inc., 655
Panix (Public Access Network
    Corp.), 694
Paranetics Technology Inc., 118
Pattern Discovery Inc., 639–40

Peat Marwick, 472
Perot Systems, 420
PHH FleetAmerica, 480
Philip Morris Co., 51
Philips Electronics, 212
Phillips Petroleum Company, 410
Pinkerton detective agency, 163
Pitney Bowes, 613
Pizza Hut, 364, 481–82, 485
Pizza Pizza Ltd., 137–39, 144
Plains Cotton Cooperative Associatin
    (Telcot), 410
Port of Oakland, 588
Pratt & Whitney, 629–31
Price Waterhouse, 472
Primrose, Mendelson, and Hansen,
    423–431
Proctor & Gamble, 90
Prodigy, 153, 156–57, 350
Progressive Insurance, 410
Provisional Airport Authority (Hong
    Kong), 595
PTT Telecom, 205
Public Access Network Corp., 694
Public Service Electric and Gas
    (PSE&G), 254, 639–40

Q

Quaker Oats, 379

R

RadioMail, 310–11
RAET, 466
RAM Broadcasting, 310
Rand Corporation, 79
Reader's Digest Association, 51, 57
Redstone Advisors, 607–8
Regency Systems Solutions, 494
Reno Air, 631
Revlon Inc., 146–47
Reynolds & Reynolds Co., 59–60
Richmond Savings, 348
Rite Aid, 308–9
Rockwell International, 668
Ross Systems, Inc., 453
Royal LePage Real Estate Service
    Ltd., 471
RSA Data Security Inc., 694

S

Saab-Scania, 456–57
SABRE Group AA, Inc., 205
Sand Dollar Management Co., 227–28
San Jose Medical Center, 579–80
Sanyo Fisher USA, 668
SAP America, 471–72
SBC Communications, 303
Schneider National, 90–91, 405, 411
Seagate Technology, 362
Sealand Transportation, 725
Sears Mortgage Corp., 261
Sears, Roebuck and Company, 30,
    48–49, 54, 58
Seer Technology, 512
Shell Pipeline Corporation, 154, 703
Sigma Imaging Systems Inc., 409
Sikorsky Aircraft, 613

Social Security Administration (SSA),
    73, 191, 400, 573–74, 712
Software Productivity Research,
    Inc., 494
Software Publishers Assocation (SPA),
    152–53
Sonny's Bar-B-Q, 260–62
Sony Corporation, 212, 329, 731
South Coast Air Quality Management
    District, 214
Southern Railway, 612
Southwest Airlines, 53–54
Southwestern Bell Corporation, 162
Sprint, 310
Standard & Poor's, 53
State Street Bank and Trust Co.
    (Boston), 43
Sundstrand Corporation, 59
Sungard Recovery Services, 697
Sun Microsystems, 348–49, 361, 694
SWIFT (Society for Worldwide
    Interbank Financial
    Telecommunications), 740
Swiss Bank Corp., 709

T

Teknowledge Inc., 655
Teledesic Corp., 308
Tetrad Computer Applications, 261–62
Texas Instruments, 282, 320
Texas Oil and Gas Corporation, 612
Textron Automotive Interiors, 52
Thai Airways, 602
Thorn EMI PLC, 185–87
Time Warner, 212, 303
Toro Co., 631
Toronto Blue Jays Baseball Club, 118
Toshiba, 212
Tower Group, 47
Toyota Motor Corp., 410
Trammel Crow Co., 452–53
Trane Co., 362
TriMark Investment Management, 204
TRW, Inc., 489

U

Ultramar Oil, 577
United Airlines, 53–54, 602, 612
United Auto Workers (UAW), 164
United Healthcare Corp. (UHC), 292
United Parcel Service (UPS), 11, 14,
    213, 411
United Services Automobile Association
    (USAA), 579
University of Colorado, 126, 728
University of Hohenheim, 620
University of Illinois, 672
University of Michigan, 671
University of North Carolina at Chapel
    Hill, 596
U.S. Air Force, 129
U.S. Department of Defense, 211, 243,
    244, 695
U.S. Department of Justice, 54, 302
U.S. Department of Transportation, 54
U.S. General Services Administration
    (GSA), 361–32
U.S. Patent Office, 151–52
U.S. Postal Service, 214
U.S. Navy, 292

International Organizations Index

A

Accor Group (Paris), 738
Airbus Industrie, 600–605
Arthur Andersen Consulting, 100

B

Barwon Water. *See* Geelong & District
    Water Board
Belgacom, 112
Bell Canada, 216–17, 303
Bell Quebec, 248–49
Black & Decker Corporation, 719–21
BGS Systems Inc., 202
Black & Decker, 719–21

C

Carp Systems International, 613
Caterpillar Inc., 95, 596, 730
Chep Lap Airport (Hong Kong), 595
Chrysler Corporation, 52, 178–82
Citibank, 46, 58, 737
Computer Associates International,
    Inc., 118
Conoco, Inc., 430
Continental Grain, 322
Corning Telecommunications Division,
    IC23–IC34
Credit Industriel et Commercial de
    Paris, 238

D

Dassault Aviation SA, 603
Deutsch Bundespost Telekom, 303
Deutsche Bank, 202
Digital Equipment Corporation (DEC),
    220, 237, 361, 652
Du Pont Merck Pharmaceutical
    Company, 443, 480

E

E. I. du Pont de Nemours & Company,
    470
Europcar Interrent, 420–21
EuroMarketing Sysems, 289

F

Financial Behemoth Corp. IC11
Festo Pneumatic, IC19–IC22
Ford Motor Company, 466
Foster Asia, 595
Frito-Lay, Inc., 612, 725
Fujitsu Ltd., 665

G

Geelong & District Water Board,
    IC2–IC10
General Electric, 360
General Motors Corporation (GM), 730
Gillette Company, 41–43, 57, 59
Ginormous Life Insurance Company,
    IC11–IC13
Groupe Colas, 241

H

Hewlett-Packard Corporation, 596
Hoechst International, 545
Human Factors International Inc., 547

I

IBM, 623, 625, 740, IC12
ICI Zeneca Ltd., 743
Israeli Discount Bank (IDB), 47

K

Kai Tak Airport (Hong Kong), 595
Kommunedata, 283
Kone Elevators, IC14–IC18

L

Logica UK Ltd., 547
Lotus Development Corporation, 583,
    587, 694

M

McDonald's, 730
Matsushita Electric Works, 594
Michelin Italia, 319–20
Mitsubishi Heavy Industries, 669

N

National Trust, 697
National Westminster Bank
    (London), 286
Nestlé SA, 324
New Zealand Inland Revenue
    Department, 395–97
Nippon Steel Corporation, 665
Nippon Telephone and Telegraph, 329

O

Odense Shipyards, 22–23
Ontario Hydro, 254–55
Oracle Corporation, IC12

P

PA Consulting, IC3
PanCanadian Petroleum, 69–71, 74
PanCanadian Railways, 89
Pizza Pizza Ltd., 137–39, 144
Plaisance Television, 303
PLC, 112
PowerGen, 112
Provisional Airport Authority (Hong
    Kong), 595

R

RAET, 466
Reuters, 547
Royal LePage Real Estate Service
    Ltd., 471
Ruhrgas AG, 112

S

Sandenbergh Pavon Ltd., 219
Sanyo Fisher USA, 668

Subject Index

Financial Manager (Azimuth Corp.), 590
Financial models, 426
    limitations of, 422
Finance and accounting information
    systems, A4-A5
Firewall, 694–95
Flexibility:
    of application software packages, 451
    of management information systems
        (MIS), 25
    of outsourcing, 463
Floppy disks, 209
Flowcharts, 502–4
    defined, 502
    joint application design (JAD), 504
    symbols, 503
FOCUS, 246
Focused differentiation, 45
Forecasting models, 617
Formal information systems, 9
Formal planning and control tools,
    541–43
Format checks, 707
FORTRAN, 239, 243, 441
Forward chaining, 650–51
Forward engineering, 511
Fourth-generation languages, 245–51,
    457–59
    application generators, 246–47
    application software packages, 247
    defined, 245
    graphics languages, 246
    microcomputer tools, 249–51, 457–59
        data management software, 250–51
        integrated software packages, 251
        spreadsheets, 249–50
        word processing software, 249
    query languages, 246
    report generators, 246
    very-high-level programming
        languages, 247
Frame relay, 323
Frames, 648–49
Franchisers, 730
Front-end processor, 314
Full-duplex transmission, 314
Function point analysis, 492–93
Fuzzy logic, 668–70
    application areas, 670
    defined, 668
    and Japan, 669–70

G

GAMIS (Glenn Asset Management
    Information System), 631–32
Gantt charts, 542
"Garbage can" model of decision
    making, 129–30
Gateway, 319–20
GDSS, See Group decision support
    systems (GDSS)
General controls, 701–5
    administrative controls, 704–5
    computer operations controls, 702–3
    data security controls, 703–4
    defined, 700–701
    hardware controls, 702
    implementation controls, 701
    software controls, 701
    See also Controls
General Problem Solver model, 645
Genetic algorithms, 670–72

commercial applications of, 671
compared to neural networks, 671
defined, 670
example of, 672
origin of, 671
Geographic information system (GIS)
    software, 632
Gigabytes, 191
Global business systems, challenges/
    obstacles to, 726
Global chief information officer
    (CIO), 733
Global coordination, 725
Global economy, emergence of, 5–6
Global markets, 725
Global Trade Point Network, 299–301
Goals:
    of ISDN, 370
    of organizations, 82
Golden Rule, 144
Gophers, 351, 353–55
Grand Design systems, rates of failure,
    536
Graphical users interfaces (GUIs),
    234–35, 742
Graphics languages, 246
Group decision support systems
    (GDSS), 618–26
    characteristics of, 621
    defined, 619
    discrete meeting elements, 619
    and group decision making, 624–25
    overview of GDSS meeting, 623–24
        activities, 624
        attendees, 623–24
        facilitator, 623
    software tools, 621–24
        electronic brainstorming
            tools, 621
        electronic questionnaires, 621
        group dictionaries, 622
        idea organizers, 622
        policy formation tools, 622
        questionnaire tools, 622
    stakeholder identification and
        analysis tools, 622
    voting and priority tools, 622
        group outlining and writing tools,
            622
Groupware, 582–89, 744
    controversy about, 588
    defined, 582
    electronic calendaring, 583
    electronic mail (E-mail), 583, 589
    electronic meeting software, 583
    functions included in, 582
    group activities, 582
    group collaboration, and the Internet,
        587–89
    Lotus Notes, 583–87
GUIs, See Graphical users interfaces
    (GUIs)

H

Hackers, 162–63, 692–94
Half-duplex transmission, 314
Handwriting-recognition systems, 213
Hard disks, 208
Hardware:
    arithmetic-logic unit (ALU), 194–95
    cathode ray tube (CRT), 214–15
    central processing unit (CPU), 192–93

evolution of, 195–99
    fifth-generation, 221
    first-generation, 195
    fourth-generation, 196–97
    input devices, 212–14
    mainframes, 199–200
    microcomputers, 199–200, 203
    microprocessors, 197–98
    minicomputers, 199–200
    output devices, 214–16
    second-generation, 196
    supercomputers, 199–200
    third-generation, 196
    workstations, 199–200
Hardware controls, 702
Harvard Graphics, 246
Health risks, 166–69
    carpal tunnel syndrome (CTS), 166
    computer vision syndrome (CVS), 166
    CRT radiation, 167
    repetitive stress (strain) injury (RSI),
        166, 168–69
    technostress, 166–67
Hertz, 313
Heuristic Dendral, 654
Hierarchical data model, 279
High-level languages, 239–42, 257
High Performance Computing Act
    (1989), 170
Home pages, 355–57
    defined, 355
    locating/tracking, 363
    updating, 360
Host country system units, 732
HTML (Hypertext Markup
    Language), 351
    See also World Wide Web (WWW)
Hub Slaashing (expert systems), 654
Human resources information systems,
    A5-A7
HyperCard, 290–91
Hyperlinks, 357
Hypermedia, 355–57
Hypermedia databases, 288–91
Hypertext Markup Language, See
    HTML (Hypertext Markup
    Language), 351

I

IBM Thinkpad, 311
ICP (Institute for Certification of
    Computer Professionals), code
    of ethics, 145
Ideal (fourth-generation tool), 458
Imaging technology, See Document
    imaging systems
Immanuel Kant's Categorical
    Imperative, 144
Implementation, 523–54
    counterimplementation, 543
    defined, 529
    designing for the organization, 544
    level of complexity/risk, 533–35
        and experience with technology, 535
        and project size, 533
        and project structure, 533
    management of process of, 535–37
    management support, 533
    managing, 539–46
        external integration tools, 540
        formal planning and control tools,
            541–43

internal integration tools, 540–41
overcoming user resistance, 543–44
problems of, 537–39
analysis, 538
conversion, 539
design, 538–39
programming, 539
testing, 539
sociotechnical design, 546
and systems analyst, as change agent, 530–31
user-designer communications gap, 532–33
and user involvement/influence, 531–33
Implementation controls, 701
Implementation stage, decision making, 122
Inaccuracy, of data, 527
Inbound logistics, 55, 57
Inconsistency, of data, 527
Incremental decision making, 124
Index, 269
Indexed sequential access method (ISAM), 269
Index server, 578
Industrial economies, transformation of, 6–7
Inference engine, 650
Informal information systems, 9
Information, 9
for general support, 44
for management, 44
as paper dragon, 44
as strategic resource, 43–45
See also Data
Informational roles, managers, 116
Information architecture:
defined, 33
development of, 87
major elements of, 33
manager's questions about, 34
planning, 32–34
Information centers, 460–61
management benefits, 461
services provided by, 461
Information partnerships, 58–59
Information policy, 291–93
Information portability, 366
Information processing, and computers, 185–226
Information providers, regulatory regimes for, 155
Information requirements:
defined, 413
enterprise analysis, 400
establishing, 399–404, 413
process/organization matrix, 400–401
strategic analysis, 401–4
Information retrieval, Internet, 350–51, 353–55
Information rights, 141, 148–50
ethical issues, 149
Fair Information Practices (FIP) principles, 148
political issues, 149–50
privacy, 148–49
due process, 148
federal privacy laws, 149
social issues, 149
Information superhighway, 302–4
Information systems:
auditing, 710–12
behavioral approach to, 15

business perspective on, 10–14
management, 13
organizations, 12–13
technology, 13–14
business value of, 421–31
capital budgeting models, 421–28
nonfinancial/strategic considerations, 428–31
as a capital project, 422
challenge of, 3–39
changing concepts of, 44
characteristics of, 19
and competitive advantage, 45–57
and competitive business environment, 5–9
computer-based information systems (CBIS), 9–10
control environment, creating, 699–710
decision-support systems (DSS), 26–27
defined, 9
electronic markets, 53
ensuring quality with, 475–521
executive support systems (ESS), 27–29
formal, 9
informal, 9
integration, 29-30
international, managing, 719-50
interorganizational systems, 53
knowledge work systems, (KWS), 21–24
linking to business plan, 399
lowering costs, systems for, 54–55
management information systems (MIS), 24–26
management issues, 34–35
globalization challenge, 34–35
information architecture challenge, 35
information systems investment challenge, 35
strategic business challenge, 34
managers' questions, 60–61
moral dimensions of, 147–71
office automation systems (OAS), 21–24
and organizations, 69–109
effect on, 94–102
outsourcing, 462–68
as planned organizational change, 397
problem areas, 526–28
cost, 528
data, 527
design, 526–27
operations, 528
products and services, 46–48
purpose of, 5–9, 88–91
environmental factors, 89–91
institutional factors, 91
and quality, 477–521
reliability of, and ethics, 141
responsibility and control challenge, 35
strategic, 43–45
strategic role of, 41–68
system applications, 16–18
knowledge-level systems, 16
management-level systems, 16–17
operational-level systems, 16
strategic-level systems, 17
system failures, 525–26
causes of, 529–39
system success:
causes of, 529–39
measuring, 528–29

system vulnerability, 691–99
technical approach to, 14–15
threats to, 691
transaction processing systems (TPS), 18–21
See also Competitive advantage; Computer hardware; Computer software; Implementation; Systems development process
Information systems department, 88
size of, 88
Information systems managers, 88
Information systems plan, 399
Information systems steering committee, 398
Information systems technology, 13–14
Information technology:
capabilities, organizational impact of, 405
changing nature of, 32
and fundamental assumptions, 101-2
and organizational culture, 102
and organizational transformation, 8–9
as threat to organizations, 82
trends, 216–21
multimedia, 216–20
superchips, 220–21
Information work:
defined, 571
groupware, 582–89
managing information, 589–90
and office automation, 574–90
and productivity, 572–74
Information workers, 571–72
examples of occupations for, 571
See also Data workers; Knowledge workers
Informix OnLine RDBMS, 631
Inheritance, 252–53
Input, 9
pen-based, 213
Input authorization, as input control, 706
Input controls, 706
Input devices, 212–14
computer mouse, 212
source data automation, 213–14
touch screens, 212–13
Installation stage, systems life cycle, 441
Instant Update (On Technology, Inc.), 588–89
Institute of Electrical and Electronic Engineers (IEEE), 365
Institutional factors, 91
Intangible benefits, of information systems, 422
Integrated circuits, 196
Integrated Services Digital Network (ISDN), 142, 369–71, 741, 744
goal of, 370
levels of service, 371
Integrated software packages, 251
Integration, 29–30
Intellectual property, defined, 150
Intellex Legal Information System (ILIS), 425
Intelligence:
as stage of decision making, 121
See also Artificial intelligence
Intelligent agents, 324–26, 328–29
Interaction theory, 543
Internal integration tools, 540–41
Internal rate of return (IRR), 428

Logic Theorist, 645
"Look and feel" copyright infringement lawsuits, 151
Loss of control, and outsourcing, 463–64
Lotus, 1–2-3, 241, 250, 583–84, 618, 627
Lotus Freelance Graphics, 246
Lotus Notes, 292, 583–87
  and compound documents, 584
  groupware capabilities of, 587
  for Windows, 424
Lowering costs, systems for, 54–55
Low-orbit satellites, 308
Lynx, 363

M

M.1 (expert system), 655
Machine bureaucracy, organizations, 77
Machine control systems, A3
Machine cycle, 195
Machine language, 239
Machine Shop Estimating System, Header Die & Tool, 56
Macintosh computers, 234–35
  System 7, 238
MAC-PAC OPEN, 486
Magic (language), 247
Magnetic disks, 208–10
Magnetic ink character recognition (MICR), 213
Magnetic tape, 207–8
Magneto-optical disks, 211–12
Mail Prospector, 654
Mainframes, 199–200
  and cooperative processing, 201–3
Main memory, See Primary storage
Maintenance:
  and application software packages, 453
  of software, 488–90
  in systems development process, 419
Major organizational functions, 13
Management:
  behavioral models, 114–15
  changing process of, 30–34
  classical model of, 113–14
  decision making by, 116–31
    See also Decision-support systems (DSS); Executive support systems (ESS; Group decision-support systems (GDSS)
  how managers work, 116
  and information system development, 13, 397–99
  managerial roles, 115–16
  middle-level, 13, 612
  myths about, 117
  and strategic information systems, 57–58
  and telecommunications, 330–31
  See also Decision making; Implementation; Project management software; Project management team; Risk
Management actions, 171
Management control, decision making for, 120
Management information systems (MIS), 24–26, 44, 441
  characteristics of, 26
  compared to DSS, 609–11
  defined, 24, 26

flexibility of, 25
  role of, 24–25
Management-level systems, 16–17
Management process, changes in, 30–34
Managerial roles, 115–16
  decisional, 116
  informational, 116
  interpersonal, 115–16
Man-months, 536
Manpower planning systems, A6
Manufacturing and producing informations systems, 796–98
Market analysis systems, A1
Market niche. systems focusing on, 48–49
Massively parallel computers, 221
Master file, 214
Material movement control system, A3
MCI Mail, 589
Medical databases, 567–69
Megabytes, 191
Megahertz, 198, 307
Memory size, 191
MESA, 486
Michelangelo virus, 695
MICR, See Magnetic ink character recognition (MICR)
Microcomputer operating systems, 235–39
  DOS, 235, 366
  functions of, 230–31
    allocation and assignment, 230
    monitoring, 231
    scheduling, 230–31
  OS/2, 237–38, 240–41, 424, 583
  selecting, 238–39
  System 7, 238
  UNIX, 238, 366, 486, 583, 738, 740
  Windows, 236, 366, 583, 740
  Windows 95, 236–37
  Windows NT, 237, 738
Microcomputers, 199–200, 203
  and cooperative processing, 203
  data storage devices in, 206
  linking, 200
  and workstations, 203
Microcomputer tools, 249–51
  data management software, 250–51
  integrated software packages, 251
  spreadsheets, 249–50
  word processing software, 249
Microeconomic theories, 91, 102
Micro marketing, 725
Microprocessors, 197–98
  PowerPC microprocessors, 199
  and reduced instruction set computing (RISC), 198–99
Microseconds, 190
Microsoft Mail, 589
Microsoft Network, 324
Microsoft Word, 249
Microwave systems, 307–8, 314
Middle management:
  and decision-support systems (DSS), 612
  and executive support systems (ESS), 627
  and information systems, 13
  See also Management
Migration, 365–66
Milliseconds, 189
Minicomputers, 199–200
MIPS, 374, 665

MIS, See Management information systems (MIS)
MIS audit, 710
Mobile data networks, 310–11
Model bases, 617
  forecasting models, 617
  sensitivity analysis models, 617–18
  statistical models, 617
Models, 617
Modem, 306
MOD (Masters of Deception), 162
Modules, 502
Monitoring:
  by operating system, 231
  See also Security
Moral dimensions:
  accountability and control, 141, 143, 153–58
  information rights, 141, 148–50
  property rights, 141, 150–53
  quality of life, 141, 159–67
  system quality, 141, 158–59
Mosaic, 357, 363
Mouse, 212
Muddling through (model), decision making, 124
Multimedia, 216–20
  business applications, 217–18
  defined, 216
  and full motion video, 219
  organizational applications, 218–19
  QuickTime software, 219
  and sales presentations, 218
Multinational strategy, 730
Multiplexer, 315
Multiprocessing, 233
Multiprogramming, 231–32
Multitasking, 232, 236
Multithreading, 236–37
MYCIN, 654

N

Nanoseconds, 190
National Crime Information Center, FBI, 286
National Information Infrastructure (NII), 364
National Research Educational Network (NREN), 142, 170
National Science Foundation Network (NSF Net), 692
Negligence, and liability, 155
Net present value, 427
Net, The, See Internet
Netware (Novell), 320
Network control software, 315
Network data model, 280
Network Notes, 587
Network operating system, 319
Networks:
  connectivity for, 365–71
  global, 299–301
  monitoring with, 325
  neural, 659–67
  See also Telecommunications networks
Network Sniffer, 325
Network topologies, See Telecommunications networks
Neural networks, 659–67
  applications, 662
  building, 665
  compared to expert systems, 662–65

Neural networks, (*Continued*)
    defined, 659
    genetic algorithms compared to, 671
    in Japan, 665
    stimulators, power of, 665
New York Cash Exchange (NYCE), 46
Nexis, 326
Nomad2, 247
Nonimpact printers, 215–16
Nonprocedural languages, *See* Fourth-
    generation languages
Nonswitched lines, *See* Dedicated lines
Normalization, 285
Normative goals, 82
NREN, *See* National Research
    Educational Network (NREN)
NSF Net, 692
NYCE (New York Cash Exchange), 46

O

OAS, *See* Office automation
    systems (OAS)
Object code, 233
Object-oriented analysis (OOA), 505
Object-oriented databases, 286–88
Object-oriented design (OOD), 505
Object-oriented programming, 252–53
    classes, 252
    concepts of, 252–53
    defined, 252
    inheritance, 252–53
    and visual programming, 252
Object-oriented software development,
    505–6
    benefits of, 505–6
    defined, 505
    disadvantages of, 506
OCR, *See* Optical character recognition
    (OCR)
Odd parity, 190
Office, roles of, within organization,
    574–75
Office activities, 575
Office automation, 574–90
Office automation systems (OAS),
    21–24, 575–77
    desktop publishing, 22
    document imaging systems, 577–78,
        580–82
    document management, 577
    index server, 578
    jukebox, 578
    role of, 23–24
    word processing, 22
    workflow management, 578–80
Oligarchies, 97–98
Omni-Desk workflow software, 409
On-line processing, 214
On-line transaction processing, 697
Open systems, and connectivity,
    365–71
Open Systems Interconnect (OSI),
    367, 740
Operating excellence, examples of, 410
Operating System/2, *See* OS/2
Operating systems, 230–31
    defined, 230
    DOS, 235, 366
    functions of, 230–31
        allocation and assignment, 230
        monitoring, 231
        scheduling, 230–31

OS/2, 237–38, 240–41, 424, 583
    selecting, 238–39
    System 7, 238
    UNIX, 238, 366, 371, 486, 583,
        738, 740
    Windows, 236, 366, 583, 740
    Windows 95, 236–37, 324
    Windows NT, 237, 738
    See also Microcomputer operating
        systems
Operating system standards, for
    connectivity, 371
Operational control, decision making
    for, 120
Operational feasibility, 412
Operational-level systems, 16
Operational managers, and information
    systems, 13
Operation Desert Storm, 699
Operations, as problem area, 528
Operations software, checks over, 702–3
Optical character recognition (OCR),
    213, 578
Optical disks, 210–12, 578
    CD-ROM (compact disk read-only
        memory), 210–12
    magneto-optical disks, 211–12
    WORM (write once/read many), 211
Oracle, 420, 430, 631
Order processing systems, A1
Organizational change, Kolb/Frohman
    model of, 530–31
Organizational culture, 76–77
    and change, 77
    changes in, 102
    and information technology, 102
Organizational decision making, *See*
    Decision making
Organizational impact analysis, 544
Organizational models of decision
    making, 127–31
Organizational politics, 76
Organizational transformation, and
    information technology, 8–9
Organizations:
    behavioral definition of, 74
    as bureaucracies, 75
    computer package, decisions about,
        86–88
    constituencies, 82
    environments, 81–82
    features of, 74–86
        adhocracy, 79–81
        divisionalized bureaucracy, 79
        entrepreneurial structure, 77
        machine bureaucracy, 77
        organizational culture, 76–77
        organizational politics, 76
        professional bureaucracy, 78
        standard operating procedures
            (SOP), 75–76
    goals of, 82
    hierarchy of authority in, 75
    as information processing entities, 73
    and information systems, 12–13,
        69–109
        decisions about role of, 86
        effect on, 86–91
        new role of, 31
        two-way relationship, 72
    leadership, nature of, 82–83
    levels of analysis, 83–86
    major organizational functions, 13
    planning information architecture of,
        32–34

resistance to change in, 102–3
structural characteristics of, 75
system applications, 16–18
    knowledge-level systems, 16
    management-level systems, 16–17
    operational-level systems, 16
    strategic-level systems, 17
technical definition of, 72–73
vertical vs. horizontal, 98
OS/2, 237–38, 240–41, 424, 583
Outbound logistics, 55
Output, 9
Output controls, 708
Output devices, 214–16
    plotters, 216
    printers, 215–16
    video display terminals (VDTs), 214
    voice output devices, 216
Outside interfaces, 497
Outsourcing, 462–68
    advantages of, 463
    defined, 462
    disadvantages of, 463–64
    managing, 465–68
    when to use, 464–65

P

Packets, 322
Packet switching, 322
Pages, 232
Paging systems, 307, 310
Papnet (Neuromedical Systems Inc.),
    663–65
Paradigm shift, 406
Paradox, 251
Parallel processing:
    commercial applications, 204–5
    defined, 205
    speed of, 204
    and supercomputers, 203–5
Parallel strategy, 418
Parity, 189
Parity checks, 702
Particularism, 725–26
Pascal, 244, 650
Passwords, 703
Patents, 151–52
Payback method, 425–26
Payroll systems, A4
PBX, 317–18
PC LAN (IBM), 320
PCS, *See* Personal communication
    services (PCS)
PDAs, *See* Personal digital
    assistants (PDAs)
Pen-based input, 213
Pentium:
    chip, 220
    microprocessor, 197
People-oriented theory, 543
Perceptron, 644
Personal communication services
    (PCS), 311
Personal computers, 199–200
Personal digital assistants (PDAs),
    311–12
Personal information managers, 589–90
PersonaLink, 329
Personal interviews, and critical success
    factors (CSFs), 402
PERT (Program Evaluation and Review
    Techniques), 542, 590

Photo Credits

CHAPTER 15

CHAPTER 16

CHAPTER 17

CHAPTER 18

CHAPTER 19